1821

HISTORY

OF

NIAGARA

COUNTY, N.Y.,

WITH ILLUSTRATIONS DESCRIPTIVE OF ITS SCENERY,

Private Residences,

PUBLIC BUILDINGS, FINE BLOCKS, AND IMPORTANT MANUFACTORIES,

AND

Portraits of Old Pioneers and Prominent Residents.

NEW YORK:
SANFORD & CO.,
36 VESEY STREET.

1878

978-1-60135-488-4

INTRODUCTORY.

To one whose own neighborhood has been the theater of events prominent in the nation's annals, the history of those events is the most interesting of all history. To the intrinsic fascination of stirring incidents is added the charm of their having occurred on familiar ground. The river has an interest independent of its grandeur and beauty to one who knows how it has affected the course of events along its banks for centuries, determining the location, first of the Indian's hamlet and then of the white man's village; the route, first of the red warrior's trail and again of a far-reaching traffic that the greatest powers of Europe fought to control; the site, now of the frontier fortress and anon of the farmer's clearing; the place where armies maneuvered and scalping parties crouched in ambuscade.

The road that has been traveled unthinkingly for years is invested with a new interest if found to have traversed an Indian trail. The field where one has harvested but grain or fruit for many a season, brings forth a crop of associations and ideas when it is understood that it was the scene of one of those sanguinary conflicts in which the land was redeemed from savagery and the character of its civilization determined. The people will look with a heightened and more intelligent interest upon ancient buildings in their midst, although venerated by them they hardly know why, when they read the authentic record of events with which these monuments of the past are associated. The annals of a region so famous in legend and record as that of which these pages treat give it a new and powerful element of interest for its inhabitants, and strengthen that miniature but admirable patriotism which consists in the love of one's own locality.

It has heretofore been possible for the scholar, with leisure and a comprehensive library, to trace out the written history of his county by patient research among voluminous government documents and many volumes, sometimes old and scarce; but these sources of information and the time to study them are not at the command of most of those who are intelligently interested in local history, and there are many unpublished facts to be rescued from the failing memories of the oldest residents, who would soon have carried their information with them to the grave; and others to be obtained from the citizens best informed in regard to the various interests and institutions of the county which should be treated of in giving its history.

This service of research and compilation, which very few could have undertaken for themselves, the publishers of this work have performed, and while a few unimportant mistakes may doubtless be found in such a multitude of details, in spite of the care exercised in the production of the work,—including typographical errors like the printing of 1768 for 1678 in the first column of page 56—the publishers still confidently present this result of many months' labor as a true and orderly narrative of all the events in the history of the county which were of sufficient interest to merit such record.

Under the sway of cause and effect, historic events cannot stand alone—they form an unbroken chain. The history of so limited a territory as a county in New York has its roots not only in remote times but in distant lands, and can not be justly written without going far beyond the county limits for some of its most essential facts. Nor can such a county history be understood in its due relation without a historical review of at least the State in which the county is a part; hence we feel that in giving such an outline we have been more faithful to the main purpose of the work, while we have added an element of independent interest and value.

It may be noticed that the present geographical names are often used in the following pages as though dating from the earliest times. One who reads of events as transpiring in the town of Cambria which occurred long before a town of Cambria was thought of, will readily understand that the present name is used to avoid the needless circumlocution involved in repeating "what is now the town of Cambria," etc.

In the preparation of this volume the standard works embracing the history of this frontier have been consulted, besides many original sources of information. We have drawn freely from that great historic fount, the Documents Relating to the Colonial History of New York, often reproducing their quaint spelling and phraseology, the more perfectly to retain the flavor of the times in which they were written.

While we have in a few cases failed of the co-operation which it was reasonable to expect in the obtaining of needed facts from individuals, we have generally found the possessors of desirable knowledge ready and courteous in imparting it, and many have signally aided us, among whom may be named Hon. Sullivan Caverno, Marcus Moses, Rev. E. P. Marvin, L. J. McParlin, Dr. A. W. Tryon, Claudius L. Hoag, Luther Forsyth, Mrs. James Goodrich, Ezra Warren, Benoni Edwards, Dr. W. A. Townsend and Miss Adeliza Griswold, of the city and town of Lockport; Albert H. Porter, A. A. Porter, Judge T. G. Hulett, C. H. Piper, Hon. William Pool, Andrew Murray, S. F. Symonds, A. M. Chesbrough, J. J. Anthony, Peter H. Porter, jr., Samuel Tompkins, Colonel John Fisk, O. W. Cutler, Hon. Benjamin Flagler and F. R. Delano, of Niagara; Captain James Van Cleve, Charles T. Hotchkiss, P. P. Barton, Thomas P. Scovell, Solomon Gillett, Dr. M. Robinson and Dr. Edward Smith, of Lewiston; S. Park Baker, Ira Race, David Burge, Peter Tower, Samuel Chubbuck, B. D. Davis and Thomas Brighton, of Porter; Captain Luther Wilson, Mrs. Sally Holmes, Richard C. Holmes, Alexander Pettit, Mrs. Curtis Pettit and Rev. Ward B. Pickard, of Wilson; H. Frost, Peter Hess, G. C. Humphrey and A. N. Dutcher, of Somerset; J. C. Gladding, Jay Rowe, Lorenzo Webster and Luther S. Hall, of Hartland; J. P. Sawyer, A. Freeman, C. Schad, C. W. Laskey, P. P. Murphy, and Dr. Cole, of Royalton; Benjamin Stout H. Armstrong, James McClew, J. Arrowsmith and W. Shaw, of Newfane.

The material for the town histories of Cambria, Wheatfield and Pendleton was chiefly furnished by Mr. Chipman P. Turner.

Our acknowledgments are also due to the editors of the county papers, from the files of which valuable information has been obtained.

TABLE OF CONTENTS.

STATE HISTORY.

CHAPTER I.
The American Aborigines—Discoveries by European Explorers—The Opening of Colonization and Trade 9–11

CHAPTER II.
The Dutch Regime in New York—Rival Claims of the English—The Latter Prevail 11–13

CHAPTER III.
The Five Nations—Their Traditions of their Origin—Iroquois Customs and Political Organization 13–16

CHAPTER IV.
French and Indian War—Dissensions in the Colonial Government—Capture and Execution of Leisler 16–18

CHAPTER V.
Count Frontenac's Campaigns—Prevalence of Piracy—Misgovernment of New York—French Trading and Military Posts 18–20

CHAPTER VI.
The Alleged Plot to Burn New York—French and English Hostilities—The Contest for the Ohio Valley 20–22

CHAPTER VII.
The Results of Four English Expeditions Against the French—Montcalm's Successful Campaigns 22–24

CHAPTER VIII.
Extinction of French Power in America—The New York Judiciary—International Contentions 24–26

CHAPTER IX.
The Approach of the Revolution—Patriotic Attitude of New York—The First Battle Fought in 1770 26–29

CHAPTER X.
The Boston Tea Party—Meeting of the Continental Congress—The Battle of Lexington—Canada Invaded 29–31

CHAPTER XI.
Hostilities Transferred to New York—The Battle of Long Island—Burgoyne's Campaign 31–34

CHAPTER XII.
The Battle of Bennington—Failure of St. Leger's Movement—Burgoyne's Defeats and Surrender 34–37

CHAPTER XIII.
Clinton's Hudson River Campaign—France Recognizes the United States—Wars with the Indians 37–39

CHAPTER XIV.
Arnold's Treason—Close of the Revolution—Adoption of the Constitution—Internal Improvements 39–42

CHAPTER XV.
Causes of the Last War with Great Britain—Expeditions Against Canada—Border Hostilities 42–46

CHAPTER XVI.
The Erie Canal and Central Railroad—The State Administration—New York in the Civil War 46, 47

NIAGARA COUNTY.

CHAPTER I.
The Word Niagara—Relics and Theories of the Earliest Population... 49–52

CHAPTER II.
Father L'Allemant's Account of the Neutral Nation—The Destruction of the Eries 52–54

CHAPTER III.
The Traditional Origin of the Senecas—Names and Locations of their Villages 54–56

CHAPTER IV.
La Salle's Vanguard Arrives in the Niagara—The Narrative of Father Hennepin 56, 5

CHAPTER V.
The Career of La Salle—He Builds the First Sailing Vessel Above Niagara Falls 58–61

CHAPTER VI.
Niagara and the Indian Trade—The Rivalry of the French and English 61–65

CHAPTER VII.
Denonville's Expedition Against the Senecas—The Building of the First Fort Niagara 65–68

CHAPTER VIII.
The Joncaires, and the French Trading House Established at Lewiston in 1720 68–71

CHAPTER IX.
The Rebuilding of Fort Niagara—It is Besieged by the English and Iroquois 71–74

CHAPTER X.
Journal of the Siege of Fort Niagara—Rout of a Relief Force—The Surrender 74–77

CHAPTER XI.
Sir William Johnson's Journal—Fort Schlosser Built—Traders Prohibited from Settling Thereabouts 77–79

CHAPTER XII.
The Devil's Hole Massacre—The Senecas Cede the Niagara Border to the English 79–81

CHAPTER XIII.
Fort Niagara During the Revolution—Its Surrender by the British—The Tuscaroras 81–83

CHAPTER XIV.
Indian Trails in Niagara County—The Portage, Military, Ridge and Lake Roads 83–86

CHAPTER XV.
The Title to the Soil of Western New York—Phelps and Gorham's Purchase—Morris' Reserve 86–89

CHAPTER XVI.
The Holland Purchase and Purchasers—Surveys, Sales and First Settlements 89–92

CHAPTER XVII.
Pioneer Experiences—Emigrating, Building and Clearing—Frontier Work and Play 92–96

CHAPTER XVIII.

Pioneer Farming—First Schools and Teachers, Meetings and Preachers—The Public Health.. 96–100

CHAPTER XIX.

Military Operations of 1812—Attitude of the Iroquois—Preparations for Invading Canada....................................... 100, 101

CHAPTER XX.

The Capture of Queenston Heights—The Assailants Overpowered, Unsupported and Taken Prisoners........................... 101–103

CHAPTER XXI.

Capture and Recapture of Fort George—Fall of Fort Niagara—Ravages of Fire and Sword... 103–105

CHAPTER XXII.

Successive Boundaries of Niagara County and its Subdivisions—Officers and Representatives... 105–107

CHAPTER XXIII.

The Projection of the Erie Canal—Its Advocates and its Construction—La Fayette's Tour.. 107–111

CHAPTER XXIV.

The Case of William Morgan—Rise and Career of the Anti-Masonic Party.. 111–113

CHAPTER XXV.

Old-time Stage Lines on the Ridge Road—Railroad History of Niagara County.. 113–116

CHAPTER XXVI.

Incidents of the Patriot War—The Old Militia System in Niagara County.. 116–118

CHAPTER XXVII.

Niagara Ship Canal Projects—The Shipping and the Commerce of Niagara County.. 118–122

CHAPTER XXVIII.

Insurance, Medical, Religious, Pioneer and Agricultural Associations—The County Farm—Statistics.......................... 122–127

CHAPTER XXIX.

The Rise and Development of the Great Fruit-Growing Interest of Niagara County.. 127, 128

CHAPTER XXX.

Sketch of the Geology of Niagara County........................ 128–131

CHAPTER XXXI.

Niagara County in the Civil War—The 28th, 49th, 100th and 102nd Infantry.. 131–136

CHAPTER XXXII.

The Record of the 23d Battery and 1st Regiment of Light Artillery.... 136–140

CHAPTER XXXIII.

The Cavalry Representation—Histories of the 8th, 3d and 15th, and the 2d Mounted Rifles.. 140–146

CHAPTER XXXIV.

Services and Sufferings of the 151st Infantry.................... 146–150

CHAPTER XXXV.

The Brilliant Career of the Gallant Eighth New York Heavy Artillery.. 150–155

CHAPTER XXXVI.

Records of the 78th, 96th, 105th, 132nd, 164th, 178th, 179th, 187th and 194th Infantry.. 155–159

CHAPTER XXXVII.

Twelfth, Nineteenth, Seventeenth and Twenty-fifth Batteries—Fourteenth Artillery.. 159–163

CITY, TOWN AND VILLAGE HISTORIES.

THE CITY OF LOCKPORT.

Main street in 1823—The Early Taverns—Completion of the Canal—The Rise of the Lower Town—Shaved by Lorenzo Dow—Early Mail Facilities—Municipal Organization—Business Establishments in 1835—The McLeod Excitement—Railroad Communications—General Scott in Lockport—Recent Events—Early Schools—The Water Power of Lockport—Flouring Mills—The Stave Manufacture—Saw-mills—Corporations and Manufactories—Hotels of the Present—The Hodge Opera House—Banks—The Stone and Marble Interests—Hydraulic Cement—Niagara Nurseries—Lockport Home for the Friendless—Union School of Lockport—The Fire Department—Societies—The Niagara Light Guards—Churches—Biographical Sketches of Lockport's Leading Citizens............ 165–226

THE TOWN OF CAMBRIA.

Early Residents of the Town—Warren's Corners—Molyneux's Corners—Cambria Center and Vicinity—Pekin and Southwestern Cambria—Churches on the Ridge—Early Schools and School-Houses—Singular Deposits—Brief Biographical Sketches........................ 227–236

THE TOWN OF HARTLAND.

First Town Meeting—Further Matters of Early Record—Principal Town Officers—Physical Features of the Town—Early Settlers—Pioneer Life in Hartland—Villages in Hartland—Industrial Beginnings—Educational—Roads and Bridges—Salt Springs—A Profitable Hurricane—An Ancient Earthwork—Taverns—Physicians—Burying Grounds—Early Preachers—Lodges—Churches—Agricultural—The Leading Citizens of To-day........................ 237–248

THE TOWN OF LEWISTON.

The French and English Occupations—Brant and the Mohawks—Tuscarora Reservation—Indian Mound—Early White Settlement—Incidents Connected with the War—Settlement after the War—Description and Civil History—Supervisors—Sanborn and Dickersonville—Seminary of Our Lady of Angels—The Village of Lewiston—Prominent Inhabitants of the Town............................. 249–264

THE TOWN OF LOCKPORT.

The Town Civil List—Outlines, Surface, Soil and Products—Ellicott Reserve and Salt Spring—Singular Antiquities—Early Settlers—Wright's Corners—The Long Causeway Turnpike—Rapids—Warren's Corners—Early Schools and School Houses—Plank and Toll Roads—Cemeteries—Churches of the Town—Biographical Notices of Lockport Citizens.. 265–274

THE TOWN OF NEWFANE.

The Pioneers—Incidents of the War of 1812—From the Early Records—Building and Beginning Business—Physicians—Antiquities—Roads and Bridges—Burying Grounds—Villages and Post-offices—Temperance Organizations—Religious History—Schools—Newfane in the Civil War—Sketches of Representative Citizens...... 275–286

THE TOWN OF NIAGARA.

Niagara River and Falls—Fort Little Niagara—The Stedman House and Farm—Porter, Barton & Co.—Early Reminiscences—Early Settlements and Improvements—Niagara in the War of 1812—Early Events—Civil History—Niagara in the Rebellion—Cemeteries—Roads—Schools—The First Religious Services—Fruit-growing in Niagara—Drainage—Population—The Village of La Salle—Pletcher's Corners.. 287–299

THE VILLAGE OF NIAGARA FALLS.

The Village in 1810—The Early Settlers—Samuel De Veaux, the First Merchant—Accessions from 1821 to 1838—General Peter B. Porter—Colonel Peter A. Porter—Business and Improvements—The Carrying Business—Further Business Progress—The Ups and Downs of 1836—The Hydraulic Canal—Mails, Stages, Railroads and Expresses—The Press of Niagara Falls—Schools—The Fire Department—Incorporation and Civil History—Oakwood Cemetery—Churches of Niagara Falls—Business Corporations—Fraternities and Social Organizations—Improvements About the Falls—Accidents and Incidents—Well Known Residents of Niagara Falls, La Salle and Vicinity.. 300–318

THE VILLAGE OF SUSPENSION BRIDGE.

Initial Events—The International Suspension Bridge Company—Business Growth and Improvements—A Great Railway Center—The Custom-House and Other Buildings—Incorporation and Civil History—Waterworks and Fire Companies—The Press of Suspension Bridge—Education—Societies—Prominent Inhabitants of Suspension Bridge.. 319–328

TABLE OF CONTENTS.

THE TOWN OF PENDLETON.

Settlement—Extracts from the Town Records—The German Inhabitants—The Enlargement of the Canal—Pendleton Village—Churches—Leading Citizens of Pendleton... 329-331

THE TOWN OF PORTER.

The Settlement of the Town—Pioneers and Early Events—Incidents During and After the War of 1812—Facts and Statistics—Ransomville—Youngstown—Sketches of Prominent Residents and Pioneers... 332-347

THE TOWN OF ROYALTON.

Settlement—Pioneer House-Building—Trails and Roads—Early Taverns—First Schools—Course of Trade and Manufacture—Professional Men—Post-offices—First Birth, Marriage and Death—Associations and Lodges—Wolcottsville—Royalton Center—Orangeport—Gasport—Reynale's Basin—Middleport—The Churches—Biographical Sketches of Prominent Residents...................................... 348-361

THE TOWN OF SOMERSET.

Pioneer Experiences—After the War of 1812—The First of their Kind—The Political Record—Salt Spring—Lodges and Associations—The Government Light-house—Statistics—Religious History—Brief Biographies... 362-372

THE TOWN OF WHEATFIELD.

Pioneer Settlements—The German Neighborhoods—Supervisors of Wheatfield—North Tonawanda—Brief Sketches of Wheatfield Citizens.. 373-381

THE TOWN OF WILSON.

Organization—Supervisors—Statistical Facts—Pioneer Experiences—Sundry First Events—Roads—The Last Wolf and Bear—The Village of Wilson—Smaller Villages—Church History of the Town—Wilson's Leading Citizens... 332-397

ILLUSTRATIONS.

Academy, St. Joseph's, Lockport..following 208
Arnold, E. E., Residence, Somerset....................................following 273
Barnes, S. M., Residence, Lockport...................................preceding 213
Barnes's Block, Store, Lime Works, etc., Lockport...........preceding 213
Barnum, H. A., Farm Residence, Wheatfield.................following 204
Bateman, V. D., Residence, Somerset.............................following 222
Beach, Cyrus, Farm Residence, Cambria.........................following 234
Bickford, H. H., Farm Residence, Hartland....................following 242
Bishop, Dr. D. F., Residence, Lockport...........................following 214
Bowen, Hon. L. F., Residence, Lockport.........................following 204
Bradley, G. H., Residence, Somerset..............................preceding 369
Brewer, S. A., Fruit Farm, Hartland................................following 244
Brigham, P. W., Residence, Somerset............................following 368
Brown, Thomas, Hartland...following 238
Brown, William, Hartland..following 238
Burge, David, Residence, Youngstown..........................following 338
Burtch, Lewis, Farm Residence, Cambria.....................following 232
Campbell, R., Farm Residence, Cambria......................following 228
Caverno, Hon. S., Residence, Lockport.........................following 190
Childs, W. H., Residence, Niagara Falls.......................following 312
Church, St. Patrick's, Church Buildings, Hartland......following 174
Coates, John, Residence, Somerset...............................following 364
Coates, Samuel, Residence, Somerset..........................following 364
Colt, H., & Son, Farm Residences, Lewiston...............preceding 263
Coleman, Aaron, Residence, Somerset........................following 362
Corwin, P. H., Newfane..preceding 283
Court-House, Lockport...preceding 165
Crapsey, M. C. & A. H., Residences, Lockport............preceding 213
Curtiss Bros., Hotel and Warehouse, Ransomville.......following 346
Davis, B. D., Residence, Youngstown............................following 340
Diez, John, Residence, Wilson......................................following 346
Eastman, Anson, Farm Residence, Cambria...............following 230
Evans, E., Residence, Tonawanda................................following 204
Faling, Dr. P., Residence, Royalton..............................following 356
Finn, A. S. & S. B., Boat Yard, Lockport.......................following 218
Finn, S. H., Residence, Lockport..................................following 218
Fitts, Hardy, Residence, Somerset................................following 362
Flagler, Hon. T. T., Residence, Lockport.....................following 214
Flanders, Hiram, Farm Residence, Cambria..............following 228
Freeman, F. B., Royalton..preceding 283
Gamble, Mrs. E. A., Residence, Newfane...................following 278
Gardner, Mrs. Judge H., Residence, Lockport...........following 212
Gardner, I. J., Somerset..following 366
Haight, J. S., Residence, Somerset..............................following 362
Haight, Mrs. L., Residence, Somerset.........................following 362

Harmony, E., Farm Residence, Cambria.....................following 340
Hayes, O. B., Farm Residence, Hartland....................following 236
Henning, John, Farm Residence, Newfane.................following 284
Hildreth, G. W., Residence, Lockport..........................following 188
Hine, G. J., Residence, Middleport...............................following 360
Hoag, Thomas, Residence, Somerset..........................following 364
Hodge Opera House...preceding 211
Holmes, D., Residence, Wilson.....................................following 394
Holmes, R. C., Residence, Wilson................................following 392
Holett, Hon. T. G., Niagara Falls..................................preceding 315
Humphrey, Hon. G. C., Somerset..................................following 366
Hyde, William H., Residence, Somerset......................following 368
Jackson, James, Jr., Residence, Lockport..................following 226
Jackson, James, Jr., & Son, Lumber Works, Lockport..following 226
Jail and Court-House, Lockport....................................preceding 165
Journal Building, Lockport..following 174
Judd, G. L., Tonawanda..following 380
Kock, Andrew, Residence, Gasport..............................following 213
Knapp, Dr. F. L., Residence, Gasport..........................preceding 359
Knapp, Silas, Farm Residence, Royalton....................following 360
Kyte, Francis, Porter..following 362
Labar, J. W., Residence, Lockport...............................following 272
Lockport in 1836..preceding 165
Loomis, G. W., Farm Residence, Wilson.....................preceding 397
McArthur, J., Residence, Newfane..............................following 280
McNeil, Hon. H. D., Store, Lockport............................preceding 187
Mann, O. E., Residence and Fruit Farm, Somerset...following 370
Mead, H. D., Residence, Somerset..............................following 356
Mighells, N. T., Farm Residence, Warren's Corners..following 274
Milliman, E. A., Farm Residence, Wheatfield............preceding 381
Morse, James M., Residence, Wilson..........................preceding 395
Niagara County Court-House, Lockport.....................preceding 165
Niagara Falls...(Frontispiece.)
Packard, Mrs. G. M., Niagara......................................following 354
Palmer, R., Residence, Wilson.....................................following 396
Parsons, A. C., Residence, Niagara.............................following 346
Partridge, C. H., Residence, Lockport........................following 218
Payne, Col. L. S., Residence, Tonawanda..................preceding 379
Pearson, William, Residence, Lockport.....................preceding 271
Pease, A. & William H., Residence, Somerset...........preceding 371
Pease, William B., Fruit Farm, Lockport...................following 274
Poole, J. A., Farm Residence, Cambria......................following 228
Rich, A. D., Hotel, Middleport.....................................following 354
Sanborn, Residence and Village, Sanborn P. O.........following 264
Scott, David, Residence, Cambria...............................following 302
Seminary of Our Lady of Angels, Suspension Bridge..preceding 259
Shafer, J. W., Residence and Fruit Farm, Royalton..preceding 359
Shaw, G. V., Farm Residence, Hartland.....................following 248
Sherwood, Elon, Residence, N. Hartland...................following 246
Shuler, Mrs. J. D., Residence, Lockport.....................following 362
Smith, Ammi, Residence, Newfane.............................following 282
Smith, S. E., Residence, Somerset..............................following 372
Snyder & Holly, Marble Works, Lockport..................following 183
Swift, E. B., Farm Residence, Cambria......................following 230
Timothy, H. B., Ransomville..preceding 345
Tower, Peter, Sen., Farm Residence, Porter.............following 344
Tower, Luke & P. S., Farm Residences, Porter.........following 344
Treichler, S., Farm Residence, Lewiston...................following 259
Union Schools, School Buildings, Lockport...............following 192
Van Horn, T. H., Drug Store, Lockport......................following 166
Van Horn, W., Farm Residence, Hartland................following 256
Walter, P. D., Residence, Lockport.............................following 204
Ward, J. A., Residence, Lockport................................following 174
Ward, N. C., Farm Residence, Wilson.......................preceding 395
Watson, James G., Farm Residence, Hartland.........following 360
Wentworth, A. P., Residence, Newfane.....................following 185
Wentworth, E. P., Residence, Lockport.....................following 224
Whitcomb, E., Farm Residence, N. Hartland...........following 250
Wilcox, O. L., Residence, Gasport..............................following 236
Williams, E. J., Residence, Wilson.............................following 392
Williams, J., Residence, Wilson..................................following 392
Wilson, S., Residence, Newfane..................................following 286
Wright, W. S., Residence, Lockport............................following 222
Wright, W. S., Farm Residence, Olcott......................following 222
Zimmerman, Nelson, Farm Residence, Wheatfield..preceding 381

PORTRAITS.

Albright, F. N., Barker's P. O., Somerset...................preceding 327
Beach, Cyrus, Cambria...following 234
Beach, Mrs. Cyrus, Cambria..following 234
Beach, Master Cyrus W., Cambria..............................following 234
Brewer, S. A., Hartland..following 244
Brewer, Mrs. S. A., Hartland.......................................following 244
Burge, David, Youngstown..following 338

TABLE OF CONTENTS.

Burge, Mrs. David, Youngstown ....following 338
Caverno, Hon. S., Lockport........................following 190
Childs, W. H., Niagara Falls.......................following 312
Clark, S. T., A.M., M.D., Lockport..............preceding 327
Colt, H., Lewiston...................................preceding 263
Colt, J. B. S., Lewiston............................preceding 263
Delano, Dr. B. L., Niagara Falls.................following 308
Ely, Rev. Foster, D.D., Lockport.................following 216
Gardner, Hon. H., Lockport.......................following 212
Henning, A. W. R., Suspension Bridge..........preceding 327
Hodge, John, Lockport.............................following 210
Holmes, D., Wilson..................................following 394
Holmes, Mrs. D., Wilson............................following 394
Hulett, Hon. T. G., Niagara Falls................preceding 315
Judd, G. L., Tonawanda............................following 380
Judd, Mrs. G. L., Tonawanda......................following 380
Labar, J. W., Lockport..............................following 272
Labar, Mrs. J. W., Lockport.......................following 272
McNeil, H. D., Lockport............................preceding 187
Morse, J. M., Wilson.................................preceding 395
Morse, Mrs. J. M., Wilson..........................preceding 395
Palmer, Reuben, Wilson............................following 396
Palmer, Mrs. Reuben, Wilson.....................following 396
Palmer, Dr C. N., Lockport.......................following 216
Palmer, Col. W. E., Lockport.....................following 216
Payne, Lewis S., Tonawanda......................preceding 379
Payne, Lewis T., Tonawanda.....................preceding 379
Pease, A., Somerset..................................preceding 371
Pease, Mrs. A., Somerset...........................preceding 371
Richardson, M. C., Lockport......................following 174
Sanborn, L. R., Sanborn P. O.....................following 264
Sherwood, Elon, N. Hartland.....................following 246
Sherwood, Mrs. Elon, N. Hartland..............following 246
Smith, S. E., Somerset..............................following 372
Smith, Mrs. S. E., Somerset........................following 372
Stewart, Z. B., Hartland...........................following 242
Timothy, H. B., Ransomville.....................preceding 343
Timothy, Mrs. H. B., Ransomville..............preceding 343
Tower, Peter, Porter.................................following 344
Tower, Mrs. Peter, Porter.........................following 344
Ward, N. C., Wilson.................................preceding 393
Ward, Mrs. N. C., No. 1............................preceding 393
Ward, Mrs. N. C., No. 2............................preceding 393
Wentworth, E. P., Lockport......................following 224
Wilson, S., Newfane..................................following 286
Wilson, Mrs. S., Newfane............................following 286

BIOGRAPHICAL NOTICES.

Albright, F. N., Somerset.. 368
Arnold, E. E., Somerset.. 369
Barnes, S. M., Lockport.. 213
Barnum, H. A., Wheatfield.. 380
Bateman, V. D., Somerset... 368
Beach, Cyrus, Cambria.. 234
Bickford, H. H., Hartland... 246
Bishop, Dr. D. F., Lockport.. 213
Bowen, Hon. L. F., Lockport...................................... 214
Bradley, G. H., Somerset.. 369
Brewer, S. A., Hartland... 245
Brigham, P. W., Somerset.. 369
Brown, Thomas, Hartland... 245
Brown, William, Hartland... 245
Burge, David, Youngstown.. 344
Burtch, Lewis, Cambria... 234
Campbell, R., Cambria... 234
Caverno, Hon. S., Lockport.. 214
Childs, W. H., Niagara Falls....................................... 312
Clark, S. T., Lockport.. 327
Coates, John, Somerset.. 369
Coates, Samuel, Somerset.. 369
Colt, H. & Son, Lewiston.. 263
Coleman, Aaron, Somerset.. 369
Corwin, P. H., Newfane... 285

Crapsey, M. C., Lockport... 272
Curtiss Bros., Ransomville.. 345
Davis, B. D., Youngstown... 339
Delano, B. L., M.D., Niagara Falls............................. 308
Diez, John, Wilson... 393
Eastman, Anson, Cambria... 235
Ely, Rev. Foster, D.D., Lockport................................ 216
Faling, Dr. P., Royalton... 359
Finn, A. S., Lockport... 217
Finn, S. H., Lockport... 217
Fitts, Harly, Somerset... 370
Flagler, Hon. T. T., Lockport..................................... 217
Flanders, Hiram, Cambria... 235
Gamble, Mrs. E. A., Newfane.................................... 284
Gardner, Hon. H., Lockport....................................... 212
Gardner, I. J., Somerset... 370
Haight, J. S., Somerset.. 370
Haight, Mrs. L., Somerset... 370
Hayes, O. B., Hartland.. 246
Henning, A. W. R., Suspension Bridge...................... 327
Henning, John, Newfane... 284
Hildreth, G. W., Lockport... 218
Hine, G. J., Middleport... 359
Hodge, John, Lockport.. 211
Holmes, D., Wilson... 394
Holmes, R. C., Wilson... 394
Hulett, Hon. T. G., Niagara Falls............................... 315
Humphrey, Hon. G. C., Somerset.............................. 371
Hunt, Hon. Washington, Lockport............................. 107
Hyde, William H., Somerset..................................... 368
Judd, G. L., Tonawanda.. 380
Keck, Andrew, Lockport... 273
Knapp, Dr. P. L., Gasport... 359
Knapp, Silas, Royalton.. 359
Kyte, Francis, Porter.. 345
Labar, J. W., Lockport... 273
Loomis, G. W., Wilson.. 395
McArthur, J., Newfane.. 285
McFarlin, L. J., Lockport.. 220
Mann, O. E., Somerset.. 371
Mead, H. D., Somerset.. 371
Mighells, N. T., Warren's Corners............................. 235
Millman, E. A., Wheatfield....................................... 381
Morse, James M., Wilson.. 395
Packard, Mrs. G. M., Niagara.................................... 317
Palmer, R., Wilson.. 396
Partridge, C. H., Lockport... 273
Payne, Col. L. S., Tonawanda................................... 379
Pearson, William, Lockport....................................... 273
Pease, Adam, Somerset... 371
Pease, W. B., Lockport.. 273
Pool, J. A., Cambria.. 235
Pool, Hon. William, Niagara Falls............................. 317
Sanborn, Hon. L. R., Sanborn P. O............................ 264
Shaw, G. V., Hartland... 247
Sherwood, Elon, N. Hartland.................................... 247
Shuler, Mrs. J. D., Lockport...................................... 274
Smith, Ammi, Newfane... 286
Smith, S. E., Somerset.. 372
Stewart, Z. B., Hartland.. 247
Timothy, H. B., Porter... 343
Tower, Peter, Sen., Porter... 343
Treichler, S., Lewiston.. 264
Van Cleve, Captain James, Lewiston......................... 264
Van Horn, W., Hartland.. 248
Walter, Hon. P. D., Lockport.................................... 224
Ward, N. C., Wilson.. 397
Watson, James G., Hartland...................................... 248
Wentworth, A. P., Newfane...................................... 286
Wentworth, E. P., Lockport...................................... 225
Whitcomb, E., N. Hartland....................................... 248
Wilcox, O. L., Royalton... 361
Williams, E. J., Wilson.. 397
Williams, J., Wilson.. 397
Wilson, S., Newfane.. 286
Wright, W. S., Lockport.. 226
Zimmerman, Nelson, Wheatfield............................... 381

OUTLINE HISTORY

OF THE

STATE OF NEW YORK.

CHAPTER I.

THE AMERICAN ABORIGINES—DISCOVERIES BY EUROPEAN EXPLORERS—THE OPENING OF COLONIZATION AND TRADE.

THE American continent, in its natural features, presents a striking and diversified display of resources and grandeurs. Bounded by oceans; indented with numerous gulfs and bays; intersected and drained by large rivers; embracing lakes equal in extent to seas, it affords every facility for commerce; while its fertile valleys and extensive plains are admirably adapted to agricultural pursuits, and its interior is stored with minerals of inestimable value. The magnificence of mountain scenery, the dashing flood and deafening roar of Niagara, the subterranean labyrinths of Mammoth Cave, are features of nature which fill the beholder with wonder and amazement. To what people were these resources offered and these grandeurs presented in the dim ages of the past? With only the shadowy and uncertain light of tradition, little else than speculation can furnish anything like a beginning to the history of the aborigines of America. The ruins of cities and pyramids in Mexico and Central America, and the numerous mounds so common in the valley of the Mississippi, are monuments which point to a people more skilled in arts and farther advanced in civilization than the Indian, found in occupancy when the first Europeans landed. Some of these mounds appear to have been erected for burial places, and others for defense. The remains of fortifications present evidence of mechanical skill, and no little display of the knowledge of engineering. Metallic implements of ingenious design and superior finish, and finely wrought pottery, glazed and colored, equal to the best specimens of modern manufacture, have been found, showing a higher degree of mechanical skill than the Indian has ever been known to possess. Some of these remains have been found twenty feet or more below the surface, showing that they must have lain there many centuries. All the investigations of the antiquarian to discover by what people these mounds were erected have ended in uncertainty. If these are the relics of a lost people, as many believe they are, it seems somewhat probable that they were from Egypt. Their pyramids and skill in the arts, together with the fact that human bodies have been found preserved somewhat similar to Egyptian mummies, support this theory. At an early age the Egyptians, who were noted for their skill in navigation, sailed around Africa, and made many other voyages, in some of which they may have reached America. Aristotle, Plato and other ancient writers appear to have been aware of an extensive body of land in the West, speaking of it as an island, greater than Europe or Africa. It is also supposed that the Egyptians may have reached America through Asia. It is related that an Asiatic people emigrated to Egypt and conquered the Mizraimites, who were then in possession; and that they became distinguished for their arts, built cities and erected gigantic pyramids, which still remain as evidence of their skill and power. The Mizraimites, smarting under their tyranny, rose against them, and after a long struggle succeeded in driving them out of the land. They retreated to the northeast, leaving mounds and walls as far as Siberia, as traces of their passage, and, it is thought, crossed Behring's strait, and eventually settled in the Mississippi valley and Mexico.

Leaving conjecture, in regard to the early inhabitants of this continent, it was found when first visited by the whites that the Indians had long been in possession. Their personal appearance, language and customs plainly indicated a distinct race. There were many points of difference among the various tribes, but in many respects they bore a resemblance to each other. The Aztecs of Mexico were found with a large and populous city, in which were temples and palaces and well cultivated grounds; while in the more northern regions a village of rude huts and a small field of corn were about the only marks of occupancy. The traditions of the Indians are so dim and conflicting as to shed little light on their origin. They obtained a subsistence chiefly by hunting and fishing, and were continually engaged in bloody wars with each other. They had no written language, no letters with which their words could be represented; but to some extent they communicated their thoughts to one another by hieroglyphics: certain symbols denoted certain ideas, and these were either drawn or painted on skins or birch bark, or chiseled on rocks. By comparing their languages they were grouped into great families, some of which contained many tribes. Of these families the Algonquin was the largest, occupying about half of that portion of the United States east of the Mississippi river, together with a part of Canada. The Huron-Iroquois was the next in importance, occupying the greater part of the State of New York and the Canadian peninsula, formed by lakes Ontario, Erie and Huron. They have rapidly diminished in numbers from pestilence and wars with the advancing whites, until only fragments remain; and their aversion to civilization, and strong attachment to a wild mode of life make their extinction inevitable. The pioneer still advances; railroads are connecting ocean with ocean, and the war whoop is silenced by the screech of the locomotive as it sounds the death knell of the once proud lords of a continent.

The discovery of America was the most important event of modern times. For the honor of this discovery several claims have been presented. Welsh historians have awarded it to Modoc, a prince of Wales, who went to sea in the twelfth century and discovered land far to the west, to which he made several voyages, but who, with all his crew, was finally lost. This claim is founded on tradition, however, and unsubstantiated. The Norwegians claim discovery and settlement on stronger evidence: Eric emigrated from Iceland to Greenland in 986, and formed a settlement. Leif, a son of Eric, embarked with a crew of men in the year 1000 on a voyage of discovery. He sailed to the southwest and discovered land, and voyaging along the coast he finally entered a bay, where he remained through the winter, calling the region Vineland. In 1007 Thorfinn sailed from Greenland to Vineland. An account of his voyage and history of the country is still extant. Other voyages were made, and the Antiquarian Society, after a careful examination of all the evidence, including the geography of the country described in these voyages, do not hesitate to locate this Vineland at the head of Narragansett Bay in Rhode Island. These discoveries, however, were so ineffectual that nothing was known in Europe of land beyond the ocean until 1492, when Christopher Columbus, believing that India might be reached by sailing westward, was at his urgent solicitation dispatched on a voyage of discovery by Ferdinand and Isabella, king and queen of Spain. He sailed from Palos, and after stopping at the Canaries, struck out upon the hitherto unknown ocean, discovering first one of the Bahama islands; then proceeding toward the south he discovered Cuba and Hayti, and returned to Spain, thus opening a highway over the trackless Atlantic. He made other voyages, and in 1498 discovered the continent near the mouth of the Orinoco river. The discovery of land in the west promised large profits, and excited maritime enterprise throughout Europe.

Henry VII. commissioned John Cabot, a Venetian, in 1497, to sail on a voyage of discovery, and take possession of new lands in the name of England. Sailing westward, in company with his son Sebastian, he discovered Newfoundland, and while off the coast of Labrador saw the main-land of North America. The next year Sebastian set sail to discover a northwest passage to China. The frozen regions at the north compelled him to change his course, and sailing toward the south he visited various points along the coast as far as Albemarle sound, taking possession of the whole region for the crown of England. John Verazzani, a Florentine in the service of Francis I. of France, arrived on the coast of North Carolina in 1524, and sailed south as far as Georgia. Turning north, he explored the coast to about 41° north latitude, and entered a harbor, which, from his description, is believed to have been New York Bay, where he remained about fifteen days, and it is supposed that his crew were the first Europeans that landed on the soil of New York. He proceeded north as far as Labrador, giving to the whole country the name of New France, which was afterward confined to Canada.

Henry Hudson, an English navigator, having failed in two expeditions to discover a passage to the East Indies, for a company of London merchants, by sailing westward, offered his services in 1609 to the Dutch East India Company of Holland, which was formed the preceding year for traffic and colonization. He left Amsterdam on the 4th of April with a small ship and a crew of about twenty English and Dutch sailors, and arrived on the American coast near Portland, in Maine, whence he proceeded south along the shore to the entrance of Chesapeake Bay. From this point he returned northward, discovered and entered Delaware Bay, and on the 3rd of September anchored at Sandy Hook. From here he proceeded up New York Bay, sending his boats to the Jersey shore and receiving on board the natives, who came in great numbers to traffic. On the 12th he entered the river which bears his name, and ascended it to a point a little above where the city of Hudson now stands, having been frequently visited on the way by the Indians, who came to traffic, bringing maize, tobacco and other products native to the country. To them he imparted a knowledge of the effects of rum, to the drinking of which in later years they became greatly addicted. Not considering it safe to proceed farther with his ship, he sent a boat with a part of his crew to explore the river higher up. It is supposed that they went a little above Albany. On the 23d he commenced to descend the river. When a little below the Highlands, the Indians made several attempts to attack his crew, who, in repulsing their attacks, shot ten or twelve of their number. Descending into the bay he immediately sailed for Europe. The following year he made a voyage for the discovery of a northwest passage to India, and discovered and entered the bay which bears his name. Continuing his search too long, he was compelled to remain through the winter. In the spring part of his crew mutinied, put him in a boat, together with his son and seven others, and left them to perish. In 1607 Samuel Champlain, a French navigator, ascended the St. Lawrence river, exploring its tributaries; and on the 4th of July discovered the lake which bears his name. Hence three nations, Holland, France and England, founding their titles upon discovery, claimed ownership in a region a part of which lies within the limits of the State of New York.

The accounts given by Hudson of his discoveries stimulated the Dutch to avail themselves of the advantages that might be gained by trading with the Indians, and accordingly in the following year another vessel was sent out to engage in the fur trade on the banks of the river he had discovered.

In 1612 two more vessels were fitted out by Hendrick Christiansen and Adrian Block, which were soon followed by others. The fur trade proving successful, Christiansen was appointed agent of the traffic, and Manhattan Island made the chief depot. He erected a small fort and a few rude buildings at the southern extremity of the island, calling the place New Amsterdam. The island was covered with giant forest trees and dense thickets, which served as hiding places for reptiles and wild beasts. In 1614 the States General granted a charter to the merchants engaged in these expeditions, conferring the exclusive right of trade in this new territory, between the 40th and 45th parallels of north latitude, for four years, and giving the name of New Netherlands to the whole region. The trade flourished, and had become so profitable at the expiration of the charter that the States General refused to renew it, giving instead a special license for its temporary continuance.

In the meantime the surrounding country was being explored. Adrian Block had passed up the East river, Long Island sound and Connecticut river, and into the bays and along the islands eastward to Cape Cod. Cornelissen Jacobsen May had explored the southern coast of Long Island and southward to Delaware Bay, while Hendrick Christiansen had ascended the Hudson river to Castle Island, a few miles below Albany, where he had established a trading post and erected a small fort. This fort was so much damaged by a flood that it was removed to the Normans-kill, a little below. Here a council was held between the chiefs and warriors of the Five Nations and the representatives of the New Netherlands, and a treaty of alliance and peace was formed.

In 1620 James I. granted to Ferdinando Gorges and his commercial associates all the land between the fortieth and forty-eighth degrees of north latitude, and extending from ocean to ocean. Captain Dermer, in the service of Gorges, appeared at Manhattan, and laid claim to all the territory occupied by the Dutch. The English embassador at the Dutch capital had been instructed to remonstrate against Dutch intrusion, but it seems his remonstrance was without effect; for in 1621 the States General granted a new charter to the Dutch West India Company, an armed mercantile association, giving them exclusive jurisdiction over the province of New Netherlands for twenty years, with power to appoint governors, subject to the approval of the States; to colonize the territory and administer justice. The executive management was intrusted to a board of directors, distributed through five separate chambers in the cities of Holland. The charge of the province had been assigned to the Amsterdam chamber, which sent out a vessel in 1623, under the direction of Captain May and Adrien Joriszen Tienpont, with thirty families for colonization. A portion of these settled on the Connecticut river, and others as far up the Hudson as the present city of Albany, where they built Fort Orange. A fort was also erected on the Delaware river, near Gloucester, and called Fort Nassau. Their number was shortly after augmented by other accessions, and colonization fairly commenced. In May, 1626, Peter Minuit arrived at New Netherlands as Director-General or Governor of the province. He purchased the whole of Manhattan Island of the Indians for trinkets the value of $24. Friendly courtesies were then exchanged with the Plymouth colony, and a brisk and profitable trade in furs was carried on.

CHAPTER II.

THE DUTCH REGIME IN NEW YORK—RIVAL CLAIMS OF THE ENGLISH—THE LATTER PREVAIL.

TO encourage immigration, in 1629 an ordinance was adopted, granting to any member of the company who within four years should plant a colony of fifty persons, upward of fifteen years old, the privilege of selecting a tract of land sixteen miles in length, on any navigable stream, and inland as far as he should choose, with the title of Patroon, denoting something lordly in rank and means. The Patroons on their part were to buy of the Indians the right to the lands selected, maintain a minister and school-master, and pay duty on trade carried on by them; but the company reserved the exclusive right to the fur trade, which was becoming extensive and attracting dealers from the banks of the St. Lawrence. Several availed themselves of this privilege, among whom were Michael Pauw and Killian Van Rensselaer, the former securing Staten Island and a large tract on the Jersey shore, and the latter a large tract on the Hudson river, now the counties of Albany and Rensselaer. Although the Patroons were excluded in their charter by the company from participating in the fur trade, their interference brought on a controversy, and Minuit, who it was thought favored their pretensions, was recalled. The vessel in which he sailed was detained by the English authorities at Plymouth, on the charge that he had traded and obtained her cargo in territory subject to England, and thus the respective claims of the English and Dutch to the title of New Netherlands were again called in question. The Dutch relied on the discoveries made by

Hudson, and their immediate occupation, ratified by charter; and the English on the prior discovery by Cabot and the grant of James I., covering the territory. No final settlement being obtained, the question was deferred; and in April, 1633, Wouter Van Twiller arrived at New Amsterdam as the new Director-General, bringing with him Everardus Bogardus, a clergyman, Adam Roelandsen, the first school-master to the colony, and a small military force, with which he subsequently made considerable display. Soon after assuming the government, he directed Jacob Van Corlaer to purchase a tract of land of the Indians on the Connecticut river, near the present city of Hartford. The English colonies earnestly remonstrated against this invasion of their territory, but without effect. The Plymouth colony secured a tract of the Indians at Windsor, and sent Lieutenant William Holmes with a force to take possession and commence a settlement. Van Corlaer being unable to oppose them with any effect, Van Twiller sent a force of soldiers to disperse them. The courage of the Dutch commander forsook him on perceiving that they were prepared to meet him, and he refrained from trying to dislodge them. Better success, however, attended him in an expedition against the Virginia colonists. A band of these, under the lead of George Holmes, had taken possession of Fort Nassau on the Delaware river. Van Twiller immediately sent a force there, which captured and brought them as prisoners to Fort Amsterdam. During his administration, Jacob Eelkins, who had formerly been an agent for the company at Fort Orange, arrived at Manhattan as supercargo of an English vessel engaged in the fur trade. Van Twiller refused to let him proceed without a license from the company, which Eelkins declined to present; but claiming a right to trade with the Indians as an Englishman, to whom the territory belonged, he proceeded up the river to Fort Orange, in defiance of the governor, and commenced trading with them. Van Twiller, in great indignation, dispatched a force after him, which took possession of his wares, and bringing his vessel back, sent it out to sea. He was so mindful of his own interests that he became the wealthiest land-holder in the province. Vehemently passionate, he became involved in a bitter quarrel with Bogardus, the clergyman, and with Van Dinklagen, a member of his council. The latter had very justly complained of his rapacity, for which he sent him a prisoner to Holland, on a charge of contumacy. His corruption and incompetency to govern becoming apparent, he was recalled, and William Kieft, in 1638, succeeded him in the government of the colony.

The company in the following year obtained a new charter, limiting the Patroons to four miles on the rivers and eight inland. Other efforts were made to encourage immigration. Settlements were extending in all directions, and the province was rapidly filling with inhabitants. The governor, however, instead of proving useful in promoting the prosperity of the colony with the opportunities presented, became involved in difficulties with the English settlements and the neighboring Indian tribes, which finally brought the colony to the verge of extirpation. By injudicious management and cruelty to the Indians, they were incited to revenge and relentless war on the whites. A robbery having been committed, a tribe of Indians, though innocent, were suspected; and Kieft sent an armed force against them, killing several of their number and destroying their property. The Indians retaliated for this unprovoked attack by murdering some settlers and burning their buildings. The chiefs refused to give satisfaction for these outrages, and Kieft resolved on a war against them. An Indian, whose uncle had been killed by the whites a number of years before, vowed revenge, and killed a Dutchman at Manhattan. Kieft sent a force against his tribe, with orders to exterminate them. Seeing their danger, they sued for peace. Before the terms of a treaty had been agreed upon, a warrior, who had been made drunk and then robbed by the whites, upon recovering his senses killed two of the Dutch. Just at this time the river Indians, in a conflict with the Mohawks, were compelled to take refuge on the Hudson opposite Manhattan, and solicit protection from their enemies; but instead of its being granted, a party under the sanction of Kieft, and against the remonstrance of the best citizens, went over to massacre them. This wicked and inhuman outrage was perpetrated at midnight, and nearly a hundred of these helpless and unsuspecting fugitives were murdered, or driven into the river to perish. A desperate and bloody war was the result. The neighboring tribes joined to avenge this outrage. The dwellings of the settlers were burned, their fields desolated, and themselves shot by their lurking foes. Their settlements were attacked in every direction, and terror, despair and death prevailed. Captain John Underhill, who had gained some notoriety in Indian warfare, was appointed to command the forces of the colonists. He finally succeeded in bringing the Indians to submission, and in 1645 a treaty of peace was concluded. An earnest appeal was made for the recall of Kieft, who had been the cause of this calamitous war. The request was favorably received, and Peter Stuyvesant, who was appointed to succeed him, took charge of the government May 11th, 1647. He had been in the service of the company as Director-General of Curacoa. The controversy between the Dutch and English settlements still continuing, arbitrators were appointed to adjust their claims. The eastern part of Long Island was assigned to the English. A line was specified for the boundary between the Connecticut and New Netherland colonies, but it was unsatisfactory to the Dutch. In 1652 a municipal government was established for Manhattan, consisting of a revenue agent, to be appointed by the company, and two burgomasters and five inferior magistrates, to be elected by the people, and to have jurisdiction in capital cases. The Swedes since the early part of Kieft's administration had been encroaching upon the Dutch territory on the Delaware; and Stuyvesant, by order of the company, went against them with an armed force, recaptured the forts, and resumed possession of the territory. While on this expedition, one of the Indians having been shot by a settler, the savages appeared at

Manhattan in canoes, killed the offender, and crossing to the Jersey shore and Staten Island, began killing other settlers and destroying their property. Stuyvesant returned, and by conciliatory measures restored peace.

In 1664 Charles II. of England, regardless of the claims of the Dutch to New Netherlands, granted to his brother, Duke of York and Albany, afterward James II., the whole country from the Connecticut to the Delaware, including the entire Dutch possessions. A fleet was sent out by the Duke under Colonel Richard Nichols, to enforce his claim and take possession of the Dutch settlements. Arriving in the bay he demanded a surrender, which Stuyvesant at first indignantly refused; but because of the unwillingness of the colonists to fight in his defense and of their insisting upon capitulation, together with the favorable nature of the terms offered, he was induced to yield, and on the 3d of September, 1664, the province was surrendered, and the government of the colony passed into the hands of the English. The names New Netherlands and New Amsterdam were changed to New York, and Fort Orange to Albany. It is supposed that at this time the province contained about six thousand inhabitants. Soon after the surrender the Duke conveyed to Lord Berkley and Sir George Carteret what now constitutes the State of New Jersey, over which a separate proprietary government was established. In 1682 William Penn purchased the settlements on the Delaware, which were annexed to Pennsylvania. Nichols, who became governor, devoted much time to confirming grants under the Dutch government by issuing new ones, and thus making a heavy expense to the land-owners. He changed the form of the municipal government of New York June 12th, 1666, by granting a city charter, placing the executive power in the hands of a mayor, aldermen and sheriff, all to be appointed by the governor. An invasion from Holland had been feared, and preparations for defense had incurred an increase of taxation, of which the colony greatly complained, in consequence of which Nichols resigned his office in 1668, and Colonel Francis Lovelace was appointed to succeed him. Holland being involved in a war with England, an opportunity was presented for the Dutch to regain their lost possessions in America, and for that purpose they sent out a squadron, which anchored at Staten Island July 30th, 1673. The fort at New York was in charge of Captain John Manning, who treacherously surrendered without making any effort to resist. The city was again in the possession of the Dutch, and Captain Anthony Clove in command of the province. Manning was afterward tried and convicted by court-martial of cowardice and treachery, and adjudged to have his sword broken over his head in front of the City Hall, and to be incapacitated from holding any office. Under Clove the Dutch claims to the province were reasserted, and preparations made for a vigorous defense in case of an attempt on the part of the English for its recapture; but by the provisions of a peace concluded February 9th, 1674, the province reverted to the English. To silence all controversy respecting his claims, the Duke of York obtained a new patent from the King to confirm the one granted in 1664, and commissioned Major Edmund Andros as governor. His arbitrary course made his administration very unpopular. He endeavored to extend his jurisdiction to the Connecticut river, but his claims were stoutly resisted by the people of that province, and he finally concluded to abandon the design. He quarreled with and disputed the right of Philip Carteret, who administered the government of East Jersey, arresting and bringing him prisoner to New York. For this act the proprietors of the New Jersey government preferred charges against him, which he was summoned to England to answer. He returned, to continue his oppressions, but the resistance of the people against him was so strong that he was recalled, and Thomas Dongan appointed as his successor, who arrived August 27th, 1683. Through the influence of William Penn he was instructed to organize a popular assembly, and accordingly, soon after his arrival, issued orders for the choosing of representatives. This, the first Colonial Assembly of New York, was convened October 17th, 1683, and consisted of a council of ten and seventeen representatives. A charter of liberties was framed, vesting the supreme legislative power in the governor and council and the people in general assembly; conferring the right of suffrage on the freeholders without restraint; providing that no freeman should suffer but by judgment of his peers, and that all trials should be by a jury of twelve men. The imposition of any tax without the consent of the assembly was prohibited. Martial law was not to exist, and neither soldiers nor seamen were to be quartered on the inhabitants against their will. The province was divided into counties, and the representatives were apportioned according to the population.

CHAPTER III.

THE FIVE NATIONS—THEIR TRADITIONS OF THEIR ORIGIN—IROQUOIS CUSTOMS AND POLITICAL ORGANIZATION.

THE greater portion of what now constitutes the State of New York, when first visited by Europeans, was found to be inhabited by five distinct and powerful tribes of Indians, who had united and formed a confederacy. The tribes that composed this confederacy were the Mohawks, Oneidas, Onondagas, Cayugas and Senecas, called by the English the Five Nations, and by the French the Iroquois. They bore among themselves the title *Aquinoshioni* or *Konoshioni*, signifying Cabinmakers, or People of the Long House, referring to their organization and territorial possessions, which extended from the banks of the Hudson to the shores of Lake Erie. Their government was, in many respects, republican, and the wisdom displayed in the management of their affairs distinguished them above all the other aborigines of the continent. At what time the confederacy was formed is unknown, its origin being as much involved in the obscurities of tradition as any other remote event of Indian history. Some as the result of their investigations have fixed the period less than a century before the Europeans came into the country, while others have placed it more than two centuries earlier. The current tradition held by the Iroquois respecting their origin was that they sprang from the earth itself:

"In remote ages, they had been confined under a mountain near the falls of the Osh-wa-kee or Oswego river, whence they were released by Tharonhyjagon, the Holder of the Heavens. Bidding them go forth to the east, he guided them to the valley of the Mohawk, and following its stream they reached the Hudson, which some of them descended to the sea. Retracing their steps toward the west, they originated in their order and position the Mohawks, Oneidas, Onondagas, Cayugas, Senecas and Tuscaroras, six nations, but the Tuscaroras wandered away to the south and settled on the Cantano or Neuse river, in North Carolina, reducing the number to five nations.

"Each of the tribes thus originated was independent of the others, and they warred with each other, as well as with the surrounding tribes. Tharonhyjagon still remained with the tribes; gave them seeds of various kinds, with the proper knowledge for planting them; taught them how to kill and roast game; made the forests free to all the tribes to hunt, and removed obstructions from the streams. After this he laid aside his divine character and resolved to live with the Onondagas, that he might exemplify the maxims he had taught. For this purpose he selected a handsome spot of ground on the southern bank of the lake called Teonto, being the sheet of water now known as Cross lake. Here he built a cabin, and took a wife of the Onondagas, by whom he had an only daughter, whom he tenderly loved, and most kindly and carefully treated and instructed. The excellence of his character and his great sagacity and good counsels led the people to view him with veneration, and they gave him the name of Hi-a-wat-ha, signifying "a very wise man." From all quarters people came to him for advice, and in this manner all power came naturally into his hands, and he was regarded as the first chief in all the land. Under his teachings the Onondagas became the first among all the original clans. They were the wisest counselors, the best orators, the most expert hunters and the bravest warriors. Hence the Onondagas were early noted among all the tribes for their pre-eminence.

"While Hiawatha was thus living in quiet among the people of the hills, the tribes were attacked by a furious and powerful enemy from the north of the great lakes. This enemy advanced into the country and laid waste the villages, and slaughtered men, women and children, until the people had no heart to oppose the invaders. In this emergency they fled to Hiawatha for advice, who counseled them to call together all the tribes from the east and from the west; saying 'Our safety is not alone in the club and dart, but in wise counsels.' He appointed a place on the banks of the Onondaga lake for the meeting, and thither the chiefs, warriors and head men forthwith assembled in large numbers, bringing with them their women and children.

"The council had been waiting for three days, but as yet Hiawatha was absent. Messengers were dispatched to hasten his attendance, but they found him gloomy and depressed. He told them that evil lay in his path, and he felt that he should be called to make some great sacrifice; nevertheless, he would attend the council. The talismanic white canoe in which he always made his voyages, and which the people had learned to reverence, was got out, and Hiawatha and his daughter took their seats. Gliding silently down the deep waters of the Seneca, the canoe reached the outlet, and entered on the placid Onondaga. As the canoe of the venerated chief appeared he was welcomed with loud shouts, but while he was measuring his steps toward the council ground, a long and low sound was heard, and instantly all eyes were turned upward, where a compact mass of cloudy darkness appeared, which gathered size and velocity as it approached, and appeared to be directed inevitably to fall in the midst of the assembly. Every one fled but Hiawatha and his daughter, who calmly awaited the issue. The force of the descending body was like that of a sudden storm; and hardly had Hiawatha paused, when an immense bird, with long distended wings, came down with a swoop and crushed the daughter to the earth. The very semblance of a human being was destroyed in the remains of the girl, and the head and neck of the bird were buried in the ground from the force of the fall.

"Hiawatha was inconsolable for several days; but at length took his place in the council, and the deliberations opened. The subject of the invasion was discussed by several of the ablest counselors, and various plans proposed to foil the enemy. Hiawatha listened to the debate, and at its conclusion bade the warriors to depart until the next day, when he would unfold his plan, which he felt confident would insure safety.

"The council again met; and with even more than ordinary attention the people listened to the words of their great chief. Hiawatha counseled them that to oppose these hordes of northern tribes singly and alone would prove certain destruction; that to oppose them successfully the tribes must unite in one common band of brothers; must have one voice, one fire, one pipe, and one war club. In the confederacy which he proposed should be formed, the several tribes were assigned the position they were to thereafter occupy, and in conclusion he urged them to weigh well his words; that if they should unite in the bond he had proposed, the Great Spirit would smile upon them, and they would be free, prosperous and happy; but if they rejected his counsel, they would be enslaved, ruined, and perhaps annihilated forever.

"The tribes received the address in solemn silence, and the council closed to deliberate on the plan recommended. Assembling the next day, the union of the tribes into one confederacy was discussed, and unanimously adopted. Pending this result, Hiawatha, warned by the death of his daughter that his mission was accomplished, prepared to make his final departure from earth. Before the council dispersed he recounted the services he had rendered to his people, and urged them to preserve the union they had formed, telling them that if they preserved it, and admitted no foreign element of power by the admission of other nations, they would always be free, numerous, and happy. 'If other nations are admitted to your councils, they will sow the seeds of jealousy and discord, and you will become few, feeble, and enslaved. Remember these words; they are the last you will hear from the lips of Hiawatha. The Great Master of breath calls me to go. I have waited patiently his summons, and am ready to go.' As his voice ceased, sweet sounds from the air burst on the ears of the multitude; and while all attention was engrossed in the celestial melody, Hiawatha was seen seated in his white canoe, in the mid-air, rising with every choral chant that burst out, till the clouds shut the sight, and the melody ceased."

This confederation, which was undoubtedly established for the purpose of common defense, was a very powerful and effective alliance. In the general council of the confederacy the Senecas, who were much more numerous than the other nations, were represented by two delegates, and each of the others by one. The presiding officer at the council was always assigned to the Onondagas, and to the Mohawks the principal war-chief. Their power was in their union, which differed from that of other nations in its perpetuity, the latter frequently securing the same results by temporary alliances in case of war. The delegates spoke the popular will of the tribes they represented, and to determine their action they were not permitted to approve any measure which the tribe had not indorsed by a unanimous vote. Each nation was governed by its own chiefs, civil and military, who might declare war and conclude peace on their own account; claimed dominion over territory defined by general boundaries, and was perfectly independent of control by other members of the confederacy, except when national or confederated action required the concurrence of all the tribes. When the united tribes in council made a decision, it was unanimous. The question then had to be referred to the warriors of each tribe, assembled in council, where a unanimous decision was also required; hence every resolve was clothed with the full popular will.

The matrons of the tribe in council could command a cessation of hostilities, and when they so determined the chiefs and warriors returned from the war-path without compromising their character for bravery. For this purpose a male functionary, the messenger of the matrons, who was a good speaker, was designated to perform an office which was deemed unsuitable to the female. When the proposition for a cessation of war was resolved upon, the message was delivered to this officer, and he was bound to enforce it with all the powers of eloquence he possessed. The following description is given of their national council. "The council-house was built of bark. On each side six seats were placed, each containing six persons. No one was admitted besides the members of the council, except a few who were particularly honored. If one arose to speak all the rest sat in profound silence, smoking their pipes. The speaker uttered his words in a singing tone, always rising a few notes at the close of each sentence. Whatever was pleasing to the council was confirmed by all by the word nee, or yes, and at the end of each speech the whole company joined in applauding the speaker, by calling 'Ho! Ho!' At noon two men entered bearing upon a pole across their shoulders a large kettle filled with meat, which was first presented to the guests. A large wooden ladle, as broad and deep as a common bowl, hung with a hook to the side of the kettle, with which every one might at once help himself to as much as he could eat. The whole was conducted in a very decent and quiet manner. Indeed, now and then, one would lie flat upon his back and rest himself, and sometimes they would stop, joke, and laugh heartily."

The Iroquois were divided into clans or families, distinguished by as many different sorts of arms or emblems, each being made to represent the clan or family to which it belonged. A sachem of one of these families, when he signed an instrument of conveyance or public paper, put his emblem upon it, representing the animal by which his family was designated. The first was that of the tortoise, and was first because they pretended that when the earth was made it was placed on a great turtle, and when there was an earthquake it was the turtle that stirred. Other families were designated by such names as the wolf and the bear.

All their affairs were under the direction of their chiefs, who obtained their authority by the general opinion of their courage and conduct, and whenever they failed to appear to the Indians in a praiseworthy light, their dignity ceased. Though the son was respected on account of valuable services performed by his father, yet without personal merit he could not attain his rank. Whatever pertained to hereditary descent was confined to the female line, and the chieftainship fell upon the son of a chief's daughter, to the exclusion of his uncle; but the chief's brother would succeed him instead of his own son in case there were no descendants through the female line. The language used by the Iroquois, both in their speeches and in ordinary conversations, was exceedingly figurative. Many of their chiefs were distinguished for their eloquence.

An early historian of New York, writing at the time when the Five Nations still constituted a powerful body, in regard to their manners and customs, says: "The manners of these savages are as simple as their government. Their houses are a few crotched stakes thrust into the ground and overlaid with bark. A fire is kindled in the middle, and an aperture left at the top for the conveyance of the smoke. Whenever a considerable number of these huts are collected they have a castle, as it is called, consisting of a square without bastions, surrounded with palisades. They have no other fortification, and this is only designed as an asylum for their old men, wives and children, while the rest are gone out to war

While the women cultivate a little spot of ground for corn, the men employ themselves in hunting. The men frequently associate themselves for conversation, by which means they not only preserve the remembrance of their wars and treaties, but diffuse among their youth incitements to glory, as well as instructions in all the subleties of war."

Before they went out they had a feast on dog's flesh, and a great war dance, at which the warriors, who were frightfully painted with vermilion, rose up and sung their exploits, or those of their ancestors, and thereby kindled a military enthusiasm in the whole company. The day after the dance they would go out a few miles, in single file, observing a profound silence. The procession being ended, they stripped the bark from a large tree, and painted the design of their expedition on the naked trunk. The figure of a canoe, with the number of men it, indicated the strength of their party; and by a deer, fox, or some other emblem, painted at its head, it was discovered against what nation they had gone. On their return, before they entered the village, two heralds advanced and set up a yell, which by its modulation intimated either good or bad news. . If the news was good the village was notified of it, and an entertainment provided for the conquerors, one of whom on their approach bore the scalps which they had taken, stretched over a bow, and elevated upon a pole. The boldest man in the village came out to receive it, and then ran at the top of his speed to where the rest were collected. If overtaken he was severely beaten, but if he outran the pursuers he was allowed to participate in the honor of the victors, who neither spoke nor received compliments until the feast was over. Then one of the victors was appointed to relate the whole adventure, while all the rest listened attentively till the close, when they all joined in a savage dance.

CHAPTER IV.

FRENCH AND INDIAN WARS—DISSENSIONS IN THE COLONIAL GOVERNMENT—CAPTURE AND EXECUTION OF LEISLER.

AT the time Champlain ascended the St. Lawrence, he found the Algonquins at war with the Iroquois, and by an alliance of his forces with the former, he enabled them, by the use of fire-arms (to them hitherto unknown), to gain a victory over their enemies. In consequence of this alliance a bitter hostility was created on the part of the Iroquois toward the French. The latter, however, were successful in gaining the confidence and friendship of the other tribes with whom they came in contact. Through the influence of their missionaries, the traders were enabled to establish their posts among them at pleasure, and navigate the lakes and rivers. Although the artful Jesuit missionaries had persistently endeavored to win back the friendship of the Iroquois, they effected but little until New York fell into the hands of the English. Since their trade and intimacy with the Dutch, they had availed themselves of fire-arms, renewed their warfare upon the Algonquins with success, repelled the invasions of the French, and, in turn, attacking them, swept over their settlements with fire and tomahawk, carrying consternation in their path even to the gates of Quebec. In 1666 the French and Adirondacks successfully invaded the country of the Mohawks, but the year following a peace was concluded, chiefly through the agency of the English colonial government, acting in obedience to the instructions of the Duke of York, to whom the colony had been granted, and who, in his bigoted and blind attachment to the Church of Rome, was desirous of securing a peace between the French and the Iroquois, with a view to handing the latter over as converts to that church.

Trade, after this peace, was profitably prosecuted by both the French and English; but the French, through their artful Catholic missionaries, were gaining a decided advantage. Through the instigation of these wily priests, hostilities had been committed on the frontier settlements of Maryland and Virginia by the Five Nations. To adjust this difficulty, a council of the chiefs met the Governors of Virginia and New York at Albany, in 1684. At this council the difficulties with Virginia were amicably settled, and Governor Dongan succeeded in completely gaining the friendship of the Five Nations. While these conferences were in progress, a messenger arrived from De la Barre, Governor of Canada, complaining of the Senecas for their hostilities against the Miamis and other western tribes, with whom the French were allied, whereby their trade was interrupted. This message was communicated to the Indian chiefs, and served to confirm their resolutions of friendship for the English, and revive their slumbering hatred of the French. Immediately on the return of the messenger, De la Barre, meditating the destruction of the Five Nations, proceeded with an army of French and Indians to Lake Ontario. The French Catholics had procured a letter from the Duke of York to Governor Dongan, instructing him to lay no obstacles in the way of the invaders; but Dongan, regardless of this command, apprised the Indians of their designs and also promised to assist them. Owing to sickness in his army, De la Barre was unable to encounter his foes, and found it necessary to conclude his campaign by offering terms of peace, which were haughtily accepted, and he was allowed to depart. He was succeeded in the following year by the Marquis de Denonville, who, with a reinforcement of troops, was sent over to repair the disgrace of De la Barre. In 1687, to prevent the interruption of trade with the Miamis, the country of the Senecas was invaded. The French, through the agency of their missionary to the Onondagas, enticed the Iroquois chiefs into their power, under pretense of making a treaty, and then seized and sent them, with others they had taken prisoners, to France, where they were consigned to the galleys. The Seneca country was overrun without serious resistance, and a fort erected at the mouth of the Niagara river. A peace was finally proposed through the interposition of Governor Dongan, who was for compelling the French to apply to him in the affairs of the Five Nations, but its conditions were rejected by the French. The Five Nations, maddened by this refusal and by the outrages committed upon them, flew to arms, and with twelve hundred warriors descended upon the French settlements with such terrible vengeance that the terms that had been offered for peace were accepted, and the whole region south of the great lakes abandoned by the French.

The Duke of York, on his accession to the throne of England in 1685, under the title of James II., directed Governor Dongan to encourage the Catholic priests who came to reside with the Five Nations, ostensibly for advancing the Popish cause, but really to gain them over to the French interests. Governor Dongan, although a Catholic, was apprehensive of the insidious designs of the French, and effectually resisted this policy, thereby displeasing his bigoted master. He also instructed Governor Dongan to allow no printing press to be established in the colony, and discouraged representative government. Catholics were appointed to fill all the offices, and Dongan, who, in his endeavors to protect the true interest of the province by opposing the Catholic missionaries, became obnoxious to the King, was recalled, and Francis Nicholson, the deputy of Sir Edmund Andros, who had been commissioned governor of both New England and New York, assumed temporary charge of the government in August, 1688. The revolution in England, resulting in the abdication of James II., and the accession of William and Mary, caused the authority of Nicholson under the dethroned king to be questioned. On one side it was claimed that the government in England did not affect affairs in the province, and that Nicholson's authority was unimpaired till the will of the new monarch was known; on the other side, that the government, extending to the colonies, was overthrown, and as no one was invested with authority in the provinces, it reverted to the people, who might appoint a person to exercise control until one had been commissioned by the ruling power. The advocates of the former of these views were mostly the wealthy and aristocratic, while the mass of the people favored the latter. The government was vested in a committee of safety, who took possession of the fort at New York, and entrusted the exercise of authority to Jacob Leisler, the popular leader, Nicholson in the meantime having returned to England. Leisler sent a statement of what had been done to King William, and dispatched Milborne, his son-in-law, to Albany with an armed force, to secure the recognition of his authority, sanction to which had been refused. A letter from the English ministry arrived, directed to Francis Nicholson, or in his absence to such person as for the time being might be in charge of the government, directing him to take chief command of the province, and to call to his aid such as he should deem proper. Leisler, considering it addressed to himself, assumed command, and appointed a council of advisers. The revolution in England which placed William and Mary upon the throne was followed by a war between England and France, and the colonies were of course involved in the conflict. Count Frontenac, who had succeeded Denonville as governor of Canada, made an effort to detach the Five Nations from the English interest. He sent a secret expedition against Schenectady, which attacked that city, near midnight, on the 8th of February, 1690, and a frightful massacre of the inhabitants ensued. The peril of Albany, from such deadly attacks, induced its inhabitants to submit to the authority of Leisler. Expeditions were fitted out against the French and Indians, and a fleet sent out for the reduction of Quebec, but all proved unsuccessful. In March, 1691, Henry Sloughter arrived as governor, having been commissioned by the King in 1689. His coming was heralded by Richard Ingolsby, who, without proper credentials, demanded the surrender of the fort at New York. This Leisler very properly refused, but consented to defer to Sloughter when he should arrive. Sloughter on his arrival sent Ingolsby with verbal directions for the surrender of the fort, but Leisler still refused, and asked for an interview with the governor. The next day he complied, but this imprudent hesitation was seized upon by his enemies, who arrested him and his son-in-law on the charge of treason. They were tried by a special committee and condemned to suffer death. Governor Sloughter hesitated to execute this sentence, but their enemies, anxious for their execution, and failing in all attempts to procure his signature, availed themselves of his known intemperate habits, invited him to a banquet, persuaded him to sign the death warrant while intoxicated, and before he recovered from his debauch, the prisoners were executed.

During the agitations attending this foul judicial murder, the Indians, from neglect, became disaffected toward the English, insomuch that they sent an embassy of peace to Count Frontenac; to counteract this, a council with the Five Nations was held at Albany, and the covenant chain renewed. In order to maintain this advantage, Major Schuyler, in whom the Five Nations had great confidence, led them in an invasion of Canada, and signally defeated the French. The intemperate habits of Sloughter brought on a severe illness, from which he died on the 23d of July, 1691, thus ending a weak and turbulent administration. Upon the death of Sloughter the chief command was committed to Richard Ingoldsby, to the exclusion of Joseph Dudley, who, but for his absence, would have had the right to preside, and upon whom the government devolved; and as Dudley, on his return, did not contest the authority of Ingoldsby, the latter governed until the arrival of Benjamin Fletcher, with a commission as governor, in August, 1692. He was a man of small ability and violent temper, active and avaricious, but prudently took Major Schuyler into his counsel, and was guided by his opinions in Indian affairs. His administration was so successful the first year that he received large supplies from the Assembly. The unamiable traits of his character were soon exhibited, however, and during most of his administration he was engaged in controversies with the Assembly, principally in regard to appropriations for his expenses, for which he made extravagant demands. He was bigotedly attached to the Episcopal form of church government, and encouraged English churches and schools in place of Dutch. He procured an act from the Assembly the provisions of which, though admitting of a more liberal construction, he interpreted as a recognition of the Episcopal instead of the Dutch church, and under this act Trinity church was organized. A printing press was established in New York city in 1693, by William Bradford, who was employed by the city to print the corporation laws.

CHAPTER V.

COUNT FRONTENAC'S CAMPAIGNS—PREVALENCE OF PIRACY—MISGOVERNMENT OF NEW YORK—FRENCH TRADING AND MILITARY POSTS.

IN 1693 Count Frontenac set out from Montreal with an army of French and Indians, and invaded the Mohawk country, capturing their castles, killing some of the tribe, and taking about three hundred prisoners. Schuyler, with the militia of Albany, hastened to the assistance of the Mohawks, and pursued the enemy in their retreat, retaking about fifty prisoners. In 1696 Count Frontenac made another effort for the subjugation of the Five Nations. With an army of regular troops and Indians under his command, he ascended the St. Lawrence to Cadaraqui, now Kingston; then, crossing to Oswego, made a descent upon the Onondagas, who, apprised of his coming, set fire to and deserted their principal towns. On retracing his march he found his progress obstructed by the Onondagas, and incursions into Canada by the Five Nations were again renewed. In the following year the war between France and England was terminated by the peace of Ryswick, and these barbarous hostilities ceased.

During the late war piracy had prevailed, and was believed to be encouraged by the governments, for the annoyance of the commerce of their respective enemies. Merchant vessels were destroyed within sight of the harbor of New York, the commercial depot of the pirates, some of whom had sailed from there, having a good understanding with Fletcher and other officers. The extinction of piracy was loudly demanded, and the English government found it necessary to resort to vigorous measures for this end; and consequently, in 1695 Fletcher was recalled, and Richard, Earl of Bellomont, appointed in his place, with instructions for the suppression of this evil. The Earl of Bellomont, whose commission included the governments of Massachusetts and New Hampshire as well as New York, did not arrive until May, 1698. Before leaving England, an armed vessel was fitted out by Bellomont and others, and placed under the command of Captain William Kidd, who sailed from England in 1696, and after cruising for a while, turned pirate himself, and became the most bold and daring of the ocean marauders. He returned to New York with his booty and concealed portions of it on Long Island. He was subsequently arrested in Boston, by order of the governor, on a charge of piracy, sent to England for trial, and there convicted and executed. Bellomont favored the Democratic or Leislerian party, and the new Assembly in 1699 being also Democratic, an act was passed by which the families of Leisler and Milborne were reinstated in their possessions. Bellomont died in 1701, and John Nanfan, the lieutenant-governor, upon whom the government devolved, succeeded him until the arrival, in 1702, of Lord Cornbury, who was appointed by King William as a reward for his desertion of James II., in whose army he had been an officer. His administration was chiefly distinguished for its intolerance, and he received the unenviable distinction of being the worst governor under the English regime. With savage bigotry he sought to establish the Church of England by imprisoning dissenting clergymen, and prohibiting them from exercising their functions without his special license, and he even robbed one clergyman of his house and glebe. With insatiable rapacity he plundered the public treasury, and opposed every measure of the people for the security of their rights. Destitute of gratitude, licentious and base, he completed the universal contempt in which he was held by appearing in public dressed in women's clothes. As he had become an object of abhorrence, the Queen, through the pressure of popular sentiment, felt compelled to revoke his commission. As soon as he was deposed he was thrown into prison by his creditors, where he remained until the death of his father, when he became Earl of Clarendon. Upon the death of King William, his commission was renewed by the Queen, who at the same time gave him the chief command of New Jersey, the government of which the proprietors had surrendered into her hands. He was succeeded December 18th, 1708, by Lord Lovelace, who died on the 5th of May following, leaving the government in the hands of Lieutenant-Governor Ingoldsby, whose administration is only remarkable for an unsuccessful expedition, under Colonel Nicholson, for the reduction of Canada. This failure was chiefly through the mismanagement of Ingoldsby, who was consequently removed April 10th, 1710, and Gerardus Beekman, the oldest member of the council, exercised the authority of governor till June 14th, when Robert Hunter arrived with a commission as governor. This year Colonel Schuyler went to England to urge the importance of subduing Canada, taking with him the chiefs of the Five Nations, who were highly gratified with their voyage and reception.

The ensuing year another expedition for the reduction of Canada was undertaken. Four thousand troops were raised in the colonies under Colonel Nicholson, to join an English fleet and land force before Quebec. Arriving in the St. Lawrence, many of the ships were wrecked, and about a thousand soldiers lost, which put an end to the campaign. Nicholson, who had proceeded as far as Lake George, on hearing this news returned, and the expedition proved an entire failure. It had entailed a heavy debt upon the province, in consequence of which the governor's influence was somewhat impaired, he having entered into it with much zeal. His request for a permanent appropriation for the government was refused by the Assembly, which brought him into several unhappy contests with that body. In March, 1713, the war between England and France terminated by the treaty of Utrecht, in which the English supremacy over the Five Nations was conceded by the French, and an end put to the infliction of Indian hostilities. The Five Nations being relieved from hostilities with the French, engaged in conflict with the Indians at the south. The Tuscaroras, a tribe kindred to the Iroquois, residing in North Carolina, having been greatly reduced by a war with the whites, and being unable to resist their encroachments, removed to the north and joined the confederacy. They settled near Lake Oneida, among the Five Nations, and the confederates were thenceforward called the Six Nations. Hunter remained at the head of the government untill 1719, when, his health failing, he returned to England. His intercourse with the Assembly was agreeable during the latter part of his administration, and his attachment to the interests of the colony made his departure regretted.

The government devolved upon Peter Schuyler, the oldest member of the council, who successfully administered affairs until the arrival of William Burnet, September 17th, 1720. A trading post was commenced at Oswego in 1722, by Governor Burnet, in order to engross the trade of the Six Nations, and with the farther design of following it up on the lakes to the westward, to obtain the trade of the more remote tribes. A congress of several colonies was held at Albany to meet the Six Nations, whereby the chain of friendship was strengthened, and trade with remoter tribes promoted. The establishment of this post at Oswego was highly displeasing to the French, and in order to intercept the trade from the upper lakes they obtained consent of the Iroquois, through the influence of the Jesuits, to rebuild their trading-house and fort at Niagara, and also decided to erect a chain of military posts to the Ohio river, so as to cut off and confine the English trade. Though not without opposition, they succeeded in erecting their fort at Niagara. Although some of the members of the Six Nations were opposed to this invasion by the French, it succeeded through the disaffection of a party of merchants and others interested in the French trading policy, who, since the peace of Utrecht, had carried on a good trade with Montreal, through the aid of Indian carriers, and were opposed to the governor's policy. The Assembly was also strongly tinctured with this spirit of opposition, and refused a renewal of supplies except for short periods. This body was dissolved in 1727, but the next was quite as stubborn, and it was likewise dissolved, and the governor could only erect a small military defense for the post at Oswego, which, to his credit and the colony's shame, was at his own expense. On the accession of George II., Burnet was, through the efforts of his enemies, transferred to the government of Massachusetts, and John Montgomery appointed to succeed him. He entered upon his duties April 15th, 1728. His short administration is not distinguished for any important event. In 1729 the King, against the wishes of the best citizens of the colony, repealed the acts prohibiting the trade in Indian goods between Albany and Montreal. A line was surveyed and agreed upon between Connecticut and New York in 1731. The establishment of this partition gave to New York a tract of land formerly on the Connecticut side, called from its figure the "Oblong," as an equivalent for lands near the sound, surrendered to Connecticut.

Montgomery died July 1st, 1731, and was succeeded by Rip Van Dam, whose administration was unfortunately signalized by the erection of a fort at Crown Point by the French, without resistance from the acting governor. The arrival of Colonel William Cosby, August 1st, 1732, finished his administration, and began one rendered memorable for its arbitrary proceedings and tumult, rather than for striking or important events. Among the first of Cosby's acts was a demand that Rip Van Dam, his predecessor, should divide equally with him the emoluments of the office before his arrival. Van Dam assented, on the condition that Cosby should reciprocate by an equal division of the perquisites received by him from the colonies since his appointment and before coming to this country. This demand on the part of Van Dam was sustained by the people generally, but Cosby, despotic and avaricious, refused, and commenced a suit against Van Dam for half of his salary. As the governor by virtue of his office was chancellor, and two of the judges his personal friends, the counsel for defense took exceptions against the jurisdiction of the court. The exceptions were overruled by the judges in the interest of Cosby, even against the opinion of Chief Justice Morris, who was immediately removed from his office and Colonel Cosby's claim ordered paid. The indignation of the public at such arbitrary proceedings found vent in squibs and ballads, aimed at the aristocracy, and placing some of the members of the legislature in a ludicrous position. The *New York Weekly Journal*, edited by John P. Zenger, in defending Van Dam published some severe criticisms on the government, arraigning the officials for assuming arbitrary power and perverting their official stations to purposes of private emolument. These papers were ordered to be burnt by the common hangman, and Zenger was arrested and imprisoned on a criminal charge for publishing a seditious libel against the government. When the trial came on, the publication was admitted, and proof offered for its justification, which was objected to by the attorney-general, on the ground that in a criminal proceeding for the publication of libellous matter, the truth of the facts alleged was not proper to be admitted in evidence, and he was sustained by the court.

Andrew Hamilton, the counsel for the defense, resisted this decision of the court, and insisted that the jury were the judges of both the facts and the law, and it was for them to interpose between arbitrary violations of law and justice and their intended victim. The jury, after a short deliberation, gave a unanimous verdict of acquittal. Cosby, although repulsed by this verdict, persistently continued to make himself odious to the people by other arbitrary measures. A few days before his death he convened his council in his bed-chamber and suspended Van Dam, the senior member thereof, upon whom the government would have devolved upon his decease. He died March 10th, 1736. The council convened immediately after his death, and George Clarke, next senior counselor, was declared president, and assumed the authority of governor. The suspension of Van Dam was declared illegal by a powerful party in his favor, and a struggle ensued between him and Clarke for the office, both exercising authority until October 30th, when Clarke received a commission from England to act as lieutenant-governor. He sought to conciliate those hostile to him, and to keep in favor with the aristocratic party at the same time. He dissolved the Assembly that had continued in existence for many years, and a new one was elected, which, to his chagrin and regret, was in sympathy with the popular party, and at its session could not be prevailed upon to grant a revenue for a longer period than one year, establishing a precedent that subsequent Assemblies did not depart from.

CHAPTER VI.

THE ALLEGED PLOT TO BURN NEW YORK—FRENCH AND ENGLISH HOSTILITIES—THE CONTEST FOR THE OHIO VALLEY.

IN 1741, several fires having occurred in New York, suspicions were awakened that a conspiracy had been formed for the destruction of the city. It was not long before it was charged upon the negro slaves, who at that time constituted about one-fifth of the population. Universal consternation seized upon the inhabitants, and a general panic ensued, in which reason and common sense were scarcely entertained. Rewards were offered for the arrest and conviction of the offenders, and a full pardon tendered to any of their number who would reveal their knowledge of the conspiracy. A weak negro girl, named Mary Burton, a servant in a low boarding house, after much importunity and full promise of pardon, implicated several negroes, by confessing to have heard them talking privately about burning the city. They were arrested and executed on this slender testimony. Others, among them several whites, were implicated by her, and suffered the same fate. Other informers appeared, arrests became numerous, and the popular fury and delusion did not subside until Mary Burton, the chief informer, after frequent examinations, began to touch characters above suspicion and known to be innocent. Then, as reason began to return, the delusion passed away, but not until one hundred and fifty-four negroes and twenty-four whites had been committed to prison, and nearly forty of these unfortunates executed. In the commencement of his administration Clarke had succeeded in conciliating both parties to a considerable extent, but managed before its close to lose the confidence of both, insomuch that his retirement, on the arrival of his successor, Admiral George Clinton, September 23d, 1743, was but little regretted. Favorable accounts of Clinton's talents and liberality had been proclaimed, and he was received with demonstrations of universal satisfaction. The election of a new Assembly was ordered, and a spirit of harmony so far prevailed that he concurred in all its measures.

In March, 1744, war was declared between England and France, and measures were again taken for the conquest of Canada. The colonies of New York and New England united in an expedition, to co-operate with a fleet under Commodore Warren, for an attack on the French fortress at Louisburg, on Cape Breton Island, which capitulated in June, 1745. The country north of Albany was seriously molested by attacks from the Indians and French. The fort at Crown Point was garrisoned with a force sufficient to enable its commander to send out detachments to destroy the English settlements. The settlement at Saratoga was burned, and nearly all the inhabitants either killed or taken prisoners. This was followed by an attack on the village of Hoosick. The fort at that place was commanded by Colonel Hawks, who was compelled to surrender, thus leaving the settlements, all the way to Albany, open to the enemy; but measures were speedily adopted for putting the frontier in a state of defense. In 1746 an expedition against Canada was resolved upon by the English government. The colonies, with the promise of assistance from England, entered upon the design with much zeal. New York raised sixteen hundred men for the forces directed upon Crown Point and Montreal. England failed to furnish the promised assistance, and the expedition proved unsuccessful. Peace was concluded at Aix la Chapelle in 1748. Hostilities ceased, and the colony enjoyed a short period of tranquillity. The harmony between the Assembly and the governor did not long continue, for, in 1745, an open disagreement occurred, and almost constant bickerings followed. In 1748 Clinton sent a message to the Assembly, demanding an appropriation for the support of the government for five years. The Assembly, justly regarding it as a direct attempt to render the crown independent of the people, indignantly refused; and after a few weeks' contention, the governor prorogued that body, and by successive prorogations prevented it from sitting for nearly two years, until the affairs of the colony were in an alarming condition for want of funds. His reiterated demands for a permanent revenue met with persistent refusal. Opposed and embarrassed by political factions, he tendered his resignation, after an administration of ten years, and was succeeded October 10th, 1753, by Sir Danvers Osborne. The new governor immediately informed the council that his instructions were to maintain the royal prerogative and demand a permanent support for the government. He was told by the members present that the Assembly would never submit to the demand, and appeared greatly depressed, the loss of his wife a short time before having already thrown him into a melancholy state of mind, bordering on insanity. Knowing the difficulties that his predecessor had experienced, and being charged with instructions still more stringent, he saw in the tempest before him a prospect which so worked upon his morbid mind that the next morning he was found dead, having hung himself at his lodgings. On his death, James de Lancey, by virtue of his commission as lieutenant-governor, assumed the administration of the government. He had formerly been a leader in the aristocratic party, but recently had opposed the demands of the crown, and consequently had become highly popular. Striving to retain his popularity by favoring the representatives in measures advantageous to the colony, while holding his office at the will of the English government, and being compelled by the instructions of his predecessor to convince the ministry that he was zealous to promote the interests of the crown, his task was peculiarly difficult; but it was performed with a shrewdness and skill creditable to his ability as a statesman.

By the treaty of Aix la Chapelle, the boundary between the French and English colonies was left as indefinite as before, and consequently those lands which both claimed the right to possess were still in dispute. The French had established their trading posts, missionary stations and fortifications from Canada to the gulf of Mexico, and were vigorously pursuing their designs for the extension of their power and dominions. The English Ohio Company, formed for settlement and trade with the Indians, obtained, in 1749, a grant from the British government of an extensive tract of land on the Ohio river. Christopher Gist was sent out in 1751 to explore this region, and found that it had already been visited by the French traders, who had so influenced the Indians that they were very suspicious of the designs of the English. The claim of the French to the ownership of this region was priority of discovery and occupancy. The English had from the first claimed from the Atlantic to the Pacific by right of discovery; but they now based their claims on the ground that the country belonged to the Six Nations, who had placed all their lands under the protection of England. Commissioners were sent to treat with the Ohio Indians and win them over to the English interest. They succeeded in obtaining a deed of the lands in question from the Indians, and a guaranty that their settlements should not be molested by them. The governor of Canada, perceiving the design of the English to occupy the Ohio valley, informed the governors of New York and Pennsylvania of the encroachments of the English traders upon what he claimed as his territory, and of his intention to seize them wherever found. Accordingly, in 1752 some English traders were seized and confined in a fort at Presque Isle, on Lake Erie. From this point the French were engaged in establishing a chain of posts to the Allegheny, opening communication to the Ohio, and keeping it clear by means of troops stationed at convenient points along the way. The Ohio Company, seeing this intrusion upon their lands, complained to the governor of Virginia, of which colony their territory was a part under the grant of the crown. He resolved to send a trusty messenger to the French commander to remonstrate against these encroachments, and George Washington was entrusted with this delicate mission. On reaching the post of Venango, he could obtain no satisfaction, the officer in command boldly declaring that the French intended to seize on the whole valley of the Ohio. He proceeded to Waterford, the headquarters of the French commandant, St. Pierre, who received him with courtesy, but did not disguise the intentions of the French. His answer to the governor of Virginia was, that he had taken possession of the Ohio valley under the authority of the governor of Canada, and by his orders should destroy all English posts therein. It was now obvious that the Ohio would not be relinquished without a struggle. The Ohio Company commenced to construct a fort at the confluence of the Allegheny and Monongahela rivers, on the site of Pittsburg. The governor of Virginia dispatched a small force to protect the laborers and aid in constructing the fort, and wrote to inform the Board of Trade of the design of the French to occupy the Ohio valley. He likewise sent to the governors of New York and Pennsylvania for aid to resist the aggressions of the French.

When the Assembly met in the spring of 1754, Governor De Lancey, in his message to that body, called their attention to the recent encroachments of the French, and to the request by Virginia for aid from the colony of New York. The Assembly voted only a thousand pounds for aid, and to bear its share in erecting forts along the frontier.

Early in the spring of 1754, Washington, with a small body of troops from Virginia, set out for the disputed territory, with supplies for the fort in course of construction at the junction of the Allegheny and Monongahela. When near Will's creek, he was met by the ensign of Captain Trent's company, which had been sent out to protect and help build the fort. From him he received the unwelcome intelligence that while they were at work on the fort the French troops from Venango came down the river with their artillery, and resistance being useless, they were obliged to surrender it to them. The French completed it and named it Fort Duquesne, after the governor of Canada. On hearing this news, Washington reported to the governors of Virginia and Pennsylvania the situation of affairs, and urged them to hasten forward reinforcements. Advancing, he soon learned that the French were on their way to intercept his progress, and not knowing their strength he fell back to Great Meadows and began to throw up an intrenchment, which he called Fort Necessity. While here, he received a courier from the chieftain Half King, who, with a party of Indian warriors was a few miles distant, informing him that a body of French were in his vicinity. He immediately set out with a part of his men for the camp of Half King. An attack on the enemy, whose position had been discovered, was at once agreed upon, and successfully executed. Receiving additional troops, Washington proceeded toward Fort Duquesne, but had not gone far before he heard of the advance of a large body of French and Indians, and returned to Fort Necessity. Here he was soon after attacked by a superior force, and after an obstinate resistance accepted the terms of capitulation offered, which gave him permission to retire unmolested to Virginia.

Thus were the French left in undisputed possession of the entire region west of the Alleghanies. The necessity of concerted action on the part of the English colonies to resist their aggressions had now become obvious, but unworthy sectional feelings often prevented harmony of action for a general defense. The Six Nations were also becoming alienated from the English by the influence of French emissaries. The English ministry, aware of this critical state of affairs, had advised a convention of delegates from all the colonial assemblies, to secure the continued friendship and alliance of the Six Nations, and to unite their efforts in the common defense. In accordance with this recommendation, a convention of delegates from the colonies of New York, Massachusetts, New Hampshire, Connecticut, Pennsylvania and Maryland, was held at Albany in June, 1754. The chiefs of the Six Nations were in attendance, and the proceedings were opened by a speech to the Indians from Governor De Lancey, who had been chosen president of the convention. A treaty with the Six Nations was renewed, and they departed, apparently satisfied. While this treaty was being negotiated, at the suggestion of the Massachusetts delegates, a plan for the union of the colonies was taken into consideration. The suggestion was favorably received, and a committee, consisting of one member from each colony, was appointed to draft plans for this purpose. The fertile mind of Benjamin Franklin had conceived the necessity of union, and before leaving home he had prepared a plan, which was adopted. It was similar in many of its features to our Federal Constitution, framed many years afterward. The provincial assemblies, considering it too much of an encroachment on their liberties, rejected it, and it was rejected by the English government because it gave too much power to the people.

CHAPTER VII.

THE RESULTS OF FOUR ENGLISH EXPEDITIONS AGAINST THE FRENCH—MONTCALM'S SUCCESSFUL CAMPAIGNS.

THOUGH England and France were nominally at peace, the frontier was desolated by savage hordes let loose upon the settlements by the French. While the English ministry were hesitating, the Duke of Cumberland, who at that time was Captain-General of the armies of Great Britain, sent over, early in 1755, General Braddock, with a detachment from the army in Ireland. Braddock, soon after his arrival, met the colonial governors in a conference at Alexandria, to devise measures for repelling the encroachments of the French. Four separate expeditions were there resolved upon: the first against Nova Scotia; the second, under Braddock himself, for the recovery of the Ohio valley; the third against Fort Niagara, and the fourth against Crown Point, on Lake Champlain. The first resulted in the complete reduction of Nova Scotia. The second and most important, under Braddock, from which much had been expected, was, through the folly of that officer, disastrous in the extreme. Washington had repeatedly urged the necessity of sending scouts in advance, but Braddock, obstinate and imperious, would listen to no warnings of danger from Indian ambuscades. When within a few miles of Fort Duquesne, the army was surprised by the lurking foe, and only saved from total destruction by the bravery of Washington, who, upon the fall of Braddock, assumed command, and conducted a retreat, but not till more than half the force had been sacrificed. The expedition against Fort Niagara, under Gen. Shirley, governor of Massachusetts, was also unsuccessful. His troops hearing of Braddock's defeat, soon after leaving Albany, were so disheartened that many of them deserted. At Oswego he was detained by having to wait for the completion of boats. When these were completed, he was further detained by heavy storms and other casualties, until the lateness of the season rendered it imprudent to proceed. Leaving a garrison at Oswego under Colonel Mercer, he led back the residue of his army to Albany, and returned to Massachusetts. The expedition against Crown Point was entrusted to General Johnson. The greater part of the troops were sent forward under General Lyman, of Connecticut, to the head of boat navigation on the Hudson, which, being the nearest point on that river to Lake Champlain, was called the carrying place, where they erected a fortification, which was afterward named Fort Edward. Here they were joined late in August by Johnson, who, advancing with the main body of the army to the head of Lake George, established a camp, and began to make some arrangements for an attack on Crown Point, but apparently was in no hurry to prosecute the enterprise. Meanwhile Dieskau, the French commander, was approaching by way of Lake Champlain, with the intention of surprising Fort Edward, cutting off Johnson's retreat, and capturing his army; but being misled by his guides, he found himself on the way to Johnson's camp on Lake George. Abandoning his first intention of attacking Fort Edward, he continued his advance on Lake George. Johnson, learning that the French were advancing to the Hudson, sent out Colonel Williams with a thousand troops, and Sachem Hendrick with two hundred Indians, to intercept them and aid Fort Edward. They had advanced only a few miles when they fell into an ambuscade, in which both Williams and Hendrick were slain, and the force hurriedly retreated, closely pursued by the enemy until they reached the camp, when the Canadian militia and Indians, who were in the advance, perceiving the artillery they would have to confront, skulked into the surrounding woods, and left the regulars to begin the attack, thereby giving the English time to recover from the confusion into which they had been thrown, and undoubtedly saving them from defeat. A severe struggle ensued, in which the French at length began to give way, upon observing which the English leaped over their breastworks and dispersed them in all directions. The French leader, Dieskau, was severely wounded and taken prisoner. Johnson was wounded in the commencement of the action and retired from the field, and the whole battle was directed by General Lyman, who proposed and urged a vigorous continuation of efforts by following up the routed enemy, preventing their escape down Lake Champlain, and attacking Ticonderoga and Crown Point; but Johnson, through fear or some other cause, not easily explained, withheld his consent, and allowed the French to intrench themselves at Ticonderoga, while he spent the residue of the autumn erecting Fort William Henry, on the site of his camp. On the approach of winter he garrisoned it, disbanded the remainder of his army and returned to Albany.

On the 3d of September, 1755, Sir Charles Hardy arrived in New York as governor. He was an admiral, and unacquainted with civil affairs. Being conscious of his deficiences in executive ability, he soon surrendered all but nominal duties into the hands of De Lancey, and in 1757 resigned the government and returned to his former profession, and De Lancey again became governor. At a meeting of the provincial governors, held at Albany in December, the plan discussed for the campaign of 1756 consisted of movements against Fort Niagara with six thousand men, Fort Duquesne with three thousand, Crown Point with ten thousand, and two thousand were to advance on the French settlements on the Chaudiere, and onward to Quebec. At this time, 1756, the population of the province of New York was 96,775. In March, De Levy, with three hundred French troops from Montreal, penetrated the forests to the Oneida portage, took and destroyed the fort at that point and returned to Canada with the garrison as prisoners. Although active hostilities had been carried on for two years in the colonies, the English ministry did not arouse from their imbecility enough to issue a formal declaration of war against France until the 17th of May, 1756. Lord Loudoun was appointed commander-in-chief and governor of Virginia, and General Abercrombie was placed second in command. General Winslow, who had been intrusted with the expedition against Crown Point, finding that he had not sufficient force for the undertaking, waited for reinforcements from England. Late in June Abercrombie arrived with troops, but at the same time blighted any hopes that might have arisen regarding a vigorous prosecution of the war, by showing his contempt for the provincials in announcing that the regular officers were to be over those of the same rank in the provincial service. On this announcement all harmony for a united effort was dispelled. The men began to desert, and some of the officers declared they should throw up their commissions if the obnoxious rule was enforced. This difficulty was finally adjusted by an agreement that the regulars should remain to do garrison duty, while the provincials should advance under their own officers against the enemy. Then, instead of making any effort for the relief of Oswego, which was in danger, Abercrombie ordered his troops to be quartered on the citizens of Albany. De Villiers had encamped with eight hundred Frenchmen at the mouth of Sandy Creek, on Lake Ontario, whence he could send out detachments to infest the water passes leading to the Oswego fort, and intercept supplies or reinforcements on the way thither. Colonel Bradstreet, however, succeeded in throwing some provisions into the fort. On his return he fell in with a party of De Villiers' men in ambush, and gained a decisive victory over them. Hearing that a large force was already on its way to attack Oswego, he hastened to Albany, and informed Abercrombie of the contemplated attack and the necessity of immediate reinforcements. But it was all in vain, as the General could not be induced to move before the arrival of Lord Loudoun. It was nearly August before Loudoun made his appearance, and affairs were not improved by this event. Instead of making an immediate effort to avert the threatened blow at Oswego, he began slowly to make preparations for a descent on Ticonderoga and Crown Point. Reinforcements were sent to forts Edward and William Henry. This procrastination proved fatal, for the opportunity of relieving Oswego was now lost. The Marquis de Montcalm, successor of Dieskau, had cut off communication with Albany, and on the 12th of August opened his artillery on Fort Ontario, nearly opposite Oswego. The fire was returned by the garrison till their ammunition was exhausted, when, spiking their guns, they retreated across the river to Fort Oswego. Montcalm immediately occupied the deserted fort and turned such guns as were yet serviceable against Fort Oswego. Colonel Mercer was killed, and a formidable breach effected in the walls. Montcalm was making preparations for storming the entrenchments, when, seeing that the defense was no longer practicable, the garrison surrendered themselves prisoners of war. By this affair sixteen hundred men, one hundred cannon, a large quantity of provisions and stores, and the vessels in the harbor, all fell into the hands of the victors, and were safely conveyed to Montreal. Montcalm demolished the forts, much to the satisfaction of the Six Nations, who afterward sent a delegation from each castle to make peace with the governor of Canada. The French sent their emissaries among them, who now succeeded in seducing them from the English interests.

The fall of Oswego did not awaken the energies of Lord Loudoun—if it can be said that he possessed any—but on the contrary he abandoned all offensive operations that had been contemplated, and contented himself with doing nothing. Having wasted the season in shameful idleness, he, on his arrival in the city of New York, billetted a part of his force for free winter quarters on the citizens, regardless of the remonstrance of the authorities against this invasion of their rights. Overawed by his profane threats, the colonists found themselves obliged to support the British soldiers, who had done nothing in their behalf. In June of the following year he made an ineffectual effort to capture Louisburg. Before leaving New York he rendered himself still more detestable to the colonists by laying an embargo upon the seaports from Massachusetts to Virginia, and impressing four hundred men from the city of New York alone. He went to Halifax, where he was largely reinforced, but instead of making any advance on Louisburg contented himself by drilling his troops in mock battles, till the complaints of his inactivity became so numerous that he finally gave orders to embark for that place. Almost as soon as the orders were given, receiving intelligence that Louisburg had been reinforced, and that the French fleet contained one more vessel than his, he countermanded his orders and came back to New York, having accomplished nothing. While he was thus trifling, Montcalm, watchful of his movements, proceeded with a large force of French and Indians against Fort William Henry, then in command of Colonel Monroe, with about twenty-two hundred men. General Webb, the English commander in that quarter, was at Fort Edward with a force of four thousand. Montcalm landed with his men and artillery at a point about two miles from Fort William Henry, where he was entirely sheltered from its guns ; beleaguered its garrison, and sent a summons to Monroe to surrender, which he defiantly disregarded, confident of being relieved by Webb. The French then opened fire on the fort, which was spiritedly returned by the garrison. Expresses were sent to Webb imploring aid; but that coward remained inactive, terrified at the distant roar of artillery. Finally, after repeated solicitations, he allowed Generals Johnson and Putnam, with his rangers, to march to the aid of Monroe; but they had proceeded only a few miles when he recalled them, and sent a letter to Monroe, advising him to surrender. This letter was intercepted by Montcalm, who forwarded it to Monroe, requesting him to follow Webb's advice and save further loss of life. Still the intrepid colonel held out until his ammunition was nearly exhausted, part of his guns disabled, and all hopes of assistance abandoned, and under these discouraging circumstances he was forced to capitulate on the 9th of August, and the sixth day of the siege. By the terms of surrender, the garrison were allowed to leave the fort with all the honors of war, and furnished with an escort to Fort Edward. On the next morning, when they began their march, the Indians, who had spent the night in debauch, began an indiscriminate massacre and robbery of the English troops. Despite the efforts of Montcalm, many of the disarmed and defenseless soldiers were slain, and only a thousand reached Fort Edward. Fort William Henry was demolished. General Webb, paralyzed with terror, prepared to retreat, although reinforced until his army was more than double that of the enemy.

CHAPTER VIII.

EXTINCTION OF FRENCH POWER IN AMERICA—THE NEW YORK JUDICIARY—INTERNATIONAL CONTENTIONS.

BY these repeated failures the spirit of the English ministry in meeting the exigencies of the occasion was aroused, and William Pitt, a very able statesman, was intrusted with the management of affairs. His accession gave a new impulse to the national energies, and the campaign for 1758 opened under more favorable auspices. Three formidable expeditions were projected for this year, against Louisburg, Ticonderoga, and Fort Duquesne respectively. Admiral Boscawen, with twenty ships of the line and fifteen frigates, together with twelve thousand men under General Amherst, arrived before Louisburg on the 2d day of June, and entered vigorously upon the siege of that fortress, and on the 26th of July the French commander, finding farther opposition useless, surrendered at discretion. The army destined for the reduction of Ticonderoga and Crown Point, under General Abercrombie, consisting of nine thousand provincials and seven thousand regulars with a fine train of artillery, assembled at the head of Lake George, where they embarked on the 5th of July for the fortress of Ticonderoga, which was held by Montcalm with about four thousand men. They landed the next day and began their march, necessarily leaving their artillery behind until the bridges, which had been destroyed by the enemy, could be rebuilt. It was the purpose of Abercrombie to hasten forward and carry Ticonderoga by storm, before re-inforcements which were expected could arrive. The advance party fell in with a body of the enemy, and Lord Howe, the second in command and the soul of the expedition, was killed. The loss of Howe was severely felt, and the incompetent Abercrombie, uncertain what course to pursue, fell back to the landing place. Colonel Bradstreet advanced, rebuilt the bridges and took possession of some saw-mills destroyed by the enemy about two miles from Ticonderoga, to which place Abercrombie advanced with his army, and sent forward an engineer with a party of rangers to reconnoitre. They reported that the works could be easily taken. Stark, who led the rangers, thought differently, and so advised Abercrombie ; but he rejected his advice and ordered an attack without artillery, which, after a desperate struggle, was repulsed with the loss of nearly two thousand men. With the great force still at his command Abercrombie, instead of bringing up his artillery to bombard the French works, sounded a retreat, and, unpursued by the enemy, returned to the head of Lake George and sent his artillery and stores to Albany.

Colonel Bradstreet, anxious to do something to retrieve the disgrace of this shameful retreat, asked to lead an expedition against Fort Frontenac, which, with the entire fleet on Lake Ontario, surrendered on the 26th of August.

The command of the expedition against Fort Duquesne

was given to General Forbes. Contrary to the advice of Washington, Forbes insisted on having a new road cut to the fort. With this and other delays, on the 5th of November the English forces were still forty miles from their destination, when it was resolved to go into winter quarters. Washington, satisfied of the inability of the garrison to resist an attack, asked and obtained permission to push forward with his Virginians, and on his approach the French set fire to the fort and fled. On the 25th Washington took possession of the ruins, and changed the name from Duquesne to Pittsburg.

Although Louisburg and Fort Duquesne had been retaken, still there could be no security for the frontier so long as Fort Niagara and the posts on Lake Champlain were held by the French, nor even while Canada remained unsubjugated. Accordingly, adequate preparations were made for the campaign of 1759. Abercrombie was superseded in the command of the expedition against Ticonderoga and Crown Point by General Amherst. General Wolfe was directed to ascend the St. Lawrence to Quebec, and General Prideaux was to take Fort Niagara and proceed to Montreal. He was joined by General Johnson at Oswego, from which point he sailed for Fort Niagara, leaving Haldimand with a force at Oswego. The latter was soon afterward attacked by a body of French and Indians, but succeeded in repulsing them. On the 7th of July Prideaux appeared before Niagara, but soon after the siege began he was killed by the premature bursting of a shell. Johnson succeeded to the command, and the siege continued without cessation. On the 24th a force of nearly three thousand French and Indian troops made an effort to raise the siege. A sharp conflict ensued, in which the relieving force was defeated, and the next day the garrison surrendered.

General Amherst, with a force of nearly twelve thousand men, arrived at Ticonderoga on the 22d of July, and in four days thereafter the garrison abandoned the post and withdrew to Crown Point, which also was abandoned on the approach of Amherst.

The strength of Quebec was well known, and General Wolfe left Louisburg under convoy of a large fleet and eight thousand regulars to capture it. It was intended that Amherst should sweep Lake Champlain, capture Montreal, and form a junction with Wolfe before Quebec, but he failed to accomplish his part, and Wolfe alone had the glory of taking that strong fortress. On the 27th of June he landed on the Isle of Orleans, a few miles below the city. Montcalm occupied the place with thirteen thousand men, and a strongly entrenched camp extended below the city from the river St. Charles to the Montmorenci. General Monckton took a position at Point Levi, opposite Quebec, with but little opposition, and erected batteries from which the lower town was considerably damaged, but no impression could be made on the walls of the city. General Wolfe crossed the St. Lawrence and encamped on the bank of the Montmorenci within cannon shot of the enemy on the opposite side, and resolved to storm their strong camp. Monckton crossed the St. Lawrence a little above the Montmorenci, and at the same time the forces on the opposite side forded that stream and joined his division. The grenadiers, impatient of restraint, rushed up the bank before the troops that were to support them could be made available, and were consequently repulsed with fearful loss, when they took shelter behind a redoubt which had been abandoned by the enemy in the commencement of the action. At this time a tempestuous thunder-storm broke over the belligerents, and before it abated night came on, and the English were obliged to recross the river. Weeks passed, and the capture of Quebec seemed as far off as ever. The arrival of Amherst was looked for in vain, and Wolfe and his officers, weary and impatient of delay, concerted a plan for scaling the Heights of Abraham, back of Quebec, and thus forcing the French into an engagement. The camp at Montmorenci was broken up and the troops conveyed to Point Levi. Admiral Holmes ascended the river with a part of the troops and artillery. At night the remainder proceeded up the river, and Montcalm, thinking they were about to raise the siege, remained in his camp, while Bourgainville marched up the river to prevent their landing. Before daylight the British, returning silently down the river, unperceived by the French, landed and ascended the precipice. The French guard was dispersed, and by daylight five thousand regulars were drawn up in battle array on the Plains of Abraham. When this intelligence reached Montcalm he saw at once the danger of his garrison, and marched his army across the St. Charles to attack the English. A fierce battle followed, in which both Wolfe and Montcalm were slain and the French army defeated, and on the 18th of September, five days after, Quebec was surrendered to the English.

In the following Spring De Levi, the successor of Montcalm, attempted the recapture of Quebec, which had been left in charge of General Murray with seven thousand men. De Levi advanced upon the city with an army of ten thousand, and Murray marching out to attack him, was defeated and forced to retreat to the city. De Levi followed up his success, but on the arrival of the English fleet in the St. Lawrence he retired in great alarm to Montreal. General Amherst appeared before that city on the 6th of September, 1760. Murray approached from Quebec on the same day, and on the day following Colonel Haviland arrived with his division from Crown Point. De Vaudreuil, the governor-general, despairing of a successful defense, capitulated on the 8th. As the result of this campaign, Canada, with all her dependencies, fell into the hands of the English, and hostilities between the colonies of the two nationalities ceased. Peace, however, was not concluded between England and France until February 10th, 1763, when France ceded to England all her possessions in Canada.

On the 30th of July, 1760, Governor De Lancey suddenly died, and Cadwallader Colden took charge of the government, being president of the council. In August, 1761, he received his commission as lieutenant-governor. The death of De Lancey left the seat of chief-justice vacant, and the remaining judges, having doubted their ability to issue processes since the death of King George II., under whom they had held their old commissions, urged Colden to appoint a successor. Colden requested the Colonial Secretary of State to nominate a chief-justice, and he not only nominated but appointed Benjamin Pratt, a lawyer from Boston, to hold the position at the pleasure of the King instead of during good behavior, as formerly. The people, regarding this as an encroachment on their rights and liberties, vigorously protested, and the remaining judges even refused to act longer unless they could hold their commissions during good behavior. When the Assembly met, Colden requested that the salary of the chief-justice should be increased, but that body not only refused to increase it, but refused to provide for it unless the judges' commissions secured them their seats during good behavior. The chief-justice having served some time without a salary, the income of the royal quit-rents of the province was appropriated to his compensation.

General Robert Monkton was appointed governor of New York, and assumed the reins of government in October, 1761, but left on the 13th of the following month to command an expedition against Martinique, leaving the administration of affairs again in the hands of Colden. In 1763 the boundary line between New York and New Hampshire became a subject of much controversy. The disputed territory was the tract of land between the Connecticut river and Lake Champlain, comprising what is now known as the State of Vermont. The patent granted to the Duke of York in 1664 included all the land west of the Connecticut river to the east side of Delaware Bay. Controversies had arisen, growing out of the indefinite character of their respective charters, between the province of New York and those of Connecticut and Massachusetts relative to their boundaries, which had been adjusted by negotiation and compromise. The line agreed upon was to extend north and south twenty miles east of the Hudson river. New Hampshire, regardless of justice or title, insisted upon having the same western boundary. Against this claim New York vigorously protested, but the protests were unheeded, and the governor of New Hampshire continued to issue grants until, in 1763, one hundred and thirty-eight townships had been granted. Alarmed at this encroachment, and in order to stop these proceedings, Governor Colden, in December, 1763, issued a proclamation claiming jurisdiction to the Connecticut river under the patent granted to the Duke of York, and commanded the sheriff of Albany county to return the names of all persons who, by virtue of the New Hampshire grants, had taken possession of lands west of the Connecticut river. This was followed by a counter proclamation from the governor of New Hampshire, declaring that the grant to the Duke of York was obsolete, and that his grantees should be protected in the possession of their lands. Through the Board of Trade the disputed question was referred to the crown, and in 1764 a decision was obtained pronouncing the Connecticut river the boundary between the provinces of New York and New Hampshire. Upon this decision the government of New York declared the grants from the governor of New Hampshire illegal, and insisted that the grantees should surrender or re-purchase the lands upon which they had settled. To this unjust demand the greater part refused to accede, and the governor of New York thereupon granted their lands to others, who brought ejectment suits against the former occupants, and obtained judgment at the courts of Albany. All attempts, however, of the executive officers to enforce these judgments met with a spirited resistance, and led to continual hostilities between the settlers and the government of New York.

CHAPTER IX.

THE APPROACH OF THE REVOLUTION—PATRIOTIC ATTITUDE OF NEW YORK—THE FIRST BATTLE FOUGHT IN 1770.

THE representative assemblies of the provinces had occasionally remonstrated against the various acts of Parliament which tended to abridge their liberties, and the regulation of the Board of Trade by which their manufactures and commerce were injuriously affected; yet their attachment to the mother country and regard for her institutions had not to any considerable extent been weakened. But now the borders of the Revolutionary struggle were reached; the time had arrived when unquestioned submission to the exactions of arbitrary power had ceased to be considered a virtue, and knowing the value of their liberties, the colonies firmly asserted their rights. They were heavily burdened by the expenses of the late war, for which they had liberally contributed, materially aiding in procuring for the English government a vast and valuable accession of territory; yet their generous support of the power and dignity of the realm the British ministry regarded as only the exercise of a duty, and before the smoke had fairly drifted away from the battle grounds began to devise plans for taxing them to raise a revenue without their consent. The first measure which aroused the colonists to a lively sense of their danger was the issuing of writs of assistance, which the English ministry had determined to force upon them. These were, in effect, search warrants, whereby custom-house officers were enabled the better to collect revenues by breaking open houses or stores that were suspected of containing concealed contraband goods. This exercise of arbitrary power created indignation and alarm, and the colonists resolved to resist it. Public meetings were held, and remonstrances sent to Parliament, but without effect. The ministry were determined to derive a revenue from the colonies, either by import duties or direct taxes, vigorously levied and collected, and the writs were granted; but the feelings of the people were such that the custom-house officers never attempted to carry their new powers into execution.

In 1764 George Grenville, then at the head of the English ministry, submitted to the House of Commons a proposition for raising a revenue by the sale of stamps to the colonists, at the same time assuring the colonial agents that he would not press its immediate adoption, but leave the plan open for consideration. When intelligence reached the colonists that such an act was meditated by the ministry, discontent was everywhere visible. The provincial assemblies strenuously refused to recognize the right of Parliament to tax them without their consent, and asserted the sole right to tax themselves. They passed resolutions of remonstrance, and clearly demonstrated that taxation without representation in Parliament was unjust and tyrannical; but, in contemptuous disregard of all respectful remonstrances and petitions, the Stamp Act was passed in March, 1765. By its provisions no legal or commercial documents were valid unless written or printed on stamped paper, upon which a price was set, according to the nature of the instrument, payable to officers appointed by the crown. The passage of this act created feelings of resentment throughout the colonies, accompanied by a determination to resist or evade its enforcement. The people of New York were among the most bitter in their opposition to the measure. An association styling itself the Sons of Liberty held meetings to discuss plans for resistance. The obnoxious act was reprinted and paraded about the streets of New York city, bearing the inscription, "The folly of England and ruin of America." A committee was appointed by the New York Assembly in October, 1764, to correspond with the several colonial assemblies, with a view to resisting the oppressive measures of Parliament. They suggested to the several colonies the holding of a convention, to remonstrate against the violation of their liberties. This suggestion was heartily responded to, and delegates were appointed, who convened in the city of New York on the 7th of October, 1765. This body continued in session two weeks, and adopted a declaration of rights, a petition to the King, and a memorial to Parliament, in which the principles by which the colonies were governed through the Revolution were clearly foreshadowed.

The Stamp Act was to take effect on the first day of November. As the appointed time drew near the excitement increased, and when the day had finally arrived flags floated at half mast, bells were tolled as on funeral occasions, and many other manifestations of public sorrow and discontent were made. The stamped paper, which had previously arrived, had been deposited in the fort for safe keeping, under the direction of Governor Colden, who had taken the oath to execute the Stamp Act, but McEvers, who had been appointed by the crown to manage its distribution and sale, seeing the manifestations of popular indignation, resigned. In the evening the Sons of Liberty appeared before the fort and demanded the stamped paper. On being refused, they repaired to the Commons, where they hung Governor Colden in effigy, and returned to the fort with his image. Not being admitted at the gate, they broke into Colden's stable, and brought out his carriage, placed the effigy in it, paraded the streets, and returned to the fort, where it was again hung. They then made a bonfire and burned the carriage and its accompaniments. A party proceeded to the house of Major James, an artillery officer who had rendered himself particularly obnoxious, destroyed the furniture, and carried off the colors of the Royal Artillery regiment. The next day Colden announced that he should not issue any of the stamped paper while he remained in office, but leave it to his successor, who was already on his way from England. But the Sons of Liberty, not satisfied with this assurance, insisted that the stamped paper should be delivered into their hands, and threatened to take it by force if it was not. The Common Council, alarmed at their ungovernable fury, requested that the paper might be deposited in the City Hall, which was done, and a guaranty given for its safe keeping. In the meantime, at a meeting called by the citizens, a committee was appointed to correspond with the merchants of the several colonies, inviting them to enter into an agreement not to import certain goods from England, which suggestion was promptly acted upon, and the trade with England almost ceased.

When the new governor, Sir Henry Moore, arrived, he was disposed to carry the Stamp Act into execution, but the unanimous advice of his council, together with the unmistakable character of public sentiment, soon convinced him of the folly of such an attempt. The Sons of Liberty seized ten boxes of stamped paper, on the arrival of a vessel containing it, conveyed it to the ship-yards, and it was consumed in a bonfire. The Stamp Act was so odious to the colonies, and their opposition to it was so effective, that it was repealed on the 18th of March, 1766; but immediately on its repeal a bill was passed declaring the absolute right of Parliament "to tax the colonies in all cases whatsoever." The repeal, however, was not owing to any appeals from the colonists, for Parliament would not receive the petitions of the Colonial Congress, because that body had not been summoned to meet by it; but it was because of the influence of London merchants, whose trade was seriously affected by the non-importation agreement. Notwithstanding the declaratory act that accompanied the repeal the news was hailed with a delirium of delight, and the city was in a blaze of illumination in honor of the event. On the King's birthday, which occurred soon afterward, the New Yorkers assembled, and with enthusiastic manifestations of loyalty erected a liberty-pole, inscribed to the King, Pitt, and Liberty. The Assembly met in June, and the Governor requested its compliance with the demands of the ministry in relation to furnishing supplies for the troops stationed in New York city. Some controversy ensued upon the subject, and only a partial compliance could be obtained from the Assembly.

The sounds of rejoicing which followed the repeal of the Stamp Act had hardly passed away before the ministry, by its unjust acts, again awakened the murmurs of discontent, and the declaratory act began to loom up and dampen all the hopes of the colonists. The partial provision of the Assembly for supporting the troops was distasteful to the Sons of Liberty, who well knew the soldiers were sent to enforce the abridgement of American liberties, and on their arrival did not disguise their feelings. Animosities arose between them, and the soldiers, believing that it was owing to the Sons of Liberty that the Assembly had not been more liberal in furnishing them with supplies, retaliated by cutting down the citizens' flagstaff. The next day, while the citizens were replacing it, they were assaulted by the troops, and several of them wounded. The officers were indifferent to this conduct of their men, and other outrages were committed. The Assembly met again in November, when the governor placed before it the instructions of the ministry, requesting that immediate provision for the troops should be made; but their outrageous conduct had so disgusted the legislators that they refused to comply, and were severely censured by the crown. Parliament declared the legislative powers of the Assembly annulled, and forbade the governor and council to give their assent to any act passed by that body until unqualified compliance with the demands of the government had been obtained.

In June, 1767, a bill was passed by Parliament imposing a duty on tea, glass, lead, paper, and printers' colors imported into the colonies. This act was shortly followed by another re-organizing the colonial custom-house system, and establishing a board of revenue commissioners. When intelligence of these acts reached the colonies the excitement was renewed, and the non-importation agreement revived. The colonists saw that Parliament intended to tax them in some way, and declared that taxes on trade for a revenue were as much a violation of their rights as any other taxes. In 1768 the Assembly of Massachusetts addressed a circular letter to the other colonies referring to the acts of Parliament, and soliciting their co-operation in maintaining the common liberties. This so offended the ministry that a letter was sent from the Secretary of State to the several colonial governors, forbidding their assemblies to correspond with that of Massachusetts. When the Assembly of New York was convened the governor placed the document before it, and requested their obedience to its mandates. The Assembly unhesitatingly refused; declared its right to correspond with any other of the legislatures; denounced the infringements upon its rights by Parliament; and was dissolved by the governor. The people sustained their representatives, and when a new Assembly convened in April, 1769, it was found that but very little change had been effected by the election.

The death of Sir Henry Moore occurred on the 11th of September, 1769. His mild and prudent course in avoiding controversy as far as possible had endeared him to the colony, and his death was much lamented. By that event the government again devolved upon Cadwallader Colden. The English merchants, suffering from the non-importation agreement, had joined their petitions with those of the colonists for the repeal of the obnoxious custom-house act, and a circular letter assured the people of the colonies that at the next session of Parliament a proposition would be made to abolish the duties on all articles except tea. This attempt at conciliation was far from satisfactory; for the right of taxation was not relinquished, and the principle was the same whether applied to one article or many. A bill was introduced in the New York Assembly in November for issuing colonial bills of credit to the amount of £120,000, to loan out as a means of revenue. The project at first met with favor from the popular party, but when it was followed by an appropriation to support the British troops in the colony, to be taken out of the interest arising from the loan, a revulsion of feeling at once took place. Shortly after handbills were circulated charging the Assembly with betraying the inhabitants of the colony, and advising the people to meet on a certain day and express their sentiments upon the subject. Accordingly, a large concourse of people gathered, and emphatically denounced the action of the Assembly. That body passed resolutions declaring the handbills libelous, and offering a reward for the detection of their authors. John Lamb, who had presided over the popular meeting, was arrested and brought before the House, but was soon after discharged.

Animosities continued between the Sons of Liberty and the soldiers. Now that their supplies were granted the latter no longer held themselves in check from motives of policy, and on the evening of the 13th of January, 1769, renewed their attack upon the flagpole of the citizens. The latter hastily gathered for its defense, whereupon they desisted. Their failure in this attempt, together with the derisive jeers of the citizens, so enraged them that they charged upon a group of people in front of a tavern which was a favorite resort of the Sons of Liberty, drove them in and destroyed the windows and furniture. On the evening of the 16th they cut down the flagstaff, sawed it in pieces, and piled the fragments before the battered hotel. On the following morning several thousands of the citizens assembled at the scene of the outrage, and passed resolutions censuring the riotous proceedings of the soldiers, and recommending that whenever found in the street after roll-call they should be dealt with as enemies to the peace of the city. The next day placards were found posted up, ridiculing the resolutions and daring the citizens to execute them. During the day the Sons of Liberty caught two or three soldiers in the act of putting up these bills, and arrested them. While conducting them to the mayor's office the citizens were attacked by a party of twenty soldiers, armed with cutlasses, and a skirmish ensued—the citizens defending themselves with clubs. The soldiers were forced back to Golden Hill, as John street, between Cliff street and Burling Slip, was then called. Here they were re-enforced, and made a furious charge on the citizens, most of whom were entirely unarmed. The latter stoutly resisted until a party of officers appeared on the scene and ordered the troops back to their barracks. Several of the citizens were severely wounded, some of whom had not participated in the skirmish. Several affrays occurred on the following day, in which the soldiers were generally worsted. The mayor issued a proclamation forbidding them to leave the barracks unless accompanied by a non-commissioned officer, and order was restored.

Thus terminated the first conflict in which blood was shed in the cause of American independence. It is usually asserted that at Lexington was the first battle fought ; but the actual beginning of the combat, so doubtful in its progress, and so glorious in its results, was the battle of Golden Hill, on the 18th of January, 1770, at least five years earlier. The Sons of Liberty purchased grounds and erected another pole, which stood until the occupation of the city by the British forces in 1776.

CHAPTER X.

THE BOSTON TEA PARTY—MEETING OF THE CONTINENTAL CONGRESS—THE BATTLE OF LEXINGTON—CANADA INVADED.

IN October Lord Dunmore arrived in New York and superseded Colden in the government of the province. Meanwhile the duties had been removed from all articles except tea, and the non-importation agreement was restricted to that article. The new governor brought the news of the royal approval of the act authorizing the emission of colonial bills of credit. This strengthened the spirit of loyalty, and affairs went on more smoothly. On the 8th of July, 1771, William Tryon was commissioned as governor in place of Lord Dunmore, who was transferred to the government of Virginia. By a recent order of the crown the governor's salary was to be paid from the revenue, thus rendering the executive independent of the people. The East India Company were suffering severely from the non-importation agreement in regard to tea, and in 1773 urgently petitioned the British government to abolish the duty levied upon that article in the colonies, offering to submit to double that duty as an exportation tariff. This would increase the amount of revenue two-fold, but the party in power, deluded by false views of national honor, would not in the least relinquish its declared right to tax the colonies. It preferred to favor the East India Company by a special act allowing them to ship their tea to the colonies free of export duty, which would enable them to sell it at a lower rate than in England. By this act the ministers imagined they had outwitted the colonists and that this appeal to their pockets would end their resistance. Ships were laden with tea and consignees appointed in the colonies to receive it, with the expectation that this new act would secure its ready sale. When information of this arrangement reached the colonies their indignation was deeply aroused. The Sons of Liberty rallied and resolved that the obnoxious article should not be landed under any pretense. The tea commissioners appointed for New York resigned in view of such decided demonstrations of resistance.

Expecting a consignment of tea would soon reach the city the citizens held a mass meeting, and regardless of the efforts of Governor Tryon to secure its reception, emphatically resolved that it should not be landed. The expected vessel was delayed and did not make its appearance until April, 1774. When it arrived off Sandy Hook the pilot, acting under the instructions of the vigilance committee, refused to bring the ship any nearer the city. Captain Lockyer, the commander, under escort of the committee, was allowed to come up and consult with the consignee, but the latter refused to receive the cargo, and advised the captain to return to England immediately. Meanwhile Captain Chambers, of New York, professing to be a patriot, arrived in the harbor. His vessel was boarded by the committee, and upon being questioned he denied having any contraband goods ; but on being informed by the committee that with the evidence they had to the contrary they should search his ship, he admitted that there was tea on board which he had brought out on a private venture. The hatches were forced open and the chests brought on deck and given air and water. The next morning Captain Lockyer was conducted by the committee to his ship, together with Chambers, his companion in the tea trade, and they were sent on an outward voyage.

The New Hampshire grants continued a source of serious contention. The civil officers were opposed by force in their efforts to enforce the judgments obtained in the ejectment suits, and the New York Assembly passed an act declaring resistance to be felony. A proclamation was issued by Governor Tryon offering a reward for the apprehension of Ethan Allen and other conspicuous offenders. This was followed by a burlesque proclamation from the proscribed, affirming their determination to resist and offering a reward for the arrest of the governor of New York. In the spring of 1775, at the time appointed for the session of court in the disputed territory, the settlers took possession of the court-house and prevented the New York officers from entering. The officers thereupon collected a force, and being again refused admittance fired into the house, killing one of the occupants, and wounding several others. Some of the officers were arrested by the enraged inhabitants and lodged in jail, and matters appeared to be approaching a crisis ; but the battle of Lexington occurring at this juncture, active hostilities between Great Britain and the colonies began and caused a cessation of these difficulties.

A cargo of tea had arrived in Boston harbor considerably earlier than in New York, and the Bostonians resolved that it should not be landed. The vessels containing the obnoxious article were boarded and the chests emptied into the water. The ministry, enraged at this spirited resistance, determined to subjugate the colonies. Various measures were determined upon which were ruinous to the liberties of the American people ; among them was the celebrated "Boston Port Bill," closing the harbor and destroying the trade of the city to punish the citizens for having destroyed the tea. The people everywhere were awakened to a lively sympathy with Boston, seeing by its treatment what was in store for them. A brisk correspondence was carried on between Boston and New York through the agency of committees appointed for that purpose. Public meetings were held for the consideration of their common grievances, and among the measures devised and recommended were the restoration of the non-importation agreement and the convening of a colonial congress. On the 5th of September, 1774, this congress met at Philadelphia and adopted a declaration of rights, setting forth wherein those rights had been violated; agreed on a petition to the King for the removal of their grievances and also on an appeal to the people of Great Britain and Canada; and then adjourned to meet again in May of the following year. The Assembly of New York was the only colonial assembly that withheld its approval of the proceedings of this congress It, however, addressed a remonstrance to Parliament, which was treated as all others had been, with disdain. The Assembly adjourned on the 3d of April, 1775, and was never again convened. Its refusal to appoint delegates to the Continental Congress gave great dissatisfaction, and a provincial convention of county representatives was called by the people to perform that duty.

At midnight on the 18th of April, 1775, General Gage sent a detachment of British regulars from Boston to destroy the military stores collected by the Americans at Concord, Massachusetts. The expedition was conducted with great secrecy, but the troops were discovered and the people warned of their coming. On reaching Lexington the following morning they found the militia assembled on the green. The latter, disregarding a command to disperse, were fired upon and several of them were killed. The British troops proceeded to Concord, but the inhabitants, having been apprised of their design, had concealed the greater part of their stores, and the British troops on their return were severely harrassed by the militia who had gathered from the neighboring towns.

When intelligence of this event reached New York the excitement was intense. The affair was in fact the signal for a general rush to arms throughout the colonies. The Sons of Liberty took possession of the arms at the arsenal in New York city and distributed them among the people. At the suggestion of the Committee of Observation a provisional government for the city was formed, consisting of one hundred of the principal citizens, who were to control affairs until Congress should otherwise order. The British troops at New York having been ordered to Boston, the provisional government allowed them to depart on condition that they should take nothing but their own arms with them. Regardless of this stipulation they attempted to carry off some military stores belonging to the city, but were defeated in their designs by Colonel Marinus Willett with a party of the Sons of Liberty, who confronted them and succeeded in retaking the property and replacing it in the fort.

While the patriots were flocking toward Boston the Connecticut Assembly was in session, and several of its members agreed upon a plan to seize the cannon and military stores at Ticonderoga and Crown Point for the use of the patriot army. They appointed a committee to repair to the frontier and raise an expedition, under Colonel Ethan Allan, to surprise and capture the posts named. A force of two hundred and seventy men was soon collected, and marched by night under Colonels Allen and Benedict Arnold to a point on Lake Champlain opposite Ticonderoga. They had but few boats, and when day began to dawn only the officers and eighty-three men had crossed. Fearful that delay would be hazardous, Allen resolved to make an attack before the rear division had crossed, and marched at the head of his men directly to the sally port. The sentinel snapped his musket at him and retreated to the parade with the patriots close at his heels. The garrison were aroused and taken prisoners. Colonel Allen went directly to the apartments of the commander and demanded and obtained a surrender of the fort "in the name of the Great Jehovah, and the Continental Congress." Crown Point was taken without resistance two days afterward, and the command of Lake Champlain was thus secured.

The Continental Congress reassembled and organized on the 10th of May, the same day that Colonel Allen captured Ticonderoga, and proceeded at once to raise and equip an army for the defense of the colonies. New York was ordered to raise three thousand men as her proportion. The population of the province during the preceding year had increased to 182,251. George Washington was commissioned as commander-in-chief of the American forces. A provincial congress of New York, convened on the 22d of May, authorized the raising of troops, encouraged the manufacture of gunpowder and muskets in the province, and projected fortifications at King's Bridge and the Hudson passes in the Highlands.

Captain Lamb was ordered to remove the cannon from the battery at the foot of the city to a place of greater security. On the evening of August 23d he proceeded to the execution of the order. The captain of the British war-ship Asia, being informed of the intended movement, sent a barge filled with men to watch it. A shot was fired from the barge into the American force, which was immediately answered by a volley, killing one of the crew and wounding several others. The Asia then opened a cannonade upon the city, doing considerable damage to the buildings in the vicinity of the battery, but the patriots were undismayed, and in the face of the cannonade, deliberately removed every gun. Governor Tryon returned from England in June and strenuously exerted himself to promote the royal cause. Finding that his position was growing more and more unsatisfactory, and having fears for his personal safety, he abandoned the city and took refuge on board a British sloop of war.

The Continental Congress directed General Schuyler to collect an armament at Ticonderoga, and put that post in in a state of defense, preparatory to an expedition against Canada. The forces under Generals Schuyler and Montgomery appeared before St. John's in September. General Schuyler was compelled by ill health to relinquish the command to General Montgomery and return to Ticonderoga. The fort at Chambly, twelve miles below, was captured on the 19th of October by a detachment of the American force, aided by friendly Canadians. They passed the fort at St. John's during a dark night in boats, with their artillery, and appeared before Chambly, which was feebly garrisoned and soon surrendered. The spoils taken at Chambly materially aided in carrying on with vigor the siege of St. John's, which after several unsuccessful assaults and numerous mishaps was on the 3d of November compelled to surrender. While this siege was in progress, Colonel Ethan Allen, acting without authority from the commander-in-chief, in a rash attempt to take Montreal with a small advance force, was taken prisoner and sent to England. General Carlton, when informed of the capture of Chambly, made an attempt to reinforce the garrison at St. John's, but being defeated by Colonel Seth Warner, only hastened its fall. General Montgomery moved forward to Montreal, which was taken without resistance. In September Colonel Benedict Arnold was dispatched by Washington with a force of eleven hundred men against Canada, by way of the Kennebec river, to aid Montgomery, who was invading that province by way of Lake Champlain. After surmounting incredible obstacles and suffering terrible privations and hardships, Arnold at last arrived at Point Levi, opposite the city of Quebec.

He was for several days prevented from crossing the St. Lawrence by tempestuous winds. On the night of the 13th of November he crossed the river and scaled the heights to the Plains of Abraham. Failing to draw out the garrison he demanded a surrender, which was contemptuously refused. Finding all his attempts useless he retreated up the river about twenty miles and awaited the arrival of Montgomery, who joined him on the 1st of December, and the combined forces then moved toward Quebec.

A bombardment of the city proved unavailing and it was resolved to storm the town, although the whole assailing force was considerably less than the garrison. The lower town was to be attacked by Montgomery and Arnold, and at the same time feigned attacks were to be made upon the upper town. Montgomery descended from the Plains of Abraham to Wolfe's Cove, and marched through the drifting snow toward the lower town, while Arnold with another division moved around to the north on the St. Charles, in order to form a junction with Montgomery and storm Prescott Gate. Montgomery in his advance encountered a block-house defended by a battery. Pushing forward in a charge at the head of his men he was instantly killed, together with his aids, by a discharge of grape-shot from the battery. Appalled at this disaster, his division fell back in confusion and made no further attempt to force a junction with Arnold. Meanwhile the latter had pressed on through the snow-drifts, and like Montgomery charged at the head of his men upon a battery, and received a wound which compelled him to leave the field. Captain Morgan took the command, carried the first battery and rushed on to a second, which was also carried, after a severe contest of three hours' duration.

Carlton sent a detachment from the garrison to attack them in the rear, and while Morgan was pressing on into the town he heard of the death of Montgomery, and finding himself unsupported and surrounded, was compelled to surrender. The rest of the division in the rear retreated. Colonel Arnold took command of the remainder of the army, consisting of about eight hundred men, and intrenched himself a few miles from the city, where he remained until reinforced by General Wooster, in April, who took command and renewed the siege. Large reinforcements having arrived at Quebec, the American force was obliged to retreat, and by the superior numbers of the enemy was soon after driven out of Canada.

CHAPTER XI.

HOSTILITIES TRANSFERRED TO NEW YORK—THE BATTLE OF LONG ISLAND—BURGOYNE'S CAMPAIGN.

IN March, Washington, having compelled General Howe to evacuate Boston, and apprehensive that New York would be the next point of attack, made immediate preparations for putting that city in a posture of defense. General Lee, with twelve hundred men, was ordered forward from Connecticut. The captain of the British man-of-war Asia had threatened to cannonade the city if "rebel troops" were permitted to enter it. It was the stronghold of loyalty to the crown and disaffection to the patriot cause, and the Committee of Safety in their timidity protested against Lee's entrance, but threats and protests were unavailing. Lee came, and the tories either fled or ceased to oppose the cause of the patriots. Sir Henry Clinton, who had been sent over on a secret expedition, appeared off Sandy Hook at nearly the same time that General Lee entered the city, but finding it in possession of the American troops, proceeded south to attack Charleston. Washington hastened forward from Boston, and on the 14th of April arrived at New York and established his headquarters in the city. General Howe went to Halifax on leaving Boston, but about the 1st of July appeared off Sandy Hook, and shortly after landed on Staten Island. He was soon after joined by his brother Admiral Howe, with a force of British regulars and Hessian hirelings, and also by Clinton and Parker on their return from an unsuccessful attack on Charleston, making altogether a combined force of nearly thirty thousand men. Howe was here visited by Governor Tryon, who had contrived a plot to capture Washington, blow up the magazine, and secure the passes to the city. The mayor also was in the conspiracy, and was receiving money from Tryon to bribe the Americans. Two of Washington's guards yielded to the temptations of the enemy, but the third, who could not be bribed, exposed the plot. The Provincial Congress of New York, seeing the hostile demonstrations toward the city, adjourned to White Plains, where it convened on the 9th of July, and passed resolutions heartily endorsing the action of the Continental Congress and approving of the Declaration of Independence.

The plan of the campaign on the part of the British army near New York was to take possession of the city and the islands in its vicinity, and to ascend the Hudson, while Carlton should move down from Canada, and thus separate the Eastern from the other States. Two ships succeeded in passing the batteries and ascended the Hudson to furnish the tories of Westchester with arms, but all their attempts to land were frustrated and they returned.

On the 22d of August a British force of ten thousand men, with forty pieces of cannon, landed on the south side of Long Island, in the vicinity of New Utrecht, and advanced in three divisions upon the Americans stationed in and about Brooklyn. The Hessians, under De Heister, formed the center. The left, along New York Bay, was commanded by General Grant, and the right, which led in the action, was commanded by Clinton and Cornwallis. While Grant and De Heister were diverting the Americans on the left and center, the division on the right was to make a circuitous march and fall upon their rear. This division left the Flatlands on the night of the 26th, and guided by a tory gained possession of the Bedford and Jamaica passes before General Sullivan, who commanded in that quarter, was aware of the movement. While this advantage was being gained Grant was making a movement toward Brooklyn, and early in the morning came into collision with the Americans under Lord Stirling on the site of Greenwood Cemetery, when an engagement took place without material advantage to either side. De Heister advanced and kept up a cannonade on the works at the Flatbush pass. In the meantime, Clinton had gained a position in the rear of the Continental army and commenced to attack them. De Heister then pressed forward, and Sullivan, perceiving the peril of his army, attempted to retreat, but it was too late. They were met by Clinton's forces and driven back upon the Hessians. Some forced their way through the ranks and reached the fortifications, but after a desperate struggle and great loss of life Sullivan himself and the greater part of the left wing of the American army were taken prisoners. Cornwallis hastened to cut off the division under Stirling, who was not yet aware of the situation. A part of his force succeeded in crossing Gowanus creek in safety, but many were drowned or taken prisoners. Stirling himself was captured and a decisive victory gained by the British. About five thousand were engaged on the side of the Americans, of whom five hundred were killed or wounded and eleven hundred taken prisoners. These were confined in loathsome prison-ships on the East river, where they suffered indescribable privations and hardships. Fortunately for the Americans, Howe did not dare to attempt an assault upon their fortifications in Brooklyn, but encamped about a third of a mile distant, and waited for the support of the fleet.

On the 28th, the day after the battle, the British began to cannonade the intrenchments. At night a heavy fog settled over the battle-field, which remained all the following day. When night had added its darkness to the mist which had obstructed the vision of the hostile parties throughout the day, Washington, with the remainder of the troops on Long Island, silently crossed the East river in safety to New York. The British forces took possession of the American works and prepared to attack New York. Washington knew that with his dispirited and undisciplined army he could not successfully oppose them, and decided to evacuate the city. On the 15th of September Howe landed with about four thousand men under cover of his fleet at Kip's Bay, on the east side of Manhattan Island, near what is now the foot of Thirty-fourth street. Two brigades of militia, stationed for defense in that quarter, were panic-stricken and retreated disgracefully despite all the efforts of their officers to rally them. Putnam, who had charge of one column of the army, was compelled to leave in great haste, and narrowly escaped being captured. The Americans retreated to Harlem, and the British took possession of New York and held it until the close of the war.

The next day an advance party of the British were attacked, and after a severe skirmish driven back with considerable loss. Howe, perceiving that the Americans were strongly intrenched upon Harlem Heights, determined to gain their rear, cut off their communication with the north and east, and hem them in. He sent a part of his fleet up the Hudson, and transferred the main body of his army in boats to Westchester county, landing them at Throck's Neck. When Washington saw this movement he sent a detachment to oppose their landing. All the passes were well guarded, and a detachment was intrenched at White Plains. The main army advanced in that direction and intrenched upon the hills from Fordham to White Plains. On the 28th of October the enemy came up and attacked General McDougal, on Chatterton's Hill. McDougal, after an obstinate resistance, was forced to fall back to intrenchments above White Plains. While Howe was preparing to storm their encampment at this place, Washington withdrew, unobserved by the enemy, to North Castle, where strong breastworks had been erected, and awaited an attack; but Howe, not deeming it prudent to assail him in so strong a position, retreated toward New York, preparatory to the contemplated reduction of Fort Washington, which was soon environed by the British forces. It was gallantly defended by Colonel Magaw until he was overpowered by a superior force and compelled to surrender. Fort Lee, on the opposite side of the Hudson, was abandoned on the approach of the enemy, and Washington, who had crossed the Hudson, retreated through New Jersey to the opposite side of the Delaware river, closely pursued by the enemy. On the night of the 25th of December he recrossed the river and gained an important victory at Trenton, and shortly afterward another at Princeton, and then went into winter quarters at Morristown.

General Gates, who had been appointed to the command of the Northern forces, apprehensive that General Carlton would follow up his success in Canada and attempt to capture Crown Point and Ticonderoga, abandoned the former, and concentrated his forces at the latter. A small squadron was formed and placed upon Lake Champlain, under the command of Arnold, in August. Carlton constructed a fleet at St. Johns. Arnold sailed down the lake, but, being ignorant of the strength of the armament preparing against him, fell back to Valcour's Island. On the 11th of October, the British fleet passed around the east side of the island and took up a position south of the American squadron. An action began about noon and continued until night. One of the schooners in Arnold's fleet was disabled, and burned to prevent it from falling into the hands of the enemy. The British force was greatly superior, and as another engagement would have been extremely hazardous, it was deemed advisable to return to Crown Point. The night was exceedingly dark, and the Americans succeeded in sailing through the British fleet unobserved, although the latter had been stationed in a line across the lake in anticipation of such a movement. On reaching Schuyler's Island, ten miles distant from the British fleet, they stopped to make some repairs, and, on being discovered at daylight, were pursued by the enemy. On the 13th, the British ships, three in number, came up with and attacked the "Washington," which, after a heroic defense, was compelled to surrender, and her commander and all his men were taken prisoners. The whole force was now concentrated in an attack upon the "Congress," which maintained the unequal contest with unflinching resolution for four or five hours, till it was reduced to a complete wreck. Arnold then ran the craft into a creek and burned it, together with the rest of his boats, and marching to Crown Point, where the remainder of the fleet was stationed, sailed for Ticonderoga. General Carlton took possession of Crown Point and threatened Ticonderoga, but, abandoning his design, he prudently withdrew to Canada.

The Provincial Congress, which had assembled at White Plains on the 9th of July and approved the Declaration of Independence, appointed a committee to draw up and report a constitution. The occupation of New York city and part of Westchester county by the British greatly disturbed the labors of the convention, and finally, in February, they repaired to Kingston, where the draft of a constitution was prepared by John Jay, and adopted on the 21st of April, 1777. George Clinton was elected governor under the new constitution, and took the oath of office on the 31st of July following.

The principal object of the British in the campaign of 1777 was to carry out their cherished design of separating the Eastern from the Southern colonies, by controlling the Hudson river and Lake Champlain. The most prominent feature of the plan was the advance of an army from Canada, under Lieutenant-General Burgoyne, who had superseded General Carlton. It was intended that Burgoyne should force his way down the Hudson as far as Albany, while Sir Henry Clinton was to proceed up the river and join him, and thus a free communication between New York and Canada would be established, and the colonies separated. In order to distract the attention of the Americans, and the more completely subdue the Western border, Colonel St. Leger was to ascend the St. Lawrence with a detatchment of regulars, accompanied by Sir John Johnston with a regiment of loyalists and a large body of Indians. From Oswego the expedition was to penetrate the country to Fort Schuyler, on the site of Rome, and after its capture sweep the Mohawk valley and join Burgoyne at Albany. Burgoyne arrived in Canada early in March. Unavoidable difficulties having greatly embarrassed his first movements, it was past the middle of June before his army was assembled at Cumberland Point, on Lake Champlain. The main army of more than seven thousand men appeared before Crown Point, and occupied that post on the 30th of June. Having issued a proclamation, intended to terrify the inhabitants into submission, Burgoyne prepared to invest Ticonderoga, then in command of General St. Clair. On the east shore of Lake Champlain, on Mount Independence, there was a star-fort, so connected with Ticonderoga, on the west side of the lake, by a floating bridge, as to obstruct the passage of vessels up the lake. For want of a sufficient force to man all its defenses the outworks toward Lake George were abandoned on the approach of Burgoyne. A detachment of the enemy, under General Fraser, took Mount Hope, and thereby cut off St. Clair's communication with Lake George; and at the same time the abandoned works of the Americans, more to the right, were occupied by General Phillips. On the south side of the outlet of Lake George, and opposite Mount Independence, is a lofty eminence, then known as Sugar-loaf Hill, which was found to completely command the works both at Ticonderoga and Fort Independence. A battery was planted on its summit by the British during the night, and St. Clair, on perceiving his critical situation, at once called a council of war, by which it was unanimously decided that immediate evacuation of Fort Ticonderoga was the only chance of saving the army. During the ensuing night such military stores and provisions as could be removed, together with the sick and disabled troops, were embarked on batteaux, and sent up the lake to Skenesborough, as Whitehall was then called, under convoy of five armed galleys and a detachment of six hundred men, under Colonel Long, while the main body of the army was to cross the lake and proceed to the same point by land. The garrison passed over the floating bridge to Mount Independence about two hours before daylight; and would probably have made their retreat undiscovered had not the house of the commander at Fort Independence been set on fire just at this time. This unfortunate occurrence threw the Americans into disorder, for the light of the conflagration revealed their movements to the British, who made immediate preparations for pursuit. St. Clair's orce made a disorderly retreat to Hubbardton. On the following morning General Fraser came up with his brigade, and commenced an attack. The conflict was for some time fierce and bloody. The Americans had almost surrounded the left wing of the British when General Riedesel came up with reinforcements, and St. Clair made a precipitate retreat. The boats which conveyed the military stores and the detachment of Colonel Long reached Skenesborough safely, but Burgoyne in a few hours broke through the boom and bridge at Ticonderoga, on which the Americans had placed much reliance, and with his fleet rapidly pursued them; and while they were landing at Skenesborough three regiments disembarked at South Bay with the intention of gaining the road to Fort Edward, and cutting off their retreat. On the approach of the British gunboats, Colonel Long's men destroyed three of their galleys and several buildings, and escaped capture by a rapid flight to Fort Anne. Two days after the battle at Hubbardton St. Clair retreated to Fort Edward. Burgoyne was joined at Skenesborough by the detachments of Fraser and Riedesel, and prepared to push forward to the Hudson. Lieutenant-Colonel Hill was sent forward to Fort Anne to intercept such as might retreat to that post, and to watch the movements of the Americans. This post was guarded by Colonel Long, with about five hundred men, mostly convalescents. Hill's force exceeded this number. Colonel Long did not wait for an attack, but marched out to give battle, and gained a decided advantage; but their ammunition giving out, they were obliged to give way; and aware of their inability to hold the fort against General Phillips, who was approaching with reinforcements, set fire to it, and fell back on Fort Edward.

CHAPTER XII.

THE BATTLE OF BENNINGTON—FAILURE OF ST. LEGER'S MOVEMENT—BURGOYNE'S DEFEATS AND SURRENDER.

BURGOYNE remained at Skenesborough nearly three weeks, while detachments were building bridges and repairing the road to Fort Anne. This delay greatly diminished his supplies, and on arriving at Fort Anne he sent a detachment under Colonel Baum to surprise and capture a quantity of stores which he had heard was collected at Bennington, and with the expectation of receiving material aid from the loyalists in that quarter. General Schuyler had not sufficient force to defend Fort Edward, and throwing all the obstructions possible in Burgoyne's way from there to Fort Anne retreated down the valley of the Hudson. Colonel Baum on his march to Bennington reached Cambridge on the 13th of August. The American General Stark in the meantime had repaired to Bennington, and was collecting the militia to join his brigade in opposing any invasion in that direction. Hearing that a party of Indians were at Cambridge, he detached Colonel Gregg to attack them; and shortly after, learning that a large body of the enemy was in their rear marching on Bennington, he moved immediately to the support of Gregg. After going about five miles he met him retreating, and Colonel Baum not more than a mile in the rear. Stark at once disposed his army for battle, and Baum perceiving its strength began to intrench, and sent to Burgoyne for reinforcements. The next day some skirmishing took place, and on the following day, August 16th, Stark arranged his army for an attack. Two detachments were sent to flank the enemy while another was attracting their attention in front. As soon as the attack on the enemy's flank began the main body pressed forward, and after two hours' fierce conflict gained a decisive victory. The remnant of Colonel Baum's force in its flight was met by Colonel Breyman with reinforcements, who pressed forward with the combined force to regain the abandoned intrenchments. Stark was also reinforced, and the conflict was renewed with vigor. The enemy at length giving way, were pursued until darkness came to their rescue and enabled them with their thinned and broken ranks to escape to the main army. Colonel Baum was mortally wounded and taken prisoner. The total loss of the enemy was, in killed, wounded and prisoners, nine hundred and thirty-four, and all their artillery and military stores. Up to this time all had gone well with the boastful Briton, and his path had been illuminated with victory; but with the failure of this expedition his glory began to wane and his sky to grow dark and threatening, where hitherto it had been bright and serene.

While these events had been taking place with the main division, the expedition under Colonel St. Leger had invested Fort Schuyler (earlier and even now more commonly called Fort Stanwix), on the site of Rome. A movement of the Mohawk valley militia to its relief was arrested by the bloody battle of Oriskany, but while most of the besiegers were engaged in this conflict their camp was sacked by the garrison; and learning that a more formidable provincial force was on its way to raise the siege of the fort, which had held out tenaciously, St. Leger abandoned his undertaking and returned to Canada.

Schuyler, with his army, marched down the Hudson to Stillwater, and finally to the mouth of the Mohawk, still keeping his headquarters at Stillwater and exerting all his energies for the augmentation of his force, preparatory to a conflict with Burgoyne. On the 19th of August, at the instigation of his enemies, he was very unjustly superseded by General Gates. On the 8th of September the American army advanced to Bemis' Heights, above Stillwater, which had been fortified under the superintendence of Kosciusko. The British detachment sent to Bennington, instead of bringing back any plunder had lost largely of what they already had, as well as most of the force, and Burgoyne had hardly recovered from this unexpected shock when the news was brought him of the defeat of St. Leger at Fort Schuyler. These disasters had a very depressing effect upon his army, and the Indians and loyalists began to desert, while the Americans were greatly inspirited. In view of these difficulties the British commander deemed it expedient to halt at Fort Edward.

Stores having been brought forward from the posts on Lake Champlain, he proceeded down the Hudson, and on the 18th of September encamped at Wilbur's Basin, two miles from the American position, and prepared for battle, and the next day advanced to the attack in three divisions. General Riedesel commanded the left column, which with the heavy artillery moved down a road along the margin of the river. The center was commanded by Burgoyne in person, and the left by General Fraser. The front and flanks of both the center and right were covered by Indians, tories and Canadians. The American right, which was the main body of their army, was commanded by Gates, and the left by General Arnold. Colonel Morgan was detached from Arnold's division and encountering the Canadians and Indians in the advance drove them back; but they being reinforced the contest resulted in both parties finally falling within their respective lines. The action soon became general, and the combined force of Burgoyne and Fraser was engaged with Arnold's division. Arnold called upon Gates for reinforcements but they were refused, and he, resolving to do what he could with the force at his command, continued the contest with the most obstinate and determined resolution, both armies alternately advancing and retreating without a decisive victory for either. The conflict did not cease until the shades of night fell upon the combatants. The Americans then retired to their encampment unpursued by the enemy. The British forces bivouacked on the field of battle. The total loss of the former was three hundred and nineteen, and that of the latter more than five hundred. Few actions have been more remarkable for determined bravery on both sides than this. The number of the British in the engagement was about three thousand, and that of the Americans five hundred less. Both parties claimed the victory. The object of the British was to advance and gain ground, which they failed to do; while it was not the intention of the Americans to advance, but to maintain their position, which they accomplished, and it is therefore not difficult to determine on which side the advantage lay. Though the British remained in possession of the battle-field through the night, they retired to their camp in the morning without advancing to renew the conflict. General Gates, in his report of the battle, said nothing of Arnold or his division, to whom all the honor was due. He was jealous of the reputation that officer had earned, and of his growing popularity with the army, and carried his meanness so far as to take from him the command of his division. Both parties strengthened their positions after the battle, but no general engagement took place for upwards of three weeks.

Burgoyne saw with painful anxiety that the American forces were rapidly increasing, while his own were daily diminishing by the desertion of his Indian allies. His provisions began to fail, and the vigilance of the Americans not only prevented any supplies reaching him, but deprived him of all communication with Sir Henry Clinton for assistance. At length he was obliged to put his troops on short allowance, and hearing nothing from Clinton, who was to make a diversion in his favor, became seriously alarmed. Amid the thickening perils he found himself reduced to the alternative of fighting or retreating. The latter was not only inglorious but difficult, and he resolved to make a reconnoissance in force, for the twofold purpose of ascertaining definitely the position of the enemy, and of collecting forage to supply his camp, of which it was in pressing need. On the 7th of October he, at the head of fifteen hundred men and accompanied by Generals Riedesel, Phillips and Fraser, advanced toward the left wing of the American position. The movement was seasonably perceived by the Americans, and the enemy were repulsed and driven back to their lines by Morgan, who, at his own suggestion, was dispatched by a circuitous route to gain the right of the British, and fall upon the flanking party of Fraser at the same time an attack was to be made on the left of the British. General Poor advanced toward an eminence upon which were stationed the British grenadiers and the artillery of Ackland and Williams. He had given his men orders not to fire until after the first discharge of the British guns, and they moved onward toward the frowning battery in awful silence until a sudden volley of grape-shot and musket balls made havoc among the branches of the trees, scarcely a shot taking effect upon the advancing column. At this signal Poor's men sprang forward and delivered their fire, and opening to the right and left pressed furiously upon the enemy's flanks and gained the top of the hill, where the struggle became fierce and obstinate in the extreme. One cannon was taken and retaken five successive times, finally remaining in the hands of the Americans, when Colonel Cilly turned it upon the retreating enemy, and fired it with their own ammunition. Williams and Ackland were both taken prisoners, the latter being severely wounded; and the grenadiers fled in confusion, leaving the field in possession of the Americans, thickly strewn with their dead and wounded.

As soon as the action was begun at this point Morgan's command rushed down like an avalanche from the ridge skirting the flanking party of Fraser, and assailed them with such a destructive fire that they were hastily driven back to their lines. Then, by a rapid movement, he fell upon the right flank of the British with such impetuosity as to throw them into confusion, and Major Dearborn, coming up at this critical moment, completed their discomfiture. The right and left of the British lines were thus broken, but the center had remained firm. General Arnold, who had so unjustly been deprived of his command, had been watching the progress of the battle in great excitement, and now mounted his horse and started for the battle-field. Gates sent Major Armstrong to order him back, but Arnold, suspecting his errand, was quickly beyond his reach, and exposed to such perils that the messenger was not anxious to follow him. Placing himself at the head of the men he formerly commanded, he rushed like an unchained tiger upon the British center, which soon began to give way under his furious assault. General Fraser, who was commanding on the right, seeing the center in such a critical situation, brought up reinforcements, and by his courage and skill restored order. He soon fell mortally wounded; dismay seized the British soldiers, and a panic spread all along the line, which was increased by the appearance of General Ten Broeck with a reinforcement of New York militia. Burgoyne, finding himself unable to keep up the sinking courage of his men, abandoned his artillery and ordered a retreat, and the whole force fell back precipitately to their intrenchments. The Americans pursued them, and scarcely were they within their fortifications when, under a terrific shower of grape and musket balls, Arnold assaulted them from right to left, forcing the outworks, and driving the enemy to the interior of their camp. Here he was overtaken by Major Armstrong, who delivered to him Gates' order to return to camp, fearing that "he might do some rash thing." He returned, but not until he had achieved a glorious victory, and put his life in great peril without a command, while Gates had remained in camp, receiving the honors that justly belonged to others. Night came on and the conflict ceased; before dawn Burgoyne abandoned his encampment, now rendered untenable, and the Americans early in the morning took possession of it.

Burgoyne, who in the beginning of the campaign had boastfully exclaimed, in general orders, "Britons never retreat," now found that there was no alternative for him but retreat, and when night came on again he began his retrograde movement in the midst of a drenching rain. This had been anticipated, and General Fellows, previous to the action on the 7th inst., had been sent with a detachment to take a position opposite Saratoga ford, on the east side of the Hudson. Another detachment of two thousand men, was now sent to occupy the heights beyond Sarotoga, to prevent Burgoyne's retreat upon Fort Edward; and still another was stationed at the ford above. On the evening of the 9th Burgoyne halted for the night at Fish creek. The main portion of his army forded the creek and encamped on the opposite bank, while he, with a brigade as a guard, passed the night rather merrily with some companions in a house belonging to General Schuyler. This delay lost him his army. Finding the ford across the Hudson strongly guarded by the detachment under Fellows, he concluded to continue his retreat up the river to Fort Edward. He sent forward a party to repair the bridges, and a detachment to take possession of the fort, but finding the Americans stationed in force upon the heights, they fell back to the main army. In the afternoon of the 10th General Gates came up, with the bulk of the American army, in pursuit, and occupied the high ground on the south side of Fish creek, opposite the enemy's encampment. The detachment sent forward to Fort Edward led General Gates to believe the rumor that the main army of Burgoyne had retreated, and he resolved to fall upon what he supposed was the rear guard. Burgoyne was aware of Gates' error, and hoping to profit by it concealed his troops for the purpose of falling upon the Americans as soon as a favorable opportunity should be afforded. Early the next morning, and in a thick fog, which both parties considered favorable to their respective designs, the army of Gates advanced. Morgan was ordered to cross the creek and begin the action, and at once fell in with the British pickets, who fired upon him and killed several of his party. His reception led him to believe that the rumor of the enemy's retreat was false; that the main body of Burgoyne's force was still near, and that the position of his own corps was critical. Another brigade had already crossed and captured a picket-guard, and another was about to follow when a deserter from the enemy came in, reporting that the entire British army was at hand, and prepared for battle, which statement was shortly after confirmed by the capture of a reconnoitering party. As the fog cleared away and exposed the position of both armies, a retreat was deemed advisable by the detachments that had crossed the creek. As soon as they turned about, the British, who were watching their movements and awaiting their advance, opened fire upon them, but they made their retreat with the loss of only a few men.

Burgoyne was now completely environed. On the opposite bank of the Hudson, Fellows was entrenched, with heavy batteries to open on him if he should attempt to cross the river. Fort Edward was held by an American force of two thousand men. On the south and west the main body of the Americans was posted, while small detachments were in all directions watching his every movement, and continually harrassing his outposts. His provisions were almost exhausted, and none could be obtained, and it was extremely hazardous to attempt to get water from the river or creek. There was no place of safety for the sick and wounded, and the women and children, as well as soldiers and officers, were constantly exposed to the cannon balls that were flying about the encampment. On the 12th he held a consultation with his generals, and it was decided to retreat that night, but the returning scouts brought such discouraging intelligence that the movement was postponed till morning. During the night the Americans crossed the river on rafts, and erected a battery on Burgoyne's left flank. Retreat was now hopeless. The next morning a general council was called, when it was unanimously decided to open negotiations with General Gates for an honorable surrender. This conclusion was hastened by the passage of a cannon ball across the table at which Burgoyne and other generals were seated. The negotiations were not completed until the 16th, when the terms of his surrender were agreed upon, and were to be signed by the commander on the following morning. During the night a tory succeeded in reaching the British camp from down the river, who reported that Clinton had taken the forts on the Hudson and ascended the river as far as Esopus. This news so excited Burgoyne's hopes that he resolved not to sign the articles of capitulation, and to gain time he wrote Gates that he had been informed that a part of his army had been sent toward Albany, which, if true, should be considered a breach of faith, and that he could not give his signature until convinced that the strength of the Americans had not been misrepresented. He was informed by Gates that his army was as strong as it had been before these negotiations took place, and unless the articles were signed immediately he should open fire upon him. Burgoyne thereupon reluctantly signed the articles of capitulation.

The surrender of Burgoyne was of the utmost importance to the Americans in their struggle for independence. The preponderance of success up to this time had been on the side of the British. The reverses on Long Island and at New York in the previous year, together with the recent defeats in Pennsylvania, had darkened the military horizon with thick clouds of doubt and dismay. All eyes were now anxiouly watching the army of the north, which had also been forced to relinquish Ticonderoga and Fort Edward at the commencement of the campaign, and shaded the prospect of successful resistance in that direction. The news of a complete victory filled the patriots with joy and hope, and appalled the tories, who now began to tremble.

CHAPTER XIII.

CLINTON'S HUDSON RIVER CAMPAIGN—FRANCE RECOGNIZES THE UNITED STATES—WARS WITH THE INDIANS.

WHEN Burgoyne first perceived the difficulties gathering around him, he urged Sir Henry Clinton to hasten the expedition up the Hudson to join him, but Clinton was obliged to wait for the arrival of reinforcements, and it was the 4th of October before he was ready to move. The first object to be accomplished was the reduction of Forts Montgomery and Clinton in the Highlands. These had been constructed to prevent the ships of the enemy from ascending the river, and each was indefensible in its rear, and feebly garrisoned. Clinton landed first at Verplanck's Point, and under cover of a fog dropped down with a part of his force to Stony Point, where he landed, and marched toward the forts. These were commanded by Governor George Clinton and his brother James. Governor Clinton, on learning that the enemy were moving up the river, sent out a scouting party to watch their movements, and from them he first learned of their having landed at Stony Point. A small force was then sent out by him, which met the advance guard of the British about three miles out. Shots were exchanged, and the Americans retreated to the forts. Governor Clinton then sent out a stronger detachment to oppose the enemy's advance, and as this was soon engaged in a sharp conflict, another was sent to its assistance. They were pressed back by a superior force, but not until the enemy had met with considerable loss. Upon nearing the forts the British were divided into two columns, and made a simultaneous assault upon them. After an incessant fire for several hours the British general demanded an instant and unconditional surrender. The proposition was rejected, and the conflict continued until evening, when part of the besieged fought their way out. Governor Clinton made his escape, and likewise his brother, though wounded. Fort Constitution was abandoned on the approach of the British, which gave them command of the river. A detachment under Vaughn and Wallace landed without much opposition and burned Kingston. On hearing of the disastrous termination of Burgoyne's campaign the expedition returned to New York.

It was obvious that France had no sympathy with Great Britain, but looked upon the revolt of her colonies with secret satisfaction, and earnestly desired their separation from England. By the war which closed in 1763 she had been compelled to relinquish her extensive possessions in North America, and she rejoiced to have an opportunity to assist in the infliction of a like dismemberment of territory upon Great Britain. The commissioners at the court of Versailles from the revolted colonies, although not always openly countenanced, were by no means discouraged, and aid was frequently extended to the Americans in a clandestine manner. When intelligence of the capture of Burgoyne reached France her vacillating policy ended, and, casting off all disguise, she entered into a treaty of alliance with, and on the 6th of February, 1778, acknowledged the independence of the United States. This event made the patriots almost certain of ultimate success.

The Indians and tories who had been dispersed at Fort Schuyler were meditating mischief, and making preparations through the winter of 1777-8 to invade the Mohawk valley. Brant, the Indian chief who had prepared the ambuscade at Oriskany, was foremost in these threatening movements. Sir John Johnson and Colonel John Butler were also active in enlisting tory refugees. A council was called by the Revolutionary authorities, to secure, if possible, the neutrality of the Indians. It met at Johnstown in March. None of the Senecas, the most powerful of the Six Nations, were present, and but few of the Mohawks. General La Fayette, who was to command a proposed expedition against Canada, attended the council. His attention was called to the exposed condition of the settlements, and he directed the building and strengthening of fortifications for their protection. The first hostile movement of Brant was the destruction of the small settlement of Springfield, at the head of Otsego lake. On the 2d of July an engagement occurred on the upper branch of the Cobleskill between an Indian force of four hundred and fifty and fifty-two Americans. The latter were overpowered. The Indians burned the dwellings, and slaughtered the cattle and horses they could not take with them. The settlers generaly were continualy harrassed by marauding parties of Indians during the summer, but on the approach of winter Brant withdrew with his forces toward Niagara, and hostilities apparently ceased. On his way to Niagara he was met by Walter Butler, a fugitive from justice. He had been arrested as a spy and condemned to death, but had been reprieved through the intercession of friends, sent to

Albany, and confined in prison, from which he made his escape. He joined his father, Col. John Butler, at Niagara, and obtained command of two hundred tories to unite with Brant in an incursion into the Mohawk valley. Upon meeting Brant he prevailed upon him to return and attack the settlement of Cherry Valley. Colonel Alden, who was in command of the fort at that place, received information of the intended attack, but treated it with unconcern. He refused to permit the settlers to move into the fort, believing it to be a false alarm. He, however, assured them that he would keep scouts on the look-out to guard against surprise, and he did send them, but they fell into the hands of the savages, who extorted from them all necessary information respecting the situation. On the morning of the 11th of November the enemy entered the settlement, under cover of a thick and misty atmosphere, and began an indiscriminate slaughter of men, women, and children. The house of Mr. Wells, of which Colonel Alden was an inmate, was surrounded, and the whole of the family brutally massacred. The colonel, in attempting to escape, was tomahawked and scalped. Thirty-two of the inhabitants, mostly women and children, and sixteen soldiers of the garrison, were slain in the most horrible manner. The whole settlement was plundered, and every house burned. Nearly forty prisoners were taken, and conducted down the valley to encamp for the night, promiscuously huddled together, some of them half naked, without shelter, and no resting-place but the cold ground. The next day, finding the women and children cumbersome, the captors sent most of them back. The infamous Butler was not only the author of this savage expedition, but he was the director of all the cruelty practiced. With the destruction of this settlement hostilities ceased along the frontier until the following spring. Through the winter Brant and his colleagues were making preparations for a renewal of their incursions, and necessity seemed to demand the infliction of severe punishment upon the savages who threatened to desolate the border settlements. Accordingly on the 18th of April, 1779, Colonel Van Schaick was sent out with a force from Fort Schuyler to make a descent upon the Onondagas. The expedition had approached to within a few miles of their villages and castle before their occupants were aware of the expedition against them. The Indians fled to the woods, leaving everything behind them, even to their arms. Their villages, three in number, consisting of about fifty houses, were burned, and their provisions and cattle destroyed. The council house, or castle, was spared from the flames, but a swivel found in it was rendered useless. Thirty-three of the Indians were taken prisoners and twelve killed. The expedition then returned to Fort Schuyler, arriving on the 24th, having accomplished its object in six days, without the loss of a man. While this short campaign was in progress, the lower section of the Mohawk was visited at different points by scalping parties, and the settlements menaced with the fate of Cherry Valley. The Onondagas, fired with indignation at the destruction of their villages, retaliated by a descent upon the settlement at Cobleskill, and more than twenty of the militia were killed in defending it. The settlement at Minisink being unprotected, Brant resolved to ravage it. On the night of the 19th of July, at the head of a party of Indians and tories disguised as savages, he silently approached the town, and had set fire to several houses before the inhabitants were aroused to the danger of their situation. All who could sought safety in flight, leaving everything to the invaders, who plundered and destroyed all their property, and retired to Grassy Brook, where Brant had left the main body of his warriors. When intelligence of this outrage reached Goshen, Doctor Tusten, colonel of the local militia, ordered them to meet him at Minisink, and one hundred and forty-nine responded to the call. A council was held, and it was resolved to pursue the invaders. Colonel Tusten was opposed to such a hazardous undertaking with so small a force, but he was overruled, and the line of march taken up. The next morning the pursuers were joined by Colonel Hathorn, with a small reinforcement. On coming to the place where the Indians had encamped the previous night, it was obvious from the number of camp-fires that the force was much larger than had been expected, and the leading officers advised return rather than pursuit, but their rash associates were determined to proceed. Soon after Captain Tyler, who was with a scouting party, was shot by a hidden foe, but this circumstance, although it gave the company some alarm, did not check the pursuit. When the party reached the hill overlooking the Delaware, they saw the enemy marching toward the fording place near the mouth of the Lackawaxen. Hathorn determined to intercept them, and arranged his men accordingly. Hills intervened between the opposing forces, and they soon lost sight of each other. Brant was watching the movements of the whites, and anticipating their design turned as soon as they were lost to view, and throwing his whole force in their rear, formed an ambuscade. Not finding the enemy where they had expected Hathorn's men were greatly perplexed, and retracing their steps discovered the Indians in an unexpected quarter and greatly superior in numbers. The latter managed to cut off from the main body of Hathorn's troops about one-third of his entire force in the commencement of the skirmish. From the summit of a hill the militia maintained the unequal conflict until their ammunition was exhausted, and then attempted to retreat, but only thirty succeeded in making their escape from their merciless enemies. When the retreat began there were seventeen of the wounded behind a ledge of rocks under the care of Doctor Tusten, and in this helpless condition they were ruthlessly murdered, together with the doctor, by the Indians.

But a fearful retribution was at hand, and soon fell on the Indians with destructive force. In the spring it was determined to send a large expedition into the Indian country, and so severely chastise the savages and their tory allies as to discourage them from renewing their depredations upon the settlements. General Sullivan was placed in the chief command of this expedition, the plan of which was a combined movement in two divisions; one from Pennsylvania, to ascend the Susquehanna, under Sullivan himself, and the other from the north, under General James Clinton. The two divisions were to unite at Tioga. On the 17th of June General Clinton commenced the transportation of his boats across the country from Canajoharie to Otsego lake, and proceeded to its outlet, where he awaited orders from Sullivan. While there he built a dam to confine the water within the lake, hoping by its sudden removal to render the navigation of the river more certain in case of a long drought. This not only facilitated the transportation of his boats upon the river, but it caused an overflow of its banks and destroyed the corn-fields belonging to the Indians, who, being ignorant of the cause of their loss, were greatly astonished and alarmed. General Clinton formed a junction with Sullivan at Tioga on the 22d of August, and the combined force moved cautiously up the Tioga and Chemung. On the 29th the enemy were discovered occupying an advantageous position near the present city of Elmira. The light infantry in the advance formed for battle, and while waiting for the main body to come up skirmishing was carried on with small parties of Indians who would sally out from their works, fire, and retreat, and make the woods echo with their hideous war-whoops. The Indians occupied a hill on the right, and Sullivan ordered Poor with his brigade to flank them, while the main body of the army attacked them in front. As Poor began to ascend the hill he was fiercely opposed by the savages under Brant and the tories under Sir John Johnson. It was some hours before the latter began slowly to give way. Having gained the summit of the hill Poor moved against the enemy's left flank, which he soon carried, and perceiving that they would be surrounded they abandoned their works and made a precipitate retreat. Sullivan's army encamped upon the battle-field that night, and the next day the wounded were sent back, together with the heavy artillery, and the march was resumed toward Catharine's Town, where the expedition arrived on the 2d of September. On the following day the place was destroyed, together with the corn-fields and orchards. The Indians fled before the invaders, who continued their work of destruction, pillaging the villages of their enemies and thus depriving them of all means of subsistence. On the 7th Sullivan's army reached Kanadaseagea, the capital of the Senecas. This they destroyed, as well as all the smaller villages on their way to the Genesee river, which was reached and crossed on the 14th. The Genesee castle was doomed to meet the fate of the rest, and the whole surrounding country, together with the town, which comprised 120 houses, was swept as with the besom of destruction. On the 16th the expedition recrossed the Genesee river, and retracing their steps arrived at Tioga, the starting point, on the 3d of October. The Indians, although subjected to great suffering, were not wholly crushed by these severe losses. Their numerical force was but slightly reduced, and they retaliated upon the frontier settlements with savage vengeance whenever a favorable opportunity offered.

CHAPTER XIV.

ARNOLD'S TREASON—CLOSE OF THE REVOLUTION—ADOPTION OF THE CONSTITUTION—INTERNAL IMPROVEMENTS.

EARLY in June of 1779 Sir Henry Clinton conducted an expedition up the Hudson, and attacked two small forts, one at Stony Point, on the west side of the river, and the other at Verplank's Point, nearly opposite. The former had only about forty men to defend it, and they retreated on the approach of the British; but the latter, with its garrison of seventy men, resisted, and was captured. Washington much regretted the loss of these posts, and although they had been enlarged and strengthened after the British took possession of them he resolved to make an effort to regain them. Stony Point was surprised on the night of the 15th of July following, and after a short and fierce conflict the garrison, of more than five hundred men, together with the cannon and military stores, were captured, and the works demolished and abandoned.

In the spring of 1780 Brant was again upon the war-path, and with a band of Indians and tories destroyed Harpersfield in April. It was his design to attack the upper fort of Schoharie, but on his way he captured Captain Harper, who represented to him that the fort had lately been reinforced, and he returned to Niagara with his prisoners. Sir John Johnson, with a force of five hundred tories and Indians, very unexpectedly appeared at Johnstown on the night of May 21st, and the next day swept the country between that neighborhood and the Mohawk. Several persons were murdered, others taken prisoners, and all buildings not belonging to the tories were burned. On the following afternoon the party retreated toward Canada. On the 21st of August Canajoharie and the adjacent settlements were attacked by Brant, at the head of a large body of Indians and tories, who did even more damage than Johnson's party.

General Benedict Arnold, wounded at the last battle with Burgoyne, and unable to take any active position, was appointed military governor of Philadelphia in the spring of 1778. Feeling the importance of his station, and fond of making a show, he began living in such an extravagant manner as to become pecuniarily embarrassed; and rather than retrench, and live within his income, he resorted to a system of fraud which brought him into unpleasant relations with the citizens of Philadelphia. By order of Congress he was tried before a court-martial, and sentenced to the mildest form of punishment—simply a reprimand from the commander-in-chief. He appeared to acquiesce in the sentence, but his pride was wounded and he thirsted for revenge. While in Philadelphia he had married the daughter of a tory residing in that place. She was accustomed to receive the attentions of British officers during their occupancy of the city, and through her intimacy with Major Andre a correspondence had been initiated between him and Arnold, by which means the latter's treacherous schemes were developed, and culminated in a most infamous treason. Still he was loud in his professions of patriotism and attachment to his country's cause, and pretended to be anxious to again join his companions in the field. He solicited the command of West Point, then the most important post in the possession of the Americans. Washington had assigned him to the command of the left wing of the army, but upon his repeated and earnest request the command of West Point was given him instead, on the 3d of August, 1780. He established his headquarters on the opposite side of the river, at the house of Colonel Beverly Robinson, whose property had been confiscated on account of his espousal of the British cause. Arnold well knew that Sir Henry Clinton would richly reward him for being instrumental in placing West Point in his hands, and hinted as much to Major Andre, between whom and himself letters passed in disguised hand-writing and over fictitious signatures. In order to settle the terms of this infamous treachery it became necessary for Sir Henry Clinton to send Major Andre for a personal interview with Arnold, not only to agree upon the conditions of his contemplated surrender but to guard against a counterplot. Major Andre sailed up the Hudson on board of the Vulture, and a meeting was finally effected. Near the village of Haverstraw resided Joshua H. Smith, who was duped by Arnold to assist in carrying out his designs. It was he who brought Major Andre on shore, where Arnold was awaiting him, and concealed in a thicket they plotted the ruin of the patriot cause from about midnight until day began to dawn, and then repaired to Smith's house to complete their plans. Arnold was to receive ten thousand pounds and the office of Brigadier-General in the British army, while West Point was to be given up on the approach of the English fleet. Major Andre was supplied with papers explaining the military condition of the fort, which were concealed in his stockings; while a pass was given him under the name of John Anderson. In the morning a cannonade was opened upon the Vulture, and she was obliged to fall farther down the river, which reminded Andre of the fact that he was within the American lines. Smith's fears were so much aroused that he refused to convey him by boat to the Vulture, but offered to accompany him a considerable distance by a land route. They crossed the river and proceeded toward White Plains. Near Pines Bridge they parted, and Andre continued his journey alone. When near Tarrytown he was stopped by three militiamen, who were watching for stragglers from the British lines. From what they said to him he was led to believe they were loyalists, whereupon he avowed himself a British officer, but upon discovering his mistake he presented Arnold's pass, and endeavored to explain his previous statements; they insisted upon searching him, and he was forced to submit, and the important papers were found. His liberal offers of money if they would release him were of no avail, and he was conducted to the nearest military post.

On the same morning that Washington arrived at Arnold's head-quarters from Hartford, where he had been to confer with some French officers, Arnold received intelligence of Andre's arrest, and hastening to his barge made his escape to the Vulture. He was apprised that Washington would soon be at his quarters, and left orders to inform him that he had gone over to West Point, and would soon return. Washington arrived shortly after, and crossing over to West Point found, to his surprise, that Arnold had not been there. After spending some time in examining the works he returned, when the papers which had been found upon Andre were placed in his hands and the whole conspiracy revealed. An immediate pursuit to overtake the traitor was made, but it was too late to prevent his escape. Unfortunate Andre was tried by a court of fourteen generals, convicted of being a spy, sentenced, and executed. Arnold wreaked his malice on the Americans by devastating different parts of the country during the war. After its close he went to England, where he was shunned and despised by all honorable men.

On the 15th of October, 1780, a large party of tories and Indians, under Sir John Johnson and Brant, invaded the Mohawk valley by way of Schoharie creek, destroying the settlements on the way to Fort Hunter, and thence up the Mohawk on both sides. As soon as intelligence of this invasion reached Albany General Van Rensselaer marched against them with a body of militia. Colonel Brown was stationed at Fort Paris, and receiving orders from Van Rensselaer to attack the enemy promptly obeyed, but his small force was dispersed, and himself and forty of his men slain. Van Rensselaer, after great delay, attacked and routed the invaders, who fled and succeeded in making their escape to Canada. The Mohawk valley continued to be devastated by the savage foe. On the 9th of July, 1781, Currytown was attacked by a party of more than three hundred Indians, commanded by a tory named Doxstader. They were pursued by Colonel Willett, and in a battle forty of their number were slain and the others routed. On the 24th of October Major Ross and Walter Butler, at the head of nearly a thousand men, consisting of British regulars, Indians and tories, made a sudden descent into the Mohawk valley and began a work of plunder and devastation. They were met by Colonels Willett and Rowley near Johnstown, and a sharp engagement ensued, lasting till dark, when the enemy fled. They were pursued, and at Canada creek another skirmish took place, wherein the cruel and infamous Butler was slain. Upon his fall their whole force fled in the utmost confusion. This was the final invasion of the Mohawk valley, and their flight the closing scene in one of the most terrible warfares on record.

While menacing an attack on New York, Washington carefully withdrew from the Hudson to attack Cornwallis in his devastating march through the South, and was far on his way to Virginia before Sir Henry Clinton was aware of the movement. Cornwallis was besieged at Yorktown, and compelled to surrender his whole army on the 19th of October, 1781. This virtually closed the war. Sir Guy Carlton was sent to take the command of the British forces in place of Sir Henry Clinton, with directions to open negotiations for peace. A provisional treaty was signed on the 30th of November, 1782, and a definitive treaty, recognizing the independence of the United States, was concluded at Paris, September 3d, 1783. On the 25th of November the British troops took their final departure from the city of New York, and on the same day Washington entered it with his army, amid the joyous acclamations of the emancipated people. Never, perhaps, was peace more welcome, for the long war had been a terrible ordeal for the patriots, and we who are living in peace and plenty, so far removed by the wheels of time from that eventful period, are not likely to properly estimate their endurance of great and continued sufferings, nor fully appreciate the liberties they obtained at so great a sacrifice, and bequeathed to succeeding generations.

The United States having been recognized as an independent nation, it was early perceived that the powers conferred upon Congress by the Articles of Confederation were in many essential respects inadequate to the objects of an effective national government. The States had been leagued together for a particular purpose, but retained their individual sovereignty, and Congress had no power to compel them to obey its mandates. The people were losing their regard for the authority of Congress; its recommendations for the liquidation of the debts incurred by the war were not promptly complied with, and financial and commercial affairs were falling into serious derangement. Each State being independent of the others in the confederacy, jealousies would naturally arise, and without concerted action on the part of the States it was almost impossible to collect revenue. In view of these increasing evils the leading minds of the country desired a closer union of the States under a general government. A convention was held at Annapolis, in September, 1786, to take into consideration the establishment of a general tariff on imports and a uniform system of commercial regulations. Commissioners were present, however, from only five States, among which was New York, represented by Alexander Hamilton. They recommended the calling of a convention of delegates from the several States in May following, and transmitted a report of their conclusions to Congress. Their recommendations were adopted by Congress, and that body deemed it expedient that the delegates should be instructed to revise the Articles of Confederation and report to Congress and the several State Legislatures such amendments and provision as should seem adequate to the exigencies of the government. All the States except Rhode Island were represented in the convention, which was held at Philadelphia. Believing that the Articles of Confederation were so defective as to be wholly inadequate to the wants of the country the delegates went to work to form a new constitution. Its plan was generally approved, but there were many in the convention who looked upon the preservation of State sovereignty as pre-eminently essential, and regarded the proposed change in this particular as an infringement of State rights. The delegates from New York, upon their appointment, had been restricted to the revision of the existing Articles of Confederation; and when the convention decided to provide a new constitution they, with the exception of Alexander Hamilton, withdrew. That body then proceeded to form a constitution, which was adopted and submitted to the several States for approval, the assent of nine being required for its ratification. A spirited contest ensued in the State of New York between its advocates and opponents, the latter being in the ascendancy; but having been adopted by the requisite number of States, it was ratified in convention by the State of New York by a close vote on the 26th of July, 1788, but with the recommendation of several amendments which however, were not adopted. The city of New York was chosen for the seat of the federal government, and George Washington was elected President.

The difficulties relative to the New Hampshire grants still continued. A convention of the people in that disputed territory in 1777 declared it an independent State, and petitioned Congress for admission into the confederacy. New York thereupon sought the interposition of Congress in her behalf, and that body recognized her claims; but the people interested in the New Hampshire grants were determined to maintain their independence, and during the following year organized a State government. This revived the discord, which had remained inactive since the breaking out of the war, and so great was the hatred of the New Hampshire people toward the State of New York, that rather than be subject to her jurisdiction they chose to return to their allegiance to Great Britain, and were secretly negotiating with the British to become a colony under the crown; but before the conspiracy was fully matured it was interrupted by the capture of Cornwallis. Hostile feelings continued after the war, but in 1790 the difficulties were amicably adjusted. New York, on receiving a stipulated sum for the extinction of land claims, relinquished her jurisdiction, and in the following year the disputed territory was admitted into the Union, under the name of Vermont.

Large tracts of wild land were in possession of the State of New York at the termination of the war. In 1786 the State granted two tracts to Massachusetts, to satisfy certain antiquated claims of that State, but retained her sovereignty over the ceded territory. The largest of these tracts, known as the Genesee country, embraced the western part of the State, and was designated by a line running south from Sodus Bay on Lake Ontario to Pennsylvania. The other embraced a portion of the present counties of Tioga and Broome. Land commissioners of the State, a few years later, authorized by an act of the Legislature, disposed of large tracts of land in the northern part of the State for very small considerations. The largest and most important of these was that granted to Alexander Macomb, containing upward of three and a half millions of acres, at about eighteen pence per acre.

In 1791 the Legislature ordered an exploration and survey to ascertain the most eligible method of removing obstructions from the Mohawk and Hudson rivers, with a view to improving their navigation by the construction of canals. The following year two companies were incorporated, styled the Northern and Western Inland Lock Navigation Companies, for the purpose of facilitating navigation by connecting by canals Lake Ontario with the Mohawk and Lake Champlain with the Hudson.

Governor Clinton in 1795 having declined to be a candidate for re-election, John Jay was chosen as his successor. The State was now rapidly gaining in population, and in 1800 had nearly six hundred thousand inhabitants. By an act of the Legislature a convention was called to amend the State Constitution in regard to the appointment of members of the Legislature. This body convened in 1801, chose Colonel Aaron Burr to preside over it, and fixed the number of Assemblymen at 100. In 1801 George Clinton was again elected to the governorship, which office he held until 1804, when he was chosen Vice-President of the United States, and Morgan Lewis was elected his successor. At this time Aaron Burr was holding the office of Vice-President, and failing to receive the nomination for re-election was nominated by his friends for the office of governor of New York. Mortified and chagrined at his defeat, he sought revenge upon those who had been the most prominent and influential in causing it. He regarded the influence of Alexander Hamilton as having contributed largely to his failure, and in desperation at his blighted political prospects determined to wreak his vengeance upon him. An excuse was presented by Hamilton's expressing political views antagonistic to his own, which having been reported to him in a distorted form he chose to consider as personal, and challenged him. The challenge was accepted and the duel fought, Hamilton falling mortally wounded at the first exchange of shots. His deplorable death produced a gloomy feeling throughout the country, as his brilliant talents and unexceptionable character had won for him the esteem of the whole community. After this occurrence Burr visited the Western States and engaged in treasonable schemes for detaching them from their present political associations, to form, in conjunction with Mexico, a separate government. He was arrested and tried for treason, but escaped conviction for want of sufficient proof. All confidence in his integrity, however, was lost, and the remainder of his life was passed in comparative obscurity. In 1807 Daniel D. Tompkins was elected to succeed Morgan Lewis as Governor of New York. In this year Robert Fulton completed the Clermont, the first boat that ever succeeded in steam navigation. It was launched at Jersey City, and made its trial trip up the Hudson to Albany.

Great Britain and France being at war, the former by a series of "Orders in Council" prohibited vessels of neutral nations from trading with France or her allies, and in retaliation Napoleon proclaimed the notable Berlin an Milan decrees, forbidding all trade with England and her colonies. The effects of these ordinances were very injurious to American commerce; and in consequence thereof Congress, on the 23d of September, 1807, laid an embargo on all vessels in the harbors of the United States, which bore heavily on the mercantile interests of the country, and excited considerable opposition.

CHAPTER XV.

CAUSES OF THE LAST WAR WITH GREAT BRITAIN—EXPEDITIONS AGAINST CANADA—BORDER HOSTILITIES.

THE country was now rapidly drifting into another conflict with Great Britain. The aggressions of the British had for several years been a subject of great anxiety and bitter animosity, which continually increased. Although the United States maintained a strict neutrality while the Napoleonic wars were raging between Great Britain and France, their rights as a neutral nation were disregarded. The embargo laid by Congress upon the shipping in American ports was found so injurious to commercial interests that it was repealed, and a non-intercourse act passed in its place. In April, 1809, the English ambassador at Washington opened negotiations for the adjustment of the existing difficulties, and consented to the withdrawal of the obnoxious "Orders in Council" so far as respected the United States, on condition that they should repeal the act prohibiting intercourse with Great Britain. Upon this basis an agreement was effected, when the President issued a proclamation declaring that as it had been officially communicated to the United States that the "Orders in Council" would be repealed on the 10th of June, trade might be resumed with Great Britain after that date. As soon as intelligence of this agreement on the part of their ambassador reached the English government, the latter refused to ratify it on the ground that he had exceeded his instructions, and immediately recalled him. The proclamation of the President was then revoked, and the two governments resumed their former relations. In addition to other injuries and encroachments upon the rights of the United States as neutrals, the English government claimed the right to search American vessels, and authorized its officers to examine their crews, seize all whom they chose to regard as British subjects, and force them into their service. All remonstrances were unavailing. The English officers in enforcing this right of search committed great outrages, and the practice became so obnoxious as to demand some decided measures for its suppression. Under these circumstances there appeared to be no alternative but war, and Congress having authorized it, war was declared against Great Britain on the 19th of June, 1812. The measure, however, was far from being universally sustained. The Federal party, then in the minority, opposed it, and their political opinions being apparently stronger than their patriotism, they loudly denounced it. It was also but feebly sustained by a portion of the Democratic party, not on political grounds, but from the belief that the country was unprepared for war. New York and New England were most prominent in their opposition, and if they did not directly aid the enemy their conduct was discouraging and injurious to those who were perilling their lives in their country's cause.

The Americans, deeming it expedient to invade Canada, directed their attention at once toward that point, and measures were taken to collect forces along the northern frontier of New York, and westward to Michigan. They were distributed in three divisions. The eastern rendezvoused in the vicinity of Plattsburg, on the western shore of Lake Champlain. The central was under the command of General Stephen Van Rensselaer, who made his headquarters at Lewiston, on the Niagara river; and the northwestern division assembled at Detroit. In connection with these armaments a naval force was fitted up on the lakes, the command of which was assigned to Commodore Chauncey. In July a small British fleet made an attack upon Sackett's Harbor, on Lake Ontario, which was defended by Lieutenant Woolsey, who, from a battery arranged on the shore, so disabled the hostile fleet that it withdrew. In October an attack on Ogdensburg by a British fleet was repulsed by General Brown. In the same month Lieutenant Elliott, by a bold movement, captured at the foot of Lake Erie the British vessel "Caledonia," laden with a valuable cargo of furs, while she lay in fancied security, protected by the guns of a British fort.

After the inglorious surrender of Gen. Hull at Detroit, the next offensive movement on the part of the Americans was assigned to the central division, which was eager to offset Hull's disgrace by a brilliant achievement. An attack on the heights of Queenston was decided on, and was made October 13th. With inadequate means of transportation about a thousand men were transferred to the Canadian bank of the Niagara, drove the British from their batteries, and took the heights. Gen. Brock rallied the enemy and attempted to recapture the position, but was mortally wounded and his force repulsed. The Americans, however, were unable to hold their ground against the British reinforcements which were brought up, having no implements for fortification; and the militia who had not yet crossed the river became panic-stricken on seeing some of the wounded brought over, and refused to go to the aid of their outnumbered comrades. The latter were therefore overwhelmed and forced to surrender, after having about sixty killed and a hundred wounded.

Nothing save a little skirmishing occurred in this quarter during the remainder of the year. The disgrace which had fallen upon the American arms on land this year was alleviated to a considerable extent, however, by their splendid triumphs on the water. Soon after the new year had been ushered in, the sanguinary conflict at Frenchtown, on the Raisin river, took place, resulting in the surrender of the American forces. The prisoners taken on this occasion were left to be tortured by the barbarous Indians under Proctor, the infamous British commander, in direct violation of his pledge for their safety. Several persons in St. Lawrence county were arrested by the British authorities and confined in Canada on charges of desertion. On the 7th of February Captain Forsyth, the commander of the post at Ogdensburg, crossed to the Canadian shore with a small force, and captured about fifty prisoners and some military stores. In retaliation Colonel McDonnell, on the 22d of the same month, crossed the river with a considerable force and attacked Ogdensburg. Only a feeble garrison was stationed there for its protection; but this, with the aid of the citizens, defended the town gallantly, although they were finally obliged to abandon it to the invaders. A large quantity of military stores came into the enemy's possession, several vessels were destroyed, and considerable damage was done to the property of the citizens.

General Dearborn had been entrusted with the command of the central division, and on the 25th of April detached a force of seventeen hundred men, under General Pike, for a descent upon Toronto, then known as York. They embarked at Sackett's Harbor on board the squadron of Commodore Chauncey, and landed on the 27th in the vicinity of York in the face of a spirited fire from the enemy, whom they soon drove back. The British before leaving their fortifications had laid a train of combustible matter, and connecting it with their magazine thus plotted the destruction of the invaders. The scheme was in part successful, for the Americans took the redoubts as they advanced, and when within about fifty rods of the barracks the explosion took place. General Pike was mortally wounded, and about two hundred of his followers either killed or injured. The troops were appalled at this disaster; but at the order of their dying commander they sprang forward and captured a part of the retreating enemy, and drove the remainder from the field. After the capture of Toronto the squadron returned, and preparations were made for an attack upon Fort George, on the Niagara river, near Lake Ontario. A descent was made upon this point on the 27th of May, and although meeting a stout resistance was in the end successful. On the landing of the troops Colonel Scott advanced to attack an advantageous position held by the enemy, and after a sharp conflict succeeded in dislodging them. General Vincent, the British commander, in alarm, ordered the evacuation of the remaining posts on the Niagara frontier, and on retreating from Fort George caused the magazine to be blown up. The greater part of the garrison made their escape, but nearly four hundred regulars and five hundred militia were made prisoners. General Vincent retreated with the view of taking a position on Burlington Heights, and was followed by a detachment of the Americans; but the British turned and attacked their pursuers in the night, and succeeded in capturing their generals, and further pursuit was abandoned. Colonel Boerstler was detached with a force of about six hundred men to dislodge a body of the enemy stationed at Beaver Dam, about seventeen miles from Fort George. Arriving in the vicinity of that place he was attacked by a body of Indians in ambush, who kept up a conflict in their skulking manner until the arrival of a reinforcement of British troops. The British officer then sent a summons to the colonel to surrender, at the same time magnifying the number of his troops. Colonel Boerstler believing that he had a superior force to contend with, and unable to obtain a reinforcement, surrendered his detachment as prisoners of war.

During these offensive operations on the part of the Americans, like expeditions were undertaken by the British. The force at Sackett's Harbor having been reduced to aid the expedition along the Niagara river, and the fleet of Commodore Chauncey being at Fort George, Sir George Prevost made an attempt to take the former post. On the 29th of May he appeared before the place with a force of about one thousand men. It had been left in command of Colonel Backus, who, aided by General Brown, so successfully resisted the onslaught that the enemy, after sustaining considerable loss, withdrew. This affair was followed by considerable skirmishing along the American side of Lake Ontario, and on the 11th of July Colonel Bishop made an attack upon the village of Black Rock, on the east side of the Niagara river. In this conflict the British force was repulsed with considerable loss, and their leader mortally wounded.

Meanwhile Commodore Perry was preparing to dispute the control of Lake Erie with the enemy. The Americans had no efficient force upon that lake, and Perry, by unremitting exertions, built and equipped a fleet of nine vessels. Of these the Lawrence and the Niagara each carried twenty guns, and the whole fleet but fifty-four. The British fleet, under Commodore Barclay, consisted of six vessels, carrying sixty-three guns. On the 10th of September, the British commander approached the American fleet with his vessels arrayed in battle order, and Perry at once prepared for action. With his flag-ship, the Lawrence, he advanced to meet the enemy, and maintained an unequal conflict until his ship was reduced to a complete wreck, and nearly all of her crew either killed or wounded. At this juncture, and when the enemy had a fair prospect of obtaining a briliant victory, Captain Elliot, commander of the Niagara, who had perceived the crippled and unmanageable condition of the Lawrence, moved forward to her aid, and Perry, although exposed to a continuous fire from the enemy, sprang into a boat and proceeded to the Niagara, to which he transferred his flag. The action was then renewed with great vigor by the remainder of the American squadron. They passed fearlessly among the enemy's ships, dealing such a destructive fire upon them that the whole fleet soon after surrendered.

This important and brilliant victory was followed by one under General Harrison, commander of the northwestern division, who on the 5th of October defeated General Proctor at the battle of the Thames. By these victories the territory of Michigan, which had been so ingloriously surrendered by General Hull at the commencement of the war, was regained. Late in the autumn of this year an unsuccessful attempt was made to invade Canada, under the direction of General Wilkinson, who had succeeded Dearborn in the chief command of the northern army. The American Generals Izard and Hampton were repulsed near the border in Franklin county. General Wilkinson descended the St. Lawrence, and on the 19th of November, at Chrystler's Farm, near Williamsburg, an indecisive engagement took place, the Americans retreating to their boats, and abandoning further operations.

The forces on the Niagara frontier had been so much reduced that they were inadequate for its defense after the British were reinforced by General Drummond. General McClure, finding he would be obliged to abandon Fort George, removed his military stores, and unnecessarily inflicted great distress upon the citizens of the villages of Queenston and Newark, reducing the latter place to ashes. The British soon after retaliated by a series of cruel barbarities along the Niagara frontier. On the 19th of December a successful attack was made upon Fort Niagara, and a large share of the garrison, together with the hospital patients, were put to death without mercy. General Rial, with a detachment of Royal Scots and a large body of Indians, crossed the river, plundered and burned Lewiston, and inflicted barbarous cruelties upon the defenseless inhabitants. Youngstown, Manchester, Schlosser, and the Indian village of Tuscarora were devastated in the same manner. On the 30th of this month an engagement took place near the village of Black Rock, between General Rial's force and the militia, resulting in the repulse of the latter under General Hall. The villages of Black Rock and Buffalo were abandoned by the Americans, and speedily destroyed by the invaders.

In February, 1814, General Wilkinson dispatched a part of his army to Sackett's Harbor, and removed from French Mills to Plattsburg. The British had collected a strong force at La Colle Mills, on the Sorel, and General Wilkinson resolved to dislodge them. On the 30th of March he crossed the frontier and commenced the attack, but was repulsed and withdrew with his force to Plattsburg. In consequence of this failure he was removed from his command, General Izard succeeding him.

The military stores deposited at Oswego Falls attracted the attention of the British, and with a view of capturing them a British squadron appeared before Oswego. As soon as it was discovered information was sent to Captain Woolsey of the navy, and the militia gathered under Colonel Mitchell and gave the enemy such a spirited reception from a battery prepared on the shore that boats approaching found it prudent to return to their ships. The fleet advanced, and the American force of only about three hundred defended their positions for several hours. A landing was finally effected, and the little band, having maintained their ground as long as it was possible against a vastly superior force, withdrew towards the Falls to defend the stores, destroying the bridges in their rear. The British disabled the ordnance of the fort, and on learning that the bridges had been destroyed returned to Kingston. It was deemed prudent, however, to remove the stores thus preserved to Sackett's Harbor, and Captain Woolsey, aided by a body of riflemen and Indians, set out for the accomplishment of this object. The British admiral was apprised of the movement, and learning their destination through the treachery of a boatman, dispatched a force to intercept them. On the approach of the enemy, Captain Woolsey's force put into Sandy Creek, and Major Appling was landed with his troops, which he concealed in ambush. The enemy followed and landed a detachment to pursue them. The British having ascended the bank of the creek to the place of concealment of Major Appling's men, the latter arose and opened such a destructive fire upon them that they fell back in confusion and left Captain Woolsey's expedition to proceed to its destination without further molestation.

On the 3d of July, 1814, Fort Erie, on the west bank of the Niagara, where it leaves Lake Erie, was surrendered to an American force of 3,500 under General Brown, who then moved on to Chippewa. Here they met and defeated the enemy in a general action, the latter retreating to Fort George, at the mouth of the river. The Americans pursued as far as Queenston Heights, whence they returned to Chippewa.

On the 25th General Scott's brigade, while reconnoitering in force, encountered the entire British army advantageously posted, and the battle of Lundy's Lane occurred. The brigade of General Ripley came to the relief of Scott's when the latter had maintained the engagement into the evening, and after the brilliant capture of a British battery the enemy gave up the field. The losses were exceedingly severe on both sides.

The next day the Americans broke up their camp and retired to Fort Erie unmolested. Here they immediately proceeded to strengthen their defenses. On the 4th of August the enemy, having been reinforced, appeared and invested the fort, then commanded by General Gaines. On the 7th they opened fire upon the American lines, and before dawn on the 15th a combined and furious assault was commenced. In their attack on the left of the American lines the enemy were repulsed four times with heavy loss, and on the right they met with no better success. In the center the conflict was desperate in the extreme, and the enemy finally succeeded in gaining possession of the bastion, but their advance was suddenly checked by its explosion, and the combat shortly after ended in their defeat at every point. They retreated to their camp with broken columns, having sustained a loss of nearly a thousand men. The Americans continued to strengthen their defenses, and both armies were reinforced. General Brown, having recovered from his wounds, resumed the command, and finding the enemy were intent on prosecuting the siege, determined to make a sortie to dislodge them and destroy their works. The British force consisted of three brigades, each of which, in its turn, was stationed at the batteries, while the others remained at their encampment about two miles distant. The object in making the sortie was to defeat the brigade on duty before it could be reinforced. On the 17th of September the sortie was made, and resulted in the capture of the British batteries and the destruction of their fortifications. A few days afterward General Drummond left his encampment before the fort, and returned to Chippewa. No further offensive operations were carried on in this quarter, and a few weeks later the fort was demolished and the troops withdrawn to the American shore.

While this siege was in progress, hostile movements of greater magnitude were being made in other sections of the country. The British army had been strongly reinforced during the summer; the city of Washington had been captured and the public buildings destroyed, and the entire coast was held in a state of blockade by their fleet. They contemplated a dismemberment of the Union by obtaining possession of Lake Champlain and the Hudson from the north, and capturing the city of New York; believing that a division of the Republic would thus be accomplished and a separate peace concluded with the Eastern States, whose discontent and opposition to the war were manifest. The people were now fully aroused, and measures were immediately taken for the defense of New York. Its fortifications were strengthened and strongly garrisoned. The invasion of New York by the way of Lake Champlain was entrusted to General Prevost with about fourteen thousand veteran troops from Wellington's army, and the aid of a strong fleet carrying ninety guns. To oppose this formidable armament General Macomb, at Plattsburg, had only fifteen hundred regular troops and about three thousand militia, hastily collected and undisciplined. Commodore McDonough, by almost incredible exertions, had in a short time constructed a fleet carrying sixty-six guns. General Izard had transferred a large portion of the troops from this quarter to the Niagara frontier. Knowing the weakness of the American force at Plattsburg, General Prevost hastily organized and put his army in motion before the fleet was ready for co-operation, and on the 6th of September his advance reached Beekmanstown, where their progress was disputed by a body of militia and a few regulars, who, however, soon retreated toward Plattsburg, and tearing up the bridge over the Saranac entered their entrenched camp. The British advanced, and having taken possession of some buildings near the river attempted to cross; but they were met with a shower of hot shot which proved so annoying that they contented themselves with preparing for an assault upon the fortifications. On the morning of the 11th the British fleet under Commodore Downie was seen advancing in line of battle, to engage the American ships at anchor in the bay off Plattsburg. A fierce and determined conflict followed, and in less than three hours the whole British fleet, excepting a part of the galleys, which had made their escape, surrendered. Simultaneously with the naval engagement General Prevost opened his batteries on the American lines, and attempted to force a passage of the Saranac at three different points, but at each place his troops were repulsed with great loss. On the surrender of the fleet, in sight of both armies, further efforts to cross the river were abandoned. When night came on, General Prevost, in great alarm, made a precipitate retreat from the town, leaving behind his sick and wounded, together with a large quantity of military stores. This expedition was the last undertaken for the invasion of this frontier, and its signal defeat materially aided in bringing the war to a close. On the 24th of December a treaty of peace was concluded at Ghent, but before the welcome news had reached our shores the British met with another disastrous defeat at New Orleans.

CHAPTER XVI.

THE ERIE CANAL AND CENTRAL RAILROAD—THE STATE ADMINISTRATION—NEW YORK IN THE CIVIL WAR.

THE construction of the Erie and Champlain canals, which had been projected just at the breaking out of the war, had been virtually abandoned by the repeal of the act authorizing the commissioners to borrow funds for the prosecution of the work. But on the termination of the war the policy was revived, and the attention of the people was again called to this great undertaking. The difficulties of the enterprise however, were formidable. The late war had drawn heavily upon the State treasury. The preliminary measures for the construction of the canals had already been attended with considerable expense, and the people were loth to engage in an enterprise which they plainly foresaw would be so insatiable in its demands upon the public treasury. They were therefore slow to encourage additional legislation for its prosecution, but through the untiring energy and perseverance of De Witt Clinton an act prepared by him was passed in April, 1817, authorizing the construction of the work. Governor Tompkins, having been elected Vice-President of the United States, resigned his office as governor; and in April De Witt Clinton, the ardent and zealous advocate of the system of internal improvements, was elected to succeed him. On the 4th of July, 1817, the Erie Canal was commenced at Rome, and in October, 1817, that portion of it between Utica and Rome was opened to navigation.

In 1821 an act was passed by the Legislature authorizing a convention to be called to revise the State constitution. This convention met at Albany, and after a lengthy session adopted a constitution, which was subsequently ratified by the people, and under its provisions the State was governed for a quarter of a century. By the new constitution the time of holding the State elections was changed from April to November, and the officers elected were to enter upon their official duties on the 1st of January. Joseph A. Yates was elected governor in 1822, and was succeeded in 1824 by De Witt Clinton. The Erie Canal having been completed, the first flotilla of canal boats left Buffalo for New York on the 26th of October, 1825. Intelligence of its departure was communicated to New York in one hour and twenty minutes by the discharge of cannon stationed at points within hearing distance of each other along the entire route. The occasion was celebrated with great rejoicing throughout the State.

The first State charter for the construction of a railroad was granted in 1826. The points to be connected were Albany and Schenectady, and the road was completed in 1831. Although the road was but rudely constructed, the advantages of this new mode of transportation were so obvious that railroads were soon after projected in various parts of the State.

On the evening of February 11th, 1828, Governor Clinton suddenly expired. This unexpected and sad event was deeply lamented throughout the community. Amid discouragements of every kind, and of a magnitude that would have filled ordinary men with dismay, he had persevered with unflagging energy, and accomplished measures which in succeeding years proved eminently beneficial to the best interests of the State. On the death of Clinton, Nathaniel Pitcher, then lieutenant-governor, succeeded to the governorship for the remainder of the term, and in November Martin Van Buren was elected to succeed him. In March following Van Buren was appointed to an office in President Jackson's cabinet, and resigned the governorship, which devolved upon Enos T. Throop, who was elected to the office at the succeeding election in 1830.

In February, 1832, the State Agricultural Society was formed at a convention of its friends in Albany, but received no support from the State until it was reorganized in 1841, and measures were adopted for raising funds and holding annual fairs. In April, 1832, an act was passed chartering a company to construct the New York and Erie Railway, and four years later the comptroller was directed to issue State bonds to the amount of $3,000,000 to aid the enterprise. In November, 1832, William L. Marcy was elected to succed Throop as governor of the State. In 1833 a legislative act was passed authorizing the construction of the Chenango Canal, connecting the Erie Canal at Utica with the Susquehanna river at Binghamton. In April, 1835, the Legislature passed an act by which the schools in the State were to be provided with libraries. Near the close of this year a great conflagration occurred in New York city, consuming property to the amount of eighteen millions of dollars.

In 1838 Wm. H. Seward was elected governor of the State, and in 1842 was succeeded by William C. Bouck. After the death of the patroon Stephen Van Rensselaer, disturbances arose in Rensselaer, Albany, and other counties from the tenants refusing to fulfill the obligation of their leases, which in 1844 assumed serious aspects. The tenants organized and arrayed themselves in opposition to the enforcement of legal proceedings, and outrages were often committed upon executive officers in the discharge of their duties. Many of the tenants on the Van Rensselaer manor were seriously aggrieved by the demands of their landlords under the provisions of ancient leases, which for a long time had been suspended and the revival and enforcement of which threatened to ruin them. Silas Wright was elected governor in November, 1844, and on assuming the duties of chief magistrate in January following called the attention of the Legislature to these anti-rent outrages, which continued to increase. Stringent laws were passed for the punishment of offenders; but the excitement still prevailed, and lawless acts were committed by members of an organization of anti-renters disguised as Indians. These occurred so frequently that it became necessary to order out the military to suppress the insurrection. In 1846 the Legislature passed laws to abolish "distress for rent," and facilitate legal remedies by extending the time for a "re-entry" on lands for its non-payment, and during the ensuing year those who had participated in these outrages were pardoned by a proclamation.

Through the energy and genius of Professor Morse the magnetic telegraph was added to our list of public facilities for intercommunication, and as early as 1845 various lines were in process of construction through the country. A constitutional convention having been called, met at Albany on the 1st of June, 1846, and continued in sessions upward of four months. The amendments to the State constitution adopted by that body were ratified by the people in November, and John Young was elected governor of the State.

The annexation of Texas to the Union led to hostilities between Mexico and the United States, and on the 11th of May, 1846, Congress declared that by the acts of the Mexicans war existed between the two nations. The Americans were victorious in all important engagements with the Mexican army, and the part taken by the troops from the State of New York was conspicuous and highly creditable to their valor. Peace was concluded on the 2d of February, 1848. In November of the same year Hamilton Fish was elected governor.

By the census of 1850 it was found that the population of the State amounted to upward of three millions, being an increase of two and a half millions in half a century. In November of this year Washington Hunt was elected to succeed Hamilton Fish as governor of the State. He was a candidate for re-election in 1852, but was defeated by Horatio Seymour. In 1854 an amendment was made to the State constitution requiring the appropriation of an annual sum during a term of four years for the enlargement of the Erie and the completion of other canals in the State. In November of the same year Myron H. Clark was elected governor. In 1855 the State contained about three thousand miles of railroad, constructed at an aggregate cost of $125,000,000. In 1856 John A. King was elected governor, and at the expiration of his term was succeeded in 1858 by Edwin D. Morgan.

The recognition of slavery in the Territories belonging to the United States having been earnestly combatted for several years, the difficulty finally terminated in a gigantic civil war. On the election of Abraham Lincoln to the Presidency in 1860, upon principles of avowed hostility to the extension of slavery, and the failure to effect a compromise by which slavery should be recognized or tolerated in any portion of the Territories, the Southern States resolved to secede from the Union and organize a separate government. The capture by the Confederates of Fort Sumter was the first overt act of the rebellion, and upon its occurrence, in April, 1861, active hostilities were begun, and before the close of the year one hundred and fifteen regiments had been put in the field by the State of New York. In July, 1863, during the execution of the draft ordered by an act of Congress for recruiting the Union army, a terrible riot occurred in the city of New York. The police were unable to check its progress, and for several days the city was convulsed and overwhelmed with tumult, rapine, and murder. The outbreak was finally quelled by the interposition of the military, but not until a large amount of property had been destroyed and a considerable number of lives lost. The war was prolonged until the spring of 1865, when it terminated with the complete success of the Union cause, and peace has since prevailed.

By the census of 1875 the State was found to contain 4,705,000 inhabitants. Within a period of two and a half centuries this immense population had accumulated, and from the almost pathless wilderness, in the beginning trodden only by wild beasts and savages, it has by industry and enterprise removed the primeval forests, reared large and numerous cities, and constructed vast and magnificent public works, which conspicuously appear in all parts of what is justly termed the "Empire State." With the full enjoyment of peace, it continues to advance with accelerated and rapid strides, in accord with its proud and becoming motto, "Excelsior."

THE HISTORY OF NIAGARA COUNTY.

CHAPTER I.

THE WORD NIAGARA—RELICS AND THEORIES OF THE EARLIEST POPULATION.

THE name Niagara is of Mohawk origin, and is interpreted by the best authorities as meaning the "neck." Like most of the Indian appellations, which were first written as they sounded to different authors, it has been spelled in several ways. Indeed, we shall best illustrate the difference of orthography in the case of this word by quoting the beginning of the article "Niagara" in the general index of the Documents Relating to the Colonial History of New York, which is as follows:

"Niagara, (Iagara, Iagare, Jagara, Jagare, Jagera, Niagaro, Niagra, Niagro, Oakinagaro, Ochiagra, Ochjagara, Octjagara, Ochinagero, Oneagerah, Oneigra, Oneygra, Oniagara, Ongagerae, Oniagorah, Oniagra, Oniagro, Onjagara, Onjagera, Onjagora, Onjagore, Onjagoro, Onjagra, Onnyagaro, Onyagara, Onyagare, Ouyagaro, Onyagoro, Onyagars, Onyagra, Onyagro, Oneygra, Oneagoragh, Yagero, Yangree.)"

This extreme variety of spelling, embracing, as it would seem, nearly all the combinations possible without entirely metamorphosing the word, could only have arisen from a wide variance in pronunciation among the aborigines themselves. Probably none of the above forms ever obtained general prevalence until, at an early day, the present orthography of the word was universally adopted. "It is," says Mr. O. H. Marshall, "the oldest of all the local geographical terms which have come down to us from the aborigines. * * * Its first appearance as Niagara is on Coronelli's map, published in Paris in 1688. From that time to the present the French have been consistent with their orthography, the numerous variations alluded to occurring only among the English writers." The name having been applied to the "neck" of land between lakes Ontario and Erie, its transfer to the river traversing that space, to the military post at its mouth, and to the great falls which have given world-wide familiarity to the word, was easy and natural.

Equally natural and appropriate was the choice of Niagara as the name of the frontier county bounded by the great lake, the famous river, its chief tributary stream and a meridian line from the last named to the first. On this fair and well defined arena a series of events has been transpiring for more than two centuries and a half richly meriting historic record. To relate these events in their order, with only such reference to occurrences beyond the county limits as is necessary to a proper understanding of those taking place within them, is the purpose of these pages.

The first question relates to the original inhabitants of the region. It is beset with difficulties and admits of no certain solution. The disturbing element in the inquiry is the discovery, throughout western New York, of relics generally considered indicative of a race inhabiting the country before the historic Indian tribes, and now long extinct. These relics include the specimens of pottery, stone implements, etc., now quite common and familiar; but their most prominent and interesting feature is the traces of ancient fortifications, usually circular or elliptical earthworks, upon whose embankments, when discovered by white men, trees had in some cases been growing for hundred of years. The Iroquois had various contradictory traditions to account for the construction of these works, but they show no more real knowledge of the subject than we possess. Mr. Schoolcraft finds in these fort-builders of centuries ago "the ancient Alleghans," who fixed their name upon the Alleghany mountain range. No author could give a more valuable opinion on the vexed question than this eminent student of the pre-historic period in America; and we shall quote a few lines from his Notes on the Iroquois as the best suggestion that scholarship has to offer on this interesting topic:

"This ancient people, who occupy the foreground of our remote aboriginal history, were a valiant, noble and populous race, who were advanced in arts and the policy of government, and raised fortifications for their defense. While they held a high reputation as hunters, they cultivated maize extensively, which enabled them to live in large towns; and erected those antique fortifications which are extended over the entire Mississippi valley as high as latitude 43°, and the lake country, reaching from Lake St. Clair to the south side of the Niagara ridge (the old shore of Lake Ontario,) and the country of the Onondagas and Oneidas. Towards the south they extended as far as the borders of the Cherokees and Muscogees. * * * If we fix upon the 12th century as the era of the fall of the Alleghan race, we shall not, probably, overestimate the event. They had probably reached the Mississippi valley a century or two before, having felt in their original position, west and south of that stream, the great revolutionary movements which preceded the overthrow of the Toltec and the establishment of the Aztec empire in Mexican America."

While the elaborate character of the relics referred to indicates a race of greater industry and resources than the savages whom the first white men found in possession of the country, the existence of such a race is not conceded by all authors. Those who reject it point to the palisades of timber which the French found defending the strongholds of Canadian and New York tribes, as requiring more skill and patience in their construction than the simple, though extensive, earthworks ascribed by Mr. Schoolcraft to the extinct Alleghans.

It would be useless to pursue the general inquiry, but nothing could be more pertinent than an account of such of these prehistoric remains as are found within the region of which we are writing. One of them is the ancient citadel in the town of Lewiston, called Kienuka by the inhabitants of the Tuscarora village, near which it is found. "There is," said the author of the History of the Holland Purchase, writing in 1849, "a burial ground and two elliptic mounds, or barrows, that have a diameter of twenty feet, and an elevation of from four to five feet. A mass of detached rocks, with spaces intervening, seems to have been chosen as a rock citadel; and well chosen, for the mountain fastnesses of Switzerland are but little better adapted to the purposes of a lookout and defense. The sites of habitations are marked by remains of pottery, pipes and other evidences." Three years earlier Mr. Schoolcraft had reported his observations on the spot as follows:—"The term Kienuka is said to mean 'the stronghold or fort from which there is a sublime view.' It is situated about three and a half miles eastward of the outlet of the Niagara gorge at Lewiston, on a natural escarpment of the ridge. * * * From the ascent of the great ridge, following the road from Lewiston to Tuscarora village, a middle road leads over this broad escarpment, following, apparently, an ancient Indian trail, and winding about with sylvan irregularity. Most of the trees appear to be of second growth; they do not, at any rate, bear the impress of antiquity which marks the heavy forests of the country. Occasionally there are small openings, where wigwams once stood. These increase as we pass on, till they assume the character of continuous open fields at the site of the old burying-ground, orchard and play-ground of the neighboring Tuscaroras. The soil in these openings appears hard, compact and worn out, and bears short grass. The burial-ground is filled almost entirely with sumach, giving it a bushy appearance which serves to hide its ancient graves and small tumuli. Among these are two considerable barrows, or small elliptic mounds, the one larger than the other, formed of earth and angular stones. The largest is not probably higher than five feet, but may have a diameter of twenty feet in the longest direction. Directly east of this antique cemetery commences the old orchard and area for ball playing, on which, at the time of my visit, the stakes or goals were standing, and thus denoted that the ancient games are kept up on these deserted fields by the youthful population of the adjacent Tuscarora village. A small ravine succeeds, with a brook falling into a gulf or deep break in the escarpment, where once stood a saw-mill, and where may still be traced some vestiges of this early attempt of the first settlers to obtain a water-power from a vernal brook. Immediately after crossing this little ravine, and rising to the general level of the plain, we enter the old fields and rock fortress of Kienuka. * * * Nothing, we think, is more evident to the observer, in tracing out the Kienuka plateau, than the evidences which exist of Lake Ontario having washed its northern edge, and driven its waters against its crowning wall of limestone. The fury of the waves, forced into the line of junction between the solid limestone and fissile sandstone, has broken up and removed the latter, till the overlying rock, pressed by its own gravity, has been split, fissured or otherwise disrupted, and often slid in vast masses down the ragged precipice. Kienuka offers one of the most striking instances of this action. The fissures made in the rock by the partial withdrawal of its support assume the size of cavern passages; they penetrate in some instances under other and unbroken masses of the superior stratum, and are, as a whole, curiously intersected, forming a vast reticulated area, in which large numbers of men could seek shelter and security. * * * Most of these fissures which extend in the general parallel of the brink appear to have been narrow, and are now covered with the sod, or filled with earth or carbonaceous matter, which gives this portion of them the aspect of ancient trenches."

On the east of the orchard which now occupies the crest of the hill at this point, there is said to have been in Indian times a castle, consisting of a stockade of logs, perhaps ten or twelve feet high, fifteen or twenty rods long and six or eight wide, with a gate at either end; surrounding a collection of wigwams, and having a more substantial lodge in the center for the head of the clan occupying it. This inclosure is reported to have had the rock ledge at the brow of the hill for its northern barrier, and a trench outside its southern wall. Some irregular masses of rock, fallen upon the slope below the ledge that formed the Kienuka citadel, are now the only representatives of the old fortress.

Dewitt Clinton, in his celebrated paper on the Iroquois, also assuming the former dominion of Lake Ontario over the northwestern border of New York, makes it an argument for the high antiquity of the pre-historic earthworks: "On the south side of the great ridge [the 'Ridge road'], in its vicinity, and in all directions through the country, the remains of numerous forts are to be seen; but on the north side, that is, on the side toward the lake, not a single one has been discovered, although the whole ground has been carefully explored. Considering the distance to be, say seventy miles in length and eight in breadth, and that the border of the lake is the very place that would be selected for habitation, and consequently for works of defense, on account of the facilities it would afford for subsistence, for safety, and all domestic accommodations and military purposes, and that on the south shore of Lake Erie these ancient fortresses exist in great number, there can be no doubt that these works were erected when this ridge was the southern boundary of Lake Ontario, and, consequently, that their origin must be sought in a very remote age."

Reviewing these conclusions, Mr. Orsamus Turner, author of the History of the Holland Purchase, makes the following remark: "Upon an elevation, on the shore of Lake Ontario, near the Eighteen-mile creek, there is a mound similar in appearance to some of those that have been termed ancient; though it is unquestionably incident to the early French and Indian wars of this region; and the same conclusion may be formed in reference to other similar ones along the shore of the lake."

In 1823 Eliakim Hammond discovered, while hoeing on his farm in the town of Cambria, some five miles west of Lockport, now owned by Mr. Ramson Campbell, the bones of a child, on the surface of the ground. "No further thought," says Mr. Schoolcraft, "was bestowed on the subject for some time, for the plain on the ridge was supposed to have been the site of an Indian village, and this was supposed the remains of some child who had been buried there. Eli Bruce, hearing of the circumstance proposed to Mr. H. that they should repair to the spot, with suitable implements, and endeavor to find some relics. The soil was a light loam, which would be dry and preserve bones for centuries without decay. A search enabled them to come to a pit, but a slight distance from the surface. The top of the pit was covered with small slabs of the Medina sandstone, and was twenty-four feet square, by four and a half in depth—the planes agreeing with the four cardinal points. It was filled with human bones of both sexes and all ages. They dug down at one extremity, and found the same layers to extend to the bottom, which was the same dry loam, and from their calculations they deduced that at least four thousand souls had perished in one great massacre. In one skull two flint arrowheads were found, and many had the appearance of having been fractured and cleft open by a sudden blow. They were piled in regular layers, but with no regard to size or sex. Pieces of pottery were picked up in the pit, and had also been ploughed up in the field adjacent. Traces of a log council house were plainly discernable; for, in an oblong square, the soil was poor, as if it had never been cultivated until the whites had broken it up, and where the logs of the house had decayed, was a strip of rich mould. A maple tree over the pit being cut down, two hundred and fifty concentric circles were counted, making the mound to be anterior to as many years. It had been supposed by the villagers that the bones were deposited there before the discovery of America, but the finding of some metal tools with a French stamp places the date within our period. One hundred and fifty persons a day visited this spot the first season, and carried off the bones. They are now nearly all gone and the pit ploughed over." The remains of a wall were traced near the vault. Some of the bones found in the latter were of unusual size. One of these was a thigh bone that had been healed of an oblique fracture. One was the upper half of a skull so large that that of a common man would not fill it. As lately as 1864, Mr. Campbell and Isaac Bonnell exhumed here an entire skeleton, which, after less than twenty-four hours exposure, crumbled to pieces.

Apropos to this general subject, Mr. Turner has the following interesting paragraph:

"At the head of a deep gorge [now closed up by the Central railroad embankment,] a mile west of Lockport, (similar to the one that forms the natural canal basin, from which the combined locks ascend,) in the early history of the country a circular raised work, or ring-fort, could be distinctly traced. Leading from the enclosed area there had been a covered way to a spring of pure cold water that rises from a fissure in the rock, some fifty or sixty feet down the declivity. Such covered paths, or rather the remains of them, lead from many of these ancient fortifications. Mr. Schoolcraft concludes that they were intended for the emergency of a prolonged siege. They would seem now to have been but a poor defense for the water-carriers against the weapons of modern warfare, yet probably sufficient to protect them from arrows, and a foe that had no sappers or miners in their ranks."

The following is from the same source:

"About one and a half miles west of Shelby Centre, Orleans county, is an ancient work. A broad ditch encloses in a form nearly circular about three acres of land. The ditch is at this day well defined, several feet deep. Adjoining the spot on the south is a swamp about one mile in width by two in length. This swamp was once, doubtless, if not a lake, an impassable morass. From the interior of the enclosure made by the ditch there is what appears to have been a passage way on the side next to the swamp. No other breach occurs in the entire circuit of the embankment. There are accumulated within and near this fort large piles of small stones, of a size convenient to be thrown by the hand or with a sling. Arrow heads of flint are found in and near the enclosure in great abundance, stone axes, etc. Trees of four-hundred years growth stand upon the embankment, and underneath them have been found earthenware, pieces of plates or dishes, wrought with skill, presenting ornaments in relief, of various patterns. Some skeletons, almost entire, have been exhumed, many of giant size, not less than seven to eight feet in length. The skulls are large, and well developed in the anterior lobe, broad between the ears and flattened in the coronal region. Half a mile west of the fort is a sand hill. Here a large number of human skeletons have been exhumed, in a perfect state. Great numbers appeared to have been buried in the same grave. Many of the skulls appear to have been broken in with clubs or stones."

CHAPTER II.

FATHER L'ALLEMANT'S ACCOUNT OF THE NEUTRAL NATION—THE DESTRUCTION OF THE ERIES.

THE realm of mere conjecture and tradition we leave with these remains of a remote age and the theories they have raised, and gladly listen to the first voice of history concerning the territory embraced in this work. Under date of May 19, 1641, the Jesuit father L'Allemant reported from St. Mary's mission, an outpost of the church near the eastern end of Lake Huron, the tour of a pair of his black-robed brethren in the preceding year, to the neighborhood of the Niagara river. His narrative is interesting chiefly as showing approximately the date at which Europeans first visited this region, and giving an account of the people whom they found in possession. Its importance in these respects is such as to demand its reproduction.

"Jean de Breboeuf and Joseph Marie Chaumonot, two fathers of our company, which have charge of the mission to the Neutral Nation, set out from St. Marie on the 2nd day of November, 1640, to visit this people. Father Breboeuf is peculiarly fitted for such an expedition, God having in an eminent degree endowed him with a capacity for learning languages. His companion was also a proper person for the enterprise.

"Although many of our French in that quarter have visited this people to profit by their furs and other commodities, we have no knowledge of any who have been there to preach the gospel, except Father De la Roche Daillon, a Recollet, who passed the winter there in 1626. The nation is very populous, there being estimated about forty villages. After leaving the Hurons, it is four or five days' journey, or about forty leagues to the nearest of their villages, the course being nearly due south. If, as indicated by the latest and most exact observations we can make, our new station St. Marie, in the interior of the Huron country, is in north latitude, about forty-four degrees, twenty-five minutes, then the entrance of the Neutral Nation from the Huron side is about forty-four degrees. More exact surveys and observations cannot now be made, for the sight of a single instrument would bring to extremes those who cannot resist the temptation of an ink-horn.

"From the first village of the Neutral Nation that we meet with in traveling from this place, as we proceed south or southwest, it is about four days' travel to the place where the celebrated river [Niagara] of the nation empties in Lake Ontario, or St. Louis. On the west side of that river, and not on the east, are the most numerous of the villages of the Neutral nation. There are three or four on the east side, extending from east to west towards the Eries or Cat nation. This river is that by which our great lake of the Hurons, or fresh sea, is discharged, which first empties into the Lake of Erie, or of the nation of the Cat; from thence it enters the territory of the Neutral nation, and takes the name of Onguiaahra [Niagara,] until it empties into Ontario or St. Louis lake from which latter flows the river which passes before Quebec, called the St. Lawrence; so that if we once had control of the side of the lake nearest the residence of the Iroquois, we could ascend by the river St. Lawrence without danger, even to the Neutral nation, and much beyond, with great saving of time and trouble.

"According to the estimate of these illustrious fathers, who have been there, the Neutral nation comprises about 12,000 souls, which enables them to furnish 4,000 warriors, notwithstanding war, pestilence and famine have prevailed among them for three years in an extraordinary manner. After all, I think that those who have heretofore ascribed such an extent and population to this nation have understood by the Neutral nation all who live south and southwest of our Hurons, and who are truly in great number, and, being at first only partially known, have all been comprised under the same name. The more perfect knowledge of their language and country which has since been obtained has resulted in a clearer distinction between the tribes.

"Our French who first discovered this people named them the Neutral nation; and not without reason, for their country being the ordinary passage by land between some of the Iroquois nations and the Hurons, who are sworn enemies, they remained at peace with both; so that in times past the Hurons and Iroquois, meeting in the same wigwam or village of that nation, were both in safety while they remained. Recently, their enmity against each other is so great that there is no safety for either party in any place, particularly for the Hurons, for whom the Neutral nation entertain the least good will. There is every reason for believing that, not long since, the Hurons, Iroquois, and Neutral nation formed one people, and originally came from the same family, but have in the lapse of time become separated from each other, more or less, in distance, interests and affection, so that some are now enemies, others neutral, and others still live in intimate friendship and intercourse.

"The food and clothing of the Neutral nation seem little different from that of our Hurons. They have Indian corn, beans and gourds in equal abundance; also plenty of fish, some kinds of which abound in particular places only. They are much employed in hunting deer, buffalo, wild-cats, wolves, wild-boars, beaver and other animals. Meat is very abundant this year on account of the heavy snow, which has aided the hunters. It is rare to see snow in this country more than half a foot deep, but this year it is more than three feet. There is also abundance of wild turkeys, which go in flocks in the fields and woods. Their fruits are the same as with the Hurons, except chestnuts, which are more abundant, and crab-apples, which are somewhat larger.

"The men, like all savages, cover their naked flesh with skins, but are less particular than the Hurons in concealing what should not appear. The squaws are ordinarily clothed, at least from the waist to the knees, but are more free and shameless in their immodesty than the Hurons. As for their remaining customs and manners, they are almost entirely similar to the other savage tribes of the country.

"There are some things in which they differ from our Hurons. They are larger, stronger and better formed. They also entertain a great affection for the dead, and have a greater number of fools, or jugglers.

"The Sonontonheronons [Senecas], one of the Iroquois nations, the nearest to and most dreaded by the Hurons, are not more than a day's journey distant from the easternmost village of the Neutral nation, named Onguiaahra, of the same name as the river.

"Our fathers returned from the mission in safety, not having found in all the eighteen villages which they visited but one, named Khe-o-e-to-a, or St. Michael, which gave them the reception which their embassy deserved. In this village a certain foreign nation, which lived beyond the Lake of Erie, or of the nation of the Cat, named A-ouen-re-ro-non, has taken refuge for many years for fear of their enemies, and they seem to have been brought here by a good providence to hear the word of God."

As this is the earliest, so it is the completest account of the first recorded inhabitants of the northwestern corner of the State. We are told of their situation; their name and the singular ground on which it was bestowed; the vegetables and fruits on which they fed; the fish and game birds which they captured; the edible and fur-bearing animals which they hunted; their style of clothing; their moral and physical characteristics; their relation with their neighbors; and the number of their villages and inhabitants, with a theory to account for the apparent exaggeration of the latter. Important as this nation appears in the "relation" of Father L'Allemant, it was overshadowed by the fame, and finally destroyed by the prowess of the Iroquois, so that, as compared with the latter, little is known of it. In 1642, says Charlevoix, "a people larger, stronger and better formed than any other savages, and who lived south of the Huron country, were visited by the Jesuits, who preached to them the kingdom of God. They were called the Neutral nation, because they took no part in the wars which desolated the country. But in the end they could not, themselves, escape entire destruction. To avoid the fury of the Iroquois, they finally joined them against the Hurons, but gained nothing by the union. The Iroquois, that, like lions that have tasted blood, cannot be satiated, destroyed indiscriminately all that came in their way, and at this day there remains no trace of the Neutral nation." The inability of the neutrals to preserve their pacific attitude is one of the reasons for considering the Jesuits' report of their numbers greatly exaggerated. It was not to be expected that they could maintain peace with such neighbors on either hand. The grain might as well hope to remain undisturbed between the upper and nether millstones. It was about the year 1643, according to Charlevoix, (none too good authority), that this aboriginal people, dwelling in part, between the Senecas and the Niagara, perished; Mr. Marshall says 1651. Students of Indian history have carefully investigated the meager sources of information relative to them, and have supplemented Father L'Allemant's statement with some interesting conclusions. They are generally considered to have been identical with the Kah-Khwas, a name applied to a nation at an early day dwelling along the Niagara, and extending perhaps half way down the end of Lake Erie. Their villages on this side of those waters were near, though not upon their banks—as that would have rendered them more easily approached and surprised by a hostile war party—and one is said to have been located on Eighteen-mile creek, near its mouth.

Along the southern shore of Lake Erie, beyond the Kah-Khwas, dwelt the powerful "Eries or Cat nation," as the French, for an unknown reason, called them. They, sharing the fate of the Kah-Khwas, about 1654 or 1655 fell victims to the conquering Iroquois.

Tradition says that the immediate occasion of the war in which the Iroquois exterminated the Eries was the defeat of the latter by the former in a series of athletic games. The Eries having learned with alarm of the confederation of the Five Nations, proposed, as a test of the power of the new alliance, that a hundred of the Seneca braves should contest with as many of their own, for a suitable prize, in the native game of ball. The challenge was twice declined, but on its third presentation the eagerness of the young warriors overcame the caution of their elders, and it was accepted. The flower of the Five Nations presented themselves. After a desperate struggle the match was won by the picked men of the Iroquois. The Eries, burning to retrieve their reputation as athletes, thereupon challenged their adversaries to a foot race, in which ten of each party should compete. The young Iroquois assented, and were again the victors. The guests now accepted an invitation to visit the Kah-Khwas at their village on Eighteen-mile creek, and a delegation of the Eries accompanied them. Smarting with mortification from their double defeat, the latter in desperation dared the champions of the Five Nations to a last and more serious contest, namely, a wrestling match, ten on each side, in which the vanquished should be slain by the victors. The first of the Eries was thrown by his Seneca antagonist, and on the refusal of the latter to dispatch his fallen adversary, the Erie chief himself brained him. Thrice was this butcherly scene repeated, when the rage of the defeated nation had risen to such a pitch that the Iroquois, to avoid a battle, for which they were not prepared, withdrew and returned to their homes.

The result convinced the Eries that the Iroquois tribes had made common cause, and their only hope lay in destroying the Senecas, by a sudden blow, before they could be supported by their confederates. Their purpose to do so was frustrated by a Seneca woman, a captive among the Eries, who escaped to her kindred in time to warn them of their danger. The Iroquois rallied, and marched out to meet the invaders. They encountered near the foot of Honeyoye lake, and after a fierce conflict the Eries were routed and almost annihilated. A remnant which escaped attacked the Senecas years after, near Buffalo, but were defeated. Such is the attempt of tradition to account for the extinction of the most powerful native foe that ever crossed the path of the all-conquering Iroquois.

CHAPTER III.

THE TRADITIONAL ORIGIN OF THE SENECAS—NAMES AND LOCATIONS OF THEIR VILLAGES.

THE destruction of the Eries brings us to the history of the nation which by that event extended its hunting grounds to Lake Erie. This was the westernmost and by far the most powerful of the Iroquois tribes, the Senecas, the immediate predecessors of the white inhabitants of this region. The name of this people is thought to have been derived from the Mohawks, the first of the Five Nations with which the Dutch and English came in contact. The Senecas themselves knew nothing of it except as applied to them by outsiders. As with other Indian proper names, the spelling for a long time varied, the nation being often called in old documents the Sinnekes, and given some sixty other names, mostly similar. The later, classical form of the word is certainly an improvement, in spite of its coincidence with the name of the Latin philosopher. Though we find the same name applied to this division of "the Romans of the New World" that was great among the Romans of the seven hills, it is pleasant to be able to consider it a slight modification of a native word, and not an instance of the stupid wholesale application of classic titles in the geography of central New York.

The French sometimes called the Senecas Tsonnontouans or Sonnonthouans. The tribe called themselves Nundowaga, the People of the Hill, in conformity with one of their traditions, which represented that the nation originated and first dwelt on a hill at the head of Canandaigua lake. While seated here, as the legend runs, the existence of the tribe was jeopardized by a snake, which grew up in their midst and assumed immense proportions and hostile attitude. This serpent, called Kaistowanea, was, while small, caught in the woods by a boy, who kept and cared for it as a pet. It grew rapidly, demanding more and more food, until the hunters had to provide it with deer ; and at length it could no longer find room in the lodge of its captor, but had to take post on a neighboring hill. Thereafter it took care of itself, sporting occasionally in the lake, and still growing, until the tribe became alarmed in view of its possible actions, and determined to flee for safety. But in the morning of their intended escape, they found the monstrous reptile coiled about their castle, with jaws gaping before the gate. Escape was impossible, and though starvation prompted the attempt, the wretched prisoners only rushed into the mouth of their terrible besieger. Most were thus devoured ; but a warrior, having dreamed that " if he would fledge his arrows with the hair of his sister the charm would prevail over the enemy," shot into the serpent an arrow so prepared. Mortally wounded, the huge reptile rolled down the hill into the lake, breaking off the trees in his way. After wallowing in agony in the water, and vomiting up the bodies swallowed, the serpent expired and sunk from sight. The remnant of the tribe immediately left the scene of their suffering, and removed to the site of Geneva. Mr. Schoolcraft considered this story of the Senecas worthy of an attempt at interpretation, and suggested the following : " Internal feuds, created by somebody brought up in their own lodge, originated hatred and hot blood. In a long and bloody war the nation was nearly exterminated ; at length the affections of a woman prevailed. Harmony was restored, and a new era of prosperity began, by removing the council fire to another place."

This tradition of the origin of the nation contradicts the legend of an original immigration from the west, and that other precious invention which represents the Iroquois as springing from the earth near the falls of the Oswego, and separating to their various stations along that river and its tributaries. These remnants of the mythology of the Indians are worthless, even as a test of their ability at legend-making ; like their printed speeches, they have been through the hands of too many fanciful white men. The search for information in aboriginal sources is vanity and vexation of spirit.

It has been customary with recent writers on the Indians to ascribe to them many and lofty excellencies and abilities, and to begin by deprecating the alleged disposition to do them injustice and ignore their claims to respect and admiration. If such a disposition ever existed, the tide of opinion has of late certainly been flowing the other way, and it may be time for the ebb. There seems to have been something like statesmanship in the formation of "the league of the Iroquois," albeit the expedient was the simplest possible, and the object success in savage warfare; also in the means by which the league was strengthened, including the complicated system of family and tribal relationship; but has not the glory of this barbarian union been exaggerated? For example (we are speaking of Red Jacket's nation), must we believe all we read of Indian oratory ? Not satisfied with the eloquent periods ascribed to the red speechmakers, their eulogists remind us that we have only white men's versions of what the orators said, and assume that the speeches suffered by the interpretation. But it is possible that they gained. The interpreters, it is said, were often illiterate men. But they were in all cases less so than the orators, and in many cases they must be admitted to have been quite adequate to the task. One of the most famous of Indian orations is the address of Garangula, *alias* La Grand Guele—Big Mouth, as Mr. Parkman translates it—to De La Barre in the conference at the mouth of Salmon river, in Oswego county; "but this," says Mr.

Clinton, in his celebrated eulogy of the Iroquois, " was interpreted by Monsieur Le Moine, a French Jesuit, and recorded on the spot by Baron La Hontan, men of enlightened and cultivated minds." The man who translated it from the French must have been a scholar, and it is not likely that the speech suffered in his hands. Mr. Parkman makes a very suggestive remark on Big Mouth : " Doubtless, as he stood in full dress before the governor and the officers, his head plumed, his face painted, his figure draped in a colored blanket and his feet decked with embroidered moccasins, he was a picturesque and striking object; he was less so as he squatted almost naked by his lodge fire, with a piece of board laid across his lap, chopping rank tobacco with a scalping knife to fill his pipe, and entertaining the grinning circle with grotesque stories and obscene jests." Fondness for speech-making does not necessarily argue eloquence, and it is not easy to believe in a phenomenal development of true oratory in a race of savages who were primarily warriors, in a skulking and brutal fashion, and whose home life, if we may use the expression, was, generation after generation alike, contentedly passed in idleness and squalor. On the whole, we may say that, questionable as may have been some of the white man's dealings with the Senecas, the extinction from their ancient territory of that people, with their doubtful virtues and indubitable barbarity, was an exceedingly good riddance.

While the Senecas shared with their allies the authority gained by their conquests throughout the south and in the Canadas, the territory of their immediate jurisdiction was confined within comparatively narrow limits. One of the first allusions to the tribe by Europeans occurs in a Jesuit "relation," dated 1664-5, and is as follows : "Toward the termination of the great lake called Ontario is located the most numerous of the Five Nations, named the Senecas, which contains full twelve hundred men, in two or three villages of which it is composed."

In 1677 Wentworth Greenhalgh passed through the "long house" of the Iroquois from end to end, and made a detailed report of his journey and observations, from which we extract the following :

"The Senecas have four towns, viz., Canagora, Tiotohatton, Canoenada and Keint-he. Canagora and Tiotohatton lye within 30 miles of ye Lake ffrontenacque, [Ontario] and ye other two ly aboutt four or five miles apiece to ye Southward of those. They have abundance of Corne. None of their towns are stockadoed.

"Canagorah lyes on the top of a great hill [Boughton hill, near Victor, Ontario county], and in that, as well as in the bignesse, much like Onondago, containing 150 houses, northwestward of Caiougo 72 miles Here ye Indians were very desirous to see us ride our horses [probably the first they ever saw], wch wee did : they made great feasts and dancing. * * *

"Tiotohattan lyes on the brincke or edge of a hill ; has not much cleared ground ; is near the river Tiotehatton, wch signifies bending. It lies to Westward of Canagorah about 30 miles, containing about 120 houses, being ye largest of all the houses wee saw, ye ordinary being 50 *a* 60 foot long, with 12 *a* 13 fires in one house. They have good store of corne, growing about a mile to the Northward of the town.

"Being at this place the 17th of June, there came 50 prisoners from the Southwestward. They were of two nations some whereof have few guns ; the others none at all. One nation is about 10 days journey from any Christian and trade only with one great house, not far from the sea, and the other trade only, as they say, with a black people, This day of them was burnt two women, and a man and a child killed with a stone. All night we heard a great noyse as if ye houses had all fallen, butt itt was onely ye Inhabitants driving away ye ghosts of ye murthered.

" The 18th going to Canagorah, we overtook ye prisoners; when the soudiers saw us they stopped each his prisoner, and made him sing, and cutt off their fingers, and slasht their bodies wth a knife, and when they had sung each man confessed how many men in his time he had killed. Thatt day att Canagorah, there were most cruelly burnt four men, four women and one boy. The cruelty lasted aboutt seven hours. When they were almost dead letting them loose to the mercy of ye boys, and taking the hearts of such as were dead to feast on.

"Canoenada lyes about four miles to ye Southward of Canagorah; conteynes about 30 houses, well furnished with corne.

" Keint-he lyes aboutt four or five miles to ye Southward of Tietehatton; contayns about 24 houses well furnished with corne.

"The Senecques are counted to bee in all aboutt 1000 fighting men."

In 1684 Father Lamberville, dissuading La Barre from attacking the Senecas, gave the number of their warriors at 1500. In 1698 there was made an official census of the Five Nations, in which it was reported that the "Sinnickes" had dwindled to 600 from 1300, their number in 1689. In 1763 Sir William Johnson estimated the men of the nation as numbering 1050, and mentioned that the tribe had " several villages beginning about 50 m. from Cayuga, and from thence to Chenussio, the largest, about 70 m. from Niagara, with others thence to the Ohio." In 1770 he reported that there were 1000 of the Seneca warriors. The fighting strength of this tribe was generally nearly equal to that of all the other Iroquois. This was stated by Governor Tryon to be the case in 1774, when, on the excellent authority of Sir William Johnson, he reported the total number of Iroquois warriors at 2000.

When the Senecas first became known to the whites their villages were scattered from Seneca lake half way to the Niagara. In 1669, when La Salle made his first visit to their country, their four principal villages were from ten to twenty miles south of the falls of the Genesee, and to the eastward of that river. Mention is made of cabins of the Senecas on the Niagara in 1678 and 1736. General Amherst, writing in 1763, mentions the Kanadaseegy and Canadaraggo castles, the former of which, more commonly spelled Kanadaseaga, stood on the site of Geneva. These are presumably the villages which Sir

William Johnson, in his enumeration of the Indians in 1763, calls Kanadasero and Kanadaragey, and mentions as being in the English interest, while the rest of the nation was hostile. There were, in Sir William's time, two castles of the tribe at Chenussio, once their western outpost, and a village, called Chenondoanah, stood on the west bank of the Genesee, some fifteen miles from its mouth.

CHAPTER IV.

LA SALLE'S VANGUARD ARRIVES IN THE NIAGARA—THE NARRATIVE OF FATHER HENNEPIN.

EUROPEANS first learned of the Niagara river and falls, as of many other of the grand natural features of North America, through the expedition of the Frenchman Jacques Cartier up the river St. Lawrence, as far as the site of Montreal, in 1535. Savages whom he met told him of a great lake, from which their river flowed, and that beyond it another lake, of similar size, might be reached through a river, by a portage round a cataract. Thus was the first intelligence of northwestern New York gained by the people whose explorers, priests and traders were to be its pioneers, and so long its only civilized inhabitants. Cartier, however, did not reach the Niagara, and it was nearly a century after his sojourn on the St. Lawrence before any of his countrymen penetrated the noble country of which he was vaguely informed.

The "many of our French in that quarter" who visited the barbarous people dwelling there, "to profit by their furs and other commodities," before the mission of the Recollet priest Daillon in 1626, as recounted by Father L'Allemant, must have been the first white men who entered the region of which we write. The exact date of their advent cannot be ascertained; we only know that more than two hundred and fifty years ago, and probably before the Puritans landed at Plymouth, a Frenchman was not a very rare spectacle at this point, four hundred and fifty miles into the wilderness from the historic beach where the pilgrims stepped ashore.

No French settlements were now made on the Niagara, although traders probably visited it occasionally for the next century, and at least three explorers saw the river in 1669. It was an event, therefore, when, on the 6th of December, 1768, a ten-ton craft sailed into the mouth of the river, bearing an advance party of one of La Salle's wonderful exploring expeditions into the west and south which pushed the boundary of New France to New Mexico, and gave to the French crown the once vast and indefinite territory in the south named by its discoverer Louisiana. The party consisted of sixteen persons, chief among them the Sieur de la Motte, commander of the little craft, and the Franciscan Father Hennepin, historian of the expedition. The latter's account of the voyage over Lake Ontario enables us to imagine the satisfaction with which the company left it for the smoother waters of the river.

"On the 18th of November," says Father Hennepin, "I took leave of our monks at Fort Fontenac [Kingston] and after mutual embraces, and expressions of brotherly and christian charity, I embarked in a brigantine of about ten tons. The winds and the cold of autumn were then very violent, insomuch that our crew were afraid to go in so little a vessel. This obliged us and the Sieur de la Motte, our commander, to keep our course on the north side of the lake, to shelter ourselves under the coast against the northwest wind, which would have otherwise forced us upon the southern coast of the lake. This voyage proved very difficult and dangerous, because of the unseasonable time of the year, winter being near at hand. On the 26th we were in great danger, about two large leagues off the land, where we were obliged to lie at anchor all that night, at sixty fathoms of water and above; but at length, the wind coming at the northeast, we sailed on, and arrived safely at the other end of the lake Ontario, called by the Iroquois Skannandario.

"We came pretty near one of their villages, called Tajajagon, lying about seventy leagues from Fort Frontenac, or Catarokouy. We bartered some Indian corn with the Iroquois, who could not sufficiently admire us, and came frequently to see us in our brigantine, which for our greater security we had brought to an anchor into a river; though before we could get in we ran aground three times, which obliged us to put fourteen men into canoes, and cast the ballast of our ship overboard, to get her off again. That river falls into the lake, but for fear of being frozen up therein we were forced to cut the ice, with axes and other instruments. The wind turning then contrary, we were obliged to tarry there till the 5th of December, 1678, when we sailed from the northern to the southern side, where the river Niagara runs into the lake, but could not reach it that day, though it is but fifteen or sixteen leagues distant, and therefore cast anchor within five leagues of the shore, where we had very bad weather all the night long. On the 6th, being St. Nicholas day, we got into the fine river Niagara, into which never any such ship as ours entered before.

"We sang there the *Te Deum*, and other prayers, to return our thanks to God Almighty for our prosperous voyage. The Iroquois Tsonnontouans [Senecas], inhabiting the little village situated at the mouth of the river, took above three hundred whitefish, which are bigger than carps, and the best relished as well as the wholesomest fish in the world; which they presented all to us, imputing their good luck to our arrival. They were much surprised at our ship, which they called the great wooden canoe."

On the following day the intrepid voyagers went up the river to where the current became too rapid for a canoe to stem it—"two leagues" Father Hennepin says—looking for a suitable building site. Not suiting themselves below the falls (which appalled Hennepin by their features of sublimity and terror), they landed and marched above the cataract (finding "no land fit for culture"), to a point near the mouth of the Chippewa river, where they encamped for the night, removing a foot of snow to make a place for a fire. "La Salle's party," says Captain James Van Cleve, "soon after entering the Niagara proceeded on their way up the river to the head of the eddy at Queenston, where lies a large rock distinguished to this day as Hennepin Rock, which is still prominent directly under the west end of the Lewiston and Queenston suspension bridge. Finding their progress by boat stopped at this point by the heavy current, and the bank of the river very steep and some 350 feet high, they crossed the river 650 feet wide) to the east side, and then the party walked to the falls," etc. The next day they retraced their course, seeing on the way great numbers of "wild goats and turkey cocks," as the translation (one hundred and eighty years old) calls the deer and wild turkeys. On the 11th Father Hennepin "said the first mass that was ever said in that country."

The result of the search for a proper place to put up buildings was the determination " to build some houses " at the point where the swiftness of the river compelled the explorers to take to the shore in their trip of the 7th, that is, at the site of Lewiston. For several days, however, the direction of the wind prevented sailing to the place, and on the 15th it was found necessary to tow the vessel up the river. "I was desired to sit at the helm of our brigantine," writes the serviceable priest, "while three of our men hauled the same, from the shore, with a rope ; and at last we brought her up and moored her to the shore with a hawser, near a rock of prodigious hight, lying upon the rapid currents we have already mentioned.

"The 17th, 18th and 19th we were busy making a cabin, with palisadoes, to serve for a magazine ; but the ground was so frozen that we were forced several times to throw boiling water upon it, to facilitate the beating in and driving down the stakes." The next four days were spent in efforts to preserve the brigantine, which " was in great danger to be dashed to pieces by the vast pieces of ice that were hurled down the river." The craft was finally got ashore, and saved "from the danger of being broke to pieces, or carried away, by the ice which came down with an extreme violence from the great fall of Niagara."

The Iroquois were always extremely suspicious of the establishment of permanent posts in their country, particularly fortifications, and it was now high time to ascertain whether the Senecas would tolerate the operations of the French party on their soil. The intruders fully realized their danger in this respect, although so hospitably received on entering the river : " Whoever considers our map," the Franciscan remarks, "will easily see that this new enterprise of building a fort and some houses on the river Niagara, besides the fort of Fontenac, was likely to give jealousy to the Iroquois, and even to the English, who live in this neighborhood [at Albany] and have a great commerce with them." As soon, therefore, as the brigantine was secured, La Motte, Hennepin and seven others of the company set out on what proved a five days' march to the Seneca village Tegarondies, the Canagorah of Wentworth Greenhalgh, on Boughton hill, near Victor, Ontario county, also called Gannagaro. There they remained more than a week, Father Hennepin preaching on New Year's day in the Jesuits' bark-built chapel, before fathers Raffeix and Garnier, missionaries stationed among these Indians. A council was held with the Seneca sachems, from which Father Garnier was excluded, as La Motte had an antipathy to him ; and Hennepin, choosing to associate himself with his aggrieved fellow priest, and " bear part of the affront put upon him," also remained without. There was the usual propitiation of the savage landlords by gifts, and La Motte then told them that the French proposed to construct " a great wooden canoe " on the Niagara, by which they would be enabled to supply the Indians with merchandise cheaper than they could buy from the English. They would also station a blacksmith and gunsmith at the mouth of the Niagara to repair the arms of the Iroquois. The Senecas acquiesced, and the embassy returned to the river, which they reached on the 14th of January, 1679, worn out with the toils of the journey, and prepared to feast with an appetite on corn and whitefish, with the broth of the latter, which were the only provisions in the camp. La Motte, "being not able to endure the fatigue of so laborious a life, gave over his design and returned to Canada."

The mention of Jesuit priests among the Senecas at this date suggests a summary of the previous labors of the order with this nation : In the spring of 1666, in a council with ten Seneca sachems at Quebec, the Marquis de Tracy, acting French viceroy in America, promised to send them Jesuit missionaries, whom they agreed to shelter and protect. Accordingly, in 1668 Father Fremin was sent to labor with the tribe. He was joined the next year by Father Garnier, who was assigned to the village of Gandachiragou, Fremin remaining in charge at Gandagarae, where he found a remnant of the Neutral nation, absorbed into the community of their conquerors. Fremin was recalled in 1671, and Father Raffeix took his place in the following year, going from the Cayuga mission, which he described as being in the most beautiful country he had seen in America, while the Senecas' domain he found comparatively rugged, and a poor hunting ground. At his arrival among them the nation numbered, according to Garnier's extravagant estimate, from twelve to thirteen thousand souls. Father Pierron was sent into this field in 1673, but had been recalled when the embassy of La Motte visited the tribe.

CHAPTER V.

THE CAREER OF LA SALLE—HE BUILDS THE FIRST SAILING VESSEL ABOVE NIAGARA FALLS.

"ON the 20th I heard, from the banks above where we were, the voice of the Sieur de la Salle, who had arrived from Fort Frontenac in a large vessel." Thus the ecclesiastic records one stage in the wide wanderings of this remarkable man. Robert Cavalier de la Salle was a native of Rouen, and belonged to a family in good social standing. He was educated in a Jesuit seminary, and in 1667, when but twenty-two years of age, emigrated to Canada. He had become possessed with the belief that China might be reached by voyaging westward through the mighty lake and river system of North America, which the French pioneers had already extensively explored; and was so enthusiastic on the subject that his neighbors mockingly called his place on the St. Lawrence *La Chine* (China), the name ever since borne by the rapids at the head of which he lived. Courcelles, the governor of New France, as the French called their American possessions, was disposed to share La Salle's convictions, and encouraged him to test them by a westward expedition, on which he embarked in the summer of 1669, accompanied by two Montreal priests, Dollier and Gallinee. The explorers expected in their tour to visit "divers Indian nations, situated along a great river called by the Iroquois *Ohio*, and by the Ottawas *Mississippi*." Traversing the St. Lawrence and Lake Ontario in canoes, they visited the Senecas in the Genesee valley, reached the Niagara, and gazed upon the great cataract. Illness obliged La Salle to return to Montreal; but his clerical comrades, remaining, explored the region between the lakes, and took possession of it for France and the church, planting the royal arms in token thereof.

La Salle, thwarted in his original project, repaired to the French court, bearing the endorsement of Count Frontenac, then governor of New France, as "the most capable for all the enterprises of discovery;" and obtained letters patent from Louis XIV. authorizing him to explore the western portion of the vast territory claimed by the French in America. "We have consented to this proposal more willingly," says the Grand Monarch, "because there is nothing that we have more at heart than the discovery of this country, through which it is probable that a passage may be found to Mexico." La Salle obtained other favors from the King, including the rank of nobility, and returned to America to prosecute his new and grand scheme of exploration, believing he could find, through the Mississippi and the Gulf of Mexico, a better route of communication with Europe than that through the lakes and the St. Lawrence. Two hundred years later found a committee of the United States Senate pondering on this same idea, balancing the relative advantages of the lakes and the Mississippi as an outlet for the products of the northwest; as a result, hundreds of thousands of dollars were appropriated for the improvement of the latter, showing the nation's faith in the commercial capacity of the mighty stream whose lower course was to be explored by the adventurous Frenchman now arriving at the mouth of the Niagara. The authority on La Salle's advent here in 1679, relied on by all historians of this series of events, is the narrative of Father Hennepin, from which we have already quoted. We cannot do better than to copy his account, as translated from the best French edition by Mr. O. H. Marshall, of Buffalo. We continue it from the opening sentence of this chapter:

"He brought provisions and rigging necessary for the vessel he intended building above the great fall of Niagara, near the entrance into Lake Erie. But by a strange misfortune that vessel was lost, through fault of the two pilots, who disagreed as to the course. The vessel was wrecked on the southern shore of Lake Ontario, two leagues from Niagara. The sailors have named the place the Mad Cape. The anchors and cables were saved, but the goods and bark canoes were lost. Such adversities would have caused the enterprise to be abandoned by any but those who had formed the noble design of a new discovery.

"The Sieur de la Salle informed us that he had been among the Iroquois Senecas before the loss of his vessel; that he had succeeded so well in conciliating them that they mentioned with pleasure our embassy, * * * and even consented to the prosecution of our undertaking. This agreement was of short duration, for certain persons opposed our designs in every possible way,and instilled jealousies into the minds of the Iroquois. The fort, nevertheless, which we were building at Niagara, continued to advance. But finally the secret influences against us were so great that the fort became an object of suspicion to the savages, and we were compelled to abandon its construction for a time, and content ourselves with buildinga habitation, surrounded with palisades.

"On the 22d we went two leagues above the great falls of Niagara, and built some stocks [at the mouth of Cayuga creek] on which to erect the vessel we needed for our voyage. We could not have built it in a more convenient place, being near a river which empties into the strait which is between Lake Erie and the great falls. In all my travels back and forth I always carried my portable chapel upon my shoulders. On the 26th, the keel of the vessel and other pieces being ready, the Sieur de la Salle sent the master carpenter, named Moyse, to request me to drive the first bolt. But the modesty appropriate to my religious profession induced me to decline the honor. He then promised ten louis d'or for that first bolt, to stimulate the master carpenter to advance the work.

"During the whole winter, which is not half as severe in this country as in Canada, we employed in building bark huts one of the two savages of the wolf tribe whom we had engaged for hunting deer. I had one hut especially designed for observing prayers on holidays and Sundays. Many of our people knew the Gregorian chant, and the rest had some parts of it by rote [Gregorian music was given by practiced European tenors, with the tremendous bass of Niagara.—*Brodhead*].

"The Sieur de la Salle left in command of our ship yard one Tonti, an Italian by birth, who had come to France after the revolution in Naples, in which his father was engaged. Pressing business compelled the former to return to Fort Frontenac, and I conducted him to the border of Lake Ontario, at the mouth of the river Niagara. While there he pretended to mark out a house for the blacksmith which had been promised for the convenience of the Iroquois. I cannot blame the Iroquois for not believing all that had been promised them at the embassy of the Sieur de la Motte. Finally the Sieur de la Salle undertook his expedition over the snow, and thus accomplished more than eighty leagues. He had no food except a small bag of roasted corn, and even that had failed him two days' journey from the fort. Nevertheless he arrived safely, with two men and a dog which drew his baggage on the ice.

"Returning to our ship-yard, we learned that most of the Iroquois had gone to war beyond Lake Erie while our vessel was being built. Although those that remained were less violent, by reason of their diminished numbers, still they did not cease from coming often to our shipyard, and testifying their dissatisfaction at our doings. Some time after, one of them, pretending to be drunk, attempted to kill our blacksmith ; but the resistance which he met with from the smith, who was named La Forge, and who wielded a red-hot bar of iron, repulsed him, and, together with a reprimand which I gave the villain, compelled him to desist. Some days after, a squaw advised us that the Senecas were about to set fire to our vessel on the stocks, and they would, without doubt, have effected their object had not a very strict watch been kept. These frequent alarms, the fear of the failure of provisions, on account of the loss of the large vessel from Fort Frontenac and the refusal of the Senecas to sell us Indian corn, discouraged our carpenters. They were moreover enticed by a worthless fellow, who often attempted to desert to New York, a place which is inhabited by the Dutch, who have succeeded the Swedes. This dishonest fellow would have undoubtedly been successful with our workmen had I not encouraged them by exhortations on holidays and Sundays after divine service. I told them that our enterprise had sole reference to the promotion of the glory of God and the welfare of our Christian colonies. Thus I stimulated them to work more diligently in order to deliver us from all these apprehensions.

"In the meantime, the two savages of the wolf tribe whom we had engaged in our service followed the chase, and furnished us with roe-buck and other kinds of deer for our subsistence ; by reason of which our workmen took courage, and applied themselves to their business with more assiduity. Our vessel was consequently soon in a condition to be launched, which was done after having been blessed according to our church of Rome. We were in haste to get it afloat, although not finished, that we might guard it more securely from the threatened fire. This vessel was named the 'Griffin,' in allusion to the arms of the Count de Frontenac, which have two griffins for their supports. For the Sieur de la Salle had often said of this vessel that he would make the griffin fly above the crow. We fired three guns, then sang the *Te Deum*, which was followed by many cries of joy.

"The Iroquois who happened to be present partook of our joy and witnessed our rejoicing. We gave them some brandy to drink, as well as to all our men, who slung their hammocks under the deck of the vessel to sleep in greater security. We then left our bark huts, to lodge where we were protected from the insults of the savages.

"The Iroquois having returned from their beaver hunt, were extremely surprised to see our ship. They said we were the *Ot-kon*, which means in their language penetrating minds. They could not understand how we had built so large a vessel in so short a time, although it was but sixty tons burthen. We might have called it a moving fort, for it caused all the savages to tremble who lived within a space of more than five hundred leagues along the rivers and great lakes."

Hennepin, accompanied by one of the Seneca hunters, next paddled up the river to Lake Erie in a canoe, taking soundings and testing the strength of the current; and returned reporting the passage entirely practicable for the new vessel. One more preparatory journey the enterprising priest had to make, namely to Fort Frontenac, to engage two of his fellow ecclesiastics to labor with him in the West. The tour of Lake Ontario was made in a bark in which a trader named La Foret had come to the mouth of the Niagara with a stock of Indian goods. On the departure of the vessel fifteen or sixteen squaws from the Genesee villages took passage, expecting a much more easy and agreeable journey home than the toilsome tramp through the forests; but, "as they were unaccustomed to travel in this manner, the motion of the vessel caused them great qualms at the stomach," and all hands wished they had gone overland. At the mouth of the Genesee, Hennepin relates, "Sieur de la Foret traded brandy for beaver skins. This traffic in strong drink was not agreeable to me, for if the savages drink ever so little they are more to be dreaded than madmen." Having reached Fort Frontenac, and associated with him Father Gabriel de la Ribourde and Zenobe Mambre, Hennepin in a few days embarked for the return in a trading craft, which stopped for traffic with the Indians at the mouth of the Oswego river; tarrying so long that the priests built a little chapel of bark "half a league in the woods," where they avoided disturbance by the crowds of savages who gathered at the water-side " to see our brigantine, at which they greatly wondered, as well as to trade for powder, guns, knives, lead, but especially brandy, for which they are very greedy."

Thus delayed, the party did not reach the Niagara until the 30th of July. On the 4th of August Hennepin and a sergeant named La Fleur visited the falls, and proceeded to the ship-yard above. The "Griffin" meanwhile had been moved up the river, to within a league of Lake Erie, and Hennepin and his companion followed in "a bark canoe, half rotten and without paddles," which they found in place of the larger craft, and devised means to navigate. "Our arrival was welcomed with joy," says the clerical annalist. "We found the vessel perfectly equipped with sails, masts, and everything necessary for navigation. We found on board five small cannon, two of which were brass, besides two or three arquebuses. A spread griffin adorned the prow, surmounted by an eagle. There were also all the ordinary ornaments which usually adorn ships of war.* * *

"On the 16th and 17th we returned to the banks of Lake Ontario, and ascended with the bark we had brought from Fort Frontenac as far as the great rock of the river Niagara. We there cast anchor at the foot of the three mountains where we were obliged to make the portage caused by the great falls of Niagara, which interrupt the navigation. Father Gabriel, who was sixty-four years old, underwent all the fatigues of this voyage, and ascended and descended three times the three mountains [the terraces of the mountain ridge at Lewiston], which are very high and steep at the place where the portage is made. Our people made many trips to carry the provisions, munitions of war, and other necessaries for the vessel. The voyage was painful in the extreme, because there were two long leagues of road each way. It took four men to carry our largest anchor, but brandy being given to cheer them the work was soon accomplished, and we all returned together to the mouth of Lake Erie.* * *

"We endeavored several times to ascend the current of the strait into Lake Erie, but the wind was not yet strong enough. We were therefore obliged to wait until it should be more favorable. During the detention the Sieur de la Salle [who, leaving Fort Frontenac, had coasted along the southern shore of Lake Ontario in a canoe, and arrived on the Niagara after another tour of the Seneca villages] employed our men in preparing some ground on the western side of the strait of Niagara, where we planted some vegetables for the use of those who should come to live in this place for the purpose of keeping up a communication between the vessels [i.e., should have charge of the portage], and maintaining a correspondence from lake to lake. We found in this place some wild chervil and garlic which grow spontaneously.

"We left Father Melithon [Watteau, who had joined the party] at the habitation we had made above the great falls of Niagara, with some overseers and workmen. Our men encamped on the bank of the river, that the lightened vessel might the more easily ascend into the lake. We celebrated divine service on board every day, and our people who remained on land could hear the sermon on holidays and Sundays."

At length a wind sprung up "strong from the northeast," and the "Griffin," bearing a company of thirty-four persons, all Frenchmen but Tonti, essayed the entrance of Lake Erie, which was only gained by the aid of tow lines from the shore. Once more hear Father Hennepin.

"We set sail on the 7th of August, 1679, steering west southwest. After having chanted the *Te Deum*, we fired all the cannon and arquebuses in presence of many Iroquois warriors, who had brought captives from *Tintonha*, that is to say, from the 'people of the prairies,' who live more than four hundred leagues from their cantons. We heard these savages exclaim, 'Gannoron!' in testimony of their wonder."

If we were among these astonished savages, and could follow with prophetic eye the course of this first sailing vessel above the great cataract, as it sinks from sight over the blue waters of Lake Erie, we should see trouble and disaster lying in wait for the pioneer bark and its sanguine crew. The outward voyage ended at Green Bay, in Lake Michigan, or Illinois, as it was then called. The "Griffin" was there freighted with furs, and with a crew of six men set out for the Niagara. No trace of crew, vessel or cargo was ever obtained, unless some cannon, with a French inscription, and wrought iron, including an anchor, which are said to have been found early in this century on the eastern shore of Lake Erie, belonged to the ill-fated craft. No other wreck is known to have occurred in this quarter so early as the discovery of these relics, but La Salle was assured by those whom he sent in search of the missing craft that it did not return to the straits of Mackinaw, at the foot of Lake Michigan; and the Indians between lakes Huron and Erie never saw it repass the waters of St. Clair, although the unlucky bark was seen at anchor near the north end of Lake Michigan after its departure from Green Bay.

After the loss of the "Griffin" La Salle built a trading post at the head of Lake Michigan, and another on the Illinois river, from which he returned on foot to Fort Fontenac, with but two companions and what provisions his rifle brought him. Repairing again to his western posts early in 1682, he descended the Mississippi to its mouth. He next returned to France, whence in 1684 he sailed for the mouth of the Mississippi direct, with a number of ships and several hundred men, to found a colony. The fleet missed its destination, and returned to France, after the storeship had been wrecked on the coast of Texas; leaving La Salle with a little company of malcontents, embittered by their misfortunes and hating him as the cause. With sixteen of them he started for Canada, after a fruitless search for gold in New Mexico, but was assassinated before he had reached the present boundary of Texas. As to the locality of La Salle's shipyard we cannot do better than print the following remarks, submitted by Captain James Van Cleve, of Lewiston:

"As there are differences of opinion among historians and others as to the locality where La Salle built the bark 'Griffin,' the following brief local historical facts are given to show conclusively that she was built within Niagara county.

"*First*, La Salle says he landed at the 'three mountains [Lewiston],' went on foot to the great falls and proceeded on to a creek two leagues (6 miles) above the falls, where he erected some cabins and shops and built the bark 'Griffin.'

"*Second*, Denonville (who was the French governor)

says in his proclamation dated July 31, 1687, that La Salle spent several years on the east side of the Niagara river, two leagues above the great falls, where he built a bark (the 'Griffin') of which the stocks were then standing.

"*Third*, Joshua Fairbanks, late of Lewiston, who first settled in Queenston in 1793 (before Lewiston, as such, was known), was well acquainted with an old French officer who came to Canada and Fort Niagara as a young lieutenant with French troops, and frequently told Mr. Fairbanks that his coming to Canada was only fifty years behind the building of the bark 'Griffin' by La Salle, and that traces of the old ship-yard at Cayuga creek were visible; that old spikes and other articles of rusted iron were frequently found, and that the place was notorious among Indians as the place where the 'big canoe' or 'Griffin' was built.

"(After the death of the old French officer, in 1794, his effects were sold at 'vendue.' Among them was a very beautiful chess and backgammon board, inlaid with Ebony and ivory, which Mr. Fairbanks bought and which is now in the possession of his grand-daughter, Mrs. James Van Cleve, of Lewiston.)

"*Fourth*, Mrs. Eli Reynolds, now (1878) residing at Niagara Falls, aged 85 years, says her father, who settled near Cayuga creek in 1808, was well acquainted with an old ship-carpenter, named Smith, who had some years before located his ship-yard upon ground where evidences appeared that vessels had been built long before, such as rusted remains of iron and various forms of chip mould, visible under the surface of the ground; and that tradition among the old Indians was that the 'big canoe' ['Griffin'] was built there. The location of the old ship-yard is about half way between the mouth of Cayuga creek and the head of Cayuga Island, upon land now known as the Angevine farm.

"Many other facts and traditions might be given to show that Niagara county is entitled to the credit of having the first vessel built upon her soil that navigated the lakes above Niagara Falls, but they are deemed unnecessary." The other operations of La Salle's company, as narrated by Father Hennepin, were on the east bank of the river; and if in all their going to and coming from the ship-yard they had had to cross the river Hennepin would certainly have mentioned it.

Thus was inaugurated in this quarter the domination of the French, which marked one of the most important eras in the early history of America. A little more than three quarters of a century later, France held every point of advantage commanding the communication between the lakes and the great rivers of the West, and possessed a controlling influence over all the Western tribes. The toil and daring by which this eminent position was gained are well illustrated in this chapter. The boldness and versatility of the explorers, the devotion of the ecclesiastics, and the hardihood of the laborers in lower ranks are as plain to the reader as to the author in the lucid narrative of Father Hennepin, and need hardly a comment. The deeds of the founders of New France, so important a portion of which was performed within the western borders of Niagara county, were worthy of the great lakes, the boundless forests and prairies, and the mighty rivers that formed the splendid arena on which they were enacted.

CHAPTER VI.

NIAGARA AND THE INDIAN TRADE—THE RIVALRY OF THE FRENCH AND ENGLISH.

THE French were now established on the upper lakes, and in friendly relations with several Indian tribes, including the Illinois, Miamis, Hurons and Ottawas, with whom they carried on a trade which was their most important interest in America, exchanging firearms, ammunition, blankets and brandy for furs, chiefly beaver, to great advantage. The establishment of their posts on the Niagara guarded transportation along that stream, and they seemed prepared to achieve a career of brilliant prosperity. Such might have been their good fortune but for a war with the Iroquois in which they now became involved, and which proved extremely disastrous to both belligerents.

The English had built up a similar trade among the Five Nations, which both parties found it for their interest to promote and develop; but the territory of New York afforded limited resources for the trapper, as compared with the boundless wilds of the Northwest, whence the French drew their harvest of furs. The great Indian confederacy was now at the height of its power, and its warriors, stimulated by a prospect of gain, as well as by the fondness for war and the lust of conquest which always animated them, determined to overcome the clans of the prairies and the greater lakes, and possess themselves of the fountain of wealth now tapped by the French, but which would in the event of their success be diverted to the English. The prosecution of this scheme must inevitably, soon or late, have driven the French to arms; but the Iroquois, contemptuous of the power of Onontio, as they called the governor of New France, whoever he might be, needlessly precipitated the conflict. Early in 1684 a war party of the Senecas and Cayugas, on a campaign against the Illinois, which in the scale of distances traversed belittles Sherman's famous "march to the sea," attacked the garrison of the post which La Salle had planted on the Illinois river, after seizing seven canoes loaded with valuable goods which the French governor, De la Barre, had expected to dispose of on the Mississippi. There was now no alternative left but war; but the power of La Barre was inadequate to avenge his injuries, and an expedition which he led against the Iroquois got no further into their country than the lake shore of Oswego county, where a parley was held with their chiefs and a disgraceful truce effected, the Indians falsely promising to make reparation for the plunder of the canoes, but refusing to grant peace to their western enemies, the allies of the French. De la Barre was recalled to France, and the Marquis de Denonville appointed to succeed him.

The situation and the demands of the hour were about this time summed up as follows, in an official communication laid before the French King:

"The Iroquois Indians have, from all time, waged a cruel war against all the other Indians of the country called Canada. Since the Dutch first, and the English afterwards, held Manatte [Manhattan—New York] and Orange [Albany], which adjoin the hamlets and villages of the said Iroquois, these have been excessively urged thereto by those Dutch and English, who clearly foresaw that they would become masters of the whole of the hunting of the country should the Iroquois destroy all the other tribes, and thereby gain a great trade and ruin that of Quebec. The English have spared nothing to accomplish that object. They have supplied those Iroquois with merchandise, and particularly with arms and powder, nearly at European prices; have given feasts and presents to their chiefs, and sometimes to the entire nation; and have finally succeeded, because, the colony of Quebec and New France being formerly governed by companies, these gave themselves very little trouble about the good or evil which might eventually result to the colony.

"Now that things are changed by the favor of God, and the King takes care of that country, it appears very easy to return the compliment to those English if, as there is reason to hope, his Majesty's arms are victorious over the Iroquois, and these are reduced; particularly by erecting a fort at Niagara, with a strong garrison for the protection of the settlers, who will establish themselves there in order to clear the land, which is most excellent, and to carry on the trade in furs with the said Iroquois Indians, who do all their hunting on the lands belonging to the King's domain. The English will thus be deprived of a trade in peltries amounting to four hundred thousand livres yearly, which will be very beneficial to the French colony. All the inhabitants of said Niagara will pay to the revenue of his Majesty's domain the duty of one-fourth of the beavers, and one-tenth of the moose, the same as at Quebec. This will increase by a large sum the King's revenue in said country, and should his Majesty think fit to lease it to a private person when the said Iroquois are pacified, inasmuch as the establishment of the said Niagara must be considered a newly discovered country, persons will be found who will give a considerable sum for the privilege of receiving the duties on the beaver and moose which will be exported from said Niagara."

Denonville further urged similar considerations upon the French government, writing as follows under date of "Quebec 8th May 1686:"

"I am satisfied the Iroquois hea'. desire peace now that they see troops, but I do not at all believe that they consent to abandon all future hostilities against the other tribes, our allies. Therefore, there remains not a doubt of the necessity of placing ourselves in a condition to humble them. The establishment of a very strong post at Niagara would, in my opinion, be the most effectual means to accomplish that object.

"The mode observed by the English with the Iroquois, when desirous to form an establishment in their neighborhood, has been to make presents for the purchase of the fee and property of the land they would occupy. What I consider most certain is, that whether we do so or have war or peace with them, they will not suffer, except most unwillingly, the construction of a fort at Niagara, whereby we would secure to ourselves the communication of the two lakes, and become masters of the passage by which the Senecas go after peltries, having none in their own country, and where they rendezvous when they hunt for game, with which, as well as with all sorts of fish, this country abounds.

"That post would be of great advantage as a retreat for the other nations who are at war with them, and who dare not come into their neighborhood in consequence of having too far to retreat. This post would keep them in check and in fear, especially were the fort made sufficiently large to accommodate a body of four to five hundred men to wage war against them. It would necessitate some expense, as it should be inclosed by ordinary palisading to protect it from insult, as the garrison would not derive any assistance from us.* * *

"I am assured the lands in that neighborhood, which is in about the 44th degree of latitude, are very fine, highly productive, and easy of cultivation. All I learn of the place confirms me in my opinion that in three years, at the farthest, the post would support itself. Fortifying it, 'tis feared, will draw down war on us if you wish to avoid it. But at the same time it is my belief that the Senecas, on seeing us strongly established, would be much more docile."

After the fashion of the Roman senator, whose constant peroration was, "Carthage must be destroyed," Denonville reiterates in closing: "The whole world here is convinced that the progress of the faith among the Indians depends absolutely on humiliating the Iroquois."

A mass of documents besides those already quoted might be cited to show the importance of Niagara as a post commanding the Indian trade, which was from this time a constant object of competition and bone of contention between Canada and New York for three quarters of a century. It was officially reported to the French government that in 1683, "in addition to the bark, there were seven or eight canoes trading at the falls of Niagara, * * * which is the place where the savages pass on their return from hunting." It was recommended to Colonel Schuyler in 1720 by Robert Livingston "that a private conference be held with a sachem of each nation to engage a party of their people to go to Onjagore [Niagara] and demolish that French settlement, and to prevent any future settlements which they may hereafter attempt to make;" also that there be "encouragement given to those that will go to the Sinnekes' country and Onyagoro to sell what Indian goods they please to the Five Nations, or the farr Indians, and moreover that some person of respect, that has influence among the Indians, may be sent with a considerable company to the Sennekes country to remain there and keep the Indians steady to the British interest and defeat the subtle artifices of the French."

"Att a Private Conference held between the Hon bll Coll Peter Schuyler Esqr President of his Majesties Council of New York and two Sachims of each of the four nations vizt the Maquase oneydes onnondages and cayouges in Albany ye 1st of Sept 1720," the report represents the Indians as saying that "as the french are making a Settlement at onjagra they are very senceable it is prejudicial to them [the Indians] as well as to us [the English] and therefore are willing if Quider [Col. Schuyler] will send some of his people thither they of the five Nations will join them and go unaniarously and pull it Down but wee must withall tell you that the selling of Indian goods to the french and their Indians of Canada is Great Inducement for the french to make that Settlement and therefore we desire you to stop that trade and then the french will not have goods so cheap to serve the farr Indians withall for we are all sencible that Goods can be aforded Cheaper here than at Canada and that the french knows very well which makes them come hither to buy to supply the Indians with out which the far Indians would be Obliged to Come hither and be Suplyed."

The report which Lawrence Clawsen made of his mission to Niagara in 1720, and consultation with the Senecas, contains the following paragraphs:

"Jean Coeur [Joncaire] the French interpreter interrupted me when I repeated the above Speach to the Sachims of the Sinnekies and young Captains and sayed you endeavour to have the House at Octjagera [Niagara] demolished only because you are afraid that you will not get any trade of this Nation and the farr Indians for when wee have and keep a house and people there Wee can stop all the Sinnekies & farr Indians but not that you are afraid that wee shall keep the Land from this Nation.

"Whereon I made answer that the French made the settlement at Octjagera to encroach on the five Nations to hinder them of their hunting and debarr them of the advantage they should reap by a Free passage of the Farr Indians through their castles and in hopes to impose on the said Nations by selling them Goods at an extravagant Rate as for a Blanket of Stronds for 8 Beavers a White blanket 6 and other Goods proportionally whereas they may have them at Albany for half which the said Indians affirmed to be true."

Governor Burnet, in a letter to the English Lords of Trade, November 20, 1720, recommended that a fort be built "at Ochiagara and a sufficient number of brisk young men posted there with proper Officers and an intelligent sencible man reside there to defeat the intreagues of the French and secure and preserve the Five nations to the British interest and likewise to keep the path open and patent for all the Far Indians to come hither [to Albany] and trade which would take off a vast quantity of goods."

The hopes of the French and the apprehensions of the English were justified; in 1738 the Commissioners of Indian Affairs had to report that the French fort at Niagara "in a great measure commands the Indian Trade from the westward, and overawes the Sinnekes." In 1741 the governor of New York assured the Lords of Trade that he held the Five Nations only by presents, and it would be "absolutely necessary" to take the fort. Sir William Johnson wrote in 1750 that an acquaintance had "read a letter from the Lord intendant of Quebec to the commanding officer at Niagara, dated sometime this last summer, wherein he desires him to supply all Indians (who pass in their way to Oswego) with Goods, at such a Price as may induce them to trade there to gain which point at the time, he said the Lord Intendant in his letter says, he will not regard the loss of 20 or 30,000 Livres a year to the Crown. He also allows said officer to supply said Indians with what quantity of Brandy or Rum they may want, which was never allowed before, for their Priests were always against selling them liquor, but finding liquor to be one of the principal articles, they trade for, they are determined to let them have it as they would otherwise go to Oswego for it I take it their view in this, is as much if not more, for preventing communication between us and said Indians, as for engrossing the trade, and in my opinion they could not have fallen upon a better scheme to accomplish."

On the hostility of the priests to the sale of liquor to the Indians, here mentioned by Johnson, Mr. Orsamus Turner, in his History of Phelps and Gorham's Purchase, makes the following important statement: "From the first advent of the French Franciscan and Jesuit missionaries in this region they were the determined opposers of the introduction of spirituous liquors among the Indians. They would suppress it in the trading houses of their own countrymen, and at the risk of their lives knock out the heads of English rum casks. They became, in some instances, martyrs in endeavoring to suppress the traffic. The first temperance essay the world ever saw, other than the precepts of the Bible, was written in this region by a Jesuit missionary, and published in Paris." Governor Colden wrote in 1751 that the improvement which the French were making in the Niagara post would, if not prevented, "be of great consequence, not only as it will keep the Six Nations at all times in awe, but intercept all the Indians to the westward of it, and where the great beaver hunting is, in their way to trade with the English."

Sir William Johnson set the importance of Niagara in a strong light in a letter which, as illustrating the commercial and political value of the post, was as true of the period we have now reached as it was in 1759, when Johnson wrote. He said: "The Reduction of Niagara, * * * will be in the light I view it a point of inestimable advantage to the security and welfare of these His Majesty's Dominions, and if the conquest is rightly improved, will throw such an extensive Indian Trade and interest, (for they are inseparable) into our hands, as will in my humble opinion overset all those ambitious and lucrative schemes which the French have projected and in pursuit of which they were interrupted by the present war in this part of the world. Whilst the French are in possession of Niagara in vain will our repossession of Oswego, and establishing an Indian Trade there enable us to hold the Balance from them either in Indian Interest or Trade. The many nations of Westward Indians in comparison with whom the Six Nations are but a handfull must pass by Niagara in order to come to Oswego, where the French stop them and their goods, secure them by negotiations, and engross their Trade. This we felt for some years before the War began when very few of those Indians came to trade with us to Oswego, and latterly the chief Trade there was rather carried on with the French than Indians, by which means our enemies procured assortments and supplies of Goods from us to support this Trade at and from Niagara."

In the sharp competition for the Indian trade of which the Niagara post was the depot, the attitude of the Senecas toward the competing powers was a matter of the highest importance. We have already seen something of the intrigues by which their favor was sought. The fickleness of the race was never more conspicuous, and never made more profitable to them. For a brief and treacherous adherence to either party they were liberally subsidized. At one time we find their representatives promising to help the English pull down the French trading house; and anon we read of a French official with "orders from the court to join the Sieur de Joncair at Niagara, and go with him and the Sieur de la Chauvinerie to the village of the Sunekees, to thank them by presents for the good will they had shown to the French." Then we have an Iroquois speech maker demanding of Governor Dongan: "What has the father to doe to examine whether they [the Iroquois] are His Majesty's subjects or not, wee have been so time out of minde and always united to this Govern', let the Gover' goe forwards and remove the French from Onyagra, Cataracque and Tyschsarondia which is the place where wee goe a beaver huntinge for if thoes forts continew in the French hands wee are always besieged." At another time writes Vaudreuil: "About fifty Senecas, headed by one of the principal chiefs of the Five Nations, on whom I can rely, arrived at Niagara. When the council assembled, that chief presented to these Senecas one of my belts, and speaking to them and the Five Nations, said:

"'Here's the axe our father has presented to us that we may avenge the continued treacheries of the English; I have accepted it, with all those who have been at Montreal. I present it to you and invite you to follow my example.' The tribes of the Bear and Beaver accepted it and offered it to the two other tribes, who received it with pleasure, and all with one accord unanimously say: 'We are going to try M. de Vaudreuil, our Father's, axe on the English, to see if it cut well.'"

About this time occurred "the examination of Mons' Belestre, a French ensign, taken before the Honble Edmund Atkyn, Esqr, His Maj^{tys} agent for, and Superintendent of Indian Affairs, in the Southern Department. In presence of Col' Washington and George Croghan, Esqr, Dep^y to Sir William Johnson."

Belestre says: "I was informed that the French at Niagara was very scarce of Provisions, that some Munsey Indians with the King of that tribe who went there this spring had differed with the French Commandant and told him that they could no longer be amused with his false speeches, for we now see your designs: You look on us only as your Dogs; for every old man who is scarce able to walk, or a young boy, who comes among you, you immediately give him a hatchet and say, here child take this and go and kill the English, while you stay at home yourselves and laugh at us, but I tell you we will be Fools no more. You put the Hatchet into our hands, and I would have you take care how you behave or perhaps you may feel it soon." It would seem that the savages were sometimes about as dangerous to their friends as to their enemies, and a French paper tells how they once sacked Fort Niagara while at peace with the garrison:

"Several Senecas going there in the month of May, after having traded their peltries there, demanded some brandy from the man named Champagne, who is the store keeper and warden. But apprehending some disorder on the part of the said Iroquois, through drunkenness, he refused them any, which obliged them to force the said fort, to make themselves masters of it, and even to pillage it. * * * They restored all the merchandise, after having given Champagne and the handful of people there a sound drubbing, and drank as much brandy as they pleased.'

The fact seems to have been that on the question of their alliance the Indians spoke as the spirit moved them; and the spirit was French brandy one day and English rum the next. When dosed with the former, they were the dutiful children of Onontio; when filled with the latter, they were the steadfast brothers of Corlear, as they dubbed the governor of New York. Whichever side was favored (?) with their adherence found it hard to get and harder to keep.

There was a standing dispute between the French and English as to the right of the former ever to have established themselves on this side of the Niagara, where the latter claimed authority under their general protectorate of the Five Nations; and even as to the question of fact whether the French ever obtained the consent of the Senecas. The Indians themselves lied freely on this latter point, as on others, when cornered by either party, but there is abundant evidence that they permitted the original settlement of the French. In a council at Fort Frontenac in 1720, the Indian spokesman said that "Father Ononthio (who is Mr. de Vaudreuil) and their uncle Sononchiez (who is the Sieur de Joncaire) were the masters of their land, and that the Indians consented not only to the building of the House of Niagara but also engaged themselves to maintain it, and if the English should undertake to demolish it they must first take up the hatchet against the Cabanes of the two villages of the Sennekas." When

Lawrence Clawsen counselled with the Senecas in the same year the "Sachims & Young Captains say'd that the French had built the House at Ocjagera without asking any of them leave and desire that their brother Corlaer may do this endeavour to have ye said House demolisht that they may preserve their Lands and Hunting or to write to the Governor of Canada that he may order his people to do it." Lieutenant Governors Colden and Clarke admitted that the French establishment was authorized by the Iroquois, the former in the following words: "After the peace of Utrecht the French changed their measures. They took every method in their power to gain the Friendship of the Five Nations & succeeded so far with the Senekas who are by far the most numerous & at the greatest distance from us, that they were entirely brought over to the French interest. The French Obtained the consent of the Senekas to the building of the Fort at Niagara situated in their Country."

In 1733 the sachems of the Six Nations assured Governor Cosby that they had "Sinnekes on the Falls of Iagara who perswade the Far Indians to trade at Oswego." It seems strange at first to read of the Indians traversing the length and breadth of the State for a slight advantage in trade, and we wonder that any of them passed Niagara to barter at Albany or Oswego; but they were about as much at home in one place as another, and had nothing to do but hunt, which they could do while journeying, so that their indifference to time and distance is not, after all, so remarkable.

CHAPTER VII.

DENONVILLE'S EXPEDITION AGAINST THE SENECAS—THE BUILDING OF THE FIRST FORT NIAGARA.

WE must return to events connected with the administration of Denonville as governor of New France.

The tribes betrayed by La Barre's treaty evidently could no longer be depended on for beavers unless something were done to protect them, and procure their respect, as well as that of the Iroquois. Denonville therefore made it his chief concern to chastise the Senecas, who were foremost in hostility to the French. For that purpose, in the summer of 1687 he assembled nearly 3000 French and Indians, including Algonquins who had come via Niagara from a thousand miles up the lakes, at Irondequoit Bay, now in Monroe county. Thence, on the 12th of July, the army took up the line of march for the Seneca village of Gannagaro, twenty-two miles inland, making but nine or ten miles that day. On nearing the town in the afternoon of the 13th, the natives, to the number of 800 as reported by the French, but probably much fewer in fact, were encountered in ambuscade, and a lively engagement took place, in which the Senecas were finally beaten off, and forced to take refuge in the forest, leaving about thirty of their dead and carrying with them nearly as many more and a larger number severely wounded. Denonville had ten or eleven killed and twice as many wounded. His army bivouacked on the field, and the next morning advanced, and took possession of the burned and deserted village, which Abbe Belmont speaks of as "the famous Babylon of the Senecas, where so many crimes have been committed, so much blood spilled, and so many men burned. It was a village or town of bark, on the top of a hill. They had burned it a week before. We found nothing in it but the grave-yard and the graves, full of snakes and other creatures; a great mask, with teeth and eyes of brass, and a bearskin drawn over it, with which they performed their conjurations." The invaders completed the work of destruction which the inhabitants had begun, by burning a great quantity of corn which they found in bins of bark, killing a large number of hogs, and cutting down the growing crop of corn. An abandoned castle, a mile and a quarter away, was also burned, and three villages in the same region met a like fate.

They were Totiakto, called by the Jesuits Conception, which Brodhead locates "on a bend of the Honeyoye creek, near what is now West Meridon, in Monroe county;" Gannogarae, some three miles and a half from Gannagaro, and in the present town of East Bloomfield; and Gannondata, situated, according to Brodhead, "near East Avon, in Livingston county." At the last named "were found the English arms, which Dongan had caused to be placed there in 1684, 'antedated, as of the year 1683.' This greatly disgusted the French, who thought it 'beyond question that they first discovered and took possession of that country, and for twenty consecutive years have had fathers Fremin, Garnier, etc., as stationary missionaries in all these villages.'" Accordingly, they now formally took possession, as they had actually before, but with the added claim of conquest.

It was not until the 24th that Denonville and his force returned to Irondequoit Bay, where they embarked for the mouth of the Niagara. Mr. Parkman has the following interesting note on this campaign:

"The Seneca ambuscade was on the marsh and the hills immediately north and west of the present village of Victor; and their chief town, called Gannagaro by Denonville, was on the top of Boughton's hill, about a mile and a quarter distant. Immense quantities of Indian remains were formerly found here, and many are found to this day. Charred corn has been turned up in abundance by the plow, showing that the place was destroyed by fire. The remains of the fort burned by the French are still plainly visible on a hill a mile and a quarter from the ancient town."

The French had now the opportunity desired by them of fortifying their position on the Niagara. Denonville, who directed the enterprise, shall tell us how it was accomplished:

"*26th [July]*. We set out for Niagara, resolved to occupy that post as a retreat for all our Indian allies, and thus afford them the means of continuing, in small detachments, the war against the enemy whom they have not been able to harass hitherto, being too distant from them, and having no place to retire to. Although it is only thirty leagues from Ganniatarontagouat [Irondequoit] to Niagara, we were unable to accomplish the distance in less than four days and a half by reason of contrary winds; that is to say, we arrived there on the morning of the 30th. We immediately set about selecting a site, and collecting stockades for the construction of the fort which I had resolved to build on the Iroquois side at the point of a tongue of land between the Niagara river and Lake Ontario.

"31st of July and 1st of August. We continued this work, which was the more difficult as there was no wood on the ground suitable for making palisades, and from its being necessary to haul them up the hill. We performed this labor so diligently that the fort was in a state of defense on the last mentioned day.* * *

"2d of August. The militia having performed their allotted task, and the fort being in a condition of defense, in case of attack, they set out at noon for the end of the lake, on their return home.

"3rd. The next day I embarked in the morning for the purpose of joining the militia, leaving the regular troops in charge of M. de Vaudreuil, to finish what was the most essential, and to render the fort not only capable of defense, but also of being occupied by a detachment of a hundred soldiers, which are to winter there under the command of M. de Troyes, a veteran officer."

This is from Denonville's journal of the expedition. In his report to the government he writes:

"I selected the angle of the lake, on the Seneca side of the river; it is the most beautiful, the most pleasing and the most advantageous site that is on the whole of this lake.* * * The post being in a state of defense, I left a hundred men there under the command of Sieur de Troyes.* * * The post has caused much joy to all our farther Indians, who, having no place of retreat, scarcely dared to approach the enemy. They have made me great promises, especially our Illinois, to harass them this winter by a number of small parties.* * * On quitting Niagara I left M. de Vandreuil there for a few days with the troops to cut firewood, after having done what was necessary for lodgings. The inconvenience of this post is that timber is at a distance from it."

A little later the Marquis wrote to the minister, Seignelay:

"The post I have fortified at Niagara is not a novelty, since Sieur de la Salle had a house there, which is in ruins since a year, when Serjeant La Fleur, whom I placed at Cataracony, abandoned it through the intrigues of the English, who solicited the Senecas to expel him by threats. My Lord, if you do not wish to lose the entire trade of the upper country, we must maintain that post; also that of Dulhu, at the Detroit, and the possession of all the lakes."

On the 31st of July Denonville promulgated a windy declaration, full of misstatements, by way of formally taking possession of Niagara. "This acte" was "executed" in his presence and that of his principal subordinates. The new stockade thus hastily constructed was christened with the name of its builder, but was always called Fort Niagara. It was armed with some small cannon, and the Jesuit Lamberville was stationed at the post as chaplain.

The western Indians, who had come the length of the lakes to assist in the destruction, as they expected, of the Senecas, and who after the battle of July 13th urged a vigorous pursuit of the flying enemy instead of the inaction which allowed them to escape, regarded Denonville's expedition as a failure; and only the building of the fort on the Niagara, which might serve their needs in future inroads, prevented them from giving over the war entirely. On leaving for their distant homes, however, they told the French governor "that they depended upon his promise to continue the war till the Five Nations were either destroyed or dispossessed of their country; that they earnestly desired that part of the army should take the field out of hand, and continue in it both winter and summer, for they would certainly do the same on their part; and, in fine, that forasmuch as their alliance with France was chiefly granted upon the promises the French made of listening to no proposals of peace till the Five Nations should be quite extirpated, they therefore hoped they would be as good as their word."

Perhaps a feeling on the part of the French that they had treated their western allies rather shabbily had something to do with Denonville's sending a French escort with them on their return voyage, to help them defend themselves against the warriors whom they would have had exterminated. They were remarkably fortunate in escaping from Iroquois ground, even with this escort, for a large force of the vengeful Senecas—a thousand, says Baron La Hontan, who commanded the French—had rallied to intercept the invaders on their way up the Niagara, and the latter had barely embarked at the upper landing when their foes reached the bank of the river. Had the pursuing party met the retiring one while climbing the heights above Lewiston, where, as La Hontan says, "one hundred Iroquese might have knocked them on the head with stones," few either of Algonquins or Frenchmen would ever have taken the war path again.

Some high authorities consider it established that La Salle's company built a fortification at the mouth of the Niagara, and Denonville's report seems to countenance this belief. Yet it does not appear from Father Hennepin's narrative, which might be expected to show it. What we learn from Hennepin is that the party with which he came to the mouth of the river on the 6th of December, 1678, halted there that night; left their brigantine there and made a tour of exploration above the falls the next day, beginning their portage at the point where "the current was too rapid for us to master," undoubtedly at the site of Lewiston; returned on the 8th to the mouth of the stream, and made it their next business to get the brigantine "up the river as far as the rapid current above mentioned [the site of Lewiston again], where we had resolved to build some houses. Whosoever considers our map," Hennepin continues, "will easily see that this new enterprise of building a fort and some houses," [plainly at the place last named] etc. On the 15th the party succeeded in getting the brigantine up the river, "and moored her to the shore with a hawser, near a rock of prodigious height lying upon the rapid currents we have already mentioned. The 17th, 18th and 19th we were busy making a cabin, with palisadoes, to serve for a magazine." The natural presumption is that this palisaded cabin was where the brigantine was moored, at the foot of "the rapid currents," and therefore at or near the site of Lewiston. The next mention of building operations is in connection with the notice of the arrival, on the 20th of January, 1679, of La Salle himself, who had come by way of the Seneca villages, whose inhabitants in council with him had "consented to the prosecution of our undertaking. This agreement was of short duration, for certain persons [agents of the governor of New York] opposed our design in every possible way, and instilled jealousies into the minds of the Iroquois. The fort, nevertheless, which we were building at Niagara, continued to advance. But finally the secret influences against us were so great that the fort became an object of suspicion to the savages, and we were compelled to abandon its construction for a time, and content ourselves with building a habitation, surrounded by palisades." Is it not natural to conclude that this structure was the same mentioned in the previous quotations? There has been no mention of a removal of operations to the mouth of the river. The first record of anything of the kind at that point is that La Salle, while there on his way to Fort Frontenac, to make final preparations for his voyage up the lakes in the "Griffin," "*pretended* to mark out a house for the blacksmith which had been promised for the convenience of the Iroquois."

All this goes to show that the palisaded post established by La Salle was about where Lewiston stands, and not on the site of Fort Niagara; in conformity with the opinion of Bancroft, who speaks of "a group of cabins at Lewiston, on the site where La Salle had driven a rude palisade." The "house" or "houses" which Denonville speaks of as having stood on the spot where he now built, need not have been the fortified post of La Salle; and on the whole we incline to agree with Mr. Marshall, that "no regular defensive work was constructed in the vicinity until Denonville" built his; and with the historian of Erie county, that this fortification was "the origin of Fort Niagara."

The bright hopes which had inspired the French in building and garrisoning the new fort were destined to bitter disappointment. Its construction was part of a campaign against the Senecas, and they of course regarded the post with the bitterest hostility. They very soon placed it in a state of siege. Without exposing themselves to its guns, they thoroughly beleaguered the feeble frontier fortress, lurking in the neighboring forests and slaying all who ventured beyond the palisades. Foul and sickening provisions were poisoning the garrison, and no one dared venture out to hunt or fish for food more agreeable and wholesome, nor could they have procured firewood to cook any game they might capture. Says Parkman: "The fort was first a prison, then a hospital, then a charnel-house, till before spring [1688], the garrison of a hundred men was reduced to ten or twelve. In this condition they were found towards the end of April, by a large war party of friendly Miamis, who entered the place and held it till a French detachment at length arrived for its relief." Immediately upon the construction of the fort, Governor Dongan, of New York, had demanded its demolition, as being built on English territory and contrary to existing treaties. The answer was: "This cannot be granted; first, because it is built there by the command of the most christian King, and therefore it must be demolished by his command; secondly, because it would not be reasonable to demolish it before there be a general peace, since in the meantime we have need of the fort to protect ourselves from the Indians until there be something concluded concerning the limits. This only I can declare and grant, that the aforesaid fort does not give us any other right to those Indians than what we pretend to have long since."

Seeing, however, that disease and the Senecas would compel the abandonment of the post, Denonville concluded to make a virtue of necessity, and wrote from Montreal August 20th, 1688, to Governor Dongan, as follows: "Regarding the fort at Niagara, of which you write me, I beg to assure you that so soon as I see some certainty as to affairs, I shall, in order to contribute to a permanent peace, withdraw the garrison that is there." Two months later he informed the New York governor that he had withdrawn the garrison. The palisades had been removed in the middle of September.

The following minute and curious account, by the French commander, of the condition in which the place was left in other respects, we judge sufficiently interesting to demand insertion:

"On the fifteenth day of September, of the year one thousand, six hundred and eighty-eight, in the forenoon, Sieur Desbergeres, captain of one of the companies of the detachment of the marine and commandant of Fort Niagara, having assembled all the officers, the Reverend Father Millet, of the Society of Jesus, missionary, and others, to communicate to them the orders he has received from the Marquis de Denonville, governor and lieutenant-general for the King throughout the whole extent of New France and country of Canada, dated the 6th of July, of the present year, whereby he is commanded to demolish the fortification of said fort, with the exception of the cabins and quarters, which will be found standing;"

"We, Chevalier de la Mothe, lieutenant of a detached company of the marine, and major of said fort, have made a *proces verbal*, by order of said commandant, containing a memorandum of the condition in which we leave said quarters, which will remain entire, for the purpose of maintaining the possession his Majesty and the French have for a long time had in this Niagara district.

"Firstly:—We leave in the center of the square a large,

framed, wooden cross, eighteen feet in height, on the arms of which are inscribed in large letters these words:

REGN· VINC· ⊕ IMP·CHRS·

[*Regnat, vincit, imperat Christus*—Christ rules, conquers governs.] which was erected on last Good Friday by all the officers, and solemnly blessed by the Reverend Father Millett.

"Item: A cabin in which the commandant lodged; contained a good chimney, a door and two windows, furnished with their hinges, fastenings and locks, which cabin is covered with forty-four deal boards, and about sixty other boards arranged inside into a sort of bedstead.

"Item: In the immediate vicinity of said cabin is another cabin with two rooms, having each its chimney, ceiled with boards, and in each a little window and three bedsteads, the door furnished with its hinges and fastenings; the said cabin is covered with fifty deal boards, and there are sixty like boards on each side.

"Item: Right in front is the Reverend Father Millet's cabin, furnished with its chimney, windows and sashes, shelves, a bedstead and four boards arranged inside, with a door, furnished with its fastenings and hinges the which is of twenty-four boards.

"Item: Another cabin, opposite the cross, in which there is a chimney, a board ceiling and three bedsteads, covered with forty-two boards, with three like boards, on one side of said cabin; there is a window, with its sash, and a door, furnished with its hinges and fastenings.

"Item: Another cabin, with a chimney, a small window, with its sash, and a door; covered with thirty deal boards; there are three bedsteads inside.

"A bake house, furnished with its oven and chimney, partly covered with boards and the remainder with hurdles and clay; also an apartment at the end of said bakery, containing two chimneys; there are in said bakery a window and door, furnished with hinges and fastenings.

"Item: Another large and extensive framed building [probably the chapel] having a double door, furnished with nails, hinges, and fastenings, with three small windows; the said apartment is without a chimney; 'tis floored with twelve plank, and about twelve boards are arranged inside, and without 'tis clapboarded with fifty-two plank.

"Item: A large storehouse, covered with one hundred and thirty boards, surrounded with pillars, eight feet high, in which there are many pieces of wood serving as small joists, and partly floored with several unequal plank. There is a window and a sliding sash.

"Item: A well, with its cover, above the scarp of the ditch.

"Item: All which apartments are in the same condition as they were last winter, and consequently inhabitable. Which all the witnesses, * * * certify to have seen and visited all the said apartments, and have accordingly signed the minutes and original of these presents."

CHAPTER VIII.

THE JONCAIRES, AND THE FRENCH TRADING HOUSE ESTABLISHED AT LEWISTON IN 1720.

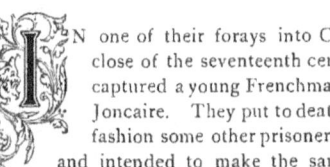N one of their forays into Canada toward the close of the seventeenth century, the Senecas captured a young Frenchman named Chabert Joncaire. They put to death in their fiendish fashion some other prisoners, taken with him, and intended to make the same disposition of him. By way of giving him a fortaste of the torture in store for him, a chief applied the burning contents of his pipe to the end of one of the Frenchman's fingers. Joncaire promptly knocked him down. This spirited action so pleased his captors that they let him live and adopted him as a member of the tribe. With all the usual readiness of the Canadian French to affiliate with the savages, he made himself at home, learned the Seneca dialect, married a young squaw, and became a favorite with the tribe. In a few years, being given entire freedom, he returned to Canada, and in 1700 entered the French service, in which he was employed during the remaining forty years of his life. He was especially useful as an agent among the Senecas, who had made him a sachem of their nation and over whom he had gained a great influence, which was inherited by his two sons Chabert and Clauzonne, who devoted it to the service of the government in a capacity similar to that of the father.

One of Joncaire's first undertakings in behalf of New France was his mission to procure the release of the French held captive among the Iroquois. His most important achievement, however, was the obtaining permission from the Senecas for the establishment of a French trading house in 1720, at the foot of the Niagara portage, where Lewiston now stands. Many papers of that early date, some of them called forth by this enterprise, are now extant, and are very pertinent and interesting in this connection. From them is to be constructed the history of this commercial venture on the soil of Niagara county more than a century and a half ago. In a "memorial of what passed concerning the establishment of a post which the French have built at Niagara for the trade of peltry," we read:

"In the year 1718 came orders from the court of France to establish a trade for the benefit of the King in the circuit of the Lake Ontario, and there to build magazines, as well upon the north as the south side thereof.

"In the year 1719, in the beginning of the harvest, the Sieur Joncaire, lieutenant of a detachment of marine troops and interpreter, was sent, in obedience to the said orders, by monsieur the Marquis de Vaudreuil and by Monsieur Begon, to try the minds of the Sinnekees and to see if they could engage them to consent to the building of a house upon their land, and to maintain that settlement in case the English would oppose it. This message which they sent there was accompanied with some belts of wampum, and other presents, consisting of powder, lead, brandy, and other small merchandise."

It need hardly be said that the request borne by the palefaced sachem, and so persuasively "accompanied," was favorably received by the "Sinnekees." The desired permission was obtained, and Joncaire returned to Canada to avail himself of it. We next read:

"The Sieur Joncaire remained only at the Fort of Catarcouy for ten or twelve days [in May, 1720], and then returned to Niagara with the Sieur de la Corne, son of Monsieur de la Corne, captain and mayor of the town of Montreal. They had with them eight soldiers, who conducted a canoe of merchandise, consisting of some pieces of blue cloth, three dozen or thereabout of white blankets for the use of the Indians, half a barrel of brandy, etc. At their arrival at Niagara the Sieurs de Joncaire and La Corne caused to be built in haste a kind of cabin of bark, where they displayed the King's colors and honored it with the name of the 'Magazine Royal.' The Sieur de la Corne had a commission of M. Begon to winter in the said post, and there to trade. The Sieur de Joncaire left him there with two soldiers, and afterward returned to Cataracouy."

"Abstract of Messrs. de Vaudreuil and Begon's report on Niagara," dated

"Canada 26 S'ber 1720:"

"Messrs. de Vaudreuil and Begon transmit a report on the post established this year at Niagara, which is required both to prevent the English introducing themselves into the upper country and to increase the trade at Fort Frontenac. This report sets forth that the above post is situated about four leagues from the entrance into Lake Erie. It is the only pass of the Indians who come by the lake from all the upper countries; the portage necessary to be made by land is four leagues, for which distance they are obliged to carry, on their backs, their goods and canoes.

"The English had proposed to an Iroquois chief, settled at Niagara, to send horses thither from Orange, which is 130 leagues distant from it, for the purpose of transporting goods, and to make a permanent settlement there, and offered to share with him whatever profits might accrue from the speculation. The English would, by such means, have been able to secure the greatest part of the peltries coming down the lakes from the upper countries; give employment not only to the Indians who go up there and return thence, but also to the French. They have a store there well supplied with goods for the trade; and have, by means of the Indians, carried on there, up to the present time and since several years ago, a considerable trade in furs in barter for merchandise and whiskey. This establishment would have been enabled to purchase the greater part of the peltries both of the French and Indians belonging to the upper country.

"Sieur Joncaire, aware of the importance of this post by the quantity of goods which could be disposed of were there a permanent establishment at that place, caused the Indians to construct last spring, by order of Messrs. de Vaudreuil and Begon, a picketed house, which they were prevailed on to do the more readily through the influence he has over them, being an adopted son of the Iroquois. [It would seem that the fragile 'Magazine Royal' was soon strengthened and improved.]

"The English, being advised of this, used all their efforts to have this house demolished, and with that view sent the commandant at Orange to the Seneca village to persuade these Indians to oppose it. He even sent an Englishman with an Indian to tell Sieur de la Corne, whom M. Begon appointed to trade at that place, to withdraw, and that they were going to pull down that house. La Corne answered them that he should not permit them to do so without an order from Sieur de Joncaire, who, on being advised thereof by an Indian, went to the Senecas to prevent them consenting to that demolition. He experienced great difficulty there, because they had been gained over by the presents of the English. Nevertheless, he prevailed on them to change their minds, and to maintain that establishment, by making them understand the advantage they would derive from it.

"Therefore, though the English should renew these attempts, Sieur Joncaire is confident that the Indians will maintain this post.

"That determined Messrs. de Vaudreuil and Begon to send Sieur Joncaire thither with some articles of trade. He left at the close of September, and is to remain there until the month of June next. No one is better qualified than he to begin this establishment, which will render the trade of Fort Frontenac much more considerable and valuable than it has ever been. He is a very excellent officer, the interpreter of the Five Iroquois Nations, and has served thirty-five years in the country."

It is interesting to read the English messenger's own account of his mission to demand the demolition of the new post. Parts of it are as follows:

"On the 24th of the said month [May, 1720] I set out with three Sachims of the Sinnekies in order to go to Octjagera where we arrived on the 30 Do & on the 31st I on behalf of the Sachims told a French Merchant who was there in a house of Forty Foot long and thirty wide with two other French, that I was sent to accompany the said Sachims and to tell you that the five nations have heard that you are building a house at Octjagera and the said Sachims having considered how prejudicial that a French Settlement on their Land must consequently prove to them and their Posterity (if not timely prevented) wherefore they have sent me and them to acquaint you with their resolution that it is much against their inclination that any buildings should be made here and that they desire you to desist further building and to leave and demolish what you have made. The French Merchant answered that he had leave from the young fighting men of the Sinnekis to erect a House at Octjagera and would not demolish it before he did write to the Governor of Canada his Master who had posted him there to trade for him and not before he received his orders for so doing.

"The said three Sachims said that they never heard that any of their young men had given such leave for making any building at Octjagera.

"On the 7th of this Inst [I returned] to Tjerondequatt where I mett a French Smith sent by the Governor of Canada to work for the Sinnikies gratis he having compassion on them as a father on his children knowing they wanted a smith since they have lay'd out a New Castle and that three French Canoes loaded with goods went up to the trading house at Octjagera."

November 20th, 1720, Governor Burnet, of New York, wrote to the English Lords of Trade as follows : " I will do my endeavors in the Spring without committing any hostility to get our Indians to demolish a trading House or Block House that is made Muskett Proof with Port holes for firing with small arms, which the French have sett up near the fall of Niagara in the Sennekees country. This is in open defiance of the Kings right the Sennekees having granted that Land to the crown of Great Britain before the French had ever been there, this place is of great consequence for two reasons. First, because it keeps the communication between Canada & Mississippi by the River Ohio open which else our Indians would be able to intercept at pleasure, and Secondly, if it should be made a Fort with souldiers enough in it it will keep our Indians from going over the narrow part of the Lake Ontario by this only Pass of the Indians without leave of the French, so that if it were demolished the Farr Indians would depend on us, by means of the goods which they want of us and which the French cannot afford to supply them with unless they get them from this Province."

Failing in his purpose, Governor Burnet, in July of the next year, wrote to Vaudreuil, then governor of Canada: "You will perceive, by the Treaty of Utrecht, that all the Indians are to be at liberty to go to trade with one party and the other ; and if advantage be taken of the post at Niagara to shut up the road to Albany on the Far Indians, it is a violation of the Treaty which ought justly to alarm us, especially as that post is on territory belonging to our Indians, where we were better entitled to build than the French, should we deem it worth the trouble."

"I have the honor to observe to you hereupon," responds Vaudreuil, "that you are the first English governor-general who has questioned the right of the French, from time immemorial, to the post of Niagara, to which the English have, up to the present time, laid no claim ; that it is upwards of fifty years since that post has been occupied by the late Sieur de la Salle, who had an establishment there and had vessels built there to navigate Lake Erie ; that his Majesty had a fort there thirty-four years ago with a garrison of one hundred men, who returned thence in consequence of the sickness that prevailed there, whithout this post, however, having been abandoned by the French, who have ever since always carried on trade there until now, and without the English being permitted to remain there ; also, that there has never been any dispute between the French and the Five Nations respecting the erection of that post, and that the latter always came there to trade with the same freedom that they repair to the other French territory, as well as to that which is reputed English.

"Respecting the report you received that the establishment of this post closes the path to our far Indians, who could no longer go to trade with the English. I have the honor to observe to you that they will always enjoy the same privilege of going to the English that they have hitherto had, and that no Indian in my government has been compelled to trade with the French rather than with the English. The proof of this is evident, for a great number of their canoes went again this year to Albany, and those domiciled in the neighborhood of Montreal and Three Rivers trade there almost altogether."

The block-house which was the bone of so much contention became dilapidated in five or six years, but in the meantime it had become surrounded with a little Seneca village and, like any place where Joncaire was, served as a powerful centre of French influence. The ready but extravagant writer Charlevoix visited the place in 1721, and from it sent a letter to Madame de Maintenon, which contains so much of local interest that we will make a long extract from it, at the risk of a little repetition.

"I have already had the honor to acquaint you that we have a scheme for a settlement in this place ; but in order to know the reason of this project it will be proper to observe that as the English pretend, by virtue of the Treaty of Utretcht, to have sovereignty of all the Iroquois country, and by consequence to be bounded on that side by Lake Ontario only ; now it is evident that, in case we allow of their pretensions, they would then have it absolutely in their power to establish themselves firmly in the heart of the French colonies, or at least entirely to ruin their commerce. In order, therefore, to prevent this evil, it has been judged proper, without, however, violating the treaty, to make a settlement in some place which might secure to us the free communication between the lakes, and where the English should not have it in their power to oppose us."

"A commission has therefore been made to M. de Joncaire, who having in his youth been prisoner among the Tsonnonthouans, so insinuated himself into the good graces of those Indians that they adopted him, so that even in the hottest of their wars with us, and notwithstanding his remarkable services to his country, he has always enjoyed the privileges of his adoption. On receiving the orders I have been mentioning to you he repaired to them, assembled their chiefs, and after having assured them that his greatest pleasure in this world would be to live amongst his brethren, he added that he would much oftener visit them had he a cabin amongst them, to which he might retire when he had a mind to be private. They told him they had always looked upon him as one of their own children, that he had only to make choice of a place to his liking in any part of the country. He asked no more, but went immediately and made choice of a spot on the banks of a river which terminates the canton of Tsonnonthouan, where he built his cabin.

"The news of this soon reached New York, where it excited so much more the jealousy of the English, as that nation had never been able to obtain the favor granted to

Sieur de Joncaire in any Iroquois canton. They made loud remonstrances, which being seconded with presents the other four cantons at once espoused their interest. They were, however, never the nearer their point, as the cantons are not only independent of each other, but also very jealous of this independence. It was therefore necessary to gain that of Tsonnonthouan, and the English omitted nothing to accomplish it; but they were soon sensible that they should never be able to get Joncaire dismissed from Niagara. At last they contented themselves with demanding that at least they might be permitted to have a cabin in the same place, but this was likewise refused them. 'Our country is in peace,' said the Tsonnonthouans; 'the French and you will never be able to live together without raising disturbances. Moreover,' added they, 'it is of no consequence that Joncaire should remain here; he is a child of the nation; he enjoys his right, which we are not at liberty to take from him.'

"Now, Madame, we must acknowledge that nothing but zeal for the public good could possibly induce an officer to remain in such a country as this, than which a wilder and more frightful is not to be seen. On the one side you may see, just under your feet and as it were at the bottom of an abyss, and which in this place is like a torrent by its rapidity, a whirlpool formed by a thousand rocks, through which it with difficulty finds a passage, and by the foam of which it was always covered. On the other the river is confined by three mountains, placed one over the other, and whereof the last hides itself in the clouds. This would have been a very proper place for the poets to make the Titans attempt to scale the heavens. In a word, on whatever side you turn your eyes, you discover nothing which does not inspire a secret horror.

"You have, however, but a very short way to go to behold a very different prospect. Behind those uncultivated and uninhabited mountains, you enjoy the sight of a rich country, magnificent forests, beautiful and fruitful hills; you breathe the purest air, under the mildest and most temperate climate imaginable, situated between two lakes, the least of which is two hundred and fifty leagues in circuit. It is my opinion that had we the precaution to make sure of a place of this consequence by a good fortress and by a tolerable colony, all the forces of the Iroquois and the English conjoined would not have been able at this time to drive us out of it; and that we ourselves would have been in a condition to give law to the former, and to hinder most part of the Indians from carrying their furs to the second, as they daily do with impunity.

"The company I found here with M. de Joncaire was composed of the Baron de Longueil, the Marquis de Cavagnal, captain, son of the Marquis de Vaudreuil, the present governor of New France; M. de Senneville, captain; and the Sieur de la Chauvignerie, ensign and interpreter of the Iroquois language. These gentlemen are about negotiating an agreement of differences with the canton of Onontague [Onondaga], and were ordered to visit the settlement of the Sieur de Joncaire, with which they were extremely well satisfied. The Tsonnonthouans renewed to them the promise they had formerly made to maintain it. This was done in a council, in which Joncaire, as they told me, spoke with all the good sense of a Frenchman, whereof he enjoys a large share, and with the sublimest eloquence of an Iroquois."

On the death of Joncaire his son Chabert succeeded him in the Seneca agency, but soon gave place to his younger brother Clauzonne. Both were in their day very prominent and influential along the Niagara frontier. They are referred to as follows in the *Maryland Gazette* of August 30th, 1759: "There are ten other officers, one of which is the famous Monsieur Joncaire, a very noted man among the Seneca Indians, and whose father was the first that hoisted French colors in that country. His brother, also a prisoner, is now here, and has been very humane to many Englishmen, having purchased several of them from the Senecas."

CHAPTER IX.

THE REBUILDING OF FORT NIAGARA—IT IS BESIEGED BY THE ENGLISH AND IROQUOIS.

THE English not only failed for the time to oust the French from their foot-hold at Lewiston, but the latter in 1725 rebuilt the fortification at the mouth of the river, on a scale of strength and permanance making it far superior to Denonville's hasty structure. The earliest reference we can obtain to the rebuilding of Fort Niagara comes from the French government archives, and reads in part as follows:

"The Marquis de Vaudreuil reported in 1725 an establishment projected by the English at the mouth of the River Choueguen [Oswego], on the borders of Lake Ontario, in the upper country, which is a part of New France, and adjacent to the French post at Niagara, among the Iroquois. It was of importance to prevent that establishment, more especially as the French have always exclusively carried on the trade with the Indians of the upper countries; as the English thought of going to trade there only since the peace of Utrecht, and as they are now trying to drive us thence by force of presents to the Indians, whom they furnish with goods at a low rate, and supply with Rum, which is their favorite beverage. M. de Vaudreuil ordered M. de Longueil, governor of Montreal, to proceed to the Iroquois, and to summon the English established there to withdraw. * * * He afterwards repaired to Onontague [Onondaga], an Iroquois village, and obtained the consent of their chiefs to the erection of a store house at Niagara, in the place of the one which fell in ruins; also, to the construction of two barks for the transportation of the materials. Messrs. de Longueil and Begon made a report on the subject, and observed that it was of the utmost importance to urge on this work, which they proposed undertaking the following spring. They transmitted a plan of it, and the estimate, amounting to 29,295 livres, and they had the two barks constructed at a cost of 13,090 livres. On the account having been transmitted to the King, his Majesty ordered these funds to be remitted, and they have been sent."

The Senecas made no serious opposition to this movement, but it probably required Joncaire's influence to obtain their acquiescence. There is some probability in the tradition that strategy was found necessary to accomplish the purpose of the French. Mr. Samuel De Veaux, writing forty years since, put the story of the origin of the Mess-house in the following form :

"It is a traditionary story that the Mess-house, which is a very strong building and the largest in the fort, was erected by strategem. A considerable though not powerful body of French troops had arrived at the point. Their force was inferior to the surrounding Indians, of whom they were under some apprehensions. They obtained consent of the Indians to build a wigwam, and induced them, with some of their officers, to engage in an extensive hunt. The materials were made ready, and while the Indians were absent the French built. When the hunting party returned, they found the French had so far advanced with their work as to cover their faces and to defend themselves from the savages in case of an attack. In progress of time it became a place of considerable strength. It had its ravines, its ditches and pickets; its curtains and counterscarp; its covered way, drawbridge and raking batteries; its stone towers, laboratory and magazine; its mess-house, barracks and bakery, and blacksmith shop; and for worship, a chapel, with a large ancient dial over the door to mark the course of the sun. It was, indeed, a little city of itself, and for a long period the greatest place south of Montreal and west of Albany. The fortification originally covered a space of about eight acres."

Whether openly or by ruse, the French built, more than a hundred and fifty years ago, the first story of the old Mess-house, as it now stands. Here was one more resort of the French soldiers, traders and bush rangers and the red hunters and warriors who formed the small and shifting population of the frontier; another bulwark of the French trade, and another link in the chain that was to connect Lake Ontario with the Ohio and the Southwest and mark the boundary of New France.

One of the traditions of old Fort Niagara was that in the center of the Mess-house there was a well, and on the curb might sometimes be seen sitting a headless French officer, who had presumably been murdered and thrown into the well. Another was that there were deposits of gold and silver buried in the fort, and it is said that persons have had at different times vainly applied to the officers for permission to dig for them.

The French fort was improved and strengthened from time to time. "Niagara is also well fortified," said an official report in September, 1736. "It had only six guns, but Choueguen [Oswego] has furnished twenty-four of the largest calibre, which are now mounted. People are busy supplying Forts Duquesne, on the Beautiful river [Ohio], Niagara, and Frontenac with provisions, in order to be no longer obliged to employ the best men at such work when they may be required elsewhere."

Yet one thing was lacking. Thirty big guns and five times thirty miles additional travel could not prevent the Indians from trading where they could get plenty of liquor; and at Niagara the supply of firewater was at this time meager. This state of things and the results are revealed in a report to the crown, of October 12th, 1736. We quote:

"As for the commerce now carried on at Fort Frontenac and Niagara, it becomes every year more inconsiderable in comparison to the expenses the King incurs there. These two posts, which produced some years ago as much as 52,000 lbs. of peltries, have these four years past returned only 25,000 to 35,000 lbs. This falling off has occurred merely since the discontinuance of the distribution of brandy to the Indians, whereof it is the King's pleasure that Messrs. de Beauharnois and Hocquart be very sparing. * * * We admit that it is difficult, and perhaps impossible, to sell brandy to the major portion of the Indians without their getting drunk. But it is equally certain that nothing deters them from trading with the French on these posts, and anywhere else in the upper countries, more than the refusal to sell them any of this liquor, for which they entertain an inexpressible passion. They find plenty of it at Choueguen, where they repair from all the posts of the upper countries, without any means of stopping them at Niagara. Sieurs de Beauharnois and Hocquart perceive, unfortunately, no means of destroying or interrupting the commercial relation this drink keeps up between the Indians and the English."

The rebuilding of Fort Niagara was but one step in the formation of a chain of posts along this frontier, Lake Erie, and the Alleghany, Ohio and Mississippi rivers, by which the French resolved to assert and maintain that line as the boundary of their domain in America. The time was coming when, if the English were ever to hold more than the Atlantic slope of the continent, they must arouse to the employment of more vigorous measures than intrigues with the Indians and remonstrances to the Canadian governor. In 1756 war between England and France was declared. Active hostilities had already been in progress for two years between the forces of the two powers in America, taking the form of a contest for the possession of the posts between Lake Erie and the Ohio. In 1755 Fort Niagara was threatened by an expedition from the east via Oswego. The expedition got no further than that point, but the French were led to have the menaced fortress reconstructed by the competent engineer Pouchot, and before it could be assailed it was in a formidable condition. Montcalm wrote in 1756: "M. de Vaudreuil employed M. Pouchot, captain in the regiment of Bearn, who has erected a good fortification at Niagara. It consists of a horn-work with its half-moon, covert-way, lunettes at the *places d'armes* re-entering from the covert-way. The front of this work is 120 toises. It is fortified according to M. de Vauban's method."

It had need to be; for an army would one day march against it which would not stop at Oswego. It was not until the 1st of July, 1759, however, that a force of 2,200 regular troops and militia, which had rendezvoused at Oswego under Brigadier-General John Prideaux, embarked for the siege of Fort Niagara, accompanied by 943 Iroquois warriors, who had been rallied for the undertaking by the best efforts of the best Indian manager America ever knew—Sir William Johnson.

This remarkable man, now and long before and after superintendent of Indian affairs for the English government, came from Ireland in his early youth, and established himself in 1738 as a farmer and trader near the site of Amsterdam, Montgomery county, N. Y., where, and subsequently on the border of the now fine old village of Johnstown, Fulton county, which was founded by and named after him, he had his home during the remainder of his life. By his genial and honest character and his intimate affiliation with the Indians, he gained an unparalleled influence over them, which he strenuously exerted in the interest of the British crown. The campaign upon which he now entered associates his name inseparably with the history of the Niagara frontier.

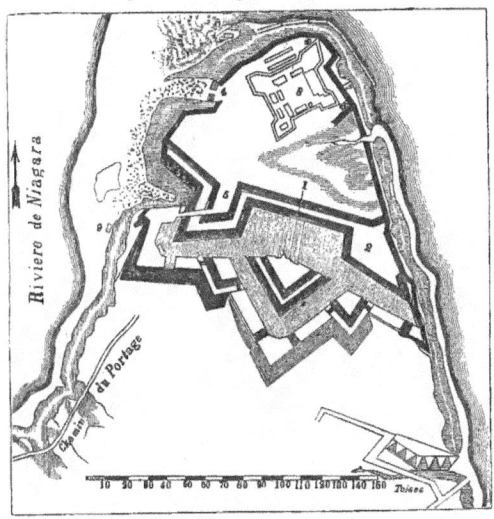

FORT NIAGARA IN 1759.

1. Galleries to communicate with the exterior works.
2. Lake Ontario Bastion.
3. Barracks, stores and vestiges of the old fort.
4. Niagara Gate.
5. Bastion at the Gate of the Five Nations.
6. Barbet Battery of 5 guns.
7. Relief Gate.
8. Another Barbet Battery of 5 guns.
9. Indian huts.

In what condition was the French fortress to resist the armament coming over the lake to its attack? Captain Pouchot, its rebuilder and commander, shall tell us:

"Fort Niagara is situate on the east point of the river of that name, which terminates in a triangle, whose base is the head of a horn-work, one hundred and fourteen toises on its exterior side, all of earth, sodded interiorly and exteriorly; with a ditch eleven toises wide by nine feet deep, one-half moon and two small lunettes or intrenched places of arms, with a covert-way and glacis proportioned to the works. The ditches have no revetment. The fort (*place*) and one-half moon are palisaded on the berm. The other two sides are a simple intrenchment, also in earth, sodded within and without, seven feet high inside and six feet thick on the summit of the parapet, with a fraise on the berm. These two sides of the intrenchment are on broken ground forty feet in height. The river side would be accessible, although with difficulty. That of the lake is more perpendicular.

"We must here enter into some details as to the condition of the fort at the time it was besieged: M. Pouchot had just completed the raising of the ramparts. The bastion batteries, which were in barbet, were not yet finished; they were constructed of barrels filled with earth. On his arrival, he set men to work at oak blindages, fourteen inches square and fifteen feet long, with which he lined the rear of the large house on the lake side, the quarter most sheltered, in order to build an hospital there. Along the faces of the powder magazine, he constructed, for the protection of the walls and to serve as casemates, a vast storehouse in pieces joined by a pinnacle at their summit, and in this house he placed the arms and armorers. 'Twill be remarked that such a work is excellent for field forts in wooded countries, and can easily serve for barracks and magazines. The shell falling on an oblique plain does it little injury, because such construction is very solid.

"The garrison was composed of 149 men detached from the regiments of La Sarre, Royal Rousillon, Guienne and Bearn, under the orders of Captain Pouchot, of the Bearn Regiment, Commandant; Captain de Villars of La Sarre; Captain de Cervies of Royal Rousillon; Lieutenant de Marambert of Guienne; Lieutenant Salvignac of Bearn; Lieutenant la Miltiere of Languedoc; of 183 Colonials, under the orders of Captain de la Roche, of that service, Lieutenants Cornoyer and Larminac; of 133 militia and 21 gunners, commanded by Lieutenant Bonnafoux of the Royal Corps. M. Pouchot increased this number to 100 drafted from the troops and the most adroit of the militiamen; in all 486, and 39 employes, five of whom were women or children, who with two Douville ladies attended the hospital, served up gun cartridges, and made earth bags."

The English force debarked at a point spoken of as the Little Swamp, a cove some distance east of Fort Niagara, where they drew up their batteaux and secured their position by an intrenchment. ["The Little Swamp is forty rods west of the mouth of the Four-Mile creek. Some of the remains of the battery are still there." *Orsamus Turner*, 1849.] In the evening of the 6th of July, a soldier of the Niagara garrison, who had been hunting in the neighboring forest, rushed into the fort and told Captain Pouchot that in the border of the woods which swept around it from lake to river, beyond a clear space that gave free range to the French guns and left no cover for an enemy, he had discovered an Indian war party, who had fired on some other hunters from the fort. The report was soon confirmed by a reconnoitering force, which encountered a volley that drove it back to the the works. A few cannon shot were fired at the enemy's position, and Pouchot, apprehensive of a surprise, stationed Captain Selviert with a hundred men in the outworks of. the fort, while "the rest of the garrison was under arms on the ramparts till midnight."

On the 7th Captain Pouchot, while communication with the outside world was still possible, dispatched runners for the French posts to the south and west, summoning to his aid their garrisons, with all the western Indians they could rally. That this had not been done before shows that the English expedition came upon him unexpected, for otherwise he must certainly have strengthened himself already by all available reinforcements.

The first point where Pouchot's carriers left their warning of the arrival of the enemy was Fort Little Niagara, otherwise called Fort du Portage, the Little Fort and Fisher's Battery (Marshall), a feeble establishment built above the falls by the French in 1750, on the point now occupied by the Stedman house, to protect the portage at its upper end. The Joncaire brothers were now stationed here, Chabert being in charge. On learning of the danger which threatened the post he transferred all the moveable property connected with it to the west bank of the river, burned the buildings, to prevent their being of service to the enemy, and retired to Fort Niagara.

CHAPTER X.

JOURNAL OF JOHNSON'S SIEGE OF FORT NIAGARA—ROUT OF A RELIEF FORCE—THE SURRENDER.

IT was on the morning of the 7th that the garrison of the fort got their first certain intimation "that it was the English come to besiege" them, by seeing "seven barges on the lake, a league and a half distance from the fort." The armed schooner "Iroquois," Captain La Force, lying before the fortress, put out with orders to destroy the English barges, in which it would seem to have failed. " All that day several savages showed themselves on the edge of the desert. Monsieur La Force fired several cannon shot at them; and perceived they were working at an intrenchment at the Little Swamp." So says the French journal of the affair. In this document we can best trace the progress of the siege:

"*Sunday, 8th July.* The schooner continued to cruise and fire on the English camp. About nine in the morning an English officer brought a letter from Brigadier Prideaux to Mons. Pouchot, to summons him, proposing him all advantages and good treatment, all of which he very politely refused, and even seemed to be unwilling to receive the English general's letter. The remainder of this day the English made no motions."

"*Tuesday*, 10th. At two o'clock all our men were on the ramparts, and at daybreak we perceived that they had opened their trenches at the entrance of the wilderness, at about three hundred toises from the fort; we made a very hot fire upon them all day. M. Chabert [Joncaire] arrived with the garrison of the Little Fort, and seven or eight savage Iroquois and Missagoes. Monsieur Pouchot went to palisade the ditches. The service, as usual, only the addition of two officers to be in the covered way. About eleven o'clock at night orders were given to make all the pickets fire from the covered way, to hinder the workmen of the enemy. M. La Force sent his boat on shore for Monsieur Pouchot's orders.

"*Wednesday*, 11th July. The works continued on both sides. At noon a party of about fifteen men, soldiers and militia, went very nigh the trenches of the enemy and perceived them sally out, between four and five hundred, who came towards them at a quick pace, but they were stopped by our cannon. They began on the other side of the swamp, which is the left of their trench, another, about twenty yards." In the evening of this day, an Iroquois chief who was with the garrison found means to introduce into the fort several of Johnson's Indians, who held a a fruitless parley with Pouchot. These fickle savages were even now wavering, and the British leaders dared not refuse them permission to visit the French, though suspicious of their purpose. Pouchot "sent them back each with a loaf, because he knew that the English army were eating only flour baked into cakes in the ashes." Johnson found it necessary to promise them the plunder of the fort to keep them to their work. At ten in the evening of the 11th the English had eight mortars in operation.

"*Night between the 11th and 12th.* The enemy ran their parallel from their first trench to the lake side, where it seemed they intended to establish a battery. * * * The enemy wrought the rest of that day [the 12th], and perfected their night's work. Monsieur La Force had orders to proceed to Frontenac and to return immediately. In the night between the 12th and 13th they fired many bombs. I went with thirty men to observe where the enemy wrought.

"*Friday, 13th July.* * * * The enemy threw a great many bombs all this day, and continued to work to perfect their trenches; we fired a great many cannon shot. * * *

"*Saturday, 14th July.* At day-break we found they had prolonged their trenches to the lake shore, in spite of the great fire from our cannon and musketry, during the night, and perfected it during the day time; they have placed four mortars and thrown many bombs. All our garrison lay in the covered way and on the ramparts.

"*Sunday, 15th July.* In the morning we perceived they had finished their works begun the night before. During the night they threw three hundred bombs; the rest of the day and night they threw a great many, but did not incommode us in any shape.

"*Monday, 16th July.* At dawn of day we spied, about half a league off, two barges, at which we discharged some cannon, on which they retired. In the course of the day they continued to throw some bombs. They have already disabled us some twenty men. All our men lie on beaver, or in their clothes and armed. We do what we can to incommode them with our cannon.

"*Tuesday, 17th July.* Until six this morning we had a thick fog, so that we could not discern the works of the enemy; but it clearing a little up, we saw they had raised a battery of three pieces of cannon and four mortars on the other side of the river. They began to fire about seven A. M., and Monsieur Pouchot placed all the guns he could against them. The fire was brisk on both sides all day; they seemed most inclined to batter the house where the commandant lodges. The service as usual for the night.

"*Wednesday, 18th July.* There was a great firing, as on the preceding day; we had one soldier dismembered and four wounded by their bombs.

"*Thursday, 19th July.* At dawn of day we found the enemy had begun a parallel eighty yards long in front of the fort. The fire was very great on both sides. At two P. M. arrived the schooner 'Iroquois,' from Frontenac, and lay abreast of the fort, waiting for a calm, not being able to get in, the enemy having a battery on the other side of the river." * * * In the evening of this day General Prideaux was instantly killed by the premature explosion of a shell, which burst immediately on leaving a gun near which he was standing, a piece striking him on the head. The command of the besiegers now devolved upon Sir William Johnson, who pressed the siege with vigor.

"*Friday, 20th July.* The English have made a third parallel, towards the lake; they are to-day about one hundred and sixty yards from the fort. They cannot have worked quietly at the sap, having had a great fire of musketry all night long which they were obliged to bear. During the day they made a great firing with their mortars, and they perfected their works begun the night of the 19th to the 20th. We had one man killed and four wounded. The fire of the musketry was very hot on both sides till eleven at night, when the enemy left off and we continued ours all night. * * *

"*Saturday, 21st.* During the night the enemy made a fourth parallel, which is about one hundred yards from the fort, in which it appears they will erect a battery for a breach in the flag bastion. They have hardly fired any cannon or bombs in the day, which gives one room to think they are transporting their cannon and artillery from their old battery to their new one. The service as usual. Their battery on the other side fired but little in the day. * * *

"*Sunday, 22d.* All the night was a strong conflict on both sides. We had one man killed by them and by our own cannon. We fired almost all our cannon with cartridges. They worked in the night to perfect all their works begun the night before. The enemy began to fire red hot balls in the night. * * * All day they continued to work to establish their batteries. They fired, as usual, bombs and cannon. The service as usual for the night of the 22nd and 23d. They worked hard to perfect their batteries, being ardently sustained by their musketry." The fort was by this time seriously feeling the effects of the siege. The batteries on the bastions had on the arrival of the English been hastily protected by barrels, and afterward bags, of earth; but the barrels were soon splintered by the enemy's guns, and the bags were now burnt or torn, or worn out by shifting them from point to point of the line where the fire of the besiegers for the time bore most severely. Wadding for the cannon also gave out, and the hay which was resorted to as a substitute did not last long. The straw and even the linen of the beds next went the same way.

"*Monday, 23d.* We added two pieces of cannon to the bastion of the lake, to oppose those of the enemy's side. At eight A. M., four savages brought a letter from Monsieur Aubrey to Monsieur Pouchot, by which we learn that he has arrived at the Great [Navy] Island, before the Little Fort, at the head of twenty-five hundred, half French and half savages. Monsieur Pouchot immediately sent back four savages with the answer to Monsieur Aubrey's letter, informing him of the enemy's situation. Those savages, before they came in, spoke to the Five Nations, and gave them five belts to engage them to retire from the enemy. They saw part of the enemy's camp, and told us the first or second in command was killed by one of our bullets, and two of their guns broken and one mortar. We have room to hope that with such success we may oblige the enemy to raise the siege, with the loss of men; and as they take up much ground, they must be beat, not being able to rally quick enough. At two P. M. they unmasked another battery of * * * cannon, three of which were eighteen pounders, the others twelve and six. They began with a brisk fire, which continued two hours, then slackened. * * * We worked hard to place two pieces, twelve pounders, on the middle of the curtains, to bear upon their battery.

"*Tuesday, 24th July.* The enemy began their fire about four o'clock this morning, and continued to fire with the same vivacity the rest of the day. At eight A. M. we perceived our army was approaching, having made several discharges of musketry at Belle Famille. At nine the fire began on both sides, and lasted half an hour. We wait to know who has the advantage of these two. At two P. M. we heard by a savage that our army was routed, and almost all made prisoners, by the treachery of our savages; when immediately the English army had the pleasure to inform us of it, by summoning us to surrender."

The journal from which these extracts are made was printed in Mr. Orsamus Turner's History of the Holland Purchase, with a paragraph appended saying that it was found with other papers, in the fort, two or three days from the date last mentioned, and soon after translated.

We have heard what a fugitive savage, just escaped from a bloody battle field, could tell of the result of an effort to raise the siege. What had really happened was this:

In response to Pouchot's appeal for help from the southern and western forts, some 1,400 French and Indians—two-thirds of them the former—rendezvoused at Presque Isle, now Erie, whence, in batteaux and canoes, they paddled for the Niagara. Halting a day or two at Navy Island, they crossed to the east bank of the river, left their boats with a guard of one hundred and fifty men, and marched to the relief of the beleagured fortress.

The woods were full of Johnson's Iroquois, who duly informed him of the approach of the French and the western Indians. The superior numbers of the besiegers enabled their commander to station an adequate force to meet the relieving army, without so far emptying the trenches that they need fear a sortie from the fort. His dispositions and the results of the encounter seem to be fairly reported in a letter written at Oswego on the 28th, as the result of an interview with Lieutenant Moncrieff, General Prideaux's aid-de-camp, who had just arrived there. From it we extract the following:

"Having intelligence from his Indians of a large party being on their march from the falls to relieve the fort, Sir William made a disposition to prevent them. The 23d, in the evening, he ordered the Light Infantry and pickets of the lines to lie near the road on our left, leading from the falls to the fort. These he reinforced in the morning of the 24th with the Grenadiers and part of the 46th Regiment, all under the command of Lieutenant-Colonel Massey. Lieutenant-Colonel Farquar, with the 44th battalion, was ordered to the tail of the trenches to support the guard of the trenches, commanded by Major Beckwith. About eight in the morning our Indians advanced to speak to the French Indians, which the enemy declined. The action began soon after with screams, as usual, from the enemy; but our troops were so well disposed to receive them in front, and our Indians on their flanks, that in less than an hour's time their whole army was ruined. The number of the slain was not ascertained, as the pursuit was continued three miles. Seventeen officers were made prisoners, among whom are Monsieur D'Aubrey, chief in command, wounded; Monsieur De Lignery, second in command, wounded also; Monsieur Marini, leader of the Indians; Monsieur De Villie, Repentini, Martini and Basonc, all captains, and several others. After this defeat, which was in sight of the garrison ['The battle ground is a mile and a half below the Five Mile Meadows, at a place called Bloody Run. Skulls and other human bones, bill-axes, pieces of muskets, etc., were strewn over the ground there long after the settlement of the country commenced.'—*Turner.*], Sir William sent Major Harvey into the fort with a list of officers taken, recommending it to the commanding officer to surrender before more blood was shed, and while he had it in his power to restrain the Indians. The commanding officer, to be certain of such a defeat, sent an officer of his to see the prisoners. They were shown to him and, in short, the capitulation was finished about ten at night of the 24th, by which the garrison surrendered, with the honors of war, which Lieutenant Moncrieff saw embarked the morning he came away, to the number of 607 private men, exclusive of the officers and their ladies and those taken in the action. We expect them here to-morrow on their way to New York."

A letter of which the following is a part was written at Fort Niagara on the day after the battle; except in the points corrected it is corroborated by the accounts of persons who were in a position to know the facts:

"Yesterday morning a party of French and Indians, consisting of 1500, of which 400 were Indians, about eight o'clock came upon our right [left], where a breastwork was thrown up, as we had intelligence of their coming; and as ten of our people were crossing the lake [river] above they began to fire upon them, which gave our people time to get all their pickets, the 46th regiment, part of the 44th [600 men of both], 100 New Yorkers, 600 Indians, ready to oppose them. We waited and received their fire five or six times before our people returned it, which they did at about thirty yards distance, then jumped over their breastwork and closed in with them, upon which they immediately gave way and broke; their Indians left them, and for a while we made a vast slaughter. * * * The ordnance stores found in the fort at Niagara when General Johnson took possession of it were two fourteen-pounders, nineteen twelve-pounders, one eleven-pounder, seven eight-pounders, seven six-pounders, two four-pounders, five two-pounders—all iron; 1500 round twelve pound shot, 40,000 pounds musket balls, 200 weight of match, 500 hand grenades, two cohorns and two mortars, mounted; 300 bill-axes, 500 hand hatchets, 100 axes, 300 shovels, 400 pick-axes, 250 mattocks, 54 spades, twelve whip-saws and a considerable number of small arms, swords, tomahawks, scalping-knives, cartouch-boxes, etc."

An express who bore from Albany to New York the tidings of the capture reported that "the number of our [English] killed and wounded in the defeat of the reinforcement from Venango [D'Aubrey's force] we cannot as yet justly ascertain, but there were five of the New Yorkers among the slain in that affair. It is said we had not lost forty men in the whole since the landing of the troops at Niagara. The Indians were allowed all the plunder in the fort, and found a vast quantity of it—some say to the value of £300 to a man. The fort, it is said, is large enough to contain 1,000 fighting men without inconvenience. All the buildings in and about it are standing and in good order, and it is thought had our forces stormed the place, which was intended, they would have met with a warm reception; and beating the Venango party will undoubtedly crown with laurels the ever deserving Johnson."

It is related that one of the Iroquois besiegers found among the captured garrison an intimate friend named Moncourt, to whom he was greatly attached. Not doubting, from his ideas of a captive's fate, that the prisoners would be put to death with torments, he approached his friend, and saying, "Brother, I am in despair at seeing you dead, but take heart, I'll prevent their torturing you," struck the Frenchman dead with his tomahawk.

CHAPTER XI.

SIR WILLIAM JOHNSON'S JOURNAL—FORT SCHLOSSER BUILT —TRADERS PROHIBITED FROM SETTLING THEREABOUTS.

IN D'Aubrey's attempt to raise the siege of Fort Niagara at least a hundred and fifty of his men had been killed, and probably many more; and more than a hundred captured. The remainder fled with all possible speed back to the point where they left their boats, and embarked for Detroit, leaving the intermediate posts to the fate which the fall of Niagara had rendered inevitable. The only force which had any chance of saving the fort, and therefore the last body of men charged with the maintenance of the French flag on the Niagara, fled from the task, satisfied and glad to have escaped with their lives. We have gleaned the incidents of the siege of the fated French fortress largely from the journal of its defender; for the events immediately following the surrender we will quote the diary of its captor, Sir William Johnson, as printed in Stone's life of the Baronet:

"The garrison of Niagara surrendered July 25th at seven in the morning. The number of which consisted of six hundred and seven men and eleven officers, besides a number of women, children, etc. The former to be sent to England by way of New York, and escorted to Oswego by a detachment of the 46th, consisting of three hundred; the latter to the first French post, with one priest. * * *

"*July 26th.* They embarked, after grounding their arms, and proceeded to Oswego. * * *

"*27th.* I divided among the several nations the prisoners and scalps [taken in the battle of the 24th], amounting to two hundred and forty-six, of which ninety-six were prisoners. The officers I with difficulty released from them, by ransom, good words, etc.

"*28th.* The greatest part of all the nations set off in boats, with a deal of plunder, for their several countries. Buried Brigadier-General Prideaux in the chapel, and Colonel Johnson, with a great deal of form. I was chief mourner. * * * Colonel Haldimand arrived here with Captain Williamette from Oswego, to claim the command, which I refused giving up, as my commission gave me rank of him. He gave up the point until General Amherst's pleasure was known, which may be soon, as Colonel Haldimand, on receipt of my letter, wrote him upon it. In order to secure this important post to his Majesty, it is necessary to leave for the present a garrison of 700 men, who are to repair the works, which have been hurt by our cannon, and put the fort in the best posture of defense they can, with the assistance of an engineer, who is to be left here for that purpose. To have the two vessels fitted out, armed and manned to escort the batteaux, with the remainder of the army, to Oswego; also endeavor to take the French schooner. Artillery and ammunition to leave here, and have Captain Stretchey's opinion in writing thereupon; also some artillerymen and gunners. The French officers and other prisoners to take with me to Oswego, and send them to [New] York in order to be sent to England. To write Governor De Lancey to send all the French prisoners to England as soon as possible. * * *

"*29th.* I gave the French officers shoes, stockings and blankets. I wrote by De Normandy to Oswego for all the ship carpenters to come here, to build two vessels of eighteen guns each. * * * I wrote a letter to the Secretary of State with a short account of the siege of Niagara; also sent him a plan of the fort, and a return of the killed and wounded in the siege, and action of the 24th, being 60 killed and 180 wounded, besides three Indians killed and five wounded—63 killed, 183 wounded.

"*August 1st.* I went to see Niagara falls, with Colonel Haldimand, Mr. Ogilvie and several officers, escorted by three companies of the eighth infantry. Arrived there about eleven o'clock. In my way, at the thither end of the carrying place, I met a flag of truce from Presque Isle, desiring to know the number of officers I had in my hands from the action of the 24th, and begging I would advance them anything they might want, they being men of fortune and credit. * * * I ordered them to stay in the woods, and left Mr. Rogers, with a guard with him, until I sent a message to them and provisions. The artillery was this day partly shipped on board the batteaux, the readier to be shipped to-morrow, with ammunition, etc.

"*Saturday, August 4th.* I was to embark at five o'clock in the morning with the troops, etc., for Oswego, but the two French schooners appearing off harbor prevented our embarkation until five in the evening, when I left Colonel Farquhar everything in charge; also some Indian goods to give occasionally to such Indians as might come upon business to him. Then set off, with all the Yorkers except one company; all the light infantry and grenadiers, and the general's company of the 44th regiment, and arrived at Oswego Tuesday about three o'clock P. M., with everything safe."

Very soon after the fall of Fort Niagara the English took possession of the portage, and at its head, some forty rods from where Fort Little Niagara had stood, built a fortification, which was named Fort Schlosser in honor of its first commandant, Captain Joseph Schlosser, a German by birth, but serving in the British army which took Fort Niagara. A flattering estimate has been placed upon his character by different writers, among them the Moravian missionary Heckwelder, who in his "Indian Narrative" wrote of him as an officer deservedly esteemed by all good men for his humanity and manly conduct. He was subsequently promoted to the rank of colonel, and died in the fort. It is said that an oak head-board bearing his name was to be seen at his grave above the fort in 1808, but this statement is received by those acquainted with the locality with considerable allowance.

The fort has been described as having the outline of a tolerably distinct fortification, with rude bastions and connecting curtains, surrounded by a somewhat formidable ditch. The interior plateau was a little elevated and encompassed by an earth embankment, piled against the inner side of the palisades, over which its defenders could fire with great effect.

In the summer of 1761 Sir William Johnson made a journey to Detroit, being, as he recorded, "directed by General Amherst to settle and establish a firm and lasting treaty" with the western Indians; "also to regulate the trade at the several posts in the Indian country." He reached Fort Niagara on the second anniversary of his decisive victory over D'Aubrey. He kept a diary of his tour, from which, as printed for the first time by Mr. Stone, his biographer, we make some extracts of local interest:

"*Friday, 24th [July]*. * * * At six in sight of Niagara Fort; stood in and made the harbor about seven in the morning. * * * Mr. Preston, formerly of the 44th regiment, came to me and told me that the Chenussios [a branch of the Senecas already referred to], with whom he lived all the winter, were not well affected to the English, neither did they like our going beyond Niagara to garrison posts, or even to trade; that it was their country, and they looked upon it that we were going to surround or hem them in; that they were very scarce of powder, and believes that if they had a sufficiency they would be ready enough to fall upon some parties of our people going to Detroit; that they have an English lad prisoner, and a great number of horses which they stole from us; and that they daily take more from Pittsburgh, etc."

"*Sunday, 26th*. At seven in the morning I set off with Colonel Eyre, Lieutenant Johnson, my son, and De Couagne, for the island whereon the vessel is building for exploring the lakes Huron and Michigan, which island is about two miles from Little Niagara on the place where Shabear Jean Coeur [Johnson's English for Chabert Joncaire] lived. There is a house built within a quarter of a mile of said place by one Stirling, for the use of the company, viz: Rutherford, Duncan, &c., who intend to monopolize the whole carrying place by virtue of a permit from General Amherst. The schooner building upon the island was in such forwardness as to be ready to launch in about ten days, but was put a stop to in order to build a boat, pinnace fashion, for Major Gladwin's service. Dined with John Dies, after which Colonel Eyre went in a boat to explore the Chippeway river, the entrance to which is about two miles above the great falls. In another branch of said river our people found a great quantity of pine planks of several dimensions, sawed by hand, which they used in making the vessels. About six P. M. we set off from the post where Jean Coeur lived, and arrived at the fort of Niagara at nine at night.

"*Monday, 27th*. * * * About twelve o'clock we took a walk into the Trader's Town."

"*Saturday, August the 1st*. * * * In the afternoon took a walk to my old encampment in 1759."

"*Tuesday, 4th*. * * * This afternoon I made out regulations for Indian trade, which is to be put up at each post where trade is carried on with the Indians.

"*Wednesday, 5th*. * * * In the afternoon went gunning with Captain Slossen [Schlosser]. Four men whipped for robbing a Seneca Indian of a keg of rum, in the irpresence."

"*Saturday, 8th*. * * * Captain Slasser [Schlosser] took me out to walk, when he let me know his desire of settling on a farm and quitting the army, and sending for his wife and family. He left it for me to choose a proper place for him, which I shall look out for on my return."

"*Monday, 17th*. * * * Loaded all the wagons and set off, myself and company, for the other end of the carrying place, or Little Niagara, where Shabear Jean Coeur lived. * * *

"*Tuesday, 18th*. Showery. I went to see the falls with Lieutenant Johnson, Johnny and Ensign Holmes. * * * Captain Slosser, Dembler, Dies, Robertson, &c., dined with me, and got pretty happy before they left me.

"*Wednesday, 19th*. * * * At four o'clock embarked."

From reaching the Niagara river on his return trip, Sir William made the following entries:

"*Sunday, 4th [October]*. * * * We went on board the schooner which lay about a mile from the entrance of the lake, in the river, where the current runs six knots an hour. * * * Captain Robinson told us that the garrison of Niagara, himself and crew, were lately within a day or two of abandoning the fort, vessel, etc., when provisions arrived from Oswego. Dined on board and left the vessel about five o'clock, and encamped about ten miles down the river. * * *

"*Monday, 5th*. * * * Arrived at Little Niagara about ten o'clock, and got over on horseback myself, and got wagons to carry over as many of my boats, baggage, etc., as I could. Then set off in an old boat for Niagara, where I was met at eight o'clock at night by the waterside by Major Walters and all the officers. Supped with the major, and took up my old lodgings.

"*Tuesday, 6th*. * * * The major, De Couagne, etc., complain of Stirling monopolizing the trade by keeping a great store of goods at Little Niagara, which will prevent any Indians coming to the fort or under the eye of the garrison, so that they [Stirling and others] may cheat the Indians as much as they please, in spite of all regulations."

The reader may have judged from the Baronet's remarks in his journal that the establishment by this Stirling, for himself and others, of the trading-house at Schlosser, was a serious matter. Further citations on this point will be found pertinent. Sir William, on his way to Detroit, having ascertained the state of things, immediately wrote General Amherst a letter, of which the following is a part:

"I see plainly that there appears to be an unusual jealousy amongst every [Indian] nation, on account of the hasty steps they look upon we are taking towards getting possession of their country, which uneasiness, I am certain, will never subside whilst we encroach within the limits which, you may recollect, have been put under the protection of the King in the year 1726, and confirmed to them by him and his successors ever since, and by orders sent to the governors not to allow any of his subjects settling thereon; with which they were acquainted by his late Majesty in your speech of the 22d of April, 1760, delivered by Brigadier-General Moncton. You then promised to prevent any person whatsoever from settling or even hunting therein, but that it should remain their absolute property. I thought it necessary to remind your excellency thereof, as the other day, on my riding to the place where the vessels are building, I found some carpenters at work finishing a large house for one Mr. Stirling, near the falls, and have since heard others are shortly to be built thereabouts. As this must greatly add to the Indians' discontent, being on the carrying place, and within the very limits which, by their own agreement, they are not so much as allowed to dispose of, I should be glad to know whether I can acquaint them that those people will be ordered to remove or not; and I hope from your excellency's answer to be able to satisfy them on that head."

Under date of January 28, 1762, twenty-seven merchants of Albany wrote to the English Lords of Trade, making a similar complaint on the same grounds, though it is hardly likely they were as disinterested as Sir William. The burden of this communication was that General Amherst had "licensed and authorized Captain Rutherford, Lieutenant Duncan and others to settle at the Niagara carrying place and given them ten thousand acres of land there." The sentiment of the King coinciding with that of the Albany merchants, and being communicated to General Amherst, he wrote that he had only granted "a permit until the King's pleasure was known, but without the least clause that could entitle them to an exclusive right of trade;" and "I have now," said the general, "in obedience to his Majesty's commands, sent orders to the commandant at Niagara to put a stop to any settlement on the carrying place."

Such were, at least for traders, the attractions of the Niagara frontier under the settled rule of the English, and such the tenure of the land, that it was then necessary for the government to discourage rather than promote settlements along the river. In the quotations we have made from original documents the reader will have caught glimpses of the state of things, and it needs but little imagination to develop the picture of the rude and vigorous life of the transient population, whose chief element was the succession of red hunters and trappers and indianized European bush-rangers arriving at Fort Niagara or Schlosser from a voyage or a tramp of hundreds of miles; trading at the latter, or trooping down the portage trail with their packs of furs; lounging about the forts brave in new blankets and jewelry, or stirring the garrison's monotonous life with their wild carousals and savage brawls over the liquor purchased with a part of their beavers; gladdening the eyes of the prosperous trader and saddening the heart of the missionary priest who must cast the good seed into such ungrateful soil.

The savage element predominated, and even yet, by thorough co-operation, might sweep the foreigners from the lake region. So thought Pontiac, King of the Ottawas, and organized his famous plot for the redemption of the land from the pale-faced intruders.

CHAPTER XII.

THE DEVIL'S HOLE MASSACRE—THE SENECAS CEDE THE NIAGARA BORDER TO THE ENGLISH.

IN the spring of 1763 nine of the twelve British posts in what was then the west were cut off at a blow by Pontiac's league of the northwestern Indians. Detroit, Pittsburgh and Niagara held out, though more or less vigorously besieged. The Senecas, whose antipathy to the English had been remarked by Sir William Johnson two years before, and who now co-operated with Pontiac, beset the land communications of the Niagara posts, and wreaked their hatred upon the new lords of the river in the frightful massacre of the Devil's Hole. The scene and the story of this terrible tragedy are probably quite familiar to our readers, but we cannot omit the sad recital.

The hostility of the Senecas made it necessary to station a guard at the foot as well as at the head of the Niagara portage, and to protect the teams and teamsters on their trips by a convoy of soldiers. On the 14th of September, 1763, a wagon train which had come up from Lewiston, loaded with supplies for Detroit, set out from Schlosser on the return, with an escort of twenty-five men, accompanied by John Stedman, who had charge of the portage. Five hundred Senecas, chiefly Chenussios, lay in wait for them in the thickets crowning the stern precipice that bounds the Devil's Hole. As the doomed company carelessly defiled along the brink of the chasm, a murderous volley was fired by the hidden savages, who then sprang forth, thirty or forty to one of the survivors, and butchered them with tomahawk and scalping knife. Crazed by the din of fire arms and the yells of the savages, part of the teams went off the rocky wall; and even the men in some cases, rather than be hacked to pieces on the spot or roasted at an inland castle, flung themselves from the cliff. Among the latter was a drummer boy, named Mathews, who fell into a tree top, from which he descended without mortal injuries. Above, John Stedman, spurring a good horse through the assailants' line and through a shower of bullets, regained Fort Schlosser. It is said that a wounded teamster, dragging himself into the shelter of the dense evergreens, escaped the knife and the hatchet. Certainly no more than these three survived the savage onset.

The firing had been heard by the guard posted at the

lower landing, and suspecting the state of the case they hastened up the portage road. The savages had time to complete the destruction of the train and its escort and ensconce themselves again in the bushes, with rifles reloaded and tomahawks handy, before the reinforcement reached the spot, when the massacre was renewed. A blast of bullets from the thicket tore through the close lines of the detachment, felling more than half the troops; again the Chenussios, sallying from their cover, swarmed round their prey, and the scalping knives, hardly dry from their latest use, were bathed anew with blood. Eight men escaping with their lives bore the horrible tidings to Fort Niagara. The garrison immediately marched to the scene of slaughter, but the triumphant Senecas, not, it would seem, expecting this detachment, which, so far as we can see, they might as well have destroyed as the other, had retired carrying eighty scalps; and only the naked and mangled bodies from which they had been torn awaited the party from the fort—these and the crushed remains of men, teams and wagons, strewn at the bottom of the dismal gulf or hanging in the treetops about the base of the cliff.

The little rivulet falling into the glen, and called Bloody Run, first became such on that dreadful day when it was crimsoned by the butchery upon its banks. The passer by now looks from his carriage down the gloomy pit, which yawns close beside the roadway, into the bristling treetops that hide its lowest depths, and shudders to think of the situation of men who judged it best to cast themselves into this deep and rugged chasm. Yet one who made this choice long outlived every other actor in the awful tragedy—the drummer Mathews, who died at Queenston, aged ninety.

The savages still haunted the neighborhood of the Niagara posts, and on the 5th of November killed two of the garrison at the lower landing, who were, with a few others, cutting wood within sight of their quarters.

In a communication to the English government dated March 1, 1777, Colonel Claus, a son-in-law of Sir William Johnson and himself officially familiar with Indian affairs, gave the following summary of the events we have just narrated:

"In the fall of 1762 a Dutch Indian trader was killed by a vagrant Indian from the Ohio, in their [the Senecas'] country, and fled for it; for which murder the commander-in-chief demanded satisfaction from them, and they not capable to give it as required, hostile measures were put on foot against them. In this situation they saw themselves necessitated to call the western Indians to their assistance; who being then unfriendly to us, through the instigation of the French traders about the upper posts and some principal people at Montreal, readily accepted their messages, and in the spring of 1763, by a well concerted plot, cut off all the posts beyond Niagara, except Detroit, which was happily discovered before executed; and the Tsinusio's cut off the communication to Niagara by land, and defeated a party of 100 men of the 80th regiment, and this brought on that destructive Indian war which cost so much blood and treasure before it could be settled again. Indians not easily forgetting injuries, the Tsinusio's still harbored ill will against those they ascribed their misfortunes and losses to, in reflecting upon their once happy days at Niagara, and could not be prevailed upon to attach themselves cordially to the British interest till after the unwearied pains and endeavors of the late Sir William Johnson."

No summary punishment was inflicted upon the Senecas for their outrages of this year. They realized that they deserved it, and on the collapse of Pontiac's bold scheme were so fearful of receiving it that they were anxious to make terms with the English. Accordingly in April, 1764, four hundred of them waited on Sir William Johnson at Johnson Hall and begged for peace. Now was the time to pay off the Devil's Hole score, and Sir William was the man to do it. The article of the concessions exacted by him with which we have most to do reads as follows:

"That they [the Senecas] cede to His Majesty and his successors for ever, in full right, the lands from the fort of Niagara, extending easterly along Lake Ontario about four miles, comprehending the Petit Mavais, or landing place, and running from thence southerly, about fourteen miles, to the creek above the Fort Schlosser or Little Niagara, and down the same to the river or strait and across the same, at the great cataract, thence northerly to the banks of Lake Ontario, at a creek or small lake about two miles west of the fort; thence easterly along the banks of the Lake Ontario, and across the river or strait to Niagara; comprehending the whole carrying place, with the lands on both sides the strait, and containing a tract of about fourteen miles in length and four in breadth. And the Senecas do engage never to obstruct the passage of the carrying place, or the free use of any part of the said tract, and will likewise give free liberty of cutting timber for the use of His Majesty, or that of the garrisons, in any other part of their country, not comprehended therein."

To this the Senecas assented, "provided the tract be always appropriated to His Majesty's sole use," and that at the definite treaty, which was to be had within three months, "the lines be run in presence of Sir William Johnson and some of the Senecas, to prevent disputes" thereafter. They further agreed "never more to make war upon the English;" to deliver up "all the English prisoners, deserters, Frenchmen and negroes amongst them" and never to harbor any more of the last three classes; to always allow the English free passage through their country and the use of all the harbors in it; to treat the Indian enemies of the English as their enemies; to give up any of their number who murdered or robbed a British subject to be tried by English laws, and not to redress their own injuries but report them to the superintendent of Indian affairs. Eight chiefs signed the articles, and the deputation went home and considered with the rest of their tribe whether they had better carry them out.

The occasion on which they were expected to ratify these preliminary articles, and enter into a permanent treaty, was a general meeting of the Indian tribes at Niagara, to which the superintendent invited them in order to readjust their relations to the English government in view of the events of the war with Pontiac's confederacy. The tribes desiring peace were to treat for terms at Niagara, while two military expeditions set out to subdue those still refractory. One of these expeditions, consisting of 1200 men under General Bradstreet, rendezvoused at Oswego in June, 1764, and was there joined by Sir William Johnson with 550 Iroquois warriors. The army set out for Fort Niagara July 3d and reached it on the 8th.

Meanwhile the distant Indian tribes which had received Sir William's summons had been flocking to the appointed place by hundreds, and Fort Niagara on the Baronet's arrival was such a center of life and activity as it had not been for many a long day. "The sight which greeted him," says Stone, " as he stepped from his boat upon the sandy beach, must have been peculiarly gratifying to his self-love. In response to his invitations he beheld, far stretched across the fields, the wigwams of over a thousand Indians, whose number but a few days after was increased to two thousand and sixty, of whom seventeen hundred were warriors. Deputations from all the nations dwelling in that vast region lying between the pine forests of Nova Scotia and the head springs of the Mississippi were here assembled. Ottawas and Hurons, Chippewas and Caughnawagas, Sacs and Foxes, picturesquely attired, strolled in groups about the fort; while here and there might be seen an Indian from tribes that trapped the beaver on the margin of Hudson's Bay, and hunted the moose on the northern shores of Lake Superior."

It required all of Johnson's skill and influence to keep the peace and preserve order among two thousand savages, who had been often hostile to each other and but lately fighting—and needing but slight inducement again to fight—the English themselves. Some of them had a fresh grievance : In coming down the portage past one of the block-houses guarding it, they had saluted and serenaded the garrison by firing a volley and singing a war-song. The garrison, considering the demonstration a hostile one, answered with a discharge of grape shot, which wounded three of the Indians. They were with difficulty pacified.

The Senecas were tardy, and trouble was had in procuring their attendance. When they finally arrived, they brought with them fourteen English prisoners and a deserter, and promptly ratified the preliminary articles drawn up at Johnson Hall. In addition they extended the four-mile cession of land on the east bank of the Niagara from Fort Schlosser to the head of the river, and gave all the islands in the river to Johnson, who shortly after turned them over to the crown. From that time forward the Senecas were in alliance with the English for nearly fifty years.

Johnson also made a treaty with the Hurons, and the other tribes renewed their engagements. The Baronet then left for the east, while Bradstreet set out for Detroit, embarking at Schlosser, August 8th. His expedition proved hardly less abortive than one which attempted the same voyage in the preceding year. In that instance six hundred regular soldiers going to help Detroit against Pontiac were driven ashore by a gale on Lake Erie, seventy-three men drowned, the artillery lost and the surviving troops obliged to march back to Niagara. Bradstreet accomplished nothing as affecting the Indians, and on his return lost by a storm on the lake six brass cannon, his ammunition and baggage, and so many of his boats that a hundred and fifty of his men had to attempt to traverse on foot four hundred miles of wilderness, from which many of them never emerged. Parts of his force straggled into Fort Niagara all through November and December.

CHAPTER XIII.

FORT NIAGARA DURING THE REVOLUTION—ITS SURRENDER BY THE BRITISH—THE TUSCARORAS.

DURING the Revolution the Niagara posts, being far from the populated parts of the country, were not the scene of any engagement, but were throughout the war in the undisputed possession of the British. Fort Niagara was the base of extensive predatory operations, the point from which the Butlers and Brant led forth their savage bands for the devastation of the eastern part of the State, marking their course with blood and ashes, and to which they brought back their booty and their wretched captives. The vicinity of the fort was during the war the most permanent station of the Mohawk Indians, most of whom, like all the Iroquois, except the Oneidas and Tuscaroras, sided with the British, and whom their great chieftain Brant led westward with the superintendent, Guy Johnson, at the opening of the Revolution, abandoning forever their ancient seat in the lower Mohawk valley.

Here was held in September, 1776, a great council, not only with the Iroquois nations favorable to the English, but with nine or ten other tribes also. The British government was represented by Colonel Butler, Lieutenant-Colonel Caldwell, commandant of the post, Lieutenants Matthews, Burnet and Kinnesley, and Ensign Butler. The chiefs all signed a manifesto declaring in favor of the crown and appealing to the Oneidas and Tuscaroras to take the same stand; portions of these tribes complied.

The infamous tory Colonel John Butler, and his more infamous son, Major Walter Butler, here consorted with the savages and planned such inhuman enterprises as the massacres of Wyoming and Cherry Valley. From the latter the marauders returned to Niagara, by way of the Susquehanna and Tioga rivers—a common route with such expeditions—driving as prisoners the family of a border patriot named Moore, having left the wife and children of one Campbell at Kanadeseaga. Mrs. Campbell was also taken to Niagara in June, 1779, by the agency of Colonel Butler, who wished to exchange her for his wife, then held by the patriots. At Niagara Mrs. Campbell found two notorious Indian women: Molly Brant, sister of the famous chief, who lived with Sir William Johnson during the latter years of his life; and that singular character Catharine Montour, a half-breed, said to have been a daughter of one of the French governors of Canada, but who always lived with the Senecas and was essentially a savage, though conversant with the manners of society. Her home, at the head of Seneca lake, was called Catharinestown. One of her sons participated in the Cherry Valley butchery, and two of them in that of Wyoming, where she herself is said to have been present as an animating spirit. It was a year before Mrs. Campbell was able to leave Niagara; during that time three of her children, who had been scattered among the Senecas, were taken to the for and delivered to her, and the fourth was recovered at Montreal, where mother and children were exchanged for Colonel Butler's family.

The capture of Fort Niagara—hive of scalping parties and incendiary expeditions—was one of the objects of Sullivan's campaign in 1779. This part of the programme was, however, for some reason hard to fathom, abandoned; and nothing was accomplished but the destruction of the villages and crops of the Senecas and Cayugas. These Indians were compelled to resort to the fort for support during the winter following, and suffered greatly by the extraordinary severity of the season.

On the 7th of April, 1780, in one of Brant's forays upon the Mohawk border, he seized Captain Harper and ten militiamen, and would have proceeded to the destruction of the settlements on Schoharie creek had not Harper led him to believe that they were well defended. Abandoning his design, the raider returned with his prisoners to Niagara, with difficulty saving their lives, which his followers were eager to take. One who now glides comfortably from the Schoharie to the Niagara in a few hours cannot conceive the captive's experience of suffering and dread, who made the distance by weeks of painful marching, shivering with cold, faint with hunger, and at the mercy of a barbarous foe. Reluctantly sparing the lives of Harper and his men, the savages would have at least compelled them to run the gauntlet at one if not both of two Indian camps before Fort Niagara had not the chieftain interposed in their behalf. Brant knew that Captain Harper, with whom he was well acquainted, was the uncle of a lady in the fort, who was Miss Jane Moore when brought as a prisoner from Cherry Valley, but now Mrs. Powell, having married an officer of the garrison. Wishing to be on good terms with Powell, he informed him by a fleet courier whom he had captured, and suggested that the Indians at the fort be got out of the way before the arrival of the party. This was accomplished by getting up a pic-nic several miles distant, so that the Indian camps were empty when the captives were conducted through them.

In May, 1780, a marauding party of Indians captured near the Hudson river a Captain Snyder and his son and took them to Niagara, where they were forced to run the gauntlet but protected by their captors from serious injury. The fort was then, according to Captain Snyder, "a structure of considerable magnitude and great strength, enclosing ana rea of from six to eight acres." Within the enclosure was a handsome dwelling-house for the residence of the superintendent of the Indians. It was then occupied by Colonel Guy Johnson. Lieutenant-Colonel Bolton was about this time the commandant of the post.

An Oneida Indian who left Niagara about the 1st of December, 1780, reported to the colonial authorities that Brant, Colonel Butler and Guy Johnson were then there, with 60 regular troops, 400 tories and 1200 Indians, who were well supplied with everything needful.

The Mohawks were located during most of the war on and east of the site of Lewiston, where they had a little log church at which the chaplain of Fort Niagara occasionally conducted the Episcopal service. A bell hung upon a neighboring tree summoned the dusky worshipers to the place of prayer. Soon after the war closed the Mohawks removed to a large tract north of Lake Erie, granted them by the British crown. While at Lewiston their notorious leader Brant lived, says Turner, in "a block-house, standing near what is called 'Brant's Spring,' on the farm of Isaac Cook." The improvements made by the Mohawks told on the price the pioneer whites had to pay for the lands which they had occupied.

At the end of the Revolutionary struggle the English government ignored the treaty of peace by refusing to surrender the lake posts within the United States, pleading that the government of this country (if it can be said that there was here a government or a country, under the contemptible notions of State rights then prevalent) also violated the treaty in some points. The controversy is thus summed up by Lossing:

"Against Great Britain it was charged that slaves had been carried away by her military and naval commanders subsequent to the signing of the treaty, and on their departure from the country. It was also complained that the western military posts had not been surrendered to the United States according to Article VII. of the treaty. Against the United States it was charged that legal impediments had been interposed to prevent the collection of debts due British merchants by Americans, and that the stipulations concerning the property of loyalists, found in Articles V. and VI. of the treaty, had not been complied with. These criminations and recriminations were fair, for it has been justly remarked, 'America could not, and Great Britain would not, because America did not, execute the treaty.'"

Thus it happened that Fort Niagara was held by the British for years after the conclusion of peace, and only given up on the fourth of July, 1796, in pursuance of a second treaty, adopted in the summer of 1794. "The treaty," says Lossing," provided for the establishment of commissions to determine the eastern boundary of the United States, then in dispute; the amount of losses incurred by British subjects by impediments being thrown in the way of collecting debts in the United States incurred before the Revolution ; and to ascertain and estimate the losses of the Americans by irregular and illegal capture by British cruisers, such losses to be paid by the British government. It was provided that the western military posts should be given up on the 1st of June, 1796, in consideration of the adjustment of the ante-revolutionary debts. The Indian trade was left open to both nations," etc.

In the beginning of June, 1793, General Lincoln, Colonel Pinckney and W. Randolph, United States commissioners, arrived at Fort Niagara on their way to a great council with the western Indians, to be held at the Miami river, on which occasion, being the King's birth-day (June 4th), the Canadian governor Simcoe gave a ball and hospitably entertained the commissioners.

The Duke de Liancourt, a French nobleman, visited the Niagara river from the falls down to Lake Ontario in June, 1795, and was entertained by Governor Simcoe, who invited him to dine with the English officers stationed at Fort Niagara.

On one occasion Simcoe remarked to the Duke that it was with great aversion he crossed the river to visit the fort, as he was well convinced it would finally have to be delivered up to the Americans.

In the spring of 1781 the Tuscaroras who had sided with Great Britain located themselves on a square mile of land on the mountain ridge, now in the town of Lewiston, which the Senecas had assigned them. They and their descendants have remained in undisturbed possession of this property, which has been increased by a grant of two square miles and a purchase (in 1804) of 4,329 acres from the Holland Land Company. For the latter tract they gave $13,722, being part of the indemnity paid them for the extinction of their interest in North Carolina. The Tuscaroras were thus the first established settlers of Niagara County who still retain their place among its people—the first inhabitants except the traders and other adventurers operating in the shadow of the storehouses and forts along the river. The first white emigrants to the county found in them friends and good neighbors. This remnant of the tribe took kindly to civilization, and has long constituted a prosperous farming community. In 1846 Mr. Schoolcraft, the eminent authority on matters of Indian history, made a report to the State government on the numbers and condition of the Iroquois then living in the State, in which he said of the Tuscaroras that they numbered 283, cultivated the preceding year 2,080 acres of land, and owned 1,300 head of various kinds of live stock. The enumeration gave "an average of six neat cattle, three horses (nearly), two milch cows (nearly), ten hogs, and 92 bushels of wheat, 966 of corn to each family," and Mr. Schoolcraft remarks: "Their capacity to sustain themselves and their advance as agriculturists will be perceived. Fifty-nine plows were found amongst fifty-three families. They cut 195 acres of meadow to sustain their cattle. They have over 1,500 fruit trees, and dwell in excellent frame or square timber houses, well finished and for the most part well furnished. * * * Of the entire population 63 are church members, and 231 members of temperance societies, which is a far higher proportion than is found in any other of the cantons." The present number of the tribe is 412.

CHAPTER XV.

INDIAN TRAILS IN NIAGARA COUNTY—THE PORTAGE, MILITARY, RIDGE AND LAKE ROADS.

IN their long journeys between the most frequented points in their domain, the Indians naturally found in course of time the most direct and easy lines of travel and adhered to them, forming permanent trails, which the white settlers in some cases located upon and adopted as their first roads. The principal trail of the Iroquois ran through their "long house" from the Hudson to the Niagara. Coming from the east via Canandaigua and Batavia, it emerged from the Tonawanda swamp, says Turner, "nearly southeast of Royalton Center, coming out upon the Lockport and Batavia road in the valley of Millard's brook, and from thence it continued upon the Chestnut ridge to the Cold Springs. Pursuing the route of the Lewiston road, with occasional deviations, it struck the Ridge road at Warren's. It followed the Ridge road until it passed Hopkins' marsh, when it gradually ascended the mountain ridge, passed through the Tuscarora village and then down again to the Ridge road, which it continued on to the river. This was the principal route into Canada, crossing from Lewiston to Queenston, a branch trail, however, going down the river to Fort Niagara." Over this road, during the last ten or fifteen years of the eighteenth century, and an equal period in the beginning of the nineteenth, herds of cattle were constantly driven from the eastern part of the country, to feed the garrison on the Niagara and the settlers on the Canadian border. About the close of the last century the Indians allowed such improvement of this trail as enabled sleighs to traverse it in winter, and a weekly mail was carried over it between Fort Niagara and Canandaigua. This road, as thus improved by the so-called Holland Company, was the first laid out north of the main road from Canandaigua to Buffalo.

"The Ontario trail," Mr. Turner tells us, coming from Oswego via Irondequoit Bay, pursued the Ridge road "west to near the west line of Hartland, Niagara county, where it diverged to the southwest, crossing the east branch of the Eighteen-mile creek, and forming a junction with the Canada or Niagara trail at the Cold Springs."

Interesting as are these long-traveled paths, on which barbarism went forth to war and the chase and civilization marched in to supplant it, no other of the old highways of the county has the historic interest of the Portage road. We have seen La Salle's party toiling up the hills at Lewiston with their ship-building materials and other burdens, and repeatedly making the portage back and forth, possibly guided by a trail over which the Indians long carried their canoes past the unnavigable section of the Niagara. The old documents relating to French and English occupancy contain frequent interesting references to the portage. In quotations from them already made the reader's attention has been called to the importance of this position in connection with the fur trade, and the efforts of the Canadian and New York governments to control it. One of the earliest accounts of the portage occurs in a "memoir on the Indians between Lake Erie and the Mississippi," written in 1718, and reads as follows:

"The Niagara portage is two leagues and a half to three leagues long, but the road, over which carts roll two or three times a year, is very fine, with very beautiful and open woods through which a person is visible for a distance of six hundred paces. The trees are all oaks, and very large. The soil along the entire of that road is not very good. From the landing, which is three leagues up the river, four hills are to be ascended. Above the first hill there is a Seneca village of about ten cabins, where Indian corn, beans, peas, and water-melons and pumpkins are raised, all which are very fine. These Senecas are employed by the French, from whom they earn money by carrying the goods of those who are going to the upper country; some for leggings, others for shirts, some for powder and ball, whilst some others pilfer; and on the return of the French, they carry their packs of furs for some peltry. This portage is made for the purpose of avoiding the cataract of Niagara, the grandest sheet of water in the world, having a perpendicular fall of two to three hundred feet. This fall is the outlet of Lakes Erie, Huron, Michigan, Superior, and consequently of the numberless rivers discharging into these lakes, as well as of other lakes towards the Sioux, with the names of which I am not acquainted."

In what sense the Portage road of 1718 could have been called "very fine," it is hard to guess. It is hardly supposable that any roadway which would now be considered tolerable was maintained for the passage of rude carts "two or three times a year." The Senecas probably had as yet very little competition from vehicles as carriers, and that they had the carrying business in their hands almost to the close of the French regime appears from the colonial documents. They were, it is said, "much caressed and indulged by the French, and had the liberty to enjoy the emoluments of that carrying place, which were so lucrative and considerable to that nation that in a short time they enriched themselves thereby, and had besides some other advantages in trade and other necessaries of life." Yet even before the French gave way to the English on the Niagara the portage business began to slip from the hands of the Indians. Montcalm, in April, 1757, reported to his government an interview with an embassy of the Six Nations, in which "the Iroquois orator spoke of the establishment of carts at the carrying place of Niagara as being prejudicial to them, inasmuch as formerly they did the transportation over that carrying place themselves." Captain Pouchot, the last defender of French power on this border, has a remark on the portage in a letter to Marshall de Belle Isle written at Montreal in April, 1758, in which he contradicts the extravagant misrepresentations of Hennepin and Charlevoix. He says:

"That country, my Lord, would be well worth being seen by experienced eyes, which has not as yet been the case; the well known carrying place of Niagara is an evident proof. The most recent accounts thereof describe it as the most rugged of alps, whilst 'tis only a rise of ground a little more elevated than that of Bellevue; below and above are very fine plains, as can be seen on my map."

On the transfer of power to the English the Senecas lost the carrying business entirely, and this was part of the account they paid with bullet and tomahawk at the Devil's Hole. "The Tsinusio Indians [Senecas of Chenussio]," wrote Colonel Claus, "had their privilege of the Niagara portage and other advantages taken from them, and having for many years entirely depended upon that for their support, they soon were reduced to a naked and starving condition, not having been accustomed to hunting from that time, besides their country being scarce of game."

Sir William Johnson, in reporting to the Lords of Trade his treaty of 1764, wrote as follows: "The cession made by the Senecas is very considerable, and will, I hope, put a stop to all future disputes about the carrying place; in fact, they have been great losers by us concerning it, as they were the only carriers made use of by the French traders; but since our possessing Niagara, carriages were made use of at a much higher rate, and even a monopoly attempted there, but for my remonstrance against it." Writing to the Earl of Halifax in regard to the cession by the Senecas the Baronet said: "The carrying place of Niagara is comprehended therein, and there are at present several little posts erected for its better security; * * * it may turn to very great use to all the posts on the communication, which is the most important of any I am acquainted with."

A few months later Colonel Bradstreet recommended that the government assume the portage. "The post of Niagara," he says, "is of great importance, and will always be an expense to the government. The principal part of the trade, if the transportation is carried on in vessels, will pass that way, and from its proximity to the Jeneseo Indians, a part of the Six Nations and the greatest savage enemies we have, it will be difficult, if not impractible, for some time to come, for private persons to keep up boats and carriages so well but that the trade will meet with delays; it would therefore be more safe and permanent in the hands of government, who only can make transportation certain, and by the traders paying a reasonable price for the carriage of their goods, etc., theer will be no stop, and the public service carried on there without expense."

After Fort Niagara had been taken and Fort Schlosser built by the British, Sir William Johnson, in the name of the government, contracted with John Stedman to reconstruct the road over the portage and to transport military supplies. The line of the road as improved by Stedman (in 1763) probably varied but little from that which had been followed all through the period of French occupancy, at least most of the way below the falls. It commenced, says Marshall, " at the Lewiston landing, and followed the river until it reached the small depression just north of the present Suspension Bridge. Diverging from this it intersected the river a short distance above the Stedman house, and followed its bank for about forty rods to the fort above. Midway between the house and fort were a dock, a warehouse and a group of square-timbered, whitewashed log cabins, used by the teamsters, boatmen and engagees connected with the portage. About half a mile below the Stedman house, the head of the present hydraulic canal, was the old French landing, where goods were transhipped when only canoes were used, and where the Portage road terminated before Fort Schlosser was built. All along the road between the fort and Lewiston block-houses were erected about a mile apart, to protect the teams from disasters such as had occurred at the Devil's Hole. The remains of some of these were quite recently in existence."

In his interesting little work on Niagara, published in 1872, Mr. George W. Holley speaks of Lewiston as follows :

"This was the commencement of the portage to the river above the falls, which passed over nearly the same route as the present road to Lewiston, and what is still called the Portage road. Here, too, the first railway in the United States was constructed. True, it was built of wood, and was called a tramway ; but a car was run upon it to transport goods up and down the mountain. The motion of the car was regulated with a windlass, and it was supported on runners instead of wheels. This was a very good arrangement for getting freight down the hill, but not so good for getting it up. But the wages of labor were low in every sense ; since many of the Indians, demoralized by the use of those two most pestilent drugs rum and tobacco, would do a day's work for a pint of the former and a plug of the latter." Captain James Van Cleve informs us that " the line of stone piers upon which the old tramway up the 'three mountains' at Lewiston was built, and by many thought to have been originated by La Salle, and afterward improved upon not only by the French but by the English during the following one hundred years (from 1680 to 1780), were nearly all undisturbed up to the year 1825."

In connection with their total withdrawal from the territory of New York in 1796, the British authorities transferred their portage to the Canadian side ; and Stedman, who had been for thirty-five years connected with it, moved over the river. An English gentleman named Maude, who visited this region in 1800, speaks thus of the new carrying place : " The Niagara is not navigable higher than Queenston ; consequently there is a portage from that place to Chippewa, which employs numerous teams, chiefly oxen, each cart being drawn by two yoke of oxen or two horses. I passed great numbers on the road, taking up bales and boxes and bringing down packs of peltry. * * * Queenston contains from twenty to thirty houses, whose fronts are east and west—the worst possible aspect, but which has been regulated by the course of the river."

Before roads from the east were opened through to Lake Erie, transportation and emigrant travel from the eastern part of the State and New England largely followed a water route, consisting of the Mohawk river, Wood creek, Oneida lake and river, Oswego river, Lake Ontario and Niagara river. The first through turnpike drew off traffic from this roundabout water route, which in any case must have been entirely superseded by the canals.

In 1801 the United States government directed General Moses Porter, then in command at Fort Niagara, to employ his troops in opening a road to connect that fort with one which it was then intended to build on the high bluff at Black Rock. This road was opened in 1802 from the top of the mountain, at Lewiston, through the town of Niagara, by a nearly direct course to Tonawanda, and thence onward two or three miles on a straight line, so far as to cut and burn the timber on a strip six rods in width ; but few bridges were built, two of them over Cayuga and Tonawanda creeks, and little other work was done to render it passable for teams. At this juncture an unfortunate misunderstanding arose between the government authorities and those of the State, which resulted in a discontinuance of the work. This left the road in an unfinished condition for a number of years, to the serious disadvantage of both parties to the contract, as was afterward admitted. In 1809 the State appropriated $1,500 toward the completion of the work, to be paid by persons who had bought lands in the "mile strip" along the Niagara and were in arrears for the same. With this sum the road was made passable from Black Rock to the falls. The State originally gave the land, while the general government undertook to construct the road ; and the name by which it is known to the present time—"Military road"—is said to have been given it because it was originally opened by the soldiers. In time it became overgrown by bushes and saplings except in places where it was kept clear by the early settlers for local travel. It was also very wet and boggy, and there was an almost impassable swamp extending for a mile along the road, beginning a little south of the farm of Jonas Young in Niagara, which was regarded as the worst on the entire route. About the year 1820 the county authorities began the work of rendering this road available to the traveling public ; but it was not in good condition until 1832 or 1833.

The Ridge road is of course one of the most interesting in the county, historically considered, as well as with reference to the singular natural formation from which it takes its name. Augustus Porter is said to have learned of the ridge from the Indians, and had the line of a road traced along it in 1798. Mr. Orsamus Turner, in his

History of the Holland Purchase, says that "the Ridge road, through all the eastern portion of Niagara, was discovered in 1805. Some of the new settlers in Slaton's settlement in 1805 were hunting cattle, and observed that there was continuous elevated ground and changed their location, settling upon it east of Hartland Corners. It was not, however, known in its full extent throughout that region until some years after."

Mrs. Warren, a pioneer settler in Cambria, contributed to the above-named work a statement of which the following is a part:

"In 1808 the Ridge road was laid out by General Rhea, Elias Ransom and Charles Harford. I remember well the arrival of the surveyors; their delight at finding a bed to sleep in, and something to eat that was cooked by a female. Previous to this there had been nothing but an Indian path through the low grounds west of Wright's Corners."

Settlements began on the ridge west of Warren's before the Holland Company cut out the old trail from Batavia into a passable road; and the ridge was used for transportation with teams between Warren's and Lewiston sooner than in any other part. East of this section there was nothing that could be called a road before 1803. John Dunn, who located on the ridge at the east line of the county in that year, had to cut his way through the woods from the Genesee river. As late as 1809 the way to his place was encumbered with logs and brush.

After other parts of the ridge had been made passable the swamp which extended some two miles between Warren's and Wright's Corners was an obstacle. In the spring of 1813 General Dearborn, representing the United States, contracted with Isaac B. Taylor to build for $2,900 a log causeway through the low ground. The work was done that season, but was early and often undone. The logs were frequently afloat in the spring and autumn, and annual repairs were made by town appropriations and subscriptions by stage proprietors until 1823, when the franchise for a turnpike was granted to David Maxwell, who subsequently sold it to the town of Newfane.

The operation of laying out the Ridge road in 1808, spoken of by Mrs. Warren, seems to have been merely a survey, and not to have affected the condition of the road for travel. The State commissioners named by her ran their lines without regard to those bounding the Holland Purchase lots, and the latter were made to conform to the course of the road, for which the Holland Company gave the land. In 1814 a State appropriation of $5,000 was expended on parts of the road west of Rochester, greatly to its improvement. It was regularly laid out under State authority in 1815 by Philetus Swift and Caleb Hopkins, and was resurveyed west of Rochester in 1852. In 1815 mail was carried on horseback twice a week between Canandaigua and Lewiston, following the Ridge road through Niagara county; the next year three times a week in two-horse wagons.

At the time of laying out the Ridge road there was no other entering the county from the east except the former Indian trail from Batavia; by the Ridge road most of the pioneers entered the county, and along or near it they first settled, except those who located at an equally early day upon the Niagara border.

Perhaps no natural feature of northwestern New York is better known or better worthy of note than the singular formation on which the Ridge road runs. De Witt Clinton spoke of it as follows:

"From the Genesee near Rochester to Lewiston on the Niagara there is a remarkable ridge or elevation of land running almost the whole distance, which is seventy-eight miles, and in a direction from east to west. Its general altitude above the neighboring land is thirty feet, and its width varies considerably; in some places it is not more than forty yards. Its elevation above the level of Lake Ontario is perhaps one hundred and sixty feet, to which it descends with a gradual slope; and its distance from that water is between six and ten miles. This remarkable strip of land would appear as if intended by nature for the purpose of an easy communication. It is, in fact, a stupendous natural turnpike, descending gently on each side and covered with gravel, and but little labor is requisite to make it the best road in the United States. * * * The gravel with which it is covered was deposited there by the waters, and the stones everywhere indicate by their shape the abrasion and agitation produced by that element."

Geologists have generally concluded that this wonderful ridge was a mammoth bar on the bed of Lake Ontario when the lake rolled over the country south to the brow of the so-called mountain ridge.

Travel between Lewiston and Fort Niagara of course began in the earliest days of French occupation, and the road between those points must be considered one of the oldest in the country. It has been the route of many military movements, which are recorded in their appropriate places in this work.

In the autumn of 1811, as the pioneer Reuben Wilson informed Mr. Orsamus Turner, "there was a road opened from Fort Niagara to Somerset; it was generally along the lake shore, though deviating at the streams; at its termination a foot path continued on to Johnson's Creek, on the Ridge road."

CHAPTER XV.

THE TITLE TO THE SOIL OF WESTERN NEW YORK—PHELPS AND GORHAM'S PURCHASE—MORRIS'S RESERVE.

IN 1684 the Five Nations, alarmed by the prospect of a French invasion of their territory, appealed to the English authorities through a council at Albany for aid, offering to put their country under the protection of the King of Great Britain. In this instance they showed the same characteristic indifference to equivalents that they manifested in the same place twenty-five years before, when they complained with indignant surprise that the Dutch, who professed to be their brothers, would only furnish them with ammunition so long as they had beavers to sell. They now expected to obtain support, but did not realize that they had parted with any of their independence, being ignorant of the effect of a protectorate. The colonial officials, however, took advantage of the opportunity to assert a claim to English sovereignty over the Iroquois territory, having the arms of the Duke of York planted even in the remotest villages of the Senecas. The French, as we have seen, always ignored this claim; and, as already related, took formal possession of western New York in 1687.

The English, however, obtained new admissions on the part of the Iroquois, as is shown by a deed reciting that "whereas the sachems of the Five Nations did on the 19th day of July, one thousand, seven hundred and one, in a conference held at Albany between John Nanfan, Esq., late lieutenant-governor of the province of New York, give and render up all their land where the beaver hunting is, which they won with the sword then eighty years ago, to Coorachkoo, our great King, praying that he might be their protector and defender," the signers ratified that agreement; "and we do also, of our own accord, free and voluntary will, give, render, submit and grant * * * unto our said sovereign lord King George, his heirs and successors for ever" the land for sixty miles inland from the southern shore of Lake Ontario, and from the southern shore of Lake Erie as far as Cleveland, "for our use, our heirs and successors." This document is dated September 14, 1726, and signed by seven Seneca, Cayuga and Onondaga sachems, who, it will be noticed, thought they were acting solely for their own benefit. It was on this deed that the Albany merchants afterward based their protest against permitting settlements to be made along the Niagara.

The next negotiation in regard to the ownership of the soil of this part of the State was Sir William Johnson's treaty with the Senecas in 1764, by which they gave up all right to the islands in the Niagara and the land adjoining the river for four miles inland, all of which went directly or indirectly to the crown.

The encroachment of the whites upon the territory of the Iroquois gave the latter great uneasiness, to allay which a very numerously attended council was held with them at Fort Stanwix (Rome) in 1768, to agree on a line beyond which settlements should not be permitted. The line decided upon in the State of New York "ran along the eastern border of Broome and Chenango counties, and thence northwestward to a point seven miles west of Rome."

The close of the Revolution left the hostile Iroquois unprovided for by their British employers and at the mercy of the United States. Couqueres after waging a long, bloody and destructive warfare against the patriots of New York, they had forfeited their territory and would have had little cause of complaint had they been dispossessed. The government, however, thought it wise to deal not only justly, but generously with them; and in a council held on the site of Rome in 1784, recognized their continued ownership of the land between the line agreed on at the same place sixteen years before, and one beginning at Lake Ontario four miles east of the Niagara river, running southward parallel with the river to Buffalo creek, thence still southward to the Pennsylvania line and following that to the Ohio river. All of New York west of this second line seems also to have been subsequently conceded to the Indians except a mile strip along the Niagara.

Every reader of English colonial history knows how ignorantly or carelessly grants of American territory were made by the crown to individuals and companies, the same tracts being in some instances given at different times to different parties, laying the foundation of conflicting claims. Thus the province of New York, when granted to the Duke of York in 1664, covered part of Massachusetts as defined by the charter given to the Plymouth Company in 1620. The territory of both provinces under their charters also extended indefinitely westward; but New York in 1781 and Massachusetts four years later relinquished to the United States their claims beyond the present western boundary of this State, and Massachusetts contented herself with claiming that portion of New York west of the meridian which now forms the eastern line of Ontario and Steuben counties—some 19,000 square miles. New York of course also asserted jurisdiction and ownership of this vast tract.

The dispute was compromised by a convention of commissioners from the two States, held at Hartford in December, 1786. It was agreed that the sovereignty of the disputed region should remain with New York, and the ownership with Massachusetts, subject to the Indian proprietorship, which had been recognized by the general government. "That is to say, the Indians could hold the land as long as they pleased, but were only allowed to sell to the State of Massachusetts or her assigns." The meridian bounding the Massachusetts claim on the east was called the "pre-emption line," because it was decided to allow that State the right of pre-emption, or first purchase, of the land west of it. There was one exception: New York retained the ownership as well as the sovereignty of a strip a mile wide along the Niagara river.

In 1788 the State of Massachusetts sold to Oliver Phelps and Nathaniel Gorham, two of its citizens, and to others for whom they acted, its pre-emption right to western New York for $1,000,000, to be paid in three annual installments, in certain securities of the State which were then worth about one-fifth of their face. The next thing with these gentlemen was to complete the title by buying the Indian interest. For this purpose Phelps held a council with the Iroquois at Buffalo early in July, 1788, and bought, for $5,000 down and a perpetual annuity of $500, about 2,600,000 acres, bounded on the east by the pre-emption line. Part of the western boundary was a meridian from Pennsylvania to the junction of Canaseraga creek with the Genesee river. Thence northward the line followed the course of the Genesee "to a point two miles north of Cannawagus village; thence running due west twelve miles; thence running northwardly so as to be twelve miles distant from the western bounds of said river, to the shores of Lake Ontario." The tract thus defined constituted the famous "Phelps and Gorham's Purchase."

The Indians were reluctant to sell any land west of the Genesee, and it is said that to induce them to do so Phelps had recourse to a fraudulent device: He told them that he needed a site on the west bank at the falls for a mill, which would be very useful to them; and when they assented, and asked how much he would need, he named the twelve-mile strip above indicated—some 200,000 acres.

In securing their vast estate Phelps, Gorham and company encountered the opposition of another set of land sharks who also had a covetous eye upon this magnificent domain. These were the capitalists forming the New York and Genesee Land Company, engineered by one John Livingston; and its branch the Niagara-Genesee Company, headed by Colonel John Butler, and consisting almost entirely of Canadians. As we have seen, the Indians were barred from selling their lands except to Massachusetts or her assigns. Butler, Livingston and their associates proposed to get possession of them by a long lease; hence they are spoken of as the "lessee companies." Chiefly through the influence of Butler they obtained from part of the Iroquois chiefs and sachems a nine-hundred-and-ninety-nine-years' lease of most of their territory for $20,000 and an annual rent of $2,000. Their scheme fell through, the Legislatures of New York and Massachusetts declaring a lease of that length equivalent to a purchase, and as such null and void. Butler, however, profited by the purchase of Phelps and Gorham. He was one of three to whom the Indians referred the question of the price they should charge those gentlemen, and is said to have had 20,000 acres placed at his disposal by the purchasers in consideration of the advice he gave the confiding red men. The "lessees" continued their intrigues until they succeeded, in 1793, in getting from the Legislature a grant of one hundred square miles east of the pre-emption line, instead of obtaining twenty thousand miles and founding a new State, as there is reason to suppose the Niagara-Genesee Company, at least, intended, with the co-operation of the Senecas, whom Butler and other Canadian officials were always embittering against the people of New York.

Before Phelps and Gorham had half paid for the entire pre-emption right they had bought of Massachusetts, the securities of that State, in consequence of the adoption of the Federal Constitution, had risen nearly to par; and finding that they should be unable to fulfill their contract they induced the State to resume its right to the portion of its original New York claim which they had not yet bought of the Indians, and release them from their contract as to that part, leaving on their hands the tract since called Phelps and Gorham's Purchase and bounded as above described. This agreement was reached on the 10th of March, 1791.

Two days later Robert Morris, the illustrious financier whose services were of such vital importance to the nation during the Revolution, contracted with Massachusetts for the pre-emption right to all of New York west of Phelps and Gorham's Purchase. About this time he also bought 1,264,000 acres of Phelps and Gorham (paying £30,000 in New York currency), which he soon sold to three English gentlemen, Sir William Pultney, John Hornby and Patrick Colquhoun, for £35,000 sterling. It was only after much difficulty and delay that Mr. Morris completed his title to the tract of which he had purchased the pre-emption right from Massachusetts. It was necessary to buy out the interest of the Indians, and this was accomplished by a council at Geneseo in September, 1797, when he was enabled to purchase all of the State west of Phelps and Gorham's Purchase, except that the Indians retained eleven reservations, amounting to about three hundred and thirty-eight square miles, including the Tuscarora reservation three miles east of Lewiston, then one mile square ; and the Tonawanda reservation, part of which formed the extreme southeast corner of Niagara county.

It was by his speeches in the councils affecting the title to the lands of western New York that the Seneca chief Red Jacket came into prominence. He figures in history as a crafty demagogue, vain, ambitious and dishonest ; a coward in war and a sot in peace ; chiefly noted for his harangues against parting with the lands of the Seneca nation, and the bitterness he usually manifested against the power by whose grace alone the nation had any lands after the Revolution.

The conveyance from Massachusetts to Mr. Morris was made May 11th, 1791, by five deeds. The first covered the land between Phelps and Gorham's Purchase and a line beginning twelve miles west of theirs on the Pennsylvania border and running due north to Lake Ontario. The next three embraced as many sixteen-mile strips crossing the State north and south, and the fifth what remained to the westward of these.

The tract covered by the first mentioned deed was what has been called "Morris's Reserve," from the fact that he retained the disposition of this section in his own hands when he subsequently sold all west of it. He sold the reserve in large tracts, though small as compared with his purchases. To Leroy, Bayard and McEvers he sold the triangle bounded by Lake Ontario, the line of Phelps's "mill seat," and a line from the southwestern end of the latter due north to the lake—about 87,000 acres. He next sold to Watson, Cragie and Greenleaf 100,000 acres in a block six miles wide and nearly twenty-nine miles long, bounded on the east by the west line of the above-mentioned triangle and the same line continued southward. This property was afterward purchased by the State of Connecticut and Sir William Pultney, and is usually spoken of as the Connecticut tract. When sold by Mr. Morris it was supposed to lie wholly within the Morris Reserve ; but on running from the south the "east transit line," a meridian which bounded the reserve on the west, the Connecticut tract was found to extend over the line one hundred and sixty-six chains and thirty links. As the east transit was meant to be the dividing line between the Connecticut tract and the Holland Purchase (which was sold by Mr. Morris at a later date and had therefore an inferior claim for remaining unchanged), the transit line was on reaching the Connecticut tract shifted westward to the distance above named, and so carried forward to the lake. It runs between the eastern and middle tiers and middle of towns in Orleans county.

This transit line was so called because it was run with a transit instrument in connection with astronomical observations, the variation of the magnetic needle disqualifying the surveyor's compass for running a meridian line. It is called the "east" transit to distinguish it from a similarly surveyed meridian passing through Lockport, which is called the "west" transit. The laying down of this line was a slow and laborious operation. It involved nothing less than felling a strip of timber three or four rods wide most of the way across the State to give unobstructed range to the miniature telescope of the transit. This required, beside three surveyors, a considerable force of axemen. On most of the line all hands camped where night overtook them in the unbroken wilderness. All the summer and autumn of 1798 was consumed in running the first eighty miles of the transit meridian, there being about thirteen miles remaining undone on the 22nd of November.

The surveyor in charge of this work was Joseph Ellicott. He was born in Bucks county, Pennsylvania, in 1756. In 1770 the family removed to Maryland and founded Ellicott's Mills on the Patapsco river. Joseph was taught surveying by his brother Andrew, who was afterward surveyor-general of the United States and professor of mathematics at West Point. He assisted the latter in laying out the city of Washington, and in 1791 surveyed the boundary line between the State of Georgia and the Creek Indian lands. The remaining years of his business career were chiefly spent in the service of the Holland Land Company, so called. His intimate connection, in this capacity, with the history of Western New York is thus summed up by the historian of the Holland Purchase:

"No man has ever, perhaps, been so closely identified with the history of any region as he is with the history of the Holland Purchase. He was not only the land agent, superintending from the start surveys and settlement, exercising locally a one-man power and influence; but for a long period he was far more than this. In all the early years of settlement, especially in all things having reference to the organization of towns, counties, erection of public buildings, the laying out of roads, the establishment of post-offices—in all that related to the convenience and prosperity of the region over which his agency extended—he occupied a prominent position, a close identity, that few if any patrons of new settlements have ever attained."

CHAPTER XVI.

THE HOLLAND PURCHASE AND PURCHASERS—SURVEYS, SALES AND FIRST SETTLEMENTS.

DECEMBER 24th, 1792, Robert Morris deeded to Herman Leroy and John Linklaen one and a half million acres of his lands west of the east transit line. On the 27th of the following February he gave a deed for a million of acres to these gentlemen and Gerrit Boon. July 20th, 1793, he conveyed to the same three parties eight hundred thousand acres; and on the same day to Herman Leroy, William Bayard and Matthew Clarkson three hundred thousand acres. These gentlemen purchased this vast tract as trustees for a number of rich merchants of Amsterdam, Holland, who have been commonly spoken of as the Holland Company and the Holland Land Company, though there was no corporation with either of those titles. The immense estate acquired by them, being all of New York west of the east transit line, except the Indian reservations and the State mile strip along the Niagara, constituted the Holland Purchase.

The purchasers bought through the above-named citizens of New York because they themselves, as foreigners, could not at the time legally hold real property in the State. The Legislature of 1798, however, changed this regulation, and the trustees thereupon turned over the property to the actual owners; all but three hundred thousand acres being transferred to Wilhem Willink, Nicholas Van Staphorst, Pieter Van Eeghen, Hendrick Vallenhoven and Rutger Jan Schimmelpenninck. The remainder went to Wilhem Willink, Jan Willink, Wilhem Willink, jr., and Jan Willink, jr. Two years after Jan Gabriel Van Staphorst, Roelif Van Staphorst, jr., Cornelius Vallenhoven and Hendrick Seye also acquired an interest in the tract.

When the Indian title to the Holland Purchase had been extinguished by Mr. Morris, in 1797, measures were immediately taken for the survey of the tract, so that it might be put in market, sold and settled. Operations were directed from Philadelphia by Theophilus Cazenove, who was the first general agent of the Hollanders. He appointed Joseph Ellicott chief surveyor, and in the autumn of 1797 he and Augustus Porter, Mr. Morris's surveyor, as a step toward ascertaining the actual area of the purchase, made a tour of its lake and river front. The running of the east transit line in the next year by Mr. Ellicott, as already related, was another step in the survey of the Holland Purchase; and at the same time "eleven other surveyors, each with his corps of axemen, chainmen, etc., went to work at different points, running the lines of ranges, townships and reservations. All through the Purchase the deer were startled from their hiding-places, the wolves were driven growling from their lairs by bands of men with compasses and theodolites, chains and flags, while the red occupants looked sullenly on at the rapid parceling out of their broad and fair domain."

The division of the land began on the plan which had been followed in Phelps and Gorham's purchase, namely, the laying off of six-mile strips reaching from Pennsylvania to Lake Ontario, called ranges, and numbered from east to west; and dividing them by east and west lines into regular townships, numbered from south to north. Each township was to be sub-divided into sixteen mile-and-a-half squares, called sections, and each of these into twelve lots, three-fourths of a mile by one-fourth, containing one hundred and twenty acres apiece. After twenty-four townships had been surveyed on this plan the sub-division was judged unnecessarily minute, and was so much so as to be often ill adapted to the surface of the ground; thereafter the mile-and-a-half squares composing a township were each divided into four three-quarter-mile squares, of three hundred and sixty acres apiece, which were sold off in quantities to suit purchasers, quite commonly going off in one-hundred-and-twenty-acre lots, as originally planned.

The mile strip along the Niagara river belonging to the State of New York was surveyed in the autumn of 1798 by Seth Pease, at the expense of the Hollanders.

The theoretically regular division of the Holland Purchase into square townships was of course in some cases broken in upon by bodies and streams of water, and was also interfered with by the Indian reservations. Town boundaries in the region we are considering have not generally been made to conform to range and township lines, but the towns are rectangular except where defined by natural boundaries, and most of the roads in Niagara and Orleans counties, running to the cardinal points of the compass, also show traces of the surveying system of the Holland proprietors.

The price at first charged by them for their lands was $2.75 per acre, one-tenth to be paid down. The proprietors found it very difficult to obtain this ten per cent. advance payment. It was extremely desirable to secure settlers for the tract, for every pioneer who located made the country more attractive to others who might be contemplating a similar movement. Lands could be had very cheap in parts of the State nearer the centers of population, and also in Ohio; while farms in Canada were offered by the British government at sixpence per acre. The competition among owners of large tracts was thus so strong that the proprietors of the Holland Purchase often waived all advance payment by actual settlers. Even so their lands at first went off but slowly. The rate of sales, however, constantly increased. In 1801 there were 40; in 1802, 56; in 1803, 230; in 1804, 300; in 1805, 415; in 1806, 524; in 1807, 607; in 1808, 612; in 1809, 1160.

It is not our purpose to give here a detailed account of the settlement of this corner of the State. The pioneer experiences of the settlers of different towns belong to the annals of those towns; but a few remarks will give such a glimpse of the progress of settlement as may properly be taken at this point. A tourist who visited western New York in 1792 gives us the following:

"Many times did I break out in an enthusiastic frenzy, anticipating the probable situation of this wilderness twenty years hence. All that reason can ask may be obtained by the industrious hand; the only danger to be feared is that luxuries will flow too cheap. After I had reached the Genesee river curiosity led me on to Niagara, ninety miles—not one house or white man the whole way. The only direction I had was an Indian path, which sometimes was doubtful. The first day I rode fifty miles, through swarms of mosquitos, gnats, etc., beyond all description. At eight o'clock in the evening I reached an Indian town called Tonnoraunto; it contains many hundreds of the savages, who live in very tolerable houses, which they make of timber and cover with bark. By signs I made them understand me, and for a little money they cut me limbs and bushes sufficient to erect a booth, under which I slept very quietly on the grass. The next day I pursued my journey, nine miles of which lay through a very deep swamp; with some difficulty I got through, and about sundown arrived at the fort of Niagara."

One of the pioneers of Lewiston furnished Mr. Orsamus Turner some reminiscences of his entrance into this region in 1793. He says:

"We coasted up Lake Ontario, going on shore and camping nights. We were seventeen days making the journey from Geneva to Queenston. The only person we saw on the route from Oswego to Niagara [the party went from Geneva to Lake Ontario by the Seneca and Oswego rivers] was William Hencher, at the mouth of Genesee river. We made a short halt at Fort Niagara, reporting ourselves to the commanding officer. He gave us a specimen of British civility during the hold-over period after the Revolution. It was after a protracted dinner sitting, I should think. He asked me where I was going. I replied, 'To Chippewa.' 'Go along and be d—d to you,' was his laconic verbal passport. There was then outside of the garrison, under its walls, upon the flats, two houses; no tenement at Youngstown."

In 1799 a gentleman familiar with western New York described the country in a series of letters. From one of them we take the following;

"Should curiosity induce you to visit the falls of Niagara, you will proceed from Geneva, by the State road, to the Genesee river, which you will cross at New Hartford, west of which you will find the country settled for about twelve miles, but after that, for sixty-five miles, to Niagara river, the country still remains a wilderness. This road was used so much last year by people on business, or by those whom curiosity had led to visit the falls of Niagara, that a station was fixed at the Big Plains to shelter travelers. At this place there are two roads that lead to Niagara river; the south road goes by Buffalo creek, the other by Tonawanda village to Queenston landing [the Batavia and Lewiston trail, heretofore mentioned]. The road by Buffalo creek is most used, both because it is better and because it commands a view of Lake Erie; and the road from this to the falls is along the banks of Niagara river, a very interesting ride."

Speaking of the Niagara or Lewiston trail, Mr. Turner says: "Add to this the two or three log and one framed hut at Buffalo, and two or three tenements at Lewiston, and the reader will have a pretty good idea of all in the way of improvement that had transpired upon the Holland Purchase before the close of 1799; and at the close of the century there was but little more than the addition of a few families along the Buffalo road, and the prosecution of surveys."

Surveying was therefore all that had thus far been done toward civilizing Orleans county. It was an unbroken wilderness, except for the impression that the surveyors' axemen had made upon it, and a multitude of wild beasts were its only inhabitants. In 1803, however, Mr. Ellicott, vainly hoping that the mouth of Oak Orchard creek would prove a practicable harbor, and the port of the northwestern part of the Purchase, had a village laid out there, which was to be called Manilla. In the spring of that year James Walsworth settled at the place. He was the pioneer settler of Orleans county, and the first on the lake shore between Braddock's Bay and Fort Niagara. His nearest neighbor to the westward lived at the Cold Springs, just east of Lockport, and in 1805 he himself removed inland, settling on the Lockport and Batavia road, where he cleared a farm on the border of the Tonawanda swamp, and kept a well known tavern. Says Mr. Turner:

"Walsworth, and the few others that located at Oak Orchard, were all the settlers in Orleans before 1809 except Whitfield Rathbun, who was the pioneer upon all that part of the Ridge road in Orleans county embraced in the Holland Purchase. It will be noticed, by tabular list of settlers, that settlement had just begun at the mouth of Eighteen-mile creek, in Niagara, and at Johnson's creek, in Orleans, in 1806. Burgoyne Kemp settled at the Eighteen-mile creek in 1808. There was then settled there William Chambers and ———— Colton, and there was one family at Johnson's creek, on the lake. At that period there was no settler between lake and ridge in Niagara or Orleans."

An interesting exhibit of the state of business at this period in western New York is afforded in "a description of the Genesee country," by Robert Munroe. From it we extract the following:

"Trade is yet in its infancy, and has much increased within a few years. Grain is sent in considerable quantities from Seneca lake and the Conhocton, Canisteo, Canawisque and Tioga rivers to markets on Susquehanna river, and flour, potash and other produce to Albany; and a considerable quantity of grain has for some years past been exported by sleighs in winter to the west of Albany. Whisky is distilled in considerable quantities, and mostly consumed in the country, and is also exported to Canada and to Susquehanna. The produce of the country is received by storekeepers in payment for goods, and, with horses and cattle, is paid for land. Several thousand bushels of grain have been purchased in the winter beginning this year, 1804, for money at Newtown and at the mills near Cayuga lake. Hemp is raised on Genesee river and carried to Albany. Droves of cattle and horses are sent to different markets and a considerable number of cattle and other provisions are used at the markets of Canadarqua [Canandaigua] and Geneva, at Niagara, and by settlers emigrating into the country. Cattle commonly sell for money at a good price, and as this country is very favorable for raising them they will probably become the principal article for market; many being of opinion that the raising of stock is more profitable as well as easier than any mode of farming. The following is a list of prices of articles and the rate of wages since January 1801:

"Wheat, from 62 cents to $1 a bushel; corn, from 37 to 50 cents a bushel; rye, from 50 cents to 62 cents a bushel; hay, from $6 to $12 a ton; butter and cheese, from 10 to 16 cents a pound; a yoke of oxen, $50 to $80; milk cows, from $16 to $25; cattle for driving, $3 to $4 a hundred pounds; a pair of good working horses, $100 to $125; sheep, from $2 to $4; pork, fresh killed in winter, $4 to $6 a hundred, and salted in spring, $8 to $10; whisky, from 50 to 75 cents a gallon; salt, $1 a bushel weighing 56 pounds; field ashes, 4 to 9 cents a bushel; —600 bushels may be manufactured into a ton of pot or pearl ash, which has been sold at market at $125 to $150, and some persons, by saving their ashes or by manufacturing them, have nearly cleared the cost of improving land; the wages of a laborer, $10 to $15 a month and board; a suit of clothes made at $4 to $5; a pair of shoes, $1.75 to $2.50. Store goods are sold at very moderate prices, the expense of carriage from Albany to New York being about $2 a hundred weight."

The progress of settlement in Niagara county during the first decade of this century is thus summed up by Mr. Turner:

"The territory now comprising the county of Niagara, it will be seen by some sketches already given was mostly a wilderness in the beginning of 1807; the few settlers in it were principally upon the Ridge road, on the Lewiston road, in Slaton's settlement and on and near the Niagara river. During the five years preceding the war of 1812, settlers broke into the woods all along upon the fine grade of land under the mountain ridge, along on the lake shore, upon the Eighteen-mile creek and in a few other localities." He also informs us that "the earliest prominent settlers west of Oak Orchard on the ridge in Orleans were Ezra D. Barnes, Israel Douglass (the latter was the first magistrate north of Batavia), Seymour B. Murdock and sons and Eli Moore. The milling of the first settlers was obtained at Niagara Falls and the Genesee river."

Up to 1821 only about half of the Holland Purchase had been sold. In that year the proprietors offered the remainder "for a consideration which would cover the original amount of purchase money and interest of four per cent." The next year they offered to sell out at four shillings per acre. "The final result," says Turner, "was probably better than would be inferred from these offers."

A frequent effect of the long credit given to settlers

was to make them feel aggrieved when pay day came; and the longer they had been in arrears with their interest the more thoroughly were they persuaded that it was an outrage to ask them to square up their accounts. They vainly called the company's title in question, and asked the interference of the Legislature in their behalf. The financial depression of 1837 rendered payments harder to make, and the harder it was to make them the less the debtors owed them, according to the idea that seems to have prevailed among them. If they could not shake the title of the Hollanders, they could terrorize the land agents and hold agrarian meetings to denounce their debt-paying neighbors as "Judases;" and they could and in some cases did stave off payment for their lands until they gained a title to them by continuance of "adverse possession." In most cases, however, this brilliant expedient was not successfully resorted to, and the Holland Company's customers for the most part finally paid for their farms.

In 1810 the Dutch proprietors sold the pre-emption right to the Indian reservations to David A. Ogden and others constituting the Ogden Company, for fifty cents per acre, the area being estimated at 196,000 acres. These gentlemen found the Senecas reluctant to dispose of the remnant of their lands; but by several councils the company at length extinguished the Indian title to nearly all of the reservations. The negotiations did not affect the territory of Niagara county to any extent.

In a council at Buffalo, September 12th, 1815, the Senecas ceded to the State of New York, for $1,000 and a perpetual annuity of $500, all the islands in the Niagara river not within the British line.

CHAPTER XVII.

PIONEER EXPERIENCES—EMIGRATING, BUILDING AND CLEARING—FRONTIER WORK AND PLAY.

TEDIOUSLY and lumberingly, through woods, across rivers, along roads that have been corduroyed and roads that sadly need to be corduroyed, over dry places and through swamps, over high hills and through tortuous mountain passes, a heavy wagon has been rolling and slipping and sliding—sometimes floating, where the fording places were not good—for many days. Did you ever see one of those heavy old Dutch wagons, with wheels that have spokes like small saplings and felloes like those in the wheels of a modern stone truck; that have poles bent across, bow-fashion, from side to side of the stout box, and covered over with a canopy of canvass to keep out the wind, the storm and the sweltering sunshine? Such is the wagon of which we write—a wagon drawn by a span of sorrily jaded horses that have seen nothing resembling the inside of a comfortable stable for weeks, and in which ride a woman and two or three small children, the husband and father, perchance, trudging by the side of the vehicle, sinking at times knee deep into the mud or staggering over a fallen log or large stone, in his desire to guide the team and at the same time lighten their burden by walking.

He is a strong, well-built six-footer, with a heart to brave every danger, the kind of man for a pioneer, leaving behind him the comforts and pleasures of civilized life, and going to endure hardships, reverses, struggles, trials, and perhaps to die in a wild country, leaving wife and children to wrest their sustenance from land uncultivated and unpaid-for, or to make their way back to civilization as best they may. But he hesitates not. For himself he cares nothing; but his wife and children? Is he doing right in isolating her from home and kindred and all of the associations of her childhood and her girlhood? Is he doing right in taking their children to the far away new country, to rear them on the outskirts of civilization, where education had not yet one rude temple and christianity no voice to proclaim its truth?

These questions he has discussed with his wife over and over again. They have been settled before leaving their former home; but somehow they will not stay settled. They have forced themselves upon his attention many times during the slow and tedious journey; but it is too late, now, to reason about them; and resolutely he sets his face toward the west—for it has, from the earliest days, been west that the sturdy pioneer has bent his steps—ever west, and further west! There is no complaint from the patient woman in the wagon.

It is nightfall—the sun sunk below the tree-tops an hour ago, and the dim shadows of approaching darkness are creeping over the forest, while afar off can be heard the cries of the owl and the whippowil, and over in the swamp at the left bull-frogs are croaking dismally and "peepers" are singing merrily. It is nightfall, and one of the children is asleep on a pile of stuff in the wagon and the baby is asleep in the mother's arms. Her eight year old boy sits beside her gazing out over the horses' heads, at the shadows dropping down, one by one, over the wood. He looks tired, but hopeful, she thinks, as she watches him a moment. She knows what kind of a life is before her—she can half realize some of its trials and hardships and disappointments, but not all of them. She knows that she and her husband will never live to have many years' enjoyment of the fruits of their sacrifice and toil, but their children will—it is for these that she has consented to risk the perils of pioneer life.

A few days more, and they have reached their destination. Again it is evening. Dimly they can see that they are in the midst of a little opening in the timber, watered by a small stream that flows through it. Here they will erect their cabin on the morrow; to-night—one night more—they will sleep in the wagon. The tired horses are watered at the babbling stream and tethered where they can get their fill of the grass that grows rankly in the opening. Then a fire is made on the ground, a

hasty meal is prepared, a few minutes are passed in conversation and many more in silent thought; after that, weariness and drowsiness overcome them and they know no more till they are awakened at dead of night by the snapping and snarling of wolves prowling about the outskirts of the opening. The fire has died down and its smouldering embers can be scarcely seen. It is the fire that has kept the wolves off till now. The man raises himself on his elbow and, lifting the corner of the canvas cover of the wagon, looks out. Presently one of the animals, more bold than his fellows, emerges from the timber and comes stealthily toward the half startled horses. He is followed in a minute by another and another! The foremost is now alarmingly near one of the horses. The man reaches for his rifle. In a moment it is at his shoulder. His quick glance runs along the barrel; there is a lurid flash, a sharp report, a howl of agony—and the wolf is stretched dead on the ground, while his blood-thirsty followers are hurrying away in the gloom. This is not the first time wolves have molested them since they came into the wilderness—it is a matter for determined action but scarcely one to keep them long awake. The fire is rekindled and they sleep again, and are only awakened by the singing of the birds in the trees over head, after the sun is up in the morning.

The preparations for the erection of a log house are begun without delay. First several trees are felled, trimmed, cut up into lengths and laid on the ground in piles on the four sides of the place where the cabin is to stand. Then the work of placing them in their proper position begins. It is no easy task, for the logs are heavy; but the man and the boy both work with a will. They have slept in the wagon so long that the thought of lying down that night in their own house, even if it is unfurnished, affords an incentive to extra exertion. The work goes briskly on through the day. So many logs have been rolled up and notched together at the corners that, by nightfall, the walls of the house are done. An opening has been left at one side for a door, and a smaller one opposite for a window. It is too late and the builders are too weary to do more than this to-night; so a couple of blankets are stretched across one end of the structure to serve as a temporary roof, another is hung over the doorway, and the house is ready for its first night's occupancy.

In the morning the work is resumed. Poles are laid across the top of the walls to support the chamber floor, a ridge pole and rafters are put up and then the roof is laid on them—a roof of broad bark strips, held in place by withes fastened at the ends with slender strips of green bark. An opening is left in the chamber floor, a rude ladder is constructed and set up, affording communication with the loft; and, with the exception of the window and the door, the carpenter work on the house is done, and the family stand and look at it with a feeling of such relief as they have not felt during all their long journey. It is but a cabin of logs, a rude hut only twelve by fifteen feet square, with a hole in the roof to let out the smoke,—not such a residence as is built in these days of elegance and luxury, but it is a home! Of course no sash and glass are at hand, but the necessity which is said to be the mother of all invention gives birth to an idea at the right moment, and the pioneer is not left without resource. The window hole is not very large, and he goes to the wagon and gets an old newspaper, one that was printed far away in New England or Pennsylvania; and with some hesitation he tears it in two—for it

will be a long time, perhaps, before another newspaper comes to him—saturates it with grease and stretches it across the opening and the window is complete ; one that will not permit the inmates of the house to look out, but will let the light in. The canvas which has afforded them shelter during the journey is taken from the wagon, folded to the proper size and suspended over the aperture left for ingress and egress, and this is the door that must serve till a more substantial one can be made of planks split out of logs—a bit of extra work that may be done in any leisure hours before cold weather comes. The openings between the logs are to be "chinked," or filled with pieces of wood split out of the proper size and secured in place by the use of a thick mortar of mud, and a fire-place is to be constructed ; but these can be dispensed with until after the house is furnished and some sort of a shelter has been provided for the horses. In our engravings our readers will recognize the edifice thus completed, and note the improvement which the rolling seasons witness in the pioneer's circumstances and surroundings.

There is no trip to a furniture store, attended with the trouble of selection and the usual banter about the price, common to these later days. The house is soon furnished "without money and without price," and as well as any other house within a circuit of twenty miles or more. And this is how it is done: For chairs, three or four blocks of the proper height are sawed from the end of a log; for bedsteads, holes are bored in one of the logs at the side of the building, a foot and a half from the ground, poles about four feet long are hewn off at one end and driven into them, the other extremity being supported on blocks similar to those used for chairs, and on these are laid some small boughs, then some blankets and some quilts; the table is constructed at one side of the place in the same manner as the frame for the beds, its top being a wide, flat piece split from a large log and hewn as smooth as possible; the fire-place, which is the most primitive of all, is simply a spot on the ground under the aperture in the roof. The cooking utensils were brought in the wagon. They are a long-handled frying-pan, a cast-iron bake-kettle and one or two tin pans, one of which serves the purpose of a tea-kettle, in the absence of the black earthen "steeper" which was broken on the way. Some knives, some tinned-iron spoons, some forks, and some cups and saucers and a few plates, all of the "blue edged" variety, now nearly out of existence, comprise the table furniture.

And thus they begin housekeeping in their new home, miles distant from any other human habitation, and beyond the reach of mails and other conveniences of the densely populated districts. Here, with faith in their God and faith in themselves, they begin to live their new life—a life of progress from the most primitive elements of civilization through all the years that shall be given them to the prosperity of the future—a life given unreservedly for the benefit of those who shall live when they are gone—a career of hardship and of unremitting toil freely devoted to the coming generation.

Here, amid such surroundings and with the most primitive appliances and the most meagre facilities, the pioneer begins to exact from Nature the fruits of honest toil. He chops, he logs, he plants and sows and gathers in with each succeeding year; and as the work goes on the little

clearing gradually extends its limits, encroaching on the surrounding forest till the patch has grown to be a small farm, with substantial rail fences and improved buildings, a door having superseded the canvas curtain, a chimney having been built of sticks plastered with mortar, and a comfortable stable having been erected for the horses. Inside the house the blocks of wood have given place to three-legged stools, the beds are a trifle easier to lie upon, and a floor of hewn planks has replaced the hard, bare earth which was the first floor.

By and by other settlers begin to come into the vicinity. One by one log cabins are erected until, within a radius of a dozen miles, there are as many habitations, and it is beginning to be common for the settlers to talk of their neighbors, but perhaps not as some people talk of their neighbors at the present time. To the lonely pioneers, the sight of a human face is so grateful that they never pause to question whether it belongs to a rich man or a poor one. In such a community all are friends, all are ready to help each other along, to do neighborly kindness, to contribute to the general prosperity and the general happiness. One's neighbors, like many other good things, are valued in proportion to the smallness of their number, and an acquaintance who lives ten or twenty miles away, and whom one does not often see, is held in higher estimation than one whom it is no luxury to see and whose frequent visits are looked forward to as inflictions ; and if one has but few neighbors, and if they all dwell inconviently distant, one is likely to contemplate the not very frequent social meetings which bring them all together with pleasurable anticipations.

Parties were few in those days, though as settlement advanced an occasional dance was participated in by the rustic belles and beaux. Not more than two or three dozen, at most, would be present, and often it was difficult to get together a sufficient number of girls to make the affair a success. On one occasion two young men walked more than twenty miles through the woods to another settlement, invited a couple of girls to accompany them to one of these frolics, and came back with them on foot, carrying them on their shoulders across a stream they were obliged to wade. At another time two young men arrived at the residence of a sylvan belle at the same time and with the same errand, that of securing her company to an approaching party. The lady had no decided choice, and as no satisfactory settlement of the difficulty could be arrived at it was finally agreed that she should go with both of her admirers, which she is said to have done, conducting herself with so much circumspection as to keep them both good-humored throughout the whole time till they returned her safe home. Those who lived on roads leading directly to the appointed place came in wagons. Others, who lived in the woods, where some of the prettiest girls were found, often mounted a horse behind a young man, with a blanket to sit upon, dressed in their every day apparel, with woolen stockings and strong shoes on. They would dash through the woods on some trail, through streams and over every obstacle in their way, carrying a bundle containing their ball dress in their hands. Upon their arrival a few minutes at the toilet put them in condition for the dance.

The pioneer fiddler was always a well-known individual

and often an original character. Sometimes he was a "jack at all trades." His music was never of a high order, but it was of the kind to suit the times—loud if not grand, and energetic if not artistic. His favorite tunes were "Walk Jaw. Bones," "Fisher's Hornpipe," "The Devil's Dream," "The Bummer's Reel," and a few others of the same kind. When the interest in the dance began to manifest itself by grotesque and original steps on the part of the dancers, he would often accompany his violin with a rollicking song, bringing in all of the "calls" in rhyme, frequently ending the "set" by singing out "Four gents forward and "—after a long pause, giving the swains time to balance in the center of the room—"ladies take your seats." This was a favorite trick of his, which invariably created a laugh at the expense of the young fellows thus unceremoniously deserted by their partners. The amusements of old and young were enjoyed with a keen relish. There were quilting, husking, apple-paring, raising, chopping, logging and other "bees," and every gathering of the kind was a joyous occasion, giving a double enjoyment from the consciousness of profitable employment and social intercourse. They were the means by which the pioneers helped each other along, and to the friendly spirit which prompted them the citizens of the county are largely indebted for the prosperity of to-day.

CHAPTER XVIII.

PIONEER FARMING—FIRST SCHOOLS AND TEACHERS, MEETINGS AND PREACHERS—THE PUBLIC HEALTH.

THE agricultural implements in use in the early days were of the most primitive order. Much of the first farming was done without the almost indispensable aid of a plow, and the earliest plows were of home manufacture, having often been made from the crotch of a tree which nature had fashioned something after the required pattern, and which the settler had only to sharpen and finish in the most unpretentious way imaginable. Afterward clumsy wrought-iron plows were introduced, which were effective only to stir up the surface of the ground, having wooden mould-boards in some cases, the point only being imported. To construct a drag was an easy matter. The settler had only to cut two round sticks of unequal length, joining them in such a manner that the end of the longer one projected sufficiently to attach the chain, and boring four holes for teeth in the longer and three in the shorter piece, the two being held apart at the rear by a wooden brace. Flails were the only threshers and hand-fans the only separators. Hoes and rakes were very heavy and very strong, for there were few forges in the country and it was no easy matter to get a broken tool repaired. Grain was cut with a sickle and hay with an old fashioned scythe, as heavy as it was unhandy.

With such tools seed was put in the ground, the work of cultivation went on and crops were harvested. Sometimes they were almost an entire failure and sometimes there was an over abundance, but the average yield was good. But there were no markets established; while grain was abundant, it could not be converted into funds with which to pay for land, but there was usually no scarcity of food. A favorite mode of money-making in the early days was that of locating and improving a claim and "selling the betterment," as disposing of the improvement at an advance was called. Some settlers repeated this operation several times, gaining a little with each transaction, and finally buying and paying for a desirable farm.

Among the few business advantages offered to the pioneers was that afforded by a market for "black salts" which was created at an early day. "All who could raise a kettle," wrote one informed as to the make-shifts of that time, "entered upon the manufacture of this new article of commerce. It brought money into the country, enabled settlers to pay taxes and buy necessaries, and promoted the clearing of land." The manufacture and sale of potash was another enterprise which proved a God-send to the pioneers. "The trade in the product of their ashes," says the writer quoted above, "for which merchants paid half in cash and the rest in goods, seemed almost providential. New settlers put up rough leaches and generally made black salts. When kettles were available, potash was manufactured. The lands timbered with elm, beech and maple supplied a value in ashes to almost pay for clearing. It was an expedient of the new settler to go into the forest, cut down trees, roll them in heaps, and burn them, having in mind no thought of clearing, but to supply a want of store trade or money. The proceeds of the burnt log-heaps in the clearings supplied many families with the necessaries of life where otherwise there would have been destitution. One must be willfully blind not to see in this relief thus afforded a providential aid." The timber, which was looked upon as a hindrance to agricultural progress, was thus removed, becoming a source of profit and making way for the work of underbrushing, grubbing and cultivation, which could not have been prosecuted until its removal. Another and a later element of progress was the sale of timber and staves.

Saw-mills were first built at a comparatively early day in the history of the county. They were small and easy of construction, and they were located on some stream whose waters provided their motive power, and conveniently to the timber the manufacture of which into lumber proved a source of profit. There was usually but one saw, and from the peculiar manner in which it was hung the mills were known as "English mills," by which title, though they have long since gone out of use, they are referred to at the present time. With the increase of the number of these mills and the gradual growth of the lumber trade the fortunes of the settlers improved. They were enabled to dispose of their timber profitably, and at the same time clear their lands and buy lumber with which to erect buildings to replace their early log houses and out-buildings.

Before grist-mills were introduced, the settlers labored under a great disavantage, sometimes being obliged to carry their grain by the single bag-full across the backs of horses to a distant mill, consuming several days in the trip and having to go often on account of the impossibility of taking much at a time. Many families kept one or two mortars or "hominy blocks" in which to pound corn. They were generally made in the stump of a tree near the house, the top of it being cut off square and burned or gouged out hollow, the cavity being large enough to receive the corn; and to relieve the laborer the pounder was frequently suspended by means of a spring-pole. The first grist-mills were small, usually having only one run of stones and often lying idle much of the time for want of water.

The early schools, though not so good as they might have been, were certainly conducive in no small degree to that intellectual growth which must precede all systematic and permanent improvement in any community. The teachers were often strangers who were travelling through the country, and who paused to replenish their purses or gain a few months of recreation in school teaching. Sometimes they were foreigners, often they were intemperate, and they were all addicted to the use of the rod. Sometimes, so uncertain and unreliable were they, three or four changes would occur in a single year, the first going away and giving place to another and he, in turn, making a place for a new comer. The school-houses were generally built by "bees," or gatherings of such settlers as had children to be educated. They were log structures, a little better, because built at a later day, than the first residence described in the preceding chapter. The seats were benches made of slabs split from logs, with legs inserted in auger holes at the corners. The desks, when there were any, were constructed after the same plan; there was no blackboard, and the entire stock of apparatus consisted of a half-dozen well-seasoned switches and a substantial ruler, and no opportunity was neglected to make use of these appliances for the general advancement of the causes of education and good manners.

In those days the question was not, "Has the teacher a good education?" but "Is he stout? Has he good government?" It was a frequent practice in some districts to smoke out the entire school or to "bar out" the teacher. Frequently there was a conspiracy among the large boys to whip the teacher and break up the school. Their attempts in this direction were successful for several successive years, and then, when the district had won a bad name and come to be shunned by the generality of pedagogues, a stranger with well-developed governing powers would happen along, open a school and speedily reduce the belligerent "big boys" to a condition of subjection and prompt if not cheerful obedience, thus setting the ball of education rolling on.

The text-books were few and scarcely up to the present standard. At first any book, be it Bible or almanac, was admissible as a reader, and there was little uniformity in the other books. Among those used most may be mentioned Noah Webster's Spelling Book, Daboll's Arithmetic, Morse's Geography, Murray's Grammar and the English Reader. In some schools the United States Speller was used, the first reading lesson in which is as follows:

"My son, do no ill.
Go not in the way of bad men,
For bad men go to the pit.
O, my son, run not in the way of sin."

The youthful readers were required to memorize such lessons, and they no doubt impressed truths that had a lasting influence on their lives and characters. Attempts were made to inculcate gentlemanly deportment and respect for the aged, and many pupils on their way to and from school would politely raise their hats on meeting strangers. It is to be regretted that Young America to-day appears to be less susceptible of such instruction, or that it is not so prominent a feature in the public schools of the present time.

The pioneer teachers were many of them very ingenious in the contrivance of original modes of punishment, which from their novelty and their untried terrors were a by no means inoperative agency in maintaining the authority which was regarded as so essential to the well-being of the school. Some of these inventive characters flourished in a certain district at a day after the introduction of the box stove. He conceived the brilliant idea of placing a brick on top of the stove over a brisk fire, and making delinquents walk around the stove, one behind the other, and turn over the rapidly heating brick once during each circuit; this was kept up until their blistered fingers goaded them into subjection.

The first religious services were held in the open air, beneath the wide-spreading branches of the forest trees and amid all the varied surroundings of wood and plain, hill and valley—not in a house reared with human hands and dedicated for the worship of a certain few in a certain prescribed way, but in God's own temple, made in infinite splendor for all mankind. How the prayers of the migratory Methodist preachers rang through the arches of the forest, as with plain words from honest hearts they knelt on the ground to intercede for their fellow men; how the great scheme of salvation was unfolded in homely yet terrific sentences, which fell from their lips with all the awful force of prophetic utterance; how their simple auditors trembled at the terribly vivid picture of the reward of sin which was presented to their view; and how they rejoiced at the declaration that salvation was "full and free" to all who sought it with broken spirits and contrite hearts! By scores they owned the saving power of the Son of Man, and crowded the open space around the preacher, asking for prayers or praying for themselves. Thus were the seeds of Christianity planted in the wilderness. They took root, they were nurtured with anxious care, they grew and flourished under the watchful and prayerful attention of the pioneers and their sons and daughters—the parents and grandparents of this generation—and they have brought forth good fruit. It is visible in all the evidences of the progress of the past and the enlightenment of the present.

Thus were a few here and there brought into the fold of the Good Shepherd. Then they organized and began to do His work. First one "class," as the religious societies were called, was formed, then another and another, till in every settlement there were at least "two or three" who regularly "gathered together in the name of the Lord." Soon meetings were held with some attempt at regularity in the school-houses. Circuit preachers would hold services in the various neighborhoods once in two, three, four or six weeks, as the case might be. By and by several districts were united in one charge and put under the pastorate of a minister who went from one to another, managing somehow to make the circuit once a week, though often obliged to preach once every week day and two or three times Sundays. After a time Sunday-schools were started, and they aided greatly to build up and strengthen the church.

One by one churches were built in the county. Some of them are standing yet. They are not like the costly edifices of the present generation. They were nearly all fashioned after the same general plan, being wooden buildings about thirty by forty feet square, with an unpretentious spire at the highest part of the roof near the front, the doors being invariably at the end fronting the street. Some of them were provided with basements which were occupied as Sunday-school rooms, and sometimes, at a later day, by day-schools. The pulpit and the pews were of the plainest and most rigidly simple style imaginable; and the family who had a cushion on their seat were regarded, if not as wickedly proud, at least as being in much danger of relapsing into the "cold and beggarly elements of the world."

The minister often preached for a simple living, which was paid to him in the shape of flour and meat from the well-to-do farmers of his congregation, wood and potatoes from those who were just getting a start on new farms, and general store trade from the early merchants and in payment of orders for the same from such as had nothing to give him but could buy something. His wife was the object of much attention and the subject of no little discussion among the ladies of the society, and was generally a worthy help-meet to a worthy husband. She set a good example to her sisters by eschewing jewelry and gay ribbons and dressing in a style of severe simplicity—which was useful in inculcating lessons of economy if not of religion. There never was a class of men who, taken all in all, were more zealous, more steadfast, more self-sacrificing, and who labored harder for a simple subsistence and the consciousness of doing good than these pioneer preachers. Their works live after them and speak eloquently in testimony of their unselfish devotion of their lives and their best energies to Christianity and humanity; and every one of the many church spires of to-day is a monument to their memory.

As the land was cleared, drained and put under cultivation the public health improved. The seasons following the first settlement were very sickly in proportion to the population. In the summer of some years little or no rain fell, the streams became nearly or entirely dry, and it has been said that "every little inlet became a seat of putrefaction; the heavens seemed on fire, the earth scorched and the air saturated with pestilence." In some places hogs were found dead in the woods. Fever prevailed to an alarming extent, the cases being more numerous than in the cities but not as fatal, and there were many cases of dysentery. This condition of things was prevalent throughout all this section of the country. An early physician, writing of diseases in the pioneer days and at a later period, said: "The summer of 1801 was warm, with frequent showers; the days hot and the nights very chilly. Intermittent fevers prevailed. Peruvian bark was generally a remedy, but was of rare use. When left to nature the symptoms became typhoid, and endangered recovery; 1802 was similar to the year previous. In 1803 intermittents declined and continued fevers prevailed. The summer of 1804 was moderately warm, while the winter was intensely cold. Much snow fell, and lay longer than ever before known. The new settlements were healthy; the winter diseases were inflammatory. These diseases continued during 1805 and 1806, and the abusive use of mercury sacrificed numbers. The character of the inflammatory fever varied with localities in 1807. Near streams whose course was obstructed by dams strong symptoms marked its attack, whereas on high ground the approach was insidious and more difficult of control. Ophthalmia prevailed in July and August. Influenza was epidemic in September. The season of 1808 resembled the one previous. A typhoid appeared in January and continued till May. The treatment was careful depletion followed by judiciously-given stimulants. In 1811 bilious fevers prevailed. In the spring of 1812 a few sporadic cases of *pneumonia typhoides*, a previously unknown disease, first came to notice. It was the most formidable epidemic ever prevalent in this country. The disease became general in 1813, and caused great mortality. By spring, 1814, it entirely disappeared. The principal disease up to 1822 was dysentery; it was most fatal to children. The change since 1828 is such that death from fevers became a rare occurrence and consumption took precedence." The section is now notably healthy, and it is difficult to conceive of the sickness and mortality of pioneer times. This happy improvement is due greatly to the removal of many of the early causes of disease by the drainage of low lands and the general improvement of the whole country, and in no small measure to the advance in medical skill and the high grade of the physicians of the present day.

The pioneer medical practitioners were no less hardy than the pioneer farmers and no less self-sacrificing than the pioneer preachers. They were men of quick decision and prompt and energetic action. The developments of science had not supplied many of the remedies and modes of treatment to which the physicians of a later day owe much of their success, and much has been said in sarcasm of the lancet and the blisters and the calomel of those times; but in lieu of something better these were employed with no small degree of success, and many a pioneer who has died within the memory of some of the youngest who read this, owed his preservation for a long and useful career to the prompt administration of those harsh but effective remedies by one or another of the unflinching frontier doctors.

Their rides extended for miles and miles in all directions, embracing much of the territory now comprised within the limits of several neighboring counties. They rode by day and by night, in answer to any call, with their saddle bags well filled with such remedies as were accessible, often traveling for hours guided only by "blazed" trees and thankful even for a cow path running in the right course. A record of their early struggles, sacrifices and adventures would make an interesting volume.

One point of deep interest to the resident and the stranger still claims our notice. It is the cemetery. If the regularly changing style of the architecture of the houses of the living indicate unerringly the period at which they were erected, so the memorial stones raised above the resting places of the dead bear evidences of their newness or their antiquity.

The first gravestones were merely flat pieces of stone placed, a large one at the head and a smaller one at the feet of the departed, to mark the place of his narrow home. In walking through the cemetery the stranger is led to the first grave. Perhaps it is at some obscure corner of the burying ground, perhaps it is grass-grown, sunken and almost obliterated by the gradual changes of many years; perhaps there is not even a bit of stone at the head of it or at the foot of it; perhaps those who walk above it have forgotten the name and the history of its occupant. He may have been an old man, wearied out with the struggles and privations of pioneer life, or he may have been an infant who was removed before he could realize them; it is all the same—the first grave is ever an object of more than passing interest to the beholder. It was made in the long ago, when the flourishing village was a little frontier settlement; and a memorable day it must long have been to the early settlers when first the earth was opened to receive one of their number, and when first in the experiences of their lives in the new country the solemn words, "dust to dust—ashes to ashes," fell on their ears. All who were connected with that burial became endowed with a peculiar interest, and all were pointed out for years afterwards—the first mourners, the preacher who preached the first funeral sermon, the man who made the first coffin, and the man who dug the first grave. The grave only remains to suggest their memory; for they lie in other graves around it.

The most important of the initial events that preceded the period of advancement which has brought forth the present flattering condition of agriculture and manufacture, and advanced the causes of education and religion, have been adverted to in the preceding pages. The changes which they heralded are but footprints left on the sands of memory by the triumphant march of civilization. Flattering as has been the progress of the past, it is not too much to say that it is but an earnest of the more perfect attainments of the future, seed planted in the soil of time to yield virtue, happiness and abundant success in the years to come.

CHAPTER XIX.

MILITARY OPERATIONS OF 1812—ATTITUDE OF THE IROQUOIS—PREPARATIONS FOR INVADING CANADA.

THE causes and preliminary events of the last war with Great Britain have already been recorded. It remains to tell what occurred during the war within and upon the bounds of Niagara county. It will be found that this county witnessed more of the incidents and experienced more of the immediate effects of the struggle than any other in the United States.

The President announced the declaration of war on the 19th of June, 1812. As soon as the British authorities in Canada were informed of it they took measures to secure the alliance of the Six Nations and the western Indian tribes. The United States government was equally prompt in efforts to neutralize the intrigues of the British. A council with the Senecas was opened at Buffalo on the 6th of July. The United States were represented by Mr. Erastus Granger, then Indian agent. He urged the savages to preserve neutrality, but offered to take a small force of their young warriors into the army if they insisted on fighting. Red Jacket was the Seneca spokesman, and for once cast his influence in favor of the United States. His nation promised not to take up the hatchet unless in alliance with the States, and sent messengers to persuade the Mohawks to neutrality. Their embassy was fruitless; the latter tribe promptly sided with Great Britain, and were active throughout the war, under the leadership of their young chieftain John Brant, son of the guerilla captain of Revolutionary notoriety.

It was found impossible for the young Seneca braves to allow a war to go on in their neighborhood without taking a hand; and their elders did not try to restrain them after the British, at an early stage of hostilities, took possession of Grand Island, which the Iroquois tribe then claimed as part of their territory. A declaration of war was made by the nation in writing—the first instance of the kind in Indian history. The United States government was reluctant to employ savage allies, addicted to barbarities not countenanced in civilized warfare; and it was not until the spring of 1813 that Major-General Lewis, commanding Fort Niagara, invited the Seneca warriors to the fort, to avail himself of their co-operation. Even then it was hoped the employment of the savages in actual hostilities would hardly be necessary; and that on the appearance of the Senecas in the field the Mohawks would withdraw from the war, rather than be involved in a bloody struggle with their kindred nation. The Senecas had no such notion. They repaired to Fort Niagara in full panoply of war, to the number of three or four hundred; and on learning that they were expected to exert a moral influence, rather than to swing tomahawks, they went away disgusted. They were required to abstain from killing or torturing any of the enemy who might fall into their hands, and from mutilating their corpses. With this understanding they rendered some rather unimportant aid during the war, while their friendly attitude was of great value to the United States.

This nation entered upon the war of 1812 with the design of making a conquest of Canada. The force assembled along the river in Niagara county for this purpose at the end of the summer consisted of a small detachment at Niagara Falls (then called Manchester), under General Amos Hall, commander of the militia of western New York, and others at several points along the line, amounting in all to less than seven hundred insubordinate men, poorly clothed and supplied. They had no heavy artillery, and no competent gunners for the field pieces, and there were less than ten rounds of ammunition apiece for the infantry.

Stephen Van Rensselaer, of Albany, a civilian of no military genius, had been made Major-General, and appointed by Governor Tompkins commander-in-chief of the detached militia of New York in order to secure for the State the benefit of the influence which his prominence in the Federalist party, as well as his great wealth and high social standing, gave him. He was accompanied to the Niagara frontier, where he was to have chief command, by Colonel Solomon Van Rensselaer, an officer of some experience, who was to do the fighting for the general. Van Rensselaer reached Fort Niagara on the 13th of August, and immediately proceeded to Lewiston, where he established his headquarters.

Sir Isaac Brock was the British commander-in-chief in Canada, and after the capture of Detroit with its garrison he marched to the Niagara frontier, reaching Fort George, opposite Youngstown, about the 1st of September, with his disciplined, well-officered and victorious little army.

It was evidently impossible for Van Rensselaer to accomplish anything in the way of invasion with the force at his command, and he was even powerless to resist an invasion which seemed to be intended by the enemy. He appealed for reinforcements to the governor and to General Dearborn, commander-in-chief of the United States forces. The latter gave him no assurance of support, but wrote insisting that Upper Canada must be conquered before winter set in. Reinforcements were sent to the Niagara, however, both regulars and militia. The latter rendezvoused at Lewiston. At that point before the middle of October there were assembled, under the immediate command of Brigadier-General Wadsworth, something over 2,500 men, with all the ignorance of militia and no superfluous courage to offset it; and with militiamen's insubordinate eagerness to precipitate a fight, and willingness to get out of it as quickly and safely as possible. At Fort Niagara there were some 300 light artillery and about 1,000 regular infantry.

The little army gathered at Lewiston reflected the anxiety that was felt all over the country for a successful aggressive movement, that should wipe out the disgrace of Hull's surrender at Detroit. The militia so hungered and thirsted for battle that they were willing to mutiny, or even desert unanimously, if they could not be led against the enemy. Something must be done.

It was determined to begin the invasion of Canada by occupying the enemy's position on Queenston Heights. Two companies of the 49th British infantry, under Captains Dennis and Williams defended the post, assisted by a considerable number of militia. Within supporting distance, at Fort George, were about a thousand infantry. At several points along the river were batteries, manned by small detachments. One of these, consisting of a single twenty-four-pounder, planted on Vrooman's Point, a mile below Queenston, commanded that village and Lewiston, and the river between them. General Brock was at Fort George, as was also General Roger Sheaffe, the latter in immediate command of the garrison.

On the 10th of October General Van Rensselaer made arrangements for attacking Queenston Heights the next morning before daylight. Thirteen boats were brought down on wagons from Gill creek, and launched at Lewiston. Lieutenant-Colonel Fenwick was ordered to bring up the flying artillery from Fort Niagara, and General Smyth to send down part of his brigade of regulars, stationed at Buffalo. During the night of the 10th Lieutenant-Colonel Chrystie arrived by the lake at the mouth of Four-mile creek, with 350 troops of the 13th infantry, in thirty boats. He proceeded as fast as possible to Lewiston, and finding an expedition on foot asked permission to join it; but all the arrangements were completed, and it was thought impracticable to change them in his favor.

At three o'clock in the morning of the 11th the troops turned out, in a cold rain storm, and assembled at the landing. One Lieutenant Sims, who had been appointed to conduct the crossing, embarked in advance, and rowed off into the darkness, carrying with him the oars of the other boats, as was found when the party would fain have followed him. It was at first thought that this leading navigator had made a mistake, and it was nearly daylight before the force destined for the attack gave up waiting for his return, and retired drenched and disgusted, concluding that they had been made the victims of treachery.

The storm continued for twenty-four hours. When it was over preparations for the attack on Queenston were cautiously renewed. The time decided upon was the morning of the 13th. As before, the command of the enterprise was given to Colonel Solomon Van Rensselaer. Lieutenant-Colonel Chrystie protested against this arrangement, claiming for himself the honor of command; but finally consented to take orders from Colonel Van Rensselaer, and in the evening of the 12th led 300 men from Fort Niagara to Lewiston. Among his subordinates were Captains Wool (afterward Major-General), Malcolm, Lawrence and Armstrong.

On the 12th three regiments of regulars which had arrived at Niagara Falls were also summoned to Lewiston. Another regiment, commanded by Lieutenant-Colonel (afterward Major-General) Winfield Scott, lay at Schlosser. Scott heard of the intended movement in the evening of the 12th, and galloping down to headquarters obtained permission to post his regiment and cannon on the mountain above Lewiston, and take part in the action if needed; by four in the morning he had taken the position indicated. One of General Van Rensselaer's subordinates, named Lovett, had charge of an eighteen-pounder planted in the same commanding situation, with which to protect the troops in crossing and landing.

At three o'clock, as on the previous occasion, the troops were assembled at the landing place, and, as then, with a cold rain pouring upon them, which, however, shortly ceased. Two bodies, of 300 each, were to cross first, commanded respectively by Colonel Van Rensselaer and Lieutenant-Colonel Chrystie. Detachments under Lieutenant-Colonel Fenwick and Major Mullaney were to follow as called for. The first movement on reaching the Canada shore was to be made against the Heights, while the supporting forces arriving later were to occupy the village of Queenston.

Not more than half the force considered necessary for the first operation could be transported at once in the thirteen boats which had been provided. The first to embark were Captains Wool, Malcom and Armstrong's companies of regulars; forty artillerymen from Fort Niagara, commanded by Lieutenants Rathbone and Gansevoort; and sixty militiamen. Lieutenant-Colonel Chrystie commanded one of the boats. Colonel Van Rensselaer took his place with the artillerymen, and the flotilla put off.

CHAPTER XX.

THE CAPTURE OF QUEENSTON HEIGHTS—THE ASSAILANTS OVERPOWERED, UNSUPPORTED AND TAKEN PRISONERS.

THE boats commanded by Chrystie and Captain Lawrence were carried down stream so far as to be obliged to return to the New York shore, Chrystie having been slightly wounded by a grape shot from Vrooman's Point. A third was still more unfortunate, striking the Canadian bank just below Queenston and being captured by the enemy. The other ten made their intended landing in a few minutes near Hennepin Rock. The boats immediately returned for another load.

The landing was attended with slight opposition and loss. The enemy had gathered at the water's edge, and as the boats drew near fired a volley, by which Lieutenant Rathbone was mortally wounded. The fire was returned by the eighteen-pounder on the heights above Lewiston; and the regulars, under Captain Wool, on landing charged and drove the British up the hill toward Queenston. On nearing the village Wool halted. At their base he was received with a severe fire from two companies of the enemy posted above, while the party which he had been pursuing fell upon his right. Turning upon the latter he forced them back upon Queenston, supported by Rensselaer, who had come up with the militia first landed, and exposed to a deadly cross fire from the heights. The encounter was severe, seven of the ten officers of the 13th being killed or wounded, and a number of the attacking party made prisoners. Colonel Van Rensselaer was disabled by several severe wounds.

The invading force at this stage of the fight retired to the river side, under the shelter of the bluff, where they re-formed and received reinforcements. Colonel Van Rensselaer before being carried back to his camp ordered Captain Wool, who was the senior of the effective officers on the ground and himself painfully wounded, to storm the heights. The order was boldly and vigorously executed. Wool's command, returning to the attack, climbed the heights—in some places only by the aid of the bushes growing on them—captured a three-gun battery and drove the enemy from the summit.

In the meantime General Brock, warned by the roar of artillery, had ridden up from Fort George, accompanied by Colonel McDonnell and Major Glegg. He reached the battery on the heights just as its defenders were compelled to fly from it to avoid capture by Wool. Retiring to Queenston he sent orders to General Sheaffe to open a bombardment of Fort Niagara and come up with reinforcements. He himself then rallied the entire British force at command, and set himself to recapture the heights by an attack on the left of Wool's line. The United States troops were at first driven toward the river, but when forced to the very verge of the precipice they repulsed the assault by a desperate rally, and turning on the enemy drove them once more from the heights.

Brock rallied his retreating troops, and, strengthened by reinforcements which began to arrive from down the river, formed for a renewal of the attack. When just beginning the ascent he was struck from his horse by a bullet in the breast, and died in a few minutes. His followers made a brave attack on the heights, but were met by an equally brave defense, and at length repulsed with the loss of Colonel McDonnell and Captains Dennis and Williams wounded, the first mortally. The defeat of the British was at this time—early in the forenoon—complete. They abandoned Queenston and retired to Vrooman's Point, leaving Wool and his 240 heroes masters of the situation. He sent out scouts and strove to bring the captured cannon to bear on the distant foe.

Reinforcements were on the way for both belligerents. All the morning troops had been slowly arriving from the New York shore under the fire of the Vrooman's Point battery, and part of them took position on the heights.

Generals Van Rensselaer and Wadsworth, Lieutenant-Colonel Scott and other officers arrived during the forenoon. Scott, as the senior regular officer, was allowed to assume the command. His force amounted to about 600, rather more than one half regulars.

The first British reinforcements to arrive were 500 Mohawks under John Brant, who early in the afternoon emerged from the forest and rushed upon the Americans with apalling yells, so frightening them that it required Scott's best efforts to make them stand their ground. The savages were beaten off, and driven into the woods and finally off the heights.

General Sheaffe with at least 800 regulars, militia and Indians, next hove in sight on the river bank below Queenston, and gathering in his march all classes of the defeated British force, approached the heights from the west by a long detour through St. Davids, and confronted Scott's weary little army with a thousand mostly fresh men.

The slowness of Sheaffe's approach gave ample time for bringing over the remainder of the New York militia and securing the victory so bravely earned. Van Rensselaer crossed the river and ordered them forward. To his unspeakable disgust, they refused to cross. The sight of the wounded, and what other evidence they could get of the severity of the conflict, had scared the manhood out of them, and inspired the brilliant discovery that they were not legally bound to serve out of the State. "Neither entreaty nor threats," wrote General Armstrong, "neither arguments nor ridicule, availed anything. They had seen enough of war to satisfy them that it was not part of their special calling; and at last, not disdaining to employ the mask invented by faction to cover cowardice or treason, fifteen hundred able-bodied men, well armed and equipped, who a week before boasted largely of patriotism and prowess, were now found openly pleading constitutional scruples in justification of disobedience to the lawful authority of their chief." "They pleaded their exemption as militia," says Lossing, "under the constitution and laws, from being taken out of their own State! and under that miserable shield they hoped to find shelter from the storm of indignation which their cowardice was sure to evoke. Like poltroons as they were, they stood on the shore at Lewiston while their brave companions in arms on Queenston Heights were menaced with inevitble destruction or captivity. All that Rensselaer could do was to send over some munitions of war, with a letter to General Wadsworth ordering him to retreat if in his judgment the salvation of the troops depended upon such movement, and promising him a supply of boats for the purpose. But this promise he could not fulfill. The boatmen on the shore were as cowardly as the militia on the plain above. Many of them had fled panic-stricken and the boats were dispersed."

About four o'clock the British made the final attack in overwhelming numbers, and the invaders, after a brave though brief stand, fled toward the landing or up the river. Those who took the latter course were soon captured by the Indians, except a number who were driven over the precipice, a very few of whom managed to let themselves down by bushes. All who escaped from the struggle on the heights were soon gathered on the river's brink. There no boats awaited them, and there was no alternative but surrender. Even this was difficult, for the Indians repeatedly shot down the bearers of flags of truce. Scott himself at length, narrowly escaping slaughter by young Brant and another Mohawk, managed to reach the British headquarters and surrendered all of the invaders on the Canadian shore as prisoners of war. He was astonished at their number. They were found to include two hundred militia who early in the day had been driven on shore below by the current and captured; and the total number of the prisoners was swelled to between eight and nine hundred by a crowd of militia who had either never left the margin of the river after landing or had returned to it as soon as possible, and remained all day hidden along the foot of the precipice.

The loss on the side of the British in killed and wounded is believed to have been 130; on the other 90 killed and 100 wounded. Although the capitulation had been arranged by Scott, the formal surrender was made by General Wadsworth in the evening at Newark, whither the prisoners were marched immediately after the battle. Young Brant and the other savage who had tried to murder Scott while bearing a flag of truce renewed the attempt at Newark, and would probably have succeeded but for the opportune interposition of a British officer.

The bodies of Brock and Colonel McDonnell were buried on the 16th in a bastion of Fort George. Minute guns were fired during the funeral service not only there but also at Fort Niagara and Lewiston; the latter rather sentimental performance is said to have been directed by General Van Rensselaer, at Scott's suggestion. The House of Commons ordered a monument to Brock erected in St. Paul's cathedral, London; and voted his four brothers twelve thousand acres of land in Upper Canada and pensions of $1,000 each. The Canadian government had a medal struck in his honor in 1816, and an imposing monument built on Queenston Heights, which was finished and the bodies of Brock and McDonnell deposited in it October 13th, 1824. This was ruined by an explosion of powder maliciously fired in it in the spring of 1840. The corner stone of the present structure was laid near the former one October 13th, 1853, and the remains removed to it.

Colonel Van Rensselaer lay at the point of death at Lewiston for two or three days. Five days after the battle he was carried on a litter to Fort Schlosser, and thence proceeded by way of Buffalo to his home at Albany.

We have mentioned that a bombardment of Fort Niagara was directed in the orders which General Brock sent down to Fort George just before his fall at Queenston. The order was energetically executed, and Captain Leonard, the commander of Fort Niagara, responded by cannonading Newark with hot shot which burned several buildings. The British had so much the best of the firing that Leonard, after bursting one of his largest guns, decided to abandon the fort. After the garrison had withdrawn it returned on seeing the enemy embarking to take possession of the deserted fortress; and the latter gave up the movement upon the fort being re-occupied by the garrison.

The militia captured at Queenston Heights were immediately discharged on parole and the regulars held for exchange. This was soon effected; and Scott arrrived at Fort Niagara early in 1813, prepared for fresh acheivements.

CHAPTER XXI.

CAPTURE AND RECAPTURE OF FORT GEORGE—FALL OF FORT NIAGARA—RAVAGES OF FIRE AND SWORD.

TEN days after the battle of Queenston Heights General Van Rensselaer resigned in favor of General Smyth. The latter issued a couple of ludicrous proclamations summoning the militia of western New York to a new attempt for the conquest of Canada, which was to be conducted on correct principles and sure to succeed. He assembled 4,500 men at Black Rock, but he never led them across the river, and the most warlike adventure in which he took part was a bloodless duel with General Porter, who had taunted him with his cowardice. Smyth's incompetence, at least, was plain, and he was soon deposed.

After the capture of York, on the 27th of April, 1813, the fleet of Commodore Chauncey, which had co-operated in that enterprise, sailed across the lake laden with troops and arms destined for an attack on Fort George. General Dearborn, who had taken command on the frontier, accompanied Commodore Chauncey and other officers in a schooner which sailed in advance of the fleet. The troops were landed and encamped near the mouth of Four-mile creek, and the fleet returned to Sackett's Harbor and brought over another installment of troops and war material. Dearborn had 4,000 or more effective men by the 27th of May, the date selected for the attack on Fort George.

A large number of boats had been built at the Five-mile meadows. When they were launched in the afternoon of the 26th, preparatory to taking them round to the camp, they were fired upon by a small battery across the river. A battery at Youngstown thereupon opened a destructive fire upon Fort George, and a general cannonade followed. During the night the boats were taken to the camp. The heavy guns and part of the troops were embarked on the vessels of the fleet, and the remainder of the force took to the boats. The armada set off shortly after four in the morning, the darkness of the night being increased by a fog. Part of the armed vessels took position in the mouth of the river, to command a battery near the lighthouse, and others before a similar battery half a mile further west, near which it was intended to land the troops. At daylight a cannonade was begun between the hostile fortifications.

The fire from the shipping in a few minutes drove out the little force manning the enemy's western battery, and the landing was effected without serious opposition. On ascending from the beach, however, the British were encountered more than one thousand strong, and the advance of the invaders was momentarily checked. After a sharp conflict of a few minutes duration, during which a very effective fire was kept up from the men-of-war, the enemy were routed by their assailants, who pursued them through Newark and entered Fort George, which had been deserted by its garrison after being very much damaged by the cannonade. The three magazines of the fort had been fired, and one of them, exploding as the victors approached, hurled a stick of timber which struck Colonel Scott from his horse, not, however, disabling him. The trains laid to the others were extinguished.

Scott renewed the pursuit; but after following the routed enemy for five miles, when just on the point of overtaking them—as though it were too much that on this border a victory should be achieved unmarred by a display of official idiocy—he was recalled by superior authority. By noon all the British positions at the mouth of the Niagara had been taken, with a loss to the victors of 40 killed and 100 wounded; and to the vanquished of 51 regulars killed, 305 wounded, captured and missing, and 507 militia taken prisoners.

The English General Vincent, who was in command on this frontier, ordered the abandonment of all the British posts on the river, and some of them were destroyed. Commodore Chauncey's fleet returned to Sackett's Harbor.

A very successful affair on a small scale was the raid of Lieutenant-Colonel Clark upon Schlosser on the night of the 4th of July. Crossing from Chippewa with a party of Canadians and Indians he captured the guard, a quantity of provisions, arms and ammunition and a brass field piece, and retired unmolested.

General Wilkinson succeeded Dearborn as commander-in-chief in the summer of 1813, and in the autumn of that year operated on the St. Lawrence, leaving General McClure, of the New York militia, to hold Fort George. Early in November that post, garrisoned by only about sixty men, was threatened by the approach of a considerable British force from the west. McClure concluded it must be abandoned, and left it for Fort Niagara on the 10th of December, the enemy being then close at hand. The last minutes he thought he could allow himself on the Canada shore he spent in burning the village of Newark, whose population of non-combatants was turned out into a deep snow, in intensely cold weather. While McClure claimed in this act to have aimed only at destroying what might prove a shelter for the enemy, he left the fort intact for their reception, and tents enough to shelter fifteen hundred men.

The British authorities resolved to retaliate severely for the wanton destruction of Newark when they had the opportunity, and they very soon made the opportunity. In the night of December 18th a thousand British and Indians crossed the river three miles above Fort Niagara. Colonel Murray, with 550 regulars, turned toward the fort, prepared to storm it. The pickets were captured without giving an alarm, and the enemy on reaching the fort about three o'clock in the morning actually found the main gate standing open and undefended, and the fortress at their mercy. For a few minutes the "southeastern block-house" and the "red barracks" withstood the entrance of the foe so stoutly that several were killed or wounded, among the latter Colonel Murray. Most of the 450 occupants of the fort only awoke to find themselves prisoners. The slight resistance was made the pretext for an onslaught in which 80 of the helpless garrison, including many hospital patients, were butchered after surrendering. Fourteen were wounded, 344 taken and 20 escaped; 27 cannon, 3,000 stand of small arms, and great quantities of ammunition, provisions and camp equipage fell into the hands of the victors. They held the fort until the treaty of peace restored it.

To the usual criminal blundering of officials on this border, treachery seems in this case to have been added, to assure the enemy's success. McClure, though anticipating an attack, had gone to Buffalo, and satisfied himself with a proclamation announcing the danger of Fort Niagara and summoning the people to its defense. Before this was twenty-four hours old the fort was in the hands of the enemy. Captain Leonard, who had been left in command, spent the night of the assault with his family, two or three miles distant, leaving without informing any one.

The portion of the British force which did not accompany Murray to the fort, including the Indians, pillaged and destroyed the six or eight houses then constituting Youngstown. They then marched upon Lewiston, where they plundered, burned and butchered to their hearts' content. Mr. Lossing understood that 500 Indians under General Riall crossed from Queenston to Lewiston on hearing a cannon fired at Fort Niagara announcing its capture. He quotes the following "extract of a letter from 'an officer of high rank,' [whom he conjectures to have been General Drummond] at Queenston," written while the devastation was going on:

"A war-whoop from five hundred of the most savage Indians (which they gave just at daylight, on hearing of the success of the attack on Fort Niagara) made the enemy [at Lewiston] take to their heels, and our troops are in pursuit. We shall not stop until we have cleared the whole frontier. The Indians are retaliating the conflagration of Newark. Not a house within my sight but is in flames. This is a melancholy but just retaliation."

The flying inhabitants of Lewiston were pursued several miles eastward on the Ridge road, and the Tuscarora village was destroyed. The savages then pushed on up the river, stoutly withstood by Major Mallory and forty volunteers from Schlosser. Along the whole length of the river the destruction and desolation were complete, the inhabitants thinking themselves happy if they could escape inland, forsaking all they possessed. Newark was bitterly avenged. On the 24th and 25th a party of sixty or eighty regulars traversed the lake shore from Fort Niagara to Van Horn's mill, near the mouth of Eighteen-mile creek, and back, burning the mill and nearly all the buildings between it and the fort and taking some prisoners.

"It is impossible now," says Turner, "to give the reader such an account of the condition of things in western New York during that ill-fated winter as will enable him to realize the alarm, the panic, the aggregate calamities that prevailed. On the immediate frontier all was desolate; the enemy holding possession of Fort Niagara, detached marauding parties of British and Indians came out from it, traversed the frontier where there was nothing left to destroy, and made incursions in some instances in the interior, enlarging the theatre of devastation and spreading alarm among those who had been bold enough to remain in the flight. West of a north and south line that would pass through the village of Le Roy, more than one-half of the entire population had been driven from their homes by the enemy, or had left them in fear of extended invasion. Entire backwoods neighborhoods were deserted, hundreds of log cabins were desolate, and the signs and sounds of life were mostly the deserted cattle and sheep, lowing and bleating, famishing for the lack of fodder there were none left to deal out to them."

A committee of safety and relief appointed at Canandaigua to minister to the homeless sufferers issued on the 8th of January, 1814, an appeal in their behalf of which the following is a part:

"Niagara county and that part of Genesee which lies west of Batavia are completely depopulated. All the settlements in a section of country forty miles square, and which contained more than 12,000 souls, are effectually broken up. These facts you are undoubtedly acquainted with; but the distresses they have produced none but an eye witness can thoroughly appreciate. Our roads are filled with people, many of whom have been reduced from a state of competency and good prospects to the last degree of want and sorrow. So sudden was the blow by which they had been crushed that no provisions could be made either to elude or to meet it. The fugitives from Niagara county, especially, were dispersed under circumstances of so much terror that in some cases mothers find themselves wandering with strange children, and children are seen accompanied by such as have no other sympathies with them than those of common suffering."

But two days before this address was issued a gentleman wrote from Le Roy as follows:

"Numerous witnesses testify to the following facts: The Indians mangled and burned Mrs. Lovejoy in Buffalo, massacred two large families at Black Rock, namely Mr. Luffer's and Mr. Lecort's; murdered Mr. Gardner; put all the sick to death at Youngstown and killed, scalped and mangled sixty at Fort Niagara after it was given up. Many dead bodies are yet lying unburied at Buffalo, mangled and scalped. Colonel Marvin counted thirty-three this morning. I met between Cayuga and this place upward of one hundred families in wagons, sleds and sleighs, many of them with nothing but what they had on their backs; nor could they find places to stay at." Mr. Lossing, who quotes this letter, remarks: "Fearful was the retaliation for the destruction of half-inhabited Newark, where not a life was sacrificed! Six villages, many isolated country houses and four vessels were consumed, and the butchery of innocent persons at Fort Niagara, Lewiston, Schlosser, Tuscarora Village, Black Rock and Buffalo, and in farm houses, attested the fierceness of the enemy's revenge."

In the campaign of 1814 the United States forces were commanded by officers of some sense and ability, and distinguished themselves by their courage in several engagements on the Canadian border, of no great permanent results, and which have no direct connection with the history of Niagara county.

This region, so afflicted by the hardships of war, was visited with unauspicious circumstances after the close of hostilities, which prevented its immediate recovery and restoration. The harvest of 1814, though it saved from starvation the pioneer families who had ventured back to their homes and clearings, was of course small; and in 1816 a series of frosts continuing far into the summer so nearly ruined the crops as to seriously threaten the country with famine. Before the belated harvest of autumn, wheat had risen to two or three dollars a bushel, and even corn brought the former figure. Some families were compelled, while the small grains were still green, to gather the milky kernels and eat them, boiled, as a staple article of food. Roots and herbs never commonly eaten came into consumption for the time being.

In the fruitful seasons that followed the great obstacle to the prosperity of the county, which neutralized the fertility of the soil and frustrated the farmer's labor, was the want of means of access to markets where surplus produce might be sold. This paralyzing influence was destined ere many years to be overcome by the noble water way whose construction forms the subject of a following chapter.

CHAPTER XXII.

SUCCESSIVE BOUNDARIES OF NIAGARA COUNTY AND ITS SUBDIVISIONS—OFFICERS AND REPRESENTATIVES.

BETWEEN 1782 and 1784 all but the eastern portion of New York was called Tryon county, having previously been a part of Albany. In the latter year the same territory took the name of Montgomery. In 1789 all of the State west of Phelps and Gorham's pre-emption line was set off under the title of Ontario county. A single town, called Northampton, swallowed up the entire

Holland Purchase. In 1802 Genesee county was formed from the portion of New York west of the Genesee river. The town of Northampton was divided into four, of which Batavia comprised all of the State west of the east transit line.

On the 11th of March, 1808, a bill was passed creating Niagara county. Its east line was as at present, but it extended southward to Cattaraugus creek. The part of the new county north of Tonawanda creek was constituted one town and named Cambria.

April 2d, 1821, the county was divided into Niagara and Erie counties, as at present bounded. It need hardly be said that this work is a history of the Niagara county of the present. The history of Erie county has recently been related with much vivacity and interest by Mr. Chrisfield Johnson, and we have no occasion to repeat it.

On the 1st of June, 1812, the town of Cambria was divided into four, the portion east of the west transit line constituting Hartland; township 13 in ranges 7, 8 and 9 forming Niagara; township 14 in those ranges retaining the title of Cambria and the remainder of the original Cambria taking the name of Porter. April 5th, 1817, Royalton was formed from the portion of Hartland south of township 15. February 27th, 1818, Lewiston was taken from the west end of Cambria, having its present lines; and on the 10th of April following Porter was restricted by its present east line and Wilson created. On the 8th of February, 1823, Somerset was formed from Hartland, having its present width but running west to the transit line. February 2d of the next year Lockport was formed from Cambria and Royalton, with its present boundaries, and on the 20th of the next month the western ends of Hartland and Somerset were joined with a slice of Wilson to make Newfane. Pendleton was laid off from Niagara April 16th, 1827, and Wheatfield May 12th, 1836.

The county seat of the original Niagara was at Buffalo, and on the division in 1821 the part which became Erie retained the existing organization. The act creating the present county of Niagara appointed the following officers: Sheriff, Lothrop Cook; clerk, Oliver Grace; judges—Silas Hopkins (first judge), James Van Horn and Robert Fleming.

The location of the county seat was one of the first questions to be settled, and of course different places were rivals for the honor. Erasmus Root, Jesse Hawley and William Britton were appointed commissioners to determine the location of the county buildings. Before they had taken action Mr. Britton died. Mr. Root favored Lewiston, or Molyneux's, in Cambria—a suggestion which gives a vivid idea of the insignificance of other villages in the county at the time. Mr. Hawley preferred Lockport, and as they could not agree nothing was accomplished by the commission. Another was appointed by the Legislature of 1822, consisting of James M'Kown, Abraham Keyser and Julius H. Hatch. These gentlemen in July selected Lockport as the county seat. A two-acre lot was purchased of William M. Bond for the site of the county buildings. The new court-house was not ready for occupancy until January, 1825, when the first court was held in it. The bench at this time included Judge Samuel De Veaux, beside the judges above mentioned. Courts had been held at Lewiston until July, 1823, when the first session in Lockport was held on the upper floor of the old Mansion House, now Miller and Sons' Exchange Hotel, which was then the most commodious room in the settlement. Judge Rochester presided. The county clerk's office was built in 1856, at an expense of $13,000.

The first election in the county was held in November, 1822, and resulted in the choice of Almon H. Millard as sheriff, Asahel Johnson clerk, and Benjamin Barlow member of Assembly. The vote cast was 1,324.

We have decided in this chapter to depart from the chronological order hitherto followed, in order to give a connected view of the civil history of the county. Below is a list of the names, with dates of appointment or election (November of the year given, unless otherwise specified,) of Niagara's citizens who have been the more important

COUNTY OFFICERS.

Sheriffs: Almond H. Millard, 1822; Eli Bruce, 1825; John Phillips, 1827; Hiram McNiel, 1830; George Rynall, 1833; Tarmerlane T. Roberts, 1836; Theodore Stone, 1839; James A. Cooper, 1842; Franklin Spaulding, 1845; Elisha Clapp, (appointed January 27th) 1851; Chester F. Shelley, 1854; Benjamin Farley, 1857; George Swain, 1860; James D. Ames, 1863; Alfred Ransom, 1866; Oscar E. Mann, 1869; Norman O. Allen, 1872; Joseph Batten, 1875.

County clerks: Asahel Johnson, 1822; James F. Mason, 1825; Henry Catlin, 1828; Abijah H. Moss, 1834; Hiram A. Cook, 1837; David S. Crandall, 1840; James C. Lewis, 1843; Edwin Shepard, 1845; John Van Horn, 1845; George W. Gage, 1848; Lewis S. Payne, 1851; Wilson Robinson, 1854; Nathan Dayton, 1857; Charles H. Van Duzen, (appointed May 7) 1859; Charles H. Symonds, 1859; William S. Wright, 1862; Lewis S. Payne, 1865; George B. Wilson, 1868; Peter D. Walter, 1871; George L. Moot, 1874; Amos W. R. Henning, 1877.

County Treasurers: Thomas T. Flagler, 1848; Alfred Van Wagoner, 1851; William J. Dunlop, 1854; John Van Horn, 1857; Morrison W. Evans, 1860; Jacob M. Chrysler, 1863; Josiah L. Breyfogle, 1866; Hiram Benedict, 1869; S. Curtis Lewis, 1872 and 1875.

District Attorneys.—Under the Second Constitution, which was adopted in 1822 and in force until the end of 1846, they were appointed by the Court of General Sessions; for the last thirty years they have been chosen by popular vote at the November elections. The list for Niagara county is as follows: Zina H. Colvin, April 2, 1821; Elias Ransom, jr, 1830; William Hotchkiss, 1833; Joseph C. Morse, January, 1836; Robert H. Stevens, May, 1836; Jonathan L. Woods, 1839; Alfred Holmes, 1843; Sherburne B. Piper, 1845, and June, 1847; George D. Lamont, 1850; John L. Buck, 1853; Andrew W. Brazee, 1856; Mortimer M. Southworth, 1859, who held the office by re-election until succeeded by Frank Brundage, who was elected in 1874. Ben J. Hunting was the successful candidate in 1877.

First Judges of the Court of Common Pleas (appointed by the governor): Silas Hopkins, February 8, 1823; Robert Fleming, April 22, 1828; Nathan Dayton, March 13, 1833; Washington Hunt, January 30, 1836; Elias Ransom, January 19, 1841; Jonathan L. Woods, April 29, 1846.

County Judges: Hiram Gardner, June, 1837; Levi F. Bowen, 1851; resigned and Elias Ransom appointed December 11, 1852; Alfred Holmes, 1857; George D. Lamont, 1865; resigned and Hiram Gardner appointed November 19, 1868; Levi F. Bowen, 1873.

Surrogates (appointed by the governor under the Second Constitution; since elected: Rufus Spaulding, April 2, 1821; Willard Smith, February 25, 1822; Hiram Gardner, March 31, 1831; Joseph C. Morse, January 30, 1836; Henry A. Carter, February 28, 1840; Josiah K. Skinner, February 28, 1844; Thomas M. Webster, 1851; Mortimer M. Southworth, 1855; George W. Bowen, 1859; Henry D. Scripture, 1863; John T. Murray, 1867; Joshua Gaskill, 1871; George P. Ostrander, 1877.

INCUMBENTS OF STATE OFFICES.

Niagara county has been represented in the chief executive office of the State by Washington Hunt, a gentleman so eminent in various honorable walks of life that a sketch of his career is called for. He was born in Windham, Greene county, N. Y., August 5th, 1811, and descended from a Revolutionary ancestry. His father, Sanford Hunt, subsequently removed to Livingston county and gave the name of Hunt's Hollow to the settlement where he established himself. In 1828 Washington Hunt went to Lockport. It that town, of which he was to become the most illustrious citizen, he began life for himself by serving two years as a clerk in the store of Tucker & Bissell, evincing in this connection the excellent business and social traits which afterward had so much to do in giving him wealth, reputation and influence. In 1830 he began the study of law with Lot Clark. He found, however, more profitable and congenial employment for his talents than the practice of his profession, in real estate transactions, which through life constituted his principal business operations. In 1833 the firm of Hunt & Walbridge was formed for the purchase of 32,000 acres of land in Niagara county from the Albany Land Company. The investment made Mr. Hunt a rich man. In the following year he married Mary, daughter of Mr. Walbridge. When but twenty-four years old he was appointed by Governor Marcy "first judge" of the county, and is said to have filled the office for five years with a dignity and ability which could not have been expected of a youth.

About the time of receiving this appointment he made an unsuccessful run for Congress on the Democratic ticket. In 1840 he left that party on a financial issue, and two years later was elected to Congress by the Whigs, who re-elected him for the next two terms. His ability and industry in the House made him prominent before the country and one of the leaders of his party. On leaving Congress he was appointed comptroller of New York. In November, 1850, he was elected governor, beating Horatio Seymour by 262 votes in a total poll of 428,966. He was renominated, and defeated by Mr. Seymour by a small majority in the next gubernatorial campaign. He was also defeated as the Congressional candidate of a coalition in 1856, and of the Democrats for the same office in 1862.

Probably no man has been more prominently identified with the business history of Lockport than Governor Hunt. He held official positions at different times in at least five banks, and was prominent in the application of the splendid water power created by the canal, which he and Governor Marcy leased from the State in 1836. Governor Hunt had much to do in the establishment and formation of the numerous industrial concerns which have been developed by the water power, as well as in other enterprises, and was a very extensive holder of real estate in the city, and interested and influential in railroad circles.

His house was that now occupied by the heirs of the late William P. Daniels. He was a pillar in the Episcopal church of Lockport, which he frequently represented in diocesan and general conventions. For several years before his death he spent a portion of his time in New York, and died there from a cancer, February 2d, 1867.

Bates Cook, of Lewiston, was appointed comptroller February 4th, 1839.

General Peter B. Porter, of Niagara Falls, was appointed secretary of State February 16th, 1815, and a Regent of the University nine years later.

George H. Boughton was appointed canal appraiser October 7th, 1839, and November 16th, 1852; and canal commissioner February 22d, 1840. Hiram Gardner was appointed to the latter office November 21st, 1858, and James Jackson November 4th, 1873. George C. Greene was appointed appraiser January 27th, 1870. All these gentlemen were citizens of Lockport.

Gaylord G. Clark, of Lockport, was elected one of the inspectors of State prisons November 4th, 1862.

George D. Lamont, of Lockport, was elected a Justice of the Supreme Court for the eighth district in 1868, and again in 1871. Nathan Dayton, also of Lockport, was appointed a circuit judge February 23d, 1838.

Hiram Gardner and John W. McNitt were members from Niagara of the constitutional convention of 1846, and Thomas T. Flagler and Levi F. Bowen of that of 1867.

The following citizens of Niagara county have served as Presidential electors: Hiram Gardner, 1836; Davis Hurd and Peter B. Porter, 1840; Solomon Parmele, 1848; William Vandervoort and Sherburne B. Piper (elector-at-large with Charles O'Connor), 1852; William Keep, 1856; Moses C. Richardson, 1872.

LEGISLATIVE REPRESENTATIVES.

State Senators.—The Second Constitution divided the State into eight senate districts, entitled to four senators apiece; Niagara county was part of the eighth. The present constitution created thirty-two districts, each to choose one senator. Of these, Niagara, Orleans and Genesee counties constituted the twenty-eighth until changed to the twenty-ninth by the act of 1857. The senators from Niagara county, with their residences and the years they were in the Senate, have been as follows: George H. Boughton, Lockport, 1829, 1830; Samuel Works, Lockport, 1837-1844; Horatio J. Stow, Lewiston, 1858, 1859; died during the session and George D. Lamont, of Lockport, filled out his term; Peter P. Murphy, Royalton, 1860, 1861; Richard Crowley, Lockport, 1866-1869; Lewis S. Payne, North Tonawanda, 1878, 1879.

Assemblymen.—Niagara constituted one Assembly district until May 3d, 1836, when it was divided. It has ever since been entitled to two members. At the adoption of the present constitution the first Assembly district consisted of the towns of Lockport, Niagara, Pendleton, Royalton and Wheatfield. In 1857 Niagara was transferred to the second district, and Cambria in 1866 from the second to the first. The members from the creation of the county have been as follows:

In the session of 1823, Benjamin Barlow, jr.; 1824 and 1825, Daniel Washburn; 1826, William King; 1827-1829, John Garnsey; 1830, Samuel De Veaux; 1831-1833, Henry Norton; 1834, Robert Fleming, jr.; 1835, Henry McNeil; 1836, Hiram Gardner; 1837, Reuben H. Boughton (who died during the session), Davis Hurd (who completed Boughton's term) and Hiram McNeil; 1838 and 1839, Davis Hurd, Peter B. Porter, jr.; 1840 and 1841, Peter B. Porter, jr., Francis O. Pratt; 1842, Thomas T. Flagler, Francis O. Pratt; 1843, Thomas T. Flagler, John Sweeney; 1844, John Sweeney, Luther Wilson; 1845, Levi F. Bowen, John Sweeney; 1846, Lot Clark, Morgan Johnson; 1847, Benjamin Carpenter, Christopher H. Skeels; 1848, Elias Ransom, Solomon Moss, Morgan Johnson (who unseated Moss on a contest during the session); 1849, Hollis White, Morgan Johnson; 1850, George W. Jermain, James Van Horn, jr.; 1851 and 1852, Abijah H. Moss, Jeptha W. Babcock; 1853, George W. Holley, Reuben F. Wilson; 1854, Robert Dunlap, Reuben F. Wilson; 1855, Linus Jones Peck, Ira Tompkins; 1856, William S. Penn, John Gould; 1857, Elisha Clapp, John Gould; 1858, Burt Van Horn, John W. Labar; 1859, James Sweeney, Burt Van Horn; 1860, Thomas B. Flager, Burt Van Horn; 1861, Henry P. Smith, Oliver P. Scovell; 1862, Benjamin H. Fletcher, Peter A. Porter; 1863, Benjamin H. Fletcher, William Morgan; 1864, James Jackson, jr., William Morgan; 1865, Albert H. Pickard, Guy C. Humphrey; 1866, Solon S. Pomeroy, Guy C. Humphrey; 1867, Elisha Moody, William Pool; 1868 and 1869, Ransom M. Skeels, Benjamin Farley; 1870, Lewis S. Payne, Lee R. Sanborn; 1871, John E. Pound, Lee R. Sanborn; 1872 and 1873, Isaac H. Babcock, George M. Swain; 1874 and 1875, Artemus W. Comstock, Orville C. Bordwell; 1876, Amos A. Bissell, Jonah W. Brown; 1877, Amos A. Bissell, Sherburne B. Piper; 1878, Joseph D. Loveland, Sherburne B. Piper.

Members of Congress.—An act of March 8th, 1808, made the fifteenth Congressional district of New York consist of Allegany, Cattaraugus, Chautauqua, Genesee, Niagara and Ontario counties. Peter B. Porter, of Niagara Falls, represented the district in the XIth Congress (1809-1811), the XIIth (1811-1813), and the XIVth (1815-1817). An act of April 17th, 1822, formed the thirtieth district from Niagara, Erie and Chautauqua counties. In 1832 Niagara and Orleans became the thirty-third district, in 1842 the thirty-fourth, and in 1851 the thirty-first. In 1862 Niagara, Genesee and Wyoming were made to constitute the twenty-ninth district, and in 1873 the thirty-first. The district has been represented by Niagara county men as follows:

Sessions of 1831-1833 (XXIId Congress), Bates Cook, of Lewiston; 1837-1841 (XXVth and XXVIth Congresses), Charles F. Mitchell, of Lockport; 1843-1849 (XXVIIIth, XXIXth and XXXth Congresses), Washington Hunt, of Lockport; 1853-1857, (XXXIIId and XXXIVth Congresses), Thomas T. Flagler, of Lockport; 1861-1863, 1865-1867 1867-1869, (XXXVIIth, XXXIXth and XLth Congresses), Burt Van Horn, of Newfane.

CHAPTER XXIII.

THE PROJECTION OF THE ERIE CANAL—ITS ADVOCATES AND ITS CONSTRUCTION—LAFAYETTE'S TOUR.

ADVOCATES of the extension of inland navigation in New York did not at first contemplate anything beyond the improvement of the natural channels from the Hudson to Lake Ontario—the Mohawk river, Wood creek, Oneida lake and river and the Oswego river. Governor Colden in 1724 even expressed the hope that the western part of the State might be penetrated by boats, independent of Lake Ontario. In his memoir of that year on the fur trade, occurs the following passage, which has been remarked as the first recorded speculation on the possibility of inland water communication between Lake Erie and the Mohawk river:

"There is a river which comes from the country of the Sinnekes and falls into the Onnondage river, by which we have an easy carriage into that country without going near the Cataracqui [Ontario] lake. The head of this River goes near to Lake Erie and probably may give a very near passage into that lake, much more advantageous than the way the French are obliged to take by the way of the great fall of Iagara." Colden seems not to have known of the Genesee, crossing what he supposed to be the course of the "Sinnekes'" river. No natural stream, indeed, could have followed the line he conjectured; but a hundred years later saw an artificial river pursuing such a line, and doing far more for interior navigation than he had mistakenly thought might be accomplished by the natural one.

The improvement of river channels being found inadequate, the construction of a canal from Lake Erie to the Hudson suggested itself to commercial and scientific minds. The first proposal, if not the original conception of such an enterprise is claimed for Gouverneur Morris. In conversation with Simeon De Witt, surveyor-general of the State, in 1803 at Schenectady, Mr. Morris suggested the project of conveying the water of Lake Erie direct to the Hudson by cutting through intervening highlands and forming an artificial river with a uniform fall of six inches per mile from west to east. The surveyor-general, in common with most to whom the scheme was mentioned, regarded it as visionary and impracticable, and so represented it to James Geddes, a surveyor of Onondaga county, in a conversation with him. Geddes, however, on reflection viewed it differently, and concluded that with some modifications the plan might be carried out, and that the work would be one of great utility. People generally, however, appalled by the magnitude of the suggested enterprise, hardly dared to consider the subject gravely, and for several years after the conception of the idea nothing was done toward realizing it.

The man who first publicly championed the idea of a canal from Lake Erie to the Hudson was Jesse Hawley. He was born at Bridgeport, Connecticut, in 1773. In 1805 and for some years after he was engaged in buying wheat in the Genesee valley, which he had ground at Mynderse's mill at Little Falls and sent the flour to Albany. His occupation suggested thoughts on the improvement of transportation facilities. "I first," said he, "conceived the idea of the overland route of the canal from Buffalo to Utica in Colonel Wilhelmus Mynderse's office, at Seneca Falls, in 1805." Mr. Hawley expatiated on the subject in his private correspondence and conversation; and, spending the winter of 1806-7 in Pittsburgh, he published an article in the *Commonwealth* newspaper of that city setting forth his views. This was reprinted on the 27th of October, 1807, in the *Genesee Messenger*, and was followed by thirteen other essays published in the same paper, the last March 2nd, 1808. In these papers, which Mr. Hawley signed "Hercules," he explained and advocated the canal idea with great originality and foresight, creating a powerful sentiment in its favor. He recommended a route very nearly corresponding with that followed in the construction of the canal through western New York, and prophesied the results to be attained with singular correctness. Having had the pleasure of seeing his views carried out, with the anticipated fruits, he exerted his influence in favor of the enlargement of the canal as earnestly as he had in behalf of its construction; but he had reason to complain that his services never received adequate recognition. He spent his last years in Lockport, where he died in January, 1842. He was buried in the beautiful Cold Spring rural cemetery, and the neighboring city, a creature of the Erie Canal, is in some sense his monument.

Mr. Geddes corresponded with surveyors and engineers on the subject of a canal, and agitated the topic in his county until it became a leading political issue, and Joshua Forman was elected to the Assembly on a "canal ticket." He was the first to propose legislation looking toward the construction of a canal, which he did February 4th, 1808. Pursuant of a resolution offered by him a committee was appointed to report on the propriety of an exploration and survey, to the end that Congress might be induced to appropriate the necessary funds. The committee reported favorably; a survey was ordered April 6th, 1808, and $600 appropriated for the expenses.

The service was performed by James Geddes. He was directed to examine the route for a canal from Oneida lake to Lake Ontario, as well as that from Lake Erie eastward. He reported in favor of the latter, which he pronounced feasible. He suggested that there might "be found some place in the ridge that bounds the Tonawanda valley on the north as low as the level of Lake Erie, where a canal may be led across and conducted onward without increasing the lockage by rising to the Tonawanda swamp."

The latter difficulty was involved in the route contemplated by Mr. Joseph Ellicott. He supposed the summit on that line would not be more than twenty feet above Lake Erie, and that upon it a sufficient supply of water might be obtained from Oak Orchard creek and other streams. In this he was mistaken; the summit was found to be seventy-five feet above Lake Erie, and to be supplied with no adequate feeder. It is probably not too much to say that the canal could never have been successfully constructed through western New York, but for the discovery of such a route as Mr. Geddes suggested, permitting a continuous flow eastward from Lake Erie and making the lake the feeder.

During the legislative session of 1810, pursuant of a resolution offered by Senator Platt, and concurred in by the Assembly March 12th, Peter B. Porter, Gouverneur Morris, Stephen Van Rensselaer, DeWitt Clinton, Simeon DeWitt, William North and Thomas Eddy were appointed commissioners to make a complete exploration of the proposed routes of water communication between the Hudson and the lakes. Three thousand dollars were voted them for expenses. Messrs. Morris and Van Rensselaer traversed the proposed line of the Erie Canal in advance of the other commissioners, and awaited them at Lewiston. The rest of the board, accompanied by Mr. Geddes, after exploring the Oswego river, paddled up the Seneca river, and held a consultation at Geneva on the 24th of July. Thence they continued to the falls of the Genesee, and from there by the Ridge road to Lewiston. A meeting of the board was held at Chippewa August 3d, when Mr. Geddes was directed to make some further surveys. On the 16th the party was at Buffalo.

The commissioners made their report March 2nd, 1811. It embodied a recommendation of a canal on the route selected by Mr. Geddes, and a warning against allowing it to be built by private parties, which would defeat cheap transportation by permitting a monopoly. The cost of the work was estimated at $5,000,000. The Legislature, on the strength of this report, continued the commission and voted $15,000 for further operations.

A year later, it having been found impossible to obtain an appropriation from Congress, the Legislature authorized the commissioners to borrow $5,000,000 on the credit of the State for the construction of the canal.

The prosecution of the work was prevented by the war of 1812, which so engrossed public attention that the canal project was abandoned and the act authorizing a loan in its behalf was repealed.

Toward the close of 1815 the enterprise was revived. An influential meeting in its favor was held at New York in December of that year, at which resolutions were adopted urging the construction of the canal. Similar meetings were held at Albany, Utica, Geneva, Canandaigua and Buffalo, and a sentiment created which expressed itself in petitions with more than a hundred thousand signers for the prosecution of the work.

The Legislature of 1816 reconstructed the canal commission, making it consist of De Witt Clinton, Stephen Van Rensselaer, Joseph Ellicott, Myron Holley and Samuel Young. A year later was passed an act prepared by Mr. Clinton authorizing the commencement of actual construction. The canal, however, was still regarded by many as a ruinous experiment, and lamentations were frequently heard on the miseries of an overtaxed people and their posterity.

The work was divided into western, middle and eastern sections, the dividing points being Rome and the Seneca river. Of the western section James Geddes was appointed chief engineer. In 1815 he surveyed the route. Up to 1820 nothing was done upon this section except to adopt the line laid down by Mr. Geddes. In 1820 he was succeeded by David Thomas, who in that year examined the line adopted from Rochester to Pendleton and modified it somewhat east of Oak Orchard creek. A more important change was made as to the point of passing the mountain ridge in Niagara county—one that determined the site of the city of Lockport. Mr. Geddes's line crossed the ridge in the gorge a mile west of Lockport. The whole western part of the canal was put under contract in 1821.

Then followed long, tedious years of labor, that must sometimes have tried the faith and hope of the most sanguine. First, a belt of the forest had in most places to be removed. Then little armies of men and teams, toiling in the lane thus made in the woods, slowly gave the ground the shape of a great ditch with its bounding embankments; or still more slowly, with drill and powder, wrought their way through ledges of solid rock. Extempore hamlets of shanties sprung up along the line, moving like miners' camps with the progress of the contractors' gangs ; and shrewd speculators were busied in possessing themselves of lots where more permanent villages seemed destined to stand.

During the autumn of 1823 the completed and navigable portion of the canal was extended westward to Brockport and Holley, and during the next season to the foot of the ridge at Lockport. In 1824, also, the adaptation of the Niagara river and Tonawanda creek to the purposes of the canal was completed, and the line excavated from the creek toward Lockport. It need hardly be said that the stupendous rock cutting extending through and west of that city was the last spot finished between Buffalo and Albany. Mr. Orsamus Turner has drawn an interesting picture of the state of things in this vicinity in 1822. He says :

"Culver & Maynard were clearing the timber from the slopes of the mountain around the ravine and excavating the first rock section ; Childs & Hamlin were excavating the second section, Darius Comstock the third, John Gilbert the fourth ; Norton, Bates, House & Boughton the fifth and last rock section. The dense forest between Lockport and Tonawanda creek looked as if a hurricane had passed through it, leaving a narrow belt of fallen timber, excavated stone and earth ; and, to complete the ragged scene, log boarding houses had been strung along the whole distance. The blasting of rocks was going on briskly. * * * As the rock excavation deepened it baffled the ingenuity of commissioners and contractors, and became expensive beyond all estimate ; no greater facilities existed for raising the rock than wheelbarrows and long runs. In this exigency Orange Dibble, * * * with a brother-in-law of his, named Olmsted, invented and introduced a simple crane, that revolutionized the work, vastly cheapened it, and in the end was the means of completing the canal one year before it could have been done in the absence of it. In the original construction of the locks the contractors, at great expense, opened a road through the woods to Williamsville to procure their water lime. At the same time, in excavating the lock pits and a portion of their rock section, they were removing immense quantities of stone capable of making an hydraulic cement equal in quality to the best that has been discovered in the United States. It was used in the construction of the new locks, and has become an article of commerce upon the canal and lakes, for use in public structures or wherever such a material is required. The credit of demonstrating its superor quality and introducing it into extensive use belongs to Mr. Seth Pierce, of Lockport."

Mr. Turner elsewhere states that among the trees cut to make place for the locks was a black walnut " a saw-log from which, fourteen feet in length, made 1,643 feet of inch boards ;" and that " an Englishman who had a nursery of forest trees in England in an early day procured in the neighborhood of Lockport a black walnut, an oak and a whitewood plank, all eighty feet in length, and measuring at their butts over five feet in breadth, clear of the wane. He took them to London for exhibition."

The commissioner who superintended the construction of the western portion of the canal was William C. Bouck, afterward governor of the State. On the 29th of September, 1825, he wrote from Lockport to Stephen Van Rensselaer, president of the canal commission, the following letter :

" Sir : The unfinished parts of the Erie canal will be

completed and in a condition to admit the passage of boats on Wednesday, the 26th day of October next. It would have been gratifying to have accomplished this result as early as the first of September, but embarrassments which I could not control delayed it.

On this grand event, so auspicious to the character and wealth of the citizens of New York, permit me to congratulate you."

By extra exertion the work of excavation was completed and the filling of the last section begun on the 24th of October. In twenty-four hours the filling was accomplished, and all things were ready for a grand celebration on the morrow, for which due preparations had been made.

In the forenoon of the 26th a flotilla of five boats left Buffalo for the first through passage from lake to seaport, bearing the highest executive officers of the State and many other dignitaries. Their departure was the signal for firing the first of a large number of cannon (some of them thirty-two pounders from Perry's fleet), stationed within hearing distance of each other along the whole line of the canal and the Hudson river and at Sandy Hook. By discharging one of these the instant its next neighbor —five or six miles away—was heard from, the momentous news of the opening of through travel at Buffalo was conveyed to the ocean in an hour and twenty minutes. A small fleet of boats which had started at the foot of the locks at Lockport about the time that the flotilla left Buffalo met the latter in Tonawanda creek and convoyed it to Lockport, where, and at Albion, Holley, Brockport and everywhere along the line, it was hailed with a jubilant enthusiasm which it is now difficult alike to imagine and to describe.

The length of the canal was 363 miles, and its original cost $7,143,780.86. It was planned to be forty feet wide at the surface and twenty-eight at the bottom, with four feet of water. The locks were ninety feet long, and twelve feet wide in the clear. The capacity indicated by these figures was soon found to be inadequate, and the necessity of enlarging the canal was made apparent. By an act passed in May, 1835, the canal commissioners were authorized to have the work performed, including the construction of double locks, as fast as they should judge advisable. Under this act the enlargement was begun, and continued with more or less activity for more than a quarter of a century before it was complete throughout. The reconstructed canal was reduced to 350 1-2 miles in length, and increased in breadth to seventy feet at the surface and fifty-two and a half at the bottom, while the depth of water was increased to seven feet. The cost of the enlargement was over $30,000,000.

It can hardly be necessary to point out the effects of the canal in facilitating communication and opening markets, breathing the breath of a new life into the agricultural interest of western New York, and stimulating the growth of population along its line. We might as well call attention to the uses of the sunshine and the air as refer at length " to the great cities that have been doubled in population, to the new ones it has created, to the large and prosperous villages that are dotted along its banks, to the new empire it has helped to create around the borders of our western lakes, and the fleets of steam and sail vessels it has put afloat upon their waters."

The canal at the outset, far from being exclusively an artery of commerce, as at present, was the fashionable avenue of western travel. The packets were elegantly furnished, set excellent tables, and outstripped the freight boats in speed by their comparative lightness, and their three-horse teams. They ran from the east as far as Lockport before the completion of the upper level of the canal. Mr. Turner informs us that " Seymour Scovell built the first packet west of Montezuma, the 'Myron Holley,' and Oliver Culver the next one, the 'Wm. C. Bouck.'"

The most famous of early travelers by the canal was the illustrious Marquis de Lafayette. After a tour in the west he reached Buffalo in the first week of June, 1825, and journeyed down the Niagara to its mouth, where he was received with a salute from the guns of the fort. At Lewiston he spent a night at the hotel kept by Thomas Kelsey. Thence he was conveyed to Lockport, an escort from that place meeting him at Howell's on the Ridge road. At Lockport he embarked for the east on a packet at the foot of the locks. At all points he was received with such honors as might be expected from a people who appreciated his services to their country during the Revolutionary war.

CHAPTER XXIV.

THE CASE OF WILLIAM MORGAN—RISE AND CAREER OF THE ANTI-MASONIC PARTY.

EXCEPTING, perhaps, the events of the war of 1812, no occurrence in the history of north-western New York ever so generally attracted the attention of the country as the disappearance of the free mason Morgan in the autumn of 1826, with the uprising against the masonic fraternity which his mysterious fate produced. No other event, therefore, more fairly demands a chapter in the history of the region where the circumstances connected with the affair occurred. These circumstances are even now a subject of controversy, from which we carefully refrain, while giving the facts as nearly as they can be ascertained. Our narrative is based largely upon an account compiled from the official reports of the trials for the abduction of Morgan, by a gentleman who thought it must be admitted that those who believe the unfortunate man was murdered "base their conclusion upon presumptive evidence of a nature which is by no means conclusive."

William Morgan was living at Batavia during the summer and part of the autumn of 1826. He was a native of Virginia, and is represented to have been a man of indifferent character and very poor. The latter fact is suggested as perhaps the chief consideration which led him to determine upon the publication of the secrets of the masonic fraternity, of which he was a member in the Royal Arch degree. The design becoming known in the summer of 1826 strenuous efforts were made by the free masons with whom he had affiliated to prevent the intended publication. A stranger obtained an introduction to Morgan, and on pretense of wishing to buy an interest in his proposed book tried to get possession of the manuscript he had written.

The revelation was to be gotten out by a Batavia printer named Miller. This was understood, and Miller's office took fire under circumstances indicating an incendiary attempt. On the 12th of September Miller himself was arrested at Batavia by a constable named Jesse French, on a justice's warrant issued by one Bartow, of Le Roy. Roswell Wilcox and James Hurlbut accompanied the constable and his prisoner to Le Roy, and their carriage was followed by a crowd who seem to have understood the signifigance of the arrest. At Stafford Miller was taken into the masonic lodgeroom, where, it is said, an armed assemblage tried to frighten him into agreeing to deliver up the obnoxious manuscript. A company of his friends outside, however, made demonstrations which led to his being brought out and carried on to Le Roy, whither the crowd followed. There was no case against the prisoner, and he was immediately discharged, and escorted back to Batavia by his partisans. In turn, French, Wilcox and Hurlbut were tried for false imprisonment, riot, and assault and battery, and sentenced to imprisonment for twelve, six and three months respectively.

On Sunday, September 10th, Ebenezer C. Kingsley obtained from Justice Jeffrey Chipman, of Canandaigua, a warrant for the arrest of Morgan on a charge of having stolen a shirt and cravat, which Kingsley had in fact lent him. On this warrant Morgan was arrested the next day at Batavia, and taken in a public coach to Canandaigua. The charge against him was not sustained and he was promptly discharged. He was immediately re-arrested, however, on a civil suit for $2, the amount of a tavern bill against him, held by one Ackley, which the latter had assigned to Nicholas G. Cheesebro, the master of a masonic lodge at Canandaigua. A judgment was given against Morgan, to satisfy which he offered his coat. The offer was refused and the unfortunate man was lodged in the Ontario county jail.

This was in the evening of the 11th. Twenty-four hours later members of the masonic fraternity called at the jail, and in the absence of the jailor advised his wife to release Morgan, telling her the judgment against him had been paid by one Loton Lawson. The prisoner was accordingly liberated, but on reaching the street he was suddenly seized, thrust into a close carriage in waiting, gagged and bound and driven rapidly out of the village to the westward. His fellow passengers were three free masons, one of whom was Lawson. This man subsequently testified that it had been decided upon by the fraternity that Morgan must be separated from Miller and his other friends at Batavia; that on being put into the carriage he at first struggled and called out, and once afterward shouted "Murder!" but otherwise was quiet and admitted his error, and that it was best he should leave Miller and not publish his intended revelations. In this frame of mind he was taken through Rochester and west on the Ridge road. It is stated that none but masons were allowed to communicate with the occupants of the carriage. No noise was heard from it except at one point. The Ridge road was followed to Lewiston, and thence the carriage passed down the Niagara river to Fort Niagara. On reaching the fort the driver was told to stop near the graveyard. Here the passengers got out and entered the enclosure, and the coachman was dismissed. This was near midnight of the 13th.

For some days before, according to testimony in court, preparations had been making for the reception of the kidnapped man, and he was now taken into the fort, blindfolded and pinioned, and thrown into the magazine, where he was confined until the 19th. He was quite "noisy" at first, and prominent masons tried to "quiet" him. Captain James Van Cleve makes the following statement bearing upon this stage of the affair:

"In September, 1826, many free masons came up the lake on board the steamer 'Ontario' [on which Van Cleve was clerk] from Rochester, to participate in the installation of Colonel William King as knight templar at Lewiston. On the steamer's return she landed (by request) at the government wharf at Fort Niagara, and many masons went into the fort for the purpose of seeing William Morgan, who was then confined there by the masons. Colonel Samuel Denison, the managing owner of the 'Ontario,' who was a mason, told me at the time that he was requested to go into the fort and see Morgan, but he declined, believing such high-handed measures in violation of the law would in the end lead to much trouble, which proved true."

Morgan was constantly visited, as witnesses represented, and threatened, to make him tell where and how his manuscript could be obtained. He begged to see his wife and children. He is reported to have said several times that he would rather stay in the magazine than be bled to death by the doctor; this was thought to indicate that his reason was giving way; it is not known that any doctor had anything to do with him.

Consultations were held in regard to the disposal of the man, as he proved obdurate on the subject of his revelations. Three propositions were discussed, if our authority may be trusted, namely, to settle him on a farm in Canada, to hand him over to the masonic commander of a British man-of-war at Montreal or Quebec, and to drown him in the river. Masons who admitted having participated in these discussions declared that they strenuously opposed the last suggestion, even to the point of high words and a quarrel.

On the 19th of September Morgan disappeared. No one who was sworn at the trials for his abduction was at the magazine when the wretched man left it, nor, as they claimed, could they ascertain his fate.

When the foregoing facts came out the conclusion that Morgan was drowned in the Niagara naturally prevailed, and the river was dragged for his body, but to no effect. A little more than a year after his disappearance a corpse was found on the lake shore in Carlton, Orleans county. A coroner's jury pronounced it that of an "unknown" person; but the anti-masons, suspecting that it was the body of Morgan, had it exhumed and procured another inquest and a verdict in accordance with their belief, on the strength of which the remains were conveyed to Batavia and buried. Thurlow Weed, who was one of the anti-masonic leaders, was among those examined at this inquest. It is charged that certain persons, politically interested in promoting the belief that Morgan was drowned, manipulated the body so as to increase its resemblance to him, one of them making the remark, which became part of the political slang of the day, that it was "a good enough Morgan till after election." Additional information having been obtained respecting the body in question, one more inquest was held, by which the corpse was proved to be that of Timothy Monroe, a man accidentally drowned near the mouth of the Niagara.

A tremendous excitement of course followed the disappearance of Morgan, and investigating committees were everywhere appointed. Eli Bruce, the sheriff of Niagara county; the commandant of Fort Niagara, and several other prominent masons were tried at Lockport and Canandaigua for abduction or kidnapping, and one or two were convicted. Others escaped by the refusal of witnesses to testify. Prominent and previously respectable citizens were seen in the attitude of refusing to give evidence lest it should criminate themselves. Eli Bruce was fined and imprisoned for contumacy, and deposed from his office by the governor. The trials, some of which were conducted by Judges Nelson, Marcy and Throop, and the ablest counsel that could be obtained, occurred during four or five years after the event that originated them, and perpetuated and intensified the interest which the disappearance of Morgan and the alleged circumstances of course created.

The hostility of feeling between masons and anti-masons was of the bitterest description. The dividing line ran through families and churches, and no relation was too intimate or sacred to be disturbed by the agitation. Even the boys in the streets took sides, and while their elders bandied hot words they satisfied themselves only by throwing stones. The masonic fraternity throughout a large section of the country was threatened with destruction, many lodges being so weakened by withdrawals and lack of applications for membership as to be disbanded for years, if not permanently.

The most notable effect of the agitation was the rise and career of the Anti-Masonic party, which immediately controlled local elections and ultimately made itself felt on a far wider scale. This phase of the subject the writer to whom we are indebted for much of the substance of this chapter sums up by saying that "at this time [1826], when the politics of the nation were in bitter and vehement controversy between the adherents of General Jackson on one side and the Republicans (designated in New York as Clintonians and Bucktails), the new party of anti-masonry subdivided and distracted all other parties, and drew thousands of adherents from them all; that in the election of 1829 its candidate for State senator in the VIIIth district of New York was elected by the unprecedented majority of 8,000; that in the general election of 1830, in a poll of 250,000 votes, it failed to elevate its candidate to the executive chair by barely 8,000, and in the election of 1832 in the same State, in a poll of 320,000, it was defeated by less than 10,000 majority; that it diffused itself like wildfire throughout the neighboring States, carrying its candidate into the gubernatorial chair in Pennsylvania in 1835, and developing an astonishing degree of strength in previous years in Ohio, Massachusetts, Rhode Island and Vermont, in which latter State it was triumphant for three years; and finally that this unprecedented outbreak of public sentiment found voice in a national convention in 1831, putting forth the most stringent resolutions against the institution of free masonry as a platform, and nominating candidates upon it who in the States named received a large support, and who in the electoral college had the seven electoral votes of Vermont."

CHAPTER XXV.

OLD-TIME STAGE LINES ON THE RIDGE ROAD—RAILROAD HISTORY OF NIAGARA COUNTY.

THE dependence for public conveyance previous to the completion of the canal was the stages running west from Canandaigua, either to Buffalo direct or by way of the Ridge road, Lewiston and Niagara Falls. The latter route was established in 1816. It was controlled at one time by brothers named Coe, living at Buffalo and Canandaigua, and at another by parties of the name of Hildreth. These stages ran one each way every day and did a roaring business, which was somewhat impaired by the completion of the canal and the establishment of the packet lines. In their palmy days they were always full, inside and out, of emigrants, business men, and tourists on the way to Niagara Falls, who would go west from Canandaigua by the Ridge road and return from Buffalo direct, via Batavia, or *vice versa*. The Coe coaches were met at Wright's Corners by a wagon from Lockport, bringing mail and passengers for the stage line. They were kept running up to about 1850. Passengers paid first or second class fare, the former only being assured of inside seats, of which there were enough for twelve persons. In winter a rectangular box on bobs took the place of the wheeled coaches. These stages ran every day in the week.

In 1828 a number of wealthy gentlemen, principally of Rochester, regretting the violation of the Sabbath involved in coaching on Sunday, established an opposition line to run on week days only, which they called the Pioneer line. Their route left the Ridge road at Wright's Corners for Lockport, where "Gid" Hersey's coffee house, which is still standing in West Main street, was the stopping place; thence it continued west to Niagara Falls, and so to Buffalo. The stages of this line aimed to leave Wright's for the east at a different hour from the Coes', both to secure a larger share of passengers and to avoid running in company with their rivals. When they did fall in with each other the drivers had a war of words, and sometimes raced their four-horse teams at the top of their speed, which the imperfect finish of the road made a dangerous proceeding. The Coe line lowered its rates, and the other failing to get the mail contract, succumbed to the competition and went down after running about two years.

At times, especially in the season of visiting Niagara Falls, neither line could accommodate the tide of travel with its regular coaches alone; both turned out extra teams and wagons, and eight or ten stages of various sorts, heavily loaded, sometimes went west in a day.

Gaines, Orleans county, was a place for changing teams and getting refreshments. The stopping place was the old Mansion House, which was succeeded by the Gaines House. Gaines was two hundred and fifty miles from Albany by stage, and the trip required about forty-three hours, including stops.

With the advent of railroads the glory of the stage and packet lines departed. Several roads were constructed about the same time, making the three or four years beginning with 1835 an era of pioneer railroad building in America. In 1835 the Lockport and Niagara Falls company began the construction of its line. The road started at the corner of Chapel and East Market streets, in Lockport, and running southwesterly a short distance turned across the canal at Cady's boat-yard, and by a grade which is still traceable reached the end of Glenwood street. Along that street, which was originally graded for the railroad, it wound its way up the mountain side, and after turning to the south to pass the head of the gorge a mile west of Lockport it bore away to the northwest through Pekin and nearly to Lewiston, and then turned up to what is now Suspension Bridge, whence it ran to the Falls along the cliff that overlooks the Niagara river. The track consisted of oak "mudsills," two and a half inches by twelve, laid lengthwise of the road, with the ties resting across them, and upon the ties four by six inch oak timbers, on which were spiked bands or straps of iron. These irons had a tendency to work loose at the ends and turn up, forming "snakeheads," as they were called, which were ready to catch in the bottom of a car, spearing the passengers and throwing it off the track. The cars were small affairs with four wheels, holding either sixteen or twenty-four persons, those of the former class being divided into two and the others into three compartments, with seats running across, stage coach fashion. They were drawn for about two years by horses, when light locomotives came into use. They often had difficulty in surmounting the stiff grade which they encountered in leaving Lockport.

Meetings were held at Lockport in 1835 in favor of the construction of railroads to Batavia and Buffalo, but nothing was done. The next enterprise of the kind in this region was the building of a horse-car line from Medina, Orleans county, to Akron, Erie county, in 1836 by the Medina and Darien Railroad Company. It was operated but a short time, as it did not pay, and the track was taken up. In the same year enterprising Medina took measures for the building of a railroad to the mouth of Oak Orchard creek. The Medina and Ontario Railroad Company was incorporated for that purpose, but the line was never built. The history of the Batavia, Albion and Oak Orchard Railroad scheme of 1875 is equally brief.

In July, 1836, the *Niagara Falls Journal* announced that the road from Lockport to that place was rapidly approaching completion, and that the Buffalo and Niagara Falls Railroad was in a similar forward state, cars being then running on some part of it. It was expected that the track from the Falls to Schlosser and from Black Rock to Buffalo would be in use by the first of August, with a steamboat completing the connection by several trips daily; and that both roads would be ready for the track throughout in September. The Buffalo road had been surveyed in 1834, and the grading partially done in 1835. The track, which was laid in 1836, was similar to that of the Lockport and Niagara Falls road, consisting of two-inch plank laid lengthwise as sleepers, ties resting on them three feet apart, and across these (and sunk into them for security) four by six inch oak scantling, thirty, thirty-three, thirty-six or thirty-nine feet in length, on which flat rails of iron, half an inch thick and two and a half wide, were fastened by spikes driven about fifteen inches apart. The frost heaved up this track so badly as to make it unsafe for engines in winter, and horses were then used to draw the cars. About 1844 the road was reconstructed, the route being also slightly changed. Heavier rails were laid, on white oak ties. The cars were like those above described, the conductor collecting fares by passing along outside on a narrow platform. The first conductor was Samuel Hamlin, and the first baggage master George Hamlin.

In the latter part of August the *Buffalo Courier* announced that the first locomotive had just been put on the track between Tonawanda and Black Rock, and a speed of about fifteen miles per hour attained. The part from Tonawanda to the Falls was not then finished, but must have been soon after. The first engine was the "Little Buffalo," and the next the "Niagara." The first was run by one Ford, and the other by an engineer named Barney.

On the 10th of December, 1850, the Rochester, Lockport and Niagara Falls Railroad Company was organized. It bought out the Lockport and Niagara Falls company in 1851, and the latter's track was abandoned and taken up. Local subscriptions were made along the proposed line amounting to $225,000. The first board of directors consisted of Joseph B. Varnum and Edward Whitehouse, of New York; Watts Sherman, of Albany; Freeman Clarke, Silas O. Smith and A. Boody, of Rochester; Alexis Ward and Roswell W. Burrows, of Albion; and Elias B. Holmes, of Brockport. Mr. Varnum was elected president, Mr. Ward vice-president, and Mr. Clarke treasurer. The directors and a few others passed over the road June 25th, 1852, and regular trains began running on the 30th. The first one between Rochester and Lockport was drawn by the engine " Niagara," and made fifty miles per hour part of the way. The new road and the other lines running through central and western New York were consolidated, May 7th, 1853, to form the New York Central. The branch from Lockport junction to Tonawanda was built by the Rochester, Lockport and Niagara Falls Company in 1852, and opened in January, 1853.

At the same time with the Central there was organized a company which built the Canandaigua and Niagara Falls Railroad. The line was opened to the Falls July 1st, 1853, and to Suspension Bridge October 1st, 1854. March 22nd, 1857, it was bought by James M. Brown and other parties in Europe, to whom it was heavily mortgaged, who changed the name to Niagara Bridge and Canandaigua Railroad, and immediately leased it for ninety-nine years to the Central company, which changed its original broad gauge to the standard gauge of four feet, eight and a half inches. The first president of the road was a Mr. Bond, of Honeoye Falls; and the first superintendent, Mr. Lapham, of Canandaigua.

The Suspension Bridge and Erie Junction branch of the Erie railway, from Buffalo to Suspension Bridge, was built in the fall and winter of 1870 and 1871. Freight trains were run over the road in the winter of 1870-1. The road was not formally opened for the transaction of all business until May 15th, 1871. Passenger trains commenced running on that day. The first train for Suspension Bridge left Buffalo at 5.55 A. M., drawn by engine 189, with A. Hale, engineer,—Kirse fireman, — Davis baggageman; — Collins brakeman and I. A. Waldron conductor, and arrived at Suspension Bridge at 7.15 A. M. The first for Buffalo left Suspension Bridge at 5.50 A. M., drawn by engine 413, James Gates engineer, A. L. Gire fireman ; — Whitman was baggageman, — Decker brakeman, and J. C. Davenport conductor. The train arrived at Buffalo at 7.24 A. M. The first superintendent of the division was H. C. Fisk, of Buffalo. The present superintendent is R. G. Taylor, of Buffalo. The first station agent at North Tonawanda after the road was opened was W. H. Upson, who is the present agent.

On the 9th of September, 1852, the Niagara Falls and Lake Ontario Railroad Company was incorporated to build a line from Niagara Falls to Youngstown. Benjamin Pringle was president, John Porter vice-president, Bradley D. Davis secretary and William S. Mallory treasurer. This road, so remarkable for the amount of rock cutting required in its construction, and for its position in part on a narrow shelf in the cliff that towers above the rapid waters of the Niagara between the Devil's Hole and Lewiston, was graded and opened down to that village in 1854. On the 21st of October, 1855, a train was run over the line to Youngstown, and soon afterward work on this part of the road was suspended and the track taken up. Had the project been carried forward and the line put in operation, Youngstown would probably have been the port for the Lake Ontario steamers, and would have taken much of the business which now centers at Lewiston and Niagara Falls. The portion of the road that was built was subsequently leased and is now operated by the Central company.

In May, 1874, the " Niagara River and Air Line Railroad Company" elected directors from Lockport, Medina, Albion, Holley, Brockport and Spencerport, and as president J. W. Helmer, of Lockport. A year later the company voted to disband.

In the spring of 1870 the Lake Ontario Shore Railroad Company was organized at Oswego. The road which the company was formed to build was intended to be part of a future trunk line from Boston to the west. The town of Kendall, Orleans county, gave its bonds for $60,000 worth of the stock; Yates, $100,000; Somerset, Niagara county, $90,000; Newfane, $88,000; Wilson, $117,000; Lewiston, $152,000. The work of construction proceeded slowly. Litigation over the town bonds checked their sale, and crippled the company so that it could not complete the road. In May, 1874, the Rome, Watertown and Ogdensburg company assumed the undertaking. The road was then principally graded, but it was more than a year later before the bridges on the western part of the line were finished. The road through Orleans and Niagara counties was graded by Hunter & Co. of Sterling Valley, Cayuga county. In the latter part of July, 1875, the track was laid twenty miles west of the Genesee river, and was carried through Orleans county during the autumn and to Lewiston in the following spring. The first passenger train ran over the western portion June 12th, 1876. The road was built at an average cost of $20,000 per mile. The wrought iron bridge over Eighteen-mile creek rests on twelve piers, and is 390 feet in length and 78 feet above the water.

In 1876 the Lockport and Buffalo Railroad Company was organized, with T. T. Flagler president, B. H. Fletcher vice-president, and Elisha Moody, Lewis S. Payne and Benjamin Carpenter in the directorship. A. R. Trew was the chief engineer, and M. Lally contractor. Lockport gave bonds for $100,000 worth of the stock. Early in 1877 the grading and bridge building were substantially finished from Lockport to Tonawanda, and ties distributed along the line. In that state the enterprise remains. The Central company resisted the crossing of its track by the proposed road, but was beaten in the courts. At a meeting of the stockholders on the 9th of July, 1877, the following board of directors was chosen: T. T. Flagler, B. H. Fletcher, J. A. Ward, John Hodge, James Jackson, jr; Benjamin Carpenter, Lewis S. Payne, J. L. Breyfogle, Josiah H. Helmer, Elisha Moody, J. C.

Jackson, L. F. Bowen and I. H. Babcock.

The first two were re-elected president and vice-president, Mr. Ward secretary, and Mr. Hodge treasurer. A road from Lockport to Olcott was contemplated in connection with the Lockport and Buffalo, but nothing was done toward its construction.

CHAPTER XXVI.

INCIDENTS OF THE PATRIOT WAR—THE OLD MILITIA SYSTEM IN NIAGARA COUNTY.

IT is time we noticed the so-called "patriot war" of 1837-8.

In 1837 a feeble insurrection against the British government broke out among the Roman Catholic French of lower Canada, and soon spread to upper Canada. There were then, as there always have been since, persons on the borders of New York who imagined the Canadians to be an oppressed people, anxious to revolutionize their government and join the United States. The excitement in this case infected the frontier population of this State, until it was estimated that one-fourth of the able-bodied men were "professed friends and abettors" of the insurgents. Emissaries were sent out in New York who formed a secret organization by which the "patriots," as they styled themselves, could be rallied and handled when their services should be required. The New York sympathizers with the insurrection were discountenanced by the better part of the citizens of the State, and the President issued a proclamation ordering the preservation of neutrality, which made no impression on the patriots.

By the middle of December, 1837, a few hundred of them, crossing from Schlosser, armed with weapons furnished by private contribution or stolen from a State depository—among the latter a number of cannon—had assembled on Navy Island, preparatory to an invasion of the Canadian mainland. They were led by one Rensselaer Van Rensselaer, who is generally said to have been a son of Colonel Solomon Van Rensselaer, though it is denied by Mr. Edward Mansfield, author of "The Life of General Winfield Scott."

On the 29th of December the little steam-boat "Caroline," belonging to Mr. William Wells, of Buffalo, made two or three trips between Schlosser and the island, transporting men and munitions of war to Van Rensselaer's camp, and finally lay up at the Schlosser landing. That night a British party crossed the river, and after a fight in which one New York man was killed and several wounded, set fire to the Caroline and cut the craft loose, so that she drifted over the falls, below which the charred fragments were afterward found. Some twenty-five men beside the crew were on the boat at the time of the attack, and as part of them were missed after the affair it was believed that they perished in the burning vessel or on the rocks beneath the fall.

The destruction of the "Caroline" was an authorized proceeding and a palpable invasion of United States territory. As such it created the greatest indignation throughout the country. A spirited diplomatic correspondence with the English government grew out of it, by which the aggrieved party obtained no redress. Captain James Van Cleve, of Lewiston, gives us the following history of the "Caroline:"

"This celebrated little steamer was built in the city of New York between the years 1820 and 1825 by Commodore C. Vanderbilt. Her engine was a square low pressure, built in New York. She was run for a time on Albemarle Sound. About 1834 she was brought from Albany through the Erie Canal to Lake Ontario at Oswego, and for a time run as a ferry boat between Ogdensburgh and Prescott, after which she passed through the Welland Canal into Lake Erie. During the Canadian rebellion in 1837 she was running between Buffalo and Schlosser landing. While on this route she was taken in the night of the 29th of December by the English at the dock, set on fire and sent over the falls. During the attack on the boat Mr. Durfee, of Buffalo, was killed and several wounded. Captain G. Appleby, of Buffalo, was in command of the 'Caroline' at the time. Her bowsprit was picked up in the river at Fort Niagara by Colonel E. Jewett, and presented by him to Mr. Molyneux, and is now a hitching post in front of Molyneux's tavern, twelve miles east of Lewiston on the Ridge road Colonel Jewett died at Santa Barbara, in California, on the 18th of May, 1877, in the 86th year of his age."

The "Caroline" outrage recruited the ranks of the patriots from a better class of citizens than had before joined them, and more energetic measures on the part of the government were necessary to keep the peace. General Scott was sent to the Niagara frontier, whither he was accompanied by Governor Marcy. A considerable force of troops, including Randall's brigade of artillery, was collected at Buffalo. In anticipation of another attack at Schlosser the army was marched to that point in January, 1838, but had nothing to do, and returned to Buffalo.

A few days later the troops took position at Black Rock. After the destruction of the "Caroline" the patriots had the steamboat "Barcelona" brought down from Buffalo to serve as their ferry boat. General Scott circumvented them by hiring the craft for the United States, and she was ordered to return up the river on the 16th. The British authorities were watching her, and had stationed three armed schooners just above Grand Island with a view to attacking the steamboat as she passed up. A British land force was under arms on the Canadian shore. Scott had on the preceding day warned the English commander that he was prepared to restrain the fillibusters from hostilities, and would consider a fire upon the "Barcelona" a breach of neutrality. The warning was repeated on the morning of the 16th, and the general had now drawn up his men and planted his cannon on the New York bank. The gunners had their matches lighted to apply if the British fired on the ascending vessel. They did not, and an international war was as narrowly avoided as ever in the history of the world.

On the previous day Van Rensselaer, seeing that he should lose the "Barcelona," gave up trying to maintain himself on the island, under a cannonade from the Canadian mainland, and his party retired to the New York shore and dispersed. They gave up their cannon to the State authorities, but five of the guns were returned to a delegation of another party of patriots on their presenting a forged order (purporting to be signed by General Scott) to Colonel Harry B. Ransom, who had the artillery in his charge at Tonawanda, where he was stationed with a body of militia. The fillibusters were soon scattered, however, by a United States marshal, and the cannon once more restored to their rightful owner. The insurrection in Canada was soon crushed. William Lyon Mackenzie, the leader, escaped to New York, and a requisition for his surrender was disregarded by Governor Marcy.

One of the ever to be remembered institutions in the earlier history of this section was the militia. There are few incidents of any nature that are recounted with more pleasure by the old men or listened to more attentively by the rising generation than those of the memorable drills and musters. The militia consisted of all the able-bodied white male citizens between the ages of eighteen and forty-five. State officers, clergymen, school teachers and some others when actively employed, were exempt from military duty. Students in colleges or academies, employees on coasting vessels and in certain factories, and members of fire companies were also exempt, except in cases of insurrection or invasion. Persons whose only bar to military service was religious scruples could purchase exemption for a stated sum annually. The major-general, brigade-inspector and chief of the staff department, except the adjutant and commissary generals, were appointed by the State. Colonels were chosen by the captains and subalterns of their regiments, and these latter by the written ballots of their respective regiments and separate battalions. The commanding officers of regiments or battalions appointed their staff officers. Every non-commissioned officer and private was obliged to equip and uniform himself, and perform military duty fifteen years from his enrollment, after which he was exempt, except in cases of insurrection or invasion. A non-commissioned officer, however, could get excused from duty in seven years, by furnishing himself with certain specified equipments, other than those required by law. It was the duty of the commanding officer of each company to enroll all military subjects within the limits of his jurisdiction, and they must equip themselves within six months after being notified.

On the first Monday in September of each year, every company of the militia was obliged to assemble within its geographical limits for training. One day in each year, between the 1st of September and the 15th of October, at a place designated by the commander of the brigade, the regiment was directed to assemble for a general training. All the officers of each regiment or battalion were required to rendezvous two days in succession in June, July or August, for drill under the brigade-inspector. A colonel also appointed a day for the commissioned officers and musicians of his regiment to meet for drill, the day after the last mentioned gathering being generally selected. Each militiaman was personally notified of an approaching muster, by a non-commissioned officer bearing a warrant from the commandant of his company; or he might be summoned without a warrant by a commissioned officer, either by visit or letter. A failure to appear, or to bring the necessary equipments, resulted in a court martial and a fine, unless a good excuse could be given; delinquents who could not pay were imprisoned in the county jail. When a draft was ordered for public service it was made by lot in each company, which was ordered out on parade for that purpose.

"General training" was usually regarded as a pleasant occasion by the men, as it gave them a chance to meet many acquaintances; and was the holiday of the year for the boys. Provided with a few pennies to buy the inevitable ginger bread from the inevitable peddler, they were happier than the lads of to-day would be with shillings to spend among the greatest variety of knicknacks. The place of meeting and the extent of the parade ground were designated by the commanding officer. The sale of spirituous liquors on the ground could only be carried on by permission of the same official. Total abstinence was not the rule, however, on such occasions; and an officer who had the right to throw away the contents of a private bottle did not always practice such extravagant wastefulness, particularly if fond of the "critter," being persuaded that if spared some of the beverage would ultimately find its way down his own throat.

Of general trainings, a veteran of those days writes as follows: "Although the companies exhibited the *elite* of our regimental splendors, glittering with tinsel and flaunting with feathers, a more heterogeneous and unsoldierly parade could scarcely be imagined. There were the elect from the mountains, who sometimes marched to the rendezvous barefoot, carrying their boots and soldier clothes in a bundle—the ambitious cobblers, tailors, and plough-boys from cross-road hamlets and remote rural districts, short, tall, fat, skinny, bow-legged, sheep-shanked, cock-eyed, hump-shouldered, and sway-backed—equipped by art as economically, awkwardly, and variously as they were endowed by nature, uniformed in contempt of all uniformity, armed with old flint-lock muskets, horsemen's carbines, long squirrel rifles, double-barrelled shot-guns, bell-muzzled blunderbusses, with side-arms of as many different patterns, from the old dragoon sabre that had belonged to Harry Lee's Legion, to the slim basket-hilted rapier which had probably graced the thigh of some of our French allies in the Revolution. The officers of the volunteer companies, on the other hand, were generally selected for their handsome appearance and martial bearing, and shone with a certain elegance of equipment, each in the uniform pertaining to his company.

There was also a sprinkling of ex-veterans of 1812, recognizable by a certain martinet precision in their deportment, and a shadow of contempt for their crude comrades, but quick to resent any extraneous comment derogatory to the service. A city dandy who undertook to ridicule the old fashioned way in which some officers carried their swords, was silenced by the snappish reply: 'Young man, I've seen the best troops of Great Britain beaten by men who carried their swords that way.' This harlequinade of equipment, costume, and character was duly paraded twice a day, marched through the streets, and put through its manœuvres on the green commons adjoining the village, much to the satisfaction of all emancipated schoolboys, ragamuffins, idlers, tavern-keepers, and cake and beer vendors, and somewhat, perhaps, to the weariness of industrious mechanics who had apprentices to manage, and busy housewives who depended on small boys for help."

The militia history of Niagara county is much the same as that of other localities, and its beginning dates back to an early day. From 1830 to 1860 the militia was an institution in this section. As early as 1835 it is said there were three regiments in the county, though it is not probable that there were more than a few hundred men in each. Among other early organizations of this kind may be mentioned a company under command of Captain Woodward, and Captain Mapes's independent company of Lockport.

The older residents of the county remember the sixty-sixth regiment, made up of soldiers from all parts of the county, many of whom had been members of the earlier regiments, which had been disbanded in consequence of changes in the militia laws. The date of the organization and the names of the first officers of this regiment are not accessible. One of the early commanding officers was Colonel (formerly Captain) Isaac Mapes, who was succeeded by Colonel Brown, with Solomon B. Moore as lieutenant-colonel and Peter Griner as major. The next who succeeded to the command of the regiment was Colonel E. D. Shuler, who had been an adjutant under Colonel Brown, with Dudley Donnelly as lieutenant-colonel. The organization of the regiment was as follows: An artillery company of Wilson, Captain Luther Wilson; an artillery company of Newfane, Captain Ira Tompkins; an infantry company of Wilson, Captain Loren D. Wilson; an infantry company of Niagara; an infantry company of Lockport, Captain James O. McClure; the Lockport light dragoons, Captain B. H. Fletcher; the "Irish Greens" of Lockport, Captain Thomas Kennedy, and an infantry company of Medina, Orleans county, under Captain Bowen.

The brigade districts were changed frequently, and at different times this regiment was in the brigades of General Gustavus Adolphus Scroggs, of Buffalo, General Burroughs, of Medina, Orleans county, and General Williams, of Rochester. During the summer and autumn months street parades were held as often as once in eight or twelve weeks. A four days' encampment, under the name of "Camp Steuben," was held at Buffalo one year, with General Scroggs in command. In July, 1858, the Lockport light dragoons went into camp for three days at Olcott, and in October of that year the sixty-sixth regiment encamped at Lockport for four days.

The Lockport light dragoons were organized in the fall of 1856. The company consisted of forty-two enrolled and uniformed members, equipped for both cavalry and infantry service. The first officers were B. H. Fletcher, captain; H. D. Oakley, first lieutenant; J. L. Breyfogle, second lieutenant, and George R. Keep, orderly sergeant. The company, like other militia organizations, disbanded at the outbreak of the late war, in which a number of its members held commissions and distinguished themselves for faithfulness and bravery. Among them were the following, whose names are well known throughout the county: Captain W. W. Bush, the first man to enlist in his Congressional district; Adjutant Charles P. Sprout, Lieutenant Samuel Sully, Captain James Maginnis and Captain William Hawkins. The career of these men in the Rebellion was of an eventful character, exhibiting all of the cruelest and most forbidding experiences of the battle-field and the prison-pen. Captain Bush was wounded at Cedar Mountain and taken prisoner, and kept in irons at Staunton, Virginia. Adjutant Sprout was killed in the same engagement. Lieutenant Sully received wounds at Cold Harbor, from the effects of which he died after his return to Niagara county. Captain Maginnis was killed at Ream's Station. Captain Hawkins was wounded by the explosion of a magazine on Maryland Heights. Recovering, he again went to the front only to receive injuries in the battle of Cold Harbor from which he subsequently died at Georgetown, D. C.

CHAPTER XXVII.

NIAGARA SHIP CANAL PROJECTS—THE SHIPPING AND THE COMMERCE OF NIAGARA COUNTY.

THE project of constructing a canal from the navigable waters of the Niagara river above the falls to the navigable waters below is one that has, from time to time, engaged the attention of civil engineers and capitalists in all parts of the Union for more than a century.

The first company having the consummation of this scheme for its object was incorporated in the year 1798, and it is stated that a survey was made soon afterward. As early as 1808, in pursuance of a resolution of the Senate, the Secretary of the Treasury submitted to that body an able and elaborate report on the subject of roads and canals, in which, among others of public interest that might require the aid of the government, was suggested a canal around the falls of Niagara.

A paper prepared by the late Amos S. Tryon, of Lewiston, and read before a national commercial convention held in Detroit in December, 1871, to consider the question of increased facilities for transportation from the west to the seaboard, contained a sketch of the history of some of the attempts to carry this enterprise to a successful end, from which the following is condensed:

In the year 1823, while the Erie Canal was being constructed, a general desire existed to see a ship canal built around the falls of Niagara. This desire took expression in the form of an organized company, which was chartered in April, 1823. It was empowered to hold all necessary property and to "open navigation from the Niagara river above the falls thereof to the heights near the village of Lewiston." The company was composed of influential persons of Lewiston and vicinity, and it sought to carry out the wishes of the people, with whom its members were daily conversant. Under the auspices of Nathan Roberts, an engineer of the Erie Canal from its beginning, a survey was made for the contemplated ship canal pursuant to charter. Beginning at the mouth of Gill creek, two miles above the falls, a line was run about due north to the brow of the mountain just above the village of Lewiston. Roberts made full and careful reports, showing that the canal could be constructed on that route, with single locks, for a trifle less than $1,000,000. The project failed, notwithstanding this favorable report, for want of means to carry it on.

The scheme had grown into national prominence in another decade, and in 1836 Captain W. G. Williams, Topographical Engineer of the United States Army, was sent by President Jackson to make surveys "preparatory to the construction of a ship canal around the falls of Niagara." Accordingly surveys were made, one of which followed that of Mr. Roberts, on a due north course from Gill creek to the top of the mountain. The cost of construction, including the locks, was estimated at $3,000,000, labor and material being more expensive at that time than in 1823. The failure of this project may be attributed in part, at least, to the financial crisis of 1837.

From that time onward till about the year 1863, the matter of a Niagara ship canal lay dormant. In that year it came before the President and Congress, and a new survey was ordered in 1868; in pursuance of this order several different lines were run and reports were prepared and the matter laid before Congress for its sanction. It was put to vote and lost by a small majority.

Such, in brief, is the history of the more important of the projects to construct a Niagara ship canal. The matter has been discussed in the leading newspapers of the United States and Europe; it has been introduced in conventions of business men and before boards of trade in the east and west, before the legislatures of different States, and before the Congress of the United States, and it is probable that no other similar enterprise has become more widely known, or its advantages more generally appreciated. In view of these facts it is confidently believed by many that a Niagara ship canal will yet be a reality, supplying to the United States a great competing line between the producers of the west and the markets of the east with the Welland ship canal of Canada.

The account of the commercial interests of Niagara county and reminiscences of the vessels connected with them which compose the remainder of this chapter were furnished us by Captain James Van Cleve, of Lewiston.

In 1780, during the American Revolution, his Majesty's ship "Ontario," of 22 guns, Captain Andrews left the Niagara river with troops, for Oswego, and foundered on the passage; 172 persons perished.

The first vessel built on the New York side of Lake Ontario after the Revolution was built by Eli Granger at Hanford's Landing, on the Genesee river, in 1797, and named "Jemima"; she was a craft of 30 tons. In 1798 Augustus and Peter B. Porter bought this vessel; the original bill of sale is in possession of Albert H. Porter, of Niagara Falls.

In 1803 the sloop "Niagara" was built at Cayuga creek.

The Niagara portage company owned or controlled many vessels plying between Oswego and Lewiston, transporting salt, merchandise, etc., to pass over the portage. Among the vessels were the schooners "Niagara," "Ontario," and "Charles and Ann." The last was named for two children of Jacob Townsend. Many other vessels, not directly owned by the portage company, ran in connection with it between Oswego and Lewiston. The following named individuals and firms were directly or indirectly connected with the portage between Lewiston and Lake Erie: Archibald Fairchild owned two vessels in Oswego; Matthew McNair & Co., of Oswego, owned a number; also Townsend, Bronson & Co. Sharp & Vaughn, of Oswego, owned a vessel named "Jane," of Genesee; Bronson & Co., of Oswego, owned many vessels, and Henry Eagle two or three; John T. Trowbridge and Captain Joseph Whitney were owners of the schooner "Mary Ann." In addition to the foregoing named parties, many individuals owning vessels at various ports on the lake employed them in transporting salt, etc., to Lewiston, to be carted over the portage.

The first steamboat that arrived in Niagara county, and at Lewiston, was the "Ontario" of about 240 tons. She was the first steamboat built upon the great North American lakes. Captain Van Cleve was clerk on board of her from 1826 to 1830. The "Ontario" was built at Sackett's Harbor in 1816; the ship carpenter was Asahel Roberts. The boat was 110 feet long, with twenty-four feet beam and eight and a half feet depth of hold. She was fitted with a low pressure engine of thirty-four inch cylinder, four feet stroke and two single flue boilers without return flues; and her rig was two masts with three fore and aft sails. She was well built. Her first commander was Captain Francis Mallaby U. S. N. She made her first trip in April, 1817. Her owners were Major-General Jacob Brown, U. S. A., Commodore M. T. Woolsey, U. S. N., Jacob Warring, Hooker & Crane, and Elisha Camp, of Sackett's Harbor; Eri Lusher, of Ogdensburg; Charles Smyth, of Oswego;

Abram Van Sanford, David Boyd and John I. De Graff, of New York. The "Ontario" was not only the first steamboat on the lakes, but was the first on waters subject to swell or waves, and determined the interesting problem whether steamboats were adapted to the navigation of open water as well as rivers. On her first appearance at the different ports about the lake and river St. Lawrence she was greeted with great joy.

In 1817 President Monroe visited Niagara county. He landed at Fort Niagara from the U. S. brig "Jefferson," from Sackett's Harbor, and continued his journey to Lewiston, Niagara Falls and Buffalo.

The first English steamer built on Lake Ontario was the "Frontenac," of 700 tons, which appeared in the Niagara river in 1818; she was commanded by Captain James McKenzie.

The steamer "Canada," built at Toronto in 1826 by Captain Hugh Richardson, ran as a packet between the Niagara river and Little York (now Toronto).

The steamer "Queenston" was built in 1824 at Queenston by John Hamilton; she came out in 1825 under command of Captain Joseph Whitney.

The steamer "Transit," owned by Captain Hugh Richardson, ran as a packet between Lewiston and Toronto from 1835 to 1842.

The steamer "Chief Justice Robinson," owned and commanded by Captain Hugh Richardson, ran as a favorite packet between Lewiston and Toronto from 1842 to 1852.

The small steamers "Queen" and "Gore" ran between Lewiston and Toronto from 1837 to 1840. They were irregular in their movements.

The steamer "Great Britain," 500 tons, came out in 1831 under command of Captain Joseph Whitney, late of Lewiston. She was owned by Hon. John Hamilton, and ran as a regular passenger packet between Lewiston and Prescott for ten years.

The iron steamer "Peerless," Captain Thomas Dick, ran as a packet between Lewiston and Toronto for a short time, about 1855 to 1857. She was sold to the United States during the Rebellion, and lost off Cape Hatteras in the Port Royal expedition.

The steamer "Zimmerman," Captain Milloy, from 1856 to 1861 ran as a packet between Lewiston and Toronto. She was burnt in the night when lying at the dock at Niagara, in 1861.

The steamer "City of Toronto" is now running upon the route between Lewiston and Toronto.

The steamer "Southern Belle" has for the past three or four years been running between Youngstown, Niagara and Toronto. She is an iron boat, built for blockade running during the Rebellion.

Soon after the war of 1812, the timber trade of Niagara county became a business of large proportions. The timber and staves were drawn out of the forest to Lewiston, Youngstown and various places along the lake shore within the county. Those collected along the lake shore were rafted off to vessels lying at anchor near the shore in fair weather. The timber and staves shipped at the various places mentioned were discharged at Cape Vincent, Carlton Island, Clayton and other points in the St. Lawrence river, formed into large rafts and floated down to Montreal and Quebec. Jesse Smith and E. G. Merick were prominent parties in this trade, also O. P. Starky, and Ainsworth & Lee of Cape Vincent.

On the trade in the products of the forest Mr. Turner gave, in the History of the Holland Purchase, the following paragraph, his informant being Mr. James Mather, an Orleans county pioneer, who understood that the business began in that county:

"In 1817 and 1818 it was extended along the lake to the Niagara river; the mouths of Oak Orchard, the Eighteen [mile], the Twelve [mile creeks], Youngstown and Lewiston were the principal depots. The trade was at first in butt staves; ship timber followed and continued until the fine groves of oak between ridge and lake have pretty much disappeared. As soon as the canal was completed as far west as Lockport the commerce in staves and ship timber commenced upon it. Daniel Washburn and Otis Hathaway first engaged in the business at Lockport, under a large contract with the eminent ship-builder in New York, Henry Eckford. The fine oak that grew in the immediate vicinity of Lockport was used to fill their contract. Since that the business of shipping staves and timber from Lockport and other points on the canal and Tonawanda creek has continued, employing in the earliest years of canal navigation a large amount of capital and labor."

The next American steamer that visited Niagara county after the "Ontario," was the "Martha Ogden," built at Sackett's Harbor in 1824. In 1827 she ran as a packet between Youngstown and Toronto (then Little York). Captain Andrew Estis was in command.

The next New York steamer of importance that appeared in Niagara county was the fine vessel "United States," of about 500 tons, under the command of Elias Trowbridge, in July, 1832; she ran as a passenger boat for ten years between St. Lawrence and Niagara counties. She was built in Ogdensburg. Captain Trowbridge was succeeded by Captain R. J. Van Dewater in 1833. Captain Van Dewater was succeeded in 1835 by Captain James Van Cleve, who in November, 1838, was drawn with the steamer into trouble during the Canadian rebellion in the attack on Prescott. A cannon shot passed through the steering room and took off the head of his steersman. Soon after this serious part of the farce the steamer was seized by the United States marshal.

The late Captain Joseph Whitney of Lewiston was in command of the "United States" in 1839, 1840 and 1841. Captain William Williams, of Oswego, commanded her in 1842, at the end of which season she was broken up.

The next steamer visiting Niagara county was the "Oswego," under command of Captain Macy, in 1834. She was driven on shore above Oswego in a snow storm, about the middle of May in that year. She was built in Oswego, and was a craft of about 400 tons.

The steamer "St. Lawrence," of about 500 tons, built

in Oswego, next appeared in Niagara county, under command of Captain John Evans, in 1839. Her engines were those formerly in the "Oswego." Captain James Van Cleve, of Lewiston, became part owner of her, and commanded her for seven years until she was broken up.

The steamer "Oneida," built at Pultneyville in 1835, ran for a short time between Oswego and Niagara counties. She was a vessel of 300 tons.

In 1843 the steamer "Lady of the Lake," Captain J. J. Taylor, commenced her regular trips between Niagara county and Ogdensburg. She was of 425 tons. She was finally sold to parties in Canada and burnt in the harbor of Toronto.

The steamer "Rochester" was the next to visit Niagara county, which she did under command of Captain George S. Weeks in 1844. She ran between Lewiston and Ogdensburg, and was for some years under command of Captain H. N. Throop.

In November, 1841, the "Vandalia," the pioneer propeller on the North American lakes, when on her experimental trip from Oswego to the head of Lake Ontario, under command of Captain Rufus Hawkins, visited Youngstown. She was built in Oswego and excited much attention.

The steamer "Niagara," 473 tons, made her appearance at Lewiston in 1845, under command of Captain R. F. Child. She was built at Clayton, in Jefferson county, and run on the route between Lewiston and Ogdensburg.

The steamer "Cataract," 577 tons, was built at Clayton in 1846, and made her first trip in June, 1847, under command of Captain James Van Cleve, from Ogdensburg to Lewiston.

The steamer "Ontario," 832 tons, was built at Clayton in 1847, and came out in 1848 under command of Captain H. N. Throop. She ran upon the route between Lewiston and Ogdensburg.

The steamer "Bay State," 1,098 tons, was built at Clayton in 1848, and came out in 1849 under command of Captain Van Cleve. She was run between Lewiston and Ogdensburg.

The steamer "Northerner," 905 tons, was built in Oswego, came out in 1850 under command of Captain R. F. Child, and ran between Lewiston and Ogdensburg. She was taken down the St. Lawrence and out to sea during the Rebellion, and sold to the government.

The steamer "New York," 1,200 tons, was built at Clayton in 1851 and the next season was under command of Captain R. B. Chapman, who commanded her for five years. Captain Van Cleve commanded her in 1859 and 1860, after which she was run down the St. Lawrence and out to sea and chartered to the government during the Rebellion. She is now (1878) running on the coast of Maine. She was the last large side-wheel passenger steamer built on the New York side of Lake Ontario.

During the existence of the New York passenger steamers on Lake Ontario the amount of wood alone consumed by them from the forests of Niagara county was enormous, and its use was of great advantage to all interests in the county.

On the completion of the railroads on both sides of Lake Ontario, the interest invested in steamers on the New York side of the lake became of no value as an investment. The capital of the company owning the nine or ten steamers was $500,000; the whole property was sold for $84,000.

The steamer "Maid of the Mist" (second of the name) commenced running as a ferry boat immediately below the Falls of Niagara in 1854; Captain Baily was in charge. Not proving a profitable investment she was, in 1861, run down the grand rapids from the Falls to Lewiston to avoid falling into the hands of the sheriff. As the trip was made at great hazard of lives and boat, this extraordinary pioneer passage caused great excitement in the community. When making her first great plunge in the rapid just below the lower suspension bridge, her smoke pipe was carried away; otherwise the boat received no serious injury from her perilous and exciting trip down the great gorge of the Niagara river. She was navigated by Joel Robinson, a ferryman at Niagara Falls.

The following schooners were built at Youngstown in the years mentioned: "R. H. Boughton," 1829 (she was the first vessel passed through the Welland Canal at its opening); "Lewis Shicklona," 1836; "John Porter," 1838; "Star," 1848; "Frank Pierce," 1853; "Cheney Ames," 1873; "Challenge," 1852. A schooner called the "Massachusetts" was owned in Youngstown in 1839, after having been on shore all winter near Wilson harbor.

In November, 1871, the schooner "W. I. Preston," Captain James Tifft, of Oswego, went on shore near Six-mile creek, east of Fort Niagara, loaded with wheat, and was got off and taken into Youngstown, where she sunk and remained all winter, when she was raised with much trouble and taken to Oswego.

The following vessels have been built at Wilson: schooners—"R. F. Wilson," 1846; "Niagara," 1847; "Emblem," 1848; "Forest," 1849; "Almira," 1849; "Enterprise," 1850; "Geraldine," 1850; "Josephine," 1853; "Belle Adkins," 1854; "Active," 1862; "Meteor," 1863; "Eureka," 1863; "Fleet Wing," 1863; "Pilot," 1866; "Plow Boy," 1875; "Trader," 1875; "Union," 1876; scow, "Live Oak," 1867.

In 1831 the schooner "Henry Clay," of Oswego, Captain Campbell, capsized off Fort Niagara. Two of the crew were saved; the captain and a young son of Captain Elias Trowbridge, of Oswego, were lost. The vessel was new and on her first trip. She was owned by Henry Fitzhugh, of Oswego.

The following schooners have been built at Olcott: the "Monterey," built in 1847; "Gem," 1849; "Conquest," 1853; "Governor Hunt," 1853; "Ruby," 1854; "Joseph Grant," 1855; "Corsican," 1862. In 1819 there were two small vessels owned at Olcott; one was called the "Crazy Jane," Captain Mark Burch; the other, the "Eliza Jane;" she was re-built in 1840 and commanded by Captain S. R. Swarthout.

A number of disasters to shipping have occurred on the lake shore of Niagara county. About 1817 the schooner "Mary," of Oswego, was driven on shore in the town of

Somerset, and went to pieces. She was loaded with merchandise from Oswego. The goods were principally for merchants in Niagara county. In 1854 the schooner "Isabell," of Cleveland, went ashore in a snow storm, near Olcott. In the same year the schooner "Minerva" went ashore below Pine Grove, east of Olcott harbor, in a snow storm; also the schooner "I. E. Rigs." In 1866 the schooner "Montana," of Clayton, went ashore in April in a snow storm near Olcott harbor. In 1862 the schooner "Helen Mar," of Port Hope, met a similar fate, and in 1861 the schooner "Sunrise," from Canada. In 1861 the schooner "Wanderer," of Sodus, went ashore while loading at a small pier east of the creek, at Olcott.

The customs district of Niagara was created by act of Congress in 1799, and included all the shores and waters of Lake Ontario and Lake Erie and the river connected therewith, lying within the State of New York west of the Genesee river, with the port of entry at Fort Niagara. The district of Buffalo creek on the west and the district of Genesee on the east were set off from the district of Niagara in 1805.

The port of entry was removed from Fort Niagara to Lewiston in 1811, and from Lewiston to Suspension Bridge in 1863. The district extends from the east bank of the Oak Orchard creek to the channel of the Tonawanda creek. It is in charge of the following officers:

Benjamin Flagler, collector of customs; Eli S. Nichols, special deputy collector; deputy collectors: F. J. Fellows, at Tonawanda; Phineas Moon, at Port Day; J. E. Whitmore, at Lewiston; H. C. Root, at Youngstown; Ralph Stockwell, at Wilson; Henry Kenny, at Olcott; A. T. Coleman, at Yates; William Fleming, inspector at Lewiston.

CHAPTER XXVIII.

INSURANCE, MEDICAL, RELIGIOUS, PIONEER AND AGRICULTURAL ASSOCIATIONS—THE COUNTY FARM—STATISTICS.

IN February, 1877, Mr. George L. Pratt, of Ridgeway, Orleans county, began publishing in the leading papers of that county and Niagara a series of articles on the subject of mutual insurance. This agitation of the topic resulted in a call for a meeting at Middleport on the 22nd of the following March. Only a few of the thirty-one signers of the call attended the meeting, and nothing was accomplished except an adjournment for two weeks. The second meeting consisted of three persons, among them Mr. Pratt, and was unanimously voted a fizzle.

The next move was to call a meeting for May 15th at the Orleans House, Albion. Six persons besides Mr. Pratt attended. Overtures for a union were made to the Farmers' Mutual Insurance Association of Orleans County, which was in session at the same time, but no response was made by the latter. The meeting adjourned to assemble at the American Hotel, Lockport, May 26th. When the hour arrived there were just enough persons present to fill the offices of chairman and secretary, to which they mutually elected each other. The effort so far had been to organize under the statute law of the State then in force, but hope in that direction was extinguished by the repeal of that law as affecting such cases during the Legislature's session of 1877.

About four months later Mr. Pratt opened a correspondence with the president of the Orleans association above mentioned, and was invited to attend a meeting of that body at the court-house at Albion in the latter part of September. Only five persons were present, however, and only three at a meeting November 10th, and nothing was accomplished.

Mr. Pratt once more renewed his efforts, and brought about a meeting at Ridgeway December 18th, at which seventeen of the twenty-two towns in Niagara and Orleans counties were represented by some of their most substantial farmers. The Farmers' Mutual Insurance Association of Niagara and Orleans Counties was organized, a constitution and by-laws adopted, and the organization began to solicit patronage.

At a meeting of the directors at Ridgeway, February 19th, 1878, it was found that the association had applications for insurance for $329,500. It was voted that the first policies issued all bear the date February 20th, 1878. The association on the 18th of July had policies in force to the amount of $1,180,000, and written, but not in force, amounting to over $150,000 There are sixty-one mutual companies in Pennsylvania and eleven in Michigan each of which is carrying less at risk than this association.

The officers are: George Bradley, of Somerset, president; A. P. Scott, of Ridgeway, vice-president; George L. Pratt, of Ridgeway, secretary; John P. Sawyer, of Royalton, treasurer. The board of directors consists of one member from each town in the two counties, holding for two years, or until their successors are elected. The business of the association is confined to the insurance against fire and lightning of farm property and other property no more hazardous, within Niagara and Orleans counties. The association is organized on the co-operative or honor plan, there being now no State law for the organization of mutual insurance companies.

The office of the association is at Ridgeway, where a stated annual meeting is held on the second Wednesday of January, to hear reports, elect officers, etc. The term of the officers is one year, and they are, *ex officio*, directors. The treasurer receives all moneys collected by assessment for the payment of losses, and pays out the same, by order of the secretary countersigned by the president, the fee for his services being one-half of one per cent. for receiving and paying out the funds. The admission fee is $1.50 plus one-tenth of one per cent. on the amount desired to be insured, and the application must be approved by the director for the town in which the property is situated, and by a majority of the executive committee, which consists of the president, vice-president and secretary.

The business is under the supervision of an auditing committee of three, appointed annually by the directors. A loss is adjusted by the secretary, and the director of the town in which it occurred; and controversies are referred to an arbitrator chosen by the association, one chosen by the property-owner, and a third selected by these two. When a loss has been adjusted the members are assessed for the payment at the rate of five or some multiple of five cents per hundred dollars of their respective policies; and members forfeit their policies so long as they refuse to pay any assessment after notification by mail, and permanently lose their membership by refusal to pay on personal solicitation by the directors. Any surplus in the treasury is used for the payment of small losses. Claims for loss must be presented within ten days of the occurrence of the loss, and within forty-eight hours in the case of death of live stock by lightning. The association may insure personal property for its entire cash value, and buildings for two-thirds. On live stock the limit is $100 per head for horses, $30 for cattle, $10 for hogs, and $3 for sheep.

THE NIAGARA COUNTY MEDICAL SOCIETY.

The statute under which all of the county medical societies of the State of New York were incorporated was passed by the Legislature during the session of 1806, and the medical society of the State was duly organized on the first Tuesday in February, 1807.

The Niagara County Medical Society was organized in 1823, and has had a continuous existence to the present time. The first delegate to the convention of the State society was Dr. Henry Maxwell, in 1830. The officers of the society were at that time as follows: Dr. J. K. Skinner, president; Dr. Lloyd Smith, vice-president; Dr. L. S. Robbins, secretary; Dr. J. W. Smith, treasurer; Dr. W. Ritter, corresponding secretary; censors, Drs. Henry Maxwell, I. Southworth, L. Smith, Jacob Chatterton and Darius Shaw. The names of the members of the society at that time are as follows: Drs. Edward Arnold, Franklin Butterfield, Alexander Butterfield, Asa Crane, Robert H. Henderson, John A. Hyde, Henry Maxwell, Myron Orton, Darius Shaw, Isaac Southworth, Willard Smith, Josiah K. Skinner, Abner Barnard, Isaac W. Smith, B. Henderson, Lloyd Smith, Ambrose Thomas, John Warner, Washington Ritter, Asa B. Brown, Jonathan Chase, Alexander S. Chase, Jacob Chatterton, Eli Hurd, Roswell Kimbell, Benjamin Sayre, B. V. Peterson, Z. Ross, George W. Graves, Luther P. Robbins, Benjamin Hardy, Edwin Cook and Archibald Baker. In 1831 the names of Drs. John S. Shuler, Luther Cross and Abraham Hogeboom were added.

The officers of the society at the present time are: President, M. S. Kittinger; vice-president, John M. Duff; secretary, A. Walter Tryon; treasurer, Peter Faling. The delegates to the State Medical Society in 1877 were Drs. Rexford Davidson and Peter Faling.

The names of the present members of the society are as follows: Drs. La Fayette Balcom, Lockport; Simeon T. Clark, Lockport; Nathan Cook, Ransomville; Electus Cole, Middleport; John W. Cormon, Beech Ridge; Rexford Davidson, Lockport; John M. Duff, Royalton; Peter Faling, Gasport; D. S. Fasset, Lockport; John Foote, Lockport; C. W. Gould, Middleport; William B. Gould, J. W. Grosvenor, D. W. Harrington, J. B. Hartwell, J. H. Helmer, Lockport; W. Q. Huggins, Sanborn; M. S. Kittinger, Lockport; M. L. Langs, Suspension Bridge; A. M. Leonard, William McCollum, Lockport; J. I. McFadden, Olcott; C. P. Murphy, D. H. Murphy, Royalton; C. N. Palmer, E. F. Ryle, W. J. Ransom, Lockport; William C. Raymond, Cambria; Charles H. Reed, Wilson; G. H. Saddleson, Newfane; C. A. Sage, Pekin; A. G. Skinner, Youngstown; E. Smith, Lewiston; N. B. Tabor, Wilson; A. Walter Tryon, Lockport; C. H. Turner, Hartland; H. A. Wilmot, Luke Woodworth, Johnson's Creek.

An annual meeting is held on the first Tuesday in June; semi-annual, first Tuesday in January; quarterly, first Tuesdays in March and September.

THE PRESBYTERY OF NIAGARA.

The Presbytery of Niagara was set off from that of Geneva in February, 1817. It originally embraced its present territory, together with that of the presbyteries of Buffalo, Rochester and Genesee. The last two of these were separated from it in 1819, and the first in 1823.

The first meeting of the presbytery, as now constituted, was held at Gasport, January 27th, 1824. The ministers present were Revs. David M. Smith, of Lewiston, and George Colton, of Gasport, and the elders, Titus Fenn, Gasport; Abel Tracy, Gaines; Daniel Holmes, Wilson; Luther Crocker, Cambria; Asahel Munger, Lockport; and Lovel Lewis, Lewiston. Rev. D. M. Smith was chosen moderator, and preached the inaugural sermon.

It was reported that the presbytery had within its bounds eleven churches besides the Tuscarora mission, and four ordained ministers, two of whom had charges. "Owing to the newness of the country and the multiplicity of religious sects," not one of the churches was self-supporting. In 1846 a total membership of 2,514 was reported, the number having been raised by a series of powerful revivals to about that of the present members. Up to 1874 about 144 ministers had been enrolled by the presbytery. At that date the church edifices were estimated to be worth $200,000 and the parsonages $33,000, with but slight indebtedness on the property.

In 1833 thirty-four Sabbath-schools were reported in Niagara county, with 214 teachers, 1,818 scholars and 1,339 library books; and in Orleans county twenty-three schools, with 282 teachers, 1,567 scholars and 1,580 books; in the presbytery, fifty-seven schools, 496 teachers, and 2,919 books.

In a historical sketch of the presbytery, presented by Rev. E. P. Marvin in the latter part of April, 1875, from which the foregoing facts have been taken, he stated that the presbytery then numbered twenty-three ministers and eighteen churches, with a membership of 2,647 in the churches and 2,841 in the Sabbath-schools. The churches are those of Albion, Barre Center, Carlton, Holley,

Knowlesville, Lewiston, Lockport, Lyndonville, Medina, Millville, Niagara Falls, Porter, Pendleton and Wheatfield, Somerset, Tuscarora, Wilson and Wright's Corners.

THE NIAGARA BAPTIST ASSOCIATION.

This body was organized at a meeting of ministers and delegates chosen for that purpose by several churches then belonging to the northwestern part of the Genesee association, convened at Hartland, June 23d, 1823. It included the churches of Lewiston, Porter, Cambria, Somerset, Royalton, Hartland, Yates, Gaines, Barre and Shelby, nine in all. At this meeting, after completing the organization, it was agreed to meet annually on the third Wednesday in June, at 10 o'clock A. M. At a subsequent meeting of the association the time of meeting was changed to the second Wednesday in June.

The first annual meeting was held with the church in Hartland, June 16th, 1824; all the churches of the association were represented by delegates and letters. The opening sermon was preached by Rev. Jeremiah Irons, from Romans XII, 1,2. Rev. William Harrington was moderator, and Elisha Bowen clerk. The association had at this time seven ordained ministers, viz: Samuel Alvord, Jehiel Wisner, William Harrington, Jeremiah Irons, James Carpenter, Simeon Dutcher and Asa Spencer, with one licenteate, Arah Irons. At the time of the first meeting the churches composing the association had a membership of 339. Besides the nine churches which first united to form the association others joined from time to time. Some of these had but an ephemeral existence, while others were dismissed to join other associations. This number continued to multiply until June, 1843, when twenty-four churches were connected with the association, namely, those of Albion, Alabama, Akron, Carlton, Cambria, Gaines and Murray, Hartland, Knowlesville, Lockport, Lewiston, Lewiston and Niagara, Medina, Porter, Royalton, Somerset, Shelby, Tuscarora (Indian church), Tonawanda (Indian church), Wheatland and Pendleton, Wilson, Yates, Pendleton and Middleport, Niagara Falls and Newfane. These churches had an aggregate membership of 2,668.

At a semi-annual meeting of the association held with the church at Hartland in February, 1844, the churches of the following localities at their request were dismissed for the purpose of forming the Orleans Baptist Association: Albion, Alabama, Carlton, Gaines and Murray, Knowlesville, Medina, Shelby and Yates.

The Niagara association now comprises fourteen churches, nine ordained ministers, three licentiates and 1,646 members. Its regular annual meetings commence on the second Wednesday in June. The officers of the association are: Moderator, Burt Van Horn, Lockport; clerk, J. C. Hopkins, Ransomville; corresponding secretary, H. P. Hunt, East Clarence, Erie county; treasurer, R. W. Noble, West Somerset.

PIONEER ORGANIZATION.

On the 14th of September, 1877, a goodly number of the old citizens of Niagara county met on the grounds of William Tenbrook, at Olcott, to form an association under whose auspices the record of the settlement of the county might be compiled and preserved, and meetings held at which the pioneers might pleasantly recall reminiscences of the eventful experience of old times. The following persons were present, the figures attached to whose names indicate their age at the time and the date of their advent in the county:

From Cambria, Harvey Beach, 77, 1801; Thomas Barnes, born in the county in 1811.

Hartland, Daniel Van Horn, 83, 1811; William Morgan, 62, 1830.

Newfane, Benjamin Stout, 75, 1815; Stephen Wilson.

Porter, Peter Tower, 86, 1815; Henry Palmer, 69, 1832.

Pendleton, Orrin Fisk, 71, 1810.

Lewiston, John Cornell, 68, 1828.

Lockport, Elisha Clapp; B. M. Edwards, 81; Ira Farnsworth, 54, 1837; Peter Aiken, born in 1816; W. W. Bush, born in 1828.

Royalton, Andrew J. Secor, born in 1817; P. P. Murphy.

Somerset, David Barker, 83, 1815; Adam Pease, 68, 1817; Leman Hoag, 81, 1825; Loran Fitts, 77, 1810.

Wilson, J. M. Newman, 65, 1818; J. S. Cuddeback, 69, 1816; Rev. A. Holsey, 84, 1830; Richard Holmes.

Niagara, Asahel Colt.

Wheatfield, Lewis S. Payne.

The Niagara County Pioneer Association was organized, and the following board of officers chosen:

President, John Van Horn; secretary, F. N. Albright; executive committee, J. S. Hopkins, Cornelius Tompkius and Willard A. Cobb.

NIAGARA COUNTY AGRICULTURAL SOCIETY.

A county agricultural society was informally organized at the court-house in Lockport in 1841. The persons most efficient in effecting the organization were M. C. Crapsey, Dr. W. A. Townsend, Daniel Pomroy, Jabez Pomroy, General Parkhurst Whitney and ex-Governor Washington Hunt. The first president of the society was William Parsons. The first fair was held at Lockport, and subsequent ones were held in most of the towns in the county except the eastern tier. The premiums were guaranteed by subscription. The oldest certificates of premiums which have fallen under our notice were issued in 1841.

Of the fair held in 1842 Henry Coleman, the distinguished agriculturist, and author of "European Agriculture," who was present, writes as follows; "We had the pleasure of meeting the farmers of this fertile county on the first day. The day began with rain and so continued until afternoon. * * * As to shaking off the dust of your feet, though one may have felt ever so uncomfortable towards the good people of Lockport, it was out of the question; one could hardly shake the mud off unless the feet went with it. The farmers of Niagara county however, turned out in great force. They are not house plants. The show of cattle was quite numerous. Some excellent animals of the improved breeds and some first rate specimens of the Dishley, Cotswold and Leicester sheep, as well as of the fine wooled varieties, were exhibited. Some excellent horses and colts were likewise on the ground. From appearances we think we have reason to infer that in no county in the State, all circumstances considered, is the spirit of agricultural improvement more rife than in this rich and beautiful county."

The third annual meeting of the society was held in the basement of the Baptist church in the village of Lockport, on the 11th of October, 1843; after the exhibition, which excelled that of the previous year, a very able address was delivered by the president, Dr. William A. Townsend.

The officers of the society for 1844 were: William Parsons, president; Parkhurst Whitney and William Freeman, vice-presidents; Chauncey Leonard, secretary; William O. Brown, treasurer.

The society held its fourth annual cattle show and fair at Lockport on the 9th and 10th of October, 1844. One who was present says: "The show of stock was unusually large and of very superior quality. The statements of several cultivators of crops showing the manner and expense of cultivation and product of wheat, corn, barley, oats, carrots, potatoes, onions, etc., were such as to show the great advantage of liberal manuring and thorough culture. There was exhibited to the viewing committee on grain crops satisfactory evidence that 58 bushels of wheat, 106 of corn, 100 of oats, 52 of barley, etc., were produced on one acre of land each, during that season, in this county." The annual address was delivered by George W. Holley of Niagara Falls, on the architecture of farm buildings, the happy influences of a rural life, and the beauties and charms of nature which always surround the husbandman.

The officers for 1845 were: James D. Shuler, president; Jonathan Ingalls and John Gould, jr., vice-presidents; Sullivan Caverno, secretary; and Silas H. Marks, treasurer. The society from that period has held a fair in the autumn of each year, down to the present time, and for the past few years a spring meeting has been held regularly for the exhibition of fine blooded stock and farm machinery.

The present agricultural society was formed by the re-organization of the one above adverted to December 2d, 1858, under the act of Legislature of April 13th, 1855, entitled "An act to facilitate the formation of agricultural and horticultural societies." The first election of officers took place January 5th, 1859, at which Willard Wild was elected president for the ensuing year, S. S. Pomroy secretary, and Roland Sears treasurer. The constitution of the society provides that the officers shall consist of a president, twelve vice-presidents, one of whom shall be designated as first vice-president, a secretary, a treasurer and six directors. All of the officers except the directors are elected annually by ballot, the election being held on the first Tuesday in January, and the board of managers consists of all of the officers named, including the directors, a majority of the managing board constituting a quorum. All residents of the county are eligible to membership for one year upon the payment of one dollar into the treasury of the society, and to life membership upon the payment of ten dollars.

The fair grounds owned and occupied by the society are situated on the corner of Washburn and Willow streets in the city of Lockport. They originally comprised about twenty acres, but additions have since been made which render the area considerably greater. The grounds are well fenced and provided with suitable buildings for the exhibition of articles of industry. The trotting course is one of the best, and the judge's stand, sheds and seats for the accommodation of visitors are substantial and convenient.

The officers of the society at the present time are as follows: W. E. Gantt, president; Solomon Ernest, vice-president; L. H. Hill, secretary. The directors and vice-presidents are chosen from the different towns in the county.

FARMERS' CLUB AND FRUIT-GROWERS' SOCIETY.

This society was organized in 1873. Its objects were the mutual benefit of its members and the collection and dissemination of information that would benefit the farmers and fruit-growers of the county, by holding weekly meetings during the winter season, and discussing the various topics connected with agriculture and horticulture; also the establishment of a first-class agricultural library; in which should be found all the best agricultural and horticultural works that have been or may be published in the English language. To this library every farmer, fruit-grower or any other person in the county has free access by the payment of one dollar per year; and all the money thus received is applied to the purchase of new agricultural works. The library that has been established by the club contains most of the best agricultural works that have been published in this country during the past twenty years. The club meets weekly during the winter months. The officers for the first four years were: Claudius L. Hoag, president; Dr. Ephraim W. Gantt, secretary; Edward Simmons, treasurer and librarian. They were succeeded by Hon. Isaac H. Babcock, president, and the previous secretary and treasurer; and this board in 1878 by the present officers, viz.: John Crowe, president; Jabez B. Woodward, secretary; and Edward Simmons, treasurer and librarian.

COUNTY POOR HOUSE AND FARM.

Previous to 1829 each town took care of its own paupers, letting the contract for their support to the lowest bidder. In that year, by legislative enactment, the maintenance of the poor became a county matter. The same year this county purchased a farm of ninety-one acres in the western part of the town of Lockport, and erected a commodious frame building, to which, in the fall, the paupers of the county, then numbering about thirty, were transferred. Hiram McNeil, Henry Norton and George Reynale were appointed superintendents of the poor, and

John Gould keeper. In 1833 the main part of the present building was erected. It is built of stone, 100 feet by 60 in size and three stories high, with a spacious basement. The following winter a school was opened in the building, for the benefit of its younger inmates, taught by David Murray, a highly educated Irishman, which many of the young people of the neighborhood attended. In 1845 two three-story stone wings were built, each forty by sixty feet; the east wing was intended for the use of the insane, exclusively. Rear wings have since been added for hospital and other purposes. In 1858 an area one hundred feet or more square was inclosed by a solid stone wall nine feet high. This yard communicates with the east wing and is known as the "crazy yard." Its name is suggestive of its use. In 1854 an addition of twenty-nine acres was made to the farm, making now in all one hundred and twenty acres.

Formerly paupers of all classes and all ages were received and kept here, and a school for the benefit of the young inmates was maintained. In 1875 the county made arrangements with the Home for the Friendless in the city of Lockport, whereby children between the ages of three and thirteen are cared for and schooled at that institution, at a cost to the county of two dollars each per week. The insane who were formerly kept here are now sent to the State Lunatic Asylum at Utica, where the incurable cases are retained, and the others transferred to the Willard Asylum in Seneca county, for medical treatment. Niagara county pays these two asylums an average of $1,200 annually for the support of the insane.

The county house and farm were under the control of a board of three superintendents until 1856, when the number was reduced to one. A keeper was always employed to take charge of the institution until 1875, when it was voted that the superintendent should reside in the house and oversee its management in person. They are elected once in three years. A. B. Lewis, the present superintendent, took control of the institution January 1st, 1878. Some much needed improvements which Mr. Lewis has already made have added at least $2,500 to the value of the property.

There is on this farm an inexhaustible quarry of soft limestone. To utilize this quarry and at the same time furnish employment for tramps, Mr. Lewis caused a building to be erected 150 by 24 feet in size and 16 feet high, into which the limestone is drawn and there broken up, when it finds ready sale at fifty cents a load for macadamizing roads.

The present number of inmates is about 180, one third of whom are females. They were maintained during the year 1877 at an average cost apiece per week of $1.56. The average annual products of the farm amount to about $3,000. Two overseers are employed on the farm. The stock consists of seven horses, seventeen cows and a fine drove of hogs of a superior breed.

STATISTICS.

The following compilation from the last State census furnishes an interesting exhibit of the population and religious and agricultural status of the county in 1875:

POPULATION.

Population in 1875, 51,399. From 1870 to 1875 the rate of increase per cent. of the aggregate population of Niagara county was 1.91; white population increase, 2.02. Decrease of colored population 10.27. Increase of native population, 2.61. Decrease of foreign population, 0.08. The males of voting age in Niagara county June 1st, 1875, numbered 13,686. The total number of males was 25,616; females, 25,783.

CHURCHES.

There were 95 church organizations: Baptist 7, membership 938; Congregationalist 3, membership 961; Methodist Episcopal 22, membership 1,792; Presbyterian 9, membership 1,335; Protestant Episcopal 7, membership 989; Roman Catholic 12, membership 5,385; A. M. E. 2, membership 46; Campbellite 1, membership 80; Christian Connection 1, membership 20; Evangelical Association 3, membership 365; Evangelical Lutheran 10, membership 1,115; Free Will Baptist 1, membership 75; Friends 2, membership 70; Methodist Protestant 1, membership 48; Union 2, membership 105; United Evangelical Church 1, membership 125; United Methodist Free Church 5, membership 165; Universalist 3, membership 185; Wesleyan Methodist 3, membership 55.

AGRICULTURE.

Niagara county is one of the five counties cultivating the largest area in barley. The wheat crop of this State in 1874 was 10,188,067 bushels, of which Niagara raised 657,822 bushels.

The number of apple trees in the State June 1st, 1875, was 18,278,636, of which Niagara had the greatest number, being 1,128,274. The four counties next in order were Monroe, Wayne, Erie and Orleans.

Farms, total number, 4,296; containing 20 to 50 acres, 907; 50 to 100 acres, 1,406; 100 to 500 acres, 1,125. Since 1870 the number of farms had increased 254. There were 257,998 acres of improved land, 35,709 acres woodland and 9,868 acres other land. The whole is valued at $26,893,511; with farm buildings other than dwellings valued at $2,766,466; stock valued at $2,449,262. The products of the farms in 1874 were:

Barley, 244,131 bushels; buckwheat, 12,260; Indian corn, 627,510; oats, 836,177; rye, 12,404; spring wheat, 4,298; winter wheat, 653,524; beans, 78,151; peas, 17,249; potatoes, 407,084; Hops, pounds, 6,722; Grapes, pounds, 933,506. The amount of butter made in families during 1874 was 1,309,860 pounds. In 1875 the amount of clipped wool was 148,402 pounds.

CHAPTER XXIX.

THE RISE AND DEVELOPMENT OF THE GREAT FRUIT-GROWING INTEREST OF NIAGARA COUNTY.

THE history of fruit-growing in this county dates from the first settlement of the county by the whites. The motives that induced its cultivation at that early day were not of a character to cause extensive planting of orchards of apples, or any other fruits. The home of the early settler and his immediate neighborhood were the limit of the demand for all kinds of fruit for many years after the first settlement of the county. The improved varieties of fruits were but little known to the inhabitants of this county in those days. The apple and peach were the principal fruits grown for many years.

The largest orchards planted by the early settlers were on the Niagara river below Lewiston, on the shore of Lake Ontario, and about Lockport. Probably the largest orchard planted at that early period was one of about seven hundred trees, set out by Nathan Comstock, within the present limits of the city of Lockport in the year 1817, on the farm now owned and occupied by Claudius L. Hoag, on Lake avenue; some four hundred of the trees in this orchard are still in a vigorous condition and produce good crops of fruit, of most of the popular varieties of those early days; among which are found the Spitzenburgh, New Town Pippin, Fall Pippin, Talman's Sweet, Rambo, Yellow Bellflower, Rhode Island Greening, and the famous Jersey Red for cider. The last mentioned variety proved the most profitable for many years, as cider was the standard and popular beverage among the early settlers, before the introduction of those modern accompaniments of civilization the brewery and distillery. The early settlers had no conception of the great change that half a century would bring about in fruit-growing in Niagara county, never dreaming of the fact that they were living in a county that was destined to become more noted in that respect than any other in the United States.

About the year 1845 there began to be a demand for winter apples in the then newly settled States of the west, which stimulated the owners of apple trees to graft the almost worthless sorts that they had in cultivation with the varieties that were in demand for shipping. From that time to the present there has been a rapid increase of apple orchards throughout the county. The trees that have been planted during the past twenty-five years were mostly Baldwins, Rhode Island Greenings, Roxbury Russets and Northern Spys; the Baldwin has probably been more extensively planted during the past twenty years than all other winter sorts, and judging from the health of the tree, great productiveness and beauty of fruit, it promises at no very distant period to supersede in this section most of the other winter varieties.

This county is blessed with climate, soil and peculiar surroundings which make it the leading fruit-growing county in the United States. Apples, pears, peaches, plums, quinces, apricots, nectarines, cherries, currants, gooseberries, strawberries, blackberries, raspberries, and grapes are all perfectly at home, and succeed admirably in all parts of the county, except on clay soils, where the peach is not a success. More attention has been given to the cultivation of the apple than any other fruit, owing to the increased demand and growing popularity of Niagara county apples, in both the Eastern and Western States, and in foreign markets wherever they have been introduced, which has stimulated to increased planting of the more popular varieties of winter fruits. From the most reliable information we are enabled to state quite accurately the number of apple trees now growing in orchards in this county to be 1,400,000, and more are being planted every year.

The marked peculiarity of the Niagara county apple is its fine grain, containing less juice and of a higher quality than the same varieties grown in many other parts of the United States. The same peculiarity may be justly claimed to exist in the character of all other varieties of fruit grown in this county, and is quite as marked in the pear and peach as in the apple; each of the many varieties of these fruits possesses its own peculiar flavor, which is brought out most distinctly by the climatic surroundings of this favored fruit-growing section. As an illustration we will take the Bartlett pear, so well known as having a peculiar strong musky flavor, natural to that variety when in perfection; which quality is fully developed in that fruit when grown in this county. Many of the readers of this work have undoubtedly eaten fine specimens of the Bartlett grown in other localities in the United States, in which they discovered not the least trace of this aroma; and the same marked deficiency of flavor will be found to exist in other fruits grown in the South and West, and in localities where the annual rainfall is much heavier than in Niagara county.

Next to the apple the peach is grown more extensively than any other fruit in this county, having been introduced with the apple by the first settlers. Most of the varieties grown for many years were seedlings, some of which were quite equal to the cultivated varieties now grown. This fruit is considered by many the most profitable crop they can grow. The most promising varieties for orchards at present are the Early Beatrice, Early Louise, Amsden, Alexander, Crawford's Early, Crawford's Late, Oldmixon and Morris's White. A large number of peach trees are planted yearly; a good crop and good prices are sure to be followed by a large planting the following season.

Many of the first settlers planted a few pear trees, some of which still remain as landmarks, but many of them have died from blight and old age. The pear is being grown to considerable extent in all parts of the county, but its mortal enemy, the blight, has found it here as well as in other places, and has swept away thousands of trees, many of which have been replaced, and a number of quite large orchards have been planted during the past few years. The most popular sorts at present are the Bartlett, Duchesse d'Angouleme, Seckel and Beurre d'Anjou. There are many other excellent varieties in cultivation, but none which have as yet attained the popularity of those that have been named.

Previous to 1865 but few quince trees had been planted; but since that time many thousand trees have been set in different parts of the county. There are at present ten times as many trees of this fruit growing in the county as there were ten years ago.

The improved varieties of plums have never been grown here to any great extent, but increased attention is now being given to the cultivation of this excellent fruit, with a prospect of many thousand trees being set during the next few years; as this fruit is very profitable at prices much below the usual sales in this market, a single crop bringing from three to five hundred dollars per acre.

The grape is comparatively a new fruit among the fruit-growers of this county, as but little attention has been given to its cultivation until within the past few years. Some who have neglected their vineyards do not consider it a profitable fruit, but when properly cared for it has proved a paying crop, and the greatly increased consumption of this healthiest and finest of all fruits, in all of our large towns and cities, will warrant increased planting of vineyards where the grape succeeds as well as it does in Niagara county. The number of acres of vineyard in the county probably would not exceed two hundred.

One of the sources of Niagara county's remarkable superiority in fruit production is the climatic influence of the winds. The southwest, west, northwest, north and northeast winds always pass during the whole year over open water before reaching this section, which accounts for the mercury seldom falling lower than five or ten degrees below zero during the winter season. These winds also serve as a protective against the late spring and early autumn frosts. The cool autumn winds blowing directly off the lakes are supposed to retard the ripening of winter fruits, leaving the ripening process to be carried out during the winter and spring following, and greatly enhancing their value for market by their long keeping qualities. Another favorable influence is the dryness of the atmosphere. The average annual rainfall given by a record kept in this county during a period of eighteen years was 22.45. It is conceded by every observant cultivator of fruit, that all fruits possess a much higher quality when the season is dry than when it is very wet; this conclusion is fully verified by the experience of many cultivators in this county, where the fruits we have named find a climate and surroundings which enable them to better develop all their high qualities than in any other section of the United States east of the Mississippi valley.

Thus soil and climate combine to render Niagara county an unequaled fruit-growing region, and the intelligence and enterprise of its horticulturists have given it the pre-eminent position it was naturally fitted to take.

CHAPTER XXX.

A SKETCH OF THE GEOLOGY OF NIAGARA COUNTY.

[By A. Walter Tryon, M.D.]

THE geology of Niagara county presents several features of more than ordinary interest, as three important groups of rocks have quite an extensive exposure within its limits. These groups compose the larger portion of the Upper Silurian age, and have been named after the localities in which they have their greatest development, or exposure. The lowest of these groups is the Medina, the second the Clinton, and the third is the Niagara.

Each gives peculiar features to the landscape along the line of its outcrop. The Niagara limestone, on account of its compactness and power to resist weathering, gives the character of a bold bluff to the terrace known as the Mountain Ridge. The Clinton forms small plateaus at the base of the shale hills, and the uniform texture of the lower portion of the Medina is the cause of the even surface of the country bordering on and extending back from Lake Ontario. But these features will be better understood by a separate study of each group.

THE MEDINA EPOCH.

The rock of this formation is exposed in the Niagara river from Lewiston to near the Falls, where it passes under the water of the river. From Lewiston eastward, it extends for several miles along the base of the escarpment formed by the Niagara limestone; afterward it spreads out wider to the northward and forms a distinct bluff from half a mile to a mile from the limestone terrace, and on a line corresponding with it. A few miles east of Lockport its elevation is lost in the general level of the country, and the rock disappears, and is not seen again in the county.

The strata of this group are usually divided into four different bands :

1. Red marl, or marly sandstone ; 2. Gray quartzose sandstone ; 3. Like the first, but to the westward becoming more sandy ; 4. The gray terminal portion.

The Red Marl, the first or lowest of these bands, is sometimes mottled with greenish spots, and it is readily decomposed by exposure. It is the source of the red clays throughout the county. No fossils are found in it.

The Gray Quartzose Sandstone.—This portion succeeds the previous, and is twenty-five feet thick on the Niagara river. It is the hardest portion of the group, and is extensively quarried north of the city of Lockport, for paving and flagging stones. This region is known as Rattlesnake hill, taking its name from the large numbers of these reptiles which formerly found secure retreats in the crevices of these rocks. The strata in this locality are in distinct layers and are easily separated. Some of these layers are very thin, being not more than an eighth to a quarter of an inch in thickness. Red bands and mottlings frequently intersperse the gray color. This band contains many valves of Lingula and a few other shells. It is ripple and wave marked and bears indisputable evidence of its deposition in a shallow, broken sea.

Red Shale, or Sandstone.—This is a red, shaly, or marly mass, mottled with circular spots of greenish gray, or is frequently marked with bands, parallel with the strata. The oxidation of the iron, which gives color to the rocks, has been altered by the presence of carbonaceous matter. As we ascend the shaly matter diminishes, and the sandy character increases, until the whole is terminated by a silicious, or in some places argillaceous, light gray sandstone.

Greenish-Gray Argillaceous Sandstone.—This band differs from the 3d division more in its color than in any of its other features. It forms a marked line, contrasting sharply with the dark red of the preceding division. It is variable in thickness, being at Lockport less than two feet, and on the Niagara river about ten feet in thickness. At Lewiston small black pebbles are found in it. Only one species of fossil is known in this division, *Dictuolites Beckii*, Conrad. It was a remarkable seaweed, having curiously reticulated branches, and fine interlaced lateral rootlets. It often covers large spaces with its curious branches, indicating that it grew abundantly during this period.

The Medina epoch affords many peculiar features worthy of special study. The intercalation of the gray quartzose band, abounding in fucoids and low orders of molusca, between the red shaly bands that lie above and below it, is an interesting fact, showing the great changes which occurred in the midst of a single period.

The lowest or first division appears to have been rapidly deposited; the material, as it was of a uniform nature, was probably furnished from the same source. It was a marly mud, charged heavily with iron, and nearly void of organic life, and it was deposited in moderately deep water. An upheaval occurs, or some change takes place, by which the depth of the water is greatly lessened, and an entirely different sediment is washed into and deposited over this shallow ocean bed. Organic life becomes abundant. In the siliceous sand the curious brachiopod *Lingula cuneata* flourished. Long, jointed, fucoid seaweeds, floating in the water, became stranded on the beaches. So near the surface, in places, lies the sandy bottom that ripple marks and wave marks are distinctly impressed on the sand, and so free from heavy winds or storms was the period, that these delicate shiftings of the sand are left undisturbed, and to-day we behold this rippled and wave marked ocean bed permanently preserved in the solid stone of this ancient Silurian age. There were places where the sand was entirely exposed at times, for rain drops have marked the surface, and sun cracks, the result of shrinkage from the drying of argillaceous sand in the sunshine, are plainly discernable. Again the scene is shifted, and nearly the same conditions prevail as at first. A red, marly mud, mixed with sand, is now washed into a deeper ocean basin, and the remains of organic life again disappear, except here and there a mass of peculiar seaweed still exists.

The extent of the Medina group seems quite limited, when compared with the remaining rocks of this period. It occurs throughout western New York, thinning out to the eastward; it is not found beyond Utica. Southward of the Appalachian region, it extends through to Pennsylvania and Virginia, where in places it attains a thickness of 1,500 feet. It is from 350 to 400 feet thick on the Niagara river, and passes into Canada, and has been traced to the northwest as far as the straits of Mackinac. Everywhere it presents the same features, indicating a quiet, shallow sea, fed by streams which for ages brought down the same sediment.

The minerals of this period are not available for economic purposes. Iron is largely diffused throughout the rocks, but only sufficient to give coloring. Salt springs abound, and in many places in the county salt water is obtained in digging, but it is too impure to be worked advantageously. Muriate of lime and iron constitute these impurities, and give to the salt obtained its sharp, brackish, unpleasant taste.

CLINTON EPOCH.

Next above the Medina group follow the rocks of the Clinton epoch. They have a wide range and are quite variable in character. The first of this series is a green shale, forming rather an abrupt transition from the sandstone below. This band is mostly devoid of fossils, but at Lockport, on the banks of the Eighteen-mile creek, the writer found a portion was full of a little crustacean, *Agnotus latus*. This band is only a few feet thick, and in places has an intermediate red stratum.

In this county the next subdivision of this group is wanting. This contains in other parts of the State a red, argillaceous iron deposit, and from the small flattened grains which compose it, is called "lenticular ore."

Next in order comes the division called the Pentamerus limestone, from the vast numbers of a shell called *Pentamerus oblongus*, which some portions of it contain. This stratum thins out in this county, and is almost devoid of this shell, only a few specimens having been found.

A green shale similar to the first is found next in other regions, but is also wanting here, and the limestone, which follows and is composed largely of broken crinoid columns and small shells, lies immediately upon the Pentamerus limestone. It is difficult to distinguish the two into separate bands. This upper layer of limestone is largely magnesian, and from the presence of iron pyrites is rapidly decomposed, producing sulphate of magnesia, or epsom salts, which is found in quite large pieces at favorable points along the river banks above Lewiston. This band of the Clinton forms the small plateau below the shale hill on which stands the residence of Mr. Whitmore; also the larger plateau on which the county house is erected, and which extends from the bluff west of the county house eastwardly to the ravine and northward to the vineyards of N. S. Ringueberg.

The rocks of the Clinton epoch are only about twenty

feet in thickness at Lockport and twenty-four feet on the Niagara river. Their outcrop is seen at various points along the base of the Niagara group, on the top of the terrace formed by the Medina sandstone, between Lockport and Lewiston, and along the banks of the Niagara river.

The Clinton rocks indicate a wide-spread ocean. It has been traced west to the Mississippi river and beyond into Iowa, and southward along the Appalachian range through Pennsylvania and Virginia into Alabama. At the West it is thin, but in some parts of New York it is two hundred feet thick.

The shale bands indicate deeper water, consequently a subsidence of the land. The limestone must have been formed in shallower water, under a tropical climate, for coral reefs abound, and brachiopod shells were common, with crinoids and echinoderms. Fucoids prevailed in great numbers and were quite variable in size, but different from those in the rocks below.

NIAGARA EPOCH.

This group terminates the series of rocks found in the county. In many respects it is one of the most remarkable of all the geological formations. It clearly marks vast changes in this great inner continental basin, lying between the Appalachian range on the east and the Rocky mountain range on the west. The uniformity of its structure, and the regularity of its occurrence, point to a vast ocean lying between these mountain ranges, and extending at least from Alabama on the south far into the arctic regions. Along the eastern portions of this vast inland sea the deposits of this epoch first occurred. In this county and immediately following the limestone of the Clinton, we have a fine, bluish-gray, argillaceous rock, known as the Niagara shale. This formation is well seen where the locks of the Erie Canal are cut through its outcrop at Lockport.

This shale readily changes, on exposure, to a gray marly clay. This character is best observed in the various shale hills, or terrace slopes, below the junction of the canal and railroad at Lockport. The lower portion is mostly a pure aluminous shale, but in the higher parts bands of limestone occur. These on exposure break up into fragments which retain many fine specimens of fossils, most beautifully preserved on their surface. These limestone strata increase till the shale ceases, and the hard, compact Niagara limestone obtains. This transition can be traced along the cut of the canal above the locks, towards Messrs. Carpenter's quarries, where the limestone is seen in its perfection, and it is extensively quarried for building material. The thickness of the shale is quite uniform. At Rochester it is a little less than 100 feet, at Lockport it is 81 feet, by actual measurement, and it is the same at Niagara Falls.

The Niagara limestone, as before stated, forms the outcrop along the summit of the escarpment known as the "Mountain Ridge," and extends from Lewiston to Lockport, and eastward to the Cold Spring Cemetery, just beyond which this rock was quarried to obtain the material for constructing the locks.

The limestone gradually increases in depth to the westward; in Wayne county it is 30 to 40 feet thick, at Rochester from 70 to 80, and at Niagara Falls 164 feet. Like the other groups of this period the Niagara limestone is very thick in the Appalachian region, through Pennsylvania and Virginia. In the former State its thickness exceeds 1,500 feet. To the Niagara limestone are we indebted for the falls of Niagara, with all their wonderful scenery. Its great solidity and thickness protect the shale beneath, which being decomposed out, leaves the projecting strata of limestone to form the edge of the vast precipice over which the immense cataract pours. It is very plain to the geologist that there was a time in the past when the falls of Niagara stood at Lewiston. By the slow process of the decomposition of the underlying shales and sandstones, till the projecting mass of limestone was compelled to break away, by its own weight and that of the mass of water which poured over it, the river has cut its way to its present bed, and the falls have receded to the position which they now occupy.

For a theory of the formation of the falls, the writer refers the reader to Mr. Holley's interesting work, "Niagara, its History and Geology," and to an article in the Popular Science Monthly, Vol. 1, No. 5, page 564, by Prof. W. D. Gunning, "The Past and Future of Niagara."

Minerals of the Niagara Group.—This county abounds in certain fine mineral specimens, which are unsurpassed, or scarcely equalled, by those of any other region of the world. These specimens are mostly obtained in the Niagara limestone. In the shale iron pyrites are abundant, but are never found in large masses. Their decomposition with the shale forms sulphate of magnesia, sulphate of allumina, and chloride of sodium. The water of wells sunk into the shale too far is sufficiently impregnated with these products to make it very unpalatable for drinking purposes.

In the limestone numerous geodes, or cavities, have been formed by dissolving out the organic remains deposited in them. Masses of corals, being porous, were readily removed in this way. The surfaces of the cavities thus formed were lined by the deposition upon them of beautiful crystals of dog-tooth and pearl spars, forming crystal grottoes of wondrous brilliancy. Fine pieces of snowy gypsum, of selenite, celestite, and rarely of anhydrite and fluor spar, are also found in these geodes. Small crystals of zinc blende, also of galena, or lead ore, prevail, more especially in the higher and darker portions of the limestone. Occasionally fine specimens are obtained, where several kinds of these minerals are most wonderfully blended and intermingled. Little pools of selenite have their depths lined with exquisite crystals of spar. Fine silvery bars of celestite lie imbeded in the transparent selenite; masses of the snowy gypsum are crowded with crystals of spar, and perhaps over all a clear layer of glassy selenite is spread. These combinations make beautiful and desirable cabinent specimens. In the large masses of rock which have been removed from the deep cut of the canal above Hitchin's Bridge, these specimens can yet be obtained abundantly by breaking them up carefully with a heavy hammer.

Prof. Asher B. Evans, principal of the Lockport Union School, has recently obtained in this way as fine a collection of these minerals as probably has ever been made in this county.

Fossils of the Niagara Epoch. The organic remains found in this group, and particularly in the shale, are very interesting. Six species of trilobites and nine species of crinoids, with as many species of shells, characterize this epoch, and occur in no other rocks found in this State. Corals abounded in great profusion, but are small and mostly branching forms in the shale. In the limestone period reef corals prevailed, with delicate crinoids of wondrous beauty. These last named creatures were rooted in the mud of the sea bottom, from which arose a long, slender, jointed stem, which suddenly expanded into a cupped, lily-like summit, made of many neatly fitting embossed plates, and around the summit of which many long, slender jointed, fingers extended. These it probably used for gathering in its food. On the top of its head, and amidst its delicate fingers, was situated its mouth, surrounded by five petal-like lips. Such a creature was *Caryocrinus ornatus*, the finest, most abundant, and characteristic crinoid of this shale ocean. In and out among the various forms of these fairy crinoids there crept and crawled a still more unique and strange form of life; these were the triobites of this ancient sea, a form of life which has passed entirely away. They were a crustacean with three-lobed, jointed, expanded flat bodies, with many-lensed eyes, a sort of prophecy of the butterfly, which should flit in the air of after ages, as they crawled through the mud of this ancient sea. Some of them were 12 inches long and several inches broad; others were scarcely an inch in length. Besides these quaint creatures many curious and exquisite mollusca dwelt in this old ocean. Orthocerae—straight-chambered shells, the forerunner of the coiled ammonites of after ages and the pearly nautilus of our day, found a home in this Silurian sea. The spirifers, a bivalve shell, were particularly abundant, and *Spirifer Niagarensis* is the characteristic shell of the group. *Rhinchonella cuneata* and *Rhinchonella neglecta* marked another class. *Ahypa reticularis*, a shell of wide distribution, being found in the upper Silurian deposit of England as well as here, flourished in the Clinton epoch and passed through all the changes of that formation, through all the vicissitudes of the Niagara epoch, to find its highest development in the Hamilton group, ages after the completion of the Niagara county rocks. A singular feature of this survival is that this shell continually increases in size. The specimens found in the Niagara group are larger than those of the Clinton, while in the Hamilton it attains a size that has made naturalists hesitate to call it a *reticularis*, believing that it must be a new species; but a careful study of a large number of them confirms the naturalist in the opinion that this species is the same through all these periods, and that it continued to find more favorable conditions of growth till the Hamilton period closed, when it was destined to pass away. Several species of *bithis*, a most exquisite and delicate shell, are found in the Niagara shale.

Though this ancient ocean teemed with a curious life, yet it was a silent, lonely waste of waters. As yet no fish sported in its deeps, no reptile crawled amid its soft ooze. No bird sported over its bosom, or dipped its crest in its slumbering surface. No animal haunted its lonely, barren shores. Many fresh water streams must have been busy carrying sediment from the land above its surface, yet no traces of any fresh water creatures are found. Not a trace of any land plant has yet been discovered. Barren and desolate indeed must have been the lonely coast which surrounded this paleozoic sea. Not a plant, not a bird, not an animal or creeping thing on the land.

Yet in these mysterious waters the processes of laying the foundations of a vast continent were going on. Slowly beneath that wide spread sea, corals, crinoids and mollusca were elaborating the rocky material of a vast tract that after the lapse of an almost infinite period of time, was to teem with a life and an activity immensely superior to the creatures which laid the stepping stones on which we tread to day. Yet such are the ways of the Infinite Creator. More than 2,500 feet of solid rock, deposited out of a sea teeming with lower forms of life, and preserving in its rocky strata the petrified forms of their existence, contain God's record of what has been, and which lies beneath the feet, and the line of ascent of him who proudly treads above them now.

If we are filled with wonder and awe when we gaze back through these aeons of the past and consider what has been, what should be one's feelings when we contemplate the vistas of the future, and think of what is yet to be? We cannot rest in the belief that the consummation of animated nature is yet reached. Rather let us reverently look forward, and work on in the faith that as an infinite past lies downward behind us, so an infinite future rises upward before us.

CHAPTER XXXI.

NIAGARA COUNTY IN THE CIVIL WAR—THE 28TH, 49TH, 100TH AND 102ND INFANTRY.

THIS county shared largely in the martial enthusiasm created by the fall of Fort Sumter in the middle of April, 1861, and President Lincoln's proclamation calling for 75,000 volunteers to re-establish the authority of the government in the South. Public meetings were held all over the county, the first at Lockport on the 18th of April, and a second at the same place on the 20th. At the latter more than $8,000 was raised, which was paid out to volunteers and their families. Large sums were also contributed elsewhere in the county.

By the 18th Captain Elliott W. Cook had opened a recruiting office at Lockport for the purpose of raising a company. Such was the spirit of the hour that in two days one hundred and forty men enlisted, and within a few days more five companies had been organized from the volunteers of Niagara county. They were commanded respectively by Captains Cook, Bush, Mapes and Paige, of Lockport, and Gould, of Niagara Falls; and were subsequently joined with two companies from Orleans county, under Captains Bowen, of Medina, and Hardie, of Albion, and one each from Genesee, Ontario and Sullivan, to form a regiment.

The Niagara men set out from Lockport for Albany on the 16th of May. Arrangements had been made for giving them a worthy start. Colonel E. D. Shuler was the marshal of the day, with D. A. Van Valkenburgh and B. H. Fletcher as his aids. At one o'clock the stores closed on the firing of signal guns at the fair ground, whither the various military and civic organizations of the city then repaired. A grand procession was formed, and the volunteers were escorted through the city between such ranks of enthusiastic spectators as never before assembled in Lockport. A halt was made at the American Hotel, where there was a flag presentation, with appropriate addresses. Thence the procession marched to the depot, where the volunteers took the cars for the capital.

It was voted on May 18th by the State Military Board "that the companies commanded by Captains David Hardie, James R. Mitchell, Erwin A. Bowen, Theodore P. Gould, Elliott W. Cook, W. W. Bush, William H. H. Mapes, H. H. Paige, T. Fitzgerald and John Waller, jr., be formed into a regiment numbered Twenty-eight; that the services of Dudley Donnelly as colonel, and James R. Mitchell as major, be accepted and the election confirmed." Charles J. Sprout, Christopher L. Skeels and Rev. C. H. Platt, of Lockport, were appointed respectively adjutant, quartermaster and chaplain.

The regiment was mustered in at Albany on the 22d of May, and on the 36th was ordered to Camp Morgan, near Norman's Kill, where it was supplied with uniforms and tents and armed with Remington rifles. It was not until the 25th of June that it left for Washington. "The expenditure by the State on account of the regiment up to August 15th, 1861, was $40,694.18, exclusive of subsistence and quarters."

The regiment reached Washington June 28th, and on the 5th of July was attached to General Patterson's command at Martinsburgh, Va. On the 11th, Company A, while on a scouting expedition, met the cavalry of the enemy, and had one man killed—Isaac Sly, of Lockport. July 24th the 28th crossed the Potomac at Harper's Ferry and went into camp near Berlin. At that point on the 10th of August companies B and F recrossed the river, and marching by night to Point of Rocks, Va., surprised a force of rebel cavalry, attacking them from both sides, killed one, wounded a number and took ten prisoners, capturing twenty-one horses and returning without loss.

August 20th the regiment moved its camp to Darnestown, and two months later to Muddy Branch. It was intended that it should take part in the battle of Ball's Bluff, but it was unable to reach the scene of that disastrous affair before the fighting was over, although it marched twenty-two miles in five hours; and could only serve in the transportation of troops across the Potomac.

The camp was removed to Frederick on the 5th of December, and to Hancock on the 6th of January, 1862. On the 1st of March the 28th crossed the Potomac at Williamsport, and as a part of General Crawford's brigade of General Williams's division of General Banks's corps (the fifth), marched to Winchester, which was reached on the 13th. On the departure of the bulk of the army, a week later, company I of the 28th was left with other forces under General Shields to guard the supply train. They were attacked on the 21st by General Jackson, but the enemy shortly retreated up the Shenandoah valley, pursued by the entire force of General Banks.

During this campaign Company E participated in a brilliant enterprise, with a detachment of the Ringgold cavalry and a company of the 5th Connecticut. By a circuitous night march of thirteen miles, from Columbia Furnace to "Cross Roads," the Union force was enabled to surprise and capture a company of Ashby's rebel cavalry, with all its equipments.

On the 27th of March Company I had a skirmish with three companies of rebel dragoons seven miles from Harrisonburgh, Va., whom they defeated and drove, inflicting considerable loss.

During the month of May General Banks withdrew his army to Maryland, pursued by the enemy. In this retreat the 28th on one occasion marched seventy miles in two days, and lost four men wounded and sixty-four prisoners. It covered the retreat near Winchester, and took part in the battle at that point on the 25th.

June 2nd the army resumed the offensive, recrossed the Potomac, and marching up the Shenandoah valley encamped near Front Royal. On the 6th of July the 28th marched to Culpepper Court-house, and on the 9th of August took part in the battle of Cedar Mountain. The following is the official report of this engagement:

"On Friday, August 8th, at about 12 o'clock, noon, we were ordered to march at once, as General Bayard's cavalry had been attacked and the enemy were advancing in force. As usual, we marched on very short notice, thinking it to be nothing but a 'cavalry scare'; the men took nothing with them but arms and ammunition. The day was extremely hot, and after a march of seven miles the command was halted, and we bivouacked for the night.

"About 12 o'clock, noon, August 9th, a cannonade was opened on our side, which continued about one hour; was opened again at half past four in the afternoon, and the action soon became general. The first brigade (General Crawford's) was brought into position (Colonel Donnelly commanding the infantry regiments, the command of the [28th] regiment falling upon Lieutenant-Colonel Brown) to drive the enemy from a skirt of woods. This the 5th Connecticut and the 28th New York succeeded in doing in gallant style. The woods were some ten or twelve rods through, and on the other side were three or four regiments of rebel infantry, 'en masse,' with two pieces of cannon.

The guns were turned upon us and discharged once, but before they could reload we were upon them. They ran off with the limbers, leaving the guns in our possession. We also captured two standards. A most perfect panic ensued among the rebel regiments beyond the woods, and we might well say with Sir Walter Scott:

> ' Our fresh and desperate onset bore
> Our foes three furlongs back, or more.'

At one time we had more prisoners than we could guard, one man having charge of half a dozen at a time, conducting them to the rear. A little help at this time would have turned the entire fortunes of the day in our favor. The enemy, reinforced, rallied and returned to the charge, and after a terrible resistance we were forced to give way, having in fact held our position too long, being at the time entirely surrounded.

"We now had to cut our way back through the woods and retreat across a cleared field some sixty rods, exposed to a most galling fire poured in from all sides. It was in crossing this field that Colonel Donnelly fell, mortally wounded. Lieutenant-Colonel Brown received a shot in the left arm, shattering it to such a degree that amputation was rendered necessary. Adjutant Charles P. Sprout was killed. Our total loss in killed, wounded and prisoners was 207. The officers and men behaved with great coolness and decision."

A participant in the battle relates that at one stage the rebels were posted behind a rail fence, hidden by berry bushes. The 28th charged under a murderous fire across a field of wheat, cut and shocked, and scattered the enemy like chaff. So close was the encounter that men were seen clinched, and fighting with their fists.

After the battle the corps to which the 28th belonged retreated to Rappahannock Station, and was in action thereabouts from the 21st to the 25th of August, and under artillery fire several times in the next five days. During the second Bull Run battle the 28th was at Manassas Junction, and after it fell back to Alexandria. It is recorded that during the three weeks' campaign thus ended "the regiment marched every day and lay on its arms every night."

On the 3d of September the 28th crossed into Maryland, and for the next two weeks moved about on the border. Then came the battle of Antietam. In that famous engagement this regiment occupied a position on the extreme right of the Union line, which it held against superior force for two hours and a half, being commanded by Captain William H. H. Mapes. "Through the whole fight the indomitable courage of the men of the 28th was conspicuous, and was appropriately acknowledged in general orders."

Two or three days after the battle the regiment encamped at Harper's Ferry, and went to work on the fortifications of the place. Early in December another advance into Virginia was made, and the 28th wintered at Stafford Court-house. The deaths in the regiment during 1862 were sixty-three.

The last battle in which this organization took part was that of Chancellorsville, in connection with which it was in action three days and lost seventy-eight in killed, wounded and missing. The regiment returned to New York about the middle of May, 1863, and was soon mustered out.

We have had difficulty in procuring a complete list and record of the men of this and the other organizations hereafter treated of. The provision of the State government for the compilation of town records was to a considerable extent frustrated by the neglect of the town authorities to carry it out, and the records in the county clerk's office are not exhaustive. The following is the roll of the men from Niagara county in the 28th, as complete as we have been able to make it. Mstd and dschd will be recognized as abbreviations of mustered and discharged.

FIELD AND STAFF OFFICERS.

Colonel, Dudley Donnelly; lieutenant-colonel, Edwin F. Brown; major, James R. Mitchell; adjutant, Charles P. Sprout; quartermaster, Christopher L. Skeels; surgeon, Albert M. Helmer; surgeon's mate, Matthew F. Regan; sergeant-major, Charles B. Wright; quartermaster sergeant, Edwin A. Swan; drum-major, John Minor; fife-major, Alonzo J. McMaster.

COMPANY A.

OFFICERS.

Captain, Elliott W. Cook; lieutenant, Daniel R. Whitcher; ensign, John Repass; 1st sergeant, Jeremiah Long; sergeants, Henry Repass, John L. Wright, Thomas Herbert; corporals, Henry Foster, Newfane, enlisted in April, 1861, promoted to sergeant, dschd for disabilty in 1864; Riley P. Butrick, jr, Wesley G. Ray, James Lewis; musicians, Benjamin F. Repass, William Baker.

PRIVATES.

James L. Atwood, Jacob M. Armstrong, Luther L. Bosserman, Chester Barry, Thomas Boodger, Sylvester Bowen, Newfane, enlisted in October, 1862, died in hospital at Albany, in March, 1864; Benjamin B. Brown, Jeremiah Babcock, William H. Chambers, John S. Chambers, Michael Casey, Francis H. Church, Patrick Carroll, William H. Crampton, John Clark, Amon Carson, Charles G. Davis, Martin W. Demerest, Orlando E. Dickerson, Bernard Englert, Alva A. Eaton, James M. Ford, William D. Fox, Samuel Farr, Lyman Field, George W. Good, John F. Gailor, Alonzo Greenman, Michael Gaffney, John Henning, John Kinardt, jr., Amos E. Kniffen, William H. Langdon, Henry W. Logan, Noah B. Lincoln, Joseph W. Little, Charles Lureman, Alexander Mehwaldte, Philip Moyer, William Merville, Adam B. Merville, John McLeland, Philo A. Watson, Daniel Noaker, Royalton, enlisted Oct. 25, 1861, dschd in June, 1865; Aaron G. Oakley, Ambrose Peacock, Nathan Z. Peterson, Thomas Pasco, Elias Reid, Charles Lowter, Isaac W. Sly, Charles B. Sullivan, Henry V. Sterling, Lyman A. Stikells.

COMPANY B.

OFFICERS.

Captain, William W. Bush; lieutenant, Alfred B. Judd; ensign, John C. Walsh; 1st sergeant, George H. Maxwell; sergeants, Peter B. Kelchner, promoted to 1st sergeant Mch. 13, 1862; William White, James F. Bush, promoted to 2nd sergeant Mch. 13, 1862; corporals, Thomas E. Bateman, Shuler T. Smedley, Royalton, enlisted in April, 1861, promoted to 4th sergeant March 13, 1862, dschd in June, 1863; Philip H. Murphy, James F. McMullen; musicians, Joseph W. Chandler, Wright Boodger.

PRIVATES.

Dewitt C. Bulmen, Alfred Bell, dschd Aug. 12, 1862, for disability; Amos M. Brown, Henry Bollow, dschd July 24, 1862, for disability; William Blackwell, Joseph Bayard, dschd July 24, 1861, lost foot by accident; Henry Burk, William T. Behan, deserted Sept. 25, 1862; John Burk, Joseph Barker, deserted Aug. 23, 1862; John Balantine, Palmer Colton, dschd Aug. 5, for disability; Henry W. Colton, Royalton, enlisted Apr. 24, 1861, dschd June 2, 1863; William Connor, James Coville, George M. Cook, James Coile, Stephen H. Chandler, James Campbell, Stephen Clark, Patrick H. Cooney, William H. Crampton, died at Winchester, Va., March 17, 1862; John Calbeck, dschd for disability; Thomas Dalton, Frederick Dohring, George Eslinger, John Finn, Michael Finegan, William Gier, James Goggin, James Garnum, Martin Horner, William Hans, Robert Hamilton, Patrick F. Hanley, John Jacobus, John Johnston (1), John Johnston (2), John M. Lacey, Thomas Leonard, John R. Mabee, Burnett Murphy, Franklin McClanathan, Henry Mitger, John Miller, Edward S. Newman, William D. Parker, Commodore O. Perry, Luther A. Russell, William Robison, dschd for disability; Peter Rollow, William Rutz, William Smith, Alexander Smith, William Siek, William Skinner, deserted Nov. 6, 1862; John Skinner, deserted Nov. 6, 1862; George Southard, James Scott, Nelson J. Tubbs, John Turner, James Turner, Arthur Woods, deserted Sept. 22, 1862; George Squires, John H. Stahl, Robert Southard, Harrison Thomas, Bergen F. Tyler, George W. Tucker, Malcomb G. Taylor, William Taylor, John F. Taylor, John R. Wright, Nathan J. Wright, William Winthrop, Edward White, John Sutton, Robert Hyne, mstd in Mch. 6, 1862, died at Strasburg hospital May 17, 1862; Robert Irving, Joel A. Lisbey, William Roach, George Suttonn, Peter Mangen.

COMPANY I.

OFFICERS.

Captain, Theodore P. Gould, died in Baltimore in 1869; lieutenant, Justin C. Ware, transferred to another regiment; ensign, George A. Bingham, dismissed from the service in Feb. 1862; 1st sergeant, Charles Brown, wounded by an accident and dschd; sergeants, John T. Sullivan, captured at Cedar Mountain; exchanged and promoted; dschd June 3, 1863; Edward G. Brooks, served his term and was dschd June 3 1863; Charles O. Ingalls, served his term and was dschd June 3, 1863; corporals, Edward H. Lampshire, died of disease in general hospital, Baltimore, 1861; Martin McMahon, killed at the battle of Cedar Mountain, Aug. 9, 1862; Francis M. Wadsworth, wounded at the battle of Cedar Mountain, and dschd; Francis Kilmer, transferred to another regiment and dschd; musicians, Homer H. Fields, served time of enlistment and was dschd; Horace L. Drake, served time of enlistment and was dschd.

PRIVATES.

Henry Appelby, deserted early in 1861; James H. Boyd, dschd in 1861 for disability, afterwards re-enlisted and served with distinction through the war; Parker Burnapp, dschd; Charles Benton, killed at Cedar Mountain, Aug. 9, 1862; George Bower, served term in 28th, enlisted in another regiment and was killed; John L. Booth, promoted June, 1862, dschd; Andrew Brennan, served term and was discharged; Edward K. Bullock, deserted in 1861; John Beuch, served term and was dschd; Lewis Bapp, died in general hospital in Baltimore in 1861; George E. Bostwick, served his time and was dschd; Matthew Barton, dschd in 1861; Richard W. Bell, accidentally shot himself and was dschd; Thomas Cooper, deserted at battle of Ball's Bluff, 1861; Alonzo W. Cline, served his time and was dschd; Lanty Conklin, served his time and was discharged; George Davy, served his time and was dschd; William Dunn, served his time and was dschd; James Dougan, wounded at Cedar Mountain, served his time; Robert Deppa, David Evans and Peter Einsfield served their time and were dschd; William H. Frank, wounded at Cedar Mountain, served his time; Thomas J. Frarey, served his time and was dschd; James Fitzgibbons, deserted in October, 1861; William O. Garner, released on writ of *habeas corpus*; Theodore A. Gould, James Hany and John Hany, served their time and were dschd; Charles R. Haight, killed at the battle of Cedar Mountain; Jacob Hagerman, dschd for disability; Oscar P. Harvey, served his term of enlistment and was afterward killed by Mosby's guerillas; George Irish, served term of enlistment and was dschd; James A. Kearns, dschd; Peter Kearns, dschd; William Killer; Michael Kilberer, killed Aug. 9, 1862, at Cedar Mountain; Simon Keefer, served his term and was dschd; Francis Lacy, transferred to another company, dschd; Gatien Liger, served his term of enlistment, afterward was a commissioned officer in 2d Mounted Rifles; Stanley Lefferty, deserted; Henry C. Miller, Edward Moody, Lawrence Metzger, William McMullen, James Morrority, John McCann, John Myers, James McClary and George Nash, served their term and were dschd; Alphonzo Pursall, deserted; Albert Price, deserted; Alvin T. Richmond and George Robinson, served their time and were dschd; James Scarrow, deserted; Charles Stephenson, served his time and was dschd; Francis L. Shipman, promoted to be sergeant, served his time; Alexander Simpson, served his time and was dschd; Matthew G. Tierany, deserted; Charles Vice, served his time and was dschd; Einst Wager, Thomas Watkins, John Walker and John Zurkee, dschd for disability.

COMPANY K.

OFFICERS.

Captain, Henry H. Paige, resigned July 16, 1862; lieutenant, Volney Farley; enisgn, James D. Ames; 1st sergeant, Hugh A. Jameson; sergeants, William F. Williams, John H. Moyses, Henry F. King; corporals, Wilber F. Lawton, Norman O. Allen, Samuel Williams, Samuel Lewis; musicians, Edmund Stoney, Byron Anderson.

PRIVATES.

Nathaniel Angevine, Charles A. Beebe, John S. Bush, Nelson H. Beebe, Kearon Brophy, William Bush, William H. Crowley, William H. Cleveland, Daniel Caton, Fredrick A. Caman, Dexter F. Carpenter, Joseph Coty, Daniel H. Davis, Ingraham D. Eaton, Franklin S. Eggart, William O. Engler, Stephen Flinn, Freeman B. Goodenough, John Griffin, Charles Harting, Royalton, enlisted Apr. 29, 1861, dschd June 2, 1863; Henry H. Helmer, Charles E. Halsted, Isaiah Harrington, Emery Hilton, William Kruskie, Alexander W. Lowrie, Gottfried Mevis, Matthew Moyres, Franklin O. McKinney, James Mason, Patrick McCann, John C. L. Moll, killed at Culpepper, Va., Aug. 9, 1862; Sylvester S. Marvin, Walter Mullen, Peter C. More, Joseph J. G. Nellis, George A. Nye, Perry Putnam, Nehemiah Pecktil, Joseph Phillips, Charles L. Pickard, James N. Phillips, William Parsons, Stephen C. Roberts, Albert Rogers, William E. Richardson, August Strasberg, Dennis Sullivan, Don C. Smith, Newfane, enlisted Oct. 5, 1861, dschd in June, 1862; John H. Smith, Charles F. Seger, Joshua B. Smith, William H. Simons, John Stacy, William H. Tenbrook, Thomas C. Tenbrook, Charles Vogt, Abram Wheeler, Hixon Woolever, Watson Swick, William C. Ward, Henry Webb, Willard White, William D. Young.

Company C included Sergeant George Brown, Newfane, enlisted in April, 1861, mstd out in Aug. 1862, and private J. Bryan Lovell, mstd out with the regiment.

FORTY-NINTH INFANTRY.

This regiment was made up of companies raised in the counties of Niagara, Chautauqua, Erie and Genesee. Company H, raised and commanded by Captain Charles H. Moss, of Lockport, was Niagara's representation in the organization, with names and rank as follows:

OFFICERS.

Captain, Charles H. Moss, Lockport; first lieutenant, Andrew W. Brazee, Lockport; second lieutenant, Henry D. Hall, Lockport; first sergeant, William D. Boughton, Lockport; second, Otis B. Hayes, Somerset; third, Charles A. Murphy, Lockport; fourth, William Tindall, Lockport; first corporal, Frank Baker, Lockport; second, Isaac N. Porter, Lockport; third, Jay Silsby, Lockport; fourth, Henry E. Barlow, Lockport; fifth, Michael Hutchinson, Lockport; sixth, William Levan, Lockport; seventh, George W. Pixley, Somerset; musician, Schuyler S. Ballou, Lockport; wagoner, Ludolphus W. Fuller, Lockport.

PRIVATES.

Willard W. Bailey, Jefferson Baylis, John R. Baylis, Garret Barry, Henry D. Blakely and Stephen Bramon, Lockport; George C. Bugbee, Royalton, enlisted Aug. 1861, dschd 1864; James A. Bugbee, William Bush, Emory E. Burton, James B. Calvin and John P. Casey, Royalton; Alphonso T. Coleman, Somerset; Thomas Curran, Newfane, enlisted Sept. 17, 1864; James Carr and Samuel B. Colt, Lockport; Francis M. Doubleday, Somerset; Henry Davis, Newfane, enlisted Oct. 1, 1864; John Evans, jr., and Elmer Fox, Somerset; Charles Freeman, Lockport; James H. Griswold, Royalton, enlisted Sept. 5, 1861, dschd July 7, 1865; Mathias Fese, Lockport; John Haight, jr., Somerset; Cornelius Hermon, Charles E. Hessel, Thomas Hughes, Samuel Johnson, William Jones and Charles A. Kendall, Lockport; Henry Krupp, Newfane, enlisted Sept. 14, 1862, dschd Dec. 9, 1863; Parnell Lawcock, William Rhodes, Joseph McCuen, Charles A. Merwaldt, Samuel A. Morris, Hiram Odell, John Ortwaine, Egbert Perry, Elias Perry, Theodore Pesirie and Fred Peters, Lockport; John Rose, Newfane, enlisted Oct. 1, 1864; John Ryan, Newfane, enlisted Oct. 1, 1864; Nathaniel I. Russell, Newfane; John Staler, Newfane; Aaron B. Severs, Hartland; Levi W. Sherman and Charles Ligwald, Lockport; John D. Silsby, Hartland; Albert Smith, Wilson; Michael Smith, Royalton, enlisted Aug. 1861, dschd 1865; Hiram P. Springstead, Somerset; Wesley B. Steele, Hugh M. Swick and George Swicker, Lockport; Thomas E. Talliday, Somerset; Robert H. Taylor and Hiram P. Thompson, Lockport; David W. Vail, Somerset; Rufus R. Waite, Alonzo D. Wilcox and Theodore C. Williams, Lockport; James White, Newfane, enlisted Oct. 1, 1864.

The regiment was raised in response to the call for 300,000 men in 1861. It was mustered in on August 22nd of that year, and went out under command of Colonel Daniel D. Bidwell of Buffalo, for three years' service.

After the organization was perfected the 49th was encamped at Fort Porter, Buffalo, several weeks, in camp of instruction. In September it was ordered to New York city to receive arms. After being furnished with equipments the regiment went direct to Washington, and remained there one night. The next morning it crossed the Potomac into Virginia and went into camp at Fort Ethan Allen, where the men were engaged for a little time in strengthening the fort, by throwing up breastworks. They were then ordered to camp Griffin, where they were attached to General "Baldy" Smith's division. They remained in camp doing picket duty during the autumn of 1861 and winter of 1862, meantime participating in the engagement at Drainesville and in several sharp skirmishes. In the spring of 1862, when the Army of the Potomac broke camp and entered upon the famous Peninsula campaign, the 49th was included, subsequently participating in the battles of Yorktown, Williamsburg, Golding's Farm, Savage Station, White Oak Swamp and Malvern Hill.

The regiment afterward fought at Crampton's Gap, Antietam, Mary's Heights, Salem Heights, Gettysburg, Rappahannock Station, Wilderness, Spottsylvania, Cold Harbor, Petersburg, Fort Stevens, Opequan, Fisher's Hill and Cedar Creek. Company H, however, did but little fighting after the engagement at Malvern Hill, having been detailed at division headquarters as provost guard, Captain Brazee acting as judge advocate.

The portion of the regiment that went through the several battles above named was cut to pieces, and when mustered out there was but a small remnant of the body of 800 men that started out. At the battle of the Wilderness every officer was either killed or wounded. After having surrendered the rebels charged upon them with terrible effect, and mowed them down like grass before the sickle. Captain Moss did not remain long with his company; he was stricken down with camp fever in 1862, and was forced to come home. He died March 25th, 1862. He was succeeded by Lieutenant Brazee, who remained in command until October 18th, 1864. His term of office having expired, he came home and Lieutenant Hayes took command. The regiment remained in the service until June 27th, 1865, when it was mustered out in accordance with orders from the War Department.

ONE HUNDREDTH INFANTRY.

This regiment was raised and organized at Buffalo, to serve three years. It was mustered in from September, 1861, to January, 1862, and retained in the field until August, 28th, 1865, when it was mustered out. It included quite a number of men from the western portion of Niagara county, all of whom but two—a musician (John Castle, Tonawanda) and a wagoner, (William Hay, jr., Tonawanda) —were privates. The following were the men, all enrolled at Tonawanda unless otherwise mentioned :

Ithainer Ackley, La Salle; John B. Atkinson, Mitchell Allair, James Ansley, William J. Bailey, Charles Butch, Myron Becker, John G. Brookman, Walter C. Bates, Andrew E. Bigsby, Wheelock T. Bates, James Berryman, Wheatfield; Christian Burgwadt, Wheatfield; John Caverno, Louis Daniels, Philip Deermere, William Dixon, John Desselberger, Wheatfield; James Ewart, Michael Enright, Franklin F. Flannery, Valentine Fix, Henry Gaslin, Wheatfield; Charles Hagen, William Hubb, Henry Hidell, Robert Jones, Philip Klein, Lawrence Keller, Henry Keller, Frederick Knobel, William K. Lounsbury, John W. Lingley, Francis Leonard, Joseph Longer, Charles Leonard, Wheatfield; Jacob Lightmire, Henry Luthso, Wheatfield; Henry Meitzinger, John Monteith, George H. Martin, Henrick Miller, Wesley McCafferly, Wheatfield; John F. McCafferly, Wheatfield; Charles Wetzdorf, Wheatfield; George Newman, Jacob Pfalegraf, James Pendergrass, Daniel W. Rundell, William Richardson, David Rappleyea, Michael Ryan, Frederick Reipstick, Henry Shultz, James W. Simson, Winfield B. Scott, George H. Stormes, Caspar Shelbeck, Thomas Schulby, Jacob Shopp, William H. Striker, John Saco, Wheatfield; Frederick Shlotman, William Smith, Wheatfield; Lawrence Torney, Charles Whitmur, John F. White, Willett P. Wilkins, William Wright, Newfane, enlisted Dec. 12, 1861, mstd out Jan. 30, 1865; David W. Williams, Wheatfield; John H. Wolfe, Wheatfield; Henry Wicker, Wheatfield; William Jahr, Wheatfield.

The battles in which the regiment was engaged were those at Yorktown, Williamsburg, Fair Oaks, Bottom's Bridge and White Oak Swamp.

ONE HUNDRED AND SECOND INFANTRY.

In this regiment, which was organized at New York city from November, 1861, to April, 1862, to serve for three years, were three men from Niagara county, viz.: Fourth Sergeant William Parker and privates Michael Barriers and William Swift, all of Niagara Falls. It did service at the battles of Cedar Mountain, Antietam, Chancellorsville, Gettysburg, Lookout Mountain, Missionary Ridge, Ringgold, Resaca, Dallas, Altoona, Pine Hill and Atlanta. On the expiration of the term of service the original members (except veterans) were mustered out, and the regiment, composed of veterans and recruits, retained in service until July 21st, 1865, when it was mustered out in accordance with orders from the War Department.

CHAPTER XXXII.

THE RECORD OF THE TWENTY-THIRD BATTERY, AND 1ST REGIMENT OF LIGHT ARTILLERY.

IT was in August, 1861, just after the humiliation at Bull Run and in response to the second call from the President, that Captain Alfred Ransom, then of Newfane, applied to Governor Morgan for authority to raise a company of volunteers. The permission was granted August 6th, 1861, and the work of recruiting at once began. It was performed under the most adverse circumstances. It was in he busy season of harvest, and there was thus a restraint upon the farmer, with nothing save loyalty to country to induce him to enlist, for no bounties were given at that time and the term of enlistment was "three years or during the war, unless sooner discharged." All this proved to be no great barrier. Niagara county was "true blue," and as early as the 16th day of October, the company was ready for inspection. Captain Ransom had associated with himself

Samuel Kittinger, of Cambria, and Lewis B. Manning, of Wheatfield, well and favorably known throughout Niagara county, and from the first the work progressed satisfactorily.

On the last named date the battery passed the inspection of State Inspector E. D. Shuler, and was mustered into service. It was ordered to rendezvous at Buffalo. Starting out with the minimum number, eighty men, whenever a man was found who would enlist he was mustered in. In November, 1861, the battery was sent to Albany, under command of Captain Ransom and Lieutenant Samuel Kittinger. There were at Albany a number of small companies and squads of men which were being consolidated into regiments and battalions. One company, recruited by J. C. Salter, of Warren county, numbering sixty odd men, was divided, one-half being assigned to Captain Ransom's battery and the other to Captain Jay E. Lee's, thus raising Ransom's to the full number for light artillery batteries. On the 7th of December, 1861, at the urgent request of General McClellan, General Barry and many other military men at Washington, and under advice of General Rathbone and Major J. F. Sprague, of Albany, Captains Ransom and Lee consented to enter into an organization with their respective companies to be designated as Battery A, Rocket Battalion, and the officers and men were mustered as such and ordered *via* New York to Washington.

Upon their arrival at Washington they at once began to drill and practice experiments in the use of war rockets, being the only organization of the kind in the service. Early in April, 1862, the rockets and carriages were returned to the arsenal, and field pieces (3-inch rifled Rodman steel guns) taken instead. The battery was then ordered to Newbern, N. C., to reinforce General Burnside; took sailing vessels, and after a fifteen days passage arrived at Newbern about April 28th. The battery was assigned to General Reno's division (2d division 9th army corps), and encamped on the east side of Trent river, having the same camp that the rebel cavalry occupied before Burnside drove them out of Newbern. It was known as the "Spaight plantation," and lay in the angle of the Trent and Neuse. The place was very unhealthy, so much so that it was sometimes called the great "North Carolina alligator nursery." Many of the soldiers succumbed to malaria, and either died or were confined to the hospitals.

During the summer of 1862, the battery was stationed at Moorehead City, N. C., and engaged in the various raids and skirmishes of the army of North Carolina, including Pollockville and Trenton. These services are fully described in Major-General J. G. Foster's report on the conduct of the war in North Carolina from July 1st, 1862, to July 15th, 1863. On the 11th of December, 1862, while at Moorehead City, orders were received by Captain Ransom to move his battery, with all of his ordnance camp and garrison equipage and stores of every kind, to Newbern, and hold himself in readiness to march from that point at 5 o'clock A. M. on the 12th, with three days' rations of cooked meals and five days' rations of hard bread, sugar, coffee and salt. The order was received on the afternoon of the 11th. The battery moved accordingly, in company with all the available forces of General Foster, on the memorable raid to Goldsboro.

The next day active skirmishing was commenced, lasting all day. On the 14th the battle of Kinston was fought, in which the battery did its full share of the work. The next engagement was the battle of Whitehall, in which this battery fired the first gun. After this the battery was moved to the southwest of the main column to strike Mount Olive, about seventeen miles south of Goldsboro, on the Wilmington railroad. At Mount Olive a large trestlework was destroyed, about half a mile of the track torn up and the rails bent so that they were useless; a large amount of cotton destroyed, and the post-office thoroughly overhauled. It was a memorable day in the career of the 23d battery.

On the following morning the battle of Goldsboro was fought, in which two bridges over the Neuse river were destroyed and a large number of prisoners taken, who were released on parole. Then, in the heart of the enemy's country, and almost out of ammunition, the expedition started on its return march for Newbern, where it arrived on the 21st instant, after having been engaged in fighting and marching for ten successive days and eleven nights. During the winter of 1862 raiding and skirmishing were kept up around Newbern, in which Ransom and his men did good service. On the 14th of March, 1863, the enemy made a desperate attempt to retake Newbern. Here again the 23rd was most conspicuous, on account of its long ranged guns, they being the only pieces that could reach the enemy's lines across the Neuse in the rear of the unfinished Fort Anderson. The fort was garrisoned by the 92nd N. Y., but they had not a gun mounted, and but for the 23rd battery must have been captured. Troops were finally sent over to the support of the little garrison, under cover of Ransom's battery, the enemy's lines were broken and another glorious day closed for the 23d, now in the 18th army corps. During this engagement, the following message was sent:

"Captain Ransom: General Foster sends to you his compliments for the magnificent firing of your battery. He never saw anything better."

Soon after this failure of the enemy to take Newbern, they undertook by a long siege to capture Washington, N. C. In this connection the 23d battery was engaged for eighteen days and nights, sometimes on the road, then in the woods, and part of the time on boats, endeavoring to break the chain that the rebel General D. H. Hill had wound about Washington, which was garrisoned by only about 1,200 men.

On the 18th of April, 1863, General Foster, having run the rebel batteries at Hill's Point and Rodman's Point in the steamer "Escort," and arrived at Newbern, made a general move outside of Hill's line around Washington, hoping to shut off and capture that portion of Hill's army then operating on the neck of land lying between Newbern and Washington. General Hill discovered the movement, and believing undoubtedly that discretion was "the better part of valor," abandoned his position.

This action concluded the siege of Washington. The battery remained at that place until April, 1864. During this time it went on numerous raids, usually in the night, against the enemy's camps established to protect their foraging parties which were supplying Lee's army. Among the many good things the 23d did while mounted as cavalry was the surprise and destruction of Major Whitford's (rebel) camp on a dark rainy night, and bringing in as a trophy Captain White's new uniform, complete from cap to boots; and on another occasion capturing and bringing in one of the pieces of the famous North Carolina "Star" battery, with four horses and limber complete.

In the spring of 1864 the enemy again attempted to take Washington, N. C. The 23d was the only light battery at that post at the time. After a siege of three days and nights the rebels abandoned the attack, and orders were given by Brigadier-General Harland, then commanding, to evacuate the place. Harland took all the infantry at the post and went with them himself on board of transports around through Pamlico Sound, while Captain Ransom, being the senior officer left in command, with the 23d, two companies of the 12th N. Y. cavalry and one company of the first N. C. cavalry, took the overland route to Newbern, making an all night's march.

The battery remained at Newbern during the summer of 1864 and until the spring of 1865, doing camp and garrison duty, provost duty, and watching the movements of the enemy until the surrender of Lee. The fighting having then ceased, Captain Ransom, being broken down in health after having served nearly three years and a half, resigned his commission and left the battery in charge of First Lieutenant Samuel Kittinger, who was afterward promoted to the rank of captain.

Captain Kittinger was ordered to report his battery to General Kilpatrick to serve as horse artillery in connection with Kilpatrick's calvary brigade, who went on a "wild goose chase" after Jeff. Davis; with them the battery moved to Mount Olive, to the very spot it had occupied nearly two and a half years previous; and after traversing the greater portion of North Carolina, finally brought up at City Point, where the men turned in their horses and battery and started for home. They were mustered out of service July 3d, 1865, after being in the field three years and eight months and taking part in the following engagements:

Kinston, December 14th, 1862; Whitehall, December 16th, 1862; Goldsboro, December 17th, 1862; attack on Newbern, March 14th, 1863; siege of Washington, N. C., April 1-19, 1863; Blount's Creek, April, 1863; siege of Washington, N. C., 3 days, 1864; Kinston, March, 1865.

As already stated, the battery started out with only the minimum number, about eighty men. While home on sick leave in 1862, Captain Ransom recruited it up to the full maximum number. Ninety-two men were sent to it from Albany county, N. Y., in 1864, thus swelling the number at that time to nearly three hundred men. The surplus men were organized into a company, and armed with rifles, with which they did provost duty in Newbern until Lieutenant Thomas Low, of the 23rd, received his commission as captain, and they were assigned to the 8th N. Y. Heavy Artillery.

The whole number of men enlisted for the 23d battery during the war was 394.

Those from Niagara county who served under Captain Ransom are named in the following compilation made up from the muster-rolls:

OFFICERS.

Captain, Alfred Ransom; first lieutenant, Samuel Kittinger; first lieutenant, Thomas Low (promoted to captain); second lieutenant, Nelson Cornell; first sergeant, Lewis B. Manning; quartermaster sergeant, Joseph Kittinger; sergeants, John K. Swick, Newfane, enlisted Nov. 11, 1861, mstd out Nov. 10, 1864; Edgar C. Balcom, Frederick F. Palmatier, Newfane, enlisted Oct. 22, 1861, mstd out Nov. 10, 1864; George W. Sprout, Newfane, enlisted Oct. 16, 1862, died in 1865; Amos Parker, Orlin S. Hays; corporals, Charles T. Saxton, William Sage, William M. Smith, Simeon H. Talbot, Newfane, enlisted Nov. 11, 1861, mstd out Nov. 10, 1864; Sylvester Perry, Edmond T. Ackerman, Edwin Saxton, James McDonald. Almon Bliss, William H. Merville, Philip Simmons, Stephen Flynn; buglers, Clark Anderson, William J. Porter; artificer, William L. Warden; blacksmith, Jedediah Biggins, Newfane, enlisted Aug. 25, 1862, mstd out July 24, 1866; wagoner, Perry McKenzie.

PRIVATES.

Lewis Alvers, William Amsdell, Charles L. Atwater, James F. Allen, Wheatfield; Adelbert Anderson, Wilson; Jothan Bliss, Wheatfield; Christian Baumann, Newton O. Baker, Andrew B. Balcom, James N. Bull, George C. Bull, John Berger, Pennel Bobst, Clark Burget, Burr A. Beebe, Porter; Perley Brown, Wilson; Sylvester G. Campbell, James H. Clow, William L. Cole, William H. Carver, Ward Chapman, Wheatfield; Robert Churchill, Wilson; Cassius M. Cole, Cambria; Samuel K. Dietrick, Nelson Defoe, William Delaney, Lewis M. Daniels, Estes E. Dake, George W. Davenport, Wilson; William H. Enderton, Anthony Enderton, Charles H. Flint, George Flint, Elihu C. Fitch, Augustus C. Fitch, Charles Ferrah, Christian Fisher, Ashley D. Francisco, John W. Gilbert, Wheatfield; James Graham, Henry J. Gregory, Wilson; Charles B. Hayes, Royal S. Hurlbert, Hiram W. Hewitt, William Hagle, Henry Hudden, William Hill, Wilson; Walter R. Hurlburt, Robert Harnott, Wilson; Milton Holley, Wilson; Cyrus Hawley, Wilson; Henry B. Hewitt, Lewiston; William H. Kline, Abraham Kraut, Levi Karchner, W. E. Knowles, Charles Keyes, Wilson; Luther Knapp, Wilson; Jacob W. Layloud, Newfane, enlisted Oct. 27, 1861, dschd June 27, 1865; William D. Lovell, Newfane, enlisted Aug. 29, 1862, mustd out July 14, 1865; Edwin Leete, Wheatfield; William Lutts, Porter; Ezra G. Lounsbury, Wilson; Henry Morris, John McCollum, Michael McCorning, Newfane, enlisted Sept. 28,

1861, mustd out July 14, 1865; George McBride, William Mayer, William Moore, George Merrill, Wheatfield; Frank B. Mallett, Wheatfield; Smith J. Newman, Augustus Nervist, Porter; Henry Niles, Wilson; Thomas O'Reilly, Lockport; David Peggs, Niagara, killed at Newbern, Feb. 12, 1864; Palmer Pierce, Edwin P. Pierce, George L. Perry, John Phalen, Benjamin C. Palmer, Daniel S. Porter, William Powley, Philomon R. Payne, Philo A. Patrick, Lorenzo R. Putnam, Wheatfield; George A. Pettit, Wilson; Cyrus M. Pierce, John Reynolds, Charles Richert, Ben J. Reynolds, Wilson; Sampson Sovereign; Eugene Slocum, Peter Smith, Lockport ; Philip H. Swick, Newfane, enlisted Aug. 30, 1862, mstd out in June, 1863; William H. Simonds, Lewiston; Jesse B. Stoughton, Porter; John H. Tucker, James E. Taylor, John Tenbrook, Thomas Tryon, George Towner, Orrin W. Towner, Albert H. Thornton, Daniel Vogle, Pliny Vanfleet, Wheatfield; Calvin Vantwormer, Wheatfield; Joseph A. White, Samuel Worden, jr., Hiram A. Worden, Jerome Worden, Alvin H. Webster, John A. Whitlock, Wheatfield; Norris Withington, Wilson; George W. Williams.

The above list was copied from an original muster-for-pay roll of September and October, 1864, according to the muster-roll on file in the office of the clerk of Niagara county. The following named persons from the county were also members of the battery when it left home in 1861:

George D. Bunleton, William M. Brulis, Daniel Dietrick, jr., Charles Depue, William Engle, Orrin L. Elwood, Milo Hollenbeck, Henry Harrington, Flanders J. Kellar, Lyman A. Levan, Michael McCormick, John N. Miller, Thomas Pike, James F. Skinner, Charles L. Spade, Edward I. Simmons, Elijah Vredenburg, Augustus Wilcox, John Wood, Edwin D. Weaver, John Wright.

FIRST LIGHT ARTILLERY.

The companies of which this regiment was composed were raised in the counties of Niagara, Orleans, Oswego, Oneida, Onondaga, Chemung, Steuben, Monroe, Wayne, Erie, Jefferson, St. Lawrence, Lewis and Herkimer. Company M was from Niagara. The regiment was mustered into the service for three years, from August 30th to November, 1861, and organized at Elmira. The following were the members of company M from Niagara county.

OFFICERS.

Captain, George W. Cothran, Lockport; 1st lieutenant, C. E. Winegar, Medina ; second, James H. Peabody, Olcott ; third, George B. Eggleston, Wilson ; fourth, John D. Woodbury, Wilson.

PRIVATES.

Amaziah Adams, Wilson; William Alger, Rapids Bridge; Willard Atkins, Pekin; Oscar Benedict and Chauncey F. Bullen, Somerset ; Byron B. Barber, Wilson ; Morris C. Bonesteel, Wilson; Stephen L. Brasington, Porter; Orla W. Burtch, Hartland; Martin Bookner, Wheatfield; William Baugh, Wilson; Henry Benson, Youngstown; Calvin E. Bedell, Somerset; Robert Brown, Wilson; Egbert Baright, Lockport ; James Burns, Wilson; George W. Draper, Lockport ; Asa L. Day, Royalton, enlisted Sept. 25, 1861, dschd in June, 1865; Robert Day, Royalton; Henry Dehn, Wilson; Erasmus Dettinger, Lockport. Joseph and John Dryer, Wilson; Elias A. Dunkleberger, Pendleton; H. W. Duffee and Albert Daily, Wilson; F. Dutcher, Somerset; Jonathan D. Elliott, Newfane, enlisted Oct. 5, 1861; Uriah H. Eshbaugh, Lockport; John H. Gormley and Egbert J. Greene, Wilson; Henry F. Houstater, Pekin; Thomas D. and Henry E. Herbert, Lockport; Joseph Haas, George A Holmes, and William H. Henning, Wilson; Amalond Hathaway, Somerset; Augustus W. Hilton, Pendleton; Timothy Hopkins, Lockport; John Hannah, Wilson; Willam Huffman, Hartland; Perry V. D. Johnson, Wilson; John L. Kinney and George Kent, Lockport; John W. Lockwood, Wilson; Washington Ludwig, Pendleton; Clark B. Lowell and Clarence H. Levan, Wilson; Eldridge Lewis, Somerset; Henry J. Liscom, Wilson; Ira S. Losier, Lockport; Solomon Levan, Wilson; John McGuern, Lockport; Peter Miller, Jeremiah McGrath, Clark McKenzie, Wilson; Schuyler McKenzie and Sanford B. Nixon, Wilson; Simeon Outwater, Newfane, enlisted Oct. 14, 1861, killed July 13, 1864, at Atlanta; Reuben W. Oliver, Wilson; Fred. A. Porter, Porter; Augustus M. Patterson, Royalton; James Robinson, Cambria; Hiram M. Ribble, Porter; Henry C. Sherrill, Lockport; Hiram Snyder, Rapids; Martin Shuck, Lockport; Christian Sholtz, Wheatfield; Hiram H. Smith, Alfred F. Stevens, Caleb Sweet, William H. Smith, Thomas M. Singer and William L. Smith, Wilson; Charles H. Schad, Royalton; Reuben A. Snyder, Rapids; George W. Shears, Wilson; John Shaw, Lockport; James A. Vanbergen, Wilson; George Vogle, Wheatfield; Almon Vanwagoner, Somerset; Emanuel Wertman, Rapids; William Winslow, Wilson; John E. Wright, Lockport; Ammon F. Webster and Thomas G. Williams, Wilson; Fred. C. Wilke, Wheatfield; Harrison H. Wright and J. Francis Webster, Wilson; John Walker, Lockport; Harry Y. Pecise, L. N. Pratt and H. Wright Harrison, Wilson.

The regiment did service by batteries, of which there were twelve in number, from A to M inclusive, and when the war was over it was mustered out by batteries. Battery M went from Lockport and joined the regiment at Elmira.

Under command of Colonel Guilford J. Bailey, of the regular army, the regiment left Elmira for Albany, where it remained about three weeks and then went direct to Washington and into camp Barry, where the men received their equipments. Here they remained until about the first of January, when they were ordered to Frederick, Md., to join General Banks. On the 22d of February they moved with Banks from Frederick to Harper's Ferry, and on via Charlestown to Berryville, midway between Charlestown and Winchester. They made a forced march from Berryville to Winchester to relieve General Shields. At Winchester they had an engagement. From Winchester the battery went with Banks to Strasburg, and from Strasburg to Edenburg, Va., meantime engaging in a sharp fight with the rebels under Stonewall Jackson.

This was in April, 1862. From this time forward until August, 1863, the battery was fighting with the Army of the Potomac, participating in the battles of Antietam, second Bull Run, Cedar Mountain, second Winchester and Gettysburg.

In the month last mentioned the battery marched under General Hooker to Chattanooga to relieve General Rosencrans, who was cooped up there. Under Hooker they fought at Lookout Mountain and Wahatchie Valley.

The following winter the regiment went to Bridgeport, Alabama, where, its term of service having expired, it was discharged. The original members re-enlisted as veterans and joined Sherman, who was then preparing to open a spring campaign at the South. Battery M was assigned to the 12th army corps in the army of the Cumberland, under General Thomas. After the capture of Atlanta Sherman divided his army and selected four corps to go with him on the march to the sea. The 11th and 12th corps had been consolidated and formed the 20th corps. This, with the 14th, 15th and 16th corps, went with Sherman, and the rest went back with Thomas to Nashville. From this time until the close of the war, Battery M was with Sherman, aiding in the capture of Millidgeville and Savannah; traversing South Carolina, destroying all that came in their way; traversing North Carolina until the capture of Raleigh and the surrender of Johnston's army; on to Virginia, stopping at Richmond; next going to Alexandria and finally arriving at Washington in time for the grand review.

The battery was mustered out June 23d, 1865. As regards casualties it was quite fortunate as compared with the experience of other like organizations. Among those who met their death in the field was Colonel Bailey, who was killed in action at Fair Oaks. The muster-in roll, as given in the foregoing columns, contains only those names enrolled in the military records on file in the county clerk's office. Many recruits were added to the battery during the service.

CHAPTER XXXIII.

THE CAVALRY REPRESENTATION—HISTORIES OF THE 8TH, 3RD AND 15TH, AND THE 2ND MOUNTED RIFLES.

THE 8th regiment of cavalry was composed of companies raised in the counties of Niagara, Orleans, Monroe, Ontario, Seneca, Wayne, Chenango, Oneida and Livingston. It was mustered into the service from November 28th, 1861, to October 4th, 1862, and the organization was completed at Rochester. Its field officers were: Colonel, Samuel J. Crooks, of Rochester; lieutenant-colonel, C. R. Babbitt; majors, W. S. Markett and W. H. Benjamin.

The regiment left Rochester for Washington November 27th, 1861, and arrived at its destination at 2 o'clock, Sunday morning, November 30th. It left Rochester without marching orders, arrived in Washington unheralded and was there two days before being recognized by the War Department. The regiment remained in Washington during the winter, and it looked very much at one time as though it would be regarded by the government as surplus cavalry and be either transferred or mustered out. Finally the men were furnished with carbines, but no other equipments.

Early in March they were transferred to a point near Conrad's Ferry, on the Potomac. Here they guarded the river for twenty-five miles. April 6th the regiment removed to Harper's Ferry and took quiet possession of that place. Then the U. S. arsenal, once the pride of the government, giving employment to over one thousand men and turning out an immense number of muskets and small arms, was a mass of ruins, having been destroyed by the Federal forces to prevent its falling into the hands of the rebels.

While doing guard duty along the railroad out of Harper's Ferry the regiment shared the rout of Banks's army by the enemy. The men had not been mounted yet, and were poorly armed, having inferior carbines and sabres. Poorly fitted as they were to enter battle, five companies of the regiment nearest Winchester were thrown forward to hold the enemy in check and cover the retreat of the worn out soldiers, and they did their duty. June 7th Captain Davis of the 2nd regular cavalry was given the colonelcy, and shortly after an order was issued giving the men their horses and equipments. The regiment was then stationed at Baltimore for some little time, preparing for active service. Early in September it moved to Harper's Ferry and scoured the country day and night capturing many prisoners.

On the 8th this regiment made a reconnoissance up the river to Shephardstown and found General White's command was retreating from Martinsburg, about nine miles away, and the rebel army reported in force at that place. Just beyond Sharpsburg they found the whole corps of General Jackson crossing into Virginia for the purpose of surrounding the Ferry. Our forces soon found themselves in a bad predicament. Colonel Miles ordered the guns to be spiked and our forces to fall back.

The whole cavalry force was put under the command of Colonel Davis of the 8th. They crossed the river on a pontoon bridge and turned the column to the left on a gallop, shooting the enemy's pickets as fast as seen. The ride to Sharpsburg was a thrilling one.

At Sharpsburg Colonel Davis learned that the rebel army was stationed at Hagerstown, and their immense wagon train moving toward Williamsport for the purpose of crossing into Virginia. He at once conceived the plan of capturing it if possible, and selected a guide who led through cornfields and ditches, over hills and through valleys, avoiding Hagerstown and reaching Williamsport just at the break of day. General Longstreet's ammunition train shortly afterward arrived. Colonel Davis rode up to a rebel major and asked him to what regiment he belonged. The major replied, "The 44th Virginia," and asked Colonel Davis what regiment he belonged to. "To the 8th New York cavalry, and you are my prisoner," was the stern reply, and Davis shouted to the rebel wagon-master, "You are my prisoner; turn that train up the first right hand road." He then called one of the companies of the 8th regiment to act as guard, and ordered that the first man who left his wagon should be shot on the spot. Colonel Davis, fearing that the alarm would be given to the rebel army before he could escape with his plunder, concluded to reach the Pennsylvania border before halting. In this daring exploit Davis's force took 81 prisoners, including several commissioned officers; over 80 wagons, comprising the whole of General Longstreet's ammunition, and over 300 horses and mules. Upon their arrival at Greencastle, Pa., the prisoners were sent to Harrisburg and the wagons to Chambersburg.

The next morning the 8th went back to Williamsport and captured sixteen more prisoners. The regiment scoured the country until the battle of Antietam, in which it took no very active part, as it was late in the day when it arrived. After the army passed into Virginia in the fall of 1862 the 8th was constantly on the advance; having almost daily skirmishes, in which it came off successful and with but trifling loss.

Immediately following these adventures the regiment went into camp near Hagerstown. It did not see much camp life during the winter, as it was doing picket duty, scouting, reconnoitering and the like.

The principal engagements of the 8th were in repelling the raids of Stuart's forces. June 9th, 1863, in the great cavalry raid near the Rappahannock the regiment was again engaged; here it won laurels again but at a great sacrifice, losing several men, among them the brave Colonel Davis, who was killed on the field at Beverly Ford; also Captain Benjamin F. Foote, of Company E, of Niagara county, Lieutenant Cutler, of Company A, and Lieutenant Rees, Company C, and having Lieutenant Elpha, of Company D, badly wounded. There was, however, but a single casualty in the Orleans company, the case of Sergeant Daniel Haskell, badly wounded. The 8th regiment sustained its hard earned reputation in the three days' battle at Gettysburg. To follow its movements from this time forward until the expiration of its term of service would be to speak principally of successful raiding here and there. On the battle-flag of the regiment, in addition to the engagements mentioned in the foregoing, are Locust Grove, Hawes's Shop, White Oak Swamp, Opequan, Cedar Creek and Appomattox Courthouse.

In 1864 the original members of the regiment were mustered out, and the veterans and recruits retained in the service until June 27th, 1865, when they were also mustered out.

Company E was from Niagara county, and most of the men were from the towns of Hartland and Royalton. It was raised by Captain Benjamin F. Foote, of the town of Hartland, and consisted of the following named men, besides himself and First Lieutenant Alpha Whiton, of Royalton, who enlisted September 5, 1861, and was discharged May 22, 1863.

PRIVATES.

George R. Achilles, Hartland; John Anstey, Middleport; John C. Ayers, Middleport, enlisted in Oct. 1861, dschd in Nov. 1863; Horace Bacon, Hartland; George W. Burdick, Royalton, enlisted Feb. 1, 1864, dschd June 29, 1865; Chester F. Barry, Somerset; Lewis Burch, Hartland; Daniel S. Brown, Royalton; Alexander H. Braddock, Hartland; Albert Marion Bristol, Royalton, enlisted in Oct. 1861, dschd July 27, 1865; F. L. Bristol, Royalton, enlisted Mch. 25, 1865; John C. Brown and Philo Burch, Hartland; Addison Barton, Royalton, enlisted Aug. 12, 1862, dschd July 14, 1865; Alexander Barton, Royalton, enlisted Oct. 19, 1861, died in Baltimore, Sept. 10, 1862; John Bremmer, Royalton, enlisted Mch. 27, 1865, dschd June 27, 1865; Henry Brickford, Almon Brightman, Amos A. Castle, Daniel Connor, John Cline and James Congdon, Hartland; Henry R. Christman, Royalton, enlisted in Sept. 1861, mstd out with regiment; William Cassidy, Royalton; William Davis, Hartland; Newton Fisk, Royalton; Charles A. Fox, Royalton, enlisted Nov. 6, 1861, promoted sergeant, dschd June 27, 1865; James N. Garrett, Hartland; Henry Griffis, Royalton, enlisted in October, 1861, died in hospital in June, 1862; Thomas Hartley, Hartland; Alexander Harrison, Royalton, enlisted Oct. 15, 1861, dschd Dec. 30, 1863; David Hinman and Willis S. Hinman, Hartland; Augustus Hause, Royalton, enlisted Oct. 12, 1861, promoted to quartermaster sergeant, fought in over twenty battles, dschd Dec. 8, 1864; Oscar Jones, Hartland; James Johnson, Royalton, enlisted Oct. 15, 1861, died at Relay House, Md., Aug. 15, 1862; Lewis Kane, Hartland; George Long, Royalton, enlisted Oct. 8, 1861, promoted corporal, dschd Dec. 8, 1864; James H. Marion, Royalton, enlisted Oct. 7, 1861, died in hospital, Mch. 12, 1862; Thomas H. Murphy, Royalton, enlisted Oct. 9, 1861, dschd Dec. 8, 1864; James O'Neil, Harrison D. Odikirk and Chester D. Owens, Hartland; George Rifenbank, Royalton, enlisted Oct. 15, 1861, dschd Dec. 8, 1864; Bailey Roberts, Royalton; James K. Robson, Hartland; Thomas Richardson, Royalton, enlisted in October, 1861, served three years; William G. Richardson, Royalton; James Reynolds, Newfane, enlisted Mch. 10, 1865; Nelson A. Rude, Hartland; Charles Ross, Royalton, enlisted in October, 1861, dschd in June, 1865; Robert Ramshaw, Hartland; George Sheriff, Hartland; William H. Shaffer, Royalton, enlisted in September, 1864, dschd in May, 1865; George Skeel, Hartland; Jacob Shaffer, Royalton, enlisted in March, 1865; Carlos F. Smith, Hartland; Albion Stearns, Royalton; Orrin Smith and Wheaton R. Southworth, Hartland; Thomas Strouse, Royalton, enlisted Oct. 19, 1861, dschd Dec. 8, 1864; John S. Schaller, Royalton, enlisted in October, 1861, dschd in July, 1865; Christian

Snyder, Royalton; George D. Tuttle, Newfane, enlisted Mch. 29, 1865; James P. Thorn, Hartland; James M. Tucker, Royalton, enlisted Dec. 1, 1861, promoted to lieutenant, stationed at Santiago, Tex.; Elijah Walton and Franklin Wright, Hartland; Charles H. Ware, Royalton, enlisted Sept. 25, 1861, killed in battle June 15, 1864; Jerome Wright, Royalton, enlisted Oct. 8, 1861, dschd Nov. 1, 1863; George A. Wilcox, Gasport, enlisted in Aug., 1862, promoted quartermaster sergeant, dschd in Nov. 1863; David Walsh, Royalton; Allen A. Willson, Robert H. Watkins, and James Watterson, Hartland; Henry Wichterman, Royalton, enlisted Oct., 1861; dschd in April, 1862; Samuel C. Ward and Albertus Wilcox, Hartland; Henry Winegardener, Royalton; Charles Wallace, Hartland; John Zimmerman, Royalton, enlisted in Oct., 1861, dischd in Jan., 1862.

The regiment was mustered in from November 28th, 1861, to October 4th, 1862. The original members were mustered out at the expiration of the term of service, and the regiment, composed of veterans and recruits, retained in service until June 27th, 1865, when it was mustered out. It participated in the battles of Winchester, Antietam, Upperville, Beverly Ford, Gettysburg, Locust Grove, White Oak Swamp, Opequan, Cedar Creek and Appomattox Court-house. At the battle of Beverly Ford, June 9th, 1863, Captain Foote was killed.

THIRD CAVALRY.

Here was a regiment raised in the counties of Albany, Schoharie, Chemung, Delaware, Oneida, Onondaga and Orleans, and organized at New York, that included in its ranks a number of men from Niagara county, among them the following Royalton men:

John Benson, enlisted Feb. 19, 1864, dschd July 12, 1865; David Boulton, enlisted July 4, 1862, dschd June 21, 1865; William Breening, enlisted Aug. 14, 1861, taken prisoner Oct. 7, 1864; Henry Breening, enlisted Oct. 14, 1861, dschd Nov. 29, 1865; John Breening, enlisted Jan. 27, 1864, dschd Nov. 29, 1865; Sergeant Sterling D. Ewington, Company F, enlisted Aug. 9, 1861, killed in action Mch. 4, 1863; Frank Griswold, Company F, quartermaster sergeant, enlisted Aug. 14, 1861, dschd June 14, 1865; George W. Proctor, bugler, Company C, enlisted Aug. 2, 1862, dschd June 10, 1865; Charles Reardon, enlisted Apr. 25, 1864, died in July, 1865; Silas S. Tucker, lieutenant, Company F, enlisted in August, 1861, taken prisoner at Jones's Landing and never heard from; Timothy Tracey, enlisted in March, 1864, now in the regular army; Edward E. Taylor, enlisted Feb. 19, 1863; Charles Wesley Perry, enlisted June 13, 1861, dschd July 17, 1864; William Wallenberg, corporal, Company F, enlisted July 21, 1861, dschd Dec. 16, 1865.

Also the following from Newfane: Sergeant Morris Harrington, Company F, enlisted Aug. 12, 1861, shot by guerillas at Swan's Quarters, N. C., Mch. 4, 1863; Corporal Dewey Hawkins, Company F, enlisted Sept. 3, 1861, dschd for disability in 1864; Sergeant Samuel Kemp, Company F, enlisted Aug. 12, 1861, killed by guerillas Mch. 14, 1863; and the following recruits to Captain Ira Holmes's company, all of whom were enrolled at Tonawanda:

Charles Sharpstone, James Tools, Patrick C. Gough, Gregory Bellinger, Thomas H. Shellots, James Johnson, Sidney J. Smith, William Ryan, Charles Seeman, Urban Kuppersmedt, Henry H. Leonard, William Anderson, William Smith, Frederick Cappel, John Mitchell, Walter Ross, John W. Forrester.

The regiment did good service at the battles of Burns Church, Young's Cross Roads, Williamston, Kinston, Whitehall, Goldsboro, Ball's Bluff, Weldon Railroad, Edwards Ferry, Stony Creek, Petersburg, Malvern Hill, Newmarket and Johnson's House.

FIFTEENTH CAVALRY.

This regiment was organized for three years' service at Syracuse, and the companies of which it was composed were raised in the counties of Onondaga, Ontario, Orange, Oneida, Chautauqua, Cattaraugus, Genesee, Tompkins and Erie. Company E, however, was made up largely of men from Niagara county, as shown in the following list of men enrolled at Lockport:

OFFICERS.

First Sergeant, Orlando E. Dickerson; commissary sergeant, George A. Bond; sergeant, Edward Bragden; corporals, George Frazier, Walter W. Smith, Royalton, enlisted July 13, 1863, dschd Aug. 9, 1865; Robert Hamilton; farrier, John G. McLean; blacksmith, John Jacobus.

PRIVATES.

John Birmingham, William Cole, William Ebert, George Emms, John German, Thomas Nogan, George C. Hollis, Royalton, enlisted July 27, 1863, dischd Aug. 9, 1855; John McGrath, John McClellan, Newfane, enlisted in July, 1863, and served through the war; Commodore O. Perry, Thomas S. Roberts, Peter Rollo; Luther A. Russell, William Scott, James Smith, Alfred H. Smith, Royalton, enlisted Dec. 26, 1863, dschd June 22, 1865; Peter Snyder, Charles Temple, William Turner, Albert Wright, Royalton, enlisted July 11, 1862, dschd in August, 1865.

Ambrose Peacock, of Lockport, belonged to Company C. The regiment was mustered in from August 8th, 1863, to January 14th, 1864. It was consolidated with the 6th N. Y. cavalry June 17th, 1865, and the consolidated force designated the "2d N. Y. Provisional Cavalry."

SECOND MOUNTED RIFLES.

In the month of July, 1863, under the head of "Governor's Guard," the following announcement was made in the papers throughout western New York, and circulated throughout the country in the form of hand bills:

"Colonel John Fisk, of Niagara, has been authorized by Governor Seymour to raise a regiment for three years' service in the U. S. army, to be known as the 'Governor's Guard.' Any person desiring to raise a company to be attached to this regiment can procure authority by applying to Colonel John Fisk, of Suspension Bridge, or Lieutenant-Colonel Cook, or Captain William P. Warren, late of the 28th New York.

"Captain Warren will act as adjutant in forming the regiment. Headquarters at Lockport."

It was shortly afterward made known that it would be raised under the title as given above, or, in other words, that it was to do mounted rifle service. The first three men mustered in were Henry F. Pierce, of Niagara Falls; Dr. Robert T. Paine, Lockport; and William P. Warren, Lockport. Dr. Paine was mustered in as surgeon and Warren as adjutant, and they at once set about aiding in the mustering in. The response to the call was encouraging from Niagara county, and it was backed up by the counties of Erie, Wyoming, Orleans, Wayne and Sullivan. The first company completed was Captain Joseph N. Rushmore's, of Lockport. Captain W. H. H. Mapes, of Lockport, was next ready with a company, and was quickly followed by Captain Henry G. Stebbins, of Lockport, with a full complement. Twelve companies were made up, and by February, 1864, the regiment was ready for the field. The regimental officers were:

Colonel, John Fisk, Niagara Falls; lieutenant-colonel, Jasper N. Raymond, New York; lieutenant-colonel, Joseph H. Wood, 2nd regular cavalry; major, William H. H. Mapes, Lockport; major, John D. Newman, Lockport; major, John H. Fralick, Little Falls; adjutant, William P. Warren, Lockport; adjutant, Franklin Rogers, Buffalo; quartermaster, Henry F. Pierce, Niagara Falls; commissary, Joseph A. Briggs, Buffalo; commissary, John M. Hill, Lockport; surgeon, Robert T. Paine, Lockport; assistant surgeon, Hugh McGregor Wilson, Lockport; assistant surgeon, Eli Woodworth, Allegany; chaplain, Washington Stickney.

W. H. H. Mapes, who started out with rank of captain, was promoted before entering the service.

The regiment first rendezvoused at Lockport, but the barracks were insufficient and the regiment was ordered to Fort Porter, Buffalo, which latter barracks were made a recruiting station and camp of instruction. The 2nd remained there from December, 1863, until the March following, when, three battalions being completed, they were ordered to Camp Stoneman, near Giesboro Point in the neighborhood of Washington. Here they remained until about May first, when they were ordered to the front to reinforce the Army of the Potomac. Instead of being furnished with the cavalry outfit for which they were sent to Camp Stoneman, or receiving instruction in cavalry tactics, which had been promised them, they were assigned to a provisional brigade, composed of dismounted cavalry and heavy artillery, commanded by Colonel Marshall, of the 14th heavy artillery, in the ninth corps, under General Burnside.

On the day following their arrival at Camp Stoneman they participated in the battle of Spottsylvania, suffering but little loss. Their next engagement was the battle of North Anna, southeast of Spottsylvania. In this their loss was light.

Returning from North Anna the regiment was placed as rear guard of the ninth corps, when it had a severe engagement at Tolopotomoy Creek, losing quite a number of men. The next day it was in the fight at Bethsaida Church, a few miles from Tolopotomoy. At this time the regiment was under command of Lieutenant-Colonel Raymond, of New York. The loss at Bethsaida was quite heavy, fifty or sixty killed and wounded. Among those killed was Lieutenant Jeremiah R. Morrison, of Wyoming county.

Hardly had the smoke of this battle cleared away before the 2nd was in the memorable fight at Cold Harbor, in early June; its loss here was not heavy. Among those wounded was Lieutenant Charles W. Flagler. From Cold Harbor the regiment moved with the Army of the Potomac and crossed the James river, arriving at Petersburg June 16th, just in time for service again. On the morning of June 17th, the 2nd made a charge over the enemy's works and captured a large number of prisoners, who were sent to the rear in charge of Captain W. Fitzer Williams. The regiment was engaged during the entire day, but its loss was light. On the morning of the 18th of June it again advanced on the enemy's works, near the Weldon railroad, and toward evening made a gallant charge, which resulted in the capture of the railroad, the 2nd, however, suffering a terrible loss.

In this action First Lieutenant Delong, of Lockport, was killed, and Captain Williams; the entire loss was between two and three hundred men killed and wounded.

From this time until July 29th, 1864, the regiment lay in the rifle pits under a constant fire, losing men day by day, among them Lieutenant J. L. Atwood, who was killed by a sharpshooter. On the morning of July 30th, the mine in front of Petersburg was exploded. A terrible struggle followed, in which the 2nd regiment was engaged, under command of Major Mapes. One division was repulsed by the rebels. The division in which the 2nd regiment fought had been held for the final charge, in case those already in the fight did not hold their ground. The order was finally given for them to charge, and they did it nobly, capturing two lines of the enemy's works, they held them about six hours, but as no relief came, they were compelled to fall back. In this engagement the regiment lost nearly one hundred and fifty men, killed, wounded and prisoners. It remained in command of Major Mapes from this time forward until the battle of Pegram's Farm.

A few days subsequent to the fight at the mine the regiment moved to the left and took a position near Fort Hell, where it remained for some time, experiencing no loss. The next battle was at Pegram's Farm, southwest of Petersburg, where Major Mapes, Captain Stebbins, Lieutenant Mansfield, Lieutenant Bush and others, in all forty or fifty, were taken prisoners. The killed and wounded numbered between fifty and seventy-five. Among the killed was Lieutenant Casey, of Lockport. The next field was the first battle of Hatcher's Run, in October, 1864. The loss was slight. From here the 2nd went back to Pegram's Farm, where it remained until the last of November. It was then ordered to dismounted camp at

City Point, where the men received their promised horses, with orders to report to General Charles H. Smith, of the 3d brigade, 2d cavalry division. The second day after reporting the regiment went on a raid to Stony Creek station, where, with the balance of the division, it assisted in destroying a large amount of stores and taking many prisoners, sustaining slight loss. It then returned to camp near Fort Stevenson, in the vicinity of South Petersburg, where it remained until December, 1864. The regiment next accompanied the celebrated Warren raiders, and assisted in the destruction of the Weldon railroad from near Petersburg to Weldon, N. C.

At this time the 2d was divided, a detachment having been sent back to the second battle of Hatcher's Run, under command of Lieutenant Newman. Upon the return of the regiment to camp it was detailed as a rear guard to the 5th corps of infantry. In this action the 2nd lost about forty men, among them Captain Watson and Lieutenant Tippling, of Wayne county. It went into camp again and remained until March 29th, 1865, doing picket duty and losing but few men. On this date it started with General Sheridan's corps in the final pursuit of Lee, and March 30th engaged in the battle of Dinwiddie Court-house, southwest of Petersburg, in which engagement Captain Eli Morse, of Little Falls, N. Y., was killed, and Lieutenant Flagler and C. A. Murphy, of Lockport, seriously wounded.

The next day the 2nd was in the battle of Five Forks, but sustained no loss. Next, at Jettersville, it lost a dozen wounded, but none killed. At Sailor's Creek it lost a few men, and again at Farmville. It was next engaged at Appomattox Court-house, where Joshua Smith was killed. After doing service at Appomattox the brigade to which the 2nd regiment belonged was detailed as an escort of General Grant from Appomattox to Burkville Junction, Va. It then returned to Petersburg, when, pending negotiations between Johnston and Sherman, it was ordered to North Carolina to reinforce Sherman. There it was learned that Johnston had surrendered, and the 2nd was ordered back to Petersburg and from there to Buckingham county, Va., where it remained on provost duty until August, 1865.

This closed the eventful career of the regiment, and its next movement was homeward. Arriving in Buffalo August 10th, 1865, it was mustered out. It left home 1,500 strong, and during the service was reinforced by upward of 300 recruits; but came back with only between seven and eight hundred men. The depleted ranks and the scars the survivors bore told the story of their service in their country's defense. They were in the field a little over a year, and took part in nineteen distinct engagements, as recorded in the foregoing narrative.

The records on file in the office of the clerk of Niagara county have reference only to those companies and parts of companies that were raised in Niagara county. From them we obtain the following partial roll of the regiment:

COMPANY A.

OFFICERS.

Captain, Joseph M. Rushmore; first lieutenant, James B. N. Delong; second lieutenant, Eli Kahler; first sergeant, Michael Casey; quartermaster sergeant, W. Roselle Pack; sergeants, John Parker, Newfane, enlisted Sept. 14, 1863, mstd out Aug. 14, 1865; George Squires, Newfane, enlisted in September, 1863; commissary sergeant, Philip Moyer; second sergeant, William T. Behan; third, Amos M. Brown; fourth, James F. McMullen; first corporal, Lafayette Randall; second, John Parker; third, James Bonnell; fourth, John Maynard; sixth, illiam Spalding; Weighth, Michael Owens; farrier and blacksmith, Enoch A. Turner; trumpeter, George W. Harrison—all of Lockport.

PRIVATES.

Samuel Avery, Lockport; George Brooks, Porter; Gustave Bistoff, Francis V. Brown, Peter Brady, Albert Baldwin, James Brady, and John Conlan, Lockport; T. Cornelius, Niagara; Frank Dunn, Oscar B. Draper (promoted to regimental quartermaster sergeant), Matthias Gough, Hiram Gay, Washington L. Hicks, Lionel L. Harrington, Frank H. Kennedy, Owen Kenyon, John Kinney, and William King, Lockport; Philip Matthias, Niagara, drowned in James river, Apr. 14, 1863; Thomas McWaters, Adam Prime, George Presby, William Pasco, James Penders, Samuel F. Robinson, Henry Smith, David Spaiel, Daniel A. Stahl, Charles Schroder, Alfred Southwick, Moses Turney, Henry W. Wright, and Burt Wentworth, Lockport.

COMPANY B.

Samuel F. Brickley and Sylvester Base, Lockport; Jacob A. Cole, Newfane, enlisted Mch. 6, 1865; Miles Caleb, Malcome Ferguson, Christian Henselin and Edgar Hoglan, Lockport; John Mergendoller, Royalton, enlisted in October, 1863; John Prime, Alfonso A. Powers, Reuben Pearce, Patrick Quinlan, Michael Riley, John Shanly, Gottfried Schramm, Henry Smith and Charles Tinney, Lockport.

COMPANY C.

OFFICERS.

Captain, Henry G. Stebbins; first lieutenant, Peter B. Kelchner; second lieutenant, Charles W. Flagler; orderly sergeant, Charles A. Murphy, Lockport; quartermaster sergeant, Lafayette Olmstead, Niagara; commissary sergeant, William P. Sheldon, Lockport; first sergeant, Augustus Hawn, Lewiston; second, William Luff, Cambria; third, Thomas C. Tenbrook, Lockport; fourth, William H. Gaskill, Wilson; fifth, John P. Murphy, Lockport; corporals, William Allan, Lockport; George Beiber, Niagara; James W. Barber, Newfane, enlisted Dec. 22, 1863, mstd out Aug. 24, 1865; L. Edward Warren, Royalton; George H. Moore, Royalton; Andrew Ackerman, Pendleton; Thedran D. Fellows, Cambria; musician, Augustus Ehler, Lockport; wagoner, Christian Sanger, Cambria.

PRIVATES.

William H. Bush, Hartland; George Birdsall, Newfane,

enlisted Oct. 18, 1864, mstd out Aug. 23, 1865; Thomas Barber, Niagara; Byron W. Baxter, Newfane, enlisted May 1, 1865, mstd out Aug. 24, 1865; Marvin Baily, Newfane, enlisted Dec. 17, 1863; William Clark, Royalton; William Cady, Royalton, enlisted Dec. 22, 1863, dschd Aug. 23, 1865; William A. Coulter, Cambria; Barneste Doran, Royalton; James Dorsey, Lockport; William H. H. Drake and Jacob Everhart, Niagara; Fred Everett, Tonawanda; John Fladd, Niagara; Jacob Freese, Lockport; William W. Fellows, Cambria; Henry J. Green, Tonawanda; Paul C. Griffis, Niagara; Charles E. Howe, Hartland; Fred Kibbler and David Kohler, jr., Tonawanda; John McDonald, Royalton, enlisted in December, 1864, dschd in 1865; William Martin and James Morton, Niagara; Earl H. Nicholas, Pendleton; Charles Olrich, Niagara; Edwin Roberts, Lockport; Alma A. Simons, Royalton; William Smith, Royalton, enlisted Dec. 26, 1863, dschd in June, 1865; Joseph Sykes, Luke E. Summers and John Summers, Royalton; Theodore Smiling, Wilson; John D. Schoonmaker, Porter; Mark A. Schoonmaker, Niagara; Lawrence Smith, Lockport; Hiram T. Walker, Royalton; Reuben Whitney, Niagara.

COMPANY E.

OFFICERS.

First sergeant, Henry V. Sterling, Lockport; sergeants, Isaiah Harrington, Somerset; Eugene A. Stottle, Newfane, enlisted Dec. 18, 1863, died of typhoid fever at Alexandria, July 9, 1864; Frederick Mahl, Wilson; Isaac Harris, Royalton, enlisted May 31, 1861, fought in fourteen battles, dschd Aug. 10, 1865; Charles P. Mapp, Lockport; corporals, Ozro Bachelder, Wilson; Truman B. Richardson, Lockport; John T. Reilly and Norman Robinson, Wilson; Alphonso T. Coleman, Somerset; farrier, Orrin E. Johnson; teamster, John Fisher, and saddler, Clark Davis, Wilson.

PRIVATES.

George H. Althouse, Royalton, enlisted Nov. 20, 1863, dschd Jan. 19, 1865; Theodore H. Brayton, Newfane, enlisted Dec. 18, 1864; Samuel Barnes, Tonawanda; William Bathrick, Lockport; Robert Burnside, Newfane, enlisted Dec. 31, 1863; William H. Clift, Wilson; Martin Congdon, Lockport; John F. Casy, Lewiston; Thomas Deckstader, Lockport; Martin Dell, Tonawanda; Thomas Elmore, Lockport; John Gibson, Wilson; William Heinerman, Cambria; Benjamin B. Hill, Lockport; James E. Hill, Newfane, enlisted Nov. 28, 1863, mstd out Aug. 10, 1865; Robert W. Hill, Lockport; William Kinney, Newfane, enlisted Dec. 22, 1863, mstd out Aug. 10, 1865; Cyrus King, Wilson; Frank C. Mead, Lockport; Robert McClellan, Newfane, enlisted Jan. 7, 1864, killed, Aug. 1, 1864, before Petersburg, Va.; Patrick Mosher, Lockport; John McGinnis, Lewiston; Charles Nellist, Somerset; Edward F. Ozard, Newfane, enlisted Dec. 16, 1863, mstd out August 10, 1865; Peter Renshaw, Somerset; Cortland Rouse, Wilson; Charles H. Schucker, Royalton; Charles A. Smith, Newfane, enlisted Oct. 6, 1863, mstd out Aug. 10, 1865, also served two years in the infantry; Aaron Sears, Lockport; Jesse A. Seward, Somerset; Millard F. Streeter, Lockport; John Shaver, Somerset; Martin H. Wagner, Niagara, wounded at Five Forks, Va., died in April, 1865; John Van Wagoner, Lockport; Walter S. Webb, Hartland.

COMPANY F.

OFFICERS.

First sergeant, Edward Wilson, Lockport; corporal, Victor Knorr, Lockport.

PRIVATES.

Albert Butts, and Eldridge T. Burchell, Somerset; John Gedre, Lewiston; Leonard James, Hartland; James Tolland, Newfane, enlisted Dec. 24, 1863, mustd out May 18, 1865; Edward Powers, Lockport.

COMPANY H.

OFFICERS.

First sergeant, Robert Erskine, Tonawanda; commissary sergeant, Oscar F. Whipple, Tonawanda.

PRIVATES.

William Day, Wheatfield; Liban W. Keith, and Charles N. Sheldon, Tonawanda.

COMPANY I.

OFFICERS.

Captain, William H. H. Mapes; first lieutenant, William F. Williams, Newfane, enlisted in August, 1863, promoted to captain, killed before Petersburg, June 19, 1864; second lieutenant, George F. Gould; first sergeant, Riley P. Buttrick; quartermaster sergeant, Nelson H. Bebee; commissary sergeant, George Woods; first duty sergeant, Charles B. Sullivan; second, Francis H. Church; third, Thomas Boodger; fourth, Christopher Holzheimer; fifth, Gatien A. Lizer; corporals, John M. Bredell, James Cole, Frank McClanathan, Joseph J. Leacount, Moses Brady, Henry T. Daggett, William Lindsley; farrier, John S. Hyman; blacksmith, Charles Hemmelman; trumpeters, John Kempter, John Yankey; saddler, Franklin S. Eggert—all from Lockport.

PRIVATES.

John Aikens and Lewis B. Atwood, Lockport; John E. Babcock, Newfane, enlisted Mch. 1, 1865; mstd out Aug. 24, 1865; Augustus Bauer, Fred Brooks, William Beitz, John Blanket and Sidney S. Buttrick, Lockport; Isaac W. Batchelder, Royalton, enlisted Oct. 17, 1863, dschd Aug. 12, 1865; James Bruce, Lewiston; Lewis H. Burtch, Hiram Brooks, Hilton Bailey and Charles E. Coryell, Lockport; Rimmon Colton, Royalton, enlisted Mch. 6, 1865, dschd Aug. 22, 1865; James Cramer and Willard Carney, Lockport; William H. Decker, Newfane, enlisted Mch. 1, 1865, mstd out Aug.

10, 1865; John Dixon, Horace L. Dickerson, Charles Daniels, Henry Darling, Fred Eccels, and John W. Gordinier, Lockport; John D. Gibson, Newfane, enlisted Sept. 16, 1863, mstd out Aug. 10, 1865; James P. Gibson, Newfane, enlisted in December, 1863, killed June 3, 1864, at Cold Harbor, Va.; Albert Gilman, Newfane, enlisted Oct. 29, 1863, promoted to corporal, mstd out Aug. 24, 1865; Albert Gould, Newfane, enlisted Mch. 1, 1865; John Hannah, Lewiston; Luther Halsted, Newfane, enlisted Mch. 1. 1865, mstd out Aug. 24, 1865; Alvia Hunt, John M. Hill, Isaac Harris, and Robert Jamison, Lockport; Keith T. McKenzie, Lewiston; Wallace Mandaville, Newfane, enlisted Dec. 29, 1863; John Murray, Silas W. Mapes, Hermann Meike, John Miller, Patrick McCann, George M. Nellist, and Fred Nye, Lockport; Millard Nye, Newfane, enlisted Nov. 26, 1863, mstd out Aug. 24, 1865; James O'Neil, Samuel Piper, Lewiston; Frank C. Palvley, Lockport; La Fayette Printup, Niagara; Isaac Johnson, John P. Ranney and Thomas Sky, Lockport; Alexander Simpson, Lewiston; Cornelius Snyder, Charles Silver, Charles A. Smith, William Silk, James W. Troley, James L. Tibbets and Franklin Thayer, Lockport; Edward E. Williams, Newfane, enlisted Apr. 1, 1864, died July 14, 1864, at Camp Stoneman, Va.; Henry L. Williams, Burt Wentworth, Newfane, enlisted Sept. 16, 1863, mstd out Aug. 10, 1865; John Wentworth, Newfane, enlisted Sept. 16, 1863, died at home, July, 1864; Fayette P. Woodruff, Newfane, enlisted Sept. 10, 1863, mstd out Aug. 24, 1865; Charles Wenkfield and Fred Ziehl, Lockport.

COMPANY L.

Second lieutenant, Henry F. Arnold, Somerset. Private, William H. Shaver.

COMPANY M.

William H. H. Sheldon, Lockport; Carl Winsch, Niagara.

CHAPTER XXXIV.

SERVICES AND SUFFERINGS OF THE ONE HUNDRED AND FIFTY-FIRST INFANTRY.

IN the month of August, 1862, immediately after the departure of the 8th heavy artillery for the front, Colonel William Emerson, of Albion, with competent aid, set about raising a regiment to do service under the title of the 151st N. Y. V.

By the middle of October it was ready for inspection. The companies of which it was composed were raised in the counties of Niagara, Orleans, Genesee, Monroe and Wyoming. Companies B, F and H, the major portion of K and a part of G were from Niagara; A, D and part of G were from Orleans; C from Genesee, E from Rochester, and I from Wyoming and Genesee. Thus in less than two months' time upwards of 1,000 men from this corner of the State responded to the call for 600,000. It was a patriot organization, composed almost wholly of young men of noble bearing. They went out when the waves of rebellion rolled highest, expecting to be called at once into perilous service. When, on the 22d of October, 1862, they left Camp Church, Lockport, where the regiment was organized, for Baltimore, the final hand-shaking was marked by a sadness never to be forgotten. But there was a glory that enshrouded the gloom, and the tears that were shed as the bereft ones turned to their depleted firesides would not have disgraced the field of battle, but would have mingled fittingly with patriot blood on hallowed sod.

The regiment went from Lockport to Elmira, where it received arms. From there it went to Baltimore, where the division under General Emory was being organized for service in the Gulf, and the 151st was assigned to it; so the regiment in less than twenty-four hours after its arrival in Baltimore was ordered out on review. Some of the men, never having had a gun in their hands, were ridiculously awkward, whereupon General Emory said that the regiment was wholly unfit for service until schooled and ordered it to go into camp of instruction. In compliance with this order the regiment rendezvoused at Lafayette Square Barracks and commenced drilling. Here it remained until spring. It is unnecessary to add that it became familiar with the tactics during its six months' practice.

On the 22d of April, 1863, the regiment was ordered to West Virginia, to reinforce Colonel Mulligan, and during the two weeks following was at Clarksburg, Buckannon and Weston, but in no engagement. It was then ordered back to Winchester to join General Millroy. It got as far back as Martinsburg, when the order was countermanded. Here the 151st remained a few days awaiting orders. It was finally sent to do guard duty on the Potomac between Berlin and Monocacy, and was there when Lee's army crossed below Harper's Ferry. Its next line of march was to Maryland Heights, where it was encamped when Hooker crossed above the ferry with the Army of the Potomac. About the first of July the Heights were abandoned and the troops, in the neighborhood of 16,000 strong, were ordered to Frederick City and were there held as a reserve force while the battle of Gettysburg was being fought. At noon on the 4th of July a dispatch was received from General Meade saying that the enemy had been repulsed, and ordering General French with his forces, including the 151st, to march to South Mountain Pass, a distance of sixteen miles. In thirty minutes the forces were in line and on the march. After tramping until dusk that night, a terrible thunder storm raging meanwhile, South Mountain was reached. Orders were given for the soldiers to sleep on their arms; and no fires were to be kindled lest they might attract the attention of the enemy. Without fire the "boys" had to go without coffee. They would have met the foe more bravely than they submitted to this. Nothing could cheer them like good coffee, and it was almost excruciating to do without it after marching all day. They, however, bore with the inevitable, and morning found them in possession of their good spirits again, likewise their favorite beverage.

On the 8th of July, the Army of the Potomac arrived, commanded by General Hooker, and commenced its march through the pass; and for the first time the 151st regiment saw the vast Army of the Potomac. All day and all night was heard the "tramp, tramp, tramp" of the "boys in blue." The sight of the scarred and bronzed veterans of Bull Run, Chancellorsville, Antietam, Fair Oaks, Fredericksburg and Gettysburg, and the sound of the dull rumble of heavy artillery trains, the clatter of cavalry hoofs and the clinking of sabres made an impression strange and thrilling, and nerved the lookers on for the warfare. The army was about two days going through the pass. In a few days the 151st regiment was assigned to the Army of the Potomac, forming a part of the 3d army corps. The experience that immediately followed was exciting. The regiment found itself among veterans, heard their thrilling description of the terrible battles they had just passed through, and eagerly discussed the results thus far of the war they believed was then about at a close.

While the Army of the Potomac was going through the pass Lee's army was at Williamsport, on the Potomac, some six or seven miles away, intrenching, acting under the apprehension that it would at once be attacked by Meade's forces. These intrenchments were thrown up on the bank of the river, in the shape of a horse-shoe, and gave Lee peculiar advantage provided he was well supplied with ammunition. Meade marched his forces to Williamsport and prepared to make an attack on the following morning. It turned out that Lee had been playing a ruse in throwing up the breastworks, for he had no ammunition. His operations, however, had the effect of making General Meade over-cautious and slow to make the attack, and so the night before it was to be made Lee with his troops quietly crossed the river on a bridge made of canal boats, thereby saving himself from destruction that at one time seemed imminent, and might have been accomplished by Meade had he understood the situation. The feeling of disappointment among Meade's men was intense; many of them declared that they would never go back into Virginia, and not a few were true to their resolves, for a large number deserted.

Lee's escape made immediate pursuit necessary, and the Federals turned their faces toward Virginia. Marching on the 15th of July, beneath a broiling sun, wearied and dispirited, scores fell out, and that night when the 151st went into camp, only twenty men of the regiment answered to their names, Lieutenant L. T. Foote, of Lockport, being the only line officer. The men came straggling in afterward, footsore and heartsick. On the 16th of July the regiment encamped in the beautiful Middletown Valley, at the base of Maryland Heights. One of the officers relates that at nightfall of that day he, with a party, ascended the heights, a distance of 1,900 feet, and looking down in the valley they could take in at one glance the whole of three army corps. The white tents glittering in the shadows of the twilight, and the thousands of camp-fires upon which they could look directly down, made a picture weird and enchanting.

The remainder of the campaign of 1863 was a series of maneuvers—one army watching the other without attacking. Each day furnished its quota of incidents. The picket, the skirmish, the march and countermarch, the grand review, kept the soldiers in continual excitement, meantime engaging in the battle of Wapping Heights, inscribed on their battle-flag.

Crossing the Potomac from the Middletown valley the route lay on the eastern side of the Blue Ridge Mountains. In the latter part of July the 151st passed through Warrenton and went into camp at Bealton, where it remained about six weeks. Here nearly every man in the regiment was sick, and many died. Lee's movements compelled the army to fall back to Centreville. He was trying to get to Washington, and the division to which the 151st belonged was trying to head him off. The two armies marched almost side by side for a time, when Lee finally abandoned the project and fell back to the Rapidan. The Union forces under Meade followed, never halting until Lee was driven to the south side of the river. On the 26th of November Meade took his forces across the Rapidan, with a view to attacking Lee, and, if successful, marching on to Richmond. On the night of the 26th the army bivouacked on the south side of the river. On the 27th the division to which the 151st belonged engaged with Johnston's division of Ewell's corps, and for two hours was in one of the sharpest musketry duels of the war at Mine Run. It was here that the gallant officer Captain Wilcox, of Gasport, Niagara county, was killed. The infernal yell of the rebels as they rushed into the fight, the sharp thud of the bullet striking the flesh, lent fury to the struggle. This was the first severe engagement in which the 151st participated. The troops remained on the south side of the Rapidan about a week without any further engagement. They then recrossed the river, and went into winter quarters at Brandy Station. The 151st encamped on the farm of the somewhat famous John Miner Botts. During the winter the men cut down and burned twenty-five acres of timber for Botts. It does not appear, however, that they were ever paid for it.

In the spring of 1864 the 3d army corps was broken up and united with the 6th corps, General Sedgwick commanding; and the diamond badge was exchanged for the Greek cross. Grant then came into command, and on the 4th of May the Army of the Potomac started once more on its march toward Richmond. On the morning of May 5th Grant, with a force 100,000 strong, including the 151st, marched across the Rapidan, and before night was commenced the hand-to-hand conflict between the two mighty wrestlers, Lee and Grant, in the memorable battle of the Wilderness. Here the 151st suffered the heaviest loss incurred during its service. Among those killed was Captain Billings, of Batavia. The regiment was again engaged at Spottsylvania, suffering severe loss, and again at Cold Harbor. Among those killed at the latter point were Captain Goodspeed, of Batavia, and Captain Shoen, of Rochester. From the Wilderness to Cold Harbor, from the Rapidan to the James, the tide of battle surged with hellish wrath, and the carnage was fearfully great. The troops fought in the daytime and threw up breast-works at night; and for eighteen days of that time there was not a single night of rest for a man in that vast army.

At the battle of Spottsylvania the fighting was so severe in front of the brigade to which the 151st belonged that the dead were literally piled up between the lines and were used for breastworks. It was this terrible sacrifice of lives that gave the field the name of the "slaughter pen." So sharp was the firing that a large part of a forest near the lines was destroyed by minie balls.

On the 15th of June the regiment crossed with the Army of the Potomac the James river for a new field of operations in front of Petersburg, going over on a pontoon bridge 2,000 feet long. Just previous to this removal the regiment was encamped, it is said, near the tree under which Pocahontas saved the life of Captain Smith. From the 15th of June until the 1st of July the 151st was in front of Petersburg. On the last named date it started for Washington to head off Early and his forces. Another division had started in advance of the 151st and saved it the trouble. In consequence of this the regiment marched to Baltimore, and from there to Monocacy, and on the 9th of July fought a hard battle. Overwhelmed by superior numbers the 151st was compelled to retreat to Ellicott's Mills, about twenty miles. The next day it went to Baltimore, and into camp at Druid Hill Park, near the very spot where it first wintered.

In the course of a few weeks the regiment was in the Shenandoah valley under command of General Sheridan. Here it participated in the eagagements of Opequan, Fisher's Hill and Cedar Creek, doing good service. In November it was ordered back to the Army of the Potomac at Petersburg. Here, near what was called the Yellow House, the 151st encamped for the winter. By the 1st of April the regiment was in line again. Our army broke through the enemy's lines and followed the retreating foe. On the 6th the regiment had a sharp engagement at Sailor's creek. It was then ordered to Danville to make connection with Sherman. After Johnston surrendered, and the final blow had been struck, the regiment went to Richmond, and from there to Washington, and thence home.

Many of those who went forth to battle in 1862 had joined the army of martyrs, and were not in the homeward march. The thin rank told its own story of war and bloodshed. It left Lockport with upwards of 1,000 men, as already stated, but mustered out at the close of the war only 306 enlisted men.

The engagements in which this regiment participated numbered fourteen, as mentioned in the foregoing account.

The following is a roll of the field and staff officers, and of the companies in which, as above stated, Niagara county was represented.

REGIMENTAL OFFICERS.

Colonel, William Emerson; major, Thomas M. Fay; adjutant, James A. Jewell; quartermaster, John K. McDonald; surgeon, A. M. Leonard; assistant-surgeons, John R. Cotes, and D. W. Onderdonk; chaplain, E. M. Buck.

COMPANY B, ENROLLED AT LOCKPORT.

OFFICERS.

Captain, F. W. Coleman; first lieutenants, James Lount, Nathaniel F. Peck, Newfane, enlisted Aug. 27, 1862, mstd out June 26, 1865; second lieutenant, J. G. Shepard; first sergeant, Fred R. Derrick; second sergeant, E. E. Russell; sergeants, John A. Maronell, Niagara, killed at Locust Grove, Nov. 27, 1863; George Horvie, John Whelan; corporals, Charles Gill, E. H. Allan, Z. S. Parsons, Niagara, killed at Monocacy Junction, Md., July 9, 1864; Paul Kline, P. P. Jackson, A. B. Kidder, William E. Walsh, J. J. Dempsey; musician, Thomas Samways; wagoner, Mark C. White.

PRIVATES.

A. Aldrich, F. Albright, E. C. Brown, M. Bartholomew, John Byron, C. O. Brown, John Brady, James Barber, H. H. Bell, H. Behmer, James Brewster, William Cooley, M. Crawford, James Clifford, Niagara, died at Dansville prison, Va., in September, 1864; Louis Crout, Niagara, killed at Brandy Station, Apr. 19, 1864; John Corbett, John Crowder, Aaron Crowder, George Crooper, A. Carrington, R. Cahill, Thomas Donnelly, Frank Demar, C. C. Dart, William Dameron, Thomas Day, James English, Jacob Fisher, Joseph Gross, William Gurin, J. L. Hoffman, William Horrock, James Haney, A. Hewitt, A. Hagle, S. Henly, E. A. Johnson, Jacob Kilberer, Niagara, killed at Opequan, Sept. 19, 1864; M. Klink, H. Kittle, J. Kruger, A. Kimball, L. Linder, L. Lichard, J. Mossy, A. Miller, R. Mahana, Thomas Maher, E. Oakley, R. Oliver, C. O'Hara, J. Pullman, John Perrigo, R. Power, George Ridgeway, D. A. Robinson, D. Robinson, W. L. Riley, Amos Smith, Niagara, died at Baltimore in Mch., 1864; D. Steiber, John Smith, Charles Stemer, G. W. Tillapaugh, Niagara, died June 21, 1864; Thomas Tarphy, R. Tarlton, U. Turk, F. O. Todd, Benjamin Udall, Niagara, died at Culpepper, Va., in Oct., 1864; H. Verhoof, S. Werner.

COMPANY F, ENROLLED AT LOCKPORT.

OFFICERS.

Captain, Luron D. Wilson; first lieutenant, Adney B. Beals; second lieutenant, John A. Wolcott; sergeants, Charles J. Carlin, John L. Carrier, Sidney O. Weston, Henry C. Willard, James Duncan; corporals, Joseph H. Parsley, Loren Warren, William Basserman, Oliver H. Warden, John P. Romig, William H. H. Goodman, Royalton, enlisted Aug. 26, 1862, dschd in Mch., 1863; William F. Disbrow, Joseph Nimblet; musicians, Enoch Pettit, Asa J. Warden.

PRIVATES.

W. H. Brooks, Edward Brown, John P. Bingham, W. T. Burke, W. H. Blosser, S. Buchanan, James W. Baldwin, John Brooks, Theodore Bragdon, Peter H. Burdick, Francis A. Brown, Barnard Cuff, William G. Coobur, Philip Cook, John Duffy, jr., Christian Dekow, D. Drake, Evan Evans, Charles Fero, Charles Furge, Charles E. Goodman, Royalton, enlisted Aug. 26, 1862, dschd June 26, 1865; John Glaney, Thomas W. Green, William D. Griffin, Lucius Greenman, Stephen Hayes, Henry Hutchings, Daniel Hoachen, Reuben Hendeliter, Harry Johnston, Christian Jacobson, William James, Daniel Kelley, Hazard Kinney, Edward Morris, Edwin F. Millard, George W. McIntosh, William Murfit, Jeremiah Noacker, Royalton, enlisted Sept. 1, 1862, died in hospital Aug. 15, 1863; Henry C. Roberts, Asa A. Reed, Mead A. Roberts, Darwin J. Soper, John Sullivan, Lamberts Z. Sturgess, George J. Sturgess, Daniel Shaft, Royalton, enlisted Sept. 2, 1862, dschd June 30, 1865; Alzon Sheaver, William Shanley, Elijah Silk, John Silk, William H. Sheaver, Francis Story, Sylvester Searles, Alfred Silk, Daniel Southard, John R. Taylor, John Trankley, Andrew Trankley, Jarvis A. White, Frank J. Walker, John E. Willard, Hulbert Whitmore, Edgar Wentworth, Milton Merrill.

COMPANY G, ENROLLED AT LOCKPORT.

OFFICERS.

Captain, A. J. Potter; first lieutenant, Edward Hart Royalton, enlisted Sept. 16, 1862, resigned Feb. 23, 1864; second lieutenant, Benjamin T. Miller; first sergeant, John M. Weatherbee; sergeants, Walter E. Secor, Royalton, enlisted Aug. 30, 1862, dschd in June, 1865; John W. Simpkins, William Rowley; corporals, Valentine Crosman, Royalton, enlisted Aug. 28, 1862, dschd Feb. 14, 1865; Harmon L. Salsbury, Francis Balcom, John Dickson, William R. Caldwell, Leander Gelispie, James Dalton, Anson Richardson, Royalton, enlisted in Sept., 1863, killed at Monocacy, Md.; musicians, Thomas H. Cheshire, Royalton, enlisted Aug. 25, 1862, dschd June 26, 1865; Peter L. Smith; wagoner, William W. DeWolfe.

PRIVATES.

James M. Baldridge, James Bullemore, Henry Bollow, Richard Butler, Royalton, enlisted Aug. 21, 1862, dschd Feb. 16, 1864; William Bowman, Royalton, enlisted in August, 1862, died in hospital in District of Columbia, July 14, 1863; John Bensonhofer, Royalton, enlisted Aug. 23, 1862, died in September, 1863; Chauncey Braddock, Abram D. Baldwin, Daniel M. Burnett, Fordyce R. Brace, Darwin E. Bronson, John T. Brady, Lafayette Baker, William P. Bamber, George J. Cheshire, Royalton, enlisted Aug. 25, 1862; William H. Cook, George D. Cramer, Russell H. Drake, Royalton, enlisted Aug. 29, 1862, dschd Jan. 30, 1865; Frederick F. Drake, enlisted in Aug. 1862, dschd in June 1865; Lewis E. Darrow, Alexander Dixon, James Fitzgerald, Herman Frolic, S. C. Francis, Thomas Glasford, E. W. Glidden, John Gwine, Isaac Hammond, A. J. Hammond, Patrick J. Hayes, George Harwood, George W. Haggard, C. Hartwig, Charles Henning, Frederick Henning, Jackson Jeffrey, Newfane, enlisted Sept. 14, 1862, mstd out July 1, 1865; John Kennedy, Royalton, enlisted in Aug., 1862, dschd July 1, 1865; John Kelly, John Langhlay, Hsoea M. Lawrence, Levi M. Lawrence, Timothy Morrissy, Thomas Mortimer, Royalton, enlisted Aug. 29, 1862, dschd Aug. 16, 1865; Loughlin McClory, Royalton, enlisted Aug. 30, 1862, dschd July 1, 1865; Edward D. Merrill, Chauncey L. Matson, William Monroe, David Miller, Edward Murphy, Hiram B. Orsland, Ransom H. Owen, Charles H. Pridman, George Plumley, Charles H. Phillips, James Roderick, H. Raymond, A. D. Riley, Daniel T. Root, Walter B. Rhodes, John O. Ross, Elijah S. Reed, James B. Sheed, George Singler, Anson Smith, Parker Travers, Royalton, enlisted Aug. 13, 1862, dschd July 13, 1865; Wellington Tibbits, Edward T. Vallence, John Whitley.

COMPANY H.

OFFICERS.

Captain, C. P. Clark, Royalton, enlisted in Aug., 1862, resigned in Dec., 1862; first lieutenant, Sylvanus S. Wilcox, Royalton, enlisted in Aug., 1862, promoted captain, killed Nov. 27, 1863; second lieutenant, Lemuel T. Foote; sergeants, William Gritman, Royalton, enlisted in Sept., 1862, dschd in Dec., 1864; Lyman T. Phillips, Watson McNall, Conrad Eggenweiller, David Montonna; corporals, William Stebbins, Thomas La Roche, Royalton, enlisted Sept. 2, 1862, dschd in June, 1865; Peter C. Moore, Daniel Long, Royalton, enlisted Sept. 16, 1862, promoted sergeant, dschd June 30, 1865; James F. Taylor, S. Widrig, Harvey E. Allen, James N. Connover.

PRIVATES.

William Appling, Royalton, enlisted Aug. 26, 1862, dschd July 1, 1865; Christopher Andrean, Israel D. Appling, Warren S. Berry, Alfred S. Boulton, Royalton, enlisted Aug. 29, 1862, dschd July 21, 1865; Charles H. Boots, Clark Barton, Royalton, enlisted Aug. 29, 1862, died in hospital Aug. 21, 1863; Nicholas Beck, John Berkler, William Buffham, William Bradley, William Blowers, Simon B. Cumming, James Cronkhite, Royalton, enlisted Sept. 5, 1862, dschd June 26, 1865; Samuel Cassidy, Christian Cook, Charles Clickner, Merrick N. Cole, William H. Chase, Newfane, enlisted Aug. 29, 1862, mstd out May 9, 1863; Jacob Carl, Royalton, enlisted Sept. 28, 1862, promoted corporal, dschd in June, 1865; Henry A. Earnest, Royalton, enlisted Sept. 6, 1862, became musician, dschd Sept. 12, 1865; Ezra S. Frank, Royalton, enlisted Aug. 29, 1862, dschd June 30, 1865; Franklin Fanning, Wilber C. Geer, Newfane, enlisted in August 1862, died in Danville prison in February, 1865; Capiner Harde, Royalton, enlisted Aug. 6, 1862, supposed died in Libby prison; Luther Hawkins, Lorenzo Hathaway, Godfrey Harbet, Royalton, enlisted Sept. 6, 1862, dschd Jan. 13, 1864; Warren A. Ives, Augustus R. Jacob, W. Kohler, Royalton, enlisted in August, 1861, died Jan. 17, 1864; Thomas King, Eli Long, Carl Lindo, George Leichtnam, Abraham Miller, Benjamin Middaugh, Royalton, enlisted Aug. 29, 1862, deserted; Thomas Moore, Jacob Nerber, Daniel Nerber, Royalton, enlisted in September, 1862, died in hospital Dec. 26, 1863; Thomas Oliver, John N. Olmstead, George Penley, Royalton, enlisted Aug. 29, 1862, dschd in June, 1865; William Rowe, Alexander Richman, John Ricord, William Rink, Royalton, enlisted Sept. 6, 1862, dschd Mch. 27, 1865; Bernard Roffe, Royalton, enlisted Sept. 6, 1862, died in hospital Aug. 7, 1864; George Snow, Peter N. Snyder, Charles B. Stanton, Royalton, enlisted Aug. 29, 1862, died in hospital Oct. 9, 1863; F. J. Schlotterback, Royalton, enlisted Sept. 6, 1862, died in hospital Apr. 25, 1865; H. Schleder, Charles Sickles, William Snediker, Henry Stamper, Edwin Stockwell, Frederick Selip, Royalton, enlisted Sept. 6, 1862, died in hospital Aug. 18, 1864; Americus Tanner, Charles Teel, Frederick Urtel, Royalton, enlisted Sept. 4, 1862, dschd in January, 1864; O. Wichteman, Royalton, enlisted in August, 1862, dschd June 30, 1865; John Wagner, Harvey P. Wilson, Newfane, enlisted Aug. 27, 1862, mstd out June 29, 1865; John Westfall, Royalton, enlisted Aug. 29, 1862, died in Andersonville prison July 13, 1864; Nelson Widridge, Royalton, enlisted Sept. 6, 1862, dschd in July, 1865; Sela Wood.

COMPANY K.

OFFICERS.

Captain, Browning N. Wiles, Newfane, enlisted Oct. 22, 1862, mstd out Jan. 14, 1865; first lieutenant, Hiram A. Kimball; second lieutenant, Theodore E. Van Wagoner; sergeants, Philip H. Messeroll, Newfane; Charles G. Bloomer, Somerset; Nathan F. Peck, and William T. Stout, Newfane; corporals, John D. Walford, Olcott, enlisted Aug. 30, 1862, promoted sergeant, mstd out Aug. 11, 1865; Henry Weaver, Lockport; John W. Todd, Somerset; Russell A. Ferris and Henry B. Howell, Newfane; William H. H. Peacock, Somerset; Seldon R. Godard, Newfane, enlisted Aug. 27, 1862, promoted lieutenant, dschd June 3, 1865; musician, Seth A. Birdsall, Olcott, enlisted Sept. 6, 1862, mstd out May 31, 1865; James M. Crownover, Newfane, enlisted Aug. 29, 1862, mstd out June 29, 1865; wagoner, John F. Smith, Olcott, enlisted Sept. 6, 1862, dschd Jan. 29, 1864.

PRIVATES.

Samuel Bullin and James M. Bangham, Somerset; Cornelius Connor, Smith Dutcher, and Merrill T. Dutcher, Somerset; Adelbert Doley, Olcott; John Dean, Sylvester Edick, Newfane, enlisted Aug. 27, 1862, mstd out June 30, 1865; John Edick, jr., Olcott, enlisted Sept. 5, 1862, mstd out June 30, 1865; Henry Ferris, Newfane; Myron H. Fisk and Henry H. Hall, Somerset; Jacob Housemann, Newfane; William H. Huie, Newfane, enlisted Sept. 1, 1862, mstd out June 27, 1865; John and George Horsefall, Willis J. Haight, Sidney Hayes, and John Hines, Somerset; Cyrenus Hathaway, Newfane, enlisted Oct. 3, 1862; Joseph James, Somerset; Thomas Lowcock, Somerset; George Murray, jr., Newfane; John Nellist and Thomas A. Nellist, Somerset; Matthew O'Connor and John O'Connor, Lockport; Henry M. Phipps, Charles E. Pettis, and John E. Quackenbush, Somerset; Charles W. Redman, Newfane, enlisted Sept. 6, 1863, killed at Cold Harbor, Va.; Harvey Randall and Byron Randall, North Collins; Silas Spalding, Newfane; Paul Sisley, Newfane, enlisted Aug. 27, 1862, mstd out June 26, 1865; George P. Shorlen, Wilson; Joseph Smith, Horace Talcott, Olcott, enlisted Aug. 30, 1862, promoted corporal, mstd out July 28, 1865; John D. Van Horn, Olcott, enlisted Sept. 1, 1862, dschd Sept. 1, 1864; Jacob Van Norton, Lockport; George Wetherald, Newfane; Julius G. Weaver, Lockport; Delbert Warren, and Joseph Wortley, Somerset; John Wilkins, Aaron Wills, I. Witmer, William Hugh, John McCoy, and Henry Williams, Lockport.

CHAPTER XXXV.

THE BRILLIANT CAREER OF THE GALLANT EIGHTH NEW YORK HEAVY ARTILLERY.

THE history that attaches itself to this regiment is a terrible one. Volumes of a story that will never be written are expressed in the appalling truth that during its services in its country's behalf it lost nearly twelve hundred men in killed, wounded and missing. Twenty-two officers and two hundred and eleven men were killed, twenty-nine officers and six hundred and fifty-three men were wounded, and five officers and two hundred and fifty men missing.

Dark and portentous were the clouds that hung over the nation at the time the regiment was organized. The fact had become thoroughly established that the South had a settled purpose to destroy the Union, and conquest or submission was all that was left; conciliation having been put out of the question. Our troops before Richmond had been checked and they awaited help in trying suspense. The demand of the hour was men. In this crisis the President issued a call for 300,000 troops, and it was in response to this that the 8th heavy artillery was organized. The companies of which it was composed were raised in the counties of Niagara, Orleans and Genesee, by Colonel Peter A. Porter, of Niagara Falls, under authority granted by Governor Fenton. It was completed and mustered into the service at Camp Church (fair grounds in Lockport), on the 22nd of August, 1862, with the following

REGIMENTAL OFFICERS:

Colonel, Peter A. Porter, Niagara Falls; lieutenant-colonel, W. W. Bates, Orleans county; major, James M. Willett, Batavia; first lieutenant E. L. Blake, adjutant, Lockport; first lieutenant George B. Wilson, quartermaster, and major James M. Leet, surgeon, Lockport; first lieutenant H. C. Hill, assistant-surgeon, Somerset; captain Gilbert De La Matyr, chaplain, Albion.

Companies B, D, E and F were raised in Niagara county, and all mustered in at Lockport; A, C and K in Orleans, and G, H and I in Genesee county. The regiment was organized as the 129th New York Volunteers, but never did service in that name, being changed to the 8th heavy artillery in February, 1863, by order of E. M. Stanton, Secretary of War. Two additional companies, L and M, were raised for the regiment in 1864; Company L officered by captain S. Dexter Ludden, Batavia; first lieutenant, A. G. Clapp, and second lieutenant, H. H. Van Dake; and Company M, captain, H. H. Sheldon, Suspension Bridge; first lieutenant, Frederick Derrick, second lieutenant, O. M. Campbell.

The following is a copy of the muster-in roll on file in the office of the clerk of Niagara county, supplemented by the town records of Royalton and Newfane, reference being had only to those companies raised in Niagara county.

COMPANY B.

OFFICERS.

Captain, Joel B. Baker, Cambria; first lieutenant, James Low, Cambria; second lieutenant, Eli S. Nichols, Lockport; sergeants, Fayette S. Brown, D. L. Pitcher, Romeo G. Burns, W. H. Crowley, N. Z. Paterson; corporals, T. C. Edwards, L. C. Harwood, Lyman A. Pyle, John Root, W. H. Bennett, Newfane, enlisted July 23, 1862, mstd out Feb. 25, 1865; Alexander Robb, Newfane, enlisted Aug., 1862, killed at Cold Harbor; Walter L. Martin, Job Cornell; musicians, William S. Pike, H. W. Olmstead; wagoner, C. Gardiner.

PRIVATES.

Stephen Aldrich, Orrin Babcock, Charles Behm, James Brewer, A. J. Bishop, Newfane, enlisted in Aug., 1862, killed at Cold Harbor; Robert Courtney, Alfred Doolittle, Edward Davis, George W. Drake, Newfane, enlisted Dec. 24, 1863, prisoner seven months, mstd out in Sept. 1865; Homer J. Elton, W. G. Green, Newfane, enlisted July 24, 1862, dschd in July, 1865; William Ireland, G. W. Johnson, Frederick Kreuzer, Andrew Lapworth, C. G. Mehwauldt, Alexander Mabin, Charles Mahl, Bernard Messing, William McGregor, William D. Parker, William F. Parker, Benjamin J. Rose, M. W. Stiles, Adolphus Stern, Frank Slavin, Emory Wilcox, William Ward, John Walker, J. W. Vedder, R. C. Harmon, W. H. Gleason, George O. Hayne, John Howell, Newfane, enlisted Dec. 16, 1863, killed at Cold Harbor; Truman Ash, Washington Elton, Franklin A. Eshbaugh, Newfane, enlisted July 26, 1862, dschd for disability in 1864; E. C. Fuller, B. F. Sawyer, J. K. Johnson, Lewis W. McNeil, Augustus Werth, Amos Worden, Andrew A. Miller, C. H. Emerson, C. J. Sherman, Newfane, enlisted July 26, 1862, died June 26, 1864, at Paterson Park hospital, Md.; G. H. Fellows, John Nagel, William Watson, Samuel Bowman, Peter Christyan, William Rogers, Charles C. Romer, Newfane, enlisted in July, 1862, killed at Cold Harbor; Henry M. Billings, John D. Capen, Newfane, enlisted in July, 1862, promoted corporal, mstd out June 13, 1865; Samuel Dean, William A. Dutton, Robert Furman, F. J. Fellows, Edward Green, Charles R. Gifford, John Healand, jr., Joseph Jacobs, James Laylond, Lynford Levan, Isaac Lockwood, Newfane, enlisted Dec. 13, 1863, dschd July 9, 1865. J. W. Longstaff, Peter Mercig, F. E. Morrison, A. J. Merwin, Albert McKenzie, Samuel McClellan, G. Francis Nye, T. Marshall Nye, Elias Orett, J. E. Ource, W. H. Saddleson, George A. Stephens, William Thornton, Samuel Traviss, E. J. Taylor, E. C. Wright, Sharon White, J. K. P. Wilson.

COMPANY D.

OFFICERS.

Captain, James McGinnis, Lockport; first lieutenant, William Gardner; second, M. R. Blodgett, Lockport; first sergeant, John E. Owens, Royalton, enlisted Aug. 22, 1862, dschd Mch. 17, 1866; second, Arthur L. Chase; third, Horace J. McDonald; fourth, William F. Spalding, Royalton, enlisted in August, 1862, dschd in March, 1865; fifth, Charles B. Lackor, Royalton, enlisted Aug. 6, 1862, dschd Oct. 6, 1864; sergeant, W. H. H. Brown, Royalton, enlisted Aug. 4, 1862, dschd June 5, 1865; first corporal, Almon Van Wagner; first corporal, J. Cooney, Royalton, enlisted Aug. 1, 1862, dschd June 22, 1865; second, William George; third, Stephen H. Sim; fourth John E. Carrington; fifth, Henry Murray; sixth, Alfred Wakeman; seventh, Hiram Carpenter; drummer, John Greber.

PRIVATES.

Ransom Aldrich, Hiram Armstrong, Royalton, enlisted Aug. 22, 1862, died in hospital Apr. 24, 1863; Calvin Baylis, Charles S. Gunther, William H. Gregory, Frederick Hagadorn, Alfred Jones, Christian Kohler, Daniel Kohler, Royalton, enlisted Aug. 3, 1862, dschd in June, 1865; Charles S. Kinder, Royalton, enlisted July 27, 1862, dschd in Mch., 1863; John A. Lyndenthaler, Benjamin Polnys, Franklin Sleeper, Caleb H. Thomas, Royalton, enlisted July 28, 1862, dschd June 6, 1865; John Whitley, Christopher Wiseman, George W. Ward, Newfane, enlisted July 28, 1862, mstd out June 5, 1865; William Walker, H. E. Bardwell, Henry Brodock, George W. Briggs, Christian Bahol, Charles Brooks, Timothy Burns, John Cörney, Henry W. Carter, Royalton, enlisted in Mch., 1863, dschd in June, 1865; Robert Bird, George W. Cutter, Royalton, enlisted Aug. 4, 1862, died Mch 30, 1865; Henry W. Churchill, Royalton, enlisted Aug. 5, 1862, dschd June 22, 1865; Richard E. Churchill, Royalton, enlisted Aug. 18, 1864, dschd in July, 1865; James Compton, Martin Cooney, Royalton, enlisted Aug. 19, 1862, dschd June 22, 1865; C. George, A. A. George, W. E. George, Miller A. Gregory, D. G. Grippen, Royalton, enlisted in Aug., 1862, dschd in June, 1865; Egbert B. Goodwin, DeWitt D. Garner, Calvin Harrington, James M. Hudnut, Royalton, enlisted July 26, 1862, promoted quartermaster sergeant, dschd in June, 1865; Merick V. Hudnut, Royalton, enlisted Jan. 4, 1863, died from wounds June 18, 1864; John Hilman, James Laylond, Royalton, enlisted in August, 1862, dschd in July, 1865; Andrew Long, Allen Lee, Royalton, enlisted Aug. 9, 1862, dschd July 1, 1865; John G. Lacey, Royalton, enlisted Aug. 4, 1862, promoted lieutenant, dschd June 12, 1865; Daniel R. Lacey, Royalton, enlisted Nov. 5, 1863, killed in battle June 16, 1864; G. A. Marshall, D. J. Morehouse, Royalton, enlisted Aug. 7, 1862, promoted corporal, died from wounds June 20, 1864; Barney A. Mackey, Royalton, enlisted in July, 1862, dschd in June, 1863; Lewis McKee, Royalton, enlisted Dec. 26, 1863, dschd in July 1865; James Pierson, James G. Proper, Royalton, enlisted Aug. 11, 1862; Mason Baymer, George E. Smith, James Sherman, Henry L. Smith, Francis E. Smith, Royalton, enlisted in November, 1863; Philo L. Sherman, Henry F. Stahler, George Stenet, George Smeeds, Elias Thorn, John Travis, Alonzo Taglo, Rupert G. Torrey, Royalton, enlisted Dec. 7, 1863, dschd Dec. 7, 1865; Dolphus S. Wisner, Richard Warren, Benjamin D. Wright, Royalton, enlisted Dec. 26, 1863, dschd July 21, 1865; James Wiffun, Edwin Wilcox, Royalton, enlisted Aug. 1, 1862, promoted corporal, dschd Aug. 10, 1865; Thomas Byan, James K. Bridlem, Bingham Burroughs, George Crampton, Royalton, enlisted Aug. 9, 1862; wounded and dschd; Frederick Clifton, George H. Chappel, Thomas Charles, Christian Doheny, Patrick M. Doyle, Royalton, enlisted Dec. 31, 1863; James Gowett, Andrew Green, Royalton, enlisted Dec. 26, 1863, dschd Sept. 26, 1864; James F. Green, Newfane, enlisted Aug. 12, 1862, killed Feb. 27, 1863; Jacob Gilbert, Royalton, enlisted Dec. 30, 1863, dschd in June, 1865; William H. Hyde, Daniel H. D. Huller, Royalton, enlisted in August, 1862, deserted in August, 1864; Gebbard J. Kingley, Martin Lynch, John Leason, Royalton, enlisted Nov. 14, 1863, dschd July 21, 1865; James E. Murray, James J. Moore, Royalton, enlisted Dec. 9, 1863, dschd July 9, 1865; John H. Moore, Royalton, enlisted in August, 1862, dschd Apr. 4, 1865; Lucian J. Niles, Royalton, enlisted Aug. 9, 1862, killed at Cold Harbor; James Fraser, Egbert Pennoyer, George Sinsel, Newfane, enlisted Aug. 12, 1882, dschd Feb. 25, 1865; James H. Theryer, Martin Van Dusen, Charles W. Van Slyke, George W. Webb, William Wentworth, John Whitley.

COMPANY E.

OFFICERS.

Captain, J. W. Holmes, Niagara Falls; first lieutenant, R. Baldwin, Wilson; second lieutenant, H. R. Swan, Suspension Bridge.

PRIVATES.

Francis Bond, W. H. Chapman, Adelbert Comstock, James Grennin, James Hyslop, Thomas Helmer, James Niven, George W. Parker, William D. Vrooman, B. R. Benton, George Dawson, W. H. Evans, Henry Frailing, Hamilton Ingalls, Niagara, died at Salisbury prison, Feb. 10, 1865; William McKearnan, Francis B. Mosier, Reuben A. Ordway, William J. Parker, John H. Quackenbush, Irving Resigue, H. S. Regle, John Sneider, Frank Sedgwick, Alfred Shirley, Eugene M. Townsend, Luther H. Warden, Henry P. Williams, Newfane, enlisted in Aug., 1862, promoted to corporal, died Sept. 17, 1864, in hospital on David's Island; Henry W. Banck, Christian C. Barton, Osborne Edwards, John J. Flanders, Jacob Finck, Grofton Gilbert, James Gamsford, Myron H. Hale, Daniel Harling, Otto Hutsberg, John M. Holden, John W. Kent, Richard Sherf, Andrew Lohrrman, Patrick Toolon, Silas C. H. West, George Biehm, Harvey A. Baker, William Carroll, Cornelius Dawlson, Albert Dietz, Fernando Henchy, Royalton, enlisted in Aug., 1862, dschd in July, 1865; Morton Heuning, Adam Lepper, Nicholas Maybee, George D. Merville, Jerry McDonald, Frank Armsby, Joseph Phipps, James Parsons, Edward Taylor, Philetus Weeks, Henry J. Arnold, Albinus Bennett, Harlem P. Hood, Silas H. Harvey, Nelson H. Harrington, David Myers, William Moore, Ezra N. Thayer, Sumner G. Barker, Charles Burke, George W. Barker, Charles F. Behan, Nelson T. Davis, Hugh Duffy, Horace Darling, Newfane, enlisted Aug. 9, 1862, mstd out May 28, 1865; Richard Faulkner, Niagara, died at Salisbury prison, Dec. 15, 1864; John Farley, Marcus S. Grannis, W. H. Holden, Robert Hiam, Hannes Colby, Charles Hugell, Samuel Lappie, Niagara, died Oct. 10, 1864; Florence McCarty, Alexander McIntosh, Delman Morris, Charles Noble, Hiram Rappleyea, John Roberts, Charles Rettenberg, W. J. Stone, Henry O. Spencer, Robert Turner, Solomon Warren, Jefferson White, Niagara, died at Salisbury prison, Jan. 2, 1865; J. W. Stimson, Joseph Hewitt, Ashley Hawkins, Wrice Fitch; Olford Wedge, George W. Blake.

COMPANY F.

OFFICERS.

Captain, William J. Hawkins; first lieutenant, Samuel Sully; second lieutenant, George W. Rector—all of Lockport.

PRIVATES.

Abram R. Everts, Newfane, enlisted Dec. 24, 1863, mstd out June 30, 1865; D. M. Fulloh, L. C. Hosmer, R. Glass, Ebin O. Seely, Frank B. Rafter, Eugene F. Pollard, Edward W. Peckham, Edward M. Lindsley, Stephen Judd, John M. Casey, Nathan Myers, Chauncey Kester, Newell Canfield, Charles E. Rector, H. C. Flagler, Samuel Kelsey, Thomas Brown, Robert Bailey, Ephraim Baylis, Charles Burroughs, Asher T. Coleman Newfane, enlisted Dec. 21, 1863, wounded at Cold Harbor; Andrew James Case, Albert J. Dwynett, Eugene N.

Gould, Warren Goodremoote, John E. Warwood, James Moore, Charles McLaughlin, Royalton, enlisted July 21, 1862, dschd in June, 1865; Robert McLaughlin, Royalton, enlisted July 21, 1862, dschd in June, 1865; Michael Morley, Irving A. Parmenter, Ora Rooker, Charles Richardson, John Sutherland, Israel Talcott, Royalton, enlisted in July, 1862, dschd in July, 1865; John Huffcutt, John King, jr., Edward D. Lewis, Peter Megel, Patrick Owens, Henry Paine, William Catlin, Sylvester Campbell, Charles S. Kilborn; Charles R. Northrop, Joseph Childs, David Cross, Charles Cross, Robert Clark, John Draper, Lester N. Farnham, James H. Hilderbrant, Douglas Jerrold, Edward Pasco, Jerome Reynolds, John Smith, Lewis Smith, Newfane, enlisted Dec. 21, 1863, died at St. John's hospital in 1864; Thomas Stimpson, Lawson L. Taylor, Thomas Burt, Reuben Burt, Hiram L Ash, Lafayette Beadley, George H. Brown, Addison Barton, Royalton, enlisted Aug. 12, 1862, dschd July 14, 1865; Stephen Balliett, William H. Burnett, Robert Colby, Peter Clapsattle, Joseph Clapsattle, Oscar Drinkwater, Charles F. Daniels, John Dove, Alexander Fox, William Hawkins, Mortimer Johnson, Royalton, enlisted Nov. 14, 1863, dschd July 14, 1865; Sylvester Johnson, Royalton, enlisted Aug. 14, 1862, dschd June, 1868; John King, Isaac Lloyd, Henry D. Lathrop, Hulbert Moore, W. H. Murray, Newfane, enlisted Dec. 25, 1863, died June 7, 1865, at Ambulance hospital; Charles Moore, George A. McArthy, Ethan Munn, Derrick Plant, Edward D. Perry, D. W. Robinson, John Risch, Albert Salph, George Snell, Frank Fulloh, Peter S. Tower, Thomas Burns, Michael Cuff, William Blain, William Bush, Joseph Brower, Jeremiah Dixon, Sylvester Moore, Charles H. Quade, Henry Smith, Edward Tenny, Frederick Van Tassel, Newfane, enlisted Dec. 22, 1863, killed at Cold Harbor.

The regiment served from the time of its muster until the spring of 1864 in the defenses of Baltimore, with the exception of a short campaign to Harper's Ferry and in western Virginia. On the morning of May 15, 1864, it is said General Grant sat in his tent door in the vicinity of Spottsylvania Court-house, smoking a cigar and reflecting on the situation. Just what he thought about it no one but himself knew, *but he wanted more men.* Sherman was in the saddle hundreds of miles away fighting his way to Resaca. In consequence of this want, which had been made known at Baltimore by a dispatch sent *via* Washington, there was great commotion in the camp of the 8th heavy artillery. On the same morning they were expecting marching orders from the front at any moment, and so the word "we are going to the front" was passed. All believed it, and so it proved. The scene in the camp was a lively one. Orderlies were hurrying to and fro, riding hither and thither at breakneck speed; officers were packing their trunks, to leave behind them, and the men packing their knapsacks to take with them; every body was filling his canteen with water or coffee, or something stronger if he could get it. All the necessaries of camp life as well as the superfluities were lying around in utter and hopeless confusion. In the midst of all this bustle some were sitting on their trunks writing hasty letters home, for they were going—they knew not where; they wrote that it was "only a question of time" and they would write all about it as soon as possible. But many of them never wrote again. This was as early as sunrise. Toward noon battalions, companies, detachments and squads were seen streaming toward the depot of the Baltimore and Ohio Railroad. When the train moved away amid shouts and cheers, the waving of handkerchiefs and the flaunting of banners, there were many thoughtful ones who looked upon the forts they were leaving with great anxiety. Some said: " Very likely some of us will never see Baltimore again; good-bye officers' balls and company's dances, Christmas festivities and Thanksgiving dinners! farewell, Porter's Life Insurance Company!"

The regiment arrived in Washington about 4 o'clock on the afternoon of May 15th. The men went to the "Soldier's Rest" for supper and remained there all night. The next day, about noon, they went on board transports and were soon off for Belle Plain, at which place they arrived about sundown. On the morning of the 17th they were all stirring at an early hour, exploring the ravines for water, drawing rations of salt pork, hard bread, coffee and sugar; and occasionally venting their patriotism in epithets (merely) upon some 7,000 rebel prisoners in the valley near them. About ten o'clock they were on the march to Fredericksburg, with three days' rations and sixty rounds of cartridges. The day was warm, and the soldiers realized for the first time something of the discomforts that attend an ordinary march. The regiment reached Fredericksburg about 5 o'clock that evening, and crossed the river on a pontoon bridge. The town still bore the marks of Burnside's bombardment. In almost every building were crowded the wounded from the recent battles of the Wilderness and Spottsylvania Courthouse. The 8th had been called to finish the work that these wounded soldiers had begun. The regiment marched through Fredericksburg and up the heights beyond the town, until at 8 o'clock it stopped for rest and supper. At 10 o'clock it started on the march again. Some expressions were used with reference to going any further that night that were more emphatic than polite, but in less than an hour after "falling in" the boys were as merry as if they had just enjoyed a night's rest. The way was enlivened with laugh, jest and song. Some were "shouting the battle cry of freedom," others were hanging "Jeff Davis to a sour apple tree;" and anon they swelled the chorus of "John Brown," as, like his soul, they went marching on. This did not last long, however—knapsacks and guns were growing heavy. Soon after 2 o'clock in the morning the welcome order to rest until day-light was given.

With the first light of the morning the dull booming of the distant cannon was heard. The 8th regiment had joined the great "battering ram"—the Army of the Potomac—and was at the front. After breakfast the regiment started in the direction of the firing, which was not heavy nor the engagement general. As they neared the scene of action they met numbers of wounded men moving to the rear, with mangled limbs and bloody faces, while near the front lines others were waiting for stretchers. Gallant Colonel Porter, who was proud of his men, rode ahead and was anxious to prove their mettle on the field. But they were not called upon to show it that day, for they soon marched several miles in another direction, and while on their way the fighting ceased. They did not see another such day in some time.

On this, the night of May 18th, 1864, they rested quietly, camped in a lovely spot. They remained there during the next day, awaiting orders. At that time the regiment was attached to Tyler's division, 2d corps. While at this encampment, on the 18th, the 151st, of Niagara county, passed them and there were many hearty greetings. The latter regiment was worn out with continuous marching and fighting, and as the boys of the 8th looked upon their decimated ranks, thinned by casualty and disease; their clothing, begrimed with dirt and grease; their haggard faces, bronzed by storm and sun, and contrasted their storm-beaten and bullet-riddled battle flag with their own bright colors, the remark was common. "This is what we are coming to."

On the night of the 19th, the 8th regiment had its first encounter with the enemy. About four o'clock in the afternoon of that day the troops heard heavy musketry firing to the northeast of them, and they immediately started in that direction on the double quick. They soon began to meet the wounded and the bullets began to whistle over their heads. The regiment took a strong position in the second line and lay down behind the crest of a ridge. At dusk it advanced across a small stream and through a cornfield, and was soon engaged. The first charge was into the woods, where it was dark. The 8th was there until about nine o'clock, directing its fire by the flash of the enemy's guns, and was then ordered to fall back. The loss was light—33 killed, wounded and missing. The wounded were carried to a field hospital, and soon all was quiet again. When morning came again it revealed only abandoned positions. The enemy had fled with the darkness. After burying its dead the regiment went back to the old camp.

On the night of May 20th the order was received to "be ready to march at 12 o'clock" that night. At the hour mentioned in the order the regiment started, and went *via* Bowling Green to Milford Station, a distance of twenty-five miles away on the Richmond and Potomac railroads, arriving there at 3 o'clock the next afternoon, after a steady march of fifteen hours. There had been a brisk cavalry fight at Milford Station that day, and some of the wounded and a few prisoners were there still. Here the 8th rested for dinner. At 10 o'clock that night it was on the march again. About five o'clock on the evening of the 23d it arrived at North Anna river, in the vicinity of the Chesterfield bridge. The rebels held an ugly fortification, which at 6 P. M., after a vigorous fire from three sections of artillery, was stormed and captured by Pierce's and Egan's brigade of Birney's division, who drove out the garrison, capturing thirty and sending the remainder across the river in such haste that they had no time to burn the bridge. The 8th lay on its arms until morning. The rebels sent their compliments with early dawn. The 8th joined in and continued to fire all day. From this time until June 2nd the regiment was most of the time on the road to Cold Harbor, meantime engaging in several sharp skirmishes.

About 11 o'clock June 2nd this regiment took the front at Cold Harbor, relieving other troops. Up to this time the 8th had been marching and countermarching in support of the fighting line, getting just near enough to the rebels to have their fire amongst them and have no chance to return it. The men were not, therefore, altogether sorry to get in the front line. Their dash at the rebels at Spottsylvania had given them confidence and made them somewhat heedless of danger. In this frame of mind they received the order to be ready to charge at four o'clock, and at that hour they were found sitting behind their breastworks, every man grasping his gun ready to spring at the command. One of the officers of the regiment says: "We were acting very much unlike the stern and silent soldiers we read of, for we were laughing and chatting, speculating upon the prospect before us as if it were a mere holiday or some bore of a parade." But it began to rain and the order was countermanded. The sun went down under a cloud, and thus night settled down on the evening of June 2nd, 1864.

Thousands beheld the dawn for the last time. The signal gun was fired at daybreak, when the men were not thinking so much about the order to advance as they were about their coffee. The distance between the lines of the 8th and the rebel lines has been variously estimated at from 700 to 1,000 yards.

The first battalion, on the left of the regiment, was commanded by Lieutenant-Colonel Bates; the second, in the center, by Captain McGinnis (Major Spalding being sick); the third, on the extreme right, by Major Willett. The batteries in the rear of the regiment opened a heavy fire simultaneously with the advance of the charging column, and the rebels replied no less vigorously. One after another went down beneath the storm of iron and lead which swept the plain. As the ranks thinned they closed up sternly, and with arms at a trail and bayonets fixed they pressed forward on a run without firing a shot. Down went the colors, the staff splintered and broken, as well as the hand that held it. Brave hands seized them again and bore them onward until the enemy's works were close at hand. Colonel Porter fell, crying "Close in on the colors, boys!" Major Willett was wounded; a large number of line officers lay dead and dying; one third of the rank and file were *hors du combat;* a part of the regiment was floundering in the mire; the rebels were pouring in double charges of grape and canister at less than point blank range, sweeping away a score every moment. The line having lost its momentum, stopped from sheer exhaustion within a stone's throw of the enemy's works.

All this transpired in a short time. The supporting line failed to come up, old soldiers declaring that it was foolhardiness to advance under such a fire; so the brave men of the 8th had to look out for themselves. They began to dig, and every man was working himself into the ground. Every stump, mole hill, bush and tree was a shelter. Thus the regiment lay all day, under the very noses of the rebels, and came away in squads under cover of the darkness. This seemed as hazardous as the charge itself, for no sooner did the rebels detect a movement in their front than they opened a murderous fire of both musketry and artillery. Some were killed in attempting to come out, among them Captain Gardner, of Company I. An officer in describing the fire says, " It was either more severe than in the morning or the darkness made it seem more terrible "

At 9 o'clock that night the regiment was in its old position and had brought away most of the severely wounded, who had been unable to get back during the day. The dead were lying where they fell; some were buried during the night following, and some lay exposed until the truce of June 6th. No one knew exactly where the body of Colonel Porter lay, and all efforts to find it during the night of the 3rd proved unavailing. It was discovered the next day, midway between the advanced pickets, about twenty yards from either. To recover it in the day time was too hazardous to attempt, for the rebel sharpshooters were always on the alert. About midnight on the 4th Le Roy Williams (afterwards first lieutenant of Company G) crept stealthily from his picket post followed by Samuel Traverse, of Company B, and in a few minutes they reached the body without attracting the attention of their vigilant neighbors. But they could not carry the body without rising to their feet, and that they dared not do. So Williams watched the body while Traverse returned to the pit and sent a comrade to the regiment after ropes. In less than an hour they had tent ropes enough to reach the body, and having fastened one end to the feet of their dead commander they lay on their faces, one behind the other, and gradually dragged the body to a place of comparative safety. From there it was taken to Colonel Bates's headquarters and then to the hospital, where it arrived about 3 o'clock in the morning of June 5th.

Greeley once said, in speaking of Colonel Porter, " He was but one among thousands actuated by like motives, but none ever volunteered with purer motives or served with more unselfish devotion than Peter A. Porter." On the evening previous to the battle he was asked, " Don't you think it very foolish to charge across there? We don't expect that many of us will ever come back alive." The colonel replied, "That has nothing to do with the matter. If I am ordered to go *I* shall go, and I *think* my regiment will follow me."

The following figures tell something of the desperate work the 8th heavy artillery performed in this action: Killed, 9 officers and 146 men; wounded, 140 officers and 323 men; misssing, 1 officer and 12 men, making an aggregate loss of 24 officers and 481 men. The material that composed the regiment was equal to any that went out, and the story of its experience June 3rd carried desolation to many a once happy home.

The regiment went from Cold Harbor to Petersburg under command of Colonel Willett, engaging in sharp skirmishes on the way. Its services from this time forward until the close of the war were in and about Petersburg. Arriving there June 16th, the 8th was in the engagement of that day, and took part again on the 18th and 22nd. It fought at Ream's Station, Deep Bottom, Hatcher's Run and Appomattox, doing its full share of duty, and suffering a loss of 13 officers and 65 men killed, 15 officers and 230 men wounded, and 4 officers and 238 men missing.

Lieutenant-Colonel Willard W. Bates died June 25th, 1864, of wounds received in action; and Lieutenant-Colonel Blake died June 19th and Captain George A. Hoyt, July 5th, from the same cause. Captain James McGinnis was killed at Ream's Station, August 25th, 1864; Captain William J. Hawkins died of wounds, June June 23d, 1864; Captain Eldridge F. Sherman died of disease at City Point, July 30th, 1864; Captain Alexander Gardner was killed at Cold Harbor; Captain Thomas Lowe died April 25th, 1865, of wounds; First Lieutenant Charles H. West, jr., was killed at Ream's Station; First Lieutenant Henry R. Swan died of disease at Cold Harbor, June 14th, 1864; First Lieutenant George W. Rector was killed at Hatcher's Run, Oct. 29th, 1864; First Lieutenant A. G. Clapp died of wounds Nov. 21st, 1864; Second Lieutenant Fayette S. Brown was killed at Cold Harbor; Second Lieutenant Arthur L. Chase was killed at Cold Harbor; Second Lieutenant Walter P. Wright in action before Petersburg, June 16th, 1864; Second Lieutenant Joseph W. Caldwell, Wallace B. Hard, Oliver M. Campbell and George W. Gladden were killed at Cold Harbor.

June 4th, 1865, companies G, H, I and K were transferred to the 4th New York artillery. Companies L and M were transferred to the 10th New York volunteer infantry and the remaining six companies mustered out June 5th, 1865.

CHAPTER XXXVI.

RECORDS OF THE 78TH, 96TH, 105TH, 132ND, 164TH, 178TH, 179TH, 187TH AND 194TH INFANTRY.

THE 78th regiment was made up in the counties of Niagara, Erie, Monroe, Steuben and Oneida, and organized at New York city. It was mustered in from October 1st, 1861, to April 12th, 1862; and consolidated with the 102nd New York volunteers June 29th, 1864. Company I of the 78th was raised in Niagara county, by Captain Peter M. T. Mitchell, of Suspension Bridge, and most of the men were from the towns of Niagara and Lewiston. Their names and rank were as follows:

OFFICERS.

Captain, Peter M. T. Mitchell, Suspension Bridge, killed at Antietam; first lieutenant, Henry F. Pierce, Suspension Bridge; second lieutenant, Myron E. Dunlap, Suspension Bridge; first sergeant, Henry Stearns, Suspension Bridge; sergeants, Thomas Mayberry, Suspension Bridge; James H. Cleveland, Niagara City; corporals, Cornelius Mitchell, William O. Butler and Henry Williams, Suspension Bridge; George H. Whitman, Lewiston; James Jones, William H. Seely, James Foster, and John B. Church, Suspension Bridge.

PRIVATES.

John S. Allen, Andrew T. Abbott, John Aegan, William Bissell, Edward Burns, Henry Boy, David Bex, George Brunner, Robert Burns, Frederick Boy, David P. Burnap, Patrick Byron and John Brown, Suspension Bridge; William F. Butler, Lewiston; Charles Buckley, John Buchannan, Lewis Crout and John Conklin, Suspension Bridge; Joseph Callahan and Stephen Carpenter, Lewiston; Duncan Durham and Theodore Dunahan, Suspension Bridge; Charles Dixon, Lewiston; Edwin Frank, John Fisher, George Gleason and Terrance Gallagher, Suspension Bridge; John Grigg and John Gillett, Lewiston; Bartholnal Goempel and Joseph Gibbs, Suspension Bridge; Josiah Higgins, Robert Herron and Michael Holley, Suspension Bridge; George Haggerty, Lewiston; William Johnson, John Jones, John Kelly, John Knox, Luther Knapp, Conrad King, John Kershaw and Edward Lynch, Suspension Bridge; George Murray, Niagara City; David Maloney, Hugh McNaughton, John Martin, John Mullen and Michael Murray, Suspension Bridge; Richard Nagle, Niagara City; James Newton, Benjamin G. Pfeiffer, James Powers, Hiram D. Partridge, Thomas Quinn, John Rooney, Nicholas M. Pyall, Patrick Reilly, John E. Roberts, James Regan and Napoleon B. Seely, Suspension Bridge; James Sammon, Niagara City; James Smith, Lewis Skinner, William Stewart, Patrick Sweeney, Charles Smith, Robert Swift, Henry W. Smith, Samuel Simpson and Stephen W. Smyth, Suspension Bridge; Henry Smith and James Scott, Lewiston; George H. Vogt, Edward Walter, Reginald T. Wing, John Willey and William H. Williams, Suspension Bridge.

The regiment participated in the battles of Manhatchie, Lookout Mountain, Resaca, Dallas, Lost Mountain, Pine Knob, Kenesaw, Peach Tree Creek and Atlanta.

NINETY-SIXTH INFANTRY.

In this regiment, which was organized at Plattsburg, N. Y., to serve three years, the companies of which it was composed being raised in the counties of Clinton, Essex, Franklin, Warren and Washington, were the following named Niagara county men: First sergeant, Alexander McLaughlin, of Niagara, promoted to captain, wounded, died in 1871; and privates John Lander, James McLaughlin, George Price, James Smith, and Robert Stover, Niagara, died in June, 1864.

The regiment was mustered into the service from February 20th to March 7th, 1862. On the expiration of the term of service the original members (except veterans) were mustered out, and the regiment, composed of veterans and recruits, retained in the service until February 6th, 1866, when it was mustered out by orders from the War Department.

Its record is a good one—it having fought at Gainesville, Second Bull Run, South Mountain, Antietam, Mine Run, Fredericksburg, Chancellorsville, Gettysburg, Wilderness, North Anna, Tolopotomoy, Spottsylvania, Bethesda Church, Petersburg, Weldon Railroad, Chapel House, Hatcher's Run, Yorktown, Williamsburg, Fair Oaks, the Seven-day battle, Blackwater, Kinston, Whitehall, Goldsboro, the siege of Newbern, Dury's Farm, Port Walthall, Cold Harbor, Battery Harrison and Charles City Road.

ONE HUNDRED AND FIFTH INFANTRY.

The companies of which this regiment was composed were raised in the counties of Niagara, Cattaraugus, Genesee and Monroe. It was organized at Rochester and Le Roy; mustered in in March, 1862, and consolidated with the 94th New York volunteers in March, 1863, which latter organization was mustered out July 18th, 1865. The One Hundred and Fifth did good service in the battles of Cedar Mountain, Rappahannock Station, Thoroughfare Gap, Second Bull Run, Chantilly, South Mountain, Antietam and Fredericksburg. The colonels of the 105th were: James M. Fuller, of Le Roy, who was commissioned Apr. 10, 1862, but resigned Aug. 6, 1862; Howard Carroll, of Rochester, commissioned Aug. 2, 1862, who did not muster in as colonel; John W. Shedd, of Le Roy, commissioned Oct. 1, 1862, mstd out at the consolidation, Mch. 17, 1863.

The representation in the regiment from Niagara county included Quartermaster Sergeant James C. Phillips, Hartland; Hospital Steward W. N. Van Buren, Pendleton; and the men named in the following list, copied from the original muster roll in the office of the county clerk; we begin with company B.

OFFICERS.

Captain, James B. N. Delong, Lockport; first lieutenant, Charles F. Rudgers, Lockport; second lieutenant, Frederick I. Massey, Lockport; first sergeant, C. V. Mesler, Royalton, enlisted Nov. 13, 1861, promoted to captain, dschd July 18, 1865; third sergeant, William M. Mesler, Royalton; enlisted Nov. 13, 1861, dschd Nov. 27, 1864; fifth sergeant, John Quick, Lockport; second corporal, Jesse M. Spears, Lockport; third, Andrew J. Taylor, Lockport; fourth, Henry H. Nicholson, Lockport; fifth, Russell G. Olmstead, Lockport; sixth, John McArthur, Lockport; eighth, Thomas W. Davenport, Lockport; musicians, Isaiah Davis, Hartland,; James E. Shephard, Lockport; teamster, Charles W. Jackson, Lockport.

PRIVATES.

Russell C. Bloomingdale, Alfred Bell, Charles N. Bust, William Barrett, William Boodgers, Patrick Burk, Alonzo

J. M. Barrett, Henry Bennett, Daniel Clark, jr., Daniel Costello and William Clapham, Lockport; Richard N. Cook, Hartland; Charles Campbell, Willis Clement, Isaac E. Conklin and Michael Donnelly, Lockport; James B. Edwards, Hartland; William Fermoil, Noah S. Green, Washington E. Hallock, Stephen Harvy, William Harvey, jr., John Hamlin and Homer Hawkinson, Lockport; Augustus Klee, Middleport, enlisted in November, 1861, promoted to corporal, killed at Antietam Sept. 17, 1862; Lewis Knotthoff, Lockport; Joseph Light, Pendleton; Charles McMaster, James Morris, John Moyer, Conrad Minnick, James Newton, James Oswald and Thomas Oliver, Lockport; James E. Phillips, Hartland; Michael Slattery, James R. Swan, Wheeler Strycland, James Stewart, Frederick Schramm, John W. Sinclair, James Smith, William Stapleton, John B. Sherman, Henry Spurr, Daniel Timms and Samuel Thorp, Lockport; Daniel B. Thorne, Hartland; Nicholas Terry, Lockport; William W. Van Buren, Pendleton; Peter Vanoter, Lockport; Nery White, Pendleton; Henry White, George Wilson and Edward Walton, Lockport; Elvin White, Hartland.

Company D included the following

OFFICERS:

Captain, Isaac S. Tichnor; second sergeant, Michael Leonard; third sergeant, James B. Chase; second corporal, Roswall Wilson; eighth corporal, Henry Ballow; teamster, James Totten—all of Lockport.

PRIVATES.

David P. Allen, Lockport; Charles N. Ashford, Wilson; John Adams, Ransomville; George Beecker, Lockport; James Barker, Ransomville; Robert H. Clapsattle, Lawrence Cline, Henry Davenport, Pardon Earl, William Fink, Martin Gage, Jacob Geiser; John Grosskopf and George Granger, Lockport; George W. Giddings, Youngstown; Norton Hornbeck and Otto Kahler, Lockport; Barnard Kaller, Pendleton; William Kahler and Patrick Leonard, Lockport; Kobert Lutze, Wilson; William McMaster, Homer Moore, Joseph Moffat and James W. McGrath, Lockport; Jehial Moore, Youngstown; Van Rensselaer Perry and George W. Post, Ransomville; Charles Reynolds, John Stewart and Daniel Stowell, Lockport; Julius Turner, Wilson; Michael Thaney, Henry Woodcock and Abram. G. Wendall, Lockport.

In Company H there were of Niagara county men: Third corporal, Joseph T. Cary, of Suspension Bridge; fourth corporal, George W. Phillips, of Niagara Falls; and the following

PRIVATES:

Bartholomew B. Benson, Youngstown; James Brewster, Niagara Falls; Calvin Cary, Lewiston; Gaines B. Clapp and James Cafferty, Suspension Bridge; Edwin Ede, Niagara Falls; Edward Green, Harvey Garner, Richard Heath, and Michael Hoy, Suspension Bridge; Alvis Hewitt, Tuscarora; Charles Kline, Lewiston; James Kelly, Niagara Falls; John Kelly, Suspension Bridge; Thomas King, Niagara Falls; John Lawrence, Albert Ladroot, and William Massey, Suspension Bridge; Edward McManis, Niagara Falls, killed at Fredericksburg, Va., Aug. 13, 1862; John McCabe, Suspension Bridge; Thomas Needham, Niagara Falls; Israel Patterson and Frederick C. Stephens, Suspension Bridge; Robert Thompson, Niagara Falls; John A. West, Lewiston; Joseph Salmon and William H. Sperry, Niagara Falls.

Company I included second sergeant William Robertson, Suspension Bridge; third sergeant, Patrick Joyce, Niagara Falls; and the following privates: Thomas Foley, John W. Green, Matthew Hardegan, Daniel Sheehan, John Sheehan, and Edward Williams—all of Lockport. Lewis Kittleman, Royalton, enlisted Feb. 13, 1862, dschd June 9, 1865, belonged to Company K.

The regiment rendezvoused at Le Roy, remaining there till spring. From there it went to New York, and staid ten days, and then to Washington. After staying at Washington one week it moved to Alexandria and camped there for three weeks. It was afterwards encamped at Catlett's Station several weeks, and finally ordered to General McDowell's corps. The first battle was at Cedar Mountain.

THE 132nd INFANTRY.

Company G, of the 132d regiment, raised principally in New York city, and organized there, contained upwards of thirty Niagara county men, all enrolled at Suspension Bridge, and Company D three, enrolled at Lewiston. The list follows:

OFFICERS.

First sergeant, John Logan; second, William A. C. Ryan; third, Henry Smith; fourth, William Rea; first corporal, Robert Harris; second, James Goss; third, John Brennan; fourth, Andrew H. Oswald.

PRIVATES:

William Blodgett, Stephen Concklin, Charles Devinger, John Dalley, John Dillon, John Filmore, William H. Fleming, Robert Gibson, William Galloway, George S. Haskill, Hiram N. Hoag, Ezra Landen, William Meadows, Patrick Mitchell, John Murphy, Joseph Maroney, Michael Reynolds, John Rogers, Jeremiah Sullivan, William Stephenson, John W. Watts, George Garlow, Jacob Hewitt, Peter Terry.

The regiment was mustered into the service October 4th, 1862, and mustered out June 29th, 1865. It participated in the battles of Blackwater, Franklin, Pollockville, Street's Ferry, Newbern, White Oak Creek, Blount's Mills, Batchellor's Creek, Jackson's Mill, Southwest Creek and Kinston.

THE 164th INFANTRY.

This regiment was made up of companies raised in the counties of Niagara, Orleans, New York, Kings, Erie and St. Lawrence. It was organized at New York, mustered in November 19th, 1862, and mustered out July 15th, 1865, when only two men of company B were fit for service. Its record was a good one; it fought in the battles of Suffolk, Blackwater, Spottsylvania, Tolopotomoy, Cold Harbor, Petersburg, Strawberry Plains, Deep Bottom, Ream's Station and Boydtown Road. Company B was raised in Niagara and Orleans counties, by Captain William Maroney, of Lockport, and contained the following men:

OFFICERS.

Captain, William Maroney, Lockport; first sergeant, John Ryan, Lockport; second, Patrick Sullivan, Lockport; fourth, M. J. Doolan, Lockport; fifth, John Eagan, Lockport; first corporal, Michael McGrath, Lockport; second, Francis Williams, Lockport; third, Peter Monahan, Somerset; fourth, John Steel, Lockport; fifth, Martin Nolan, Lockport; seventh, Dennis Cary, Lockport, eighth, Edward O'Neil, Lockport.

PRIVATES.

Philip Burns, Newfane, enlisted Aug. 23, 1862, killed at Cold Harbor, Va; George Baker, Lockport ; James Bradley, Lockport; Thomas Corrigan, Newfane, enlisted Aug. 23, 1862, mstd out in Aug., 1865; Daniel Connolly, Somerset; John Dunnigan and Patrick Doolan, Lockport; Horace Every, Somerset; John Ellarel and Michael Fox, Lockport; Michael Finnegan, Newfane; John Garrity, William Gleason, James Hickey, Patrick Hyland, Thomas Hornsby, Matthew Hardigan and Patrick Kane, Lockport; Thomas Kerrigan, Newfane; John Kingston, Lewiston; James Kinsler, Lockport; Richard King and James Lunneen, Lockport; James Meagher and Patrick Monahan, Somerset; Thomas Mahar, Newfane, enlisted Aug. 23, 1862, killed at Cold Harbor; Patrick Meagher, Somerset; Thomas Meagher, Newfane; John A. McAllister, Michael McMahon and Daniel McGrath, Lockport; Charles Maguire, Newfane, enlisted July 1, 1863, killed at Suffolk, Va, in 1863; Andrew Rea, Jeremiah Reardon, Robert Shortley and Martin Shine, Lockport; William Tracy, Somerset; John Welch and John Williams, Lockport.

THE 178TH INFANTRY.

In Company A of this regiment, which was raised in the county of New York, were three Niagara county men, viz: Riley P. Buttrick, James Dow and Joseph Mottershed. The regiment was mustered into the service from June 18th to Oct. 17th, 1863. It was mustered out April 2nd, 1866. It was engaged in the battles of Fort De Russy, Pleasant Hill, Nachitoches, Coultersville, Kane River, Alexandria, Moore's Plantation, Chambers's Plantation, Marksville Prairie, Yellow Bayou, Lake Chicot, Hurricane Creek, Franklin and Nashville.

THE 179TH INFANTRY.

In this regiment, which was raised in the counties of Chemung, Erie, Steuben, Tioga and Tompkins, there was also a small representation of Niagara county volunteers, as follows:

COMPANY A.—Timothy W. Buckland, Almeron C. Howell and John Marshall.

COMPANY C.—William Doharty and Graham Crawford, Niagara; Charles E. Hogan and Charles F. Hagar, Royalton; Michael Kelley and Duncan McKay, Niagara.

COMPANY D.—John P. Atchworth, Lewiston; Arthur P. Powell, Lockport.

COMPANY F.—Karl Frederick, Wheatfield; John Riley, Porter; George A. Zimmerman, Royalton, enlisted June 8, 1863, dschd Mch. 20, 1865.

COMPANY H.—Thomas Cairns, Niagara; Abraham Isbery, Lockport; Francis Lovett, Niagara; Henry Miller, Wheatfield; Henry Maxwell and James Young, Niagara.

The regiment was engaged in the battles of Petersburg, Weldon Railroad, Poplar Spring Grove and Hatcher's Run.

THE 187TH INFANTRY.

This organization was made up principally of men from Erie, Chautauqua and Cattaraugus, and was organized at Buffalo, to serve one year. It was mustered into the service in October, 1864, and mustered out in July, 1865. The muster-rolls on file in the Niagara county clerk's office show it to have included Anthony Wesser, Niagara, in Company C; John H. Smith, Lockport, in Company E, and the following members of

COMPANY G:

Henry Ames, Wilson; Peter Brocklehurst, Niagara; Charles Bennett, Lewiston; John Bugbee and Alexander H. Clark, Lockport ; James Dempsey, Porter ; James Downing, Niagara; Joseph A. Dersey, Manly Fox, and Joseph Gibbs, Lockport ; Lorenzo Hill, Wilson; John Haskins, Royalton; Monroe Haskins, Lockport; Henry Hall, Somerset; Harrison Harvard, Wilson; Simms King, Lockport; Frank Lily, Royalton; James Morrow, Porter; John Marshall, Wilson ; Joel McCall, Royalton ; George A. Otis, Lockport; Chauncey C. Robinson, Wilson ; George Sporbeck, Lockport ; Charles Smith, Royalton ; Francis M. Shelp, and Samuel Smith. Lockport; William O. Webster, Somerset; Gottreil Weiler, and L. W. Van Slyck, Lockport.

The principal engagement in which this regiment participated was at Hatcher's Run.

THE 194TH INFANTRY.

This regiment was organized at Elmira, to serve one and three years. The companies of which it was composed were raised in the counties of Niagara, Chemung, Gates, Allegany, Seneca, Ontario, Onondaga, and Cattaragus. It was mstd in from February to April, 1865. On the 3rd of May, 1865, without ever having left the State, it was mustered out in accordance with orders from the War Department.

Company G of this regiment was from Niagara county, and consisted of the following men, all enrolled at Lockport:

John Adams, Albert Anderson, John Berlet, William Bell, Harlow Bartholf, Charles Belan, James Barrett, Austin E. Bigelow, Hiram Bevans, Edward Birmingham, Ebenezer Birmingham, Adolph Catnoir, Samuel Center, John Clark, John Conlon, Jacob Chase, Robert Cleland, John Clere, Charles Carr, Perry M. Cottrell, Charles Doyle, Joshua Davis, William Dixon, Chapin Davy, Charles Dutcher, John Edmonds, Legnon Erlgeng, Luther M. Finn, Frederick Fonea, George Fuller, Thomas Flack, William R. Gillings, Michael Gorman, James Gregory, Charles Guenzler, Joseph Howard, Melvin C. Hawley, Elias Hoffman, Almon Glena, John Hoffman, Almo B. Hixson, James W. Jones, Patrick Katon, Ole Kragering, Joseph Kelly, Patrick Lennon, James Lewis, John Martin, Joseph Murphy, William H. McKimm, William F. Munn, Henry Minett, Henry Moore, George Manzier, John McIntyre, Samuel Nelson, George O'Camb, Edward Parker, Henry Pansier, Timothy Ray, Thomas Ryan, Thomas Riley, Joseph Reed, Corey Smith, William Stone, John Thompson, George B. Thompson, John R. Tibbets, George Wheeler, John Wheeler, Peter Ostrander, Alfred Roberts, Samuel Tenny, Peter Neason.

CHAPTER XXXVII.

TWELFTH, NINETEENTH, SEVENTEENTH AND TWENTY-FIFTH BATTERIES—FOURTEENTH ARTILLERY—TOWN RECORDS.

ALTHOUGH the 12th battery was organized at Albany, by Captain William H. Ellis, of Troy, there was in it a fair sprinkling of Niagara county "boys." The battery entered into the service January 14th, 1862, for three years. On the expiration of its term, in accordance with orders from the War Department, the original members were mustered out, and the battery, composed of veterans and recruits, retained in the service until June 14th, 1865, when they too were mustered out. The career of the 12th was an eventful one, it being engaged in the battles of Petersburg, Ream's Station, Kelly's Ford, Mine Run, North Anna, Tolopotomoy and Cold Harbor. Those who enlisted in this organization from Niagara county, are mentioned in the following list:

OFFICERS.

First lieutenant, Walter Shaw, Newfane, enlisted Oct. 7, 1861, honorably dschd Mch. 31, 1863; orderly sergeant, Elijah Ewing, Newfane, enlisted in August, 1861, mstd out with regiment; sergeants, Rollin G. Steele, Newfane; George Outwater, Newfane, enlisted Oct. 11, 1861, mstd out Dec. 19, 1865; corporals, William T. Slocum, Cambria; Charles Frink, Wilson; Matthias Hoffman, Hartland; bugler Charles H. Newell, Newfane, enlisted Oct. 12, 1861, mstd out July 21, 1865; carpenter, Elijah Dodge, Newfane, enlisted Aug. 18, 1862, dschd Aug. 28, 1863.

PRIVATES.

William H. Anderson, Newfane; Charles D. Avery, Newfane, enlisted Nov. 20, 1861, mstd out June 17, 1865; John Adriance, Wilson; Alvin Austin, Hartland; Franklin Brown, Lockport; Lester W. Babcock, Somerset; Asahel Brown, Newfane, enlisted Dec. 10, 1861, mstd out June 14, 1865; John M. Clark, Somerset; Cyrus A. Deming, Newfane, enlisted Nov. 20, 1861, mstd out June 17, 1865; Hiram A. Folsom, Newfane, enlisted Oct. 7, 1861, mstd out April 25, 1865; Charles O. Gregory, Newfane; Arnold Harris, Wilson; Henry Kinney, Newfane, enlisted Oct. 7, 1861; promoted to corporal, prisoner eleven months, mstd out June 14, 1865; Gustavus V. Kendall, Newfane, enlisted Oct. 11, 1861, dschd March 27, 1863; Peter Krupp, enlisted Oct. 10, 1861, and served three years; John King, Newfane; John H. Lewis, Newfane, enlisted Oct. 12, 1861, mstd out Dec. 19, 1864; Abraham Liddle, Newfane, promoted to first lieutenant; Jesse Lefever, Newfane, enlisted in October, 1861, mstd out, re-enlisted and died Nov. 16, 1864; Joseph Lewis, Newfane, enlisted Nov. 20, 1861, mstd out June 17, 1865; John Mulor, Cambria; Andrew Marquot, Hartland; Peter Nerber, Frederick Odiron and Patrick O'Brien, Lockport; Nicholas Parton, Hartland; William Shaver, Hartland; John Tyler, Royalton, enlisted Nov. 30, 1861, dschd June 26, 1865; Elijah Talcott, Somerset; Alexander Thompson, Newfane; Zenas Tracy, Newfane; Ira E. Thompson, Newfane, enlisted Oct. 7, 1861, mstd out June 17, 1865; Cornelius C. Tice, Newfane, enlisted in November, 1861, mstd out March 21, 1862; Charles Van Horne, Newfane, enlisted Oct. 7, 1861, and served three years; Wentworth, Newfane; Henry W. Wright, Newfane, enlisted in October, 1861, died at home April 5, 1865.

NINETEENTH INDEPENDENT BATTERY.

It was in 1862, during the darkest hours of the rebellion, that the 19th independent battery of artillery was organized. Fresh sacrifices had been made on the fields before Richmond, and the President had issued an immediate and imperative demand for 300,000 more men, 50,000 of whom were to be raised in New York. This was in July, when the harvest fields were whitening, the farm laborer was hard pressed and help was at a premium. The abstract idea of soldiering presented no attractions, and all things considered, the appeal could only be made to patriotism.

On the 9th day of August, while the call yet awaited response, Captain William Stahl, of Lockport, made his initial endeavor to raise 142 men to do service under his command and under the above mentioned title. Despite the discouragements under which he labored, the month of September found him in command of 162 men, upward of 100 of whom were sturdy farmers. The military regulations allowed him only 142 men, and those in excess were by authority transferred to other organizations. Immediately following its formation the battery was encamped on the fair grounds in Lockport about two months. On the evening of October 23d the brave fellows bade their friends adieu and left, *via* Rochester, for Washington, where they went into camp of instruction and remained during the winter.

During this time they were officered by Captain William H. Sthal, First Lieutenant Edward W. Rogers, and Second Lieutenant Peter McGraw, all of Lockport The eventful career of the battery commenced in April, 1863, when it was sent to Suffolk, Virginia, to reinforce the forces under General Peck, who were holding that place when its capture was attempted by the rebels under General Longstreet. It participated in several of the actions in that siege and in the pursuit of Longstreet, who in May fell back and abandoned the attempt. Up to this time the battery suffered the loss of but one man. Its services during the remainder of the campaign were of a promiscuous order. Captain Stahl died in September, 1863, of fever, near Washington, and the command of the battery was assumed by Lieutenant Rogers.

The battery encamped near Washington for the winter. April 27th, 1864, it broke camp and marched with the 9th corps, General Burnside's, to join the Army of the Potomac. (The 9th corps held the Orange and Alexandria Railroad until the Army of the Potomac commenced its advances, when the railroad was abandoned and the corps made a forced march to join the Army of the Potomac in its attack upon Lee). On May 5th the battery and its corps crossed the Rapidan river and joined the Army of the Potomac while it was engaged in the battle of the Wilderness. The 19th battery participated in the whole of that terrible campaign, which commenced May 5th, 1864, and terminated with the surrender of Lee April 9th, 1865. It was engaged in many fierce struggles, not only suffering severe loss but enduring long continued and unremitting privation and hardship. Being placed in a much exposed position at the battle of Spottsylvania, it was charged by a rebel brigade with desperate energy and determination. Its support consisted of only one small regiment 115 strong. The rebels charged almost to the very muzzles of the pieces, but the sturdy sons of Niagara and Genesee held their guns and their dead and wounded comrades. Only a portion of the battery (about fifty men) was engaged in this action, yet in the few minutes of this charge they lost ten killed and eight wounded. Of the latter only two were able to do service with the battery again.

The gallantry of the 19th was not unobserved by its division and corps commanders, as was evidenced in the fact that its commanding officer was given a brevet of major for services on that date. Again during the siege of Petersburg the 19th battery did its full share of active service, suffering loss daily. Its position was close to the mine that was exploded under a rebel fort, July 30th, 1864, at which time an assault was made in attempt to carry the defenses of Petersburg. On that memorable morning this battery was steadily engaged until the assault was repulsed. It took part in many of the movements by "the left flank" in the operations before Petersburg, and was engaged in the defense of Fort Steadman when it was assaulted by the rebels, March 25th, 1865, under command of General Gordon. In this attack it again suffered severe loss.

After the surrender of Lee the battery went to Alexandria, Va., where it remained until June 5th, taking part meantime in the grand review. June 8th it left Washington for Elmira, where it was mustered out and discharged, June 16th, 1865, after nearly three years' service. On the battle-flag which the battery bore through its career are inscribed Suffolk, Spottsylvania, North Anna, Cold Harbor, Weldon Railroad, Petersburg and Hatcher's Run.

In the following compilation are given the names and places of residence of those who did service in battery 19, together with remarks showing who died or were wounded, and who returned to tell the story.

OFFICERS.

Captain, William H. Stahl, Lockport, died Sept. 15, 1863; first lieutenant, Edward W. Rogers, Lockport, promoted captain Oct. 23, mstd out June 17, 1865; second lieutenant, Peter McGraw, Lockport, dschd Sept. 29, 1863; first sergeant, Henry J. J. Fassett, Lockport, dschd in January, 1863; quartermaster sergeant, George N. McCoy, Lockport, died Dec. 9, 1862; sergeants, Henry H. Moore, Lockport, promoted to lieutenancy; Michael Long, Lockport, promoted to lieutenancy; Gardner Corliss, Pendleton, wounded and dschd; corporals, Oratus F. Pierce, Lockport; Alvin B. Baker, Lockport, deserted; James Richards and Willard Heath, Lockport; John W. Haskell, Porter; Lockwood S. Sherwood, Lockport, killed July 29, 1864; W. Scott Hovey, Newfane, enlisted Aug. 16, 1862, died Dec. 8, 1862, at Washington; musicians, Richard A. Perry, Porter; Charles A. Bowen, Lockport, deserted Feb. 8, 1863; artificers, Elijah Dodge, Newfane, enlisted Aug. 18, 1862, dschd August, 1863; W. C. Beck, Lockport.

PRIVATES.

John A. Ashton, Newfane, enlisted Aug. 15, 1862, promoted corporal, mstd out June 13, 1865; William H. Atchinson, Newfane, enlisted Aug. 15, 1862, mstd out June 14, 1865; Hawley Abbott, Pendleton; Nicholas Bowers, Pendleton, dschd in April, 1863; Werner Bellinger, Lockport, killed May 12, 1864; James Benton, Lockport; William T. Bush, Lockport, died Nov. 8, 1862; S. F. Baylis, Lockport; I. Barnes, Porter; J. Bixler, Newfane, enlisted Aug. 14, 1862, wounded July 17, 1864, mstd out May 26, 1865; Jacob Braucker, Newfane, enlisted Sept. 2, 1862, killed May 12, 1864, at Spottsylvania, Va; Charles W. Beebe, Newfane; John Beach, Lockport; Ransom E. Bigelow, Hartland, dschd Dec., 1863; Edmond Brotherton, Newfane; William F. Clark and Edward J. Cady, Lockport; William W. Clement, Newfane, enlisted Aug. 15, 1862, mstd out June 13, 1865; John W. Carter, Porter, died July 20, 1863; Timothy C. Cox, Lockport, wounded; Lewis W. F. Cole, Lockport; DeWitt C. Collier, Newfane, dschd Sept., 1863; William Coan, Wilson; George Coyle, Lockport, killed in June., 1864; George

E. Dutton, Hartland; John E. Declute, Porter; William A. Douglas, Newfane, enlisted Aug. 16, 1862, mstd out June 13, 1865; Edward Dunkleburger, Lockport; George W. Eaton, Lockport, dschd Mch. 8, 1863; Solomon A. Eshbaugh, Newfane, enlisted Aug. 15, 1862, mstd out June 16, 1865; George Evans, Pendleton; Sylvester Esterly and Henry Egan, Lockport; William A. Fuller, Pendleton, deserted; David H. Frink, Wilson; Theron Goodspeed, Newfane, enlisted Aug. 13, 1862, killed May 12, 1864, at Spottsylvania, Va; Jesse Goddard, Pendleton; Joseph Golias, Pendleton, killed May 12, 1864; George Humphrey, Hartland; Edwin A. Hoffman, Lockport; Alexander Halstead, Newfane, enlisted Aug. 15, 1862, mstd out June 17, 1865; John Hall, Lockport, killed May 12, 1864; James Hill and Theodore O. Hayne, Wilson; Louis A. Halstead, Newfane, enlisted Aug. 29, 1862, dschd Dec. 24, 1864, for disability; John A. Hamlin and William H. H. Hotchkin, Wilson; James H. Hotchkin, Wilson, wounded and dschd; Seth Jillson, Porter; Willis Johnson, Newfane, enlisted Aug. 13, 1862, promoted corporal, mstd out June 18, 1865; Jesse E. Kieffer, Lockport; Ansel Kayner, Lockport, dschd in April, 1863; George B. Kinne, Lockport, wounded and dschd; Thomas Kelly, Lockport; John Kelly, Porter; Francis King, Pendleton; Joseph Kiltz, Lockport, dschd March, 1865; Richard Lansom, Lockport, died Oct. 2, 1863; Alfred P. Lake, Newfane, enlisted Aug. 19, 1862, mstd out June 16, 1865; John Lanigan, Newfane, enlisted Feb. 22, 1864; Andrew Linck, Lockport; Joseph Linck, Lockport, wounded and dschd; David O. Lewis, Newfane, enlisted Feb. 22, 1864, killed May 12, 1864, at Spottsylvania Court-house; John E. Loyd, Porter; Daniel Lehn, Wilson, wounded; Mark McKenzie, Wilson; Thomas Muldoon and Narcise Montray, Lockport; George K. Mosher, Newfane, enlisted Aug. 18, 1862, mstd out June 18, 1865; Christian Murr, Lockport, died Sept. 9, 1864; Joseph L. Morris, Porter, dschd June 10, 1863; Joseph W. Morris, Porter, dschd June 17, 1863; Caleb C. McKee, Newfane, enlisted Aug. 18, 1862, mstd out June 13, 1865; Peter Morton, Lockport, killed June 2, 1864; James Mount, Pendleton; Charles Muchaw, Lockport; John Mahoney, Pendleton, taken prisoner; Harmon Moyer, Pendleton; James A. Martin, Newfane, enlisted Aug. 11, 1862, mstd out June 14, 1865; James Morrison, Wilson; James Moran, Newfane, enlisted Sept. 30, 1864; George Morrison, Lockport; William McGory, Newfane, enlisted Aug. 15, 1862, killed May 12, 1864, at Spottsylvania, Va.; Edwin H. Northrop, Porter; Michael Donahoe, Newfane, enlisted Feb. 22, 1864; Robert O'Hara, Cambria; William F. Parsons, Wilson; William D. Pierce, Newfane, enlisted Feb. 22, 1864, died July 21, 1864, at Davis Island, N. Y.; William Roe and William Roberts, Lockport; William Retchless, Hartland, wounded and dschd; Gideon Richtmeyer, Wilson; Clark M. Riddle, Pendleton, wounded, transferred to veteran reserve corps in 1863, mstd out Aug. 23, 1865; James Robbins, Newfane, enlisted Aug. 29, 1863; Ephraim Robinson, Lockport, dschd Mch. 9, 1863; John V. Rector, Pendleton, wounded; Frederick Schurz, Lockport, died Sept. 4, 1863; Christian Schurr and Charles A. Smith, Lockport; Chauncey Stone and Joseph B. Stone, Lewiston; Seymour Stace, Hartland; Thomas Turner, Porter; Albert Talcott and Philip Van Norman, Lockport; Ormel Valentine, Hartland; Philip S. Williams, Newfane, enlisted Aug. 15, 1862, mstd out June 13, 1865; George H. Weaver, Pendleton, killed; Daniel Wertman, Pendleton, dschd in March, 1863; Sheldon M. Weatherbee and George Weatherbee, Lockport; Delevan C. Waters, Lockport, died in hospital; Nimrod White, Lockport, died September, 1863; Franklin Zimmerman, Lockport.

The following is a list of the names of men who were not original members of the battery but joined it during the service:

Theodore D. Hallet, Charles H. Stocking, David Shepard, George H. Tuite, Adelbert Thompson, Arthur Thompson, William Hepner, G. R. Hawkins, Jacob D. Irish, John Jameson, Elias Kelsey, John Horn, John Lanagan, Henry Lord, Thomas Mahoney, Charles Miller, Jacob Moore, Isaac Martin, Nelson Matieson, Orrin Mills, E. Mills, W. Mills, R. Northup, Michael O'Donohue, Charles Pletcher, Joseph Rogers, Robert G. Wilson, Michael King, John Murray, Jared Goodrich, David O. Lewis, William D. Pierce, J. Wesley Johnson, Jeremiah Everhart. Of these Michael O'Donohue, Charles Pletcher, Joseph Rogers, Robert G. Wilson, Isaac Martin, John Lanagan, Elias Kelsey, John Jameson, Jacob D. Irish and William Hepner are known to have gone from Niagara county.

In addition to these there were many men who did duty with the battery by being detached from other organizations to fill its depleted ranks. For instance, at the battle of Spottsylvania a detachment of twenty-five men from a heavy artillery regiment was ordered to the battery to take the place of the men lost in that battle. It should be added that the detachment did good service with the 19th during most of the campaign of 1864, and lost many of its number, killed and wounded.

SEVENTEENTH BATTERY.

This battery was organized in Lockport, but raised in Orleans county by Captain George J. Anthony. It was mustered into service August 27th, 1862, and mustered out June 12th, 1865. Its ranks included from Niagara county John Normille, Anthony T. Weaver and Alanson Kimball, of Lockport, and from Royalton: Franklin R. Axtell, enlisted Aug. 22nd, 1862, dschd June 12, 1865; Silas J. Flinn, enlisted Sept. 10, 1864, dschd June 12, 1865; Murdo McDonald, enlisted Aug. 26, 1862, dschd in June, 1865.

FOURTEENTH ARTILLERY.

This regiment was raised in the counties of New York, Queens and Erie, and was organized at New York city, to serve three years. It was mustered into service from November 24th, 1862, to July 8th, 1863. August 1st, 1863, it was formed into a battalion of six companies, which were consolidated with the Eighteenth New York cavalry June 12th, 1865. In Company B of this regiment therewas the following representation from Niagara county:

OFFICERS.

Second lieutenant, Charles A. Vedder, Suspension Bridge; fourth sergeant, B. S. Fall, Niagara; third corporal, Thomas H. Henderhan, Niagara; fourth, Patrick Rineham, Niagara.

PRIVATES.

Lester Atkins, Lewiston; James M. Abbott, Joseph Carley, Isaac L. Caursen, William A. Dunlap, Edwin E. Elliott and Thomas Gannon, Niagara; George O. Powley, Porter; Charles A. Poole, Lewiston; Nathan Smith, Porter; Russell H. Titus, Lewiston; John Wiseman, Niagara; George W. Whittaker, Porter; Griggs Holbrook, Niagara.

Company G included Sergeant William Walker, of Suspension Bridge, and William E. Phillips, of Royalton, and Company F the following:

William Berryman and Cains Blanchard, Lockport; William Berry, Suspension Bridge; Thomas Dalton, Lockport; Michael O. Holleran, Suspension Bridge; — McPherson, Suspension Bridge; Patrick O'Neil and Charles Payfair, Lockport; Philip H. Proper, Royalton, enlisted July 9, 1863, dschd in June, 1865; William Smith and Edward Williams, Lockport; John Wheeler, Suspension Bridge; William Young, Lockport.

25th BATTERY, LIGHT ARTILLERY

This battery was organized at Lockport in 1862, to serve three years. It was raised in the counties of Niagara, Orleans and Genesee, by Captain John A. Grow, of Medina, and mustered into the service December 12th, 1862. It was in the field nearly three years, being mustered out August 5th, 1865. The principal engagement in which the battery took part, as shown in the adjutant-general's report, was at the battle of Lafourche. The representation of Niagara county in the battery is shown in the following roll:

OFFICERS.

First sergeant, James P. Boyd, Lockport; sergeant, Charles White, Hartland; corporals, Allen M. Mudge, Hartland; George O. Strain, Royalton, enlisted Sept. 1, 1862, killed at Pleasant Hill, La., April 9, 1864; artificers, Thomas A. Lusk, Hartland; Daniel G. Walters, Lockport; Wagoner, William H. Pease, Hartland.

PRIVATES.

Ira M. Allen and J. P. Andrews, Hartland; Joseph Anna, Lockport; Albert Sentley and William Brownell, Hartland; Robert Cook, Somerset; Lyman A. Curtin, Albert B. Dean, Owen Donohue and Patrick Farrell, Hartland; Adam Gardner, Lockport; James S. Harrington and Myron S. Hills, Hartland; Thomas Irwin, Lewiston; Allen Lount, Lockport; John W. McCandish, George Papworth, William W. Ross, George Shorten, William Shorten and Henry Shorten, Hartland; William Smith, Lewiston; Philip Swick and Andrew B. Stewart, Lockport; Joseph A. Thomas and M. Darwin Williams, Hartland; William Wilkinson, Lewiston; Henry Waterson, Lockport; Andrew Welsher, Hartland.

NEWFANE AND ROYALTON RECORDS.

In the town records of Newfane and Royalton, which have been freely used in preparing the foregoing lists, a number of men are named who belonged to organizations in which this county was so slightly represented that we could not afford space for their histories. Besides the Newfane and Royalton men, therefore, whose records appear in their proper places, we have the following volunteers to record :

NEWFANE.

John Adams and Thomas Artis, 6th cav., enlisted Oct. 1, 1864; Sergeant Henry A. Bailey, 7th cav., enlisted Sept. 9, 1861, mstd out Mch. 31, 1862; Morris A. Bailey, 12th inf., enlisted Sept. 3, 1861, dschd; Jeremiah Babcock, 12th heavy art., enlisted Dec. 25, 1862, died in Salisbury prison, Dec. 22, 1863; J. D. Birdsall, 10th inf., enlisted Dec. 16, 1863, mstd out June 30, 1865; Second Lieutenant Charles W. Baxter; Corporal Joseph R. Barrell, 26th inf., enlisted Nov. 7, 1861, missing after the battle of Cedar Mountain; Theodore Butcher, 12th bat., enlisted Dec. 26, 1861, mstd out June 17, 1865; Lewis Brooks, enlisted Sept. 24, 1864; James M. Barnum, 61st inf., enlisted Aug. 4, 1864, mstd out July 20, 1865; Second Lieutenant Oliver M. Campbell, Co. M, 8th heavy art., enlisted Jan. 3, 1864; died in Libby prison, June 24, 1864; John Dewger, 136th inf., enlisted Sept. 27, 1864; Henry Davis, 49th inf., enlisted Oct. 1, 1864; Calvin Davis, 6th inf., enlisted Oct. 1, 1864; George Dorty, 126th inf., enlisted Mch. 11, 1865; Almon Gallup, 108 inf., enlisted Aug. 16, 1862, dschd Dec. 9, 1864; J. A. Glassoway, 7th cav., enlisted Sept. 7, 1861, mstd out Mch. 31, 1862; Martin Gage, 94th inf., enlisted in October, 1861, died May 6, 1865, at Mower Hospital, Philadelphia; Owen Gage, 12th bat., enlisted Mch. 18, 1862, mstd out Mch. 20, 1865; John Gafney, 60th inf., enlisted Aug. 22, 1862, mstd out July 28, 1865; Sergeant David Gammer, Co. D, 129th inf., enlisted Aug. 18, 1861, prisoner ten and a half months, mstd out June 17, 1865; Benjamin Greenfield; Ezra H Harwood, 147th inf.; David B. Halsted, 12th inf., enlisted Sept. 2, 1861, mstd out Sept. 1, 1864; Charles C. Halsted, 26th inf., enlisted Nov. 23, 1861, mstd out in July 1865; First Lieutenant Henry B. Howell, 30th inf., enlisted in Aug. 1862, served through the war; Norton Hornbeck, 5th Maine, enlisted Nov. 6, 1861, dschd Dec. 3, 1864; Dorman C. Johnson, 7th cav., enlisted Sept. 9, 1861, mstd out Mch. 31, 1862; John Jones, 8th heavy art., enlisted Jan. 9, 1864, killed June 2, 1864, at Ream's Station, Va; Emmons Johnson, 15th U. S. inf., enlisted Jan. 20, 1865, mstd out Dec. 1, 1865; Hiram Kelley, 16th cav., enlisted July 1, 1864; John Keyser, enlisted Sept. 16, 1864; C. C. Lockwood,

7th cav., enlisted Sept. 9, 1861, mstd out Mch. 31, 1862, afterward in the navy; Marcus Lafler, 147th inf., enlisted July 28, 1863, mstd out July 14, 1865; Seth M. Lovell, 140th inf., enlisted July 23, 1863, prisoner seven and a half months, dschd June 7, 1865; Quartermaster Jacob Leonard, served two years and a half in the army and afterward in the navy; Morris Marquet, 10th veterans, enlisted Jan. 20, 1863, served twenty months; First Lieutenant Philip Messaroll, Co. D, 161st, enlisted Aug. 27, 1862, mstd out June 26, 1865; Orderly Sergeant George Murray, Co. A, 27th inf, enlisted Mch 12, 1864, killed June 18, 1864, before Petersburg; Marcus Mandeville, 60th inf., enlisted Sept. 6, 1862, mstd out July 17, 1865; James H. Mandeville, 12th bat., enlisted Feb. 8, 1864, mstd out July 3, 1865; James A. Maxwell, 12th bat., enlisted Sept. 6, 1864; George McGlynn, 91st inf.; Henry Miller, 91st inf.; Henry Marshall, 6th col'd; William N. Oxley, Michael O'Neil, 91st inf.; Milton E. Perigo, 147th inf., enlisted July 28, 1863, mstd out July 19, 1865; James Porter, 7th cav., enlisted Sept. 9, 1861, mstd out Mch. 31, 1862; David Phillips, second lieutenant 12th bat., enlisted Oct. 7, 1861, dschd Mch 31, 1862; Earle Pierce, 151st inf., enlisted Aug. 13, 1862, mstd out June 29th, 1865; William Parker, 7th cav., enlisted Sept 29, 1861, mstd out Mch 31, 1862; Lorenzo N. Pratt, bugler, 1st bat., enlisted Oct. 14, 1861, mstd out June 26, 1865; John Porter, 6th U. S. col'd; John Phillips, Lawrence Prentice, 1st bat., enlisted in March, 1863, died in hospital at Chattanooga, July, 26, 1864; John Quinn 91st inf.; David Richards, 34th N. J., died at home on furlough, Dec. 26, 1864; Reuben H. Redman, 1st light art., enlisted Mch 27, 1864, mstd out June, 1865; James Raling, 6th U. S. col'd; First Lieutenant W. J. Rabo, Co. D, 10th cav., enlisted in September, 1861, killed at Beverly Ford, Va, June 9, 1863; George E. Reynolds, navy, enlisted Aug. 29, 1862, dschd Nov. 22, 1862; Sergeant W. F. Stout, Co. K, 151st inf.; Hugh M. Swick, 5th veteran cav., enlisted Aug. 1, 1861, mstd out with regiment; George Spencer, 10th inf., enlisted Dec. 24, 1863, mstd out in June, 1865; Charles and James Smith, 6th U. S. col'd; John Slater, 49th inf.; William H. Shiefner, enlisted Mch 20, 1865, died at Hart's Island, N. Y., May 6, 1865; William Taylor, 9th cav.; Charles Van Horn, 12th bat., enlisted Oct. 7, 1861, served three years; John Vreeland, 110th inf., enlisted July 5, 1861, supposed to have died; William Vreeland, 12th bat., enlisted Nov. 10, 1861, died at home, April 13, 1864; Levi Vaughan, Ind. Co. 35, enlisted Mch. 2, 1865, mstd out in May, 1865; William Wentworth, 10th cav., enlisted Aug. 11, 1862, mstd out Aug. 30, 1865; John Wilson and Dennis White, 6th U. S. col'd.

ROYALTON.

William Bridgen, 37th art., enlisted April 10, 1864, dschd June 30, 1865; William H. Brookins, 2nd cav., enlisted Oct. 1, 1863, dschd Aug. 10, 1865; George C. Bugbee, 49th inf., enlisted in August, 1861, served 2 years; James A. Bugbee, 49th inf., enlisted in August, 1861, died in hospital in October, 1862; Peter B. Burgo, 7th cav., enlisted Sept. 12, 1861, dschd in March, 1862; Corporal James Compton, 129th inf., enlisted Aug. 5, 1862, dschd Feb. 27, 1865; James H. Cleveland, 11th inf.; Simeon Corey, 33d art., enlisted June 9, 1863; dschd June 25, 1865; John Congdon, 7th cav., enlisted Sept. 9, 1861; dschd in March, 1862; Truman A. Drake, 2nd cav., enlisted Jan. 12, 1864, killed in action in June, 1864; Charles P. Dutcher, 2nd cav., dschd in May, 1865; Sergeant Franklin Dutcher, enlisted Oct. 15, 1861, served three years; Milton A. Fellows, 22nd cav., enlisted Nov. 18, 1863, dschd May 18, 1865; Albert Green, corporal in the regular army, enlisted in June, 1864; William Griffis, 17th art., enlisted Sept. 10, 1864, dschd June 20, 1865; James A. Henry, 8th art., enlisted July 19, 1862, dschd June 5, 1865; Charles W. Harch, 105th inf., enlisted Jan. 14, 1862, dschd July 29, 1864; Quartermaster Sergeant James Hudnut, 8th art., enlisted July 26, 1862, dschd in June, 1865; First Sergeant H. C. Jennings, 19th inf., enlisted April 20, 1864, died from wounds Aug. 6, 1864; William Jargo, 5th inf., enlisted in September, 1862, dschd in June 1865; Henry G. King, 104th inf., enlisted Aug. 6, 1864, dschd July 17, 1865; Henry S. Ketcham, 17th art., enlisted Sept. 10, 1864, dschd June 12, 1864; Henry Luth, 8th art., enlisted Jan. 5, 1864, dschd June 30, 1865; Sergeant Watson C. McNall, Co. H, 151st, enlisted Sept. 6, 1862, dschd Dec. 21, 1864; Martin Murphy, 15th art., died at home, Dec. 29, 1864; Charles Martin, 8th art., killed in battle May 9, 1864; Andrew Nelson, 8th art., enlisted in January, 1864, wounded and sent to hospital. Daniel and Samuel Nerber, 10th cav., enlisted in October, 1864, former dschd in June, 1865, latter killed in battle Nov. 18, 1864; Rudolph Newmoda, 10th inf., enlisted Jan. 5, 1864, dschd June 30, 1865; Thomas Oliver, 151st inf., enlisted Aug. 20, 1862, dschd July 1, 1865; William E. Phillips, 14th inf., enlisted Oct. 29, 1861, served three years; Henry Rush, 8th art., enlisted Jan. 4, 1864, died at home, Nov. 17, 1864; Christian and Godfrey Rehwaldt, 8th art., enlisted July 21, 1862, former dschd June 5, 1865, latter June 29, 1864; John Russell, 49th inf., enlisted in May, 1862, died in hospital in Nov. 1863; Jacob Stadley, 8th art., enlisted in November, 1863, dschd Nov. 10, 1864; Alfred Southwick, 2nd cav., enlisted Oct. 13, 1863, dschd Aug. 10, 1865; Sergeant Michael Smith, 49th inf., enlisted in August, 1861, dschd in May, 1865; Charles H. Schad, 1st art., enlisted Oct. 8, 1861, dschd April 13, 1864; Charles Stock, 8th art., enlisted in July, 1862, killed at Cold Harbor; Henry Stock, 8th art., enlisted Oct. 4, 1863, died in Libby prison; Jay Silsby, 49th inf., enlisted in August, 1861, died in hospital Feb. 3, 1863; John D. Silsby, 49th inf., enlisted in August, 1861, dschd for disability; Captain John H. Tucker, 2nd cav., enlisted July 13, 1861; William H. Taylor, navy, enlisted Aug. 27, 1864, dschd Aug. 21, 1865; Frederick Urtel, 151st inf., enlisted Sept. 4, 1862, dschd January, 1864, Christopher F. Wallenberg, 8th art., enlisted July 21, 1861, dschd Aug. 22, 1865.

NIAGARA COUNTY COURT HOUSE — JAIL — CLERKS OFFICE

LOCKPORT IN 1836 FROM AN OLD PRINT

1 Aunt Edna Smith Place
2 Geo. W. Roger's Res.
3 Berkshire Block (Canal Bank)
4 Spalding Saw Mill & Foundry
5 Spalding Grist Mill
6 Joseph Center's Block
7 Eagle Hotel
8 Safford's Hall
9 Jonathan Ingalls Warehouse
10 Locks
11 M. E. Church
12 Woodward Bdg.
13 Presbyterian Church
14 Court House
15 Hydraulic Canal

CITY, TOWN AND VILLAGE HISTORIES.

THE CITY OF LOCKPORT.

IT may be claimed that the city of Lockport originated from a fortuitous circumstance. Considering the natural features in the primitive condition of its site this may be true, but this fact would render it more apparent that its growth and prosperity are the result of industry and enterprise.

In all ages it has been the pride of a city or community to preserve a record of the events associated with its formation and progress. There is always an interest connected with the initial movements, and an importance given to the characters at this primitive stage of action, which posterity is loath to consign to oblivion.

Great and rapid changes frequently take place along the highways cut for the onward march of civilization. The traveler upon his journey may pass an unbroken and secluded forest at one period, and returning at a later behold thereon a large and populous city, replete with the agricultural products of the surrounding districts and resounding with the continuous hum of its manufactories. This can truthfully be said of Lockport, for in less than three score years this vast and varied change has been effected. The primeval forest in its solitude and gloom has been removed, and in its place reared, first a village, and then a city which has grown to its present extent and population.

It is pleasantly situated on a commanding eminence, with wide streets, the greater part of which are beautifully ornamented with shade trees. The dwellings are neat and rendered cheerful and inviting by artificial surroundings, while the huge granite manufacturing establishments, standing boldly out upon the precipitous banks give the city a charming and picturesque appearance.

The location of the Erie Canal through the mountain ridge at this point gave the first impetus for forming the nucleus from which Lockport has grown, and that commercial artery, combined with the industry and public spirit of the inhabitants, has wrought the wondrous change, and achieved for the city the position it now holds. Previous to the location of the canal the dense forests had scarcely been touched by the hand of civilization.

The land upon which the city is built was purchased from the Holland Company by Esek Brown, Zeno Comstock, Nathan Comstock, Webster Thorn, Daniel Smith, David Fink, Almon H. Millard, Reuben Haines, Joseph Otis, John Comstock, Asahel Smith, Nathan B. Rogers, Daniel Washburn and James Conkey. In 1820 there were but two or three unfinished log houses upon the whole tract now embraced within the city limits, and not a hundred acres of the land under cultivation.

It was early in 1821 when the commissioners decided upon the exact location of the canal through the mountain ridge, and announced that they were ready to receive proposals for the construction of the locks and the excavation of the canal in the vicinity. Movements for the commencement of the village followed immediately. The owners of the land at once made arrangements for the sale of village lots. Among the land proprietors at this time was Otis Hathaway, who in the spring of this year employed Jesse P. Haines to survey and map some lots. While this initial movement was yet in progress the question arose as to what name should be given to the embryo village. It was agreed to call a council of the land proprietors in the vicinity to consider the matter. This was accordingly done, and Mr. Haines proposed the name of Locksborough as one that would correctly indicate the origin of the place. Dr. Isaac W. Smith offered an amendment proposing Lockport. The merits of the two were discussed, and the latter finally adopted; and the village had a name, though a stranger would have needed a guide to find it.

This want was in a measure supplied by Esek Brown, who about this time opened his unfinished log house as a tavern. He procured his license at Lewiston, preparatory to opening his house to the public, but to fill the requirements of the law he must first hang out his sign. To meet this demand was not so easy a matter as might be supposed; for, although at that very time he was building, a board of sufficient dimensions for a sign was not to be found on the premises. Necessity suggested invention, and Ebenezer Mix, a temporary guest, taking a door sill, attached to it a basswood bolt, which was planed off sufficiently smooth to inscribe upon it with a piece of coal, "Lockport Hotel, by E. Brown." This was put up between the ends of the projecting logs of the pioneer tavern, as an announcement, if not a guide to the weary traveler, that rest and refreshments could be found therein. This building stood about forty rods west of Transit street, near Main; and being the head-quarters of the canal contractors was for a short time the head and center of the new-born village.

Capitalists, always watchful and ready to purchase where the prospect appears favorable to growth, were attracted to the spot, and the energetic merchant and mechanic, ever ready to locate where there is promise of a demand for their wares and labor, soon found their way to the village site; and before the summer was past log houses in the course of construction could be seen on either hand peeping out from among the forest trees. Morris H. Tucker opened a store during the summer. This was the first in Lockport, and Mr. Tucker gave to the author of the History of the Holland Purchase a graphic description of the primitive state of things at that period. He represents, among other things, that "Jared Comstock and Esek Brown were selling village lots on Main street. Brown's land was cleared from Genesee street to a little north of Caledonia street, and extended from Prospect street to Transit. Jared Comstock's land was cleared from his south bounds to the north side of Niagara street. From the north side of Niagara street the land of Comstock was uncleared; and the land from the head of the locks, around the ravine, embracing all the lower town and extending as far east as the residence of Judge Dayton, was a dense forest." * * * *

" I brought with me from Batavia an old stock of goods, which I stored at Esek Brown's until I could build a store. There was no store nearer than Hartland Corners. When it became known to the women that I had good tea stored at Brown's, no excuse would answer; have it they would, and I was obliged to open shop. In two or three weeks I moved my goods into a new framed store, an imposing building at that time, twenty-five feet square, a story and a half high. Here for several weeks I had no opposition in trade. Soon, however, House & Boughton got their new store finished, and Lebbeus Fish brought on goods from Batavia, and Lockport began to be a place of no little importance. That summer the rattlesnakes were so numerous that they occasioned much alarm to the villagers."

Toward the close of 1821 William M. Bond, a man of speculative proclivities, came from New Hampshire and procured some land of Esek Brown. In glowing terms he represented the advantages and consequent growth of the village to result from the erection of a glass factory. Brown was charmed, and while in this happy state of expectancy Bond obtained his title to the land for a nominal consideration, on condition that the glass factory should be forthcoming. John Comstock was called to draw up the instrument of conveyance, and, contrary to Bond's actual wishes, insisted upon a condition in the agreement making it obligatory upon Bond to erect the factory within a stated period of time, since Brown had given the land for that express purpose. Bond was unwilling to be bound to any time, but the notary's logic could not be overcome and Brown held him to the provision. To get that part of the contract annulled and still retain the land now taxed the inventive genius of the speculator. This was successfully accomplished through a friend of his representing to Brown that the dense smoke and dirt from the factory would ruin the town. Brown was now as much alarmed as he had before been elated at the presence of the glass factory in the center of the village. No other place would do at all for Bond, and Brown, in ignorance of the schemers's plot, agreed not only to release him from building the factory, which he never intended to build, but also agreed to sell to Bond at a low figure another valuable piece of land, which he was desirous to obtain, to end the smoky controversy.

The farm of Esek Brown grew smaller rapidly to supply the wants of the incoming tide of immigration, or at least the wants of the real estate dealers in anticipation of it. A large portion of it was speedily mapped out into streets and village lots, and passed into the hands of Jesse Hawley and John G. Bond, who were associated with William M. Bond, of whom mention has already been made.

Associated with the Comstocks—Jared, Darius and Joseph—were Otis Hathaway and Seymour Scoville, and these gentlemen were interested in laying out and selling lots east of Transit street. Zeno Comstock had purchased the land in this vicinity from the Holland Company, as Brown had west of Transit street, but had conveyed it previous to the founding of the village, and invested in the vicinity of the head of the gulf, a mile and a half to the westward, in expectation that the canal would be located there.

At the end of a year a very perceptible change had been wrought, and the infant village had made considerable advance. The forest in the immediate vicinity, mangled and hacked, bore undeniable evidence of the struggle. Rattlesnakes were becoming less numerous, and the bear and wolf, which had hitherto held almost undisputed sway, were getting cautious and finding more secluded resting places. The deer, too, which had been quite plenty, found their favorite haunts unsafe, and moved with faltering steps and sensibilities awake to the dangers that beset them in pursuing their accustomed pathway, which from the east descended the mountain slope, near where now stands the Douglas Mills. Active and adventurous spirits were not slow in coming forward. The anvil could be heard ringing from the sturdy strokes of George W. Rogers, the pioneer blacksmith. A shoeshop was indispensable, and the want was supplied by Shepard and Towner, and the demand for harnesses and saddles by Elliott Lewis. John Jackson had established a bakery, and the prospect was favorable for an early establishment of all branches of business requisite. The great amount of labor needed in the construction of the canal at this point promised a good field for business until the great work should be completed, and at that time was the most attractive feature in bringing business men forward.

Early in 1822 the post-office was established, but to procure the mail was a matter yet attended with many inconveniences. It was brought from Molyneux's Corners, usually on horseback. This inconvenience was somewhat obviated the next year by the opening of a road through the howling wilderness to Wright's Corners, connecting at that point with the stage route. A wagon then took the mail over this road, or rather through this opening in the woods.

A printing press had likewise been brought forward and set in motion about the time the post-office was established. The pioneer printer was Bartemus Ferguson, but he soon sold his establishment to Orsamus Turner. Mr. Turner, who became the editor of the village paper in August, 1822, observes that at that time the work of excavating the canal was under headway on each of the five rock sections, and that "the blasting of rocks was going on briskly on that part of the canal located upon the village site; rocks were flying in all directions; framed buildings and roofs of log buildings were battered by them, and huge piles of stone lay upon both banks of the canal with a narrow opening to admit the passage of teams over a log bridge on Main street."

As before intimated, people were actuated in a great measure in making Lockport their abiding place by the chance of helping to supply the various wants of contractors and laborers in opening the canal. Many believed that when this work was completed the village, which had been of mushroom growth, would decline correspondingly. But another impetus, more potent in its bearing, was given it in the summer of 1822. In July of this year the commissioners appointed to locate the capital of the county fixed upon Lockport. Two acres of land were deeded to the county by William M. Bond upon which to erect the county buildings. By becoming the county seat, in addition to its other advantages, both growth and permanency were assured.

The public peace was considerably disturbed during the latter part of 1821 by the rows of the Irish laborers, growing out of a demonstration of the Orangemen. On such occasions clubs and stones were freely used as weapons for attack or defense. On Christmas Eve a serious riot occurred, originating from a fight which happened at a tavern kept by a man named Law. So great was the commotion that Captain Howell's rifle company was called out by the sheriff to suppress the rioters. In this affray one man, named Jennings, was killed, and many injured. One man had his skull fractured by a stone which penetrated to the brain. A physician living at Batavia was sent for to extract it, but it was dug out with a jack-knife before his arrival.

MAIN STREET IN 1823.

The advancement which the village had made within two and one half years from its first incipiency, particularly in the amount and variety of business, is faithfully exhibited in the following sketch, prepared for this work by Marcus Moses, Esq., an early pioneer and still a resident of Lockport:

"When I came to Lockport, in the fall of 1823, the greater part of the business doing in the village was on the west side of the canal. On the northeast corner of Main and Transit streets was a small building occupied as a store, and there also William Fox kept a barber shop. Going east from this point, along the north side of Main street, there was one and perhaps two buildings, occupied as stores, before reaching the Lockport Hotel, kept by Samuel Jennings. This hotel was somewhat celebrated, and quite spacious for those days, though but a one story building. Adjoining this, on the east, Dr. Maxwell had an office, and next was the blacksmith shop of Allen Skinner. These two buildings were about where the Judson House now stands. The next building east was the store of House & Boughton, in which the post-office was kept by George H. Boughton, who was the first postmaster. A little further along A. T. Prentice had a small building, in which he repaired watches and kept a small stock of jewelry. From there down what is now Canal street huge piles of stone lay all along the way. Where the Congregational church now stands was a small building used for a tavern.

"About opposite Prentice's jewelry store the canal was crossed by a bridge. This primitive structure consisted of two log stringers reaching from shore to shore, across which were thrown split logs with the bark side up, and was only wide enough for one team. East from this bridge, and on the ground where the Bristol fountain now stands, Alexander Pound kept a meat market. Near this market was a small building in which Judge Birdsell had an office. There was no other building between this and a yellow store kept by William Parsons & Co., which stood upon or near the ground now occupied by the Moyer block. The next was a stone building, a part of which was used for a store and was occupied by Sidney and Thomas Smith. This building is still standing and but little changed. The ground between this and the store of Lyman A. Spalding, which stood where the Farmers' and Mechanics' Savings Bank does now, was vacant and used as a passage way to the locks and to the front of a building which stood on the bank at the head of the locks. In this a grocery was kept, and it was afterward used as an office by Asa W. Douglas, the first toll collector.

"The next building east of Spalding's store was a small law office occupied by James F. Mason, who was county clerk and kept the records of the county in his office; and adjoining that was a store kept by H. Kimberly & Co. On the corner of Main and Pine streets, where the Exchange Bank stands, was a two-story frame building, a part of which was occupied by the canal commissioners and engineers and the residue by Orsamus Turner as a printing office. Up 'the hill' from here, as it was then called, and on the bank of what is now the mill race, near where the Murray block is, stood a log cabin owned and occupied by Dr. Isaac W. Smith. This dwelling was neat in every respect, and in perfect keeping with Dr. Isaac and Aunt Edna. It was built of small logs, nearly equal in size, with the bark peeled off, and whitewashed both inside and out. Who of our old citizens do not remember Aunt Edna, with her checked apron, always sociable and cheerfully smiling as she said, 'How does thee do?' At the top of the hill, where the Hodge Opera House stands, was the residence of M. H. Tucker. The triangular block now encompassed by Main, Market and Elm streets was occupied by the Quakers as a burying ground. Their meeting-house was built of logs, and stood in the rear of the brick block facing Main street. I well recollect attending a wedding there. Two couples were united on that occasion, the parties performing the marriage ceremony themselves.

"Where the American House is was a log building used as a tavern. Timber was standing close about this building, and great stumps were yet in the street. Lyman A. Spalding lived on the corner where the Hosmer block stands. From there down to Pine street, on the south side of Main, not much improvement was made, as it was quite away from the business portion of the village. I well remember Isaac Price having urged me to buy a lot of him about where the Breyfogle building stands; but the location was too far out of town. It was then thought that the business would be done west of the canal. It was about in front of Breyfogle's that I paid my first highway tax. There was a gigantic stump standing in the street at this place, and myself and several others were two days busily employed in removing it. Before the street was graded, the surface where the American House stands was about up to the floor of the stoop on that building, as it is now, and continued nearly level westward to where Breyfogle's store stands, where it was higher than the second floor of that building; from that westward it fell away quite abruptly. Morris H. Tucker had a store about where Simmons & Walter's jewelry store is now. Next east was the "Green store," occupied by Nathan B. and George W. Rogers as a grocery. Adjoining this, Elias Ransom had his law office; and there was Dr. Isaac Smith's office. From there west was a vacant lot enclosed by a stone wall. Then came the "Red store," kept by William Kennedy, who died soon after on a canal boat near Rome, while on his way home from New York. West from the "Red store" was a passage way for teams to the yard of the Cottage Hotel. The Cottage was a log house, of much renown in those days, kept by Joseph Langdon. He always kept a good fire when needed. In cold weather, in the old-fashioned Dutch fireplace would be seen a large back log, and on the andirons a large fore stick, and heaped upon these about a quarter of a cord of wood. The Cottage stood upon the ground where the spacious Ringueberg block now stands. On the corner of Main and Cottage streets Harvey W. Campbell kept a store in a small building, and adjoining that Price & Rounds kept a grocery. The next building was John Jackson's bakery, which did a pretty large business. West of this was Gillett Bacon's grocery; and there were some other small buildings and a blacksmith shop along what is now Buffalo street, but in front were piles of stone so high that the buildings on the opposite side of Main street were hidden from sight.

"On the point of ground between the canal and Main street, about opposite where the Judson House stands, was a stone building. In one part Hiram Gardner had a law office, and in another part a shoe store was kept. In the upper story the masonic hall was first established. The next west was the tin shop of Pardon D. Richardson. A little further along was the Mansion House, kept by Captain McKain. It is now the Exchange, and has been made one story higher, with some other slight alterations. The first court held in Lockport was in the second story of this building. The members of the bar residing in Lockport at that time were John Birdsell, Hiram Gardner, J. F. Mason, Elias Ransom, Harvey Leonard and Theodore Chapin. On the corner of Main and Transit streets, where the Mansion House now stands, was a small bakery, kept by a man named Woodard, and Moses Goble kept a meat market west of Transit street.

"Of those who were residing in Lockport when I came there are yet living here only Lyman A. Spalding, Alexander Pound, Daniel Price, Moses Goble, N. B. Rogers, J. G. Gustin and P. G. Richardson.

THE EARLY TAVERNS.

Judging from the number of public houses that sprung into being in a few years, it would seem that ample accommodation and entertainment suitable to those rustic times could be furnished. It seemed to be settled beyond question that the business would center around the county buildings, and hotels were built in their vicinity in quick succession. On the northwest corner of Main and Transit streets the Washington House was erected in 1823, which continued to exist until 1865, when it was destroyed by fire. On the northwest corner of New Main and Hawley streets the Exchange Coffee House was reared. The house as constructed still remains, but is not used for the accommodation of the public. The name was painted in large letters upon the side fronting Hawley street. The ravages of time have not fully effaced them, and though dim they are sufficiently distinct to be read. The Niagara House of those early days was located on the north side of Niagara street, between Transit and Hawley. It was erected by John Gooding, who came to Lockport early in 1823. The same building, remodeled, is now No. 81, the residence of Mrs. R. J. Cass. On Niagara street, at the corner of Prospect, was the Eagle Hotel, kept by one Holmes. From an uncouth drawing on the sign to represent the eagle it obtained the name of the "Black Eagle."

The Cottage, on the corner of Main and Cottage streets, mentioned by Mr. Moses, was rather peculiar in its style of architecture. The landlord's fancy led him to enlarge his log house for the accommodation of his guests by additions on the ground instead of in height. In this way he kept adding room after room, each built of logs, until it covered considerable ground, and in that view was in fact roomy. It is related that a man on his first visit to Lockport arrived in the evening and put up at the Cottage, which was then very popular. He found his quarters comfortable and highly satisfactory. In the morning the full extent of the structure was before his gaze, and curiosity prompted him to inquire after its dimensions. The landlord, delighted at having so good an opportunity to explain, quickly replied: "My house is fourteen stories, sir." "High?" inquired his guest, somewhat amazed. "No," was the rejoinder, "on the ground."

THE COMPLETION OF THE CANAL.

The canal was opened for navigation eastward from the foot of the locks for a considerable time previous to its completion through the mountain ridge, and a portage became necessary. It was cut across the country to Pendleton, and the freight unshipped and transported on vehicles between these two points. An engine for one of the earliest steamboats launched on Lake Erie was taken over this carrying place on an ox sled.

In the summer of 1825 Lockport was honored by the presence of the "nation's guest," General Lafayette. He was escorted into the village by the committee appointed for the occasion. The Washington House, at the corner of Main and Transit streets, was the place chosen for his reception. A bower was arranged from the door of the hotel to where the carriage would stop for him to alight, and the pathway underneath carpeted with boughs. Every thing was rendered as cheerful and befitting as the primitive times would permit. The citizens of the village and surrounding country turned out *en masse* and collected here, and to their intense delight were introduced to the friend of Washington and his co-worker in the struggle for the nation's independence. The universal demonstrations of joy on the occasion fully attested the people's grateful appreciation of the defender of their liberties. His visit was brief, and at the conclusion of the appropriate ceremonies he was escorted to a packet awaiting him at the foot of the locks, followed by a great crowd of admiring citizens.

While the memory of this passing scene was yet fresh in the public mind, an event long sought and longer to be remembered occurred. Scarcely had the green leaves of the summer changed to the various tints of autumn when the last obstructions to the uninterrupted navigation of the Erie canal were removed. Perhaps no work of a similar character was ever attended with greater rejoicing upon its completion. The mountain ridge was the only place remaining to finish, and all were intently watching for the signal to prepare for celebrating the event. On the 29th of September, 1825, it was announced by William C. Bouck to the president of the board of canal commissioners that the canal would be in a condition to admit the passage of boats on the 26th of October following. The forces were increased on this unfinished part in order to have it in perfect readiness on the appointed day. On the evening of the 24th, the work having been completed, the guard gates were raised and the Lake Erie level was filled with water sufficient for the passage of the boats on the morning of the 26th. The first glimmering rays of the sun on that morning were greeted by the roar of cannon, resounding along the hills and valleys adjacent to Lockport. One of the cannon belonging to Perry's fleet was brought here and fired in honor of the event so full of promise. General Whitney was marshal of the day, and under his direction the procession formed at nine o'clock, marched to the foot of the locks and embarked on boats lying there in readiness for the occasion. The officers and some of the most prominent citizens of Lockport and vicinity went on board of the packet "William C. Bouck," which had been chosen to take the lead in passing the locks. The remaining boats were filled with men and women anxiously waiting to hear signal guns announcing that the fleet had left Buffalo *en route* for the Atlantic seaboard. At ten the signal passed eastward with the speed of sound; the lock gates flew open and the boats, burdened with human freight, commenced the passage. The ascent of this fleet to the Lake Erie level is thus graphically described by an eye witness of the scene:

"As it ascended the stupendous flight of locks, its decks covered with a joyous multitude, it was greeted with the constant and rapid discharge of heavy artillery, thousands of rock blasts or explosions prepared for the occasion, and the shouts of spectators that swarmed upon the canal and lock bridges and upon the precipices around the locks and basin. As soon as the two forward boats had passed out of the upper lock, they were drawn up side by side, and after a prayer by the Rev. Mr. Winchell, an address was delivered by Judge Birdsall. Stepping upon an elevated platform upon the deck of one of the boats, in the stillness that had succeeded the earthquake sounds and shouts of human voices, he exclaimed: 'The last barrier is passed! We have now risen to the level of Lake Erie and have before us a perfect navigation open to its waters.' When his address, glowing with cheering prophecies of prosperity in the future, was concluded, the boats moved westward to meet the fleet approaching from Buffalo and act as an escort in passing through Lockport."

THE RISE OF THE LOWER TOWN.

The work on the canal being finished, the tide of a laboring population, as a matter of course, ceased to flow into the village, and a portion of this class removed to other places, where labor of a kindred nature was in demand. Nor was removal confined to this class alone. There were others who believed that when the State expenditure for excavation ceased, business would decline, and sought other localities.

The idea was erroneous, for besides all the other resources of the village a reliable water power, which had hitherto been wanting, was now supplied from the canal, and was found so valuable that all fears of a decline were speedily dispelled. The village continued to flourish, and so encouraging were the prospects that in 1827 movements were in progress for laying out and building up the lower town, or East Lockport as it was called. Nathan Comstock conveyed three hundred acres of land lying in that quarter to Joel McCollum, Otis and S. R. Hathaway, and Seymour Scoville, who had it sur veyed and a village plat made of it. In advertising it for sale capitalists were specially invited to give it their attention.

It was represented as being a very eligible location, "lying below the locks and the grand natural basin," and in a position highly advantageous for mills and mechanic shops, as well as for stores and dwelling houses. It was further argued that the location was desirable from the fact that although it had been surveyed but a few months, there was already a grist-mill in operation upon it, besides three saw-mills and other machinery. To show why there was such a noticeable disparity in improvements between the two portions of the village it was claimed—and not unjustly—that the improvements in that part of the village about the locks "were commenced and had extensively advanced previous to the completion of the canal, and in a considerable degree were indebted for their rapid progress to the expenditures made in the construction of the locks and the excavation of the rock through the mountain." A full and impartial examination, however, would "exhibit the fact" that the locality was in all respects fully equal and in some superior to that portion of the village above the locks.

Brought before the public with so favorable a notice, some lots were disposed of to purchasers who erected dwellings upon them and made considerable improvement. The proprietors soon after sold out to Lot Clark and others constituting what was termed the "Albany Company." The efforts of this company to make the investment a lucrative one were extremely vigorous. To enhance the value of property in that section of the village and obtain ready sale of lots, it was represented that the surplus water would be brought there and the upper town deprived of its use, a matter which at the time did not seem improbable. The growth of the village would then necessarily have extended in that direction; but in the attempt to carry that project out a contention was engendered which did not very quickly subside. In addition to the controversy about the water power, there was considerable rivalry between the two sections for several years after the lower town began to thrive, lest one should gain more honor or outgrow the other; but as time passed on their territorial limits were brought in close proximity, and they gradually became united in one common interest.

SHAVED BY LORENZO DOW.

The youthful village seems not to have been overlooked by distinguished characters in their travels. Those who could not well go abroad to see curiosities occasionally have their desire in that respect satisfied at home. It was in the summer of 1828 that no less a curiosity than Lorenzo Dow made his appearance and delivered one of his peculiar discourses in the woods in the rear of the court-house. Impelled by curiosity, a large concourse assembled to see and hear him. An anecdote, characteristic of his strange peculiarities, is preserved in connection with his advent in the village on this occasion. It was early in the morning when he took passage on a westward-bound packet near Medina. He was a stranger to all the passengers; but he displayed his eccentricities in such a manner that he was soon a target toward which all eyes were aimed. Perceiving that he was the center of attraction, he represented to his fellow-travelers that he was poor; that he was bound for the West, but was so destitute that he had not money to pay his traveling fare. But he was a barber, and it would be a favor if they would allow him to shave them, as he was in great need of a little money to help him along; and, furthermore, he had an entirely new mode of shaving—he shaved "right and left." He had no difficulty in finding several quite willing to submit themselves to a trial of his new process. Arranging them in a row, he lathered them thoroughly, and commenced shaving a little on each in succession, until the boat reached the foot of the soks; when, having the right side fully completed, he hurriedly disembarked, saying, "You must excuse me, gentlemen, for I have an appointment to preach." As his customers wrenched their gaze from his departing figure, they found to their astonishment that they were shaved "right" surely, "*and left*" in an uncomfortable plight.

EARLY MAIL FACILITIES.

When the road from Lockport to Wright's Corners became in good condition for travel, a daily stage brought the mail and passengers, Sundays included. Sunday travel and traffic were highly displeasing to that portion of the community imbued with "blue-laws" doctrine. They clamored for reform in this particular; but preaching availed not, and "the way of the transgressor" remained unchanged. Other means, therefore, were brought into use to assist in effecting a reformation by this extremely scrupulous class.

Stages were started in opposition, running six days only, and called the Pioneer line. It was supposed by the originators of the measure that it would be a lever of sufficient power to pry over the seven-day mail traffic, as it was termed. A great many of the most prominent citizens of Lockport, however, were strongly opposed to having the mail discontinued on Sunday, and put their objections on record by calling a meeting to remonstrate against it. It was held on the 9th of December, 1828, and was well attended. The call, to which a goodly number of names were attached as signers, declared that at the time in question there were within the village four or five hundred buildings of various kinds, a population of about two thousand, and twenty-five respectable mercantile establishments. It emphatically denied that a majority of the business men favored the project of discontinuing the Sunday mail.

Deacon John Gooding was one of the stockholders in the Pioneer line, residing at Lockport, near the intersection of Washington and Gooding streets. The stages of this line stopped there on their way to and from the Niagara frontier. He had stables fitted up for their accommodation, and a blacksmith shop was near at hand to do any work needful in the way of repairing at this point on the route. Mr. Gooding owned quite an extensive tract of land in the vicinity, extending back toward the branch of the Eighteen-mile creek, and from this fact, and the circumstances already enumerated, that portion of the village received the name of Pioneer hill, by which it was familiarly known for a long time after. The opposition line of stages continued for about two years, without accomplishing the object for which they were started, and not proving a paying investment closed up their business and withdrew from the field.

MUNICIPAL ORGANIZATION.

The increase of population was so rapid that it became necessary to have a more convenient system for regulating local affairs, and the village was consequently incorporated. The petition was favorably received by the Legislature, and that body on the 26th of March, 1829, passed the act for incorporating the village of Lockport. The boundaries established for the village under the original charter encompassed an extent of territory quite inconsiderable, compared with the limits at the present time. The original lines of incorporation described a parallelogram. The commencing point was in the center of the canal, under the bridge which connects East Market street with Lake avenue. From this point the line extended sixty chains each way, at right angles with the canal, forming the eastern boundary. It ran westward along both sides of the canal at the distance of sixty chains from it, or parallel to it, as far as the natural basin. The canal bearing more to the south, left a larger portion on the northwest side of the canal westward from this point. The whole distance on either side of the canal was one hundred and forty chains. The parallelogram was therefore one mile and three-quarters in length. It was divided into two wards.

The charter provided for the election of five trustees, a treasurer and collector, two constables, five assessors and five wardens. Three of the trustees were to be elected from the ward containing the greater number of inhabitants, and two from the other.

The first board of trustees elected under the village charter consisted of Joel McCollum, Levi Taylor, Levi E. Rounds, Joshua G. Driscoll and James F. Mason. Their first meeting was at the office of James F. Mason, on the 13th of May, 1829. Joel McCollum was chosen president of the board and Henry R. Hopkins clerk. On the 18th of May following, the board of trustees met for the appointment of officers. Eben Griswold was appointed pound master; Samuel Learned and Luke Draper, fence viewers; N. W. Gardner, surveyor; and George W. Rogers, chief engineer of the fire department. The charter allowed them to appoint any number of firemen not exceeding forty, and hook and ladder men not exceeding twenty. They appointed sixteen men to form a company of each. The firemen appointed were Sylvester Seeley, John Hallock, Amos Bigelow, George Hildreth, Charles F. Mitchell, Washington Hunt, Caleb Kniffen, Alfred R. Benedict, Stephen Bush, Norman Shephard, Samuel G. Hamilton, Stephen Story, George Richardson, William T. Lewis, Saxton Burr and Joseph Pound.

The company of hook and ladder men consisted of Richard Southard, Horace Comstock, Erastus O. Smith, Elisha Heacock, Edwin A. Cooley, William F. Stickney, Sanford L. Collins, John Scarborough, Darius Bucklin, A. G. White, William P. Slocum, Randolph Comstock, S. B. Conley, Jacob Flint, William Pound and Charles D. Woodard.

The massive stone piles along what is now Canal street were not all removed for many years after the canal was finished. In 1831 a portion of the heap near the head of the locks was removed to give place for the foundation of some buildings. The body of a gigantic black walnut tree which had been cut down in 1822 was uncovered and found in a perfect state of preservation, the second log selling for ten dollars. It is said that objections were made to cutting it down, and it was urged that it might remain till the canal should be completed, when a monster canoe could be made from the trunk in which as many as wished could go on a pleasure excursion in honor of the event.

BUSINESS ESTABLISHMENTS IN 1835.

Statistics were prepared in 1835 showing the position of Lockport as a business center. In the first ward was Spalding's flouring mill, with eight run of stones and a capacity for manufacturing one hundred and twenty thousand barrels of flour annually. At the price of wheat at that time it was estimated to amount to the sum of $607,500, and the cost of barrels, expense of labor, etc., $40,000 more. The other manufacturing and mercantile houses in the first ward of the village were as follows:

A wool carding and cloth dressing establishment, giving employment to six persons and an expenditure of about $4,000 annually; an iron foundry, employing a capital of $3,000, and turning out work to the amount of $10,000 yearly; two saw-mills, one doubled geared, capable of sawing 1,500,000 feet of lumber annually, and employing nine persons to operate it, and the other doing about one quarter as much; one turning and machine shop; a sash factory doing work to the amount of about $6,000; from fifty to sixty mercantile establishments, employing a capital respectively of from $1,500 to $50,000, selling in the aggregate $600,000 worth of goods annually; five boot and shoe manufactories, making and selling about $50,000 worth of these articles; a tannery making $30,000 worth of leather; six clothing shops, a hat manufactory, two harness and saddle shops, all of which made and sold about $50,000 worth of goods annually; four cabinet and chair shops, two jewelry shops and various establishments for making carriages, wagons, and blacksmith work generally; a brewery, several cooper shops, a book-bindery and two newspapers, published weekly.

In the second ward there were three flouring mills, the largest of which contained eight run of stones, the next largest four run and the smallest two, making about $1,000,000 worth of flour yearly; seven saw-mills, making in the aggregate about $40,000 dollars worth of lumber;

a cotton factory in operation, though not fully completed; a woolen mill and cloth dressing establishment, doing work to the amount of $8,000 yearly; two distilleries, one furnace and plough factory, a soap and candle factory, an ashery, and a tannery; five mercantile establishments, selling in the aggregate goods to the amount of about $50,000 yearly; two tailoring shops, a boot and shoe factory, a hat factory, a harness and saddle factory and a printing office.

THE McLEOD EXCITEMENT.

Lockport was the scene of much excitement during the latter part of the autumn of 1840 and winter of 1841, in regard to the arrest and trial of Alexander McLeod. He was one of the men in the expedition sent out from Canada by Sir Allan McNab for the destruction of the steamboat "Caroline" during the patriot war. In the affray Amos Durfee was killed, and the grand jury of Niagara county indicted McLeod for his murder. In September, 1840, nearly three years after, he was found on the New York side and arrested upon a warrant issued upon that indictment and lodged in the jail at Lockport. A writ of *habeas corpus* was issued, and McLeod was brought before Judge Bowen, and after a hearing was discharged upon the ground that the indictment was against Angus instead of Alexander McLeod. About two months after he was arrested again, at Lewiston, under a warrant issued by a justice of that place, and after an examination was held to await the action of the grand jury of the county. He was again brought before Judge Bowen, and after a thorough examination was held for trial, but was allowed to give bail in the sum of $5,000 himself, and two securities in an equal sum. Two men were finally found in the county who consented to become his bondsmen, and the bail was perfected.

The release of McLeod in this manner was highly displeasing to the citizens generally, and before he was set at liberty a public meeting was held in Lockport, attended by a large assemblage, to express the prevailing indignation toward his bondsmen. Speeches were made, bells rung and cannon fired. A cannon was placed in front of the jail, and bands of music marched back and forth, playing the "Rogue's March" with vigor. The spirit of indignation was so much aroused that one of the prisoner's bondsmen withdrew from the bond, and although the other remained firm amid the tempest of excited passions, the prisoner was not released.

In February following, the grand jury found a bill of indictment against the prisoner for arson and murder, charging him with having engaged in the burning of the "Caroline" and murder of Durfee. The British government, upon hearing of the arrest of McLeod, demanded his release. While a diplomatic sparring between the two nations was in progress, McLeod remained confined in the jail at Lockport. The insecurity of the jail caused much apprehension lest he might be rescued by his friends, or taken out and lynched by those enraged by the memory of the murderous assault on the "Caroline," until his removal to New York in May following.

During the "patriot war" and the excitement consequent upon the imprisonment of McLeod, Benjamin Lett, who was implicated in the disturbances in Canada, fled across the line and made his headquarters in Lockport, stopping sometimes at a tavern kept in a stone house near Hitchin's bridge, and also making "Our House" a place of resort. This was a hotel standing in the rear of the Exchange Bank, and was then kept by a Mr. Griswold. The building is now used as a blacksmith and wagon shop. In April, 1840, Lett blew up Brock's monument with gunpowder. He was engaged in a number of desperate acts. With an accomplice named William De Field, he fired the steamer "Great Britian" at Oswego. He went to the house of Captain Fisher, in Chippewa, and calling him to the door, shot him. He blew up a lock on the Welland canal and attempted to blow up the locks at Belleville, in Canada. He was finally sentenced to imprisonment and served a number of years, and was at last found dead on the beach at Mackinaw, Lake Michigan. He claimed to have been incited to such desperate deeds in consequence of his two sisters and mother having been brutally treated by two British officers.

RAILROAD COMMUNICATIONS.

The opening of the railroad from Lockport to Niagara Falls, rude and imperfect as it was, did much toward giving an impetus to the business of Lockport and served to encourage further works of the kind. The construction of the Rochester, Lockport and Niagara Falls Railroad cast this primitive line into the shade, and afforded much greater facilities for intercourse and commerce. It was so far completed in the summer of 1852 that on the 25th of June an engine, with a passenger car attached, passed over it for the first time. It was only an excursion, for the purpose of inspection on the part of the directors and others interested in the road; but the screech of the locomotive whistle and approach of a train from the east, hitherto without communication of this kind, produced quite a stampede among the citizens of the village. It was hailed as a harbinger of deliverance from isolation and confinement—for the old line to the Falls had suspended operations nearly a year before. The old road ran some distance upon East Market street before crossing the canal, and the business men in that vicinity were glad that they were no longer molested by the terminus of a railroad in their midst. It had driven trade away, in consequence of the liability of horses to become frightened by the presence of cars in motion. When the last trip had been made, the down-towners, as they were called, demonstrated their joy by illuminating the streets with bonfires, anticipating that a return of trade would follow. The first cattle train passed over this road for New York on the 8th of September, 1852, and before the close of the year the receipts on the road from Rochester to Niagara Falls amounted to upwards of a thousand dollars daily. In January, 1852, the branch from Lockport to Buffalo was completed, and trains commenced running on it. These facilities brought Lockport to the notice of capitalists from abroad, who were seeking favorable localities to invest their money and engage in business, and many of them availed themselves of the advantages it offered. This proved beneficial in a high degree in various ways. The tillers of the soil in the rural districts found a more ready sale and ample remuneration for the products of their labor, and real estate was enhanced in value, both in the village and the surrounding country.

GENERAL SCOTT IN LOCKPORT.

In the autumn of 1852 General Winfield Scott, whose valuable military services on the Niagara frontier and elsewhere in fighting the nation's battles had rendered his name familiar in every household, made a visit in Lockport. He came from the Falls on the morning of October 14th over the new railroad, which had been in operation but a few months. His coming had been duly heralded, and thousands of citizens had assembled at the depot awaiting the arrival of the train. Unusual interest was manifested from the fact that it was almost upon the eve of a Presidential election, and Scott was one of the candidates. As the train approached the station its rattling noise was drowned by the shouts of the multitude and the roar of artillery. A carriage was awaiting the illustrious passenger, and accompanied by a committee of welcome he proceeded to the American Hotel, around which was a surging sea of humanity eager to get a sight of the honored veteran. Upon the balcony of the hotel he was introduced to the citizens of Lockport by Hon. T. T. Flagler. Great changes had indeed been wrought since he had periled his life in repelling the enemy upon the Niagara frontier. The canal was only an enterprise contemplated in the future, and Lockport was an unbroken wilderness. He had been called to the frontier during the "patriot war," but happily it proved through his discretion a bloodless campaign. The onward march of progress in this vicinity was strongly impressed upon his mind, as his remarks to the crowd plainly indicated. The canal that had been drilled through the stubborn rocks he alluded to as a monument of lasting fame. It was doubtless pleasing to his memory to review the scene so replete with evidences of prosperity, when in his earlier days he had seen it in nature's mould, untouched by the hand of civilization. Such may be readily inferred from his remark that "the rapid changes which seem to mark your onward progress are truly astonishing. Indeed, to know and appreciate your position it would seem necessary to pay you a visit every few years."

A number of old soldiers who had been with him on the battle field were present on the occasion, and the general received them in the drawing-room of the hotel. Among the number was Major Mallory, then a resident of Lockport. He was an aged veteran who had done service in the Revolutionary war under Washington. He was at the battle of Chippewa, where he was severely wounded. He was so old and infirm at the time of Scott's tour that he was unable to walk, and was carried into the room by his friends. He died a few months later, carrying to his grave the scars from his wounds received at Chippewa.

General Scott remained but a few hours in Lockport, but before taking his departure rode through the principal streets of the village, and halting at the Union School he made a short address to the teachers and pupils, and then repaired to the depot and resumed his journey eastward.

RECENT EVENTS.

The immense business carried on through the canal soon caused it to become taxed beyond its capacity, and made enlargement a necessity. Only ten years had elapsed since its completion ere measures were adopted by the Legislature for the performance of the work as fast as advisable. This was not fully completed until nearly a quarter of a century after. The rebuilding of the locks and excavating through the rocks at Lockport gave employment to a great amount of labor, and beneficial results to the business prosperity of the village.

The village was visited with a destructive fire on the night of the 2d of November, 1854. The fire commenced in a building a few rods west of the Judson House. It spread rapidly, and within a few hours a great number of buildings were swept away by the destructive element. This was the most extensive and disastrous conflagration that ever occurred in Lockport. On the following day might be seen the blackened walls and smouldering remains of three hotels, eighteen stores, two churches and a large number of other buildings. The loss was severe, but notwithstanding the discouraging outlook the debris was soon removed and the cheerless scene enlivened by men employed in erecting other structures upon the same foundations.

In 1865 Lockport became a city. The legislative act incorporating it as such took effect on the 11th of April of that year. The city was divided into four wards. The officers elected by ballot under the provisions of the charter consist of a mayor, clerk, police justice, treasurer, tax collector, superintendent of streets, one chief and two assistant engineers of the fire department; and in each ward two aldermen, a supervisor, three inspectors of election, one constable, assessor, poor master, and fire warden. These officers were to be elected annually in the years succeeding 1865, on the second Tuesday in April; the mayor and aldermen constitute the common council.

Benjamin Carpenter was the first mayor of the city. He was elected in 1865, and re-elected in 1866. James Jackson, jr., was elected in 1867, and re-elected in 1868. Albert F. Brown was elected in 1869, John Van Horn in 1870, Origen Storrs in 1871, Elisha Moody in 1872 Peter D. Walter in 1873, John H. Buck in 1874, Freeman H. Mott in 1875, and re-elected in 1876, Hiram D. McNeil in 1877, and Richard B. Hoag in 1878.

The census of 1875 showed a population of 12,553 in the city of Lockport alone. Its progress has been interesting in the past, and its steady and constant growth makes the prospect in the future flattering.

THE PRESS OF LOCKPORT.

Lockport is well supplied with the means for the diffusion of general knowledge. The large and fully equipped printing establishments would be creditable to a city of much greater population. This fact furnishes a correct criterion of the amount of business performed, as well as of the enterprising spirit of the citizens. The press chronicles the events through successive years, a comparison of which in local affairs indicates the progress made. When only a small hamlet had sprung into existence at Lockport, there could be found the printing press, its type busily clicking to the echo of the woodman's axe in the receding forest. In the newspaper every event is recorded and every change noted, so that in its files the history of the locality is embodied and preserved. Since the first printing press was established a great improvement has been made in the art, as well as in the facilities for obtaining the news for general diffusion. At that time there were no telegraph wires over which news could be conveyed in advance of time itself, nor was there yet a railroad in the land. Intelligence of events in distant parts of the country would be a month old on its reception. The dingy impressions received from the old Ramage press (inked by sheep skin balls), upon the diminutive weekly sheets, compared with the issues of the present time, display a wondrous change and improvement.

Now, eight-column folios are issued daily, each number replete with items from foreign shores, and circulated through the land through the agency of the fleeting locomotive. It was fortunate for Lockport that in its infancy it had an editor of undoubted ability. The pioneer paper, soon after it had been started, passed into the hands of Orsamus Turner, who conducted it and was connected with the press of Lockport the greater part of the time until his death, which occurred March 21st, 1855. It was in his printing establishment that a fortuitous incident occurred worthy of being recorded for all time. It was here, in a remote village, that the first composition roller seen in this country was made and used. Previous to this occurrence, balls covered with sheepskin were used. This process of inking the form was slow and toilsome. A man used these balls, to which a short handle was attached, to place the ink on the type, and the impression was made by a hard pull of the arm. The introduction of the composition roller, now universally used, was altogether accidental. An itinerant from across the Atlantic came along one day, and reported that a great improvement had been made in the "old country" in inking the form by means of the composition roller; and under his direction the first in this country was made and used, and their utility discovered.

The *Niagara Democrat* was the first newspaper published in Lockport, and also the first in Niagara county. It was started at Lewiston in 1821 by Bartemus Ferguson. During the ensuing winter the printing materials were purchased by some of the enterprising citizens of Lockport, and together with the editor were removed to the latter village. William Carney was engaged to transport the press and accompaniments. The venerable pioneer is still living to relate the difficulties under which he labored in the undertaking. The road was in a most wretched condition. Deep mud was prevalent, in a partially frozen state, and such obstructions as logs, brush and stones were plentiful. With two yoke of strong oxen and a heavy lumber wagon he was enabled, after two days of diligence and hard labor, to accomplish the task. On his arrival the interested inhabitants gathered about to gaze on the scene as if a caravan was approaching. The advent of this old printing press marked an important era. The name of the paper was changed to *The Lockport Observatory*, and a copy of the first issue was preserved by M. H. Tucker and subsequently deposited in the corner-stone of Grace Church. Though but a diminutive weekly sheet it was for many years far from self-sustaining, and relied on voluntary contributions to a considerable extent for support, as did succeeding newspapers for many years. It was removed from Lewiston in consequence of the citizens not contributing to its support liberally enough to guarantee its continuance at that place. In August, 1822, it passed into the hands of Orsamus Turner, who became editor and publisher. In his own language, Lockport was at that time "as rough and primitive a village as any, perhaps, that ever gloried in an old Ramage press and a few fonts of worn out type." In 1823 another paper was started at Lewiston, bearing the name of *The Lewiston Sentinel*, and published by James O. Daily. It soon passed into the hands of Oliver Grace, who removed it to Lockport and changed the name to *The Niagara Sentinel*. In 1828 it was united with the *Lockport Observatory* and issued as the *Democrat and Sentinel*. The same year it was purchased by Peter Besancon, who changed the name to *The Lockport Journal*. In 1829 it was re-christened and took the name of *The Lockport Balance*. In 1833 the *Lockport Gazette* was started by Pierpont Baker, and in the following year the two were united and issued as the *Lockport Balance and Gazette*. It afterwards was divested of the *Gazette* part of its name, resumed the name of *The Lockport Balance* and was published by D. C. Coulton for a short period, and subsequently by T. H. Hyatt. Orsamus Turner in 1835 started a new paper, giving it the name of *The Niagara Democrat*, and in 1837 purchased the *Lockport Balance*, united the two in one and issued it as the *Niagara Democrat and Lockport Balance*. It, however, soon resumed the name of *The Niagara Democrat*. Mr. Turner remained editor and proprietor until 1839, and during part of the time he was connected with it, it was published at the lower town, between which and the upper town there was a rivalry for village honors.

In 1839 the *Niagara Democrat* passed into the hands of Thomas P. Scovell, who owned and published it until 1846, when it was transferred to Turner & McCollom, who were succeeded by Ballou & Campbell, and then the paper again passed into the hands of Orsamus Turner, who published it until his death. John Campbell then became proprietor of the paper and published it until

MOSES C. RICHARDSON.

JOURNAL BUILDING, LOCKPORT, N.Y.   RES. OF JOSEPH A. WARD, COR. HIGH & WATERMAN STS. LOCKPORT, N.Y.

1858, when it was purchased by A. S. Prentiss. Mr. Prentiss had since 1853 been publishing a free advertising paper called the *Lockport Daily Advertiser*. After purchasing the *Niagara Democrat*, he enlarged the *Advertiser*, and continued its daily publication, and the weekly was called *The Democrat and Advertiser*. In 1860 it was conveyed to Gaylord J. Clark. On the 9th of April, 1859, the *Lockport Chronicle* was established by S. S. Pomroy & Co.; it was a weekly paper. In the following year the *Lockport Daily Union* was issued from the same office. In 1862 a consolidation of the above papers was effected. A compromise upon the various nomenclatures was also agreed upon, the daily taking the name of *Lockport Daily Union* and the weekly that of *The Niagara Democrat*, which names they still retain. Pomroy & Chamberlain became editors as well as owners when they were united. In 1863 Mr. Pomroy retired from the paper, and in the ensuing year Chamberlain sold his interest to Henry E. Shaft, who had commenced the publication of *The Lockport Bee*, a daily and weekly paper, which was merged in the *Union and Democrat*. Mr. Shaft did not long remain connected with it. It was then under the management of Wolcott & Chamberlain until June, 1867, when Chamberlain sold his interest to R. M. Skeels, who in 1870 bought Wolcott's interest likewise. On the 1st of October, 1871, William C. Olmsted became a partner, the firm name being R. M. Skeels & Co. On October 1st, 1876, a stock company was formed, with John Hodge as president and James Jackson, jr., treasurer, which remains unchanged at the present time. The paper is under the editorial management of R. M. Skeels.

On the 1st of May, 1827, M. Cadwallader commenced the publication of a weekly paper to which he gave the name of *Niagara Courier*. It was subsequently published by George Reese, who, however, remained connected with its publication but a short time. T. T. Flagler became his successor, and under his able management it gained very much in public estimation and attained to a susbtantial and permanent basis. He was its editor until 1843, when it was purchased by Crandall & Brigham. It subsequently passed into the hands of David S. Crandall, who in 1847 issued a daily, the first of a permanent character in Lockport. In 1851 both daily and weekly were purchased by C. L. Skeels and John Williams. In 1846 Robert H. Stevens commenced the publication of *The Niagara Cataract*; he continued it for a short period and then sold to Humphry & Fox, and subsequently the paper was bought and continued by Charles J. Fox until June, 1851, when M. C. Richardson, who as associate editor had during the three preceding years been connected with the *Courier*, having determined to start a free soil Whig paper, purchased the material of the *Niagara Cataract* of Mr. Fox for that purpose. The material consisted of only a hand press and some worn out type, but Mr. Richardson speedily added new type, and in the latter part of the same month issued the first number of the *Lockport Journal*. It was published weekly, and within three months attained to a circulation and patronage unprecedented by any weekly paper which had ever been published in the county. In 1852, in compliance with the solicitations of many friends, Mr. Richardson commenced the publication of the *Lockport Daily Journal*. The population of the village at that period was not large enough to warrant a pecuniary success, and for about three years it was unremunerative. It required much hard work and money sacrificed before it returned an adequate compensation for the labor bestowed upon it, and during these years it was customary for the proprietor to work assiduously from twelve to sixteen hours each working day throughout the year, thus carrying a burden which with larger receipts would have been shared by two or three persons. In 1852 Cornelius Underwood, an experienced printer, but destitute of capital, became a partner in the business. The largely increased expenditure arising from the publication of the daily rendered the prospect gloomy to Mr. Underwood, dissolution was effected by mutual consent, and Mr. Richardson again became the sole proprietor. In 1863 he purchased at the expense of eight hundred dollars a power press, the first ever introduced in Lockport, and placed it in the establishment. It was run by means of a crank turned by hand, as the office at the time in question could not afford the expenditure for steam power. In November, 1854, the building in which the *Journal* was located caught fire, and although the flames were extinguished the printing material was mostly destroyed. Of the insurance only about five or six hundred dollars were realized. The office was then in the second story of No. 9 Main street. Not disheartened by the disaster the proprietor ordered more type, and issued the *Journal* again; occupying part of the second and all of the third story of a building owned by John Alexander, on the ground where Breyfogle's store now stands. New and more valuable presses were obtained in due time, and by means of economy and vigilance the establishment became prosperous and profitable.

As before stated, the *Niagara Courier* was purchased in 1851 by Skeels & Williams. In the same year S. S. Pomroy became editorially connected with it, and in 1855 became its proprietor. In 1857 John G. Freeman took an interest in its publication, and it was issued under the firm name of Pomroy & Freeman; the latter subsequently became the sole proprietor. The *Courier* and the *Journal* politically were now occupying a similar position, and the friends of each urged the union of the two papers as a measure of political harmony and success. Accordingly, in February, 1859, the two were united under the proprietorship of Richardson & Freeman. The daily was issued as the *Journal and Courier* and the weekly as *The Niagara Intelligencer*. The name of the weekly was afterward changed to *The Niagara Journal* and that of the daily to *Lockport Daily Journal*, which names they still retain. In 1861 Mr. Freeman sold his interest to A. Holly, who within a few months in turn sold to James W. Barker. On the night of May 3d, 1863, the building occupied by the *Journal* caught fire in the basement, filling every room before discovered with a dense, suffocating smoke, rendering an entrance into any part of it impracticable. Soon a lurid flame arose, and in a few minutes extended from basement to roof. The means at command were inadequate to extinquish the flames, the Holly system not then being in operation. All of the books, paper, presses, and the large accumulation of material were totally destroyed. The loss was about $9,000, only one-third of which was covered by insurance, aside from accounts, papers, etc. After this unfortunate event, the proprietors purchased the lot on which the *Journal* building now stands of George W. Rogers, on time, the payments extending ten years; but occupied temporarily as a publishing and business house the dwelling in which Mr. Rogers and family for many years had resided. They purchased type and presses, and the *Journal* was soon again in full operation, with a larger patronage than ever before. In July, 1864, Mr. Barker sold his interest to M. C. Richardson, who continued to run the establishment as sole proprietor, occupying the same quarters until 1869, when he erected the building in which the *Journal* is now published, with its ample accommodations. In 1870 Joseph A. Ward, who for several years had been connected with the Exchange Bank of Lockport, purchased one-fourth of the business interest of the *Journal*, including printing materials, and became the business manager, the duties of which position he has successfully continued to discharge. In the spring of 1871 Willard A. Cobb, who for several years previous had been proprietor of the *Dunkirk Journal*, purchased of Mr. Richardson a one-fourth interest in the business, material, etc., and became associate editor, Mr. Richardson retaining the other half interest in the *Journal* office and all of the real estate connected with it. Since the formation of the present firm the presses and other facilities have been multiplied and the business largely increased. It is generally conceded that no city in the State, unless considerably larger and more advantageously located, produces a daily which in the labor and expenditure bestowed upon it excels the *Lockport Journal*.

The Lockport Times.—On the 1st of January, 1871, *The Lockport Times* was started by the Lockport Publishing Company. It was issued as a weekly only until April of the same year. *The Morning Times* was then issued daily from the same office. It was under the editorial management of John Ransom until July 1st, 1871, at which time S. S. Pomroy took that position. Mr. Pomroy was thus connected with the paper until May, 1873, when he withdrew and was succeeded by J. H. Murphy. In October, 1875, S. S. Pomroy again became the editor, and continued as such until the 1st of May, 1878, when E. W. Gantt took the editorial management of the *Times*, and he still holds that position.

The Catholic Visitor was started on the 7th of July, 1875, at No. 311 East Market street, by Wilber Brothers. When its publication was commenced it was only a small two-column paper. At the end of six months it was enlarged to four columns. In about a year from the time the first number was issued the paper was again enlarged, taking its present size, which is five columns and double its original length. It is published on Wednesday of each week.

The *Lock-City News* is a five-column weekly newspaper, published in the same office with the *Catholic Visitor*. The first number of the *News* was issued on the 29th of September, 1877. It is published every Saturday by Joshua Wilber, and occupies the position of an independent newspaper, replete with current news and a variety of local events and incidents.

Two other newspapers have been started in Lockport and existed for a short period, whose history is disconnected with those of the present and consequently not mentioned in connection with them. The first bore the name of *Priestcraft Exposed*. It was an anti-masonic journal, published from 1828 to 1830 by Lyman A. Spalding. The other was started in 1837, during the "patriot war" excitement, by T. P. Scoville, and was called *The Frontier Sentinel*. They sprang into being by dint of circumstances then existing, and when the cause needed no further defense they dropped out of existence.

EARLY SCHOOLS.

The first school was taught within the limits of what is now the city of Lockport in 1821. The pioneer settlers in the vicinity, feeling the need of a school, made use of the Friends' meeting-house for a school-room until other accommodations could be obtained. The first teacher was Miss Pamelia Aldrich. The rapid increase of population which followed immediately after that date made it necessary to provide for a district school. A district was set off, but there was yet no school building. This deficiency was for a time supplied by R. L. Wilson, who in the fall of 1822 erected at his own expense a log building near where the Free Methodist church now stands. The trustees made him the proposition to open a school on subscription, which he accepted. He taught by the quarter and was furnished with board and fuel, receiving a stipulated sum per scholar. In 1823 David Nye erected a building which he used for a private school a short time, and then sold it to Charles Hammond, who continued to use it for the same purpose.

The first meeting of the school commissioners after Lockport was set off as a town was on the 17th of April, 1824. School district No. 1 was formed, extending over a large tract of territory on the west side of the canal, and on the 19th of August following school district No. 2 was formed, embracing an extent equally large on the east side of the canal. In 1825 the public money for support of the schools was first distributed in the town. The total number of scholars at that time was 542, and the amount drawn $132.49. The two districts formed in 1824 as before stated were variously sub-divided, until in 1848, when the Union school system was adopted, the number of districts had increased to seven in the city.

THE WATER POWER OF LOCKPORT.

The supply of water which could be employed as an agent for driving machinery was scanty previous to the completion of the Erie Canal. The branch of Eighteen-mile creek which meanders in a northwesterly direction through the city offered the only facility, and that in dry weather dwindled to such insignificance as to be for the most part unreliable. The surplus water, or water that could be spared from the canal and used in propelling machinery without injury to navigation, was a matter that had not been overlooked by the canal commissioners. Where its use was practicable the result would be beneficial in numerous ways. It would not only bring a revenue to the State from the sale of the surplus water along the line of the canal, but would give growth to villages at such points and thereby an increase in commerce.

By an act of the Legislature passed on the 20th of April, 1825, the canal commissioners were authorized to advertise and sell the surplus water where practicable to the highest bidder. The water is drawn from Lake Erie to supply the lower or Genesee level, extending from the foot of the locks to Montezuma, a distance of more than one hundred miles, and in order to do this it is necessary to pass a large quantity around the locks at Lockport. This was a well known fact, yet fears were entertained that this water privilege would be of but little value. It was thought it would be so affected by the working of the locks that it would be irregular and consequently unreliable. Darius Comstock was owner of the land around the locks and canal basin when the water power was advertised for sale. It appears that he entertained such an impression, from the fact that his bid for the use of the water was only fifty dollars; and a few days previous to the completion of the canal he sold all the land on the southeastern side of the canal, extending along Pine street to the passage way which now leads to the Spalding mill, and thence along the brow of the hill back of Main street and as far down the canal as the present railroad bridge, excepting a small reservation, for the consideration of $3,500. Lyman A. Spalding was the purchaser, and shortly after that transaction gave $2,000 to obtain the reservation. When the canal was finally opened for navigation and the water for the first time passed around the locks in the race prepared for it and discharged into the basin near where the Spalding mill now stands, it was at once perceived that its value was far greater than had been anticipated. Immediately after Spalding commenced removing the earth preparatory to laying the foundation of a flouring-mill, and the water in the race was first made use of by him to wash down the earth and carry it into the canal basin.

On the 25th of January, 1826, the canal commissioners on the part of the State conveyed to William Kennedy, of Lockport, and Junius H. Hatch, of New York city, the surplus water, as it was termed, at the village of Lockport. It was to be sold to the highest bidder, and Mr. Kennedy put in a bid of $200 per annum, which being the highest the lease was accordingly executed under his directions to himself and Hatch. The conditions of the lease put them in possession of all the water that could be spared from the canal without injury to navigation or to the canal itself. The water thus leased was to be discharged into the lower or Genesee level, so that virtually no water would be diverted from the canal by the lessees. In the winter of 1825-6, Lyman A. Spalding built a saw-mill a few rods below where the Pound Manufacturing Company's buildings are now located, and constructed out of timber a conduit extending from the canal race to it. About the same time Jabez Pomeroy and William Bass erected a building near the Spalding flouring mill, which they used for carding wool and dressing cloth. These buildings were both in operation in the summer of 1826, and were the first in which machinery was propelled by the water taken from the canal.

When the real value of the water power was fully demonstrated its control was an object of strong competition. The efforts put forth to secure this prize in a few years afterward resulted in a spirited controversy between the parties concerned. A large flouring mill had been erected by Lyman A. Spalding, depending upon the water from the canal to run it. He had also purchased the land on the opposite side of the canal, which left no way open for conducting the water around the locks except through his premises. In the meantime, that part of Lockport known as the lower town had been laid out into village lots and sold to parties anxious and determined to get control of the surplus water, and convey it there in such a manner as to deprive that portion of the village in the vicinity of the canal basin of it to a considerable extent. But a formidable obstacle in perfecting this design was presented in the fact that the land through which it must be conducted was owned by Mr. Spalding, with whom the lower town proprietors could not agree upon terms of purchase.

In 1829 the lease from the State for the surplus water passed from the original holders into the hands of what was known as the Albany Company. This company by purchase had become the proprietors of more than half of the lower town. One of the canal commissioners was an interested party in the transactions, which made affairs still more difficult to adjust in a pacific manner. To render the real estate investment at the lower town remunerative, it was necessary to convey the surplus water there to use in driving machinery. The lease conferred the right to the use of the water as it fell from one level to the other, without land or right of way. The lessees now wished to take the greater part of the water to the lower town, and in their efforts to obtain a right to take it through the land belonging to Mr. Spalding were aided by the canal commissioners. One of the commissioners was directly interested, and coercive measures were introduced. An order was granted by them putting the sole control of the canal and locks at Lockport into the hands of the lessees, and regardless of protest a party of men were set to work to cut a ditch along the side of the canal. The citizens, indignant at the proceedings, assembled and drove them away. When the canal closed for the winter in 1829 the water was turned out of the race and through the locks by order of the commissioners. This of course stopped the mills. Hostile feelings which had been engendered continued, and the water was forced through the locks, to the detriment of navigation when the canal opened in the spring of 1830. This practice was continued through the season, only admitting water enough into the race to run Bissell's flouring mill, to the great inconvenience of the boatmen and lock tenders. In this unhappy condition matters continued until the intervening land was bought by the Albany Company, who paid liberally for it. This ended the controversy, for it placed both the land and water power in the hands of one company, and it was to their interest now to use the water whenever it was required. In 1832 the race was completed as far as the then newly erected cotton factory, now known as the Franklin Mills.

In 1856 Washington Hunt and William Marcy came in possession of the water power, and on December 1st of the same year the Lockport Hydraulic Company was organized, with Washington Hunt as president, Charles A. Morse secretary, and George W. Rogers treasurer. To this company was conveyed the land and all right of way acquired for the construction of the necessary raceways for the passage of the surplus water. In 1857, the enlargement of the canal being considered completed, the raceway was enlarged, to supply the increased demand for water power at the manufacturing establishments erected and prospective. This quadrupled the available water power, and the race has since been otherwise improved so that the supply of water in it is continuous, and ample to furnish with water power many more manufacturing establishments than at present exist. In 1864 and 1865 the company constructed, at a large expenditure, a tunnel through solid rock on the north side of the canal, extending from the head of the locks to the Holly Manufacturing Company's buildings, a distance of one thousand feet, to furnish that establishment with water power, and to supply the city water works. In 1869 this tunnel was extended to the manufacturing establishment of James Richmond. It has been estimated that the various owners of the surplus water since the lease was granted to Kennedy & Hatch have expended a hundred thousand dollars in constructing and enlarging raceways for conducting the water to establishments requiring it.

The supply of water is plentiful, being at all times of the year as much as may safely be permitted to flow unobstructed from the harbor at Buffalo. There is a lockage fall at Lockport of nearly sixty feet, and by the computation of State engineers it requires 32,899 cubic feet of water to pass around the locks each minute to supply the Genesee level. That quantity is actually required, but to insure safety a much larger quantity is passed around and wasteweirs are provided in case it is not needed to supply the lower level. The waste water finds an outlet through the branch of the Eighteen-mile creek. This stream also furnishes a reliable water power and adds materially to the prosperity of Lockport. Although there are various mills and machine shops in active operation not more than one-fourth of the water supply is utilized for power. The present directors of the Lockport Hydraulic Company are J. H. Helmer, T. T. Flagler, T. N. Van Valkenburgh, B. Holly, N. P. Currier and S. R. Daniels. J. H. Helmer is president, and N. P. Currier secretary and treasurer of the company.

FLOURING MILLS.

The extensive flouring mills at Lockport are widely known and justly celebrated for the excellent quality of flour which they manufacture. The city is abundantly supplied with buildings fitted up for carrying on this branch of business. The facilities for pursuing the business at the present time, when compared with the early days of Lockport, exhibit an immense improvement. There was no mill for flouring grain until several years after the village was founded. To get any work of this kind done, the people were obliged to make a journey of several miles. It was only a part of the year that the primitive mills were supplied with water, and at such times as they were not it was necessary to go all the way to Niagara Falls. An alternative was offered to this long and tedious journey, and accepted by some at the most busy season of the year. This was at a large oak stump, on what is now Saxton street, which was hollowed out on top, and a wooden pestle suspended from a spring-pole horizontally arranged overhead. Into the cavity of the stump the Indian corn was poured, and the muscular arms of the man supplied the power which kept the machinery in motion until the corn was crushed into meal. A mill, affording greater convenience, was erected and put in operation by Otis Hathaway about 1824. It was built upon the branch of Eighteen-mile creek, and stood near the wasteweir, a short distance from where the Niagara mills are now located. Hathaway gave out notice that he would build a grist-mill in thirty days, and take the material from the trees then standing in the surrounding forest. He accomplished the undertaking and ground corn on the thirtieth day. Another tradition of the affair asserts that it was reared in "eighteen days from the stump." The citizens were so elated that the day upon which it was first put in operation a large party gathered at the mill, and expressed their gratitude to Mr. Hathaway, the good-natured miller, by rolling him in the first meal that was ground. In the evening the event was celebrated by a grand jollification, on which it is said that " a caldron kettle, filled with meal from the 'first grinding,' was cooked into mush, placed on an oxsled, and all hands getting aboard were drawn through the village to 'the Cottage,' the jolly crew meantime plying vigorously their spoons in devouring mush and molasses."

This rudely constructed mill, which had caused so much joy, was in a few years eclipsed by one on a much grander scale, erected by Lyman A. Spalding. This, however, was not until the Erie Canal had been opened, which furnished an adequate water power—a thing which hitherto could not be supplied. In the spring of 1826 Mr. Spalding began to erect this mill, on a foundation forty by fifty feet, and carried it to the height of seven stories, which was looked upon as a gigantic monument of enterprise. The ensuing winter it was put in operation, doing both merchant and custom work. Flour was first shipped from this mill in May, 1827. It went on the canal boat "Chief Engineer." The charge for freight to Albany was one dollar per barrel, and the best quality of wheat could be purchased at that time for fifty cents per bushel. The mill ran without interruption until the winter of 1829, when the water was shut off from the race by the lessees of the water in consequence of the difficulty arising about its use. It was purchased by the Albany Company in 1832. Mr. Spalding after selling leased it of the company, and continued to run it as before. It was destroyed by fire in 1840 during the excitement caused by the arrest of Alexander McLeod for the part he had taken in the destruction of the steamboat "Caroline," and it was supposed that his friends were the incendiaries. The site was then purchased by Mr. Spalding, who in 1841 erected over the ruins another mill, fifty by sixty feet and also outreaching the former in height, having a capacity for making about four hundred barrels of flour a day. It was purchased in 1857 by N. H. Wolf, and the same year was consumed, like its predecessor, by fire. The massive stone structure which now bears the name of the Spalding Mill was reared upon the same foundation in 1858. It was run by Harmon & Cope and D. Cope until 1866, when it was leased by A. H. Smith. It afterward passed into the hands of N. E. Moore & Co., who, in April, 1873, sold it to Thornton & Chester, the present owners. Since it fell into their hands it has been fitted up for making flour by means of the latest invention. Within a few years the process of manufacturing flour has been almost revolutionized, commencing with the Haxall process, of Hungarian invention, and perfected by later improvements. By means of the purifying process the quality of flour is much improved, and the amount made from a bushel of wheat increased. It takes considerably longer time, however, to make it, the quantity turned out being from one-third to one-half less than in the same time formerly. The machinery for making the improved quality is quite simple, the wheat being first ground in the ordinary way and the flour separated from the middlings. The former is what has heretofore been known as the best brand of flour. The middlings, which consist of the harder portions of the wheat broken and mixed with the bran, if ground again without being purified, produce only a very inferior brand of flour, and a large portion of the middlings could not be used, except for feed. It was well known that the middlings were the most nutritious portion of the wheat, if they could be separated from the bran. Every attempt to accomplish this had failed, for any bolting-cloth that would allow the middlings to pass through allowed the bran to go also. Now, the middlings are first divided into two or more portions, according to their fineness, which is necessary in order to prevent the blowing away of the finer portions when submitted to a purifying blast strong enough to remove the bran from the coarser parts. The middlings are then dropped upon a shaker of bolting-cloth, and a blast, the power of which is regulated for each grade, is forced upward through the cloth. The bran, being the lighter, is thus raised above the surface of the cloth and carried away, while the middlings s through. Such small quantities of the bran as do go through the cloth are held by the blast on the under side and brushed off by an attachment of the machine invented for that purpose. The purified middlings, when ground in the ordinary way, make the best and whitest flour known. Nearly all the mills in the city are now fully or in part fitted up for making flour in this manner. The Spalding Mill contains eight run of stones and does merchant trade entirely, manufacturing on an average about two hundred and ten barrels of flour per day. The machinery and fixtures are of the best quality, and it has facilities for taking wheat directly into the mill from the canal boats and returning the flour to them in barrels.

On the ground where the Douglas Mill now stands Edward Bissell erected a flouring mill in 1828. It was a spacious wooden building, containing eight run of stones. Mr. Bissell remained in possession of it until 1837. After that it was run by C. G. Jones, W. P. Daniels and others, before being purchased by Douglas & Jackson. In 1853 a pail factory in close proximity to it took fire, and the flames spread to the mill and reduced it to ashes. In the following year the present mammoth stone building was erected over the ruins. In 1868 it was sold to Saxton & Thompson for $50,000. They still own it, and have since purchasing expended about $30,000 more upon it. In 1874 it was fitted up for making flour by the purifying process. It is seven stories high, and contains twelve run of stones. It does merchant work exclusively, and makes about three hundred barrels of flour a day. The wheat is taken into the mill directly from the canal boats by means of an elevator.

The Niagara Mill was erected about 1832 by Henry Walbridge. It contained four run of stones, and was for several years operated by Mr. Walbridge. It was afterward run by A. Torrence & Co. and others until about 1846, when it was purchased by Charles Evans. While in his possession a large store-house was added to it and it was otherwise improved, so as to make it more convenient for conveying wheat from the boats to the mill. It was afterward owned and run by W. W. Bird. On the 31st of December, 1862, Alfred H. Smith, the present owner, came into possession of it. From forty to fifty thousand barrels of flour are manufactured at this mill annually. It now contains five run of stones, doing merchant work entirely, and is fitted up for making flour by the purifying process. It stands upon the north bank of the canal, just below the wasteweir discharging the water into the branch of the Eighteen-mile creek.

On the ground where the Empire Mills stand there was erected in 1826 a building which was first used by Pomroy & Bass for carding wool and dressing cloth. In 1850 Gridley & Brown turned it into a grist-mill containing three run of stones. It was a few years subsequently purchased by B. Draper, who operated it until 1857, when it was destroyed by fire, along with the Spalding Mill. In 1861 J. K. Gridley put up the substantial stone building which is still standing and known by the above name. After its erection it was operated for several years by

Gridley & Glass, and subsequently by Henry Thornton. In 1873 it passed into the hands of the present proprietor, Richard Becker. It contains four run of stones, and has a capacity for making two hundred barrels of flour per day. It is doing both merchant and custom work, and is partially fitted up for making flour by the purifying process.

The Lockport City Mill, immediately adjoining the Spalding Mill was erected in 1863 by David Cope, and like the Spalding and Empire, which are huddled close by it, is a substantial stone structure. In 1866 Mr. Cope commenced enlarging it, but before the work on it was completed he died. It was run for some time after by his executors and subsequently sold to N. H. Wolf. In 1870 the present owners, Messrs. Gibson, Arnold & Little, came into possession of it. It contains three run of stones, and does both custom and merchant work. The capacity is about one hundred barrels per day, and the mill is kept running the greater part of the time both day and night. It was among the first in the city to make flour by the purifying process.

The Pine Street Mill, situated near the iron bridge which crosses the canal at the locks, was built in 1861 by N. E. Moore. It contains four run of stones, doing both custom and merchant work. It makes about one hundred barrels of flour per day. Its advantageous locality adds to its value. It is operated by W. K. Moore & Co., who are doing a very successful business.

The Model Mill, situated on East Market street, was originally a plaster mill. In 1865 it was purchased by B. and N. E. Moore, who converted it into a flouring mill. Mr. Willey a year or two afterward purchased the interest of B. Moore, and the mill was then run under the firm name of Moore & Willey. It was enlarged by them so as to greatly improve its facilities, by extending it to the canal. In 1873 it began running under the present firm of J. H. Willey & Co. It contains four run of stones and does both merchant and custom work, making about one hundred barrels of flour per day.

The Franklin Mills.—The elegant and substantial five-story stone building, one hundred and twenty by fifty-four feet, known as the Franklin Mills, stands on the corner of Garden and Spring streets, and was erected in 1833 at a cost, including the water power attached, of nearly $45,000. It was erected by Seymour Scoville, George Field, M. Fisk, Joel McCollum, Nathan Dayton, Edward Bissell, Samuel Works, James D. Shuler, Henry Walbridge, Lot Clark and others, associated under the corporate name of The Lockport Manufacturing Company, with a capital stock of $100,000. It was operated by them as a cotton factory until 1841, at which time Washington Hunt became the sole owner. In the following year Mr. Hunt conveyed it to the Niagara Manufacturing Company. This company continued to run it as a cotton factory until 1854. For sixteen consecutive years prior to this date the water for power to propel machinery in this factory had been withheld by the State for the enlargement of the Erie canal during the suspension of navigation, which was about half of the year. In consequence of this the business was rendered unprofitable. The machinery was removed and the building and real estate sold to B. C. Moore, Washington Hunt and Henry Walbridge, who converted it into a merchant flouring mill. In 1857 Henry Walbridge and Washington Hunt became joint owners, Mr. Walbridge operating the mill on his own account until his death. After this event Mary H. Hunt, an heir of Mr. Walbridge, became joint owner with her husband, Washington Hunt. In 1864 Hiram Finch purchased the interest belonging to Mrs. Hunt and leased the other half from Mr. Hunt. Mr. Finch rearranged and increased the machinery, giving the mill a capacity of five hundred barrels of flour per day. In 1867 he purchased the remaining half, of the executors of Washington Hunt, becoming sole owner, and conducted the business until 1872, when it came into the possession of Mary H. Hunt, who, in 1878, conveyed it to Ambrose S. Beverly, Nathan P. Currier, J. Carl Jackson and William S. Camp. They are the owners at the present time, and are engaged in refitting for the manufacture of what they term "whole wheat flour" and other food specialties. The water power belonging to this mill, which is rent free, is a quantity sufficient to propel eight run of mill stones, and is taken from the race of the Lockport Hydraulic Company, under a fall of 53 feet. All of the above mills, together with the Cable Mill, which has been in operation about four years, with one run of stones for grinding feed, are propelled by the water from the hydraulic race.

The Farmers' Mill, located on the branch of Eighteen-mile creek, a few rods east of where it is crossed by the transit line, was erected about 1833, by a man named Gooding. It was afterward owned and operated by Ezra Howard. The original building was destroyed by fire, and the stone part of the present building was erected by Elliott & Robinson. It was run by them for several years, and afterward by Lowler & Playter. In 1865 Henry Thornton became proprietor, and in company with Mr. Moody operated the concern for one year; and the three succeeding years it was operated under the firm name of Thornton & Brace, during which time it was enlarged to its present dimensions. It was afterward owned and run by G. B. Elliott, and still later passed into the hands of Mrs. Sarah Elliott. It was purchased by M. E. McMaster, the present owner, early in 1877. It now contains six run of stones, four of which are employed for merchant milling, and the other two for various kinds of custom work. It is fitted up for making flour by the purifying process, and manufactures about five hundred barrels per week for the merchant trade.

In connection with this mill it is proper to state that Mr. Gooding, soon after disposing of it, built another mill just below, on the site of the present paper-mill. When it was first erected it contained but three run of stones. It passed into the hands of John Stahl, who so enlarged it that it had a capacity of seven run of stones. In November, 1852, it was completely destroyed by fire, together with the saw-mill and other buildings attached. The Rock Mills, situated below the Farmers', on the

Eighteen-mile creek, was erected by Henry Thornton in 1872. It contains three run of stones. It does custom-work chiefly, and is still owned and operated by Mr. Thornton.

THE STAVE MANUFACTURE.

The manufacture of staves at Lockport constitutes an important feature in the industrial resources of the place. It formed an item of much importance at a very early period in the settlement of the country, for even at that time they were manufactured for exportation as well as for home use. At first they were made entirely from oak timber, none other being considered suitable. The white oak was used to make barrels and larger vessels for holding liquids, and the red or black oak for flour barrels. The staves were riven or split from the blocks of timber by hand, and this labor was principally done by farmers engaged in clearing up their land. Part of the staves were purchased by the coopers to make up into barrels to supply the home market, and the remainder were shipped to eastern cities. Oak timber was quite abundant, and the stave trade gave the farmers employment through the long winters, and at the same time it enabled them to realize a fair compensation for valuable timber which they were obliged to cut down in clearing their land. It was also at a time when other means for turning the timber to good account were not only inconvenient but impracticable. In a few years, however, white oak became more profitable for use in other ways, and the manufacture of that class of staves which had been made chiefly for exportation almost ceased.

The manufacture of red oak staves continued to be be carried on extensively to supply the flour mills with barrels. The rapid consumption of this kind of timber to supply the constantly increasing demand at length caused some alarm among millers and those interested in the business, and led to inquiry respecting the practicability of using other kinds of timber, and methods of making staves more rapidly than by riving and dressing them by hand. The first method in which machinery was employed was sawing the staves, and was resorted to in 1846 by Lyman A. Spalding, elm timber being used. This mode did not answer the purpose fully, and was finally supplanted by the cutting process, using the knife to cut the stave from steamed blocks of timber. It was first introduced by C. A. Lowber in 1847. His shop stood on the corner of Adams and Van Buren streets. In 1846 W. H. Fursman succeeded to the business. In the summer of that year an article appeared in the *Lockport Courier* descriptive of this branch of manufacturing, in which it was stated : " The machinery now in operation is capable of turning out sixty thousand flour barrels per week on an average, although a larger quantity can be made if required. The staves sell on the spot at $6 per thousand, and the demand for them is always in advance of the supply." It was some time, however, before the strongly fixed prejudices of millers and dealers generally could be removed so as to lead them to look favorably upon cut staves; and for a long time after they began to be used flour of the same brand put up in barrels made of riven oak staves sold at a higher figure in the market than that put up in barrels manufactured from the cut staves. Time and their cheapness, together with the improvements for their adaptation, silenced objection.

Since the cutting process was first brought into use improvements have been made upon it until it has arrived at its present state of perfection. The staves are manufactured from bolts or blocks of timber sawed the desired length. These bolts are put into steam vats and kept there six or seven hours, then taken out and conveyed to the cutting machine, which is propelled with such velocity as to cut one hundred and twenty staves per minute. When sufficiently dry they are jointed and packed in bunches of fifty each, ready for shipping. For several years after the manufacture of staves by cutting, the farmers from the surrounding country delivered the bolts at the mills. By this means they were enabled to realize a considerable income from the elm timber, which was plentiful, and hitherto had been destroyed as often as utilized when clearing land.

Heading was riven out in the same way that staves were, and that practice continued for some ten or twelve years after the mode of cutting staves had been adopted. They are now sawed out of blocks, and the pieces planed and turned by machinery ready for packing.

During the war, and several years after, the business was carried on very extensively, making such havoc with the timber that large quantities of it were brought from Canada to supply the demand. Timber such as could be bought at an earlier time in the history of the business for $2.50 per cord, sold readily for three times that sum. At one time there were five establishments manufacturing staves, which used up in the aggregate about fifteen thousand cords of bolts per year. Although there are but two establishments of the kind at the present time, yet the immense stock of staves and timber which burden for a considerable distance the space between the canal and Van Buren street, is evidence that it is still an important business. These two are both on Van Buren street; that of Fursman & Dunvill was formerly owned by J. G. Norman, who conveyed it to the present owner in 1866. Fursman & Dunvill have since that time used up on an average about eighteen hundred cords of timber for heading a year, and about twenty-two hundred for staves. The establishment of S. D. Hooper was originally started by David Ritson. Mr. Hooper keeps from twenty-five to thirty men employed, and cuts on an average about three thousand cords of bolts into staves, and from two thousand to twenty-five hundred cords into heading.

SAW-MILLS.

The pioneer saw-mill was erected by Zeno Comstock in 1819. It was located on the branch of Eighteen-mile creek just below the brewery of Anthony Ulrich. It was small and rudely constructed, and could not be kept running in dry weather, as the stream failed. It was at this primitive mill that the first machinery of any kind used in Lockport was employed. David Frink erected a saw-mill soon after near the site of the mill occupied by Steele, Wells & Co. These mills cut lumber for the canal contractors, and for some of the first buildings erected in Lockport. That built by Comstock was short lived, giving way to more extensive structures of the kind. That erected by David Frink remained much longer, and the site has continued to the present time to be occupied by mills of the kind, which have supplanted it. It was afterward owned by Warren Saddler, and in 1853 was conveyed to George Wells, who still owns the property, and was for some time connected with the business. W. H. Edwards & Co. occupied it, and were succeeded in 1859 by Edwards & Wells. From 1870 to 1874 the firm name was Edwards, Wells & Hoag, since which time it has been conducted by the firm of Steele, Wells & Co. In 1865 the sash and blind manufactory was erected which constitutes a part of the business. Previous to that time there was a woolen-mill connected with it. The business in the woolen-mill was discontinued in 1860, but the building is still standing. The saw-mill cuts about 400,000 feet of lumber a year, and the number of men employed in that and the sash and blind factory will average about twenty.

The first saw-mill erected after the Erie Canal was completed, giving a more ample water power, was put up in the winter of 1825-6 by Lyman A. Spalding, and stood a few rods below the Pound manufacturing establishment. In 1836 it was taken down to give place to one of much greater capacity, which contained two gangs of twelve saws each. This mill was subsequently converted into a corn-dryer, and in 1866 was destroyed by fire, leaving nothing but the granite wall, the crumbling remains of which still mark the tomb of this once noted structure. In 1828 Edward Bissell built a saw-mill of considerable importance on the ground where Trever & Co's. machine shop now stands. In 1836 there were eight saw-mills in operation within the present city limits, and although some of them were of small capacity they all togethe did an extensive business.

In 1848 a saw-mill was built upon East Market street, near the present city limits, by Stevens, Doty & Pease. In 1850 it was destroyed by fire; in the same year Robert Stevens, of the above-mentioned firm, rebuilt it upon the same site, and shortly after sold to Van Valkenburg & Mack. While in their possession it was considerably enlarged. In 1872 it passed into the hands of James Jackson, jr., & Son, and in 1874 the firm became J. C. Jackson & Co., the present proprietors. About eighteen men are kept in constant employment at this mill, and about two million feet of lumber are sawed out yearly, most of which is boat plank and shipped to New York, Boston, and some even to San Francisco.

About 1855 H. F. Cady commenced building the docks for his boat yard, and about two years later the gang saw-mill near by was erected by him. Thirteen saws may be used at one time, and there are accommodations for sawing plank the full length of a canal boat. About ten years since the mill was enlarged, or rather another mill built immediately adjoining it, and a muley saw placed in it. In 1872 it was still further enlarged, and fitted for circular sawing in addition to the two methods already in operation. The dry docks for building and repairing canal boats are in close proximity to the mill; the number of men employed varies from twenty-five to eighty according to the demand in that line of work.

CORPORATIONS AND MANUFACTORIES.

LOCKPORT GAS LIGHT COMPANY.

This company was organized through the enterprise and influence of James G. Porter, on the 1st of February, 1851, with a paid up capital of about $15,000. The first officers were James G. Porter, president; George Reynale, treasurer; and Joseph T. Bellah, secretary. The first board of trustees consisted of James G. Porter, William Keep, George Reynale, Rensselaer S. Wilkinson, Thomas T. Flagler, Benjamin Draper, Silas H. Marks, Joseph T. Bellah and Stephen Meredith.

The present site, at the corner of Transit and Lagrange streets, was selected for the location of the works, and the contract for their construction and the laying of the pipes was let to Stephen Meredith, who completed the job before the close of the year, and on the night of the 30th of December, 1851, the village of Lockport was illuminated with gas for the first time along the following streets: Main and West Market to Union street, Church street to the railroad, Ontario and Niagara streets from Church street to Prospect street.

For the first few years gas was manufactured from resin. About the year 1855 the capital of the company was considerably increased, the works enlarged and arranged for producing gas from coal. The company has kept pace with the growth of the city, increased the capacity of the works and extended pipes from time to time as the demand required, until nearly fifteen miles of the streets are traversed by them.

The present officers are Thomas T. Flagler, president; Charles Keep, secretary; H. J. Chadwick, treasurer; and Charles F. Shelley, superintendent, who, with J. Carl Jackson, also compose the present board of directors.

MERCHANT'S GARGLING OIL.

In the year 1833 Dr. George W. Merchant, a graduate of a Philadelphia college of pharmacy, a skillful and painstaking druggist of Lockport, after a long series of experiments in the way of improvements upon recipes he had collected, brought out a medicine to be used in the treatment of certain named diseases of the horse. At that time horse power was extensively used in this section, in propelling boats on the canals, and in drawing post coaches over established mail routes. Diseases among the overworked horses being common, injuries, the result of accidents, being frequent, Merchant's Gargling Oil was submitted for inspection and trial to all classes, noted farriers and horse-coursers included. Among those whose opportunities offered an early test of the medicine were

Richard Dale, Esq., and Hon. Hiram Walbridge, the former a Niagara county stock raiser and a graduate of one of the London veterinary colleges, the latter a large owner and admirer of horses. Both gentlemen being well known and highly esteemed in western New York, their certificates gave to the local public, at once, great confidence in the efficacy of Dr. Merchant's discovery. Upon assurances thus furnished, Dr. Merchant at once commenced preparations for the manufacture of his oil on a large scale. An extensive department was added to his mammoth drug store, corner of Main and Cottage streets, and the necessary apparatus put up and set at work. An advertising bureau soon became a necessity and was added, though it was a miniature affair compared with the one now existing. The famous trade-mark, the beautiful picture of an Arab steed under treatment with Gargling Oil, was devised, and not long after all newspapers of commendable circulation, and the better class of taverns and stores, bore a semblance of the Arab horse with a recommend to use Gargling Oil added. From these beginnings, the sale of Merchant's Gargling Oil became extensive, and in 1853 Dr. Merchant found himself worn out, in want of rest, and wealthy enough to satisfy a moderate ambition. In that year he disposed of his business to M. H. Tucker, Esq., Dr. B. L. Delano, and Hon. H. Walbridge. Under the skillful management of Mr. Tucker the sale of the oil was largely increased, demands for it coming from many of the States and territories of the South and West. The adaptability of Gargling Oil to the human flesh having been discovered, it was introduced in 1854. Its sale for such purposes has steadily increased ever since. In 1858 a stock company was organized under the law authorizing the formation of corporations for manufacturing, mining, mechanical and chemical purposes, etc. Mr. Tucker was chosen secretary, and was given the exclusive management of all details of the company's affairs.

In 1860 Mr. Tucker died, and was succeeded by Mr. John Hodge, to whom really belongs the credit of making Merchant's Gargling Oil familiar with the people of nearly all the civilized nations of the earth. He is not only gifted with large comprehension and an unerring judgment, but possesses genius and foresight to aid him in presenting the merits of the commodity in connection with which his name has become so widely and so popularly known.

The changes in the proprietorship of Merchant's Gargling Oil since it passed from the control of Dr. Merchant have been few. On the death of Mr. Walbridge, a portion of the stock wandered for a while, but finally returned to the narrow circle where most of it is now held. The interest of Mr. Tucker at his death was purchased by Mr. Hodge, and Francis R. Delano, Esq., the Niagara Falls banker, holds the interest of his father, the late Dr. B. L. Delano. The laboratory is situated on Market street, is constructed of Lockport granite, is composed of four lofty stories, and is highly finished in a favorite style of modern architecture. Here the oil is compounded, and from three to four millions of almanacs, besides tens of millions of other documents which tell of its virtues, are printed.

The officers of the company, chosen from the most reliable and substantial citizens of the county, are: President, Francis R. Delano, Niagara Falls; secretary and general manager, John Hodge, Lockport; treasurer, James Jackson, jr., Lockport.

POUND MANUFACTURING COMPANY.

The business now conducted by this company was started in 1835 by Lyman A. Spalding, who commenced the manufacture of agricultural implements. About ten years later he commenced making steam engines.

In September, 1869, the Pound Manufacturing Company was formed, with L. Austin Spalding president, and Alexander Pound superintendent. The company is engaged in manufacturing stationary and tug engines, dredges, water-wheels, mill-gearing, etc. From twenty to sixty men are kept employed, and the company does an annual business of from $50,000 to $100,000.

GLENWOOD CEMETERY.

The Glenwood Cemetery Association was formed in May, 1865, with the following officers: President, Joseph Ballard; vice-president, J. H. Helmer; treasurer, J. H. Helmer; secretary, George W. Bowen. The first trustees were Jason Collier, D. M. Mather, Peter B. Aiken, Silas H. Marks, Calvin Haines, J. H. Helmer, Joseph Ballard, George W. Bowen, William B. Gould, Daniel Van Valkenburgh, John Hodge and B. L. Delano. The superintendent, from the beginning to the present time, has been Mr. George Woods, to whom we are indebted for the data from which this article is written.

An attempt was made to purchase land to enlarge the Cold Spring Cemetery. Failing in this project, it was found necessary to open the Glenwood Cemetery, in order to keep pace with the growth of the city. About one hundred acres of land, situated north of the road known as the "old railroad," a mile from the center of the city, were purchased of Michael Wheaton at $80 per acre. The locality selected is admirably adapted to such an object, being only conveniently removed from the business portion of the city. The extensive grounds seem to have been formed in all their picturesqueness by some convulsion or upheaval from beneath, or a violent sundering of masses of earth from the brow of the mountain, to shape the hills and valleys with which they are broken, and which afford an opportunity for the display of skill in improvement which has been seized upon and profited by by those who have had the grounds in charge.

The association secured the services of Frederick E. Knight, the accomplished civil engineer who laid out the Central Park grounds in New York. He planned the drives and general form of the cemetery, and the work was carried forward under the supervision of the superintendent, who directed the workmen in the laying of pavements and the construction of sewers. Improvements are in progress all the time. A large vault was built in 1875, and a fountain is partially completed which, when finished, will add much to the beauty of the grounds. Many fine monuments have been erected, the most conspicuous being those bearing the names of Daniels, Keep, Bowen, Fox, Richmond, Moody, Marks, Hodge and other prominent families of the city. Perhaps the most imposing monument in the cemetery, and the one to which attaches the greatest interest, is that of ex-Governor Washington Hunt, erected to his memory by influential political friends in all parts of the Union, at a cost of $6,000. It is twenty-two feet high from base to top, and all the dies are bronze. The following is a copy of the inscriptions and a description of the devices on the different sides. South side: "In grateful remembrance of the public services and the private virtues of Washington Hunt, who departed this life February 2nd, 1867, aged 54 years. Many friends have united in erecting this monument." East side: "Conscientiously attached to the Protestant Episcopal Church in the United States, he was a distinguished member for the last fifteen years of his pure and honored life." North side: "With eminent ability and patriotism, he successively filled the offices of First Judge of Niagara county, Representative in the Congress of the United States, Comptroller and Governor of the State of New York." West side: Coat of arms of the State of New York in bronze relief, and the word "HUNT" in large, square letters near the base.

Glenwood cemetery is open for the interment of people of all classes, sects and religions, a portion of it being set aside for the use of the Jews, who are seldom buried in the same ground with people of the different Christian denominations. It is justly the pride of the citizens of Lockport. Few cities possess so creditable an improvement, and its founders deserve a permanent memorial upon the grounds so properly selected and so tastefully beautified.

LOCKPORT COTTON BATTING COMPANY.

The manufacture of cotton batting was commenced in Lockport in 1870, by George M. Hamlin, who continued the business until October, 1876, when he was succeeded by the present firm of LeVan & Gritman. The factory is a three-story stone building, located at number 247 Market street. The machinery is run by water power from the hydraulic canal. This establishment is the second in size in the United States, has a capacity of about two thousand pounds daily, employs eight hands constantly, and manufactures all weights of batting from four ounces to sixteen ounces. It was the first factory in the country to put up batting in wooden cases.

LOCKPORT GLASS WORKS.

These works were first established on a small scale in 1840 by Hildreth, Marks, Keep & Hitchins, changing owners a number of times, until 1872, when Alonzo J. Mansfield, the present owner and operator purchased them. A portion of them have several times been destroyed by fire, having been twice burned in the early part of 1878. Their capacity has been enlarged from time to time as the demand required, until the capital now invested is about $40,000, employing sixty-five hands and doing a business amounting to about $75,000 annually. The principal ware manufactured here is druggists' glassware, bottles, fruit-jars and flasks. The works are located on Green street, between Transit and Hawley streets.

RICHMOND'S MILL FURNISHING-WORKS.

These works are located near the canal, on the corner of Caledonia and Gooding streets. The business was established here in 1869 by James Richmond, who, dying in 1874, was succeeded by his nephew, William Richmond, the present proprietor. The building is a substantial stone structure, containing four floors, 60 by 100 feet each. At these works is manufactured a variety of gristmill machinery, including the combined beater and adjustable brush smut machine, Richmond's improved upright and horizontal smut machine, Richmond's grain-separator and oat-extractor, the Empire Conical and the Niagara bran dusters. Pulleys and cables for transmitting motive power long distances are also made here.

The machinery in these works is propelled by a water-wheel, at the lower level of the canal, with which it is connected by a shaft. The water is supplied from the hydraulic tunnel on the north side of the canal. Nine different establishments, such as cabinet shops, printing offices, foundries, elevators, etc., in different localities and each using from five to twenty horse power, receive their power from these works by pullies and wire cable. This establishment employs fourteen hands and does an annual business amounting to nearly $40,000.

PENFIELD BLOCK WORKS.

These works were established in 1864 by Charles R. Penfield, who commenced and carried on the business alone, occupying various places in the lower town until about 1870, when Messrs. Martin and Gaskill became interested in the business, which was somewhat enlarged and prosecuted under the firm name of Penfield, Martin & Gaskill. This firm was succeeded in 1874 by Myron H. Tarbox and Jesse Peterson, who still continue the business under the firm name of M. H. Tarbox & Co., occupying three floors, each 50 x 150 feet in extent, in a massive five-story stone structure on East Market street.

This establishment ranks among the largest of the kind in this country, and manufactures every kind, size and style of tackle blocks and sheaves, making every conceivable part thereof from the raw material. This firm are the sole manufacturers and proprietors of an all-steel, anti-friction roller bushing for sheaves, and also of the "Common Sense" hoisting block, besides many other minor articles, including a patent lock faucet. They have about $40,000 invested in the business, and give constant employment to thirty-seven hands. They have increased and extended their business until they are now known and patronized in every port and inland town in the United States and Canadas and in many foreign ports.

TREVOR MANUFACTURING BUILDINGS.

This establishment, located on Market street, is a four-story stone building, 30 by 75 feet in size, with an addition 40 feet square and two stories high. It was erected in 1858 by Joseph and J. B. Trevor, who the same year commenced the manufacture of shingle, heading and stave machinery, continuing the business until about 1864, when it passed into the hands of the present company, composed of W. W. and F. N. Trevor, who keep from fifteen to thirty mechanics employed and turn out from $30,000 to $80,000 worth of machinery annually. Their manufactures find a market in all parts of the United States and Canada.

LOCKPORT SAW WORKS.

These works, located on Market street above the railroad bridge, were established in 1869, by William Cocker, W. W. & F. N. Trevor, under the firm name of Cocker & Trevor, the present proprietors, who manufacture saws of every size and description. At these works are made all the various kinds of saws used on the machinery manufactured by Trevor & Company, and this may properly be considered a branch of that establishment. It turns out about $15,000 worth of saws annually.

THE HOLLY MANUFACTURING COMPANY.

This company was organized agreeably to the laws of the State, with a cash capital of $20,000, on the 2nd of May, 1859. The original stock-holders were Thomas T. Flagler, Charles Keep, Silas H. Marks, L. F. Bowen, Washington Hunt, G. W. Bowen and Birdsill Holly, with Thomas T. Flagler as president, and Charles Keep secretary and treasurer. They engaged in the manufacture of sewing machines, pumps and hydraulic machinery of various kinds, leasing the two upper stories of the large stone building which extends from Market to Garden street and is now used as a block factory. In addition to the rooms leased in this building, they erected for their foundry the stone building which stands upon the bank a few rods in the rear of the railroad station. After considerable time had been spent in experimenting by Birdsill Holly, a complete plan was devised to supply the city with water for household and kindred purposes, and at the same time serve as a fire protection in such a manner as to dispense with reservoirs or stand pipes and expensive fire engines. This plan was brought into practical use in 1864. Its essential feature is placing appropriate pumping machinery in a fixed position, with regulating apparatus attached, so that the motion of the machinery will be controlled by the pressure of water in the main pipes, which are directly supplied by it, and the velocity of the machinery increased or diminished in exact ratio to the increase or diminution of the draught from the main pipes. The pumping machinery thus responds to the ever varying demands of the community for water, and never fails to produce a uniform and reliable supply, conveying it to all points in the exact amount required either for the daily supply or for extinguishing fires, for which latter use it is taken directly from the fire hydrants.

The Lockport Water Works were constructed by the company under a contract with the city corporation in 1864, and about six thousand feet of pipe were laid and twenty-seven hydrants set, the highest being at an elevation of seventy-two feet above the stationary power. The machinery was propelled by a turbine water wheel under a head of nineteen feet, enclosed by a circular brick building, twenty feet in diameter, standing near the Pine street flouring mill, and which has been kept as a reserve since the new set of machinery was put in. From there a ten-inch pipe leads up an elevation of about forty feet to Main street, a distance of thirty rods, and from there the water is distributed through smaller pipes to all parts of the city supplied with water from these works; the water wheel gate being so controlled by the pressure gauge as to give a pressure if required of two hundred pounds, equivalent to a reservoir four hundred and sixty feet high. When the water works were completed a test was given of their power to fill the requirements of the contract. It proved so satisfactory that the works were promptly accepted by the city authorities.

Three years later the company supplied Auburn with their system of water works, and since that time seventy cities and villages have adopted it, located in twenty States of the Union, the works varying in capacity from one to twelve million gallons of water daily. Among the most important and efficient works constructed by the company were those at Rochester, which were made in 1873. The contract was for two independent sets of pumping machinery, one propelled by steam and the other by water power, either set furnishing twelve streams or both sets together twenty streams, each one inch in diameter and one hundred feet high, for extinguishing fires.

In 1864 the company purchased the triangle formed by Lock and Caledonia streets with the precipitous bank of the canal, at the point directly overlooking the basin and locks. Upon these grounds massive stone buildings were erected, which were completed for occupation in February, 1866. The machine shop is three stories high above the basement, and is 245 feet long by 35 wide; the foundry is 100 by 60 feet, and this and a brass foundry, boiler, pattern, paint and blacksmith shops, store houses, etc., extend over a surface of 41,800 square feet. This manufacturing establishment is regarded as one of the most important in the country, the company being extensively engaged in the manufacture of various kinds of machinery, such as water-wheels, engines, steam boilers, fire hydrants, and pumps for all kinds of mills and factories, which are loaded into the cars at the building and shipped to all parts of the country. The establishment is supplied with tools and machinery to keep 275 men employed. In addition to the work done here the company takes contracts for the construction of water works in various parts of the country. It has a nominal capital of $120,000, with a large surplus, and its manufactured products amount to three-fourths of a million dollars annually.

In 1867 seventeen hundred and fifty feet of pipe were laid down in Lockport in addition to the original quantity, and the number of fire hydrants correspondingly increased. In 1872 the capacity of the water works was enlarged by the erection of a new and more extensive set of machinery, which was placed near the foot of the locks on the opposite side of the canal from the first. The water-wheel of the new set is under a head of fifty feet, and is equal to 240 horse power. Since then the company has operated the water works under contract for the city, and can supply fifteen one-inch streams for putting out fires. There are now more than five miles of pipe laid and upwards of one hundred fire hydrants set.

The officers of the company are Thomas T. Flagler, president; C. G. Hildreth, secretary and treasurer; Birdsill Holly, consulting engineer, and H. F. Gaskill, superintendent.

THE HOLLY STEAM HEATING WORKS.

The advantages already acquired through the agency of steam are so many and so significant of utility that every one is familiar with its wonder-working power, yet the extent of its effective usefulness has probably never been fully ascertained. The truth of this statement is exemplified by the recent adaptation of steam to the distribution of heat in cities. The method of heating by means of steam, which seems destined to come into general use, was recently invented by Birdsill Holly, a citizen of Lockport. He was impressed with the idea that steam might be conveyed from a central point and made serviceable in the heating of buildings, and by practical experiment demonstrated the feasibility of the plan. The result was the organization of the Holly Steam Combination Company of Lockport, in January, 1877, with a capital sufficient to test the scheme in a manner commensurate with the fullest requirements. Pipes were laid under ground to serve as conductors, and a series of experiments solved the problem satisfactorily and proved the utility of the plan. Its adaptation to general use was manifest, for it was found that houses at the distance of a mile were heated as readily as those near the boiler-house, which is located on Elm street. Stock companies are now forming in various cities throughout the country for the purpose of affording heat by steam, and it appears an established certainty that it will ultimately be adopted in general use to as great an extent as gas and water are. The Holly Steam Combination Company of Lockport has for a board of directors: D. F. Bishop, Samuel Rogers, F. N. Secor, J. H. Babcock, Birdsill Holly, D. B. Hall and M. M. Southworth, with D. F. Bishop as president.

BREWERIES AND MALT HOUSES.

The first brewery in the city was established by David Pye in 1832. The building stood on the site of the present malt-house of Mott, Jenney & Company. It burned down in 1835, and was rebuilt by Mr. Pye in the same year. In 1839 he sold his business to Benjamin Draper, removed to East Lockport, and established a brewery there, which was soon afterwards purchased by Mr. Draper. The latter now had a monopoly of the business, which he carried on on an extensive scale till the opening of Gibson's brewery in East Lockport about ten years later. The next brewery was George Stainthrop's. Mr. Draper disposed of his business in East Lockport to Joseph Dunvill, and in 1861 established Draper's Spring Brewery, between Saxton and Transit streets, which he operated till his retirement from the business about two years since. There are three establishments of this kind in the city at the present time, that of J. G. & W. L. Norman, Ulrich's and the Dunvill brewery. The business now conducted by J. G. & W. L. Norman was established by William Norman in 1857. The present firm established the malt-house in connection with it in 1868, and are extensive manufacturers of ale and malt, employing ten men, and turning out about 3,500 barrels of ale and 55,000 bushels of malt, making an annual business of $100,000.

Anton Ulrich came to Lockport in 1863 and engaged in the brewing business on a small scale, with a capital of about $3,000, manufacturing from two to three hundred barrels of lager. The business has gradually increased, until at present he employs eight hands and manufactures about 4,000 barrels, doing an annual business of about $32,000.

Stephen Bush, father of Captain Bush, one of the oldest residents and earliest coopers in the city, made the first beer barrel ever manufactured in Lockport at his shop on High street.

There are four malt houses at present in Lockport, including J. G. & W. L. Norman's, already mentioned in connection with their brewery. The Ontario Malt House, located on East Market street toward the eastern extremity of the city, was originally a saw-mill, which was owned and operated by George Reynolds. In 1866 it was transformed into a distillery, and used as such by Norman Lacker & Co. It was fitted up for malting purposes in 1872 by S. R. Daniels, and in the following year J. E. Mack became his partner in the manufacture of malt and the business was conducted under the firm name of Daniels & Mack. For several months past it has not been in operation.

The Lock City Malt House was erected in 1858 by Humphrey & Jenney, upon the ruins of the brewery of the Lockport Brewing Company on South Transit street. It was for several years occupied as a brewery. In 1867 it passed into the hands of William E. Jenney & Co., and in 1870 it was converted into a malt house by Mott, Jenney & Co., the present proprietors. The structure is built of stone, is about 100 feet square and has a capacity for malting about 60,000 bushels of grain annually.

The spacious malt house on Grand street was erected in 1876 by J. W. Steele and Richard B. Hoag. It is a brick building, four stories high with basement. The two lower stories are used for malting purposes. The floors are covered with water lime and sand prepared for the purpose, and made smooth for handling the barley with wooden shovels. It has a capacity for holding sixty

HON. H. D. McNEIL, EX MAYOR.
LOCKPORT, N.Y.

"NEW YORK TEA STORE" NO. 1, OPERA HOUSE BLOCK, LOCKPORT, N.Y.
HON. H. D. McNEIL, PROP.

thousand bushels of grain, which is handled by means of elevators; these take it to the top of the building, where it is deposited in bins whence it is drawn into the steeping tubs, of which there are ten, holding 1,050 bushels each. It remains in the tubs until it becomes soft, or in a suitable condition to place upon the water lime floor, where the roots and blades of the barley are pressed out. It is then taken by an elevator to the fire-proof dry kiln, where within ten days it is thoroughly dried, and if properly stored will keep for ten years. The power for running the machinery and elevators is obtained from the street water pipes. The water is conducted to a turbine water-wheel of six horse power, which is driven at the rate of one thousand revolutions per minute.

HOTELS OF THE PRESENT.

The leading hotels of Lockport at the present time are the Judson House, on Canal and West Main streets, C. B. Stewart proprietor; the Niagara House, at the corner of Niagara and Transit streets, A. H. McLean proprietor; the American Hotel, at the corner of Main and Locust streets, A. Ten Brook proprietor; the Mansion House, at the corner of West Main and Transit streets, P. J. Collins, proprietor; the Union House, Main street, near Elm, Horace S. Darling proprietor; European, 89 Main street, H. H. Cram proprietor; Bush's Hotel, 34 Main street, W. W. Bush proprietor.

THE HODGE OPERA HOUSE.

The Hodge Opera House is one of the best finished structures of its kind in the State. It was begun in the year 1871, and for over a year a large body of architects, stone-cutters, carpenters, finishers and artisans, skilled in their departments, were employed upon it. The building is located in the angle of Main and Market streets, and marks very nearly the geographical center of the city. It is about 185 feet front by 124 feet wide. It uses three stories above a spacious basement, and is crowned with a tower twenty-five feet high. The basement is occupied by a boiler and heating apparatus, and the first floor by the post-office, stores, Christian Association rooms and a restaurant, with a barber shop in the rear. The second floor is occupied by lawyers' offices, insurance offices and the United States District Attorney's office; and the third floor, and a portion of the second, are devoted to the Opera House, the Common Council chambers and music rooms. The auditorium is located high enough from the street to avoid noise, is approached by spacious and easily ascended stairways, and the corridors are wide, with high ceilings, and present a cheerful finish. The body of the house is 92 by 73 feet, with four proscenium boxes and a parquette, dress circle and family circle. In the center is a dome, 38 feet high, the inside of which is ornamented with beautifully executed figures of the nine muses. The designs are from Raphael. Beneath the dome, and surrounding its base, are portraits of Washington Irving, Clay, Webster, Morse, Franklin, Fulton, Longfellow and Lockport's lamented citizen, Washington Hunt. Under the center of the proscenium arch is the portrait of Shakespeare, flanked on either side by Schiller and Goethe. The effect produced is grand, and the auditorium may be regarded as a model. An engraving of this elegant building may be seen on another page.

BANKS.

The first bank in Lockport was the Bank of Lockport, which was incorporated in 1828. The Lockport Bank and Trust Company and the Canal Bank were organized about 1838. In 1850 the Western Bank was established, and the Cataract Bank about 1862. The Lockport City Bank was incorporated in 1858, and was in existence till 1866. All of these banks have since ceased to exist. The present banking institutions of the city are among the best and most reliable in western New York.

The National Exchange Bank was incorporated as a State bank in 1844 and as a national bank in 1865. The officers are: L. F. Bowen, president; M. A. Nichols, cashier; George G. Moss, assistant cashier; William E. McComb, teller; George T. McComb, book-keeper; Mark J. Lovell, assistant book-keeper. The banking house is at the corner of Main and Pine streets. Capital, $150,000.

The First National Bank.—This bank was organized in December, 1863, and has a capital of $200,000. George W. Bowen was the first president and John O. Noxen the first cashier. The present officers are as follows: George W. Bowen, president; M. W. Evans, vice-president; H. W. Helmer, cashier; J. J. Arnold, teller; F. B. Leonard, book-keeper; E. E. Van Horn, clerk.

The Niagara County National Bank, at the corner of Main and Pine streets, was organized December 6th, 1864. Its capital is $164,000 paid-up, and $34,000 surplus. The first president was Thomas T. Flagler, the first vice-president, Daniel A. Van Valkenburgh, and the first cashier, James R. Compton. The present officers are Thomas T. Flagler, president; Thomas N. Van Valkenburgh, vice-president; James R. Compton, cashier; William R. Chaffin, teller; William W. Blanchard, book-keeper; W. H. Moyer, clerk; Charles N. Robinson, messenger.

The Lockport Banking Association (private bankers), 57 Main street, commenced business April 8th, 1872. The partners in the corporation are Jason Collier, Origen Storrs and Edward H. Collier, Jason Collier being president and Edward H. Collier cashier.

The Farmers' and Mechanics' Savings Bank was chartered May 11th, 1870. Its first officers were elected the eighteenth of the following month. They were Jason Collier, president; Silas Osgood and John Hodge, vice-presidents; Edward Voke, secretary and treasurer; and George C. Greene, attorney. The bank was opened for business at No. 18 Main street, August 1st, 1870. The following December the lot and building now occupied were purchased. The building was repaired, remodeled, and was ready for occupancy in the spring of 1871. There have been two runs on the bank, which did not seriously affect it. Since its organization up to January 1st, 1878, it has paid its depositors $91,382.46, an average yearly interest of $14,058.84. The present officers are as follows: President, James Jackson, jr.; vice-presidents, W. W. Whitmore and F. H. Mott; secretary and treasurer, J. H. Babcock; attorney, John T. Murray. The banking house is No. 31 Main street.

The banking office of S. Curt Lewis, at the corner of Main and Pine streets, is a private bank doing a healthy and flourishing business.

THE STONE AND MARBLE INTERESTS.

Only next in importance to the great water power of Lockport are its inexhaustible stone quaries, which have attracted attention abroad and become a source of considerable wealth to the business interests of the city, the splendid quality of the stone furnished by these quarries having extended the reputation of the place to such an extent that orders are received and filled daily from New York, Chicago and other cities in the Eastern, Middle and Western States. Of the varieties of stone which the quarries in this section supply, Professor James Hall, State geologist, writes as follows: "One of the best limestones in the country in relation to freedom from clay seams is the encrinal limestone of Lockport, which at that point constitutes a portion of the lower part of the Niagara limestone. The Medina sandstone formation, from its eastern extension in Oswego county to the Niagara river, furnishes building stone, in some of its beds, which, in some localities, is good and reliable, while in other parts of the same formation it becomes rapidly disintegrated upon exposure to the atmosphere. It is quarried at Fulton and other places in Oswego county, and at a few points in Wayne county. It has been heretofore quarried on the Genesee river below Rochester; but the more reliable quarries are at Holley, Albion, Medina and Lockport; and again it crops out in the bank of the Niagara river above Lewiston, where it can be worked with facility. The formation furnishes valuable flag-stones in the neighborhood of Lockport."

One of the first quarries was that of George Reynale, who had facilities for sawing stone. The following firms are engaged in the business at the present time: B. & J. Carpenter, William W. Whitmore and Thomas Watson. B. & J. Carpenter, proprietors of the Lockport Limestone Quarries and dealers in cut and sawed stone, commenced quarrying in 1840, and were extensively engaged in cutting stone and laying mason work on the Erie Canal at its enlargement. Their operations have extended to all parts of the Union, the firm having erected, among other buildings, the original Chicago court-house, the jail and county clerk's office, Lockport; two pavilions for the New York State Woman's Hospital, at the corner of 49th street and 4th avenue, New York; the Merchant's Gargling Oil building, Lockport; the administration building and two wards for the Presbyterian Hospital, at the corner of 71st street and Madison avenue, New York; the Manhattan Market building, at the corner of 34th street and 10th avenue, New York; the Lenox Library building, at the corner of 71st street and 5th avenue, New York, and the second Woman's Hospital building, New York.

W. W. Whitmore is the pioneer of sandstone quarrying in this section of the State, and in fact has opened and run almost every quarry on this range between Lockport and Rochester. He first discovered and opened what is called the Rattlesnake Quarry in the year 1830. This quarry covers an area of about one hundred acres, and is properly the whole of Rattlesnake Hill, which received its name in 1834 from having been infested with rattlesnakes, and which is now included in the second ward of the city. Sylvester Mathews was admitted as a partner in the business in 1836. The firm put down a sandstone pavement on the main street in Buffalo, from the Canal to Buffalo creek, which was the first of the kind in use and which remains to the present time, showing conclusively the great durability of sandstone for such purposes. In 1839, on the decease of Mr. Mathews, Thomas Rathbun assumed his interest, and the firm continued as Rathbun & Whitmore until 1854. They operated stone yards in Buffalo, Rochester and Lockport, also shipped stone to Toledo, Detroit, Cleveland and various western cities. On the retirement of Thomas Rathbun, C. H. Rathbun and William Carson bought an interest, and the firm continued as Whitmore, Rathbun & Carson until the decease of Mr. Carson. Gilbert Brady then assumed his interest, and the firm still remains W. W. Whitmore, Charles Rathbun & G. Brady. They have furnished stone for several large buildings, among them the City Hall, the House of Refuge, St. Mary's Hospital, and a large number of churches in Rochester and vicinity, besides furnishing and contracting for street work, a prominent contract having been the permanent platform walk in front of the Powers Block, said to be the finest in the country. They have furnished stone for several large jobs in Buffalo, such as churches, and walks around many private residences, the City Hall, Gleney's buildings and numerous others equally prominent. In 1874 the firm sold out their stone business in Lockport, including the Rattlesnake Hill quarries, to Charles Whitmore. The firm now own and operate one of the largest quarries in the State at Albion. Under the present proprietorship, the quarries at Lockport are turning out as good a quality of stone as those which made their reputation years ago. Mr. Whitmore's office is at No. 26 Market street.

The marble finishing business was established in Lockport during the year 1844 by Norman S. Field, now residing at Albion, N. Y. Mr. Field was identified with this branch of manufacture from the time of its commencement until the year 1875, when his interest in the house of Snyder, Holley & Co., which was formed in the year 1865, was purchased by his partners. Since this purchase the business, in all branches, has been conducted under the firm name of Snyder & Holley.

HYDRAULIC CEMENT.

A superior quality of this article is obtained in great abundance from a portion of the rocks found at Lockport. When the locks were originally constructed the fact that the rocks which it was necessary to remove in immense quantities was capable of making water lime or

cement was not known. The contractors therefore were under the necessity of opening a road through the woods at a large expenditure all the way to Williamsville, in Erie county, to obtain water lime. It was found at that point and was drawn that long distance on "stone boats," as termed in common parlance among farmers. That the rock at Lockport possessed the properties for making cement was first discovered and demonstrated in 1863 by Seth Pierce, who is still a resident of the city. His attention was first called to it by the perusal of geological reports, and after a little time spent in experimenting, he was satisfied that hydraulic cement could be made from the rock at this point. A committee which had been appointed to test the various kinds of water lime or cement, of which there were nine offered, found that that produced by Mr. Pierce excelled any of the others in resisting pressure and was equal in quality to any in the country. In the enlargement of the canal it was used in constructing the locks. It is now used wherever buildings are erected requiring hydraulic cement, and has become an article of commerce.

NIAGARA NURSERIES.

The Niagara Nurseries were established by Elisha Moody in 1839. Only a few acres were at first devoted to the propagation of trees, but the quantity has increased so that at the present time about four hundred acres are used for that purpose, employing from one to two hundred men some portions of the year. These nurseries make a specialty of propagating standard pear trees, and have undoubtedly sold more of this variety of fruit than any other nursery in the world. The seed for propagating pear trees are imported from Germany and France. When one year old the trees are grafted, and two years later they are large enough for sale, and are shipped to every State in the Union, and also to the British provinces. Upon these spacious grounds may be found about 350 varieties of pear trees. There are also 300 varieties of apple and about 80 each of plum and cherry trees. At the exhibition of the American Pomological Society held at Boston in 1873, the Niagara Nurseries were awarded the "Wilder silver medal" for a collection of 112 varieties of pears; and afterward at the exhibition of the Society at Chicago, for the best collection of apples, pears and plums, over 400 varieties of which were exhibited. E. Moody & Sons are the present proprietors of the Nurseries, and have also about two hundred acres of orchard and are extensively engaged in fruit growing.

LOCKPORT HOME FOR THE FRIENDLESS.

The need of some charitable institution for the support of young orphans, and to meet the wants of those whom old age or infirmities had rendered incapable of providing for themselves, led some of the more enterprising citizens of Lockport to found this institution. The initial steps for its organization were taken in 1871. On the 2nd of February of that year, pursuant to legislative acts, a charter was issued from the Supreme Court of the State upon the petition of Hiram Gardner, John Hodge, Horatio Kilborne, Gustavus P. Hosmer, Joseph W. Helmer, M. W. Evans, J. L. Breyfogle, Thomas Hall and Dr. D. F. Bishop.

The charter defines the object for which the society was formed, and provides that the institution should be located in the city of Lockport and exist for a term of fifty years. The petitioners above mentioned were the trustees for the first year, and at their first meeting, March 1st, J. W. Helmer was elected president of the board and John Hodge, secretary.

The board of managers chosen consisted of Mrs. J. T. Bellah, president; Mrs. W. J. Dunlap, vice-president; Mrs. A. J. Mansfield, treasurer; Mrs. Calvin Haines, corresponding secretary and Miss Annie Gardner, recording secretary.

The following ladies were chosen directors:

Mrs. George W. Rogers, Mrs. Burt Van Horn, Mrs. M. H. Webber, Mrs. James Jackson, jr., Mrs. C. L. Hoag, Mrs. M. W. Evans, Mrs. C. R. Parker, Mrs. E. P. Wentworth, Mrs. Martha White, Mrs. George H. Douglas, Mrs. W. S. Wright, Mrs. P. B. Aiken, Mrs. Dudley Glass, Mrs. E. P. Marvin, Mrs. J. L. Breyfogle, Mrs. Rev. M. Ort, Miss Addie McClew, Miss Addie Currier, Miss Margaret Snell, Miss Maria Chrysler.

These were chosen for one year, their duty being to meet at the Home weekly to look after the inmates. The organization perfected, spacious grounds were purchased on High street, upon which commodious buildings were fitted up for the society's use. The board of supervisors appropriated to it $3,437.47, the amount in the treasury, on condition that it and an equal amount raised by voluntary contribution should be used in fitting up the institution. The property secured was the residence of F. N. Nelson, and was purchased in December, 1871, and the services of Mrs. Empson secured as matron. The first year there were admitted two adults and seven children. During the year 1874 there were twenty-seven inmates, of whom nine were adults and eighteen children.

Shortly after the Home was founded the young ladies of Lockport organized a society called the "Home Circle" for the purpose of making articles to be sold, the proceeds of which were to be placed in the Home treasury. They held their meetings weekly, and the result was a valuable aid. Entertainments were also given for the benefit of the Home, with gratifying results. During the year 1875 the number of inmates was fifty-four. This increase was due to the enforcement of the law requiring the removal of the children of pauper parents from the county house. At the present time there are three adults and forty-four children inmates of the institution.

UNION SCHOOL OF LOCKPORT.

The Union School has been justly called the pride of Lockport. Nature has done much to give to Lockport advantages possessed by few other places; the State of New York built the Erie Canal, which offered great inducements to local business; the county of Niagara made it her shire town and business center, and the market place for the abundant, rich, and varied products of her fertile soil; corporate and private enterprise have, with a public spirit highly commendable, and a taste and discretion truly admirable, helped to render it one of the most pleasant cities of the State. Lockport as a municipal corporation can claim no credit for these advantages and developments. But she may rightfully claim a credit for that which has given her an enviable reputation and rank among the cities of the State. Her Union School system has given her such character, and contributed, in a large measure, to her material prosperity. No inconsiderable part of her present population has been brought here, or has remained here on account of the superior advantages for gaining an education, afforded by her schools. No city or community in the State can claim a more highly educated class of citizens than is that portion of her population who have enjoyed the privileges for acquiring an education which her schools afford. A large portion of the citizens, not only of the city of Lockport, but also of the county of Niagara have been educated here.

The benign influences of these schools have been felt far and wide, by high and low, rich and poor, old and young. They have imparted to thousands a sound and useful education. Hundreds who now occupy the highest positions in the learned professions, and business pursuits of the country, were fitted and prepared in these schools for those stations. Within their walls the rich and the poor have sat, side by side, and enjoyed equal privileges, with no distinctions but such as real merit makes. Children of the poorest parents, who otherwise would never have seen the inside of any but the commonest kind of a common school-house, who would never have received any other than a common education, have enjoyed opportunities for acquiring an education equally with those of the richest parents; and have thereby been enabled to contend with them, and oftentimes successfully for mental superiority, and the highest positions in society.

Community of education creates community of feeling. Attachments formed in the school-room are most lasting. That society will generally be found to be most harmonious whose members have been brought up and educated together. A very striking proof of the truth of these aphorisms is afforded in this very city. The Union School has dissipated those local prejudices and class distinctions which prevailed before its origin. Who can measure the extent of the influence, or calculate the value, of this community of education!

This was the first union school in this or any other State. Many of the cities and most of the villages of the State have adopted this plan; and many of them have almost literally copied this act. In some instances academies have been changed to union schools, but never the converse.

Until 1848 Lockport contained no academy, seminary, or other educational institution, except seven common schools, some of them kept in houses unpleasant, uncomfortable, unhealthy, dark, and gloomy; and a few so-called *select* schools. To obtain a respectable degree of education for their children, parents were obliged to send them away, at great expense, and at an age when they most need the watchful supervision, the fostering care, and the salutary restraints of parents, and the genial influences of home.

In 1846 Sullivan Caverno originated the plan of this Union School system. He submitted the plan to Professor Sandborn of Dartmouth College, Horace Mann of Massachusetts, Mr. Bishop of Rhode Island, and other eminent educators, and received from them many valuable suggestions. He framed an act to be passed by the Legislature, and, by the aid of the Honorable Samuel Young in the Senate, and the Honorable Benjamin Carpenter in the Assembly, the same was passed, being Chapter 51 of the session laws of 1847. The provisions of this act were substantially as follows: Sullivan Caverno as trustee of primary district number one, William G. McMaster as trustee of primary district number two, Joseph T. Bellah as trustee of primary district number three, Silas H. Marks as trustee of primary district number four, Isaac C. Colton as trustee of primary district number five, John S. Wolcott as trustee of primary district number six, Edward L. Boardman as trustee of primary district number seven, and Nathan Dayton, Samuel Works, Jonathan S. Woods, Lyman A. Spalding, and Hiram Gardner, as trustees of the Union district, and their successors in office, were constituted a corporation, by the name of "The Board of Education for the Village of Lockport." The successors of these trustees were so classified that the terms of office of four of them expire each year. This board of education was vested with all the powers, and was subject to all the duties of trustees of common school districts; and many other powers were conferred, and many other duties were imposed upon them by this act. For certain purposes the seven common school districts were consolidated into one union district; for certain other purposes they were to remain distinct as primary districts. Provision was made for a class of intermediate, called secondary, schools; for which purpose afterwards in one case three, and in two cases two, of the primary districts were formed into secondary districts. The Union School was divided into two departments, junior and senior. Provision was made for establishing a separate school for the education of colored children; also for a normal department in the Union School for the instruction of teachers. Generous and liberal provisions were made for the exemption from tuition fees, in favor of the indigent.

The schools in the several districts were divided, arranged and graded as follows: In the primary schools the lowest grade of studies is pursued, until the pupil attains a certain age and degree of proficiency. Upon attaining such age, and passing a successful examination, the pupil is promoted to a secondary school. Here a higher grade of studies is pursued, until a certain other age and degree of proficiency are attained. Then upon a like examination the pupil is promoted to the junior department, and from thence, by like process, to the senior department of the Union School. Pupils prepared

HON. SULLIVAN CAVERNO.

RES. OF HON. SULLIVAN CAVERNO, ONTARIO ST. LOCKPORT, N.Y.

for any department or school above the primary, may be admitted thereto upon passing the required examination.

The degree of education attainable in the secondary schools is equal or superior to that usually acquired in the common schools of the State. The course of studies prescribed for the senior department of the Union Schools was as follows: For the classical course, in the Latin, the grammar, lessons, reader, Viri Romæ, Cæsar, Virgil, Cicero, Sallust, Ovid, Livy, Horace, Tacitus, prose compositions and Roman antiquities; in the Greek, the grammar, lessons, reader, Testament, Anabasis, Homer, tragedies, prose compositions and Grecian antiquities; for the English course, ancient and modern geography, higher arithmetic, algebra, Bourdon, grammar, book-keeping, natural philosophy, chemistry, physiology, history of the United States, universal history, Botany, rhetoric, logic, elements of criticism, mineralogy, geology, Constitution of the United States, science of government, political economy, geography of the heavens, astronomy, mental philosophy, moral philosophy, natural theology, evidences of Christianity, mensuration, geometry, trigonometry, surveying, navigation, music, drawing, mapping and painting.

The courses of studies which are now prescribed, from which students are annually graduated, are three in number; the classical, the English and the commercial. The classical course fits students for the higher grade of colleges. It requires four years for its successful completion. Graduates from this course have entered Yale, Dartmouth, Hamilton, Amherst, Hobart, and Genesee Colleges, and Michigan, Boston, Wesleyan, Cornell, and Rochester Universities. The English course also requires four years for its completion. The studies taught in this course are as follows: Arithmetic, grammar, geography, physiology, book-keeping, algebra, natural philosophy, analysis, rhetoric, physical geography, geometry, chemistry, general history, mental philosophy, geology, criticism, astronomy, history of English literature, and botany. The commercial course extends through two years. The German and French languages, vocal and instrumental music, drawing, and painting are also taught. A student who should complete the whole of these courses would acquire a higher and more useful education than is usually acquired in the four years course in most colleges.

At the first meeting of the board of education and annually thereafter for four years, Mr. Caverno was chosen president of the board. He drew up a code of rules, regulations, and by-laws, which were adopted by the board. For five years he devoted a large portion of his time and his best energies, without fee or reward, to the interests and business of the schools; doing duties, performing labor and services in amount greater, and in character more important than has been annually done by, or required of those who have held offices since created therefor, and for which the board have paid, annually, $1,000 to $1,400.

The teachers' wages were paid in the primary schools by the money received from the common school fund of the State; in the secondary schools and Union schools, by money received from tuition fees. These fees were fixed for residents of the Union district at $1 per quarter of three months; in the secondary schools at $1.50 in the junior department of the Union School, and at $3 in the senior department of the Union School; for non-residents of the Union district at $2 in the secondary schools, at $3 in the junior department, and at $4 in the senior department of the Union School.

Immediately after organizing and adopting the by-laws, the board of education purchased a lot, centrally located, for the Union School-house, and commenced to build the large and commodious house now thereon. For the purchase of the lot, building the house, furnishing it with proper fixtures, furniture, bell, and chemical, philosophical, and mathematical apparatus, it became necessary to levy a tax upon the whole taxable property within the Union district, the boundaries of which were substantially the same as are those of the city of Lockport, amounting to the sum of $13,000. To this time all seemed to be harmonious. The petition to the Legislature for the passage of the law, had been signed by more than eight hundred of the most prominent citizens and largest property holders. No opposition was manifested.

Upon the levying of this tax an excitement arose; an indignation meeting was called, at which a motion was made by a very prominent citizen and advocated by others, that the further building of the Union School-house be abandoned, that the walls, which were then nearly completed, be torn down, and that measures be taken to procure a repeal of the law. Threats of violence towards some of the friends of the system were made, and it seemed at one time that a fearful riot would follow. For a long time afterwards the opponents of the school used to cast it as a term of reproach upon its friends, that they had been instrumental in bringing this system into operation, as if it were a calamity upon the community. A very prominent citizen, who afterwards became its warm friend, and was for many years connected with it in an official capacity, used to threaten his children, as a punishment for disobedience or misconduct, that he would send them to the Union School.

Opposition gradually died out. Men who had been its enemies became its warm friends and patrons. Within the last ten or fifteen years there have been built, within the Union district, five school-houses, costing, with their fixtures, furniture, and apparatus, little less than $100,000; two of them costing $25,000 each, one costing $20,000, one of the others costing as much as the Union school-house cost, and the remaining one costing more than half as much. These amounts were respectively assessed upon the taxable property in a single district; yet the tax-payers had become so favorable to a system which afforded such good schools that little or no complaint has been heard about the taxes therefor. The schools offering such facilities, and affording such superior advantages for acquiring an education, few parents are so blind to the best interests of their children that they would deprive them of these privileges. A man who should now avow himself an enemy of the Union School would manifest a hardihood and want of candor that would bring him into contempt. Few parents who desire to give their children a good, sound, useful, and finished education, send them abroad for that purpose.

The new system went into operation July 4th, 1848. Among the advantages secured by this system are these: The primary and secondary schools are under the care of female teachers, who, it is generally conceded, are better constituted for managing and controlling children than male teachers are; and a great saving in expenses is thereby gained.

The board of education receives annually a share of the common school fund, and of the literature fund; and also a large sum from the State treasury towards the salary of the superintendent, and on account of the normal department; in addition to these a large sum for tuition fees of pupils who are not residents of the Union district.

The primary schools are in the immediate vicinity of the pupils; none are obliged to travel a great distance.

Pupils of nearly the same age and size are brought together, and many troubles, difficulties, and inconveniences, arising from bringing into the same house those of different ages and of all sizes, are thus prevented.

Frequent changes of teachers are avoided. There is now in one of the grades, a teacher who has been continuously a teacher from the commencement of the system.

Each teacher in each grade makes the teaching of the branches for that grade a specialty.

As they progress, and rise from grade to grade, the pupils come under the instruction of teachers of higher and higher qualifications, until, in the senior department, they come under the instruction of those who will compare favorably with the professors in colleges.

Large classes are formed, and thus the stimulant of competition and rivalry is obtained.

Children well brought up at home will, generally, yield ready obedience to the laws, rules, and regulations of the schools, and the influence of their example cannot fail to produce salutary effects upon the others.

The time for the election of members of the board of education is in September for trustees of primary districts, and in October for trustees of the Union district; thus avoiding the contaminating influence which sometimes follows when these elections are held at the same time with political elections. It is believed that neither personal, local, political or sectarian considerations have ever disturbed the harmony of the system, or the usefulness of the schools.

By the act of the Legislature of 1850 the Union School became subject to the visitation of the regents of the university, as academies are, and entitled to receive, and does receive annually from the literature fund a share proportionate to the number of pupils taught therein, who have pursued the course of studies, and to the extent prescribed for that purpose by the regents of the university.

Twenty pupils annually attend the sessions of the normal class. This department is under the direction and control of the board of education, subject to the visitation of the commissioners of common schools of the county of Niagara.

The greatest number of different pupils in any year, registered in the senior department, is four hundred and fifty; in the junior department three hundred and eighty-five; in the primary and secondary schools, two thousand two hundred and thirty-nine, making a total of three thousand and seventy-four.

The average attendance in the senior department of the Union School, during the past year, has been two hundred and twenty; in the junior department, two hundred and fifty; in the secondary and primary schools, twelve hundred. The attendance of pupils has increased on an average in the primary and secondary schools from six hundred to twelve hundred; in the junior department of the Union School, from one hundred and fifty to two hundred and fifty; and in the senior department of the Union School, from one hundred and twenty-five to two hundred and twenty; making a total increase of eight hundred and seventy-five pupils, or more than ninety-six per cent. During this period the population of the territory included in the Union district has increased from nine thousand to twelve thousand five hundred, making a total increase of only three thousand five hundred, or less than forty per cent.

Pupils from all parts of the county, and from other counties, have sought the advantages afforded by the Union School; and for many years past the attendance, in the senior department, of non-resident pupils has exceeded that of resident pupils, and the amount of tuition fees received from non-resident pupils is greater than the tuition fees received at any like institution in the State. Their average number is one hundred and thirty; the tuition fees from $8 to $10 per term; amounting, annually, to more than $2,500. The board of education also receives, annually, from taxes $20,000; from the common school fund $8,000; from the literature fund $700; from the treasury of the State towards the salary of the superintendent $800; and for the normal department $200; amounting in all to $32,200. During the year 1877, in all the schools there were forty-three teachers employed, to whom was paid the sum of $22,338. The average expense for each pupil was $17.

There is a well selected library of three thousand five hundred volumes, the use of which is free to all residents of the Union district. This library has been purchased with that portion of the common school fund which the statute prescribed for that purpose. This is the only public library in the city.

There is a department in which are taught the natural sciences. It is furnished with an extensive and choice chemical and philosophical apparatus, and a museum rich in rare specimens of geology, mineralogy, botany, palentology, conchology, and other specimens of natural curiosities.

The act creating the Union School system remains

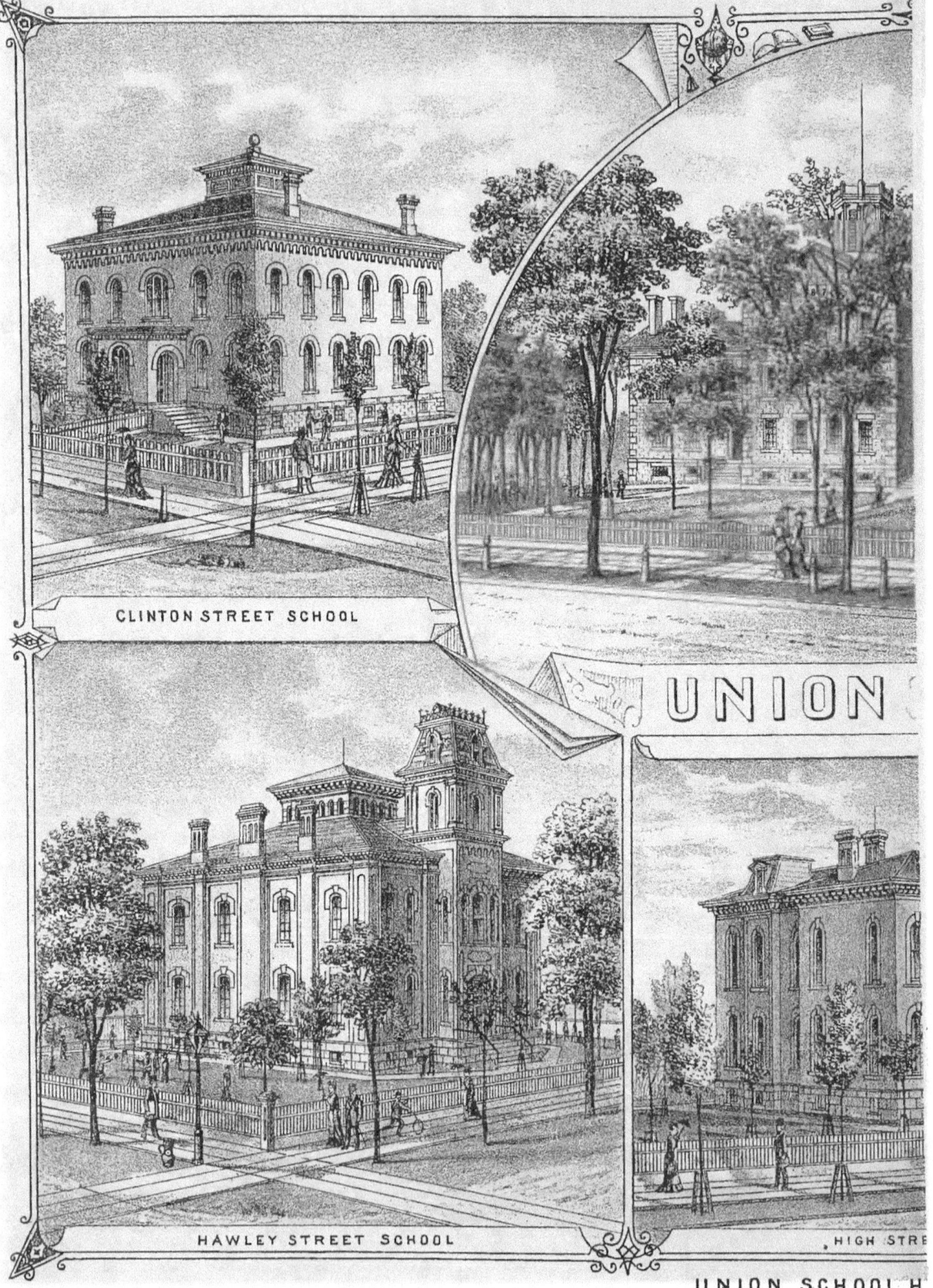

substantially as passed in 1847. The only material changes are as follows :

1. By Chapter 77 of the session laws of 1850, tuition fees in the secondary schools were abolished; the regents of the university were authorized to declare the Union School to be an academy for certain purposes; "subject to, and to be governed by, the provision of the act authorizing said Union School, and subject to such rules and regulations as the regents may prescribe;" and the office of superintendent of the Union School was created. To the office of superintendent, without any extension of his territory, there has recently been added that of commissioner of common schools.

2. By Chapter 378 of the session laws of 1866, the boundaries of the Union district were conformed to the boundaries of the city of Lockport; the power to raise money by taxation was transferred to the common council of the city; the board of education fixing, by resolution, each year, the amount of money which it will be necessary to raise by taxation for the purposes of education for the year, and the common council causing the same to be raised accordingly.

3. By Chapter 406 of the session laws of 1867, tuition fees in all the common schools of the State were abolished. The Union School still retaining its common school features, tuition therein became free to residents of the Union district. Before this time the amount raised annually by taxation for all purposes of all the schools, except for buildings, was on an average the sum of $5,000, being one mill on the dollar of valuation, according to the town assessment roll. Since that time the sum so raised has been $18,000 to $20,000, being more than three mills on the dollar of such valuation.

4. By Chapter 729 of the session laws of 1868, authority was given to the board of education to unite and consolidate, for certain purposes, any two or more of the primary districts. In the exercise of this authority the board has so united and consolidated these districts that there are now, except for the election of trustees, only five. In each of these there is a large, commodious, and substantial school-house, in which are brought together all the pupils that were formerly included in the seven primary and three secondary schools. The gradation is by classes, and comprehends, substantially, the same studies as were formerly prescribed for the primary and secondary schools.

The names of the presidents of the board of education, the order of their succession and the time during which they held that office, respectively, are as follows : Sullivan Caverno, four years ; William G. McMaster, two years ; Stoughton Pettibone, one year ; John Van Horn, five years ; B. S. Delano, three years ; M. L. Burrell, two years ; John L. Buck, four years ; C. G. Palmer a few months; Samuel Wright, two years ; James Atwater, three years ; James Jackson, jr., who now holds the office, five years.

The second president, William G. McMaster, deserves more than a mere mention. He has always been a strong advocate of universal education; he gave his influence and rendered important and valuable services in putting the Union School system into operation; and, what can be said of few other men, if any, in the State of New York, *he was a trustee of a common school district for more than fifty years consecutively; forty years of which time he was such trustee of the district where he now resides.* He was a member of the board of education from its organization until 1878, when, on account of ill health, he declined a further election.

The names of the principals of the Union School, the order of their succession, and the time during which they held that office, respectively, are as follows : Frederic R. R. Lord, three and a half years; Nathan Britton, two years; Moses H. Fitts, one year; William P. Eaton, two and a half years; Edwin A. Charlton, four years; Benjamin M. Reynolds, five years; Asher B. Evans, who now holds the position, twelve years.

The names of the superintendents, the order of their succession, and the time during which they held that office respectively, are as follows : M. S. Burrell, one year; George W. Jermain, one year; Sampson Robbins, one year; Hezekiah W. Scovell, one year; James Atwater, eleven years, during which time he was teacher of mathematics in the senior department, and for a short time acting principal of the Union School; James Ferguson, ten years; M. J. Keeler, one year; Arthur A. Skinner, who now holds the office, two years.

The members of the present board of education are as follows : James Jackson, jr., James O. King, John H. Buck, James Atwater, and Freeman H. Mottt, as trustees of the Union district, Lewis Harmony of primary district number one, John S. Stahl of primary district number two, William S. Wright of primary district number three, Joseph B. Boyce of primary district number four, Lewis H. Hill of primary district number five, David Woods of primary district number six, and John McCue of primary district number seven, as trustees of those primary districts respectively.

THE FIRE DEPARTMENT.

Lockport, as has been stated, was incorporated a village in the year 1829. Before it had a fire organization a rotary engine was used, which was purchased by Lyman A. Spalding for the sum of $350. It was christened the "Tuscarora," and a company was subsequently organized under that name. The old engine was too large for practical purposes, taking sixteen men to operate it in case of fire. It was then necessary to have a relief corps of sixteen more near at hand, for one force could work the engine but a few moments at a time. The headquarters of the firemen at that time were in the rear of the site of the Farmers' and Mechanics' Savings Bank. The "Tuscarora" was finally abandoned, and a new engine, called the "Niagara," purchased. The former is now stored in a barn on the premises of Dr. A. R. Chase, on Transit street.

Shortly after the village was incorporated the Tuscarora company was formed. Jonathan G. Gustin was foreman, Joseph S. Pound assistant foreman and Alfred

Holmes clerk. The members included John Bagley, Stephen Strong, Erastus Ransom, Benjamin Long, Robert N. Steele, Theodore Stone, William T. Lewis, George W. Winchester, Alexander H. Spalding, Norman Leonard, Charles H. Spalding, Elijah Edson, Dwight A. Darwin, N. Wilbur Gardner, William A. Goodrich, Jerome Petre, Benjamin Carpenter, Ellis F. Pierce, Joseph T. Bellah, Ezra P. Wentworth, Benjamin Blake, Jonathan Gilbert, Frederick A. Spalding, John McCadd and Nelson D. Elwood.

The first hook and ladder company was organized in 1833. Henry Backentoe was the first foreman. Among his successors were William Carpenter, W. Swan, John Jenney and Walter Williams. Their first quarters were in the rear of Rogers & Brown's dry goods store, near the site of McMahon's meat market. They afterward removed to a building on the lot on which is now located the Protection Hook and Ladder truck house, on Locust street. Among the members were William Bachman, S. R. Daniels, M. W. Evans, Colonel D. Donnelly, Francis Johnson and Elnathan W. Lewis.

In the year 1836 a company was formed in the lower town, under the title of Tuscarora Engine Company No. 2. William Dixon was foreman and Arnold C. Brown assistant foreman.

Some years later a company known as the Osceola Engine Company No. 1 was formed. It served under this name until May 26th, 1873, when it was reorganized and took the name of Spalding Hose Company No. 1.

About the same time that the "Osceola" was organized another company was formed, known as the Rescue Engine Company No. 3. The first foreman was Colonel E. D. Shuler, who served up to the time of the old Eagle fire in 1854. The company remained in the department until January 27th, 1868, when it was disbanded and Washington Hose Company No. 2 was organized from it. After the Eagle fire alluded to a new engine was purchased. Dr. L. W. Bristol became foreman.

DE WITT CLINTON ENGINE COMPANY.

In 1853 Tuscarora Engine Company No. 2 was reorganized and became what is now the DeWitt Clinton Engine Company. An engine was purchased at the World's Fair in New York city. The lamented Governor Hunt donated the company ground upon which to erect an engine house, and he was therefore tendered the honor of giving the company a name, the foremen visiting his residence and taking their apparatus with them for that purpose. The first foreman was Benjamin H. Fletcher. The company uses the same engine still, and is among the foremost in the department. The engine house is located on Market street in East Lockport.

PROTECTION HOOK AND LADDER COMPANY NO. 1.

The organization of Protection Hook and Ladder Company was consummated June 15th, 1863. It was regularly formed with thirty-five charter members, among whom were such men as Hon. George W. Bowen, Captain B. H. Fletcher, Hon. George C. Greene, Hon. John H. Buck, George R. Keep and other prominent citizens. The first quarters were upon the site of the company's present house on Locust street, near the central portion of the city. The first officers were elected June 15th, 1863, and were: Foreman, George R. Keep; assistant foreman, William E. Jenney; secretary, George W. Hall; treasurer, S. Curt Lewis.

The average membership since the date of the formation of the company has been forty. The active members now on the company's roll are thirty-four. It may be truthfully said of the organization that of its kind no finer exists in western New York. The present officers are: Foreman, John H. Leach; secretary, R. Hudson Bond; treasurer, John B. Arnold; steward, Albert M. Mather.

HYDRANT HOSE COMPANY NO. 1.

This company made itself in due form a factor in the city fire department November 24th, 1865. It had then only twelve members. At a regular meeting held a week later it was reinforced by the enrollment of eight members. The city council then recognized and accepted the company, principally upon the recommendation of H. F. Cady, then chief engineer. The first officers of the company were elected November 24th, 1865, as follows: Foreman, H. K. Wicker; first assistant foreman, S. C Condon; second, S. B. Armstrong; secretary, W. F. Wicker, jr.; treasurer, A. J. Duquette. The company's headquarters for a short time were in a building on the triangle at the junction of Ontario and Canal streets. In due time suitable buildings were furnished by the city on Cottage street, and the company has since occupied them. The average membership of the company has been twenty-four. It now has twenty-eight members. The present foreman is E. C. Ayling. His associates in office are: First assistant foreman, Willard F. Wright; second assistant foreman, Charles F. Wellish; president, T. J. McMaster; secretary, J. T. Darrison; treasurer, J. P. Devereaux; steward, Isaac Ellis.

ACTIVE HOSE.

The Actives are the youngest fire company in Lockport. They were organized February 5th, 1878, with a charter membership of fourteen. The first officers were: Foreman, James Doyle; assistant foreman, John Carney; secretary, D. W. McRae; treasurer, O. T. Markey; steward, William Pelham. The company purchased its own apparatus, which consisted of an elegant four-wheeled hose carriage, built by S. M. Steward of Rochester, and with quarters on the corner of Elm street and East avenue, in the office formerly occupied by the lumberman P. M. Ranney, was at once in full trim and considered a valuable addition to the city department.

WASHINGTON HOSE COMPANY NO. 2.

Washington Hose Company No. 2 was organized January 27th, 1868, immediately after the disbanding of Rescue Engine Company No. 3. The charter members were: Michael Dempsey, foreman; Richard Golbally, Edward F. Clifford, Thomas G. Mangua, Daniel Lundy, W. W. Doyle and Robert Cochrane, all of whom had been members of said Rescue Engine Company up to June 1st, 1869. They used the same carriage that the disbanded Rescue had on that date. They purchased a new four-wheeled apparatus. For about nine years they occupied a hose-house on Church street. In June, 1877, they moved into new and elegant quarters on Niagara street, where they remain. The average membership has been thirty.

SPALDING HOSE COMPANY.

This company had its origin in the Osceola Engine Company No. 1, in the month of May, 1873. The first officers were: J. Gardner, president; F. J. Le Valley, foreman; A. Thompson, first assistant foreman; Robert Graham, second assistant foreman; William H. Conklin, secretary; Joseph Lambert, treasurer; James Covill, steward; F. P. Lambert, assistant steward. The company started with nineteen members, and the average membership since has been twenty-four. The quarters have been on Pine street, and are ample, commodious and well furnished. The following named persons served as foremen from May 26, 1873, to 1879: F. J. Le Valley, W. H. Conklin, Joseph Lambert, and Max Starck.

HODGE HOSE COMPANY (JUVENILES).

Hodge Hose Company was organized in 1875, and consisted of eight active members. Their first carriage was a two-wheeled one that cost them fifteen dollars. In 1876 Mr. John Hodge, after whom the company was named, presented them with a spider-built hose-cart that cost one hundred and fifty dollars. At this time there were twenty-five active members. Irving H. Wilson was foreman and Albert R. Helmer assistant. In 1877 the company had forty active members and upwards of two hundred honorary members. It was in this year that the company commenced holding regular meetings, occupying room 27, Hodge Opera House Block. Here it transacted its business and drilled for parades. At this time Frank W. Shaw was foreman and Clelland A. Ward assistant. The officers for 1878 were the same as the previous year, with the exception of Curtis B. Campbell, president, and Benjamin W. Jellings, assistant foreman. Mr. Hodge, the founder of the company, took a deep interest in its welfare, making generous contributions to the treasury from time to time, and entertaining the members occasionally. The company was organized with a view to one day becoming an important factor of the fire-department.

THE WATER SUPPLY.

The organization of good, active fire companies was only a secondary movement to getting the necessary supply of water in case of fire. The earliest means was a Silsby rotary pump, which Mr. Lyman A. Spalding purchased to use in case of a fire in or about his flouring-mill on Pine street. This he put in on the south side of the mill, and it was operated by a water-wheel in the mill. But this could only be of service in the mill and immediate vicinity. Shortly afterward the city entertained a proposition made by a company to construct a reservoir at a point where the American Hotel now stands. The reservoir was built and the supply of water obtained from the canal by means of the Spalding pump, already referred to—the water being conveyed through hose. The reservoir plan was confessedly imperfect. The gravitation pressure did not meet the varying wants so far as quantity was concerned, and was only of value in supplying fire engines. It was, withal, expensive. The frequency of fires which fire engines were lamentably incompetent to check or control led Birdsall Holly of Holly water works fame, to turn his thoughts in the direction of providing a better method of protection. Thus the Holly system, referred to on a preceding page, came into use. In the contract for the works it was stipulated by the Holly company that from a hydrant set at a point fifty feet above the pump a stream of water should be thrown through 100 feet of hose 100 feet high. Upon the trial the stream was not only thrown over the test pole, but fully seventy-five feet higher. The works were promptly accepted by the city, and are in use at the present time. Among those who have served the city in the capacity of chief engineer of the fire department, have been the following named persons: George W. Rogers, Benjamin Carpenter, B. S. Pease, Isaac Dolu, John Jenney, Dudley Donnelly, J. T. Bellah, L. Austin Spalding, Dr. L. W. Bristol, B. H. Fletcher, John E. Mack, M. Dempsey, H. F. Cady, William Spalding, Robert Madden and John Hodge, serving in the order given.

SOCIETIES.

MASONIC.

Lockport Lodge, No. 73, F. and A. M. is one of the oldest masonic lodges in western New York, having been organized, under a dispensation from the Grand Lodge of the State, at the Niagara Hotel, in the early part of 1824, with twenty-one members, among whom were Harvey W. Campbell, Hiram Gardner, Orsamus Turner, Joel Gould, William Buell and Eli Bruce. The first leading officers were Daniel Washburn, W. M.; Alfred Barrett, S. W.; Isaac Southworth, J. W.; Stephen M. Potter, secretary. It was chartered by the Grand Lodge on the 5th of June, 1824, and numbered 401. During the "anti-masonic war," which followed the abduction of Morgan in the fall of 1826, when hundreds of masonic lodges became extinct, this organization maintained an existence and annually elected its officers. On September 4th, 1839, the then existing lodges in this State were renumbered according to their ages, by the Grand Lodge, when this one became No. 73. Over six hundred persons have been made masons in this lodge since its organization. The present membership is 170. Its regular communications are held on the second and fourth Tuesdays of each month, at Masonic Hall. Annual elections occur in

December. The present officers are: Frank W. Holly, W. M.; William Cocker, S. W.; David Bruce, J. W.; Andrew R. Ferguson, treasurer; Warner H. McCoy, secretary; Rev. Sumner C. Smith, chaplain.

Ames Chapter, No. 88, R. A. M. was organized under and by virtue of a charter issued by Ezra Ames, Grand High Priest of the Grand Royal Arch Chapter of this State, dated February 6th, 1824. The petitioners for his charter number twenty-three. The first leading officers were: Harvey W. Campbell, high priest; Almond H. Millard, king; Seymour Scovill, scribe; its regular convocations are held on the first and third Thursdays of each month at Masonic Hall. The present number of members is 150. The present officers are: C. P. T. La Roche, M. E. H. P.; George A. Torrance, E. K.; Peter D. Walter, E. S.; Warner H. McCoy, treasurer; Van N. Douglas, secretary; Jason Collier, chaplain.

Bruce Council, No. 15, Royal and Select Masters.—This council was organized in December, 1859, and chartered on the 5th of June, 1860. The charter members were nine in number. The first officers were Charles H. Platt, Th. Ill. M.; Charles Craig, Rt. Ill. D. M.; Daniel O. Knapp, recorder. Regular assemblies are held at Masonic Hall on the first Wednesday in each month. The present number of members is forty. Annual elections occur in December. The present officers are as follows: Charles Craig, Th. Ill. M.; Jason Collier, Rt. Ill. Dep. M.; Perry Stowell, Ill. P. C. of W.; Peter D. Walter, treasurer; Van N. Douglas, recorder; G. A. Torrance, captain of guard; E. P. Holly, cond. of council; David E. Snyder, steward; H. H. Servoss, marshal; L. King, chaplain.

Genesee Commandery, No. 10, Knights Templar.—This encampment was organized under a "letter of dispensation," granted November 21st, 1825, by DeWitt Clinton—then Most Eminent Grand Master of the Grand Encampment of Knights Templar of this State—to Henry Brown and eight others, authorizing and empowering them to "form, open and hold an encampment of Knights Templar in the Village of LeRoy," Genesee county, to "be known and distinguished by the name of Genesee Encampment". Henry Brown was appointed the first grand commander, Orange Ridson the first generalissimo, and Frederick Fitch the first captain-general. On the 16th of December, 1825, it was chartered by the Grand Encampment of the State, under the name of Genesee Encampment, No. 10; and on January 28th, 1826, it was duly consecrated. It was one of the first encampments organized in western New York. Sometime during the years when anti-masonry was at its height it was moved to Batavia, where it remained until 1839, when, by authority of the Grand Commandery, it was removed to Lockport. The grand commanders have been Henry Brown, Ebenezer Mix, Peter P. Murphy—who was elected in 1841 and served until 1863, was then followed by E. D. Shuler for two years, and was again elected and served two years longer—Charles Craig, elected in 1867; C. P. T. La Roche, elected in 1873; and George A. Torrance, elected in 1877. This commandery celebrated its semi-centennial anniversary January 28th, 1876, with appropriate exercises, festival and so forth. It now has a membership of about 110, with fifty fully uniformed and equipped. The present officers are: George A. Torrance, E. C.; Perry Stowell, Gen.; Van N. Douglas, Capt.-Gen., Jason Collier, prelate; Edgar P. Holly, S. W.; W. J. McElroy, J. W.; P. D. Walter, treasurer; Andrew J. Morse, recorder. Regular conclaves are held on the first and third Fridays in each month, at Masonic Hall.

Niagara Lodge, No. 375, F. and A. M. was organized January 27th, 1855, and chartered by the Grand Lodge of this State July 7th, 1855. The original members were Myron L. Burrell, E. D. Shuler, Ira S. Howe, J. B. Chase, Charles J. Fox, G. W. Gould, N. S. Ringueburg, J. Ringueburg and W. W. Douglas. The first leading officers were Myron L. Burrell, W.M.; E. D. Shuler, S.W.; Ira S. Howe, J.W.; W. W. Douglas, secretary. Its regular communications are on the first and third Wednesdays of each month at Masonic Hall, corner of Main and Cottage streets. It has a present membership of 185. Annual elections occur on the communication next preceding the festival of St. John the Evangelist. The present officers are Edward Beck, W.M.; R. W. Case, S. W.; John Hosbury, J.W.; C. P. T. La Roche, secretary; Rev. Foster Ely, chaplain.

Red Jacket Lodge, No. 646, F. and A. M. was chartered and organized with twenty-six original members on February 27th, 1867. The first officers were: Jason Collier, W.M.; S. M. Robbins, S. W.; James D. Ames, J.W.; S. T. Clark, S.D.; E. B. Weaver, J.D.; J. R. Compton, secretary; B. H. Fletcher, treasurer; Rev. L. S. Stevens, chaplain; B. Bunnell, tiler.

Its regular communications are held on the second and fourth Wednesdays in each month at Masonic Hall, Ringueburg Block. Annual elections occur upon the last meeting in December. The present officers are: Charles Rakes, W.M.; Hiram D. McNeil, S.W.; Theodore D. Babcock, J. W.; James R. Compton, treasurer; Henry Goodman, jr., secretary; Eugene M. Ashley, S.D.; Waterman S. Pound, J. D.; Rev. Foster Ely, chaplain. The present number of members is 94.

Lock City Lodge of Perfection, A. A. Rite.—The organization of this lodge was effected on the 25th of December, 1875. Its charter was granted August 16th, 1876. The number of charter members was eighteen. Its first officers were: John Hodge, T. P. G. M.; Otis Cole, D. G. M.; Charles Craig, V. S. G. W.; A. H. Robinson, V. I. G. W.; Rev. Foster Ely, gr. orator; C. P. T. La Roche, gr. treasurer; John H. Leach, gr. secretary; George A. Torrance, G. M. of C. Meetings are held at Masonic Hall on the second and fourth Thursdays of each month. Elections occur on 3rd, Adar, A. M. The present membership is fifty-six. The present officers are: John Hodge, T. P. G. M.; Charles Craig, D. G. M.; D. T. Stevens, V. S. G. W.; C. P. T. La Roche, V. J. G. W.; Rev. Foster Ely, gr. orator; O. C. Wright, gr. treasurer; John H. Leach, gr. secretary; George F. Smith, G. K. of S.; George A. Torrance, Gr. M. of C.; William J. Robb, Gr. C. of Guard.

ODD FELLOWS.

Cataract Lodge, No. 54, I. O. O. F.—This lodge was instituted by W. L. G. Smith, Past Grand Master, under a dispensation granted by the Grand Lodge of this State September 6th, 1844. The charter members were N. Titus Wakeman, S. J. Sweetland, S. Pettibone, John A. Bassett and E. G. Wolcott. The first officers were: John A. Bassett, N. G.; Stoughton Pettibone, V. G.; E. G. Wolcott, secretary; S. J. Sweetland, treasurer; P. L. Ely, conductor; L. W. Bristol, warden; E. Thomas, guardian.

P. L. Ely of this lodge was appointed the first district deputy grand master for the district of Niagara. Lodge meetings are held Wednesday evenings at Odd Fellows' Hall, over 100 Main street. The present officers are: T. M. Weaver, N. G.; G. W. Sutton, V. G.; J. H. Murphy, recording secretary; J. P. Bishop, permanent secretary; Dr. L. W. Bristol, treasurer.

Constellation Lodge, No. 184, was organized August 19th, 1859, by District Deputy Grand Master E. C. Williams, with eleven charter members. The first officers were: Crumel J. Lloyd, N.G.; Thomas R. Bailey, jr., V.G.; Hiram Benedict, recording secretary; S. D. Hooper, permanent secretary; Demeritus M. Trowbridge, treasurer. Regular meetings are held at the lodge's hall, at the corner of East Market and Exchange streets, every Tuesday evening. Semi-annual elections occur at the last meeting in June and December, and installation of officers on the first meeting in July and January. The present officers are Robert W. Duncan, N.G.; Theron Baldwin, V.G.; William J. Graham, recording secretary; William Chambers, sen., permanent secretary; Lewis H. Hill, treasurer. The board of trustees consists of George L. Smith, Edwin Sexton and William Cocker. The present number of members is 84.

Niagara Union Encampment was instituted March 12th, 1852. It now has fifty-three members.

TEMPERANCE.

Temperance organizations are fairly represented in this city, there being two Good Templars' lodges, one division of Sons of Temperance, one lodge of Royal Templars of Templars and a Women's Christian Temperance Union.

Lock City Lodge, No. 75, Good Templars was organized in 1866. Regular meetings are held every Monday evening at Good Templars' Hall, corner of Main and Pine streets. The present leading officers are: L. A. Dietrick, W.C.T.; W. C. Phillips, secretary; William Whittaker, treasurer.

Porter Lodge, No. 66, Good Templars was organized in 1866. It meets every Friday evening on Market street, East Lockport.

Lockport City Lodge, No. 12, Royal Templars of Templars was organized October 22d, 1877. Regular meetings are held every Thursday evening at Good Templars' Hall. The present officers are: Lyman A. Dietrick, S.C.; Dr. J. W. Grosvenor, V.C.; Seth M. Lovell, P.C.; Walter E. Doty, secretary; O. E. Moody, treasurer; Joseph Harst, chaplain.

Sons of Temperance, Niagara Division, No. 109.—This organization was instituted January 26th, 1846. It has a present membership of 156. The present officers are: George P. Rignal, W.P.; Mrs. Carpenter, W.A.; Harvey Weaver, recording secretary; James F. Dunning, financial scribe; O. E. Moody, treasurer.

UNITED WORKMEN.

Columbia Lodge, No. 20, was instituted in Lockport on April 5th, 1876, with thirteen charter members, and its organization fully completed by the election and installation of its first officers, as follows: John Hodge, P.M.W.; William E. Jenney, M.W.; George R. McChesney, recorder; S. D. Hooper, receiver; L. J. McParlin, treasurer; J. Franklin Gill, overseer; W. W. Stevens, general foreman. Regular meetings of the order are held on Thursday evenings, at Columbia Hall, in the Murray block on Main street. Regular elections are held at the last meeting in December of each year. The present number of members is 143. The present leading officers are: William E. Jenney, M. W.; H. Craig, G. F.; J. B. Boyce, recorder; Edward Beck, P. M. W.; Drs. M. S. Kittinger and J. W. Grosvenor are the medical examiners.

This lodge, since its organization, has lost two of its members by death: Ernest M. Rogers in August, 1876, and James D. Caton, October, 1877, the families of the deceased promptly receiving from the order $2,000 each.

Lock City Lodge, No. 63, A.O.U.W. was organized with twenty-seven members on February 7th, 1877. The first officers were: Charles Whitmore, P.M.W.; Edwin Saxton, M.W.; George L. Smith, G.F.; William McElroy, overseer; James W. Little, financier; W. H. Andrews, receiver; Abram Walker, recorder. Its regular meetings are held every alternate Wednesday evening at Columbia Hall, over 69 Main street. Annual elections occur at the first meeting in January. The present membership is about fifty. The present officers are: George L. Smith, P.M.W.; H. H. Walker, M.W.; Joseph W. Little, general foreman; Charles Whitmore, recorder; James Duncan, overseer; Abram Walker, financier; W. H. Andrews, receiver. No deaths have yet occurred among its members.

John Hodge Lodge, No. 69, was organized February 23d, 1877, with fifty-six members. The first officers were: Horace H. Servoss, P. M. W.; Van N. Douglas, M. W.; Andrew Tenbrook, general foreman; Charles Watts, overseer; Andrew J. Morse, recorder; Edward J. Wakeman, financier; Demont A. Hixson, treasurer; Theron Baldwin, guide. It now has a membership of 146. It has sustained one loss since its organization, that of Wright L. Patterson, December 31st, 1877. Stated meetings are held on Tuesday evenings, at its hall in the Hodge Opera House. Regular elections occur at the last meeting in December. The present officers are: Van N. Douglas, P. M. W.; Andrew Tenbrook, M. W.; H. C. Hill, G. F.; Thara Willard, overseer; A. J. Morse, recorder; E. J. Wakeman, F.; C. P. T. La Roche, receiver.

LOCKPORT SAENGERBUND SOCIETY.

This society was organized on the 3d of May, 1864, with nine active members. Its object is to cultivate musical talent, both vocal and instrumental, and its rise and progress are largely due to the exertions of George F. Smith. The members at the date of organization were: George F. Smith, William F. Knorr, G. L. Winten, Henry Weber, Henry Primassin, Joseph Kurtz, John Zwirlem, Matthew Fritton, Joseph Oswald. William F. Knorr was chosen president; G. L. Winten musical director; Joseph Oswald secretary, and George F. Smith treasurer. The meetings for the first year were held at the house of Joseph Kurtz, during which time the members increased to about twenty-five. The society then rented what is now known as "Checkered Hall," which it occupied for three successive years and then removed to a room in Webber's Hall, and afterwards to a room in the building in which the *Morning Times* is published, which was occupied till 1872, when it rented the spacious room which it now occupies in Lambert's block, on Locust street. When the society was first organized the fee of admission to membership was one dollar. The admission fee has steadily increased, and at the present time is $2.50 for active members and $5 for others, the latter being admitted to all the entertainments given by the society.

The members meet every Friday evening for rehearsal. The election of officers takes place on the first Tuesday in May, annually. The presidents of the society have been William Knorr, William Dunka, Frederic Walter, Henry Levi, and George F. Smith, the latter having been elected the ninth time to the office. In 1876 the society provided itself with a magnificent silk banner, ornamented with exquisite taste, at a cost of nearly three hundred dollars. The various musical instruments and fixtures are valued at about $2,000. The society at the present time numbers 96 members, 24 of whom are active.

LOTOS CLUB.

This association was formed under the auspices of L. C. Breyfogle, and organized on the 5th of April, 1878. Its object is to provide for the members a place where they can meet and exercise their musical talents, and also engage in a game of billards and kindred amusements without being exposed to the bad influences brought to bear on young men in general who frequent saloons for recreation of this kind. There are about twenty charter members belonging to the club, occupying as their place of meeting the hall in the third story of the Moyer block. The officers are as follows: L. C. Breyfogle, president; E. S. Morey, vice-president; L. B. Holton, recording secretary; J. F. Parkinson, financial secretary; and Joseph Arnold, treasurer. The board of trustees consists of G. T. McComb, William Huston and George Ballew.

C. M. B. A.—L. J. McPARLIN BRANCH, NO. 3.

This branch of the Catholic Mutual Benefit Association of the United States and Canadas was organized on the fourth day of April, 1877, previous to which time, for a period of three months, an invitation was extended to all male Catholics between the ages of eighteen and fifty-five, to meet in the basement of the Church of St. John the Baptist, on Chestnut street, from January 1st to the day above named. Four or five men met weekly at the designated place, until finally, on the fourth day of April, 1877, the necessary thirteen members were secured, examined, elected and initiated. On that evening grand president Daniel Barrett, grand deputy John Clifford, and grand secretary Joseph MacKenna, from the grand council, at Niagara Falls, N. Y., were present, and installed the officers and instituted the branch. The total membership in the association at this time numbered about fifty. The charter members were as follows:

Louis Bushman, William Brown, Frank S. Brookshaw, Thomas Gallagher, Thomas J. Murphy, Thomas M. McParlin, George A. Wilber, John McParlin, William C. Long, Peter H. McParlin, John T. Tully, Lawrence J. McParlin, jr., and Oliver D. Long.

The society held its regular weekly meetings, but did not increase in membership until the first week in December, when three new names were added. From that time forward the society rapidly gained in numbers, and on the first of January, 1878, there were one hundred and fifty-seven members. The present membership of the branch is one hundred and ninety. The charter members are known throughout the order as the "gallant thirteen" on account of their struggle for organization as a society.

On the first day of March, 1878, on account of the rapid increase in membership, the branch removed to room 32 in the Hodge opera block, which was furnished in such good taste and elegance that it is acknowledged that this society has a more attractive session room than any other in the city. A library will soon be added. The regular meetings take place every Thursday evening. It is the intention of the members to invest the surplus money of the branch to create a sinking fund, and in a few years the interest from the investments will pay all beneficiary dues, so that members will have to pay nothing but general dues. The affairs of the society are very carefully and economically manged. On the first day of April, 1878, the branch was named in honor of its president L. J. McParlin Branch, No. 3. The first officers of Branch No. 3 were as follows: Rev. M. J. Darcy, spiritual director; Lawrence J. McParlin, jr., president; Frank J. Brookshaw, first vice-president; Thomas J. Murphy, second vice-president; Louis Bushman, treasurer; Peter H. McParlin, recording and corresponding secretary; George A. Wilber, assistant secretary; William C. Long, financial secretary; John T. Tully, marshal; Thomas M. McParlin, guard. The first trustees were Owen Cain, chairman; John B. Sullivan, Louis Bushman, William C. Long and Thomas J. Murphy.

The officers of the branch at the present time are as follows: Rev. M. J. Darcy, spiritual director; L. J. McParlin, president; Owen Cain, first vice-president; Peter Golihar, second vice-president; Louis Bushman, treasurer; Peter H. McParlin, recording and corresponding secretary; George A. Wilber, assistant secretary; W. C. Long, financial secretary; J. P. Tully, marshal; Thomas Gallagher, guard; William Brown, chancellor; Dr. Frank

Gallagher, medical examiner; trustees, Patrick Powers, J. R. Cummings, John McGovern, Edward O'Brien, John Connolly, jr.

The fee for admission is three dollars for those between the ages of eighteen and forty-five, and six dollars for those between the ages of forty-five and fifty, and the dues are seventy-five cents per quarter; on the occasion of the death of a member of the association in this beneficiary jurisdiction, one dollar and ten cents must be paid within twenty-one days thereafter.

L. J. McParlin, jr., represented the branch at the last grand council meeting, and is elected to represent it at the next session of that body.

C. M. B. A.—BRANCH NO. 27.

This branch was organized by members of L. J. McParlin Branch, No. 3, who were allowed withdrawal cards for the purpose of organizing this branch in and for St. Patrick's parish, of the city of Lockport. The former branch kindly allowed the withdrawing members the ownership of one half of all their property, as several of them had been a long time in the old branch. Branch No. 27 is composed exclusively of members of St. Patrick's parish, and holds its meetings in the hall of Branch No. 3 every Wednesday evening. It was duly instituted and its officers installed June 18th, 1878, by grand deputy John Clifford, of Niagara Falls. The charter officers were as follows:

Rev. P. J. Cannon, spiritual director; Robert Madden, chancellor; John M. G. Colville, president; Daniel McCarthy, first vice-president; Thomas Powers, second vice-president; John B. Sullivan, treasurer; John J. McGrath, recording and corresponding secretary; Robert Madden, assistant secretary; Michael Ryan, financial secretary; John Carney, marshal; Thady Conroy, guard.

Trustees:—James Clifford, chairman; Thomas Conroy, John Carney, Thomas Powers and Michael Ryan.

The regulations of this branch respecting dues, fees and benefits, are identical with those of L. J. McParlin Branch, No. 3, which are fully set forth in the preceding sketch of the history of that society.

CATHOLIC LITERARY UNION.

This society was organized December 26th, 1871, by a meeting of about thirty Catholic young men at what was then the common council chamber, in the old Arcade building on Pine street. Dr. E. J. Brennan presided, and L. J. McParlin jr., acted as secretary. A committee was appointed by which a constitution and by-laws were reported at the second meeting. They were promptly adopted and the following officers were elected:

Spiritual director, Rev. Patrick J. Cannon; president, P. H. Linneen; vice-president, E. J. Brenan, M.D.; recording and corresponding secretary, Lawrence J. McParlin, jr.; financial secretary, James Kehoe, jr.; treasurer, M. C. Feeney; librarian, John Johnston; marshal, William Brown; trustees—Hiram McCollum, chairman; Owen Cain, Michael Lally, James C. Feeney, Thomas Powers, Edward Clifford, Daniel Lundy, Patrick Griffin, John B. Sullivan.

A lecture was delivered in St. Patrick's Church by Rev. Father Caughlin, a Jesuit missionary, on the 13th of February following, from which about $360 was realized. This started the society on the high road to success, and it at once purchased a library of well chosen books, paying down $500 for the same; since that time constant additions have been made thereto.

The association occupied the old common council chamber but a short time, and from there moved to the hall at No. 35 Main street, which was occupied for two years. Thence the union moved to Chrysler's Hall, over 15 & 17 Pine street, which it occupied three years, and from there to the large hall on Main and Pine streets over the Niagara County National Bank, which place it now occupies.

The society has a very large circulating library, a large list of periodicals and a beautifully furnished reading room, meeting hall and parlor. The members are particularly educated in debate and parliamentary law. On the 16th of April 1873, the Union was chartered. The charter officers of the corporation are as follows: Patrick H. Linneen, president; John D. Welch, vice-president; Lawrence J. McParlin, jr., recording and corresponding secretary; John M. Smith, financial secretary; Michael C. Feeney, treasurer; John Johnston, librarian. Trustees: Owen Cain, chairman; James C. Feeney, James D. Caton, Owen Coyne, John B. Sullivan, Edward Clifford, Patrick Griffin, Michael Lally and Thomas Powers. The corporation is allowed to hold $100,000 worth of property.

Since the formation of the society the following gentlemen have held the office of president: Patrick H. Linneen, three terms, and John D. Welch, Patrick Griffin, John M. Smith and Thomas Markley, each one term.

Lawrence J. McParlin, jr., has been secretary three terms. The secretary of the Union is also secretary of the board of trustees, and the duties of that office are laborious. The method of keeping its accounts was the work of Mr. McParlin, and most if not all Catholic organizations in the city have adopted it.

THE NIAGARA LIGHT GUARDS.

That constitution which declares that "a well regulated militia is necessary to the security of a free State," was plainly accepted by the citizens of Lockport, when, in the summer of 1876, they lent encouragement and support to the organization of a company that became the 6th separate company of the 31st brigade N. G. S. N. Y. They recognized the fact that the offices of the National Guard in repressing insurrection and assisting in the enforcement of the laws were as important and necessary as any repulse of foreign hostilities; open manifestations of which importance they saw in the riots of 1877, when this company was called into service.

The initiatory steps for the formation of the company were taken by a few of the spirited young men of the city, and they invited to their aid old war veterans. A majority of these young men were members of a society known as the Alert Gymnastic Association, and in their rooms the first meeting was held. Among those who were first to second the movement was Captain Benjamin H. Fletcher. He attended the preliminary meetings, and gave assurance that all that was needed to bring about the desired consummation was to go ahead with energy. The meetings were well attended for a time, and a majority of the first young men of the city pledged themselves to become members. Others showed reluctance, deeming the maintenance of a company objectionable, as not only being onerous, but interfering with business pursuits and social pleasures.

Finally the meetings were held in Arcade Hall, and when the enlistment roll showed about one hundred names William Bruce Douglas, upon solicitation, consented to become the captain; Horace H. Flager, first lieutenant, and J. William Collier second lieutenant. Drill meetings were then held, as often as practicable, in Arcade Hall, and in an almost incredibly short space of time the company was thoroughly schooled in military tactics. All this transpired by and with the advice and consent of Governor Tilden.

In the fall of 1876 the company appeared on their first parade, full fledged and thoroughly equipped, 102 men strong. The showing they made was highly complimented by the thousands who were out to see them as they filed through the streets. As recognition of their efforts they were in due time provided with elegant quarters on Locust street, near the central portion of the city. Captain Douglas was subsequently promoted to the rank of major of the brigade; Lieutenant Flagler succeeded him; P. M. Ranney became first lieutenant; Second Lieutenant Collier resigned, and First Sergeant John Quadlander succeeded him. Captain Flagler finally removed to Chicago, and Ranney became captain, which position he held at the time of writing this history. S. A. Dietrick, a veteran of the war of the rebellion, was first lieutenant, and Dr. A. J. Allan second lieutenant.

On the occasion of the railroad riots of 1877, the company was ordered to Buffalo, where it did guard duty until order was restored. During the spring of 1878 the company was reinforced by an addition of about twenty-five new members, eighteen of whom enlisted as musicians, forming an excellent band. From the first the organization was known by a name of its own adoption, viz., "The Niagara Light Guards." Its order in the brigade was changed to the 6th separate company in the spring of 1878.

CHURCHES.

The first building erected in Lockport for the purpose of public worship was a log meeting-house built by the Society of Friends. The lot contained two acres, and was the same that is now embraced in the triangular shaped block formed by Main, Market and Elm streets. This lot, a portion of which was used for burial purposes, was purchased at a cost of twenty-four dollars, and the meeting-house built under contract for two hundred dollars.

The Holland Land Company, from whom all titles to land in this section were originally obtained, had a rule or regulation under which the society that should erect the first house of worship in any town was entitled to locate and take one hundred acres of land for the support of its minister. The Society of Friends, being the first to erect such a building in Lockport, was advised to select the specified quantity of land, but declined because the object seemed to be a provision for paying ministers for preaching, to which they were conscientiously opposed.

FIRST PRESBYTERIAN.

This church was formed through the instrumentality of the Rev. David M. Smith, who had been installed pastor of the church at Lewiston in 1817. The church which had been organized at Lockport was taken under the care of the Niagara Presbytery on the 28th of January, 1823. The members at that time were Aaron, Ward, Lucy and Martha Childs, Alpheus and Lucina Saunders, Reuben Brockett, Elliott Lewis, Jeremiah Price, John Gooding, James Bosworth, Elphia B. Knowlton, David A. Holt, Nicholas Holt, Samuel Horn, Betsey Horn, William Parsons, Abigail Bosworth, Sylvia Bitely, Oressa Lewis, Susan Davenport, Sally Bond, Anne Knowlton, Mary A. Gooding, Dolly McLean, Philena Whaley, Amanda Parsons, Norman Shepard, Lorina Shepard, and George W. Cotton.

The society erected a small church on the court-house square, and availed itself of the Holland Land Company's offer, which had been declined by the Society of Friends, and selected its tract of a hundred acres on the transit, about two miles south of the city, which was afterwards sold for one thousand dollars and the proceeds applied toward liquidating the expense of building. Abatus Kent became the first settled pastor, early in 1825. During that year the membership was so much increased that the whole number amounted to fifty-five, and a year later this number was a little more than doubled. Mr. Kent was succeeded by William F. Curry, who was installed pastor on the 12th of February, 1828. He has been represented as a zealous worker, holding religious services three times every Sabbath and delivering a sermon at each.

In 1830 the society built a brick church on the corner of Ontario and Church streets, the site of their present edifice, and the house which they had formerly occupied on the court-house square was used for a long time afterward as a female seminary. The society increased rapidly in membership, and in 1832 reached the large number of three hundred and fifty-five. Mr. Curry's pastoral relation with the church was dissolved on the 31st of January, 1832, and he was succeeded by the Rev. Joseph Myers, who was installed pastor on the 8th of November following and remained until the 8th of July, 1834. He was succeeded by Rev. Gilbert Crawford as a stated supply, who remained nearly three years, when the church was left without a pastor by his accepting a call to the First Presbyterian church in Milwaukee. In 1836 the board of village trustees, of which Deacon Scovell of this church was president, refused to license a circus exhibition, which resulted in considerable excitement for a few days. The manager of the circus was arested, but that night both the Presbyterian and Methodist churches were disfigured by a coat of tar, the leading members of the Methodist society having sustained and commended the decision.

After Mr. Crawford left the pastorate the society employed as a stated supply, for a single year, the Rev. John Keep. For several years previous to Mr. Keep's ministry there was growing up a difference of opinion in regard to the form of government in the church.

The line of demarkation continued to grow more visible, until it was evident there were two distinct elements in the church, which could not be harmonized. At the close of the ministry of Mr. Keep, the disagreement culminated, and resulted in the minority requesting letters to form another church, which were granted, and the dissenters organized what has since been known as the First Congregational Church of Lockport. After the separation the Presbyterian church was supplied, for a few months, by the Rev. Timothy Hopkins, after which the congregation secured as their pastor the Rev. Nathaniel W. Fisher, who took the pastoral charge of the church on the 10th of July, 1839, and remained until the 11th of May, 1842, when he accepted a call to the pastorate of the church at Palmyra, in this State. The Rev. William C. Wisner, who had been for several years pastor of the church in the lower town, but was at this juncture about to separate from that church, received a call to become the pastor of the First Presbyterian Church, which he accepted, and commenced his labors in May, 1842, and continued them through a third of a century. At the commencement of his pastorate, the congregation was comparatively small, numbering only about two hundred. The number increased, however, though slowly for several years, and in 1846 reached two hundred and eighty-six. At length the church was found too small for the congregation, and in 1855 the present spacious edifice was erected upon the same site, and the old building moved back and used for a chapel.

The thirtieth anniversary of Rev. William C. Wisner's pastorate with the church was commemorated by a grand re-union of members and those who had been, accompanied by jubilee exercises. This was on the 15th of May, 1872. On the Sunday evening preceding, the pastor delivered to a large audience his thirtieth anniversary discourse, in which he gave a somewhat extended review of his long ministry. In alluding to the kindness he had received from his official board, he remarked upon "the unbroken and abiding unity which had subsisted for so long a period," and showed that the society had never been more prosperous than at that time. "We have," said he, "a church of over six hundred members. We report to the General Assembly 687, but a portion of these are not on the ground. We have a large and increasing society, and by no means the least interesting feature of our prosperity is to be found in the flourishing condition of our Sabbath-school. It never was larger and more flourishing than now, and I trust that it will ever have a large place in the hearts of this people, and continue to be more and more the nursery of piety to the Church."

Mr. Wisner continued his ministry until 1875, when he retired from the pasrorate and Rev. Henry T. Miller was engaged as a stated supply and remained five months. The Rev. John N. Freeman was called in 1876, and is pastor at the present time.

BAPTIST CHURCH.

In 1816 there were but five persons residing in what is now Lockport entertaining Baptist sentiments. On the 13th of April in that year, under the sanction and direction of John Uptold, missionary from the Hamilton Baptist Missionary Society, they met, formed themselves into a conference, and signed a covenant to devote themselves to the service of God, and make His word their only rule of faith and practice. Thereafter the conference met once a month, and was usually presided over by Samuel Alvord. The meetings were continued in this manner until March, 1817, when, having their number augmented to twelve, they were duly organized into a church. On the 26th of April of that year the society adopted the name of Cambria Baptist Church, and Samuel Alvord was licensed to preach, and was ordained by a council of delegates from the Gaines and Hartland churches, and also from Clinton church, in Canada. He remained the pastor until it was voted that Deacon Garrick Stoughton should take the lead in the meetings, and the society was without a minister until the 27th of December, 1820, when Mr. Alvord was again called to the pastorate, and remained until the 11th of December, 1824. During these early times the meetings were held at different places. The society met for the first time in Lockport on the 6th of December, 1824, at which time about fifty persons constituted the entire membership. In April, 1825, the Rev. R. Winchell was called to the pastorate, and on the 30th of July following the name of the church was changed to the "Lockport Baptist Church."

On the 5th of August, 1825, a committee was appointed to procure a site upon which to erect a house for worship, but the work of building was deferred for several years, the meetings in the meanwhile being held in the second story of a building on Main street, in the court-house and in the old seminary building.

Mr. Winchell remained pastor till 1829, and during his ministry the society had so increased that the membership was upward of a hundred when his pastoral relations with the church ceased. He was succeeded by the Rev. Ichabod Clark, who took charge on the 26th of December of the same year and remained until August 16th, 1831. On the 29th of October following the Rev. R. M. Taggert became the pastor, remaining one year. In 1833 a stone church on Pine street was erected at an expenditure of about five thousand dollars. After the close of Mr. Taggert's ministry no pastor was employed regularly until the 29th of September, 1833, when the Rev. William E. Waterbury became pastor of the church. At the close of his ministry the membership numbered 198. The Rev. T. L. Caldicott became pastor on the 27th of December, 1835, and after a successful ministry of nearly five years resigned and was succeeded on the 23rd of February, 1840, by the Rev. A. Tucker. He remained until 1842, and after the close of his ministry the church was for a considerable time without a pastor.

The deficiency was at length supplied by the society's obtaining Rev. Elon Galusha as its pastor. Up to this time the membership had steadily increased, and the church was in a harmonious and flourishing condition. This happy state of affairs, however, was soon changed to tumult and division, growing out of a course of lectures which was delivered in the church on the "second advent." These lectures were given by the Rev. Mr. Miller, and his doctrine was accepted by Mr. Galusha, the pastor, who commenced advocating it himself. The larger portion of the members were unfriendly to this doctrine, and the pastor and his followers withdrew from the church and held service in another place. This division, which took away about one-third of the members and caused dissatisfaction in various ways, gave the church such a shock that many years elapsed before it recovered.

The Rev. S. B. Webster was called to the pastorate, and remained about two years. The Rev. Mr. Sullivan next became pastor, but the discord was so great that he remained but a few months. Mr. Winchell, who had been the successful pastor in the past, was again called, but he remained less than a year, and the Rev. Mr. Murdock, who succeeded him, did not remain as long as he. The Rev. S. R. Mason became pastor in 1850, but in the following year the discord reached the culminating point; the church withdrew the hand of fellowship from a portion of the members, and shortly after disbanded, giving letters to the remainder.

But a short time elapsed, however, before a movement was made to reorganize it; at a meeting held in November of the same year a portion of those holding letters, thirty in number, organized themselves as a church under the name of the Second Baptist Church of Lockport, and Mr. Mason resumed the pastorship, remaining till 1854. He was succeeded by the Rev. B. D. Marshall, who remained nearly five years. Under his charge the affairs of the church became more harmonious, and the society began to increase in members and influence. In 1860 V. R. Hotchkiss was engaged as stated supply, and held that position satisfactorily for three years. The Rev. S. G. Smith was then called, and took the pastoral charge in September, 1863. In 1867 the congregation had become so large that arrangements were made for building a larger house for its accomodation. The site upon which the present edifice is erected was procured and the old one sold. While the new house was in course of construction the meetings were held in the second story of Strong's block on Pine street.

The reorganization under the name of the Second Baptist Church in 1851 was void in law, and in order to transact business with legal authority it became necessary to have the name of the church changed by an act of the Legislature, which was accordingly done on the 23d of April, 1867, when it received the name of The Baptist Church of Lockport.

The building of the new church left the society with a debt of $14,000. Mr. Smith continued his ministry for nearly seven successive years, and was succeeded by the Rev. J. M. Harris, who commenced his labors in December, 1870, but before the end of his second year ill health compelled him to retire from the ministry, and for about a year thereafter the church was without a settled pastor. During this time the Rev. Dr. Sager supplied the vacancy a portion of the time. In the summer of 1873 arrangements were made with R. B. Hall to serve as a stated supply, and on the 17th of February, 1874, he was ordained and settled over the charge. He remained until April, 1877, when he resigned and was succeeded by the Rev. W. P. Hellings, the present pastor.

NIAGARA STREET METHODIST.

The first preaching by a Methodist minister of which there is any record was by the Rev. Daniel Shepardson, who during the year 1816 and the succeeding year traversed a large region of country, extending from the Genesee to the Niagara river. He came around about once a month, and preached at the school-house about two and one-half miles east of the village of Lockport, and also near Warren's Corners. In the year 1823 Lockport was included in the Buffalo and Lewiston circuit. It was in October of this year that the society was incorporated. The trustees elected were: Samuel Leonard, Austin Atchinson, Ira Smith, Peter Aikin, William Hattan and Laban Smith. This corporation was afterward dissolved, but a reorganization was effected on the 30th of April, 1827. A small building was erected for a church in 1824, which stood at the edge of what was then a forest, now Genesee street, between Pine and Cottage.

Previous to this the meetings were held in a school-house near where the Baptist church now stands, in the court-house, and sometimes in the Presbyterian church. The congregation soon became too large for the diminutive church, and additions were made to its length, making it so long in proportion to its width that it was sometimes called the ball-alley. In a few years it became apparent that this building was still too scanty in its seating capacity, and movements were made for the erection of a house adequate to the wants of the constantly increasing congregation. The old church and its grounds were disposed of, and the site procured which the society still retains. A brick edifice of convenient proportions was erected at a cost of about $10,000. It was completed and dedicated in 1833, during the pastorate of Dr. Seager. A revival followed shortly after the occupation of the new church which considerably increased the membership, but notwithstanding this evidence of prosperity there was still a lack of harmony in some respects.

The building of the new edifice had devolved a debt upon the society, and measures for its liquidation had, of course, to be taken. In the old church the seats were movable benches, but in the new a more fashionable system was adopted, and the benches had been supplanted by pews. These were rented by the trustees, much to the dislike of a portion of the congregation. The agitation of the slavery question found its way into this church, in common with others throughout the country, causing a division in sentiment, and finally a separation. The trustees in 1838, having under consideration a motion opening the church for an anti-slavery convention, it was lost by a tie vote. The trustees were evidently fearful of the results if the motion was carried, for they passed a resolution requiring those who should demand the house for the use of the anti-slavery advocates to sign a bond, making them responsible for any damages it might sustain. The discussions which followed were characterized by bitter denunciations, and in 1840 resulted in a second organization. The dissenters maintained a separate organization, which existed till 1846, when they disbanded, and the members of the denomination were again united in one society.

In the general conflagration which occurred in 1854, the flames extended to and destroyed the Methodist church. The indebtedness of the society had continued to increase, rather than diminish, since the church had been erected, and the amount of insurance that could be collected to apply toward building another church amounted to less than seven hundred dollars. Disheartening as affairs were, four days after the fire a resolution to rebuild was passed. The efforts for this purpose, however, were met with financial embarrassments on every side, which so impeded the progress of the work, that the new house was not dedicated until the 22d of February, 1857.

The membership at the present time numbers upwards of three hundred. The Sabbath-school, which was established in the early days of the society's existence, is in a flourishing condition, numbering two hundred scholars, with a library of two hundred and thirty volumes.

The ministers who have held pastoral charge over the society, in order of succession, are as follows:

D. Shepardson, P. Buell, Z. Paddock, J. B. Alverson, P. Jones, B. Williams, P. Jones, Richard Wright, Isaac Puffer, Sylvester Carey, Ira Bronson, E. Herrick, John Copeland, Andrew Prindle, John Copeland, Wilber Hoag, B. F. Roa, Levi B. Castle, E. O. Fling, John W. Nevins, S. Seager, John E. Cole, Jonas Dodge, John Copeland, J. W. Kent, — Blanchard, A. Steele, Philo E. Brown, E. Thomas, S. Lonckey, J. M. Fuller, W. M. Ferguson, W. B. Sloughter, I. C. Kingsley, Schuyler Seager, Loren Stiles, E. M. Buck, Schuyler Parker, Griffin Smith, E. M. Buck, H. R. Smith, E. E. Chambers, S. Hunt, J. B. Wentworth, S. Seager, K. P. Jarvis, J. N. Brown, C. C. Wilber.

CHRIST CHURCH.

The Rev. David Brown was the first clergyman of the Protestant Episcopal Church to locate in Lockport. He came as a missionary in 1830. Services were then held in the upper story of a brick building on Market street owned by Judge Joel McCollum, which is still standing.

The labors of Mr. Brown were so acceptable and developed so much interest that the members of the congregation resolved to organize themselves into a parish. An incorporation was effected September 28th, 1832. Mr. Edward W. Raymond and Dr. Josiah H. Skinner were elected wardens, and Messrs. Nathan Dayton, Henry Walbridge, Lot Clark, Seymour Scovell, Edward Bissell, Leverett Bissell, Joel McCollum, and George Field were elected vestrymen. The parish took the corporate name of "The Rector, Church Wardens and Vestrymen of Christ Church, Lockport."

In 1832 a church edifice was erected, and was consecrated by Bishop B. T. Onderdonk in the autumn of that year. It stood upon the site of the present church, but farther back, its front being where the chancel of the present church is. It was constructed of sandstone, in the Grecian style of architecture, the interior being nearly square and about as high as wide; four large wooden columns in front supported a wooden gable, in appearance very pretentious, but very unchurchly. It was built as a union meeting-house, but funds falling short, application for aid to complete it was made to Trinity Church, New York. A loan, which was practically a gift, was granted on condition that it be used for Episcopal services only. This condition was agreed to, and carried out. At that time about forty families and thirty-five communicants were connected with the parish.

The following clergymen have been successively rectors of the church:

David Brown, from 1830 to 1833; Orange Clark, from 1834 to 1836; Russell Wheeler, from 1836 to 1837; Ebenezer H. Cressey, from 1837 to 1841; Origen P. Holcomb, from October, 1841, to August, 1843; Erastus B. Foote, from October, 1843, to December, 1845; Henry Stanley, from December, 1846, to 1849; Orlando F. Starkey, from December, 1849, to 1855; Andrew Mackie, from April, 1856, to 1857; Martin Moody, from February, 1860, to November, 1860; Albert C. Lewis, from August, 1861, to July, 1863; James Abercrombie, D. D., from August, 1863, to May, 1874; Frederic S. Hyde, from July, 1874, to April, 1877.

It was during the rectorship of the Rev. Mr. Starkey that the present church was erected. The plans and specifications were procured of Mr. Frank Wills, of New York. The old edifice was pulled down and its materials used in the construction of the new one. The cornerstone was laid early in May, 1854, by the Rev. Henry W. Lee, D. D., rector of St. Luke's Church, Rochester, afterwards Bishop of Iowa. It was consecrated on November 16th, of the same year, by Bishop William H. De Lancey, D. D., LL.D. It is of stone, Gothic in architecture; cost about $5,000, and will seat about 300.

The rectory was built during the rectorship of the Rev. Dr. Abercrombie. It stands in the rear of the church on a lot the gift of the Hon. Washington Hunt. It is of stone, Gothic in design, elegant and commodious, and cost about $3,000. It was completed and occupied in November, 1864. In 1869 a bell for the church was presented by Dr. B. L. Delano, a former parishioner.

The Hon. Washington Hunt, LL. D., was connected with this church from the time he took up his residence in Lockport till his death. Besides being a vestryman, and repeatedly representing the parish in the convention of the diocese, he was for twelve years a deputy from the diocese to the General Convention. He was always deeply interested in the welfare of the parish, a most generous contributor toward its support, and in his will left it a legacy of $1,000.

The present rector is the Rev. George W. Southwell, who took charge in May, 1877. There were reported to the convention of the diocese in September, 1877, as connected with the church, sixty families, one hunredd and ten communicants, eleven teachers and seventy-five pupils in the Sunday-school, and three hundred volumes in the library.

SECOND WARD PRESBYTERIAN.

The Second Ward Presbyterian Church of Lockport was organized June 5th, 1832, with a small membership, as the Second Presbyterian Church of Lockport.

The first elders were Sampson Robbins and Willis Peck. The first trustees were Joel McCollum, Nathan Dayton, Willis Peck, William Kline, John Harris and John Gooding.

The congregation worshiped for about five years in a brick block on Market street. In 1836 a doctrinal defection occurred under the pastorate of Rev. Samuel Beaman. Mr. Beaman seems to have lived a blameless life, and in many respects to have held the orthodox faith most sincerely. Fault was found with him for teaching a certain kind of perfectionism, disregarding the special sanctity of the Lord's day, teaching that believers might get above the need of "ordinances," teaching too strictly the literal interpretations of the Bible and rejecting all creeds.

The Presbytery of Niagara, on February 23d, 1837, prescribed some articles of faith to test the soundness of the church. Only seven members subscribed to them, six women and one man, and these persons were declared to be the church. The total membership had been about 30. Mr. Beaman soon removed to New York city and ceased preaching.

The present stone edifice on Van Buren street, seating about 400, was erected at a cost of about $5,000, and dedicated January 8th, 1838. Rev. William Wisner, of Ithaca, preached the dedicatory sermon.

The name was changed to the Second Ward Presbyterian Church, and on December 30th, 1846, the property was sold for debt and bought by a member of the society for $900. The society has always been financially weak. About 500 members have been connected with the church since its organization. Many revivals have prevailed in it. After one conducted by the eccentric Rev. Jedediah Burchard, over 100 persons united with the church, but a very large portion of them soon proved themselves spurious converts. The church reported a membership of 125 in 1878.

The Sabbath-school has been well attended and prosperously conducted from the first. It has been a constant nursery of wisdom and piety, furnishing materials for the church and continuing its services when the voice of the preacher was temporarily suspended.

Dr. J. H. Helmer, the children's pastor, has labored zealously as superintendent of this school for about 25 years, and has thus been the religious instructor of full two generations of children and youths. His natural force seems yet unabated, and his zeal in the study and teaching of the word of God undiminished, so that he may yet instruct another generation.

The following ministers have successively officiated: E. B. Coleman, R. G. Murray, J. Hovey, F. W. Graves, E. H. Adams, S. Beaman, William C. Wisner, Mr. Loomis, A. Van Wagner, W. Rosevelt, George P. Pruden, D. Cushing, William C. Boyce, W. S. Parsons, E. W. Kellogg, Robert Norton, J. W. Marcusson and E. P. Marvin. The Rev. Robert Norton has just been called to serve the church a second time and is now its pastor.

GRACE CHURCH

was duly organized on the 8th day of February, 1835, under the name or title of "The Rector, Church Wardens and Vestrymen of Grace Church, Lockport." Edmund Raymond and John Bagley were elected church wardens, and Hezekiah Thomas, Lathrop Fellows. Edward I. Chase, Elias Ransom, jr., Alexander Ralston, John S. Shuler, Stephen B. Bond and George H. Boughton were elected vestrymen. The number of vestrymen to be annually chosen was fixed at eight; and Tuesday in Easter week was designated as the day for the annual elections. Efforts were made to procure the services of a minister, but so small was the number of members, and so limited their pecuniary means, that these efforts were ineffectual until October, 1835, when the Rev. Beardsley Northrup accepted a call at a salary of $550 for six months. He officiated as minister until March, 1836, and then resigned. During the first three years the services were held in a room in the third story, over the store of Mr. George H. Boughton. For the first two years the services were mostly conducted by lay readers.

In August, 1836, the vestry resolved to build a church, and for that purpose bought of Messrs. Elias Ransom & George H. Boughton a lot on Buffalo street, at a price exceeding $2,000. A subscription paper to raise funds therefor, and for building the church was started. The building was to be 35 by 56 feet, to be built of wood; and the cost of it was estimated at $2,000. In February, 1838, the church edifice was finished, with a capacity to seat two hundred and fifty persons. The slips were generally rented at prices varying from $8 to $35 for the remainder of the year, amounting in the whole to the sum of $840. A debt was created, which long hung over and embarrassed the society, and retarded its growth and prosperity.

In June, 1837, the Rev. George Denison was invited to become the minister of the church at a salary of $500 a year, and a small missionary stipend. He accepted the call, took charge in August following, and continued in charge until December, 1841.

The Right Reverend Benjamin T. Onderdonk, D.D., Bishop of New York, consecrated the church edifice on the 12th day of August, 1838. At the annual renting of

slips in 1840 the amount realized therefrom was less than $600. In 1848, being the second year of the rectorship of the Rev. Charles H. Platt, the slips were all rented, the proceeds of which were $1,224. The congregation began to experience inconvenience for want of room in the church. In August, 1848, Mr. Platt tendered his resignation, but, at the earnest solicitation of his parishioners, withdrew it. During the time of the rectorship of Mr. Platt, a period of more than thirteen years, the most kindly relations existed between him and the parish, and the church steadily increased in numbers and prosperity.

In 1852 the inconvenience for want of room had induced competition in the renting of slips to such an extent that some, being unable to procure sittings, or becoming offended by such competition, left the congregation. The subject of enlarging the church edifice was again brought up; committees were appointed to inquire into the matter, and to devise ways and means by which this great inconvenience could be obviated. After much discussion and deliberation was had upon the subject, the vestry on the 13th day of March, 1852, resolved to purchase a lot and build a new church thereon. Accordingly the location on the corner of Genesee and Cottage streets was selected, and the large and elegant church edifice now thereon was built. The building is of stone, seventy-two feet in front, and one hundred and twenty feet deep; has a capacity to seat five hundred persons, and, including the lot, cost about $20,000. The vestry resolved that the money therefor be raised by subscriptions, payable in installments; that when completed permanent valuations be put upon the slips; that subscriptions, when paid, should entitle the subscribers to apply the amount thereof towards the purchase of permanent leases of slips, subject to an annual tax of not more than ten per cent. upon such valuations, and subject also to such rules and regulations as the vestry may, from time to time, prescribe; and that the vestry would not proceed further therein unless good subscriptions therefor should be secured to the amount of $12,500 before the first day of June then next. Gillett Bacon, George W. Davis and Sullivan Caverno were appointed a committee to solicit subscriptions, and in time, largely through the perseverence of Mr. Caverno, good subscriptions were obtained to an amount greater than that prescribed by the vestry. A large amount was also promised on which the committee thought it would be safe to rely.

In November, 1852, the work of building the new church was commenced. The corner stone was laid on the 2nd of May, 1853, according to the rites of the Protestant Episcopal Church. This stone was a cube, measuring twenty inches on each surface, and was laid at the southeast corner of the chancel wall. It was marked with a cross on the upper surface; a Greek cross, incised, and Roman numerals denoting the year, on the south face; and a Greek cross incised on the east face. An opening was made on the north side, and in the cavity, which was afterward closed with a marble slab, was deposited a leaden box, soldered, which contained the customary papers, etc. The church was finished, and the use and right of occupation of the slips were sold on the 12th of March, 1855. Divine services were thereafter held in the new church. The purchase of the new site and the building of the edifice again involved the parish in debt, which, however, was removed in a few years. Its consecration was delayed until the 12th of August, 1857, in consequence of a rule which the bishop had adopted, that no church should be consecrated until all legal incumbrances thereon were removed. To encourage the removal of incumbrances the Rev. Charles H. Platt, in addition to a liberal subscription, refused to accept an increase of his salary, which had recently been raised from $1,000 to $1,200.

When the church was completed, nearly every slip, except those that were reserved as free sittings, was rented. The number of communicants has been increased from about twenty to five hundred and twenty-five; the number of families belonging to the congregation from about forty to two hundred and fifty; the average attendance on the services from about fifty to three hundred; the annual slip rents from about $700 to $3,870; the annual salary of the rector from $500 to $2,260. In number of families and number of communicants, Grace Church parish stands higher than any other parish in the diocese. The office of deaconess, as an assistant to the rector, has been created, and Miss Harriet M. Dayton now holds that office at a salary of $250 a year.

The Honorable Peter D. Walter is and for twenty-six years has been superintendent of the Sunday school. Under his efficient and popular administration, the school has been increased in number from about thirty to two hundred and sixty scholars. It now comprises ten officers, twenty-four teachers, and two hundred and sixty catechumens and scholars. The average attendance is more than two hundred.

The value of the church edifice and furniture is not less than $35,000; that of the rectory $6,000, subject to a mortgage of $1,200.

In addition to $3,870 slip rents, above mentioned, there was raised, during the past year, by the Ladies' Guild of Grace church, toward church repairs $1,200, and by offerings for parochial, diocesan, and general objects, about $2,000, amounting in all to about $7,070.

The names of the clergymen, the order of their succession, and the time of their administration or rectorship respectively, are as follows:

Rev. Beardsley Northrup, minister, from October 12th 1835, to March 9th, 1836; Rev. George Denison, minister, from July 1st, 1837, to December, 1841; Rev. Lloyd Windsor, rector, from February 13th, 1842, to June 24th, 1846; Rev. Charles H. Platt, rector, from July 14th, 1846, to December 21st, 1859; Rev. William A. Matson, D. D., rector, from May 1st, 1860, to September 1st, 1866; Rev. Lawrence S. Stevens, rector, from September 1st, 1866, to October 1st, 1870; Rev. Charles G. Gillit, Ph. D., rector, from December 18th, 1870, to October 1st, 1875; Rev. Foster Ely, D.D., rector, from December 15th, 1875, to the present time.

The names of the wardens, the order of their succession, and their term of office, respectively, are as follows:

Edward W. Raymond from February 9th, 1835, to April 1st, 1840; John Bagley from February 9th, 1835, to March 28th, 1837; Hezekiah Thomas from March 28th, 1837, to April 17th, 1838; Hezekiah W. Scovel from April 17th, 1838, to May 25th, 1855; George W. Merchant from April 1st, 1840, to April 18th, 1843; Elias Ransom from April 18th, 1843, to April 10th, 1860; James Ferguson from June 22d, 1855, to April 14th, 1857; Sullivan Caverno from April 14th, 1857, to April 6th, 1858; Peter D. Walter from April 6th, 1858, to the present time; James Ferguson from April 10th, 1860, to April 2d, 1861; Peleg B. Peckham from April 2d, 1861, to April 22d, 1862; Samuel N. Edwards from April 22d, 1862, to April 7th, 1863, D. Fowler Bishop from April 7th, 1863, to the present time.

The Reverend Foster Ely, D. D., rector; Hon. Peter D. Walter and D. Fowler Bishop, M. D., wardens; and Timothy E. Ellsworth, Thomas N. Van Valkenburgh, John E. Pound, John Hodge, Freeman H. Mott, Samuel Rogers, George C. Green, and William E. Jenney, vestrymen, compose the present vestry.

THE UNIVERSALIST CHURCH.

The doctrine of God's impartial grace was first proclaimed in Lockport by missionary efforts as early as 1835, but the names of the preachers of that time have been forgotten. The first preacher of whom any record can be obtained was Rev. Job Potter, though Rev. Luther Knapp also preached in the then village, but at what time the records do not disclose. Rev. Job Potter was in the village in the winter of 1836 and 1837, and held meetings in the court-house which resulted, soon after, in the formation of a society under the name of the First Universalist Society of Lockport; but for some cause unknown at this time some of the members lost their interest, and finally the attempt to sustain preaching was abandoned for a time. Those who were the real friends and advocates of the doctrines of the Universalist church, then everywhere spoken against, were discouraged and disheartened by the failure of their efforts, and in this condition affairs remained until early in the summer of 1841, when Rev. Charles Hammond, a preacher of considerable ability, afterwards editor of a Universalist paper, called *The Western Luminary*, published at Rochester, came to the village "determined," to use his own words, "to make a trial" and see what could be done for the cause of truth as he understood it. The friends of the cause, though discouraged and burdened with a debt incurred in their previous efforts, came together at his call and again hired the court-house, and held several meetings. Feeling encouraged by the attendance at the services, the meetings were continued.. Being at last refused the use of the court-house, they hired a hall that would seat about one hundred and fifty, and continued their meetings upon every alternate Sunday. In February, 1842, the Conference of the Niagara Association of Universalists met in the village, the Methodist church being engaged for the services during the two days' session of the association. A number of converts were made to the faith in universal salvation, and united in the bond of church fellowship. About this time the hall occupied for religious worship proved too small to accommodate the congregation, and they moved to Franklin Hall.

On the eleventh day of April, of the same year, a society was organized in accordance with an act passed in 1831, entitled "An act for the incorporation of religious societies," and the following named persons were elected as trustees, to serve in classes as the act provided: For one year, Daniel A. Van Valkenburgh, Harlow V. Wood; for two years, Samuel C. Stevens, David S. Crandall; for three years, Stephen B. Ballou, Abial Eastman. On the fith day of May, 1842, Elliott Lewis and Samuel C. Stevens appeared before Judge Elias Ransom and certified to the act of incorporation. Steps were immediately taken toward building a meeting-house. A lot on the corner of Church and Ontario streets was purchased at a cost of $800. The records do not state when the erection of the building was begun or when the corner-stone was laid. There were various delays in the work. Rev. Mr. Hammond closed his labors with the society, and in the spring of 1843 they called the Rev. B. B. Bunker. During his pastorate the church was completed and dedicated in the fall of 1843.

Rev. S. R. Smith, late of Buffalo, preached the dedicatory sermon. Mr. Bunker continued with the society until December, 1844; then there was a period of supplies, until in April, 1845, Uriah Clark, a young man, was called to the pastorate, and was ordained to the work of the ministry in the church at Lockport, May 23rd, 1845, Rev. S. R. Smith preaching the ordination sermon. The records are silent as to the length of time he served the society, but probably about fifteen months. He was succeeded for a portion of a year by his brother, Rev. George Clark. After this the society called Rev. J. J. Austin, and he remained about six years. A good degree of prosperity was enjoyed under this pastorate. He was succeeded by Rev. Nelson Snell, now of Rochester. This pastorate extended from 1854 to 1862. In November, 1862, Rev. Richmond Fisk, jr., now of Syracuse, became pastor of the church. His pastorate extended over a period of great political excitement, and a sermon preached by him on the eve of the second election of Abraham Lincoln to the presidency of the United States divided the society; a large number left the church and entered other communions, and the church has never fully recovered from the effects of that division. In August, 1865, Mr. Fisk was followed by Rev. E. W. Reynolds, who remained only eight months. The next pastor was Rev. William N. Van De Mark, who begun his labors in August, 1866, and closed them in April, 1869. During his pastorate the church building was remodeled and enlarged at an expense of about $6,000. He was a man of much power as a speaker, and drew together a large and admiring congregation. He was followed in July, 1869, by Rev. L. D.

Cook, an able and earnest preacher. During his pastorate a large number of persons united with the society, the accession of members being greater than under any previous pastor. He remained about two years, and after a season of candidating, during which many men of note were heard, Rev. Charles F. Lee, now editor of *The Christian Leader*, a Universalist paper published at Utica, was called to the pastorate. He began his labors September 29th, 1872, and resigned in December, 1873. Although a young man, he possessed marked abilities as a speaker and sermonizer, and was well liked by his people, who parted with him with more than ordinary regret. His immediate successor was Rev. H. B. Smith, now of Stoughton, Massachusetts, who came January 1st, 1874, and remained until June, 1876. After a month's interim, during which time the pulpit was supplied by Rev. A. P. Reiss, a student from the Canton Theological School, Rev. George Adams was called, and became pastor of the society July 1st, 1876, and remained thirteen months. After this, with the exception of an occasional supply, the church was closed until April, 1878. December 23rd, 1877, the present pastor, Miss E. E. Bartlett, preached to a small congregation. She preached again January 20th, 1878, and for three successive Sundays in February, when she was unanimously called to the pastorate of the society, and she began her labors April 7th, 1878. Miss Bartlett is a native of New Haven, Conn., and a graduate of the Theological School at Canton, St. Lawrence county, N. Y. This completes the list of pastors of this society, extending over a period of forty years. The present official control of the society is vested in a board of six trustees, as follows: J. M. Chrysler, J. B. Boyce, Frederick Crosby, John McCue, J. S. Breyfogle, John Reando; clerk, J. Dunham; treasurer, C. C. Parker.

A Sunday-school was organized in 1841, and has continued with varying success since that time. It is now in a healthful and growing condition. The first pastor received a salary of $500. Others have received as high as $1,500. The society has always been burdened with more or less debt. Efforts have been made from time to time to cancel the indebtedness, though without success; but at present the outlook is hopeful, and the end so much to be desired by all interested in the welfare of the church seems likely to be attained.

ST. JOHN THE BAPTIST, ROMAN CATHOLIC.

This church has existed over forty years; its history is the history of the Catholic Church in Lockport. The first stone of St. John's Church was laid in August, 1834. A brother of James Mooney, of Lockport, had the job of building, and by Christmas the walls were up, the roof on, and though the windows were boarded up, and there was no floor, the members then attended mass in the new church.

The land on which it stands was donated by Edward Bissell and Hon. Joel McCollum, and Lyman A. Spalding gave a lot in another part of the town, which was sold, and the proceeds applied to paying for the balance the church ground.

The stone was quarried on the bank of the creek where George Stainthrop's house now stands. The cut stone corners of the front were supplied by men who worked on the rock sections of the canal enlargement, the contractors generously permitting them to select such stones as they chose.

These masons and stone cutters would give a day or two's work, occasionally; others would send a load of lime or sand, others would assist as laborers, while a few donated money. One Scotch Catholic, living on the ridge, gave $150, and it was to gratify his whim that the rear of the original building was constructed in a semicircular shape, giving a curious appearance to it as seen from below the hill. Something less than $200 was collected in New York city. The roof was put on by Colonel Mapes. Previous to Christmas a priest, whose name we have not ascertained, came once a month to say mass in the courthouse. Now Father Managan came to be the resident pastor of the little flock.

The little congregation was divided—the men on one side, the women on the other. One old lady states that they would kneel upon a flat stone to keep them from contact with the ground. A few seats were supplied by using the plank that had done service as scaffolding. Father Managan's stay was not long, and but few reminiscences of his pastorate are preserved. Father Costello was the second resident priest of St. John's, an energetic, learned, and influential man, working for the advancement of his congregation. It was discovered, however, early in 1842, that he had a Protestant wife in town, to whom he had been married in Buffalo by a justice of the peace, six months before the discovery. There was living in Rochester a fine old priest, Rev. Bernard O'Reilly, afterwards second bishop of Hartford, Connecticut, who was a sort of vicar-general for western New York, and who was, even then, spoken of by old residents as Bishop O'Reilly. He was immediately communicated with, and the matter laid before him. The following Sunday he appeared in Lockport, bringing with him the third priest of St. John's, Father McMullen, a newly ordained ecclesiastic, who then commenced a long and honorable course of service and whose name is held in reverence and benediction until this day. Father Costello was degraded from the priesthood and permitted to quietly depart.

He had commenced and carried well forward the erection of the fine, substantial stone house nearly opposite to the church, which was designated as a pastoral residence. This property was held in his wife's name, and when his action was discovered she exchanged it for a farm in the West, to which place she and her parents removed. This house is now the tasteful residence of the family of the late Judge Lamont.

Father McMullen's pastorate extended over a period of seven years and a half, beginning with March, 1842, during which time the church was enlarged to its present size. Previous to enlarging the church the priest's house was built. When Father McMullen came he boarded at a hotel, which was so inconvenient that the people united to build the stone house on the site of the present residence. After the addition to the church was completed it was consecrated by Bishop Timon, who had recently entered upon his episcopal duties. The congregation continued to increase, and the pastor discharged his duties acceptably. His successor, Father McEvoy, came to Lockport in October, 1850, and remained only two years. He had a large and flourishing congregation. He formed a total abstinence society, and exerted himself to forward his parishioners in the spiritual life. Rev. M. Creedon assumed the pastoral charge in October, 1852, and continued four years. He was an educated, gentlemanly man, a good speaker, and of a social, genial turn. He was a faithful, zealous priest, highly regarded by his people and respected in the community. During his term of office the Know-Nothing party was in existence, and a story was started that the Catholics were secretly collecting arms and ammunition, which they intended using to overpower the Protestants. It was definitely stated that the basement of St. John's Church was the depot for such articles in Lockport. So high did the excitement run during a political campaign, that a deputation of Know-Nothings waited upon Father Creedon to ascertain if any such deposit of weapons had been made. They were civilly received, and shown through the church premises, when they departed satisfied that the report was a slander.

Not long after, one Sunday evening, the church took fire from the furnace, but by timely and well directed efforts the fire was easily subdued.

One Sunday afternoon in the fall of 1856, Father Creedon called a meeting of the parishioners to consider some subject which he wished to bring before them. They convened in the basement, in which he had two flourishing schools, supported by voluntary monthly collections. The matter to be considered was the building of a new church—the initiatory steps for the construction of the present St. Patrick's. It was favorably considered, pledges of aid were given, and Father Creedon introduced his successor—Father Bede—to whom the task of building was committed.

Father Bede officiated as priest until 1860, carrying forward the construction of the new edifice in the meantime, when he was removed to Elmira, where he afterward died.

His successor was Father Gleason, the present vicar-general of the diocese of Buffalo. Under his administration, the new church on Church street was completed, and consecrated by Bishop Tinon, under the invocation of St. John the Baptist, the church on Chestnut street being given up to the Sisters of St. Mary for a school, they having just arrived from Belgium.

The sisters resided in the priest's house, and used the church for a school-room, the pews having been removed.

In 1866 the bishop decided to re-open the old church, the sisters having purchased the land on which their academy is located on Church street, and removed to the frame house then standing upon it. There was doubt as to whether the sisters could use the old church for a school, as the land on which it stood was originally donated to the Catholics of Lockport for a Catholic church; if it ceased to be used for a church, it would probably revert to its original donors, or their heirs.

Besides, it was apparent that one church was not enough to contain the English-speaking Catholics of the parish.

Father Quigley was sent to say mass in the old church, and to gather the nucleus of a congregation in that part of the town. Repairs of the old church were commenced, but Father Quigley stayed only a few months, the bishop transferring him to Buffalo, where he has since remained.

Father Fitzpatrick succeeded him. He was a young man, and also staid but a short time. Under his administration repairs were continued, a new roof being put on and new pews built.

Father Byrnes came in 1867. He had the walls frescoed, a new altar erected, and the interior put into a respectable shape. In the meantime an organ had been procured, which is still in use. Soon after Father Byrnes's arrival, Bishop Timon came and rededicated the old church, restoring to it the former name of St. John's, and giving the name of St. Patrick's to the edifice on Church street.

In 1869 Father Byrnes was transferred to Rochester, where he died recently, and Father Mulholland came from Seneca Falls in his place. He applied himself assiduously to his duties, and had the satisfaction of seeing the church prosper under his pastoral care. He was plain and unostentatious, a firm friend, and zealous for the honor of religion. He spent five years in the faithful service of St. John's.

One of his last works was the rebuilding of the pastoral residence. The church basement had previously been put in order for the use of the school.

On the evening of the last Saturday of November, 1873, as he was going from the church, where he had been hearing confessions, to take his tea, by a misstep on the stairway leading to his dining-room he was precipitated to the bottom, striking his head against the door frame there and fracturing his skull. He was taken up insensible, and remained so until his death, which took place about midnight on the following Sunday. His funeral was attended by many of his brother clergymen and by a great concourse of people. He was interred in the new Catholic cemetery on Gooding street.

On the death of Father Mulholland the bishop sent Rev. Edward Kelly from Buffalo to take temporary charge of the parish. Father Kelly at once endeared himself to the people by his earnest labors for their welfare, and by his plain and instructive discourses. In June, 1874, he returned to Buffalo to resume his duties as chancellor of the diocese.

Rev. Matthew J. Darcy, the present incumbent, was transferred from Bath immediately on the retirement of Father Kelly. He soon established his reputation as an

ST. JOSEPH'S ACADEMY, LOCKPORT N.Y.
Directed by the Sisters of St. Mary

energetic and zealous priest, an earnest and effective speaker, and an able financier. Under his administration the church indebtedness has been nearly cancelled.

Father Darcy made a visit to his parents in Ireland in 1875, and remained absent about four months. His place was filled during his absence by Rev. J. C. O'Reilley, now of Middleport, N.Y.

Hiram T. McCollum and Lawrence J. McParlin, jr., are trustees of the church at present. The latter gentleman inaugurated the system of giving receipts and statements for pew rents, which no doubt will be followed by the other churches.

Rev. Fathers Gleason, O'Farrel and J. Cannon have been the pastors of St. Patrick's Church since its formation from St. John's.

From the latter has also been formed St. Mary's Parish, for the German Catholics of the city, who have a neat frame edifice on Buffalo street.

FIRST FREE CONGREGATIONAL.

This church was brought into existence in consequence of adverse opinion as to the line of policy and conduct to be observed in the government of the First Presbyterian Church of Lockport. An attempt to harmonize these difficulties seemed quite futile, and separation finally became the inevitable result. The dissenters requested letters of dismissal from the First Presbyterian Church, which would allow them to form themselves into a separate society. These were granted, and they proceeded to organize a Congregational church. A meeting for this purpose was called on the 7th of June, 1838, presided over by the Rev. H. G. Nott, of Buffalo. Upwards of forty letters were presented, and by a resolution the bearers were formed into a body denominated the First Congregational Church of Lockport, adopting a constitution which embraced the articles of faith and form of government agreeable to their principles.

On the 16th of August following the society leased the third story of a store on Main street, at an annual rent of $100, where the meetings were held. The society engaged Rev. William Bacon as a stated supply. The members at the time of the organization numbered forty-five, which number was increased to ninety-two at the close of the year, about six months later.

On the 7th of January, 1839, a committee was appointed to select a suitable piece of ground upon which to erect a house for worship. The site selected was on the corner of Church and Niagara streets. It was purchased of Mrs. Millard, and on the 20th of May, 1839, the trustees were instructed to build the church. It was constructed of lime stone, fifty by seventy-five feet, and was so far completed that the congregation met for religious services within its walls for the first time on the 12th of January, 1840. The society had at this time increased to one hundred and fifty members. Though Mr. Bacon was not settled as a pastor he remained as a supply until August, 1841. Washington Roosevelt was afterward engaged for an indefinite time, and remained until May, 1842. William F. Curry was then called to the pastorate, and remained till August 7th, 1844.

On the 11th of January, 1844, a committee was appointed to report on the obligations of the church in regard to slavery. The report denounced the institution in very bitter terms, declaring it the work of darkness; and a resolution was shortly after adopted refusing to receive into membership or communion any person who justified it. This measure caused no division in the church, as opposition to slavery was one of the causes which actuated the original members in separating from the Presbyterian church. After the departure of Mr. Curry the church was without a settled pastor until the 15th of January, 1845, when the Rev. Edgar Perkins, who had been a supply for about two months, was called to the pastorate. He was ordained on the 25th of June following, and was succeeded by the Rev. Edward W. Gillman, who was called on the 15th of October, 1849.

On the 2d of November, 1854, the church edifice was destroyed by fire. The society received but $1,000 from insurance, and was at the same time twice that sum in debt. Only a week passed, however, before it was resolved to rebuild, and the brick chapel was so speedily erected that in January following meetings were held in it. The present stone church was erected upon the foundation of the old one, at a cost of about $16,000. The chapel cost about $1,800.

Mr. Gillman continued his pastorate until the 17th of June, 1856. After this the Rev. F. W. Braums was a stated supply for six months, closing that relation with the church on the 16th of April, 1857. The Rev. Zacharias Eddy then acted as pastor for a few weeks, when Rev. Joseph L. Bennett was engaged as a stated supply. On the 23d of August, 1857, the society extended a call to Mr. Bennett to become the settled pastor, which he accepted and was installed shortly afterward After a successful pastorate, extending over a period of more than thirteen years, his resignation was accepted on the 12th of January, 1871. At the commencement of his ministry the membership of the church was about one hundred and fifty; it had increased to near five hundred at the close. His successor, the Rev. J. W. Cooper, commenced his pastorate on the 10th of June, 1871, and was installed shortly after. In August, 1877, the membership was reported to be 468, and that of the Sabbath-school, including the Bible class, 466. The Sabbath-school was established when the society was first organized, and has since been under able superintendents, and is in a very flourishing condition. The pastorate of Mr. Cooper closed on the 21st of February last, since which time the society has had no regular pastor.

CALVARY PRESBYTERIAN.

The city of Lockport, from the first, has extended its growth in a southeasterly direction more than any other, and hence most of the older churches are not now centrally located. About ten years ago, a religious service was started on Sunday afternoon, chiefly by the efforts of a zealous and godly man, now deceased, Mr. Henry Harrington, first in his own house and then in the stone school-house on South street. The city pastors and others alternated in preaching there, so that the service seldom failed from year to year, and much spiritual good was accomplished. A few persons met on May 15th, 1877, for mutual conference about the interests of the cause of Christ in the southeastern part of the city, and concluded it best to organize a society and church upon the doctrinal basis of the World's Evangelical Alliance, and with the Presbyterian form of government, making the officers elective for a specific term. On September 28th the South street school-house was rented for one year, and Rev. E. P. Marvin began preaching there October 7th, 1877. Professor Everett Earle led the singing and Miss Libbie Pickard played the organ. The room was well filled, and thirty-four persons attended the first prayer-meeting, which was held on the following Thursday evening. A Sabbath-school was organized, with the following officers: Willard H. Wild, superintendant; Edward G. Parker, assistant superintendent, and Willie Saraw, secretary and treasurer.

On October 23d a committee negotiated with the Board of Education to purchase the school-house for $900, by paying $100 down, and the Calvary Religious Society, organized November 2d consummated the bargain. The first trustees were William Glover, Charles R. Parker, James Dickson, J. J. Winne, John Woodyer and George Burch. The building, 24 by 33 feet, soon proving inadequate to the congregation and Sabbath-school, was extended to 50 feet in length at an expense of $400, all of which was soon paid. The building was dedicated on December 10th, with a sermon by the pastor.

A series of meetings were held during the winter, in which 25 or 30 persons were converted to God. It was then proposed to organize a church, and an independent constitution was presented, with a confession of faith and covenant based on the doctrines of the Evangelical Alliance, and these were approved by the congregation. Upon ascertaining afterward that nearly all the persons who intended to join the church preferred the Presbyterian order of government, the society recommended this instead of the independent order, with the same confession and covenant.

Accordingly a committee appointed by the Presbytery of Niagara, consisting of Rev. Robert Norton and Elder Thomas Scovell, met the congregation on Sabbath evening, May 5th, 1878, and regularly organized the Calvary Presbyterian Church, with 28 members, 26 joining on profession of faith and by letters.

The following officers were elected: Elders—William Glover and Willard H. Wild; deacons—James Dickson, J. J. Winne and George Burch. The sacrament of the Lord's Supper was then administered.

Mr. Marvin preached his first sermon in the school-house on the wonderful character of Christ, from Isa. lx, 6, and the dedication sermon, upon the household of God, from Eph. ii, 19. Mr. Norton preached the organization sermon, upon the church as the body of Christ, from 1 Cor.

xii, 27. In May, 1878, the officers of the society issued the following statements, in an appeal for aid to build a plain brick chapel, to hold four or five hundred persons.

"In the southeastern quarter of the city we have a population of about 2,500 people, mostly Americans, within whose bounds no church edifice stands. In October, 1877, we procured a school-house and lot for $900, paying $100 down. This building, 24 feet wide, we lengthened to 50 feet, at an expense of $400, all of which is paid. The attendance on the preaching services, E. P. Marvin pastor, has comfortably filled the room, and the Sabbath-school, Mr. W. H. Wild superintendent, has been much straitened for room, the average attendance having been about 170 persons. We believe that both congregation and Sabbath-school can be largely increased if we have more room. * * * We desire and design to make it a church for the people, and a light-bearing, Christ-witnessing missionary body. We are in favor of free pews, congregational singing, plainness and simplicity of church architecture, dress and worship, the sacredness of the sanctuary, and only the simple scriptural method of raising money for the Lord. We pay all current expenses as we go, by weekly offerings, the last offering of the month going to the pastor."

FREE METHODIST.

A formal organization of a Free Methodist class was effected by Rev. C. D. Brooks, of Pekin, in 1862, with about twenty-five members, among whom were Lewis E. Chase and wife, Justus Southworth and wife, William Pawling and wife, William R. Little and wife, J. H. Blosser and wife, D. Snediker and wife, and James Payne.

Rev. Levi Wood of this denomination had held meetings in private houses for some time previous to the organization of a church. Jacob H. Blosser was chosen the first class leader. Rev. C. D. Brooks remained as pastor one year, and was followed, in the order named, by Ichabod White, 1 year; A. A. Phelps, 3 years ; George W. Marcellus, 2 years; M. M. Downing, 1 year; E. P. Salem, 1 year; A. B. Mathewson, 2 years; G. W. Coleman, 1 year; Nathaniel Brown, 1 year; C. C. Eggleston, 2 years; and Rev. William Manning, the present pastor, who commenced his labors in September, 1877.

Meetings were held in private houses and public halls until the erection of the church edifice, which was commenced in 1865 and completed and dedicated by the Rev. D. W. Thurston, of Syracuse, in the spring of 1866. It is built of brick, 38 by 68 feet in size, and cost about $5,000.

The present number of members is thirty-eight. The trustees are Washington Carl, William R. White and — Brown. This class belongs to the Buffalo district of the Genesee conference.

A Sunday-school was formed soon after the organization of the church. L. Lewis was the first superintendent The present number of scholars is about thirty.

ST. MARY'S GERMAN CATHOLIC.

St. Mary's German Catholic Church was organized

John Hodge

> "Lives of great men all remind us
> We can make our lives sublime,
> And, departing, leave behind us
> Foot-prints on the sands of Time."

It is peculiarly fitting that the above-quoted lines should introduce a chapter from real life, in which are furnished incidents strikingly illustrative of what energy will do if well directed. The subject of this sketch is one of the few self-made men of the times, and no man on the American continent has achieved greater success in corresponding time. Self-made men have in all ages been special objects of mark, and not infrequently proven material aids, giving tone and shape to those principles which underlie the social and political fabric. Unassisted, save by the impulse of a precocious nature, they come to the surface unheralded, stamp the age in which they live with their identity, and leave an example for honorable emulation for those who come after them. Of this type is John Hodge. But it is often asserted that the surroundings make the individual—that the possession of rank, wealth and power is the result of chance. Quite evident it is that the ease and rapidity with which certain persons attain position and wealth almost compel full credence in the fabled skill of the goddess Fortune; but in this individual case the fact must be recognized that the man shaped and moulded his circumstances—that not chance, but labor, judgment, foresight, determined purpose and the exercise of intelligent reason accomplished the desired results, and made him the architect of his own fortune.

Mr. Hodge was born in Jefferson county, N. Y., in 1839. He left his father's house at an early age, before attaining his majority, and located in Lockport, then a village, with the determination to build up his fame and fortune there. He had inherited, not money, but what was far better, an unsullied family name and strong manly character. Realizing the importance of being educated, as soon as able to command the requisite means he entered an academy near his native place. By diligent application to his studies and improvement of spare time when out of school, he accumulated ideas and acquired habits as the foundation of that symmetrical character which ever commands respect and insures success. The persistent industry and singleness of aim of the *boy* are strikingly seen in his career as a *man*.

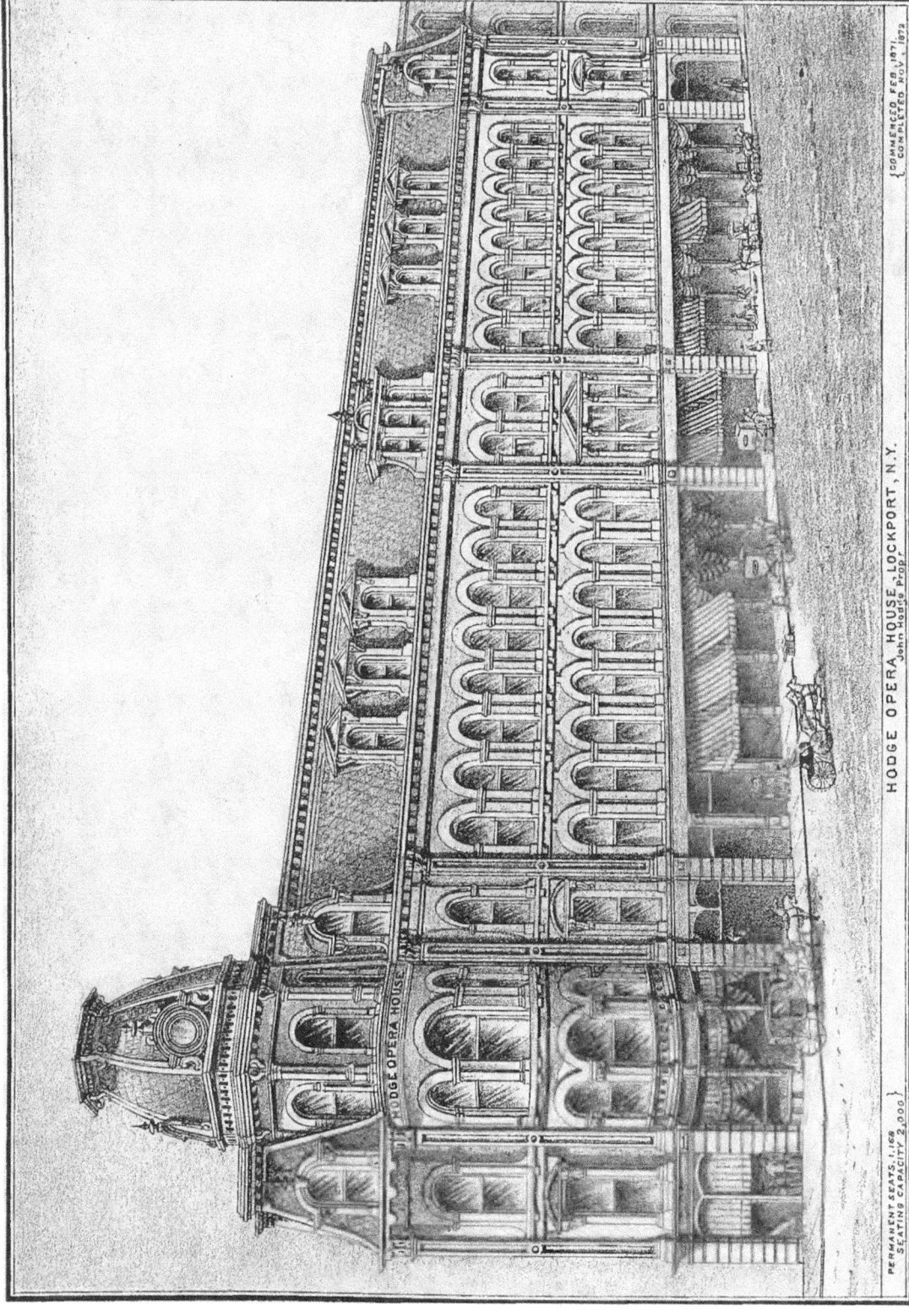

He started out into his busy life with nerve, indomitable will, persevering industry, and great fertility of resources, confident of worldly success if he wisely chose his avocation. What this should be perplexed him somewhat, as it does most talented young men. Thinking at last that possibly duty and interest pointed to the legal profession, he entered as a student the law office of an eminent practitioner.

He afterwards concluded that an active business life, with its untold opportunities for usefulness, was better suited to his tastes, as giving a wider scope to his abilities; he therefore abandoned his profession, and at once entered a business sphere that long since gave him distinction and wealth, and, what is far better, the opportunity he coveted for so utilizing the ideas of his academic days as to contribute to the prosperity and fame of the "City of Locks."

Engaging as clerk with the proprietor of a liniment of which but few had heard—called "Merchant's Gargling Oil"—he evinced such fidelity to the interests of his employer, and aptitude for the discharge of his clerical duties, that he soon became the controlling spirit of the business, and gave it an impulse and direction which have developed the greatest magnitude and yielded compounded profits. Mr. Hodge in 1866, on the death of M. H. Tucker, Esq., succeeded him as secretary and manager of the oil company. In 1871 he erected the famous Hodge Opera House, described elsewhere in this history. This was his private enterprise, and cost $125,000. It is a stately monument to his success in business and his public spirit.

Notwithstanding the arduous duties devolving upon him as the sole manager of the Gargling Oil Company, Mr. Hodge has found time to promote the good of various business, social and benevolent associations; his quick perception, power of organization, invincible energy and ready dispatch may perhaps account for his successfully managing interests of a number and variety that would break either the will or constitution of most business men; this may be inferred from the simple statement that in the year 1877, when only 38 years of age, he was treasurer of the Lockport and Buffalo Railroad Company, grand receiver of the Ancient Order of United Workmen of the State of New York, director of the Masonic Life Association of Western New York, president of the Union Publishing Company, director of the Cataract Bank, Niagara Falls; chief of the Lockport Fire Department, president of the Firemen's Life Association of the State of New York, president of the Driving Park Association, president of the Firemen's Association of the State, and last, but not least, an influential trustee of one of the two largest churches in Lockport.

In the spring of 1878 he declined the nomination for mayor tendered him, feeling that the duties of the office demanded more attention than he was able to give them. Of the educational interests of the city he is ever jealous. To him belongs the honor of having in 1874 taken the initiative in the matter of presenting a medal annually to the member of the graduating class of the Lockport Union School whose record for scholarship and deportment should best entitle him or her thereto, he himself presenting the medal, which contained over ninety dollars worth of gold and was known as the "Hodge Prize Medal."

Conceiving a favorable opinion of masonry through the worthy exemplars of the sublime art in Lockport, he sought admission to its mysteries, and was initiated in Niagara (symbolic) Lodge on attaining his majority. His superior clerical abilities were acknowledged at the first succeeding election by his being chosen secretary, which office he filled acceptably for five years, when he was obliged to decline a re-election by reason of pressing private business.

Mr. Hodge's progress on the masonic ladder was rapid, and characterized by the proficiency of a true craftsman. In the year 1878 he was member of Ames Chapter, R. A. M.; Bruce Council, No. 15, R. S. M.; Genesee Commandery, K. T.; Thrice Potent Grand Master Lock City Lodge of Perfection, Ancient Accepted Rite; Rochester Chapter, Rose Croix, and Rochester Consistory, S. P. R. S. Ill. Mr. Hodge was invested with the sublime grade of 32° May 4th, 1875, and was in 1878 an officer of the Council of Deliberation in the State of New York.

He by labor and largess has steadily contributed to the prosperity of the city of Lockport. He has been faithful to every business and social duty. His efficiency for work, strong infusion of common sense and fertility in resources, are conceded by all who know him best. He blows no trumpet in the market-place, nor in the church, with hypocritic smile, supplies with cant the lack of Christian truth; loathing pretense, he does with cheerful mood what others talk of when their hands are still, while modest reserve and native dignity mark his daily walk and conversation; yet

"—— a merrier man,
Within the limits of becoming mirth,
We never spent an hour's talk withal."

about 1860. The following is the succession of pastors: Revs. F. S. Urich, Joseph Zoegel, A. Hechiniger, Joseph Zoegel, Charles Wensiersky, F. X. Koffier, F. S. Urich and Vincent Scheffels. The society bought the old Episcopal church at the corner of Buffalo and Saxton streets about the time of its organization. At present there is a membership of between sixty and seventy families.

THE FIRST EVANGELICAL LUTHERAN CHURCH

was organized in 1837, with about one hundred members, and Rev. John Selsmer as pastor. The Sunday-school was under charge of Charles Barnes, with seventy-five pupils. The first meetings of the society were held in the court-house. In 1838 the society built a brick church edifice at the intersection of what are now West Main and New Main streets. In 1850 the present church was built, at a cost of about $4,000. Since Mr. Selsmer the following clergymen have been engaged to minister to the spiritual wants of this people:

In 1845, Rev. N. W. Goertner; 1847, Edward Meyer; 1849, Thomas Lape; 1850, H. L. Dox; 1855, W. H. Lukenbach; 1858, P. A. Stroebel; 1860, H. L. Dox; 1863, S. R. Griffith; 1867, M. Orb; 1875, D. M. Moser, the present pastor.

There are at present about fifty-five members. The Sunday-school contains about thirty pupils, with Samuel Basserman as superintendent. The value of the church property is $4,000.

CLINTON STREET METHODIST CHURCH

was formally organized October 16th, 1855. The following persons were appointed stewards: D. W. Ballow, W. R. Ford, D. B. Ingraham, J. McDonald and D. Thurber. W. R. Ford was chosen recording steward.

The church was finished at a cost of $4,000, in 1856. The names of the pastors who have served the church since its organization are as follows: Rev. John C. Nobles, Rev. John Kennard, Rev. C. P. Clark, Rev. J. M. Simkins, Rev. D. M. Buck, Rev. George W. Coe, Rev. Peter Stover, Rev. C. P. Clark (second term), Rev. J. M. Simkins (second term), Rev. A. S. Staples, Rev. Sumner Smith and Rev. C. B. Sparrow, the present pastor. The information used in writing the above was furnished by Mr. and Mrs. W. R. Ford, of Clinton street, who are among the oldest members of the church. There is a large and flourishing Sunday-school in connection with this society.

THE GERMAN UNITED EVANGELICAL CHURCH

was organized in 1862, and the following year had sixty-two members. A church edifice was erected at the corner of South and Locust streets in 1863, at a cost of about $4,000. The pastor at that time was Rev. William I. Cutter. The present pastor is J. J. Abele.

OTHER CHURCHES.

Besides the churches whose histories have been given, there are the African Methodist Episcopal, the Advent Christian Union Society, Main street, and the Rhoder Sholem congregation, A. Walker president, Henry Goodman, sen., treasurer; Henry Goodman, jr., secretary.

BIOGRAPHICAL.

LOCKPORT'S LEADING CITIZENS.

HON. HIRAM GARDNER.

Hon. Hiram Gardner was born in Dutchess county, N.Y., February 9th, 1800. He carved out his own fortune with his own hands. After pursuing his academical studies as far as circumstances would permit, in 1818 he became a student of law in Rensselaerville, N. Y., where he studied about two years, and removed to New York, where he finished his law course. In 1822, about a year after he began to practice in the lower courts, he was admitted as a practitioner in the Supreme Court. In October of the same year he came to Lockport. The next year he was appointed to the office of justice of the peace, and in his official capacity he took cognizance of nearly all the business transacted in the Court of Common Pleas. In 1825 he was appointed associate judge of the Court of Common Pleas. In 1827 he was appointed Supreme Court commissioner, and was admitted as a master in chancery. In 1831 he was appointed surrogate, which office he held for five years, and then resigned it that he might represent his district in the State Legislature, to which position he had already been elected. In 1845 he was elected a member of the constitutional convention which revised the second and framed the third State constitution. In 1847 he was elected county judge and surrogate; in 1858 canal commissioner for the term of three years. In the fall of 1868 he was appointed to the office of county judge to supply a vacancy, and was elected in November, 1869, to the same position. Judge Gardner was for more than half a century a legal practitioner, and his conspicuous ability and talent were successfully directed to the elevation of the judicial office and of the legal profession. He was not a politician. His ideas of political honor were of the most elevated character, and though holding public offices more than twenty-five years, he never sought official preferment or solicited the vote of any man. Judge Gardner's benevolence, and devotion to the interests and prosperity of Lockport during his fifty years of citizenship, endeared him to the entire community. In the church he was a pillar of strength, reflecting in his life the beauty and power of Christianity. He died at his residence on Niagara street March 13th, 1874, and we copy from the Lockport *Journal* in commenting upon the event: "Never before in Lockport history has one gone down to the grave amid such generally expressed tokens of sorrow and respect as yesterday surrounded the burial of the late Judge Hiram Gardner."

Rev. John J. Abele is pastor of the German Evangelical Church of Lockport.

Peter B. Aikin, real estate and insurance agent, Lockport, was born in Athens, Greene county, N. Y., March 7th, 1810, and came to Lockport from Porter in 1822. Mr. Aikin has creditably held a number of responsible offices, among them that of deputy sheriff of Niagara county in 1843, 1844, and 1845; justice of the

H. Gardner

RES. OF MRS. JUDGE H. GARDNER, LOCKPORT N.Y.

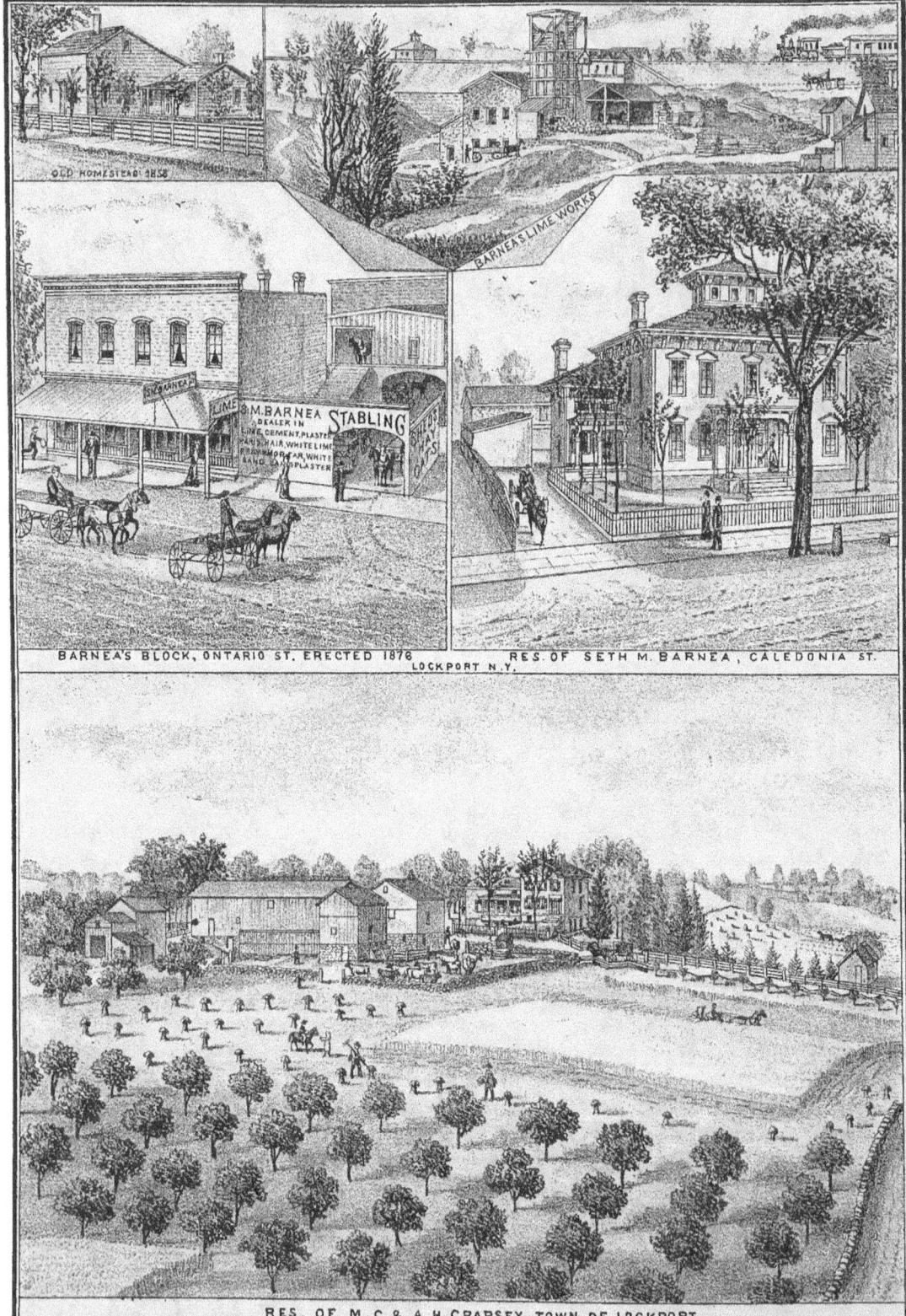

peace of the village of Lockport from 1846 to 1853; associate justice of Niagara county in 1852; canal collector at Lockport in 1854 and 1855; deputy provost marshal in 1863 and 1864, and assistant revenue collector in 1866, 1867, 1868 and 1869.

Alfred W. Allen was born in Cayuga county, and came to Niagara county and located at the Falls in 1836. He remained there until 1865, holding many public offices in the village of Niagara Falls and town of Niagara, and in that year came to Lockport, where he has since been in business as a merchant tailor, over 102 Main street.

George Arrowsmith, a native of Monroe county, located in Lockport in 1857, and was for some time employed as a wheelwright. Since 1872 his time and energies have been devoted to the invention and introduction of a turbine water-wheel, which was patented in 1874, and which he is now manufacturing.

Henry W. Axtell, superintendent with James Jackson, jr. & Son, manufacturers of sash, doors and blinds, Lockport, was born May 4th, 1831, at Winsor, Massachusetts, and came to Lockport in 1834.

Seth M. Barnea was born July 23d, 1822, at Canandaigua, N. Y., and came to Lockport in 1850. October 8th, 1856, he was married to Sarah P. Church, of Lockport. Mr. Barnea keeps a large and varied stock of groceries and a large quantity of lime, land plaster, cement and building material generally, and has a convenient barn and sheds for stabling, to accommodate farmers driving into the city on business and wishing to feed their horses. His place of business is on Orleans street.

Charles A. Barnes was born in January, 1834, in the town of Cambria, and removed to Lockport in 1856. He is engaged in the sale of groceries at Lockport, and dry goods, groceries and general merchandise at Ransomville.

T. R. Bailey, jr., son of the late T. R. Bailey, sen., who came to Lockport from Vermont, in November, 1842, is located as a merchant at 198 Market street. The business was established in 1851 by the elder Bailey, who was the inventor and patentee of the Bailey gauge lathes. The establishment provides work for a large number of hands in busy times. Mr. Bailey, sen., died in Iowa in 1868.

Lafayette Balcom, M. D., was born in the town of Lewiston, N. Y., June 12th, 1840, and married April 13th, 1864, to Libbie M. Mack, of Lockport. Dr. Balcom came from Ransomville, N. Y., to Lockport in 1865, and is actively engaged in the practice of his profession. In 1864 he was assistant-surgeon at Hampton Hospital, N. C. Dr. Balcom is the author of several dramatic works, the one entitled "Thrice Saved" being most prominent and of some considerable local interest.

A. F. Balliett, successor to Martin Webster & Co., coal merchants, located in Lockport in 1851. He was married to Miss S. E. Babcock, in 1869. Mr. Balliett is a native of Northumberland county, Penn. Office and yard, Hawley street, near the N. Y. C. & H. R. R. R.; branch office, No. 1 Hodge Opera House building.

William D. Balliett was born in Limestone, Penn., October 29th, 1845, and came to Niagara county in 1847. After residing at Pekin for a time, he removed to East Lockport, where, for the past nine years, he has been engaged in the sale of drugs and medicines.

J. W. Beek, a native of St. Johns, N. B., came to Lockport in 1833. He was married to Miss C. McMichael, a native of Niagara county. Mr. Beek has held the office of street commissioner two years.

R. W. & E. Beck, manufacturers of frames.—This enterprise was established as a distinct business in 1865, having previously been conducted in connection with the manufacture of furniture. The furniture business of this firm was established in 1840.

Henry M. Belding was born June 29th, 1821, at Marcellus, N. Y. and was married January 6th, 1851, to Lucia S. Allen, of Lockport. Mr. Belding came to Lockport from Pekin in 1847, having moved from Marcellus to the latter place in 1829. Business, livery; post-office address, Box 886.

Thomas Bell, a native of Cambridgeshire, England, came to Niagara county in 1836 and located in Lockport. He followed the business of drayman ten years and that of boatman fifteen years, and about 1853 he commenced buying real estate. In 1863 he removed to his farm in the town of Lockport and remained there till 1869, when he came to the city, where he has since lived at No. 4 John street.

Joseph T. Bellah, a native of Claymont, Delaware, where he was born in 1811, has been a resident of Lockport since 1831. In 1833 he was married to Elizabeth Warner, of Philadelphia. He has been engaged in the manufacture of sash and blinds, and also in the hardware trade. He was superintendent of the gas works at one time, and was known as one interested in the cause of education. He died in April, 1877, and Mrs. Bellah, his widow, resides at his former home at the corner of East avenue and Elm street.

John & Louis Bendinger, marble dealers.—John Bendinger resides at 48 Saxton street, and Louis Bendinger at 312 Walnut street.

A. S. Beverly, hardware merchant, corner of Market and Exchange streets, established his business in 1857, and has so managed it that it has constantly increased since. He deals extensively in boat builders' materials, stoves, tinware etc, etc.

G. W. Bird was born in England. He located in Lockport in March, 1853, since which time he has worked at blacksmithing. Mr. Bird was married in 1852. He was a fire marshal of the city six years.

D. F. Bishop, M. D., president of the Holly Steam Combination Company, was born in Paris, Oneida county, in 1829, and came to Lockport from Philadelphia in 1855. He was the organizer and for four years president of the Niagara County Medical Society, and has held various offices in the State Medical Society, besides being surgeon of the 66th regiment for ten years, and city physician about half the time during the past twenty years.

J. P. Bishop is one of the leading coopers in Niagara county, having an extensive manufactory in Lockport and employing eight men. He is a native of England, and came to America in 1852. After spending ten years in Buffalo, he was in the navy a year. He was married to Anna M. Begy, a native of Canada, in 1865, and located in Lockport in 1866.

Hon. A. A. Bissell is a native of Oneida county. He came to Lockport in 1856 and engaged in the transportation business, which he increased to such proportions that in one year he shipped over the canal as high as 50,000 barrels of flour, 100,000 bushels of grain and apples, and a large quantity of stoves and heading. Mr. Bissell has represented his district in the Legislature two years. In 1868 and 1869 he was a partner in the flouring business with Asa W. Douglas.

Hon. Levi F. Bowen was born in Homer, New York, in 1808, and married March 27, 1840, to Sylvia De Long, of Cornwall, Vermont. He came to Lockport in 1832, and has been a prominent citizen of the county ever since. He was judge of the old Court of Common Pleas, member of Assembly in 1845, justice of the Supreme Court of the 8th judicial district, member of the constitutional convention of 1867 and 1868, and provost marshal of the 28th district of New York during the rebellion. Judge Bowen is engaged in the practice of law, and is the present county judge of Niagara county.

J. W. Bramley, of the firm of Bramley Brothers & Co., manufacturers of patent cast steel plows and agricultural iron work. This business was established in 1875 and the company formed in 1877. The company's works are near Hitchin's bridge, southwest of the city.

Ira Briggs, a native of New York, located in Newfane, Niagara county, about 1847. After a residence of five years there, he removed to Erie county, where he remained four years, after which he lived in Pendleton until 1871, when he removed to Lockport, where he has since lived retired.

Lawrence Brink, carpenter and joiner, was born in Lehigh county, Pennsylvania, and married Miss Addia Mott, a native of Vermont.

Charles N. Brizse was born in Lockport, October 28th, 1854. Business, plumbing and gas and steam-fitting.

G. L. Brockett, a native of Herkimer county, N. Y., graduated at Hamilton college in 1851, since which time he has been engaged as a teacher in Cortland county, N. Y., Albany, N. Y., and Flint, Mich., till 1875, when he removed to Lockport, where he has lived retired. He was married in 1875 to Miss Caroline A., a daughter of the late H. W. Campbell and a sister of Mrs. Edward R. Graves, of Lockport. Mrs. Brockett has also had much experience as a teacher, having taught at Clinton, Hamilton and other places, besides several years in the Union School at Lockport.

Hon. John H. Buck was born in Northfield, Vermont, November 22d, 1827, and came to the city of Lockport February 14th, 1851. He has been for many years actively engaged in the practice of his profession as attorney-at-law. In 1874 and 1875 he was Mayor of the city.

George H. Burch was born December 10th, 1841, at St. Catherines, Canada, and came to Lockport in 1863. Mr. Burch is a machinist by trade, and has sold tin, glass, and china ware in Niagara county for the last ten years.

Charles L. Burgess, a native of Pennsylvania, came with his mother and settled in Porter, Niagara county, when he was two years old. At the age of fourteen he went to sea, and was absent thirteen years. On his return he located in the town of Wilson, and in 1857 he was married to Miss Lucinda A. Wilson, a native of that town. Mr. Burgess engaged in lake navigation till 1867, in which year he removed to Lockport. He has served three years as chief of the city police. Residence, No. 6 John street.

Benjamin Burridge, house and stair-builder, No. 6 Spalding street, Lockport, was born in Dorsetshire, England, July 10th, 1810, and came to Niagara county in 1850.

Arthur L. Burtis, tin and copper smith, was born in Macedon, N. Y., February 22d, 1842. Post-office box, 172 Lockport.

Miss Eliza J. Butler was born in Schoharie county, N. Y., and came to Lockport with her mother's family about 1834. Her mother, Mrs. Electa Butler, died in 1860. Miss Butler resides at No. 22 Gooding street.

R. H. Button was born in Sheffield, England, and came to Lockport in 1848. Mr. Button is a machinist, and is connected with the business of T. R. Bailey.

W. W. Buttrick was born in Berkshire county, Mass., in 1830, and came to Lockport with his father in 1833. He was married in 1855 to Miss Maria L. Steel. For several years Mr. Buttrick worked as a machinist for the Pound Manufacturing Company. In 1872 and 1873 he held the position of superintendent of the 13th section of the Erie Canal. Afterward he was foreman in the Pound Manufacturing Company's works for three years, since which time he has held the office of gauger for districts 28 and 30.

Mrs. R. S. Cass, whose maiden name was Drake, was born in Montgomery county, N. Y., in 1811. In 1826 she was married to James Brott, a native of Schenectady, N. Y., and with her husband removed to Niagara county and located in Lockport, where he died in 1850. In 1852 Mrs. Brott was married to James Stevenson, a native of Pennsylvania, at the time a resident of Lockport. Mr. Stevenson died in 1865, and in 1870 Mrs. Stevenson married John Cass, a practicing physician in Lockport. Dr. Cass died in May, 1873, since which time his widow has resided at No. 81 Niagara street.

Hon. Sullivan Caverno was born in Stratford, N. H., in 1807, and came to Lockport in 1831, having graduated at Dartmouth College that year. He received from Dartmouth College his degree of A. B., and from Hobart College the degree of A. M. Mr. Caverno was principal of the Lewiston academy two years, and in 1834 and 1835 he finished his preparatory legal studies in Judge Gardner's law office and was admitted to the bar. In 1836 he was appointed master and examiner in chancery which office he held for four years, and in 1844 he was appointed police justice of Niagara county, which office he held for four years. He was president of the board of education

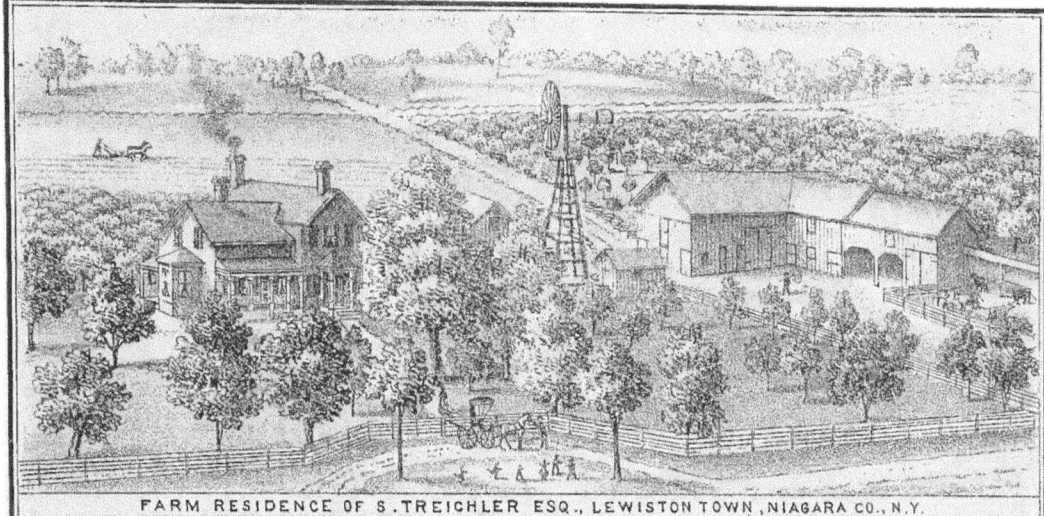
FARM RESIDENCE OF S. TREICHLER ESQ., LEWISTON TOWN, NIAGARA CO., N.Y.

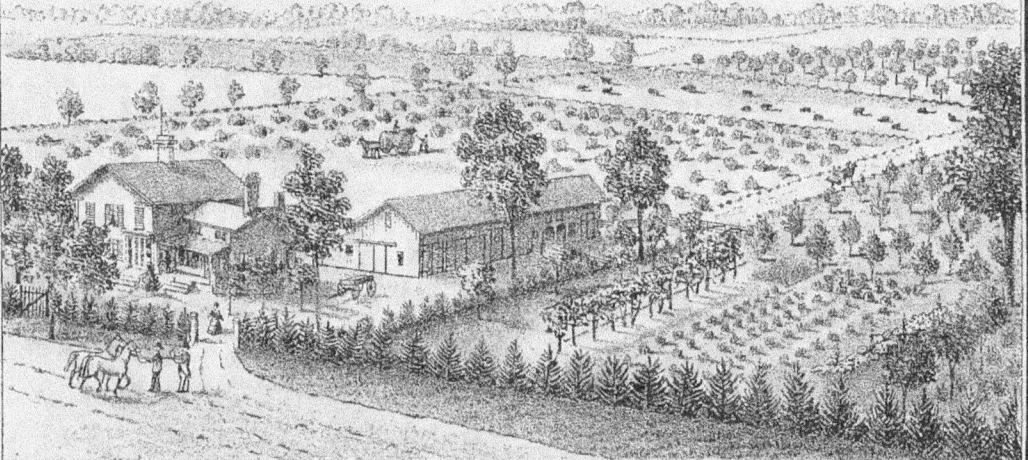
FARM RESIDENCE OF ANSON EASTMAN ESQ., CAMBRIA TOWN, NIAGARA CO. N.Y.

FARM RESIDENCE OF E. B. SWIFT ESQ., CAMBRIA TOWN, NIAGARA CO. N.Y.

RES. OF DR. D. F. BISHOP, 252 GENESEE ST. LOCKPORT, N.Y.

RES. OF HON. T. T. FLAGLER, LOCUST ST. LOCKPORT, N.Y.

for several years, and from 1846 to 1851 was engaged in originating and perfecting the Union school system of Lockport and carrying it into operation. In 1875 Mr. Caverno was appointed as one of the commissioners to revise the statutes of the State of New York.

Mrs. A. B. Chapin, formerly Miss Anna B. Hills, daughter of the late John Hills who died in March, 1878, was married in 1837 to Mr. Alvin Chapin, a native of Cortland county, N. Y., at that time a resident of the town of Niagara. In the year 1841 they removed to the old Hills homestead in Cambria, where they remained till 1854, when they removed to Wilson. In 1873 they came to Lockport, where Mrs. Chapin now resides; Mr. Chapin having died in September, 1876.

Oramel S. Chapin was born in Hampden county, Mass. He came to Niagara county in 1834, and has been a resident of Lockport since 1871, having lived in Royalton several years previous to that date.

H. J. Chadwick, a native of Cattaraugus county, N.Y., came to Lockport in 1861, and was engaged in the drug business till 1877, when he was elected treasurer of the Gas Company, and he is at present acting in that capacity. He was married in 1873 to Miss Ida D. Flagler.

Warren Chrysler is proprietor of a toy and variety store. The business was established in 1869, and has since been so successfully managed that it has steadily increased. Mr. Chrysler was born in Guilderland, N. Y., June 10th, 1832, and came to Lockport in 1835. He is the inventor of Chrysler's Patent Peanut Roaster, and in connection with his other business is extensively engaged in its sale throughout the United States.

Hon. Elisha Clapp was born in Hampshire county, Massachusetts. He came to Niagara county in 1829 and located in Lockport, engaging in the business of cabinet making. In 1851 he was appointed by Governor Hunt as sheriff of Niagara county, in place of Alvah Hill, deceased, and was elected to the same office for a term of three years in 1856. Residence, 73 Clinton street.

Joseph Clark was born in England, and came to America and settled in Lockport in 1850, where he has since resided, following the occupation of machinist and pattern maker. Mr. Clark is now in the service of George W. Hildreth & Co.

F. B. Clench was born at Black Rock, July 17th, 1838, and came to Lockport from Niagara, Ontario, in 1863. Mr. Clench is well known as a photographic artist.

Cocker & Trevor, saw manufacturers, Market street, business established in 1857 by William Cocker. Mr Trevor became a partner in 1869. The amount of business has gradually increased, and from five to ten hands are employed.

William Cocker, a native of Sheffield, England, came to Lockport in 1857, and established himself as a saw manufacturer. In 1869 he took in Mr. Trevor as partner, since which time the firm of Cocker & Trevor have gradually increased the business, till they now employ from five to ten hands.

Mrs. Esther Comstock, whose maiden name was Hayward, came to Lockport in 1820. In 1822 she was married to Horace Comstock, a native of Saratoga county, New York, who came in 1821. Mr. Comstock, who was a miller, followed his business until his death in 1862. Mrs. Comstock's residence is at No. 2 Elm street.

Mrs. E. W. Cook, formerly Miss Malvina L. Littlefield, is a native of Rochester. She was married in 1841 to the late Colonel Elliott W. Cook, who was born in Cumberland, Rhode Island, June 13th, 1818, and became a resident of Lockport in 1837. The colonel raised a company of soldiers for the Mexican war, but did not go to the front. In 1849 he was elected treasurer of the Niagara and Calafornia Mining Company, and spent one year in California. Afterwards he was engaged in the mercantile business in Lockport till the war of the rebellion, in which he served as captain of Company A, 28th New York Volunteers, afterwards being promoted to a colonelcy. At the close of the war he returned to Lockport, where he resided until his death, in the spring of 1877.

Hiram A. Cook was born in Rutland county, Vt., and removed to Genesee county, N. Y., from whence he came to Lockport in 1827. He was engaged in the lumber business seven years, and in 1837 was elected county clerk. He held that position three years, and in 1849 was appointed deputy county clerk, serving in that capacity ever since, during a period of nearly thirty years.

William Bryant Cook, engineer and surveyor, was born in Cambria, N. Y., January 6th, 1834. and came to Lockport in 1870. Office over No. 2 Main street.

George H. Conover, proprietor of saloon and billiard hall, No. 1 Central block. Mr. Conover succeeded to the business in 1877.

D. D. Crosby is proprietor of the railroad elevator. This was built and the business established in 1874. It was the first elevator erected on the railroad in the city, and does a business of about $50,000 annually.

H. Craig was born at Three Rivers, in Canada East, and came to Lockport in the summer of 1865, since which time he has continued to reside in the city, following his trade of carriage trimmer. He is at present located at No. 25 New Main street.

John Craine, nurseryman and grower of grape vines. Business established in 1853.

H. H. Cram, proprietor of Cram's Hotel, on the European plan, at No. 89 Main street, located there in 1877, having previously been in the same business on Pine street.

H. H. Daniels, painter and machinist, was born in Ohio, and located in Lockport in 1869.

H. S. Darling, proprietor Union House, East avenue.

J. T. Darrison & Son, dealers in flour and feed, No. 5 Buffalo street; business established in 1851.

Dr. Luther T. Dickinson, dentist, corner of Main and Pine streets. Business established in 1871 by Dickinson & Balcom. Dr. Dickinson succeeded to the business in 1874. He was born November 9th, 1841, in the town of Somerset, N. Y.

John Devereux located in Lockport in the fall of 1854. He was engaged in the grocery trade till his retirement in 1872.

Benjamin S. Davenport, a native of Elmira, N. Y., came to Lockport about 1822. In 1834 he was married to Miss Phoebe Allen. Mr. Davenport has for many years followed the trade of carpenter and builder.

J. B. Davison, a native of Jefferson county, N. Y., located in Lockport in 1866. He has long been engaged in the sale of gentlemen's furnishing goods, and in 1872 he established his insurance agency at No. 2 Opera House block.

Joseph Donnelly was born in Lockport in 1840, and began to practice as an attorney in the fall of 1872. Office, No. 20 Hodge Opera House.

J. W. Doty was born in Lockport, December 20th, 1820, and is probably the oldest resident of the city who was born within its limits. He followed the business of farming till 1873, since which time he has been engaged in the sale of agricultural implements. Mr. Doty was married in October, 1841, to Emily Wildman, a native of Danbury, Conn.

Robert Dorman, dealer in groceries, No. 33 Locust street. Business established in 1869.

Mrs. D. A. Douglas, whose maiden name was Dickinson, was born in Lewiston, N. Y. In 1847 she married Uriah E. Douglas, a native of Columbia county, N. Y. Mr. Douglas died in 1877, in the fall of which year Mrs. Douglas came to Lockport, where she has since resided at No. 154 Locust street.

Mrs. B. Draper was born August 27th, 1813, in Yorkshire, England, and came with her husband to Lockport in 1837. Mr. Draper, until his retirement, was engaged as a brewer.

Jacob A. Driess, attorney, was born July 10th, 1849, in Bavaria, Germany, and came to Lockport in June, 1856, from Rochester, N. Y. He is a justice of the peace of the city of Lockport.

Charles F. Dudley was born in Lockport in 1845. He was married in 1866 to Miss Alice A. Sutton. Mr. Dudley is engaged in the foundry business at 56 and 58 Market street. He is the inventor of Dudley's fluting machine, which was patented November 2d, 1876.

Duncan & Wilson, general book and job printers, over No. 51 Main street. This business was established by Leonard & Murphy in 1868, and came into the possession of the present firm in 1876. George W. Duncan was born June 28th, 1857, in Lockport.

Mrs. Ellen M. Dunn, widow of the late Michael Dunn, resides at No. 82 Niagara street. Michael Dunn was married to Miss Ellen Brennan, a native of England, in 1859, and removed to Lockport in 1868, where he was well and favorably known in business circles as a coal dealer till his death, September 16th, 1877.

Mrs. Robert Dunlap, a native of England, came to America in 1839, and resided in Elizabeth, N. J., eight years, and afterwards in Geneva, N. Y., till 1855, when she was married to Robert Dunlap, and came to Niagara county.

Ambroise Dupont is of Canadian nativity. He removed to Rochester in '1840, afterwards lived in Pennsylvania and Canada, and in 1864 came to Lockport and was employed by B. & J. Carpenter at his trade as stone-cutter. Mr. Dupont was married in 1843 to Miss Amy Austin, a native of Chautauqua county, N. Y.

Frederick Eckensperger, jr., butcher, No. 5 Pine street, is a native of Wertemberg. He came to Niagara Falls in 1852, and removed from there to Lockport in 1872. Residence west of the city.

Thomas Edwards is a native of Wayne county. In 1841 he was married to Cornelia Ann Porter. He came to Niagara county and settled in Wilson in 1847. In 1873 he removed to Lockport, where he has since resided.

Frank J. Eighme, attorney at law, was born in Buffalo, N. Y., October 2, 1850.

Mrs. Frank A. Elton, dressmaker, was born in Rye, Sussex, England, in 1845, and was married to Washington W. Elton, of Cambria, N. Y., April 19, 1859, her maiden name having been Brooks. She came to Lockport from Suspension Bridge in May, 1872.

Ellsworth Ely was born in Lodi, Seneca county, N. Y., in 1827, and came to Lockport in 1861, having been engaged previously in the dry goods business in Brooklyn; and was in partnership with John Van Horn in the hardware trade until 1874, since which time he has been connected with Pratt & Letchworth in the hardware business, at Buffalo.

Rev. Foster Ely, D D., LL. B., was born May 21st, 1836, at Watertown, Jefferson county, N. Y. He was the eldest son of Adriel and Evelina F. Ely. He graduated at Hamilton College in 1858, and at the State Law School, at Poughkeepsie, N. Y., in 1859. From the latter institution he received the degree of LL.B., and from the former that of A.B., and recently the honorary degree of D.D. In 1860 he was admitted to the bar as an attorney-at-law, after which he practiced a short time, and then devoted himself to the study of theology, and was ordained to the deaconate of the Protestant Episcopal Church in 1864, and became assistant minister of St. John's Church, Mobile, Ala. In 1866 he assumed a similar relationship to Calvary Church, New York, and during that year was ordained to the priesthood, and soon afterward became rector of the Church of the Holy Spirit, Kingston, N. Y. He resigned three years later, and after spending two years in European travel returned and accepted the rectorship of St. Paul's Church, of Newport, Ky., continuing in charge till December, 1875, during which time he was mainly instrumental in erecting a costly church edifice, in reference to which the presiding bishop said that he might well regard it as his monument. In 1873 Dr. Ely was married to Sarah Olive Brewster, widow of Samuel C. Brewster, Ph. D., late of Syracuse, N. Y. He resigned the rectorship of St. Paul's Church in December, 1875, and became rector of Grace Church, Lockport, N. Y. As a Christian minister, an elegant and forcible speaker, and a scholar of profound erudition, Rev. Foster Ely, D. D., is widely and favorably known.

Asher B. Evans, A. M., principal of the Lockport Union School, and maker of astronomical calculations, was born in Hector, Tompkins county, N. Y., September 21st, 1834, and married May 13th, 1869, to Sarah Elizabeth Haines,

REV. FOSTER ELY, D.D.

COL. W. E. PALMER, LOCKPORT, N.Y.

DR. C.N. PALMER. LOCKPORT, N.Y.

of Lockport. He came to the city in 1866 from Wilson, N. Y. For the last twenty years Prof. Evans has been a regular contributor to different mathematical periodicals in the United States and England, and has received notices of commendation from various influential journals in both countries.

C. W. Evans was born in Lockport in 1842. He served two years as sergeant in Company H of the 21st N. Y. cavalry. He is a barber. Residence, 441 Green street.

Leonard Everett was born in Canton, Mass. He came to Niagara county in 1848 and located in Pendleton, being engaged as a contractor in the widening of the Erie Canal till 1855, after which he resided at Clifton a year, at the expiration of which time he removed to the town of Lockport and worked on the canal. In 1857 he became a resident of the city, his family having since lived at 121 Cottage street. During the past twenty years Mr. Everett has been engaged on public works in the East and West. At present he is connected with the Holly Steam Combination Company.

A. S. Finn, a native of Waterloo, Seneca county, N. Y., removed to Lockport in 1862, where, with the exception of two years spent in the oil regions, he has been engaged in business as a boat-builder. He was married in 1872 to Miss Kate E. House, of Lockport.

S. H. Finn, boat-builder; yard on the canal at the railroad bridge. The business was established by A. S. & S. H. Finn in 1862, and carried on in partnership until 1865, since which time each member of the former firm has conducted a separate business.

Hon. Thomas T. Flagler was born in Pleasant Valley, N. Y., in 1811, and came to Lockport in 1836, where he has since been known as an energetic, enterprising and public spirited citizen and business man. He represented his district in the Legislature in 1842 and 1843 and again in 1860, and was a member from this Congressional district of the thirty-third and thirty-fourth Congresses. In 1867 and 1868 he was a member of the New York State constitutional convention, and was county treasurer from 1849 to 1852. Besides these political offices he has held many trusts of high responsibility in business circles, having been prominently identified with the leading interests of Lockport and the surrounding country. He is president of the Holly Manufacturing Company, president of the Niagara County National Bank, president of the Lockport Gaslight Company, president of the Lockport and Buffalo Railroad Company, and a director of the Lockport Hydraulic Company.

J. Fleming was born in Ireland, and came to America in 1845, locating for a time in Lockport, and then removing to Canada for a few years. Returning to Lockport he became a permanent resident, following his business as contractor for stone work, ditching and similar jobs.

John J. Frazer, carriage manufacturer, was born in Lockport, April 19th, 1849.

Rev. John N. Freeman, of Lockport, was born in Allahabad, N. India, July 18th, 1844. His parents were missionaries of the Presbyterian church in India, and his father and stepmother were martyred during the Sepoy mutiny in 1857-58. He came to Lockport from Peekskill N. Y., in February, 1876.

Julius Forhsee, C. E., a native of Germany, where he was born in 1835, came to Lockport in 1868, where he served seven years as city surveyor.

Benjamin F. Gaskill was born on the old Gaskill homestead in Royalton, in 1822. He was married in 1843 to Miss Olive Freeman, of Royalton. In 1847 he removed to the town of Lockport and purchased the farm now owned by Theodore E. Van Wagoner, where he remained till 1876, when he removed to the city of Lockport, where he now resides at 155 Genesee street.

H. F. Gaskill was born in 1845 in the town of Royalton, and removed to the city of Lockport in 1865. He was married in 1873 to Miss Mary E. Moore, of Lockport. Mr. Gaskill was engaged for three years in the manufacture of sash and blinds, and has been employed since 1873 as mechanical engineer for the Holly Company.

Joshua Gaskill was born in Royalton, Niagara county, N. Y., in 1835. He graduated at the University of Rochester in 1859, and was admitted to the bar of Niagara county in the following year. He has been a resident of Lockport since 1859, and has held the offices of city clerk, city treasurer and tax receiver, clerk of the board of supervisors and county surrogate.

Frank Gibbie established the business of the Niagara Reservoir Company, Transit street, in 1874. Messrs. Cook & Moore became partners in 1877.

O. C. Gibson, a native of England, came to Lockport in 1851, and has been a resident of the city since that time. He is of the firm of Gibson, Arnold & Little. Mr. Gibson has been for three years superintendent of the poor of Niagara county, and for the same period overseer of the poor of the city of Lockport.

Edward R. Graves, a son of the founder of Amherst College, is a native of Amherst, Mass. He was married June 5th, 1844, to Miss Mary S. Campbell, a daughter of the late H. W. Campbell, a well known citizen of Lockport. Mr. Graves lived in Ohio about six years, at the expiration of which time he returned, with his wife, to Lockport, and followed the photographic business several years. He is at present employed as a salesman for a New York paper house.

George Gregg, miller, was born in England, in 1831, and came to Lockport in 1864.

M. W. Griffin is of Irish parentage. He came to Lockport when one year old, and graduated from the Union School in 1861. He spent some time subsequently in a telegraph office, and was book-keeper for a time at the Lockport City Bank. In 1868 he became manager of the Western Union telegraph office, since which time it has been under his management.

Joseph W. Grosvenor, M.D., was born in 1837, in South Brookfield, Mass., and came to Lockport in 1868, from Providence, R. I., and has since been engaged in the practice of his profession. During the late war Dr. Grosvenor served two years as a surgeon in the U. S. army.

William B. Gould, M.D., was born in Cambria, October 28th, 1821, and came to Lockport in 1844. Dr. Gould was appointed by Governor Hoffman one of the commissioners to locate the Buffalo State Asylum for the Insane, and received an appointment as one of the managers of the same from Governor Dix for the term of six years, expiring August 26th, 1879. The doctor devotes his leisure time to his farm near the city, fifty acres of which is in fruit culture.

Cornelius S. Guild was born July 25th, 1840, at Utica, N. Y., and came to Lockport May 12th, 1847. Mr. Guild is a leading dry goods merchant and has been president of the Young Men's Association twice, and of the Young Men's Christian Association twice.

Roscoe L. Gulick was born at Pascoag, R. I., February 9th, 1853, and was married October 14th, 1874, to Ella E. Ransom, of Lockport. He came to the city from Boston in 1863. Business, woolen mill and hat store.

Albertus Haskins was born in the town of Lockport in 1839 and removed to the city in 1866. He was married in 1868 to Miss Eliza Dancer, a native of Clarence, Erie county, N. Y. Mr. Haskins is foreman for Steele, Wells & Co., lumbermen.

Otis Hathaway was born in Ontario county, N. Y. He came to Lockport in 1821, having taken a contract to open the canal through the locks, and brought his family on the following year.

John Hawkes is a native of England, and was born September 15th, 1832. He came to Lockport in 1851, and is engaged in butchering and the general stock trade. Mr. Hawkes served as an alderman of the city in 1875 and 1876, and was elected supervisor in 1878.

S. S. Hallady, a native of Montgomery county, N.Y., removed to Niagara county in 1843 and located in Lockport, where for eight years he has engaged in the livery business, and one year in hotel keeping at the Gothic Hotel, when he removed to Canada and was in the distillery business twenty-five years, returning to Lockport in 1871, since which time he has been engaged in buying hops for a New York firm. Residence on Cottage street, corner of Pine.

Hall & Downer, dealers in dry goods, No. 74 Main street. This business was established in 1866 by the present firm, previous to which time Mr. Hall had been connected for sixteen years with the firm of Shaeffer, Bouck & Co.

Dr. J. H. Helmer was born in Canajoharie, Montgomery county, N.Y., and came to Lockport in 1853, having previously lived for a time in Jefferson county.

George W. Hildreth was born in Boston, Mass., December 20th, 1805. After the death of his father, in 1809, Mr. Hildreth resided for a time in Keene, N. H., and in 1812 removed to Montpelier, Vermont. In 1819 he commenced learning the builder's and machinist's trades, and served an apprenticeship of seven years. After his majority he made astronomical apparatus for the use of schools, and sold them to institutions in the East and West, disposing of one to the Washington Institute, in New York. He spent the fall of the year 1827 in the lumber and iron regions of northeastern New York, but removed from there to Lockport in the following July. In October of that year he married Miss Abigail Pauline Baldwin. Mrs. Hildreth bore him four sons and five daughters, and died in 1872 at the age of sixty-five. Mr. Hildreth has been for many years prominently identified with the manufacturing interests of the city of Lockport. In the year 1833 he established Hildreth & Co.'s manufactory of school and opera-house furniture, and agricultural and contractors' machinery, which is the oldest manufactory of the kind now in operation in the city. In 1837 Mr. Hildreth introduced the heating of houses by steam in Lockport and other cities, and some of his apparatus is now in use. About 1845 Mr. Hildreth assumed control of the glass-works, and carried on the enterprise in connection with his other business for about ten years. Mr. Hildreth, now an old man, looks back over a half century and more of active business life with that pleasure which must always arise from the consciousness of having done something to render the world prosperous.

The well known fruit-grower Claudius L. Hoag, of Lockport, was born January 26th, 1825, at Pittstown, N. Y., and removed from that place into Niagara county in 1834. In September, 1853, he married Elizabeth C. Weld, of Lockport. He has been for the last thirty years engaged in the nursery business and fruit-growing.

Lewis H. Hill, merchant, was born in Lewiston, N. Y., September 2d, 1834, and came to Lockport from Niagara Falls in 1841. Mr. Hill has been secretary of the Niagara County Agricultural Society, a member of the board of education and city treasurer, holding the last named office two years.

Charles G. Hildreth was born in Lockport in 1838, and has always been a resident of the city, being well known as the secretary of the Holly Manufacturing Company.

F. W. Holly, a son of B. Holly, was born at Seneca Falls, N. Y., 1851, came to Lockport at the age of seven years and has since been a resident of the city. He has acted for the Holly Company for several years in the capacity of mechanical and erecting engineer. In 1870 he was married to Miss Carrie Clark, a native and resident of the city.

E. Adam Holt, insurance agent, was born in Cambria, N. Y., September 14th, 1823.

Hon. Alfred Holmes, attorney, was born in Albany county, N. Y., in 1804. In 1832 he came to Lockport, where he has since been engaged in the practice of his profession. Mr. Holmes was district attorney from 1842 to 1845, and county judge of Niagara county from 1858 to 1866.

Sherman D. Hooper was born at Rome, N. Y., in 1835, and came to Lockport in 1845. Since 1864 he has been engaged in the manufacture of staves and heading, employing about forty hands, and doing a business of from $15,000 to $20,000 yearly.

Mrs. Mary A. Jackson came to Lockport in 1825. In 1838 she married Adolphus Tibbits, of the city. Mr. Tibbits died in 1857, and in 1860 she married Cyril M. Jackson, who was a resident of Lockport to the time of his death, May, 1867.

RES. OF ANDREW KECK, TOWN OF LOCKPORT, N.Y.

BOAT YARD OF A. S. & S. H. FINN, LOCKPORT, N.Y. RES. OF S. H. FINN, 55 WALNUT ST.

RES. OF CHESTER H. PARTRIDGE, TOWN OF LOCKPORT, NIAGARA CO, N.Y.

PROMINENT RESIDENTS OF LOCKPORT.

Edwin Jakeway, a native of England, located in Canada in June, 1835, and remained there three years. He afterward lived in Orleans county a few years, and for a short time in Ohio. He located permanently in Lockport in 1848. Business, millwright.

William E. Jenney, malster and contractor, was born in Lockport, August 9th, 1830, and was married in November, 1855, to Kate Whitbeck, of Lockport. Mr. Jenney was major in the 66th regiment, N. Y. S. militia. He was supervisor of Lockport in 1869, and has held many other official positions.

C. W. Judd, liquor dealer, 31 Locust street. Business established in 1871.

Jacob Kelley, a native of Maine, located in Lockport in 1860. He is a carpenter and carriage maker. Shop on East avenue, east of Central block.

James O. King was born in Otsego county, N. Y. He came to Niagara county with his father in 1835 and settled in Hartland. He removed to Lockport in 1854 and has since been engaged as a bookkeeper, having been in the employ of B. & J. Carpenter since 1863. Mr. King was supervisor of the first ward for the years 1869, 1870, 1871, and 1873, and has been six years a member of the board of education.

Dr. M. S. Kittinger was born in Erie county, N. Y., and graduated at the College of Physicians and Surgeons, at New York, in 1853, having read medicine with doctors Gould and Fassett. He commenced the practice of his profession with Dr. Fassett in 1853. In 1856 he went to Europe, where he passed two years in the hospitals of England, Germany and France. Returning in 1858, he resumed his practice with Dr. Fassett. The partnership was terminated in 1861 by Dr. Kittinger's entering the army as surgeon of the 100th N. Y. S. volunteers Since the war he has lived at Lockport continuously.

Wells Knowles was born in Genesee county, N.Y. He came to Somerset, Niagara county, about 1855. He was in the war of the rebellion three years, and came to Lockport in 1865. In 1875 he succeeded Ashely Rowel in the brick manufacturing business.

Walter L. Lamont, deputy collector of customs, was born in Lockport, N.Y., September 26th, 1848.

Captain John Larkin, a native of Ireland, came to America in 1832 and lived in Troy, N. Y., till 1840, when he removed to Lockport, where he has since resided with the exception of three years spent in California. Captain Larkin followed boating till within the last ten years, and has since been engaged in boat building.

C. P. T. La Roche, dealer in hats and caps, 55 Main street, entered business life as a clerk in the employ of Jacob Seyler, in 1858. He was afterwards in the service of Willett Boune & Howard Strong, and in partnership with his brother he begun business for himself in 1867, since which time he has been a leading dealer in his line.

Lerch & Williams, dealers in dry goods, 68 and 70 Main street, Lockport, N. Y. Jeremiah E. Lerch was born in the city, July 22d, 1842. William A. Williams is a native of Uckermark, Germany. He came to Lockport December 1st, 1862.

Edwin Le Van, proprietor of planing mill and manufacturer of cotton batting, was born in Cambria, N. Y., in 1835, and has been a resident of Lockport for many years, having lived in Hartford, Conn., about ten years.

Mrs. A. A. Lewis was born in Watertown, Conn., in 1812. In 1828 she was married to E. W. Lewis of Stratford, Conn. Mr. Lewis and family came to Lockport in 1832, from Canandaigua, N. Y., where he resided until his death, having been engaged in business as a tinsmith and hardware merchant.

A. B. Lewis, of the firm of Humphrey & Lewis, manufacturers and dealers in harnesses, was born in Auburn, N. Y. In 1843 he removed to Orleans county, from there to Newfane in 1849, and to Lockport in 1859. Mr. Lewis is superintendent of the poor of Niagara county.

Elliott Lewis, a native of Connecticut, came to Lockport in 1822. He soon afterward opened a harness shop—the first in the city—where he made the first saddle ever made in Niagara county. He retired from business in 1846. Owning twenty acres of land on Washburn street, he began to improve it, and opened a street through it, which was named in his honor Lewis street.

E. B. Lewis, a native of Connecticut, came to Lockport from Hartland in 1867, and has since been engaged in the cultivation of flowers, plants, vegetables and small fruits. Residence and grounds on Locust street in the south part of the city.

J. W. Little, cooper, established his business in Lockport in 1867. He employs thirty-five hands and does a business amounting to about $30,000 annually, manufacturing on an average 80,000 barrels per year. Mr. Little was alderman two years, and has served as supervisor, and as a corporal in the 28th regiment N. Y. S. V,

F. Loosen, bone-dust manufacturer and dealer in hides. tallow, furs, etc., No. 6 Pine street, came from Buffalo and established his business in 1870.

Danforth W. Lyor, dealer in hats, caps and ladies' furs, Lockport, N. Y., came to the city in 1837, from Buffalo, N. Y. He was born at Stafford, Conn., April 12th, 1807.

Mrs. Eliza J. Mackey, whose maiden name was Mericle, is a native of New Jersey. She married Barnett Mackey, also a native of that State, in 1843. They removed the town of Lockport in 1836. In 1867 they moved into the city. Mr. Mackey died in March, 1871. Mrs. Mackey lives at No. 215 Ontario street.

W. H. Mapes was born in the city of Lockport, January 19th, 1838. He was in the rebellion, serving as captain and major for four and one-half years, and he has been seven and one-half years in the civil service, holding a responsible official position at the present time.

Rev. E. P. Marvin, pastor of the 2nd Ward Presbyterian Church, was born at Bethany, N. Y., in 1834, and came to Lockport from Black Rock in 1866.

A. H. McLean, proprietor of the Niagara House, Lockport, was born in Sullivan county, N. Y., September 11th, 1818. The Niagara House is one of the most popular hotels in the city.

William McGill is a native of Ireland. In 1849 he came to America, and took up his residence in Lockport on the site of his present residence, No. 25 Washington street. Mr. McGill's oldest son, William, was killed in the war of the rebellion at the battle of Cedar Mountain. In former days Mr. McGill was a carpenter and builder, but for the past few years he has been employed at William Richmond's as a machinist.

M. McKenny, No. 135 East avenue, is a native of Schenectady county, N. Y. He came to Lockport in 1826, where he has since resided and followed his trade as a mill-wright.

Daniel McKim was born in Lockport in 1831. In 1854 he was married to Miss Eliza Allen, a native of Ireland. McKim is a moulder by trade, and since 1864 has been a partner with George W. Hildreth & Co. in the foundry business.

William McLean, blacksmith, No. 2 Ontario street, located in Lockport, and commenced business in May, 1836. He has moved only once since then, when he located at his present place of business in 1851.

M. E. McMaster, proprietor of the "Farmers' Flouring mills," bought the property and succeeded George Elliott in the business in February, 1877. Mr. McMaster was born at Argyle, N. Y., September 22d, 1831. October 10th, 1854, he was married to Laura A. Brown, of Attica, Ind. He has been a resident of Lockport most of the time since 1836.

Lawrence J. McParlin, jr., has always resided in Lockport, where he was born November 14th, 1848. After leaving school at the age of fourteen he worked at the stave-mills in East Lockport, and afterward entered a telegraph office and became manager for the Atlantic and Pacific company. He subsequently studied law with Hon. Richard Crowley two years, and with Thomas M. Webster three years. He was admitted to the bar at Rochester in 1875. Besides his legal practice, he represents Martindale's Collecting Agency in the county, also the International Law and Collecting Agency, and is agent for the Inman line of ocean steamers, and for C. B. Richards & Boa's Banking Association, in which connection he sells drafts on all parts of the world. He founded the Lockport Catholic Literary Union, and was for three years secretary of it; president of the C. M. B. A. branch which bears his name, and was first grand vice-president of the grand council of that association for New York; and was for three years president of St. John's Total Abstinence Society. He was chairman of the second ward Republican committee five years, and secretary of the county committe two years, and has been chairman of the greenback county committee.

T. O. Markey was born in Ireland, and came to Lockport in 1849. He succeeded C. Pennoyer in the manufacture of bolts in 1870. Manufactory at 172 Market street.

Hugh Marshall was born in Belfast, Ireland. He came to the city of New York in 1836 and remained there till 1847, when he came to Niagara county and located in Lockport, where he has since followed his business as a custom tailor. Residence No. 125 Saxton street.

Mrs. D. Merritt was born in Newfane, Niagara county, in 1813. She is a daughter of William Wisner, formerly of Seneca county, who came to Newfane in 1810, taking possession of the farm now owned by Jacob Outwater, two and a half miles east of Olcott. Mrs. Merritt came to Lockport in 1871.

J. E. Merritt was born in Newfane, and, after living in Somerset, came to Lockport in 1866. In 1870 he begun the manufacture of agricultural implements on a small scale, since which time the business has gradually increased till at present he employs from twelve to fifteen hands, doing a business averaging $25,000 to $30,000 annually.

George F. Miller, barber, at the Judson House. Business established in the fall of 1877.

James Molyneux, No. 47 Main street, wholesale and retail dealer in tobacco and cigars. Business established in 1875.

John W. Moran was born in Lockport, March 31st, 1854. He is a grocer, his place of business being at 8 Exchange street.

Marcus Moses, residing at No. 135 East avenue, was born in Hartford county, Conn., September 30th, 1800. He came to Lockport from Rochester in 1823, and has lived here most of the time since, engaged in mercantile pursuits, from which he has now retired. He lived in Ohio from 1828 to 1838, and during 1835, 1836 and 1837, was appointed a captain in the militia of that State and promoted to the office of colonel.

Hon. Elisha Moody, senior member of the firm owning the Niagara Nurseries, has been closely identified with the interests of the county for the past forty years, having been president of the western New York Horticultural Society, and of the Niagara County Agricultural Society, alderman from the fourth ward, mayor of the city of Lockport and member of Assembly from Niagara county. In 1867 he was tendered by Governor Fenton the appointment of horticultural commissioner from New York State to the world's fair, at Paris, which appointment he was obliged to decline on account of other business engagements.

Orange C. Moody was born in Stowe, Vermont, December 11th, 1820, and came to Lockport in 1847. In 1856 Mr. Moody served as a volunteer in Kansas with John Brown, of anti-slavery fame.

Henry H. Moore, No. 16 Main street, is a wholsale and retail dealer in cigars and tobacco. Business established in 1866.

Thomas Moore was born in Monroe county and came to Lockport in May, 1825. He has been in the painting and the sash and glass business. He is at present engaged in the manufacture of pumps, in the rear of No. 36 East avenue.

James A. Morgan was born in Royalton, came to Lockport in 1848, and has since lived there and been engaged at his trade as carpenter. His father, Thomas Morgan, a native of Wales, located in Royalton in 1830. In 1848 he also removed to Lockport, where he died in 1852. Mrs. Morgan is still living with her son on Chestnut street.

Mrs. Sarah Howe Morris, M. D., was born in Maine.

She studied medicine at the New England Female Academy (now Boston University), and graduated from that institution in 1869. She interested herself in the study of drunkenness in its various conditions, and came to the conclusion that it was a curable disease; and for several years she devoted her time and energies with much success to the improvement in the condition of inebriates of all classes. The proper credit will be given her for boldness and originality in this project, when it is understood that she devised and put her scheme into operation before the establishment of the Baltimore and Binghamton Asylums as medical institutes. She was married in 1871 to James Morris, a native of Carlisle, England. They left Brooklyn in 1873, and were not permanently located until February, 1875, when they came to Lockport, where Mr. Morris follows his business as an engraver, and Mrs. Morris has since practiced her profession. Residence, 135 Washington street.

Elias Moyer was a native of Berks county, Pa. He removed to Lockport in 1850, where he was engaged in the grocery trade till his death in 1862. He was married in 1849 to Miss Louisa M. Watterson, who survives him, living at 103 Ontario street.

James P. Murphy, agent for the Workingmen's Grocery Association, was born in Minden, Montgomery county, N.Y., May 9th, 1816, and came to Lockport in 1832 from Starkville, Herkimer county, N. Y. Mr. Murphy occupied the position of assessor of internal revenue, 29th district, N. Y., from 1862 to 1871.

James E. Murray was born in the town of Lockport, February 28th, 1832. After his marriage with Miss Morden he removed to the city of Lockport, where he has become very proficient in running a steam-engine for various purposes, but principally for threshing, and predicts that before many years it will almost entirely supersede the various powers now employed.

Mrs. Luman H. Nicholls, formerly Miss Ann Minerva Hallady, was born in Amsterdam, Montgomery county N.Y. In 1838 she was married to her late husband. Luman H. Nicholls was a native of Albany county, N.Y. In 1837 he became a resident of the city of Lockport, where for several years he practiced his profession as an attorney and dealt somewhat in real estate. He died September 2d, 1864, since which event Mrs. Nicholls has resided at 160 Cottage street.

John Noble, proprietor of Noble's steam bakeries, located and begun business in Lockport on a small scale in 1868. He has gradually increased it until he employs ten hands, running three bakeries in the city and doing a business of about $20,000 annually, consuming about 21,000 pounds of flour per annum.

William L. Norman was born in 1848. In 1857 the business now carried on by J. G. & W. L. Norman was established by William Norman. For further information see history of the brewing interest.

Rev. Robert Norton, pastor of the Second Ward Presbyterian Church of Lockport, was born February 18th, 1822, at Goshen, Conn. He came to Lockport in July, 1857, from Rushford, Allegany county, N. Y.

Charles Augustus Olmsted, civil engineer, was born in Onondaga Valley, Onondaga county, N. Y., May 30th, 1811, and came to Lockport from Kentucky in 1860. Mr. Olmsted has been assistant, resident and division engineer on the Erie, Champlain and other canals of the State of New York.

George P. Ostrander was born in the town of Royalton, Niagara county, N. Y., February 25th, 1847, and has been a life-long resident of the county. He is a lawyer by profession and is at present surrogate of Niagara county.

Timothy Paige, a native of Bennington county, Vt., removed, at the age of two, with his parents to Oneida county, N. Y., where they lived till 1814, when he went to Jefferson county and remained there till 1817, when he came by schooner to Fort Niagara and walked from there to Lewiston, and from Lewiston to Wright's Corners, and thence to Slayton Settlement. Here and in other places round about he worked by the month in clearing land and at similar work. In 1824 he was married to Mrs. Eliza Wright, also a native of Vermont. In the meantime he had bought a farm near Orangeport of Joseph Ellicott. He located upon it, and in 1826 was elected constable, and he served as constable and sheriff till 1836. In 1846 he removed to Michigan and remained there eight years, after which he was for twelve years a resident of Buffalo. Mrs. Paige died in 1855, and two years later he was again married, to Mrs. Mary M. Rogers, of Buffalo. In 1865 he removed to Lockport, since which time he has served as constable, health-inspector and in other capacities, and for seven years has been crier in court. Residence, 259 Pine street.

W. H. Paine was born in Rhode Island. In 1856 he located in Rochester, since which time he has been in the service of the New York Central Railroad Company and is at present acting as baggage-master at Lockport, where he has resided since 1865. Mr. Paine was married in 1851 to Miss Laura S. Webster, of Monroe county, N. Y.

Asa F. Payne was born September 5th, 1839, at Perryville, Madison county, N. Y. He came to Lockport April 1st, 1848, and is engaged as a milk dealer. Residence on Clinton street.

G. W. Penfield, a son of A. B. Penfield, was born in Monroe county, and removed with his parents to Lockport in 1850. He was for six years book-keeper at the Niagara County National Bank. In 1866 he engaged, in company with Jesse Shaeffer, in the produce business and continued in it till July, 1877.

H. L. Penfield, carpenter and builder, No. 191 North Transit street, is a native of Monroe county. He came to Lockport in 1840 and was married to Miss Jane F. Oliver in 1842.

Jesse Peterson was born in Belfast, Allegany county, N. Y., October 1st, 1850, and came to Lockport in 1860. He is a manufacturer.

Hiram A. Phillips was born in Ontario county. He located as a farmer in Royalton in 1847, and removed to Lockport in 1871, where he has since lived retired.

James C. Phillips was born in Sweden, Monroe county, N. Y., March 22d, 1816. In 1838 he was married to Miss

Sarah Ferrce, of the same town, and a year or two later removed to North Hartland, Niagara county. Mrs. Phillips died in 1850, and in the following year Mr. Phillips married Miss Louisa A. Fortia, of Orwell, Rutland county, Vt. He died February 7th, 1865.

H. C. Pomroy has been a life-long resident of the town and city of Lockport, having been born in the town in 1825. Mr. Pomroy, who resides at 144 Locust street, is engaged in the hardware trade at 44 Main street, corner of Pine, and is a stockholder and trustee of the Holly Manufacturing Company, and a director of the Niagara County National Bank.

Hon. Solon P. Pomroy was born September 22d, 1830, in Bennington, Wyoming county, N. Y., and came to Lockport in 1838. Mr. Pomroy became early known in political and public life, having been connected editorially with the press of Lockport while a young man, and continuing in that relation twenty-eight years in the city and elsewhere. He was captain and afterwards major in the N. Y. National Guards. In 1855 and 1856 he was canal collector; in 1856 member of Assembly; and he is now clerk to assistant canal superintendent Hon. Linus Jones Peck.

G. C. Pool, a native of Lewiston, removed to Lockport in 1869, and, after butchering two years, engaged at his trade of carriage trimming and painting. Shop, 58 and 60 Market street.

Thomas Powers, carriage blacksmith, was one of the aldermen of the city of Lockport from 1874 to 1876. He was born in Ireland, November 14th, 1835, and came to Lockport from Suspension Bridge in 1857.

Mrs. Paulina Pratt, whose maiden name was Parsons, was born in Goshen, Hampshire county, Mass., and came to Niagara county in 1832, with her husband, Mr. G. W. Pratt, to whom she was married in 1826, and settled in the town of Wilson. In 1860 they removed to Lockport. Mr. Pratt died in January, 1870, since which time Mrs. Pratt has resided at No. 66 Genesee street.

Daniel Quinlian, jr., manufacturer of cigars, No. 56 Main street (up stairs), successor to Ogden & Quinlian. The business was established in the spring of 1875. Mr. Quinlian does an extensive business; employing six hands in the winter and a larger force in the spring and summer.

Alfred Ransom was born in Colchester, Sullivan county, N. Y., February 16th, 1823. He came to the town of Wilson in 1840, and from there to Lockport in 1867. Mr. Ransom is an architect and builder, and devotes a portion of his time to farming. He has served as commissioner of highways and town clerk of the town of Wilson, and as sheriff of Niagara county three years. Taking an active part in the late rebellion, he acquitted himself with much credit as captain of the 23rd battery from November, 1861, to April, 1865.

Lewis Ransom, builder and machinist, was born in Ulster county, N. Y. He came to Niagara county in 1840, and located at Ransomville, where he resided continuously till 1846, and has resided a portion of the time since, having spent some time in the South. He came to Lockport in 1866, and has been a resident of the city ever since. In 1866 Mr. Ransom was married to Miss Mary Estes, a native of Addison county, Vt., at that time a resident of the town of Porter.

Walter J. Ransom, M.D., was born in the town of Porter, N. Y., April 3d, 1853. Dr. Ransom was assistant surgeon at Bellevue Dispensary during the winter of 1874 and 1875, and a member of Charity Hospital medical staff from April, 1876, to March, 1877, when he resigned on account of ill health. Residing in East Lockport he is engaged in the practice of his profession.

Mrs. Rhoda Judd Raymond, daughter of Ozias Judd, an early settler of the county, sister of Orange Judd, publisher of the *American Agriculturist*, New York city, and widow of Augustus E. Raymond, who died in 1874, was born in Lewiston, Niagara county, July 17th, 1829, and married to her late husband in September, 1849.

George W. Rector is a native of Montgomery county. He came to Niagara county and located in Lewiston in 1824. In 1846 he removed to Lockport, where he has since resided.

William Richmond, No. 4 Gooding street, was born in Worcestershire, England, October 7th, 1847, and came to Lookport February 3d, 1868, from Perry, Wyoming county, N. Y. Mr. Richmond is a manufacturer of patented improved machinery for flouring mills.

Victor W. Ringueberg was born in Lockport in 1849, and has been a life-long resident of the city, where he is largely interested as a farmer, grape-grower and wine manufacturer.

Daniel Rodenbach, liquor dealer, was born in Lyons, Wayne county, December 29th, 1840, and came to Lockport April 16th, 1867.

J. W. Rogers, produce and commission merchant, No. 79 Market street. Business established in 1857.

Edwin Saxton, No. 303 Market street, successor to Slocombe & Saxton in 1877; in 1875 Slocombe & Saxton succeeded H. M. Brundage, who established the business in 1870.

E. W. Scott, superintendent of agencies for the Equitable Life Insurance Company, Broadway, New York city, was born in Cambria, Niagara county, in 1845, and came to Lockport in 1863, where his family have since resided.

Thomas Scovell, loan and insurance agent and notary public (residence 198 West Main street), was born in Orwell, Vermont, October 2d, 1383. He came to Cambria in 1836, and from Cambria to Lockport in March, 1867.

George Seaver, cigar manufacturer, over No. 82 Main street, employs from ten to fifteen hands, manufacturing from 25,000 to 40,000 cigars per month, and doing a business of about $15,000 annually. This business, which was established in 1873, is the most extensive manufactory of the kind in Niagara county.

Jesse Shaeffer, dealer in grain, beans, wool and other produce, was born in Dauphin county, Pa., January 22d, 1112, and came to Lockport in 1824.

Edward Simmons is a native of Madison, N. Y., where he was born August 1st, 1815. He came to Lock-

port in April, 1838, from Galesburg, Ill. He has been for many years a silversmith and jewelry manufacturer, and lately has engaged somewhat extensively in the sale of music. In 1856 Mr. Simmons was one of the trustees of the village of Lockport, and he has been treasurer of the Niagara County Agricultural Society o ur years, and treasurer and deputy of the Niagara Bible Society for thirty-eight years.

Hon. R. M. Skeels, managing editor of the *Lockport Daily Union*, was born in Hartland in 1825. He was elected member of Assembly from this district in 1868 and 1869, serving with credit to himself and satisfaction to his constituents. Under his management the *Union* has greatly improved in editorial ability and influence, and its circulation has largely increased.

Arthur A. Skinner was born in Greene county, Ind., December 19th, 1847, and came to Lockport in September, 1876, from the city of New York, where he had been for three years employed as a teacher. Mr. Skinner has been for the past two years superintendent of the public schools of Lockport.

Alfred H. Smith, merchant miller, Niagara Mills, was born in Chili, N. Y., June 25th, 1828, and came to Lockport in 1863, from Buffalo.

T. Frank Smith, a son of Thomas Smith, who settled at Lockport in 1821, was born in the city in 1831. He has always been a resident of Lockport, and having retired from active business is living quietly at his home at 368 East avenue.

George F. Smith, a native of Germany, located in Lockport in 1857, and followed his trade as harness-maker until 1863, when he opened a saloon and restaurant under the Niagara County National Bank, at the corner of Main and Pine streets, which he has conducted to the present time.

Rev. S. C. Smith is of Canadian nativity, having been born in the town of Carter, District of Gore, Ont., May 21st, 1819. He moved from Canada into the town of Porter, Niagara county, in 1828. For thirty years and more, Rev. Mr. Smith has been actively engaged in the duties of a clergyman of the M. E. Church, having served the churches at Youngstown, Wilson, Somerset, Middleport and Clinton street, Lockport, regular terms.

Lyman A Spalding was born in Scipio, Cayuga county, N. Y., February 28th, 1800, and came to Lockport in December, 1822, from Canandaigua, Ontario county, N. Y. Mr. Spalding is one of the most enterprising business men of Lockport. His time is divided between the duties of a merchant, a miller, a broker and a manufacturer of iron machinery. For years Mr. Spalding was interested in the construction and operation of saw and gristmills, building and owning in whole or in part a number of each in different parts of the county. He was treasurer of Niagara county from 1836 to 1838, United States assistant assessor in 1864, and postmaster of the city of Lockport from November, 1866, to March, 1871.

George Specht, cooper, was born in Bavaria, Germany, and came to America in 1855. In 1856 he was married to Miss Kunigynda Uber, also a native of Bavaria. In 1857 he engaged in business as a cooper, which he continues in the same shop.

Steele, Hoag & Company, malsters. This business, which is very extensive, was established in 1875. A large brick malt house was erected, four stories high, 120 feet by 50 feet, capacity for malting about 60,000 bushels per annum, employing only four men, the use of elevators taking the place of more hands.

Origen Storrs, a native of Mansfield, Conn., came to Lockport from Seneca Falls, N. Y., in 1839, and was for several years engaged in the sale of general merchandise. He is at present connected with the Lockport Banking Association. He has, during his residence in the city, held a number of responsible offices, among them those of supervisor, magistrate, and mayor. He was mayor at the time of the Chicago fire, and took a leading part in raising money for the relief of the sufferers.

J. B. Sullivan, grocer, No. 11 Pine street, succeeded Sullivan & Hyer, who established the business in the spring of 1870. Mr. Sullivan is a native of Montreal, Canada, and located in Lockport in 1852.

William Sullivan, a native of Toronto, Canada, came to Lockport in 1858, and was for several years engaged in the bakery business. Since 1873 he has conducted a saloon.

Stephen Sult was born in Columbia county, Penn., and came to Lockport in March, 1836, as foreman in laying the track of the Lockport and Niagara Falls strap railroad. He has remained in the city since, and has for many years been in the employ of the N. Y. C. & H. R. R. R. Company, as road-master. He is one of the oldest railroad men west of Rochester, if not the oldest.

Samuel R. Talbot, carriage manufacturer, was born in Rochester, N. Y., in the year 1836, and came to Lockport in 1840. He was married to Mary C. Young in 1871.

Alexander Tenbrook, hotel keeper, was born in Pottsville, Schuylkill county, Pa., June 4th, 1838. He came to Lockport thirty years ago, and has lived in Niagara county ever since, being known as an enterprising citizen, and an active worker politically, in the Democratic party.

James O. Tenbrook was born July 20th, 1850, at Lockport, N.Y., and married June 5th, 1874, to Franc H. Raymond, of Cambria, N. Y. Judson House.

John P. Tenbrook was born February 10th, 1848, at McEwensville, Pa., and is now engaged in hotel keeping in the city of Lockport. He served in the rebellion as a member of battery M, 1st N. Y. Light Artillery.

L. H. Tenbrook, a native of Northumberland county, Pa., came to Niagara county in 1849. He kept a hotel in Somerset two years, and at Youngstown one year, and after living in Waterloo, Seneca county, a year, he removed to Lockport, and kept the Tenbrook House about a year. He remained in the city till the spring of 1877, when he assumed control of the Gothic Hotel, west of Lockport.

A. L. Tennant was born in Lockport, and has resided for several years in Cambria. In 1865 he returned to

Lockport, where, in 1867, he established a shirt front manufactory. The business has gradually increased since then, and at present the factory turns out 60,000 fronts per annum, furnishing employment during the busy season to about fifty hands. In 1867 Mr. Tennant added the manufacture of shirts to his previous business. He occupies the third floor of the Central Block.

Windsor Trowbridge was born in Monroe county, N. Y., in 1825, and was married to Miss Mary R. Heath in 1846. Mr. Trowbridge removed to Lockport in 1853, and located permanently, engaging in the manufacture of brick till 1865. In 1867 he purchased the greenhouses and vegetable gardens of Joseph Duquette, which business he has successfully conducted ever since.

A. Walter Tryon, M. D., was born in Durham, N. Y., in 1840, and came to Lockport in 1854, where he has since been engaged in the practice of his profession. During the late war he served three years as an army surgeon, being for two and a half years in charge of the U. S. general hospital in Alexandria, Va.

William C. Tucker, a native of Boston, Mass., removed to Niagara county in 1832, and located in Lockport. He was by trade a wood turner and cabinet-maker, which business he carried on with different partners and in different locations in the city till his retirement in 1871, when the business passed into the hands of Messrs. Wright & Rogers. Mr. Tucker's residence is at old No. 59 Pine street.

Anton Ulrich, a native of France, came to Buffalo in 1858. In 1863 he removed to Lockport and established himself in the brewing business. For particulars see history of that interest.

C. E. Underwood, dealer in dry goods, No. 6 Main street. Business established in 1877.

Hon. Burt Van Horn was born in the town of New-fane, N. Y., October 28th, 1823 and came to Lockport in 1865. He has for many years been engaged in agriculture and fruit-growing. Mr. Van Horn served three years in the Assembly of the State of New York, and six years in Congress. He is now the United States internal revenue collector for the 28th New York district, embracing nine counties, with headquarters at Rochester, N. Y.

Hon. John Van Horn is a native of Ovid, Seneca county, N. Y., and was born March 7th, 1813. Mr. Van Horn's father located in Niagara county in 1810. He built mills in the following year, and in May, 1819, brought his family from their former home in Seneca county. Mr. Van Horn has been a dry goods and hardware merchant in the county for forty years, and besides being a well-known business man, he has been prominent in public life. In 1845 he was elected county clerk and served three years. He was chosen county treasurer in 1856, and held the office for one term. Always interested in the cause of education, he was elected trustee of the board of education of the city of Lockport, and served six years, and he was president of the board for five years. He was appointed by the governor of New York a commissioner for building the State blind asylum at Batavia, and served until its completion. In 1870 he was elected mayor of the city, and justice of the peace in 1875, and still holds the latter office.

T. H. Van Horn, druggist, 69 Main street.

M. P. Van Valkenburgh was born in Canaan, Columbia county, N. Y., and came to Lockport with his father's family in 1838. In 1835 Mr. Van Valkenburgh was married to Caroline Worden, a native of Wayne county, N. Y. Mr. Van Valkenburgh has been engaged in the manufacture of lumber for many years.

Thomas N. Van Valkenburgh, vice-president of the Niagara County National Bank, Lockport, was born December 23d, 1842, at Lockport. He was married June 15th, 1865, to Francis A. Lewis, also of Lockport.

William A. Van Valkenburgh was born at New Canaan, Columbia county, N. Y., and came to the town of Lockport with his father in 1825. About 1831 he came to Lockport, where he was engaged in the lumber business till 1848, when he bought a farm near the rapids, in the south part of the town. Remaining there till the spring of 1878, he removed to the city, where he now resides. He was one year inspector of lumber for Niagara county.

Alfred Van Wagoner was born in Milan, Dutchess county, N. Y., January 26th, 1812. In April, 1833, he came to the town of Somerset and purchased a farm on the lake shore. At present he is a resident of the city of Lockport. He was appointed postmaster in 1844 and held the office till removed by President Tyler, and he has held various town offices, besides that of county treasurer, to which he was elected in 1852. In 1872 and 1873 he was an alderman from the 3d ward.

Morgan Van Wagoner was born in Dutchess county, N. Y., and came to Niagara county in 1833 and located in Somerset. In 1867 Mr. Van Wagoner removed to Lockport, where he has since lived retired. He was commissioner of highways in Somerset for several years, and supervisor of that town three years.

Charles Watts, dentist, was born in Birmingham, England, January 7th, 1841, and came to Lockport October 7th, 1862, from Rochester, having come from England in 1842.

Hon. P. D. Walter was born September 15th, 1817, in Springfield, Otsego county, N.Y., and came to Lockport from Richfield Springs, N.Y., in 1845. Mr. Walter, who is known as one of the most enterprising jewelers of western New York, has occupied many positions of trust and responsibility, among which may be mentioned the following : In 1841 and 1842 he commanded a regiment of militia; in 1853 he was trustee of the then village of Lockport; in 1860 and 1861 he was secretary, in 1862–64 treasurer, in 1865 and 1866 vice-president, and in 1867 president of the Niagara County Agricultural Society; in 1865 and 1866 he served as city treasurer and tax receiver; in the fall of 1871 he was elected clerk of Niagara county and served three years, and in 1873 he was chosen mayor of the city of Lockport. He is connected with Grace Church, and is now one of the trustees of De Veaux College, at Suspension Bridge.

RES. OF E. P. WENTWORTH, 109 CHURCH ST. LOCKPORT, N.Y.

EZRA PERRY WENTWORTH. (DEC)

Thomas G. Watson, dealer in paving and building stones, was born in Rochester, N. Y. Quarry north of the city of Lockport, on Price avenue.

Mrs. E. M. Webber was born in Orwell, Addison county, Vt., in 1813. In 1836 she was married to her late husband, Mr. A. C. Webber, a native of Worthington, Berkshire county, Mass., who had come to Niagara county with his father's family while young, and who was at the time of his marriage a dry goods merchant in Lockport. He died in December, 1849.

M. H. Webber, a native of Cambria, N. Y., was born in 1824. He has always lived in Niagara county and is now a hardware dealer in Lockport.

Williard Wild was born in Berkshire county, Mass., in 1808, and in 1810 came with his father's family to Genesee county, where he resided till 1830, when he moved to Lockport and settled on the farm now owned by J. H. Mosier. In 1862 he removed to his present location on South Transit street.

Rutlege Wells, foreman of Wells's lumber yard, 18 Caledonia street, was born December 29th, 1827, at Stratford, Conn., and came to Lockport in 1853.

Ezra P. Wentworth was born in Jefferson county, N. Y., in 1810 and came to Lockport in 1825, afterward purchasing the farm where his son A. P. Wentworth now lives, where he remained for two years and then removed to the city of Lockport. In 1832 he engaged in the lumber business, in which he continued till 1875. He removed to Buffalo, and after a residence of six years there returned to Lockport. In 1833 he was married to Olivia Ann Sweet, who died in 1851. In 1853 he was again married, to Phebe L. Flagler, who still survives him, residing at No. 109 Church street. Mr. Wentworth was prominently identified with the Congregational church of Lockport. He was actively engaged in business until about two years before his death, which occurred January 24th, 1877.

Alexander White established a hoop skirt and corset manufactory in Lockport in 1866. In 1868 it was changed to a trade in millinery and fancy goods. The business is rapidly increasing, and is now one of the most extensive in the city.

W. W. Whitmore is a member of the firm of W. W. Whitmore & Company, proprietors of sandstone quarries. This business was established in 1830 by Whitmore & Robins, and several times changed hands until 1872, since which time it has been under the management of the present firm, consisting of W. W. Whitmore, Charles H. Rathbone and Gilbert Brady. Branch yards are located at Rochester, under the management respectively of Whitmore, Brady & Company, and Whitmore, Rathbone & Company. The first use made of sandstones for street paving was on the lower end of Main street, Buffalo, in 1836.

Frank W. Wicker was born in Erie county, N. Y., and came to Lockport in 1845, and engaged in book-keeping and carpenter's work. In 1861 he enlisted in the 28th Regiment N. Y. S. Volunteers. After three months he was detailed for signal service duty, and in 1863 received a lieutenant's commission. He was discharged in 1865, and was appointed second in command of the land laying forces of the Atlantic cable, and at its completion returned to Lockport. He was appointed special agent for Alaska in 1869, and in 1873 collector of customs at Key West, Florida, where he still remains, having been re-appointed in 1878. Mr. Wicker was married in 1860 to Miss Hattie, a daughter of Z. M. P. Spalding.

Joshua Wilber, editor and publisher of the *Lock-City News*, was born in Norwich, Conn., in 1824. He was married in 1856 to Mary Hickey, of Lockport.

S. A. Wilcox was born in Madison county, Vt. He conducted a cheese factory at Sanborn three years after coming to Niagara county, and afterwards had control of one in St. Lawrence county for four years. In 1877 he came to Lockport and bought out Palmer's Laundry, over numbers 15 and 17 Pine street. This business, which is now so extensive as to keep about fifteen hands constantly employed, was established in 1874, by W. E. Palmer.

Daniel Willard is a native of the city. In 1876 he established a furniture manufactory, which he has conducted since with increasing success, employing at the present time six hands.

Ebenezer W. Williams, of the firm of Williams & Co., livery stable keepers, was born in Shoreham, Vt., in 1817, and came to Lockport in 1834. Mr. Williams has held several offices of trust and responsibility, having been alderman, police justice and canal superintendent.

John C. Williams, a Canadian, came to Lockport in 1860, and has since worked at his trade as a cooper. In the spring of 1878 he was appointed on the city police force.

Mason B. Williams, of the firm of Williams & Co., liverymen, was born in Royalton, N. Y., October 3d, 1821, and was married to Mary J Dunlap November 19th, 1850. Mr. Williams has resided in the city during his life, excepting four years' residence at Whitewater, Wisconsin. He is now superintendent of section 10 of the Erie Canal.

George Woods was born in England. In June, 1835, he came to America and located in Lockport, following agricultural pursuits for a livelihood until he became superintendent of Glenwood Cemetery, which position he holds at the present time. He was married in 1834 to Miss Mary Ann Little.

Samuel Works was born in New Hampshire, and came to Rochester in 1816, removing from there to Lockport in 1831, and began farming on the site of D. M. Mather's tannery. Mr. Works has been called to a number of official positions, having been State Senator two terms and superintendent of the canal one year.

O. C. Wright established himself in the city as a bookseller in 1841. The present firm of O. C. & E. C. Wright was formed in 1851, since which time the junior member has been the active manager in the book department. A stock of pianos and organs was added about 1850, and that branch of the business has been under the management of Mr. O. C. Wright. This house, which is one of the oldest of its class in western New York, does a business of from $35,000 to $40,000 per annum.

W. S. Wright was born October 15th, 1824, at Granville, Washington county, N. Y., and was married November 19th, 1847, to Maria Lockwood, of Olcott. Mr. Wright was justice of sessions in 1859, and clerk of Niagara county from 1863 to 1866, and has held many minor offices, being at present a member of the board of education of the city of Lockport. He is a dealer in furniture and frames at No. 67 Main street, and devotes much of his time to fruit culture on the lake shore at Olcott, N. Y.

Edward A. Young, designer and engraver on wood and metals, was born at Rochester, N. Y., in 1852, and came to Lockport in 1861, from Somerset, N. Y. Mr. Young was elected town clerk of Lockport in 1878.

Stephen Young, a native of Onondaga county, N. Y., came to Lockport in 1833. In 1839 he purchased and settled on the farm that he at present owns.

Among other prominent residents and business men of the city of Lockport the following are conspicuous: C. A. Barnes, grocer, No. 30 Main street; Joseph Batton, sheriff of Niagara county; Edward D. Bennett, saloon-keeper, No. 11 Main street; R. H. Bond, attorney, over No. 37 Main street; J. L. Breyfogle, merchant, Nos. 68 and 70 Main street; Albert F. Brown, No. 66 Walnut street; Charles L. Burgess, No. 6 John street; B. and J. Carpenter, proprietors of stone quarries and dealers in cut and sawed stone, Transit street and State road; P. J. Collins, Mansion House; Rev. P. Cannon, pastor of St. Patrick's Church; Rev. J. W. Cooper, pastor of Congregational church; Fred. Crosby, canal forwarder, No. 23 Gooding street; J. Crosby, No. 33 Gooding street; James R. Compton, cashier Niagara County National Bank; Mrs. Annie Culver, No. 189 Genesee street; Mrs. W. J. Daniels, Lake avenue; Mrs. J. G. Disinger; L. Duquette; Dr. R. Davison, No. 55 Main street; Mrs. Mary S. C. Graves, Mrs. C. A. Brockett, No. 216 West Main street; Henry Grigg, manager of Saxton & Thompson's mill; Edgar P. Holly, assistant superintendent Steam Combination Company; John Hodge, secretary Merchant's Gargling Oil Company; John A. Hubbard, postmaster; Hon. R. B. Hoag, No. 233 Lock street; B. Holly, consulting engineer Holly Manufacturing Company; M. T. Haney, of the firm of M. T. Haney & Company; R. F. Holly, of the firm of Snyder & Holly; John T. Joyce, of the firm of Ransom & Joyce, attorneys; Hon. James Jackson, jr., president Farmers' and Mechanics' Savings Bank; Charles Keep, No. 436 Locust street; George R. Keep, corner of High and Waterman streets; Mrs. Chauncey Keep, East avenue; Augustus Keep, No. 13 East avenue; Eugene Kearns, publisher and proprietor of the Niagara *Industrial Advocate*, over 51 Main street; P. H. Linneen, canal contractor; S. J. Dibble; S. Curt Lewis, banker and county treasurer; Frank Lackor, dealer in flour, feed and grain, corner of Buffalo and Saxton streets; Myron C. Ludlum, proprietor of boarding and livery stables, corner of Cottage and Center streets; Mrs. E. S. Mack, 154 Locust street; S. Wright McCullum, market gardner, ice dealer and wine manufacturer, corner of North Adam and Vine streets; Thomas McMahon, proprietor of meat market, No. 27 Main street; Miss M. E. McCullan; Rev. D. M. Moser, pastor of the Evangelical Lutheran Church; Hon. H. D. McNeil, proprietor of the New York Tea Store, No. 1 Hodge Opera House Block; Mark McDonough, police justice and United States commissioner, office No. 14 Hodge Opera House Block; Colonel William McRae, contractor, No. 25 Gooding street; Robert T. Paine, M. D., 171 Ontario street; Waterman S. Pound, manager for Owen Pixley & Company, No. 58 Main street; Hon. Linus Jones Peck; Abraham Pettit, carpenter, No. 8 Spalding street; W. E. Shaeffer, dealer in produce, wool, grain and seed, Nos. 22 and 24 Market street; David E. Snyder, of the firm of Snyder & Holly, No. 111 Chestnut street; Rev. G. W. Southwell, rector of Christ Church; W. W. Steele, of the firm of Steele, Torrance & Co., No. 69 Niagara avenue; Frederick Specht, barber, Hodge Opera House; George A. Torrance, of the firm of Steele, Torrance & Co., No. 135 Ontario street; Charles H. Van Dusen, proprietor of the Opera House news room; Robert Van Valkenburgh, dentist, over No. 72 Main street; John C. Williams, No. 75 Van Buren street; Mrs. Ann Eliza Young, 422 Walnut street.

JAMES JACKSON JR. AND SON, LUMBER DEALERS, LOCKPORT, N.Y.
1 OFFICE 3 SASH FACTORY & PLANING MILL
2 SAW MILL 4 LUMBER YARD
James Jackson Jr.
J. Carl Jackson

RES. OF HON. JAMES JACKSON JR., COR. PINE AND WALNUT STS., LOCKPORT, N.Y.

THE TOWN OF CAMBRIA.

THE act of the Legislature, passed March 11th, 1808, to form Niagara county from Genesee, included the following lines:

"And be it further enacted that that part of the county of Niagara lying north of the main stream of the Tonnawanta creek, and of a line extending west from the mouth of said creek to the boundary line between the United States and the dominion of the King of Great Britain, be erected into a town by the name of Cambria; and that the first town meeting in the said town be held at the house of Joseph Hewitt."

"And be it further enacted, that so much of this act as relates to the forming of towns, shall take effect from and after the day preceding the first Tuesday of April next."

Tuesday, April 5th, 1808, according to the town records, "the freeholders and inhabitants of the town of Cambria, by the authority aforesaid, met in town meeting at the house of Joseph Hewitt; and Robert Lee, Esq., a justice of the peace in and for the county of Genesee, presided, superintending the same. The said town meeting being thus organized, proceeded to the election of a town clerk. James Harrison was duly elected; Joseph Hewitt supervisor; Robert Lee, Benjamin Barton and Charles Wilber, commissioners of highways; Lemuel Cook, Silas Hopkins and John Dunn, assessors; Stephen Hopkins, collector; Philemon Baldwin and Thomas Slayton, overseers of the poor; Stephen Hopkins, Ray March, Stephen A. Baldwin and Alexander Haskin, constables; Enoch Hitchcock for the eastern district, and Thomas Hustler for the western, pound-masters."

Then followed the necessary legislative enactments:

"Ordered, that there be erected one other pound in addition to the one ordered by a former town meeting of the then town of Erie, in the eastern district, near the school-house, on the land of Gad Warner, Esquire." This location was at Orangeport, the other near Lewiston.

Sixteen overseers of highways were elected and assigned their routes. By reference to the established highways it may be judged that some of the districts imposed a rather tedious duty, for example, one from Fort Niagara to the main street of Lewiston—seven miles.

It was further ordered that a reward of five dollars be paid for each and every wolf killed in said town, on proof before a magistrate, accompanied with the production of the skull with the entire skin thereon;" and "that one hundred dollars be raised for the destruction of wolves, by a direct tax on the said towns." Also " that one hundred dollars be raised for the support of the poor, and two hundred and fifty dollars for the 'reperation' of the highways."

The meeting adjourned to meet the next season at the house of Stephen Hopkins. The following items of record will be acceptable to such as interested in the details of pioneer management:

"Marks of cattle, sheep and hogs: Daniel Howell's marks, half penny on the left ear, the half penny on the under side of the said ear, and a slit on the end of the right ear. Joseph Howell's, a crop off the end of the left ear and a half penny on the under side of the same ear. Charles Wilber's, a slit on the end of each ear. John Beach's, a slit in the right ear. Elijah Doty's, a swallow fork on the left ear." Similar devices were resorted to by all the owners of animals, that of necessity must run at large until clearing could be done and pastures fenced. For any one other than the owner to meddle or appropriate was a violation of the cardinal law of community. This first town meeting also "ordered that the lawful fence in said town shall be five feet six inches high, and the overseers of highways shall act as fence-viewers."

The aggregate vote in the town for five candidates at the first election of State senators, was sixteen. For member of Congress, Peter B. Porter had forty-three votes, Nathaniel W. Howell twenty-eight, and Archibald Clark two. For member of Assembly, S. Clark had forty-four votes, Phineas Stephens two, and Peter B. Porter two.

We have reason to admire the concert of action that prevailed among the first settlers, in forming and regulating communities. "Men in high estate" did not pride themselves on former position or favored condition, nor hesitate to become subordinates if services were required to advance the prosperity of all. Benjamin Barton, before in the position of sheriff, wielding power over all western New York, becomes a highway commissioner or pathmaster. Peter B. Porter stands in rank with him, for any duty imposed; also Jonas Harrison, an educated and qualified lawyer, the first established in the county, and for several terms the efficient town clerk. Wherever the most reliable men were found, they freely submitted and were freely used.

At a meeting held at the house of Ira Harris, August 14th, 1815, the commissioners divided the town into nine school districts. There are now twelve. The amount of public money for 1878 was $1,421.31. District No. 3 received the largest amount, $166.64; No. 4 the smallest, $81.77. The scholars between the ages of five and twenty-one number five hundred.

EARLIEST RESIDENTS OF THE TOWN.

The origin and record of those who lay the foundation of communities is a part of the most interesting history. It would almost seem a hereditary spirit of advance that controls the acts of most who settle the wild localities of a new country. Inspirited by laudable enterprise, it is often the case that a halt is made only to see settlement commence.

Philip Beach and his family were the leading pioneers of Cambria. In the spring of 1801 their tent was pitched on the bank of Howell's creek, by the side of the Indian trail they had been for days traversing. At this point was built the first log house to shelter reclaimers of the waste places and subduers of the forest. Mr. Beach had become acquainted with the country by having been the earliest mail carrier from Batavia to Fort Niagara. He followed obscure Indian paths, directed by an Indian guide. As there was no white man's habitation to enter when night overtook him, the ground was his bed, the forest trees his covering, the sky his window to disclose the light of day. It was the diligent work of several days to complete the round trip. Relief from the arduous duty was only had by the voluntary aid of his brother Jesse.

This service was performed for Ganson and Hosmer, who had the mail contract during the years 1799 and 1800.

During the same season Philip's wilderness home was made less lonely by the welcome arrival of his two brothers, Jesse and John, with their families. Strange as it may now seem, when they sought and found a new home, within the distance of a hundred miles, it was upon the outer boundary of the same county and town in which they had been living; they only moved through the county of Ontario and town of Northampton; marked trees indicating a road for them from Batavia. Emigrating from Vermont in 1789, Isaac Scott, father of Mrs. Jesse Beach, purchased a tract of land from the notorious Ebenezer Allen, at the outlet of Allen's creek into the Genesee river. The place was named from him Scottsville. Hinds Chamberlain, a brother-in-law of Scott's, locating at Avon the year previous, and William Hencher, at Scottsville, were the first white settlers west of the Genesee river. The Beaches, when they located in the unknown Niagara county, had been residents of the Scottsville neighborhood about ten years.

It may be noticed, as showing the condition of a county that now embraces the wealth of eight populous counties, that in 1800 Philip Beach, one of the assessors of the town of Northampton, levied a tax, upon the basis of a valuation of all the real and personal property, amounting to $4,785,368. The amount of tax to be collected over an extent of country reaching west of the Genesee river to Lake Erie and the Pennsylvania line, and north and south from the shore of Lake Ontario to the Allegheny river, was $8,387.11; and it was collected from one hundred and ten tax-payers.

To provide against destitution, the Beaches brought into the woods what they supposed would be a year's ample supply of provisions for their families. The draft of others upon them, who had not their means, or who failed to exercise their forethought, early exhausted their stores. To replenish them was not an easy undertaking. David, the eldest son of Jesse Beach, and some others, were detailed for the mission. Making their way to Lake Ontario, they embarked in a small skiff and coasted along the southern shore to the mouth of the Genesee river, and thence proceeded to Scottsville. A cargo laid in, the return voyage was accomplished by long days and nights of fatigue.

Philip attempting to locate before surveys had been perfected, Mr. Ellicott, to encourage settlement, directed him to "stick a stake," and promised to survey a piece for him, which he did, regardless of any other survey, and gave him possession. This was the Howell place. Mr. Beach sold to Joseph Hewitt, who exchanged with William Howell for the present Joseph P. Hewitt farm on the Falls road, above Lewiston. Mr. Beach next located on the Sparrow Sage farm, which he sold to William Molyneux, and settled next on what is now the See farm, east of Molyneux's Corners. He finally located on the North Ridge, half a mile from the South. He died August 1st, 1840, aged sixty-eight; and his wife Lois March 28th, 1842, aged sixty-seven.

In 1810 Jesse Beach made his final location, west of Molyneux's Corners, on the place that has since been retained by his son Cyrus Beach. Here he died December 5th, 1815, aged forty-seven. His wife, Lovinia, a daughter of Isaac Scott, mentioned in connection with Scottsville, survived her husband forty-three years, and died August 29th, 1858, aged ninety.

An older brother of the Beach pioneers, Aaron Beach, located on the South Ridge, near his brother, in 1811, and in 1815 on the North Ridge, where he died January 17th, 1846, aged eighty-five. His wife Rachel died March 13th, 1849, aged seventy-nine. Mr. Beach was a settler at Scottsville, Monroe county, from 1791 to 1794, but in consequence of Indian troubles returned to Vermont, and from there removed to Cambria. He was taken prisoner in the Revolutionary war, and confined in Montreal prison eighteen months.

Olive Beach is a name familiar to the earlier and more recent inhabitants, among whom for sixty-five years she sustained a marked character for her many virtues. She was a pioneer in religious missionary work. At a time when there were no religious services within distance to be reached, she walked through the woods from the home of her father, Aaron Beach, on the North Ridge, to the mouth of Four-mile creek (ten miles), to procure a minister to form a class of the small number of Methodists that could be collected for the purpose. The services of the Rev. Mr. Ash were available, and he organized the first class that existed in the county. The memory of "Aunt Olive" will live in memory as though it were engraved

FARM RESIDENCE OF JAMES A. POOL, ESQ. CAMBRIA TOWN, NIAGARA CO. N.Y.

FARM RESIDENCE OF RANSOM CAMBELL ESQ., CAMBRIA TOWN NIAGARA CO. N.Y.

FARM RESIDENCE OF HIRAM FLANDERS ESQ. CAMBRIA TOWN NIAGARA CO. N.Y.

upon marble. She was, in 1815, the superintendent of a Sunday-school, which must have been the first in the county. She died April 14th, 1876, at the advanced age of 88.

Joseph Hewitt was the successor of Philip Beach on the premises first taken up by him. Mr. Hewitt often related to Nathaniel Cook, who now states the fact, that he set twenty-five apple trees when he first located, buying them of a man from Canada at twenty-five cents each. Such as are interested to learn the location of what was unquestionably the first bearing orchard in the county may, in passing along the South Ridge, to the west side of Howell's creek, look at the first trees on the right, included in Mr. Nathaniel Cook's orchard; twenty of them are now standing, bearing a pleasant quality of fruit, greenings and Newtown pippins. Mr. Hewitt, it is thought, only remained about two years, when, by an exchange with Howell, he became a resident on the mountain above Lewiston.

In 1808 William Howell, by the last mentioned transaction, became the permanent occupant of what for seventy years has been widely known as the "Howell place." Mrs. Harriet Cook, an only daughter, advanced to the age of sixty-nine years, who was born on the premises where she now resides, states with clearness and vigor of mind the oft-repeated story of the journey of her father and mother, with their parents, into the county. They found their way from New Jersey by Indian paths, through southern New York, *via* "Painted Post" to Batavia, and thence followed the Indian trail afterward adopted as the Niagara road, intersecting the ridge at Warren's Corners, and following it to Lewiston. Four horses carried bedding, clothing, provisions and persons upon their backs.

The travelers did not see a house after passing the Genesee river until they reached the Niagara. The night before coming to the latter they made their camp on the westerly bank of the branch of Eighteen-mile creek, where the stone road now passes to the ridge. Turning out the horses after securely hampering them, upon a favorable spot of wild grass, they cooked supper and lodged under a large black walnut tree. Pursuing the journey the next morning, they traversed the ridge, crossed the Niagara river at Lewiston, in bark canoes, swimming their horses, and landed to look for an abiding place in Canada. Before leaving their last camp they enjoyed the relish of some Jersey apples, and planted the seeds on the camping ground, the product of which remained for many years afterwards. They shortly returned from Canada, and located two miles up the river from Niagara Falls, and soon after on the Hewitt farm, next to his residence on the ridge. "My mother said," remarked Mrs. Cook, "when on the mountain months would pass away without seeing a white man or woman." Mr. Howell built the first saw-mill (on Howell's creek) in that section of the town, and his tavern stand was the next successor of those placed at Molyneux's and Warren's Corners. There were but two children, George and Harriet. The latter (now Mrs. Nathaniel Cook) is now the oldest woman living born in the county. William Howell died in Pulaski, Ill., October, 1847; his wife, Sally, March 11th, 1854, aged 85.

Nathaniel Cook married Harriet Howell December 26th, 1824. He was a native of Onondaga county, and first came to Lockport at the time of the letting of the rock sections of the Erie Canal, and the original locks, where he engaged with John Gilbert, contractor on the upper or last section, as a purchaser of supplies. He remained until the canal was finished, and in 1824 purchased the farm he now resides on of the Holland Land Company, paying $5.50 per acre for one hundred and nineteen acres. "It was," said he, "all wet and swamp, hard to subdue in consequence of what was called cat-holes. I had to contend with a beaver dam for as much as ten years, when the work of the animal was still visible. Could only get fifty cents per bushel for my wheat, the only resource to pay for my land, that I had run in debt for."

Joash Taylor located at an early date on the South Ridge, one mile east of Molyneux's Corners. He was a resident there previous to the war of 1812.

Mrs. Adelia Taylor, wife of Homer, son of Joash Taylor, who died October 7th, 1874, states that her father, Harry Steadman, came from Lima, Livingston county, in 1807 or 1808, and purchased one hundred and ninety acres of the Holland Land Company, on the north side of the eastern terminus of the South Ridge, where the turnpike intersects. Her father boarded the hands building the log road over the swamp, between Wright's and Warren's; they looked like an army when coming to his log house. There were daily calls upon Mr. Steadman, to help some one out who had got a team stuck in the mud. He died in August, 1815; his wife, Sally, in November, 1832.

Pomeroy Oliver moved to Cambria in the summer of 1815, and cleared a piece of land, which is now on William Mackey's farm. In 1816 John Hitchcock settled on the farm now owned by Josiah Balliet and Mrs. Douglas. The mountain road, from near the Cold Springs in Lockport to the Deacon Chamberlain farm, was then only defined by marked trees, and had not been cut out. John Ingersoll and Jason Lane settled on the part of lot 20 north of Daniel Oliver; Pomeroy Oliver on the same lot under the mountain ridge, on a road now discontinued. Lot 28, west of lot 20, was settled by Russell Weaver and Joshua Cowell some time previous to 1810; Weaver locating on the farm now owned by his sons-in-law, D. W. Bristol and J. S. Hyman, and Cowell on land now occupied by William Hoover and James Thrall. In 1810 Philo Cowell located on what is now the farm of Hiram Richardson.

Mrs. Fanny F. Longmate, aged 78, states that she located with her husband, Daniel P. Oliver, on the mountain ridge, four miles west of Lockport, in 1817. They followed a woods path from Warren's Corners, with a horse team, until they reached the mountain. Not able to get any further with the team, each took as much of the scant household effects as they could carry up the ledge. A chest made the most trouble, but it had to be taken, as they had no other table to eat from. Their log house was without a door or window. Two acres of land had been partially cleared. The neighbors west were John Miles, Hezekiah Hill and Elijah Smith; east, Coonrod Keyser. Mrs. Longmate's father, Samuel Faxon, located on the road leading from the mountain to the railroad junction in 1820.

Colonel Andrew Sutherland, with his wife, Naomi, removed to Cambria in 1810, and bought land on the Ridge road between Molyneux's Corners and Warren's Corners, where, excepting his absence in the war of 1812, he resided until his death, in 1836. Fletcher Sutherland still resides on the homestead.

Andrew Budd, born in Kinderhook, N. Y., in 1816, moved to Cambria in 1842, locating near Slocum's tavern, then bought 99 acres on the Ridge road, where he now lives. The present grave yard near his place was originally a part of his farm.

There is a divergence of an arm of the main or South Ridge in an irregular westerly course at Molyneux's Corners, that adds to instead of unfolding the problem of the formation of the wonderful bars or ridges. For three miles it takes a course to leave a flatiron shape between the two ridges, varying in width from the eastern point to near a mile at the western extremity, embracing some of the most desirable farming land in the county. In a state of nature, as the floods left the perpetual deposits, it was heavily timbered, wet land, or a series of marsh and swamps.

Reuben Hurd was the first to break into the wilderness and chose a location on so desirable a spot as the present residence of Mr. O. B. Averill. The time cannot be fixed, but is supposed to have been about 1805. James Barnes located in 1810, taking an article from the Holland Company for three hundred and fifty-seven acres at $2.50 per acre, advancing but a small payment. Drafted into the service in 1813, he had but little opportunity to make improvements. He was taken prisoner at the battle of Newark, and never returned.

WARREN'S CORNERS.

John Forsythe, in 1805, located at what is now Warren's Corners, and opened a tavern in 1806. His wife was among the first pioneers of the "Genesee country," a descendant of the Gansons, prominent in local history. She journeyed to her new home on horseback, carrying two small children. When Mr. Forsythe located on the ridge there were but three or four settlers between Dunham's and Lockport. East of his place there was no neighbor nearer than beyond the "eleven-mile woods" (Morehouse's Corners). The widow of this isolated pioneer wrote as follows to the author of the History of the Holland Purchase: "We brought in a few sheep with us; they were the only ones in the neighborhood; they became the especial object of the wolves. Coming out of the Wilson swamp nights, their howling would be terrific. Two years after we came in, with my then small children, one day when I heard the sheep bleating, I went out to see what the matter was. A large wolf had badly wounded a sheep. As I approached him he left the sheep, and walked off snarling, as if reluctant to leave his prey. I went for my nearest neighbor, Mr. Stoughton, to come and dress the sheep. It was three-fourths of a mile, through the woods. On my way a large grey fox crossed the road ahead of me. Returning with my neighbor, a large bear slowly crossed the road in sight of us." Similar was the experience of others and the common lot of all, in the early days of Niagara's history. Mr. Forsythe died June 2d, 1812, aged 31; his widow, Mary, February 23d, 1857, aged 74.

Ezra Warren, a Vermonter by birth, served on the Niagara frontier in the war of 1812. His company was divided into squads of three or four each, which were stationed along the Ridge road to arrest deserters and act as messengers. Mr. Warren and three others were posted for four weeks at the tavern kept by the widow of John Forsythe. Warren returned home when discharged, but having formed a strong attachment to the young landlady he went west, married her and became the landlord of the tavern, which he kept until 1825. From him the place took the name of Warren's Corners.

Artemus Baker, who was the first physician in the town, located on the main ridge near Warren's Corners in 1815; Darius Shaw at Molyneux's Corners in 1820.

The first established religious organization at Warren's Corners was a class of Methodists, formed by the then young circuit preacher John Copeland. Ira Bronson was on the circuit at the same time. Rev. Mr. Fillmore was the presiding elder. A small church was erected, which the present brick church replaced about eighteen years since, at a cost of $2,300. Ezra Warren donated the land.

MOLYNEUX'S CORNERS.

Molyneux's Corners has always been an important point in the Holland Purchase. Mr. Ellicott, influenced by frequent applications, caused a lot to be surveyed here before other surveys were completed, to meet the pressing necessity of shelter for such as were prospecting for locations, Hence the irregular lines of the lot, not corresponding with the section lines. This arrangement is understood to have been made with Plant and Clink.

In 1809 John Gould purchased of Plant, and kept a tavern in the original log house. In 1811 he sold to one Odell, and he to Silas Hopkins in 1812. Soon after the property passed to William Molyneux, who continued in possession up to his death, November 7th, 1830. His sons, Charles, William and Robert, were in interest with him in conducting the tavern and large farm. The primitive log tavern was superseded by the present hotel in 1826.

The first post-office in the town was established at the first tavern house. William Molyneux was the earliest postmaster, and was succeeded by Colonel Charles Molyneux, and the office was kept on the premises until the death of the latter; it has since been removed to different private houses on the North Ridge, and retains the original name Cambria. About half a mile east of the west end of the North Ridge another post-office is located, bearing that name.

The first and only store at Molyneux's Corners was es-

FARM RESIDENCE OF LEWIS BURTCH ESQ., CAMBRIA TOWN, NIAGARA CO., N.Y.
This Farm for Sale, 110 Acres, a Spring of Living Water

tablished by Hamlin & White immediately after the close of the war; it was located in front of George Gould's residence. The same building is now standing a few rods west on the North Ridge, occupied by Mr. Boll.

Many of the pioneers may be traced to the primitive burying-ground that arrests the attention of the most casual observer passing by a well-selected, quiet, rural spot on the west side of the ridge, near Molyneux's Corners. The enclosure of one acre was an individual appropriation, according to the best advice by Silas Hopkins, in 1812 or 1813. Two stranger soldiers dying in the neighborhood, it was provided as the place of interment. They were the first laid in it. The early pioneer Jesse Beach was the third.

CAMBRIA CENTER AND VICINITY.

The earliest settlers at Cambria Center and vicinity were Benjamin and Suchel Silly, Peter Nearpass, William Scott, Enoch Hatch, Asel Muroy, David Waters and one Crowell. They formed the majority of the community previous to 1812.

William Scott purchased from the Holland Company five hundred acres, located immediately at the Center, paying but a small advance, having the foresight to reserve his money for clearing and improving, which, it appears, was energetically done. He cleared for a crop sixty acres the first season. He early built a tavern, which was a popular resort. Prominently located, this house still remains, the private residence of William Scott's son, Homer, who remains at the place of his birth.

The alarm of the burning of Lewiston in 1813, and the prevailing consternation, caused a general flight from this as well as adjoining neighborhoods. Mrs. Scott, to escape and save an infant child, rode on horseback, carrying it to Lima, Livingston county, in her arms. William Scott died October 16th, 1841, aged 59, his wife, Sophina, died April 4th, 1868, aged 77.

John Gould, living at the Molyneux location, in 1812 became a resident, purchasing of Nearpass 240 acres, nearly the same farm now owned by his grandson, John B. Gould. He early became one of the largest grain growers and fruit producers in the county. The remains of his original dwelling and long known public house still stand, to suggest the simplicity and economy that resulted in his success. Some old people remember seeing Lafayette standing in the west room, greeted by all ages and both sexes, the landlord's animated bearing showing his appreciation of being honored by so distinguished a guest. Mr. Gould died June 15th, 1850, aged 76; his wife, Elizabeth, died September 16th, 1854, aged 77.

Christopher Howder purchased from the Holland Company 150 acres in 1812, one and a half miles east Cambria Center. Adam Houstater located in 1813 near Howder, purchasing of him. Philip Houstater, son of Adam, came with his father. His son, Alvin, is on the original homestead in Cambria.

William Campbell located in 1817 and purchased of Enoch Hotchkiss 138 acres, the premises now owned in part by Luther Campbell and M. C. Crooker. John M. Eastman located two miles east of the Center, on the stone road leading to Lockport, in 1821, purchasing of John Howder fifty acres. He had a family of eleven children, several of whom, including his son Anson, are now living in Cambria. Mrs. Eastman is still, at the age of eighty-seven, vigorous and industrious. Jacob Flanders, from New Hampshire, bought of Elias Rose in 1820 150 acres, two and three-fourth miles west of the Center, and afterward purchased of the same gentleman the farm and stone grist-mill on the mountain east of Pekin. His son Hiram is now living in Cambria.

The first burial-ground was donated by William Campbell, and was known as the "Campbell burial-ground." It was located on the Lockport stone road, one mile east of the Center. The second established is upon an elevated slope of the mountain ridge, a short distance south of the Corners; the land was a gift of William Scott. Both grounds contain the remains of the earliest inhabitants.

The First Congregational Church of Cambria was organized in the year 1817, by Rev. David M. Smith, the pastor of the then Congregational church of Lewiston. The original members were Josiah Owen, Susan Owen, Thomas Chamberlain, Jonas Chamberlain, Rachel Mills, and Hannah Crocker. In one year their numbers had increased to 23.

It was through Mr. Smith that the Holland Company granted 100 acres of land to this church as being the first organized church in Cambria. This land was situated in what is now the town of Lockport, near the present city limits. In 1827 it was sold by vote of the society, and the avails applied to the purchase of land nearer the center of the town.

The church had no resident pastor till 1827—until this time they had occasional preaching, at first by Rev. D. M. Smith, of Lewiston, and afterward by Rev. James C. Cram, who was the missionary of the American Board of Foreign Missions to the Tuscaroras, on their reservation, a little west of the town. The following is a list of the pastors of the church, with the years in which their pastorates here began:

Revs. Silas Parsons, 1827; Hiram Halsy, 1831; J. H. Rice, 1836; J. Thalheimer, 1837; W. Bridgeman, 1840; E. Parmelee, M.D., 1845; S. Johnson, 1857; D. D. Hamilton, 1859; Isaac R. Bradnack, 1863; George A. Hood, 1870; S. Wolfson, 1872; H. P. Bake, 1873; J. W. Grush, 1877.

There have been connected with the church from the beginning 563 members, and there is a present total membership of 120. The deacons at the present time are: Lewis Daggett, Artemus W. Comstock and Henry Roads.

On the 7th day of May, 1824, the ecclesiastical society in connection with the church was formally organized by the adoption of a constitution. Josiah Owen was the first chairman of the society meeting, and the following were elected the first trustees: Eliakim Hammond, Wiley Bancroft, Joash Taylor, Luther Crocker, Thomas Chamberlain and John Miles, jr. Thomas Webber was the first clerk, and William Scott the first treasurer.

Previous to 1836 the church had no house of worship. Meetings were held in the school-houses or in private houses, according to convenience, and during the ministry of Rev. Hiram Halsey, previous to the erection of their church edifice, by the generosity of William Scott, they occupied the hall of his hotel at Cambria Center for all church meetings. At length, however, they erected a house of worship, and dedicated it on March 1st, 1836. This they occupied till October, 1877. At that time the society, at a special meeting appointed for the purpose, resolved to remodel and modernize the meeting-house. The work was carried on and completed during the following winter, and on April 2d, 1878, the new church was dedicated with appropriate services; Rev. Myron Adams, of Rochester, preaching the sermon, and Rev. I. R. Bradnack, a former pastor, offering the dedicatory prayer.

The entire cost of remodelling the house was $4,400. The building was raised so as to allow of a good basement for various church purposes; the galleries in the main audience room removed and a vestibule built in front, so that the present audience room has a seating capacity of 350. The finish and furnishings are such as to do credit to the church and society.

PEKIN AND SOUTHWESTERN CAMBRIA.

The southwest part of the town was next in order of settlement. In 1809 John Carney purchased of the Holland Company five hundred acres in a body. It embraced all of the site of Pekin on the east side of the dividing line between Lewiston and Cambria.

Jairus Rose was the next settler, locating in 1811. His first purchase of the Holland Company was six hundred acres, at $4.50 per acre, to which he soon added at $5 per acre enough to make two thousand acres, which would now include the extreme southwest corner of Cambria and southeast corner of Lewiston, being lots 17, 25, 26, 32 and others. Canandaigua was the former residence of Mr. Rose. Soon after making his first purchase, in May of the same year, the difficult task of planting his family upon it was undertaken. An ox cart and a one-horse wagon completed the transportation outfit. The journey of the pioneer, with his young family and three hired men, took over one week to perform. They came by the way of Rochester, on the ridge to Dickersonville, where the family stopped with a man by the name of Harris, while Rose and his men advanced and put up a log house in three days. The way had to be cut from Dickersonville up the mountains, to the small open spot in the woods that indicated the beginning. The fields, in a state of nature, were stocked with forty head of cattle, that had before them a hard winter, with the prospect of having to live on twigs of birch and soft maple. There was considerable valuable pine timber on the purchase, that was relied upon for several years for building purposes. In 1813 Mr. Rose sowed two acres with apple seeds, thus starting the first nursery in the county. When fit for selling they were sold for twelve cents each, and taken in all directions to start the first orchards in the county.

In the Indian foray upon the Niagara border in 1813 Mr. Rose was made a prisoner; his horse was taken from him and he was stripped of his clothing, except shirt, pantaloons and boots. While his captors were taken off his overcoat, he succeeded, unobserved, in changing his pocket book, containing $400, from the side pocket to his bosom, whence it luckily passed into his boots, which proved to be a safe deposit. Two Indians, one on each side, locked arms with the captive, forcing a slow run the entire five miles to Lewiston, and often accelerating his speed by raps over the head with the handle of a tomahawk and the ramrods of their guns. The party crossed into Canada, where a British government agent by the name of Nellis tried to buy Rose. Three times the bargain was completed and a hundred dollars paid, and as often the Indians failed to give up the prisoner, clamoring for the death of the "Yankee," whom Nellis was concealing in a garret, denying his whereabouts. Finally, extorting another hundred, the Indians went off and got drunk. They then returned and threatened the life of Nellis if the prisoner was not surrendered to them. He was not, however, and after six weeks' confinement, receiving his food during the time through a scuttle, Rose was sent in care of a private escort of soldiers ot Buffalo, from where he joined his family in Canandaigua, to which place they had escaped. Peaceable possession of his land was again had after the close of the war, where he remained, clearing, improving and disposing of smaller farm lots, until his death, January 31st, 1828, aged 59; his wife, Zedpha, died April 3d, 1859, aged 88. They had a family of seven children, of whom George P. Rose, aged 70, occupies one hundred acres of his father's original purchase, where he has lived since three years of age. As commandant of the 163d regiment during the patriot war, he was called out for twenty days at different places on the frontier.

Myron Orton was born September 20th, 1784. He was married to Mary Hoyt, of St. Albans, Vt., in 1811, and moved into St. Lawrence county, N.Y., where he practiced medicine till the troubles on the frontier consequent upon the war of 1812 caused a pretty general flight of the inhabitants, when he went to Middlebury, Genesee county, N.Y., from which place he moved in March, 1815, to Cambria, Niagara county, where he spent the remainder of his life. During part of the time he was engaged in the practice of his profession, being one of the founders of the Niagara County Medical Society. His later years were devoted to agricultural pursuits. In common with the mass of early inhabitants they had little means, except strong hands and tireless perseverance, and were subject to the struggles, vicissitudes and hardships incident to pioneer life. They brought up a large family to habits of industry. Dr. Orton died June 20th, 1873, aged 89; his wife, Mary, died February 25th, 1867. Three years after he settled, his father and mother performed the journey from Vermont in a lumber wagon to visit him; arriving at Scott's, within two and a half miles, they dared not risk the rest of the journey, as the roads were so bad, and staid there for the night.

William Crosier was a leading citizen for over sixty years. He was a pioneer school teacher in the town of Cambria, the district of his labor for several years spreading over a large portion of the town. He located in 1821 on a farm one and a half miles east of Pekin village. He was the father of W. H. Crosier.

In 1822 a post-office was established, by the title of Mountain Ridge; John Jones was postmaster. In 1831, it was changed to Pekin, when the prospects of a village were flattering, and hopes of future prosperity attracted business enterprise. The earlier days were the most encouraging. Divided by the town line between Cambria and Lewiston, business operations commenced on both sides. Jones opened a store on the Lewiston side. In 1832 the growth of the place was more active. John Cronkite erected a large hotel; a smaller one was soon after erected by Benjamin Thrasher. Cronkite was also largely engaged in the mercantile business, and had an extensive ashery. James McBain kept a dry goods and grocery store. Josephus Taylor started a store on the Lewiston side. Calvin Hotchkiss in 1832 supplied a store in the building put up by him, now the tavern stand of George Beber. On the Lewiston side, a grocery, hardware store and tin shop are combined with the post-office, kept by E. H. Cox. On the Cambria side there are two general stores and three blacksmith shops. Another well-remembered business man of Pekin was the late Peter F. Loucks, who came to the town between 1830 and 1840 and bought a farm, which he sold after a time and removed to Pekin, where he embarked in trade. He continued there twenty-five or thirty years, and finally disposed of his property and went to the city of New York. He died in Jersey City, February 9th, 1877. His son Addison D. Loucks, of the firm of Tompkins & Loucks, lumber dealers in the village of La Salle, is one of the most enterprising of the younger business men of the county.

The first burying ground, located on the east side of the street in the village, was appropriated by Samuel Carney, and ultimately deeded by William Carney, John Jones and William Earl, trustees of Elam Carney, to the town of Cambria about 1830. As near as can be ascertained, the ground was first occupied in 1817. Henry Dill was the first person interred.

The land upon which the cemetery of the Mount View Rural Association is located, 6 1/10 acres, was originally owned by Amos H. Pyle. The organization took place April 20th, 1864, under the general statute. Pyle conveyed to the trustees, John Robinson, Lee R. Sanborn, Abraham Le Van, Amos H. Pyle, Thomas Root and Sumner Burns. Funds for fencing and repairs are created by the sale of lots, and have been sufficient to keep the grounds in the present creditable condition. An appropriate white marble monument has been conspicuously erected to commemorate the valor of soldiers from the neighborhood in the late rebellion. Of the Soldiers' Monument Association Abraham Le Van was president; A. H. Pyle vice-president; Samuel Schmeck treasurer, Thomas Root secretary; William O. Rogers and Pennel Schmeck trustees.

Elias Rose built a grist-mill, one and a half miles east of Pekin, which was depended upon by a large extent of country.

Major John Beach built a saw-mill on Cayuga creek, one mile from the head, the first that was built in that locality. Cayuga creek heads in a marsh one mile from the south line of the town, and two miles from the west.

Thomas Comstock located on the Pekin road, one mile west of the railroad junction, in 1822, purchasing one hundred acres of the Holland Company. He moved from Susquehanna with an ox team. His son Artemus W. Comstock owns the original homestead.

The Comstock cheese factory was established on the farm as a private enterprise, in 1848. It has been and continues popular for the best quality of cheese manufactured, meeting a ready sale.

CHURCHES ON THE RIDGE.

There are four churches located upon the ridge. The Methodist was the first built now existing. Near the middle a handsomely constructed cobble-stone edifice stands upon a gravel bank elevation, that could not be more suitably provided. It was built in 1845. The land was donated by Reuben Wilson. The present membership is 43; the church is in an advancing condition. H. L. Newton is the present pastor.

Near the west end of the ridge the churches form a cluster. The First Universalist Society of the Town of Cambria was organized in 1867, consisting of 34 members; at the present time it has 50. The first trustees were T. S. Elton, N. B. Peterson, George W. Bolt, Darius Ferris, Samuel Saddeso and John M. Easman. The first pastor was Charles H. Dutton; he is now dead. The present trustees are T. S. Elton, Christian Sanger, N. B. Peterson, Samuel Adams, Herrick Halsey and R. L. Lamb. Benjamin Brunning is the officiating clergyman. The church lot was a donation by H. C. Denison, and a brick church was erected in 1868, costing $6,000.

In close proximity, on the north side of the street, stands a neatly arranged, unpretending Catholic church, of wood. Opposite, in like style, is a German Lutheran church. Both accommodate wide-spread congregations.

The cemetery of the North Ridge Burying Ground Association is located on the same elevated ground, in the rear of the Universalist church. The entire ground, of six acres, has a crowning surface of regular grade, so that but small expense is required for suitable improvement of individual lots, which in many instances is creditably done, by the erection of substantial monuments. The first grant, of two acres, was by a deed of gift from Harry C. Denison and wife, in trust to Moses Barstow, Thomas Barnes, Isaac Van Dozen, John G. Webster and Josiah Pratt. The control is by a board of nine trustees. February 10th, 1877, D. A. Jeffrey, Thomas Barnes, Darius Ferris, Cyrus Beach, F. J. Webster, John R. Peterson, T. S. Elton, S. L. Town, and Samuel Allen became trustees; John R. Peterson, president; Cyrus

Beach, vice-president; Thomas Barnes, treasurer; T. S. Elton, secretary; and S. J. Rogers, sexton. The first burial was that of Mrs. Timothy Tuttle.

EARLY SCHOOLS AND SCHOOL-HOUSES.

The first school established, other than the Indian mission, which provided for the white children as well as for the Indians until other schools were started, was kept in a log house in what is now district No. 1. It was one of the buildings that had been temporarily used for an arsenal, in the war of 1812, on the ridge, west of Howell's creek; a Mrs. Neal was the teacher. The first framed school-house was built opposite. District No. 2 was the next formed, midway between Warren's and Molyneux's Corners, a log school-house was buil in 1815; the school was kept by a Scotchman, named Watson. At Molyneux's Corners the first school-house was built in 1819, in district No. 2; it was soon after burnt. A disagreement caused the district to be abandoned, the district at Warren's Corners was set off as No. 2, and the former No. 2 was made No 10.

Mr. George P. Rose states that the first school-house in Pekin was built on the brow of the hill, at the northeast corner of the mountain road and the one leading to the ridge. It was a log structure fifteen feet by twelve; here he attended school, two miles and a half from his home. A Mr. Hill and Miranda Finch were the first teachers. This was long before there was any other school. Meetings were held in the same house. The first minister remembered was the Rev. Mr. Briggs.

SINGULAR DEPOSITS.

Mr. Nathaniel Cook states that a man chopping for him, on the south side of the North Ride, found in the body of a white oak, eighteen inches in diameter, a common sized vest button, embedded in the solid timber, four inches from the surface; there was no other mark but a dead spot where it lay. Examined by a silversmith in Lockport, it was pronounced a fair quality of gold. It was only battered on one side.

In a locality of two or three acres, on the north side of the South Ridge, on the farm of Cyrus Beach, while he was clearing, in a majority of the trees, mostly in the center, musket balls were found in the solid wood four inches from the outside, in large number, and also in plowing the ground. A musket barrel was plowed up, containing a charge of powder.

On the north side, near the west termination of the North Ridge, there was during early settlement a limestone quarry, available to quite an extent for the building of fire-places and other uses. It was a deposit in regular layers, that were taken out in blocks of required sizes, and the only one that existed between the mountain ridge and the lake. The stone have long since been entirely exhausted.

BRIEF BIOGRAPHICAL SKETCHES.

Athur A. Ashford was born April 24th, 1852, at Drummondsville, Canada, and married April 24th, 1873, to Anna B. Robinson, of Lockport, N.Y. Mr. Ashford is proprietor of Molyneux's Hotel, in the town of Cambria.

David W. Bagley, farmer and merchant, was born in Lewiston, N. Y., August 14th, 1835, and has lived in Cambria for the past twenty years.

Cyrus Beach, the youngest son of Jesse Beach, who is referred to in other parts of this work, was born at Dickersonville, May 7th, 1808. When but two years old he was brought by his parents to the place where he has since lived, and which is the only abiding place he has ever known. As early as 1824, when he was only 16 years old, he began the life of a farmer, which business he has followed successfully ever since, having connected with it in latter years the fruit-growing interest. In 1844 he erected a saw-mill in Cambria, on his farm, which burned in 1876, it having been in operation most of the time during its existence. Too busy to engage in politics, Mr. Beach has repeatedly refused proffered offices of trust and emolument, preferring rather the life of a farmer. His farm consists of two hundred and fifty acres.

D. L. Beach was born in Cambria July 14th, 1812. In 1849 he was married to Miss Lucinda Hutchins, who was born in Canada August 16th, 1822. He now resides at the old Beach homestead.

Lewis Bevier was born at Fayette, Seneca county, N. Y., August 5th, 1825, and came to the town of Cambria in April, 1831. He was married to Miss Angeline Wright, a native of Lewiston, in 1853. His business is fruit-growing.

Tyler F. Blackstone was born April 12th, 1836, at Morristown, N. Y., and came to Cambria and settled at Warren's Corners in 1872. Mr. Blackstone is a well-known farmer.

Henry Bristol, father of D. W. Bristol, a native of Columbia county, N. Y., came to the town of Cambria in June, 1853. D. W. Bristol was born June 19th, 1821, at Gainesville, Wyoming county, N. Y., and was married in 1851, to Lydia Ann Weaver, a native of the town of Cambria. He is a farmer; post-office, Lockport.

Nathaniel Brockway, a native of Rensselaer county, N. Y., came to the town of Cambria in 1833. His son, D. S. Brockway, was born in Rensselaer county in 1820. He was married to Miss Eliza Slocum in 1866.

One of Cambria's prosperous farmers is David S. Brockway, born in 1821, at Schodack, Rensselaer county, N. Y., whence he removed to this town in 1833. Post-office, Cambria.

Lewis Burtch was born in Newfane, N. Y., October 13th, 1816, and came to the town of Cambria, where he has since resided, in 1851. He was married January 26th, 1842, to Louisa Curtis, of Newfane. He is a farmer. Post-office, North Ridge.

Ransom Campbell was born May 5th, 1833, in the town of Cambria, Niagara county, where he resides at the present time, engaged in farming. Post-office address, Hickory Corners.

Nathaniel Cook was born January 25th, 1792, at Scovell's Hill, Schoharie county, N. Y., and came to Cambria in 1819, from Manlius, Onondaga county, N. Y. He is a

FARM RESIDENCE & PORTRAITS OF CYRUS BEACH, WIFE & SON, CAMBRIA.TOWN, NIAGARA CO., N.Y.

farmer. Post-office, North Ridge, Niagara county, N. Y.

Anson Eastman was born in Wyoming county, N. Y., September 11th, 1823, and came to Cambria, Niagara county, at the age of four. He is a farmer. Post-office, Warren's Corners.

Joseph Eighme, deceased, a native of Dutchess county, N. Y., located in Erie county in 1817. He was in the war of 1812. George W. Eighme, a native of Monroe county, married Miss Catharine Halifax in 1846, and came to Cambria in 1853.

Benjamin Farnsworth, father of Hunt Farnsworth, and a native of Connecticut, came to Genesee county in 1810. He died in 1822. Hunt Farnsworth was born in Vermont in 1806, and came to Cambria in 1846. He was married in 1832 to Amanda Pierce.

Hiram Flanders was born in Cambria, N. Y., September 24th, 1833. He was married to Miss Maria Elton, of Cambria, April 25th, 1860. Mr. Flanders is a well-known and enterprising farmer. His post-office address is Pekin, N. Y.

John B. Gould was born in Cambria in 1839. He was married to Miss Frances L. Hall, a native of Massachusetts. He is a farmer and fruit-grower; post-office address, Cambria Center.

Rev. James A. Grush is pastor of the Congregational church, Cambria.

Richard Hall was born in Liverford, Oxfordshire, England, August 28th, 1824, and came to the town of Cambria in 1845. Mr. Hall is a well known farmer.

Henry Hoag was born February 13th, 1812, at Palmyra, N. Y.; he came to the county and located at Lockport in 1822, and remained there until April 1st, 1878, when he removed to Cambria. Mr. Hoag was foreman in Carpenter's stone quarry for thirty-three years, and served as alderman of the city.

Philip Houstatter, father of A. H. Houstatter, and a native of Pennsylvania, came to the town of Cambria when he was but sixteen years of age. A. H. Houstatter was born in Cambria in 1827. He resides on the old homestead.

William S. Howe, farmer, post-office address, Sanborn, N. Y., was born in Ridgefield, Connecticut, September 17th, 1815, and came from there to Cambria in 1824.

Nelson T. Mighells, the only surviving son of Thomas Mighells who settled at Warren's Corners in 1810, was born there in 1818. In 1849 he married Miss Harriet P. Forsyth. Mr. Mighells owns and works the place settled by his father.

Myron Orton was born in Cambria, August 14th, 1831. Mr. Orton is an enterprising farmer. He has held the position of postmaster. Post-office, Pekin.

Josias T. Peterson was born May 19th, 1824, in Ridgeway, Orleans county. He came to Niagara county in 1831. He was married to Miss C. R. Andrews, a native of Niagara county. He is engaged in farming and fruit-growing, and his post-office is North Ridge.

A. L. Peterson, son of N. B. Peterson, senior, was born in the town of Cambria January 29th, 1850, and now resides on the old homestead. N. G. Peterson, his brother, was killed at the battle of Cold Harbor. He was a member of the 129th regiment N. Y. S. Vol. infantry, but was transferred to the 8th heavy artillery in December, 1862.

N. B. Peterson was born in Canada, June 30th, 1826. He was married to Miss Sarah E. Andrews in 1849. Miss Andrews was born in Cambria in 1829.

James A. Pool was born in Lewiston, May 5th, 1836. April 2d, 1862, he was married to Permelia Woolson, of that town. In 1862 he became a resident of the town of Cambria. Mr. Pool, who is one of the most enterprising farmers in the town, has often been chosen to official positions of trust and responsibility; in 1872 and 1873 he was supervisor of Cambria, town clerk in 1874 and 1875, and in those years and 1876 and 1877 he was justice of the peace.

George W. Rose was born May 1st, 1808, at Canandaigua, Ontario county, N. Y., and came to Cambria and settled on the farm where he has since lived in 1811. He was colonel of the 163rd regiment during the patriot war, taking an active part in the occurrences of that time.

J. K. Sabin was born in Cambria January 24th, 1824. He was married to Miss Mary A. Porter in 1855. Miss Porter was born in Cambria in 1825.

Christopher Saddleson, father of Ransom Saddleson, and a native of Pennsylvania, came to Cambria in 1812. He was married to Cynthia Holmes in 1833. Ransom Saddleson was born in Cambria. He was married to Miss Laura Pardee, of Erie county, in 1859.

C. See was born May 1st, 1815, in the town of Greenwood, Crawford county, Pa., and came to Cambria in March, 1853. He is a farmer. Post-office, Warren's Corners.

A. E. Vandusen is a farmer, residing in the eastern part of the town, and having his post-office at Hickory Corners. He was born July 19th, 1848, in the town of Wilson.

Joshua Worrill was born in Bennington connty, Vt, in 1809, and came to Niagara county in 1831. He was married to Miss Margaret Butts in 1837.

We might also name the following persons (whose post-offices are also given) as among the more prominent and enterprising citizens of the town:

William H. Skinner, Cambria; David Scott, Lockport; E. B. Swift, Cambria; Samuel Treichler, Sanborn; W. H. Crosier, Pekin; William Martin, jr.; J. Bingham, North Ridge; Rev. H.L. Newton, Methodist pastor, North Ridge; Homer Scott, Lockport; Itha J. West, Hickory Corners; George Rikert, Pekin; Homer Manning, Lockport; Edwin Harmony, Lockport; A. W. Comstock, Lockport; George S. Freer, Warren's Corners; Joshua G. Rockwood, Cambria; Henry L. Taylor, Warren's Corners; Andrew Budd, Warren's Corners; Charles M. Crocker, farmer, Lockport; Hiram Richardson, Lockport; Marshall Martin, hotel keeper, Cambria; Julia Pomroy, Lockport; and Hunt Farnsworth, Hickory Corners.

THE TOWN OF HARTLAND.

THIS town derives its name from one of the same name in Vermont, from which many of the early settlers migrated. It is one of the three towns on the eastern border of the county, and was formed from Cambria in 1812. It originally embraced the towns of Royalton and Somerset, and a part of Newfane, covering an area of 143,855 acres of land, according to the assessment roll of 1813.

At that time there were no printed blanks, but the books were of the same shape and ruled about as at present. The number of taxable inhabitants in Hartland in 1813 was one hundred and twenty-six, and the number of acres assessed to them at that time was 19,487, the assessed valuation of which was $19,487, and the rate of tax was one per cent.

The lands of non-resident proprietors were assessed as follows: Holland Land Company, 107,851 acres; Joseph Ellicott, 6,201 acres; Benjamin Ellicott, 5,791 acres; David E. Evans, 2,395 acres; James W. Stevens, 1,077 acres; William Peacock, 339 acres; David Goodwin, 714 acres; making 124,368 acres owned by non-residents, having an assessed valuation of $110,620.50. The total valuation of the real estate in the town was $130,107.50. The personal property was assessed at $902.50. Total valuation for 1813, $131,010.

The certificate attached to the assessment roll of 1813 is as follows:

"Completed according to the most equal and exact way we could find, and go agreeable to the new act. Done this 10th day of July, 1813. Signed,

"JAMES WELCH,
JOHN C. DVE, } Assessors."
DANIEL CORNELL,

In 1817 Royalton was taken off from Hartland, Somerset in 1823, and a part of Newfane in 1824, leaving, according to the assessment roll of 1877, 31,145 acres of land, valued at $1,647,194, and equalized by the board of supervisors at $1,679,066. The personal property was assessed in 1877 at $76,400. Total valuation $1,755,466, against a total of $130,010 in 1813, with only 31,145 acres in 1877, against 143,855 acres in 1813.

The following paragraphs are copied from a volume in the town clerk's office, entitled:

"Book of records containing an accurate enrollment of the legal, business and prudential affairs appertaining to the town of Hartland, in the county of Niagara, and State of New York, April 7th 1812."

"An extract from the act of the Legislature of the State of New York, entitled an act to divide the town of Cambria, in Niagara county, into several towns:

"And be it further enacted that all that part of the town of Cambria bounded east by the meridian line dividing the said town of Cambria from the county of Genesee, betweeen the fourth and fifth ranges of townships, and south by the main stream of the Tonawanta creek, be erected into a separate town by the name of Hartland, and that the first town meeting in said town of Hartland shall be held at the house of Gad Warner, in said town."

FIRST TOWN MEETING.

"Tuesday, April 7th, 1812, the freeholders and inhabitants of said town of Hartland, by the authority aforementioned, met in town meeting at the house of Gad Warner, and John Dunn, Esq., justice of the peace in and for the county of Niagara, presided at said town meeting and superintended the same.

"The said town meeting being thus organized, proceeded, and adjourned the same to the barn of Enoch Hitchcock, forthwith, where they resumed the business of the day.

"Met according to adjournment and proceeded to the election of town clerk. On counting the votes it appeared that William Smith was duly and legally elected to said office and qualified.

"The town meeting then proceeded to the election of supervisor. On counting the votes it appeared that Ephraim Waldo was duly and legally elected to said office.

"The town meeting then proceeded to the election of assessors, whereupon, on counting the votes, it appeared that Samuel Jenks, Harry Ellsworth, and David Weasner were duly and legally elected to said office.

"The town meeting then proceeded to the election of commissioners of highways. On counting the votes, it appeared that John Dunn 2d, John Bates and Benjamin Wakeman were duly and legally elected to said office.

"The town meeting then proceeded to the election of a collector. On counting the votes it appeared that Amos Brownson was duly and legally elected to said office.

"The town meeting then proceeded to the election of overseers of the poor. On counting the votes it appeared

FARM RESIDENCE OF O. B. HAYS, ESQ., HARTLAND TOWN, NIAGARA CO., N.Y.

RESIDENCE OF O. L. WILCOX, ESQ., GASPORT, TOWN OF ROYALTON, NIAGARA CO., N.Y.

FARM RESIDENCE OF W. VANHORN ESQ., HARTLAND TOWN, NIAGARA CO., N.Y.

that James Lyman and Stephen Wakeman were duly and legally elected to said office.

"*Ordered*, that the town meeting elect one constable. Proceeded to the election thereof, and on counting the votes, it appeared that Amos Brownson was duly and legally elected to said office.

"*Ordered*, by said town meeting, that Enoch Hitchcock officiate as pound-keeper.

"*Ordered*, by said town meeting, that the persons a catalogue of whose names is immediately subjoined officiate as path-masters in their several respective districts in said town of Hartland, viz: James Weasner for district No. 1; Lyman Godard for district No. 2; Jeptha Dunn for district No. 3; William Taylor for district No. 4; Joshua Slayton for district No. 5; Stephen Wakeman for district No. 6.

"*Ordered*, by said town meeting, that swine run at large.

"*Ordered*, by said town meeting, that no money be raised for support of the poor.

"*Ordered*, by said town meeting, that one hundred and fifty dollars be raised to be appropriated to the use of the highways in said town.

"*Ordered*, by said town meeting, that one hundred dollars be raised for the purpose of destroying obnoxious animals and birds.

"*Ordered*, by said town meeting, that three cents per head be paid for blackbirds, and a certificate from any justice of the peace then residing in said town, testifying that such person or persons appeared before him with a certain number of blackbirds' scalps, and made satisfactory proof that they were killed within the said town of Hartland, such certificate shall be good against the treasury of said town.

"*Ordered*, by said town meeting, that the next annual town meeting be holden at the present dwelling house of Enoch Hitchcock. Signed,

"WILLIAM SMITH, *Town Clerk*."

FURTHER MATTERS OF EARLY RECORD.

"This is to certify that at an annual election holden in and for the town of Hartland, in the county of Niagara, and State of New York, on Tuesday, Wednesday and Thursday, being the 28th, 29th and 30th instants, Francis G. Bloodgood, Russell Atwater and Henry Hager had nine votes each for senator. Peter B. Porter had sixty-five votes for member of Congress, and Jonas Williams had three votes for member of Congress; and that Jonas Williams had 51 votes for member of Assembly, and Peter B. Porter had three votes for member of Assembly. Given under our hands at Hartland, this 30th day of April, 1812. Signed,

"EPHRAIM WALDO,
WILLIAM SMITH,
HENRY ELLSWORTH,
SAMUEL JENKS,
} Inspectors of Election."

"At a special town meeting on the 7th of November, 1812, for the purpose of electing a supervisor instead of E. Waldo, deceased, * * * James Lyman was duly and legally elected to said office."

In 1813 it was ordered by a town meeting that the lawful fence be four and a half feet high; and that five dollars be paid out of the treasury for each wolf caught in the town.

January 20th, 1818, a special town meeting was held, and resolutions were unanimously adopted that a petition be immediately forwarded to the Legislature, "for a new county to be erected, embracing the towns of Niagara, Cambria, Hartland and Porter, in Niagara county, and Ridgeway and Gaines in Genesee county; and firmly to remonstrate against any division of said county of Niagara, unless such new county shall contain as great extent of territory as above described." Robert Edmunds, Samuel B. Morehouse, Hiram Allen, Titus Fenn, Almon H. Millard, and William Smith were appointed "a committee to form said petition and carry the aforesaid resolution into execution."

The first election of justice of the peace by the people was in the spring of 1830, when Christopher L. Taylor was elected.

PRINCIPAL TOWN OFFICERS.

SUPERVISORS.

The following is as complete a list of the supervisors and clerks of Hartland from 1812 to 1878, inclusive, as can be obtained:

1812, Ephraim Waldo and James Lyman; 1813–16, James Lyman; 1817, 1818, Dexter P. Sprague; 1820, 1821, Asahel Johnson; 1822, James Wisner; 1823, Smith Darling; 1824–27, Daniel Van Horn; 1828, 1829, Dexter P. Sprague; 1830–33, Franklin Butterfield; 1834, Christopher H. Skeels; 1835, Daniel Chaplin; 1836, 1837, James C. Lewis; 1838–45, Christopher H. Skeels; 1846, Daniel Seaman; 1847, John Dunigan; 1848, A. H. Jameison; 1849, 1850, Christopher H. Skeels; 1851, G. L. Angevine; 1852, William Wheeler; 1853, F. A. Wright; 1854, G. Angevine; 1855, 1856, Linus Spalding; 1857, Curtis Root; 1858, William Morgan; 1859, Thomas Brown; 1860–63, William Morgan; 1864, 1865, Linus Spalding; 1866–68, William Morgan; 1869, 1870, Linus Spalding; 1871, William Morgan; 1872, Edward O. Seaman; 1873, John L. Beardsley; 1874, Edward O. Seaman; 1875, George B. Taylor; 1876–78, John L. Chase.

TOWN CLERKS.

1812–15, William Smith; 1816, Dexter P. Sprague; 1817, William Smith; 1818, Hiram Allen; 1820, 1821, Dexter P. Sprague; 1822, 1823, Daniel Van Horn; 1824–27, Daniel Seaman; 1828, Thomas Bills; 1829, 1830, Daniel Seaman; 1831, Thomas Bills; 1832, 1833, Daniel Seaman; 1834, Truman E. Pomeroy; 1862–64, Hiram G. Dean; 1865, Cyrus A. Lewis; 1866, Hiram G. Dean; 1867–76, Eber Kendall; 1877, 1878, Charles A. Kendall.

JUSTICES.

In 1831 Christopher H. Skeels was elected justice of the peace, and in 1832 Daniel Seaman and Reuben Seymour were elected justices, making the four in the town which the law required.

Dexter P. Sprague was appointed justice of the peace by the State council of appointment from 1809 to 1830, after which he was elected by the people for several terms.

PHYSICAL FEATURES OF THE TOWN.

The surface of this town is gently undulating, the greatest inequality being along the Ridge road, which crosses from east to west, nearly through the middle of the south half of the town. The ridge ranges from fifteen to thirty feet above the surface of the country on either side of it, and the only stream that breaks through it is Johnson's creek, at the village of that name.

The farms south of the Ridge road are mostly of a stiff clayey soil. There are a very few exceptions, where portions of some farms are mixed with a sandy loam. North of the ridge the farms are mostly of a sandy loam, in some cases mixed with clay.

Johnson's is the principal creek, so called from a family of that name living upon its banks in the early days of the town. It enters the town from Royalton, in school district No. 3, running in a northerly direction to the middle of district No. 15, where it turns and crosses districts 10 and 9, in a northeasterly direction, and flows into Orleans county. It has five branches flowing into it, three from the west and northwest and two from the east and south, the largest of which is Mud creek, rising in the southeast corner of district No. 18.

Eighteen-mile creek enters the town in school district No. 10, from Royalton, flowing northerly for a short distance, thence westerly and southwesterly, and leaving the town in the southwest corner, flowing into Newfane.

Oak Orchard creek comes in through the village of Middleport, and flows into Ridgeway, Orleans county, about half a mile south of the Ridge road.

EARLY SETTLERS.

The first settlement was made in this town in 1803, by John Morrison, David Morrison, Zebulon Barnum, Jedediah Riggs, Isaac Southwell, and Daniel Brown. In 1805 Abel Barnum and Oliver Castle located in this town. Castle settled nearly two miles southwest of what is now known as Johnson's Creek village, and was the first preacher on the Holland Purchase, uniting with the Christian church at Slaton settlement, now Orangeport. John Morrison located on the farm now owned and occupied by Colonel Weaver and his son R. B. Weaver, the colonel purchasing the farm of Morrison, on the Ridge road, one mile east of Hartland Corners. Others soon came in and settled, and among them was Jephtha Dunn, in 1807, locating on the Ridge road, two miles east of Johnson's creek, where H. N. Hand now lives. Benjamin Cornell arrived in 1809, locating just west of Johnson's creek. Mr. Crane located on the Ridge road in 1810. Daniel Van Horn in 1811 settled at Johnson's creek. Benjamin H. Benson in 1811 located where he now resides, and James Shaw in 1812 on the Ridge road, two miles east of Johnson's creek. Dexter P. Sprague came in 1809, Colonel Richard Weaver in 1814, and J. W. Seaman in 1816.

Benjamin H. Benson located in 1811 near where he now resides, near the town line, south of Hartland Corners. Daniel Van Horn came to this town from New Jersey in 1811. George Garbutt, born April 5th, 1792, in England, came to Hartland in 1832, and lives at the village of Johnson's creek.

Colonel Richard Weaver, a native of Clarendon, Rutland county, Vt, was born April 19th, 1792. He came to Hartland in 1814, engaged with Mr. Edmunds in the pioneer agricultural pursuits of those times, and in due time became the owner of the farm occupied by the first settler, Isaac Southwell, where he has lived ever since. The old log-house stood a little east of his present dwelling. Colonel Weaver during his early and middle life was an ardent lover of fine stock, especially horses, and at times was engaged in raising and training horses for the old fashioned race course. He was also prominently identified with the early military operations of this section. In 1820 and 1821 he was commissioned by Governor Clinton as major, lieutenant-colonel, and finally colonel of the militia regiment in his district.

Mary, widow of Elisha Brownell, and daughter of Jesse and Phebe Birdsell, was born November 4th, 1815, in a log house that had neither doors nor windows, other than those made by hanging up blankets. There was no chimney, and the under floor was made of basswood logs, split and spotted down. The upper floor was of narrow poplar boards, drawn from Oak Orchard Creek, a distance of twelve miles, where was the nearest sawmill. The cradle in which she was rocked was a hollow log, adzed out, with ancient rockers attached. She is the oldest woman in the town who lives upon the farm on which she was born, which is on the Quaker road, three miles northwest from Johnson's Creek, and she was the first child born in that settlement. Her father, Jesse Birdsell, died in 1825. Her mother remained a widow until her death, aged 77.

Mrs. Baker, widow of the late Stephen Baker, was born June 4th, 1800. She resides with O. T. Bachelor in the southeast part of the town. Her mental and physical faculties are far above the average of her age and sex. She came to this town with her parents in 1809, and remembers distinctly many of the incidents of pioneer life.

Miss Maria Deuel is the oldest maiden lady in town. She was born in Stamford, Dutchess county, N. Y., January 12th, 1797. She located at Johnson's in 1817. She retains her mental faculties to a wonderful degree, and still does sewing for her younger neighbors, without the aid of glasses.

PIONEER LIFE IN HARTLAND.

With but slight exceptions, it was a territory presenting to the pioneer a rugged forest of heavy timber. Except by the resolute and determined, the task of securing a home was undertaken with a faltering step. To make even passable roads required a great amount of labor and

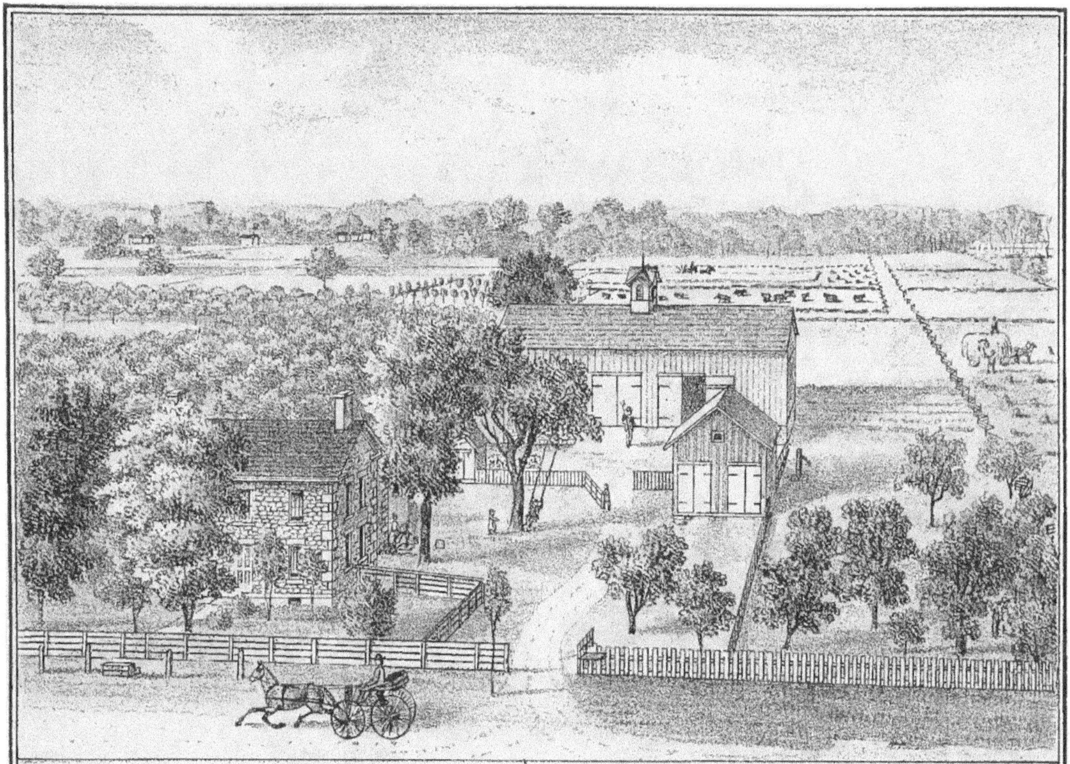

RES. OF WM BROWN ESQ, TOWN OF HARTLAND

RES. OF THOMAS BROWN ESQ., TOWN OF HARTLAND

time. The want of them was a serious drawback upon the efforts of the beginner, and a check upon rapid emigration. Before the determined and resolute adventurer the forest has melted away, and nearly the whole face of the country changed. Where the dense forest once stood there is now the waving field of ripening grain, and instead of the sturdy old oak, chestnut and beech, there is a forest of apple, peach and pear trees, remunerating the industrious husbandman, and gladdening his heart with their fruits.

Seventy-five years have passed since the first pioneer located in this town. Industry and indomitable enterprise have achieved their triumphs over sickness, privations and hardships. Comfortable homes have been reared where stood the rude accomodations incident to pioneer settlement. Luxury is found where stinted subsistence once prevailed. Church spires loom up, and school-houses are in abundance. An incident or two of pioneer life may be of interest, and also carry down to future generations the privations, dangers and great inconveniences under which the early settlers toiled and suffered.

Benjamin Cornell located near Johnson's creek in 1809. Pasturage being scarce near where he settled, he kept his span of horses at Oak Orchard Creek, that being the nearest pasture ground, a distance of ten miles. His milling, like his neighbors', had to be done at Rochester or Niagara. The first wheat he sowed he had to travel a distance of sixty miles to procure, and after stacking his first crop of wheat, his hired man, good clever soul, attempted to and did destroy a bumble-bees' nest near the stack, by fire, and in doing so burned the entire crop of the first wheat raised.

Some of the pioneers, like Edmunds, had the necessary means to pay for their land and support their families for a year, while Jephtha Dunn was at the other extreme, he having just two shillings with which to buy a home in the wilderness. With an honest, manly courage, equal to the emergency, he walked up to the land office and was "booked" for a tract of land in Hartland, the price of booking being just equal to the amount of his cash capital. With a determined will he went to work, and soon became not only "booked" and "articled," but possessed a deed for the land for which he had at first been "booked." This was a term used at the land office for those who only had money enough to have their names placed on file, as desiring land.

Jephtha Dunn, although starting with only two shillings, and experiencing all the hardships of pioneer life, was honored by his townsmen, and his name will go down to posterity as one of the bright pioneer stars of western New York.

Polly, wife of Isaac Southwell, who came here in 1803 with her husband, was the heroine of at least one "bear story." Hearing their old hog, their only one, squealing in the pen, she knew only too well the cause, and arming herself with a piece of an old chair as a club, she soon declared war on a bear she found in the pen, who defended himself nobly for a while, but was forced to retreat, leaving Mrs. Southwell mistress of the situation. The hog was so injured by the bear that it died, and the next day an old-fashioned figure-4 trap was set and baited with a piece of the dead porker, and the bear captured.

"Mrs. Morrison, wife of John Morrison, who settled in this town in 1803, gives a relation of the events of a night, which no doubt will interest the reader. In the summer of 1804 Mr. M. had gone to Batavia to get some provisions, leaving her alone with her children over night. A pack of wolves came near the cabin and set up a terrible howl—such as is usual with them when scenting prey. Mrs. M. got up from her bed, and heard them for a long time, apprehending no danger until she found they had approached within a few feet of the door place. There was no door—a blanket supplied the place of one; this, as she was aware, afforded but a poor protection. Careful not to wake up her sleeping children, lest the sound of their voices might excite the wolves to a bolder seige, she took her husband's axe, and stood sentry for hours and hours until, daylight approaching, the wolves retired into the depths of the forest."

Those who settled in the town in 1803 are supposed to have built log houses, but where most of them stood neither history nor tradition gives any statement that could be relied upon. A few of them, however, can be definitely located. Major John Morrison established himself in the south part of the town, near Eighteen-mile creek, chopped five acres, and in the spring brought his family from Niagara, U. C.

Isaac Southwell, located in 1803 near the Ridge road, on the farm now owned and occupied by R. B. Weaver, one mile east of Hartland Corners. Here he built a log house, in the lot where Mr. Weaver's peach orchard is now growing, which was the first land cleared in the town. In 1805–6 Mr. Southwell cut oak timber, split it into rails and built the first rail fence in this town. In 1878 Mr. Weaver took up the old fence, and some of the rails were still in good condition; they are serving the third generation, and seem to be good for the fourth.

Daniel Brown located in 1803 about eighty rods west of Johnson's creek, on the Ridge road. Here he built the usual style of log house, without chimney, floor or windows, and some sort of a blanket was hung in place of a door.

In 1805 Oliver Castle located on what is still known as the "Castle farm," two miles southwest from Johnson's Creek. Mr. Castle, with the assistance of his wife, cut trees and put up a small log house, which they occupied for a number of years. The farm remained the property the Castle family until the spring of 1878, when it was sold to a Mr. Robinson.

Christopher H. Skeels purchased, in or about the year 1817, the first wooden clock sold in this town, and for many years this was the neighborhood time-keeper.

Jephtha Dunn built a frame house on the Ridge road in the east part of the town in 1811. Thomas R. Stewart was the owner of the first frame house at Hartland Corners, built in 1814. Samuel B. Morehouse built the present hotel building at Hartland Corners, in 1815.

Mr. Elijah Austin tells how, in 1835 or 1836, while living in the neighborhood of Slaton's Settlement, George Angevine, returning from an evening visit about 11 o'clock, when near Maybee's mill, heard the howling of wolves. He and Mr. Austin raised all the force they could, joined by others at Hartland Corners, numbering at least one hundred and fifty, armed with guns, and such as had none with clubs. Thus organized they surrounded the woods that lay south of the ridge in the direction of Gasport. Rationed by scouts, they lay and stood sentry until day-light, when the wolves began to run and make the most daring and desperate attempts to break through the hunters' line, sometimes coming as near as three and four rods, when the men would drive them back, firing the few guns in their possession, while others attacked with pieces of rails or anything they could get hold of, at the same time making all the noise they could to frighten the beasts. A thousand shots or more were fired, but no wolves were killed until 3 o'clock in the afternoon, when four of them fell; two others were known to escape and cross the ridge to the north. There had been for a long time disturbance and slaughter among the sheep, in which vicious dogs united with the wolves.

In 1837 and 1838 two destructive wolves, a male and female, infested the more northern towns, proving to be prolific breeders; three distinct litters of whelps were killed by different individuals. Mr. Freeman N. Warren, of Lewiston, stated that about one year before the last old one was known to be killed, he found an old one with six young ones; the parent escaping, he dispatched four of the whelps, and George Warren and John Van Tassel the other two. Near the place four middling sized hogs were found, covered with leaves, and one partly devoured.

The veteran hunter John Peterson, who for a series of years and to advanced age, by the unerring aim of his rifle, spread dismay among the fiercest and most nimble of the forest, stated that he once found and killed six young wolves, and was one of the party engaged in the last onset upon the old ones.

VILLAGES IN HARTLAND.

HARTLAND CORNERS is located on the Ridge road, at the crossing of the Somerset and Gasport road, in the west part of the town, and ten miles east of Lockport. This place in the early history of the town was called "Morehouse's," from the fact that Samuel B. Morehouse built a very large and commodious hotel here, and was celebrated throughout the country as one of the sharpest, shrewdest and trickiest landlords extant. This and Johnson's Creek are the oldest settled places in the town. There are at the Corners one hotel, one church, two stores, a post-office, one blacksmith and machine shop, a shool-house, about twenty-five dwellings, and one hundred and fifty inhabitants. The first frame house at this place was the hotel. The building is still standing and occupied as a hotel. Buildings were put up on the other three corners at about the same time. The land on which the village is located was formerly owned by Samuel B. Morehouse, on the east side of the Gasport road; on the northwest corner by George Reynolds, and on the southwest corner by James C. Lewis. The "eleven-mile woods," noted in pioneer times, began at William Bradford's place, about a mile and a half west of Hartland Corners.

JOHNSON'S CREEK, a village of about four hundred inhabitants, located on the Ridge road, derives its name from the creek that passes through the ridge at this place. The land upon which the village stands was formerly owned, on the north side of the Ridge road, east of the creek road, by Henry Taylor for about eighty rods from the corner east, containing one hundred and twenty acres. Mr. Taylor located on this land June 16th, 1816. He built a log house on the east side of where the west store stands. He afterward built the house now standing on the east side of the hotel. Mr. Taylor was born in New Jersey in 1792, and died May 13th, 1870, at Johnson's Creek. The land that he owned is now all in village lots, and owned and occupied by different proprietors. The land on the south side of the road, east of the creek, was owned by Thomas F. Stewart, John Secor and others, and west of the creek by Stewart and others. The first frame house in the village was built by Thomas F. Stewart, just west of Johnson's creek, on the farm now owned by John L. Chase. The same building is now used by Mr. Chase as a horse barn and wagon house. John Secor had a small grocery store in this place as early as 1812. He also kept a tavern on a small scale for the accommodation of the weary traveler. Mr. Secor was also a surveyor, and a man of business generally. James and Daniel Van Horn opened a general grocery and dry goods store on the corner, in the east end of the village, in 1815. This firm was succeeded by George Reynolds in 1818. George C. Pease built the store in 1815. There are in this village at present two stores, a church, a grist-mill, a saw-mill, a carriage manufactory, a school-house, a tin shop, three blacksmith shops, a post-office, three physicians' offices, a cooperage and a hotel, with about eighty-five dwellings.

NORTH HARTLAND, located in the northwest corner of the town, is a small hamlet of about one hundred inhabitants. There are a church, post-office, store and blacksmith shop.

INDUSTRIAL BEGINNINGS.

George Robson and two other men opened blacksmith shops at Johnson's Creek in 1815. A Mr. Carrington had a blacksmith shop at Hartland Corners in 1816. There are at present six shops in the town.

Johnson's saw-mill was located on Johnson's creek, where it crosses the county line. It was built as early as 1820. There is a mill at the same place yet, but no dam. There was also a mill built at Johnson's Creek village, in 1818, by Ebenezer Seeley. The timber in this section was mostly chestnut, ash, oak, elm, baswood and buttonwood. Before mills were built here, people had to go to Oak Orchard creek, in Orleans county, for what little lumber they wanted for doors and floors. At present there is but one mill in running order in the town, and that is at Johnson's Creek village, and built by Mr. Seeley.

The first grist-mill in this town was about three-quarters of a mile east of where R. B. Weaver now lives, on the Ridge road. It consisted of the top of a white oak stump, sawed off square and dug out in the shape of a mortar. The pestle was attached to a spring pole, which raised it, and the customer at the mill had only to pull down hard enough to break and pulverize the grain. This was rather a slow process of grinding corn and wheat, but for a small grist was rather quicker than to go to Rochester or Niagara Falls, a distance of from thirty to thirty-five miles. When large grists were to be ground, the neighbors would take turns in going to Schlosser to mill, carrying each other's grists. In about 1818 or 1820, some of the most enterprising of the old pioneers turned their attention to the wants not only of themselves but of their neighbors, and built a mill on Johnson's creek, where it crosses the ridge. The one at the Creek is the only one in the town, and was built originally by Ebenezer Seeley, who still resides at that place. The first and only tannery in Hartland was built at Johnson's Creek in 1818, and went to decay several years ago.

The early merchants were James and Daniel Van Horn, John Secor, Martin Miner, and George Reynolds. The two first named carried on a general dry goods and grocery business, just east of the village of Johnson's Creek, in 1815. They were succeeded by George Reynolds in 1818. Miner and Secor each kept a grocery store at the Creek.

In 1813 Mrs. Burnett, who lived a short distance west of Johnson's Creek on the Ridge road, worked at weaving for her neighbors.

EDUCATIONAL.

The town meeting of 1814 elected as commissioners of common schools, Samuel Colton, James Welch and Samuel B. Morehouse; and ordered that Daniel Cornell, John Leach and William Smith be inspectors of common schools.

The first school in this town was taught by Miss Nancy Judson, in the summer of 1813. Mrs. Stephen Baker, now living in the southeastern part of the town, is one of the surviving pupils, and probably the only one in the town. In 1816 the town was divided by the commissioners of common schools, into six districts. In the same year, it was voted at town meeting to raise sixty dollars for the support of schools. In 1878 there were eighteen school districts, with an average daily attendance of four hundred and seventy-one, and the amount of school money apportioned to the town for 1878 was $2,411.16.

The following is an extract from the records of school district No. 5, showing the original bounds of the district: "Beginning at the southwest corner of lands now owned and occupied by Zenas Seaman, at the Ridge road, thence north to the north line of section 2, in the sixth range, thence west to the town line, thence south along the town line to the southwest corner of section 6, in the seventh range, thence east to the place of beginning. April 26th, 1828." The school-house was built of logs, and in the highway, as no one that occupied land could give a good title for a lot upon which to build. Absalom Ladner, John Scovell and Levi Hall were the first trustees. The school-house was built of logs, in 1831; size, 18 by 24 feet, and cost, $15.

In October, 1832, school district No. 5 voted to raise $10 to repair the school-house and to buy firedogs and shovel. The board for the teacher was sold at auction to the lowest bidder, James Slaton bidding off the job at one dollar and fifty cents per week.

The "Quaker road" school-house was built about the year 1818, of logs, with a stick chimney, and a sufficient opening between that and the logs to store away the necessary number of blue beeches to enforce proper order and discipline in the school-room. The first school in the district was taught by Rachael Pease, in 1819. The first male teacher was Jesse Aldrich, who taught about 1820. The district is now known as No. 12.

ROADS AND BRIDGES.

The Ridge road, or rather the ridge, was discovered in 1805 by some of the new settlers around Slaton Settlement, who, while hunting after their cattle, observed that there was a continuous ridge or elevated ground running nearly east and west across the town, and that upon it was heavy timber of a valuable kind. They therefore changed their location and settled upon this ridge, east of Hartland Corners.

Among the first to settle upon the ridge in this town were Isaac Southwell, Jedediah Riggs, Daniel Brown and others. In a very few years the Ridge road was celebrated as one of the best roads in the State, settlers began to come in and locate, stages began to go over it, heavily loaded, business revived, and Hartland soon became noted for its numerous hotels (one every mile), where the traveler could rest and refresh his wearied body, and from which he could start out afresh on his pioneer pilgrimage or tour of inspection of the many natural wonders that presented themselves at the falls of Niagara.

The several roads running north and south from the Ridge road were hewed out by the sturdy pioneer; patches of ground were cleared on either side, and the beginning of future homes established by the building of a rude log hut, the raising of a little grain and a few vegetables; and in a few years the paths that were followed only by marked trees became the turnpikes, including the celebrated Ridge road, over which, in 1816, four-horse stages, with their additional baggage or express wagons, heavily loaded, began making daily trips between Rochester and Lewiston.

Jesse Aldrich and wife, in company with Asa Baker and wife, moved from Perinton, Monroe county, into the town of Hartland June 6th, 1815, and became the first settlers of that part of the town now known as the Quaker Settlement, and are believed to have been the first settlers north of the Ridge road in what is now known as Hartland. These families were accompanied by Joseph Birdsall, Daniel Baker and Esek Aldrich, and helped to clear a road from the Ridge, a distance of a mile and a half, to the lands that had been "articled" to Jesse Birdsall, sufficiently to pass a team through; also to clear a site and put up a log house. These labors being accomplished, those persons returned to their homes, leaving these two families to the solitude surrounding their new home. During the time the house was being built the women were left at the house of John Cook, on the Ridge road. No other settlers came to this place until the following year, 1816, when Jesse Aldrich, Joseph Birdsall, Joseph Baker, Hugh Jackson, Jesse Jackson, William Jackson, Richard Earl and Christopher H. Skeels, with their wives, moved in, all being members of the Society of Friends—commonly called Quakers—except the two last named. With their united industry the wilderness was soon being transformed into cultivated fields and pleasant homes, and the neighborhood was soon known as the "Quaker Settlement," and the road passing through it as the "Quaker road."

The town records contain the following:

"A survey of a road beginning at the south side of the Ridge road, at the corner of lots No. 4 and No. 2, being, as is supposed, about three-fourths of a mile west of the east bounds of the now county of Niagara, running thence southerly along the line of Linus Spalding's land, to the north line of township No. 14, in the 5th range of townships of the Holland Company's land; turning thence a course south, 40° west, striking again the line between quarter sections, thence a straight course with the line until striking the west branch of Oak Orchard creek, and crossing with the line until meeting with the creek again; then running with the bank of the said creek two chains, turning thence an easterly course, fifty-six chains, to the county line; making a route of four miles and a half, and seventy-two rods.

"JOHN SECOR, Surveyor."

There are in this town about fifteen bridges crossing the three principal streams, the most important of which are the Johnson's Creek, county line, and Hartland Corners bridges. The one south of the Corners is a construction costing about $500. The one at Johnson's Creek village is a stone arch bridge, built in 1878, costing $850, contract price, besides the filling in at the ends and widening the roadway and wings. The county line bridge, crossing Johnson's creek, was rebuilt in 1878. The first bridge in this town was at the site of Johnson's Creek village, and was built of logs, in 1813, and covered with earth.

SALT SPRINGS.

On the farm of P. Newton, about one and a half miles southwest of Johnson's Creek village, there is a salt spring, or well, about twenty feet deep. For a large space around, reaching over on to the farm of William Wheeler, there is so much of the saline property in the ground that no vegetation whatever will grow upon it. At one time salt was quite extensively manufactured. The troughs used were made from large basswood trees, and some of them are still in existence. When the Erie Canal was opened, salt was brought from Syracuse and sold cheaper than the Hartland salt, and in a few years the words were abandoned, probably about 1830.

A PROFITABLE HURRICANE.

Some time previous to the settlement of this town by Barnum, Riggs and others in 1803, a hurricane passed over this town, from southeast to northwest, and about half a mile wide, apparently destroying everything in its course. Isaac Southwell and Oliver Castle settled upon this "windfall," as it was called. Mr. Castle cut from the fallen timber the logs to build his cabin, and Mr. Southwell cut from the same streak, about two miles northwest from Castle's, logs for rails to make his fences, and also logs for his wilderness mansion.

AN ANCIENT EARTHWORK.

Neither history nor tradition furnishes any account of Indian trails in or passing through what is embraced in the present boundaries of Hartland. But on the Castle farm, many years before the red man of the forest retreated before the advance of his white foe, some people build an earthwork, evidently for defensive operations. It was similar to those hastily thrown up in modern times. The works were circular in form, with an opening on the northeast side for ingress and egress. In 1828, Mr. William Wheeler, who now owns and lives on the adjoining farm, assisted in clearing away the timber, then growing in, upon and around these works, which was as large as any of the timber surrounding the fort. He afterward assisted in plowing down the embankments, which were at that time from two to four feet high. In plowing and cultivating this piece of ground, which was about twenty rods in diameter, a large number of pieces of earthen ware, apparently of some ancient or foreign make, were found. Arrow heads and some other small relics of ancient warfare were also found. The place has been cultivated since 1828, and the first road west of Johnson's creek, running south from the Ridge road, passes over what was the east side of the fort, just south of the old Castle mansion. For many years the place was known locally as "Fort Peace." There is now scarcely any trace of the works left.

TAVERNS.

Jephtha Dunn was the first inn-keeper in the town of Hartland. He opened his house for the accommodation of travelers in 1809. He was located about two miles east of Johnson's Creek, on the Ridge road.

Daniel Brown was also a tavern-keeper in the early history of the town. He kept in a log house about eighty rods west of Johnson's Creek, on the Ridge road.

Samuel B. Morehouse, one of the most noted men in this part of the country in his day, built a hotel at Hartland Corners about 1813. He was postmaster at that place in 1816. He was a character, and could his career be written out in full it would fill a volume.

At present there are but three hotels in the town, viz.,

at Hartland and Johnson's Creek, and one on the east side of the town, on the Ridge road, locally known as the "Break o'Day Hotel."

PHYSICIANS.

Dr. Asa Crane settled in Hartland in 1810, and was the first physician in the town. Dr. Moore soon followed. Dr. Butterfield came in 1812 or early in 1813, and located at Johnson's Creek. Drs. Crane and Moore located on the north side of the Ridge, at the corner of the Quaker road. Dr. Butterfield was a graduate of the Fairfield Medical School, and located in Canada. Upon the declaration of war in 1812 the doctor and a friend of his took a skiff and struck out across Lake Ontario for their native land, landing at Sackett's Harbor. The doctor located early in 1813 at the Creek, and remained there during life. He had a very extensive ride. He rode what was known in those days as a circuit, and would often be from home for several days at a time. While absent from home he shared the hospitality of the pioneers, partaking of their frugal meals, and after tying his horse to a tree would find shelter for himself under the wide-spreading branches of another tree close by. Thus the good old man worked for his fellow men, spending his health and life for the good of others.

BURYING GROUNDS.

There are some half dozen in the town, but the most prominent is the "Skeels burying ground," between the Skeels and Weaver farms, on the Ridge road, a little west of the Quaker road. Skeels and Weaver donated half the land, and caused a substantial stone wall to be put around the whole lot; and as long as Mr. Skeels lived, the grounds were kept in good order.

EARLY PREACHERS.

Oliver Castle, who settled here in 1815, although not ordained, was the first to preach the gospel in this and adjoining towns. Elder Mairo, a Methodist itinerant, came here in 1814. In about 1816 Elder Harrington, a Baptist, came here and organized a Baptist society. In 1811 the Universalists held services at the house of Benjamin Cornell.

LODGES.

MASONIC.

Hartland Lodge, No. 218, F. and A. M. was organized in 1825, at Hartland Corners. In 1826-7, when the anti-masonic agitation swept over over this State, the lodge suspended labor, and the master's gavel was not heard again until 1850, when labor was resumed at Johnson's Creek, with the following charter officers: B. K. Cornell, M.; Robert Dixon, S. W.; Richard Weaver, J. W. The officers for 1878 are: N. L. Wallace, M.; E. F. Mather, S. W.; John Long, J. W.; E. H. Whitman, treasurer; R. S. Hawkins, secretary; 86 members were reported June 1st.

I. O. OF G. T.

A lodge of Good Templars was organized at Hartland Corners January 6th, 1869, with sixteen charter members, and Dr. E. H. Elliott as W. C. T. The lodge is in a flourishing condition, and has at present about seventy members.

A. O. U. W.

Beneficiary Lodge, No. 101, Ancient Order of United Workmen, located at Hartland Corners, was instituted July 28th, 1877, by D. D. G. M. W. William E. Jenney. The following is a full list of officers installed at the organization:

Andrew Welcher, P. M. W.; Alfred Deuel, M. W.; Dexter Wheeler, G. F.; Joseph Garbutt, O.; Dr. H. A. Wilmot, recorder; Stephen Dennie, financier; W. R. Bronson, receiver; W. H. Marshall, guide; James Bryant, I. W.; Charles A. Kendall, O. W.

The present officers were installed in January, 1878, as follows: A. Welcher, P. M. W.; Alfred Deuel, M. W.; C. D. Silsby, G. F.; John Gow, O.; Dr. H. A. Wilmot, recorder; Robert Bardwill, financier; W. R. Bronson, receiver; W. H. Marshall, guide; Albert J. Dean, I. W.; Albert Carlin, O. W.; James Bryant, Andrew Welcher, Stephen Dennie, trustees. The lodge meets at Hartland Corners on Saturday evening of each week.

CHURCHES.

The first "meeting-house" of the Friends, or Quakers, was erected about the year 1818, and was built of logs. It stood on the Ridge road, at the corner of the Quaker road. This building was occupied for a meeting-house up to 1835, when the society built their present house of worship, constructed of cobble stone. It is located about three-quarters of a mile east of the old one, on the Ridge road. This society for a number of years was quite large, but of late has become considerably reduced by deaths and removals. Its members were industrious and temperate in their habits, and a people peculiarly addicted to minding their own business.

Among the most prominent and leading of the members of this society was Jesse Aldrich, who took an active part in all the measures calculated to enhance the prosperity of the church. He was a man much respected for his intelligence, and moral and religious standing. He held various town offices, although frequently declining on the ground that the duties required the administering of oaths. He built the first frame house and barn on the Quaker road. He died at the advanced age of 88 years. The Society of Friends most of the time have had no resident minister. The only ones now remembered were Robert Comfort, Mead Atwater, and Huldah, his wife.

FIRST BAPTIST.

The First Baptist Church of Hartland had its rise in the hearts of a few earnest christians from Vermont, who settled in the town in February, 1875. They were James Edmunds and family, of whom four were Baptists, and Deacon Horton and wife.

As soon as Mr. Edmunds had cleared a few acres of land and built him a log house, he began looking about for others of a like faith, with a view to organizing a Baptist prayer meeting. He found Mr. and Mrs. Green and Mr. Abial Tripp on the mountain ridge, who gladly united with him in establishing weekly prayer meetings, held alternately at their homes, with occasional preaching by Elders Bennett and L. Hatt, of the missionary convention, and Elder Dutcher, of Gaines.

These services were continued a little more than two years, during which time several converts were received, the first one being Mrs. Lydia Le Valley. In December, 1817, the little band of believers, numbering only twenty-two, was formally recognized as the First Baptist Church of Hartland, Niagara county N. Y., by Rev. Simeon Dutcher, pastor of the Gaines church, and Rev. Timothy Shepherd, missionary of the State convention. The ensuing May, Daniel Bateman joined the church by letter, was licensed to preach and supplied the pulpit two years. The first deacon was James Edmunds. The first pastor was Rev. William Harrington, of Vermont, who was induced to settle in this vicinity by Deacon Edmunds, in 1820. He served the church faithfully and acceptably until the time of his death, December 2nd, 1830.

On April 10th, 1822, the church resolved itself into a body corporate, agreeable to the law of 1813, to be known as The First Baptist Church of Hartland. This title was changed in 1832 to The Society of the First Baptist Church of Hartland. The first trustees were: James Edmunds, Otis Leland and Holden Le Valley.

Up to this time, seven years, services had been held alternately in the house or barn of Deacon Edmunds, the "Green" school-house, on the mountain ridge, and the house of Holden Le Valley, three-quarters of a mile north of Middleport. The society then raised $100, and with it added ten feet to the length of a school-house being built at Johnson's Creek, and thus secured a commodious place of worship, which served until 1833, when, during the labors of their second pastor, Rev. Roswell Kimball, the church succeeded in building, at the cost of $2,700, a church edifice. This being the first church organized in the town, it was entitled to and applied for the government apportionment of fifty acres of land, and received the southwest corner lot of the town. This not being eligible for building purposes, was disposed of, and the proceeds devoted to the erection of the house on its present site at Johnson's Creek. In 1868, during the pastorate of Rev. G. C. Walker, the society rebuilt and enlarged the church at a cost of $6,000.

In 1877, during the ministry of Rev. B. L. Van Buren, the members purchased the adjoining property north, for a parsonage, for the sum of $1,000.

The church has had in all thirteen pastors, viz.: Elders William Harrington, Roswell Kimball, James Handy, Peter Robison, W. I. Crane, J. E. Maxwell, D. D. Chittenden, Cantine Garrison, Elon Galusha, G. C. Walker, S. S. Utter, S. I. Lee and B. L. Van Buren, who has just entered upon his fourth year.

The church has called councils for the ordination of three of her sons, viz.: Roswell Kimball, J. Olin Edmunds and Edward B. Edmunds, the two latter being the son and grandson of the honored instrument of the organization of the church.

The deacons of the church have been: James Edmunds, Otis Leland, Joseph Worthen, Jeremiah Turner, Orlando Bates, Silas Gilbert, Archibald McClay, F. L. Weston, James Edmunds, jr., S. M. Kingman, H. B. Stewart, Garret Spoor, Platt Betts and Charles Williams, the three latter now serving the church.

ROMAN CATHOLIC.

Saint Patrick's Roman Catholic Church is located on the Quaker road, near the north line of the town. Previous to 1856 this society held its services in private houses within the limits of the parish, and in that year, under the labors of Rev. T. Shehan, who resided at Newfane, the society erected a frame church, thirty by forty feet, at a cost of $750, which was dedicated in 1877 by the Right Rev. John Timon, D. D., bishop of Buffalo.

In 1865, under the pastorate of Rev P. A. Mulloy, the church building was enlarged, and in September, 1872, the Rev. T. P. Brougham came in charge of the mission; and through his efforts the transept, sanctuary and vestry were built, and finished inside and out, in modern style, at a cost of $2,200.

The rededication took place July 7th, 1875, the Right Rev. S. V. Ryan, D. D., bishop of Buffalo, officiating on the occasion.

The presbytery was erected in the fall of 1876, costing $2,000. Rev. Thomas P. Brougham is the first resident priest, he having moved here in 1877 from Newfane.

At the organization of the society there were less than forty souls in the mission, and at the present there are seven hundred. The value of the church property is $6,000.

METHODIST PROTESTANT.

The Methodist Protestant church is located on the Quaker road about two miles north of the Ridge road. The society was organized in the spring of 1842, with fifty members, and Rev. O. C. Paine in charge. It built a church in 1843, of wood, costing $1,000, which was burned in 1872. In 1873 the society erected the present edifice of brick, 30 by 40 feet, costing $2,500, which was dedicated in July of that year, by Rev. Mr. Hurd, of Lockport. The present pastor is Rev. Nelson H. Becker. The number of members is eighty-five. The society built a parsonage in 1877, on the lot adjoining the church lot, costing $1,100. The Sunday-school of this society is in a flourishing condition. The value of the church property is $4,000.

METHODIST EPISCOPAL.

A Methodist Episcopal church is located at Hartland Corners, and another at north Hartland, Rev. Mr. Sharp in charge. We were unable to obtain either history, or material for one, from any reliable source.

EVERGREEN FRUIT FARM. RES. OF S. A. BREWER, TOWN OF HARTLAND, NIAGARA CO., N.Y.

AGRICULTURAL.

In 1873 probably not more than five per cent. of the land then embraced in the town was improved, while in 1875 more than eighty-five per cent. was under improvement. The cash value of farms as estimated by the assessors in 1873 was $19,487; in 1875 the cash value, as given by the land owners and holders to the United States census marshal, was $2,809,600. In 1875 the value of farm buildings was $263,090; value of stock, $263,200; farm tools, $97,150; gross sales from farms, $263,444; bushels of barley, 16,400; of buckwheat, 2,122; corn, 69,575; oats, 97,840; rye, 3,563; winter wheat, 39,840; beans, 18,895; potatoes, 59,267; apples, 114,739; grapes, 53,450 pounds; butter, 122,979; averaging 109 pounds to each cow in the town; number of farms of all sizes, 528; number of families in the town 721; total value of dwellings in town, aside from farm buildings, $593,265.

The first orchards were set out on the Bennett and Edmunds farms, and others west of them in 1815. The trees were brought from Lima, Livingston county. Mr. Edmunds, who had just come from the Green Mountain State, wanted fruit trees; and not having the money with which to buy them, traded the only feather bed his family had for some trees, thus starting an orchard that has spread all over the town.

THE LEADING CITIZENS OF TO-DAY.

H. P. Alvord was born in Hartland, N. Y., April 1st, 1832, and in 1855 he was married to Eliza J. Robinson, of Hartland. Mr. Alvord is a well-known farmer. Post-office, North Ridgeway.

O. T. Bachelder, farmer, was born in Hartland, N. Y., July 23d, 1825. He was married October 10th, 1848, to Louisa Baker, who was born October 10th, 1828. Post-office, Middleport.

Ezra K. Banker was born in Clinton county, N. Y. October 16th, 1812, and was married to Eliza Whiten, a native of Montpelier, Vt. Mr. Banker is a farmer and blacksmith. Post-office, Johnson's Creek.

Enoch W. Bardwell was born in Ontario county, N. Y., January 31st, 1807, and was married in Middlesex, Yates county, N. Y., in 1829, to Malah Stebbins, who was a native of Franklin county, Mass.

A. J. Bickford was born October 17th, 1843, in Hartland, N. Y., and married March 20th, 1867, to Susan Van Nortwick, of Yates, N. Y. He is a farmer. Post-office address, Johnson's Creek, N. Y.

H. H. Bickford, a native of Michigan, was born March 13th, 1838. He came to Hartland in 1840, where he has since resided. He is a nurseryman, farmer, and gardener, by occupation. He served in Company E, 8th N.Y. cavalry, during the war. Post-office, Johnson's Creek.

M. W. Bigelow, farmer, Johnson's Creek, was born in Hartland, March 29th, 1831. He was married March 23d, 1859, to Caroline Swift, who was born in Yates, Orleans county, March 10th, 1831.

Charles H. Boyd, of Johnson's Creek, a native of Bennington, Vt., was born September 13th, 1818, and married October 15th, 1838, to Charlotte Nelson, of Hartland N. Y. Mr. Boyd came to Hartland from Erie county in 1837. He is a farmer and fruit-grower.

Samuel A. Brewer was born in Yates county, N.Y., October 12th, 1831. He was married November 15th, 1853, to Salina Hinman, who was born January 5th, 1830, at Le Roy, Genesee county, N. Y. Mr. and Mrs. Hinman have four children, three sons and one daughter. Mr. Brewer is known as an enterprising farmer and fruit-grower. Post-office address, Johnson's Creek.

Thomas Brown, farmer, Johnson's Creek, was born in Ontario county, N. Y., January 27th, 1808. He was married February 6th, 1833. Mrs. Brown is a native of Albany; she was born April 13th, 1822.

William Brown was born January 12th, 1836. May 10th, 1859, he was married to Elizabeth Curtis, who was born November 28th, 1837. Mr. Brown is a farmer. Post-office, Johnson's Creek.

James Bryant was born in Royalton, N. Y., June 11th, 1836. He married Lovisa S. Crandall, of Newfane, Niagara county, N. Y.

C. O. Chaplin, of Ridgeway Corners (post-office, Ridgeway), was born December 19th, 1848, in Hartland, and married October 19th, 1867, to Miss E. J. Warren, of that town. He removed from Middleport March 28th, 1878, to his present place of residence, where he keeps a hotel.

John L. Chase was born in Franklin, New London county, Conn., December 11th, 1829. He was married November 27th, 1850, to Sarah C. Taylor. He has been supervisor of the town for 1877 and 1878.

J. W. Cleghorn was born near Edinburgh, Scotland, March 18th, 1821. He was married at Lockport, January 1st, 1854, to Rebecca P. Moore, who was born at Mooresburgh, Pa., July 2nd, 1826.

John G. Cook is a native of Orleans county. He was born October 28th, 1829. In 1856 he was married to Ruth Ann Smith. Mrs. Cook was born in Hartland, August 5th, 1837. Mr. Cook has lived in the town forty-two years.

Harvey Cook was born September 17th, 1827, in Allegany county. He was married on New Year's day, 1849, to Eliza Goodman, a native of Royalton. He is a farmer. Post-office, North Hartland.

Samuel Curtiss was born in Columbia county, N. Y., May 27th, 1805. May 14th, 1842, he was married to Margaret Delany.

William T. Curtiss, farmer and fruit-grower, was born in Hartland, N.Y., November 30th, 1833. He was married April 25th, 1865, to Jane E. Ashley, a native of England.

John W. Davis was born June 17th, 1824, and was married March 16th, 1848, to Mary A. Waterman. Mrs. Davis was born in Hartland, October 6th, 1829. Mr. Davis is a farmer. Post-office, Middleport.

Stephen Dennie, a native of Mayfield, Fulton county, N. Y., was born September 25th, 1832, and married March 21st, 1853, to Emlinda Swartwout, of Mayfield. Mr. Dennie removed from Mayfield to Hartland, N. Y., in 1868. He is a farmer, and also deputy collector and inspector of customs at Suspension Bridge. He was also first lieutenant in the 10th cavalry. Post-office, Hartland, N. Y.

John Drum was born May 11th, 1825, in Wayne county, N. Y. September 11th, 1855, he was married to Susan Doty, of Madison county, N. Y. Farmer; post-office, Johnson's Creek, N. Y.

Hosea Dunbar was born in Vermont, May 5th, 1812, and married October 16th, 1834, by Squire Seymour, to Laura Chaplin.

Reuben D. Feagles was born in Seneca county, N. Y., February 15th, 1812, and was married April 18th, 1838, to Polly Doty. He is a farmer. Post-office address, West Somerset.

Joseph Garbutt was born at Bilsdale, England, February 13th, 1831. He married Caroline Bradley, who was born in Hartland April 24th, 1855. Mr. Garbutt is commissioner of highways of the town of Hartland. His mother, Mrs. George Garbutt, who lives at Johnson's Creek, brought the first hair cloth sofa into the town in 1840.

Lloyd A. Gardner was born in Royalton, March 18th, 1849, and was married to Margaret McCandlish September 29th, 1875, at Eagle Harbor, Orleans county, N. Y.

Jesse A. Gladding was born April 8th, 1820, in that part of the town known as the "Quaker Settlement," and in the same school district in which he now resides. His parents were born in Massachusetts, and came from there to Ontario county, N. Y., and from there to the town of Hartland in 1818. The father died in 1834. The mother still survives. Jesse was brought up to farm work. Besides the common school, he had the advantage of several terms in the academy at Millville, Orleans county, in 1840-41. He taught school winters from 1841 to 1850. He has held the offices of school inspector, town superintendent of schools, assessor, justice of the peace, and justice of sessions, and loan commissioner for the county of Niagara, and has done much of the legal business of the town for the last twenty-five years, but has devoted his time mostly to farming, and has been a daily witness of the transformation of the town from an almost unbroken wilderness to its present state of clearing and cultivation. Mr. Gladding was married to Adeline C. Gardner, May 1st, 1849, who was born in Batavia, Genesee county, N. Y., February 6th, 1824. Their children are Ada C., born June 30th, 1850; Cora A., born February 5th, 1853; and Milton S., born June 22d, 1856.

Levi Hall, father of Luther S. Hall, was born December 9th, 1790, at Cape Cod, Barnstable county, Mass., and came to Niagara county in 1815. Luther S. Hall resides on the old homestead, and was born there March 11th, 1821. He was married November 16th, 1843, to Harriet S., daughter of Elisha S. and Lovina B. Fassett, of Hamburgh, Erie county, N. Y.

O. B. Hayes was born in the town of Somerset, Niagara county, N. Y., on the 6th day of February, 1835, and was married March 22d, 1869, to Grace M. Fuller, a native of Saratoga county, where she was born September 22nd, 1845. Mr. Hayes came to Niagara county about nine years ago. They have had four children, one of whom is dead.

Eli F. Hill, a native of Wallingford, Vt., was born April 27th, 1810. January 29th, 1844, he was married, Mrs Hill being a native of Saratoga county, N. Y., where she was born December 11th, 1815.

B. F. Hoffman came from Newfane, N. Y., to Johnson's Creek, N. Y., in 1874. He was born in Somerset, Niagara county, N. Y., September 26th, 1836. He was married September 10th, 1862, to D. Cornelia St. John, of Victory, Cayuga county. Mr. Hoffman served as lieutenant in the 9th N. Y. artillery during the late war.

Orrin L. Hudnut was born in Cayuga county, N. Y., November 1st, 1818. He married Catharine Vandoran March 22nd, 1840. Mrs. Hudnut was born August 11th, 1819.

George Humphrey was born February 15th, 1844, in Cambridgeshire, England, came to Hartland in 1853, and is now engaged in farming and fruit-growing. He was in the late war for three years, and in twenty-four battles. Post-office, Hartland Corners.

D. W. Hunt, farmer, Johnson's Creek, is a native of Hartland, where he was born April 3d, 1835. He was married August 17th, 1861, to Ellen O. Smith, who was born August 17th, 1845.

H. B. Ingersoll, farmer and fruit-grower, who was born December 6th, 1852, is a son of Levi H. Ingersoll, a native of Broome county, who was born December 7th, 1815. Mr. Ingersoll was married to Mary E. Pollard, October 29th, 1845. H. B. Ingersoll was married September 21st, 1875.

Irena Jameson was born February 22nd, 1816, in Genesee county, and lived in that county and Orleans until locating at her present residence in Hartland. Her deceased husband, Alexander H. Jameson, was born October 22nd, 1805, at Barnet, Vt., and removed to Genesee county, N. Y., and thence to Niagara. They were married May 11th, 1834. Mr. Jameson was a lawyer by profession, but was connected with the army for two years as sutler for the 28th regiment.

M. L. Jones was born in Otsego county, November 18th, 1803. He was married at Westport, N. Y., to Eliza White, September 16th, 1826. Mr. Jones is a farmer.

James Kinnabrook was born in Ovid, N. Y., July 18th, 1815, and was married to Rachel Dunn, September 18th, 1838. Mrs. Kinnabrook was born June 10th, 1814, in Columbia county, N. Y.

John Kinyon, jr., was born at Marcellus, Onondaga county, N. Y., May 3d, 1832, and was married March 22d, 1859, to Edith Sheldon, who was born in Royalton, N. Y., June 19th, 1833.

Isaac Kittredge, farmer, was born at Danville, Vt. December 12th, 1799. February 5th, 1834, he was married to Matilda J. Hitchcock, of Royalton, N. Y.

M. B. Knapp, a native of Oneida county, was born June 27th, 1829. His wife, formerly Miss M. E. Kellogg, was born July 28th, 1830, in Oneida county.

M. W. Leach, farmer and fruit-grower, was born Octo-

FARM RESIDENCE OF ELON SHERWOOD ESQ. NORTH HARTLAND, NIAGARA CO., N. Y.

ber 7th, 1825, in Meadville, Pa., and was married September 9th, 1852, to Almira Chaplin, a native of Clarendon, Vt., February 8th, 1833.

James H. Manchester was born September 24th, 1809, at Broadalbin, Fulton county, N. Y. He was married November 26th, 1835, to Margaret De Pui, who was born in Cayuga county, N. Y., July 31st, 1812.

'John Mather was born in Middleport, January 18th. 1837, and was married November 9th, 8170, to Jane E. Bradley, a native of Hartland, N. Y.

James W. Mead was a native of Somerset, where he was born September 7th, 1847, and settled in Hartland in 1851. In 1876 he was married to Sarah A. Cook.

William H. Mead was born in Somerset, N. Y., in 1840, and was married to Martha Wicks in 1864. Mr. Mead located in the town in 1849. They have four children, two sons and two daughters.

William Morgan was born June 18th, 1814, at St. Braivals, Gloucestershire, England. He came to New York in 1830, and to Hartland in 1848 from Rochester, where he had been married to Miss Margaret Parks, May 1st, 1838. He is an architect and builder, and has built over thirty church edifices in Niagara and the three neighboring counties; and more of them and school-houses than all other builders now living in Niagara county. He has served the town ten years as supervisor (first in 1857) and was elected to the Assembly in 1862 and re-elected in 1863 from the first district. He has served eight months as revenue assessor, and is now serving his sixth year as one of the loan commissioners of the county. He has been more than any other man identified with reclaiming the swamp lands of Hartland, with the possible exception of Elijah Mather. He has four children : boys, Charles and William, and girls, Flora Isabella and Emma Ione. Post-office, Somerset.

Ephraim Randolph was born in Hartland, N. Y., July 29th, 1826, and married November 9th, 1853, to Altheda Southworth, who was born February 6th, 1831. Mrs. Randolph died September 12th, 1859, and Mr. Randolph was married June 10th, 1862, to Martha L. Randall.

Mrs. S. A. Ransom was born January 6th, 1817. Farmer, district No. 9. Post-office, North Ridgeway, N. Y.

James Robinson was born in Columbia county, N. Y., April 1st, 1809. He was married in Hartland January 1st, 1835, to Elsie W. Seaman, who was born April 25th, 1818.

James K. Robson, Johnson's Creek, was born May 14th, 1832, in Hartland. Mr. Robson is a farmer. He served three years during the rebellion in the 8th N. Y. cavalry.

Alvira L. Root, formerly Alvira L. Kittredge, was born November 3d, 1831. She was married to Joel E. Root February 10th, 1852. Mr. Root was born August 7th, 1829, and died November 13th, 1859, aged thirty years, two months and six days.

Gordon Rowe was born in Onondaga, N. Y., September 20th, 1822, and was married April 15th, 1846, to Maria Spalding. Mr. Rowe is a well known farmer, and holds the office of justice of the peace.

Mrs. Alanson Saxon was born in 1826. Mr. Saxon was born in Monroe county, N. Y., in 1825.

David P. Seaman was born in Hartland July 15th, 1822. He was married February 18th, 1846, to Betsey Ann Drum. Mrs. Seaman died May 12th, 1851. February 28th, 1861, he was married to Miss Ann Reneghan.

William Seward came to Hartland in 1854 from Yates, Orleans county. He was born June 3d, 1849, in Lincolnshire, England, and married July 2nd, 1873, to Alice E. Sharpstein, of Hartland. He is a farmer and fruit-grower; post-office, Hartland Corners.

G. V. Shaw, a well-known farmer of the town of Hartland, was born in a log house near the site of his present residence, November 29th, 1812, and is the oldest native resident of the town. He was married January 19th, 1837, to Betsy Edmunds, who was born May 1st, 1813, in Clarendon, Vt. Mr. and Mrs. Shaw have had eight children, four of whom are dead. Two of their sons, Philander F. and William O., are married.

O. W. Sherman, a native of the town of Hartland, was born February 25th, 1822. June 16th, 1856, he was married in Michigan to Margaret Gilsen, of Shelby, N. Y. Mr. Sherman is a farmer and carpenter.

Abel S. Sherwood was born in Connecticut, New Year's day, 1823. November 10th, 1847, he was married to Mary Ann Dewhurst, a native of England.

Elon Sherwood, farmer, was born in Clarkson, Monroe county, N. Y., May 10th, 1827. March 9th, 1852, he was married to Susana Dewhurst, a native of Somerset, Niagara county, who was born September 11th, 1832. Mr. and Mrs. Sherwood have four sons. Mr. Sherwood has lived on the farm where he now resides twenty-seven years. He has greatly improved it, adding many modern conveniences, including a wind-mill for grinding feed, pumping water, and similar services.

Austin J. Spalding was born June 25th, 1853, in Hartland, N. Y., and was married November 29th, 1876, to Sarah McDonald, of Middleport, Niagara county, N. Y. Mr. Spalding is a farmer, carpenter and builder. Post-office address Middleport, N. Y.

Z. B. Stewart was born at Venice, Cayuga county, N.Y., February 2nd, 1805. In 1808 his father, Benjamin Stewart, came to Johnson's Creek and cleared the first land at that place, and spent the winter with his family at Hartland Corners. There were but three or four families living there at that time. In the spring of 1809 he removed with his family to his own house at Johnson's Creek. The Ridge road was not then open. The nearest neighbor east was at Gaines, about ten miles distant. In 1812 Mr. Stewart sold his place at the creek to a Mr. Secor, and again removed to Hartland Corners, where the family lived until 1814. When Lewiston was burned by the Canadians and Indians, the family removed to Monroe, then Ontario county. Z. B. Stewart returned to Hartland and taught school for a time, and in the fall of 1833 bought the farm now owned and occupied by H. H. Bickford. He resided here with his family for forty years, a much respected member of society. He died March 18th, 1873, and was buried in the grounds near his home. A portrait of Mr. Stewart appears on another page.

Abraham Taylor was born in Hartland, N. Y., January 18th, 1832. He is a son of Christopher L. Taylor, who was born in Sussex county, N. J., October 11th, 1791. Abraham Taylor was married to Emma Joice January 16th, 1866.

George B. Taylor was born August 13th, 1826, in Hartland, N. Y. He was married February 15th, 1854, to Amelia Crocker, of Le Roy, Genesee county, N. Y. Mr. Taylor is a farmer and dealer in fruit evaporators. He has served as supervisor and justice of the peace for his town and justice of sessions for the county.

George P. Taylor was born in Hartland, N. Y., April 29th, 1833, and married Helen J. Congdon November 29th, 1866, at Lockport, N. Y. Mrs. Taylor was a native of the town of Hartland.

Jasper J. Taylor was born at Johnson's Creek, Hartland, N. Y. He was married to Ida L. Strimbeck April 2d, 1861, at Albion, Orleans county, N. Y.

L. R. Vanderwarker was born November 23rd, 1849. He was married October 14th, 1869 to, Fayetta Shippen, who was born August 23d, 1850. Post-office, Johnson's Creek.

William Van Horn was born in Hartland, N. Y., May 31st, 1820, and was married September 10th, 1845, to Debby Ann Maker, of Benton Center, Yates county, N. Y. Mr. Van Horn is one of the enterprising and successful farmers of this town, owning and managing a farm of one hundred and sixty-seven acres, on the east side of the town, south of the Ridge road. His father, Hon. Daniel Van Horn, who is still living, was born May 6th, 1794. He located at Johnson's Creek in May, 1815, and engaged in the mercantile business. He was married in the summer of 1816, to Sarah Taylor, of Hartland, who was born September 6th, 1798.

Clara Vedder, wife of James S. Vedder, formerly Clara Goodman, was born in Niagara county, June 2nd, 1837, and married to Mr. Vedder March 29th, 1854. He is a farmer and fruit-grower.

James G. Watson, farmer, a native of Hartland, N. Y., was born June 16th, 1844. In the year 1865 he was married to Emily A. Compton, of Middleport, N. Y. His father, Robert, settled in the town in the year 1843.

Richard Reynale Weaver, of Hartland, resides on and works the farm on which his parents settled in 1806, when the nearest mill was at Chippewa, Canada. He was born April 25th, 1822. On the 14th of November, 1844, he married Mary A. Mackey, of Royalton.

Albert S. Webb was born in Berkshire, England, February 17th, 1833, and was married to Elizabeth Fisher, of Orleans county, N. Y., April 1st, 1860.

Lorenzo Webster, son of William Webster, was born August 27th, 1820, in Ogden, Monroe county, N. Y., and married November 30th, 1842, to Mary A., daughter of Amos Webster, of Parma, N. Y., who was born in 1824. He is now a retired farmer, and resides on the Ridge road, one mile west of the Corners. Mr. Webster has served his town twelve years as justice of the peace, and the county one term as justice of sessions.

William Wheeler, jr., was born May 2nd, 1811, in the town of Stratton, Bennington county, Vt., and came to Hartland and settled on the farm where he now lives. He was married March 6th, 1834, to Louisa, daughter of Dexter P. Sprague. Mrs. Wheeler was born January 9th, 1811, in Hartland, N. Y., and died September 16th, 1877. Mr. Wheeler served one term as supervisor.

Charles White was born in Schoharie county, February 11th, 1837, and was married March 29th, 1875, to Mary Smith, who was born June 5th, 1847.

Edwin Whitcomb was born in Henrietta, Monroe county, N. Y., September 27th, 1830. He was married to Mary A. Goodman, who was born in Royalton, October 28th, 1829. Mr. Whitcomb has resided on his present farm for more than thirty years. Mr. and Mrs. Whitcomb have had five children, one of whom is dead.

M. D. Williams was born January 17th, 1843, in Hartland, N. Y., and was married August 20th, 1867, to Mary V. Starks, of Burlington, Mich. Farmer; post-office, Johnson's Creek. Charles Williams, father of M. D. Williams, was born March 12th, 1809, at Taghanic, Columbia county, N. Y., and came to Hartland in 1831. He was married April 19th, 1837, to Rachel Robinson.

Luke Woodworth, M.D., a native of Watertown, Jefferson county, N. Y., was born September 2nd, 1807. At the age of sixteen he attended the academy at Lowville, N.Y., and then was a student at Bellville academy two years. He attended medical lectures at Fairfield medical college in 1832-34, and in the latter year located and commenced the practice of medicine at Johnson's Creek, N. Y., where he has practiced nearly forty-four years.

The following list gives the names, occupation and post-offices of some of the other prominent and more enterprising citizens of this town:

James C. Gray, farmer, Hartland; A. J. Spalding, farmer and carpenter, Middleport; C. B. Jennings, farmer, fruit-grower and real estate agent, Jeddo, Orleans county; Esek Aldrich, farmer, Johnson's Creek; B. F. Huffman, farmer, Johnson's Creek; S. B. Bennett, farmer and fruit grower, Johnson's Creek; Charles H. Turner, physician and surgeon, Johnson's Creek; Seth Warren, farmer, Johnson's Creek; George Martin, farmer, Middleport; William Seaman, Johnson's Creek; Rev. B. L. Van Buren, Baptist minister, Johnson's Creek; Jacob Rafter, Johnson's Creek.

THE TOWN OF LEWISTON.

THERE is no town in the county richer in picturesque scenery and historical interest than Lewiston. The site of the village of Lewiston has been an important point since men below the falls of Niagara began to exchange merchandise with men above. During the French occupation of the New York frontier, during the English occupation, and during all the years since the triumph of the arms of our patriot forefathers down to the present time, this spot has been regarded as one destined to have no small part in carrying on the commerce between the East and the West. Situated at the head of the navigable portion of the Niagara river below the falls, on the direct line of water communication *via* the great chain of lakes and their connecting rivers from the Atlantic ocean nearly half way across the western continent, it was designed by Nature as an important commercial point. Just when this place was first used as a point of transfer in transporting property between the navigable waters of the river above and below the falls cannot be certainly known, but that it was the terminus of a rude portage around the falls previous to the exploration of this region by white men there can be no doubt. This portage was in use by the Indians at a very early day, but it was not until after the occupation of the country by the French that it was used regularly as an established means of transportation. The facilities employed were of the most primitive kind, such of the supplies for the military posts and trading stations as were not too bulky, and the peltries purchased of the western Indians, being transported over the portage on the backs of Indians, during the greater part of the French occupation, while heavy articles were moved up and down the mountain by means of a tramway, or rude railway, which was without doubt the first railway constructed in the United States. Starting at the ferry landing, it traversed the side of the steep mountain diagonally, reaching the summit near the site of Fort Gray, on the brow of the mountain overlooking the village.

In building this tramway, said Mr. James L. Barton in an address delivered before the Young Men's Association of Buffalo, in 1848, the French "did not level the ground where it was too high or fill up the hollows. Where the ground was level, hewn timbers, with a rabbet or shoulder projecting upwards from the outer edges, similar to log railways in saw-mills, connected with cross pieces, were laid upon and rested firmly on stones laid under them; in passing over hollows, instead of filling them up, stone pediments were built up to the proper level and the timber ways laid on them, and in this manner it was carried to its completion. The power made use of in raising the cars was capstans or windlasses." Mr. Barton added that when a boy he had often traced the line of the old tramway, where could be seen the decayed timbers lying for many rods in continuation, and in many places the stone pediments were perfect. At the present time no traces of this structure are to be seen, the changes wrought by time and advancing civilization having swept them all away.

THE FRENCH AND ENGLISH OCCUPATIONS.

This initial enterprise was instituted during the period of Joncaire's stay at the lower landing, which begun as early as 1719. He built a substantial log house, thirty by forty feet in size, encompassing it with a strong palisade, on the lower river bank at Lewiston, which served the double purpose of a protection to the landing and a place for carrying on traffic with the Indians. Professor Kalm, a Swedish naturalist who visited this region in 1750, mentions "seeing Joncaire at the carrying place, and a settlement there of about two hundred Senecas, who were employed in carrying on their backs over the portage packs of bear and deer skins, at twenty cents a pack." So successful were Joncaire's efforts in behalf of his employers that it was not long before Lewiston became the center of French influence. There was no regular fort erected there, but a detachment of French soldiers was stationed at the landing, at least a portion of the time. The location of the stockade was near the ferry landing, up the river bank from the American Hotel and some distance below the suspension bridge.

After the events of 1759, which transferred the control of the Indian trade and the responsibility of pushing forward the work of civilization on the Niagara frontier from the hands of the French to those of the English, the latter improved the facilities for transportation over the portage, introducing the general use of teams and wagons, which measure was provided for by the construction of a more available road between Lewiston and Schlosser, though carts and teams had been used by the French to some extent during their possession, to the displeasure of the Indians, who complained to the French governor in 1757 that their long enjoyed rights and privileges were being thus violated. The English, on taking possession of the French works on the frontier, stationed soldiers in the fort at the mouth of the river, at the upper and lower landings of the portage, and in the several stockades they had built along the road to protect their trains in the transportation of goods. They were fully aware of the extent of the hatred with which the Indians regarded them, and while they doubtless strove to conciliate them and win their confidence, they took every available precaution to guard against any injury that might result from their bad feeling and their treachery. In transporting their supplies from Lake Ontario to their possessions in the "upper country," the English employed teams of horses or cattle, attached to heavy, old-fashioned wagons, and the vehicles went in caravans over the portage, under convoy of guards of soldiers of sufficient numerical strength, as was supposed, to insure the safety of the train and their attendant teamsters. Their precautions, however, as we have seen, did not save them from the bloody massacre of the Devil's Hole.

Old residents of the vicinity state that the appearance of the Devil's Hole has changed considerably within the last half century. In former days a clear, cold spring was to be seen at the bottom. A saw-mill, which has since gone out of operation and been removed, was erected on Bloody Run, near where it plunges off into the hole. In quarrying stone, on the highest part of the bank above the pit, to construct the wall around Fort Niagara, since the last war with Great Britain, large quantities of rocks, loosened earth and other rubbish have been thrown down, covering the spring and materially reducing the depth of the hole. Not many years ago pieces of bent and rusted iron, portions of wagon hubs and other reminders of the massacre were often found near the bottom of the abyss. Mr. Hetzel Colt, a well-known resident of the town of Lewiston, has one of these relics—an old chain of peculiar construction and appearance, which was undoubtedly in use on that memorable day of 1763. It is said that rattlesnakes abounded there in large numbers many years ago.

BRANT AND THE MOHAWKS.

Just where the Mohawks stopped, after leaving their country on the river which bears their tribal name, with Guy Johnson and Brant, or if they found any temporary abiding place before reaching Lewiston, is not known. In his History of the Holland Purchase, Turner says: "In an early period of the border wars, Brant's residence was at Lewiston—his dwelling, a block-house, standing near what is called Brant's Spring, on the farm of Isaac Cooke. His followers, forming a considerable Indian village, were located along the road between the Academy and the road that leads up to the Tuscarora village. There were remains of the huts standing when white settlement commenced. It would seem by reference to the books, that for several farms there the purchasers were charged an extra price in consequence of the improvements the Mohawks had made during their residence there. There was a log church in which the Episcopal service was usually read on Sundays by some one attached to the British garrison at Niagara, and occasionally a British army chaplain or a missionary would be present. That church, in any history of its origin and progress in Western New York, may well assume that beyond the garrison at Niagara, Lewiston—Brant's rude church—was the spot where its services were first had. Upon an humble church there could, of course, then be no belfry or steeple. The bell that was brought from the Mohawk was hung upon a cross-bar resting in the crotch of a tree, and rung by a rope attached. The crotch was taken down by the Cooke family after they had purchased the land. In 1778, John Mountpleasant (then but eight years old) says, his Tuscarora mother used to take him down to the church, where he remembers seeing his father, Captain Mountpleasant, then in command of the garrison at Niagara. He speaks of the crotch and the bell as objects that attracted his especial attention."

Shortly after the close of the Revolutionary war, the Indians under Brant captured a man named James Pemberton, and conducted him to the site of Lewiston village. After a brief council it was decided to burn him at the stake, and the place selected for the deed was the strip of level land on the bank of the Niagara, near the ferry and a little north of the remains of the Lewiston and Queenston suspension bridge. He was compelled to gather the wood for the fire, after which he was bound to the stake; and the torch was about to be applied when Brant, evidently interested in his behalf, turned to some squaws standing by, with the remark that the intended victim was a good looking man and would make one of them a good husband if she would avail herself of the privilege of claiming him as such. It is related that one of the women acted upon this suggestion, choosing Pemberton to be her husband and saving his life. There are several versions of this story, but it seems that such evidence as can be brought to bear on the subject is in favor of the one here recorded, which is verified by a woman named Cusick, a daughter of Pemberton by his Indian wife, who lives on the Tuscarora reservation.

TUSCARORA RESERVATION—INDIAN MOUND.

Driven from their original seats in North Carolina, the Tuscaroras came to New York in 1712, and joined the confederacy of the Five Nations, after which the Iroquois were called the Six Nations. During the struggle for American independence, a part of the tribe joined the forces of the British and a part maintained a strict neutrality. Such of the Tuscaroras and Oneidas as had allied themselves with the English, and fled before the approach of Sullivan's army, sought refuge with the British garrison at Fort Niagara, reaching that point via the Oneida lake, Oswego river and Lake Ontario. During the early part of the following year, part of them returned to their hunting-grounds in Central New York, and part of them took possession of a mile square on the mountain ridge, which was given them by the Senecas, who owned the territory there. At a later period the Holland Land Company granted them two square miles adjoining their possessions, and in 1808 they purchased of the company an additional tract, amounting to between four thousand and five thousand acres; and the aggregate of these tracts constitutes their present reservation.

The village, which has been so often described in history, has not been in existence during several generations. It was located near the nuorthern bondary of the reservation, which now has the appearance of a quite thrifty agricultural neighborhood, a good share of the land being under improvement. The present population of the reservation is a little over four hundred.

The chief is John Mountpleasant, third son of Captain Mountpleasant. The latter was born on the island of Mackinaw in 1779, and came to the reservation two years afterward. He was an officer in the British army during the war of 1812, and took part in the battle of Queenston Heights. He acted also as interpreter, being the only one who could speak the language of the different tribes. After the war he returned to the reservation, where he remained until his death, October 9th, 1854. John Mountpleasant, jr., was born January 18th, 1810, and was elected chief in 1827, when he was only 17 years old. He was married in 1831, to Jane Green, a daughter of the tribe, who subsequently died, and he married Caroline G. Parker, a Seneca woman, and a sister to General Eli Parker, who was appointed Indian commissioner during Grant's administration.

On the 18th of June, 1878, William and Philip Johnson were installed as Tuscarora chiefs, with elaborate Indian ceremonies. Representatives were present from all of the Six Nations, and a concourse of several thousand interested spectators.

Two churches—Baptist and Presbyterian—the latter of which was organized in 1805; two schools, one of which was formerly a boarding school, and the council house are the only public buildings. Some of the most well-to-do of the Tuscaroras are educating their children at Lockport.

About thirty rods northeast from the old ferry house, at the ferry ravine, Lewiston, is a mound where the boys, in 1824, dug out human bones. Captain James Van Cleve, who was one of the number, states that, judging from the size of the oak trees growing upon it, the mound must have been at that time two hundred years old. It probably contained the slain of some Indian battle in that locality long before the beginning of the French occupation, or those who have written of that period would have gleaned from the French some Indian tradition of it. The mound is quite perfect at the present time, with small oak trees upon it, and the little excavation made by the boys in 1824 is still plainly to be seen.

EARLY WHITE SETTLEMENT.

The first permanent settlement in the town was made on the site of the village of Lewiston, about the beginning of the present century. Among those who were there in 1800 were Frederick Woodman, William Gambol, — McBride, Thomas Hustler, Henry Hough, Henry Mills, — Middaugh, and Joseph and John Howell. Hustler was a tavern keeper, his tavern standing on the north side of what is now Center street, opposite its junction with Portage street. Few were better known than Mr. and Mrs. Hustler in the pioneer days, and their memory has been perpetuated by J. Fenimore Cooper in his "Spy," he having been the model of Sergeant Hollister and she of Betty Flanagan. Middaugh kept a tavern as early as 1788, and McBride built a tannery about 1799. In some reminiscences of John Mountpleasant, which have been published, he says: "The Middaughs came from North river. When they came they occupied one of the old houses left by the Mohawks. Hough had a Mohawk wife, and used to live in the house that Brant left." "I spent most of the summer of 1788 at Lewiston, purchasing furs," said Silas Hopkins in some recollections of the pioneer days which were published in the History of the Holland Purchase. "The only white inhabitant then in Lewiston was Middaugh. He kept a tavern—his customers the Indians, and travelers on the way to Canada." Of an event which took place in Lewiston the following year, he wrote: "In 1789, on one of our droving excursions, there was an unusual number of drovers collected at Lewiston. We clubbed together and paid the expenses of a treat to the Indians—gave them a benefit. They were collected there from Tonawanda, Buffalo, Tuscarora, and some from Canada; there were two or three hundred of them. They gave a war dance for our amusement. We had as guests, officers from Fort Niagara. The Indians were very civil. After the dance, rum was served out to them, upon which they become very merry, but committed no outrage. We had a jolly time of it; and I remember that among our number was a minister, who enjoyed the thing as much as any of us."

In 1802 Captain Lemuel Cook came. He was one of the best known of the early settlers of Lewiston. Previously he had been a surgeon in the army. His sons afterward became prominent men. Bates, who was an attorney, becoming comptroller of the State of New York. He died at Lewiston May 31st, 1841. Judge Lathrop Cook was long a resident, dying in July, 1855. Isaac Cook, another son of the captain's, died in 1810.

Another prominent early settler of Lewiston, and one who had much to do with the leading interests of the town, was Benjamin Barton. Major Barton was born in Sussex county, N. J., in 1771. His first visit to the Niagara frontier was in 1787, when he accompanied his father to assist in driving a drove of cattle and sheep, purchased for the use of the English commissariat at Fort Niagara. Subsequently he became a property owner near Geneva, and was married at Canandaigua, in 1792. In 1807 he removed to Lewiston, having become one of the partners in a company under the title of Porter, Barton & Co., which was formed in 1805, for the purpose of carrying on the business of the portage, in connection with a system of transportation by means of vessels on lakes Ontario and Erie. This firm had purchased lands of the State at Lewiston and Schlosser, and leased the upper and lower landings of the portage, with the stipulation that they should "erect docks and storehouses at Schlosser and Lewiston, and surrender them to the State at the termination of the lease, without compensation" other than the profits of the carrying business, of which they were given exclusive control. The provisions of the lease relative to the building of the storehouses and docks were complied with, and considerable money was expended on the improvement of the road. Before the war of 1812, several storehouses at Lewiston had been swept away by ice jams and replaced by others. The business of the company began in 1806, and "was the beginning of the first regular and connected line of transporters on the American side," that ever did business on the lakes. "They were connected with Jonathan Walton & Co., of Schenectady, who sent the property in boats up the Mohawk river and down Wood creek and other waters to Oswego ; thence Matthew McNair carried it over Lake Ontario ; Porter, Barton & Co. took it from Lewiston to Black Rock, where were some small vessels to distribute it up the lakes.

John Latta came to Lewiston four or five years before the war, and built the first tannery there, which he operated till the burning of the settlement. The appearance of the village in 1807 has been thus described by one who saw it : " It contained two small frame and five or six log houses. The ground on either side of Main [now Center] street, for a short distance, was cleared and fenced in, and corn and other grain was grown upon it. There were many old dry trees standing, and thick woods bounded it on the north and south sides." It has been impossible to obtain a complete list of the men doing business in the settlement at an early day, but the following are the names of some of those who were there previous to 1813 : Thomas Hustler, tavern-keeper ; John Latta, tanner ; Caleb W. Raymond and — Hull, blacksmiths ; Joshua Fairbanks and Alexander Millar, merchants ; — Dorman, an apothecary ; Dr. Alvord, the first physician, and Dr. Willard Smith, who came in 1810. A school had been taught by a Scotchman named Watson in 1806, and another the following year by Jonas Harrison, who was the pioneer lawyer, in a log building on Center street. There were two rooms in the house, one of which was occupied as a dwelling, the other as a school-house. Solomon Gilbert was an early settler.

Silas Hopkins settled in the town the first year the lands of the Holland Purchase were offered for sale. He was afterward a colonel in the American army in the war of 1812, and subsequently one of the judges of Niagara county. In 1803 Jesse Beach, who had come into the town in 1801, located two miles east of Lewiston on what is now known as the Ways farm, where he chopped the first timber. Afterward he was in possession of the farm of the late Colonel Dickerson, at Dickersonville, building the first house and blacksmith shop at that place, and having for his customers not only the scattered white settlers, for whom he sharpened plow points, but also the Tuscaroras, whose guns he repaired, as well as their other hunting implements, and making the forging of wrought nails a specialty. John Robinson came from Mifflin, Pa., and settled on the west third of lot No. 11 in 1806. When Asahel Sage moved on to his farm in Lewiston in 1807, he had as his neighbors—and neighbors were appreciated in those days—John Gould, — Bragbill and — Smith, who had settled on the first tier of lots east of the Mile Reserve. There were no settlers further east on the mountain. Sanders, Doty, Goodwin, Hawley and Webster were the pioneers in the neighborhood since known as Sanders Settlement.

Joseph Hewitt came into the town several years before the war. He was originally from Connecticut, but had lived since 1803 in Genesee county, and subsequently in the town of Cambria, until he exchanged farms with William Howell and became the owner of the place on the mountain where his son, J. P. Hewitt, now lives. He was a captain during the war. In 1809 Isaac Colt came from Sussex county, New Jersey; bringing with him his wife and six children, making the trip with two yoke of oxen. For a short time he lived on lot 24, on the military road, but soon took up lot 25, where he opened a tavern. Another comer in this year was Aaron Childs, who, with his wife and four children, two sons and two daughters, came from Livonia, in Livingston county, and settled on the Ridge road, where he kept a tavern for a number of years, finally removing to Niagara, where his son, William Childs, now lives.

Accompanied by his wife and two sons, Thomas and William, the eldest only eleven years old, Achish Pool made the journey from Massachusetts in 1811, arriving in Lewiston October 13th. Their conveyance was a covered wagon, drawn by a yoke of oxen and one horse. They settled at Dickersonville.

The names of most of the more prominent settlers in the town and village prior to the invasion of our frontier by the British and Indians in the winter of 1813, have been given. The town and village have been treated together thus far, for the reason that they were both identified with the events of the early history of Lewiston, and both so closely connected with the scenes of devastation and death which followed the capture of Fort Niagara as to render their separate consideration impossible. After detailing some of the incidents and experiences in the settlement at the landing and along the Ridge road, at the time of the invasion, the town and the village will be considered separately in their re-settlement after the war.

INCIDENTS CONNECTED WITH THE WAR.

Lewiston bore a conspicuous and a memorable part in the war of 1812. The horrors of the invasion by the British and Indians were enacted here in all their barbarous and vengeful cruelty, and Lewiston was the headquarters of General Van Rensselaer and the militia under his command in 1812, there being, not far from the site of the American Hotel, a building where arms and ammunition were stored—a sort of rude arsenal which had been improvised to meet the requirements of the time. A small battery was built on the brow of the mountain, opposite Queenston Heights, in 1812. The selection of the spot and the construction of this work were done by a Colonel or General Gray, an Irishman, who had distinguished himself during the rebellion of 1798, and in whose honor the battery was called Fort Gray. The remains of this fortification are plainly to be seen at the present time.

The incidents of the period beginning a few years before and terminating shortly after the close of the war, which are related in the foregoing paragraphs, are mentioned as nearly as possible in the order in which they occurred.

The British soldiers of the 41st regiment were stationed at Fort George in 1808, and some of them deserted from time to time, seeking safety on the New York side. In order to check this, if possible, the Indians on this side were employed by the British officers to arrest them, carry them back, and deliver them to the English authorities. "I have seen," wrote an early resident of the settlement, "a large number—twenty or more—British soldiers sent over the river, tramping with impunity up and down the main street in Lewiston, inquiring and searching for deserters. The Indians caught two, and took them down past Lewiston in the night, over the river. They were severely flogged, and it was reported that each received five hundred lashes. The feelings of our people became aroused at this insolent mode of capturing deserters, and they determined to stop it. For two or three miles on the road running east of Lewiston the people had ten hours to give notice to each other of trouble. I remember that one bright moonlight night we were all aroused by the blowing of the horns, and men armed came rushing in with the information that the Indians had got some deserters and were coming in with them. The alarm proved false. About the same time Sergeant McDonald, who had charge of some twenty-five men at Queenston, came over with three or four men to hunt for deserters. This party the citizens captured, and were about starting them off to jail at Batavia, when a committee of some of the leading men in Canada came across the river, and an agreement was made with our people that no more soldiers should be sent to our side, or Indians employed to catch deserters." And so the matter rested for some time, the English faithfully keeping their compact with the pioneers of Lewiston.

On the same authority we give the following incident of the days of the embargo, in which Dorman, who has been referred to as an apothecary in the village at an early day, was an interested party. "He had goods and potash that were of great value in Canada, but the embargo prohibited their being taken over. On town meeting day, which was on the first Tuesday of April, when every man in the place was attending the meeting, some twelve miles distant, Dorman had three boats come from Queenston with twenty or twenty-five men, armed with clubs swinging at their wrists. They opened the store, and rolled the ashes and carried the other property down the hill, and took it over the river. Having so much to do, they did not quite get through until the men began to return from the meeting, where they had got information of what was going on." The upshot of the matter was that the project was a failure, as the gang from Canada had to leave a good share of the property, which fell into the hands of the citizens of Lewiston.

The boys of those early days were no less warlike and patriotic than their elders, and their deeds ought not to be lost sight of in connection with other incidents of pioneer life which are here related. That the boys of Lewiston deserved full credit for these qualities will be admitted, when it is understood that several years before the war they began a war with Canada upon their own responsibility. There were less than a dozen of them, but under the leadership of Alexander Millar (son of the pioneer merchant of that name, who came from Scotland, bringing to the settlement one of those regular old-fashioned stocks of merchandise, principally hardware, which is said to have included about everything "from a cambric needle to a beetle ring, with several kegs of powder, shot and lead"), they formed themselves into a military company, young Millar furnishing the powder necessary to fire salutes at sunrise and sunset. "We constructed a regular battery on the bank of the river," wrote Mr. James L. Barton, who was a member of the company, "with embrasures for cannon; went into the woods and chopped down some maple saplings about five or six inches in diameter, cut them into pieces about two and a half feet long, bored them out with a two-inch auger, and put on each end a beetle ring, mounted them on blocks and garnished our battery. We had some eight or ten of them. We had been into the forts at the mouth of the river, and seen the manner of piling up the cannon balls along side of each gun. We then made as many as a barrel full of balls of the clay in the bank, and dried them in the sun, and piled up in proper order by the side of each cannon a sufficient number of balls. Here we went through our military evolutions, mounted guard, and did garrison duty every leisure day we could get. The general rode a small sorrel pony which he called Stirling, but speaking in rather a broad dialect, he pronounced it *Studgel*, and we gave this name to the horse. One afternoon, while we were all present, each with his shot gun on his shoulder, and having much to do that day, we did not get through until dark. About twilight, we discovered a British schooner bound to Queenston, coming up the river under full sail, with her flag flying, and keeping very close to our side to avoid the current. We manned our battery, and when she came opposite the work, peremptorily ordered her to strike her colors and come to. She not obeying our orders, we opened our wooden cannon at her. The mud balls striking the water made considerable splashing; she 'up helm' and ran down the river, and losing that wind did not get up for three or four days." This affair caused considerable excitement in Canada, and soon a deputation came over, representing that "if the officer having charge of the troops along the river to guard the revenue laws, followed up his reckless conduct of firing into unarmed vessels coming up the river on their lawful business and having no design or intention to violate the laws of the United States, some one would be killed, shots would be returned from the other side and serious consequences follow." Upon learning that the belligerent act of which they had complained was simply the sport of a few small boys, the gentlemen from Canada were no less amazed than chagrined, and they returned to their own soil without further threats of war. Ludicrous as this affair was, it was only the foreshadowing of what afterwards occurred, and in which some of those who were members of the company that manned the battery of wooden guns were called to take part.

After the investment of Fort George and Fort Erie, in the spring of 1813, by the United States forces, and while the Canadian frontier between the lakes was in their possession, they established a ferry just below the site of the Lewiston and Queenston suspension bridge. Solomon Gillet, jr., relates that upon one occasion a gang of Canadians gathered at the ferry wharf and attempted to kidnap or harrass such of our people as crossed the ferry, and that a party of small boys, himself among the number, with the assistance of one man, secured a four-pound gun, and dragging it to a place opposite the party of Canadians loaded it with grape shot, and, young Gillet touching it off with a fire brand, discharged it among them, driving them up the bank and into a stone house, not far distant, owned by a man named Hamilton. Reloading the piece, he says, they fired several times, using balls, one of which went through a window, routing them and driving them away; and that the mark made by one of the balls was visible on the inner wall of the house long afterward.

The battle of Queenston was witnessed by the residents of the settlement at the landing, as was also the dastardly conduct of the militia in refusing to cross the river, on the plea that the general had no authority to lead them beyond the boundary of the United States. It is related by early settlers that balls from the heights across the river were fired into the settlement, one of them passing through the corner of a store which stood on the ground now occupied by the residence of Mrs. Amos S. Tryon, demolishing a barrel and spattering its contents about the place, besides otherwise damaging the building and the stock. The British had batteries planted on the side of the heights. Miles Gillet, a son of Solomon Gillet, was one of a number who went across the river with the intention of participating in the fight, not as regular soldiers, but as skirmishers. He hid behind a large stump, and placing his hat on top of it drew the fire of some of the British Indians, which he returned, but with what effect he never knew. After the adventure his hat was riddled with bullet holes. No place on the frontier suffered more severely than Lewiston on the ever-to-be- remembered nineteenth of December, 1813—the deeds and sufferings of that day will be recounted by father to son for generations to come. The attack was after the Indian fashion, a sudden surprise. There was little or no warning. The Indians, preceding by a few minutes a detachment of British soldiers, swarmed out of the woods and commenced an indiscriminate shooting down of flying citizens. Full license was given by Riall to his Indian allies, and the place was sacked, plundered and destroyed. When the work of devastation was completed, the settlement was a perfect desolation. Only a small force, under the command of Major Bennett, was stationed there, and they retreated under fire from the attacking party, with a loss of about half a dozen men.

A small volunteer force had been raised a few days before, composed of whites and friendly Indians, to protect the frontier against the anticipated attack by guarding the river between Lewiston and Five-Mile Meadows; but they were not prepared to resist the sudden onslaught, and, not being together, it being a little too early for their regular drill, they were taken as completely by surprise as the unsuspecting residents of the village. The elder Gillet, who was a member of the company, was coming up the street from Benjamin Barton's, on the top of the hill in the western part of the village, where he had been for cartridges, and making his way along Center street, when he met a party of Indians, at a point a little east of Mrs. Tryon's residence, whom he greeted and passed by, thinking them friendly. Meeting a second party soon afterward, he spoke to them and entered into conversation with some of their number. One of the party, whom he recognized as a white man dressed and painted as an Indian, asked him, "Where are you going with that gun?" "I am going to drill," he replied. "Don't you know the fort has been taken?" asked the other, pointing down the river. Gillet glanced up the street and saw the British forces about the middle of Center street, and before he realized his position he was made a prisoner. In the meantime, his son, Miles Gillet, met the first party of Indians as he came around the corner of a building on the site of Mrs. Tryon's house. He had often heard of the atrocities of the savages to their captives, and had determined never to be taken by them alive; and, without delaying a minute, he raised his musket and shot a chief through the bowels. As soon as he fired, he turned and attempted to escape around the corner of the building, but before he could do so he was shot through the head and died instantly. At this moment his father was being escorted by his captors along the street, and seeing Miles fall, requested that he might be led down the same side of the street. This request was granted, and he had an opportunity to look upon the body of his son, but he did not inform the Indians of the relationship between them.

Among the slain were two men named Tiffany and Finch, Thomas Marsh, Jarvis Gillet, only seven years of age, who was shot while escaping with his mother, and the pioneer physician, Dr. Alvord. The latter had just mounted his horse before his house, at the corner of Sixth and Center streets, and started to ride away, but he was shot before he had gone far. A peddler who lived with the family of Isaac Colt was in the village at the time of the arrival of the invaders. Seeing the people fleeing for the mountain, he brandished a sword which he had picked up, and, pointing toward those who were escaping, said, as if he had been one of the attacking party: "There they go, d—n 'em. I'll catch 'em!" And, brandishing the sword, he escaped, by means of the ruse, to the cover of the woods, where he had a pack of goods concealed. In attempting to save this, his progress was impeded, and he was soon overtaken and killed.

Reuben Lewis lived at the foot of the mountain, at the outskirts of the present village. He had agreed with a neighbor that he would never be taken alive by the Indians; and when he was attacked, he fought until he was wounded, and fell down behind a log. Unable to stand, he still managed to load, and continued to fire until the Indians came up to him and dispatched him with their knives or tomahawks. This was one of the most desperate hand-to-hand conflicts of that day. Marsh, who lived on the mountain near the Hewitt property, tried to save his life by claiming protection as a British subject; but he was shot.

The killed at and near Lewiston numbered nearly a dozen, who when found were all scalped except one, and he was decapitated. Among the bodies was that of a boy (probably that of Jarvis Gillet), stripped and scalped.

The Tuscarora village shared the fate of Lewiston. "The Ridge road," says Turner, "presented one of the harshest features of war and invasion. The inhabitants upon the frontier, *en masse*, were retreating eastward, men, women and children, the Tuscarora Indians having a prominent position in the fight. The residents upon the ridge who had not got the start of the main body fell in with it as it approached them. There was a small arsenal at the first four corners west of Howell's creek, a log building containing a number of barrels of powder, several hundred stand of arms and a quantity of fixed ammunition. Making a stop there, the more timid were for firing the magazine and continuing the retreat. The braver counsels prevailed to a small extent. They made sufficient demonstrations to turn back a few Indian scouts who had followed up the retreat to plunder such as fell in the rear. The mass made no halt at the arsenal, but pushed on in an unbroken column, until they arrived at Forsythe's, where they divided, a part taking the Lewiston road, and seeking asylums in Genesee county and over the river, and a part along the Ridge road and off from it in the new settlements of what is now Orleans and Monroe counties, and in what is now Wayne and the north part of Ontario counties. All kinds of vehicles were put in requisition. It was a motley throng, flying from the torch and the tomahawk of an invading foe, with hardly a show of a military organization to cover their retreat."

The above general description of the scenes of terror on the mountain is so comprehensive that but few incidents are deemed necessary in this connection. John Robinson, living three miles east of the village on the Ridge road, being apprised of the invasion about nine o'clock, hastily gathered together such useful articles as he could conveniently collect, and placing them on a sled drawn by cattle carried them to the site of the village of Pekin. Meanwhile Mrs. Robinson took the children and crossed the mountain to a place south of the Indian reservation, where she remained for three days concealed in the woods before she was found by her husband, who, not finding her sooner, thought her dead. Returning to the house after the removal of the goods, Robinson was surprised by a party of Indians and captured, but subsequently escaped and found his family as above described.

At the time of the invasion Lathrop Cook was an invalid, having only recently had one of his legs amputated. "He was laid on an ox-sled," says the History of the Holland Purchase, "and accompanied by his brother, the late Hon. Bates Cook. When they had proceeded but a few miles on the ridge, a scout of five Indians overtook them and ordered a halt. Bates Cook seized a gun that was lying upon a sled directly behind them, fired and shot one of the Indians through the neck. He fell from his horse, jumped upon his feet, and after running about fifteen rods fell and died. Mr. Cook, having no further means of defense, ran, the Indians making two ineffectual shots at him in his retreat." Some Tuscaroras, hearing the report of Bates Cook's gun, hastened to the spot and repulsed the British Indians, and the sled, with its intrepid though crippled passenger, passed on in safety. A paper addressed to the Indian agent at Niagara was found on the person of the dead Indian, stating that the bearer, who was an Ottawa warrior, was worthy to be entrusted with any mission requiring daring and fidelity.

Aaron Childs, a settler on the ridge, was on guard at the Meadows the night before. Seeing the approach of the fleeing settlers, Mrs. Childs ran out and inquired for her husband. She was told that all were killed on the river, and for some time believed him dead; but he finally appeared uninjured, and they made good their escape. The farthest advance of the enemy was to the eastern boundary of Hopkins's marsh. There is a lone grove there, where a teamster is buried who was shot by a party of Indians, who overtook him at that place while he was conveying some goods away from Lewiston.

A number of persons were made prisoners, and kept in captivity during a longer or shorter period. Solomon Gillet was taken to Montreal, and held there a prisoner until the early part of the following March. All that time he slept on a bare stone floor, and was obliged to use his shoes for a pillow.

During the following summer, the British being in possession of Fort Niagara, small marauding parties, generally Indians, occasionally visited the settlers who had ventured back to their homes in the neighborhood. An Indian who was passing through the woods, one day, came out upon the Ridge road at the house of Sparrow S. Sage, about three miles east from Lewiston. Mr. Sage was absent, and his wife and another woman were in the house unprotected. The Indian made them prisoners and started away with them in the direction of the fort. Before they had gone far, the companion of Mrs. Sage made her escape, and finding Mr. Sage, she informed him of his wife's captivity. He started in pursuit, and overtaking the Indian he wounded him seriously and effected the rescue of his wife.

In 1816 a contractor with a number of men in his employ was engaged in quarrying stone on the river bank above the village. For some reason the workmen became displeased with a British officer who had command of a small detachment of soldiers on Queenston Heights, and to annoy him, every time he sounded his bugle, the sound would be imitated as nearly as possible on a tin horn by some of the men among the rocks. This made him so indignant that it was reported that he threatened in case the insult, as he called it, was repeated many more times he would fire cannon shot into the village. Whether or not this report was true is uncertain, but it was the cause of a brisk business to the man who had a little tin shop in the settlement, for all the boys, many of the men and not a few of the women had little tin horns made, with which to blow back defiance to the choleric military man across the water. No serious consequences ensued.

Among incidents of pioneer life those of wild animals have always held a favorite place. The wolves used to howl in the village; there were so many that they were a great annoyance to the settlers in all parts of the town killing calves, sheep and other domestic animals. Frequently they would be heard about the houses at night and the men would fire guns to frighten them away. Sometimes bears were seen, and there were many panthers and wild cats; deer were plenty, as well as other wild game.

SETTLEMENT AFTER THE WAR.

Some few of the residents of the town who had been driven out by the invasion ventured back in the summer of 1814. In 1815 many came, and nearly all had resumed their old habitations, and begun the disheartening work of retrieving their fallen fortunes, before the close of the year 1816. Isaac Colt, who received a wound in the leg at the time of the raid, returned with his family, and bought lots 24 of the Mile Reserve and 30 of the Holland Purchase. Aaron Childs, John Robinson, Silas Hopkins, Achish Pool, Joseph Hewitt and their families and others had come back before 1816, and there were several new settlers at that time, among them the father and grandfather of Arthur Gray, with whom he came, in 1815, and Richard Ayres, in 1816, on the Ridge road. Jairus Rose, — De Foe, — Springsteen and the Carneys went in at and west of Pekin after the war. The Carneys and the Reynolds family were the first settlers at Pekin. Bliss, the Earls, Dr. Orton, Bridge, Beamer and Wilson were first between the ridge and mountain west of Scott's, not long after.

Between 1815 and 1825 many settlers came, among whom were G. P. Nichols and Andrew A. Farley. Nichols had formerly lived in Vermont. In 1816 he settled in the county, at Niagara Falls, and came to Lewiston in 1819. Farley, who was a native of New Jersey, came in 1823, and Thomas Balmer in 1825. Among those who came between 1825 and 1835 were Abel White, in 1826; the Pletchers, in 1829; and Peter Spickerman, in 1835. Between 1835 and 1845 the following were some of the prominent settlers: In 1836, Joseph Shippy, Sanford White and John Cleghorn; in 1838, James Buckley; in 1841, Erastus Downer; in 1842, Charles McConnell and Reuben M. Doty; in 1845, Lewis W. Hull and Hartwell Haywood. The town had by this become quite thickly populated. The interest which is always felt in those who are pioneers in any community does not attach to those who settle at a later day, and for this reason only a few of those who came into the town after 1845 will be mentioned, and no attempt will be made to continue the list so as to embrace even the more prominent of those who have come into the town during the past few years. In 1848 Gideon Shippy came; in 1852, Peter Munch and Simpson Moyer; in 1854, John Ganantz; in 1855, William J. Moss; 1857, David Pletcher. In the account of the early settlement of the town, attention was given to the location of the pioneers, in order to show what parts were first occupied. The changes since then have been so numerous that it has not been thought advisable to record the numbers of the lots where the later settlers located. Some of them bought out earlier residents, who have since moved away, and others chopped, burned, plowed, sowed and improved new land in different parts of the town, re-enacting some of the more peaceful scenes of the pioneer days.

DESCRIPTION AND CIVIL HISTORY.

Lewiston was formed from Cambria, February 27th, 1818. It is the central town of the western tier, being bounded on the north and south by Porter and Wilson and Niagara and Wheatfield, and west and east by the Niagara river and Cambria. The mountain ridge extends through it, dividing it into two nearly equal parts. The surface is broken and rolling along the base of the ridge; elsewhere it is level. Gill creek, Six-mile creek, and several smaller streams rise within its limits. The soil is sandy loam, and very productive for fruit and all kinds of grain. The assessed valuation of real estate in the town is $1,910,624; of personal property, $71,150; the amount of all taxes is $10,810.17, $1,319.57 of this amount being for the maintenance of schools. The total number of acres of land in the town is 22,231½. The number of school districts is twelve. The town was named in honor of Governor Lewis. The population in 1875 was 2,823.

The act setting off the town of Lewiston reads as follows:

"Be it enacted, by the people of the State of New York, represented in Senate and Assembly, that from and after the first day of April next, all that part of the town of Cambria lying west of a line beginning at the northwest corner of section number thirty-two, township fourteen, in the eighth range of townships, thence running southerly on the west line of said section thirty-two in a direct line to the south bounds of said town of Cambria, be and is hereby erected into a separate town by the name of Lewiston, and the first town meeting in the said town of Lewiston shall be held at the house of Sparrow Sage; and that the remainder of the said town of Cambria shall be and remain a separate town by the name of Cambria, and the next town meeting shall be held at the house of John Gould.

"And be it further enacted, that as soon as may be after the first day of May next, the supervisors and overseers of the poor of the respective towns of Lewiston and Cambria, on notice being first given for that purpose by the said supervisors, shall meet and divide the poor and money belonging to the said towns, according to the last tax list." Dated February 27th, 1818.

The first town meeting was held, in accordance with the provisions of the above act, April 7th, 1818, being presided over by Rufus Spalding and Gideon Frisbee, justices of the peace. The following list of town officials was elected: Supervisor, Rufus Spalding; town clerk, Oliver Grace; assessors, Benjamin Barton, Amos M. Kidder, and William Miller; highway commissioners, John Beach, Aaron Childs, and Reuben Reynolds; overseers of poor, Jacob Townsend and Arthur Gray; school commissioners, Joshua Fairbanks, William Miller, and Rufus Spalding; inspectors of common schools, Amos M. Kidder, Reuben Reynolds, and William Hotchkiss; constable and collector, Eleazor Daggett; sealer of weights and measures, Amos S. Tryon; and eleven overseers of highways, one for each of the eleven road districts into which the town was divided at that meeting.

It was voted that hogs should "be free commoners when hampered with good and sufficient yokes;" that "the sum of five dollars be paid for each bear scalp taken in the town," and that "the sum of two hundred dollars be raised for road money, and seventy-five for poor money." The present supervisor and town clerk are William P. Mentz and Thomas P. Scovell.

SUPERVISORS.

Rufus Spalding was elected supervisor April 7th, 1818. Benjamin Barton was chosen at the next town meeting, and re-elected annually until 1828. On one occasion he resigned, and at special town meeting, February 10th, 1823, Nathaniel Leonard was chosen to fill out the term. Jacob Townsend held the office three successive years, being first elected April 1st, 1828. Sheldon C. Townsend was elected April 4th, 1831, and Lathrop Cook at the next town meeting. Alexander Dickerson served for the next eight terms, and Sherburne B. Piper the succeeding four, being first elected in April, 1842. Benjamin Hewitt was elected in 1846 and 1849, and Seymour Scovell in the intervening years. In 1850 Arthur Gray, jr., was chosen; in 1854, John L. Whitman; 1852 and 1853, Andrew Robinson; 1851, Leander K. Scovell; 1855, John Robinson; 1856, Reuben H. Boughton; 1857, 1859 and 1860, Franklin Spalding; 1858, Benjamin Hewitt; 1861, Isaac C. Cook, who served the next term also, there being 216 votes each for him and Moses Bairsto and no election. The latter was elected for the next three terms, and served a fourth, there being a tie vote of 192 each for him and Silas S. Hopkins in 1866. Hopkins was next elected, then Bairsto. Sherburne B. Piper was chosen at the election of 1869, and those of the next five years. William J. Moss was elected in 1875, and has been annually re-elected since.

SANBORN AND DICKERSONVILLE.

SANBORN is a small but flourishing village in the southeastern corner of Lewiston, on the line of the Central railroad, which crosses that part of the town. It contains two stores, a hotel, a grist-mill, a saw-mill, two wagon shops, two blacksmith shops, a drug store and other business buildings, including a cheese factory, a warehouse and the depot. The first settler there was Seth Lyon, who took up lot 33, in March, 1826.

Rev. E. C. Sanborn came in 1846. He was a Methodist clergyman, and had preached in different parts of the county for the previous nine years. Rev. Griffin Smith came into the town in 1863, and lived at Pekin. In 1864 he associated himself with Lee R. Sanborn, a son of Rev. E. C. Sanborn, for the purchase of land where the village now stands. The purchase embraced ninety acres, lying on both sides of the railroad. The following year the tract was divided, Mr. Sanborn retaining about thirty-five acres, Rev. Mr. Smith ten, and the balance being deeded to Ryan Smith, a brother of the latter. The portion going to the Smiths was fenced in as farm land, and Mr. Sanborn, in pursuance of a plan which had been previously formed, laid his portion out into village lots and offered them for sale, John Dutton being the first purchaser.

Since that time the village has had a steady and a healthy growth. Lee R. Sanborn built a saw-mill in 1854. It was burned July 3d, 1861, and immediately rebuilt on a larger scale. The post-office was established between 1856 and 1858. The first postmaster was John Starr; the present is Mrs. E. S. G. Dutton. Mr. Lee R. Sanborn held the office from 1861 to 1877. Sanborn Union Hall was erected in 1865.

The Sanborn Cheese Factory was built by a stock company in 1867. It is a wood building, 35 by 70 feet, three stories high, with a stone basement, and is one of the largest manufactories of the kind in this part of the State, having two vats, heated by steam, and fifteen screw-power presses. The basement is used for manufacturing purposes, the upper floors being intended for curing rooms. E. W. Barber, who owns a controlling interest, has managed the business for the past four years. In 1876 the product of the factory amounted to 56,000 pounds of cheese, and in 1877 to about 45,000 pounds.

In 1868 Mr. Sanborn built a grist-mill, about one hundred rods distant from the steam saw-mill, and for some time it was run by a cable from the latter. It was purchased early in 1875 by John Mower, who put in a new 35 horse-power steam engine and otherwise improved it; and being a man of energy and perseverance he has succeeded in building up a good reputation for the mill, which has a large patronage, there being no other mill within a circuit of ten miles.

The warehouse on the railroad track was erected by Mr. Sanborn in 1869. It is now owned by John Douchy.

The M. E. church of Sanborn was organized February 8th, 1868. Rev. George Kittenger was the first preacher. Rev. Messrs. E. M. Buck, L. T. Foote, R. C. Leek, — Hammond, James Hill and A. A. Craw have officiated since, the latter being the present pastor. The church edifice was completed in the autumn of 1873, at a cost of $6,000. The present membership is eighty-five.

In the northeast portion of the town is an enterprising settlement known as DICKERSONVILLE, which name it received in honor of Colonel Alexander Dickerson, who settled there at an early day and kept a tavern. The settlement contains a Methodist church, a school-house, a store and post-office, several shops of different kinds and a number of dwellings.

Colonel Dickerson came into the town in 1811, and lived for a time on the river road, afterward removing to Dickersonville. He was born in 1790, in New Jersey, and died at home October 31st, 1858.

PEKIN is situated at the eastern boundary of the town, half in Lewiston and half in Cambria. A sketch of its history and present condition will be found in the history of the town of Cambria.

SEMINARY OF OUR LADY OF ANGELS.

In 1855 Rev. J. J. Lynch, C. M., present archbishop of Toronto, conceived the idea of erecting, on the shores of Lake Erie, an institution in which the young should be carefully trained, and in which, also, those whose purpose it was to study for the Catholic ministry might be properly educated. Various causes, however, induced the abandonment of this site, and the consequence was that the place whereon now stands the Seminary of Our Lady of Angels was chosen instead. Previous to this, in the same year, 1855, the Seminary of Our Lady of Angels, after having been removed from its location on Lake Erie, was, for a while, situated in the city of Buffalo. There Father Lynch filled the office of president, and the students were in number but sixteen.

In Buffalo the Seminary of Our Lady of Angels continued its mission until May 1st, 1857. Father Lynch, not satisfied with the meagre pecuniary returns from the institution as then located, conceived the idea of its removal to the vicinity of Niagara Falls. Generous persons in Buffalo assisted him to the means with which to purchase an old roadside inn that stood on the highest point of Mont Eagle Ridge, midway between Suspension Bridge and Lewiston, which was transformed into the Seminary of Our Lady of Angels, and in May, 1857, twenty students entered its walls, Father Lynch being the first president. In the government of the institution there were associated Father Monaghan, who died about one year ago, and Father Smith, at present in New Orleans, La.

Yearly the number of students increased, and on the 20th of April, 1863, a charter was obtained. The power of conferring degrees was granted by the Legislature. About this time, or prior to it, Rev. R. E. V. Rice, C. M., assumed the management. He had already, in various capacities, given evidence of possessing marked ability. His predecessors in the office were, besides Father Lynch (in the meantime elevated to the episcopacy), Fathers Reilly, Asmuth, and Smith. A new era of prosperity seemed to be dawning, when, on December 5th, 1864, the building was almost entirely destroyed by fire. In the flames perished Thomas Hopkins, a theological student of Brooklyn, N. Y. Upon this mishap studies were discontinued, and the collegians returned to their homes. Active measures were immediately taken for the building of the newly designed seminary. The late Pope Pius IX. contributed $1,000, and gave the institution its name.

At the re-opening of studies in September, 1865, one hundred and fifty names were entered on the rolls. At this time only one wing of the present building was ready for occupancy, and the insufficiency of accommodation pointed out the necessity of still further enlargement. In 1866, a main building, 214 feet front, was projected, and in the following year it was completed. In 1869, another wing was added. During all this time Father Rice officiated as president and superior, and in the spring of 1874 he planned the erection of a college chapel, 120 by 78 feet, which is now in process of construction.

The faculty, in the spring of 1878, comprised Very Rev. R. E. V. Rice, C. M., president; Rev. P. V. Kavanagh, C. M., vice-president; Rev. M. J. Kircher, C. M., librarian and assistant superior; Rev. Felix Guedry, C. M.; Rev. J. T. Landry, C. M., prefect of studies; Rev. M. Cavanaugh, C. M., treasurer; Rev. E. J. Lefevre, C. M., director of seminarians; Rev. P. Carroll, C. M., Rev. J. J. V. Talley, C. M., assistant director of seminarians; Rev. B. V. Driscoll, C. M., prefect of discipline; Rev. E. M. Hopkins, C. M.; Rev. C. J. Eckles, C. M.; Rev. N Redmond, C. M., assistant prefect of discipline; Rev. L. I. Miller.

In March, 1878, owing to failing health, Father Rice was obliged to take a leave of absence. He died on Monday, July 29th, 1878, near Dublin. On his departure Rev. P. V. Kavanagh, C. M., was appointed superior. As his assistant Rev. M. J. Kircher, C. M., was delegated. Up to the present, success has attended the workings of the new administration. The college has six literary societies, the same number of athletic associations and a perfect gymnasium. The library contains 7,000 volumes, and the laboratory and museum are complete. The average number of students since the establishment of the seminary has been one hundred and seventy-five. The students at the college begun the publication of the *Niagara Index* in 1878. Its original title was *Niagara's Tribute*, which was changed to *Index Niagarensis* in 1874. Circulation 958.

THE VILLAGE OF LEWISTON.

The location of the village was selected in 1798, by Joseph Elicott, at the request of Simeon De Witt, then surveyor-general of the State. It was first surveyed into lots by Joseph Annin, in 1805. In 1822 it was chartered. It is situated on the Niagara river, at the base of the mountain ridge, at the head of navigation from Lake Ontario, and on the line of the Lake Ontario Shore division of the Rome, Watertown and Ogdensburg Railroad, and the Lewiston and Niagara Falls branch of the New York Central and Hudson River Railroad, of which it is the terminus. Two telegraph lines pass through the village, the Montreal and the Western Union. A daily line of steamers runs to Toronto, Hamilton and other

BROCKS MONUMENT   NIAGARA RIVER   SEMINARY OF OUR LADY OF

ANGELS, SUSPENSION BRIDGE N.Y. 2 MILES FROM SUS'P BRIDGE

points on Lake Ontario, connecting with the steamers on the St. Lawrence and with the regular passenger trains at Lewiston; and there is convenient communication with interior villages by lines of daily stages.

The principal business interests of the village are the fruit and grain trade, peaches, apples and barley being the principal products finding a market there; a considerable commerce in stone, which exists in large quantities in the land at the outskirts of the place, near the base of the mountain; and the marketing of fish, which are caught in great numbers in the river, by means of nets and fishing machines.

The causes of education and religion are in an advanced condition, there being in the village three churches and a good public school. The amount of the Lewiston school fund is $5,600, which is invested in bonds and mortgages yielding $392 interest, payable semi-annually, which is appropriated to the support of common schools in the village of Lewiston, under the direction of the commissioners of the Lewiston school fund. The present commissioners are Messrs. Bairsto, Josiah Tryon and Oliver P. Scovell.

AFTER THE WAR.

The history of the village from its earliest occupation by white men to its destruction by the British and Indians, in the winter of 1813, has been included in the early history of the town. The only structures left standing at the time of the raid were a log stable belonging to Solomon Gillet, and the walls of the stone house of Jonas Harrison, which he built in 1810 and in which he lived at that time. The inside was completely burned out of the building, and the walls remained only because they were not combustible. They now form part of a house on the north side of Center street, owned by J. Haskell.

The village did not grow very fast for some time after the war. The warehouses of the Portage Company were rebuilt, and transportation between Lewiston and Schlosser resumed, after an interval of about three or four years. Other business enterprises were resumed or introduced at different times.

The following is a list of the tavern-keepers in the village after the war, with the date at which each began business, as nearly as can be now ascertained: Thomas Hustler, who returned as soon as safety permitted; —— Hart, 1816; Josiah Shepard, opposite the present brick store of A. S. Bairsto & Co., 1817; Sol Hersey, 1823; Samuel Chubbuck, at the river side, 1824, and Thomas Kelsey, in the "Kelsey Tavern," in the same year; the Frontier House, built by Benjamin and Samuel Barton, opened in 1826; American Hotel, at the boat landing, built by N. Cornell, and opened about 1850; Exchange Hotel, by J. T. Beardsley, 1865. The merchants were: Joshua Fairbanks, who returned; Amos S. Tryon, 1815; Sol Hersey, and Crosier & Parish, 1816; Fairbanks & Thompson, 1817; Calvin Hotchkiss, 1818; Townsend, Bronson & Co., 1819; John Wyner, druggist, 1820; N. Tryon & Co., 1823; Norton Tiebout and L. & A. Woodruff, 1825; Joseph A. Norton, 1826; William Hotchkiss, F. J. Hotchkiss and Guy Reynolds, about 1830; Hugh Frazer, 1838. Miscellaneous: Tailor, Josiah Tryon, 1825; blacksmiths, Harvey Shepard, 1817 or 1818; Leonard Shepard, 1823; Alfred Twy, about 1835; tanner, Samuel Macklin, 1820; butcher, ——Balmer, 1816. Benjamin Barton was one of the earliest, if not the first postmaster.

PHYSICIANS AND ATTORNEYS, PAST AND PRESENT.

The first physician was Dr. Alvord. He was in the settlement when Dr. Willard Smith came, in 1810. They became partners, which relation was continued until the death of Dr. Alvord, at the time of the invasion. After the war Dr. Smith came back and carried on the practice, having been an army surgeon during the struggle, by appointment of the governor. At the time of the battle of Queenston, many wounded soldiers were brought across the river to him for surgical treatment. His ride was a very long one, extending, when he was summoned to counsel with other physicians, to Buffalo and Batavia, and to points remote from the river in Canada. He died in 1835.

Dr. Frisbee came next after Dr. Smith, and they were partners. Dr. Hill came to the village quite early, and removed to Detroit in 1834. Dr. William McCollum came from Porter in 1834, and entered into partnership with Dr. Smith, continuing the ride after the death of the latter, and removed to Lockport about 1845. Dr. Ambrose Thomas, who was the pioneer practitioner at Niagara Falls, took up his residence in Lewiston about 1837 or 1838, and remained till 1854 or 1855. In 1843 Dr. George P. Eddy, sen., came. He subsequently removed to Niagara Falls, where he died in the fall of 1877. About 1854 Dr. Cole came. Dr. Whittaker was a partner of his. They both went to Buffalo about 1856. Other physicians who have practiced at Lewiston in the past were Doctors Coon, Cresswell, Walch and Graves. There were still others, whose names cannot now be obtained.

There are three physicians in the village at the present time. They are Dr. Edward Smith, a son of Willard Smith, a student with Dr. McCollum and the oldest resident practitioner; Dr. George P. Eddy, jr., a son of the late Dr. George P. Eddy, and Dr. Milton Robinson, a son of John Robinson, an early pioneer in the town.

The first attorney in the place was Jonas Harrison, who came before the war. Judge William Hotchkiss settled in the year 1810, and remained till his death in 1848. Bates Cook is said to have been a student with Jonas Harrison. Zina Calvin was at the time a law partner of Judge Hotchkiss. Hon. Sherburne B. Piper, a native of New Hampshire, at this time the only attorney in the village, came to Lewiston in 1833 and has been a resident since. Among other lawyers who have practiced in the place at different times were Judge Birdsall, James H. Paige, Leonard Bennett, John V. Berry and Judge Horatio Stow, for some years a partner of Cook and afterwards recorder of the city of Buffalo. Judge Noah Davis, of New York, and the poet Saxe were at different times law students in Lewiston.

SCHOOLS.

One of the first enterprises in which the citizens of the village engaged after peace was declared was the erection of a stone school-house, a work for which some preparation had been made before the war. It was finished and a school opened in it by a man named Jonas Chamberlain in 1816. It stood inside of the plat now known as the "academy square." The present commodious school building was erected about 1844 or 1845, to replace an old brick school-house, which had been erected on the present public school lot, to supersede the stone one finished after the war.

The Lewiston Academy was incorporated April 17th, 1828. The building committee consisted of Benjamin Barton, William Hotchkiss, David M. Smith and Robert Fleming, and through their efforts the building was completed some time during the year of incorporation. The proceeds of the ferry had been appropriated for the establishment and maintenance of the school, by an act of Legislature in April, 1826. The first principal is said to have been Rev. David M. Smith. The following named gentlemen, among others, afterward had charge of the institution: Jacob H. Quimby, Sullivan Caverno, Sherburne B. Piper, Moses H. Fitts, Rev. Robert G. McGonegal, Seymour B. Phelps and a Mr. Close. The school enjoyed a successful career for a number of years. It received it first serious blow at the time of the Navy Island war, many pupils having come from Canada, who were now withdrawn in consequence of the difficulties growing out of that affair. After that date it had a fitful existence for quite a length of time. But its last financial dependence was cut off by the discontinuance of the ferry in 1851, in consequence of the erection of the ill-fated suspension bridge, and it was finally abandoned as an academy.

MEANS OF COMMUNICATION.

From the year 1832, when the steamer "United States" came out, the number of vessels multiplied and steamboat business increased, with an advantageous influence on the general prosperity of the village and surrounding country, creating a market for wood and agricultural products.

Previous to the completion of the Lockport and Niagara Falls Railroad, in 1836, the only mode of travel to and from Lewiston, in connection with the few steamboats that were running on the river before that time, was by stage. The business of staging was inaugurated here in 1816, when a line was established over the ridge between Rochester and Lewiston. It is said that as many as eight stages arrived at Lewiston daily. They were heavy, old-fashioned vehicles, drawn by four horses. The business often changed hands, and there were, at various times, a number of stage proprietors. Among them was Samuel Barton, who bought of Jeremiah Sherwood stage routes, with all facilities for carrying on the business, between Lewiston and Gaines, connecting with the Rochester stages, and between Lewiston and Niagara Falls, to connect with those from Buffalo. This business Barton controlled till 1833, when he disposed of it to E. S. Butler; and after that it several times changed hands, until the business was replaced by railway facilities.

The first survey for the Lewiston and Junction horse railroad, to connect with the Lockport and Niagara Falls railroad, was made in 1835, and its construction was begun soon afterward. The company, which was known as the Lewiston Railroad Company, embraced among its members the following gentlemen, who were its incorporators: Bates Cook, Jacob Townsend, Oliver Grace, Leonard Shephard, Joshua Fairbanks, Calvin Hotchkiss, Amos S. Tryon, Seymour Scovell, Benjamin Barton, and Lathrop Cook.

Leaving the river bank at the steamboat landing, on the site of the American Hotel, the road followed the course of the river to a point a little above Tuscarora street, where it turned, crossing that street again, and thence up Fourth street to Center, which it followed to its intersection with Portage, from which place it crossed the farms now owned by Michael Burke, L. K. Scovell, Mrs. I. C. Cook, L. W. Hull and the Miller place, the junction being on the farm of Robert Cleghorn, about two and a half miles from the landing. The circuitous route was chosen to avoid high ground. It was finished some time in the early part of 1837, and business begun June 14th of that year. According to a report made to the Secretary of State March 15th, 1838, as certified to by Bates Cooke, the cost of the road and its outfit was $27,023.04.

The cars were odd-shaped affairs, being open at the sides, and some of them having a structure on top, somewhat smaller than the roof and presenting the appearance of small observatories, for the accommodation of such passengers as desired a good view of the village in passing through from the landing to the junction, or *vice versa*. Two or three horses, driven tandem, would draw the cars up singly, and they were allowed to run down under control of the brakes in trains of two or three. At times excursion parties would call more cars into requisition, as many as ten or twelve being employed, and the trains, on such occasions, are said to have presented a pleasing sight, loaded with merrymakers, the clatter of the wheels almost drowned by the music of a band, which was invariably placed on the front car.

About 1851, when the Rochester and Niagara Falls Railroad was built, the charter of the horse railroad was sold to the Buffalo and Niagara Falls Railroad Company, the road being no longer necessary to the convenience of the public. In 1850 it was leased to Messrs. Bouton, Hotchkiss & Ways, who operated it until its abandonment. From April 1st to December 1st, 1850, 46,493 passengers went over the road. About one-fouth of this number were emigrants, and three-fourths of the others were southern travelers going from Niagara Falls to Montreal and back. The grade of the "old horse railroad," as it is now referred to, is still to be seen in many places.

The construction of the Lewiston and Queenston suspension bridge was begun in 1849, under direction of the Lewiston Suspension Bridge Company and the Queenston Suspension Bridge Company. The first board of directors of the Lewiston company were: James Van Cleve, president, and Joseph E. Ways, Calvin Hotchkiss, Seymour Scovell, and William Fitch, directors. E. V. A. Hotchkiss was secretary and treasurer. The engineer having charge of the work was Edward W. Serrell. The structure was completed at a cost of $56,000, and opened for business in the spring of 1851. The distance between the towers was 1,042 feet, and the length of the carriageway 850 feet, there being five cables on each side. The guys having some of them been removed to admit the passage of ice, the bridge was weakened to such an extent that in January, 1864, the woodwork of the carriage and foot ways was destroyed by a storm. During the day upon which this occurred a boy, whose parents resided in Canada, but who was at work in Lewiston, went over to Canada on a short visit to his parents. Just before the bridge was destroyed, the boy proposed starting for his place in Lewiston. His father was to accompany him, and as they reached the bridge it was swinging to and fro over the foaming waters. The boy hesitated a moment, but as this motion of the bridge was not unusual, they stepped upon the bridge and proceeded to cross. When they had reached the middle of the bridge, its motion rapidly increased, which caused them to fear for their safety; when the father turned around and the boy went ahead, both running at the top of their speed for the shores. They had just time to reach them, when the noble structure was borne down by the severe gale. The want of this important work seriously affects the business of Lewiston and the surrounding country, and it is said that the delay in making the necessary repairs has been caused by lack of co-operation on the part of the Canadian company; but at the present time negotiations are in progress looking to its reconstruction at no distant day.

BUSINESS ENTERPRISES.

The period beginning about 1845 and ending twenty years later seems to have been prolific of enterprising projects for the advancement of the business prosperity of the village. In the year 1851 the Legislature granted a charter for the construction of the "Lewiston Water Works," having reference to a small canal for the purpose of bringing water from the Niagara river above the falls to a convenient point on the brow of the mountain near Lewiston, for the purposes of manufacture. The canal was to have been twelve feet wide and four feet deep, having a current of five miles an hour, and a fall of two hundred feet at Lewiston. Mr. Blackwell, a competent engineer, was employed to make surveys, having completed which he offered to construct the works for $175,000. Money being dear at that time, such a sum could not be easily raised by the citizens of the village, and the project failed.

The business men and residents of Lewiston were active in all attempts to secure the construction of the Niagara Ship Canal, and to them is to be ascribed the credit of projecting and pushing forward more than one of the numerous efforts which have failed for one reason or another in the past; and there are some among their number who still predict the ultimate consummation of this splendid scheme, to the incalculable benefit of—not Lewiston, simply—but the whole frontier, with a far-reaching commercial influence, that will be felt in all parts of the Union.

In 1824 an association of gentlemen built a large stone steam-power grist-mill on the bank of the river at the foot of Center street. It had only been completed and in successful operation about a year when it was accidentally burned. A water-power grist-mill was afterwards erected on the river bank between the steamboat landing and the suspension bridge, which was carried away by an ice flood in 1844.

DAMAGE BY FIRE AND FLOOD.

There have been several fires in the village which did more or less damage to property, one of the first notable ones being the destruction of the steam flouring mill in 1826. The most sweeping fire occurred about 1867, burning the Lewiston Hotel, where it originated, and all of the buildings between that point and the tunnel on the railroad, including the cabinet shop and dwelling of Lemuel Cook, on the west side of the hotel, and the dwellings beyond. One man was burned to death. A fire company, with a hand engine, was organized about 1838 or 1839, which went out of existence after a time.

Much property has been destroyed by the ice at different times. The first ice flood doing any considerable damage since the war, occurred in 1819. In 1844 there was another very destructive ice jam, which, like others that preceded it, did much to injure the prosperity of the place by the taking away of warehouses, wharves and other property. The water-power grist-mill on the bank below the ferry was swept away at that time.

SOCIETIES OF LEWISTON.

The first lodge of Free and Accepted Masons in Niagara county was instituted at Lewiston, August 8th, 1822, under the name of Niagara Lodge, No. 345. William King was the first master, and Oliver Grace the first secretary. The successive masters were chosen as follows: December 11th, 1823, John A. Webber; December 2d, 1824, Timothy Shaw; December 14th, 1826, Gustavus N. Pope. At a communication held February 20th, 1823, it was "resolved unanimously that the petition of the brethren of the village of Lockport for a charter of a lodge to be held at that place, be recommended to the Grand Lodge of the State." There is no record of any meeting of this lodge after May 10th, 1827.

Lewiston Frontier Lodge, No. 132, met for the first time April 5th, 1848. Caleb W. Raymond was the original master, James H. Paige being secretary. J. T. Beardsley was master in 1849, A. Thomas in 1850, A. Lyon in 1851, and J. T. Beardsley in 1852 and 1853. This lodge was removed to Niagara Falls in 1853, and the name changed to Niagara Frontier Lodge, No. 132.

Sacarisa Lodge, No. 256, I. O. O. F., of Lewiston was

organized November 19th, 1846, with the following charter members: R. H. Boughton, S. B. Piper, S. P. Babcock, O. Grace, J. E. Ways, M. Randall, L. K. Scovell, J. D. Byrne, and Elias Ettenheimer. The officers were S. B. Piper, N. G.; R. H. Boughton, V. G.; M. Randall, secretary. The lodge ceased to exist September 24th, 1857. It was re-instated March 27th, 1872, as Sacarisa Lodge, No. 307, I. O. O. F., with L. K. Scovell, M. H. Bacon, B. Cornell, J. E. Ways and M. Robinson as charter members. The first officers were L. K. Scovell, N. G.; M. H. Bacon, V. G.; B. Cornell, secretary. The present officers are: N. G., James Buckley; V. G., H. M. Smith; secretary, J. H. Childs. The regular sessions of the lodge are held every Thursday evening in Hewitt's block, the present membership being fifty-six. Lewiston also has a flourishing lodge of the Ancient Order of United Workmen.

CHURCH HISTORY.

The First Religious Society of Lewiston was formed June 12th, 1817. The trustees were: Erastus Park, Josiah Shepard, Aaron Childs, Augustus Porter, Rufus Spalding, Elijah Ransom and Benjamin Barton. A meeting was held June 25th, for the purpose of choosing officers of the society, which resulted in the election of Amos S. Tryon as clerk; Bates Cook as treasurer, and Lathrop Cook as collector.

The name of the organization was afterwards amended to be the First Presbyterian Society of Lewiston. The first minister was Rev. David M. Smith, who was called to the charge August 25th, 1817. He resigned in 1821, and afterwards preached occasionally in the school-house. The first pastor was Rev. Joel Byington. The names of those who have been in charge since, either as supplies or regular installed pastors, are as follows: Rev. N. W. Fisher, Rev. —— Ingalls, Rev. Rees C. Evans, Rev. N. Bull, Rev. A. McCall, Rev. N. S. Allen, Rev. Joshua Cook, Rev. Charles Marvin, Rev. S. T. Street and Rev. Jeremiah Odell, the present pastor.

Between 1826 and 1835 a building known as "the stone church" was erected by the society, which is in excellent condition to-day, being in good repair and seating about three hundred people. The church was re-organized in 1854. The present membership is one hundred and forty-nine, with a large Sunday-school.

As early as 1822 there was a desire on the part of some residents of the village to form a Universalist society, but there being few of that belief there, no organization was effected until a later day, when a church was erected and regular services held for several years.

St. Paul's Protestant Episcopal Church was organized January 16th, 1832, the applicants for organization being Rev. John M. Robertson, Jonathan Bell and John E. Lasher. The first wardens were Asahel Lyons and Oliver Grace, and the first vestrymen Samuel Barton, George W. Shockey, Obed Smith, George W. Hawley, O. Hill, H. L. Franklin, Guy Reynolds and Horatio J. Stow.

Steps were immediately taken toward the erection of a church, which was completed in 1835, costing, with a fine organ, $3,663. The first rector was Rev. John M. Robertson. Those who have succeeded him in the charge of the parish have been as follows: Rev. Samuel McBurney, Rev. Rufus Murray, Rev. Amos C. Treadway, Rev. L. W. Russ, Rev. Israel Foote, Rev. —— Stevens, Rev. J. H. Havens, Rev. R. O. Page, Rev. G. M. Skinner, Rev. —— North, Rev. —— Mueller and Rev. George Pine. During vacancies, which have occurred from time to time, the church has been supplied with rectors from De Veaux College.

There is a Sunday-school connected with the church, the rector in charge being the superintendent.

The wardens at the present time are Alexander Miller and L. K. Scovell. The vestrymen are: J. E. Ways, A. S. Baristo, M. Robinson, A. H. Miller, L. W. Hull, Thomas Lyons, George E. Hotchkiss and C. J. Hooker. The present membership is about fifty.

There is a Catholic society at Lewiston, having a chapel and a resident pastor. The charge is connected with that at Youngstown.

CIVIL HISTORY.

Lewiston village was incorporated April 18th, 1843, the following being a copy of the act:

"The district of country in the county of Niagara comprised within the town of Lewiston and bounded as follows: Bounded on the north by lot number twenty of the Niagara tract; on the east by lots number forty-one and forty-two, township fourteen, ninth range, of the Holland Land Company's land; on the south by lot number twenty of the Niagara tract; and on the west by the western limits of the jurisdiction of the State of New York, shall hereafter be known by the name of the village of Lewiston, and the inhabitants residing therein shall be a corporation by the name of the village of Lewiston.

"The said village shall be divided into two wards, as follows: That part which lies east of the middle of Fifth street shall be the first ward, and that part which lies west of the middle of Fifth street shall be the second ward."

The first village election was held on the second day of May, 1843, at the collector's office, at which the following persons were chosen officers for the ensuing year:

President, William Hotchkiss; clerk, Jonathan Bell; collector, George W. Shockey; treasurer, Carlton Bartlett; constable, John T. Beardsley; trustees, Lathrop Cook, E. A. Adams, R. H. Boughton, N. Cornell.

The president and board of trustees at the present time are as follows: Benjamin Cornell, president; Thomas P. Scovell, clerk; J. E. Whitman and Thomas Phelan, trustees of the first ward; John Fleming and James H. Kelly, trustees of the second ward.

MISCELLANY.

The village of Lewiston was the place where the first court was held in Niagara county; and it was at one time strongly advocated as the most fitting location for the county seat, which was finally located at Lockport.

Three newspapers have been published in the place at different times. The first, *The Niagara Democrat*, was

FRUIT FARM & RESIDENCES OF HETZEL COLT & SON. J.B.S. COLT, LEWISTON, NIAGARA COUNTY, N.Y.

established in 1821 by Benjamin Ferguson. In the following year it was removed to Lockport, where it was afterwards published as *The Lockport Observatory*. The initial number of *The Lewiston Sentinel* was issued by James D. Daly, September 20th, 1822. It passed into the hands of Oliver Grace in the following April, and was issued by him for two or three years. *The Lewiston Telegraph and Ship Canal Advocate* was established in the spring of 1837, and had a short existence, under the charge of Messrs. Harrison & Mack.

The part which the town and village took in the late rebellion was creditable alike to the patriotism and the liberality of their citizens. The exposed position of the village on the frontier gave rise to many apprehensions of a raid from Canada during the war, but no difficulty was experienced from that source.

The port of entry of the customs district of Niagara was removed from Fort Niagara to Lewiston in 1811, and from Lewiston to Suspension Bridge in 1863.

PROMINENT INHABITANTS OF THE TOWN.

Edgar W. Barber, merchant and cheese manufacturer, Sanborn, was born in Lewiston August 11th, 1847.

James Buckley, farmer, was born in Moriah, N. Y. October 3d, 1833, and came to Lewiston with his parents about 1835, from the former place.

Jeremiah G. Campbell was born July 2d, 1810, at Grand Island, Vermont, whence he removed to Niagara county at the age of nine years. He was married May 11th, 1837, to Emily M. Parker, of East Bloomfield, Livingston county, N. Y. He lives in Lewiston and follows the calling of a farmer. He was for more than twenty years an assessor in the town of Cambria, and now holds the same office in the town of Lewiston.

Thorret J. Campbell, carpenter and farmer, was born in Cambria, N. Y., July 19th, 1847, and came to Lewiston in 1874.

John A. Cleghorn, farmer and carpenter and joiner, is a native of Scotland, having been born June 11th, 1799. He came to Lewiston in 1828 from Peebles, Scotland.

Hetzel Colt, one of the oldest and most honored citizens of Lewiston, was born October 16th, 1809, in the town where he has lived his life long. He was married May 29th, 1830, to Susan Hetzel, of Florida, Orange county, N. Y. She died, and May 25th, 1836, Mr. Colt married Clarissa Post, of West Hampton, Mass. He was again left a widower, and was again married, July 20th, 1842, to Juliett Scovell, of Orwell, Vt., who is still living. Mr. Colt has had four children, two of whom died in infancy. One son, C. H. Colt, a member of Company D., 44th regiment, "Ellsworth Avengers," was killed at the battle of the Wilderness, May 19th, 1864. Another son, J. B. S. Colt, is still living, at the age of thirty-five. Mr. Colt, who is next to the oldest living native-born resident of the town, was in Tufford's company on the frontier during the Radical war in Canada. For forty-two years he has been a ruling elder in the First Presbyterian Church of Lewiston.

W. J. Cook is a prominent resident and farmer of the town of Lewiston.

Ziba A. Downer is a native of Lebanon, N. Y., and was born December 4th, 1825. He was married in 1854 to Lucy A. Newton, of Norwich, Vt. Mr. Downer came to Lewiston in 1832, and has been engaged in farming for many years.

Alexander Garlow is a native of the Tuscarora Reservation in the town of Lewiston, being now fifty-five years of age. Post-office address, Suspension Bridge, N. Y.

Joseph P. Hewitt was born September 20th, 1803, in Le Roy, Genesee county, N. Y. December 20th, 1826, he was married to Lydia Waggoner, of Dunham, Canada. He came to Cambria in 1805, and to that part of that town which is now known as Lewiston, in 1809. Mr. Hewitt is a large property owner, having five farms and a good deal of village property. In earlier years he was prominently connected with the militia organizations, and he was extensively engaged in lumbering, owning several mills, in whole or in part. He also was a heavy contractor for government and canal work. He has been highway commissioner about three years, and has served several years as school trustee.

Lewis W. Hull was born in Montague, N. J., November 8th, 1822, and was married June 1st, 1852, to Miss Jane Robinson, of Lewiston, N. Y. Mr. Hull has been a resident of Lewiston since April 11th, 1845.

William Q. Huggins, M.D., was born August 9th, 1842, at Mount Morris, N. Y., and came to Sanborn from Buffalo in the early part of 1870. Dr. Huggins served in the army with great credit during the late war as sergeant, first lieutenant, and captain, and was coroner of Niagara county one term.

James Kelley, fruit-grower and produce-dealer, Lewiston, was born December 22nd, 1840, at Alleganie, N. Y., and came to Lewiston in 1841. He was married July 6th 1864, to Helen Herr, of Lewiston.

Walter Latta was born in Lewiston, August 4th, 1826, and was married August 13th, 1849, to Mary Elizabeth Jones, of Ithaca, N. Y. Mr. Latta is a farmer by occupation.

John Mower was born in Lincolnshire, England, March 1st, 1837, where he learned the miller's trade, and served an apprenticeship as engineer. He emigrated to America in November, 1869. After one year's stay at Shelby Center, he went to Medina and from there to Lockport. In March, 1875, he located at Sanborn, purchasing the grist-mill at that place, which he still owns and operates. He was married in England, in February, 1862, to Eva Smith.

A. J. Nichols was born June 24th, 1830, in Lewiston, Niagara county, N. Y., and married November 20th, 1851, to Miss Mary Beggs of that town. Mr. Nichols is a well known farmer and fruit-grower, and he has served the town as school trustee, highway commissioner and assessor.

Robert Nichols was born in Lewiston, June 10th, 1820. In 1845 he married Catharine B. Tufford, of the town of Niagara. Mr. Nichols, who is a farmer and fruit-grower by occupation, has served in an independent company for seven years.

Leander K. Scovell, farmer, who has been supervisor and assessor of the town of Lewiston, and who now holds the position of president of the Lewiston and Queenston Suspension Bridge Company, was born in Palmyra, N. Y., March 5th, 1817, and came to Lewiston in 1833, having previously lived at Lockport.

Hon. Lee R. Sanborn was born in Sweden, Monroe county, August 8th, 1831, his parents having been of the honest and sturdy New England stock. On the 9th day of September, 1849, he was married to Julia C. Crawford, of Lewiston, N. Y. Mr. Sanborn has held several town offices, has been justice of sessions, and was member of the Legislatures of 1870 and 1871. The following is an extract from "Life Sketches of Members of the Legislature of 1870:":" He was educated at that most elevating of institutions, the home circle and the common schools. His father was a clergyman, and both of his parents were school teachers. He is a gentleman of superior culture. * * * * His sterling probity of character and exemplary habits commend him to the community in which he dwells. * * * * He was a liberal supporter of the war, * * * and has contributed largely to the business success and moral improvement of the village which was named in his honor." Mr. Sanborn is now engaged in farming at his homestead at Sanborn, and extensively interested, with his sons, in lumbering in Michigan.

Thomas Smith was born September 16th, 1810, in Oxfordshire, England. In 1838 he was married to Mary Shepard, of Worcestershire, England. He came to Lewiston in 1875 from Liverford, England. He is a farmer. Post-office address, Suspension Bridge, N. Y.

Samuel Treichler was born in York county, Pa., December 8th, 1825. In the spring of 1833 he came from Pennsylvania to Wheatfield, Niagara county, and removed from there to Lewiston in 1857. Mr. Treichler is a well-known farmer of the eastern part of the town. Post-office address, Sanborn.

Captain James Van Cleve was born in Lawrenceville, Mercer county, N. J., November 12th, 1808. He was married February 9th, 1842, to Harriet S. F. Barton, of Lewiston, N. Y. Captain Van Cleve came to Lewiston in 1824, and in 1826 became a commander of a vessel in the lake service, and was in that capacity, and otherwise connected with lake commerce, till 1861. He was president of the Lewiston Suspension Bridge Company at the time of the construction of the bridge, and has been connected with the company ever since. The captain has also been in various ways connected with railroads, and was prime mover in the introduction of the propeller on the lakes in 1840 and 1841. Though always deeply interested in the public welfare, he was, as he says, "never so indolent as to seek or hold a public office," but has been untiring in his exertions as a private citizen in behalf of the general good.

George Coit Winslow, farmer and ex-quartermaster sargent of the 74th regiment New York National Guards, was born in Buffalo, October 16th, 1844, and came to Lewiston in 1875.

Among the other residents of this town the following, whose post-office is Lewiston where not otherwise specified, are well known:

Charles McConnell, farmer; Albert M. White, A. D. Cott, William P. Mentz, Samuel Burns, Pekin; Mrs. J. Houstater, Pekin; Philip Bechtel, D. Bush, farmer, Sanborn; D. H. King, hotel-keeper, Sanborn; William Legg, J. N. Babcock, farmer; Mrs. H. Newman, farmer, Pekin; J. W. Pleasant, Suspension Bridge; Miles Parker, farmer, Pekin; Asa Thompson, farmer, a Tuscarora sachem, Suspension Bridge; James Johnson, farmer, Pekin; Isaac N. Jack, farmer, Pekin; William Patterson, farmer, Sanborn; Mrs. H. L. Hitchcock, Samuel B. Russ, farmer; J. W. Murray, Christian F. Sattelberg, farmer; C. T. Hotchkiss, Charles A. Bairsto, farmer; A. Gray, farmer; George Collord, E. Smith, M. D.; W. S. McCollum, Youngstown; Mrs. H. F. Hotchkiss, J. O. Hooker.

RESIDENCE OF THE HON. LEE R. SANBORN & BIRDSEYE VIEW OF THE VILLAGE OF SANBORN, NIAGARA CO., N.Y.

THE TOWN OF LOCKPORT.

THE town of Lockport, although comparatively early settled and most numerously populated, was among the last to be organized in the county. It was not until February 2nd, 1824, that a special act was passed in the Legislature "to erect the town of Lockport," and for this purpose the eastern part of Cambria and the western portion of Royalton, including an area of 35,397 acres, were set off and combined; and the passage of this act was ratified and the township organization fully completed by the election of its first officers "at a town meeting held in pursuance of the statute, at the house of Michael D. Mann, on the first Tuesday in April, 1824, in and for the town of Lockport in the county of Niagara. Present, James F. Mason, Hiram Gardner, and Joel M. Parks, justices of the peace in said town." They were: Daniel Washburn, supervisor; Morris H. Tucker, town clerk; Eli Bruce, collector; David Pomroy, Henry Norton and John Gooding, assessors; Henry W. Campbell and Nathan Comstock, overseers of the poor; Eli Bruce, William A. Judd, Joel Herrington and Levi B. Pratt, constables; Jonathan Willett, Henry Gregory and John Williams, commissioners of highway; Jonathan Willett, Joel M. Parks and Oliver L. Willard, commissioners of common schools; William Van Duzer, George H. Boughton and Orsamus Turner, inspectors of common schools.

There were at that time twenty-five road districts, and an overseer was elected for each district, who was also constituted a fence-viewer. At this town meeting $100 was voted for the support of the poor, and $50 for building a pound for the town. Ezekiel Fulsom was appointed pound master. It was also voted "to raise as much money as the supervisor is obliged to raise for the support of the common schools," which for that year amounted to but little. That year and the year following, thirteen entire and fractional school districts were erected. According to the school commissioners' report made April 19th, 1825, the amount of public school money raised from various sources was $132.49, which was distributed among 542 scholars.

THE TOWN CIVIL LIST.

The following is a complete list of supervisors from the organization of the town to the present time :

Daniel Washburn, 1824, 1826; George H. Boughton, 1827, 1828; Morris H. Tucker, 1829; Henry Norton, 1830, 1832; Samuel Works, 1833, 1834; Asa W. Douglas, 1835, 1836; Alonzo T. Prentice, 1837; Jacob Gaunt, 1838, 1839; George W. Rayers, 1840; Timothy Backus, 1841; Robert H. Stevens, 1842; Timothy Backus, 1843; Benjamin Carpenter, 1844, 1845; Asa W. Douglas, 1846; Solomon Parmelee, 1847; Isaac C. Cotton, 1848; Abijah H. Moss, 1849; Rensselaer S. Wilkinson, 1850, 1851; Robert White, 1852; Alonzo T. Prentice, 1853; Charles Evans, 1854; Daniel Van Valkenburgh, 1855; John Jackson, 1856-1858; Benjamin Fletcher, 1859; Jacob Gaunt, 1860; Benjamin Fletcher, 1861; James Jackson, 1862; Richard B. Hoag, 1863-1865; Isaac H. Babcock, 1866, 1867; John W. Alberty, 1868, 1869; Ira Farnsworth, 1870; Luther Forsyth, 1871-1873; S. Clark Lewis, 1874, 1875; Seneca B. Frost, 1876; Nathan S. Gilbert, 1877, 1878.

The justices of the peace previous to 1830 were: James F. Mason, Hiram Gardner, Joel M. Parks, Elias Ranson, jr., Henry Norton, Joseph Carter and Daniel Alvord, jr. The following is a list of those who have since served as justices in the town, with the years in which they were elected:

Joseph Carter, 1830; Otis Hathaway, 1831; Solomon B. Connelly, 1832; Theodore H. Chapin, 1833; Henry W. Campbell, 1834; Henry A. Carter, 1835; Henry K. Hopkins, 1836; Wright Lattin, 1837-1841; Alonzo T. Prentice, 1838, 1843, 1857; Lathrop Fellows, 1839; Joseph T. Bellah, 1840, 1844; Lloyd Smith, 1842; Phineas L. Ely, 1845; Myron H. Davis, 1846, 1850, 1854; Peter B. Aiken, 1846, 1849; Alpheus Clark, 1847, 1852, 1856; Erastus Newton, 1848; Dudley Donnelly, 1851, 1855, 1859; Mortimer M. Southwick, 1853; John Bons, 1855, 1858, 1867; Walter Simmons, 1856; Myron L. Burwell, 1860; Job W. Vail, 1861; William R. Ford, 1862; Edwin Shepard, 1863; Asher Tarrance, 1864; Henry F. Cady, 1865; S. S. Pomroy, 1866; S. B. Floyd, 1868; Leander Bickford, 1869, 1873; Luther Forsyth, 1870, 1874, 1878; Philo S. Smith, 1871; Seneca B. Foot, 1872; Henry Stevens, 1875; George F. Green, 1876; John E. Linebough, 1877.

OUTLINES, SURFACE, SOIL AND PRODUCTS.

The town derived its name from the then village of Lockport, located near its geographical center. It is bounded on the north by Newfane and Hartland, east by Royalton, south by Pendleton and Tonawanda creek—which also forms a portion of the southern boundary of the county—and west by Pendleton and Cambria. Mud, creek, which flows across the southern part of the town, and Eighteen-mile creek, in the northern part—a branch of which runs through the city—are the principal streams. The mountain ridge extends across the northern portion of the town, presenting a broken and uneven surface in that part.

The Niagara limestone crops out along this ridge, and extensive quarries have been opened in and near the city of Lockport. This limestone is a very excellent building material, and large quantities have been shipped to distant places. The locks and numerous culverts on the canal are built of it. Underlying this limestone is a stratum of hydraulic limestone, from which water lime is made. The surface, both above and below the ridge, in some localities is gently rolling, but generally level. The soil is variable. In the northeast it is a gravelly loam; in the west and northwest gravelly and somewhat stony. In the south part a stiff clay prevails. It yields remunerative crops of most kinds of cereals, and is well adapted to the raising of fruit. Apples, pears and grapes are grown in abundance. Some very extensive and popular nuseries are located in this town.

ELLICOTT RESERVE AND SALT SPRING.

Joseph Ellicott, the surveyor and agent for the Holland Land Company, reserved for his own benefit, by stipulation, several tracts of land in this town. Six thousand acres stipulated for in his contract with the company were located in what was long known as the "Eleven Mile Tract," a portion of which lay in this town along the Ridge road. A tract of twenty-five hundred acres in the northeastern part of the town, which has usually been considered as a part of the "Ellicott Reserve," was a separate purchase, made jointly by Joseph and Benjamin Ellicott. Another tract which was purchased by Joseph Ellicott was on the north side of the Tonawanda creek, embracing the site of the old "Fishing Ground," or present village of Rapids, in this town. He at one time intended to secure the erection of a saw-mill at this point, by raising a dam and constructing a race across the land below.

About the year 1813, he commenced the manufacture of salt at a point known as the Salt Springs, about two miles northeast of Lockport city. From these works the inhabitants of this region were mainly supplied with salt previous to canal navigation.

SINGULAR ANTIQUITIES.

Some remarkable traces of ancient occupancy of this section were visible just outside the southern limits of the city when the first settlers appeared. On an irregular space, covering about ten acres, there were noticed over one hundred circular pits, arranged without any appearance of regularity. These pits were from twelve to fifteen feet in diameter across the top, and had an average depth of four feet. The material thrown out was composed of sand, forming a circular rim or embankment, upon which were growing large oak trees. The origin of these singular excavations and the purpose for which they were designed will probably ever remain the subject of conjecture. The fact that the sand which constituted the material of the encircling banks is found only in the stratum beneath the surface, at a depth of from three to six feet, in the above locality, affords satisfactory proof that these singular pits were not "pot-holes" formed by water, but were most probably the work of human hands. Improvements have long since obliterated them.

EARLY SETTLERS.

As early as 1802 a mail route existed between Canandaigua and Fort Niagara, the mails being carried on horseback. The route was along an Indian trail, which led from the former to the latter place, running through this town, and passing near Cold Spring, just east of the city. At this point Adam Strouse, in 1802, built a shanty by permission of Joseph Ellicott, which was applied for by the mail contractor, Stephen Bates, who wanted a place at which his postman could shelter, warm and refresh himself and horse. This shanty was without doubt the first structure of any kind erected in the town.

Charles Wilber is credited with making the first settlement within the boundaries of Lockport He is said to have located in 1805 at Cold Spring, and undoubtedly at first occupied the mail carrier's building. He afterward opened a tavern at this point. He was followed by Jedediah Darling, who settled in the town in 1808.

David Carlton came from New Hampshire in 1809, and located on what is now known as the "Hampshire farm," about half a mile east of Cold Spring. Among the first things which he did after arriving here was to plant an orchard in the forest, with seeds brought with him from New England. The apple trees still standing on this place show the irregular form in which the seed was deposited. In 1813 he left this place and took up his abode near Warren's Corners, where Alanson Bradley now resides.

Joseph Carlton also came from New Hampshire, and in 1810 settled near Warren's Corners, on the farm now occupied by his grandson, Alonzo B. Carlton. Upon this place, which he procured direct from the Holland Land Company, he built the largest log house ever erected in the town, it being 30 by 40 feet in size and two stories high. Rev. Thomas Carlton, the well known agent for the "Methodist Book Concern," was a son of this pioneer and once resided here.

David Pomroy, a native of Connecticut, came from Hamilton, Madison county, N. Y., obtained an article from the Holland Land Company to one hundred acres of land, and located in 1810 on the farm now owned by his son, Norman Pomroy, about half a mile west of the county farm. Here he remained until his death, November 1st, 1867.

Thomas Mighells, a native of Deerfield, Mass., came from Ontario county to Lockport in March, 1810, and was the first settler on the farm now owned and occupied by his son N. T. Mighells, at Warren's Corners. Phineas Burchard, of whom he bought the land, had previously obtained an article for it from the Holland Company, but had not begun an improvement. Here Mr. Mighells built up for himself a permanent house, reared a family of ten children, and here he died July 25th, 1858, at the age of 73 years.

Stephen Wakeman located in 1810 in the eastern part of the town, and George Miller, also, settled in the town the same year.

Thaddeus Alvord emigrated from Madison county, N. Y., and became a resident of this town in 1811. He procured an article for 145 acres of land, upon which he located and began improvements; this farm is now occupied by Patrick Stapleton, and is located near the county farm.

Alexander Freeman came into the town in 1811, and the same year built the first saw-mill. It was situated on a branch of the Eighteen-mile creek, near the present residence of Nathaniel Lerch.

Alexander Haskins settled about 1812 in the northeast part of the town, on the farm now occupied by Bradford Pease.

Jesse Griswold was among the first pioneers in the northeastern part of the town. He came to Lockport in the employ of Joseph Ellicott in 1813, and had charge of the salt works at the salt springs. He was for several years in Mr. Ellicott's employ, a portion of the time cutting out and constructing roads in different parts of the Holland Purchase. In July, 1817, he settled on the farm now owned and occupied by his daughter, near Millard's Bridge, where he resided until his death, November 26th, 1869. He was a drummer in an independent rifle company commanded by Captain Ellicott. He was at the battle of Queenston Heights, where he was taken prisoner, detained for three or four days and then paroled.

Jacob Loucks became a settler in 1813, on the farm now owned by George F. Green, in the eastern part of the town, and John Williams located the following year a short distance further east. Henry Norton came in 1815, and settled on the farm next west of the one now occupied by Charles Keep. Jabez Pomroy came from Madison county in April, 1815. He at first took up 120 acres of land in Cambria, but, disposing of it before making any improvements, he, the same year, procured an article for the same amount near the present county farm in this town, upon which he located. In the spring of 1826, Mr. Pomroy built and operated the first wool-carding, cloth-dressing and fulling-mill in the town. It was located just below the Spalding grist-mill. He is still a resident of the town, is 84 years of age and in the enjoyment of perfect health.

The pioneer settler on the county farm was Josiah Richardson, who came from Madison county in 1816.

Luther Crocker, from Barnstable, Maine, purchased a piece of land in the northwestern part of the town in 1812, and the same year started to move to it, but rumors of the war in this vicinity caused him to halt in Ontario county, where he remained until 1816, when he came on and settled on his land, where he continued until his death, February 14th, 1861. The farm is now occupied by his daughter-in-law, Mrs. Sarah Crocker.

John Gibson settled about three-fourths of a mile east of Warren's Corners, where, in 1815, he opened the first blacksmith shop in the town.

The first settlements in the vicinity of the city were made as early as 1815. According to a narrative given by Nathan B. Rogers, the following log houses were up in the spring of 1816 : Zeno Comstock had a house on Saxon street; Reuben Haines, a house on the old John Pound place, near the depot, and Webster Thorn lived in a house on the Transit, where Arza Lounsbury now resides; Daniel Smith built a house opposite Thorn's that spring. Those who came in 1816, were Esek Brown, who built a house near West Main street, which afterwards became a tavern; Asahel Smith, who erected a house on the Transit; John Comstock, who put up a dwelling near "the Cave," and Nathan Comstock, who located on the farm now occupied by C. L. Hoag, and in the fall of 1816 put in ten acres of wheat—this was the largest clearing in the neighborhood at that time, the balance of the settlers having barely made a beginning.

Nathan B. Rogers came from Massachusetts to Lockport in the spring of 1816, walking the entire distance. He at first worked for Nathan Comstock. In 1817 he purchased 160 acres just south of the present city limits.

Charles Smith was the first settler on the farm now owned by Jacob Gaunt, in the east part of the town. He located here in 1817.

Oliver L. Millard came from Washington county, N. Y., in 1817, and located in the northeast part of the town the same year. The farm which he purchased from the Holland Company had been occupied for one year previous by a squatter named Nathan Wilder, who had commenced a clearing and built a log shanty, and whose interest Mr. Millard bought, erecting a log house the same season, clearing and improving the farm, and making this his permanent home until his death, which occurred November 11th, 1877. Mr. Millard was a sub-contractor on the Erie Canal, constructing a portion of it between his place and Lockport city. He was general superintendent of the canal after its completion, under the resident commissioner, for six or seven years, and was connected with it in different capacities for fifteen years. He was a prominent and influential man in his time, and often held offices of trust in his town and county.

Jared Tyler, who was one of Mr. Millard's nearest neighbors on the east, located as early as 1815 on the farm where Theodore Van Wagner now resides. He had on this place a chestnut orchard. He was an odd genius, peculiar and eccentric in his ways. He was a "Jack-at-all-trades," being farmer, doctor, blacksmith, cabinet-maker, millwright, musician and clock tinker. He wore his hair long, twisted up and fastened with a silver comb of his own make; was always attired in buckskin breeches and leather apron, and in a leather belt which always encircled his waist he wore a tomahawk and brace of pistols. His grotesque and savage appearance was a terror to the younger portion of the inhabitants.

Dr. Ezekiel Webb was the pioneer physician of the town; he came as early as 1818, and lived on the N. B. Rogers place, south of the city. Dr. Isaac W. Smith came from Ontario county, and settled on what is now Main street, in the city of Lockport, in 1821, where he resided until his death, in the spring of 1842. Socially and professionally, he was a citizen of conceded worth.

Jesse P. Haines, the pioneer surveyor in this section of the country, landed in Lockport October 2d, 1818. He came from Columbia county, Pa., by wagon, and was twenty-seven days accomplishing the journey.

Edward W. Raymond located about 1826 on lot No. 88, in the south part of the town, on what was then known as the "Salt road." Here he erected a log building which he opened as a tavern, and continued to run it as such until about 1845.

Helam and Hiram Mead were early settlers in the northeast part of the town. They located in 1820 on the farm now owned by the Mackey heirs, and occupied by George Wood.

WRIGHT'S CORNERS.

Among the first settlers of WRIGHT'S CORNERS was a man named Barber, who built and kept the first hotel there. He died there at an early day, but the business was continued by the family until the building was destroyed by fire, which occurred about the year 1820. Two of Mrs. Barber's daughters—young ladies—were consumed in the flames. Another hotel was erected at the Corners soon after, of which Alva Buck was proprietor. The latter hotel, however, stood over the line, in the town of Newfane. Solomon Wright came as early as 1822 and settled on the Ridge road, at the corners which subsequently took his name. Here he opened a hotel, and continued to run it for twenty years or more. A post-office was established at this point in 1828, and Mr. Wright was appointed the first postmaster, which office he held for many years. His hotel was burned in 1861.

David Maxwell came from New Jersey in 1819, and settled at Johnson's Creek, where he purchased a farm of one hundred acres, and also kept a hotel for about one year. While here in 1821, he, being a practical surveyor, was employed to survey and lay out the well known Hess road, running from the Ridge road through Hartland and Somerset to the lake shore. In 1824 he purchased a farm at Wright's Corners, built a house, and the following year moved his family thither. Here he continued to reside until his death, June 15th, 1878. He was from the first a leading citizen of the Corners. Through his influence a post-office was established here. He opened the first and only store at Wright's Corners in 1832, but abandoned the business in 1840. In 1824, by special act of the Legislature, he obtained a charter for the construction of a toll road from Wright's Corners to Warren's Corners—a distance of four miles—which was known as

THE LONG CAUSEWAY TURNPIKE.

This road was originally cut through and a log causeway laid the entire length by Gen. Dearborn, in behalf of the government, during the war of 1812-14. Mr. Maxwell let the contract to John Dixon, of Pennsylvania, to remove the old causeway and construct a turnpike twenty-two feet wide, at one dollar per rod. Dixon completed his contract in the summer of 1825. This was the first toll road in the county; upon it only one toll gate was licensed. It was soon found that the soil out of which this pike was constructed was too soft for the ponderous four-horse coaches and heavily laden freight wagons which daily passed over it, and it became necessary to cover it deep with gravel in order to make it acceptable. This enterprise proved financially disastrous to Mr. Maxwell, as in after years the canal and Central railroad drew freight and travel in another direction. The road was, however, kept up as a toll road until about 1870, when it was sold for a nominal sum to the towns of Lockport and Newfane, and became a free highway.

RAPIDS.

The village of RAPIDS, situated in the south-east part of the town on Tonawanda creek, took its name from the fact that the stream at this point is much more rapid than at any other, and a bridge across it here, which was built in the early part of the present century, was known throughout the country as the "Rapids bridge." It contains a hotel, store, church, blacksmith shops and about 80 inhabitants. The first settlements at this place were made by Amos and S. B. Kinne, who bought the land from the Joseph Ellicott heirs in 1839, and at once platted a portion of it into village lots and placed them in market. But little was done, however, toward building up a village until 1849, when Orange Mansfield built a steam saw-mill near the creek. G. H. Utley erected and opened a two-story frame hotel, and Horace Cummings built a store and put in it a small stock of groceries, which was in 1853 sold to Mr. Williams, who opened a general store.

Among the first to locate in this vicinity was Merrit Johnson, from Montgomery county. He settled on lots 18 and 20 in 1823, and in 1835 sold out to Robert Kinne, also from Montgomery county.

WARREN'S CORNERS.

This hamlet is located on the Ridge road, in the northwest corner of the town, and a part of it lies in Cambria. It is one of the first settled localities in the town, and took its name from Ezra Warren, who became a resident of the place in the spring of 1813, and kept a tavern for many years. Previous to the opening of the Erie Canal, and for several years after, this was an important point on the Ridge road from Lewiston to Rochester.

EARLY SCHOOLS AND SCHOOL-HOUSES.

The first school-house in the town was at Warren's Corners. It was a frame building about 18 by 24 feet in size, and stood on ground donated for school purposes by Ezra Warren. It was built by subscription in the spring of 1814, and the following summer Amanda Rice—afterward the wife of Joash Taylor, of Cambria—taught the first school. The school district at that time included all the settlements within walking distance of the school-house. The pioneer school-building, although removed from its original site in 1836, is still standing at the Corners, having been converted into a dwelling. A stone school-house was built in its stead in 1836, which, in 1861, was torn down and the present commodious building erected.

The first school-house in district number 5 was built of logs, in 1818. Lyman Lyscomb was the first male teacher. The building stood just over the line, in the present town of Cambria. It was abandoned after two years, and in 1820 a frame school-house was erected on the Lockport side of the town line.

The pioneer school-house in district No. 11 was constructed of logs, in the spring of 1822. School district No. 16 was formed in 1830, and a school-house built the same year. Mary A. Pomroy taught the first school here. The first school-house at Wright's Corners was not erected until 1837. Previous to that time the nearest school was kept in a part of Benoni Edwards's dwelling, one and a half miles east of the Corners.

The town—exclusive of the city—is at present divided into twenty school districts and fractional or joint districts, with sixteen school-houses within its borders:

PLANK AND TOLL ROADS.

LOCKPORT AND BUFFALO PLANK ROAD COMPANY.

By a special act of the Legislature, passed April 29th, 1844, a company was chartered for the purpose of constructing a plank road from Lockport to intersect the macadamized Buffalo road at Williamsville, in Erie county. The corporation was known as the Lockport and Buffalo Plank Road Company. The Lockport members of the first board of commissioners were William O. Brown, William S. McMaster, Charles S. Sanford and Joseph Center. The company was allowed four years in which to complete the road. It commenced on the Transit road just south of the present city limits, and ran south on that road ten miles. This was the first plank road chartered or constructed in Niagara county. (The toll road known as the "Long Causeway Turnpike," previously mentioned, was constructed of gravel). It proved an unprofitable investment, and as the planks wore out, repairs were omitted and the road abandoned to the public.

LOCKPORT AND MANSFIELD CORNERS PLANK ROAD CO.

This company was organized under the general act for the incorporation of plank road companies, soon after its passage, May 7th, 1847, and the road, running from Lockport, through the village of Rapids, to Mansfield Corners, in Erie county, was constructed in 1848, 1849 and 1850. It was commenced with flattering prospects, but, like its cotemporary above noticed, it suffered for the want of profitable patronage and eventually experienced the same fate.

LOCKPORT AND CAMBRIA PLANK ROAD COMPANY.

The articles of association of this company were filed in the office of the Secretary of State on the 27th of December, 1849, with the following named persons as directors: Rivera Stevens, Hiram McNeil, Enos Steel, Moses C. Crapsey, Abijah H. Moss, John G. Freeman, Daniel Alvord, Joseph Center and Charles Keep. There were originally fifty-one stockholders in the company. The road was constructed the following year, of oak plank, in the place of which, as they wore out, was substituted crushed limestone. The road is now and has been for many years macadamized its entire length. It has always been kept in repair by the company and operated as a toll-road. The present officers are Jerome E. Emerson, president, and John G. Freeman, secretary, treasurer and general superintendent.

OTHER CHARTERED ROADS.

The Lockport and Wright's Corners Plank Road Company was organized in 1849, under the general law for the incorporation of plank road companies, and the following year the Lockport and Warren's Corners Plank Road Company was also chartered. Both of these roads were originally constructed of oak plank, which in time gave way to stone or macadam pavement, and they are now known as the "stone" roads. The three last mentioned thoroughfares are the only toll-roads in the county, and are all within the limits of the town of Lockport.

CEMETERIES.

COLD SPRING.

Cold Spring Cemetery is located on an undulating slope, facing the north, near the Cold Springs—from which it takes its name—about two miles east of the city. It is artistically laid out, and shaded by trees of natural growth. Considerable labor has been expended in ornamenting and transforming the naturally picturesque grounds into an appropriate place for the repose of the dead.

The plan of the cemetery was conceived as early as 1838, and an organization effected with the following named gentlemen as trustees: Joel McCollum, Wright Lattin, Joseph T. Bellah, William C. House and Samuel G. Hamilton. By an act of the Legislature the Cold Spring Cemetery Association was incorporated May 7th, 1840. The following is an extract from the act of incorporation: "Asa W. Douglas, Asahel Scovill, Horace Birdsall, James D. Shuler and Freeman Kilburn, and such other persons as may hereafter associate with them, are hereby constituted a body corporate by the name of 'The Cold Spring Cemetery Association,' with power to take, hold and convey real and personal estate for the use of said corporation to the amount of $10,000. By the conditions of the same act the five persons mentioned above were constituted a board of trustees, who the same year (1846) purchased 10 acres of land of Stephen Wakeman—adjoining an old burying ground which had been in existence for many years previous—paying $649 for the same, and platted them. The lots at first sold as low as from five to fifteen dollars. In 1844 a tax of five hundred dollars was levied upon the village of Lockport, and three acres purchased from the association for a "potter's field" or free burying place, subject, nevertheless, to the control of the trustees of the Cold Spring association. In 1855, right of way through these grounds was granted to the Rochester and Niagara Falls railroad, which cut off the potter's field from the main grounds. In 1876 the association purchased an addition of five acres, at a cost of $300 per acre, and in the fall of 1877 erected a stone vault, near the main entrance, at an expense of about $800.

The first sexton appointed to take charge of these grounds was Jonas Hartzell in December, 1841. The present superintendent is John H. Clark, appointed in January, 1876.

The present officers of the association are John H. Buck, president, and Peter D. Walter, secretary. The trustees are John H. Buck, Peter D. Walter, James Jackson, jr., George H. Elliott and Hiram Benedict.

Many of the most distinguished of the early settlers and residents of Lockport and vicinity are buried there, and many of the tombstones recall thoughts of the days of the early existence of the village. Jesse Hawley, the honored projector of the Erie Canal, is interred in Cold Spring Cemetery, and there, also, rest the remains of the mother of the late George Peabody, the great banker and philanthropist of London.

CHESTNUT RIDGE.

This cemetery is pleasantly located on the east line of the town, a portion of it lying in Royalton. It is tastefully laid out, and presents an attractive appearance of tidiness and care. An association was organized in the latter part of 1835, of which Warren Carpenter, Smith Lackor, Sylvester Flagler, Jacob Gaunt and Eben Thomas were trustees. On January 5th, 1836, they bought the grounds of Henry Lacy, and they were at once laid out into lots. The original owner of the ground, Henry Lacy, was one of the first to be buried there. On the 10th of March, 1859, the association was re-organized under the general law of the State. The present board of trustees consists of Daniel Bosserman, president; Dyer D. Denison, vice-president; Jacob Gaunt, treasurer; Charles S. Flagler, secretary; Andrew Keck, Jeffrey Bennett and Daniel Carl.

CHURCHES OF THE TOWN.

THE M. E. CHURCH OF WARREN'S CORNERS.

A Methodist Episcopal class was organized at Warren's Corners in 1825 by Rev. John Copeland, with about twelve members. The male members were: Ezra Warren, Isaac Warren, Josiah Warren, Edwin Warren, Thomas Carlton, German Bush, Jonathan Benson and Thomas Fowler. Jonathan Benson was chosen the first class leader. Elder Copeland was their first pastor. Religious meetings were occasionally held here as early as 1818, by ministers of this denomination. The circuit at that early period included Lewiston, Buffalo, Batavia, Le Roy and Rochester; and from the latter place along the Ridge road to Lewiston. Rev. Mr. Shepardson was the minister in charge of the circuit at that time, and six weeks were occupied in completing his tour of it, preaching in many places on week day evenings. Rev. John Copeland had the pastoral care of the class for two years after its organization, when he was followed by Revs. Langthon, Paddock, Cozart, Asa, Abel and others.

The first church building was erected of wood in 1833, at a cost of about $800, on grounds donated to the society for that purpose. In 1858 the building was sold to Nelson T. Mighells, removed and converted to other uses, and the present brick structure erected on the same site. The latter was completed in the spring of 1859, at an expense of $2,200, and dedicated by the Rev. H. Ryan Smith.

The pulpit is at present supplied by M. W. Ayers, a licentiate from New Jersey. The present membership is about forty, with a large number of probationers.

A Sunday-school was organized in connection with this church about thirty years ago. Farrand Stedman was the first superintendent.

THE FIRST METHODIST SOCIETY OF CHESTNUT RIDGE.

A Methodist Episcopal society was organized at the school-house in district number three, in the east part of the town, on the 27th of January, 1834, at which time Sylvester Flagler, Theodore Stone, Titus Hall, Moses Rummery and Elijah Gibbs were chosen trustees. The number of original members was 37. Their meetings were held in the above mentioned school-house until 1835, when they erected a meeting-house in that vicinity at a cost of $1,350, which was appropriately dedicated by the Rev. Glezen Filmore.

The society was legally incorporated as "The First Methodist Society of Chestnut Ridge," under the general act for the incorporation of religious societies, on the 5th of July, 1841, at which time Henry Norton, Jacob Gaunt, Sylvester Flagler, Samuel Wakeman and John Sybrandt were constituted a board of trustees.

In 1843 a division occurred in the Methodist denomination, caused by the agitation of the questions of episcopacy and slavery, the result of which was the formation of the "Wesleyan Methodist Connection," which was organized at Utica, N. Y., May 31st, 1843. This church soon after adopted the discipline of that connection, but is still known in law as "The First Methodist Society of Chestnut Ridge."

In 1866 the church building was enlarged, remodeled and repaired at a cost of $1,900, and, when completed, was rededicated by the Rev. Adam Crooks, of Syracuse, N. Y.

The following is a complete list of preachers who have served this church, the labors of the first commencing in 1836: Revs. William D. Jewett, David Nichols, Levi B. Castle, two years; William Buck, Philo E. Brown, two years; Henry Norton, John Johnston, Lyman Lovell, Henry Norton, second term; George Wilson, two years; Asa Warren, Marshall Frink, two years; Samuel Phillips, two years; John Thompson, two years; Henry Norton,

RES. OF WM PEARSON, TOWN OF LOCKPORT, NIAGARA CO. N.Y.

third term; John Johnston, second term, of three years; Jonathan Sibley, two years; Asahel Staples, four years; D. B. Douglas, four years; Joseph Bennett, H. L. Dox, five years; W. W. Willihan, two years. The church is at present without a pastor.

The present trustees are John McNeil, Jacob Gaunt, John Hall, Jeffrey Barnet and John Labar. The present number of members is about twenty-five. The present value of the society property is estimated at $2,700. Its value was considerably enhanced in 1877 by the erection of commodious sheds near the church.

RAPIDS FREE CHURCH ASSOCIATION.

An association was formed at Rapids and incorporated under the above title in the year 1850, of which Alonzo J. Mansfield, Robert B. Kinne, —— Williams, James Kinne and Sylvester Collins were chosen the first trustees. This association embraced all the religious creeds represented in that vicinity. There existed here at that time a Methodist Episcopal class and a Wesleyan Methodist society, the latter of which was organized by Elder Warren about the year 1840. Soon after its formation the association commenced the erection of a free or union church edifice, which, after being inclosed, stood several years without being finished inside. When it was, at length, completed, it was dedicated by Rev. Mr. Stiles, a Free Methodist minister from Medina, assisted by Rev. Mr. Bennett of the Congregational church of Lockport. This is the only meeting-house in the village, the use of which is free to all religious denominations.

UNITED BRETHREN CHURCH OF RAPIDS.

A society of this denomination was organized at Rapids about the year 1860, by the Rev. Mr. Snyder, of Lockport, who served as its pastor for two years thereafter. The organization absorbed nearly all the religious element then existing in the vicinity. Rev. Mr. Badgley, a minister of this persuasion, had preached at this place for three or four years previous to the formation of the church. Elder Snyder was followed by Revs. Peckham, Pierce, Luce, Bennihoff and King, the latter being still in charge, holding regular weekly services at the free church. A society of Seventh Day Baptists also holds services here every Saturday.

FIRST EVANGELICAL CHURCH OF THE TOWN OF LOCKPORT.

The church edifice is situated on lot number eighty-eight, in the southern part of the town. A religious society was formally organized in this vicinity by the Rev. Michael Lehn, at a meeting held at his house May 27th, 1857. Among the constituent members were John Dunkelberger, who was chosen the first class-leader, Solomon Dunkelberger, sen., William and Jeremiah Dunkelberger, Adam Schreiber, and Adam Roeder. Religious services had been frequently held in dwelling houses in the neighborhood by ministers of the Evangelical denomination for five or six years prior to the formation of the church. On the 5th of February, 1858, this society was legally incorporated under the name of "The First Evangelical Society of the Town of Lockport," and Adam Roeder, John Dunkelberger and Adam Schreiber were elected the first trustees.

A frame church edifice was erected in the summer and fall of 1857, on ground donated for that purpose by Rev. M. Lehn, and dedicated the following winter by Bishop J. Seybert. The buildings and lot, about one-third of an acre, are valued at $2,000. A long row of carriage sheds has been erected on the same lot.

Rev. Michael Lehn, through whose influence the society was organized, was a resident of the neighborhood, and for a long time officiated as pastor. He was followed by Rev. Messrs. Schneider, Fisher, M. Pitzinger, A. Klein, J. Granzebach, F. Lohmeyer, N. Sauch, G. F. Buesch, and Jacob Eberling, who is the present pastor, having commenced his labors in the spring of 1878.

This church belongs to the New York Evangelical Conference.

BIOGRAPHICAL NOTICES OF LOCKPORT CITIZENS.

Bernard P. Alberty was born June 10th, 1815, at Durham, Greene county, N. Y., and came to Lockport in 1838 from Prattsville, N. Y. Mr. Alberty is a leading farmer, and has served as highway commissioner of the town of Lockport for six years.

Jeremy Angevine, a native of Orleans county, removed to Niagara county in 1844 and located on the farm that he at present owns, on the town line road between Lockport and Newfane, and which consists of about 400 acres of good land. In 1847 he built the hotel at Wright's Corners, and kept it two years, when he sold it to a man named Youngs.

Hon. Isaac H. Babcock was born in Rensselaerville, Albany county, N. Y., September 20th, 1830, and came to Somerset, Niagara county, in 1833. In 1863 he removed to the town of Lockport, where he has since resided, having been for many years engaged in farming. Mr. Babcock is treasurer of the Farmers' and Mechanics' Savings Bank, and of the Holly Steam Combination Company. He was supervisor of the town in 1865 and 1866, and member of Assembly in 1871 and 1872.

Asa Baldwin, a native of Shelden, Wyoming county, located at Warren's Corners in 1867, where he has since been engaged in farming and fruit-growing.

Joseph W. Barron, of English nativity, came to Lockport in 1852, and in 1869 removed to the farm on which he now resides, southwest of the city.

R. A. Barnes was born in Cambria. He lived in Orleans county at the breaking out of the rebellion, and in 1862 he enlisted in the 151st N. Y. volunteers, and served in the army in different positions for three years and a half, after which he came to Lockport and settled on the farm he now owns.

J. W. Bramley, a native of Derbyshire, England, was born February 18th, 1849, and came to Lockport in May, 1870. For the past three years he has been connected with the firm of Bramley Brothers & Co., manufacturers of patent cast steel plows, and all kinds of agricultural and ornamental iron work.

William F. Carl was born on the farm where he now resides, December 24th, 1849. He is engaged in farming. In 1875 he was elected town clerk of the town of Lockport.

S. A. Carson, a native of Ireland, came to Lockport in 1865, since which time he has been employed as superintendent and agent of the Lockport Fruit-Growers' Association.

James B. Conkey, a son of James Conkey, who was born in Orwell, Vermont, and removed to Niagara county in 1815, with his brother, Holmes A. Conkey, and his sister, Mrs. Sarah A. Segar, occupies his late father's old homestead, east of the city of Lockport. Mr. Conkey, sen., died in July, 1857.

B. W. Clark came from Cayuga county, N. Y., and located in Lockport in 1856, living in the city till 1870, when he bought a part of the Stephen Wakeman farm, where he has since been engaged in the cultivation of fruit and grape nurseries. Residence on Canal road, east of Lockport.

M. C. Crapsey was born March 11th, 1802, at Smithfeld, Madison county, N. Y. January 31st, 1825, he was married to Mary Southworth, of Palmyra, Wayne county, N. Y. He removed to Lockport in January, 1822. Mr. Crapsey is a well known and enterprising farmer of the town of Lockport. By honesty, perseverance and economy he has amassed a sufficiency of this world's goods, and his home is one of the pleasantest and most attractive in the vicinity.

Robert L. Crocker, a son of Joseph Crocker who at the age of twelve came to Lockport with his father, Luther Crocker, in 1816, was born in the town. His grandfather, Luther Crocker, was one of the pioneer settlers of Lockport.

S. Frost Cushman, a son of John E. Cushman, a native of Rensselaer county, N. Y., who came to Niagara county in 1838, was born in Somerset, N. Y., in 1845, and came to Lockport in 1848 from Newfane. He is a farmer and a teacher, and resides at Wright's Corners.

S. A. Disinger was born in Niagara county. He was married in 1854 to Miss Nancy Dollinger, of the town of Lockport. He is agent for the Johnson Harvester Company, of Brockport, N. Y.

George W. Dodge, a native of Cambria, removed to Lockport upon the farm which he has since occupied and where he now resides, in 1856.

Benoni H. Edmunds was born in Rodman, Jefferson county, N. Y., in 1816, and two years later he came with his father's family to Niagara county and settled near Hartland Corners. He married Martha F. Matteran, of Hartland, in 1843. In July, 1876, he removed to Wright's Corner's, where he has since resided, carrying on the business of farming. Benoni Edwards, sen., was a pioneer, and one of the jurymen in the trials resulting from the disappearance of William Morgan, in 1826.

S. Ernest, a native of Perry county, Pa., came to Lockport with his father's family in 1831. He moved on to his present farm in 1864, and is known as an enterprising farmer and fruit-grower; location, on the Hinman road, southwest of the city of Lockport.

William Ernest, a son of John Ernest, a native of Perry county, Pa., who came to Lockport in 1831, was born in 1833. Mr. Ernest, sen., located on a farm east of Lockport, on what is now known as Johnny-cake Ridge, where he resided until 1847, when he was killed by an accident while chopping down a tree. William Ernest now owns a farm of one hundred and fifty acres—seventy-five of the old homestead and some land purchased of Wait Smith in 1871—on which he has recently erected a fine residence.

Jacob Frantz was born in the town of Fayette, Senaca county, N. Y., July 6th, 1839, and came to Lockport in April, 1843. He was married February 24th, 1870, to Mary Ellen Basserman, of the town of Lockport.

John Frazer, a native of Ireland, located in Lockport in 1851 and kept the old Washington Hotel till 1864, when he removed to his farm in the west part of the town of Lockport, where he has since resided.

A. N. Furgason was born in Newfane, and resided there until about 1857, when he removed to Lockport. In 1865 he located at Wright's Corners, where he has since lived. For the past four years he has been engaged in the insurance business.

Jacob Gaunt, who is a native of Perry county, Pa., came to Niagara county in 1830 and located in the east part of the town of Lockport, where he has since followed the business of farming and fruit-growing. He was supervisor in 1838 and 1839, and again from 1860 to 1865. He has also been school commissioner, and served as excise commissioner and inspector of election four years each.

N. S. Gilbert is a native of Orleans county, N. Y. He came to Niagara county in 1861. In 1852 he was married to Miss Mary E. Lane. Mr. Gilbert was supervisor of the town of Lockport in 1876 and 1877, and was re-elected for 1878.

Mrs. James Goodrich (formerly Miss Amanda Mason) was born in the town of Moriah, Essex county, N. Y., in 1809. February 10th, 1831, she married James Goodrich, who removed to Lockport in the following May, settling on the farm now occupied by Mrs. Goodrich the first of June, of that year. Mr. Goodrich died July 14th, 1864, and his widow has since managed the farm.

Miss Adeliza Griswold, daughter of Jesse Griswold, was born April 24th, 1824, in the town of Lockport. Her father was a pioneer in western New York, having been in the employ of Joseph Ellicott at an early day, cutting out and constructing roads in different parts of the Holland Purchase.

W. A. Harrington was born in Columbia county, N. Y., and came to Niagara county in 1844. He was married to Miss Amanda Mason, a native of Madison county, Vt., in 1848. He follows the business of carpenter and joiner.

E. J. Hinman was born in Niagara county. He was married to Miss Mary E. Gardiner, of Monroe county, in 1864. Mr. Hinman is connected with the Cataract Nurseries.

JOHN W. LABAR.   MRS. JOHN W. LABAR.

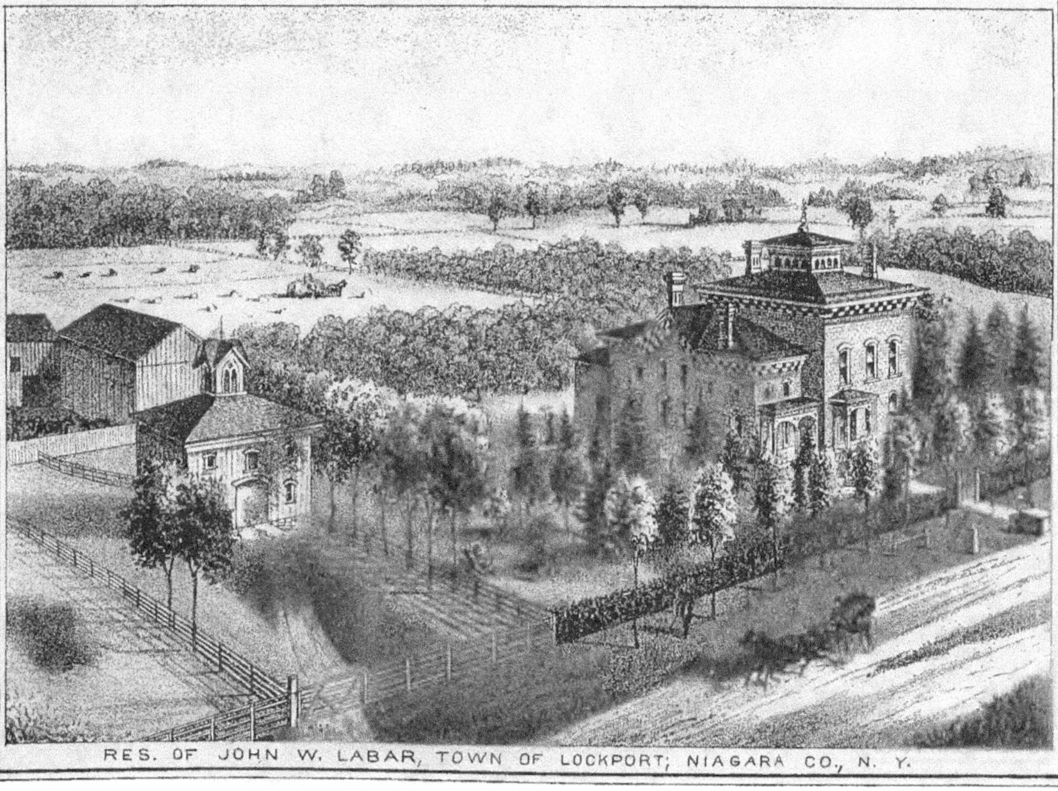

RES. OF JOHN W. LABAR, TOWN OF LOCKPORT, NIAGARA CO., N. Y.

De Witt Hinman, son of the late Charles Hinman, is proprietor of the Cataract Nurseries, on the Hinman road, southwest of the city of Lockport. He commenced planting trees in 1872, and has gradually increased his business until he has now about thirty acres of trees. These nurseries are well known, and receive a large patronage in this section and abroad.

Mrs. Emily N. Hixson, a daughter of Titus Atwater, deceased, is a native of Schoharie county, N. Y., and removed from that county to Lockport with her father's family in 1837. She has been a resident of the town ever since, and has lived on her present farm, on the Hinman road, since 1850.

Abraham Jones was born in Perry county, Pa., and removed to Genesee county in 1826, and from there to Lockport in 1834. He purchased a farm on what is now a continuation of High street, east of the city, where he has since resided, following his trade, as carpenter and builder, until his retirement from active business, a few years since.

Andrew Keck was born in Perry county, Pa., and came to Niagara county in 1832. He was married in 1846 to Miss L. C. Owen, of Canada. He is a resident of the town of Lockport, south of the city.

Hon J. W. Labar, though American born, is of French descent, his father having been a commissary in the army of the Marquis de La Fayette, and having come with that distinguished general to America during the struggle for independence. Mr Labar was born September 5th, 1807, in the town of Northampton, Montgomery county, N. Y. He removed to Orleans county in 1834, and from there, in 1836, to Royalton, Niagara county, and in 1860 he came from Royalton to the town of Lockport, where he has long been engaged as a farmer and fruit-grower. Mr. Labar is a well known and influential citizen and business man, and the confidence of the people in his ability and integrity was manifested by his election from this district as a member of the State Legislature for the years 1857 and 1858. He was married July 14th, 1832, to Miss Almira Palmer, of Northumberland, Saratoga county, N. Y.

Nathaniel Lerch, orchardist and wholesale fruit dealer, was born August 13th, 1835, in Cambria, N. Y., and married December 22nd, 1859, to Francis L. Leonard, of Pendleton, N. Y.

M. B. Lewis, whose parents were natives of Connecticut, was born in Orange county, N. Y., in 1812. He removed to Wyoming county in 1823, and from there to Lockport in 1855, where he has since followed farming, fruit-growing and stock-raising.

Mrs. J. Long, formerly Miss Susannah Disinger, is a native of Seneca county. She was married in 1825 to J. Long, deceased, a native of Pennsylvania, who came to Niagara county in 1825.

William Mackey was born in Williamsport, Pa., and came with his father's family to Niagara county in 1829, and located in Royalton, where he resided till 1868, when he removed to Buffalo, and after remaining there four years came to Lockport, where he has since devoted his time to farming and stock dealing.

John McMaster was born in Toronto, Canada, in the year 1844, and came to Lockport about 1856. Mr. McMaster, who has done top-grafting in the orchards of Niagara county for the last eighteen years, is a practical grafter and orchardist, and is agent for D. W. Hinman & Co.

John Miller was born in Schenectady county, N. Y., came to Niagara county in 1828, and in 1830 bought and settled on a farm in Newfane. He removed to Lockport in the spring of 1850, and located on the farm he at present owns and cultivates.

Eli Moore was born in Oneida county, N. Y. He came to Orleans county in 1811, and was a prominent early settler there. In 1836 he removed to Johnson's Creek, in the town of Hartland, Niagara county. Afterwards he lived in Lockport, then at Black Rock, and finally returned to Lockport and located in 1865 on the farm where he has since resided.

J. H. Mosher was born in Somerset, Niagara county, in 1827, and came to Lockport in 1863. He is a farmer by occupation.

Mrs. Ordelia Niles, whose maiden name was Ordelia De Lozier, was born in Whitesville, N. Y., in 1810. July 3rd, 1825, she married B. H. Whitaker, who established the first shoe and leather store in Lockport. Mr. Whitaker was killed by the cars in 1865, and in 1871 his widow was again married, to Joseph Niles, who died in 1874. Mrs. Niles survives him and lives in the old homestead, which has been owned in the family for forty-four years.

Chester H. Partridge was born January 24th, 1833, in Galway, Saratoga county, and came thence to his present place of residence in 1851. He is engaged in farming; post-office, Lockport. He was married February 11th, 1858, to Miss Philena Raymond, of Lockport, and August 18th, 1867, to Miss Phebe A. Morey, of Lagrange, N. Y.

William Pearson, a son of George Pearson, was born in the county of Durham, England, in 1821, and came with his father to Lockport in 1831, and located on the Slaton Settlement road, on the farm now owned by Mrs. Henry Pearson, whose husband was a son of George Pearson, who resided there till his death in 1855. In 1846 William Pearson purchased the farm he now owns and occupies. It consists of 400 acres of land on the Slaton Settlement road, and Mr. Pearson is one of the most extensive farmers in the town.

William B. Pease, farmer and fruit-grower, was born July 31st, 1830, in Somerset. On the 4th of October, 1856, he was united in marriage to Usuula Hathaway, of Lockport. Mr. Pease came from Girard, Erie county, Pa., to Lockport March 1st, 1856. His post-office is Lockport.

Norman Pomroy, farmer, was born in the town of Lockport in 1829. In 1857 he was married to Rachel Oliphant.

Orsemus Reasoner, farmer, was born in Hartland, N. Y., November 11th, 1827, and was married November 4th, 1854, to Alvina Maxfield, of the same town.

William Robinson was born in Washington county, N. Y. He removed to Niagara county in 1844, and bought a farm on the Canal road, where he has since lived. Mr. Robinson's son, Charles Robinson, lives on the adjoining farm, also owned by his father, and manages both places.

M. C. Sheehan, a native of Ireland, came to Canada when three years old, remaining there until 1849, when he removed to Lockport. In 1862 he purchased the farm where he now resides, engaged in farming and the cultivation of fruit.

Mrs. J. D. Shuler is the owner of a fruit farm of fifty acres located a mile east of the city of Lockport. She grows some of the finest fruit raised in this section.

D. Stahler, a son of Henry Stahler, who came to Niagara county in 1830, was married in 1856 to Miss A. Westman, a native of Pennsylvania. Mr. Stahler is a well known resident of the town.

Henry Stevens was born in Lockport in 1839. In 1860 he bought and located on a farm previously owned by his father, Rivera Stevens, west of the city on the Shawnee road, where he has since resided.

Mrs. P. S. Smith, daughter of the late Asa Randall, was born in Genesee county and removed with her father's family, in 1827, to the town of Wilson, Niagara county, where she remained until 1838, and then removed to the city of Lockport, remaining there until 1867, when she removed with her husband, Mr. P. S. Smith, to the farm where she now resides. Mr. Smith, who was a native of Warren county, N. Y., died in 1873.

James D. Taylor, farmer, is a native of the town of Hartland, where he was born in August, 1820. He came to Lockport in 1853, having lived in Pennsylvania from 1842 to 1849, and in Pendleton from the latter date to the time of his removal to Lockport.

Patrick H. Twohey, Michigan street, town of Lockport, general dealer in stone and in lime and sandstone of any dimensions, was born in Lockport in 1855.

Dr. W. A. Townsend was born in 1792, in Hebron, Tolland county, Conn. He removed to western New York in 1815, shortly after graduating from the medical department of Yale College; and after living in Onondaga, Livingston and Seneca counties for a number of years, was obliged to relinquish the practice of medicine on account of failing health, when he came to Lockport and purchased a farm just outside the city, where he has continued to live to the present.

Harvey H. Wakeman, a son of Stephen Wakeman who located in the town in 1811, and took up the farm where his son now lives, on the Canal road, east of the city, in 1819, was born on the homestead in 1822. He is a farmer and fruit-grower.

James E. Wakeman, farmer, was born in Lockport, in 1852, on the farm on the Warren's Corners Stone road where he now resides. He is a well known resident of the town.

Barney Warren is a native of Clinton county, N. Y., where he was born in 1817. He removed to Lockport in 1868 from Newfane, Niagara county. In the spring of 1878 he located on the Seneca B. Foote farm, east of the city, where he has since resided.

Isaac Wilson, a native of Watertown, N. Y., came to Lockport in 1861, and located on the farm he now occupies, on the Stone road, north of the city. He is an energetic and enterprising farmer.

Robert Wilson is a native of England. He was born November 28th, 1826. Mr. Wilson, who is a farmer, residing at Slaton Settlement, in the town of Lockport, came to the county in 1832, and took an active part in clearing the dense forests of this region.

Jabez S. Woodward was born April 4th, 1831, in the town of Phelps, Ontario county, N. Y., and came to Lockport in the spring of 1832. Mr. Woodward is a dealer in hardware in the city of Lockport, and owns a fine fruit farm of 192 acres in Newfane, 75 acres of which is in fruit. He has always been actively engaged in the fruit interest of Niagara county and western New York. He has been and is now vice-president of the Western New York Horticultural Society.

C. D. Worrell is a son of Daniel Worrell, a native of Vermont, who came to Lockport in 1832. Mr. Worrell, sen., had stopped one year in Royalton before coming to Lockport. He died in the fall of 1874. C. D. Worrell follows the business of farming at the old homestead on the Warren's Corners and Lockport Stone road.

Charles Wynkoop was born in Moreland township, Montgomery county, Pa., September 24th, 1804, came to Lockport in 1823, and has since been engaged in farming.

The following are the names of a few of the most prominent citizens of the town not already mentioned:

Luther Forsyth, Mrs. Hannah S. La Roche, W. E. Palmer, E. Ashley Smith, F. Steadman, Mrs. A. M. Willetts.

FRUIT FARM OF WM B. PEASE ON THE SLAYTON SETTLEMENT ROAD 3½ MILES N.E. FROM LOCKPORT.

FARM RESIDENCE OF NELSON T. MIGHELLS ESQ. WARRENS CORNERS NIAGARA CO. N.Y.

THE TOWN OF NEWFANE.

NEWFANE was so named by Mrs. James Van Horn. It was formed from Wilson, Hartland and Somerset in 1824.

William Chambers and John Brewer, who came to the town in 1807, from Canada, were the first white settlers of whom we have any account, either in history or tradition. They located at or near the mouth of Eighteen-mile creek. Mr. Chambers met his death in 1825, while attempting to cross the Niagara river above the cataract in a skiff, being drawn into the rapids and carried over the falls. A Mr. Cotton settled in this town the same year with Chambers and Brewer.

The next settlers were Burgoyne Kemp and Peter Hopkins in 1808, William and James Weisner in 1810, and Levi Lewis in 1811. These all came from the east or southeast, as Kemp was a native of New Jersey, and the others from that State and Pennsylvania. The family to which Mr. Kemp belonged journeyed from New Jersey to Canada West in 1786, before settling in this town. They and their effects were carried on pack horses, and no white person was met between Tioga Point and Lewiston. Their horses were stolen by Indians if not kept close to the camp at night, and the savages murdered a young man whom the Kemp party met on their way. A small drove of cattle and sheep which accompanied the pioneers was obliged to swim the Genesee river.

Benjamin Coomer, Ira Tompkins, Benjamin Halsted, Alvin Buck, Charles McClew, Benjamin Stout, William Cooper, Silas Mead, James Hess, Solomon C. Wright, and others, came to this town soon after the close of the war of 1812, taking an "article" of the Holland Land Company for their lots, and locating them in different parts of the town—Hess in the east, Buck and Wright in the south, Coomer in the west, Halsted, Stout and others in the north, McClew, McKie, Patterson and others in the center of the town, along Eighteen-mile creek.

INCIDENTS OF THE WAR OF 1812.

During the trying period of the war of 1812, this town, as well as others, suffered severely from British, Indians, and tories, the latter seeming to vie with the savages in their inhuman outrages upon the peaceful and unoffending pioneer settlers, who, having thus far succeeded in keeping the beasts of prey from their doors, were now set upon by a new foe, that threatened the destruction not only of property, but of life also.

Those who had gathered up all their worldly effects and left their eastern homes and kindred, hoping to find a permanent place of abode in this then western country, were ruthlessly stripped of every thing, and driven into the wilderness, away from their new homes, without food or shelter, to become food for the savage beasts of the forests, or subjects of charity should they be fortunate enough to reach a settlement beyond the reach of the invading British soldiery, or their ferocious ally, the treacherous Indian scout of the war of 1812. Not only were the few inhabitants great sufferers, but that portion of the brute creation that depended upon human aid for sustenance also, to a great degree, suffered for want of proper food.

During the war, the British having control of the lake, it was necessary in keeping up the supplies for our little army to use flat boats, propelled by oars or setting-poles, working their slow way along as best they could, dodging into bays and creeks to keep out of the way of the British cruisers. A boat loaded with salt had worked its way up to near the mouth of Honeoye creek, when it was discovered by one of His Majesty's cruisers, which at once gave chase. Our boys, thinking discretion the better part of valor, ran their boat into the mouth of the creek, gathered a few settlers who were near at hand, and returned to the boat just in time to give the red-coats a warm reception. Just how many of the British were killed and wounded is not known, as those who were unhurt picked up their dead and wounded, and retired from the scene quite as briskly as they came.

The cruiser soon discovered the mistake it had made, and opened a cannonade with solid shot, which came crashing through the tops of the trees, over the heads of our men. The shore of the lake at that point is quite high, and the creek, running almost parallel with the shore for some distance, forms a small ravine, making one of the best natural defenses on the lake. The "Yanks," being behind this, were out of all danger from any of the solid shot. The British vessel soon saw the folly of wasting ammunition in that direction, and soon disappeared in the distance, when our boys went on their way rejoicing with their cargo of salt.

In after years, when Mr. Bullard was clearing up his farm, in sawing a log his men found that the saw would not cut; and on taking it from the tree they found the teeth were badly battered. With an ax they soon found they had captured one of Johnny Bull's blue plums, that had lodged in the tree when the enemy were trying to capture Brother Jonathan's salt. Mr. Benjamin Stout, who now owns the farm upon which this pleasant little affair occurred, has plowed up several of the round shot fooled away that day by His Majesty's cruiser.

In no situation were courage and resolution so much required in woman as in the wilderness, during the settlement of western New York.

In the British raid upon the lake shore in this town in December, 1813, it was through the cool bravery of a shrewd woman that her house and furniture, as well as some of the flour at Van Horn's mill, were saved. A sergeant, with a squad of men, was sent up Eighteen-mile creek to burn Van Horn's mill and the dwellings of the settlers. Arriving at the house of Joseph Pease, a little north of Van Horn's mill, the officer in command informed Mrs. Pease of his mission, and told her she could carry her goods out of the house, which would be but a small job. Her remonstrances were of no avail, and after clearing the little log house of all she could carry, she finally asked the soldiers to help her carry out a couple of barrels of brandy, which were in the potato hole under the floor. They readily consented, and in the operation got a taste of the "critter," which Mrs. Pease did not object to, and soon another, and another, until, either forgetting their mission or becoming a little humane under the influence of the brandy, they left her house standing, and also, at her request, released her son Enoch, who was a prisoner in their hands, and allowed his brother to save several barrels of flour from the burning mill, before they left for Fort Niagara with a few prisoners.

Soon after the close of the war, and then only after the people generally had been assured of safety by the proper authorities, in a public manner, settlers began to come, and some who had been driven away to return; soon this part of the county began to assume an air of independence, and in April, 1824, a new town was formed, and all the machinery incident thereto put in motion.

Of the soldiers of the war of 1812 there are now living in the town Benjamin Halsted, David Weisner, Moses Lovell and —— Richardson.

FROM THE EARLY RECORDS.

The following information was taken from the records of the town:

At an annual town meeting held at the house of James Van Horn, on the 6th day of April, 1824, the following votes were passed:

For town officers: Supervisor, James Weisner; town clerk, Jonathan Coomer; assessors, Cornelius Van Horn, Solomon C. Wright, Jacob Albright; collector, at 2½ per cent. fees, John B. McKnight; poor masters, Ezra Barnes, Zebulon Coates; commissioners of highways Robert McKnight, Archibald McDonald, Jacob Albright; commissioners of common schools, Alexander Butterfield, John Warner, Archibald McDonald; school inspectors, Simon Newcomb, jr., Peter Hess, Heman Pratt; constables, John McKnight, George Bennett.

Voted, to raise a sum of money in the town equal to what the State affords for the use of common schools.

Voted, to have no pound. Voted, that the legality of fences shall be submitted to the fence-viewers of the town.

Voted, that every road district shall nominate their own overseers of highways.

At the general election held November 1st, 2nd and 3rd, 1824, there were 119 votes cast for governor, of which 63 were cast for Samuel Young, and 56 for De Witt Clinton; scattering, 8 votes.

At a meeting of the school commissioners of the town, held at Dr. Butterfield's on the 19th day of April, 1824, the town was divided into eight districts.

In 1825 it was voted that all hogs weighing over 30 pounds shall be free commoners.

Voted, that any man having Canada thistles on his land, and letting them go to seed, shall pay five dollars.

Voted, that Peabody shall be discharged from a fine of twelve dollars and fifty cents for suffering spirituous liquors to be sold on his premises.

The following have served as supervisors and town clerks from 1825 to 1878, in the years indicated:

SUPERVISORS.

1825–27, James Weisner; 1828, Stephen Hays; 1829–31, James Van Horn; 1832, Stephen Hays; 1833, James Weisner; 1834, Cornelius Van Horn; 1835, John U. Pease; 1836–40, James Weisner; 1841, David Kemp; 1842–44, Henry A. Reynolds; 1845, James Weisner; 1846, John W. Pulver; 1847, James Van Horn, jr.; 1848, John Henning; 1849, 1850, Peter McCollum; 1851, John Henning; 1852, Walter Shaw; 1853, John Henning; 1854, James Van Horn, jr.; 1857–60, James Van Horn; 1861, 1862, John McCollum; 1863–65, Marcellus Washburn; 1866, 1867, Alexander Campbell; 1868, 1869, Charles S. McCollum; 1870, Ziba Richardson; 1871, John McCollum; 1872, Benjamin S. Laughlin; 1873, 1874, Anthony McKie; 1875–77, William V. Corwin; 1878, James A. McCollum.

TOWN CLERKS.

1823–25, Jonathan Coomer; 1827, Elisha Newman; 1828, Nathaniel Church; 1829–31, Almeron Newman; 1832, James Van Horn, jr.; 1833, James D. Cooper; 1834, Abraham Smith; 1835, George Mann; 1836, 1837, Daniel Dix; 1838, James A. Cooper; 1839, I. B. Ransom; 1840–48, Anthony McKie; 1849, Henry Eshbaugh; 1850, George Mann; 1851, Daniel T. Odell; 1852, Henry Eshbaugh; 1853, Anthony McKie; 1854, Alden C. Heith; 1855, Ezra Post; 1856, Anthony McKie; 1857–61, Ezra Post; 1862–65, James M. McKie; 1866, Augustus B. Kenall; 1867, 1868, James Maxwell; 1869, William T. Follett; 1870, William S. Pike; 1871, 1872, Walter Shaw; 1873, R. J. Wilson; 1874, Claudius C. Hilson; 1875, Anthony McKie; 1876, Duncan R. Maxwell; 1877, 1878, James H. Patterson.

BUILDING AND BEGINNING BUSINESS.

William Chambers and John Brewer built their log houses, in the vicinity of Lockport and Main streets, in 1807, and the next year Burgoyne Kemp built a double log house three or four rods northwest from where the Grove House now stands, at Olcott. Kemp also built the first log barn, which stood a short distance northwest from the house. Up to 1810, Chambers's, Brewer's and Kemp's were the only buildings east of the creek; but in that year, Albright and the Weisners and others came in and settled east of the creek, on what is now the Lake road. Albright settled on the farm now owned by S. Wilson. At that time there were no settlers, except Fitts, in Somerset, for several miles east of Newfane. Between this and the Ridge road was a dense wilderness, where are now, along the Hess road, some of the most fertile farms in this section of country. In 1809 Mr. Hopkins built a log house near the mouth of what is now known as Hopkins creek, and about 1811 Benjamin Halsted built his house at the mouth of Eighteen-mile creek.

Martin Burch built the first frame house in this town, on the Lake road, near where it crosses Honeoye creek; it is now owned by Mr. Chapman. The building now known as the James Cooper House, at Olcott, was the second frame house in this town.

The first brick house in this town was built by James Van Horn, on the Creek road, one and a half miles south of Olcott, where W. Van Horn now lives. At present there are several brick buildings in the town. The first frame barn built in the town stands on the south side of the road, on the bank of the creek, opposite the Cooper House in the village of Olcott, and was built in 1814.

In 1816 Stout and Albright each built a frame barn. Albright's was on the Wilson farm, and the other on the farm now owned by Benjamin Stout, on the Lake road, east of the Eighteen-mile creek. Mr. Benjamin Stout laid the floor in his father's barn when he was thirteen years old. The barn is still standing, on the south side of the road, opposite Mr. Stout's residence, and is as good as new, and has the original floor and siding.

STORES.

In 1812 Asa Douglass kept a small store at what was then Kempville, and is now Olcott, and in 1816 he was succeeded by Mr. Eddy, who kept a store in the old red building west of the Cooper House, Olcott. There was also a store opposite Cooper's, kept by Boyce & Falwell. In 1821 Archibald McDonald opened a store in the rear of where Thurber's store now stands, and at that time it was the only one in the place. Soon after Van Horn built his mills, he opened a store at that place, one and a half miles south of Olcott. At that time all goods and groceries were brought by water from the mouth of the Genesee river in sailing vessels; but at the present time all goods are transported by the R. W. & O. railroad, as the station on that line is but one and a half miles distant. There are at present six stores in the town.

TAVERNS.

Halsted, Brady, Butterfield, Nichols, Harris and Cooper were the early Kempville tavern-keepers. Benjamin Halsted was the first man to open an inn, or tavern, at Kempville, which, according to tradition, he did as early as 1812. His was what was known as a double log tavern, or, in other words, a log house with two rooms, with a chimney of sticks or other ancient material at each end of the house. The tavern was on the site of the Cooper House.

Halsted was succeeded in 1815 by Mr. Brady, who was followed by one Harris, and he by one Nichols, and then came William D. Cooper, who built the present hotel. In 1819 Alexander Butterfield, M. D., kept tavern in the building now standing on the opposite side of the road from the Cooper House. The doctor was one of the justices of the peace in the then town of Wilson. The west room of the house was the bar-room, and the east room the parlor; and in this room, in 1819, the venerable old doctor, or rather justice of the peace, performed the marriage ceremony uniting Mr. Silas Mead and his future wife in the bonds of holy wedlock. Mr. Mead is still living in the village of Olcott.

There was also a tavern kept by Asa Douglass in a double log house, where John Morquett's house now stands, in the village of Olcott.

In the early history of this town, there was an old log tavern just south of W. V. Corwin's, between the house and the little creek, on the road from Wright's Corners to Olcott, kept by William Cooper, familiarly known as "Uncle Billy," and the jolliest landlord in the country.

Alvin Buck located at what is now Wright's Corners in 1817, and kept a tavern in a double log house. Solomon C. Wright suceeded Buck in 1823, and was postmaster at that place for forty-five years. In 1823 Arthur Patterson opened a hotel at Charlotte, near the center of the town. His was a frame, two-story house, and is still standing.

There are at present three hotels in the town, all located at Olcott—the Lake Shore Hotel, Grove Hotel, and Cooper House.

PHYSICIANS.

Alexander Butterfield was the first resident physician at what is now Olcott, locating there in 1814. He had a very large practice during his long and useful life. Doctor Butterfield died November 19th, 1867, aged 73 years. During his illness, Mrs. Butterfield was taken sick, and died in about thirty minutes after the death of the doctor, aged 69 years.

Doctor John Warren located soon after Doctor Butterfield, and died at Olcott, May 24th, 1834.

At present there are three physicians in the town, Doctor McFadden at Olcott, and Drs. Crane and Saddleson at Charlotte.

GRIST-MILLS.

In 1810 Levi Ellis came from Seneca county, N. Y., and commenced a grist-mill on Eighteen-mile creek. The dam was located almost directly under the railroad bridge, where it crosses the creek. Before completing the mill dam, Mr. Ellis and nearly all his men were taken sick with fever and ague, and returned to Seneca county. Mr. James Van Horn finished the work and put the mills in operation.

In 1813 the British authorities, learning of the mill, and claiming that it was working for the United States government, sent a sergeant and eighteen men to burn it, which they did, destroying everything, except a few barrels of flour, which they very kindly left for the benefit of the few poor settlers who had not taken up arms against the British government.

In 1817 the grist-mill was rebuilt by Mr. Van Horn, with Ira Tompkins as millwright; it was fitted with two run of stones, and located on the site of the present mills.

In 1839 the two mills were destroyed by fire; immediately work was commenced, and in 1840 the present mills were put in operation, with three run of stones. Since then extensive repairs have been made, flouring machinery has been put in, and the mill is now known as the "Lake Shore Mills," owned and operated by Mr. Arrowsmith. The present mills are located one and a half miles south of Olcott, and but a few rods above where the original mills were built.

Tompkins Mill (grist-mill) is on the Eighteen-mile creek, about six miles from its mouth. This mill was erected in 1869 by Hon. Ira Tompkins, and is now in good condition and doing a good business. There was an old mill on the same site in 1835, known as Adams Mills, but it went to decay long before the present mills were built.

Charlotte Grist-Mill was built in 1835, and is located at Charlotte village, on the Eighteen-mile creek, four miles south of Olcott. It is a custom mill, doing a good business.

Burgoyne Kemp built a grist-mill in 1814, at or near the mouth of Honeoye creek, east of Olcott, on the lake shore, on the farm now owned by Benjamin Stout. It had but one run of stones, and went to decay in 1835.

SAW-MILLS.

In 1811 Jacob Albright built a saw-mill on Keg creek, a little south of the Lake road. This mill was burned during the war of 1812, and afterward rebuilt by Mr. Albright.

In 1827 there was a saw-mill on Honeoye creek, on the farm now owned by James Chapman, east of Olcott; it was known at that time as the "Stout and Weisner" mill, and was destroyed about 1830.

Shubal S. Merritt owned a saw-mill on Keg creek, north of the Lake road, in 1827. There are the remains of an old mill still standing.

There was also a saw-mill at Van Horn's in 1812, and it was burned with the grist-mill, in December, 1813, by the British. There were also saw-mills at Tompkins's Mills, and Charlotte.

There is at present a saw-mill at Arrowsmith's (late Van Horn's), one at Charlotte, and one at Tompkins's mills.

SHOPS AND MANUFACTORIES.

Nathaniel Swartwout was the master builder in the town up to 1817, when Ira Tompkins came from Seneca county, N. Y. Swartwout built the barns for Albright and Stout in 1816. Mr. Tompkins is also a mill-wright by trade, and has built nearly all the mills in the town. He has probably built more buildings than any other one carpenter and builder in the county of Niagara.

Thomas Armstrong opened a blacksmith shop at Olcott in 1814, on the bank of the creek, just east of where the Cooper House now stands. A Mr. Hartwell was also an early blacksmith in the town.

There are at present, blacksmiths at Coomer Road, Hess Road, Charlotte, Ridge Road and Olcott.

In 1842 Mr. Van Horn built a woolen factory on the Eighteen-mile creek, about two and a half miles south of Olcott. The mill was closed in 1874. Van Horn & Co. also had a clothier's shop at the same place. Mr. Newman operated a clothier's shop on the Eighteen-mile creek, nearly opposite A. McClew's. James Van Horn worked a distillery near his house in 1825.

The Charlotte Woolen Mills, located at Charlotte village, were built in 1863 by Niles & Van Ostrand, and operated by them, and in 1866 by H. B. Gulick, when they were purchased by Swift, Osgood & Co., and sold in 1869 to Clark & Ingraham, who sold in 1876 to H. B. Gulick & Son, and R. L. Gulick purchased the property of them in 1877.

TANNERY.

The only tannery in this town was in 1820-21 owned and operated by John D. Cohler. It was located on the west side of the mouth of Eighteen-mile creek. Whiting followed Cohler in the business, and it was soon abandoned.

ANTIQUITIES.

Some time previous to 1700, or during the French and Indian war, the French, as is supposed, built a small redoubt, or fort, on the point on the lake shore at the west side of the mouth of Eighteen-mile Creek. The land is now owned and cultivated by Mr. Wright. From traces of the works that are still to be seen it is thought they were about one hundred and fifty feet in diameter, if circular, or the same distance on either side, if square.

During the process of cultivating this spot of ground and its surroundings, many relics have been found, plainly indicating its occupancy by the French.

In 1825 a Frenchman came here and made diligent search for gold, which he said was put inside of a long cannon and buried. Whether he ever found any or not is unknown, as he disappeared quite as mysteriously as he came.

In 1813 there was an Indian camping ground on the west side of the farm now owned by Benjamin Stout, near the mouth of Honeoye creek. The Indians here in 1813 claimed that this spot was one of the camping grounds of their fathers and chiefs, when opposing their French enemies. They were in the habit of camping here for several weeks at a time, devoting the time to hunting and fishing.

RES. OF EDWIN E. ARNOLD, TOWN OF SOMERSET.

RES. OF MRS. E. A. GAMBLE, TOWN OF NEWFANE, NIAGARA CO., N.Y.
THE ABRAM PHILLIPS HOMESTEAD.

ROADS AND BRIDGES.

The following is a record of the first road laid out after the town of Newfane was erected:

"Survey of a road beginning at the Transit line, at or near the center of lot No. 4, in the 14th section; thence east on William Cooper's north line, 60 chains, to the east line of said lot No. 4; thence south on said line, 80 links, thence east to a line dividing the 10th section on the Hess road.

"JACOB C. ALBRIGHT, } Commissioners of
ROBERT McKNIGHT, } Highways.

"June 11th, 1824."

The Coomer road, on the west side of the town, running from the Lake road, on a line parallel with the west line of the town and three-quarters of a mile east of it, to the south line, was established in the early history of Newfane by Benjamin Coomer, who lived upon its line and was quite an influential man in the town. He died October 26th, 1817, and was buried in the village cemetery at Olcott. A common field stone marks his resting place, and only his name and the above date can be traced, the rest having scaled off by the action of the atmosphere.

The Hess road was laid out in the fall of 1821, by the commissioners of highways and surveyor, Mr. Peter Hess assisting in cutting out the logs and brush. The first path was indicated by marked trees; it ran from northwest to southeast, and struck the Ridge road west of Hartland Corners. The road derived its name from the Hess brothers, living on its line. James Hess chopped the road out, three rods wide, for one mile on its line, receiving pay for three-quarters of a mile, and donating the other quarter. This road is on the east side of the town, running parallel with the east line of the town, and three-quarters of a mile from it, from the Lake road on the north, to the town line on the south.

The Creek road runs from near Wright's Corners, on the south line of this town, to Tompkins's Mills, where it strikes the Eighteen-mile creek, thence to Olcott, on the lake. This is one of the oldest roads in the town, having been used as early as 1808 or 1809.

The original road went along the east bank of the creek as it winds and turns, and that portion of it between Tompkins's Mills and the ridge was, in early times and in rainy seasons, almost impassable on account of the mud, while at the present time, with ditching, turnpiking and drawing on gravel, it has become one of the good roads of the town

The Ewing road, on the west side of the Eighteen-mile creek, runs from the lake shore half a mile west of Olcott, in a southerly direction, to the town-line of Lockport. It was named from families living along the road.

The Lake road runs across the north end of the town, nearly parallel with the lake shore, and a little south of the road that Burgoyne Kemp cut along the lake shore for the Holland Land Company east to the county line.

The first bridge of which we could gain any information of importance, was the one at Kempville, now Olcott, in 1811. There was at that time the frame of a bridge, but no plank on it finished.

In 1825 General James Weisner contracted with the town authorities to built a bridge across the Eighteen-mile creek at Olcott. The bridge was to be 400 feet long, in twenty spans of twenty feet each. The frame was to be of white oak, the timbers to be twelve by sixteen inches, and the bridge twenty-seven feet wide. The contract price was five hundred dollars. Mr. Peter Hess, now living in Somerset, worked on the bridge for General Weisner, and scored most of the timber, ready for hewing.

Previous to this, there was only a foot bridge at the mouth of the creek. Since then about three hundred feet on the east side of the creek has been dyked, sufficiently wide for teams to pass, and a fine row of willows is growing upon the north, or lake side of the dyke.

The old bridge at this place was taken down in 1878 and an iron bridge built, for which the town board appropriated $4,000. The iron structure is one hundred feet long and twenty-two feet wide, with a roadway in the middle and a foot path on each side.

There are seven bridges crossing the Eighteen-mile creek, and fifteen crossing the other creeks and their branches in this town.

BURYING GROUNDS.

Previous to the year 1817, there was a burial place near the west bank of Keg creek, south of the Lake road, on the farm now owned by Stephen Wilson, but it has all been washed away by the action of the water upon the bank of the creek.

The grave-yard at Olcott was occupied as early as October 26th, 1817, when one Benjamin was buried there. The following are a few of the oldest persons buried in the Olcott yard: Elizabeth Shaver, born 1760, died 1864, aged 104; Daniel Andrews, aged 75; Peter Hess, aged 85 years, 7 months and 14 days; Dr. Alexander Butterfield, aged 69. There are burial grounds at Charlotte, Wright's Corners, and on the Hess road, Ewing road, and Lake road, and several family burying grounds in other parts of the town.

VILLAGES AND POST-OFFICES.

CHARLOTTE derives its name from a former owner of the land upon which the village stands, Hon. George R. Davis, of Troy, N. Y., who named the village after his daughter Charlotte. It is located on Eighteen-mile creek, four miles north of Olcott, and has a population of about four hundred. It contains a post-office, two churches, grist-mill, saw-mill, store, blacksmith shop, cooperage, school-house, woolen mills, and the manufacturing establishment of the Newfane Box and Basket Company.

OLCOTT is pleasantly located at the mouth of Eighteen-mile creek, on the shore of Lake Ontario. The high banks, and the well preserved groves, beautiful walks and enchanting scenery, with the cool, bracing air from the lake, go to make it an agreeable locality for summer resort. It has one of the best harbors on the lake, with sufficient water and room for the largest vessels. It is also a port of entry, and has its custom-house officer, in the person of Henry Kinney, Esq.

At this place there are two piers, built by the United States government, for the accommodation of lake commerce, projecting from either side of the mouth of the creek, into the lake, a distance of eight hundred and eighty feet, and twenty feet wide. Upon the outer end of the west pier is located the government light-house, with Mr. Charles Mathews as keeper. The light is fifty feet the water, with a patent reflector. Geographically this above light is located in latitude north 43° 20' 04", and longitude west 78° 41' 30". There is a line of steamers running from this port to all points on the lake.

This place, it is said, was a scene of warfare during the French and Indian war. The land upon which the village is located was owned in 1808 by William Chambers on the west side of the creek, who subsequently sold to Benjamin Halsted, and on the east of the creek by Burgoyne Kemp, who named the place Kempville. The land on the east side of the creek was afterwards owned by J. D. Cooper.

For quite a number of years, the whole of the business was done on the east side of the creek, where stood the church, two or three stores, as many taverns, and other business establishments.

When J. D. Cooper came into possession of the land upon the east side of the creek, it was surveyed into building lots and streets, and sold at prices that brought in a population; and at present, the whole business of the village is carried on upon the east side of the creek, with the exception of one hotel.

There are at present three churches, a school-house, three hotels, two stores, a post-office, blacksmith, wagon and cooper shops, a cider-mill, etc., with a population of about 400.

About the year 1828 or 1830, the sailing vessel owned by Captain Mark Burch, called the "Crazy Jane," was very mysteriously sunk in the harbor at this place, near the south end of the east pier, or between that and the warehouse at the east end of the bridge; and in 1874, while the government dredge was dredging out the harbor, most of the "Crazy Jane" was raised, and pieces of her are in the hands of relic hunters.

Olcott post-office was the first in the town, and was established as early as 1817, when Doctor Alexander Butterfield was postmaster, and then received the mail from Hartland Corners as often as some kind neighbor would volunteer to bring it down. This office is now under the charge of Mr. Lombard as postmaster, and receives the mails daily from Lockport.

COOMER ROAD post-office, located on what is known as the Coomer road, on the west side of the town, was established February 3d, 1863, with Theodore M. Titus as postmaster. The present incumbent is Simon P. Clement.

NEWFANE STATION post-office, at the railroad crossing, one and a half miles south of Olcott, on the east side of Eighteen-mile creek, was established August 26th, 1876, with J. H. Mandeville as postmaster.

HESS ROAD post-office, located at the crossing of the Rome, Watertown and Ogdensburg Railroad, in the northeast corner of the town, receives its mail nine times per week; six by railroad, three by stage. F. H. Ferguson postmaster.

RIDGE ROAD post-office, located on the Ridge road, in the southeast corner of the town, and northeast of Wright's Corners, receives daily mail. Cornelius C. Tice postmaster.

WRIGHT'S CORNERS, on the Ridge road, on the south line of the town, three miles from Lockport, receives its mail daily; Mrs. Briggs postmistress.

TEMPERANCE ORGANIZATIONS.

Newfane Lodge, No. 722, I. O. of G. T., located at Charlotte, was instituted June 11th, 1874, with sixteen members and the following officers: W. H. Staats, W. C. T.; Mary A. Staats, W. V. T.; J. P. Warren, secretary. The present officers are: J. P. Warren, W. C. T.; Bertha E. Maxwell, W. V. T.; Jennie McClew, W. S.; with seventy members reported in June, 1878.

Charlotte Division, No. 100, Sons of Temperance was instituted in February, 1874, and surrendered in May of the same year.

RELIGIOUS HISTORY.

Elder Mairs, a Methodist itinerant preacher, preached here in 1816.

Rev. Jehiel Weisner was the first Baptist preacher in the town. He preached here in the year 1812. Many pleasing stories are related of elder Weisner's sayings and doings.

Elder Shepherdson was one of the early itinerants in this section of country. He was born in 1812, when the first circuit covered a large extent of country.

The house of Silas Mead was the home of the Methodist itinerants, and was known throughout this section as the "Methodist tavern."

THE WESLEYANS.

The Wesleyan Methodist church, located at Olcott, was organized in 1849, with about ten members, with William Henderson as the first class-leader. In 1850 the society built its present church edifice. It is of cobble stone. The size of the building is 30 by 40 feet, and it cost about $1,300. The first preacher was Asa Warren. He was followed by Revs. Samuel Phillips, D. B. Douglas, William L. Krale, John Watson, Henry Norton, William Pepper, William P. Ray, C. F. Hawley, A. N. Hudson, Thomas Ewing and Jonathan Sibley, the present pastor. The present membership numbers twenty-five. The Sunday-school was organized in 1851, with Rev. D. B. Douglas as superintendent.

UNIVERSALIST.

The Universalist church on Lockport street, in the village of Olcott, is of brick, about 40 by 50 feet, with

RESIDENCE OF JAMES WILLIAMS, TOWN OF WILSON.

RES. OF JAMES McARTHUR, TOWN OF NEWFANE

basement, and was built and dedicated in 1859. Rev. J. H. Tuttle, of Rochester, preached the dedicatory sermon. The society was organized on the 20th day of April, 1858, with forty-two members. The first meeting was held in the Wesleyan Methodist church. The first preacher was Rev. R. H. Pullman. The Sunday-school connected with this society was organized in 1859, with sixty scholars. The pastor of the church was the first superintendent. The present average attendance of pupils is thirty-five. W. T. Stout is superintendent. The volumes in the library number 500. The first trustees of this society were: James D. Cooper, Benjamin Stout, and A. T. Lane. The present board consists of W. T. Stout, R. A. Ferris, and S. Messeroll.

METHODIST EPISCOPAL CHURCHES.

The first organization of this denomination at Olcott was in 1815, as we find by an old record that Mrs. Alexander Butterfield was a member of a class in that year. The same record, although imperfectly kept, gives the following as among the early members of the society: John Billings, Lina Armstrong, M. Billings, Maria Bowers, Mary Crownover, Elijah Foote, Oliver Foote, Elizabeth Henderson, Nancy Holmes, John B. Kemp, Maria Kemp, Fanny Kemp, John M. Lindsay, Eliza A. Lindsay, Samuel Lockwood, Vashti Lockwood, Hester Lane, William Lindsay, Talcott Merwin and Abram Phillips. The records fail to give the name of the first leader, but tradition gives Samuel Lockwood the honor.

On the 29th of October, 1832, Nathaniel Church and Lucy B. Church, his wife, gave to the society by deed the lot upon which the church now stands, on the west side of the village, about eighty rods from Eighteen-mile creek. Thomas Ewing and Daniel McClellan were witnesses to the deed.

In 1833 the society built a frame church, forty by forty-five feet, finishing it the same year at a cost of $1,300.

The first board of trustees named in the deed consisted of William Henderson, Samuel Lockwood, Nathaniel Pease, Enoch Pease, Abram Phillips, Nathaniel Corey and Talcott Merwin.

The following ministers, and in the order named, as near as could be ascertained, have served this people: Revs. John H. Wallace, Joseph Atwood, Josiah Breakman, James H. Whalen, Samuel Saulsbury, John B. Lankton, Matthew Henderson, Salmon Judd, William B. Slaughter, William H. Scism, Henry R. Smith, Hiram May, William B. Cooley, William D. Jewett, M. W. Ripley, J. Vaughn, F. W. Conable, —— Watts, C. D. Burlingham. P. W. Gould, —— Kellogg, C. T. Foote, Z. Hurd, H. Van Benschoten, P. N. Leake, A. Staples, C. W. Swift, J. McClellan, and E. J. Whitney, the present pastor.

The Sunday-school was organized in 1833, with Ezra Foote superintendent, and seventy scholars. The present superintendent is I. W. Allen. There are fifty scholars, and 250 volumes in the library.

The Methodist Episcopal church at Charlotte was organized April 22nd, 1844. The first class was formed at Adam's Mills, with James Mathews as leader, in 1832. There was preaching at this place every two weeks, in the old log school-house that stood where Mrs. Tolen's house now stands. The records do not give the names of preachers until 1835, when S. Judd and W. D. Jewett were on this circuit; in 1836, W. O. Jewett and John Johnson; in 1837-38, D. Nichols; 1839, 1840, J. B. Lankton; 1841, A. P. Ripley.

In 1842 the place of preaching was changed to Charlotte, with W. D. Buck preacher in charge, followed in 1843-44 by William B. Cooley, under whose administration the society was fully organized by the election of the following board of trustees: James McKinney, George Steele, Walter Shaw, Reuben Godfrey, Samuel C. Brown, Oliver Lewis and Daniel Shaw.

The present church edifice was built in 1844, of cobble-stone, at a cost of $2,000, Hon. George R. Davis of Troy, N. Y., giving a deed, free of cost, for the lot upon which it stands. The size of the church is 40 by 50, and it will seat 300.

In 1845 Rev. J. W. Vaughn was the pastor; in 1846, S. H. Baker; 1847, W. B. Slaughter; 1848, 1849, R. C. Foote; 1850, J. McEwen and J. Latham; 1851, F. H. Conable and James Watts; 1852, 1853, William B. Cooley; 1854, J. Kennard and J. Latham; 1855, H. May; 1856, E. P. Clark; 1857, 1858, William Scism; 1859, W. H. Kellogg; 1860, 1861, C. D. Burlingham; 1862, S. M. Hopkins; 1863, 1864, G. W. Terry; 1865, Z. Hurd; 1866, B. Van Benschoten; 1867, 1868, B. N. Leake; 1869, 1870, Asa Staples; 1871-73, C. W. Swift; 1874-76, J. McClelland; 1877, 1878, E. J. Whitney.

The Sunday-school connected with this church was organized in 1836, with about forty scholars, and Oliver Lewis superintendent. The present school numbers one hundred pupils. The average attendance is seventy-five. Walter Shaw is superintendent.

PRESBYTERIAN CHURCH OF WRIGHT'S CORNERS.

Wright's Corners is a hamlet three miles north of Lockport, on the Ridge road. It was early supplied more or less with preaching in the school-house, by Methodist ministers. A small Sabbath-school was also carried on.

In the autumn of 1871, the place being unsupplied, and there being no religious organization in it, several of the citizens engaged the Rev. E. P. Marvin, of the Second Ward Presbyterian Church of Lockport, to preach in the school-house on Sabbath afternoons. The truth preached seemed at once to engage the attention of the people, and during the winter of 1872, Mr. Marvin, assisted by Elder William Glover, held a series of meetings which resulted in the conversion of about thirty persons. On April 16th, 1872, the Presbyterian society at Wright's Corners was organized, with the following board of trustees: Benoni Edwards, A. B. Snyder, J. W. Alberty, J. Angevine, John Henning, Sherman Beach, Alexander Campbell, David Welcher and Albert Johnson.

A Presbyterian church of thirty members was organized May 12th, 1872, by Rev. E. P. Marvin and Elders William Glover, William C. Boyce, William Hart and George Wood. The first officers were: Elders—John W.

Alberty, Charles Farnsworth, and Dewey Angevine; deacons—Joseph Morrow, James Moyne and David Welcher.

It was understood that the doctrine and polity of the church should be characterized by such liberty and charity that christians of all evangelical denominations might unite and feel at home in it. The term-elective system of officers was adopted, and a confession and covenant which all evangelical christians would approve was accepted.

The present church edifice, of brick, about forty by fifty feet, was built in 1873, and dedicated by Rev. W. C. Weisner, January 29th, 1874, and cost $4,000. Miss Janette Henning gave the lot upon which the church stands. The present membership of the church is 132. Rev. E. P. Marvin, of Lockport, is still the pastor of the church. Mr. C. C. Tice is superintendent of the Sabbath-school.

ROMAN CATHOLIC.

Saint Bridget's Roman Catholic Church, located on the Ewing road, in the southwest part of the town, was organized in June, 1859, by Thomas Mulloy, John Mulloy, Bernard Grist, John Brennan, Patrick North, James Reynolds, and David McGuire, under the direction of Rev. Thomas Shehan.

One acre of land, upon which to build the church, was donated to the society by John Mulloy, and the edifice was dedicated November 30th, 1859, during the pastorate of Father Shehan.

The following priests have ministered to the spiritual wants of this flock: Fathers Hugh Mulholland, Petrie A. Mulloy, Michael O'Dwyer, Thomas Brougham, and John Long, the present occupant of the pulpit. The congregation averages about 250.

FIRST BAPTIST CHURCH OF NEWFANE.

This society was organized May 27th, 1829, with twenty-five members, and Elder Jehiel Weisner as their pastor, who presided over them until 1832. During his pastorate, he received into the church fifty-three persons, and received for his services the sum of $24. The meetings of the society were held at private houses, and at the school-house near Judge Van Horn's.

From January, 1832, to August, 1833, the pulpit was supplied by preachers from other places. Elder Amos Reed was the next pastor, and in 1834 the church organized as a religious society under the statutes of the State. Elder Gershom B. Day, became pastor in 1835, and through his efforts the preaching services were changed to Kempville, which caused a division of the society. At a special meeting held at Olcott on the 20th of July, 1839, the society was again united.

In 1840 Rev. John Halliday became pastor, and remained about two years. November 6th, 1842, Elder Burtt became the pastor, and during his labors the society built its present church edifice, which is of cobble-stone. In 1856 it was repaired at a cost of $1,400, and June 9th, 1857, it was rededicated, Rev. Dr. Robinson, of Rochester Seminary, preaching the sermon. Besides the above mentioned, the following clergymen have served this people as pastor: R. D. Pierce, N. Sherwood, Hull Taylor, Elder Blaine, Dr. Irons, E. J. Scott, T. Fuller, A. C. Kingsley, —— Waldron, E. F. Craine, S. P. Barker, A. G. Bowles, C. S. Sheffield, J. S. Webber, W. Pike, C. H. Ham, T. G. Wright, G. W. Meade. There have been received into this church since its organization 371 persons. The church property is valued at $7,000.

SCHOOLS.

The first school in this town was held at Olcott (then Kempville), in 1815, and was taught by Bezaleel Smith. The school-house was located in the northeast corner of H. Strong's lot, on Main street.

In 1818 a log school-house was built in what is now district number four, and Martin Burch taught the school.

The old log house was located opposite where Stephen Wilson's young orchard now stands, sixty rods west of his house, on the north side of the Lake road. The following are some, if not all, of the surviving pupils of the above school: F. Newton Albright, Benjamin Stout, Asa Coates, Shuhal S. Merritt, Charles Halsted, Ransom Halsted, Silas Mead, and Delilah Merritt.

In 1824 there were eight school districts in this town. In 1830 there were 370 children taught in the common schools of the town, at a cost of $427.10. The town raised $319.11 of the amount, and $107.99 was appropriated by the State. The length of time taught in the town during that year was 44 months and 7 days. The number of children between five and sixteen years of age was 415.

In 1878 there were eighteen school districts in the town, and 1095 children between the ages of five and twenty-one, with an average attendance of 469⅓ daily. The school moneys appropriated for the use of common schools in this town for 1878 was $2,484.26.

NEWFANE IN THE CIVIL WAR.

At a special town meeting held in 1864 it was resolved, "that the town of Newfane will pay a bounty of five hundred dollars to each man that has volunteered, or that may volunteer hereafter, and also to each man that may hereafter procure a substitute to fill the quota of said town now called for by the President of the United States; and also five hundred dollars to any man who shall be drafted under said call, and accepted as a soldier, and credited to said town. And also that any person who has furnished or may furnish a substitute, who is already or who may be credited on the present call upon said town, shall receive so much and no more of this bounty of five hundred dollars, as he has expended or may expend over and above the county bounty of five hundred dollars now offered and paid." This resolution was passed by 195 for, and 16 against.

Two hundred and fifty-two soldiers from Newfane are enrolled in the records of the town. They are named in the closing chapters of the general history of the county.

SKETCHES OF REPRESENTATIVE CITIZENS.

Hannah Babcock was born in Wayne county, N. Y., in 1811, and removed to Newfane in 1835 and settled on her present place, then a wilderness. Her husband cleared the land, and they lived for some time in a log house. Wild animals were abundant in the surrounding forest at that time.

John Baker was born in Germany in 1831, and came to America in 1832, having been forty-one days on shipboard. He landed in New York, and came from there direct to Niagara county, and is now living in Newfane, being a well-known farmer of that town.

Richard Barber was born in Washington county, N. Y., in 1807, and came to Newfane in 1822, with his father, William G. Barber. In 1845 he settled on his present place. He is a farmer and fruit-grower. Post-office, Coomer Road.

Mrs. C. M. Barrell was born in Seneca county, N. Y., in 1815, and came with her husband, Joseph Barrell, to Niagara county in 1853. Her father, Benjamin Titus, was in the war of 1812, and her grandfather, Timothy Titus, who was six feet and six inches tall, was a captain in the Revolutionary war. Mrs. Barrell is a farmer. Her post-office is Olcott.

H. B. Bateman was born in Connecticut in 1819, and came to Niagara county in 1836. He was married in 1845 to Miss Hannah Mead. He located on his present place in Newfane in 1861. Mr. Bateman's father, Stephen C. Bateman, was born in Connecticut in 1770, and died at the age of eighty. Ezra C. Mead, father of Mrs. Bateman, died in 1870 at the age of sixty-eight.

John Bixler, farmer and fruit-grower, was born in Pennsylvania in 1813. He was married in 1839. When he settled on his present place of 114 acres it was a wilderness, and he has made all the improvements.

Jacob Bixler (son of Jacob Bixler who came from Pennsylvania to Seneca county, N. Y., in 1821, and after removing several times finally settled in Newfane, where he died in 1874, aged 84 years) was born in Pennsylvania in 1819. Business, farming and fruit-growing.

John T. Bird was born in England in 1848, and came to America in 1871. He settled at his present place, Newfane, in 1875, where he carries on the business of horseshoeing and carriage-ironing.

William S. Bird, carriage-maker, was born in England in 1854, and came to America in 1875, and settled where he now lives.

David Breckow, son of John Breckow, (who was born in England in 1775, and came to Niagara county, where he died in 1846, at the age of 71,) was born in England in 1820, and came to America with his father and settled on his present place in Newfane in 1854. He married Sally Morey in 1854.

Hon. Orwell C. Bordwell, son of E. W. Bordwell, who was born in 1807 and came to Niagara county in 1838, was born in Yates county, N. Y., in 1832. He settled on the Coomer road, Newfane, in 1867. Mr. Bordwell was member of Assembly from the second district of Niagara in 1874 and 1875. For several years he was engaged in the practice of medicine, and is known as an extensive farmer and fruit-grower.

Joseph H. Borst, a native of Schoharie county, N. Y., removed to Niagara county about 1843, locating in Lockport, where he engaged in trade. He left the county after remaining four years, and returned to Lockport in 1851, buying a farm, on which he resided till 1862, when he removed to Canada, and remained there two years. In 1864 he located on his present farm in Newfane, near Wright's Corners.

William Bradshaw was born in Lincolnshire, England, in 1834, came to America in 1863, and in 1870 located where he now lives, on a farm of one hundred acres. Post-office, Coomer Road.

James G. Breckow was born in Niagara county in 1844, and moved to his place near the Ridge road in 1867, and from there to his present residence in 1873.

George A. Brown, son of Samuel C. Brown, was born in Wayne county, N. Y., in 1827, was married in 1847, and settled on his present place in 1853. He put all the present improvements on the farm, and has 500 apple, 500 pear, and 1,500 peach trees. Business, carriage making, farming and fruit-growing.

Leverett A. Campbell was born in Lockport, Niagara county, in 1841, and removed from there to the Ridge road with his father, in 1846.

A. Craw was born in Greene county, N. Y., in 1819, and came to Niagara county in 1840, and settled in Lockport. He married Catharine E. Atwater. He was ordained a Methodist preacher in 1864, at Filmore, Allegany county, N. Y.

William Carmer was born in Erie county, N. Y., in 1828, and came to Niagara county in 1855, and afterwards settled on his present place on the Coomer road, where he is extensively engaged in farming and fruit-growing.

James Christie was born in Monroe county, N. Y., in 1828, and came to Newfane with his father in 1836. He owns 242 acres of land, much of which is devoted to fruit culture.

E. A. Clapp was born in Livingston county, N. Y., in 1847, and came to Niagara county in 1867, and settled on the farm of ninety-eight acres where he is now engaged in business, farming and fruit-growing. His father, Henry Clapp, was born in Connecticut, in 1817, and is now living in Livingston county, N. Y.

David Cole was born in Monroe county, N. Y., in 1811, and married in 1845 to Miss Melinda Whiting. He settled on his present place in 1845. Mrs. Cole died in 1850, and Mr. Cole married again in 1853. He is engaged in farming and fruit-growing.

Phineas H. Corwin was born in Newfane in 1835. In 1861 he was married to Mary A. Phillips, and settled where he now lives in 1864. Mr. Corwin, who is the present assessor of the town, is extensively engaged in farming and fruit-growing.

William V. Corwin, son of Phineas H. Corwin, was born in Michigan in 1832, and came to Niagara county and settled on the Hess road. After buying and selling several times, his father finally bought the property now owned by the subject of this notice, who also owns the old homestead below Charlotte. He was married in 1853. He was supervisor in 1875, 1876, and 1877.

Catherine I. Culver, daughter of George Van Vleet (who was born in Seneca county, N. Y., in 1785), was born in Tompkins county in 1819, and came to Niagara county in 1828, and settled on her present place in 1835. Her father was in the war of 1812, and took part in the battle of Fort Erie, and her grandfather served as a soldier in the Revolutionary war.

George Dole (son of George Dole, who was born in England in 1800, came to Niagara county in 1828, and died in 1860) was born in Niagara county, N.Y., in 1838, and married in 1862.

Daniel Dix (son of Ozias Dix, who was in the Revolutionary war) was born in Vermont in 1797. He settled in Newfane in 1834, and married his present wife in 1835. Her father was a captain in the war of 1812, was town clerk, and justice of the peace for twelve years, and supervisor one term. Mr. Dix is a farmer. His post-office is Newfane.

P. F. Dix, a native of White Creek, N. Y., was born October 19th, 1821, and was married on the 18th of December, 1861, to Maria A. McKie, of Newfane. He located in Olcott, in June, 1834, coming from Norway, Herkimer county, N. Y. He is a nurseryman and fruit-grower. He has held the office of town superintendent of common schools, and served two terms as justice of the peace, and two terms as railroad commissioner.

Lyman W. Drake, farmer, was born in Niagara county, N. Y., in 1851, and was married in 1876.

H. S. Earl was born in Rutland, Vt., in 1842, came with his father, Homer, to this town in 1844, and located where he now lives. His father and mother were both born in 1800. His father died in 1866, and his mother is still living. Mr. Earl is a farmer and fruit-grower. Post-office, Coomer Road.

Sylvester Edick, of Olcott, was born December 29th, 1842, in Shelby, Orleans county. He served three years in the Union army, and is now a farmer.

J. K. Fellows, a native of New Hampshire, came to Niagara county in 1836, with his father, Jonathan, and settled in Wilson. He located on his present farm in 1860. Post-office, Coomer Road.

Benjamin Fisk, son of James Fisk, jr., was born in Niagara county in 1837, and settled where he now lives in 1867. He is a farmer and fruit-grower. Post-office, Coomer road.

Bunham county, C. E., was the native place of William C. Fuller. He was born April 23rd, 1830, removed from the town of Sutton, C. E., to Newfane in February 1852, and was married December 30th, 1858, to Mary Ann Harrington, of Olcott. His post-office address is Newfane Station, and his occupation that of a mechanic and farmer.

Mrs. E. A. Gamble was born in Tompkins county, N. Y., in 1838, and came to Niagara county with her parents in 1853. She was married to Abram Phillips in 1855, and settled where she now lives. Her husband died in 1866, and she has since married Mr. Gamble.

Alexander Halstead was born in Newfane in 1843, and in 1872 located where he now lives. He enlisted August 15th, 1862, in the 19th N.Y. Battery, was in the battles of the Wilderness, Cold Harbor, Spottsylvania, Petersburg, and discharged June 17th, 1865. Post-office, Newfane.

Ransom Halsted was born November 28th, 1809, at Ovid, Seneca county, N. Y. He was married November 3rd, 1833, to Mary McClew, of Newfane. His second marriage was on November 1st, 1867, to Elmira Howell, of Newfane, who was born August 7th, 1822. Mr. Halsted is a farmer; post-office, Newfane.

Anna Halsted was born on the west branch of the Susquehanna river in 1786, and in 1791 moved to Seneca county, N. Y., and from there, in 1808, to Olcott, Niagara county. During the war of 1812 she, with her husband and family, was driven from their home, and their house and contents were burned by the British. They fled with an ox-team and sled to Seneca county, and her husband returned to take part in the war. After the war she returned, and lived in the town of Newfane until her death at the age of ninety-two. Her daughter Mary married Mr. A. Bailey.

Mrs. T. A. Harwood was born in Iowa in 1855. In 1863 she removed with her mother to Niagara county, and located where she now lives. Her father, Mr. Perigo, enlisted in Iowa, and served with credit in the late war. He returned to Iowa, and died there. Mrs. Harwood was married to T. A. Harwood in 1876.

Ezra Hayes was born in Niagara county in 1818. In 1840 he was married to Miss Hannah H. Drake, of Massachusetts. In 1852 he settled on his present place, and has since cleared land, erected buildings, and planted orchards, being now extensively engaged in farming and fruit-growing.

John Henning was born in Niagara county in 1834. At the age of ten he went to live with his uncle in Newfane, and after the death of his uncle and aunt in 1870 and 1877, respectively, inherited their farm of 270 acres. He was married in 1876.

M. H. Jaques, son of Osman S. Jaques, who was born 1818 and died in 1829, was born in Niagara county in 1840. He was married to Miss Eliza Fish in 1864. He settled on his present place in Newfane in 1874. His farm consists of 192 acres, devoted to the cultivation of fruit.

Dr. Nathan P. Johnson, son of Stephen B. Johnson, who was born in Washington county in 1794 and settled in Orleans county in 1817, was born in Orleans county in 1827. He has practiced medicine for twenty years in Orleans and Niagara counties. He settled on his present place in 1875, and has 2,600 peach, 500 apple, 250 plum, and 200 quince and cherry trees.

A. G. Johnson was born in Vermont in 1808, and came to Niagara county with his father, Clark Johnson, in 1825, and settled in the south part of Lockport. He was married in 1831. His wife died, and he was again married in 1845, and settled where he now lives in 1847, and has since been engaged in farming and fruit-growing. His father died July 15th, 1860, at the age of 79 years.

FARM RESIDENCE OF JOHN HENNING ESQ., TOWN OF NEWFANE, NIAGARA CO., N.Y.

Dr. Alden C. Keith, son of Alden and Rebecca Keith, was born in New Hampshire in 1808, and was educated at Middlebury Academy, Wyoming county, N. Y. He commenced the practice of medicine about 1835, and continued in practice till 1874, when he purchased a farm in Newfane, where he has since resided, giving his attention to fruit-growing and farming, and attending to professional business only at urgent calls. He was married in 1840 to Caroline Joslin.

W. J. Ketchum was born in Niagara county, in 1853. He married Miss Delphine M. Stratton in 1875. Business, cooperage and farming.

Peter Krupp is a native of this town, where he was born in 1838. He enlisted November 1st, 1861, in the 12th New York battery. He was in the battles of Gettysburg, Chancellorsville, Spottsylvania, Wilderness, North Anna, Cold Harbor, Hatcher's Run, and Weldon Railroad; post-office, Newfane.

George A. and John Lamont, both born in Niagara county, are the sons of James Lamont, who was born in Knearden, Scotland, in 1814, and came to America in 1857, and in 1869 located where he now lives.

H. B. Leonard was born in Seneca county, N. Y., in 1823, came to Niagara county in 1829, and was married in 1844 to Mary Woodard, of Lima, Livingston county, N. Y. Post-office, Newfane.

William Lewis was born in Germany in 1834, and came to America in 1852, being on the sea 52 days. He landed at New York and came to Niagara county, and after living at Suspension Bridge for a time, settled in 1866 on the Coomer road in Newfane, where he now resides, carrying on the business of blacksmithing and farming.

James W. McArthur was born in Albany county, N. Y., in 1821. When ten years of age he went to live with Stephen Wilson in Niagara, until he was twenty-two years old; after which he located in the Southern States. He was in the grocery and dry goods business in Canada several years, and then bought his saw-mill, afterward adding the lumber trade to his business. He settled where he now lives in 1870, having owned the property two years while living in Canada. He was married to Mrs. Emily Mulatt, who was born in England in 1831.

James McClew was born March 10th, 1876, in Duanesburgh, Schenectady county, N. Y. He was married October 11th, 1859, to Sarah Maria Ferris, of Cherry Valley, Otsego county, N. Y., who was born March 28th, 1813, and lived in Lockport at the time of her marriage. Mr. McClew came to this town in 1826, and by honest industry and strict attention to business has acquired a competency.

Mrs. Sarah A. McKee was born in Orange county, N. Y., in 1822, and came to Niagara county in 1826 with her father, William P. Johnson, who settled in the Drake Settlement, Newfane, on what is called the " Wall farm." She was married in 1845 to Archibald B. McKee.

Dr. James J. McFadden was born in Jefferson county, N. Y., in 1850; from there his father removed to Canada. In 1869 and 1870 Dr. McFadden attended lectures at McGill College, Montreal, finishing his medical course at Bellevue Medical College, N. Y. He was married in 1874, having settled in Olcott in 1873. He took an honorary degree in 1875.

A. E. Miller was born in Niagara county, N. Y., in 1850, and settled on his present place in 1874. He married a daughter-in-law of Benjamin Stout, one of the oldest settlers in the town of Newfane.

Peter D. Miller was born in Montgomery county, N.Y., in 1820, and came to Orleans county in 1834, and to Niagara county in 1835. He settled on his present place in Newfane in 1846. Mr. Miller was highway commissioner six years. He is very extensively engaged in fruit-growing, having sold as high as $6,000 worth of fruit in a single season.

Gilbert T. Miller, a farmer by occupation, was born in Newfane in 1840, and married in 1862, to Miss Julia V. Peckham. He located where he now lives in 1866. Post-office, Ridge Road. Mrs. Miller is the daughter of Dr. Peckham, a practicing physician on the Ridge road.

Mrs. E. S. Morse, daughter of W. S. Wright, was born at Olcott in 1847. She was married in 1875, and after living in Massachusetts one year, removed to her present place in Newfane.

James L. McKee was born in Orange county, N. Y., in 1818, and came to Niagara county in 1825. He was married in 1851. He settled on his present place in 1825.

Robert Mount, a native of England, was born in 1808, came to America in 1857, and located on his present farm in 1875. Mr. Mount is a farmer and fruit-grower. Post-office, Coomer Road.

John Mulloy was born in Ireland in 1814, and came to America in 1836, and to his present residence in 1845, and cleared the land and erected the buildings. The place consists of 134 acres, and Mr. Mulloy owns other land to the amount of 309 acres. His barns, full of produce at the time, were burned in 1871. His father, William Mulloy, accompanied him from Ireland, and died in 1871, at the age of ninety-two.

Stephen Pettit, son of Benjamin D. Pettit, was born in Saratoga county, N. Y., in 1837, and came to Niagara county with his father. He is a miller by trade, and is now running the Tompkins Mill. He was married in 1858, and finally settled where he now lives in 1869.

Thomas Plane, farmer and fruit-grower, was born in England in 1810, came to Newfane in 1851, and located on his present farm in 1859. Mr. Plane was married in England in 1838, to Miss Sarah Anchor. Post-office, Newfane.

S. A. Price was born at Olcott in 1841, and was married to Miss Albright in 1861. Mrs. Price's grandfather was once the owner of a large tract of land in the vicinity of Olcott. Post-office, Olcott.

Timothy J. Richardson was born in Niagara county in 1823. His father, Joseph K. Richardson, died in 1875, at the age of seventy-nine. Mr. Richardson is extensively engaged in farming and fruit-growing.

Jonathan D. Rumery, a native of Lockport, was born in 1821, and located where he now lives in 1864. His grandfather, Jonathan, served through the Revolutionary war. Mr. Rumery is a farmer. Post-office, Coomer Road.

Silas Sawyer (son of Amos Sawyer, who came to Niagara county from Vermont about 1830 and settled on the Hess road in Newfane, where he died in 1840) was born in Vermont in 1821. In 1848 he was married to Eliza Jane Leonard, and settled in 1859 on his present place, 40 acres, which he cleared; he still resides there, carrying on the business of farming and fruit-growing.

Amos Sawyer is a son of Amos, and grandson of Benjamin Sawyer, who were born in New Hampshire. Amos Sawyer, sen., located in Newfane in 1823. Amos, jr. located where he now resides in 1877. He was born in 1830, and married in 1854. He is a farmer and fruit-grower. His father built the first house on the Charlotte road.

H. H. Sears, son of Heman Sears, was born in Niagara county in 1840. His father came to this county in 1834, and settled on the place now owned by H. & H. H. Sears. H. H. Sears took up 117 acres of the Holland Land Company, and is now living on the farm of 120 acres once owned by his father.

Walter Shaw, of the firm of Shaw, Vincent & Co., was born April 13th, 1814, in Saratoga county, N. Y. He came with his father, Daniel, to Niagara county in 1832. He was married January 14th, 1840, to Margaret Demorest of Newfane. He served as first lieutenant in the 12th independent battery in the civil war. He is a manufacturer of fruit boxes and baskets. Post-office, Newfane.

George Sinsel was born in Germany in 1841, and came to America with his father's family in 1862. They came to Niagara county and settled on the Transit road, where his father died at the age of sixty-three. Mr. Sinsel bought his present place in 1871. He is an extensive fruit-grower. During the late war he served in the army with credit, receiving wounds which confined him to the hospital for some time.

Ammi Smith, son of David Smith, was born in St. Lawrence county, N. Y., in 1824, and in 1835 located on his present farm. He was married to Sophia Sears, in 1849. Mr. Smith is one of the enterprising farmers and fruit-growers of this town. He is pleasantly located on the east side of the Hess road, about one mile south of the post-office.

William Spalding, a native of Montgomery county, N. Y., was born in 1819, and in 1858 located in Newfane. He is a farmer and fruit-grower. His father, Dwelly Spalding, was in the war of 1812. Post-office, Hess Road.

John Stickels was born November 8th, 1818, at Duanesburg, Schenectady county, N. Y., and came to Newfane in September, 1825. Mr. Stickels is a farmer and fruit-grower. He has served his town as collector and assessor, one term each. He was also a captain of militia under Governor W. H. Seward. Post-office, Newfane.

Martin Stout, son of Benjamin Stout, was born in Newfane, Niagara county, in 1839, and settled where he now lives in 1861.

M. C. Swarthout was born December 23d, 1819, in Newfane, and was married January 1st, 1850 to Agnes E. Everts, of Newfane. Mr. Swarthout has always resided at Olcott, and has been master of vessels for fifteen years, inspector of harbor work for seven years, and master of engineers.

Wesley C. Taylor was born in Niagara county, August 6th, 1856. He is a blacksmith and wagon-maker.

Albert Tompkins, millwright, a son of Ira Tompkins, of the first settlers in the town of Newfane, was born in Niagara county in 1822. He was married in 1857, and in 1867 came to his present place.

Henry Van Wagoner was born in Monroe county, N. Y., in 1830, and came to Somerset, Niagara county, in 1840, and removed to his present place in Newfane in 1865.

Adelbert Van Horn, son of L. Van Horn, was born in Charlotte, Niagara county, in 1853.

W. Vickers, son of George and Hannah Vickers who came to Niagara county in 1850, was married in 1868 to Mary Ann Lewis, of Canadian birth. Mr. Vickers is engaged in the manufacture of lumber at his steam mill on the Ridge road in Newfane.

Jonathan Vincent was born in Saratoga county, N. Y., in 1819, and came to Niagara county in 1844. He was married in 1845, and settled on his present place in 1858. Mr. Vincent is one of the firm of Shaw, Vincent & Co., proprietors of the Charlotte saw-mill and fruit box manufactory.

Mrs. Irene Walford, daughter of W. J. Ferris, was born in Livingston county in 1826, and lived there until her marriage, when she removed to Wyoming county, and from there to Niagara county in 1860, settling at Olcott, where she keeps the Cooper House.

Benjamin C. Warren, a native of Niagara county, was born in 1844, on the farm he now owns. He has 130 acres of land, twenty-two of which are in fruit. Post-office, Coomer Road.

Allen P. Wentworth was born in Niagara county in 1834, and was married in 1864 to Miss Mary Mattison. He settled on his present place in Newfane in 1852.

Miss Lafy Ann Whiting, a native of Wayne county, N. Y., was born in 1825. She came with her parents to Olcott in 1835, where her parents have both since died. Miss Whiting is a capitalist and teacher.

R. J. Wilson, postmaster at Newfane, village of Charlotte, was born in Newfane in 1850. His father, Claudius Wilson, was born in Seneca county in 1820. Mr. Wilson is a merchant.

Stephen Wilson was born in Saratoga county, N. Y., in 1800. His father, Alexander Wilson, was an early settler of the town of Wilson. Mr. Wilson settled in Somerset at an early day, and cleared one hundred acres of land. Some of his reminiscences of that time are interesting. He subsequently removed to Wilson, and from there to Newfane in 1850. His farm contains over 460 acres, and he owns one of 185 acres adjoining.

John A. Wilson, son of Steven Wilson, an early settler of this county, was born December 6th, 1830, in Somerset. Mr. Wilson is a well known farmer of Newfane.

James Wilson, son of Lorenzo B. Wilson, who came to Niagara county in 1850 and located in Drake Settlement was born in Seneca county in 1831, and in 1867 settled on his present farm in Newfane.

The following named persons are among the other prominent citizens of the town—the places named are their respective post-offices:

H. Wyman, Hess Road Station; E. C. Decker, Hess, Road; Harvey Wilson, Hess Road; John Mack, farmer, Coomer; Samuel Knox, Coomer; P. W. Meseroll, farmer, Olcott; Sylvester Edick, farmer, Newfane Station; J. H. Warner, Olcott; Dewitt W. Drake, Olcott; Mrs. J. T. Ferguson, Olcott; Mrs. William Huie, Newfane Station; W. Tenbrook, hotel keeper, Olcott; W. H. Tenbrook, hotel keeper, Olcott; J. Arrowsmith, miller, Newfane Station; V. Arrowsmith, miller, Newfane Station; Mrs. R. F. Cooper, Olcott; W. H. Everts, Olcott.

MRS. S. WILSON. RES. OF S. WILSON, TOWN OF NEWFANE, NIAGARA CO., N. Y. S. WILSON.

THE TOWN OF NIAGARA.

THIS town was formed from Cambria, June 1st, 1812. It was originally called "Schlosser," in perpetuation of the name applied to the fort and landing above the Falls of Niagara. February 14th, 1816, the name was changed to Niagara. The town was reduced in area by the formation from it of Pendleton in 1827, and was again divided by the erection of Wheatfield in 1836.

It is the southwest corner town of the county, lying in the abrupt bend of the Niagara river at the falls; and, including Goat Island and the small islands between it and the mainland, all of which, with Cayuga Island, belong to it, contains 12,842¼ acres of land, much of which is improved. It is bounded on the north by Lewiston, on the east by Wheatfield, and on the south and west by the Niagara river. The principal streams flowing through it are Cayuga and Gill creeks. The first rises in Wheatfield and flows across the southeastern quarter of the town, emptying into the river at a point opposite the center of Cayuga Island; the second has its source in Lewiston, and taking a course a few points west of south, crosses the central portion of the town and mingles its waters with those of the Niagara about two miles above the falls.

The soil is a heavy clay. Its color is dark, and while it is wet in most parts of the town, it is very productive. Wheat is the leading grain, but corn and barley are extensively cultivated. In former years hay was an important crop; and though the local markets are not as good as they have been, considerable quantities are cut every year. The cultivation of fruit is a leading industry; potatoes are raised in good quantities and considerable butter is made. The surface of the town is level, and all parts are accessible by good roads, principal among which are the River road, the Portage road, the Military road and the Lockport road.

According to the assessment of 1877, the valuation of real estate in the town was $4,490,235; personal property, $137,175; total valuation, $4,627,410; showing it to be in these respects second in importance in the county only to Lockport.

The census of 1875 shows that there was within the boundaries of the town at that time a total population of 6,861. Of this number, 6,691 were whites and 170 were colored; 595 were aliens, and 2,216 were between the ages of five and eighteen, including 1,063 males, and 1,153 females.

Niagara possesses unsurpassed railway facilities, which are alike advantageous to her traveling population and her producers and manufacturers.

NIAGARA RIVER AND FALLS.

The Niagara river, with its tossing rapids, its maddened whirlpool, and its mighty cataract, from which the town derived its name, is one of the greatest of nature's wonders, and an object of world-wide celebrity. In all the world there is probably no other point of interest more widely known than Niagara, and none that has been so generally visited by travelers of all nations. In foreign lands people who could not correctly locate more than a very few of the great cities, mountains, lakes and rivers of the world, mention Niagara Falls with an air of familiarity that, as much as anything else, indicates the universality of their fame. From the time when it first became possible to reach the great cataract in safety, if not with comfort, it has been an object of interest which no traveler over the western continent has passed by unnoticed. Its first extravagant description from the hand of Father Hennepin, and the subsequent exaggerated account of it by La Hontan, excited the wonder and admiration of the world. It has been stated that the first stage coach that came to the frontier brought a visitor to the falls. However true this may be, it is certain that in the old days of canal and stage travel this locality was the objective point of many a sight-seer, who viewed the majestic waterfall and its accompanying attractions, and went away satisfied with the result of the slow and tiresome journey. With the rapid growth of the railway interest in the United States and the gradual extension of its lines, the number of visitors has constantly increased, keeping pace with the growing facilities for general travel; and for years past thousands have thronged here annually from all the nations of the earth.

To mention even a fraction of the most notable visitors at the falls would take up too much of the time and space devoted to this part of our work. Probably so great a collection of interesting autographs is to be found nowhere else in the world as upon the registers which have received the names of guests at the hotels at Niagara Falls; the pages of which bear the signatures of sovereigns and rulers of lands civilized and uncivilized; men high in official position from countries christian and heathen; and characters of celebrity in art, in literature and in science, in almost every language spoken and written. The first white man who saw the falls, and left any authentic record, was Father Hennepin, who visited this locality in 1678—two centuries ago. He was a Franciscan missionary sent out by the French among the Indians.

"Ah me! What myriads of men, since then, have come and gone;
What States have risen and decayed, what prizes lost and won—
What varied tricks the juggler Time has played with all below;
But the waters fall as once they fell, two hundred years ago."

Hennepin's description, as the first on record, deserves to be quoted. Its interest is not lessened by the quaintness of the old English into which it was translated a hundred and ninety years ago. It is as follows:

"Betwixt the lakes Ontario and Erie there is a vast and prodigious cadence of water, which falls down after a surprising and astonishing manner, insomuch that the universe does not afford its parallel. 'Tis true Italy and Switzerland boast of some such things, but we may well say they are sorry patterns when compared with this of which we now speak. At the foot of this horrible precipice we meet with the river Niagara, which is not above a quarter of a league broad, but is wonderfully deep in some places. It is so rapid above this descent that it violently hurries down the wild beasts while endeavoring to pass it to feed on the other side, and not being able to withstand the force of its current, which inevitably casts them headlong above six hundred feet high. This wonderful downfall is compounded of two great cross streams of water, and two falls into an isle sloping along the middle of it. The waters which fall from this horrible precipice do foam and boil after the most hideous manner imaginable, making an outrageous noise, more terrible than that of thunder; for when the wind blows out of the south their dismal roaring may be heard more than fifteen leagues off. The river Niagara, having thrown itself down this incredible precipice, continues its impetuous course for two leagues together, to the great rock above mentioned [Hennepin Rock, Queenston], with an inexpressible rapidity. * * * From the great fall unto this rock, which is to the west of the river, the two banks of it are so prodigious high that it would make one tremble to look steadily over the water, rolling along with a rapidity not to be imagined."

Since Hennepin wrote, the children of genius from all over the world have toiled for words to adequately praise the peerless cataract of Niagara. We shall not compete with them, nor with the guide books in describing the features of this famous locality, with which our readers are doubtless familiar.

The historical events of Niagara in the early days are too important for treatment in a town history, and they were so intimately associated with those which made the frontier the *locale* of occurrences of more than national interest, that they have been fully depicted in the general county history on preceding pages of this work. As in the case of all other towns, the modern history of Niagara begins with the first settlement of white men within its borders; and this, as being one of the earliest in the county, has been mentioned in the general history, but will be more fully set forth in this connection.

FORT LITTLE NIAGARA.

It has been seen that the first occupation of lands within the boundaries of the present town of Niagara was by the French, in connection with the business of transportation *via* the river and the portage. Father Hennepin mentions that some of their number were left at the upper landing when the "Griffin" sailed on her ill-starred western voyage.

In 1750 Fort Little Niagara was built on the river bank, about a mile and a half above the falls. Joncaire, the French officer captured and adopted by the Senecas, had established a trading point at Lewiston, the lower landing of the portage, thirty years before, and erected buildings for the storage of goods in transit there and at the landing above the falls. It was to protect the latter that the fort was built, and at a later day the portage was further guarded by a number of stockades erected at different points between the two landings. Fort Little Niagara is described as a wooden work, encompassed by palisades, with ditches and angles in the usual form. A small saw-mill was also erected, about 1750, on the shore a little below the head of Goat Island. Supplies for the trading stations and military posts, and the peltries purchased of the western tribes, were transported around the falls, over the portage, on the backs of Indians, with the exception of such heavy articles as were moved up and down the mountain at Lewiston by means of a tramway, and carried over the portage in wagons. During the siege of Fort Niagara by the British under Prideaux and Johnson in 1759, the French set fire to Fort Little Niagara and abandoned it. The outlines of this structure were to be seen not many years since, on the river bank, between the upper landing and the mouth of Gill creek. The French cleared a limited extent of land about it.

THE STEDMAN HOUSE AND FARM.

Sir William Johnson, superintendent of Indian affairs, visited this region in 1761, spending some time at Fort Niagara and in the vicinity of the falls. He says in his journal that he quartered in a tent, which would be evidence that there was at that time no fort or other building at the landing above the falls; but at the same time he states that Sir Jeffrey Amherst had permitted a company of Indian traders to establish themselves at the upper landing, and granted them the exclusive use of the means of transportation and the privilege of the Indian trade, and that a large house was then being erected for their use, which was without doubt the same afterwards occupied by the Stedmans. There is a tradition that this building was originally erected in Fort Niagara for use as a chapel by the French, and that it was taken down and put up again at the time and place above mentioned; and there is so much evidence in support of this theory as to render it more than probable. This house was two stories high, and rested on a solid foundation. The main part was long enough for five windows, and it had two chimneys, and was surmounted by a low, pointed steeple. At the southwestern end was a one-and-one-half-story wing, of sufficient length to admit three windows side by side; and at the extremity of this was a large stone chimney, with a wide fire-place at the base, which extended a little higher than the gable. This chimney is still standing.

The first permanent settlement was made by John Stedman, who, accompanied by his brothers Philip and William, took possession of the large house above described and the adjoining lands, probably in the latter part of 1759 or the early part of the following year. He enlarged the clearing at the landing, and also made a clearing of considerable extent on the river bank opposite the island now known as Goat Island, and another of about ten acres on the upper part of the island. This island derived its name from the fact that Stedman placed some goats upon it, which froze to death during the winter of 1779 and 1780. Among his other improvements, he set out an orchard of nearly one hundred and fifty trees west of the house. A few of these trees are still standing. This was the first orchard set out in this region. In 1796 it was spoken of as "a well-fenced orchard containing 1,200 trees." Though there was undoubtedly a considerable increase in the number of trees, it is doubtful if there were ever so large a number standing at the same time. At the present time there are not more than forty or fifty remaining. From this orchard were gathered the first apples raised in Niagara county.

The Stedmans were spoken of by early visitors to the falls and to Fort Schlosser, as friendly and hospitable. They were in possession until 1795, when, upon the removal of the British portage to the Canadian side, they went away, leaving as their representative Jesse Ware, who, as Stedman's agent, claimed all the rights that had been assumed by the latter, including the proprietorship of the falls and between four and five thousand acres of land in the bend of the river. Philip Stedman's health failed, and he went to New York for medical treatment, dying there in the year 1797.

It has been related how John Stedman escaped from the Devil's Hole massacre, spurring his horse away through the forest amid a rattling fire from the Senecas. Unscathed, he passed beyond range of the Indians' fire-arms, and bearing away in an easterly direction, he struck Gill creek about two miles distant, and made his way to Fort Schlosser. He afterward laid claim to all the land lying within the circuit of his flight, between the Devil's Hole and the mouth of Gill creek, by authority of a pretended Indian grant, made on account of his bearing a charmed life, as they believed after that bloody affair. There is evidence to show that it is extremely improbable that any such grant of the said property was ever made by the Senecas to Stedman, and that, admitting that it was made, there were certain conditions which would have rendered it invalid.

The portage had furnished about the only business up to this time; and, with the exception of the few improvements which have been mentioned in connection with the occupancy of the Stedmans, such as the clearing of a few acres of land, the planting of an orchard, the attempt to raise goats, and the manufacture of a limited quantity of lumber—which was probably carried on in the old French saw-mill after it had undergone repairs at the hands of the Stedmans, and which they are known to have used as late as 1797—there was nothing else in the town to indicate that civilization was advancing. No other buildings were erected or improvements made previous to 1805, and the Stedman farm, as it is called to this day, was, up to that date, the only property occupied or improved in this vicinity.

Stedman, himself or by his agent, retained possession of this property until finally removed by legal process. In 1801 he applied to the Legislature of New York to confirm the alleged Indian title, which has been referred to, to about five thousand acres of land, "bounded by Niagara river, Gill creek, and a line extending east from Devil's Hole to said creek." He represented in this petition that at the council of 1764 between the Indians and Sir William Johnson, the Indians executed a conveyance of the said property to him; that he had placed the deed in the keeping of Sir William for safety, and that it was afterwards lost with his papers; but the Legislature disregarded this claim, and subsequently sold the property to other parties. As late as 1823, the heirs of Stedman brought a number of actions against the purchasers, and a test suit was tried in Albany, and defended by Attorney-General Talcott and Judge Howell, of Canandaigua, which resulted in the establishment of the claim of the purchasers and the withdrawal of the Stedman heirs from the contest.

PORTER, BARTON & CO.

Augustus Porter first visited the falls in 1795. His second visit to this locality was made the following year, during his engagement as chief of a company of surveyors, on their way to the territory which has since been known as the Western Reserve, which they had been commissioned to explore and lay out into townships.

The Portage Company was formed as early as the beginning of the year 1805. It consisted of Augustus Porter, Peter B. Porter, Benjamin Barton, jr., and Joseph Annin. In February of the year mentioned they leased of the State the portage and the Stedman farm, and purchased lots 1, 2, 3 and 4 of the Mile Reserve, which included the falls on the American side, and extended half a mile above and three-fourths of a mile below. The lease of the portage was for ten years, but on its expiration, in 1815, it was extended for five years in consideration of the interruption of the carrying business caused by the war on the frontier. During the same year Augustus Porter erected a saw-mill and a blacksmith's shop at the falls, as a preparatory step toward the introduction of other improvements; and in 1806 he removed his family from Canandaigua, and took up his residence in the old Stedman house, near Fort Schlosser. The Stedman house has been described as having been in 1806 a substantial frame building. There were also several tumble-down log cabins, far on the road to decay. All that remained of Fort Schlosser was the barracks, then in a dilapidated condition, a number of pickets and the entrenchments, the latter tolerably distinct.

EARLY REMINISCENCES.

For a number of years the land in the vicinity of the falls remained in a wild state, cedars and dense masses of bushes growing down to the water's edge; and it is said that stately oaks, some of them four or five feet in diameter, were standing along the course of Main and Buffalo streets. One of these, the only living thing that flourished two hundred years ago, is standing on the old Porter homestead, at the corner of First and Buffalo streets, in the village of Niagara Falls. Prior to the arrival of Judge Porter, little had been done to change the wild aspect of the country. In the forests near by bears were common, and wolves so numerous as to prevent the raising of sheep. It is said of the latter that they were so bold as to approach within a short distance of the Stedman house and that "their hideous nightly howlings were familiar sounds in all the region about the falls." Ducks and geese abounded in the river, and deer and smaller animals were very plentiful. The Indians were quite numerous, and were frequently seen in their canoes passing up and down the river, fishing and hunting, and in small encampments along the shore. Their costume consisted of a shirt, clout, leggins and moccasins in summer, with the addition of a blanket-coat and cap in cool weather, and they were armed with a knife and tomahawk stuck in their buckskin belts. "The leading chiefs retained some importance in the estimation of the old settlers, and were treated with kindness and hospitality, always with good fare and a bed of blankets and buffalo skins." At different times, Farmer's Brother, the celebrated Seneca chief, with his wife, and the renowned Red Jacket, with his interpreter and two young chiefs, were guests at the fireside of Judge Porter; and when the visit of the latter party was ended they went away in their canoes with presents of provisions and whiskey.

Rattlesnakes were very plenty in the neighborhood, though none were ever known to approach within half a mile of the cataract, probably on account of the trembling of the earth for that distance. Near the whirlpool there was a large den of them of uncommonly large size; and above the falls, betwen Schlosser and the mouth of Gill creek, there were large numbers of a smaller and entirely different species. Not long before the beginning of the war of 1812, Joshua Fairbanks, who resided near the whirlpool, killed more than a hundred rattlesnakes in a single day as they ascended the rocks at that place, which was the only point at which ascent was possible, on account of the precipitous character of the river bank. Ant-hills abounded until removed by improvements of the land.

EARLY SETTLEMENT AND IMPROVEMENTS.

It has been seen that Augustus Porter was the first to settle in the town after the Stedmans. He was a native of Salisbury, Connecticut, where he was born in January, 1769. His father, Dr. Joshua Porter, was known there for half a century as a practicing physician and surgeon. Though his early advantages were limited he acquired the rudiments of an education, to which he added in after life a practical knowledge of mathematics and surveying. After acting in the capacity of chief of surveyors for a number of years, part of the time in connection with the boundaries of Phelps & Gorham's Purchase, Mr. Porter took up his residence in Canandaigua in 1800, where he lived till June, 1806, when, with his wife and three sons, Albert H., Peter B., jr, and Augustus S., he came to Niagara and domiciled himself in the Stedman house. He has related, concerning his journey from Canandaigua, that after the fashion of emigrants in those days he was his own teamster. They were four days making the trip, with all the advantages vouchsafed by favorable weather.

At this time the inhabitants along the frontier, in Niagara, were, besides Augustus Porter, at Schlosser: James Everingham, Jesse Ware, William Miller, William Howell, Stephen Hopkins, Philemon Baldwin, Joshua Fairbanks, Joseph Howell, Erastus Parks, Isaac Colt, James Murray, between the falls and Lewiston; between the falls and Black Rock there was only "Big Smith," at Cayuga creek; and Isaac Swain lived on the Military road near where it crosses Gill creek, having located there in 1805. During the year 1807, the following named persons settled at the falls: Adoram Everingham, a miller; John M. Stoughton, a cloth-dresser; Joshua Fairchilds, who became the first tavern-keeper; and Jacob Hovey, a carpenter; at Fort Schlosser, William Voluntine and John Sims, boat-builders; on the Portage road, Gad Pierce, a pioneer farmer and inn-keeper on the river road.

During 1807 Porter, Barton & Co. built a grist-mill of two runs of stones at the falls. There were not settlers enough along the river to raise it, and Lieutenant Armistead, with a detachment of soldiers, came from Fort Niagara and assisted to get the frame up. In 1808 Augustus Porter erected a commodious dwelling house, and between this year and 1812 other improvements were made; among them the establishment on a somewhat extensive scale of a rope-walk, in which cordage was manufactured for lake vessels, both American and English, from hemp raised on the flats of the Genesee; and a carding mill and cloth-dressing establishment, something less than a dozen comfortable dwelling houses, a small tannery and a commodious log tavern were erected at an early date.

In 1808, James Field settled in the town. He had formerly lived in Seneca county, but for a short time previous to his advent here he had been a resident of Canada. He rented a farm of Judge Porter, and after working it awhile bought land between Schlosser and Cayuga creek, and moved on to it in 1810. He kept a tavern, which was well known along the frontier, until his death in 1823, after which the business was carried on by his widow, Mrs. Anna Field. In the early days Field's tavern was a favorite place of meeting among the pioneer residents of Niagara, and, with the exception of an occasional meeting at the house of one of the settlers in some other part of the town, the town meetings were held there for a long time. Mr. Field was frequently honored by the choice of the people to places of trust and responsibility; and when he died the town lost one of its most enterprising and useful citizens. He left four sons, none of whom are now living. His daughter, Mrs. Reynolds, is living in Clarksville, at an advanced age. His oldest son, Spencer Field, was for many years a well known citizen of the town. Two of his children, a son and a daughter, now old people, are residents of Niagara, and another son is living in the South. Eldad Field was also a life-long resident of Niagara. He died some years ago, as did also his brothers James and Ira.

In 1809 Enos Broughton came and opened a tavern in the Stedman house, which had been vacated by the removal of Augustus Porter to his new residence, and William Chapman and David Lindsay, rope-makers, James Armington, a carpenter, William Van Norman, a blacksmith, and Ebenezer Brundage, a sawyer, settled at the falls and engaged in their respective avocations; and in 1810 came a shoemaker named James Cowing, Ezekiel Hill, who taught school in the early days, Ralph Coffin, who kept books and accounts for Judge Porter, Joshua Fish, a carpenter, Oliver Udall, a farmer, and Parkhurst Whitney, a man who soon became prominently known along the frontier, who came from the town of Phelps, Ontario county, and purchased lot No. 53 of the "Mile Strip," nearly opposite the western point of Cayuga Island.

Probably the earliest permanent settlers in the town remote from the river were John Young and his family, who came from Lancaster county, Pa., in 1810, arriving in Niagara township June 1st. The party consisted of John Young and his wife, their two sons Christian and Samuel and their families, John, Jacob and Charles (unmarried) and two daughters, Polly and Catharine. A heavy Pennsylvania wagon, drawn by five horses, furnished them a means of conveyance for themselves and such of their household goods as they brought with them. They came up the Susquehanna river and *via* Painted Post, Dansville, Genesee and Avon to Batavia, and from there to Williamsville, which place they left on the morning of the first of June, arriving some time that day at a point in the "Mile Strip" a little east of the mouth of Gill creek. From there they were obliged to cut a road through the timber in advance of their wagon to lot No. 17 of the Holland Purchase. When they arrived at the place of their destination it was late in the day or early in the evening; and they slept in the wagon and under it the first night, keeping off the chill by means of a fire built against a large log, at which they also cooked the first meal of which they partook within the present limits of Niagara county. The next morning they set four crotched sticks up in the ground and covered them with large pieces of bark stripped from a fallen tree, and this was their only protection from the sun and the rain till they could erect a log house. In 1811 Samuel Young purchased the land now owned by his son Jonas, and Christian bought the adjoining improvement of a man named Stevens, who left the country soon afterward.

In 1813 both families removed to Livingston county, and remained there till after peace was declared, the men coming back during the summer months to attend to their farming interests, and going away again after harvest. John Young lived only two years after his settlement in Niagara. His sons Samuel and Christian lived many years, to make great improvements about their pioneer homes and to rear large and respectable families. The former died in 1871 at the age of 83 years, 7 months and 10 days; the latter February 28th, 1875, aged 89 years and 10 months. Mrs. Samuel Young died in 1856, and Mrs. Christian Young December 28th, 1875, aged seventy-seven. Jonas Young, son of Samuel Young, was only six weeks old at the time they left Lancaster county. He is still living on the property purchased by his father. Charles Young, his brother, is a resident of Cambria, and his sister, Mrs. Elizabeth Hittel, lives in Wheatfield.

Christian Young worked in the early days at the cooper's trade, manufacturing flour barrels for Judge Porter, for use at his mill at Niagara Falls. He had six children, four sons and two daughters. William, the oldest, married a sister of Henry Wagner, of Niagara, and died leaving a widow and several children. The former and most of the latter reside in this township. Sally, the next in order of age, died while yet a young woman. Three sons, John, Samuel, and Benjamin, and the remaining daughter Mary Ann Kline (widow), live at the old family home. Catharine, sister of Samuel and Christian Young, is the only surviving member of the family of John Young.

The Witmers, John and Abram, also Pennsylvanians, were the next to settle in Niagara. The first, with his family, came in 1810. They departed from their home about six miles west from Lancaster, Pa., about the middle of August, and arrived here eighteen days later, early in September. Their mode of travel was the same as that employed by the Youngs, and indeed the only one available in those days, only they had four horses instead of five. Their route was up the Susquehanna to Harrisburgh, from there to the mouth of Lycoming creek, and *via* the Williamson road through Block House and Blossburg and down the Tioga valley to Painted Post, from which point they proceeded to Dansville, and from there down the Genesee river to Avon, and thence by way of Batavia to Black Rock. They came down the Niagara as far as the Devil's Hole, from which point Isaac Swain had chopped out a road to his clearing where the Military road crosses Gill creek, near the northern boundary of the township. Swain had partially cleared thirty or forty acres, and erected a good-sized and substantial log house. This improvement Mr. Witmer purchased, and Swain removed to Porter and settled near Fort Niagara. This improvement and one belonging to a man named Stevens, which was afterward bought by Christian Young, were the only ones at that date on that portion of the Military road which is within the present town of Niagara.

Mr. Witmer had come to remain; and he was foremost among those hardy and enterprising men who have toiled in the days gone by, amid the disadvantages and discouragements of pioneer life, more for the benefit of the present generation than their own. In the year 1817 he built a small saw-mill on Gill creek, near his residence, and he began to manufacture lumber the following spring. It has been in operation much of the time since, and in the early days it supplied lumber of which were built most of the frame buildings in that part of Niagara and contiguous portions of adjoining towns. He died in 1842, at the age of eighty-two. His family consisted of his wife and nine children, all but one of whom were born in Pennsylvania, previous to their settlement in Niagara. There were seven sons, Christian, Benjamin, Abram, John, Samuel, Henry and Rudolph, and two daughters, Barbara and Nancy. The elder sister was married in Pennsylvania and did not accompany the family here, but with her husband, a man named Jacob Wissler, she came a little later. At the time of the war of 1812, they returned to Pennsylvania, where they remained for a time and then removed to Indiana, where Mrs. Wissler is now living at the age of ninety. Nancy married, and now lives in Kansas. After remaining in Niagara two or three years, Christian returned to Pennsylvania. He married there, and with his family subsequently came back to Niagara. Ten years later (1834) he went west, and died in Iowa three or four years ago. Benjamin was six years old at the time the family came from Pennsylvania. He was twenty-two at the time of the erection of the mill, and performed much of the labor in its construction. In 1823 he put up a mill in Wheatfield for J. Schenck. He was married in Erie county in 1825. Mrs. Witmer died in 1871, having borne him thirteen children, only one of whom is dead and four of whom, John, Benjamin, jr., Martin and Simon, reside in this township. Benjamin Witmer is still living, hale and hospitable, at the age of eighty-three. Abram is living in Illinois, John in Indiana and Samuel in Iowa. Henry died of cholera in Hamilton, Ontario, in 1832. Rudolph, the youngest, who was born in Niagara, is still living. He served with credit in the late war.

Abram Witmer came in 1811. At that time his family consisted of his wife and four children, Christian H., Abram, jr., David and Joseph. Four others were born in Niagara, viz.: Esther, Tobias and Elias (twins) and Fanny. Christian H. married and reared a family. He was engaged in milling at Suspension Bridge and Niagara Falls for many years, and was drowned September 17th, 1859, while superintending some repairs on his mill at Suspension Bridge. His sons have since carried on the business, in connection with banking and other enterprises. Abram, jr., is living in Niagara township at the age or seventy, and his son, Joseph, lives on an adjoining farm. David and Joseph are both heads of families, both reside in Niagara and both are substantial farmers. Esther died unmarried at the age of twenty-two. Tobias is a resident of Erie county; he is a surveyor by profession, and not many years since he published a map of Niagara township which is highly regarded for accuracy. Elias is unmarried, and lives with his brother Abram.

NIAGARA IN THE WAR OF 1812.

The war of 1812-14 was a very serious impediment to the settlement, improvement and progress of the town and village, and subjected the pioneers to innumerable sacrifices, inconveniences and hardships. Immigration ceased, and most of those who had begun to rear up homes in this then new country, left them and removed to the interior, upon the declaration of war in June, 1812; but a majority returned and remained until December, 1813, when the British and their Indian allies invaded and laid waste the defenseless frontier, destroying buildings and property of all kinds, and killing many unresisting persons. Those who escaped with their lives saved nothing, and many were reduced to extreme want and suffering. Nothing was saved at the Falls except two or three small dwellings and the log tavern, set on fire, but extinguished by persons at hand after the hasty departure of the enemy. With the close of the war came an influx of settlers, and in 1815 the partially paralyzed hand of enterprise began to exhibit its wonted vigor. Among the new comers, in this year, was James Ballard, a cloth-dresser and wool-carder, on the River road. Samuel Tompkins, a Canadian volunteer, having been banished from Canada and his property there having been confiscated because of his participation with the United States against the British in the war of 1812-14, came to Niagara Falls in 1815, and purchased lot No. 52 of the "Mile Reserve," two years later, of General Parkhurst Whitney. At that time there were little more than a score of families residing on the territory embraced in the present town of Niagara, and nearly half of these were at the Falls. Mr. Saddler lived on the land now owned and occupied by A. M. Chesbrough as early as 1816. Before the war he had been at Schlosser. Besides those mentioned, several other settlers came this year, among them Philip Tufford, with his family, on lot No. 7 (Holland Purchase), near the Lockport road.

Niagara Falls was the only trading point nearer than Black Rock or Lewiston. There was only one store in the town (that recently opened by Judge De Veaux at the Falls). The judge was also postmaster. The mail arrived with some irregularity. It was carried on horseback from Buffalo to Lewiston, *via* Niagara Falls. The only school in the town was at the Falls, and previous to 1818 it was open only in the winter. The frame buildings in the town numbered less than ten, and several of these were at the Falls.

Of pioneer taverns there were three—General Whitney's, at Niagara Falls, one at Clarksville, kept by Gad Pierce, and James Field did the honors of the third in a substantial frame house between Schlosses and Cayuga creek. There were at that time two grave-yards in the town, the larger one at Niagara Falls, and the other the family burial place of John Osborne, further up the river. Until the arrival of Dr. Thomas, in 1820, there were no physicians nearer than Lewiston, at which place Drs. Smith and Frisbee had settled some time before. There was a blacksmith at the Falls.

At the time of which we write the carrying business between Schlosser and Lewiston provided the settlers of this section employment for themselves and their teams. and afforded them an opportunity to earn money which it would have been difficult for them to obtain otherwise —in fact it is said to have been about the only means of getting ready money. One old resident says this business was a "God-send to the people."

EARLY EVENTS.

As has often been the case in new countries, there was for some years a scarcity of provisions on the frontier; and as Canada was further advanced in agriculture, the pioneers here crossed the river for a great portion of their supplies of pork, flour, apples and cider. To show the scarcity of these staple necessities it will only be necessary to state that Samuel Tompkins, sen., went to Canada in the spring of 1818, and paid thirty-six dollars per barrel for pork, and twenty-two dollars per barrel for flour. Such was the aspect of affairs in Niagara before the county had recovered from the effects of the war; but by the beginning of the year 1816 the wave of emigration began to roll back, and before 1820 most of those who had sought safety elsewhere during the war returned, and began the work of rebuilding their burned cabins and redeeming their land from the wilderness; there was a considerable influx of new comers, and buildings were erected, enterprise fostered and encouraged, and the evidences of growing prosperity became apparent everywhere.

One of those who settled in the town in 1816 was Eli Bruce, on the Lockport road. He was a man of some little education and was one of the early schoolmasters. Rev. David M. Smith came during this year, and preached at the Falls and Lewiston alternately. He was one of the earliest regular preachers on the river.

Ferris Angevine, father of Jackson Angevine, came in 1818 and bought a place on the Tonawanda road, a little above the mouth of Cayuga creek. He subsequently purchased land on the Military road, made a clearing and erected a log house, in which he began housekeeping after his marriage to Miss Elizabeth Remington, in 1826. Three years later they removed to his place on the "Little river" (as that part of the river between the mainland and Cayuga island was called), where he resided until the time of his death.

Epaphroditus Emmons, an early justice, town clerk and tavern-keeper, settled at Fort Schlosser in 1818 or 1819, and put up a slight two-story wooden building around the chimney which had been at the end of the wing of the Stedman House, previous to its destruction in December, 1813. This he occupied as an inn three or four years, and then it was taken down and set up again at another place, where its remains are still standing.

Isaac Smith settled on the Portage road previous to 1819, and during that year Aden Gay and Nathaniel Bowles, two blacksmiths, came to Schlosser, and Thomas W. Fanning a tavern-keeper, James Pierce, a miller, and Arah Osborn, a carpenter, came during the following year; and William Bradner, a cloth-dresser, Dr. Ambrose Thomas, the first resident physician, and two carpenters. Peter Cowan and Andrew Huff in 1821.

Aaron and Stephen Childs came into the town in 1822, These two men were not brothers, as has been sometimes supposed; but they had long been neighbors and warm personal friends. The first was a church-member and the other, though in every way a moral man and a good citizen, was not a professor of religion. In consequence of this difference they were for many years distinguished as "Deacon" Childs and "Sinner" Childs. Stephen Childs settled near the Whirlpool rapids. Aaron Childs came from Lewiston and settled on land now within the limits of the village of Suspension Bridge. He remained there a few years and sold out to Orson Childs, son of Stephen Childs, and removed to a point now within the village of Niagara Falls. In 1836 he disposed of his property to his son W. H. Childs, and removed to Oberlin, Ohio, where he afterwards died. Stephen Childs long remained a resident of the town.

Theodore Whitney, a nephew of General Parkhurst Whitney, at that time twenty-one, came from Ontario county in 1823. After cutting logs for a cabin, he returned to Ontario county, and married Miss Experience C. Warner. Returning with his bride he boarded with the family of Samuel Young until the completion of his cabin, on the site of the present residence of his son, John Whitney. Mr. Whitney met with an accident in 1850 which resulted in his death.

In 1825 a number of new-comers found a home in Niagara, among them Henry H. Hill, who settled on the Military road, and James Ward and Peter D. Bachman, on the River road. Daniel Remington and family came from Livingston county in April, 1825, and moved in with the family of Charles Goff, who owned the only house at that time between Cayuga creek and the clearings of the Youngs. There was only one settler between the Youngs and the Witmers. The Remingtons came with four wagons drawn by horses.

One afternoon, about three o'clock, Miss Elizabeth Remington (afterwards Mrs. Angevine) and a Mrs. Rowland where lost while attempting to cross over from the Military road to that on which was the cabin of the Goffs and Remingtons. They wandered in the forest, alarmed by the darkness and the howling of the wolves, until nearly midnight before they finally reached home. Mrs. Angevine, who is yet living, states that game was very plenty in those days, and there were many fish in the river and creeks. At one time she saw twenty-four deer cross the marsh and swim the river over to Grand Island. It was customary for the settlers to so arrange their work as to hunt in company on Saturday afternoons. George Shipman, from Canada, brought his family and settled in the town in 1825. They were obliged to domicile themselves in a school-house near the Military road till a cabin could be erected for them.

In 1826 Rev. Horatio A. Parsons came to the town of Niagara and settled on the River road, between the Falls and Cayuga creek. He was born in Granby, Mass., in 1797, and previous to his coming married Miss Harriet Shepherd, of New Orleans, La. He was at one time pastor of the Presbyterian church at Niagara Falls, and for years divided his time between the duties of the pastorate and the scientific pursuit of agriculture, contributing many valuable and interesting articles on agricultural topics to the *American Agriculturist*, *The Cultivator*, *Rural New Yorker*, and similar publications. He was also the author of a guide-book to Niagara Falls. Anne Hammond became Mr. Parsons's second wife. He died in 1873, leaving a large family. Mrs. Parsons survives him, and with other members of the family lives on the old homestead, where Mr. K. P. Parsons, one of his sons, is extensively engaged in farming and fruit-growing.

Another former resident of Lancaster county, Martin Vogt, with his family, came to Niagara in 1828. They left their previous home the second of July, and arrived at the Falls August third. Mr. Vogt soon afterward purchased fifty-two acres of land—part of lot No. 17, range 9—of the Holland Company, and made himself a home, where he lived until 1836, when he disposed of his property to Rev. Horatio A. Parsons, and renoved to Upper Sandusky, Ohio.

Mr. Vogt's family numbered eight sons and daughters. The oldest daughter married in Lancaster county, Pa., and remained there. The remainder of the family, excepting one son, Jacob J. Vogt, accompanied their father west. After renting several farms in different parts of the town until 1844, Jacob J. Vogt purchased of Gardner Chapman lot No. 30 of the "Mile Strip," adjoining the Lewiston line. In 1834 Mr. Vogt was married to Miss Catherine Beaver, of Erie county. He has a son and three daughters, all of whom were born in the town. The former, Jacob B., married one of the daughters of John Whitney; one of the daughters is the wife of William E. Shafer, on the Lockport road; another, of William P. Mentz, of Lewiston; and the third, of H. G. Tompkins, of La Salle.

Mr. Vogt has seen many changes in this vicinity since 1828. At that date a great portion of the town was covered by a growth of timber, and the southeastern part was very wet. It was called "Pike Swamp," because of the great numbers of fish of that name which came up the river *via* Gill creek and Pike creek. Sometimes as many as twenty-five deer would cross the swamp in a herd. In the woods there were wild cats, wolves and bears, though the latter were not plenty. The last wolf caught in the town was trapped near Binkley's mill by Barnes Brooks, about 1828 or 1830. The last bear was killed between 1855 and 1860 at Suspension Bridge, opposite where the Presbyterian parsonage stands. It was seen in town, and dogged till it climbed a tree, when it was shot by Nelson Sanders. The roads were few and almost impassable. In the earlier days Mr. Vogt has cultivated all the land on which the village of Suspension Bridge now stands.

There was a failure of the wheat crop, causing great scarcity of bread-stuffs, in 1828, and a good deal of suffering among the people was the consequence. Such of them as were able bought corn of the Tuscaroras. The price was about a dollar a bushel.

During the next four or five years there was a steady though not large accession of settlers in different parts of the town. Among those who came in 1832 were Christian Binkley and his family, from Lancaster county, Pa., who were about three weeks making the journey, their means of conveyance being three teams. Mr. Binkley lived in an old log house a little south of where the residence of his son, Uriah Binkley, now stands, till the following spring, when he moved into a house on the farm of Ferris Angevine, further down Cayuga creek. In the autumn of the same year he removed from the town. Uriah Binkley, settled on Cayuga creek in 1855, where he has since been engaged in farming. At that date the land in the town of Niagara was generally cleared; and many families have come into the southern portion since and built houses on the different roads. Another son of Christian Binkley's, Jeremiah Binkley, is a prominent business man of Niagara Falls.

In 1833 Joseph Graves came from Massachusetts and settled at a place now within the corporate limits of Niagara Falls. His family consisted of his wife and three children, Lyman C. Graves and two sisters. Lyman C. Graves resides on what is known as the Packard road, on a part of lot No. 17, range 9, the same tract originally purchased of the Holland Land Company by Martin Vogt, and sold by him to Rev. H. A. Parsons, who sold it in turn to Mr. Graves. When he removed to this place in 1845, Mr. Graves found a log house upon it which had been erected during Mr. Vogt's occupancy, and which he replaced by a frame dwelling in the following year. Since that time he has been successfully engaged in farming and fruit-growing, and, in connection with the late Ambrose Packard, in the manufacture of lime.

Henry Ortt, a mason by trade, who has resided for a number of years on the Tonawanda road, near the line of Wheatfield, came from Lehigh county, Pa., in 1833, accompanying the family of his father, being at that time nine years of age. The Ortts settled on the Lockport road, on the farm now owned by A. Farnwalt, which constituted part of lot No. 3. At that time there were only three houses between that point and Pletcher's Corners, and only a few settlers in that part of the town. A man named Hanly kept a tavern in an old double log house standing on the ground now occupied by the residence of A. Kroening.

William Garrett came into the town from Monroe county in 1835, and purchased part of lot No. 14, his farm being the same now owned by C. Wolfe.

In 1838 Daniel Dietrick, sen., came from Pennsylvania. He was a carpenter by trade, and soon made friends and found employment. He owns property at La Salle, where he has resided for a number of years and reared a large family, some of whom are residents of this town. Between 1840 and 1850 the population of the town increased with considerable rapidity, by the accession of settlers in all parts.

Among those who settled at La Salle about 1850 was John Mason, a native of Switzerland. He married Elizabeth, daughter of John Bollier, of Niagara, in 1851. He was a wheelwright by trade. He held the position of postmaster at La Salle for a number of years, resigning about ten years ago, on account of failing health, and removing to his farm of 100 acres (part of lot No. 60) and following the life of a farmer till his death, March 16th, 1873. Mrs. Mason died March 5th, 1877, leaving two sons and two daughters, who now carry on the business of farming and fruit-growing conjointly, under the supervision of the eldest son, Joseph.

CIVIL HISTORY.

The first town meeting was held at the house of James Field, the seventh of April, 1812. The supervisor was authorized to build one pound at or near Schlosser. It was determined that Joseph Hadley's yard, or such enclosure as he might erect, should be considered a legal pound. It should be the duty of overseers of highways to act as fence-viewers. A fence five feet high, the rails not more than four inches apart, was declared a lawful fence. Hogs under four months old were permitted the privileges of "free-commoners." One dollar fine was imposed for each horse taken up on the commons. A bounty of five dollars was offered for each wolf killed in the town. The sum of two hundred and fifty dollars was voted to improve the highways, and twenty-five dollars for the support of the poor. Adjourned to meet at the same place.

The commissioners of highways divided the town into seven road districts.

A full ticket was elected at this first town meeting, consisting of Silas Hopkins, supervisor; Ezekiel Hill, town clerk; James Fields, Ebenezer Hovey and William Scott, assessors; Parkhurst Whitney, Joshua Pettit and Augustus Porter, commissioners of highways; John Sims, constable and collector; Gad Pierce and John W. Stoughton, poormasters; Amos Park, Warren Saddler, John Patterson, Abner Hull, John Witmer, William Scott and Abram Witmer, pathmasters.

At the next meeting, in 1813, horses were made "free-commoners," probably on account of the insufficient means of keeping them confined at the time. The premium on wolves was offered for a number of years. The following year the meeting was at the house of George Burger. A sum of money, the amount of which was not specified, was voted for the establishment of common schools. In 1816 the sum directed to be raised for a school fund was twenty dollars. The records of the town bear a copy of the following enactment, dated the first Tuesday of April, 1818 : " Resolved, that three times the amount of money appropriated by the State for the schools to this town be raised for the support of the schools, amounting in the whole to about twenty-four dollars." In 1816 it was directed that the number of pounds should be increased to two, and money was voted to pay for their erection. Horses belonging out of the town were declared not "free-commoners," and a fine of ten dollars was imposed on their owners in case they allowed them to go loose in the highways of this town.

In 1818 the record book was opened for the registry of "ear-marks" for the identification of sheep. Four years later a bounty of seventy-five cents was offered for foxes, and at a later period similar inducement was offered to encourage the killing of wildcats.

In April, 1827, at the annual town meeting, the supervisor and town clerk were directed to procure a map of the town, and also to prepare and circulate a petition for the division of the town and forward the same to be presented to the Legislature. Pendleton was taken from Niagara in this year. "It was agreed that after paying all of the debts due by the said towns while the same were united in the town of Niagara, two-thirds of all the accounts should belong to Niagara and one-third to Pendleton." The roads were again re-districted this year, and the number of districts reduced in consequence of the division of the town.

The town of Wheatfield was taken from Niagara, by an act of the Legislature dated May 12th, 1836.

SUPERVISORS.

Owing to the loss of a portion of the town records, it has been impossible to obtain the minutes of the town meeting for 1835 and the name of the supervisor elected at that time; and for the same reason the name for 1839 is also wanting; otherwise the following list is complete:

For 1812, Silas Hopkins; 1813, Ebenezer Hovey; 1814, James Field; 1815, George Burger; 1816, Silas Hopkins; 1817, James Field; 1818, Parkhurst Whitney; 1819, Gad Pierce; 1820, James Field; 1821, Augustus Porter (resigned and James Field chosen to fill vacancy); 1822, Augustus Porter; 1823-25, Alexander Dickerson; 1826, Samuel De Veaux (resigned. David Chapman chosen); 1827-30, Henry W. Clark; 1831-34, N. M. Ward; 1836, Henry W. Clark (resigned and William Bradner chosen to fill vacancy); 1837, Parkhurst Whitney; 1838, Henry W. Clark; 1840, Albert H. Porter; 1841-43, P. Whitney; 1844, 1845, P. B. Porter; 1846, N. W. Robinson; 1847, 1848, P. B. Porter; 1849, George W. Holley; 1850, P. D. Bachman; 1851, Samuel De Veaux; 1852, Parkhurst Whitney; 1853, 1854, Augustus S. Porter; 1855, 1856, Parkhurst Whitney; 1857-60, James F. Trott; 1861, Henry W. Clark; 1862, James F. Trott; 1863, 1864, William S. Watson; 1865-68, H. N. Griffith; 1869-71, H. F. Pierce; 1872-74, James B. King; 1875, O. W. Cutler; 1876-78, T. V. Welch.

NIAGARA IN THE REBELLION.

During the late war of the rebellion the town of Niagara was duly enterprising and patriotic, as the records show. The first man who enlisted in the town was John J. Sullivan. Three companies of volunteers went from the town to mingle in scenes of danger and carnage on the southern battle-fields, and measures were taken for the relief of soldiers' families which precluded the possibility of their suffering for any of the necessities of life, and relieved the men at the front of much anxiety concerning the dependent ones they had left behind. At a meeting for this purpose of the board of town auditors, held June 27th, 1863, the board adopted a plan to issue certificates of indebtedness. These certificates were printed on heavy blue tissue paper, and passed as freely as the money of the United States among the business men of the town, and were all redeemed when due, despite the croakings of those who opposed their issue and nick-named them "Hulett's Blue-backs" because of their prominent advocacy by Squire T. G. Hulett, in opposition to a proposition to issue town bonds. At the organization of the board for the purpose of granting this relief, Theodore G. Hulett was appointed to issue certificates in district No. 1, and Jacob Henning in district No. 2; and during 1863 and 1864 they issued to the families of soldiers about $10,000 worth of these, which were audited and paid each year. The following is a copy of one of the certificates so issued and redeemed:

"No. 804. *Town of Niagara, Dist. No.* 1, *May 30th,* 1864.
"BOARD OF RELIEF OF THE TOWN OF NIAGARA.

"Two Dollars is due the bearer from the Town of Niagara, for relief by him furnished the family of Patrick Joice, who is now in the military service of the United States. Such relief furnished by order of said board, under and by virtue of an act of the Legislature of the State of New York, entitled 'An Act providing for relief to the indigent families of volunteers and persons who may be ordered into the military or naval service of the United States,' passed May 17, 1863. This Certificate to be presented to the Board of Town Auditors of said town at their next annual meeting, to be audited by them for payment according to law, and payable when the tax is levied and the funds appropriated and placed in the hands of the Supervisor of said town for that purpose by the Board of Supervisors of Niagara County, according to law. Interest will be allowed and audited on this Certificate from the date thereof to the first day of January, 1865. By order of the Relief Board of said town. $2.00.
"(Signed) T. G. HULETT, COM'R DIST. NO. 1."

In August, 1864, the town auditors met to consider the best method for raising money for bounties, and for the payment of the certificates above described; and to prevent any public dissatisfaction it was resolved to call a meeting of the citizens to determine what course should be pursued, although the law legalized the issue of bonds by the board of town auditors at their discretion. This meeting was held at the Niagara House, in the village of Niagara Falls, on the 25th of the same month and was largely attended. T. G. Hulett was chosen chairman, and offered the following preamble and resolution, which were adopted by acclamation:

"*Whereas,* At the last annual town-meeting * * * * a resolution was passed requesting and authorizing the supervisors of the county of Niagara, under the law before referred to, to levy a tax sufficient to pay all the certificates that have been or may be issued for military purposes, such levy not to exceed the sum of $400, and to be paid out under the direction of the board of town auditors; therefore,

"*Resolved,* That the said resolution (with others of a subsidiary character) be adopted as the sense of this meeting."

The fund raised in accordance with the foregoing resolution was called the "town military fund of the town of Niagara." A fund called the "contingency fund" was also raised by legal authority.

Briefly as we have referred to the above mentioned efforts of the people of Niagara to bear their part in the great struggle for national existence, it will be seen that they lacked neither patriotism, money, nor executive ability.

One of the most sightly and attractive evidences of the patriotism, liberality and enterprise of the people of the town of Niagara, is the soldiers' memorial monument at the junction of Falls and Canal streets, in the village of Niagara Falls, where it was placed in the Centennial year in commemoration of the heroes who went from the town to do battle for their country's honor, and, to the number of fifty-three, yielded up their lives in their country's defense. The monument cost $1,976.04, $238.17 of which was subscribed by the people of the town. It was dedicated August 22nd, 1876, with religious and literary exercises, and a parade of firemen and military organizations, attended by a great concourse of spectators, including many distinguished visitors. Judge T. G. Hulett was chiefly instrumental in procuring the construction of the monument, and was the chairman of the board of commissioners having the matter in charge.

CEMETERIES.

Probably the earliest grave yard in the town was that at Fort Schlosser, though there may have been one made still earlier by the French at Fort Little Niagara. There was one at the Falls early in the present century, and John Osborne had a family burial place on the river road above the Falls.

Fifty years or more ago, the late Judge Augustus Porter donated a tract of land in the village of Niagara Falls to the town of Niagara for a town burying ground. After the incorporation of the village and the extension of its boundary lines, it was found that this cemetery was within the limits of the incorporation, and that it was yearly becoming too circumscribed for the use of the town at large. A little more than twenty years since, the Erie and Central railroad companies made propositions for the purchase of the right of way through the old grave yard. The supervisor of the town, by direction of a vote at a town meeting, sold the desired privilege for the construction of two tracks through the grounds, upon condition that the railroad companies should bear all the expense of the removal of the bodies, and with the proceeds of the transaction purchased two tracts of land for town burial purposes, one near Jonas Young's and the other adjoining Oakwood Cemetery on the south. A fine residence was erected on the latter, for the occupancy of the keeper of the grounds, and sufficient means was left to fence in and beautify the premises. A few years ago the town leased the public burying ground adjoining Oakwood Cemetery, together with the buildings thereon, to the Oakwood Cemetery Association for twenty years, upon condition that the town grounds should be free to any who might wish to make use of them for purposes of sepulture, and that the association should keep them in repair. A portion of what was left of the old grounds, after the construction of the railroad tracks through them, as above described, was sold to private parties, and a part reserved for the use of the town. The proceeds of this sale, amounting to $800—$300 of which was paid at the time—were placed in a fund designated the "old cemetery fund."

ROADS.

No efforts were put forth to open a road between Fort Schlosser and Black Rock after the abandonment of the Military road, until 1809, when the Legislature granted an appropriation of $2,000 for that purpose, and appointed Augustus Porter, Peter Vandeventer and Joseph Landon to lay out a road between the two places. This sum was so inadequate to the construction of a road over a well chosen and direct course, that the commissioners were obliged to follow the winding course of the river, and this road—on the American shore of the Niagara—was in such bad condition that for many years the greater part of the travel to the Falls was on the Canadian side.

The other principal roads of the town are the River road—which is a continuation of that last mentioned, though of earlier construction, passing through the villages of Niagara Falls and Suspension Bridge and following the course of the river to Lewiston, Youngstown and Fort Niagara—and the Lockport road, from Suspension Bridge in an easterly direction across the town, and through the intervening townships to Lockport. This road is of more recent date.

The Cayuga creek road, through the eastern part of the town, part of the way along the bank of the creek of the same name; the Packard road, from the river road, near the Gill creek bridge, to the Lockport road in the northwestern corner of the town; the road extending from Pine street, at the northeastern corner of the village of Niagara Falls, along the northern boundary of the mile strip to the Cayuga creek road, at the corner of the farm of J. Bollier; and a number of shorter roads have been opened from time to time, as the settlement of the town advanced and the convenience of the traveling public demanded.

SCHOOLS.

The first school in the town was opened at Niagara Falls in 1807, and before the clouds of war had lifted from the Niagara frontier, the law establishing common schools in the State of New York was passed by the Legislature, the act bearing date June 19th, 1812; and a year later (April, 1813,), before the destruction of the settlements along the river by the British, at the annual town meeting money was directed to be raised for the establishment and maintenance of common schools. This amount was necessarily small, but the demands of the time were perhaps correspondingly inconsiderable, and three years later the amount appropriated for this purpose was only twenty dollars. In 1818, as we have seen, the amount of school money had been raised to twenty-four dollars, and that was three times the sum appropriated by the State to the schools of this town. Other appropriations have followed from time to time. The amount of public money received at different periods for this purpose was as follows: 1819, $88.80; 1824, $37; 1828, $35.48; 1834, $127.50; 1840, $132.30; 1849, $226.80, and $340.17 raised by the people to help pay teachers. The amount of funds expended in the town for educational purposes has steadily increased, until in the year 1877 the school tax paid in Niagara was $3,092.84. In 1820 the school was kept nine months, and only thirty-seven children were taught; in 1823 there was a school for the same period, and the number of children in the Falls district between the ages of five and fifteen was fifty. The next year there were only forty-seven children of the school age. In 1834 the number had increased to one hundred and twenty-two; in 1840, to one hundred and eighty; in 1849, to two hundred and four. The number of children of the school age in the township at the present time is 2,800, divided among the different districts as follows: No. 1, 65; No. 2, 1,257; No. 3, 57; No. 4, 188; No. 5, 75; No. 6, 78; No. 7, 1,007; No. 8, 73. There were frequent changes of teachers in the early days, in some cases as many as four different ones having taught the same school in a single year. In the year 1816 the school districts of the town were originally erected. They then numbered five. There are now eight.

Previous to 1840 there had been but a few of the original log structures designed for educational purposes erected in the town, outside the village of Niagara Falls, and those by the gratuitous efforts of such of the settlers as chose to assemble and make "bees" for that purpose; and it was not till 1844 that a school-house was put up by a public tax, near Cayuga creek. It is related that on the evening of its completion the shavings were swept out of it, and it was first used that same night as a place of worship, Rev. John Cannon, of Niagara Falls, holding religious services there; and that the next morning the first school was opened in it by Miss Louisa Danforth, who afterward became Mrs. Samuel Tompkins. In the Young neighborhood, the first school-house was built near the Tufford farm, east of the Military road, in 1824, by Samuel and Christian Young and a few others. Daniel Smith was the first teacher. During the next season the family of a new comer named Shipman occupied it as a dwelling, and Mrs. Shipman taught the summer term. What was the fate of this building does not appear; but in 1827 the school was kept in the cooper shop of Christian Young, and in the same year a log school-house was erected out on the Military road, on the land of Samuel Young. Some time subsequent to 1840 this was replaced by a stone building. A man named Eldridge opened the first term in this building, but was obliged to abandon the work on account of ill-health, and was succeeded by a Mr. Fields. In 1867 land was bought across the road from this edifice, and the present building was erected. It is a substantial structure, well finished and furnished with patent desks and fixtures, affording quite a contrast to the style of school-house put up in the early days. The foregoing, repeated with some slight variations as to date and circumstance, would be the history of every school-district in the town.

THE FIRST RELIGIOUS SERVICES.

ever held in this town were conducted by Father Hennepin, during the sojourn of La Salle and his followers at Cayuga creek. Public worship was of rare occurrence previous to 1815, and the services were conducted at times in the open air, oftener in the school-house, and occasionally in barns, by the circuit preachers, who went from settlement to settlement planting the seeds of religious truth in the minds of the pioneers. But the little settlements were widely scattered, and the ever-welcome visits of these unlettered but zealous men, were not of much frequency; and it is credibly stated that there were less than a score of sermons preached in the town before the close of the war of 1812–14. The first church organization was formed in 1815, and others followed at various periods, under the auspices of different religious denominations. The celebrated pioneer evangelist Lorenzo Dow made a circuit of the Niagara frontier in 1823, preaching at the Falls on the evening of Monday, September 1st. Among the earlier local preachers who held meetings in the town was the Rev. John Cannon, still living, at a very advanced age.

FRUIT-GROWING IN NIAGARA.

John Burdette came to Niagara, from Buffalo, in 1849, and purchased an undivided half of Cayuga Island, which was at that time wild and uncultivated, consisting of about one hundred and sixty acres, only ten acres of which were tillable. He engaged in the cultivation of peaches and strawberries, becoming the pioneer in this business, which has since grown to be one of the most important interests in Niagara county. The first year he set out one acre of strawberries, and was successful in maturing and gathering the crop, clearing from it the sum of $1,000. Since that time he has been constantly increasing his facilities for the production and marketing of peaches and strawberries, and he gathered from the ten acres devoted to the first mentioned product about thirteen years ago a crop from which he received a gross income of $11,000; and since then he has been so extensively engaged in the business that he has had forty acres of strawberries growing at one time. Mr. Burdette's brother came from Buffalo a year or two later, and until his death was engaged with him in the business of fruit-growing. The above facts are mentioned to show from what a small beginning has grown an interest which is one of the most important and profitable in all this section of the State, and which has attained to its present prominence with a rapidity surpassed by no other industry. Encouraged by the success of Mr. Burdette, many of the older residents of the township embarked in the business of fruit-growing, and men of enterprise from abroad came to Niagara, purchased lands and threw all their energies into this pleasant and profitable employment. Prominent among the former were: Samuel Tompkins, J. Angevine, Ambrose Packard, Rev. Horatio Parsons, L. C. Graves, and a few others; and of the latter class, Mr. A. M. Chesbrough, Hiram D. Munson, who came over from Grand Island in 1865, and others.

Although fruit is extensively cultivated in most parts of the town, the land owners in the vicinity of La Salle make a specialty of the business, and it is stated on good authority that in 1876 there were 83,500 apple, peach, quince and pear trees growing in the township within two miles of that village; the proportion of the different species being as follows: Apple, 37,300; peach, 42,400; quince, 1,800; pear, 2,000. The fruit raised on the level reaches of Niagara orchard-land is of fine quality; and connoisseurs assert that they can select it from among that of other localities by its peculiar richness.

DRAINAGE.

A. M. Chesbrough came from Buffalo in 1850, and erected a log house at a point a little down the river from the present village of La Salle. This has since been replaced by one of the largest and finest residences in the town. Mr. Chesbrough at once became closely identified with the leading interests of Niagara. At that time much of the land in this section was wet, boggy and unfit for profitable cultivation; and he was the first person who turned his attention to its improvement by means of systematic and expensive drainage. Mr. Chesbrough went to Buffalo and contracted for 10,000 brick tiles, and began the work of tiling and draining. This was at that time looked upon by some of the earlier residents as an impracticable innovation that could, at best, result only in the loss of money to the experimenter; but like many projects that are looked upon with disfavor at their inception, this one had all the elements of success, and it was not long before the demand for tiles was so general that their manufacture at La Salle became a reliable and well-paying industry.

Formerly a great portion of the land in the southern part of the township was unfit for cultivation, being low and covered with stagnant water, which was at the same time detrimental to the advancement of agriculture and the general healthfulness of the people. Following the inauguration of the system of drainage above mentioned was the enforcement in this section of "an act to drain certain low lands in the State of New York," resulting in the reclaiming and enhancement of the value of large tracts of land, not only in this township but in other portions of the county. The earlier residents of Niagara all have reminiscences to tell of the days before the drainage of the land. All of them show against what disadvantages the pioneer farmers struggled, and some of them afford evidence of that happy temperament of some of the men of early days which extracts a joke from the most adverse circumstances. Perhaps the best story of the latter class is that told of one of the pioneers near Cayuga creek. An old acquaintance from the East called on him one day and found him out in the field plowing. After watching the wet, rich soil for a moment as it rolled up from the mould-board, the visitor remarked: "Pretty wet plowing that." "Oh, no; this ain't very bad," was the farmer's reply, as the plow went still deeper into the muck. "Well, what do you call bad?" asked the man from the East. "When I can't see anything of my plow but the tips of the handles!" was the reply.

POPULATION.

The population of the town in 1830 was 1,401; in 1840, 1,277; in 1850, 1,951; in 1860, 6,603; in 1870, 6,832; in 1875, 6,861.

THE VILLAGE OF LA SALLE.

This village is situated at the mouth of Cayuga creek. The first settler was "Big Smith," who lived there as early as 1806. In 1850 the place consisted of two dwellings, an old saw-mill, the property of Henry W. Clark and Samuel Tompkins; a blacksmith shop owned and occupied by Andrew White, and a small country tavern, standing on the ground now occupied by Nusbaum's shoe store, and kept by a man named McCulloch. A school-house stood just north of the village limits, which had been built in 1844. The settlement went by the name of Cayuga Creek.

The post-office was established about 1852. The first postmaster was Henry Clark, son of Henry W. Clark. A new building, which he had just erected, served the double purpose of store and post-office. He was succeeded by John Mason, who held the office until 1866. A man named Whitney was appointed, but only remained in office nine months. Mr. Mason was again appointed, and resigned on account of ill health in 1868, being succeeded by Alexander C. Leonard, the present incumbent.

The village received its present name in honor of the builder of the "Griffin," about the time of the establishment of the post-office.

The present business interests of La Salle may be summed up as follows: Planing mill and lumber yard, Tompkins & Loucks; manufacturer of brick and drain tile, H. S. Tompkins; grocery and post-office, Alexander C. Leonard; manufacturer and builder, Daniel Dietrick, sen. Besides these, there are a general store, a hotel and grocery, a boot and shoe store and a blacksmith shop, besides a builder, a cooper and representatives of other trades and industries.

METHODIST EPISCOPAL CHURCH OF LA SALLE.

This charge was formerly connected with that at Niagara Falls, and subsequently, for a time, with that at Tonawanda. The society at La Salle was formed in 1856. John Cannon was the first class leader. The first stewards were A. M. Chesbrough and John Kent.

Previous to this, in the fall of 1854, a number of persons met in the school-house of district No. 4, to consult with a view to the erection of a church. A building committee was appointed, consisting of the following members: Samuel Tompkins, A. M. Chesbrough, John Cannon. The project was carried rapidly forward, and William Philpott, of Niagara Falls, contracted to build the church for $1,100. It was erected in 1855, and subsequent expenses brought the cost up to about $1,400. In 1859 there was a division in the church, which resulted in the withdrawal of some of its members, who identified themselves with the Free Methodists. The ground on which the church stands belonged to some of these disaffected members, and the edifice was, after some difficulty, relinquished to them. It was purchased back in 1877 by the Methodist Episcopal society, and has since been occupied by them. Since the erection of the church the pulpit has been filled by a number of preachers of various denominations. The present pastor in charge is Rev. Albert Osborne. It has been a separate charge since 1874.

PLETCHER'S CORNERS.

Pletcher's Corners received its name in honor of the late William Pletcher. It is a farming neighborhood at the crossing of the Military and Lockport roads, in the northern part of the town. For the accommodation of the farmers in the vicinity a blacksmith's shop has been established there, the business of which is conducted by John Mailey, and a wayside tavern is kept by P. Hoehn, which is known as the "Military House."

THE VILLAGE OF NIAGARA FALLS.

THIS village was incorporated July 7th, 1848. In the early days of its history the village at the falls was called Schlosser; after it had gained some early prominence as a prospective manufacturing point, it was named Manchester, after the manufacturing town of that name in New England; and when it had become celebrated as a place of resort it received its present appellation.

The village, which has a population, according to the census of 1875, of 3,360, 1,257 of whom are of the school age, is situated in the southwestern corner of the town, on the point of land around which the river makes its abrupt change from a western to a northern course, and at the side of the cataract to which it owes its existence and from which it has derived its name.

Its chief claims to distinction are its unrivaled attractions as a place of resort, presenting as it does to the tourist natural scenery scarcely paralleled in the whole world, and affording facilities for personal comfort and enjoyment unsurpassed by those of any large city in the Union. Its streets are wide, well kept, well drained and well lighted; its residences many of them elegant and situated in the midst of spacious and beautiful grounds; its hotels palatial in their extent and appointments; its churches numerous, the edifices conveniently located, substantial and tasteful in architecture, and freely opened to the stranger in the village; and its railway facilities are unequaled by those of any place of its size in the United States, which is a convenience appreciated alike by the visitors from abroad and the local business men and manufacturers.

But Niagara Falls takes no unimportant standing as a place of thriving industry, profitable enterprise and home-like attractions. Its unequaled water power renders it peculiarly adapted to the purpose of manufacture, the uncommon railway advantages of which mention has been made enhance its natural claims in this direction, and the efforts now being put forth by the proprietors of the hydraulic canal promise to result in further stimulating manufacturing enterprise and rendering it operative and profitable. In no part of the county are the interests of education more thoroughly and systematically advanced; and those twin messengers of enlightenment and civilization, the church and the press, are sustained with an honorable and flattering liberality.

THE VILLAGE IN 1810.

A commission, consisting of DeWitt Clinton, Gouverneur Morris, Stephen Van Rensselaer, Simeon DeWitt, William North, Thomas Eddy and Peter B. Porter, left Schenectady July 4th, 1810, to explore the route for a canal from the Hudson river to Lake Erie. Clinton kept a daily journal of their progress and experiences, which is very interesting and valuable to the student of the general history of the State, parts of it especially so, as being descriptive of life on the frontier at that time; and a few paragraphs devoted to this locality will be found of interest in this connection. He wrote as follows:

"We arrived at the village, one quarter of a mile above the falls, and three-quarters of a mile from Fort Schlosser. It was established by Porter, Barton & Co., and it is the best place in the world for hydraulic works. Here is a carding machine, a grist-mill, a saw-mill, a tannery, post-office, tavern, and a few houses. An acre lot sells for fifty dollars. The rope-walk is sixty fathoms long, is the only establishment of the kind in the western country, and already supplies all the lake navigation. The hemp used in this manufactory is raised on the Genesee flats."

THE EARLY SETTLERS.

In the town history we have already described how, from the time of the purchase of the Portage Company in 1805, and the settlement at the Falls of Judge Augustus Porter in 1806, a thriving little manufacturing village grew up—small, it is true, and rude, and lacking the appliances and conveniences of a later day, but busy and full of promise for the future. Previous to 1812, the following persons were householders at the Falls:

James Everingham, John W. Stoughton, William Van Norman, Adoram Everingham, Joshua Fairchild, Ebenezer Hover, Ezekiel Hill, Ralph Coffin, Ebenezer Brundage and Oliver Udall. The landlord at the first tavern was Joshua Fairchild, and he was succeeded in 1814 by Parkhurst Whitney. There was a tavern at the end of the Portage road, at Schlosser, kept by Warren Saddler.

Parkhurst Whitney was a man who afterwards became prominently identified with Niagara Falls and its business and social interests, and a peculiar interest attaches to him as having been one of the early settlers at this point. Mr. Whitney was born in Conway, Mass., in 1784. In 1791 he removed with the family of his father, Jonathan

Whitney, to the "old Castle" farm, near Geneva, Ontario county. They came with ox teams, and were about two weeks on the road. Until he was eighteen or nineteen years of age he lived with his brothers and sisters. After that he went on to some land which he had inherited at the death of his father in 1792. He came from Phelps, Ontario county, in 1810, as has been stated in the history of the town, and settled on the farm now owned by Samuel Tompkins. In 1812 he removed to the Falls and rented Porter's saw-mill.

At the burning of the village by the British, in 1813, nothing was saved but two or three small dwellings and the tavern, in which cases the fire was extinguished after the departure of the invaders. The people were obliged to flee for their lives, and they were given insufficient warning to enable them to gather together such necessaries as would have nurtured and comforted them in their defenseless wandering from their devastated homes. For a time enterprise was paralyzed, but it was not dead. The arm of enterprise was nerved anew, and the short time between the declaration of peace and the opening of the year 1815 was sufficient for the work of reanimation to take a strong hold on the village and its people, who returned and began the bitter task of retrieving their broken fortunes as soon as the dictates of safety permitted.

The year 1814 had witnessed a considerable advance in this direction, and among other events which occurred during that year was the occupation of the Eagle Tavern by Parkhurst Whitney. The house was a log one, and occupied part of the site of the present International Hotel; but no buildings were erected at the Falls till 1815.

That the business interests of the village were advanced considerably during this year, is shown by the fact that a number of persons came in then, some of whom were mechanics and laborers, and one or two of whom were pioneer men of business. Among these were Samuel Hooker, a carpenter, who appears to have been a man of merit, as he afterwards won the confidence of his townsmen to such an extent that his name often appears among the lists of town officers in the early records; and

SAMUEL DE VEAUX, THE FIRST MERCHANT,

a man who in later years became prominent in the affairs of the town, and who died in 1852, leaving an enduring monument to his memory, which has been spoken of more fully in the history of the village of Suspension Bridge. He was born in the city of New York in 1789. On the revocation of the Edict of Nantes, in 1685, his great-grand father, Louis De Veaux, fled from his native city, Paris, and came to America; and thus it will be evident that Samuel De Veaux descended from the Huguenots, a band of persecuted men and women whose names have been perpetuated in the annals of Church and State, as those of honored and illustrious christians and citizens. His childhood was passed in New York. In 1803 he entered the land office of Phelps & Gorham, at Canandaigua. In 1807 he was appointed commissary at Fort Niagara, and in 1813 married Maria Woodruff, a Canadian lady, and went to Le Roy and remained there two years. His wife died in 1815, and in 1817 he married her sister. At Niagara Falls he engaged in trade, and by attention to business and the subsequent rise in property values at this village, became very wealthy. He was often chosen to town offices in the early days, having been elected supervisor in 1826, and to the position of town clerk for nearly a dozen terms, and he served both as judge and legislator with much credit to himself and satisfaction to those who selected him.

His store was of the old, pioneer kind. His trade was confined to no particular class of customers, and his stock in trade consisted of anything and everything that was likely to be needed by a people in a new country. These things were traded off for agricultural produce, skins and small articles of home manufacture. In those days storekeepers studied the demands of the public fully as closely as they do now, and their system of traffic was so extensive that they frequently exchanged one article of merchandise for another, so that with due diligence there was little danger of their stocks running low. Tradition says that Judge De Veaux's store, far from being an exception to the general rule, was a striking illustration of it; for he had anything that might be called for, from a yard of cloth for ladies' and children's wear to goose-yokes, ox-bows and sap-buckets for use on the farms round about.

As the village grew and advanced toward its present state of enlightened elegance and civilization, the judge kept pace with it; he was always careful, though enterprising, always up to the times, always had desirable goods at going prices and was regarded as an honest, energetic and prompt man of business. Among those who came in 1818 were Stephen and David Chapman and William Murray. The former were woolen manufacturers and cloth dressers, and afterward engaged in business enterprises in the village; and the latter was a carpenter and builder, one of the most efficient of those early days, and the father of S. T. Murray, a prominent manufacturer and citizen of Niagara Falls at the present time.

ACCESSIONS FROM 1821 TO 1838.

Settlement continued, and in 1821 came the pioneer physician, Dr. Ambrose Thomas; and in 1822 Enos Clark, a mason, John Bradner, a shoemaker, Ansel B. Jacobs, who was one of the early gate-keepers at Goat Island bridge, Ziba Gay, a blacksmith, Solomon L. Ware, a tanner, and a tailor named B. H. White; and in 1823, Henry W. Clark, Charles Clark and Jesse Symonds, paper-makers.

Among those who came in 1824 were Christopher H. Smith, who engaged in trade, Richard Ayer, a farmer, and Timothy Shaw, a cloth-dresser; and in 1826 came a cabinet-maker, a blacksmith and two wagon-makers, named respectively Ira Cook, William G. Tuttle and Thomas Chapin and A. M. Swallow. Another cloth-dresser, Aaron Parsons, came in 1829, and another of the same trade, John McDonald, in the following year, during which the population and enterprise of the now growing village received new accessions by the arrival and settlement of Charles Parsons, a merchant, and another physician, Dr. Edwin Cook, besides several persons who engaged in operating the saw-mill and labored in different capacities about the place, among the latter three sawyers named Amasa Butler, John Feehan and Robert White; and a painter named Theodore S. Whitney came in 1831.

Evidences of progress began to be apparent on every hand. Settlement continued with unabated rapidity, and the sounds of life and industry were becoming more and more plainly heard above the ceaseless roar of the cataract. Business had taken root; it was growing and flourishing under the care of diligence and enterprise; and prosperity was the ripening fruit it was bearing. The trades were by this time well represented in the village, and it had grown to be quite a center of traffic. Visitors were coming from abroad in increasing numbers, and it is not strange that the attraction which could draw men to the village for a few days to look upon the grand panorama which nature has there spread out, could induce them to linger and to seek for a life-work and a home beside the grand old river of the restless waters. The year 1834 saw still further accessions to the number who had previously settled in the village, and of those who came that year perhaps few are better remembered than two mechanics, named Oramel G. and Lucien Johnson; and none are better known at the present day than the venerable Judge Theodore G. Hulett, who came from Pittsfield, Mass., and who since that time has been conspicuously and actively identified with the best interests of the village and the town at large. He was a practical mechanic and engineer, and combined with his skill as a workman a sound judgment and a native Yankee "push" and energy that made him prominent in whatever enterprise he interested himself, and has vouchsafed to him a series of business successes which mark him one of the eminently self-made men of the county. In 1835 came Hard Munns, who will be remembered as a furnaceman; Rev. John Cannon, an aged resident of the village at the present day, who was active in the cause of religion, and devoted much of his time and energy to the salvation of his fellow-men; and Dexter R. Jerauld, well known as a wealthy and influential citizen, and one of the proprietors of the Cataract Hotel.

Of those who came in 1836, several have since become well known as business men and citizens, among them Samuel D. Hamlin, long prominent in the stage and livery business; Seth L. Burdick, William Griffith and F. C. Ford, carpenters; and James Davy, whose sons are engaged in the livery and fancy goods trade; and in 1837 came George Holland, a cabinet-maker, George E. Hamlin, now the keeper of a grocery at the corner of Falls and First streets; Joel R. Robinson, whose daring adventures on the river have caused him to be celebrated as the "Hero of the Whirlpool and the Rapids," and Andrew Murray, since well and favorably known as the passenger agent of the Erie Railway. In 1838 W. E. Hulett and A. W. Allen, since well known, took up their residence at the Falls.

Among those who came in 1840, Hon. G. W. Holley, a graduate of West Point and a man of means and literary culture, is conspicuous. He at once became interested in Niagara and its wonders and attractions, and in 1872 he published from the press of Sheldon and Company, New York, a work which he had long had in careful preparation, entitled: "Niagara, its History and Geology, Incidents and Poetry." This is one of the most thorough and exhaustive works about Niagara ever written. Michael Walsh, Charles Wilcox and John Doty also came this year; and between this date and 1855, Daniel J. Townsend, now of Buffalo, came and started a factory for the manufacture of screws, and the following well known persons settled in the village: James F. Trott, one of the firm of Whitney, Jerauld & Co.; Morris L. Fox, now a groceryman on Falls street; Dr. Gennett Conger, now of Geneva; John Geagan, a blacksmith; William Sturdy, now engaged in the manufacture of harnesses on Cherry street; A. K. Fasset, dealer in hardware; Alva Cluck, proprietor of the Spencer House; Worthy Curtis, Dayton G. Canfield, since removed to Michigan; Osborn Canfield, of the firm of Clark & Canfield, coal dealers; John D. Hamlin, afterwards proprietor of Hamlin's Banking House, and now in business in New York; William F. Evans, Charles H. Piper, attorney; Thomas Tugby, proprietor of Tugby's fancy goods bazar, and William Pool, editor and publisher of the *Niagara Falls Gazette*.

GENERAL PETER B. PORTER.

In the following year, General Peter B. Porter, a younger brother of Hon. Augustus Porter and one of the firm of Porter, Barton & Co., with his family, removed to the village from Black Rock, where he had lived since 1810. General Porter was born in Salisbury, Conn., in 1773, graduated from Yale College, and studied law in Litchfield. He was admitted to the bar in 1794, and the next year took up his residence in Canandaigua for the practice of his profession. He was appointed clerk of Ontario county in 1797, and elected a member of the Legislature in 1802. He removed to Black Rock in 1810, and was elected to Congress that year and in 1814, and in 1815 he was Secretary of the State of New York. The next year he was one of a committee to run a boundary line between the United States and Canada, and in 1828 appointed Secretary of State under John Quincy Adams. He was active in Congress pending the war of 1812, and advocated the declaration of war; and when the war came he was in the midst of it, doing a soldier's part manfully. In 1814 he was made brigadier-general of volunteers, receiving his appointment from Governor Daniel D. Tompkins, and he was brevetted a major-general soon after the battle of Lundy's Lane; in 1815 he was by President Madison appointed major-general in the United States service, and had another campaign been demanded by the exigencies of the times, he would have had command of the northern division of the army. He was married late in life to Mrs. Letitia Groyson, of Kentucky, daughter of ex-Attorney General Breckenridge. She died at Black Rock in 1831, aged forty-one years. General Porter died at Niagara Falls in 1844, having lived two years beyond the allotted three-score-and-ten.

COLONEL PETER A. PORTER.

General Porter left two children, who were afterwards known and loved by the citizens of the village, Colonel Peter A., and Miss Elizabeth Porter, both of whom are dead, the latter dying unmarried, a few years since. Peter A. Porter was born in Black Rock in 1827. He was educated at Cambridge University, and afterwards spent two years at Heidelberg University, in Germany, and in European travel. Returning, he married Miss Mary Cabell Breckenridge. She died two years later; and after a second European tour, he married Miss Josephine Morris, of New York, in 1859. In 1861 he was elected to the State Assembly, and at the outbreak of the rebellion he contributed largely toward the raising of a cavalry regiment known as the Porter Guards. The next year he organized the 8th regiment of heavy artillery, of which he was commissioned colonel. While in Baltimore, awaiting orders to join Grant's army before Richmond, he was tendered the nomination for Secretary of State of New York, but declined it. He took part in all the varying experiences of his regiment up to the time of his death, June 3d, 1864, at the battle of Cold Harbor. He held several places of trust in the western part of the State, having been for many years one of the trustees of Hobart College, Geneva, and he was appointed by the late Judge De Veaux trustee of De Veaux College, and executor of his will. His widow, two sons, Peter A. Porter, jr., a resident of the village, and George M., now a youth, and a daughter survived him; but the latter has since died.

BUSINESS AND IMPROVEMENTS.

In 1805 Augustus Porter built a saw-mill and a blacksmith's shop at the Falls, as has before been stated, and a grist-mill in 1807, the circumstances of the raising of which have been described in the early history of the town. This has been spoken of by pioneers as the only mill in the county at this time, and the people in parts of Erie and Orleans counties brought their grain here too. In the following year he built his dwelling house, afterwards destroyed by the British, and rebuilt it on the same ground and on a similar plan, in 1818. The erection of the ropewalk, tannery, carding-mill, several shops of different kinds and a number of small dwellings soon followed. Augustus and P. B. Porter purchased Goat Island in 1816. The history of this island is an interesting one. It was one of those ceded to Sir William Johnson in 1764 by the Senecas.

The after history of the island on the brink of the falls is connected with that of the other land in this section, until it became the property of the Messrs. Porter, who made an attempt to purchase it as early as 1811, but could not gain the consent of the Legislature. The manner in which they finally effected their purpose is thus described in Turner's History of the Holland Purchase:

"Samuel Sherwood, a lawyer of considerable eminence in his day, had a *float*, as it is now called in our western States. It was an instrument given him by the State of New York (such as are often issued from the General Land Office of the U. S.) allowing the bearer to locate two hundred acres of any of the unsold or unappropriated lands of the State. * * * The brothers (Porter) bought this instrument of him, and during the next year settled Goat Island and the small islands about it, in all about seventy acres, as a part of the two hundred acres." In 1816, they received their "patent," or deed, a grant from "the people of the State of New York" of "a certain island called Goat Island, situated in the rapids of Niagara river, the northwestern side of which island terminates with the perpendicular rock or precipice forming the * * falls, together with several small islands according to a plan and survey of the same, and now on file in the secretary's office."

The first time Judge Porter succeeded in getting on the island, previous to 1810, there were old dates upon the trees, the earliest of which was 1742; there were evidences that there had been a tree cut there and a canoe built, and in early years parts of several human skeletons were found there. In 1817 a bridge was constructed to the island, some distance above the site of the present iron structure. In March, 1818, a large portion of it was swept away by masses of ice which had been driven down from the lake by a heavy wind.

The first lady visitors to Goat Island were three young girls, who crossed the first bridge while it was only partially finished. One of these girls afterwards became Mrs. Murray, mother of S. T. Murray of Niagara Falls, and another the wife of Rev. S. C. Townsend. In 1818 the second Goat Island bridge was erected. It was a wooden structure. The location proved a secure one, and in 1856 the elegant and substantial iron bridge was constructed in its stead.

THE CARRYING BUSINESS.

As has been stated, in connection with their purchase of land in the vicinity of the falls, the firm of Porter, Barton & Co. took an extended lease of the landings at Lewiston and Schlosser, and the exclusive use of the portage. They purchased and built a number of vessels on the lakes, and smaller craft, called Durham boats, on the river. For a number of years transportation between the east and west *via* the lakes was largely controlled by this company. The following reminiscences of this business are extracted from the journal of ex-Governor Clinton, and they are inserted here as descriptive of the manner in which transportation on the river was carried on: "We set out from Fort Schlosser in a Durham salt boat, drawing two feet of water, twenty-five tons burthen, and able to carry one hundred and fifty bushels of salt, between seventy and eighty feet long and seven and eight feet wide. She had six men who pushed her up against the stream. * * * * The current was sometimes three miles an hour."

Before the war of 1812, Porter, Barton & Co. were

the owners in whole or in part of as many as seven vessels on Lake Erie and two on Lake Ontario. After the declaration of peace the United States government disposed of such vessels as were suitable for the purposes of commerce. In 1815 Porter, Barton & Co. and Townsend, Bronson & Co., of Oswego, consolidated under the title of Sill, Thompson & Co., and increasing their facilities for transportation, carried on the business between Oswego and the upper lakes until the expiration of the lease of the portage, in 1821. After the completion of the Erie Canal in 1825, the lines of through transportation *via* the Niagara river and the portage around the falls were discontinued.

FURTHER BUSINESS PROGRESS.

In 1816 a cloth-dressing and wool-carding establishment was erected by James Ballard, and afterwards enlarged and improved by D. and S. Chapman, for the manufacture of woolen cloth and satinet. In 1819-20 Parkhurst Whitney erected a substantial addition to his tavern, calling it the "Eagle Tavern," and on the fourth day of July of the latter year gave a grand public dinner in celebration of the completion of the frame part of the structure. It was one of those thoroughly enjoyable affairs of the early days which the old people of the village and town have looked back upon as one of the bright spots on the pages of memory; and the thought of the hilarity and good cheer of that pioneer gathering of friends and neighbors has lived with some of the participants to their latest days. Mr. Whitney continued to make improvements on the Eagle Hotel, which at the time he purchased it consisted of one room, which served as bed-room, bar-room, kitchen, dining-room, public hall and office, until 1831, when he bought the Cataract House, using it as lodging rooms for the surplus business of the Eagle. In 1835 he moved into the Cataract House and began a four-story addition. Other additions were erected in the years that followed and adjoining buildings, one of them the old stone factory purchased and connected with the Cataract House. And from this beginning has grown the present Cataract Hotel. Of the growth and progress of this business, General Whitney says in a private memoir: "During the above period I changed my circumstances from making my own fires, being ostler, tending bar, waiting on the table, my wife doing the cooking, with, all together, four or five servants, to the employment of one hundred servants, and giving up the establishment to the children and returning to my old calling, farming," which he did in 1846, at which time the firm became Whitney, Jerauld and Trott, the first two members having for a number of years previous been connected with the firm of P. Whitney & Sons.

In 1821 a forge, rolling-mill and nail factory were built by Bolls & Gay, who conducted a manufacturing business at the Falls for some time. The following year Augustus Porter erected a large grist-mill on the rapids. It is the same now owned and operated by the Witmer Brothers. In 1823 a paper mill was built near Goat Island bridge by Jesse Symonds; and in 1826 a larger one was erected on Bath Island by Porter & Clark. In 1848 it was sold to Benjamin and Chester Bradley, and afterwards purchased and enlarged by L. C. Woodruff, of Buffalo. August 12th, 1858, it was burned. The estimated loss was $75,000, part of which was covered by insurance. The work of rebuilding it was begun immediately. The business, which has grown to large proportions, is conducted by the Niagara Falls Paper Manufacturing Company.

The Cataract House was originally built in 1825, by David Chapman. Its after history has been referred to in connection with the remarks concerning the late General Parkhurst Whitney.

In 1826 the upper race, familiarly referred to as the "wing dam," was extended, it having been built in parts at different dates, and William G. Tuttle, Ira Cook, Chapin & Swallow and other parties erected works of different kinds upon it.

To follow the course of enterprise in the village, and attempt to give in detail a record of the rise and progress of its business interests—to mention names and dates and particulars—would be a task as pleasant to perform as it would be difficult, from the impossibility, because of the numerous changes wrought by Time and Death, of obtaining reliable data upon which to base our statements. The leading events in the commercial and manufacturing progress of Niagara Falls have been recorded, and with sufficient attention to detail and description to mark the rise and advancement of these interests from the time when, in 1805, the initial steps were taken tending to the establishment of general business prosperity, to a later period when that prosperity had become assured. Building went on, enterprise after enterprise was started, to fall or flourish, as in the history of every town in the country. Beginnings from which little was expected have resulted in grand successes, and brilliant projects which gave flattering promise of future profit have gone down, and are dead and buried among the failures of the past, and remembered only as a warning and a lesson.

THE UPS AND DOWNS OF 1836.

The year 1836 will be remembered as a year of wild speculation, of visionary schemes and brilliant failures throughout the country. Among the geniuses who enacted their parts in that financial drama was a well known builder, banker, hotel-keeper and speculator, named Benjamin Rathbun, and he chose Niagara Falls as his stage of action. He made contracts for the purchase of much valuable real estate in the village and vicinity. He erected a large addition to the Eagle tavern, and made preparations to put up a very large hotel on the square now occupied by the International, at the corner of Falls and Main streets. There seemed to be a disposition on the part of many of the citizens to join him in his speculations, for he was a man of plausible address and had the reputation of being an experienced man of business; and he succeeded in inspiring their confidence in his plans to such a degree that many of them afterwards saw cause to remember with regret the "ups and downs" of '36.

The village limits were considerably extended, and Rathbun commenced the sale of village lots at auction, and with the best apparent promise of success. For a time all went well; but suddenly the hopes which had been so quickly raised of easily gained profits were as unexpectedly dashed to the ground by the failure of Rathbun, entailing lasting injury to the progress of the village, loss to some of its citizens and still greater financial reverses to some of his friends in Buffalo and elsewhere, who were involved with him, as endorsers or as sharers in his projects; and teaching over again the lesson that permanent prosperity is the reward of steady, systematic and persistent labor, and not of wild-cat speculation and bonanza schemes for sudden opulence.

But gradually confidence was restored, and business went on in the legitimate channels and prospered in so doing; and from that time on till about the year 1850 there was a constant advancement; enterprise was strenghening steadily and surely; and between the latter date and 1860 the village received an impetus which gave it an increase in growth and population unprecedented in all its former history and unequaled since.

Most sightly and costly among the buildings erected in the village previous to 1860, which have not already been mentioned, were the residence of General P. B. Porter, on Falls street, erected previous to 1840 and since reconstructed and now known as the Park Place Hotel; the International Hotel, built by B. F. Childs in 1853, on the site of the primitive log tavern, and afterward enlarged by Hon. John T. Bush; and the "Frontier Mart," a row of business houses in one continuous brick block, one hundred and thirty-two feet long by sixty feet deep and three stories high, erected in 1854 by A. S. & P. B. Porter. The first floor is occupied by stores of different kinds. The apartments are large, well lighted and ventilated, and an iron front extends the entire length of the row. The second story is occupied by town and private offices, and the Niagara Falls Shooting Club has rooms there. The apartments on the third floor are used for club and lodge rooms and the like. The Spencer House was opened in 1867, two hotels having previously burned on the same site. March 1st, 1877, Messrs. Hill & Murray started their pulp mills on Cascade street.

The Hotel Kaltenbach was erected in 1877 and 1878, and opened to the public in the early part of the last mentioned year. It is a commodious brick structure, elegant in design and first-class in finish and appointments. It is rapidly growing in favor, and takes rank among the first-class hotels of the place.

THE HYDRAULIC CANAL.

This canal, extending from navigable water above the rapids to the high bank below the falls, is three-quarters of a mile long, about forty feet wide and ten feet deep, terminating in a long basin which lies parallel with the course of the river at that point, from which the water is emptied into the Niagara a quarter of a mile below the falls.

The manifest advantages of Niagara Falls for purposes of manufacture have long been recognized the world over. It is mentioned, as we have seen, in the journal of De Witt Clinton (1810) as "the best place in the world for hydraulic works." Since then the favorable natural conditions here have been commented on by the general public, and made the basis of calculations by civil engineers and manufacturing capitalists.

Augustus Porter, who owned the land through which the canal passes, early saw its importance, and for many years before his death made favorable offers to capitalists to undertake the work; and his heirs, having firm confidence in his estimate of the great utility of the enterprise, aided it by a gift of the water power and as much land in the village, adjoining the lower part of the canal, as was deemed desirable to insure the ultimate success of the project, amounting in all to about seventy acres.

The hydraulic canal was the agency which was chiefly instrumental in increasing the population of the town from 1,951, in 1850, to 6,603, in 1860, and to which is to be ascribed in no small degree the unexampled growth of the village between those years. As with all similar works, the labor of a large number of men was required in its construction, and the great accession of population during the time mentioned was consequent, in a great measure, upon the influx of laborers seeking, and many of them finding, employment on the hydraulic works, and subsequently becoming permanent residents of the village and contiguous portions of the town.

During the period of its construction, the canal constituted to men of business nearly as great an attraction as do the falls to pleasure-seekers. The history of the conception, commencement, progress and consummation of this work is a peculiar one, and one that is marked by the occurrence of changes, embarrassments, delays and vicissitudes unequaled, perhaps, in the prosecution of any other similar enterprise in the country. The work was begun in 1853, and notwithstanding all the above-mentioned adverse conditions, brought to its present degree of completion ten or twelve years since; but for various reasons it has been only recently utilized and its practical value demonstrated. In 1874 C. B. Gaskell erected a large grist-mill, the first manufacturing establishment receiving its motive power from the hydraulic canal. It was completed in the spring of 1875, and was in constant operation during the extremest cold weather of that very cold winter, with no interruption from ice, or any of the other disadvantages that usually affect water-powers of the ordinary kind; affording the most unequivocal proof that the project was from the first entitled to all the advantages claimed for it by its most ardent abettors. Another flouring mill, which will contain twenty-two runs of stones, with provisions for the addition of ten more, and which, when completed, will be one of the largest establishments of the kind in the United States, is now in course of erection by Messrs. Schoellkopff & Matthews. It will be a large and substantially built stone structure when completed; and the enterprise bids fair to be one of the most important in the place.

MAILS, STAGES, RAILROADS AND EXPRESSES.

In the early days mails arrived with little frequency and considerable irregularity. They were carried by men who rode on horseback, on the route from Buffalo to Lewiston, and the amount of mail matter was so small that it is said the bag was often carried in the coat-pocket of the postman. The first postmaster at the Falls was Judge Porter; the second was Samuel De Veaux. The present incumbent is William B. Rice, M. D.

After the era of the post-rider came that of the stage-coach. The staging business was carried on by different parties at different times and over different routes, one of the best known stage proprietors at the Falls having been Samuel D. Hamlin, who came to the village in 1836, at the time of the operations of Benjamin Rathbun, and the consequent rise in real estate, and started a line of stages with several branches, which he ran with considerable success in connection with the railroads from Buffalo and Lockport.

These railroads, the Buffalo and Niagara Falls and the Lockport and Niagara Falls, were completed in 1836. They were, like all railways at that date, slightly and insecurely built, with wooden stringers and "strap" or "snake-head" rails; the rate of speed was very slow and, owing to numerous mishaps, annoyances and delays, the running of the trains was very irregular, it being no very uncommon thing for them to be four, five or even seven hours late in coming from Buffalo or Lockport, and only one trip was made down and back per day. But though these roads were slightly built, they answered a good purpose for the light travel and traffic of that period, and served greatly to relieve the village in the general reaction of 1836, and the embarrassments of the following two or three years.

An idea of some of the disadvantages incident to travel in those days may be obtained from a perusal of the following extract from a letter written by a correspondent of the New York *Mercury*, descriptive of a trip from the metropolis to the Niagara frontier, which, though it is pervaded by a humorous vein, we are assured is very little exaggerated, if any:

"I went by the way of Lockport, on the Erie Canal, at which place I left those raging waters and took passage on one of the everlastingist railroads anywhere on top of the earth. Would you believe it, those cars, only two—one for passengers and one for baggage and jack-screws, levers and handspikes, to 'straighten up' the train when we ran off the track, and that was often enough, anyway—were just seven hours and twenty-six minutes going from Lockport to Niagara Falls, a distance of only twenty-one miles. Well, we got there, at last, and I stopped at the Falls a day or two to see the rushing fluid, and then took one of Sam Hamlin's hacks for Lewiston."

The depot was near the head of Main street in those days. Subsequently the railroads mentioned passed into the control of the N. Y, C. & H. R. Railroad Company.

The present railway connections of Niagara Falls are first-class, it being on a branch of the Erie Railway, with a commodious depot at the outskirts of the village, and on the various northern branches of the New York Central and Hudson River Railroad, this company's large and well appointed stone depot being situated conveniently to the business portion of the place. The local passenger agent of the Erie Railway is Andrew Murray, his office being in the International Hotel, on Main street; and of the Central, Francis C. Belden, with headquarters in the company's depot on Falls street, opposite the Spencer House. The Erie Railway Company's local freight agent is Mr. C. B. Hyde, and Mr. T. E. Clark fills a similar position in the employ of the Central.

There are two express companies represented—the American, with an office in the Central depot, under the charge of Mr. John Salt, and the United States, whose office is at the corner of Falls and First streets, Daniel Barrett, agent. Here also are located the extensive repair shops of the Central.

THE PRESS OF NIAGARA FALLS.

The first paper published in the village was *The Niagara Falls Journal*, which was issued in 1837 by Francis & Ward. Its publication ceased after a few months. The publication of the *Niagara Chronicle* was begun by J. Simpson in 1838. *The Iris* was issued between 1846 and 1854, by George H. Hackstaff. In 1855 *The Niagara Times* was started by W. E. Tunis, and it was issued regularly until October, 1857. *The Niagara Falls Gazette* was established May 17th, 1854, by Messrs. Pool & Sleeper. During portions of 1859 and 1860 it was issued daily and weekly. William Pool became the sole proprietor in 1864. The *Gazette* is a well-printed seven-column paper, ably edited and devoted to the principles of the Republican party. It is read extensively throughout the county and elsewhere. Rupert M. Pool is the local editor, and the printing and jobbing department is in charge of D. C. Collins.

SCHOOLS.

The first school was opened in 1807. The first school-house was of logs, and stood by the road side north of Ontario street. The present three-story stone school-houses were erected between 1850 and 1855, and in the year last mentioned the common schools were made free. In 1852 Albert H. Porter built an academy, which was conducted with much success for several years. In 1864 it was sold to the Catholics, and has since been managed under their auspices. The common schools of the village are under the management of Prof. W. S. Hall, as principal, assisted in the various departments by an able corps of teachers.

Writing of the early teachers at the Falls, Mr. Albert H. Porter asserts that some of them had peculiar characteristics, readily understood by the pupils and not easily forgotten. The first was a bachelor, and not a young one either, with a fair English education and a superficial knowledge of Latin. His vision was defective, and he looked kindly on the big girls. Next came a younger man, with a happy temperament and a pleasant smile, who, in addition to his other accomplishments, was an amateur artist of no mean taste and skill, which he made useful by drawing penciled representations of men, animals, fishes and birds, that served the purpose of the modern elegantly designed "rewards of merit." He was quaintly humorous, and this trait exhibited itself in original and, in general, very efficacious modes of punishment. Another of these pioneer pedagogues was a man of more than common amiability, who, besides being a thorough teacher, was something of a musician, and had a way of making himself generally useful in the household where he boarded in the old itinerant fashion, by aiding in the performance of the housework, and attending to babies that had a habit of rendering themselves unnecessarily noisy. Of course these qualities secured for him the good opinion of the women of the families who passed him around.

THE FIRE DEPARTMENT.

The first fire company was formed in 1834. It was called the "Belchertown Company," which name it took from the old-fashioned hand-engine which was purchased at Belchertown, Mass. Then, as now, the leading property owners and business men were identified with the fire department, which, at present, consists of the following organizations: Cataract Engine and Hose Company No. 1, Niagara Hose Company, No. 2, Rescue Hook and Ladder Company No. 1, and Protection Fire Company No. 1, recently organized. These organizations are well officered and very efficient. Their engines, hose-carts, ladder-trucks, hose and other property are of the best manufacture and material.

There are two substantial stone buildings devoted to the use of these companies, one of which, at the corner of Second and Niagara streets, erected in 1875, is large, elegantly finished and would do credit to a city. It is used by Rescue Hook and Ladder Company and Cataract Engine and Hose Company, the rooms on the second floor being fitted up expensively as club apartments for the members of the organizations. The other building, on Third street, near Falls street, was erected a number of years ago, and is occupied by Niagara Hose Company, No. 2.

INCORPORATION AND CIVIL HISTORY.

The petition for the incorporation of the village of Niagara Falls was filed by Judge Samuel De Veaux and other citizens at a court of sessions in Lockport on the 6th of July, 1848. The village was incorporated under the general village law of 1847.

The first president was Parkhurst Whitney; clerk, Charles H. Smith; trustees, Parkhurst Whitney, Augustus S. Porter, H. W. Clark, W. E. Hulett, G. Conger.

The present village officers are as follows:

President, James F. Fulton, jr.; clerk, S. T. Murray; trustees, James F. Fulton, jr., George S. Hanes, Daniel Barrett, E. M. Clark, H. N. Griffith.

OAKWOOD CEMETERY.

This cemetery, situated at the outskirts of the village, is large, well kept and remarkable for the taste and elegance of some of its memorial monuments. The Oakwood Cemetery Association was organized February 9th, 1852. The first board of officers consisted of the following persons: President, P. Whitney; vice-president, John Cannon; secretary, J. G. Callahan; treasurer, H. W. Clark; trustees, P. Whitney, H. W. Clark, A. Packard, E. P. Graves, P. A. Porter, A. S. Porter, John Cannon, G. Conger, H. H. Hill.

The grounds have been enlarged and improved from time to time. A comfortable residence for the use of the keeper has been erected within the enclosure.

CHURCHES OF NIAGARA FALLS.

FIRST PRESBYTERIAN.

This church was organized April 3rd, 1824. The first board of trustees consisted of Augustus Porter, Isaac Smith, Aaron Childs, Samuel DeVeaux, Ira Cook and Ziba Gay; and Aaron Childs and Isaac Smith constituted the first board of elders. The pulpit was at first supplied by Rev. D. M. Smith, of Lewiston. The first pastor was Rev. H. A. Parsons. The church has been served by eleven pastors. The longest pastorate was that of Rev. Thomas Doggett, which extended over a period of eleven years. The present pastor is Rev. J. S. Bacon. The church was organized with five members, and the present membership is about one hundred and sixty. The largest accession of membership was in 1831, when sixty persons were added on the profession of their faith.

The present substantial stone edifice was erected in 1849. The parsonage was given to the society by Miss Lavinia E. Porter, in 1863.

FREE METHODIST.

This organization is of recent date, having been formed in 1877, with a membership of twelve. As yet this society has no church edifice, and their meetings are held in the Baptist church on First street. The pastor in charge is Rev. W. F. Requa. This church has not as yet been incorporated.

BAPTIST.

The Baptist church of Lewiston and Niagara constituted the following members, living at Niagara Falls, a branch of that organization November 17th, 1841: William B. Dartt, Catherine Dartt, Joseph Nixon, Hard Munns, Elizabeth Munns, Maria Waite, Minerva Lyon, Sarah Hand, Sarah Collett, Charles Patterson, Peter O. Bronson, Jane Bronson and Rhoda A. Chamberlin.

The first deacon was Hard Munns, the first clerk Joseph Nixon, and the first trustees, Hard Munns, John Kelly and William B. Dartt. Rev. A. Claghorn was the first pastor.

The branch was recognized as the Baptist church of Niagara Falls, February 21st, 1842, by a council called from sister churches. In the early days many of the meetings were held in private houses. In the spring of 1843 the society begun the erection of a meeting-house, of good building stone, size 36 by 40 feet, with a basement. This structure was enclosed and the floors laid, and in the autumn of the same year, though it was as yet unplastered, the society occupied it as a place of worship, continuing work upon it until its completion late in 1854. It was formally dedicated January 10th, 1855. Since its organization the church has been ministered to by seven different pastors, but it has been without a pastor since January, 1874. The present board of trustees are S. F. Symonds, Matthew Jackson and William A. Philpott, jr.

ROMAN CATHOLIC.

The mission of Niagara Falls was occasionally visited by the priest of Lockport until 1847. In that year Rev. John Timon, having been appointed first bishop of Buffalo, formed Youngstown, Lewiston and Niagara Falls into a parish.

Father John Boyle, the first pastor, resided in Lewiston, then the largest place. He remained in charge until 1850, and built a small stone church, now replaced by the larger edifice called the Church of Our Lady of the Cataract. He was succeeded by Father Nolan, and he by Rev. William Stephens.

In 1854 the pastoral residence was changed from Lewiston to Niagara Falls. In 1859 the Lazarist Fathers assumed control of the mission, and continued in charge for three years, the pastors meanwhile being Rev. Edward Maginnis, C. M.; Rev. John Monaghan, C. M.; Rev. Edward Hennessy, C. M.; and Rev. William Ryan, C. M.

In 1862 Father Stephens again took charge of the parish, and at his death, in September of that year, was succeeded by Rev. Patrick Cannon, who built a large addition to the church in 1863 and another in 1865. July 12th, 1869, Father Cannon was succeeded by the present pastor, Rev. Patrick Moynihan. During the pastorship of Father Moynihan, the church has been again enlarged and a bell placed in one of the towers.

There are several flourishing societies connected with the church, which has a membership of about one thou-i sand five hundred.

The Academy of Our Lady of the Cataract is connected with this church. The school edifice was erected by Albert H. Porter, in 1852, and a classical school was organized in it and conducted successfully for several years. In 1864, while Father Cannon was in charge of the church, this building was purchased of the original proprietor for use, under the auspices of the church, as a day and boarding school; and it has been conducted with satisfactory results ever since. The patronage has been large, as many as forty to sixty boarders having been in attendance during the most prosperous period of its existence, besides a large daily attendance at the free school. This nstitution is in charge of Miss Bridget Fitzgerald, a very capable and successful principal, who is assisted by a corps of efficient teachers, who control the different departments.

During the pastorate of Father Moynihan, the interests of this academy have been advanced, other school property has been purchased, and the cause of education has been fostered in the parish.

METHODIST EPISCOPAL.

We are without data in regard to the introduction of Methodism at Niagara Falls. A conference was held at Lundy's Lane in 1820, before the church in Canada and the United States was divided, and there was occasional preaching at the Falls and vicinity from that time.

For a number of years the Methodists, in common with the Episcopalians and other denominations, occupied a small union building which stood on the site of the present International Hotel. In 1849 the house on the corner of First and Falls streets, which had been used by the Presbyterians, was purchased, and occupied until 1864, when the present site of St. Paul's M. E. Church was purchased. This edifice, which, with the parsonage, cost about $25,000, is one of the most elegant in the county. The Methodist society was organized in 1815.

It has been impossible to obtain the names of the early pastors in charge at this place. Following will be found the names of those who have served since 1847: Rev. D. Nichols, Rev. Z. Hurd, Rev. S. Hunt, Rev. E. R. Keyes, Rev. H. K. Hines, Rev. R. L. Waite, Rev. W. Gordon, Rev. R. Cooley, Rev. J. N. Simpkins, Rev. J. McCreery, jr., Rev. J. McEuen, Rev. P. Woodworth, Rev. J. Alabaster, Rev. J. Zimmerman, Rev. B. F. McNeal, Rev. G. Smith, Rev. S. Williams, Rev. A. L. Backus, Rev. E. M. Buck, Rev. S. Seager, Rev. J. T. Humphreys, Rev. A. F. Colburn, Rev. G. W. Loomis.

ST. PETER'S EPISCOPAL.

The first clergyman of the Protestant Episcopal Church who preached in the county of Niagara was Rev. Mr. Hopkins, of the Diocese of New Jersey, who, in the summer of 1823, officiated in the school-house at Niagara Falls.

In the winter of 1828 and 1829 Rev. Moses P. Bennet came to the village. He proposed to officiate at Lockport, Lewiston and the Falls, but failing to obtain adequate support was obliged to remove from the county.

January 5th, 1829, the first church was organized, under the title of "Christ's Church." In 1831, 1832, and during several succeeding years, Rev. William Shelton, of Buffalo, officiated several times. He is spoken of as the father of the church. From 1832 to 1840, services were performed by missionaries stationed at Lewiston.

With varying fortunes, the church progressed, until on June 17th, 1846, a subscription was raised for the erection of a church. Bishop De Lancey having given his opinion that the old organization had become invalid from lapse of time, in order to effect a new organization the following named persons met for the purpose of incorporating themselves as a religious society: Samuel De Veaux, Michael Walsh, Christopher H. Smith, Berry Hill White, Abel M. Swallow and George W. Holley. Rev. Amos C. Treadway, the rector, was in the chair. The consent of the bishop

DR. B. L. DELANO (DEC.)

Few names have been more widely known in Niagara county, or their memory more truly honored, than that of the subject of this memoir.

He was born in Williamstown, Vt., January 5th, 1807, and his boyhood was passed amid the healthful surroundings of a rural life on his father's farm. His early educational advantages were limited to those afforded by the country school of that day.

His tastes led him to the choice of a professional career, and his ambition to prepare himself for the life of a physician was at last gratified by his admission to membership of the medical department at Dartmouth College. Upon his graduation from that institution, his attention was directed to the promising facilities for the accumulation of property offered by the remunerative enterprises of western New York, which was included in the "Far West" of that time; and in 1833 he established himself in his profession in the growing village of Lockport, and for more than thirty years enjoyed a highly successful practice therein. He afterwards formed a co-partnership with Morris H. Tucker, Henry Walbridge and ex-Governor Hunt for the purchase of the liniment since so extensively known as "Merchant's Gargling Oil." He retained his interest in that enterprise, and upon the organization of the "Merchant's Gargling Oil Company" was chosen its president, which position he held during life.

Having been honored with a responsible and desirable appointment as medical examiner for the Boston branch office of the New York Life Insurance Company in 1864, he removed to that city, where he remained until, in 1870, his desire for a life of quiet retirement, within convenient distance of his property in Lockport, prompted him to return to this county and take up his residence in Niagara Falls.

Although he never afterward actively engaged in business, he was a partner with his son in the banking house of F. R. Delano & Co., and upon the organization of the Cataract Bank, July 9th, 1877, to succeed the above mentioned firm, he became a large stockholder, filling the offices of vice-president and director until his death.

Dr. Delano never aspired to political preferment; he never sought or held office other than such as he accepted at the hands of his fellow townsmen in recognition of their confidence in his ability and integrity, or because of his well known interest in the cause of education and the prosperity of the community in which he had a home. He was chosen president of the board of education of the city of Lockport, and was one of the village trustees before that place arrived at its present importance.

He was married September 25th, 1835, to Lavinia W. Ralph, of South Woodstock, Vermont. F. R. Delano, of Niagara Falls, born September 6th, 1842, was the only issue of this marriage. Mrs. Delano died in Boston, December 29th, 1866. October 20th, 1868, he was again married, to Mrs. C. H. Burke, of Boston, who survives him, together with the son above mentioned.

Dr. Delano died at his residence in Niagara Falls, October 24th, 1877, from general physical exhaustion, after an active and well spent life of more than seventy years.

was given to the formation of the corporation. In pursuance of that permission, at a meeting of the male members of the congregation, held December 28th, 1846, the church known as St. Peter's Church, Niagara Falls, was duly organized. The original wardens were Samuel De Veaux and George W. Holley; the vestrymen were Christopher H. Smith, Michael Walsh, John Tellyea, Abel M. Swallow, Hollis White, Cyrus F. Smith, Walter E. Hulett and Richard H. Woodruff.

At the same meeting Samuel De Veaux, George W. Holley and John Tellyea were chosen building committee for the purpose of erecting a church edifice. At a meeting April 5th, 1847, the same committee were authorized to collect and expend a subscription. The church was completed in 1848. A parsonage was erected in 1852.

The following is the succession of rectors: 1848, Rev. S. Reed; 1850, Rev. Edmund Roberts; 1853, Rev. Joseph M. Clark; 1859, W. O. Jarvis; 1863, Rev. Orlando F. Starkey; 1870, Rev. Myron A. Johnson; 1874, Rev. Edward Ingersoll, D.D. Rev. Stephen H. Battin was called March 1st, 1878.

The plans of the new stone church on the corner of Union and Second streets were made by Mr. Henry Dudley, architect, of New York city. The corner stone was laid in 1873. The edifice is not yet completed.

BUSINESS CORPORATIONS.

THE NIAGARA FALLS PAPER MANUFACTURING COMPANY

was organized in November, 1855, with L. C. Woodruff as president and S. Pettebone secretary and treasurer. The paper-mill of this company, on Bath Island, was originally erected in 1826, by Porter & Clark. It was destroyed by fire August 12th, 1858. The company, with characteristic energy, rebuilt it at once, and December 25th, less than five months after its destruction, resumed the manufacture of paper. Since then extensive and valuable improvements have been introduced, and the facilities for business greatly extended. The large increase in the number of manufactories, and the diminution of the consumption of paper within the past few years, have had the effect of reducing prices to a point so low that the industry ceases to be remunerative for fine grades, and the business of the N. F. P. M. Co. is confined to the manufacture of news papers of various qualities and in large quantities, forty-two male and ten female employees being engaged in the different departments of the establishment.

The present officers of the company are: President, L. C. Woodruff; secretary and treasurer, S. Pettebone; cashier, Lauren W. Pettebone.

These mills are supplied with one of the best water-powers in the world, being situated on the rapids of the Niagara river, just above the falls.

THE CATARACT BANK OF NIAGARA FALLS.

Although this corporation is of comparatively recent formation, its history dates back to 1869, when A. M. Chesbrough opened a private banking-house in an office in the International Hotel. He was succeeded in 1871 by N. K. Van Husen, from Buffalo. In 1873 F. R. Delano, of Niagara Falls, became an equal partner with Van Husen, and the firm name became Van Husen & Delano; and during the same year the firm erected and moved into their present elegant and attractive bank building on Main street.

In November, 1874, Van Husen retired, and the business was continued by F. R. Delano & Co., the partners then being Dr. B. L. & F. R. Delano (father and son). July 9th, 1877, the present institution, the Cataract Bank, was chartered under the laws of the State of New York, and began business with a paid-up capital of $50,000. Its officers and board of directors were the same as now, with the exception that Dr. B. L. Delano was vice-president, director and one of the largest stock-holders to the time of his death, October 24th, 1877.

The present officers are: President, Stoughton Pettebone; vice-president, Alvah Cluck; cashier, F. R. Delano; directors, Stoughton Pettebone, Alvah Cluck, George L. Hanes, F. R. Delano, Hiram E. Griffith, Moses Einstein, John Hodge; attorney, H. N. Griffith.

NIAGARA FALLS GAS COMPANY.

The Niagara Falls Gas Company was organized December 21st, 1859. The first board of officers was made up as follows: S. Pettebone, president; James F. Trott, secretary; M. Walsh treasurer; George W. Parsons, of the Rochester, N. Y., Gas Light Company, superintendent and constructing engineer.

The original capital of the company was $20,000. By subsequent improvements and extensions it was nominally increased to $75,000, and stock issued to the amount of $63,000.

Since the construction of the works, the mains have been extended to the village of Suspension Bridge; and during 1866 a gasometer was erected at that place, and the mains extended to De Veaux College; and gas is now supplied to the various churches, hotels, depots and other public buildings, and the streets are well lighted.

The present officers are: President, S. M. N. Whitney; secretary and treasurer, S. Pettebone; superintendent, G. M. Harrington; and the present board of directors consists of S. M. N. Whitney, S. Pettebone, Edward Woodruff, J. S. Minton, M. L. Fox, M. Federspeil, C. H. Symonds, W. F. Evans, A. W. R. Henning.

THE NIAGARA FALLS WATER WORKS COMPANY.

The organization of this company was effected January 10th, 1877, and it begun business under the management of the following officials: President, Franklin Spalding; secretary, Benjamin Rhodes; treasurer, F. R. Delano; trustees, Franklin Spalding, Stoughton Pettebone, Alvah Cluck, Francis R. Delano, D. R. Jerauld, William F. Evans, Benjamin Rhodes. During 1877 three and one half miles of main were laid, with twenty-seven hydrants. The water is supplied from the Niagara river by the Holly pump of the Suspension Bridge Water Works, under an ordinary pressure of sixty pounds to the inch, which may be increased in case of fire to one hundred and sixty pounds. This company, which has a paid-in capital of $25,000, has been instrumental in materially reducing the rates of insurance in the village by the additional security its works afford to property.

THE NIAGARA FALLS SUSPENSION BRIDGE COMPANY.

The Niagara Falls Suspension Bridge Company was chartered March 31st, 1855. The first board of directors consisted of the following named persons: Augustus S. Porter, of Niagara county; Alonzo S. Upham, of Genesee; A. B. Williams, of Wayne; Delos De Wolf, of Oswego; Vino W. Smith, of Onondaga; John L. Schoolcraft, of Albany; Henry L. Willis, New York; Henry A. King, Orleans; John E. Devlin, New York. Nothing was done by the company, and by act of April 3d, 1867, the charter was revived and the number of directors reduced to five.

The Clifton Suspension Bridge Company, with its office at Clifton, Ont., was chartered by the Canadian Parliament May 22nd, 1868, and John T. Bush, Samuel Keefer, William O. Buchanan, Delos De Wolf, William G. Fargo, Vino W. Smith and Hollis White were named first directors. The two companies entered into an agreement July 21st, 1868, by which they have the same stockholders and their interests are made common. The suspension bridge, belonging conjointly to the two companies, was opened for business January 1st, 1869.

The present officers are as follows: Delos De Wolf, president of the Niagara Falls Suspension Bridge Company; John M. Hutchinson, president of the Clifton Suspension Bridge Company; secretary and treasurer of the combined companies, C. H. Smyth; directors: Delos De Wolf, Oswego; Samuel B. Johnson, Oswego; Charles H. Smyth, Clinton; John M. Hutchinson, Buffalo; Warren Bryant, Buffalo; superintendent, Benjamin Rhodes.

FRATERNITIES AND SOCIAL ORGANIZATIONS.

NIAGARA FRONTIER LODGE, NO. 132, F. AND A. M.

This lodge was originally formed in Lewiston, April 5th, 1848, as Lewiston Frontier Lodge, No. 132, to succeed Niagara Lodge, No. 345, which was the first lodge in the county, having been instituted at Lewiston in 1822. A detailed history of this first lodge and of Lewiston Frontier Lodge, No. 122, prior to its removal to Niagara Falls, will be found in the history of the village of Lewiston. The latter organization was removed to the village of Niagara Falls and its name changed to Niagara Frontier Lodge, No. 132, in the year 1853. The masters of this lodge since that date have been as follows: 1854, Parkhurst Whitney; 1863, 1864 and 1865, Francis H. Johnson; 1856, A. Thomas; 1857 and 1858, H. H. Sheldon; 1859 and 1860, S. S. White; 1861 and 1862, J. W. Holmes; 1865, 1866 and 1867, James McFeggan; 1868, 1869, 1870, 1873 and 1874, Benjamin Flagler; 1871, 1872, J. B. King; 1875, W. P. Mentz; 1876, 1877 and 1878, F. Luippie. The present membership is one hundred and twenty-six.

NIAGARA FALLS LODGE, NO. 369, I. O. O. F.

was organized in 1849, by S. M. N. Whitney, R. H. Woodruff, Walter E. Hulett, F. C. Ford, Hollis White and others. It was a flourishing lodge for several years, but for various causes ceased to exist sometime since. It has been succeeded by

BELLEVUE LODGE, NO. 316, I. O. O. F.

This lodge was instituted at Suspension Bridge, May 3rd, 1872, and removed by dispensation of the Grand Lodge to Niagara Falls July 20th, 1877. The following is a list of the charter members: L. C. Oatman, Denby Waud, R. R. Sutton, R. R. Henderson, John McKay, A. M. Roell, M. Roell, George E. Brock, S. B. Eschelman, George A. Cross, M. S. Lang, C. Dutcher, George W. Schwartz, Jacob Wolf, R. Aberdein, William Bolles, J. Smith, W. Shaine, H. Behmer, L. Elsheimer.

The first officers were: L. C. Oatman, N. G.; Denby Waud, V. G.; R. R. Sutton, secretary; A. M. Roell, treasurer; George W. Schwartz, P. S.; John McKay, W.; R. R. Henderson, C.; M. Roell, O. G.; W. Bolles, I. G.; L. Elsheimer, R. S. N. G.; C. Dutcher, L. S. N. G.; J. Smith, R. S. V. G.; George A. Cross, L. S. V. G.; M. S. Lang, R. S. S.; W. Shaine, L. S. S.

The present list of officers is as follows: R. G. Paige, N. G.; J. H. Metcalf, V. G.; Charles Zieger, secretary; John Potter, treasurer; John S. Root, P. S.; Robert Barr, W.; R. R. Henderson, C.; Jeremiah Binkley, O. G.; Henry Ellenbaum, jr., I. G.; R. D. Wing, R. S. N. G.; Michael Norris, L. S. N. G.; Samuel Smith, R. S. V. G.; William Peel, L. S. V. G.; J. M. Locher, R. S. S.; H. White, L. S. S.; George A. Cross, P. G.

The regular meetings of the lodge occur at 7:30 o'clock, Friday evening of each week, from October 1st to April 1st, and from April 1st to October 1st at 8 o'clock, P. M., at their hall on the corner of First and Falls streets. Since the date of organization there have been three deaths of members and three of the wives of members. The amount paid for funeral benefits is $135; sick benefits, $1,952.33. The present membership of the lodge is eighty.

THE NIAGARA FALLS SHOOTING CLUB.

This is an association of about sixty gentlemen of Niagara Falls and vicinity. The club was organized in October, 1862, with the following officers: President, D. R. Jerauld; vice-president, John G. Pierce; secretary, William Pool; treasurer, H. H. Sheldon; board of directors, J. S. Minton, George B. Hamlin and S. T. Murray. The club has been represented at all of the State conventions of the State association, of which it is a member. A reorganization is being perfected under the laws of the State of New York (1875: chap. 267). William Pool has held the office of secretary from the beginning. The present officers are: James T. Fulton, president; H. Neilson, vice-president; William Pool, secretary; George S. Hanes, treasurer; board of directors: A. Cluck, Andrew Murray and George Barker. The meetings of the association are held in their own well appointed rooms in the Frontier Mart building.

THE NIAGARA FALLS LIEDERTAFEL.

This is a German society, having for its object the promotion of self culture among its members and the cultivation of vocal music. The by-laws provide that a candidate for membership shall be a German, able to speak and understand the German language. The organization was effected March 13th, 1865, and the following officers were chosen at the first meeting : M. Brooks, president; G. W. Schwartz, vice-president; R. C. Veidt, treasurer; John B. Mayer, musical director; J. Janisch, secretary; J. J. Anthony, librarian. The meetings of the society are held monthly, and the officers are elected annually by ballot. The present list is as follows : President, Antoine Biron; vice-president, D. Elsheimer; treasurer, John P. Fitsch; secretary, F. Locher; librarian, J. J. Anthony.

The society have a hall of their own, tastefully fitted up and furnished with an elegant and costly piano. They give an annual masquerade ball and many private social entertainments; and they have often appeared in concerts in different cities, with credit to themselves and satisfaction to critical audiences. In the great peace jubilee in Buffalo, in 1871, this association took a leading part.

The financial exhibit of the N. F. L. is a most flattering one, there being no outstanding obligations against the society, with a clear balance of several hundred dollars in the treasury.

CATARACT LODGE, NO. 793, I. O. G. T.

The Cataract Lodge, No. 793, I. O. G. T., was formed January 1st, 1869, having been instituted by L. S. Freeman, of Middleport. The regular meetings of this organization are held at their hall, in Frontier Mart, every Friday evening. The number of charter members was twenty-seven, and the present membership is one hundred and thirty-five. The first officers were as follows : W. C. T., H. W. Barnes ; W. S., T. Isbester ; W. T., F. M. Bush ; W. M., D. C. Collins ; R. S., Lucy Pratt ; assistant secretary, Mrs. George Davy ; W. V. T., Mary Pratt ; W. F. S., G. R. Philpott; W. Ch., V. R. Canfield ; D. M., Miss E. Canfield ; L. S., Maggie Cannon ; I. G., Jennie Davy; P. C. T., W. H. Philpott. The present official members of the lodge are : W. C. T., Addison Pratt ; W. V. T., Miss Sarah Smith ; W. S., J. G. Shepard ; assistant secretary, Carrie Wright ; W. F. S., F. C. Parchart ; W. T., George W. Wright ; W. M., William Collins ; assistant M., Miss L. Fair ; W. Ch., L. H. Burdick ; I. G., Sarah Collins ; O. G., John Higgins ; R. S., Nettie Murray ; L. S., Ada White ; P. C. T., M. Norris.

CATHOLIC TOTAL ABSTINENCE AND LITERARY SOCIETY.

The Niagara Falls Catholic Total Abstinence and Literary Society was organized January 11th, 1872. The following were the first officers of the society: Rev. P. Moynihan, spiritual director; Henry F. McBride, president; Patrick Timbs, vice-president; Thomas V. Welch, recording secretary; Robert Joyce, treasurer; John J. McIntire, financial secretary ; James Tierney, marshal; John Reilley, sergeant-at-arms.

The society occupied the hall in Chesbrough's brick block on Main street for one year, and then removed to their present apartments in the Frontier Mart building on Falls street. The members of the society have established a reading and billiard room in connection with their hall, open every day and evening, summer and winter. In the principal room, capable of seating three hundred persons, musical and dramatic entertainments are frequently given. The hall of the society also contains the parish library, consisting of four hundred volumes. The members of the society are nearly all young men, whose object is mutual intellectual improvement and the extension of the principles of temperance. The society is now in its seventh year. It is firmly established and bids fair to have a long and prosperous career.

INTERNATIONAL LODGE, NO. 6, A. O. U. W.

was instituted October 27th, 1873, by W. H. Comstock, D. D. G. M. W., of North East, Pa., as " Frontier Lodge, No. 6," with sixteen charter members, as follows: George Rowe, O. Canfield, John Potter, A. V. Simpson, Alexander McKinnon, John Tierney, George W. Howie, George Potter, Thomas Potter, M. Topping, George H. Salt, W. R. Senior, John Chambers, H. Hubbs, A. W. Olheiser and William S. Flay. The name of the lodge was changed, on account of the masonic lodge being similarly designated, November 3rd of the same year, since which date it has been known by its present title. The initial officers were: A. V. Simpson, M. W.; M. Topping, G. F.; John Potter, O.; George Rowe, P. M. W.; P. Olheiser, recorder; George H. Salt, F.; O. Canfield, receiver; W. R. Senior, W. The first two or three meetings of the lodge were held in Chesbrough's Hall. After that the lodge convened in the sitting-room of the International Hotel for four months, then two or three times in A. V. Simpson's bed-room, from which the meetings were removed to an unfinished hall belonging to Henry Clark, where they were held for about a year, since which time the sessions have been held regularly in Chesbrough's Hall. The present membership of the lodge, after four deaths, is one hundred and twenty-five, and it is rapidly gaining in numbers. Some time since twenty members, residents of Suspension Bridge, withdrew and established a lodge at that place.

CATHOLIC MUTUAL BENEFIT ASSOCIATION, BRANCH NO. 1.

Niagara Falls Branch, No. 1, of the C. M. B. A. was organized January 2nd, 1876. The first officers were: Rev. P. Moynihan, spiritual director; John Clifford, president; Sebastian Geyer, vice-president; John McAntire, recording secretary. The following officers were chosen December 26th, 1876: Rev. P. Moynihan, spiritual director; Daniel Barrett, president; John Clifford, first vice-president; Sebastian Geyer, second vice-president; John McAntire, recording secretary; Thomas Durkin, assistant recording secretary; Patrick Welsh, treasurer; Joseph George, financial secretary; Owen McCabe, marshal; Patrick Glynn, guard. The actions of the society are directed by the following board of directors: A. Biron, James Martin, James McGraw, S. Geyer, John Clifford, their term of service being limited to one year. The object of the association is to "create and disburse a fund on the death of its members, by an assessment of one dollar and ten cents on each surviving member, and not to exceed two thousand dollars to be paid to the widow or legal heirs of deceased member."

SOLDIERS' AND SAILORS' MEMORIAL DAY ASSOCIATION.

This association was formed in April, 1877, for the purpose of providing suitable yearly observances in memory of the soldiers and sailors of the town of Niagara who lost their lives in the rebellion. The present membership is fifty-eight. The first officers were as follows: President, J. G. Shepard; vice-president, James Low; 2nd vice-president, George Davy; treasurer, Charles Kugel; secretary, Harry ap Rees; captain, E. E. Russell; first lieutenant, N. E. G. Wadhams; second lieutenant, J. J. Sullivan.

NIAGARA FALLS COUNCIL, ROYAL TEMPLE OF TEMPLARS,

was organized by C. K. Porter, Supreme Councillor of the Order of R. T. of T., November 23rd, 1877, with thirty-two active and twenty-two life charter members. The original officers were: S. C., W. A. Philpott, jr.; P. C., C. M. Young; secretary, Addison Pratt; H., E. A. Butler; S., C. A. Blakeslee; V. C., W. F. Evans; chaplain, Rev. J. S. Bacon; treasurer, William Shepard; G., E. V. Root; medical examiner, F. A. Rice, M.D. The object of the R. T. of T. is to encourage the principles of temperance, and mutual assistance to members in case of death or permanent injury. On the death of an active member the heirs will receive $2,000; or should he be incapacitated to provide for himself and family, $1,000 will be paid to him, and $1,000 to his heirs at his death. The membership of this Temple has increased rapidly since its organization. It now numbers 92. The present officers are as follows: S. C., W. A. Philpott, jr.; P. C., C. M. Young; secretary, Addison Pratt; H, E. A. Butler; G., S. A. Burdick; V. C., A. P. Burdick; chaplain, Rev. J. S. Bacon; treasurer, William Shepard; assistant H., Mrs. H. E. Hermance; S., J. G. Shepard; medical examiners, William B. Rice, M.D., and F. A. Rice, M. D. Regular meetings, Friday evening of each week, at the Good Templars' Hall, in Frontier Mart.

THE NIAGARA FALLS GLEE CLUB.

The Niagara Falls Glee Club was organized in the spring of 1878. The object of the club is the cultivation of music. The officers are as follows: Director, W. A. La Mont; secretary and treasurer, L. W. Pettebone. The following named gentlemen are members: Robert O. Fulton, G. Henry Howard, William B. Rankine, George E. Curtis.

IMPROVEMENTS ABOUT THE FALLS.

TERRAPIN TOWER.

This was once one of the most pleasing points of observation about the Falls. From its summit could be obtained a magnificent and comprehensive view of the rapids, the falls, the islands and the landscape round about. It was erected in 1833 by Judge Porter, and taken down by the proprietors in 1843, being regarded as unsafe. It stood on the very brink of the Canadian Fall.

THE NEW SUSPENSION BRIDGE

is one-eighth of a mile below the American Fall. It is the property of a stock company, and was opened to the public January 1st, 1869. It is one of the longest suspension bridges in the world, and was constructed at a cost of $250,000. The span between the centers of the towers is 1,268 feet—446 feet longer than the lower suspension bridge. Height above the surface of the river 190 feet. Height of towers above rock on Canada side, 105 feet, and on American side, 100 feet. Base of towers 28 feet square, and top 4 feet square. The bridge is supported by two cables, composed of seven wire ropes each, which contain, respectively, 133 No. 9 wires. The weight of these wire ropes per lineal foot is 9 pounds, and the diameter of the cable is 7 inches. The total weight of the suspended portions of the cable is 82 tons net. There are 48 stays, weighing 15 tons net. There are 56 guys connected with the bridge. The aggregate breaking strain of the cable is 1,680 tons.

GOAT ISLAND BRIDGE.

The first bridge was built in 1817. It was swept away the following spring, and replaced in the same year (1818) by another wooden structure. The present iron structure was erected in 1856, on the plan of Whipple's iron arched bridge, and is 360 feet long, having four arches of ninety feet span each. The width is 27 feet, embracing a double carriage-way of 16½ and two foot-paths 5¼ feet each, with iron railings. This is probably one of the largest and most costly bridges in the world owned by private parties.

BIDDLE'S STAIRS,

at the precipitous end of Goat Island, between the American and the Horse-shoe Falls, were erected by Nicholas Biddle in 1829. They are secured to the solid rocks by ponderous iron bolts. The perpendicular height of the bank at this point is 185 feet. There is quite a descent, by means of a series of steps, from the level of the island, and the staircase itself is 80 feet high, and the number of steps is said to be ninety.

PROSPECT PARK.

This was formerly known as "Ferry Grove" and "Point View." The grounds were purchased by the Prospect Park Company in 1872, since which time they have been greatly improved and beautified. Near the

William H. Childs was born in Livonia, Livingston county, N. Y., April 1st, 1807. He is a son of Deacon Aaron Childs, a well known early settler and resident of Niagara county, who, with his family, settled on the Ridge road in Lewiston in 1809, and kept a pioneer tavern. At the age of seventeen Mr. Childs became a christian, and united with the Presbyterian Church; and for many years held the office of deacon where he resided, and for thirty years or more was superintendent of Sunday-schools. Soon after his conversion he felt a growing desire for a liberal education, left his clerkship and became a student at the academy at Auburn, N. Y. Owing to failing health he was obliged to relinquish a professional career, and turn his attention to mercantile pursuits. In 1827 he removed to Niagara Falls and became one of the early merchants of that place. In 1828 he was married to Miss Laura Amsden, of Seneca, Ontario county, by whom he had seven children, only two of whom are now living. Mrs. Childs died in 1865, and in the same year Mr. Childs married Mrs. Elizabeth A. Blake, of Chicago. Mr. Childs was for many years engaged in mercantile pursuits, and for the last thirty years has been actively engaged as general insurance agent, in which capacity he has been very successful. He has been a life-long advocate of the principles of temperance, and is widely known as a zealous anti-slavery man, standing in the front ranks in the early "days that tried men's souls." Mr. Childs, now past the age of seventy-one, has a step as elastic as in youth, and is still actively engaged in business.

W. H. CHILDS

RES. OF W. H. CHILDS, COR. ONTARIO & WALNUT STS. NIAGARA FALLS, N. Y.

center of the grounds is the ferry house, from which there is a descent cut in the bank to the water's edge, below the American Fall, a distance of 360 feet, down which a car is run on an inclined plane. The first descent was by means of rude stairs, put down in 1817 by P. Whitney. Spiral stairs were erected in 1825, and being regarded as unsafe the present ingenious contrivance was introduced in 1845.

THE ELEVATOR AT WHIRLPOOL RAPIDS

was constructed by Professor A. A. Smith, for the proprietors, in 1869, at a cost of $20,000. There are two carriages or elevators, with comfortable seats, similar to those used in the largest city hotels, worked by machinery which is propelled by a water-wheel three hundred feet below the level of the bank. The descent by the elevator to the reception parlor is 192 feet, and from there a graveled walk leads down to the water's edge. Formerly the descent was by means of winding stairs, the ruins of which are still to be seen.

ACCIDENTS AND INCIDENTS.

THE HERMIT OF NIAGARA.

During the afternoon of June 18th, 1839, a young man made his appearance in the village of Niagara Falls who has since become known to the world in story and song, and whose memory is retained by some of the older citizens of the place to the present day. He is described as tall, thin almost to emaciation, with hollow eyes, bright with an unnatural brightness; and it is said that his strange appearance was rendered still more striking by his peculiar dress, consisting of a long, loose and flowing robe of some brown stuff. He went to a small and not crowded hotel, in the outskirts of the village, and engaged a room for a few days, stipulating that he was to remain undisturbed in its possession and that he was to cook part of his food himself. Not long after, he came into the village and entered his name at the village library and borrowed books. He also made some small purchases about town, the most expensive of which was a violin. Soon afterward he applied for and was refused permission to erect for himself a rude hut on Moss Island. Near the head of Goat Island there was an old and dilapidated log cabin. In this he took up his residence, and for more than a year and a half remained a lonely occupant of the wooded and water-girt island, with no companions but his old violin, his books, his dog and the crows who came at nightfall to mingle their weird chorus with the never ceasing roar of the rapids and the cataract and the low, wild music of the hermit of the falls. Backward and forward through the shadows of the trees he would wander in the long hours of the night, at times going out on Terrapin bridge, to a point beyond the tower, where a small square stick of timber projected over the falls. On this he would walk with folded arms, apparently oblivious of danger and thoughts of the awful death that seemed to be reaching up for him out of the mighty depths below, at times sitting carelessly on the outer end of the timber, and it is said suspending himself from it, over the cataract, by holding to it with his hands or legs. By and by he seemed to tire of the place; for he came over on the mainland, and going to "Point View," now within Prospect Park, constructed a rude cabin of boards on the bank beside the American Fall. Although his new location brought him into nearer relations with the people of the village, he was never communicative, though he talked at times, with a precision of expression and grace of manner that surprised and charmed his listeners. He made no confidants, and was more intimate with the late Judge De Veaux than with any one else. Various opinions have been expressed as to the quality of his music, ranging from those of highest praise to severest condemnation. After he removed to Prospect Point he was in the daily habit of descending the ferry stairs and bathing in the water at the river's edge. Venturing too far he lost his footing, and was drowned, June 10th, 1841. His body was not found till ten days afterward, and then it had been carried to the mouth of the river. It was recovered and brought back to the Falls, and buried within sight of the place where he had lived so long. During his life he was one of the attractions of the place, and after his death the log hut which he had occupied on Goat Island was, for many years, pointed out to the curious visitor. It has long since gone to decay. Little is known of his history, except that he was Francis, son of John Abbott, of Plymouth, England, and that in his youth he had led a life of dissipation. These facts were learned from relatives of his, who visited the falls sometime subsequent to his death.

THE SHIP "MICHIGAN."

In 1827 large and extravagantly worded hand-bills announced that, on the 8th of September, "the pirate Michigan" would "pass the great rapids and the Falls of Niagara, with a cargo of furious animals." Arrangements were made to furnish entertainment to all visitors to the Falls on that occasion, to witness a remarkable spectacle described as "unequaled in the annals of infernal navigation." The vessel, having become unseaworthy, had been purchased by a few interested parties, and the unique entertainment promised was a scheme to attract people to the Falls. That it succeeded is small cause for wonder; the people in that day were not used to sensations of a similar kind, and though the Falls could be reached only by carriages the gathering was very large. The voyage was made with much success, and the cargo of "furious wild animals" plunged over the brink of the cataract, except a bear which escaped from the vessel and gained the shore, where it was afterward recaptured. Tables were spread on Goat Island. There was much delay in getting the ship down the river, and before it was accomplished the waiting people grew hungry and filled the tables. Before they had finished eating, word came that the "Michigan" was coming, and, as if moved by a single impulse, the whole crowd hurriedly departed, forgetting, in their excitement, to pay for their dinners, and the result was a loss to the enterprising caterers. In 1841 another condemned vessel, the "Detroit," was sent over the falls. She became fixed on some rocks in the rapids, and remained until beaten to pieces by floating ice.

ACCIDENTS AND CASUALTIES.

Visitors to the falls are surprised at the number of persons who have met their death here by their carelessness, their foolhardiness or by deliberate suicide; and the number of the latter class is astonishingly great. Though we shall make no attempt to give a complete list of these casualties, a brief mention of a few may be interesting. Many have probably met a watery grave here whose bodies have never been found and whose fate has never been known.

In 1810 the boat "Independence," laden with salt, sunk between Schlosser and Chippewa, and the captain and two of the crew went over the falls. Two men in a scow were driven into the rapids by the wind in 1821, and went over the falls, and in 1825 two men from Grand Island went over; and at other times during the same year three others, in three separate canoes, met a like fate. Two men engaged in smuggling, in 1841, were precipitated into the river above the cataract by the upsetting of their boat, and one of them swept over. One lodged on Grass Island, and his body was recovered. In the same year two of a number of British soldiers who were attempting to swim across the ferry were drowned. In 1844 a gentleman was washed off a rock under the fall, and in 1846 another was killed by falling from a rock below the Cave of the Winds. The following year a lad in the employ of A. H. Porter was drowned while attempting to row across above the rapids. In 1848 a man passed under Goat Island bridge in a boat, which soon upset, and he went over the falls, feet foremost. In the same year a small boy and girl were playing in a skiff, which was drawn into the rapids. The girl was rescued by her mother, and the boy, sitting in the bottom of the boat, with a hand on either side, was carried over.

A man fell from the tower bridge in 1852, and was borne by the rapids to the brink of the fall, where he lodged between two rocks, and was rescued by means of a rope. Probably the best known incident of this character is the Avery affair, which occurred July 19th, 1853. Avery was discovered clinging to a log which had lodged on a large rock, in the middle of the American rapids, thirty rods below Goat Island bridge. Many attempts, some of which came near being successful, were made to rescue him during the day. Thousands of people stood on the banks of the river in the utmost anxiety and suspense; men offered large rewards to any one who would save him; but all to no purpose. In attempting to avail himself of one of the various plans to which recourse was had, he was precipitated into the rapids, and was borne over the falls, just at nightfall. In 1870 a lady of Chicago, who was deranged, threw herself from Goat Island bridge and was hurried over the rocky descent to the precipice. The next year three men unacquainted with the river were drowned while attempting to make a crossing in a boat above the rapids; and a little later two others met a like fate under similar circumstances.

The second of the bridges to the Three Sisters was the scene of one of these exciting incidents in June, 1874. A painter named William M'Cullogh, while at work upon the bridge, fell by accident into the stream beneath, which at that point rushes and rages irresistibly toward the fall. But he was able to get a standing place upon a little rock which is visible above the water, scarcely more than forty feet above the brow of the cataract. A stout-hearted guide—Thomas Conroy by name—ventured into the rapids, and swam down to the rock, carrying one end of a rope. This he tied to himself and the now nearly exhausted painter, and by means of it they were both drawn safely ashore.

On the 9th of August, 1875, occurred an accident which will be long remembered by the residents of the village. Mr. Ethelbert Parsons, accompanied by Miss Lottie Philpott and some friends, descended the Biddle stairs, and, passing through the Cave of the Winds, approached the American Fall and paused to bathe in one of the sheltered eddies which are so numerous there. Too venturesome, Miss Philpott isolated herself from the others and was carried into a dangerous current. Seeing her insecurity, Mr. Parsons went to her, and while attempting to draw her away, she lost her footing and both were carried out into the river. Mr. Parsons struggled desperately to save her, but both were drowned. This affair has a peculiar interest to the people of the village, from the fact that both unfortunate victims were well known as members of two of the most respected families. Many other similar accidents have occurred, of which there is no satisfactory record. The last, to the present time, was that of April 1st, 1878, when two brothers named Reilly, of Chippewa, were lost in an endeavor to cross the river in a boat above the head of the rapids.

FEATS OF DARING AND PHYSICAL ENDURANCE.

This locality, from its world-wide fame, the depth and turbulence of its waters and the consequent danger attending the performance of such feats, has been chosen by foolhardy adventurers as the scene of their exhibitions of gymnastic skill or physical daring. Among the first of these adventurous persons was the celebrated "Sam Patch," who, in 1829, made his famous leap from a scaffolding ninety-six feet high erected in the water, between Biddle's Stairs and the central fall. The years 1859 and 1860 were signalized by the daring and startling performances of M. Blondin, the great tight rope artist, on a cable stretched across the river at different points. A year or two later these performances were equaled, if not surpassed, by those of Signor Farini. Other persons have since that time given similar exhibitions, among others Mlle. Spelterina, in the autumn of 1876; and in the fall of the year 1877, Captain Rhodes repeated the feats of Sam Patch, with some variations, from a scaffold erected near the high bank in Prospect Park.

JUDGE THEODORE G. HULETT, NIAGARA FALLS N.Y.

RES. OF JUDGE T. G. HULETT, FIRST STREET, NIAGARA FALLS, N.Y.

JUDGE T. G. HULETT.

Theodore G. Hulett was born in the town of Williamsburgh, Mass., June 13th, 1811. His mother had five children, the subject of this narrative being the youngest. When he was but one year of age his mother moved to Pittsfield, Mass., and united with a society of Friends at that place. When twelve years of age, taking a fancy that he was old enough to "paddle his own canoe on the ocean of life," he left the maternal roof at 8 o'clock, P.M., with his worldly goods, consisting of one shirt and one pair of stockings, tied up in a bandanna handkerchief, without the knowledge of his mother, who he fancied would interpose objections.

He arrived quite late at the house of a benevolent farmer, where his wants were provided for until the next morning, at which time the wanderer pursued his journey, and the farmer took the opposite course to apprise the mother of the probable whereabouts of her boy. At 9 o'clock the following morning the youthful adventurer was negotiating with the late Jason Clapp, the noted carriage maker at Pittsfield, for a situation, and before the contract was concluded the anxious mother arrived on the scene and became one of the parties to the transaction. The result was that the three negotiators went to the court then in session at the county seat, and the party returned, and the subject of this biography found himself a bound apprentice to Jason Clapp for the term of nine years, to learn the blacksmith's trade, at a salary of $50 per annum, to furnish his own clothing, and to receive one quarter's schooling.

After three years' service he made application to his employer for an order on a book-store for $50 worth of books. This being a large amount, a whole year's salary and in advance at that, and Mr. Clapp not being of a literary turn of mind, he at first hesitated, but afterwards made the order on the bookstore of the late Phineas Allen, and took a note for the amount. The apprentice took the order to the store and commenced the selection of his library, which consisted of a Bible, Josephus's Historical Works, Rollin's Ancient History, Murray's Grammar, Daboll's Arithmetic, Hedge's Logic, Telemachus, Tacitus, Plutarch's Lives, Dryden's Virgil, Homer's Iliad and Odyssey, Pope's, Pollock's and Milton's poetical works, and a bundle of quills for pens, a bottle of ink and some writing paper, the whole costing $48. The bill was returned, and the balance of the order was traded out at a grocery store, the purchase there being a box of tallow dip candles. This was the starting point of the educational advantages of this 'prentice.

In the last year of his apprenticeship the "quarter's schooling" nominated in the bond was demanded and received, and his school days began and ended in one quarter's tuition at the Pittsfield Academy. After the expiration of his apprenticeship he remained with his employer for six months, then went to the city of Albany and worked four months, and then went to Troy and remained a year, working at his trade during the summer months and studying law during the winter. From Troy he returned to Pittsfield, at the request of his former employer, for a special service, and remained there six months, at the end of which time he was married to Mercy Amelia Bailey, of that place. During the same year he removed to the city of Buffalo, where he worked at his trade for one year, and then went to Niagara Falls, where he worked two years, during which time he was engaged in the manufacture of carriage-springs and other mechanical pursuits; and at the expiration of that time he went into trade. In 1849 he was elected a justice of the peace of the town of Niagara, and continued in office for thirty consecutive years, during which time he has held the honorable position of judge of the courts of sessions and oyer and terminer of the county, as justice of the sessions, for two terms.

In 1847 he was engaged as superintendent of the first suspension bridge that spanned the Niagara river at the now village of Suspension Bridge, and built with his own hands the fairy iron basket that now hangs suspended beneath the railway suspension bridge, and made and put across the first wire cable, on which this basket was used for two years.

In the year 1849 he was engaged by Canal Commissioner Beach to construct the wire suspension bridge that spans the basin of the canal at the village of Fort Plain, N. Y. In 1850 and 1851 he was engaged by the Fort Hunter Bridge Company, and built the wire suspension bridge that spans the Mohawk river between the villages of Fonda and Amsterdam. In 1852 he was engaged in building a wire suspension bridge across the Tallapoosa river, in the State of Alabama. In the year 1860 he organized the company, obtained the capital stock, and built the Niagara Falls gas-works, and managed them successfully for twelve years. In the year 1865 he was engaged by the new suspension bridge company to superintend the erection of the massive trusses of that celebrated structure, during which time he invented and obtained a patent for the cast-iron shackle fastenings that secure the cables of the bridge to the anchors. In the year 1870 he rebuilt the gas-works at Dansville, Livingston county, for the manufacture of naphtha gas. The following year he built the gas-works at Warsaw, Wyoming county, N. Y. In 1873 he built the wire suspension bridge that spans the Mohawk river and Erie canal at Fink's Ferry, near Little Falls, N. Y.

In the year 1874 he was employed by the Buffalo Oxyhydric Gas Light Company, of Buffalo, to construct their works, on plans furnished by a French engineer.

The foregoing incidents in the life of Judge Hulett are obtained from his statements, and we have had to rely upon the public records of the town and statements of prominent citizens for his more recent public acts. Judge Hulett's grandfathers were both Revolutionary soldiers, having drawn pensions for that service until their deaths, one living to be one hundred and two and the other ninety-eight years of age.

It was only after a great deal of solicitation that the consent of Judge Hulett was obtained to have his portrait and biographical sketch placed with those of other well-known persons in this volume. From the foregoing it will be seen that his life has been a varied and active one, and he is even now an acting justice of the peace. He is in his sixty-eighth year, hale and hearty, and bids fair to equal the longevity of his ancestors. The Bible that formed a part of his ancient library has lain upon his official desk for thirty years, upon which he has administered judicial oaths for that period, and he holds his ancient library as a loved relic and reminder of his youthful struggles for an education.

Judge Hulett is regarded as a sound elementary lawyer, a forcible writer, an able debater and ready public speaker, and a skillful and ingenious civil engineer. In short, his whole career has marked him as a man born to lead rather than to follow. The public records of the town show that he was an active participant in the busy scenes of the late rebellion. He was commissioned, with twelve other gentlemen of western New York, by Governor Morgan to raise, equip and to lead to the field the 8th regiment of heavy artillery—Colonel Peter A. Porter's regiment—which was accomplished in thirty days from the date of Colonel Porter's commission. These records also show that he devised and executed a system by which the families of soldiers were relieved to the extent of $28,000, without bonding the town or creating any indebtedness; and that he also initiated a fund for the erection of a soldiers' monument. This fund was originally but $35. Sums were added to it from year to year for twelve years, and in the Centennial year, from this fund alone, was erected the beautiful soldiers' monument at the foot of Falls street, in the village of Niagara Falls, which was dedicated, and delivered by the committee of construction to the town authorities in an eloquent and patriotic speech by Judge Hulett, the president of the commission, on the 20th day of September, 1876.

Looking back over a long life of usefulness—a life devoted to enterprises of more than ordinary magnitude and public benefit, and largely given up to the welfare of the community in which, by his conspicuous ability, energy and honesty, he has won a home and a competence—it is probable that Judge Hulett sees little to cause regret in his mind for the past, and much to render him happy in the present, and hopeful as to the future. He is emphatically a self-made man. Starting with the most meager advantages, and the most unpromising prospects, he has surmounted every obstacle, and having laid as his foundation stones integrity, industry and frugality, he is firmly established on the rocks of honor and prosperity; and when he is called to a better life he will be remembered for what he has done.

WELL KNOWN RESIDENTS OF NIAGARA FALLS AND VICINITY.

Gertrude M. Andrews was born at Albany, N. Y., February 21st, 1832. In May, 1840, she came to Niagara Falls, and married Ambrose Packard, of that place, December 20th, 1866. Mrs. Packard, has one daughter, Gertrude R. Packard. Her post-office address is Maple Grove Farm, Niagara Falls.

Jackson Angevine, son of Ferris Angevine, an early settler of the town of Niagara, was born at Cayuga Creek, in that town, August 24th, 1828. He was married about eighteen years ago, and has a family. He resides on the old homestead, and is extensively engaged in farming and fruit-growing.

Francis C. Belden, of Niagara Falls, was born April 20th, 1849, at Cleveland, Ohio. He was married to Miss J. Maude Wright, of Schenectady, N. Y., December 22nd, 1869, and removed to Niagara Falls July 14th, 1875. He fills the position of ticket agent and telegraph operator at the depot of the N. Y. C. & H. R. R. R. Mr. Belden is master workman of International Lodge, No. 6, A. O. U. W., of Niagara Falls.

Charles Bierstadt, landscape photographer, Niagara Falls, was born in the town of Solingen, Prussia, November 18th, 1819, and came to Niagara Falls about fourteen years ago.

Antoine Biron was born in Luxembourg April 15th, 1842, and came to Niagara Falls, from Paris, France, in December, 1866. Mr. Biron is a leading dealer in wines and liquors. He is president and leader of the Niagara Falls Liedertafel.

George L. Brown was born July 28th, 1833, at Pittsfield, Mass., and came to Niagara Falls April 11th, 1853. He is a locomotive engineer.

Wesley P. Brown, a well known locomotive engineer, was born in Peru, Berkshire county, Mass., October 15th, 1838. May 27th, 1863, he was married to Miss Hattie Sackett, of Adams, Mass. He came to Niagara Falls September 10th, 1855.

Osborn Canfield, for thirteen years a deputy sheriff in Niagara county, was born at Youngstown, July 25th, 1823. He was married to Betsey Hathaway, of Youngstown, December 1st, 1845. In October, 1850, he removed to Niagara Falls, where he has for a long time been a leading coal dealer.

Abram M. Chesbrough was born November 14th, 1814, at Dorset, Vt., and was married May 17th, 1842, to Esther Eliza Rice, of Tinmouth, Vt. Mr. Chesbrough came to the town of Niagara June 10th, 1850, from Buffalo. He is closely identified with a number of important business interests, being half owner of the great water power at Niagara Falls, and interested in mill property and flouring-mills.

Charles E. Clarke, machinist and railroad engineer, Niagara Falls, was born at St. Catharines, Ontario, March 4th, 1831. He was married December 30th, 1856, to Annette D. Hathaway, youngest daughter of Olaf Hathaway, of Youngstown. Mr. Clark was drafted in the late war, but furnished a substitute.

Henry Clark, of Niagara Falls, was born in that village October 29th, 1826. Address, Post-office Box 146.

Alvah Cluck, proprietor of the Spencer House, Niagara Falls, was born in Westfield, N. Y., March 11th, 1824. April 1st, 1852, he married Margaret Fraser, of Inverness, Scotland. He came to Niagara Falls in 1846.

D. H. Cross, druggist, Niagara Falls, was born at Youngstown, N. Y., in December, 1853, and came to Niagara Falls in 1860.

Ephraim Damon, Niagara Falls, well known as an engineer on the N. Y. C. & H. R. R. R., was born in Chesterfield, Mass., December 16th, 1829, and married November 12th, 1856, to Miss Susan E. Robinson, of the town of Niagara.

Francis R. Delano, cashier of the Cataract Bank, Niagara Falls, treasurer of the Niagara Falls Water-Works Company, and president of the Merchant's Gargling Oil Company, of Lockport, N. Y., was born in Lockport September 6th, 1842, and married to Elizabeth Grant, of Niagara Falls, October 19th, 1871. Mr. Delano came to Niagara Falls from Boston, September 1st, 1870.

James T. Fulton, jr., president of the village of Niagara Falls, was born at Richmond Hill, Ontario, September 19th, 1836, and came Niagara Falls in 1864, from Cincinnati, Ohio. Mr. Fulton is the owner and manager of the International Hotel, Niagara Falls, and is at present organizing the Windsor Hotel Company of Montreal, Canada.

Louis Henry Fetigue Hamilton, proprietor of Hamilton's dining hall, Niagara Falls, N. Y., was born in Washington, D. C., October 2nd, 1824. He was married at Geneva, N. Y., in 1845, and came to Niagara Falls in May, 1847.

G. M. Harrington, Niagara Falls, was born February 13th, 1850, at Rochester, N. Y., and married to Sarah G. Wood, of Rochester, October 17th, 1872. Mr. Harrington came to Niagara Falls June 20th, 1872. He has been identified with the fire department. He is a machinist, and gas engineer and superintendent of the Niagara Falls Gas Company.

Rowland F. Hill, of the firm of Hill & Murray, pulp manufacturers, Niagara Falls, was born May 24th, 1839, at Niagara Falls, and married October 7th, 1874, to Louisa Baker, of New York city.

Mrs. Henry H. Hill was born near Fort George, Canada, in 1812, and came to Niagara in 1815. In 1836 she was married to Henry H. Hill. Post-office, Niagara Falls.

Hon. George W. Holley, Niagara Falls, is the author of a popular work entitled: "Niagara, its History and Incidents, Geology and Poetry." While a member of the Legislature of the State of New York, in 1852 and 1853, he originated and secured the passage of a law requiring the compulsory education of all children between eight and fourteen years of age in all towns and cities containing a certain number of inhabitants, which, with certain amendments, is still in force. It was the first law of so decided a character passed in any State in the Union.

O. G. Johnson, of Niagara Falls, was born in Norwich, Vt., June 21st, 1873. He was married to Jane A. Symonds, of Manchester, N. Y., February 9th, 1843. Mr. Johnson came from Vermont in 1834. He is a builder.

Addison D. Loucks, of the firm of Tompkins & Loucks, was born in Pekin, N. Y., November 19th, 1850. His post-office address is La Salle, where the firm is extensively engaged in the sale of lumber, having a planing-mill and lumber yard. Mr. Loucks's father was for a long time a prominent merchant of Pekin.

Joseph Mason, farmer and fruit-grower, La Salle, was born at that place December 17th, 1851. He is a son of the late John Mason, for many years postmaster at La Salle.

Rev. P. Moynihan, Catholic priest, Niagara Falls, assumed the pastorate of the Church of Our Lady of the Cataract in 1869. He was born in Killarney, Ireland, August 20th, 1844.

Henry Ortt, mason, La Salle, was born in Lehigh county, Pa., August 23d, 1824, and has lived at La Salle since 1833.

Charley B. Osterhout, for the past twenty-five years passenger agent at Niagara Falls of the New York Central Railroad, was born in Victor, N. Y., February 22nd, 1830, and came to Niagara Falls in 1853.

Ambrose Packard, deceased, husband of Mrs. G. M. Packard, of Maple Grove Farm, in the town of Niagara, was born February 13th, 1826, at Enfield, Mass. December 20th, 1866, he was married to Gertrude M. Andrews, of Niagara Falls. Mr. Packard came to Niagara from Massachusetts about 1832, and until his death, which occured January 18th, 1870, was extensively engaged in farming and fruit-growing, and also, in partnership with Mr. Lyman C. Groves, in the manufacture of lime.

Charles H. Packard, of Niagara Falls, was born in Springfield, Mass., July 7th, 1832, and came to Niagara Falls in May, 1849. December 3rd, 1874, he was married to Celia A. Burns, of Rochester. Mr. Packard has held a number of village offices, and is a dealer in building and paving stone.

Kirk P. Parsons, farmer and agent for agricultural implements, post-office address Niagara Falls, was born October 10th, 1851, in the town of Niagara. April 21st, 1877, he married Martha J. Dodd, of Buffalo. Mr. Parsons was engaged for some months in the relief of sufferers by prairie fires in Kansas, in 1871 and 1872.

John S. Pierce was born March 10th, 1827, at Niagara Falls. He was married September 12th, 1855, to Laura Smith, of Ogden, N. Y. He is a resident of Niagara Falls, where he is the proprietor of a meat market. Mr. Pierce has been a deputy custom-house officer for three years, and served eight years as chief of police of the village of Niagara Falls.

Henry F. Pierce, banker and wholesale coal merchant, Niagara Falls, was born October 11th, 1840, in Wheatfield, and came to Niagara Falls in 1850. He was married to Jane Samways, of Niagara, September 25th, 1866. He served with credit through the late war, taking rank as first lieutenant and major, and was brevetted lieutenant-colonel for meritorious conduct on the field. He has served three terms as supervisor of the town of Niagara, and as trustee and president of the village of Niagara Falls.

Charles H. Piper, attorney and U. S. Circuit Court Commissioner, was born in Northwood, N. H., April 3d, 1824. He came to Lewiston while yet young, and removed to Niagara Falls May 6th, 1850, where he was married, June 29th, 1858, to Charlote C. Hulett, daughter of Judge Theodore G. Hulett.

Hon. William Pool, of Niagara Falls, is a native of Lewiston, having been born in that town on the 15th of May, 1825. His father was one of the pioneers of Lewiston. Mr. Pool married Wealthy Woolson, of Lewiston, December 20th, 1848. He removed to Niagara Falls in May, 1854, and has since been engaged in the printing and publishing business, being at the present time the editor and publisher of the *Niagara Falls Gazette*. During the administration of Millard Fillmore he was postmaster at Dickersonville, and from 1867 to 1875 held the same position at Niagara Falls. In 1867 he was a member of Assembly from his district, and was a delegate to the last Republican national convention from this Congressional district.

Benjamin Rhodes, civil engineer, came to Niagara Falls in 1874, and has since been employed as superintendent of the Niagara Falls and Clifton Suspension Bridge.

Fred A. Rice, physician and surgeon, Niagara Falls, was born at that place February 3rd, 1856.

Stephen V. Saleno was born November 22nd, 1833, at Montreal, Canada, and came to Niagara Falls August 25th, 1849. He was married December 25th, 1856, to F. Jeanette Tompkins, of the town of Niagara. Mr. Saleno is engaged in the sale of hardware. Post-office, Niagara Falls. He was captain in the N. Y. S. N. G. and southern recruiting agent in Mississippi, for Niagara county, in 1864.

William Samways, who has been justice of the peace at Niagara Falls since 1860, was born at Littleberry, Devonshire, England, September 19th, 1810, and came to Niagara county from Buffalo June 10th, 1844. Mr. Samways served in 1863, 1864 and 1865 as justice of sessions for Niagara county. He has been three times elected president of the village of Niagara Falls, having served in that capacity in the years 1875, 1876 and 1877.

Hazard H. Sheldon, who has been president of the village of Niagara Falls and justice of the peace of the town of Niagara, was born March 8th, 1821, at Bridgewater, Oneida county, N. Y. He was married November 23rd, 1852, to Martha A. Judd, of Frankfort, Herkimer county, N. Y. In May, 1854, he removed to Niagara Falls, where he has since been engaged as an attorney and counsellor at law. Mr. Sheldon was captain of Company M, 8th heavy artillery, N. Y. Vol's, and major in the N. Y. N. G.

James B. Smith, agent American Express Company, at Clifton, Ontario, was born in Scotland February 6th, 1838, and came to Clifton July 16th, 1857. He was married July 3rd, 1866, to Mary F. Webster, of Detroit, Michigan.

Franklin Spalding, of Niagara Falls, was born at Lewiston, N. Y., August 8th, 1815. He was married October 10th, 1839, to Sarah C. Jackson, of Lockport. Mr. Spalding was sheriff of Niagara county from 1826 to 1829, and collector of customs for the district of Niagara from 1861 to 1870.

Samuel F. Symonds, agent for Mrs. Colonel Peter A. Porter, of Niagara Falls, was born February 10th, 1816, at Lee, Mass., and came to Niagara Falls March 5th, 1823. He was married March 4th, 1838, to Daphne Johnson, of Niagara Falls.

H. S. Tompkins, of the firm of Tompkins & Loucks, owners of planing-mill and lumber yard at La Salle, was born at La Salle, February 3d, 1848. March 2nd, 1871, he was married to Marie, daughter of Jacob Vogt, of Niagara. In connection with the business of the firm, Mr. Tompkins is individually engaged in the manufacture of brick and drain tile, and in farming and fruit-growing.

Samuel Tompkins was born March 9th, 1808, at Bay Quinte, Canada West, and came to Niagara in February, 1815, and has lived in the town ever since. He is engaged in farming and fruit-growing, the sale of lumber, and the manufacture of brick draining tile, at La Salle, and in coal mining operations in Utah. He was deputy United States marshal in 1863, and is the present highway commissioner of the town of Niagara.

Thomas Tugby, proprietor of Tugby's *Bazar*, Niagara Falls, was born in Leicestershire, England, November 3d, 1826, and came to Niagara Falls in 1852, marrying Miss Jennie Shepard, of that village, January 21st, 1863.

Jacob J. Vogt, retired farmer, was born February 3d, 1812, at Philadelphia, Pa. He came from Lancaster county, Pa., to the town of Niagara in 1828. During the past few years Mr. Vogt has dealt in real estate to some extent. For a period of twenty-five years he has served the town as highway commissioner or assessor.

Thomas V. Welch was born October 1st, 1850, at Camillus, N. Y. Mr. Welch is a member of the firm of Welch & Ryan, dry goods merchants of Niagara Falls. From 1873 to 1875 he was freight agent of the N. Y. C. & H. R. R. R., at Niagara Falls. He was clerk of the village for the years 1874 and 1875, and supervisor of the town of Niagara for the years 1876-78. He has been a notary public since 1874, and served as treasurer of the soldiers, and sailors' monumental commission for the erection of the soldiers' monument, Niagara Falls.

Mrs. F. West, manufacturer of mineral waters, Niagara Falls, was born June 18th, 1822, in Bath, England. She was married March 19th, 1842, to Mr. F. West, of Tumbridge, England, and came to Niagara Falls May 1st, 1852.

E. L. Whittaker, teller in the Cataract Bank, Niagara Falls, was born in Youngstown, Niagara county, September 26th, 1855, and came to Niagara Falls April 14th, 1875.

S. M. N. Whitney was born October 7th, 1815, at Niagara Falls. He was married in 1840 to Frances E. Drake, of Saratoga, N. Y. Mr. Whitney is one of the firm of Whitney, Jerauld & Co., proprietors of the Cataract Hotel, Niagara Falls. In 1835 he was appointed quartermaster of the 5th brigade of infantry, and April 30th, 1838, he received the appointment of *aide de camp* to the major of the 24th division of infantry.

John Williams was born in Buffalo, May 22nd, 1849, and married to Mary Zeiger, of Niagara Falls, October 31st, 1872. Mr. Williams became a resident of Niagara Falls in 1858, where he is a leading grocer.

Jacob M. Witmer, miller, farmer and banker, Niagara Falls, was born in the town of Niagara, July 23d, 1835.

George W. Wright was born in England on the 25th of March, 1830, and came to Niagara Falls December 19th, 1859, from Canada. Mr. Wright is an architect, and the present lessee of the "Cave of the Winds," Goat Island.

John Young, farmer, was born January 16th, 1814, in Sparta, Livingston county, N. Y. He came to the town of Niagara in 1817, and has continued to reside there since, his post-office being Niagara Falls.

Samuel P. Young was born December 18th, 1836, in the town of Niagara, N. Y. For a number of years Mr. Young has been a dealer in Europe in American agricultural implements, having gone to Russia in 1859 and introduced there the first reaping machine of American manufacture. He holds the position of U. S. consul at Moscow, Russia, having been appointed during the administration of President Lincoln.

To the foregoing list may be added the following names:

Cornelius Campbell, W. R. Robinson, Daniel H. Ford, S. G. Baldwin, T. W. Robinson, J. F. Trott, S. Pettibone, E. J. McKenna, William Walker, William Cannon, Mrs. G. W. Sims, J. W. Laflin, G. G. Davis, D. J. Townsend, Dr. F. A. Rice, J. Binkley, John Fetsch, William Landreth, W. Shepard, Joseph Sturdy, Bernard Pfeiffer, Thomas E. Clark, D. Philips, G. C. Clark, M.D., J. H. Isbister, G. E. Curtis, Mark Wells, George S. Hanes, insurance agent; S. T. Murray, A. Kaltenbach, Mrs. George P. Eddy, H. N. Griffith, Mrs. M. Wheaton, Joseph Mackenna, Bridget Fitzgerald, Aaron Shrimpton, A. F. Nussbaum, L. C. Graves and G. M. Packard, farmers and fruit-growers, and George Davy, whose post-office is Niagara Falls; John Burdett, fruit-grower, Alexander C. Lanard, merchant and postmaster, Hiram D. Munson, fruit-grower, Daniel Dietrick, carpenter, all of La Salle; John Bender, Clifton, Ont.; and Mrs. H. W. Clark, Clarksville.

THE VILLAGE OF SUSPENSION BRIDGE.

THE history of this village is coincident with that of the great railway suspension bridge, from which it has derived its name. Its name previous to its incorporation, June 8th, 1854, was Bellevue. From that date it was known as Niagara City for some years. It has since been called Suspension Bridge, which name it will probably bear for a long time, or until the great international railway bridge ceases to be the attractive object of interest which it has ever been since its completion.

The village is pleasantly located on the Niagara river about two miles below the falls, within plain view from the village of Niagara Falls and opposite the pleasant little Canadian railway town of Clifton. It participates with its sister village of Niagara Falls in the patronage of the large yearly visitation of people from abroad to view the wonders and attractions of the Niagara. It is a thriving place of business and industry, one of its greatest interests being that of the several railway lines which pass through it. It is also a port of entry, and the business connected with the collection of customs forms no insignificant portion of its commercial activity.

It is well supplied with churches and schools, and has its newspaper, which is well supported.

INITIAL EVENTS.

In 1845 there were but two houses within the present limits of the village, and these were the farm houses of Elihu P. Graves and Orson Childs. The only other building of any kind is said to have been quite a large but inexpensive structure over a sulphur spring on the river bank a little north of the end of the suspension bridge, which in former times was much resorted to by the people in the vicinity, and formed an object of interest to visitors from abroad. The vein which supplied it was cut off or turned from its course at the time the anchor plates of the first suspension bridge were being put down, and since that date the supply has been very small and the water weaker in medicinal qualities.

The land upon which the village stands was owned in three parts by E. P. Graves, Orson Childs and an Englishman named Williamson. The tract of the last named person was the central one, and embraced the point of landing of the suspension bridge. In 1845 Colonel John Fisk, a prominent railroad man, of Rochester, N. Y., General Charles B. Stuart, of Schenectady, J. V. E. Vedder, of Geneva, and Roswell G. Benedict, of Saratoga, formed a copartnership under the title of the Bellevue Land Company.

The object of this company was to purchase a portion of the land occupied by the present village, preparatory to the inauguration of a series of enterprises and improvements at that point. The first work done was the construction of a narrow, though safe, road down the river bank, beginning at a point near the end of the bridge and terminating at a landing at the water's edge a little further up stream. In 1846 the "Maid of the Mist" was constructed in the eddy above the bridge, for the accommodation of pleasure parties and for use as a means of ferriage across the river at that point. In 1854 a larger and stronger craft was built at Buffalo for the proprietors by Messrs. Bidwell & Banta, and was launched July 14th of the same year. For a time the result of the outlay of the proprietors seemed to promise all that they had hoped for; but in consequence of strong opposition from parties having opposing interests, resulting in a change of regulations detrimental to the success of the venture, the business was attended by so considerable a loss that Mr. W. O. Buchanan, who owned the "Maid of the Mist" at that time, decided to sell her in 1861. In pursuance of this plan he decided to accept an offer for her delivery to parties at the mouth of the river, provided he could find some man daring enough to navigate her through the Whirlpool, down the swift descent to Lewiston and thence to Niagara, opposite Youngstown. This difficult and hazardous undertaking was under consideration for some time; and it is said that some of the most experienced navigators of the rapids of the St. Lawrence came to consult with the proprietor, and to view the Whirlpool and decide upon the practicability of the venture. Used as these men were to dangerous navigation, they utterly declined to risk their lives in an undertaking promising only death to any man foolhardy enough to attempt it. In this emergency, Joel R. Robinson, whose daring has caused him to be remembered as "the hero of the rapids," came forward and offered to run the craft through the Whirlpool and land her safely at the mouth of the river; and James McIntyre and James H. Jones volunteered to accompany him, the former to assist him at the wheel and the latter as engineer. It has been claimed that these two men were not aware of the nature of the danger they were about to encounter, and that they were induced to embark by misrepresentation on the part of Robinson and Buchanan, one of whom had long been possessed by an insane desire to make an attempt to navigate the Whirpool in a vessel, and the other of whom was in such a desperate financial strait as to be willing to resort to any means, however dishonorable, to reap the benefits which would accrue from the sale of the vessel on Lake Ontario. But upon investigation much evidence appears to induce the belief that, like Robinson, both McIntyre and Jones were fully aware of the peril they were about to encounter, and went aboard of the "Maid of the Mist" with full knowledge that they were to navigate her through the Whirpool, where no vessel had ever passed before, and where it is probable no vessel will ever pass again. She left the landing at Niagara City a few minutes past three o'clock, and heading up stream for a short distance, described a graceful curve and bore down the river. Soon she was struggling with the rapids, and after an unsuccessful attempt to keep her on the Canada side, out of the most violent current, she darted into the Whirpool. It was dangerous to attempt to manage her by means of the wheel, and for a brief time she was almost entirely at the mercy of the terrific eddies of the Whirpool, in whose waters she was almost submerged and damaged to some extent, losing her smoke-stack in the passage. It was a moment of awful peril, unparalleled in the history of steam navigation; but it was soon passed, and the gallant little "Maid" was galloping down the swift descent to Lewiston, darting like a feather borne on the wind around the sudden windings of the stream. She landed at Queenston, opposite Lewiston, in the incredibly short space of seventeen minutes from the time of her departure from the landing. Here several friends of the daring navigators were taken on board, and then the boat headed out into the channel, and after touching at Youngstown crossed over to Niagara, the place of her destination.

It is said that Mr. Robinson declared that one such experience was more than enough to satisfy him, and that he would not engage to repeat it. It is stated by one who knew him that the effect of this trip upon Robinson was decidedly marked. Mrs. Robinson asserted to the same person that "he was twenty years older when he came home that day than when he went out!" She further said that he sank into his chair like one exhausted by great fatigue. He decided to abandon the water, and often expressed a wish that his sons should do the same.

With characteristic enterprise, the Bellevue Land Company began to make propositions to capitalists, with offers of land upon which to erect manufactories or other buildings, for use in business that would tend to establish the place on a solid foundation and inaugurate a heathful enterprise, leading to its ultimate prosperity.

In 1846 or 1847 the grist-mill since known as Witmer's mill was erected.

THE INTERNATIONAL SUSPENSION BRIDGE COMPANY

was organized August 21st, 1847. The board of directors was made up as follows: William H. Merritt, Thomas C. Street, J. Cummings, Charles B. Stuart, J. Oswald, Samuel Zimmerman, Washington Hunt, Samuel De Veaux, Charles Evans, Isaac C. Colton, Lot Clark; superintendent, William O. Buchanan.

The first suspension bridge was built under the supervision of Mr. Charles Ellet, in 1848. The following interesting account of this work, and the greater one which followed it, is from "Niagara," a book recently written and published by Hon. G. W. Holley, of Niagara Falls:

"Mr. Charles Ellet, in 1848, built the first suspension bridge over the chasm. He offered a reward of five dollars to any one who would get a string across it. The next windy day all the boys in the neighborhood were kiting, though not in the Wall street manner, and before night a lucky youth landed his kite in Canada and received the reward. Of this little string were born, so to speak, the large cables which support the present vast structure. But the first iron successor of the string was a small wire cable, seven-eighths of an inch in diameter. To this was suspended a wire basket in which two persons could cross the chasm. The basket was attached to an endless rope, worked by a windlass on each bank. The ride down to the center was rapid and delightful. The pause over the center of the abyss was apt to make the coolest persons a little anxious, and the *jerky* motion up the opposite side was rather annoying. The engineer was bold and brilliant rather than profound in his profession. At an entertainment given on the occasion of the completion of the bridge the good people of the embryo village, elated with their new acquisition, were inclined to regard their neighbors at the Falls with rather a patronizing sympathy. One of the latter said to Mr. Ellet, 'This bridge is a very clever affair, and you only need the falls here to build up quite a respectable village.' 'Well,' he replied, 'give me money enough and I will put them here.' He had great faith in dollar-power, even to the adding of the supreme adjective.

"This bridge was an excellent auxiliary in the construction of the present railway suspension bridge, buil, by Mr. John A. Roebling. It was commenced in 1852. and the first locomotive crossed it in March, 1855. It is one of the most brilliant examples of modern engineering, It is unique, and stands unrivaled for its grace, beauty and strength. It is one of the few structures that not only harmonize with the grand scenery of the vicinity. but even augment its impressiveness. It is eminently appropriate to the locality, and admirably fitted for the purpose it was designed to serve. Its plan is original, apt and excellent in every way. It was necessary that its railway track should be as high as the secondary banks of the river. It was also desirable to have a carriage way. It was wholly inexpedient to have the two side by side. Frightened horses and careless people would cause many serious accidents. Besides this, the terminus of the carriage way would be too far from the banks of the river.

"Seizing at once upon the natural capabilities of the location, the engineer resolved to combine the advantages of two systems of construction, those of the tubular and suspension bridges. The carriage way was placed level with the banks of the river at the edges of the chasm.

The railway track was placed eighteen feet above, on a level with the top of the secondary banks across which the two railroads were to approach it. The plan was perfect, and perfectly and faithfully executed in all its details. It is practically a skeleton tube. As the traveler passes over it in the carriage or the railroad car, from the almost total absence of any vibratory motion he feels at once that he is on a safe basis, and his sense of security is complete. While contemplating the grand scenery which may be viewed from its floor, we may reverently rejoice that the Creator has given to man, his creature, the capacity to comprehend, admire, utilize and adorn it.

"One feature in the construction of the bridge may be noticed as having a bearing on the question of its durability. It is well known that when wrought iron is exposed to long continued or oft repeated and rapid concussions, its fibres after a time become granulated, whereby its strength is greatly impaired and finally exhausted. It is also known that the effect of rhythmical or regular vibrations is more destructive than the effect of those which are inharmonious or irregular. Because of this no body of men is allowed to march to music across the bridge, nor a large number of cattle allowed to cross at once, lest they should, by accident, fall into a time step and so overstrain or break down the bridge. It is the difference between a single heavy blow and an irregular succession of light ones. Hence, when harmonious, regular vibrations can be broken up, the destructive effect is greatly modified and retarded.

"The bridge is supported by two large cables on each side, one pair above the other, the lower pair being nearer together horizontally than the upper pair, so that a cross section of the skeleton tube would be shaped somewhat like the keystone of an arch. Each of these large cables is ten inches in diameter and is composed of seven smaller ones called strands. These smaller strands are made of number nine wire, and each one contains five hundred and twenty wires. Each of these wires was boiled three several times in linseed oil, so that it was covered with an oleaginous coating of considerable thickness and great adhesive power. Each wire was carried across the river separately, from tower to tower, by a contrivance of the engineers, the chief feature of which was a light iron pulley about twenty inches in diameter, suspended on what might be called a wire cord. This apparatus was called a traveler, and curious and interesting was its performance as seen from below. It looked like a huge spider weaving an iron web that might—perhaps will—defy the fates.

"Six of the seven strands forming a large cable were laid around the seventh as a center, and when all were properly placed they were again saturated with oil and paint. After this, by another contrivance of the engineers, they were wound or wrapped with wire, like winding a rope cable with marlin, and thus the whole cable was thoroughly compacted laterally and made into a huge, round iron rope. This is covered with numerous coats of paint, so that the oxidation of the inner wires would seem to be impossible. The oft recurring succession of iron wire and its oleaginous coating, together with the small triangular spaces between the wires, would seem to reduce the destructive power of the vibrations to zero. But the vibrations are very greatly reduced, and the stiffness of the structure is greatly increased, by the use of a series of triangular stays, the triangle being the only geometrical figure whose angles cannot be shifted. There are sixty-four of these triangles. Their hypothenuses are formed by over-floor stays of wire rope reaching from the tops of the towers to different points in the lower floor, this latter, of course, forming their common base and the towers their altitude. The stays are fastened to the suspenders so as to form straight lines. As the towers and the floor are rigid and solid in the direction of the lines they represent, it follows that the intersections of the hypothenuses with the common base form so many stationary points in the latter. These stationary points present a powerful resistance to vibrations. The side trusses, with their system of diamond work braces, and the weight of the railway track on the upper bridge, also help much to stiffen the structure. There are likewise fifty-six under stays, or guys of wire rope fastened to the rocks below, designed to prevent upward and lateral vibrations. A heavy locomotive with twenty full-loaded cars produced a depression of the cambre or upper curvature of the track of nearly ten inches. The ordinary loads produce or depression of only five inches.

" * * * * Attention is directed to a point on the American side of the river, just below this bridge, where the disintegration of the shale and abrasion of the superposed rock is very strikingly exhibited. A singular phenomenon was presented here in 1863. A mass of rock and shale, about fifty feet long, twenty feet wide and sixty feet deep, fell with a great crash on to the hard bed of the river. Directly following the fall a remarkable motion was developed in the bridge itself. A strong wave of motion passed through the whole structure from the American side to the opposite shore, and returned again to the same side.

"Some twelve or fifteen mechanics who were at work on the upper or railway track were so alarmed that they fled with all speed to the shore. The motion imparted to the bridge was incalculably greater than, and of a different character from, any motion imparted by the crossing of the heaviest trains. The rocky mass which fell was forty rods below the bridge, and the hard floor on which it struck more than two hundred and thirty feet beneath it. The mass itself fell about sixty feet average distance, and might have weighed five thousand tons. The extraordinary motion imparted to the bridge by the concussion must have been transmitted along the subterranean rock to the anchorages on the American side, thence through the cables and the bridge across to the anchorages on the Canadian side, whence it reacted or returned again to the American side.

"Mr. Donald McKenzie, the most capable and intelligent master carpenter and superintendent of repairs, who has been connected with the bridge constantly since its erection, and all the men under him at the time, make and confirm this statement, and declare it is impossible to exaggerate or describe the wave-like motion which they experienced while escaping to the shore."

There is no history of early settlement at this point which has not been included in the history of the town of Niagara. Settlement was quite slow until after the commencement of the construction of the first bridge, and from that time on, to the completion of the second structure, the growth of the village was rapid.

BUSINESS GROWTH AND IMPROVEMENTS.

The first hotel was the New York Central, west of the site of Atwood's Western Hotel; it was burned a few years since. It was erected during the time consumed in the completion of the Mont Eagle Hotel, one of the largest, most elegantly furnished and most expensive houses among the many opened to visitors to Niagara. This structure was begun in 1847 or 1848, and completed in 1855. Among the hotels built in the village since, may be mentioned the following: Atwood's Western Hotel, Exchange Hotel, John Durwin proprietor; the American Hotel, N. Y. Central Hotel, by Felix Nassion; the Frontier House, by J. Gudbrodt; George Stoll's Hotel and Gibbs's United States Hotel. The old springhouse was converted into a hotel at an early day in the history of the village, and a barn was attached to it This, though but an inn, and not entitled to the dignity of a hotel, was, it is said, the first house of entertainment opened to the public. There was a small building which afterwards became a wing to the American Hotel, which was used as a public house in the infancy of the village. It will be remembered as the "O. K. Tavern," which title it received from an old oak tree that stood before the door, on the bark of which had been cut an inscription something like this: "O a K."

Among the small groceries, eating-houses and similar business ventures during the construction of the first bridge may be mentioned the following, concerning the existence of some of which there is some contradictory evidence, but which undoubtedly flourished for a season, at least: The refreshment store of B. H. White and his wife, at a place near the entrance to the descending roadway to the water's edge; White lived there and still lives at the Falls, and was known as a prominent general agent for the sale of village lots at the time of the initial growth of Suspension Bridge. Another refreshment saloon, it is said, was kept by an eccentric Frenchman named Joe Goentel (as nearly as the orthography of the name can now be obtained). He had formerly been a bar-tender at the Eagle Hotel at Niagara Falls. He was very loquacious, very polite and otherwise remarkable in manner and appearance. He is said to have slept in his shop and done his own cooking. Among the first merchants, it is said that Collis & Boyd were prominent. The mercantile business of Messrs. Vedder was established early, and it has since grown to be one of the most important in northern New York. Their trade is wholesale and retail, and they supply retail stores throughout the county, and at points beyond, with their stocks of general groceries.

The extensive milling business of Witmer Brothers was begun as early as 1848 by the father of the present proprietors, Mr. C. H. Witmer, who continued it until 1859, when, in September, he slipped into the river back of the mill and just above the bridge, and was drowned. Since then the business has been conducted by his sons, under the firm name of Witmer Brothers, with a mill and store at Niagara Falls. The business of this firm surpasses in extent that of any other house in this section. They are also the proprietors of Witmer Brothers' Bank at Suspension Bridge, which was established October 19th, 1874. The first school was kept in a small wooden building which stood on Niagara avenue, on land now owned by Dr. Rogers. The teacher was Miss Vedder, afterward Mrs. Pierson. The same building answered the purpose of a church also. The post-office was established in 1848 or 1849. Dr. Collier was the first postmaster. Colonel John Fisk succeeded him, and there have been several changes since. The present postmaster is A. M. Witmer.

A GREAT RAILWAY CENTER.

Suspension Bridge is one of the best known railroad points in the East. It presents a scene of constant bustle and activity in all the departments of the railroad, express, freight and telegraph interests. In former years the business transacted at the cattle yards at this place was immense. The yards were established about 1860, and did a very large business until a regular stock market was established in Buffalo, at which time the trade gradually fell off at Suspension Bridge. The building of the international bridge at Buffalo, connecting that city with the Canadian railroads, drew the trade off to a considerable extent, and since then the business has declined. Trains are passing between the East and West by way of the great international bridge in numbers that are surprising to the stranger unaccustomed to the amount of business done here. All through the day, every day in the week, there is scarcely a quarter of an hour during which cars are not crossing and recrossing the suspension bridge, between this village and Clifton. The following railways pass through the village, all except the Erie using the commodious depot belonging to the Central company: Erie railway, New York Central and Hudson River Railroad, Rome, Watertown & Ogdensburg Railroad, Great Western Railroad, and Canada Southern Railroad.

The express companies represented in the village are the American, C. E. Woodford agent; and the United States. The telegraphic facilities of the place are unrivaled.

THE CUSTOM-HOUSE AND OTHER BUILDINGS.

The custom-house is one of the finest buildings for business purposes in the village. It is large, conveniently arranged and well lighted and ventilated. It contains, besides the offices of the customs department, the post-office, which is one of the most attractive and convenient in the county. Suspension Bridge is one of the most important ports of entry in the State. The collector is Benjamin Flagler; the deputy collector, Eli Nichols. Under their supervision the large business of the port and its many dependent offices along the frontier is carried on by a large number of minor officials. The port of entry was removed to this village from Lewiston in 1863. Besides the government building there are several other fine structures in the village, among them Colt's block, Vedder's block, Lang's block and a number of smaller buildings. Like Niagara Falls and Lewiston, Suspension Bridge would have shared in the benefits that would have followed the construction of the proposed Niagara ship canal. Some of its citizens, notably Colonel John Fisk, its first president and one of its founders, and others, were prominently identified with it from first to last.

INCORPORATION AND CIVIL HISTORY.

The petition for incorporation was dated April 21st, 1854, and signed by Marcus Adams, Elihu P. Graves, Lewis E. Glover and Rodney Durkee. May 30th an election was held for the purpose of ascertaining the public sentiment in relation to the proposed incorporation, resulting in eighty-four votes for and two votes against the measure. According to a census taken by Rodney Durkee in the spring of the same year, the population of the village was 827. The village was incorporated as Niagara City June 8th, 1854, its limits including farm lots 33, 34, 35, 36, 37 and half of 38 of the Mile Reserve, comprising nearly one and one-half square miles.

The first officers were: John Fisk, president; H. P. Witbeck, Rodney Durkee, George Vogt and James Vedder, trustees; E. Stanley Adams, clerk.

The present village officials are as follows: W. H. Wallace, president; La Beaum W. Wilson, clerk; M. S. Langs, H. J. Delmage, L. Schmidt and James Low, trustees.

The village has in recent years been universally called Suspension Bridge.

WATER-WORKS AND FIRE COMPANIES.

By general consent the credit of the conception and realization of the idea of water-works for the village is accorded to O. W. Cutler, a prominent and well known resident of the place. In 1872 or 1873 a special bill was introduced in the Legislature to enable the village to avail itself of the advantages accruing from the improvement mentioned, which was defeated in the interest of certain corporations paying heavy taxes in the town of Niagara. In 1875 the general act was passed, enabling villages to supply themselves with pure and wholesome water; and soon afterward a public meeting of the citizens of the village was called at Colt's Hall, where a sentiment was declared in favor of the project, and a subsequent meeting of the tax-payers resulted in a majority favoring the prosecution of the enterprise. The New York Central and Hudson River Railroad Company, through its attorneys, procured an injunction on account of alleged irregularities. New proceedings were instituted, which, in November, 1875, prevailed in spite of much strenuous opposition. In the spring of 1876 the work was begun, and completed August 1st of the same year.

The following particulars with respect to the description and extent of the works will be of interest: The Holly system was adopted. The pumps of the Suspension Bridge works are at the hydraulic basin at Niagara Falls, the water-works company of that village using them as a source of supply, and paying for the privilege thirty per cent. of their gross receipts. There are in Suspension Bridge four and one-half miles of pipe, and twenty-seven double-discharge fire hydrants.

The advantages following the introduction of the water-works have been many, among them the reduction of rates of insurance from fifteen to one hundred per cent., and a radical change in the organization of the fire department, with a reduction of expense in its maintenance. It is said that before the system had been in operation a month there was a fire in McMann's block which was extinguished with a saving of a sufficient amount of property to nearly pay the expense of the improvement, which amounted in the aggregate to about $60,000. The village was bonded to raise the required amount, the first payment falling due in 1881, and $3,000 each year for twenty years thereafter. Strong as was the opposition of some parties to the water-works at first, time has demonstrated their practical utility to the satisfaction of the great majority of the tax-payers of the village. The annual revenue is fast increasing, and it is confidently believed that the day is not far distant when they will not only be self-supporting but profitable to the corporation, not alone for their great convenience, but in a business point of view.

The fire department of the village was organized in 1856. A bucket company was formed during that year, and a hook and ladder company in 1857. Before the close of the latter year a Hunniman engine was purchased at an expense of $1,700, inclusive of a hose cart; and a bucket wagon was procured at a cost of $150, with a hook and ladder wagon, with ladders and other accessories, costing about $250. The original organization was known as "Rapids Engine and Hose Company." The following is a list of the officers at the time of organization: President, John Brazee; foreman, John D. Hilliard; assistant-foreman, Louie Oatman; secretary, Luther Graves; treasurer, F. Weidemann. This organization was kept up till after the completion of the water-works in 1876, when the department was reorganized as follows, the date of organization being September 1st:

Rapids Hose Company, No. 1.—Foreman, James Finn; assistant-foreman, James Watters; president, George A. Stricker; secretary, William Schlisinger; treasurer, Denby Wand.

Bellevue Hose Company, No. 2.—Foreman, John Zeiger; president, Gottlieb Muir; secretary, Julius Miller; treasurer, J. Gutbrodt.

Excelsior Hook and Ladder Company.—Foreman, R. A. Perry; assistant-foreman, George Howie; president, John Shoemaker; secretary, Marcus Swan; treasurer, John Hennessy.

THE PRESS OF SUSPENSION BRIDGE.

The first newspaper published in the village was the *Niagara City Herald*, the initial issue of which appeared in October, 1855, under the business and editorial management of G. H. Hackstaff. In the following year it passed into the hands of N. F. Hackstaff, by whom it was published for a time, until it was purchased by C. B. Gaskell, now in the milling business at Niagara Falls. Mr. Gaskell continued to issue it for some time, and its publication finally ceased.

The *Suspension Bridge Journal* was established in 1870 by A. G. Liscom. In 1873 it was purchased by John Ransom, who improved it greatly, both typographically and editorially. The circulation has been increased considerably since that time, the list running as high as one thousand in 1878. The *Journal*, which, under the management of Mr. Liscom, was independent in politics, is now favorable to the interests of Democracy, but is chiefly devoted to local and vicinity news, being known as one of the most spicy and gossipy papers in Niagara county.

EDUCATION.

There is an efficient and well-equipped public school at Suspension Bridge, of which our best endeavors have not been able to procure a history.

DE VEAUX COLLEGE.

This institution was endowed by the will of the late Samuel De Veaux, made August 3d, 1852, in which, after providing for relatives and others whom he wished to remember, he left the balance of his estate, amounting to $174,652.52, to Bishop De Lancy, Rev. Dr. William Shelton, Peter A. Porter and Richard H. Woodruff, as trustees, "for the purpose of establishing, founding and maintaining a benevolent institution, to receive and support orphans and destitute children; to train them up to industry; to learn them trades and professions; to give them a mental and manual, and a social and religious education." It was further provided that the institution should be under the fostering care of the Protestant Episcopal Church, and it was placed in charge of the convention of the diocese of western New York, with the earnest request that the convention would take the same under its care as a dependency of the church. De Veaux College was incorporated April 15th, 1853. The erection of the buildings was begun in 1855, and they were completed about 1857 or 1858. The school was opened in March, 1857, with Rev. Henry Gregory as president, Rev. Israel Foote as professor and Edmund S. Wells as tutor. Elijah Ford, Esq., of Buffalo, acting as agent for the trustees, increased the fund by judicious management to $187,135.40 in 1856.

The *Register* for 1877 says: "The college domain consists of three hundred and sixty-four acres of land at Suspension Bridge, N.Y., extending for half a mile along the most picturesque part of the Niagara river, and devoted to the immediate use of the college.

"The college edifice is most beautifully situated, spacious and commodious, well ventilated, warmed by the most approved low pressure steam apparatus, lighted with gas, provided with ample bathing facilities, and in all particulars equipped with a view to health, comfort and efficient administration; it contains chapel, school and recitation rooms, library and reading room, dormitories, and commons room. A large gymnasium, designed as a play and drill room, has been lately built and fitted with suitable apparatus.

"The campus is admirably laid out for use as a parade ground, and for base ball, cricket, or other out-door sports.

"The location is proverbially healthful, and the different railways centering at Suspension Bridge make it easy of access from all parts of the country."

The present board of trustees is as follows: Rt. Rev. A. C. Coxe, D. D.; Rev. William Shelton, D. D.; Hon. James M. Smith, LL. D.; Hon. Asher P. Nichols, P. D. Walter, D. J. Townsend, Rev. Theodore M. Bishop, D. D.; Edward M. Smith, Samuel G. Cornell; with Rt. Rev. A. C. Coxe as president, and Robert P. Wilson as secretary and treasurer. Officers of the college: President, Rev. G. H. Patterson, A. M., LL. B.; head master, J. W. Craig, A. B.; masters: Rev. G. A. Mueller, A. M., German, French and book-keeping; Lieutenant J. L. Tiernan, U. S. A., military tactics; G. F. Kelly, A. B., Latin, English and elocution; L. G. Chaffin, A. M., music and composition; G. S. Pine, A. B., mathematics, and R. H. Gardner, jr., A. B., physical science and English.

CATHOLIC SCHOOL.

The Catholic school at Suspension Bridge was opened in 1866. The Sisters of the Visitation were the first teachers, remaining about two years. They were succeeded by the Sisters of St. Joseph, who have conducted the school successfully to the present time. The average attendance at the school is one hundred and eighty. The present property was purchased by Very Rev. Robert Rice, president of the Seminary of Our Lady of Angels. The school is in a very prosperous condition, and the course of instruction is one of the most thorough in the village.

SOCIETIES.

NIAGARA FALLS LODGE, NO. 81, I. O. O. F.

This lodge was organized with five charter members, viz.: C. F. Miller, Louis Elsheimer, Christian Barthan, Adam Risley and Louis Lipp. The original officers were as follows: N. G., C. F. Miller; V. G., Louis Elsheimer; secretary, Christian Barthan; treasurer, Adam Risley. The following are the names of the present officers: Gottlieb Muir, N. G.; M. S. Long, V. G.; F. W. Geiger, secretary; Louis Elsheimer, treasurer. The names of the past presiding officers are as follows: Louis Elsheimer, Conrad Fink, Louis Lipp, Charles Ransom, George Stoll, Jacob Fink, Jacob Pefesterer, John Thurecht, Daniel Elsheimer and Christopher Roller.

The lodge was formerly worked in the German language, but the English language has been in use in its sessions since August 9th, 1877.

"OUR SOCIETY."

This society was organized April 18th, 1874, with the following officers: President, E. Rommel; vice-president, R. W. Watson; treasurer, S. P. Colt; secretary, S. Z. Harroun. The object of the association is pleasant social intercourse and the cultivation of a knowledge of literature and the drama. The society is in a very prosperous condition; the members number about sixty ladies and gentlemen, who meet semi-monthly in a neatly fitted room in Colt's block, furnished with a piano and a fine library. The election of officers takes place semi-annually. The present presiding officer is Mr. S. Z. Harroun.

WHIRLPOOL LODGE, NO. 19, A. O. U. W.

Whirlpool Lodge, No. 19, A. O. U. W. was organized April 4th, 1876, with six charter members. The original officers were as follows: P. M. W., N. P. Browning; M. W., William Carr; G. F., D. P. H. Rose; O., John Brown; recorder, N. E. G. Wadhams; financier, S. B. Eshelman; receiver, M. Silberberg; I. W., Jacob Weil; O. W., Edward Oakley. The present officers are: N. E. G. Wadhams, P. M. W.; Earl Buttery, G. F.; M. Silberberg, O.; J. W. Van Horn, recorder; Jacob Weil, financier; John Brown, receiver; J. Nussbaum, I. W.; Edward Oakley, O. W. The following named persons have filled the chair of master workman: N. P. Browning, William Carr and D. P. H. Rose.

CATHOLIC MUTUAL BENEFIT ASSOCIATION, BRANCH 2.

Suspension Bridge Branch, No. 2, of the C. M. B. A. was organized March 1st, 1877, with fourteen charter members. The first officers were as follows: President, Henry Smith; 1st vice-president, Michael Hannan; 2d vice-president, James McNally; treasurer, James Holohan; recording secretary, Henry J. Delmage; assistant recording secretary, Frederick Regenhardt; financial secretary, Daniel Durwin; marshal, John Travis; guard, Peter Muldoon; board of directors, Richard Hartigan, Alexander McDonald, Daniel Durwin, James Madigan and Frederick Regenhardt. These officers were installed by the officers of the Grand Council at Niagara Falls, D. Barrett, president; J. Clifford, 1st vice-president; Joseph Mackenna, grand recording secretary. The following are the names of the present officers of Branch No. 2: Rev. D. J. Daly, spiritual director; Henry Smith, president; Richard Hartigan, 1st vice-president; August Weber, 2d vice-president; Peter Muldoon, chancellor; J. F. Muldoon, treasurer; H. J. Delmage, recording secretary; Frederick Regenhardt, assistant recording secretary; D. Durwin, financial secretary; J. Dunigan, marshal; E. Maloney, guard; board of directors, Richard Hartigan, Ignatz Reiss, J. F. Muldoon, D. Lynch and D. Durwin. The present membership of the branch is thirty-five, and the prospect for a continued accession of members is flattering in the extreme, and the treasury is in a fair condition. All together, those who were instrumental in establishing Suspension Bridge Branch, No. 2, of the C. M. B. A. may congratulate themselves on the success which has attended their efforts.

CHURCHES OF SUSPENSION BRIDGE.

THE EVANGELICAL UNITED ZION'S CONGREGATION.

This society was formed about twenty-five years ago. The membership at the time of organization was about eighteen. The following is the list of successive ministers as furnished by the present pastor: "The first minister was Althaus, two years in service; the second was Bochard, one year in service; the third was Schifterling, one year in service; the fourth was G. Ade, two years in service; the fifth was D. Blesene, three years in service; the sixth was B. Dietrick, two years in service; the seventh was Fr. Heinle, seven months in service; the eighth was C. A. C. Brandt, four years and three months in service (died January 13th, 1873); the ninth, J. J. Dietrick, from April 1st, 1873, to the present time." There is a large and flourishing Sunday-school connected with the church. The present minister is the presiding officer. The number of scholars is one hundred and forty-five, and the number of teachers is twelve. The church edifice of this society is a rock building, erected at a cost of $2,000. The congregation is not in connection with any synod. The annual election of church officers is held the first Monday after Easter.

ST. RAPHAEL'S ROMAN CATHOLIC.

St. Raphael's church was organized in 1855. The number of members at that time was about one hundred. In 1849 there were but two Catholic families in the village. Amongst the more prominent Catholic families living there at the time of the organization of the church were those of William Delahunte, Michael Maloney, Thomas McMahon, Patrick Duffy, Anthony Walsh, Michael Barrett, John and Thomas Downes, Michael Rohan, James McInerney, Michael Marrum, Michael Sheehan, Charles Waters, George Heany, Thomas O'Rourke, Charles Darrow, Martin and Michael Ryan, John and Daniel Durwin, Bartholomew Tinn, Patrick Burns, Edward Lyons, James Dunnigan, Patrick McCrone, John and Patrick McKnight, Patrick McCormack, John O'Donnell, Michael Devitt, Richard Hartigan, James Keilt, Henry Kitchen, James and Michael Hannan, Thomas O'Brien and Edward Murphy. The number of Catholics now living in the village is about 1,100. The present brick church was built in 1855, at a cost of about $3,000. In 1864 there was an addition attached to it which cost about $3,000 or more. A parochial residence and convent were afterwards erected at a cost of $3,500. The ceremony at the laying of the corner stone of the church was private. The ground on which the church and parochial residence stand was donated to the few Catholics living in the village at that time by General Stuart. The first pastor was the Rev. Father Stevens, who also had to attend Niagara Falls and Lewiston. His time of service at the Bridge was three years. The priests of the Seminary of Our Lady of Angels then attended the mission two years; Father Purcell one year; Father McMullen about six or eight months; Father Fitzpatrick one year and a half. It was afterwards attended by the college priests for over one year and a half. They were then succeeded by Father Maloy, who remained about two years. Those who followed were: Father Wells, three years; Father Flannigan, six months; Father Fitzpatrick, ten months. The present pastor, Father Daly, has had charge of the church three years, and since his coming the church edifice has been renovated and beautified.

CHURCH OF THE EPIPHANY.

It having been ascertained that there were a sufficient number of persons in the village interested in the establishment of an Episcopal church in Suspension Bridge, a meeting was called in the autumn of 1857 by the Rev. Israel Foote, D.D., professor in De Veaux College, at which it was arranged to hold regular services in Colt's hall. In accordance with the canons of the church and the laws of the State of New York, the congregation was duly incorporated and received the sanction and approval of the bishop of the diocese. On the 6th of January, 1858, it was determined and declared that the church should be known as "The Church of the Epiphany," of Suspension Bridge, N. Y. The following named persons constituted the first officers of the parish: Wardens, J. H. Crump and Anthony W. Hicker; vestrymen, J. W. Doukler, R. Durkee, A. D. Lampkins, R. B. Monroe, R. D. Cook, H. G. Stuart, D. H. Thomas and G. P. Leap.

The Sunday-school comprised about fifty scholars.

From the 6th of January, 1858, until November, 1864, the following named clergy (residents of De Veaux College) officiated for periods of from six months to a year or more each: Rev. I. Foote, D.D., Rev. E. R. Welles, Rev. M. Van Rensselaer, D.D., Rev. L. S. Stevens. Rev. R. Henry W. Wye.

In November, 1864, the Rev. Warren W. Walsh received and accepted a call to the rectorship of the parish. The following year a subscription list was opened to raise funds for building a church. Two lots were given as a site for the building; one, on the northeast corner of Lewiston and Lockport avenues, was presented by Messrs. James and Henry W. Ford, of Albany, N. Y., and the other, on Lewiston avenue, by Mrs. William H. Wallace. August 8th, 1866, Rt. Rev. A. C. Coxe, D.D., attended by seventeen clergymen, laid the corner-stone of the new church, which was to be built of stone, and on the 29th of December, the same year, the edifice was completed and opened for divine service. Value of church and lot, $7,000.

The following gifts were presented to the church: A baptismal font, by Colonel Charles B. Stuart, of Geneva; a bishop's chair, by Rev. M. Van Rensselaer, D.D., president of De Veaux College; a pulpit, by Messrs. H. J. and G. M. Walsh, and a credence table, by Rev. George Worthington.

June 29th, 1868, the church being free from debt, Rt. Rev. Arthur Cleveland Coxe, D.D., bishop of the diocese, consecrated the building, twenty-one clergymen being present.

March 29th, 1869, Rev. Warren W. Walsh resigned the rectorship of the parish, and was succeeded, July 18th, by Rev. George W. Knapp, who continued in charge till December 5th, 1872. For the next six months, Rev. George H. Patterson, president of De Veaux College, assisted by Rev. James Van Voast and Rev. W. Van Gantzhorne, supplied the parish. June 12th, 1873, Rev. Walter North accepted a call to the rectorship, which he resigned May 15th, 1875, and was soon succeeded by Rev. Gabriel Alfred Mueller, who continued in charge until February, 1877. March 19th, 1877, Rev. F. W. Raikes accepted a call to the rectorship of the parish, and entered upon his duties on Easter Sunday.

The vestry of the parish elected the following day consisted of the following persons: Wardens, Messrs. Benjamin Flagler and James Tattersall; vestrymen, Messrs. A. Witmer, H. E. Woodford, A. H. Robinson, E. Buttery, A. Henning, J. Willis, E. Nichols, W. Leap. About fifty or sixty families are now connected with the parish. The average attendance at the Sunday-school is one hundred and fifty. There are four officers and nineteen teachers.

FIRST CONGREGATIONAL.

This church was organized in March, 1855, as the First Congregational Church of Niagara City. The original members numbered eighteen, prominent among whom were W. H. Childs, E. P. Graves, James Watson, Aaron Vedder and others. The first pastor was Rev. J. D. Knapp. The succeeding ones have been W. H. Webb, B. F. Bradford, A. S. Wood, George Anderson and Joseph L. Bennett, the present incumbent. The church edifice is a substantial stone building with steeple and bell. It is conveniently arranged, having a lecture room and Sunday-school rooms. It is worth about $15,000. The Sabbath-school is one of the most flourishing in the village, having about two hundred and fifty members. The first superintendent was James Watson. He was succeeded by William H. Childs, and he by N. P. Browning. Mr. Watson is the present superintendent.

PROMINENT INHABITANTS OF SUSPENSION BRIDGE.

Henry C. Adams came to Suspension Bridge (where he now carries on a drug store) from Adams Basin, Monroe county, April 1st, 1852. He was born at the last named place, November 28th, 1844.

Jacob Bingenheimer has been president and trustee, and member of the board of education, of Suspension Bridge, and has held several State and county offices. He was born in Germany in 1825. He was married to Miss E. Eberhardt, of Germany, in 1852, having come from his native land two years before. His post-office address is Suspension Bridge, and he is an extensive coal dealer and builder.

N. P. Browning was born in Pendleton, September 28th, 1837. He removed to Suspension Bridge seven years ago. He was married July 7th, 1870, to Hattie E. Shelden, of Wheatfield. Mr. Browning is an efficient and

AMOS W. R. HENNING.
COUNTY CLERK NIAGARA CO.
RES. SUSPENSION BRIDGE, N.Y.

F. NEWTON ALBRIGHT,
BARKERS P. O. TOWN OF SOMERSET, N.Y.

S. T. CLARK, A.M. M.D.

SIMEON TUCKER CLARK, A.M., M.D.

The subject of this sketch was born in Canton, Norfolk county, Massachusetts, October 10th, 1836. He is a son of Rev. Nathan Sears Clark, his mother's maiden name having been Laura Stevens Swift. Dr. Clark graduated as M.D. at the Berkshire Medical College in 1860, and received the degree of A.M. from Genesee College in 1866. He was married in 1857 to Ruth Jennie Mendall, of Marion, Plymouth county, Massachusetts. In 1861 he came to the city of Lockport, where he has since resided, actively engaged in the practice of his profession. He was pension examining surgeon for ten years. In 1872 he was elected a permanent member of the New York State Medical Society, and in 1876, at the twenty-fifth annual meeting of the American Association for the Advancement of Science, he was chosen a member of that society. He has been for three years president of the Niagara County Medical Society, and has served as a delegate to the American Medical Association.

Dr. Clark is corresponding secretary of the Jewett Scientific Society, and is recorded in the Naturalist's Directory as a conchologist. He has been especially identified with the poetical literature of the past twenty years, his poems having been published in many of the best magazines and extensively copied in the newspapers, while his Masonic poems have given him a transatlantic reputation, and his religious verse has found a permanent place in several popular collections.

Having obtained an enviable reputation in his profession, Dr. Clark is regarded as one of the most successful physicians and surgeons and has a very extensive practice. In questions of medical jurisprudence he has few equals, and his opinions on questions in that department are regarded as the very highest authority. His command of language and the ready, clear and lucid manner in which he gives his opinions as a witness upon the stand, give to his testimony a force which carries great weight with courts and jurors, and produces a conviction in the minds of all that hear it that he is not only learned in his profession but a general scholar, well known teacher, and has held the office of commissioner of public schools for nearly four years.

Mrs. John Buttery (formerly Miss Priscilla Nichols) was born in Roxbury, Vt., March 13th, 1813, and married to John Milton Buttery, of Lewiston, N. Y., April 7th, 1835. Mrs. Buttery is the proprietor of the Whirlpool Rapids double elevator. Post-office address, Suspension Bridge, N. Y.

Leander Colt, of Suspension Bridge, was born August 28th, 1824, in the town of Lewiston. May 7th, 1856, he married Mary Helen Saxe, of Chazy, N. Y. Mr. Colt is a leading hardware merchant, and holds the position of postmaster at Suspension Bridge.

William Cornell, furniture dealer at Suspension Bridge, was born in 1841 at Lewiston, N. Y., and came to Suspension Bridge July 5th, 1865. May 5th, 1874, he married Frances E. Pew, of Stamford, Canada West. Mr. Cornell was a U. S. custom officer from 1865 to 1869. He enlisted in the 3rd N. Y. cavalry July 31st, 1861; was discharged July 21st, 1865; was taken prisoner at South Side Railroad, Va., June 25th, 1864, and confined in Andersonville prison, Ga., till April 28th, 1865.

O. W. Cutler, of Suspension Bridge, was born April 1st, 1846, at Newbury, N. H., June 1st, 1866, he married Mary Ann Tallant, of East Conrad, N. H. In 1867 he removed to Suspension Bridge, and engaged in the drug business for ten years. He has held a number of official positions, having been president of the village of Suspension Bridge in 1875 and 1876, treasurer in 1872 and 1873, and supervisor of the town of Niagara in 1875. Mr. Cutler was the proprietor of the Suspension Bridge Water-Works, an account of his connection with which enterprise will be found in the history of the village. He always has taken an active part in politics, being a zealous member of the Democratic party. Mr. Cutler fitted for college at the New London, N. H., Literary and Scientific Institute. He is at present engaged as traveling agent for the Holly Manufacturing Company.

Rev. D. J. Daly, pastor of the Catholic church at Suspension Bridge, was born in Ireland, November 14th, 1846, and came to Suspension Bridge from Buffalo in the latter part of 1875.

Samuel B. Eshelman, who has officiated as village clerk, treasurer and collector and policeman of the village of Suspension Bridge, was born July 6th, 1839, in the town of Clarence, N. Y. He came to Suspension Bridge in 1863. July 23rd, 1872, he was married to Harriet Metz, of Clarence, Erie county, N. Y.

Konrad Fink was born in Germany, August 3rd, 1835 and came to Suspension Bridge in February, 1854. Mr. Fink, who is the proprietor of a grocery and saloon, has been town assessor and water commissioner, and president of the village of Suspension Bridge.

Benjamin Flagler, collector of customs for the district of Niagara, was born December 10th, 1833, at Lockport, and married November 9th, 1859, to Martha J. McKnight, of Newfane. He removed to Suspension Bridge, his present residence, in 1862. He served as captain in the 28th volunteers during the late war, was appointed inspector of customs in 1863, deputy collector in December, 1864, special deputy in January, 1872, and collector in February, 1878.

Amos W. R. Henning, whose portrait appears elsewhere, was born at Annville, Pa., May 5th, 1842, but removed to the town of Niagara, with his parents, in 1847. He is unmarried. He graduated at Eastman's Commercial College in 1859, entered the New York Central R. R. freight office in 1860, and remained with the company at Suspension Bridge seventeen years, until October, 1877, when he resigned his position, and accepted the Democratic nomination for county clerk. After a warmly contested election, Mr. Henning was elected by about two hundred majority, carrying his home town of Niagara by the unprecedented majority of five hundred and twenty-five. His term of service will expire in 1880.

William Legg was born April 19th, 1849, at Thames Dilton, Surrey, England. He was married October 25th, 1873, to Catharine White, of Greenwich, Kent, England, and came to Suspension Bridge, where he is engaged in gardening, in 1875.

James Low, farmer and coal merchant, Suspension Bridge, was born in Toronto, Canada, January 24th, 1836, and married to Amanda Barnes, of Cambria, March 25th, 1858. He removed to Suspension Bridge in 1861. Mr. Low served in the 8th artillery from August 22nd, 1862, till March 22nd, 1865, as first lieutenant, then as captain, and finally as major, and held the position of postmaster at Suspension Bridge for seven years, beginning 1865.

James McFeggan was born at Beauharnois, Canada, March 23rd, 1829, and came to Suspension Bridge, N. Y., where he has since resided, June 1st, 1864, from Canandaigua, N. Y. Mr. McFeggan is agent at Suspension Bridge for the New York Central and Hudson River Railroad.

Samuel H. McLaughlin, proprietor of the Railroad Eating-house, Suspension Bridge, was born in Jersey City, N. J., November 5th, 1840. He married Miss H. M. Allen, of Jersey City, June 20th, 1866, and removed to Suspension Bridge April 27th, 1870. Mr. McLaughlin was a soldier in the 21st regiment N. J. volunteers.

Eli S. Nichols removed to Suspension Bridge from Lockport April 1st, 1870, and holds the office of deputy collector of customs. He was born June 24th, 1835, in Cambria. His wife was Frances R. Harwood, of Lockport; they were married January 30th, 1867. Mr. Nichols served in the late war as second lieutenant, first lieutenant and captain in the eighth heavy artillery, from July, 1862, to July, 1865.

J. A. Palmateer, of Suspension Bridge, N. Y., was born at Prattsburgh, N. Y., August 19th, 1845, and married to Kate L. Granger, of Gainesville, N. Y., August 5th, 1875. Mr. Palmateer holds the position of ticket agent and telegraph operator for the Erie Railway Company.

Rev. George Herbert Patterson, president of De Veaux College, Suspension Bridge, was born in Buffalo, December 26th, 1836. February 8th, 1865, he was married to Frances Amelia Bolles, of Syracuse, and came to Suspension Bridge September 1st, 1869. From February 1st, 1866, to April 1st, 1869, he was head master of St. Mark's school, Southboro, Mass.

George H. Pierce, retired lumberman, Suspension Bridge, for many years identified with the business and political interests of Wheatfield, where he held the office of justice of the peace for seven years, and was town clerk, assessor etc., was born in Stockbridge, Mass., January 28th, 1816, and was married in 1838 to Abigail S. Roberts, of Wheatfield; removed to Suspension Bridge in 1852.

John Ransom, publisher of the *Suspension Bridge Journal*, was born in Wurtsboro, Sullivan county, September 17th, 1830. He was married June 10th, 1856, to Sylinda M. Brown, of Wilson, N. Y. Mr. Ransom has always been prominently identified with the interests of education, having been a member of the board of education of Suspension Bridge, and has given much time to the study of free masonry, in which he is widely known.

Emmanuel Rommel, druggist, of Suspension Bridge, was born there October 14th, 1854.

George Stoll, hotel keeper, Suspension Bridge, was born at Schaffhausen, in Switzerland, August 21st, 1822, and was married to Sally Ann Young, of Niagara, January 16th, 1856. Mr. Stoll came from Switzerland to the United States and settled at Suspension Bridge in 1849.

Dr. M. Talbot, of Suspension Bridge, was born May 12th, 1846, in Parsontown, Kings county, Ireland. He came to Suspension Bridge October, 1872, and April 13th 1875, married Mary Teresa Bampfield, of Clifton, Ontario. Dr. Talbot is well known as a physician and surgeon, having served two years as health officer of the village of Suspension Bridge.

David Hulett Thomas was born August 25th, 1826, on board the ship "Ann," then in New York harbor. He was married October 28th, 1849, to Sarah A. Pierce, of Niagara Falls, N. Y. Mrs. Thomas died, and on September 29th, 1854, Mr. Thomas was again married, to Olive N. Brower, of Syracuse. He came to Suspension Bridge, where he has since resided, from Lewiston, N. Y., in 1837, and has served four years in the United States navy and been a member of the board of education of Suspension Bridge thirteen years.

Thomas J. Walker, jr., was born January 21st, 1850, in the town of Beadle, Yorkshire, England, and came to Niagara Falls in 1853. In 1872 he was married to Miss Hattie Harris, of that village. At present Mr. Walker is inspector of customs at the port of Suspension Bridge.

Cornelia L. Wadhams was born at Lockport, February 18th, 1852. May 1st, 1871, she removed to Suspension Bridge, where she is engaged as a teacher in the public school.

John Whitney, farmer, was born in the town of Niagara, April 24th, 1824. He married Elizabeth A. Garrett, daughter of William Garrett, April 6th, 1848. Mr. Whitney served as lieutenant in the 163rd regiment, N. Y. S. militia. His post-office address is Suspension Bridge. Mr. Whitney was not drafted during the rebellion, but sent a substitute.

Reginald D. Wing, a native of Stevington, Bedfordshire, England, was born September 16th, 1841, and came to Suspension Bridge from Baltimore, Md., in August, 1873. He is cashier of the N. Y. L. E. and W. R. R. Co.

A. M. Witmer, postmaster, Suspension Bridge, was born in the town of Niagara, May 26th, 1837.

Joseph Witmer, farmer, post-office, Suspension Bridge, was born September 21st, 1812, in Niagara. He married, in 1846, Catherine Kauffman, of Mannor, Pa.

H. E. Woodford, agent for the American Express Company at Suspension Bridge, was born in Tipton, England, May 23rd, 1835. He came to Suspension Bridge September 1st, 1863. He was married to Kate Hoffman, of New York city, May 22nd, 1867.

Samuel Zimmerman Harroun, telegraph operator, was born at Suspension Bridge, where he now resides, April 30th, 1857.

Besides the foregoing we might also mention the following names:

W. Alexander, A. Atwood, of Atwood's Western Hotel, F. Weidermann, Eugene T. Enos, Van R. Pearson, I. and T. Vedder, E. Dean, James A. Waldron, I. H. Arnett, George Hacherle, Benjamin Witmer, farmer and lumberman, and Daniel Pletcher.

THE TOWN OF PENDLETON.

THIS is the central town on the southern border of the county. The land is level, with the exception of Beech and Bear ridges, located in the north part of the town. Roads follow both, running southwest and northeast. The ridges are nearly parallel, three miles long, and three-fourths of a mile wide. The soil of both is gravel mixed with sand, which furnishes a fertile soil for the production of all kinds of crops, and adapted to all varieties of fruit. The elevation of the ridges above the low land on both sides of them furnishes the most desirable building locations, which have been pleasantly and permanently improved. The Beech Ridge, it is stated, became a legal highway by right of possession; marked trees first indicating the path, which was improved and followed for over twenty years, legalizing a public road.

Beech Ridge post-office was established at Hall's Station in 1853; William M. Beebe was the first postmaster. Pendleton Center is a post-office on Bear Ridge. At Pendleton village a post-office was established as early as 1823. Pendleton Clark was the first postmaster.

The Tonawanda creek forms the southern boundary of the town; Sawyer's creek crosses the western part. Neither of the creeks furnishes in the town available power for mill purposes.

The New York Central railroad on the northern extremity, and the Erie Canal in the more central part, furnish the town facilities to reach market for its increasing products.

The town is divided into twelve school districts, accommodating 621 scholars between the ages of five and twenty-one. The amount of public appropriations for 1878 was $1,142.35. The public schools are in a prosperous condition, having generally good school-houses, especially the one of brick at Pendleton village.

SETTLEMENT.

Vigilant eyes intently watched the movements of the engineers who were adopting the route of the first Erie Canal. Points of prospective advantage were eagerly sought and readily secured. The junction of the artificial channel with the Tonawanda was considered one of the mose desirable. Twelve miles of a large stream were to be turned backward, to form a river of easy navigation and a feeder for the canal. An unbroken wilderness in 1821 everywhere surrounded the spot where the junction was to be made. Pendleton Clark and Jerry L. Jenks the same year obtained by contract from the Holland Company possession of the land upon which to found a village.

The first settlement in the town was on the Tonawanda creek, near the western bounds. Martin Van Slyke and Jacob Crisman locating there in 1807 or 1808. The venerable widow Elizabeth Van Slyke states that she visited her uncles Van Slyke and Crisman when she first came to Tonawanda in 1808. Marrying Garrett Van Slyke in 1812, she became a resident on the farm now owned by De Witt Denison, and has lived in the neighborhood since. Mrs. Van Slyke, now in her eighty-third year, makes her own clothes, and is otherwise a diligent worker, exhibiting a patch-work quilt consisting of 2,800 pieces. She raised a family of six children. Her husband died in 1837. Mrs. Margaret De Cou, a granddaughter of the pioneer Crisman, resides on the farm first taken up, on which the earliest fruit trees were planted and the first fruit grown in the region. The first deaths remembered were those of Martin Van Slyke and his eldest son, John. The first marriage was that of James Van Slyke and Margaret Crisman.

Lawrence Pickard located with his father, Hartman Pickard, in 1816. His enterprises identified him with the improvements of the country. Adding to his landed possessions from time to time, he was a patron of his locality. Albert H. Pickard is one of his living children. The father died February 15th, 1861. Mrs. Lucy, the companion of his youth, now living, was the daughter of Philip Woolever, who located three miles east of Tonawanda in 1816, and one mile west of Pendleton in 1823, clearing farms at both places. Mr. Woolever was a contractor for the first improvement of the Tonawanda creek. He died February 29th, 1829, aged 49; his wife, Elizabeth, February 17th, 1851, aged 75.

Cunrod Richard located on the Tonawanda creek in 1816. His son Henry is now living in the town. The father died February 16th, 1859, age 69; his wife, Eva, December 2nd, 1873, aged 79.

Garrett Van Slyke located in the west part of the town in 1822, where his son John B. now resides. The father located in the county first on the Niagara river, three miles below Black Rock, in 1817. He was captured by the Indians in the Revolutionary war, at the age of sixteen; taken to Canada, and adopted as a child by Molly Brant, of whom he was purchased by his uncle for a gallon of rum, and restored to his parents. He died in April, 1824, aged 53.

Beech and Bear ridges, in the central part of the town,

it appears were the next locations to attract the early settlers. On them was found an elevation above the sea of water that in an early day covered the face of the country. Widow Elizabeth S. Leland states that her father, Asa Andrews, bought his farm on Beech Ridge in 1824, and was the first that settled thereabouts. Her husband, Luther Leland, settled in 1827.

Thomas Leonard located on Bear Ridge in 1833; remaining there ten years, he removed to Mapleton, where his son Allen W. Leonard now resides. He died May 20th, 1863, aged 80. Mrs. A. W. Leonard is a daughter of Samuel B. Crosby, one of the earliest citizens of Lockport, connected with the construction of the Erie Canal, and now living in extreme old age in the village of Sanborn.

Henry Tripp, eighty-one years of age, resides on the farm where he located in 1824, on Beech Ridge, Alfred Pool became a resident on Beech Ridge in 1826, on the farm where he died March 18th, 1870, aged 68. Silas Hall made a location at the northern limit of Beech Ridge in May, 1835, when it was yet a wilderness, and cleared up a farm of two hundred and forty acres, in one of the most desirable locations. At the time of his settlement it seems there was still a prevalence of wild animals; he states that two years later he had hogs killed by bears, and that wolves and deer were plenty; the former disappearing in four or five years, while the deer remained about ten years.

In the south part of the town no settlement was made until 1812, when Adam Folmer took a deed from the Holland Company for two hundred and fifty-two acres; the expressed consideration was $757.50. A part of the premises is now owned by Charles Longmate, whose father located on the "transit," four miles south of Lockport, in 1834, and removed to his home of recent years in 1839, where he died February 11th, 1878, in his ninety-third year. At the time Mr. Longmate settled, the Transit road had not been improved further than three and a half miles south of Lockport; it was opened to the Buffalo road about two years after. The location alluded to is known as Millport. It was a place of prominence, from the extensive transactions in timber and staves; and the point where a lock was originally constructed by Samuel Wilkinson to extend the navigation of the Tonawanda creek for about five miles above.

The first resources of the town were those of a lumber country; the lumbering business was the dependence of the most enterprising who ventured to undertake the earliest improvements. The village, during the construction and after the completion of the canal, was the point of attraction. There was but little to induce settlement for agricultural purposes; the country had to be made dry land out of wet places. It has been accomplished, and the town made one of agricultural prosperity.

FROM THE TOWN RECORDS.

The village obtained its name previous to the town. They are said to have been called after the first name of Pendleton Clark. The town was formed from Niagara in May, 1827. The first town officers elected were: L. Thayer, supervisor; G. Van Slyke, town clerk; Nathaniel Sykes, David Chandler and James Hawley, assessors; Kimball Feroin, collector; Willard Sykes, Lawrence Pickard and John Baker, commissioners of highways; Baily Curtis and Rossal Richards, overseers of the poor; Henry Keyes, Alanson Sykes and John Schuyler, school commissioners; J. Henderson, A. King and Asa Milliken, school inspectors; Horace Thatcher, collector. The amount of school money voted was fifty dollars. It was "voted that no road money be raised;" "that overseers of the highways be fence-viewers and damage-appraisers;" and that "this meeting is rejourned to the house of David Chandler, April, first Tuesday, in the year 1828." Fourteen road districts were established, and eight school districts.

A memorandum on the town record book gives an exhibit of the condition of the town at that time: "On examination of the tax-list, we find the amount of property taxed in the seventh range is 572.51 dollars; the amount of property taxed in the present town of Niagara is 1,630.25 dollars."

The present principal town officers, elected at the late annual meeting, are Amos A. Brown, supervisor; William Butler, town clerk; John Beebe, William B. Lewis, Morris Wire and Selden B. Graves, justices.

THE GERMAN INHABITANTS.

The German population, which occupies so large a portion of the southern and eastern parts of the town, commenced the first settlement on Tonawanda creek, west of Pendleton village. Philip Woock landed there, with his family, in August, 1832, coming from Bavaria. John Adam Koepfinger and wife and Joseph Schimp located at the same time. Orin Fisk located on the east side of the canal in 1844. His father had previously settled as early as 1810 in the town of Royalton. The only other settler at the time was John Baker. William Woods was the first adventurer between the canal and transit, settling in 1849. Henry W Goodian came in the next year.

Emigrants from Germany must be largely credited with the most permanent agricultural improvements in the town. They laid the siege and have won the victory, where others had shrunk in despair. They have overcome difficulties and suffered privations that courage failed others to undertake or endure. Seeking the most thoroughly cultivated farms, comfortable homes and enjoyment of luxury, their diligent, patient application of labor and economy has secured them.

THE ENLARGEMENT OF THE CANAL.

The enlargement of the canal through the town, commencing in 1850, proved to be an important aid in bringing into use the swamp lands. The ample ditches constructed by the State on both sides enabled the farms to be sufficiently drained for all practical purposes.

The work for the construction of the enlarged canal through this town was contracted for in October, 1850.

The contractors were Chamberlain & Edgerton, and Ryon & Aiken (a firm of which Linus Jones Peck was a member, who afterwards completed the work), Anthony & Enos, Collins & Hilton, Lee Hitchcock, and Buell & Oswald. The guard-lock was built by Duane Shuler. One mile from the village the enlarged canal takes nearly a direct course to intersect the Tonawanda creek, shortening the distance at least one-third.

PENDLETON VILLAGE.

The completion of the canal gave birth to the village of Pendleton as a timber and stave market, employing a large amount of capital to transact the business that was annually done. Austin Simons was identified with the business of the village as a merchant, and of the country as a timber and stave purchaser in 1831, and for thirty-five years afterward. William B. Lewis, who located as a merchant in the village in 1834, has held the position of postmaster for sixteen years, and that of justice of the peace over thirty years.

The first building erected was the log tavern of Pendleton Clark, built in 1821, when the place was a wilderness. This first tavern was followed by a framed building of his construction in 1822. The first store goods were brought in by Jerry S. Jenks, who died soon after locating.

There are two hotels at Pendleton village, with groceries connected. The Sulphur Spring Hotel, located on the bank of the canal near the guard-lock, was built by Reuben Fuller and Marshall Martin in 1850. It has been owned and occupied for the last seventeen years by Truman Nichols. At this place the town elections are held and town business transacted.

CHURCHES.

The Roman Catholic Church of the Good Shepherd was erected in 1854, being substantially built with brick. The officers at the time were: John Staebel, cashier; Martin Woock, secretary; Michael Mayer, John Adam Koepfinger and Jacob Danna, trustees. The church was consecrated by Bishop Timon.

St. Paul's German Lutheran church, located three miles up the creek, west of the village, was built in 1859.

The Presbyterian church at Mapleton originated on Beech Ridge, in 1835, when there were but four families interested, who used a school-house for meetings, or, as often, private dwellings. Rev. Samuel Leonard was the first pastor, and held the position for several years. The first members were: James Thompson, Nathaniel Sykes, George Oliver, Thomas Leonard, George S. Welton, Alanson Sykes, Aaron Parsons, Silas Hall, and members of their families.

In 1844 a church was formed in Shawnee, the members at Beech Ridge joining. It was under the charge of Rev. Roswell Brooks for two years, and he was followed by Rev. Harvey Chapin. In 1847 a movement was made to erect a church, which was completed the following year. The society having been formed from two towns, the name adopted was "First Presbyterian Church of Pendleton and Wheatfield."

At the organization of the church at Mapleton, the first trustees were James Thompson, Silas Hall and Isaac H. Smith. The number of members was eighteen. It is under the charge of the Rev. A. T. Rankin. The society is in a prosperous condition, as is evinced by the present number of communicants, which is given as fifty-six.

The Methodist church of the village of Pendleton, the only Protestant place of worship in the village, was organized March 17th, 1858. The trustees were Miranda Root, Morris Wire, Lewis Abbott, Francis King and William Blowers. Rev. John B. Jenkins was the pastor. The church was built in 1860. The lot was given by Willet Clark, for the use of all evangelical congregations.

The church of the United Brethren was organized in March, 1874.

LEADING CITIZENS OF PENDLETON.

W. C. Andrus came from Vermont in 1823, with his father, Asa Andrus, and located in the town of Royalton. He removed to Pendleton in 1824. He married Miss Sophia C. Hills in 1841. Post-office, Beech Ridge.

George E. Andrus, a native of the town of Southington, Conn., came to Pendleton in 1838, with his father, Warren Andrus, being six years old at that time. He settled on the Wort farm, and resided there until 1850; then engaged in the lumber business until 1855, when he resumed farming, and has lived on his present farm twelve years. Post-office, Pendleton Centre.

James H. Andrus came from Hartford county, Conn., in 1837, and located in the village of Pendleton. He was married to Susan Gillings, a native of England, in 1856. He has resided on his present place since 1844. Post-office, Beech Ridge.

A. H. Ellis, formerly from New Jersey, located on Beech Ridge with his father. He was married to Elizabeth L. Richards in 1845. He has occupied his present farm, part of the Andrus place, for fourteen years. Post-office, Lockport.

Rev. R. C. Foote and son are engaged in farming. Rev. R. C. Foote, a native of Washington county, N. Y., first moved to McNall's Corners, in the town of Royalton. He entered the Methodist Episcopal ministry in 1836, and retired in 1869 and moved to his present residence. In 1864 he was married to Electa Taylor. His son, Clark R. Foote, occupies a portion of the homestead. Post-office, Pendleton Centre.

Lyman Goodridge was born in Vermont, and moved to Monroe county in 1830. He married Mary Burditt in 1845, and in 1846 he removed to Hartland, then, again, a few years later, to his present place, a part of the Douglass tract. Mr. Goodridge was elected supervisor of the town in 1859 and 1860. Post-office, Pendleton Centre.

Hon. A. H. Rickard was born on the homestead where he now resides. He was married in 1861. He was elected supervisor in 1863, and has served six years in that capacity. He has also been a member of Assembly. Post-office address, Pendleton Centre.

Henry Richard, postmaster at Pendleton Centre, came to Pendleton with his grandfather in 1816 from Madison county, and settled on Tonawanda creek. He was married to Margaret Van Slyke in 1842. He has been postmaster twenty-five years, and town clerk two years.

Mrs. W. Swackhamer, a native of Vermont, was married in 1860 to W. Swackhamer. He died in 1877. Mrs. Swackhamer's post-office address is Pendleton Centre.

James Tripp is the son of Henry Tripp, a native of Pennsylvania, who settled in the town in 1825. He married Lydia Guthrie in 1826. Of a family of ten children all are scattered throughout the West, except James, who has settled on the old homestead on Beech Ridge. Post-office, Lockport.

THE TOWN OF PORTER.

THE early history of the territory embraced within the limits of this town is of national importance. The point of land extending out into the water at the mouth of the Niagara river has been the scene of events which have marked an era in the history of the world's commerce, and done much to shape the destinies of four nations—the French, the English, our own people and the tribes of savage aborigines whose wigwams were once erected in the shadows of the forests that bordered the lake and the river, in whose waters they paddled their primitive canoes. These events are too important for treatment in the history of a town, and have been detailed in the chapters of general history which precede this department of this work.

THE SETTLEMENT OF THE TOWN.

The modern history of the town of Porter dates back to the beginning of its general settlement, about the year 1800. Transient settlements were made at early periods by the French at Fort Niagara, but no permanent settlement was made until the beginning of the present century. John Lloyd, who had been a soldier, and a member of the garrison at Fort Niagara in 1799, settled about three miles from the fort, in 1801. After the war he became a resident of the farm near Peter Tower's known as the "Lloyd farm," and forming part of lot No. 27. The following are the names of those who took up or settled on the lands of the Holland Purchase within the boundaries of the present town of Porter from the commencement of land sales to the year 1807, the names being mentioned in the order in which the contracts were taken each year: 1803, Elijah Doty, John Waterhouse, Silas Hopkins, Peter Hopkins, Obadiah Hopkins, Conrad Zittle, Ephraim Hopkins, John Clemmons, Robert Bigger, James Benedict, and William McBride; 1804, Peter and Ephraim Hopkins took articles for more land, and the new comers were Samuel Hopkins, John Freeman and John Wilson; 1805, William Coggswell, Jonathan Jones, Abijah Perry and Samuel Shelly; 1806, Peter Ripson and John Brown. William McBride took up more land this year. A few of those just mentioned, among them Silas Hopkins, were not actual settlers, having taken up the land for purposes of speculation. Conrad Zittle, who was known among the early settlers as "Coonrod" Zittle, came from Lancaster county, Pa., and located at the place now known as "Zittle's Corners." John Brown, who was one of the early officers of the town, was called "Farmer John," afterward, to distinguish him from another John Brown, who built a mill and went by the name of "Steam-mill John." Abijah Perry was the father of William Perry, whose birth, August 11th, 1811, was the first that occurred in the town after general settlement begun, and who is the oldest person living in Porter who was born there. William Coggswell, who was probably a man of some educational attainments, taught the first school in Porter, in 1806, a year after he came. Jonathan Lutts came in 1806, and bought a farm of one hundred and sixty acres of the Holland Land Company. He improved it and continued a resident of the town for thirty years.

In 1808 Isaac Swain, who had previously settled on the Military road in Niagara, removed to the town of Porter and purchased eighty acres of land of John McBride, his purchase being the southern half of lot No. 3 of the Mile Reserve. This pioneer passed through many exciting adventures in the war of 1812. His sons, William and George, are well known citizens of the town at the present time. Jacob Lutts was the first settler on lot No. 22 of the Holland Purchase. He came from Wyoming county in 1808, driving his team the whole distance. His brother, Michael Lutts, came about the same time, and William Arbuthnot came before or during the war.

Owing to the same causes which impeded the progress of civilization along the frontier between the years 1812 and 1815, settlement was slow in the town during this period, only two settlers of importance in the history of Porter having come in 1814. These were Rudolph Clapsaddle and Joseph McCullum. Clapsaddle located on lot No. 4, and McCullum on lot No. 9, being the first settler on that lot. Afterward, Clapsaddle removed to the same lot, having his residence where Christopher Clapsaddle lives now. McCullum was originally from Pennsylvania, and he had lived for a while at Canandaigua. Another who settled in Porter at the close of the war was John Vrooman, with whose early life there is some history connected which has reference to this locality. He was stolen from Schoharie county by the Indians under Brant, during the Revolution, and brought to Two-mile creek, where he was kept in captivity a number of years. His grandmother and an aunt were killed at the time of his capture. He was rescued by some officers at the fort and sent to Montreal, from which place he subsequently made his way home, returning to Porter after the war of 1812 to take up a farm, upon which he continued to live during life. John McLoughlin came from Canada and settled in Porter in 1815. His son, James G. McLoughlin, was clerk to the sutler at Fort Niagara and was afterwards appointed sutler by Secretary Spencer.

Peter Tower came this year, accompanied by his brother Otis. The Tower brothers made their journey from Massachusetts with two horses and a wagon, and the trip consumed four weeks or more. At that time the town of Porter was a wilderness, with occasional choppings of three or four acres, where earlier settlers had erected their cabins. There were living within the present town limits at that time the following named persons, many of whom had families : John Lloyd, the widow of Dr. West, Elijah Doty, William Doty, Michael Helms, John Brown, Nathaniel McCormick, Conrad Zittle, Abijah Perry, Judge Hinman, —— Gilbert, Elijah Hathaway, widow Guernsett, Isaac Swain, —— Burton and others.

Peter Tower bought an article for one hundred acres of land of Conrad Zittle, and Otis became a pioneer farmer in Wilson. Michael Helms had become a resident of Porter before the war, and Mr. Tower lived in his family until his marriage, renting his land and employing himself at his trade as a carpenter. He was the first carpenter in the town, and his services were in good demand in all the country around. He was a cabinet-maker as well as a carpenter, and he made most of the coffins in which were buried those persons who died in this section in the early days. Mr. Tower early identified himself with the interests of the town. He caused to be opened and assisted to construct the first road east from Four-mile creek to the line of Cambria.

In 1816 William and John Clapsaddle came from Herkimer county, N. Y., and settled in Porter, the latter locating on lot No. 9. It is said that the journey was made with an ox team, which was the first ever driven attached to a wagon over the five miles of road between Youngstown and Four-mile creek. He built the first saw-mill and grist-mill in the town about the year 1817, and he was also the keeper of a pioneer tavern.

David Baker settled in Youngstown in the same year. After working there as carpenter for three years, he removed to that part of the town now known as Porter Center, and purchased a portion of a lot that had been articled to Gideon Curtiss, afterward receiving a deed for it from the Holland Land Company. The following year Gideon Curtiss came to Porter and took up land now comprised within the boundaries of the settlement known as Ransomville. He cut the first timber felled in that part of the town, and afterwards helped to lay out the main road through the village and the one from the ridge to the lake. Mr. Curtiss came from near Litchfield, Conn. G. W. Curtiss, a brother of Gideon, well known as Captain Gilbert W. Curtiss, came from Connecticut. He tried to make a clearing near that of his brother, but was unable to do so on account of the scarcity of provisions and money. It is related by a descendant of the captain that he had only one dollar in money, with which he went to Canada to purchase bread. After he had paid his ferriage across the river, he had only sufficient money left to buy two or three small loaves, with which he returned, and kept on with his attempts at clearing till he was obliged to stop from sheer want of necessary food, leave his land and engage to serve out a part of the time of a soldier at Fort Niagara. After a time, success so far crowned his efforts to establish a home in the wilderness, that he considered himself warranted by his circumstances in going back to Connecticut and marrying a girl to whom he had been betrothed before first leaving his native State. The bride and groom returned in a one-horse covered wagon of the old lumbering style. When they arrived at the ridge he was obliged to cut a road through the woods to the location of Ransomville, ahead of the vehicle which contained his bride and such of their meager domestic wealth as they could carry. Many times, when old age had whitened the captain's locks, he told the story of his bridal trip, and laughingly compared it to the luxurious and expensive tours of the newly wedded couples of to-day; and the contrast was not weakened by the fact that the journey of the bridegroom from Porter to Connecticut was made on foot. The captain was commander of a company under the old militia law, and from this fact originated the official title by which he was known through life. At the time the captain and Mrs. Curtis came from Connecticut they brought apple seeds, which he planted, transplanting the young trees afterward and starting an orchard, which is to be seen at the present time at the rear of the grain warehouse of his sons, the Curtiss Brothers, at Ransomville. From this primitive beginning has grown the fruit interest of the eastern portion of the town, now a source of considerable profit to the farmers there.

Among prominent settlers in the town between the years 1820 and 1830 the following are the names of some of the best known: Stephen Eaton, who settled on the farm now owned by his son, A. J. Eaton, about the year 1820; Charles Quade, who located sixty acres of lot No. 51, and was the first settler on said lot, and who in 1830 built a hotel at Quade's Corners, as the site of Ransomville was called at that time (Mrs. Quade had been a resident of Canada, her father's house being the only one not burned at the time of the destruction of Niagara by General McClure, May 27th, 1812); Jonathan Moss, who came from Vermont in 1823, and took up one hundred and eighty-six acres of land at the place since known as Moss's Corners, a mile and a half west of Ransomville; David Force, who settled on part of lot No. 26 in 1825; H. D. Jeffords (then ten years old), who came from Oswego county with his father in 1826 (Mr. Jeffords purchased of Richard Cuddaback the farm now owned by James Warren); Jehial C. S. Ransom, an uncle of W. H. H. Ransom, of Ransomville, a former resident of Ulster county, N. Y., who came into the town about this time, making the journey on foot (he was afterwards the first postmaster at Ransomville, which was named in his honor); L. C. Beals, William Kyte and John Hutchison, who came in 1829. J. B. Clark came with his family from Seneca county, in 1830, and settled in the town. His son, P. C. Clark, is a well known resident of Porter at the present time, owning a portion of lot 55, on the lake shore. Charles G. Willie settled on lot No. 11 during the following year. There was a log house on the ground, which had been erected by an earlier settler. Lyman Whittaker and Erastus Downer also became residents of the town in 1831. The former located on a farm owned by David Burge. He afterward removed to the farm of Ira Brown, from which place he again removed to lot No. 2, where he had purchased a piece of land. David Johnson and family came in 1832, and S. C. McCormick, accompanied by his father's family, came the same year. Among others who came in that year were William C. McCormick, John Robertson and David Johnson, all of whom were accompanied by their families. McCormick drove his teams from Northumberland county, Pa., by way of Williamsport, Painted Post, Batavia and Lockport, and soon after his arrival in Porter bought of James McCormick the place where he now resides. Robertson settled on part of lot No. 8 of the Holland Purchase, where his widow lives at the present time. His two sons, John and Christopher, live close by. Johnson located on lot No. 5, where there was no clearing at that time. He drove from Vermont, making the journey in fifteen days.

Chester Balcom, John Powley and William and John Whitfield came in 1834. Balcom, who had formerly resided in New England, settled on lot No. 46. His son, Milo C. Balcom, is an influential citizen and prominent business man of Youngstown. In company with his brother Edward, who came with him, John Powley purchased land of the Holland Land Company, his choice being part of lot No. 42. He is still a resident of the town. The Whitfields settled on lot No. 45. They came from Rochester. In 1836 James Warren came. He owns part of lot No. 6. Henry Balmer became a resident of the town during the same year, purchasing of Jesse Smith, a former settler, a portion of lot No. 42. George Kyle located on lot No. 1 of the Holland Purchase in 1837. Dayton G. Johnson and family settled on lot No. 5, and William Kyte, accompanied by Francis Kyte and other members of his family, on lot No. 52, in 1838. W. H. H. Ransom came to Ransomville from Sullivan county, N. Y., in 1839, and worked at the trade of carpenter and joiner for a number of years, and Thomas Simmons came during this year also.

During the next ten years several well known families settled in different parts of the town, prominent among whom may be mentioned the following: N. D. Mesler, from the town of Niagara, in 1840; Levi Brookins, in 1845; H. B. Timothy, in 1848; Robert Owen, in 1849, and Dr. A. G. Skinner, in 1850.

CIVIL HISTORY.

The town of Porter was formed from Cambria, June 1st, 1812. Wilson was taken off in 1818. It has been stated that the first town meeting for the town of Porter was held at the house of Peter Tower, in 1819. This would seem to have been true from an inspection of the books of record in the office of the town clerk; but there is an earlier record book of the town of Porter, to which access has been granted by courtesy of S. Park Baker, Esq., an attorney of Youngstown, which opens with a transcript of the "proceedings of the annual town meeting held in the town of Porter, on the 11th day of April, A.D. 1815." The minutes of the proceedings of one or two annual meetings, together with other entries, are to be found in this book, but they do not embrace a sufficient period to make an unbroken record to the date of the town meeting before mentioned as having taken place in 1819. It does not seem improbable that the war of 1812 might have prevented the regular order of town business previous to 1815; yet there is nothing in the records of the meeting of April 11th, 1815, to indicate that it was the first one ever held in the town, and the absence of records for two or three years previous to 1819 could scarcely be attributable to the same cause. The following is a copy of the minutes of the proceedings of the town meeting of April 11th, 1815:

"The following persons were chosen officers of said town, viz.:

"Dexter P. Sprague, supervisor; Elijah Hathaway, town clerk; Joseph Pease, Nathaniel McCormick and Thaddeus N. Sturges, assessors; Conrad Zittle and Zebulon Coats, overseers of the poor; Benjamin Kemp, John Martin and John Brown, commissioners of highways; David Porter, constable and collector; Thaddeus McIntyre, constable; Conrad Zittle and David Porter, pound keepers." For some reason unexplained by the records, it became necessary to supply the place of Dexter P. Sprague, as is attested by the following, which is a literal copy of the entry: "At a special town meeting of the town of Porter, held on the 20th day of June, A. D. 1815, was chosen Reuben Wilson, supervisor." Reuben Wilson was a prominent early resident of that portion of Porter which was afterwards erected into a separate town, taking its name from him—Wilson.

The proceedings of the town meeting of 1819, which has been several times described as the first town meeting in the town of Porter, appear in the records as follows:

"At a town meeting held at the house of Peter Tower the sixth day of April, 1819, Elijah Doty, Esq., justice of the peace, presided.

"The following persons were chosen officers for the ensuing year, viz.: Michael Helms, supervisor; Thomas Brown, town clerk; Jonathan Bell, George Ash and William Doty, assessors; John Dunlap, collector; Conrad Zittle and Daniel Kelly, overseers of the poor; Conrad Zittle, Daniel Kelly and Richard Cuddaback, commissioners of highways; Moses Barto, A. G. Hinman and John A. Hyde, commissioners of common schools; Jonathan Bell and Isaac Swain, inspectors of common schools; John Dunlap, constable; Daniel Kelly, pound keeper."

The following rules and regulations were adopted at the said meeting, viz.: It was provided that certain animals should not be permitted to run at large. "Any person having Canada thistles growing on the farm that he owns or possesses, and does not cut them off near the middle of June and the middle of August, shall forfeit the sum of five dollars, one half to the complainant and the other half to the use of the poor." The following sums of money were ordered to be raised for the purposes specified: For repairing roads and bridges, two hundred and fifty dollars; for the support of the poor, forty dollars; to build a pound in Youngstown, thirty dollars.

Fourteen path masters were chosen to have supervision of the different road districts.

Later, the following entry appears on the record:

"Mch. 4th, 1820. Settled all accounts between the towns of Porter and Wilson. Copy of certificate: 'This may certify that the supervisors and poor-masters (overseers of poor) of the towns of Porter and Wilson settled all accounts and divided all the money in the supervisors' and port-masters' hands, and made a final settlement according to the act.'

"(Signed,) REUBEN WILSON, } Supervisors.
MICHAEL HELMS, }
BURGOYNE KEMP, } Overseers of Poor.
CONRAD ZITTLE, }
THOMAS BROWN, Town Clerk."

The names of the present town officials, elected April 9th, 1878, are as follows:

Supervisor, Richard D. Balmer; town clerk, James P. Marshall; justices of the peace, Rensselaer Ward, N. D. Mesler, Warren Jackman, George D. Eaman; commissioner of highways, Samuel Baker; collector, Joseph Thompson; overseers of the poor, James Canfield, Richmond B. Johnson; constables, Frank L. Powley, John L. Whittaker, J. T. Warren, George W. Perry; assessors, John Kelly, Francis Kyte, William Swain.

PIONEERS AND EARLY EVENTS.

Interest always attaches to those who were earliest in different occupations or professions in any community. The first inn ever kept in the town of Porter was kept by Robert Guernsett where Youngstown now stands. Guernsett died, and his widow kept the inn open some time afterward. Colonel Hathaway, a well known early resident of the town, kept a tavern in a building on the ground now occupied by the Ontario House as early as 1815, and for some time afterward. There was a small grocery connected with it. Peter Tower opened his house for the accommodation of the public as early as 1818 or 1820. His residence and public house was then a small log building east of Youngstown, near the present dwelling. John Clapsaddle was also an early tavernkeeper in the town. The first tavern where Ransomville now is was opened by Captain Curtiss in 1825. There were several other houses of entertainment opened in different parts of the town in the early days, but those of which mention has been made were the best known. A man named Daggett, from the Mohawk country, had the first blacksmith's shop in Youngstown.

Dr. John A. Hyde, who came in 1818, was the first physician giving his attention to general practice, though there were surgeons at Fort Niagara at a very early day. One of the best known among them was Dr. West, who was stationed there about the time of the war. He died during or soon after the close of the war, and his family were residents of the town subsequently. A little north of the residence of Peter Tower lived an old woman named Woods. She was a widow who had devoted considerable time and trouble to the study of the medicinal qualities of roots, herbs and barks. She is said to have been quite successful in her treatment of some diseases, having been preferred by many of the pioneers to any other physician within reach. The first grave-yard in Porter, and one of the oldest in the United States, is the burying-ground at Fort Niagara. Interments were made there as early as 1687. Until 1759 it was the burial place of the French garrison, from that date until 1791 that of the English garrison, and since that period that of the American garrison. Here are buried those who fell in the siege of Fort Niagara in 1759, those who were killed in the war of 1812, and many who during all this time, running back through nearly two centuries, have died of disease. Judge De Veaux wrote of this burial place: "A few rods from the barrier gate of Fort Niagara was the burying ground. It was filled with memorials of the mutability and poverty of human life, and over the portal of entrance was painted in large and emphatic characters the word '*Rest*,' and this word *Rest*, in its relation to the ancient place of sepulture, formed the theme of a beautiful poem by the late William H. C. Hosmer, of Avon, New York."

The first mail carrier to the places on this part of the Holland Purchase was Philip Beach, who was employed about the beginning of this century to carry the mail from Fort Niagara to Batavia, traveling the route on foot and keeping his course by blazed trees. The bag contained letters principally, and was so small that he carried it in his coat pocket. From Canandaigua his route lay across the great bend of the "Tonewanta" to Tonewanta village, where he halted over night at the house of Poudrey, a Frenchman. Thnce he followed the Indian trail to the ridge, near Warren's Corners, and along the ridge to the "Landing," as Lewiston was then called, and thence along the old Military road to the fort. Such were the primitive mail facilities of the Holland Purchase, the settlement in Porter being one of the earliest served with a post delivery.

The first carpenter in the town was Peter Tower. The first school, taught in 1806, by William Coggswell, has been adverted to. This was opened in Yongstown. One of the earliest schools in the town outside of the village was kept in 1824, or 1825, in a log house at the end of Peter Tower's lot, by Sally Totten. The building had formerly served as a residence for the family of Philip McIntyre, who, previous to the time mentioned, had sold out to Mr. Tower and gone to Michigan. There were no public school-houses then. There was a tannery on lot No. 9 of the Mile Reserve at an early date. It was built before the war, and was owned by Burton & Son. Clapsaddle's grist-mill, erected in 1817, was the first mill built in the town. The water power is said to have been insufficient to keep it in operation more than two or three months in the year. It finally went out of use, and there was an interval of several years, during which the settlers were obliged to go to mill at Niargara Falls and down to the Eighteen-mile creek. The present large mill at Youngstown superseded it. The first store in the town of Porter was kept in Youngstown by John Young. Judge Hinman was the first postmaster at Youngstown.

The first religious services were held at the fort at an early date, but worship in the village or in the town was of rare occurrence previous to the organization of the Presbyterian church at Youngstown, in 1823. Judge Hinman often led in divine worship, holding meetings at the cabins of the early settlers, and at times there would be preaching by Methodist itinerants. After the erection of the first school-house in Youngstown, meetings were held there. At one time regular meetings were held in the school-house by a circuit preacher once in three weeks. The first saw-mill in the town of Porter was erected by John Clapsaddle, the builder and owner of the first grist-mill, about the time of the erection of the grist-mill. It has gone to decay.

INCIDENTS DURING AND AFTER THE WAR.

Although the leading events of the war of 1812 have been detailed in the general history of the frontier and the county, there are a few which properly belong to that department of our work which is devoted to a record of the historical characters and incidents of the town of Porter. No character of the early days is better remembered than Michael Lutts, and no narratives of danger and bloodshed in those adventurous times have been oftener referred to by the early settlers, than those of his implacable hatred and sanguinary vengeance upon the British for one of the greatest wrongs one man can suffer at the hands of another. Michael Lutts is represented by those who remember him as a man of more than ordinary domestic affection, and one uniformly kind and tender of heart, except toward those whom he knew or imagined to be related in some manner to those who had wronged him so deeply. While the British held Fort Niagara after its capture, a party of soldiers, members of the English garrison, went to the house of Lutts, not far distant, and brutally insulted and outraged Mrs. Lutts and her daughter, in the absence of the husband and father.

Lutts swore vengeance on the British soldiery, and for years devoted his life to a consummation of that oath. Soon after the occurrence first mentioned he sent his family down toward Rochester, where they remained until the establishment of amicable relations between the United States government and Great Britain, and the withdrawal of the English troops from our frontier. But Lutts remained, and, accompanied by his brother Jacob, who aided him in his work of death, was almost constantly roaming through the woods in the vicinity of the fort, watching for his victims. They would shoot a man in the British uniform on sight. When a gang of soldiers was detailed to chop wood, or for the performance of any other duty remote from the fort, it was necessary for them to post sentinels about them while they worked, to guard against an unexpected and deadly attack by the Lutts brothers. It is said that the sight of a red coat would throw Michael Lutts into a frenzy of uncontrollable anger, and no man's life was safe in his presence if he presented even a suggestive appearance of an English soldier. William Arbuthnot, an early settler, had rendered some service to the British officers in return for which they desired to shield him from an attack by their Indian allies. As a means of affording him this protection they gave him the coat of a British soldier to wear, with the assurance that it would insure him safety from the Indians; but it was the means of subjecting him to a danger as great as that from which he sought to escape. It is related that he barely escaped being shot by Lutts, while passing through the woods one day.

While the British held possession of the fort, Michael Lutts, John Lloyd and a man named Martin were at one time together in the timber about a mile east of the mouth of the river. Emerging upon a little cleared space on the lake shore, where an old log shanty stood which had long been empty, they heard sounds that indicated that some one was inside. Lutts approached the cabin cautiously, and peering through a chink in the wall saw a dozen English soldiers within, lying on the ground in various stages of intoxication. He informed his companions that he meant to kill them, and despite their expostulations and entreaties he went inside, and quickly shooting one or two who were in a condition to resist, fell upon the helpless soldiers with his knife, and killed them all before his companions had sufficiently recovered from their surprise to do anything to prevent the wholesale slaughter.

Early one midsummer morning the Lutts brothers came out through the woods to the bank of the river about midway between Youngstown and Fort Niagara. A Canadian vessel was lying at anchor out in the bay. There was but one man in sight on the vessel. He was in the uniform of a British officer, and was lying asleep on the deck. Michael Lutts raised his rifle, and taking deliberate aim at the unconscious officer shot him fatally. In a moment the brothers had gained the cover of the timber, and made good their escape before the men on board the vessel, who had been aroused by the report of the rifle, had ascended to the deck.

Many incidents of a similar character are related of Michael and Jacob Lutts. Others might be mentioned in this connection, but enough have been narrated to give the reader an idea of the persistency with which they prosecuted their work of vengeance. To suppose that they were permitted to hunt down and murder the soldiers of the British garrison without any opposition would be folly. Their lives were doubtless in danger often, but they were wily woodmen, well trained in all the tricks and make-shifts of border life, and in this respect doubtless had an advantage over the British soldiers. The hatred of the English by Michael Lutts lived while he lived. Years after the war the sudden appearance of a man in a red coat was sufficient to arouse in him the old insane desire for blood, and it is said of him that he gloried in his sanguinary achievements of the past, often referring to them with evident pride.

As late as 1828, an incident occurred that showed how strong was his ruling passion. The people of Youngstown had decided to celebrate the anniversary of our national independence in a fitting manner. No Fourth of July celebration would be complete without a cannon, and of course a cannon was brought into requisition on this occasion. It was planted on the river bank between the village and the fort, its muzzle pointed toward the village of Niagara, on the Canadian side. Of course it was intended to load it with powder and wads in the usual way, the report being the only object sought. In the process of loading the first time, Michael Lutts, who was present, was detected in an attempt to put a six-pound ball into the piece. He was prevented from carrying out his purpose, which he relinquished quite unwillingly, and only after much expostulation. "Put it in, boys!" he said, pointing toward the village across the river. "Give it to 'em! D—n 'em! Fire on 'em!"

Jacob Lutts rescued one of the three survivors after the surrender of Fort Niagara to the British. It is related of him that he saw him coming through the woods clad only in a bloody shirt. He had been bayonetted and left for dead. Mr. Lutts took him home, nursed him and cared for him till he was able to go to the hospital at Batavia.

The Lutts brothers remained in Porter until the end of their lives. They were well known and respected citizens. Harry Lutts, an enterprising farmer in the town, is the only survivor of the family of Jacob Lutts. Terrible as was the vengeance of Michael Lutts, there are few who will say that it was without commensurate provocation.

FACTS AND STATISTICS.

The town of Porter was named in honor of Judge Augustus Porter, of Niagara Falls. In 1814 the population of the town was only 148; in 1875 it had increased to 2,098. It is the northwest corner town of Niagara county, its western and northern boundaries being the Niagara river and Lake Ontario, and its eastern and southern boundaries the towns of Wilson and Lewiston. Its surface is level. Four-mile and Six-mile creeks and the west branch of Twelve-mile creek, cross the town in a northerly course, and some smaller creeks having their sources within its boundaries empty into the lake at its northern limit; and a short creek known as Two-mile Run rises in the western part of the town and empties into the Niagara river within the limits of the village of Youngstown.

There are within the boundaries of the town 19,050 acres of land, of which 14,711 are improved and 4,339 are unimproved. When the land was surveyed along the lake shore, about sixty years ago, an allowance of thirty or forty rods wide was made for the probable wearing away by constant contact with the water. To the present time this average diminution of area along the lake has been attained, the land having washed away in places to a distance of fifty or sixty rods. The land skirting the river has also been worn away to a considerable extent, the former site of the road from Youngstown to the fort now being under water, and other changes no less marked having been wrought almost imperceptibly through a considerable period of time.

The soil is generally a rich gravelly loam. A strip in the northern part of the town, on the lake shore, is a stiff clay, superior for wheat. The land in all parts of the town is excellent for crops of every kind. The principal grains are wheat and barley, but cereals of all sorts are extensively cultivated. Apples are a staple product, and peaches are successfully grown in some parts of the town.

According to the journal of the board of supervisors of Niagara county for the year 1877, the assessed valuation of property in Porter was $1,405,310, of which amount $1,333,310 was assessed on real estate and $72,000 on personal property. The total amount of tax was $9,424.77; $998 being school tax.

RANSOMVILLE.

The land where Ransomville stands was first occupied by Gideon Curtiss in 1817. He chopped the first clearing and erected the first log shanty at that place, and he afterwards kept the first tavern there, in a log building standing on the ground where Taylor Brothers' store burned a few years ago. His brother, Gilbert W. Curtiss, came in 1819. (An account of his journey and settlement has been given in the preceding pages.) In 1825 he opened a tavern in a log house which stood in front of the site of the present Ransomville House, his brother having given up tavern-keeping before that date; and in 1840 he built the Ransomville House, which he conducted to the time of his death, which occurred December 1st, 1868.

PRESENT BUSINESS ESTABLISHMENTS.

Since the death of Captain Curtiss the Ransomville House has been kept open by his sons, who, under the firm name of Curtiss Brothers, are well known business men of the village. In 1877 they erected a large grain warehouse, called the "Excelsior Elevator," on the track of the R. W. & O. R. R. This is one of the most sightly buildings in the place, being thirty by sixty feet in size, with twenty-four-foot posts, and having a storage capacity of at least 25,000 bushels. The Curtiss Brothers are doing an extensive and constantly increasing business in the purchase and shipment of wheat, barley and other kinds of grain. Their purchases in the early part of the year 1878 amounted to more than 20,000 bushels.

Prominent among the business men of Ransomville may be mentioned the firm of W. H. H. Ransom & Son. W. H. H. Ransom, who has been mentioned as having settled in Porter in 1839, is a nephew of Jehial C. S. Ransom, the first postmaster in the village, who came to Ransomville from Ulster county, on foot, about the year 1826, and for whom the village of Ransomville was named. The other member of the firm of W. H. H. Ransom &

Son is Elton T. Ransom, late supervisor of the town of Porter. The firm deal heavily in general merchandise and do considerable business in grain, having a side track on the R. W. & O. R. R., upon which they erected a substantial brick warehouse in 1877. The finest building in the village is the large brick store of W. H. H. Ransom & Son, which was built in 1872. The brick store building now owned by James Bullock was erected several years since by Messrs. Fowler & Harwick. A saw-mill was built some years ago by Joseph Fowler. It has been twice burned and rebuilt. It is now in the possession of James Bullock.

There are four general stores in Ransomville, those of W. H. H. Ransom & Son, James Bullock, G. I. Eaman and C. A. Barnes; two wagon shops, C. Sanger's and that of W. W. & H. H. Helms; four blacksmith shops; two dress-making and millinery establishments; a saw-mill and stave factory, owned by James Bullock; a lumber yard kept by James W. McCormick, and two or three physicians and a veterinary surgeon.

The village is on the line of the R. W. & O. R. R., and has a commodious and well appointed depot for a place of the size. Edward Dillingham is the local agent. The stage route from Lockport to Youngstown passes through Ransomville, and there is a baggage express between Ransomville and Youngstown. The present postmaster is Mr. G. I. Eaman.

The Union Cornet Band of Ransomville, under the leadership of Mr. W. A. Curtiss, is a fine musical organization.

CHURCHES.

There are three churches in the village, the Wesleyan, Baptist and the Free Methodist. The Baptist church of Ransomville was organized March 5th, 1834. The original membership was thirty-seven. The first pastor was Rev. Samuel J. Olney. Other clergymen who have served the church have been: Rev. William Sawyer, Rev. Benjamin Warren, Rev. Allan McDougal, Rev. Isaac C. Seely, Rev. Philander Reynolds, Rev. S. T. Thacher, Rev. John Gilchrist, Rev. Dutger Dox. The services of the church were held for several years in the school-house on Four-mile creek. The first meeting house was erected in 1840, and dedicated May 20th, 1841, Rev. Amos Tucker preaching the dedicatory sermon. The church was a wooden building, worth about $2,000. It was repaired and remodeled in 1870 at a cost of $1,800, and rededicated May 3rd, 1871, Rev. William Ruse preaching the sermon. The name of the original organization was the Porter Baptist Church. It was changed by act of Legislature in 1858.

The Free Methodist church of Ransomville was organized in 1860. The church edifice was erected in 1877. The present membership is sixty-seven. The pastor is Rev. William Ingleby. Data for the history of the Wesleyan church have not been received.

LODGES OF RANSOMVILLE.

Two secret societies have lodges in Ransomville, the Free Masons and the Good Templars.

Argentine Lodge, No. 441, I. O. G. T., was organized December 11th, 1877, with twenty-seven members. The first W.C.T. was E. B. Prudden. It is in a flourishing condition and is steadily gaining in numbers and influence

Ransomville Lodge, No. 551, F. and A. M. was chartered June 8th, 1865. The number of charter members was thirteen. The present membership is ninety-seven. The first W. M. was T. D. Miller. The present officers are as follows: W. M., R. D. Balmer; J. W., Allen Jeffery; secretary, T. D. Miller; J. D., Dudley Frink; S. M. C., T. Hewitt; S. W., W. A. Curtiss; treasurer, W. H. H. Ransom; S. D., James M. Foster; J. M. C., N. Bradley; organist, H. H. Helms; tiler, C. Brookins.

OTHER CHURCHES IN THE TOWN.

The M. E. church of Porter Center was organized in March, 1838, as the First M. E. Society of Zittle's Corners. The original number of members was forty. The first place of meeting was in the log school-house at Zittle's Corners, now Porter Center. The church edifice was erected in 1851, and dedicated January 14th, 1852, by Rev. Glezen Filmore. It is a wooden building, valued at $1,800. Commodious sheds were erected near the church in 1870 at a cost of about $600. The first pastor was Rev. William Buck. The present incumbent is Rev. Z. Hurd.

The M. E. church of the town of Porter is of early organization. The first class was formed about 1821, at the house of George Ash, who was the first pastor. The original members were fourteen in number. This church is on the Porter Center charge, and Rev. Z. Hurd is the present pastor. The church was erected in 1852, and dedicated by Rev. S. Seager, D.D. The first Sunday-school was established about 1835, with fifty scholars.

YOUNGSTOWN.

Youngstown is one of the oldest villages on the frontier, its proximity to Fort Niagara having influenced its early settlement. That this locality was early regarded as an important one is evident from the fact that at the establishment of the customs district of Niagara, in 1799, the port of entry was located at Fort Niagara, where it remained until its removal to Lewiston in 1811.

There was nothing more than a small settlement on the location of the present village at the time of its destruction by the British and Indians in December, 1813, and little of interest concerning Youngstown previous to the settlement after the war can be learned at this time. The widow Guernsett and Colonel Hathaway were early tavern keepers. The pioneer business man was John Young, of Niagara, Ontario. He is said to have been the proprietor of the first store in the village, besides being prominently identified with its early interests. The village was named in his honor. The pioneer physician, Dr. John A. Hyde, came in 1818. The first school ever taught in Porter was opened in Youngstown in 1806, by William Coggswell.

The following is a description of Youngstown in 1823:

DAVID BURGE

MRS. DAVID BURGE

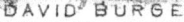
RESIDENCE OF DAVID BURGE ESQ. YOUNGSTOWN, NIAGARA CO., N.Y.

The woods grew down to the rear of the lots on Main street, and between this place and Lewiston the road passed through a forest that extended miles to the eastward and to the edge of the river on the west. There were not more than a dozen frame houses within the limits of the present corporation. There was only one store, which from the color of the building in which it was kept was called the "red store." It was conducted by two young men named Chittenden and Woodruff, but John Young furnished the merchandise, and the business was carried on in his interest. Of taverns there seems to have been more than the business of that time demanded, there being no less than three. The first was located at the north end of Main street and was kept by Phillips & Williams; the second, about midway of the street, was that of Colonel Elijah Hathaway, and the third, which stood at the south end of the street, was conducted by Robert Campbell. The accommodations were good for that day. There was one wagon shop and one blacksmith shop; the first being the property of two men named Squires and De Wolfe, and the second that of Nathaniel Brown. Judge A. G. Hinman was the postmaster, the post-office being in his house, near the center of the settlement. Mail arrived daily by stage from Lewiston and points east and south.

Gordon Davis came from Connecticut in 1823, and soon established himself in Youngstown in the shoe and leather business. Mr. David Burge, who came from New Hampshire during the same year, subsequently entered into partnership with Mr. Davis. They added such other merchandise to their stock as was necessary to the early settlers, and did a flourishing business for a number of years. In the year 1830, Mr. Davis retired from business, leaving it to the management of Mr. Burge, who became sole proprietor not long afterward. There were very few shoemakers at that time, and Mr. Burge did a somewhat extensive business, supplying the people of the surrounding country with much merchandise for a number of years, his trade, which was by no means restricted to the town of Porter, extending ten or fifteen miles to the east and south. After his retirement, Mr. Davis did not engage in any business. His health being poor, he spent his winters in the South. While on his way north in June, 1849, the steamer on which he had taken passage was wrecked on the Gulf coast, exposing him to the vicissitudes of the weather and bringing on an attack which terminated in his death.

Jason Davis, a brother of Gordon Davis, and his sons, Bradley D. Davis and Nelson R. Davis, came in 1835. They had come to Lewiston in 1830, remaining there one year and then returning to New Hampshire. Soon after their arrival at Youngstown, Jason Davis and Bradley D. Davis opened a grocery. B. D. Davis went to New York to purchase the stock, carrying $2,500 in United States bank bills, secreted in each of his stockings as a measure of safety, the facilities for exchange at that time being limited, and going to Rochester by stage and from there to New York by way of the Erie Canal. The firm of J. Davis & Son did a successful business in general merchandise for about twenty years, when the partnership was terminated by the death of Mr. Davis, sen. Since that time the business has been conducted by Bradley D. Davis until quite recently, when the style of the firm was changed to B. D. Davis & Co., in consequence of Mr. Davis's admission to partnership of a young man in his employ. W. H. Doyle, another prominent business man of the village, settled in the place in 1835. A. Emerson, a leading merchant, has been a resident of the village for half a century. Alexander Barton came to Youngstown in 1823, and Ira Race in 1826. The former worked as a painter till 1840, when he embarked as a hotel keeper, remaining in the business ever since. Mr. Race was a farmer till 1833. In that year he was chosen deputy sheriff, which position he held four years. He has filled the position of deputy collector of customs at the port of Youngstown, and has been a justice of the peace for many years. He has been called to other official positions at different times, and is a well known resident of the village. Another of the well-remembered early residents of Youngstown was ex-Sheriff Phillips, who, with his son, came to the village from Monroe county. Mr. Phillips became the first anti-masonic sheriff of Niagara county. He was at one time proprietor of the Ontario House. His son, Thomas Phillips, afterwards purchased a portion of lot No. 31 of the Holland Land Company, and became a resident of the town of Porter.

A man of more than local celebrity, for many years a resident of Youngstown, was Edward Giddings, who deserves more than a passing notice here. He was a native of New England, having been born in Connecticut in 1785. At the commencement of the last war with Great Britain he enlisted, and served until peace was declared. He was promoted to the grade of sergeant near the close of the war, but owing to its unexpected termination he did not receive his commission. After the war he was appointed keeper of the light-house at Youngstown, and placed in charge of the fort and military stores. At the time of the excitement in consequence of the alleged murder of William Morgan, he took such part as his conscience dictated, making revelations of transactions that came under his observation. Through his connection with this celebrated affair his name became widely known. Subsequently he removed to Lockport, where he remained until August, 1861, when he was again appointed keeper of the light-house at Youngstown. For several years in succession he issued an almanac, which bore the impress of his originality and exhibited his varied and extensive knowledge, and for a year or more he was editor of the *Niagara Courier*. He died at Youngstown, April 21st, 1862.

BUSINESS, PAST AND PRESENT.

A brief mention of the causes to which the village owes its prosperity in the past, and its business standing at the present time, cannot fail to be interesting in this connection. In the early days the business of lumbering was the most important interest in this section. The cutting down of the oak timber on the new lands, and its manufacture into staves and square timber, which were shipped *via* the lake to Montreal, from which place much of the timber was re-shipped to England for use in ship-building, afforded about the only means of livelihood to many of the settlers, and constituted the most prominent commercial interest of the place for some years. About 1830, a wheat market was established at Oswego, making sale for such quantities of that grain as were raised in the vicinity at that time, and providing an incentive to the settlers to improve their land and engage in farming as extensively as possible; and from that date down to the present there has been a gradual growth in the value of lands and the amount of produce. The leading merchants of Youngstown deal extensively in all kinds of grain and fruit, and the home market of the farmers and fruit-growers, whose trade centers at that place, is second to none in the county. The following figures exhibit the amount of traffic in fruit at this point: Nearly 30,000 barrels of apples are shipped per annum, and in 1877 10,000 baskets of peaches were shipped.

Considerable business has been, and is still, done in the manufacture and shipment of flour. The stone grist-mill was erected in 1840 by Hezekiah H. Smith. It was burned on the night of February 22nd, 1851, and soon afterward repaired. From this time it was operated by Jason and N. R. Davis, until the death of the former. It was subsequently controlled till 1871 by N. R. Davis. At that date it passed into the hands of B. D. Davis, who has since controlled it. The present lessee is Mr. W. D. Clark, who is also the owner of the machinery. This mill has done a very extensive business.

The principal merchants of the village are B. D. Davis & Co., W. H. Doyle & Co., and Alfred Emerson & Co., all of whom combine the purchase and shipment of grain and fruit with their trade in general merchandise.

The prominent manufacturers are William Ripson & Co., foundrymen; D. & J. Onen, manufacturers of barrels, and Jackman & Holden, manufacturers of cider and vinegar. The last mentioned firm buy apples in large quantities.

Another branch of enterprise not already mentioned is the fishing interest. Considerable business has been done during a few years past in the sale of fish, which are caught in large quantities in the Niagara river. They abound in great numbers, the different species being those common to Lake Ontario and other fresh water lakes and large rivers throughout the Union.

The village is well supplied with wagon, blacksmith, boot and shoe and other shops, and there are a number of smaller stores and groceries not designated above. The ferry at this place is managed by Mr. James P. Marshall, who owns the boats and other facilities for carrying on the business.

What the village most needs to assure its permanent prosperity is good railway communication with the markets of the outside world. Once this advantage seemed almost within reach; but owing to numerous causes, too well understood to require mention in this connection, the Niagara Falls and Lake Ontario Railroad was abandoned, and the track taken up soon after its completion.

The line of steamers which plied between Ogdensburg and Lewiston, in former years, touched at Youngstown, which was an important landing. These steamers will be remembered by the older residents of the village. They were the "Ontario," the "Cataract," the "New York" and the "Northerner." They began to run about 1845, and the business was continued until some time in 1856 or 1857.

BUILDING, AND VICISSITUDES BY FIRE AND FLOOD.

The first school-house built in the village was erected about 1823 or 1824. It was subsequently removed to give place to the substantial brick school building of the present day. The original structure is now occupied as a dwelling.

The stone hotel at the corner of Main and Lockport streets was erected by Alexander Lane in 1842, on the ground formerly occupied by the old Hathaway tavern. This hotel subsequently became the property of Robert McKnight, and is owned by his heirs at the present time. The hotel is known as the Ontario House, and under its present manager, Mr. H. C. Root, enjoys a liberal patronage.

The large brick block owned and occupied by B. D. Davis & Co. was erected in 1855. It is the finest business block in the village. The saw-mill on Second street was built by W. D. Clark in 1866. "Pickwick Hall," a large building used for dramatic and other public entertainments, is made up of several old buildings, one of which is that in which Judge Hinman kept the post-office in the pioneer times, and it stands as a silent but expressive link between the past and the present.

The dates of the erection of the several church edifices in the village are given elsewhere.

Youngstown has suffered considerably both by fire and flood. There have been, at different periods, a number of destructive ice-jams in the Niagara river, which have done much damage to the steamboat landings and the buildings near the water's edge, at the villages on its banks. One of the most notable of these ice floods occurred in 1844, filling the river from shore to shore and damming the water, which raised the masses of broken ice, piling it up, in places, as high as twenty or twenty-five feet, and crushing away the wharves and store houses at Youngstown and otherwise seriously damaging boats, buildings and other exposed property. A few days later a road for sleighs was made across the blockade of ice by the people of the village, which was used as a safe and convenient public highway between the American shore and Canada for two weeks or more, entirely doing away, for the time being, with all necessity for a ferry at that point.

The destruction of the village by the British and Indians on the 19th of December, 1813, and the burning of the grist-mill, February 22nd, 1851, have been mentioned elsewhere. On the night of April 19th and 20th, 1863, occurred a sweeping fire, the effects of which were felt

RESIDENCE & PROPERTY OF B. D. DAVIS, ESQ. YOUNGSTOWN, NIAGARA CO. N. Y.

FARM RESIDENCE OF E. HARMONY, ESQ. CAMBRIA TOWN, NIAGARA CO., N. Y.

for some time. A number of valuable buildings were consumed, among them Ontario Hall, Barton's Hotel, Connor's Hotel and the old McKnight tavern. Barton's present hotel was built on the site of the one destroyed. Connor's residence occupies the ground where his hotel stood, and the old McKnight property was not rebuilt, the proprietors having previously come into possession of the Ontario House. At different times other fires have visited the village, but none as destructive as this.

SOCIAL AND RELIGIOUS PROGRESS.

In the early days of the history of Youngstown the society seems to have been of a rude order. The men who went about the streets were watermen and discharged soldiers, whose time was largely devoted to drinking, gambling, horse-racing and kindred amusements. There were no churches, schools were illy encouraged, and in no less than three out of the dozen or so of frame buildings in the village liquor was sold freely to all who could pay for it, and its comparative cheapness at that time placed it within the reach of all, old and young. Perhaps it is true that this aspect of society is not peculiar to Youngstown in its pioneer days. The traveler through the new States and territories of the West will find the same conditions prevailing in the frontier settlements there. But this does not elevate the primitive social status of Youngstown, and besides the evils already mentioned it is said that some of its citizens carried on a regular and systematic trade in smuggling across the river.

There is said to have been only one man in the place during a great part of the first quarter of the present century who had any settled religious convictions and who did not hesitate to avow them. That man was A. G. Hinman, who seems to have been a very useful man, raised up especially to meet the exigencies of the time and place. He was postmaster, custom-house officer, town clerk and justice of the peace, and he went by the title of "Deacon" or "Judge" Hinman, at the fancy of the speaker, the first designation having been given him on account of his religious sentiments and the other from the fact that in the performance of his duties as magistrate, he was obliged to decide upon the respective merits of the claims of his neighbors. He was about the only man in the settlement who "remembered the Sabbath day to keep it holy." With many of his fellow citizens it was a day set apart for hunting, fishing, drinking, wrestling, jumping and general amusement.

Previous to 1823 there had been no religious services held at Youngstown, except occasionally by Methodist itinerants. In a sermon prepared by Rev. John Reid, pastor of the Presbyterian church of Youngstown, and delivered September 10th, 1876, to which the writer is largely indebted for the facts which appear in this department of the history of the village, it is stated that a preacher named Everett came along in the year 1823, and finding there a few persons, most of them women, who were inclined to form a religious society, appointed a meeting at the house of Judge Hinman for the purpose of effecting an organization, which was attended by those who had promised their aid; and the purposes for which they had met were carried out with appropriate religious observances. The little church thus planted in the wilderness had no pastor for some time, but its members met as "two or three gathered together in the name of the Lord," at the dwelling of some one of their number, as often as practicable, to sing and to pray, to exchange christian testimony and to listen to the reading of a sermon by Judge Hinman. At times others would take charge of the meetings, but he was the most faithful, the most untiring and reliable of the male members.

After the school-house was built, services were held there, and from time to time the people of the village were afforded opportunities to listen to sermons delivered by traveling Methodist preachers on their tours through the county, and for a while a circuit preacher held meetings in the school-house once in three weeks. A Sunday-school was started, in time, with Judge Hinman as superintendent and principal teacher. Of course the attendance was small at first. The population of the village was not large enough to insure a large school. An interest in the Sunday-school was induced; prominent men in the settlement began to drop in to the meetings at the school-house; in time some of them, Dr. Hyde among the number, occasionally took part in the services. The doctor would sometimes read a sermon and conduct the meetings in the absence of Judge Hinman. He was a man of ability and of exemplary character, though not a christian. In time he became identified with the society, as did Gordon Davis, David Burge, Hezekiah H. Smith and others. These men were influential citizens—they were the most prominent business men of the place, and their example was not without due weight and influence. Gradually—perhaps almost imperceptibly at first—but surely, the social and moral condition of the village improved. The Sabbath was respected, at first out of fear of public censure, after the inauguration of the new condition of things, and afterward because it was the Sabbath; the loose habits of the men began to improve, the inflowing tide of enterprise diverted their minds from their coarse amusements, and what had been once a place with a bad name began to take on the appearance and win the name of an enterprising and flourishing village. And from such a beginning and with such instrumentalities has grown the creditable social and religious sentiment of the present day.

CIVIL HISTORY.

Youngstown is pleasantly situated on the American shore of the Niagara river, about a mile from its mouth. In plain view from the village are Fort Niagara, on the point of land between the river and Lake Ontario, and the Canadian village of Niagara, across the river. The village was incorporated April 18th, 1854. The petitioners for incorporation were: Ira Race, A. G. Skinner, W. H. Doyle and L. P. Babcock. The limits of the village include lots No. 1 and No. 2, and parts of No. 3 and No. 4 of the Mile Reserve, with an area of four hundred and twenty-five acres.

The first village election occurred on the 4th day of October, 1854, at which time the following named officers were chosen:

President, George Swain; trustees, George Swain, Samuel Fosdick, Nelson R. Davis, Lewis C. Beals and Alfred Emerson; clerk, S. Olney; assessor, David Burge; collector, Paul Durfee; treasurer, George C. Hotchkiss; poundmaster, John Hart.

The present board of trustees is as follows: Joseph Thompson, Frank Powley, Joseph Onen, Byron W. Moore and Norton Porter. The present clerk is N. D. Haskell; C. S. Spencer, treasurer; P. G. Barton, collector; William Hutchinson, L. C. Beals and J. P. Marshall, assessors; John Hart, poundmaster.

THE PROFESSIONAL LIST OF YOUNGSTOWN.

Attorney, S. P. Baker; physicians, A. G. Skinner, M. D., William J. Falkner, M. D., and F. J. Baker, M. D.

OFFICERS OF THE GARRISON OF FORT NIAGARA.

General G. A. De Russy; Captain J. L. Tiernon; First Lieutenant Edward Davis; Second Lieutenant Charles Sellmer; Doctor C. L. Heizmann. The number of privates stationed at the fort at the present time is about forty-five.

HISTORY OF THE CHURCHES OF YOUNGSTOWN.

The First Presbyterian Church of Porter was organized in Youngstown in 1823, with the following original members: Mr. and Mrs. Bartol, Mr. Kelly, Mrs. Lutts, Mrs. McCormick, Mrs. Rebecca Hathaway and her daughter Pauline, and Judge A. G. Hinman. The early meetings were held in the houses of the members. After the erection of the school-house it was used by the society as a place of worship. The church was organized under the leadership of Rev. Mr. Everett. The succeeding clergymen who have officiated in the early days and at a later period were: Rev. E. H. Stratton, Rev. John Elliott, Rev. R. L. Hurlburt, Rev. T. J. Hodgekin, Rev. Hiram Gregg, Rev. Josiah Partington, Rev. Charles Burdick, Rev. Edwin Hall and Rev. John Reid, who is the present pastor.

The erection of the church edifice was begun in 1836. The building committee were: Hezekiah H. Smith, Obed Smith, John A. Hyde, Gordon Davis and David Burge. The contractor was Samuel Chubbuck. The church was completed in 1837 at a total cost of $2,600. It was dedicated September 10th, 1837, President Mahan, of Oberlin College, officiating. The constantly increasing interest in the church, and its growing membership, necessitated the enlargement of the edifice as soon as 1844, when two dozen extra slips were put in and the steeple built.

The number of members at the present time is about one hundred and forty, and the church is progressing spiritually and financially.

St. John's Episcopal Church was organized on the 27th of October, 1868, when the following named persons met at the brick church in Youngstown, pursuant to a notice duly given, for the purpose of incorporating themselves as a religious society, under the acts of the Legislature of the State of New York: Benjamin M. Root, Thomas Balmer, John Carter, N. E. G. Wadhams, Francis Powley, Charles M. Pyne, S. Park Baker, Lewis Leffman and Robert Patterson.

The original officers were as follows: Wardens, Benjamin M. Root, John Carter; vestrymen, Charles M. Pyne, S. Park Baker, Lewis Leffman, James S. Lawrence, Francis O. Dee, Thomas Balmer, William Mendham, Robert Patterson. The first rector was Rev. G. M. Skinner. The first delegates to the diocesan convention were Charles M. Pyne and John Carter.

St. John's parish, having no church building, remained for a number of years without a rector; but in the winter of 1878 a new interest was developed, mainly through the efforts and influence of General G. A. De Russy and Lieutenant Edward Davis, of Fort Niagara. Regular services were again instituted, conducted by Rev. G. H. Patterson, president of De Veaux College, Suspension Bridge, and his assistants, Rev. J. W. Craig and Rev. G. S. Pine, and steps were taken to build a church.

Sergeant Lewis Leffman, a veteran of Waterloo, and for many years past an ordnance sergeant at Fort Niagara, a devoted churchman and generous hearted man, donated a lot for the church, and in a few weeks about $1,500 was subscribed towards a building fund; and under the energetic and efficient management of a building committee composed of Lieutenant Davis and Messrs. Thomas Brighton and William Ripson, a beautiful and commodious church was shortly completed and opened for divine worship. The present church wardens and vestry of the parish are: General G. A. De Russy and John Carter, wardens; and S. Park Baker, Sergeant Lewis Leffman, Thomas Brighton, Edward Calvert, Peter S. Tower, William Ripson, Henry C. Root and William Mendham, vestrymen.

The Catholic church of Youngstown was organized some time ago. The chapel was instituted about 1830. There is no resident pastor. The services have been led by priests from the Seminary of Our Lady of Angels, Suspension Bridge, or by the pastor of the church at Lewiston, with which charge this has been connected.

The first regular organization of the Methodist Episcopal Church of Youngstown was effected June 29th, 1852, with a membership of twenty. Until 1854 the meetings were held in the school-house. The erection of the church was begun in 1853, and it was dedicated about the first of August, 1854; the cost, including the price of the lot, being $3,500.

The division of 1860 in the Methodist church which prevailed to some extent throughout the Union, was painfully felt on this charge. A debt still remaining on the church, it was sold at auction for $1,000, Mr. John Carter, a member and trustee of the society, being the purchaser with the intention of permitting its continued use as a place of worship. From this time until 1869, there was regular preaching by different pastors; but the

RES. & PROPERTY OF H. B. TIMOTHY, ESQ. RANSOMVILLE, TOWN OF PORTER, NIAGARA CO., N.Y.

charge was finally given up and no stated services held. In July, 1872, Rev. William C. Wilbor, then a local preacher, began to hold regular meetings in the church, and in October of that year, when the Western New York Conference met for the first time at Rochester, Youngstown and Porter Center churches, which had formerly belonged to one charge, were re-united; but they were again separated by the conference in October, 1876. During that year Mr. Carter deeded the building back to the society, with the stipulation that an amount equivalent to his claim (between $400 and $500) should be expended in repairs upon it. Alterations and improvements were made on the edifice to the value of $800, putting it in a good condition. It was re-opened May 8th, 1877. The present pastor in charge is Rev. W. H. Barnhardt.

A HURRICANE.

As dates are remembered, in 1856 a tempest of wind passed through a belt of country about two miles wide in the town of Porter, eastern part of Lewiston and western part of Cambria. The direction of the wind was from northwest to southeast. A large amount of damage was experienced, the storm prostrating acres of forests, parts of orchards, buildings and fences. On the farm of Mr. Cornell twenty-five acres of heavy timber was laid in promiscuous piles. The wind in some cases tore up trees, the roots of which were anchored under rocks from one thousand to two thousand pounds in weight. Cattle and horses drifted before the wind as if forced by a wave of the sea, over fields without the obstruction of fences. The barn of Colonel Dickerson was unroofed; also Sheldon Townsend's, whose orchard was uprooted and timber blown down.

SKETCHES OF PROMINENT RESIDENTS AND PIONEERS.

H. B. TIMOTHY.

H. B. Timothy was born at Williamstown, Berkshire county, Mass., on the 22nd of November, 1812. He is the son of Elkanah and Clarissa Timothy, who were originally from Hampshire county, in the same State. Mr. Timothy remained with his parents until 1827, when he went to Cummington, in his native State, and engaged as an apprentice in the manufacture of broadcloth, under the supervision of Theophilus and Chester Packard. In this position he remained six years, when, having become proficient in the business, he received the position of overseer. From Cummington he went to Glenham, Dutchess county, N. Y., and engaged as overseer in the finishing department of the same business, for Peter H. Schenck. He had twenty-three hands under his supervision, and remained there two years. From there he went to Pittsfield, Mass., and engaged with D. Pomeroy & Co., as overseer in making broad and narrow cloths, having twenty-one hands under him. At the end of seventeen months he removed to Millbury, Mass., and engaged with Colonel Sheppard in the manufacture of broadcloth. He was overseer in the finishing department two years, and then went to Oxford, in the same State, and engaged with E. Denny & Co., in the same business. He remained there three years, and next removed to Northfield, Vt., and engaged with the Northfield Manufacturing Company in the same business, with twenty-five hands under him. He remained with that company three years, and then went to Barre, Mass., and again engaged with Mr. Denny, who had transferred his business from Oxford to that point. From there he went to Utica, N. Y., and engaged in the Globe Mills, which turned out five hundred yards of broadcloth daily. There he remained one year.

In 1835 Mr. Timothy, while visiting his father in the town of Porter, purchased some land there, and at a subsequent time another tract, making in the aggregate 125½ acres. On the 10th of November, 1844, he was married to Miss Louisa, daughter of Elijah and Anna Smith, of Northfield, Vt. In the spring of 1847 Mrs. Timothy came and located on the farm which her husband had purchased and commenced farming, while he was yet engaged at his occupation as overseer in the Globe Mills at Utica. In the following year Mr. Timothy, having concluded to abandon the manufacturing business, retired to his farm, where he still remains in the quiet pursuit of agriculture. In 1859 he purchased of David P. Allen 124½ acres of land adjoining what he already owned, making a homestead of 250 acres.

Mr. Timothy has had six children, five of whom are still living: one daughter married and residing at Montpelier, Vt. As will be seen, Mr. Timothy is now 66 years of age. He has until quite recently enjoyed excellent health; of late he has been afflicted with a disease of the kidneys, but previous to that never lost a day's time in consequence of ill health. He has a remarkably good memory, reciting the events of his life clearly and precisely.

PETER TOWER.

Peter Tower was born in Cummington, Mass., July 10th, 1791. He came to Niagara county in 1815, and settled in the town of Porter, having lived two years previously in Clinton, Oneida county. Previous to his departure from Massachusetts Mr. Tower had learned the carpenter's trade. After his arrival in Niagara county he did a good many jobs in different places, building a hopper in Porter's grist-mill at Niagara Falls, and houses at Eighteen-mile creek and elsewhere. He also worked some time in Canada. Mr. Tower was married April 5th, 1819, to Hannah Bailey. Mrs. Tower died December 29th, 1831, and Mr. Tower was married June 13th, 1833, to Olive Baldwin Smith. By his first wife he had six children, by his present wife seven. Nine of the number are living. Most of them have married, and Mr. Tower has lived to have sixty-three grandchildren born, of whom fifty are living. Mr. Tower has always commanded the respect of his fellow-townsmen, having been chosen to a number of responsible offices. He was highway commissioner ten or twelve years, and for several years he had charge of the government lands about Fort Niagara, it being his duty to prevent persons from trespassing on them and cutting the timber or otherwise injuring them. William Morgan, of masonic fame, was once an inmate of Mr. Tower's house, and he entertained for him the warmest personal regard. Mr. Tower was much interested in his behalf at the time of his arrest and disappearance, and has ever since been an active anti-mason. Though he has attained to an advanced age, he appears hale and happy, and takes a lively interest in passing events. His post-office address is Youngstown.

David C. Baker was born in Porter, November 9th, 1821. April 24th, 1849, he was married to Delia H. Cobb, and they have three sons and one daughter now living. Mr. Baker is the proprietor of a fine farm of one hundred and seventy-five acres, at Porter Center. His post-office address is Youngstown.

F. J. Baker, M.D., of Youngstown, was born July 18th, 1843, in the town of Andover, Allegany county, N. Y. In 1862 he entered college at Lima, N. Y., but was called home before completing the course. A year later he began the study of medicine, and graduated from the medical department of the New York University in the spring of 1867. Since that time he has been actively engaged in the practice of his profession, the greater part of the time in Andover, N. Y., having spent, besides, about a year at Suffern, N. Y., and a year and a half in Buffalo. He became a resident of Youngstown October 3d, 1877. Dr. Baker is a member of the Allegany County Medical Society, the Buffalo Medical Association, the Hornellsville Academy of Medicine and the Erie County Medical Society, and an occasional contributor to a number of medical journals and of papers before the several societies. His standing as a physician is first-class, and he is a member of the Presbyterian church of Youngstown.

Horace M. Baker was born in Porter, February 17th, 1839, and married in 1865 to Miss Elizabeth Whitefield. Mr. Baker is a farmer, being proprietor of about one hundred and forty acres of land. He has spent about two years in travel. His post-office address is Ransomville.

S. Park Baker was born March 28th, 1832, at West Monroe, Oswego county, N. Y. October 21st, 1858, he was married to Ada C. Bentley, of Constantia, Oswego county. He removed to Youngstown, N. Y., May 16th, 1857, where he has since been engaged in the practice of his profession, as attorney at law, and in horticultural pursuits.

Milo C. Balcom was born in Vermont in 1825. In January, 1853, he was married to Miss Laura A. Johnson. Mr. Balcom is a farmer, and a dealer in agricultural implements. His post-office address is Youngstown.

Henry Balmer was born in Ireland. He came to America in 1832. In 1836 he purchased the farm where he now resides. He was married in 1838 to Eleanor Mack. Post-office address, Ransomville.

Silas Barrett, one of the oldest residents of the town of Porter, was born in Hinsdale, N. H., in 1789. He has been a citizen of the village of Youngstown for many years.

Frank G. Barton, son of Alexander and Elizabeth Barton, was born at Youngstown, March 27th, 1852. He has been engaged in business at Youngstown as a merchant since 1869, with the exception of two years, during which he was employed as a commercial agent by a firm in Cincinnati, O. November 28th, 1877, he was married to Miss Ida Emerson.

Levi Brookins was born June 3rd, 1826, in Montgomery county, N. Y. He came to Porter in April, 1845, and was married to Miss Caroline Simmons, November 19th, 1851. Mr. Brookins, who is a member of the Methodist church, is the recording steward of the East Porter organization, and has been elected to several town offices. Post-office, Ransomville.

David Burge, Youngstown, was born in Alstead, N. H., in 1799, and came to Youngstown, N. Y., August 23rd, 1823. He engaged in the shoe and leather trade in partnership with Gordon Davis, and in 1830 succeeded him in the management of the business. In 1829 Mr. Burge was married to Miss Sophronia Davis. In 1832 Mrs. Burge died of cholera. One son, Francis J. Burge (now in California), was the issue of that marriage. Mr. Burge married in 1834 Miss Susan Ladd. Four children were the result of this second marriage, two of whom died in infancy. The surviving two are S. Amanda, who resides in California, and Marion L. who remains with her father to comfort his declining years. Mrs. Burge died January 16th, 1876, at the age of seventy-six. Mr. Burge retired from the shoe and leather trade in 1843 and engaged in farming, which he followed till his final retirement from business, since which event he has traveled considerably in the South and West. During his long residence in Youngstown Mr. Burge has been repeatedly chosen to offices of responsibility. His life has been spent in active business, in which he has acquired a competency. He has been a christian during the greater portion of his active career, having united with the Presbyterian church on profession of his faith in 1838.

Abram S. Canfield, farmer (post-office Youngstown), was born in the town of Lewiston June 9th, 1839, and removed to Porter soon after. He served in the army during the rebellion. September 16th, 1868, he was married to Miss Frank Moss, of Porter.

John Carter, builder, Youngstown, was born at Tooley Park, Leicestershire, England, November 1st, 1814. He came to Buffalo in 1832, and from there to Youngstown in 1840.

P. C. Clark, farmer (post-office Ransomville), was born in Seneca county, N. Y., November 11th, 1820, and came to Porter with his father in 1830. In 1850 he married Ann Dawson. She died in 1863, and in 1866 or 1867 he married her sister, Margaret Dawson. Mr. Clark has one hundred acres of land, valued at $7,000.

W. D. Clark was born in the town of Lumberland, Sullivan county, in June, 1820. He came to Youngstown in 1823. He was married December 11th, 1845, to Miss Sarah E. Chubbuck, of Youngstown. For a number of years Mr. Clark has been engaged in the milling business. He is the present lessee and operator of the large stone flouring mill at Youngstown.

FARM RESIDENCES OF PETER TOWER SENR.-LUKE & P. S. TOWER, TOWN OF PORTER, NIAGARA CO., N. Y.

Daniel W. Cuddaback, farmer (post-office Ransomville), was born in Porter in 1831. He was married in 1856, to Miss Sarah Gaskill. Mr. Cuddaback has remained on his father's old homestead, consisting of about seventy-three acres.

W. A. Curtiss was born November 7th, 1843, and married October 20th, 1870, to Miss Celeia G. Ward, of Newfane. Curtiss Brothers do an extensive business in grain and general farm produce. They are proprietors of the "Excelsior Elevator," at Ransomville.

John J. Curtiss was born at Ransomville, May 14th, 1846. In 1874 he married Miss Emma Pierce. He is the proprietor of a farm at Ransomville, which he cultivates succesfully.

Lieutenant Edward Davis was born at Louisville, Ky., July 7th, 1845, and received common school education in his native city. In 1862 he joined the 5th Kentucky cavalry volunteers as a lieutenant, and served fifteen months as a staff officer of General R. M. Johnson. In 1863 he reported at the U. S. Military Academy, West Point, N. Y., as a cadet, by the appointment of President Lincoln, upon the application of Major-General W. S. Rosecrans, and graduated in June, 1867. Subsequently he served at different posts until April, 1875. On the first of May of that year, he entered the artillery school at Fort Monroe, Va., where his class of lieutenants of artillery was graduated. He came to Fort Niagara in May, 1876, where he has remained since, except while absent during the election troubles in the South and the labor riots of 1877. Lieutenant Davis was married September 18th, 1867, to Margaret Davis, of Washington, D. C.

General G. A. De Russy; post-office address, Youngstown. General De Russy is the officer in command of the garrison at Fort Niagara.

William J. Falkner, M.D., of Youngstown, N. Y., was born in Whitehaven, Cumberland, England, in March, 1855. He came to Buffalo in 1866, and graduated from the Buffalo University February 22nd, 1876, and was resident physician of the Buffalo hospital during that year. He came to Youngstown in June, 1877, where he has since resided, engaged in the practice of his profession.

William H. Gaskill was born in Porter, November 20th, 1843. He served in the army during the rebellion and was wounded. In 1867 he was married to Miss Ettie M. Gifford. Mr. and Mrs. Gaskill are both members of the Baptist church. Mr. Gaskill is a farmer and the owner of seventy-two acres. Post-office address, Ransomville.

A. A. Gatchell was born October 1st, 1846, at Camden, N. Y., and removed to Lockport in 1869, to Cambria in 1872 and to Ransomville in 1876, where he has since resided. He was married in 1872, to Miss Hannah Gallup.

Lawrence Harwick, farmer (post-office, Ransomville), was born in Caledonia, Livingston county, N. Y., June 2nd, 1820. He married Miss Mariam A. Roberts in 1848. After living in Michigan and in Lewiston, Niagara county, for some time, he removed to Ransomville and purchased the place where he now lives.

W. W. Helms, of Ransomville, carriage maker and painter, employs several hands and does a somewhat heavy business in his line. He was born in Wilson, February 2nd, 1836, and married in 1868, to Miss Josephine Reux La Comb, of Louisiana. Mr. Helms has spent several years in various parts of the South, having conducted a carriage manufacturing business in New Orleans.

Elizabeth Holden, widow of Ezra Holden, came with her husband to Youngstown in 1833. In 1835 Mr. Holden was elected justice of the peace, and held the office for several years. He was chosen to other official positions and taught school several terms. In 1853 he bought the farm where his widow now lives, of "Farmer" John Brown. He had twelve children, seven sons and five daughters. Several of his sons served in the late war, and one of them was killed. Mrs. Holden's post-office is Youngstown.

Abram Howe McCollum, farmer (post-office Youngstown), was born May 4th, 1820. He served in the U. S. army about six months in 1840. In 1837 and 1838 he was on duty on the frontier with the troops called out at that time to resist the Radical invasion. In 1841 he married Miss Susan Zettle, by whom he has had several children, eight of whom are now living. One of their sons served with honor in the late rebelllon, and died at Wilmington from the effects of starvation while confined in Salisbury prison. Mr. McCollum is a member of the Free Methodist church at Ransomville.

Warren Jackman, of the firm of Jackman & Holden, manufacturers and dealers in pure cider and cider vinegar, and general shipping and commission agents, Youngstown, N. Y., was born in Alexander, Genesee county, N. Y. March 20th, 1822. He was married May 6th, 1844, to Melinda Blodgett, of Genesee county, and came to Youngstown March 29th, 1867, from Elma, Erie county. Mr. Jackman was postmaster at Elma, N. Y., from 1855 to 1867; and he is now one of the justices of the peace of the town of Porter. He has been instrumental in building up the fruit interest in the vicinity.

Royal A. Johnson was born November 2nd, 1846, and married Miss Anna Perry, of Porter. They have one daughter. Mr. Johnson is a farmer. Post-office, Ransomville.

Charles W. Johnson was born in Porter, February 14th, 1841. He was married to Maria French in 1864. Mr. Johnson is a member of the Presbyterian church of Youngstown. Post-office, Ransomville.

Francis Kyte was born in the town of Hopewell, Ontario county, N. Y., in 1825, and came to Porter with his father in 1829. In 1849 he was married to Miss Clarinda Corwin. He has filled in a very acceptable manner several town offices. Post-office, Ransomville.

Mrs. Catharine M. Lloyd (formerly Miss C. M. Sanderson) was married to Thomas Lloyd in 1852. Thomas Lloyd was born in Porter, February 22nd, 1820. In former years he was a steamboat engineer on the lakes. In 1866 he took up his residence in Porter as a farmer. Post-office, Youngstown.

A M. McCollum, farmer (post-office Youngstown), was born in Porter October 29th, 1842. He enlisted in Company F, 8th N. Y. H. A., in December, 1863, and served until he was discharged, in October, 1864; taking part in the battles of Spottsylvania and Cold Harbor, receiving a wound in the arm in the last mentioned engagement, which necessitated its amputation above the elbow. He was married February 8th, 1869, to Almira Sanborn, of Orleans county.

James W. McCormick was born in Northumberland county, Pa., in 1825, and came to Porter in 1832. He has lived at Ransomville since May, 1875, where he has carried on a good business in the sale of lumber. Mr. McCormick learned the machinist's trade in early life with John D. Shepard & Co. (now King Iron Works), Buffalo, N. Y. He assisted to build the Collins line of steamships, at New York, worked in the locomotive works at Toronto, Canada, and has been engaged in other large manufactories at different times.

William C. McCormack, farmer, was born in Northumberland county, Pa., in 1797, and came to Porter in 1832. He was married February 19th, 1822, to Miss Margaret Kirk, who bore him three sons and a daughter, and died June 9th, 1872, at the age of seventy-two. In October, 1872, Mr. McCormack married Miss Porter, of Youngstown, who subsequently died, and he was again married May 23rd, 1876, to Miss Josephine Myer, of Buffalo. Mr. McCormack has held several town offices. Post-office, Youngstown.

S. C. McCormick was born in Cumberland county, Pa., December 16th, 1822, and came with his father to Porter in 1832. In 1846 he was married to Susan C. Moore. He is a farmer, and proprietor of eighty-six acres of land. Post-office, Ransomville.

Mrs. John Thompson, widow of John Thompson, deceased, owns a farm of one hundred and thirty-five acres. Post-office, Ransomville. John Thompson was born in Scotland in March, 1816, and came to Porter in 1856. He married Miss Elvira Cornell. He held several town offices, and was a soldier during the late war, and was a member of the M. E. church for several years prior to his death, which occurred February 19th, 1874.

James G. McLaughlin was born in Little York (now Toronto), Canada, in 1809, and came to Porter with his father in 1815. At one time he was sutler at Fort Niagara. January 17th, 1847, he was married to Miss Burch. In 1858 he purchased the farm on which he now lives of Chapman Hawley. Post-office, Youngstown.

Francis C. Morris, post-office, Youngstown, was born in Porter, February 3d, 1836, and married Miss Ann Schoonmaker in 1861.

Isaac B. Moss was born in Porter in 1826, and married in 1855 to Miss Jane E. Kerr. Mr. Moss owns one hundred and eight acres of land. Post-office address, Youngstown.

Robert G. Newton, fruit-grower (post-office, Youngstown), was born in England, and came to Buffalo in 1867, removing to Porter in 1872. In 1873 he married Miss Emma White, of Syracuse, N. Y.

Charles N. Owen was born at Perry, N. Y., October 23d, 1846, and came to Ransomville in 1850. In 1870 he married Miss Josephine McDonald, of Cambria. Mr. Owen is extensively engaged in the manufacture of harness, employing two assistants, and turning off an average of $3,500 worth of work per annum.

Robert Owen, of Ransomville, was born in Wales in 1819. He came to America in 1820. He lived in Oneida, Genesee and Erie counties till 1849, when he came to Ransomville. In 1833 he was married to Sarah Slocum. Three of his sons were soldiers in the late war.

George Parker was born in Massachusetts, June 14th, 1779. At the age of twenty-seven he was married to Lucretia Griswold, and in 1866 he came to Porter, where he has followed farming as a business. Mr. and Mrs. Parker have been life-long members of the M. E. church. Post-office address, Ransomville.

George P. Parker was born May 3d, 1850. He was married in December, 1874, to Deborah Holden. Post-office address, Youngstown.

William Perry was born in Porter, August 17th, 1811, being the first child born in the town after the general settlement begun. He was married in 1834, to Miss Martha Clark. Mr. Perry is the owner of a good farm, and despite his advanced age, is in the enjoyment of good health. His oldest son, Edward D. Perry, was a soldier in the rebellion, and died in Salisbury prison. Mr. Perry's post-office is Youngstown.

John Powley, a native of England, came to America in 1832, when he was thirteen years of age. In 1834 he came to Porter, and in company with his brother Edward purchased a farm of one hundred and eighteen acres. In 1836 he was married to Sarah Whitfield. He has held several town offices. Post-office, Ransomville.

Ira Race came to Youngstown in 1826. In early life he was a farmer, but he retired from that business in 1833, since which time he has been elected or appointed to several responsible official positions, having been a custom house officer, a justice of the peace, and a school commissioner, besides serving the town and county in various other official capacities. Few men can show a more extended or a clearer official record than Mr. Race. He was born in Washington county, in 1807. He was married in 1834, to Miss Maria Follett, who died in July, 1837, and in 1861 Mr. Race was again married, to Mrs. Charlotte Hawkins. Post-office, Youngstown.

Elton T. Ransom, of Ransomville, was born in the town of Porter, N. Y., February 20th, 1846. He is a member of the firm of W. H. H. Ransom & Son, dealers in general merchandise, and has been supervisor of Porter from 1871 to 1877, and was a delegate to the Baltimore convention in 1872.

William H. H. Ransom was born in Ulster county, N. Y., October 11th, 1816. He was married February 22nd, 1843, to Miss Eliza Estus. He came to Ransomville in 1839, and worked at the trade of carpenter and joiner till 1843, when he purchased the business of his uncle Jehial C. S. Ransom, and engaged in trade. Mr.

RES. OF JOHN DIEZ, TOWN OF WILSON, NIAGARA CO. N.Y.

HOTEL & WAREHOUSE OF CURTISS BROS, RANSOMVILLE, N.Y., SHOWING DEPOT ON R.W. & O. R.R.

'VINE COTTAGE' THE RESIDENCE OF H.A. PARSONS, 2½ MILES ABOVE NIAGARA FALLS

Ransom is the leading merchant and general business man of Ransomville. His son, E. T. Ransom, is associated with him, the firm being W. H. H. Ransom & Son.

Walter M. Richardson is a music teacher at Ransomville. He was born May 29th, 1860, in the town of Wilson.

William Ripson was born in Porter, September 15th, 1834, and was married March 15th, 1853, to Miss Marcelia Lloyd. Mr. Ripson has one son, who is junior partner of the firm of William S. Ripson & Co., founders and dealers in agricultural implements, Youngstown.

Christopher Robertson, of Porter, is well known as a farmer and a patriotic citizen. He served faithfully in the rebellion, having gone with Sherman in his march "through Georgia." His brother Daniel Robertson, deceased, also served in the army about three years, participating in the engagement at Cold Harbor and in the battle of the Wilderness and several other hard fought battles. They were sons of John and Susannah Robertson. Christopher Robertson's post-office address is Ransomville.

Henry C. Root, hotel-keeper and fruit-grower, was born in the town of Porter, November 18th, 1843. He served one year in the navy during the war, and is now deputy collector and inspector of customs of the port at Youngstown.

Dr. A. G. Skinner, of Youngstown, is a native of New Hampshire. He came to Niagara county in 1850, and has since been engaged in the practice of his profession. His standing as a medical man is high.

Richard Smithson was born in Yorkshire, England, in 1814, and, with his parents, came to the United States in 1828, and his parents died in the following year. In 1841 he married Miss Mary A. McCollum, by whom he has had eight children, five of whom are married. Mr. Smithson is one of the leading farmers of Porter, having a farm of 204 acres. His post-office is Ransomville. For years he has been a consistent member of the M. E. Church.

William M. Smithson was born in the town of Porter in 1843. He was married in December, 1870, to Miss Sarah Carter, of Youngstown. He is the owner of 140 acres of land. Post-office, Youngstown.

Mary Rudd Spencer was born April 9th, 1801, at Leyden, Lewis county, N. Y. On the 7th of October, 1819, she was married to Oliver Spencer, of Madrid, N. Y. They came to Youngstown, from New York city, in 1837. Her daughter, Mrs. Mary E. Spencer, is one of the best known and most successful educators in the county, having taught in Youngstown fifteen years, since the death of her husband in the army. Eight years of this time she was in the public school, and for several years past she has kept a private school, which has increased in members from six pupils to twenty-four. Post office, Youngstown.

Christopher Spickerman, of Porter, was born in Schoharie county, N. Y., in 1813, and removed to Lewiston in 1834, and from there to Porter in 1852. He was married at the age of twenty-six to Miss Minerva Shippy, Mr. Spickerman is a well known farmer and business man of the town. Post-office address, Youngstown.

George Swain, a son of Isaac Swain, a pioneer on the Holland Purchase, was born at Youngstown, August 9th, 1819. January 15th, 1857, he was married to Miss Cordelia Cornell, of East Henrietta, Monroe county, N. Y. In 1852 Mr. Swain purchased the farm of ninety-one acres where he now resides, of Bruce Ainsworth. At the age of twenty-one, Mr. Swain was elected inspector of common schools, chosen supervisor of the town of Porter in 1856, elected sheriff of Niagara county in 1860 and appointed deputy collector at the port of Youngstown in 1870, which position he held till 1878. William Swain, his brother, a well known and influential citizen of Porter, was born in 1821. The brothers Swain are extensively engaged in fruit-growing. Their post-office address is Youngstown.

Captain John L. Tiernon, commander of battery B., 3rd U. S. Artillery, at Fort Niagara, was born January 18th, 1840, in the township of Madison, Madison county, Indiana. He was educated at St. Mary's Seminary, Missouri, graduating in 1856. From that date to 1861, he was engaged in the mercantile business in Nebraska. In 1861 he was elected a member of the Legislature of Dakota Territory, and Speaker of the House of Representatives in 1862. February 19th, 1862, he was commissioned second lieutenant of Battery B., 3rd U. S. Artillery, a promoted to be a first lieutenant in 1864. He was again promoted, this time to the captaincy and command of the battery, July 7th, 1877. He was married February 1st, 1865, to Miss Harriet V. Pickett, of San Francisco, Cal. Post-office, Youngstown.

H. B. Tower, farmer (post-office Ransomville), was born in 1838, in the town of Porter. He was married in 1861 to Miss Harriet Henry. He is the owner of one hundred and forty-four acres of land. He has been collector and assessor of the town for several terms, and has been a teacher twelve years.

J. W. Whitfield, farmer and owner of about one hundred acres of land (post-office Ransomville), was born in Monroe county, February 14th, 1843.

John L. Whittaker was born in New Hampshire in 1830, and came with his father's family to Niagara county, and settled in Porter in 1831. He was married January 1st, 1850, to Emeline Huntington. He was a farmer until 1876, when he sold his farm to Charles Jeffords. He was elected constable in 1867, and has been re-elected each successive year since. Post-office, Youngstown.

The following are also among those who have represented Porter in the various honorable walks of life:

Samuel Shippy, Youngstown; Miss P. Barrett, Youngstown; M. L. Burton, Ransomville; Heber I. Quade, Ransomville; A. Brookins, Ransomville; Nathan Cook, Ransomville; Peter P. Barton and M. Robinson, post-office Lewiston; B. D. Davis and Thomas Brighton, Youngstown.

THE TOWN OF ROYALTON.

THIS town, like all others, is blessed with its advantages, as well as hindered by its disadvantages, although the first predominate to such an extent that the latter are rather looked upon as blessings in disguise. In its very early days, even before it assumed a name or ranked among the towns that go to make up a county, the sturdy yeomanry from New England had trod its virgin soil; and that portion of them from the old Green Mountain State, longing for something by which to perpetuate the memory of their native State, and more particularly the town from which many of them had migrated, embraced the first opportunity of christening their adopted town by the name of the one of their nativity, viz., Royalton, Vt.

This town was taken from Hartland in 1817, and a portion of it was annexed to Lockport in 1824; still it comprises 38,820 acres of land. It is located in the southeast corner of the county.

The town was fully organized on the first Tuesday in April, 1818, when the first set of town officers was elected. The population at that time was about 1,500, while at present it is 4,726, and the aggregate valuation is $2,945,269, against a mere nominal sum in 1818.

The surface is generally level or undulating, except in the northern half, where a ridge crosses the town from east to west. The soil in the northern part of the town is a reddish clay loam, in the center a gravelly and sandy loam, while in the south it is a stiff, heavy clay.

While the town was once a wilderness waste, it now boasts of some of the finest farms in the State, as well as the best improved farm machinery to be found any where.

SETTLEMENT.

Those who came to this town at the earliest date were Joshua and Thomas Slaton. The following incident shows why Mr. Slaton settled where he did:

"He was on his way to Canada with his family; broke his wagon down, about two miles east of the Cold Springs; stopped in consequence, liked the country, took up land and chopped an acre or two. His horses having strayed away from his log cabin, he went into the woods in pursuit of them, and in his rambling saw the fine soil and black walnut groves below the mountain, and soon changed his location, becoming the founder of Slaton Settlement."

Those who now pass through that beautiful, highly cultivated region, will conclude that the early pioneer made a good selection This was in 1800, and Slaton was the first settler in what is now Royalton. He and his brother came from Windsor, Vt.

In 1802 Stephen Bugbee and Andrew Brown moved in, and in 1803 Varney Gaskill and William Smith; in 1804, Benjamin Hale, Varnum Treadwell and Marvin Harwood, all from the same town in Vermont. This place is located in the northwest corner of the town.

The first clearing of land, sowing of wheat and planting of orchard of any kind was done from 1800 to 1805 by the Slaton brothers, Mr. Bugbee and Mr. Lyman, at the Slaton Settlement.

Asher Freeman, father of the present citizen of that name, was born in Washington county, N. Y., in 1774. In 1811 he purchased 500 acres of land for $3.25 per acre, located about one and a half miles south of Middleport, then an unbroken wilderness. In 1813 he sowed a piece of wheat upon the tract, and on the 18th of March, 1815, he moved on to his land, and built a log house. The floor was made of split basswood logs, hewed smooth on the upper side. The upper floor was of basswood bark, peeled the length of the house and laid down when green, with the smooth side down, and weights laid on until it was seasoned. It was so strong that Mr. Freeman put several hundred bushels of grain on it. It lasted until he built his saw-mill in the following year, when he sawed boards to take the place of the bark. The roof of the house was made of bark. At first the only board around the house was the door, which was made of an old sleigh box. In 1811 there was not a bridge from the Buffalo road to the mouth of the Genesee river. In 1824 Mr. Freeman built his brick house. In 1815 there was no house between him and the Buffalo road. Asher Freeman, now living one and a half miles south of Middleport, has a wooden-mould-board plow that was made in 1820 by Linus Spalding, of Hartland. It is in good order and can do now as good work as it ever did; compared, however, with the pulverizers of the present day, the old woooden mould-board would stand about the same chance for a premium as Robert Fulton's mud turtle would with the floating palaces upon the Hudson river at the present time.

Among the early settlers in the southern part was Severus Swift, who came in from the opening along the old Indian trail, traveled by Sir John Johnson, Brant and Butler, and settled on the farm now owned by his son, J. C. Smith, half a mile north of what is now Wolcottsville, the trail crossing the farm. He settled here in

1818, when all south of him to Tonawanda creek was a dense wilderness. Like other early settlers, himself and family had to encounter all the hardships allotted to seekers of new homes in the then western settlements. The scanty fare of potatoes and salt, or a crust of coarse bread, was to them many a time a bountiful feast. Their crops, small in acreage, and their stock, small in numbers, were often the prey of the wild beasts that inhabited the dense forests surrounding their little cabins. Fearful at night and watchful by day, they encountered and surmounted hardships that at the present time and by the present generation would be unendurable. The Swift family suffered severely, as the bears and wolves would capture their stock by night, and the redskins their crops by day.

Soon after their arrival other families began to come in and clear up the land. The first after Swift was Daniel Benedict, who settled on the farm now owned by S. B. Bratt, on Tonawanda creek. Soon another settler came in, and settled on the farm now owned by G. D. Wisterman, on the road east from Dysinger's Corners.

The facilities for milling and trading were of about the poorest kind. The nearest grist-mills were at Niagara, west, and Rochester, east, while at Batavia was the most convenient store, where a bushel of wheat would just pay for a pound of tobacco, or a yard of cotton cloth, or a gallon of cheap molasses.

Chauncey McKie settled in 1816, north of the Lewiston or Niagara road, on the farm now owned by A. B. Sherwood, on Griswold street. At that time he had to go in from the ridge guided by marked trees. Eliphalet Edmunds located the same year on the farm now owned by Barney Rinn, on Griswold street, and the farm south of his was occupied by John Griswold, and is still in the Griswold family.

PIONEER HOUSE-BUILDING.

Joshua Slaton built the first log house in this town in 1800. Soon log houses began to show themselves in different parts of the town.

The first frame house was built by Stephen Bugbee in 1804, also at the Slaton Settlement. This house has gone to decay. Soon after this John Carrington built a frame house at Royalton Center.

Two brick houses in the town are claimed to be the oldest, viz., Bugbee's, at Orangeport, and McNall's, at McNall's Corners. No exact date can be given for either, but they are supposed to have been built about 1820.

Andrew Brown built the first frame barn in this town in 1804, at Slaton Settlement. This barn is still in good repair, and in use. As early as 1816 frame barns were built in different parts of the town.

TRAILS AND ROADS.

An Indian trail showing evidences of much usage passed through Royalton long before the war of 1812. This was the well known path of Johnson, Brant and Butler during the Revolution in leaving or approaching their rendezvous at Fort Niagara. It entered the town very near the southeast corner, in the Tonawanda Reservation, and ran in a northwesterly direction, crossing the farm now owned by J. C. Smith, just north of what is now Wolcottsville, going thence to the farm of Zimmerman, where the trail divided, branches going north and south of a swamp and coming together again just south of McNall's Corners; striking the Niagara road at the residence of J. W. La Barr, jr., and following the course of the present Niagara road until it left the town. This is the only Indian trail of which history or tradition gives any account in this town. We are indebted to Heman Smith, Esq., who lived with his parents upon the trail in 1815, for information as to its course.

Probably the first road laid out was through the Slaton Settlement, in the northwest corner of the town. But the most prominent of the early roads, and one that is yet traveled as much as any other, and the one over which troops and munitions of war were moved during the trying times of 1812-14, is that originally opened by the Holland Company, and improved during the war, running about on the line of the trail above described, and known as the "Old Military road," "Lewiston road" and "Niagara road."

In 1815, the year that Severus Smith came into the town, he assisted in building a causeway, or corduroy road, across the Tonawanda swamp, on the Lewiston or Niagara road. In this way Mr. Smith obtained a little money, which he used in the purchase of a few of the necessaries of life, such as tobacco, snuff, tea and molasses.

EARLY TAVERNS.

Carrington Fisk was probably the first tavern-keeper in the town. He came in from the Ridge road in 1808, and opened a tavern at Royalton Center.

In 1816 Benjamin Barlow kept tavern half a mile south of what is now Middleport. The locality was called by turns "Peeneyville," "Pucker," "Tea Pot Hollow," "Barlow's Corners," "Taylor's Corners," "Ewing's Corners," and is at present "Freeman's Corners."

In 1818 John McNall opened a tavern at what is now McNall's Corners, west of Royalton Center, on the old Niagara road.

In 1820 Alexander Lafferty kept tavern southeast of Royalton Center, on the old Lewiston road, where John Weyand now lives.

About this time Levi Cole opened a hotel in a little log house that stood where the drug store now stands at the corner of Main and State streets, Middleport. Soon after this a frame house was put up on the opposite corner, when Squire Cole changed locations, and kept there until after the canal went through the place.

FIRST SCHOOLS.

The first school-house in the town was probably in the Slaton Settlement, or near it, as that was the neighborhood earliest settled. In those days schools were few and far between. In 1818 there was a school-house on the farm now owned by S. Weyand, in what is now district No. 23, and it was the only one south of the old Military road at that time. The first teacher was Margaret Pixley; she taught during the summer, and Dr. John McLoth during the winter of the same year. Among the surviving pupils are Heman Swift and his brothers and sisters.

COURSE OF TRADE AND MANUFACTURE.

In 1804 Marvin Harwood, from Vermont, opened a small store in the Slaton Settlement. He had to haul his goods, what few he had, from some eastern point by ox-teams, on carts, wagons or sleds, as circumstances and the condition of the roads would permit.

About 1818 a store was opened at McNall's Corners, also one at Barlow's, now Freeman's Corners.

James Northam was the first merchant at Middleport, beginning business in 1822.

The exact date cannot be obtained of the building of the first saw-mills in this town, but enough is known to warrant saying that previous to 1820 there were saw-mills at Mabee's and Asher Freeman's, and a Mr. Sleeper had a mill where the paper-mill now stands in Middleport. Mr. Bennet also had a mill in the early days of the town on the site of De Lano's mill in Middleport, and Welch worked one near Green's burying ground.

Mabee's, a little east of Gasport, was probably the first grist-mill in the town, yet Middleport also claims the honor, while some of the oldest inhabitants say the first mill was southwest from where Colonel Odell now lives, on J. Richardson's farm. F. B. Lane and James Northam had mills here quite early. The earliest date is probably about 1820.

In 1828 there was a carding-mill on the mill-site now occupied by the Heading mill in Middleport. Mr. Welch also operated a carding-mill near the Green burying ground, on the farm now owned by J. Richardson.

Mr. Benjamin B. Barlow operated a distillery in 1817 at Barlow's Corners. He also had an ashery, and was extensively engaged in the manufacture of potash. John Mabee, at what is known as Mabee's Station, ran a distillery in 1821.

G. and E Mather operated a small tannery, and also carried on the boot and shoe trade, at Middleport in 1824.

In 1840 John Van Brocklin built and operated the first and only blast furnace in this town, located at the corner of Vernon and State streets, Middleport. It is still standing, and operated by his son.

Varney Gaskill opened the first shop for blacksmithing in the town in 1803. Asa Scott carried on the blacksmith business at Barlow's Corners in 1817. In 1820 or 1821 Smith & Calkin's did a large business at blacksmithing at what is now Middleport.

[The first man who made tailoring a business in this town, was John Macker, in the year 1830. His shop was in Middleport. He was succeeded in turn by Brideman, Snell, Stone and Charles Wilcox.

Mrs. Bentley and Mrs. Colton, both living near McNall's Corners, were the first in the town who made a business of weaving for their neighbors, thus earning a large share of the support for their families.

PROFESSIONAL MEN.

Dr. Packard was the earliest resident physician in this town. He located here in 1817. He lived about a mile southwest of what is now Middleport. Dr. Chatterton soon followed Dr. Packard, and resided here for some time.

In 1820 Dr. John McLoth was the resident physician for the south end of the town, and boarded at Lafferty's tavern on the old Niagara road.

Dr. Peter P. Murphy located at Royalton Center in 1835, and has been a practicing physician at that place ever since.

Dr. P. Faling is the oldest physician at Reynale's Basin, on the Erie Canal, and resided there for many years.

Dr. F. L. Knapp resides at Mabee's, on the canal, east of Gasport.

Dr. Moore, an old and respected physician, resides on the mountain opposite Mabee's.

Dr. E. Hurd was one of the early physicians of this town. Dr. John Duff located at Royalton Center in 1874, and is still in the line of his duty.

Doctors Cole, Gedney, Gould and Garbeck are located in Middleport.

William Smith came to the settlement in 1804. For a while his services as surveyor were not required; but as soon as the country began to be settled, and large land holders began to divide up their tracts, and new settlers came in, Mr. Smith's compass and chain were brought into requisition, when he soon gained a reputation second to none, as a surveyor in this section of country.

POST-OFFICES.

Previous to the establishment of post routes in this town, which was not until 1826, Batavia was the nearest office. The neighbors would club together, put a boy on a horse, and about once a month he could be seen wending his way through forest and stream, around the swamps, and along the seldom-used trail, to get, perchance, half a dozen letters and papers for four times that number of families. Patiently the longing settlers waited the return of their faithful post rider, and when he returned, if no tidings came from loved ones, they did their best to suppress the silent tears that would often betray their sadness. But the advent of the Erie Canal, with its swift-floating packets, gave the post-office department a new lease of life, and post-offices were established all along its banks. The first in this town was at Reynale's Basin, and was called Royalton post-office. In a very few years the office was moved to Royalton Center, by which name it is still known; while Reynale's Basin was dignified with a post-office by that name, which it still retains, although receiving its mail through the Gasport office. Since then the mail facilities have increased, so that the town is well supplied. There are now six post-offices in the town, viz., Middleport, Reynale's Basin, Orangeport, Royalton Center, Gasport and Wolcottsville.

FIRST BIRTH, MARRIAGE AND DEATH.

Daniel Vaughn was the first male child born in this town, about 1806.

The first matrimonial affair in the town was in the spring of 1810. Henry Ellsworth and Polly Cornish were the contracting parties.

The first death that occurred in the town was that of Mr. Ellsworth, in 1804.

ASSOCIATIONS AND LODGES.

CEMETERY ASSOCIATION.

The Mountain Ridge Cemetery Association was organized on the 16th of June, 1848. The cemetery is located on the ridge, four and a half miles southwest of Middleport, on the east side of the road leading to Royalton Center, and contains eight and two-tenths acres of land.

At the first meeting of the association Mr. Pynchon Dwight was made chairman, and Hathaway Hurd secretary. The trustees were divided into three classes, as follows: first class, Philip Freeman, Alanson T. Odell, N. W. Baldwin; second class, Oliver Brown, James Culver; third class, E. Odell, Stephen Green, Franklin Knapp.

At a subsequent meeting, A. T. Odell was elected president of the association, and has held the office ever since. Silas Knapp is the treasurer, and Linus S. Freeman secretary.

The association about the 1st of August, 1878, contracted for an iron fence in front of the cemetery, the expense of which was to be about $1,000.

MASONIC.

Cataract Lodge, No. 295, F. and A. M., located at Middleport, was organized June 11th, 1853, with the following charter members: Charles Craig, W. M.; Avery S. Delano, S. W.; William S. Fenn, J. W. In October following, twenty-two members appear on the roll of the lodge. From that time to May, 1878, two hundred and six had been raised to the degree of master mason in this lodge.

The officers for the present year are: L. H. Spalding, W. M.; E. J. Tuttle, S. W.; E. L. Downey, J. W.; B. F. Freeman, treasurer; H. A. Robertson, secretary. The present number of members enrolled is one hundred and ten.

LIBRARY ASSOCIATION.

The Middleport Library Association was instituted in 1873 by Rev. James H. Dennis, who was then a resident of that place. The first officers of the association were: President, C. W. Gould; secretary, E. L. Downey; librarian and treasurer, E. A. Phillips. The following were the members: Rev. J. H. Dennis, Rev. W. McGovern, Rev. H. H. Baker, H. K. Taylor, J. Densmore, Dr. Downey, Dr. Gould, H. A. Wilmot, E. A. Phillips. Their first books were donated by the citizens of Middleport. In order to procure a library worthy the cause a course of lectures was inaugurated, and quite a sum was added to the treasury. In the winter of 1874-75 the same means was resorted to, and home talent put upon the lecture course, which resulted in quite an addition to the library, making in all 144 volumes of choice reading matter. The present officers of the association are: President, C. W. Gould; librarian and treasurer, Charles W. Laskey; trustees, Linus Spalding, A. D. Filer, L. E. Chubbuck.

A. O. U. W.

Middleport Lodge, No. 54, Ancient Order of United Workmen was organized January 3rd, 1877, by E. M. Clark, D. D. G. M. W. This is a beneficiary institution on the life-insurance plan. The heirs of a third degree member receive two thousand dollars at his death. The present officers are as follows: C. M. Garlock, W. M.; C. W. Laskey, P. M. W.; S. S. Ballou, G. F.; G. Pew, R.; C. M. Garlock, F.; C. W. Platts, Rec.; James Lucor, G.; G. E. Smith, O.; Henry Armstrong, J. W.; Charles Hinman, O. W.; Dr. C. M. Garlock, medical examiner. The number of members May 4th, 1878, was 34.

Cataract Lodge, No. 94, located at Gasport, was instituted June 4th, 1877. At present there are thirty members, and the following are the officers: Thomas Sterritt, P. M. W.; C. H. Mitchell, M. W.; C. V. Mesler, recorder; H. H. Bugby, receiver; I. W. Hayner, F.; Ruthvan Kill, G.; J. S. Maynard, G. F.; E. Hunt, O.; J. R. Shafer, J. W.; A. J. Smith, O. W. The lodge meets on the first and third Tuesdays of each month.

TEMPERANCE.

Middleport Council, No. 23, Royal Templars of Temperance, was instituted January 12th, 1871, with the following members, viz.: Linus S. Freeman, A. S. Freeman, W. J. Sterritt, John Sage, A. D. Filer, R. B. Oliver, G. H. Ohlendorf, B. V. Oliver, Henry McClean, George King, C. W. Gould and H. R. Webber.

Middleport Lodge, No. 396, I. O. of G. T., was organized September 4th, 1867, with the following charter members: L. S. Freeman, Mrs. L. S. Freeman, James S. Wilkins, M. E. McKie, G. P. Stirling, C. J. Eddy, Jennie Le Valley, Mary McDonald, Josephine Reynolds, H. O. Gregory, W. Bowman, J. Seaman, J. Johnson, R. Hunt, Letty Gregory, Mrs. Hiram Porter, Myra Duncan, C. Hinchey, J. Bennett, W. Youngs, S. Stride, W. Downs, C. B. Strain. The following were the charter officers: L. S. Freeman, W. C. T.; Jennie Le Valley, W. V. T.; S. C. Church, W. C.; John Seaman, W. S.; Mrs. L. S. Freeman, W. A. S.; H. O. Gregory, W. F. S.; C. S. Eddy, W. T.; W. Young, W. M.; Mary McDonald, W. D. M.; Josephine Reynolds, W. I. G.; John Johnson, W. O. G.; Letty Gregory, W. R. S.; Myra Duncan, W. L. S.; J S. Wilkins, P. W. C. T.

WOLCOTTSVILLE.

This village is located in the southern part of the town, a little northwest of the Tonawanda Reservation. The land upon which the village is located was formerly owned by Anson Wolcott, who purchased two thousand acres of the Holland Land Company, and located upon it in 1847 and 1848. Previous to this, a Mr. Ehrick Sutherland had "squatted" upon the southwest corner of the same land. When Mr. Wolcott settled, he built a steam saw-mill on the lot opposite, where Mr. Charles H. Schad now has his store and residence. The well which he dug for a supply of water for his mill is still in good condition and ready for use. He employed a large number of men in the manufacture of lumber, and the building he used for a boarding house is now used by Mr. Schad as his store, he having added a dwelling house to it.

At that time this place was a dense wilderness. Cleared spots soon began to show themselves, and in 1851 Mr. Wolcott deeded his whole tract of land to four trustees, viz.: Frederick Moll, Christian Moll, Frederick Weiland and Carl Martins, who divided it into small lots, and in 1872 and 1873, seventy-five families of Germans from Prussia settled here and located on such pieces of the land as they drew by lot, as that was the way in which the different parcels were disposed of, they being all of the same price per acre and equally well located. About this time Mr. Wolcott removed his saw-mill to Erie county. The first hotel in the village was opened by Joseph Rhodes in 1866. The village contains two churches, seven hotels, one cigar manufactory, five stores, three school-houses—one a district school and two belonging to the two churches; five wagon and blacksmith shops, one saw-mill, about an equal number of log and frame houses, and about one thousand inhabitants.

ROYALTON CENTER

is located near the center of the town, on the Niagara road, and was settled as early as 1808. A post-office was established here soon after opening the Erie Canal. The land upon which the village is located was formerly owned by Mr. Fisk on the east of the corners, and on the west of the road running north and south by Mr. Dewey.

In 1837 an academy was established at this place. The means for putting up the necessary building was raised by subscription, and when it was completed, Dr. Peter P. Murphy, Anson Baldwin and William Sibley were elected trustees. The building was forty by eighty feet and two stories high, with a wing. The average attendance of pupils was ninety. Donald G. Frazer was the principal. In 1847 and 1848 the school was closed for want of pecuniary aid, and the building taken down.

This village contains, beside dwellings, one church, one hotel, two stores, a post-office, a school-house, a blacksmith and wagon shop, and a population of about three hundred. The resident physicians are Dr. P. P. Murphy and Dr. J. Duff. Mrs. Lewis is the oldest person living here, being in her ninety-second year, with all her faculties well preserved.

ORANGEPORT

is located in the northwest corner of the town, on the Erie Canal, about one mile west of Gasport, and contains one church, a hotel, store, a post-office, wagon and blacksmith shop, and was once a railroad station. There are about fifty dwellings, and some two hundred inhabitants.

The post-office at this place was established about 1850, with Mr. Hart as postmaster. The present postmaster is Garret Gifford.

The land upon which the village stands was formerly owned by Joshua Slaton and his brother Thomas. About half a mile north of this place is the Slaton Settlement. The Erie Canal and Central railroad also pass through the lands formerly owned by the Slatons. The two places are so near each other, and their interests so closely allied, that one post-office answers for both places. Joshua Slaton, who was really the founder, and whose name should have been perpetuated in the name of the village, was, perhaps, the most public spirited man in the settlement. He first gave land and shop to Mr. Gaskill, the first blacksmith in the town. The same old shop, with its four roofs, is said to be standing yet, upon the old site, closed up, and kept as a memento of the past. Mr. Slaton also gave the land upon which the church stands and the land where the graveyard is located, both the oldest in the town.

Joseph Slaton, the present owner of a large portion of the original Slaton property, was born here in 1811, and is the oldest person living at this place who was born here. The school lot at this place is the oldest in the town, and the gift of Mr. Slaton.

The graveyard at Orangeport is the oldest one in the town. Mr. Ellsworth was buried here in 1804.

GASPORT.

Gasport is situated on the Erie Canal and Central railroad, about five miles east of Lockport. It derives its name from two sources: First, from the fact of its being a port or stopping place for canal boats, where they receive large quantities of grain and other farm produce for transportation; and, second, from the discovery of flowing springs containing large quantities of gas. About the first experiment tried in using this gas was by a scientist from Albany, N. Y. Having procured a large cask, he set it over one of the springs, and at the proper time, as he supposed, he applied a match. The next seen of our scientific friend, he was making a "spread eagle" in a mud hole near by. Other experiments, however, being satisfactory, the proper arrangements were made, pipes laid, burners attached, and one large warehouse and store were lighted by gas from this spring, with a sufficient quantity for the use of fourteen burners in the two buildings. When the canal was enlarged, it took in the gas springs, as they were situated on its south bank at this place, west of the bridge, thereby destroying the Gasport gasworks, and leaving the warehouse and store to return to tallow dips, as in days of yore. The village at the present time contains one church, a hotel, a blacksmith and wagon shop, two warehouses, three stores, one steam shingle factory, cider and vinegar works, a railroad depot, canal station, and a population of three hundred and thirty.

Samuel Hitchcock built the first house in this place about 1824, on the north side of the canal, and he also kept the first hotel or tavern.

Alfred Colwell erected the first warehouse at this place, on the west side of the bridge and south side of the canal. Samuel Hitchcock also built one about the same time, where Martin's ware house now stands.

Among the early settlers at this place were a Mr. Woolworth, wagon-maker; Mr. Marcy, blacksmith, and Timothy Y. G. Page, first physician. The first flouring mill and saw-mill was built by Colonel John Mabee, a little northeast of the village, on Johnson's creek, while Andrew and Amos Brown had a saw-mill south of the village about the same time. The first store in this place was kept by Sextus Shearer in 1823. A. Colwell was the first postmaster at Gasport. The railroad station was located here in 1854.

The land upon which the village stands was owned by Melick, Mabee and Hitchcock. In 1850, an organization was effected, a stock company formed, and an academy built. The building is of brick, about twenty-five by forty feet, two stories high, with grounds suitable for such an institution. William Crocker was the principal, and taught all the branches of an academic course of study. Alfred Colwell, Elisha Smedley, O. L. Wilcox, Jason Sawyer and Lewis Griffin were the trustees. The attendance of pupils averaged about seventy. In or about the year 1870 the institution was closed, and the property sold to the Congregational society for a parsonage.

REYNALE'S BASIN.

Reynale's Basin is about five miles west of Middleport, on the Erie Canal. The first post-office established in the town was at this place.

At one time this place was of some importance, having the only post-office, and doing quite a large business in shipping farm produce. But the young America of Middleport and Gasport, one on each side of it, soon drew the trade. It still retains a post-office by the name of the place.

It is a large hamlet, beautifully located, with schoolhouse, cheese factory, driving park, etc. Dr. P. Failing is the resident physician, and one of its most prominent citizens. There are about one hundred inhabitants. This place derived its name from the first settler, George Reynale, who settled here as soon as the canal was opened for navigation and transportation, and put up a small frame building on the north side of the canal, and west side of the road crossing at this place. Here Mr. Reynale opened a small grocery, and soon became a large dealer in staves and heading, which he purchased of the settlers north of the canal.

MIDDLEPORT.

Middleport, the only incorporated village, is located on the Erie Canal, and in the northeast corner of the town, the corporation extending over into the town of Hartland, which joins this town on the north. Previous to the construction of the Erie Canal, this was known only as a wilderness, all the business being done at what is now Freeman's Corners, half a mile south of this place. But the advent of the canal brought the business all to this point, and from the fact of its being equi-distant between Lockport and Freeport, now Albion, it was christened Middleport.

It soon became quite extensively known as a good grain market, and soon began to assume the appearance of a village. On the 25th of December, 1858, an order was issued from the Niagara County Court of Sessions, empowering certain parties to hold a corporation election, February 26th, 1859. Notices were posted for the purpose, and on the 22nd day of March A. J. Baker, B. P. Barnes, Horace Pierce, Thomas F. Smith and F. S. Taylor were elected trustees of the village of Middleport. On the 28th they held their first official meeting, and elected Francis S. Taylor president of the board for the ensuing year, and Peter B. Knower was appointed village clerk.

The trustees were elected annually, and continued to appoint one of their own number president, as follows: In 1860, Milton Seaman; 1861, Francis S. Taylor; 1862, 1863, Allen H. Pierce; 1864, A. S. Baker; 1865, 1867, Milton Seaman; 1868, Avery S. Delano; 1869, John Todd; 1870, John N. Dunn; 1871, A. H. Pierce; 1872, Henry McClean, jr., who was appointed March 26th, and served until June 3rd, 1872, when, under their new charter, the people voted directly for a president of the village, and Avery S. Delano was elected by popular vote.

At this time the number of trustees was reduced to three, and Henry McClean, jr., Bruce V. Oliver and Jeremiah Tracy were elected.

Since then the presidents of the village have been: In 1873, C. R. Blakslee; 1874, H. McClean, jr.; 1875, Charles H. Francis; 1876, J. H. Dunn; 1877, 1878, Charles H. Francis. Charles W. Laskey has been clerk of the village for the last three terms.

At the present time the population is estimated to be about one thousand four hundred. The assessed valuation has increased from $129,422 in 1859, to $320,800 in 1878, which shows a healthy state of affairs.

The business enterprises of the place are various. The lumber, grocery, warehouse, and the dry goods trades are doing a large business. The live stock and produce trade is the means of leaving a large amount of money at this point. A dry dock, for the building and repair of canal boats, is one of the live institutions of the place. All other trades are doing a good business.

There are four churches in the village, viz.: Methodist Episcopal, Protestant Episcopal, Universalist and Roman Catholic, and a movement is on foot for a fifth—Presbyterian. There are two hotels, one opera house, several civic societies, foundry and machine shops, heading-mill, and one paper-mill, turning out a ton of manilla paper per day. There was at one time a banking institution here, but the financial pressure of 1877 caused it to suspend operations, since which the experiment has not been tried. The village has but one lawyer, Charles W. Laskey, Esq.

The land upon which the village now stands was formerly owned by Messrs. Bennett, Taylor, Lane and Mather. Arunah Bennett owned the land on the west side of Main street, south of the canal; William Taylor on the east side of Main street, south of the canal; Gad Mather on the east side of Vernon street, north of the canal, and F. B. Lane on the west side of Vernon street, north of the canal. James Northam was the first to open a store in Middleport. In 1822, when the trees had just been cut, and the brush was piled up on either side of where the canal now is, and where Main street crosses the canal and not a shovelfull of earth had yet been moved, Mr. Northam erected a small frame building on what was to be the bank of the canal, and opened a store, employing A. S. Baker as clerk. Soon after this Baker went as clerk with Lane, who had a contract on the canal. Subsequently Mr. Northam sold to Messrs. Craig & Dunlap, who continued the business at Middleport. They were afterward followed in the business by Lane & Baker, at Middleport. As soon as the canal was opened for use, others entered the arena as rivals of the old merchants, and still remain in business at this place.

A FATAL AFFRAY.

The first homicide at Middleport was committed by Levi Cole, keeper of the log tavern, while the canal was being built. A party of Irishmen were in his tavern one evening, and becoming somewhat noisy from the two free use of fire-water, and indulging in language not generally used by sober men, one of the party insulted Mrs. Cole; upon learning the facts, Cole knocked the man down, when the whole party assaulted Cole, and he fled, running up the street to where Mr. Bentley lived. His pursuers following closely, he stopped, picked up a club, and struck and killed the first one that came up, and badly injured the next. Mr. Bentley and Mr. Northam, who was at Mr. Bentley's house, hearing the noise, went out and took Cole in for his safety. When the excited crowd demanded Cole's delivery, Messrs. Bentley and Northam gave themselves as hostages that Cole should be delivered to the proper authorities. Mr. Cole was finally sent to State prison for a short time for this act.

SUPERVISORS.

The act creating the town of Hartland directed that the first town meeting should be held at the house of Almond H. Millard on the first Tuesday in April, 1818. That gentleman was elected supervisor, and the list from that time to the present has been as follows:

In 1818–20, Almond H. Millard; 1821, Nathan Comstock; 1822, 1823, Daniel Washburn; 1824–27, John Garnsey; 1828–30, Asher Freeman; 1831, D. S. Fenn; 1832, Asher Freeman; 1833, Ethan Fenn; 1834–37, James Baldwin; 1838–40, Davis Hurd; 1841, John McNall; 1842, Davis Hurd; 1843, Peter P. Murphy; 1844, 1845, Samuel Z. Ross; 1846, Grandus Davenport; 1847, William S. Fenn; 1848, 1849, Alfred Colwell; 1850, Samuel Z. Ross; 1851, 1852, Alonzo W. Newcomb; 1853, John Thorn; 1854, 1855, Oliver R. Brown; 1856–59, Alonzo W. Newcomb; 1860, Alfred Colwell; 1861, 1862, Rufus W. Briggs; 1863–5, Robert F. Pierson; 1866, 1867, Orrin L. Hudnut; 1868, Chauncey Sheldon; 1869, 1870, Marcus Mabee; 1871, 1872, Elijah H. Woodworth; 1873, 1874, Orrin L. Hudnut; 1875, 1876, John P. Brown; 1877, 1878, Francis Hunter.

THE CHURCHES.

FIRST CHRISTIAN CHURCH OF ROYALTON.

We are largely indebted to Rev. Thomas Taylor for material for the history of this church, which is located at Orangeport.

Here is where the gospel was first preached in Niagara county, away from the river, and the first church organized west of Genesee river in this State.

The person who took the lead was a Mrs. Wilder, who lived north of the canal, on the farm now owned and occupied by George Kayner; and the second was Prudence Bugbee, who lived where her grandson Henry now lives. These two women finally started a female prayer-meeting. There was not a man in the community to take part in a religious meeting, or who made any religious profession; but the two women appointed a public meeting at the house of Louden Andrews, just south of what is now Orangeport. It was a log house, that stood back near the foot of the " mountain," by the spring.

As these two faithful servants of their heavenly Master rode up to the meeting on horseback, they saw a number of men standing about the house. Mrs. Wilder said to Mrs. Bugbee, " Now, Prudence, don't you flinch; trust in God, and he will sustain us." The meeting was duly opened and conducted, and some of the men were deeply affected, and soon a Mr. Ailsworth was added to this little praying army.

The first preacher who labored in this community was Oliver Castle. His labors were not immediately blessed of God, yet the bread cast upon the waters was found after many days. "About the first of January, 1813, the Lord began to move upon the hearts of the people; the rude cabins reverberated with the praises of God, the wilderness and the solitary places were made glad, and the desert began to rejoice and blossom as the rose." About the 1st of June, the same year, elders Joel Doubleday and Nathaniel Brown visited this settlement, and on the 14th six persons were baptized, and in a few days after, a few more were added to their numbers. In July and August, 1817, a revival commenced, under the labors of elders Joel Doubleday and John Blodgett, and numbers were added to the church, and saints who had long prayed for a refreshing from the Lord were made to rejoice, thank God, and take courage.

During this year seventy-three persons were baptized, including Stephen Bugbee, who was for many years deacon of the church. It was during this revival interest that the church was formally organized, on the 20th day of September, 1817, by Elder Doubleday. On the 4th and 5th of October, in the same year, a general meeting was held in the barn which is still standing on the Kayner farm, and was then owned by William Smith, one of the members of the church. This is one of the oldest frame buildings west of Rochester.

MAPLE GROVE FARM, the RESIDENCE of MRS. M.G. PACKARD, TOWN of NIAGARA N.Y.

PIERCE HOTEL MIDDLEPORT, NIAGARA CO, N.Y.
FREE BUSS TO ALL TRAINS.   A. D. RICH. PROPRIETOR.   GOOD LIVERY ATTACHED.

The ministers present at that time were, Joel Doubleday, John Blodgett, Hubbard Thompson, Levi Hathaway, and Joseph Badger. At this meeting William Smith was appointed to the office of deacon, by prayer and the laying on of hands by the elders. He was the first deacon of the church.

During the summer of 1818, a frame meeting-house was raised and enclosed, but not plastered, seated or painted, until about six years after. This was the first house built for public worship on the Holland Purchase.

On the 19th of July, 1818, Russell Weaver and Stephen Bugbee were appointed to the office of deacons. Elder David Millard, who was then present, says in a letter: "The meeting-house was up, without windows or a regular floor. Boards placed on blocks made the seats, and a work bench placed in the east end made a very good pulpit."

The church was legally incorporated on the 5th day of February, 1825, under the name of "First Christian Society of Royalton," with William Smith, Benjamin Hale, and Nathan Stone the first trustees. During this year Elder Badger was preacher in charge, and had the church finished off, doing a large share of the work himself. He had the building painted red, and as long as it stood it was known as the "red meeting-house on the hill." In the winter of 1845, the meeting-house was burned, and during the following summer the society built the present house, at a cost of $1,600. The new church was dedicated in February, 1845, by Rev. W. R. Stowe.

In the spring of 1861 the society purchased of D. D. Day the property immediately south of the church for a parsonage, paying therefor $550.

We find upon examination that upward of one hundred and twenty Christian ministers have each preached one or more sermons to this people, since the days of Oliver Castle.

The church is in a flourishing condition under the present pastor, Rev. Thomas Taylor. The total membership is 86. The salary paid the pastor is $850.

The Sunday-school numbers 116, with an average attendance of 80. There are 150 volumes in the library. The superintendent is Fayette Day.

This church can say with Joshua of old, "The Lord hath blessed me hitherto."

UNIVERSALIST CHURCH OF MIDDLEPORT.

The first time that the doctrine of this denomination was ever preached in or near Middleport, Judge A. S. Baker procured the services of Rev. Linus S. Everett, who preached in a little frame school-house, at what was then called Ewing's Corners, half a mile south of Middleport. The text on that occasion was Acts ii., 39; and the first hymn sung was, "Come, Holy Spirit, Heavenly Dove," etc.

After this the Universalists met for worship in the brick school-house, which is now standing opposite the M. E. church, and occupied by Dr. E. L. Cole as a residence. They continued to meet here until their church was built.

When the society was finally organized, Rev. Mr. Whitnall was in charge. He was formerly a sailor; was on board Nelson's flagship at the battle of Trafalgar, and helped to carry Nelson below when mortally wounded. He was one of those eccentric ministers not often met with. He was succeeded by Rev. Messrs. Hammond, Knapp, Kelsey, Van Campen, Chase, and others.

For a long time Mrs. Judge A. S. Baker was the only woman who would or did attend the Universalist meetings, and she was for a long time the only female member of the society.

In 1841 the society built the present church edifice, which is of stone and brick, located at the corner of Main and Church streets. The cost of the building was $10,000. The society has a sinking fund of $5,000.

In 1871 the society repaired the church at a cost of $2,000, putting in a pipe organ, costing $800.

There are at present thirty communicants, forty-five families connected with the congregation and an average attendance of 112. The value of the church property is $15,000. Rev. Mr. Hutchins is the present pastor.

The Sunday-school connected with this church is also connected with the County Sunday-school Institute, which meets every two months. The following have been superintendents of the school: B. F. King, James Baker, Lucy Hurd, E. J. Swain, Samuel Ward, Ira Congdon, Violetta Spalding. There are eighty-four scholars on the roll, and the average attendance is fifty-three. The library has 177 volumes. Linus S. Freeman is the present superintendent.

MIDDLEPORT M. E. CHURCH.

On the 18th of April, 1827, a Methodist organization was effected, and Francis B. Lane, James Williams, John Bickford, Arunah Bennett and Abijah Terry were duly elected trustees.

Rev. John Copeland, who was then preacher in charge, and presided at the election of trustees, also gave them and their survivors in office a warranty deed of the lot upon which the church now stands, and the church was built the same year. The church is forty by sixty feet, of wood, and built after the fashion of that day. Before the church building was completed, a revival meeting was held in it, boards and planks taking the place of pews. A large addition was made to the membership of the church at this time.

The society owns a valuable parsonage, located on Main street. The well upon the parsonage lot was dug by Rev. Isaac Puffer, who was preacher in charge at the time. The old man dug the well and stoned it up, doing all the work nights, by the light of tallow candles. He did this in order not to employ any of the day time, which might be occupied in visiting his flock and attending to pastoral duties. This was one of "Chapter-and-verse" Puffer's eccentricities.

The following preachers have served this church since the days of Copeland and Puffer: Arunah Bennett, H.

May, James Dunham, William Jarrett, Chauncey S. Baker, Philander Powers, M. W. Benedict, S. Saulsbury, D. D. Buck, H. R. Smith, D. J. B. Hoyt, William Cooley, B. F. McNeil, F. M. Warren, P. W. Gould, G. W. Kittenger, G. Fillmore, P. E. Woodruff, S. C. Church, Orrin Abbott, M. Harker, J. Vaughn, J. Timmerman, Milo Scott, L. Packard, H. Van Benschoten, L. T. Foote, S. C. Smith, William Magovern, W. S. Tuttle, and the present pastor, S. S. Ballou.

The present membership is sixty-five. The church property is valued at $6,000. The Sunday-school connected with this church is under the supervision of George J. Hine, Esq., and is in a flourishing condition. The total number of members is 120; average attendance 80; volumes in library 200.

SECOND FREE-WILL BAPTIST CHURCH OF ROYALTON.

The church edifice is located on what is known as Griswold street, about two and a half miles south of Middleport. The building is of wood, about thirty by forty feet, cost five hundred dollars, and was built and dedicated in 1839.

Elder Gilman was the first pastor, and was followed by Elder Wilder, who was succeeded by Elder Draper, who occupied the pulpit until 1871 or 1872, when he died. Since that time the church has been occupied by Methodists, Baptists, Christians and others, as there is no regular or stated preaching at the church at present. The real estate was conveyed by Adam Miller to the "Second Free Will Baptist Society" of Royalton, by warranty deed.

FIRST BAPTIST CHURCH OF ROYALTON.

This church is located four miles south of Gasport, near Dysinger's Corners, on what is known as Locust street. The society was organized August 20th, 1822, by F. Holdridge, S. J. Olney, R. W. Berry, David Pettit, G. Sprean, J. Albin, Debora Holdridge, Sally Berry, Sally Durfee, Olive Albin, and Elijah Holdridge. The first meeting for organization was held in the school-house in district No. 13, in which the church is now located.

From 1822 to 1836, elders Parsons and Waterbury were the pastors. From 1836 to 1847, there was no stated preaching, but the church was supplied by preachers from the surrounding churches. From 1848 to 1852, Elder Browning Hunt was in charge, and during 1852 was succeeded by Elder Pettit, who resigned in 1856. Elder G. W. Porter preached from 1856 to 1859; Elder Gilbert in 1860, and Elder Way in 1861. Between 1861 and 1868, Elder S. G. Smith, of Lockport, preached here occasionally.

During this time the old church was burned, and the present edifice erected and dedicated in 1866, by Elder S. G. Smith, who also supplied the church for nearly one year, when, in 1871, Elder J. P. Bates was placed in charge. Rev. R. B. Hull, now of the Tabernacle Church, New York, supplied the church in 1872; Elder J. R. Smith in 1873, and Elder E. F. Owen from 1874 to 1876. The church was closed for about a year, when, on November 1st, 1877, Elder I. N. Pease, the present pastor, was settled as shepherd of the flock.

The first church building was erected in 1823, of wood, at a cost of about $500. The present edifice, also of wood, was built and dedicated in 1869, at a cost of $3,000 for lot and building. The parsonage adjoining the church lot cost the society $2,000. The present value of the church property is $5,000.

The first Sunday-school connected with this church was organized by L. B. Horton, as superintendent, in 1826, who conducted the school until 1856, with an average attendance of twenty-five pupils. The present superintendent is W. I. Ward. The whole number of scholars is seventy, and the average attendance fifty.

ROMAN CATHOLIC.

This church property was purchased from C. W. Platts and others, trustees of the Presbyterian church of Middleport, in February, 1875, for $1,700. Since then the Catholics have expended as much more in repairs and painting, making a valuation of $3,400. This is a "mission," with Father O'Reily in charge. They have a Sunday-school, averaging about thirty scholars, connected with the mission.

GERMAN LUTHERAN TRINITY CHURCH.

This church is located on Main street in the village of Wolcottsville. The society was formed in 1854, with the following named persons as elders and deacons: F. Sarow, A. Voelker, F. Voelker, William Lindke, C. Webber, A. Hellert, L. Nemvede, P. Sy, C. Mann; and Rev. Mr. Boehm, as pastor, for the first four years.

In 1867 the society decided to build a new church, of brick, 35 by 58 feet. The brick were made on the lot on which the church stands, by members of the church, they doing the whole of the work, making the brick, furnishing all the material, building the church and completing it, all within themselves, not counting the cost, or knowing the exact value of the church when completed and dedicated in 1868, making a free will offering to Him whom they worship. The present value of church and parsonage is probably about $5,000.

The ministers since Rev. Mr. Boehm, have been: Rev. Messrs. Lemhuis, nine years; Mueller, nine years; K. G. Krebs, the present pastor, one and a half years.

This church is under the care of the Synod of Iowa. The communicants number 318.

METHODIST EPISCOPAL CHURCH OF ROYALTON.

The first Methodist class in Royalton was formed on the 25th of April, 1818, by Daniel Shepherdson and Cyrus Story, who were circuit preachers. Joel Bixby was appointed the first leader. There were sixteen members, and the preaching services were held at the house of the leader, once in four weeks. The first trustees of the society were elected in 1836.

The church is of brick, and was built and dedicated in 1838, and rebuilt in 1862. The original cost was $3,000.

RESIDENCE OF DR P. FALING, ROYALTON TOWN, NIAGARA CO., N.Y.

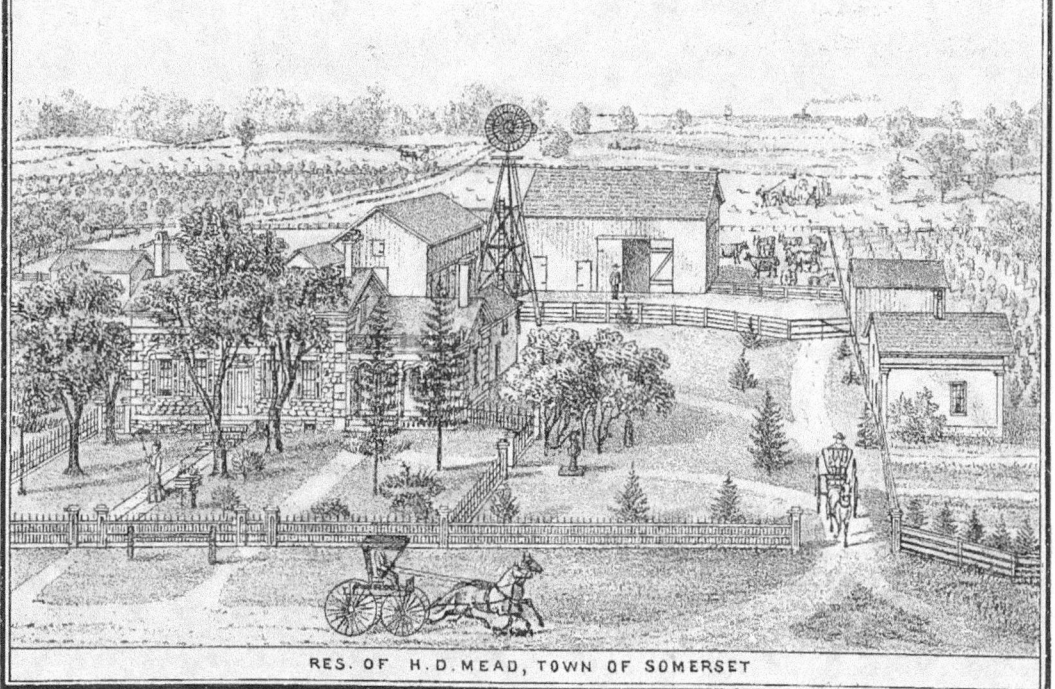
RES. OF H.D. MEAD, TOWN OF SOMERSET

The first Sunday-school was organized with fifty scholars, and Simon Bixby superintendent. The present superintendent is C. E. Bixby. The number of scholars is 123, and the average attendance 82. There are 200 volumes in the library. The value of the church property at present is $6,000. The present pastor is Rev. A. Staples.

PRESBYTERIAN CHURCH OF MIDDLEPORT.

The Presbyterian church in this village was organized June 11th, 1833, by Rev. Messrs. Rawson, Reed, Mead and Page, and was received under the care of the Presbytery of Niagara on the 25th of the same month. As stated supplies under the patronage of the American Home Missionary Society we find in succession the names of Revs. Adino Stanley, Herman Halsey, Beaufort Ladd, Richard Dunning, Samuel A. Rawson and Elisha B. Sherwood. None of them, except Mr. Sherwood, appear to have staid more than one year. Mr. Sherwood was there three years. He left in June, 1845, and was succeeded by Revs. Bridgeman, Kennedy, Clute, Beardsley, Markinson and Dox. The last named was a Congregationalist minister, located at Gasport, and supplied this place from there. He was in charge during 1874, and until February, 1875, when the church property was sold to the Roman Catholics, for $1,700.

There were then about eighty members belonging to the church, and the property was comparatively free from debt. The trustees at that time were Messrs. Boyd, of Johnson's Creek, Smith, of Jeddo, and Platts, of Middleport.

There was a very prosperous Sunday-school connected with the church, with Stephen Griswold as superintendent, an average attendance of thirty-five scholars, and two hundred and thirty volumes in the library.

CONGREGATIONAL CHURCH OF ROYALTON.

This is one of the Gasport churches. It was organized October 5th, 1817, by Rev. Eleazer Fairbanks, a member of the Connecticut Missionary Society, with the following members: Titus Fenn, William Welch, Paul Sawyer, Nehemiah Brown, James Smedley, Ethan Fenn, Samuel Hitchcock, Ruth Welch, Rhoda Fenn, Matilda Hitchcock, Thankful Barrett, Hannah Sawyer, Polly Meade, Mary Harwood, Abbie Fenn and Martha Mead. Titus Fenn and William Welch were chosen deacons, and Titus Fenn clerk of the society.

It does not appear upon the records how long Mr. Fairbanks remained with this society. He was succeeded by Rev. James C. Crane, who supplied the pulpit occasionally until near the close of 1821, when Rev. James Colton became the settled pastor. He was succeeded in 1830 by Rev. Mr. Rawson; 1832, Rev. David Page; 1833, Rev. Isaac Crabb; 1834, 1845, Rev. N. L. Yeoman; 1836, Abram Ingersoll; 1837, 1838, Rev. N. L. Yeoman; 1839-42, Rev. Richard Dunning; 1843, 1844, Rev. Elisha Sherwood; 1846-48, Rev. Roswell Brooks.

During the year 1848 the society built the present church edifice, at a cost of about $1,500. The proceeds of land donated by the Holland Land Company aided materially in the building of the church.

The society was now without regular preaching, and was supplied by Methodist itinerants, and by Rev. J. L. Bennett, from the Congregational church of Lockport. In 1859 and 1860, Rev. H. L. Dox was the supply, and he was succeeded by Revs. J. L. Bennett and John W. Markinson, and he himself again supplied the pulpit until July, 1876. In March, 1877, Rev. Edward Harwood became the settled pastor of this society.

The church building is of wood, about 36 by 50 feet. The parsonage is of brick, and was built and used for an academy until this society purchased it, in 1870, for a parsonage. The church property is valued at $3,000. The number of members at present is fifty.

The Sunday-school connected with this church numbers seventy scholars, with an average attendance of fifty. George Kayner is superintendent.

TRINITY CHURCH, MIDDLEPORT.

The services of the Protestant Episcopal church were first introduced into the village of Middleport in 1864, by Rev. W. A. Matson, D.D., and Rev. J. Abercrombie, D.D., both of Lockport, and Rev. R. D. Stearns, of Medina, who officiated in rotation on Sunday evenings during the summer and autumn of that year. These occasional services developed so much interest that a few of the leading citizens determined if possible to secure the services of a resident minister. Accordingly, Messrs. A. S. Delano, and W. H. Cornes engaged Rev. G. W. Southwell, the rector of Christ Church, Albion, to locate in Middleport, which meeting with the approval of Bishop DeLancy, he commenced permanent labor on January 1st, 1865. At that time Mrs. W. H. Cornes and Mrs. George Sage were the only communicants of the church in the village. The first baptism was that of Mrs. A. S. Delano, who was baptized by Rev. J. Abercrombie December 4th, 1864. The first confirmation was held by Right Reverend A. C. Coxe, D.D., then assistant bishop of this diocese, on January 20th, 1865, when Mrs. A. S. Delano, Mrs. E. B. Delano, and Mrs. Charles B. Lane were confirmed, and soon after became communicants.

Thirteen others were added to the communion during the year, so that on the first of January, 1866, the number of communicants was eighteen. On August 1st, 1866, the parish was organized by the name of "Trinity Church," when Messrs. A. S. Delano and C. R. Blakslee were elected church wardens, and Messrs. James Lobbett, J. Cornes, A. F. Pierce, J. Biddick, H. Pierce, W. S. Fenn, E. H. Woodworth, and E. B. Delano were elected vestrymen. At that time twenty-two communicants and about thirty families were connected with the parish.

For four years, services were held in the Presbyterian church, now owned and used by the Roman Catholics. Later, in 1868, the Presbyterian society resolved to revive their services, and re-occupy their church. This necessitated the building of a church. Plans and specifications were procured of Mr. H. Dudley, of New York, and the corner-stone was laid by Bishop Coxe on May 31st, 1869, on a beautiful lot, the gift of Mrs. A. S. Delano. The church is of brick, with stone trimmings, Gothic, with nave, porch, chancel, tower, and a basement chapel, and will seat about 250. It was completed in 1873, at a cost of $9,600.

The Rev. G. W. Southwell was compelled by ill health to resign in March, 1873, and was immediately succeeded by Rev. J. H. Dennis, who resigned in September, 1874. Rev. A. Wood succeeded in February, 1875, and remained about two years, when Rev. Mr. Southwell again became rector, in connection with his labors for Christ Church, Lockport, and is now in charge. About forty families and eighty communicants are now connected with the church. The present vestry is composed of Messrs. A. S. Delano and O. E. Seaman, church-wardens, and M. J. Sterritt, A. D. Filer, G. Cheshire, R. Pearce, and G. W. Eddy, vestrymen.

The Sunday-school was organized in January, 1865, and had, during that year, eight teachers and sixty pupils. The attendance has not varied greatly since. The superintendent at present is W. J. Sterritt. The teachers number eight; pupils, 55; volumes in library, 150.

ST. MARY'S ROMAN CATHOLIC CHURCH.

This society was organized in 1858, with about fifty members, and in that year they built a frame church, thirty by forty feet, located at Gasport, and costing about $800, Michael Brady donating the land upon which the building stands. Since then the improvements on the church property have cost about $500. The present membership is about fifty. The pastors have been: Fathers O'Conner, Vahey, Shehan, Mulholland, Dwyer, Mulloy, O'Mara, Brougham, O'Leary and O'Riley, the present pastor. A catechetical school is held every Sunday for the children.

EVANGELICAL ASSOCIATION OF ROYALTON.

This society was organized in 1858, at Gasport, with about thirty members. The discipline and doctrines of this association are similar to those of the Methodist Epsicopal Church. For nearly thirty years the society held its meetings in the old school-house at Gasport. In 1878 it built a new church of wood, twenty-six by thirty-eight feet, costing $1,000.

At present the membership numbers about thirty. The trustees of the society are, Louis Pandel, Gilbert Otto and Henry Stouth, sen. The Sabbath-school numbers about thirty pupils, with Louis Pandel as superintendent.

The following are among the pastors who have served this church: Revs. D. Fisher, Theobald Schneider, J. Granzibeck, F. Lohmyer, A. Kline, —— Pfitzinger, and Jacob Eberling, the present pastor.

There is also a German Lutheran church at Wolcottsville, for the history of which we could obtain no material.

SOLDIERS OF THE UNION.

Two hundred and twenty-nine men from Royalton are enrolled in the town records as having served in the army during the civil war. They are named and credited to the town on the rolls printed in the county history in connection with the organization to which they belonged.

BIOGRAPHICAL SKETCHES OF PROMINENT RESIDENTS.

Timothy Bray, one of the principal grocers of Middleport, was born in Tipperary county, Ireland, November 30th, 1837. He came to America and settled in Niagara county in 1858, and in 1871 removed to Middleport, where he engaged in the grocery business, which still occupies his time and attention.

Thomas H. Cheshire, a farmer by occupation, was born in Rochester December 23d, 1837. In August, 1862, he enlisted in Company G., 151st N. Y. infantry. He was regimental and brigade bugler, and was in the battles of Locust Grove, Va., and the Wilderness, Va., and discharged in July, 1865, when he located in Middleport.

S. H. Clark is the publisher of the *Middleport Mail*, a weekly paper. Post-office, Middleport.

Avery S. Delano, a native of Orleans county, was born August 20th, 1820. Mr. Delano has resided in the village of Middleport since 1850, when he came here from Eagle Harbor, N. Y. He was formerly very extensively engaged in the milling business, but at present is manufacturing barrel heading and lumber. At the spring election of 1878 he was elected justice of the peace to fill a vacancy, also for the long term.

John Duff, M.D., is a native of this county, having been born at Johnson's Creek, August 29th, 1843. At the breaking out of the late rebellion, he enlisted in the 8th artillery, where, at Cold Harbor, Va., he won for himself the lasting regard of his comrades for his bravery, which was recognized by them in the presentation to him of a gold medal, costing $100, with the following inscription beautifully engraved upon the obverse side: "A tribute of the century to John Duff, for a rare act of heroic devotion, in rescuing the body of Colonel Peter A. Porter, 8th N. Y. artillery, from under the guns of the enemy, Cold Harbor, Va., June 3d, 1864." On the reverse is a squad of soldiers in the act of carrying a wounded or dying comrade from the field of battle. Around the edge, or rim, are the words, "Valor and affection triumphant in life and death." In February, 1870, Dr. D. graduated from the Buffalo Medical College, and commenced practice at once. He came to Royalton Center in May, 1874, where he has acquired a large practice.

Henry Dysinger, a native of Perry county, Pa., was born in 1821. He came to Royalton in 1849, and located on the farm he now owns. He has served his town as assessor for one year, and is now commissioner of highways. Post-office, Lockport, N. Y.

John Ernest was born in Perry county, Pa., in 1822, and came to Lockport with his father in 1830. He owns one hundred and ninety-one acres of land, and has been assessor two years. Post-office, Lockport, N. Y.

William Ewing, who was born in the same year with

RESIDENCE & FRUIT HOUSE OF J.W. SHAFER ESQ., TOWN OF ROYALTON, NIAGARA CO., N.Y.

RESIDENCE OF DR F. L. KNAPP, GASPORT, NIAGARA CO., N.Y.

the election of the first set of officers of this town,—1818—has now but two seniors who were born here, viz., J. Slaton and E. S. Williams. Mr. Ewing's father was born in Rhode Island in 1785, and came with his family to Royalton in 1815, and located on lot No. 4, two and a half miles southwest of what is now Middleport. Mr. Ewing lives at Freeman's Corners, half a mile south of Middleport. He was born on the farm on which he now resides. Post-office, Middleport.

Dr. Peter Faling was born March 12th, 1833, at Clifton Park, Saratoga county, N. Y. He was married September 8th, 1864, to Miss Emily Robinson, of Lockport, N. Y. He located at Gasport April 1st, 1839, coming from Saratoga county. He is a physician and surgeon, and has also been engaged in milling and farming, mostly stock raising, for over twenty years. His only child, Emma D. Faling, was born June 5th, 1866. Dr. Faling graduated at Albany Medical College December 26th, 1855. He received his preliminary education at the Holley Academy, and at the Lockport Union School.

Linus S. Freeman was born in this town on the 27th of September, 1839. He is engaged in a general mercantile and insurance business. He is fully identified with the temperance work in this county; is one of those wide-awake Sunday-school men seldom met with, and is superintendent of the Universalist Sunday-school at Middleport, where he lives.

J. C. Good's post-office is Royalton. His father, George Good, was born in Lehigh county, Pa., in 1800. In 1819 he traveled on foot from Lehigh to Niagara, through the woods, where he established the first tailor shop in Niagara county. He came to Royalton in 1847, and died February 1st, 1875.

Milan A. Gregory was born in the town of Lockport in 1842. He enlisted June 7th, 1862, in Company D., 129th N. Y. infantry, and took part in the battles of Spottsylvania, Cold Harbor, and Weldon Railroad. He was wounded twice, and discharged in June, 1865. Soon after the war he located in Royalton, where he is engaged in farming. Post-office, Reynale's Basin.

Fred Hagardon, jr., enlisted in Company B., 8th Heavy Artillery, in August, 1862. He was in the battles of North Anna, Cold Harbor and Petersburg, where he was wounded, and discharged in August, 1865. His post-office is Royalton.

George B. Holdridge resides in Royalton, and his post-office is Middleport.

Gilbert J. Hine, a native of New Haven, Conn., was born March 13th, 1813. Early in life he espoused the cause of temperance, and is still its earnest advocate in all its forms. He was a radical abolitionist, which finally cost him dearly, financially, as he was for many years an extensive manufacturer of carriage springs, and had a large trade in the Southern States, which was cut off as soon as his political views were well known. He was for many years a member of the city government of New Haven. He came to Middleport in 1871, and purchased an interest in the boat yard and dry dock of Mr. Dunton, and is now sole proprietor. He is one of the leading members of the M. E. church, and superintendent of its Sunday-school.

Leander T. Huntley came to Royalton in 1845, from New London county, Conn., where he was born in 1819. In 1848 he purchased 100 acres of land. He married in 1853. He has taught school for fourteen years, and has been school commissioner five years; was elected justice of the peace in 1861, and held the office of justice of sessions one term. Post-office address, Royalton.

Thomas W. Jackson was born at Hendersonville, near Nashville, Tenn. He came to Middleport in 1873, and is the senior member of the firm of Jackson & Eddy, who are large lumber dealers, also selling paints, oils and building material.

Shedrick J. Jackson was born January 15th, 1842, at Canandaigua, N. Y. Mr. Jackson was a member of Company H, 140th regiment New York volunteer infantry, and served three years during the late war. He came from Lockport January 20th, 1870, to Middleport, where he pursues the occupation of a barber.

Silas Knapp came to Royalton from Westchester county, N. Y., May 5th, 1838, and is by occupation a farmer. He was born at Phillipstown, Putnam county, N. Y. August 4th, 1822. Post-office address, Middleport.

Dr. Franklin L. Knapp was born in Genesee county, N. Y., in 1817. His father was a pioneer Universalist minister. The son's common school education was obtained in Monroe county. Afterward his father's family moved into Niagara county, where he received his academic education, and in 1844 and 1845 attended the medical college at Geneva, N. Y. While there attending lectures he became acquainted with Dr. Williams, who advocated a new philosophy in the therapeutic action of remedies, holding that God had created special laws governing all particles of matter, and there were no exceptions in disease. Fifteen years after the first introduction of the new mode of applying remedial agents in disease in this country, by Dr. Gram in New York city, Dr. Knapp received his diploma and is now in practice at Gasport, N. Y.

Charles W. Laskey is a rising young lawyer of Middleport, where he located October 1st, 1874, coming from Albion. He was born July 28th, 1852, in Barre, Orleans county. October 2nd, 1877, he married Sarah E. Greeno of Newark, N. Y. He has been for two or three years clerk of the village of Middleport, and clerk and tax collector of the school district. He received his general and professional education at Albion, where he studied law with Reynolds & Crandall in 1871 and 1874. He was admitted to the bar in 1874.

Mrs. Polly Lyman, relict of the late A. Lyman, who died in this town April 19th, 1852, is a daughter of William Ewing, and was born in the town of Whiting, Addison county, Vt., in 1814, whence she came to Royalton in 1816 with her parents. Her post-office address is Middleport.

James Mackey came to Royalton in 1831, with his father. In 1852 he purchased a farm one mile west of the Center, but now lives on the farm purchased of Justice

Dunn. He has served his town six years as assessor. Post-office, Gasport.

Sidney McKnight was born in Berkshire county, Mass., June 24th, 1816, and came to Royalton in 1853 and purchased the farm he now lives on, which is one of the oldest settled farms in the town. Post-office, Middleport.

Mrs. Sarah McChesney, Middleport, is a daughter of Samuel and Dorothy Kittenger, and wife of George McChesney.

Charles Volney Mesler is a postmaster, notary public, and lumber dealer, and was born October 13th, 1836, in Barre, Orleans county, and married to Hattie E. Ward, of Gasport, N.Y., November 13th, 1868. He enlisted in Company K, first Michigan infantry, April 19th, 1861. He was at the capture of Alexandria, Va., when the lamented Ellsworth was murdered by the notorious Jackson. Mr. Mesler served the three months for which he enlisted, and was mustered out at Detroit, Mich., August 1st, 1861. Returning to his native State, he re-enlisted in company B, 105th N. Y. volunteers, October 13th, 1861. He was appointed orderly sergeant of the company at its organization and was commissioned second lieutenant for meritorious conduct at the second Bull Run battle. At Cedar Mountain his daring and bravery on the field of battle won for him a first lieutenant's commission; which he received November 23rd, 1863; and on January 1st, 1865, for meritorious service he was commissioned as captain of his company. Taken prisoner August 19th, 1864, he was for six months and three days a victim to the outrages practiced upon Union soldiers by the inhuman keepers of the rebel prison hells of Libby, Salisbury, and Dansville. On leaving prison, he was sent to Camp Parole, Annapolis, Md., where he received the first prize for re-enlisting veterans for the war. Captain Mesler was in nearly all the engagements of the Army of the Potomac, and was four times severely wounded. He was mustered out of service with his regiment at Albany, N. Y., July 28th, 1865. Post-office address, Gasport, N. Y.

William B. Munsee, was born in Clinton county, N. Y., in 1806. He went to Orleans county in 1822 with his father. He married in 1832, and in 1835 located on lot No. 6, in Royalton. He moved to Middleport in 1877, where he still resides.

Peter P. Murphy, M.D., was born in the city of Albany in 1801. He graduated as a physician at Fairfield, N. Y., in 1825. He represented Herkimer county in the Assembly in the winter of 1835, and in the spring came to Royalton and located where he now resides. In 1860 and 1861 he represented this district in the State Senate. Dr. M. is a prominent free mason, in the degree of Kt. of M. He was U. S. examining surgeon during the war for this provost district. He is first in all the enterprises in his town, and especially the educational interests. He has practiced for fifty years, and is still advised with in critical cases. His post-office is Royalton.

Bruce V. Oliver located in the village of Middleport in the spring of 1864. He was born in Pendleton, N. Y., on the 8th of February, 1830. He has served several terms as trustee of the village, and is foreman of the dry dock and boat yard at Middleport.

Robert J. Pearson, a native of Durham, England, came to Lockport in 1831, with his father, and built on a part of the old homestead where he now resides and follows his business of farming. He was supervisor of his town for three years, and three years assessor of Royalton. Robert J. Pearson is a son of the late George Pearson, who was a native of England, and who came to this county in October, 1831. Mr. Pearson, sen., bought a farm there and lived in the town until his death in 1855. Robert J. Pearson is a well known citizen of the town.

W. W. Ross is a son of Samuel Z. Ross, who came to Royalton about the year 1823, having graduated at Fairfield Medical College, and commenced the practice of medicine at an early date. He was born in Newport, Herkimer county, N. Y., in 1802, and died in Royalton in 1847. He was supervisor of the town three terms. The post-office address of W. W. Ross is Royalton Center.

John P. Sawyer, a life-long resident of this town, was born on the 16th day of December, 1821. He is a farmer by occupation. He has been town superintendent of common schools three years. His post-office is Gasport.

Charles H. Schad was born in this town on the 23rd day of August, 1842. He enlisted October 8th, 1861, in Company M, 1st artillery. Having lost his right leg at the ill-fated battle of Chancellorsville, in the latter part of 1863, he was honorably discharged April 13th, 1864. Returning home, he located in Wolcottsville, in the south part of the town, in 1864, and opened a general dry goods and grocery store, where he is still engaged in that business, and farming. He has been justice of the peace for four years, and for the last eight years postmaster at Wolcottsville.

Joseph Sheldon, son of Elijah and Clarisa, was born in this town in 1818. Mr. Sheldon has served as inspector of common schools, overseer of poor, commissioner of highways and assessor, each for one term. Post-office address, Royalton.

H. D. Spalding was born June 13th, 1832, in the town of Hartland, and located in Middleport April 1st, 1851. He is a farmer and salesman. He is now postmaster at Middleport.

Linus Spalding is an old resident of the town, and a merchant in the village of Middleport.

Charles B. Strain is by trade a ship carpenter and caulker, but at present is engaged in agricultural pursuits. He was born on the 9th day of March, 1851, at Lockport, N. Y. He located in Middleport (which is his post-office address) in October, 1862; has been collector of the village.

Heman Swift was born in Junius, Seneca county, N. Y., April 5th, 1813. In 1819 he came with his parents, Severus and Rebecca, to Royalton, and settled on the old Indian trail, about half a mile north of what is now Wolcottsville, on the farm now owned by J. C. Swift. Mr. S. has seen and experienced the rough side of pioneer life. Batavia was the nearest trading point, while Rochesterville and Schlosser were the nearest milling places.

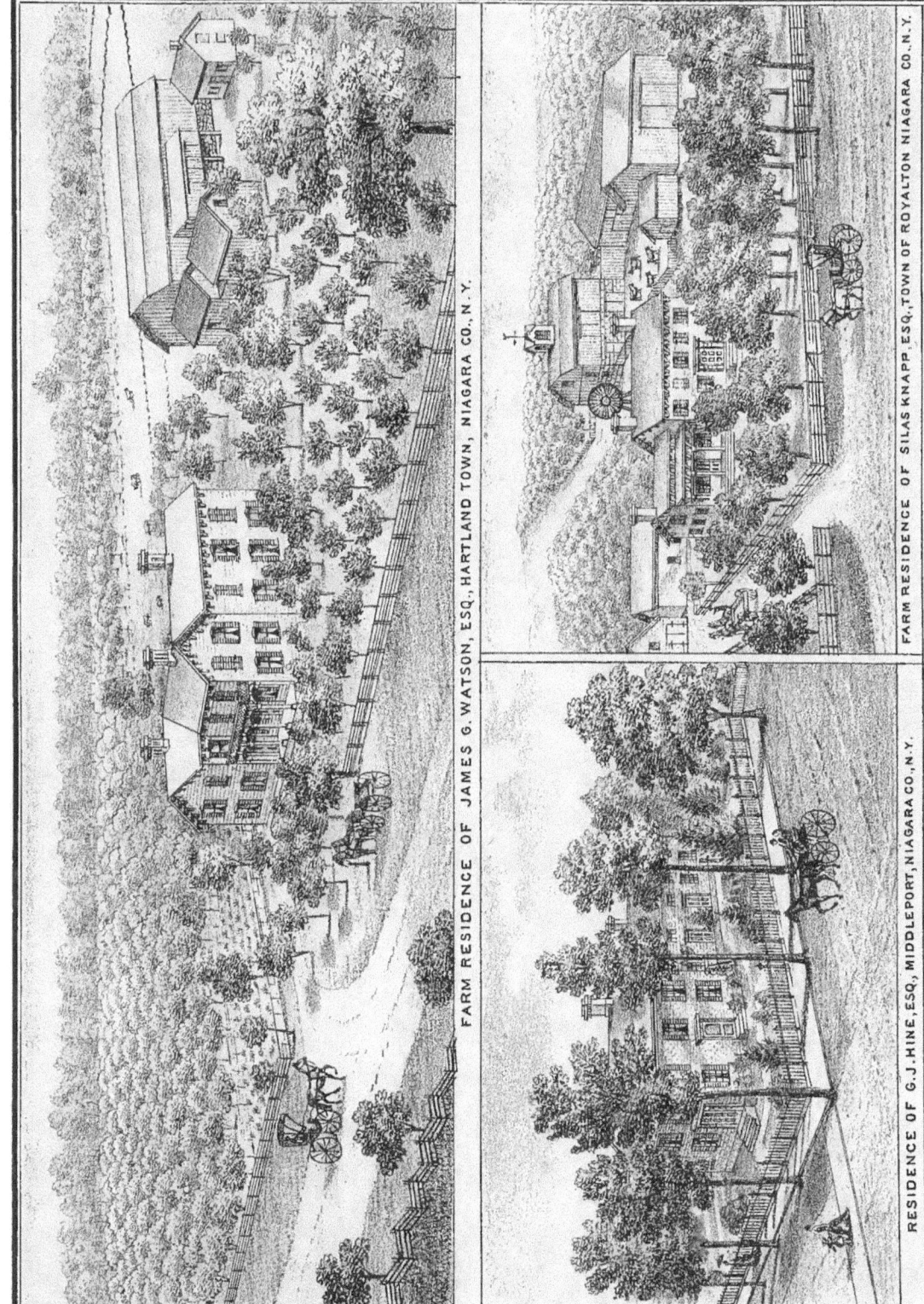

Mr. S. has lived to a good old age, and is now enjoying the fruits of his labors at Middleport.

Spellman Underwood, who is eighty-one years of age, located in Royalton in 1819, and when young made milk pans from the trunks of birch trees, dug out for troughs, and about the same time pulverized corn in an iron kettle with an iron wedge, and lived on that for three weeks. He used to go to Niagara Falls, a distance of twenty-five miles, with an ox team to get a grist ground. He never took medicine of any kind until 1877, and now enjoys good health, and has cleared one hundred acres of land. He was born in Berkshire county, Mass., May 12th, 1797. Post-office, Royalton Center.

John Weyand, a native of Union county, Pa., was born in 1831, and came with his parents to Royalton in 1835, making the journey of 330 miles in covered wagons. Mr. Weyand located about two miles east of Royalton Center, on the Lewiston road. He is a carpenter and joiner. In 1877 he purchased the farm where he resides. Post-office address, Middleport.

Oliver L. Wilcox was born June 26th, 1809, in Glen, Montgomery county, N. Y., and married October 2d, 1833, to Miss Adeline Shuler, of Florida, same county, who was born in that town August 13th, 1811. Mr. Wilcox located at Gasport, N. Y., in July, 1843, and is a farmer and fruit-grower, and has been commissioner of highways for the town one term. He is the father of eleven children, only one of whom, George A. Wilcox, who was born in Glen, N. Y., July 23d, 1839, is living. Sylvanus S. Wilcox, one of his sons, was a captain in the 8th N. Y. cavalry in the late war, and was killed at Mine Run, Va., on the 27th of November, 1863. Mr. Wilcox's father was an officer in the war of the Revolution. Post-office, Gasport.

Erastus L. Williams was born September 16th, 1814, in what is now the town of Royalton. He is one of the oldest natives of the town. The only one older is Joseph Slaton, born in 1811. Mr. Williams's present residence and post-office address is Middleport. He is a farmer by occupation, and has lived to see the Williams family grown up and settled upon farms around him.

Gotlob D. Witterman is the son of George Joseph Witterman, a Lutheran minister from Wirtemberg, Germany. He was born in Montgomery county, N. Y., on the 2nd day of May, 1803. In 1833 he located on the farm where he now resides. In 1858 himself and wife united with the M. E. church at Royalton Center. Post-office address, Royalton.

To the foregoing list may be added the names of John Pierce, Middleport; C. O. Chaplin, Middleport; W. P. Squires, Middleport; Samuel Larkin, post-office, Middleport; T. A. Lusk, whose post-office is Gasport; W. H. Cornes, Middleport; O. M. Lapp, post-office, Gasport; C. W. Gould, M. D., of Gasport, a member of the medical fraternity of the town, and doing a flourishing business; Caroline W. Wilson, post-office, Royalton Center; James C. Smith, farmer, post-office, Wolcottsville; and Mrs. A. M. Judson, farmer, Reynale's Basin.

THE TOWN OF SOMERSET.

IN the spring of 1810, Jacob Fitts and family left their quiet home in the "Jerseys," to seek their fortune in the wilds of western New York. Mrs. F. having a relative at what is now Olcott, N. Y., that place was made the objective point while they trudged over the many weary miles, passing along the Ridge road in Hartland, until they reached what is now Wright's Corners, thence turning northerly to the lake, where they found their relative, a Mr. Kemp, who kindly received them.

In locating Mr. Fitts, his friend Kemp took him over a road he had cut along the lake shore for the Holland Land Company, to a point opposite what is now Somerset Corners, about one and a half mile distant from it. Here Mr. Fitts located, and was the first settler in what is now Somerset. The farm is still in the Fitts family, being owned by Jacob's son, Loran Fitts.

Archibald Whitton, Philip Fitts, Truman and David Mudgett and Zachariah Patterson soon came in and settled. These few families made up the population until after the war of 1812. During this trying period one of their number was drafted, and served until sickness released him from the army, and death soon followed.

The trials incident to the severest experience of pioneer life were the lot of this little band of settlers, who had at times to eat raw pumpkins for want of something better, and sometimes to travel ten miles to a neighboring settlement for three pecks of potatoes, which was done by Mr. Loran Fitts, who is still living. At other times there was nothing to eat except leeks, which grew in abundance, which they would gather and boil, and occasionally they would catch a raccoon, which was the only meat they tasted for a long time. They knew what it was to live in log huts covered with bark, with barns of the same material, and to keep cattle alive through the winter by felling trees daily for them to browse upon the twigs. This last operation helped to feed the pioneer families as well as the live stock, for the deer came out of the woods to share the cattle's fodder, and the best of them were easily shot. Mr. Adam Pease can tell of many adventures with the more savage beasts—bears, wolves wildcats and panthers.

A neighbor whose hogs were running in the woods, as was the custom in those days, heard one of them squeal, ran out to see what was the matter, and to his surprise, found one of them in the arms of a large bear, and by clubbing the latter caused him to drop the hog. Then the bear made for the owner, who fled to the first small tree that he came to and climbed for his life. When he had climbed some ten or twelve feet, he felt the tree giving way, as it proved to be rotten at the roots. Down he and the tree came pell mell to the ground, where the man expected to have a tussle with the bear. But what was his surprise, when he came to look up, to see the bear running as for dear life. He said his hair stood up at the time.

AFTER THE WAR.

Immediately upon the close of the war upon the Niagara frontier, others began to come in and settle near those who had previously taken up, or "articled," as it was called, tracts of land.

Among the number who first came, were James Matthews, Samuel Palmer, David Barker, Adam Pease, Samuel Coleman, Asa Coleman, E. C. and E. Meade, M. and J. Sherwood, H. Pratt, F. N. Albright, Peter Hess, and a few others. Their experience in pioneer life was not much different from that of those who had preceded them, except that their arrival made more neighbors and rendered their lonely existence more endurable.

The following extract from the pen of one of the early settlers gives a graphic description of the good and bad times enjoyed by the pioneers years before there was any Lockport, Newfane, or Somerset:

"If it is not taxing your good nature too much I will give you a short history of our troubles and trials in subduing the wilderness I have just led you to, intermixed with some of the pleasures of living in, and subduing a wilderness. * * * Humphrey Sharpsteen, then just married, came in with his wife and his wife's sisters; Isaac Starbuck with his family; then young Captain Ezra Meade, two sisters, young women, and some other very respectable ladies who were not afraid or ashamed to rough it in the woods, for the sake of being independent, and several young unmarried men, as well as myself, helped to make up an assortment.

"We were all brothers and sisters and friends, and when we could have a good yoke of oxen and a sled, with some straw for a seat, we could all enjoy a ride as well as if in a coach, and we could get more fun out of it, as we had most all seen the time when we had ridden in what would be called better style. And when we visited some friend, if the house was small, the parlor was extensive, consisting of the whole forest. * * * With so much to enjoy, we could not help putting up with the rough. But the worst for us was when we got out of flour and meal, and no mill to grind short of Niagara

RES. OF MRS. J.D. SHULER, LOCKPORT N.Y.

RES. OF FRANCIS KYTE ESQ, TOWN OF PORTER, NIAGARA CO. N.Y.

RES. OF MRS. L. HAIGHT, TOWN OF SOMERSET

RES. OF HARDY FITTS, SOMERSET N.Y.

RES. OF AARON COLEMAN, TOWN OF SOMERSET

RES. OF JACOB S. HAIGHT, TOWN OF SOMERSET.

Falls. * * * John Flavington carried eighteen bushels of wheat to Olcott, and gave it for a barrel of salt. * * *

"When I commenced clearing, which was just after the war, and the cold season of 1816 came on, wheat was worth twenty shillings per bushel, and pork thirty-five dollars per barrel. When I raised some wheat to sell, it was worth twenty-five cents per bushel. I once had a tax of twenty shillings to pay, and I carried butter sixty miles and sold it for one shilling per pound, to pay that tax.

"But one thing we had in plenty was pure whisky; that was cheap, and one bushel of corn would pay for six quarts of whisky. The distance to the ridge, where we did most of our trading, was so great that some persons formed a company and placed a jug of whisky in a hollow tree about half way there, and each one took a drink as they passed, and when it was gone took turns in filling it. They called it the 'tree tavern.'" Others remember the "tavern" as having been a sound cherry tree of great size.

During the period between the first settlement by Mr. Fitts, before the war, and that of the Meades and others after the war, the pioneer path was a rough and rugged one, literally in a howling wilderness, infested by bears and wolves, making it necessary to institute a day and night watch in order to preserve the hogs and sheep. The bears were the most destructive enemies, not unfrequently approaching the hog pens by day, and selecting as a prize the fattest inmate, leaving a sorry chance for a well-provided pork barrel in the fall.

THE FIRST OF THEIR KIND.

The first wedding in what is now the town of Somerset occurred in 1817, when John Sherwood married Miss Rebecca Meade.

Delilah, daughter of Jacob Fitts and wife, was born in 1811. This was the first birth in this town.

Mr. Philip Fitts, who was drafted in 1813, served with his regiment until taken sick, when he was sent home, and died in 1814. He was buried on his farm, now owned by V. D. Bateman, north of Somerset Corners. This was the first death in the town, and no other person has been buried near the grave of Mr. Fitts.

The first plot of ground laid out or set apart for burial purposes in this town is the one a short distance east of Somerset Corners. The first person buried in this ground was a Mr. Amsbrey.

About 1820 James Matthews opened a small grocery store at what is now Somerset Corners, in the first frame building erected in the town.

Josiah S. Bailey opened and kept the first tavern in the town in 1817, at Bailey's Corners. Accommodations were very limited, and the old familiar jug was tipped at the modest request of his thirsty customers. This ancient hostelry was located one and a half miles east of the Corners.

Two and a half miles west of Somerset Corners Mr. James Stevens commenced blacksmithing, which he carried on successfully for several years from 1825. There are at present seven blacksmith shops in the town, and all doing a prosperous business.

Archibald McDaniels built and operated the first gristmill in the town, in 1825. It was located on Fish creek, on the lower Lake road, two miles northeast of the Corners. The mill was afterward burned.

The "Novelty Steam Grist-Mill" was built at Somerset Corners in 1845, by Stephen Peckham. The people having long been without a grist-mill, felt the necessity of one, and thinking they saw their opportunity, subscribed $2,500 towards this one, Mr. Peckham paying the balance, which was about as much more, and one of the best custom mills, with all the modern appliances, was put in operation. It did a very satisfactory and successful business for about fifteen years, when it changed hands, and the new proprietor carried on an extensive flouring business for some time; which resulted disastrously, and the town is again without a grist-mill. The "Novelty" is now in other hands, and is turned into a cider-mill, and is doing a large business.

In 1825 Guy Griswold built and operated a small tannery a short distance west of the Corners, which after a few years was abandoned, and the buildings went to decay.

The first saw-mill in this town was built by John Randolph in 1822, three-quarters of a mile north of the Corners, and after several years went to decay. There are at present two steam saw-mills in the town, one at Somerset Corners, and the other at South Somerset. These mills also manufacture staves and heading, for flour and fruit barrels.

The first bridge was built in 1822 across Fish creek, three-quarters of a mile north of the Corners, near Randolph's saw-mill.

The first log house was built by Jacob Fitts, the first settler, in June, 1810, on the farm now owned by his son Loran Fitts, about one and a half miles north of the Corners on the lake shore.

Silas Meade was the builder of the first frame barn in Somerset, which was put up in 1819, about one and a half miles northwest of the village.

In the fall of 1810 Jacob Fitts sowed three bushels of wheat on a patch of ground he had cleared during the summer, which was the first ground cleared and wheat sown in this town.

The Baptist church, located on the east side of the village of Somerset Corners, the first brick building in the town, was built in 1833.

At present there are quite a number of brick buildings. Probably the Friends' meeting-house was the second, as that was built in 1836.

The first road marked out was probably the one over which Jacob Fitts traveled from Olcott, along the lake shore, to the place where he settled. The Holland Land Company paid Mr. Kemp for making this road, although it was rather a rough one for this country. The first road marked out and used to any extent is the one running east and west through the village of Somerset. The first road of which the town records give us any knowledge is that mentioned in the report of the "survey of township line road, beginning at the Lake road and running north on the township line, between the 5th and 6th ranges of township No. 16 to the lake, one mile and twenty-five rods, to a large beech tree that stands on the beach of the lake, with a blaze on both sides, and three hacks therein. This road was laid out on the first day of May, 1824."

A Mr. Benson was the first man in this town who made a business of working at the carpenter's trade, and was the only man who had tools enough to finish a job when he undertook it. Although his tools were of the old "pod auger" style, he was considered a good workman. He built the first frame barn in the town for Mr. Silas Meade in 1819.

Before improved machinery for making all kinds of cloths was introduced into this country, weaving was done by hand, and to a certain extent by the members of almost every family; yet in many instances the want of a loom, or in some cases the lack of knowledge of its use, demanded a substitute. Thus the families of Adam Pease and Daniel Landers became the principal weavers, and to a large extent used this trade as a means of earning a livelihood.

The first resident physician was Dr. Brown, who settled at the Corners in 1826. Since then physicians have come and gone, and at present there are two in the town, Drs. Hotaling and Bigford.

In 1817 the first school was organized in a small log school-house, that stood one and a half miles west of the Corners. The first teacher was Masten Sherwood. The surviving pupils are: Loran Fitts, Silas Meade and Huldah Meade, now Huldah Bush, wife of German Bush. On the 31st day of December, 1823, there were six school districts in the town, a description of which is upon the records in the town clerk's office. In 1826 the whole number of scholars taught in this town was 165; there were between the ages of five and fifteen 144. In 1877 there were fifteen school districts.

THE POLITICAL RECORD.

Somerset was formed from Hartland, February 8th, 1823, and in 1824 a part of Newfane was taken off. On the 1st day of April, 1823, was held the first town meeting at the house of Silas Meade, and the following officers were elected: Supervisor, James Wisner; town clerk, Samuel Palmer; assessors, Nathaniel Pond, jr., Ezra Meade, James Hess; collector, John Sherwood; overseers of the poor, Samuel Coleman, James Stevens; commissioners of highways, James Hess, Samuel Coleman, Joseph S. Bailey; commissioners of common schools, David Barker, Heman Pratt, Jacob Albright; inspectors of common schools, Peter Hess, William Mosher, Josiah Bullen; constables, John Sherwood, William Palmer.

At this first town meeting it was ordered that a tax of $150 be raised for roads and bridges, and that the town be divided into three equal districts, viz.: eastern, middle and western.

"A true canvass and estimate of the votes taken at an election in the town of Somerset," in November, 1823, gives the following results: For senator, James McCall received 39 votes; John Bowman, 39; Robert McCay, 21; James Norton, 21; for member of Assembly, Daniel Washburn received 35 votes, and Benjamin Barlow, 25.

The complete list of supervisors is as follows:

In 1823, James Wisner; 1824-26, Samuel Palmer; 1827, 1828, John Sherwood; 1829-33, Roswell Downer; 1834, David Barker; 1835, John McNitt; 1836, John Sherwood; 1837, 1838, David Barker; 1839-42, Jeptha W. Babcock; 1843, 1844, Morgan Van Wagoner; 1845, Johnson Aldrich; 1846-48, Charles B. Lane; 1849, Samuel S. Rising; 1850, Stephen T. Peckham; 1851, Emmor K. Gardner; 1852, Samuel S. Rising; 1853, George K. Hood; 1854, Morgan Van Wagoner; 1855, Pixley M. Humphrey; 1856, Vernon D. Bateman; 1857, Morgan Van Wagoner; 1858, Guy C. Humphrey; 1859, Samuel S. Rising; 1860, 1861, Guy C. Humphrey; 1862-64, George M. Swain; 1865, Henry B. Miller; 1866-69, Oscar E. Mann; 1870-72, George K. Hood; 1873, Oscar E. Mann; 1874, 1875, George M. Swain; 1876-78, Guy C. Humphrey.

The town clerks have been as follows:

1823, Samuel Palmer; 1824, Nathan Pond, jr.; 1825, Albert M. Hastings; 1826-28, Heman Pratt; 1829, James Mathews; 1830, Heman Pratt; 1831, 1832, Francis D. Pratt; 1833, Solomon Marse; 1834, Jonatthan N. Shurtliff; 1835, 1836, Samuel Kemp; 1837-39, Francis O. Pratt; 1840-42, Albert Van Wagoner; 1843-48, Francis O. Pratt; 1849, Guy C. Humphrey; 1850, William Sherwood; 1851, James Matthews; 1852, Stephen T. Peckham; 1853, Joseph Hess; 1854, George L. Pratt; 1855, 1856, Joseph Hess; 1857, 1858, Willard Nye; 1859, Marvin S. Perkins; 1860-62, Willard Nye; 1863-67, Joseph Hess; 1868-70, Henry H. Frost; 1871, Joseph Hess; 1872-78, Henry H. Frost.

In the Assembly for eleven terms the member from the second district of Niagara has been from Somerset. Ex-Sheriff Oscar E. Mann is also a Somerset man.

SALT SPRING.

About half a mile west, or up stream, from where Fish creek crosses the road that runs from Somerset village to the lake is a salt spring or well. There is, or was a few years ago an old hollow buttonwood log sunk in the middle of the creek, with one end just above the surface. This salt spring must have been operated by some one before white settlers occupied the country, as it has not been worked since 1810.

LODGES AND ASSOCIATIONS.

ODD FELLOWS.

Ontario Lodge No. 373, I. O. of O. F. was organized in Somerset village in 1847, and continued to work until 1855, when labor was suspended and has not been resumed.

TEMPERANCE ORGANIZATIONS.

The Somerset "Temperance and Literary Association" was organized in 1875, with about fifty members, and the

following officers, designated as directors: Rev. William McCartney, Edwin A. Arnold, Rev. E. H. Bonney, with Charles Wilcox as treasurer, and Mrs. Julia Frost secretary. The name denotes the object of the association. The regular meetings are held monthly, alternately in the Methodist and Presbyterian churches. The present directors are: Rev. J. T. Humphrey, George H. Bradley, and J. Wickham; treasurer, Mrs. Julia Frost; secretary, A. H. Haight. The members number three hundred and seventy-five.

Fountain Union, No. 107, Daughters of Temperance was organized in 1850, under the supervision of John B. Gough. The number of members at the organization was about fifteen. The union continued to increase in numbers and interest until 1856, when it suddenly closed its doors and ceased its labors.

In 1850 a division of the Sons of Temperance was organized at Somerset Corners, and did run well for a season, and in 1867 finished its good work with about two hundred members.

Somerset Lodge, No. 144, Independent Order of Good Templars, was organized at Somerset Corners in 1867, and continued to work for about five years, when this institution followed in the wake of the "Sons" and "Daughters."

MASONIC.

Somerset Lodge, No. 639, F. & A. M. was organized in 1866, and worked under dispensation for about a year, when it received a charter from the Grand Lodge of the State of New York, with the following officers and twenty-two other charter members: C. P. Clark, W. M.; H. C. Hill, S. W.; Irving W. Hotaling, J. W.

Some of the members formed a stock company, purchased a lot on the corner of South and East streets, and erected a two-story brick building, thirty by forty-eight feet, at a cost of $1,490. The lower part of the building is rented and used as a store, while the upper floor is used for lodge purposes. The lodge now owns the property and is out of debt. The following are the present officers: Loran Church, W. M.; Henry Brown, S. W.; S. J. Porter J. W. The membership numbers seventy-eight.

A. O. U. W.

Somerset Lodge, No. 141, Ancient Order of United Workmen, located at Somerset village, was instituted in April, 1878, with the following officers and nineteen members: Oscar E. Mann, P. M. W.; J. W. Wing, M. W.; W. L. Atwater, G. F.; George B. Hood, O.; A. E. Bennett, recorder; G. H. Bradley, receiver; O. J. Thayer, financier; David Huntington, I. W.; J. A. Hill, J.

POST-OFFICES.

Previous to 1825 the people in this section received their mail, if any, by sending out by some neighbor who was going to Buffalo, Rochester or Batavia. About this year Mr. James Mathews was appointed the first postmaster for the town, and he was the only one for several years. The contents of mail bags in those days were not very burdensome to either carrier or postmaster, as but few expected any mail matter, and still fewer received any. At the present time a large, well-filled mail pouch arrives daily, and almost everybody is disappointed if they are not favored with a letter or a newspaper.

Otis Nye was the first man to run a stage from Lockport to Somerset, in or about the year 1848. The exact date of the appointment of Mr. Mathews as postmaster, or of running Mr. Nye's first stage, we are unable to obtain.

The West Somerset post-office was established in 1844, and Marvin S. Hess appointed postmaster. The present postmaster is William Hoffman.

Sidney Smith is the present postmaster at Somerset Corners. The land upon which this village stands was formerly owned by Samuel Palmer, upon the northeast corner of the streets; Isaac Lockwood, on the northwest corner; Isaac Starbuck, on the southwest corner; and William Herrington, on the southeast corner.

The Lake Road post-office is located in the northwest part of the town. The first postmaster was Joseph Babcock. The present postmaster is Lawton Pettit.

THE GOVERNMENT LIGHT-HOUSE,

known as the Thirty-mile Point Light-house, was lighted for the first time in April, 1875. A very handsome sexangular reflecting revolving light was put in, costing about $15,000, and weighing 2,000 pounds. The light shows at a distance of eighty miles. The building in which it is placed is of stone, gothic style, and cost the government about $75,000. It is arranged for two families. The light is operated by Hiram A. Vaughn and James Penfield. It is about seventy-five feet above the water-level.

STATISTICS.

The area of the town is 23,314 acres. The aggregate valuation of the real estate for 1877 was $1,441,844. The assessed valuation of personal property was 76,230.

RELIGIOUS HISTORY.

METHODIST EPISCOPAL CHURCH.

The first class in connection with this church was organized at the house of Silas Meade, west of what is now the Corners, in 1817. Masten Sherwood was appointed leader, and the other members were Tryphena Sherwood, Rebecca Sherwood, Bettie Meade, John Emmons, John Bangham and wife, Silas Meade and Miranda Meade.

For nearly two years the class meetings, as well as the public service, were held at the house of Mr. Meade, and for about five years following, in the little log school-house on Mr. Meade's farm.

Rev. Daniel Shepherdson was the first preacher in charge of this part of what was then a large circuit. He began his ministrations here in 1817. Rev. Messrs. Wright and May supplied this charge for about two years after Mr. Shepherdson, and then for two or three years there was no regular preaching.

The first quarterly meeting ever held in this town was held in Silas Meade's barn, in 1818. In 1829 Rev. Isaac

Puffer was sent to this charge. He was quite aged, as well as eccentric, and in quoting passages from the Bible would invariably give the chapter and verse; and he soon became familiarly known as "old Chapter-and-verse Puffer."

The following is taken from an old record: "1831, July 4th. At a meeting of the male members of the first Methodist Episcopal church of Somerset, held pursuant to public notice, at Alanson Sherwood's, John Sherwood and John Bangham presided, and made choice of Allen Burnham, clerk; and Ezra Meade, John Sherwood, John Randolph (1st class); Masten Sherwood, Martin Dutcher, Alanson Sherwood (2nd class); John Bangham, William Morford and German Bush (3rd class) for trustees. Ezra Meade was made choice of for treasurer.

"*Resolved*, unanimously, to build a meeting-house, to be thirty-two by forty feet on the ground, and that the trustees purchase a site for said meeting-house.

"*Resolved*, That the trustees circulate a subscription for the purpose of raising money for building said house, and purchasing a site for the same."

The lot for the church was purchased in 1831. The church was built in 1839, of wood, and cost $2,000. Over the front door, in a semi-circle or arch, are the words "Methodist Episcopal Chapel, 1839."

In 1870 the society built a parsonage, of wood, costing $2,800, on the lot adjoining the church lot.

In 1878 the society sold the old church to Dr. Irving Hotaling for $300, and built a new church edifice on the site of the old one. The new building is of wood, forty by sixty-nine feet, and cost when completed about $4,500. The corner-stone was laid on the 21st of June, 1878, by Rev. A. F. Morey, presiding elder of the Niagara district of the Genesee Conference, assisted by Revs. C. V. Sparrow and C. C. Wilber of Lockport, A. Staples of Royalton, and J. T. Humphrey, the pastor of the church. The usual deposit of subscription list, papers, coin, etc., was placed in a copper box and laid in the corner-stone. W. L. Atwater, of Somerset, was the architect and builder. The church property is valued at $7,300. The whole number of members and probationers in 1878 was one hundred and ninety-nine.

Since the days of Chapter-and-verse Puffer the following ministers have served this society, viz.: A. Ripley, W. Buck, H. Ripley, Bonn, Luce, Conable, Gridley, Timmermann, Chase, Wilkinson, S. Smith, Fillmore, J. Knapp, May, William Cooley, Gordon, Thomas, Foote, Derr, Plumbley, Scism, C. P. Clark, S. Y. Hammond, A. Staples, W. McGavern, William McCartney and J. T. Humphrey, the present very efficient pastor, under whose labors nearly one hundred have been added to the church during the last year.

At a meeting of the members and friends of the church, on the 10th of November, 1832, it was unanimously resolved to establish a Sabbath-school society. A constitution and by-laws were adopted in conformity to the discipline, making it auxiliary to the Sunday-school Union of the Methodist Episcopal church. Alanson Sherwood was chosen president; Ezra Meade, vice-president; Allen Burnham, secretary; John Bangham, treasurer; and German Bush, Caleb Martin, Oliver Earl, Martin Dutcher, Elijah R. Meade, John Sherwood, Masten Sherwood, Daniel T. Bush, Lassen Hix and Jackson F. Randolph, managers.

The following appear as scholars: Elizabeth Earl, Oliver Burnham, Dolly B. Sherwood, Hannah Martin, Miranda Meade, Arzulah Meade and Syntha Dutcher. In 1878 the Sunday-school in connection with this church numbered one hundred and fifty scholars, with an average attendance of ninety, and had one hundred and forty volumes in its library. Henry H. Frost was superintendent.

WEST SOMERSET BAPTIST CHURCH.

The first meeting preliminary to the organization of this society was held in Mr. Dickinson's barn in 1843, just west of where the church now stands.

At this meeting it was decided to purchase the house and one acre of land of S. J. Colby, on the corner of the road, for a parsonage, which was done at a cost of $200. Subsequently the society built an addition to the house for the use of the preacher and family, and for seven years held public service and social meetings in the main part of the parsonage.

The first covenant meeting of this society was held on the 12th day of April, 1845, when the following persons were recognized as members: Reuben D. Feagles, J. B. Hoffman and wife, Henry Niles and wife, C. Dickinson and wife, Isaac Raze and wife, Thomas Briggs and wife. On the 20th of April the society was fully organized. Mr. Feagles, Mr. Dickinson and Mr. and Mrs. Hoffman are the only surviving members of the original number.

On the 28th of May, 1845, the society was reorganized by the Baptist association, and known as the West Baptist Church of Somerset.

June 18th, 1845, Thomas Briggs was ordained as the first deacon of this church. October 11th, 1845, Thomas Briggs, Marcus Noble and Reuben Raze were elected trustees of the society. January 10th, 1846, elder Harvey Pettit was admitted as the first ordained minister for this society.

In the latter part of 1849 the society decided to build a brick church, forty by sixty feet with basement, which was completed in 1850, at a cost of $1,850. Elder Jesse Colby gave to the society the acre of land upon which the church stands, on the corner of the highway opposite the parsonage. The money for building the church was raised by subscription.

The following persons have served this church as pastors from its organization to the present time: Elders Pettit, Mosher, Berry, Smith, Atwater, Brown, Olney, Gardner, Islip, Parsons and Fenner, the present pastor.

The Sunday-school connected with this church was organized in 1845, with Ephraim Judson as superintendent and about thirty scholars.

The present superintendent is Romeyn Noble. The whole number of scholars is one hundred; average attendance, seventy; volumes in library, one hundred.

RES. OF GUY C. HUMPHREY, TOWN OF SOMERSET

RES. OF I. J. GARDNER, TOWN OF SOMERSET, NIAGARA CO.

FRIENDS.

The Society of Friends was organized in this town in 1821, with twenty members. For about fifteen years they held their meetings at private houses in the bounds of the society.

Mrs. Miriam Winslow was the first settled preacher, and she died in 1828. She was followed by David Gardner, who died a few years after. David Haight followed Gardner as settled preacher, and still remains with this people.

Charles Haviland, from Royalton, and others from Lockport, supplied the intervals between the pastorates of Mrs. Winslow and Mr. Gardner, and between those of Gardner and Haight. In 1836 the society built a brick church, twenty-four by thirty-six feet, costing $400.

The membership of this society at present numbers twenty-five. They pay no salary to their preacher.

Adjoining the church is a burying ground belonging to the society. In 1852 they built a stone wall around the ground at a cost of $160.

BAPTIST CHURCH, SOMERSET.

This body was first known as a Baptist church on the 23d day of January, 1820. It was formally recognized by an ecclesiastical council, which was held at the residence of James Stevens, then in Hartland, now in Somerset.

For three and a half years after its recognition the society met from house to house, frequently visited by Elder Jehial Wisner, then a Baptist missionary, visiting from place to place,

In September, 1823, Elder Wisner received and accepted a call to become pastor. His labors were in a very marked degree attended with interest and success. In the month of November following an extensive revival occurred, and a considerable number were added to the church.

On the 13th of June, 1830, a council was called by the church, for the purpose of ordaining R. L. Wilson, he having received a call from the church to become the pastor. The newly ordained pastor on this day baptized eleven persons.

In 1832 the necessity of a suitable place of worship was felt by the church and community. On application, the avails of fifty acres of land, a gift from the Holland Land Company, were applied to the building of the meeting-house, which is still standing, located at the village of Somerset.

In October, 1839, Elder Wilson resigned the charge of the church, having labored over ten years successfully as its pastor. In 1839 Elder Arah Irons supplied the church. In 1840 Elder S. J. Olney became the pastor He remained three years. During his labors eighty were added to the church. In May, 1846, the Rev. G. C. Walker received and accepted a call from the church. He remained the pastor over five years. The church then called L. M. Woodruff, a licentiate. He was ordained pastor on the 30th day of June, 1852, and remained about three years, when he resigned. During his pastorate twenty were added to the church. In May, 1855, John Gundy accepted the call of the church, and served it for three years. During this period Mortimer Willson and J. H. Denton, members of this society, were licensed by the church to preach the gospel.

In 1857 the church expended $1,400 in remodeling the house of worship.

For about one year the church was destitute of a pastor. On the 25th day of August, 1861, a council convened to ordain I. H. Denton as pastor. He served the church for about three years, and was followed by Rev. George Willson. On the 1st day of May, 1866, Rev. B. W. Rogers accepted the call of the church, and labored successfully for nearly three years, a number being added to the church through his ministry. In June, 1869, Rev. Samuel Smith became pastor of the church; he served two years and resigned.

The church has licensed twelve of its members to preach the gospel. Since the resignation of Mr. Smith, there has been no regular preaching, if any, in the Baptist church at Somerset Corners.

PRESBYTERIAN CHURCH, SOMERSET.

The Presbyterian church of Somerset was organized January 26th, 1824, at Stephen Sherwood's house. The original members, who were regularly constituted a Presbyterian church at that time, were Stephen Sherwood, Mrs. Diana Sherwood, Jesse Sherwood, Mrs. Mary Bangham, Mrs. Lydia Brown, and Mrs. Lucy Sherwood.

The Rev. E. Everett officiated at this organization. June 5th, 1832, James Hess, Elijah Arnold and Anselmo Tenny were ordained as elders, and Peter Hess and Lorenzo Thayer deacons of the church, by the Rev. David Pratt.

February 10th, 1834, at a meeting of the male members held at Dr. A. B. Brown's office, it was "resolved, that this society be known by the title of the First Presbyterian Church and Society of Somerset." The following persons were then elected as trustees, viz.: J. W. McNitt, Elijah Arnold, James Matthews, Asa B. Brown, Ezekiel Merritt and Alva Foster. James Matthews was chosen clerk, and Elijah Arnold treasurer.

In 1832 Rev. David Pratt was pastor, supplying the desk half the time. In 1833 and 1834 Rev. David Page was pastor, preaching here half the time. On the first Sabbath in July, 1837, Rev. Truman Baldwin commenced preaching on a salary of four hundred dollars per year.

February 17th, 1839, twenty-three persons joined the church on profession, and on February 28th, 1841, fifty more united. Rev. W. C. Wisner, of Lockport, assisted in the services.

During the four years' ministry of Mr. Baldwin one hundred and thirty-one persons were received as members of the church.

The church was built of wood, and dedicated October 1st, 1840. Previous to this the meetings had been held in James Matthews's store chamber; afterwards the society worshiped in the old brick school-house. The church lot (½ acre) was purchased of Isaac Starbuck for one hundred dollars. Alfred Van Wagoner built the church for $2,000. In 1852 the society bought a house and lot for a parsonage, costing seven hundred and fifty dollars. It was repaired soon after at a cost of two hundred dollars. In 1860 the church was repaired at an expense of about four hundred dollars. In 1871 the parsonage was remodeled at a cost of about one thousand eight hundred dollars. The late Mrs. Lucy Thayer bequeathed to the society one thousand dollars for the purpose of building a chapel for the church, and now the society is about to raise another thousand for remodeling the church in connection with building the chapel, which is to be known as the "Thayer Chapel."

The pastors since Mr. Baldwin have been as follows: Thomas Paine, two years; David L. Hume, one year; E. H. Stratton, five years; J. J. Ward, four years; Ezra Jones, two years; James M. Van Wagoner, five years; Eusebius Hale, two years; D. D. Hamilton, one year; Lewis B. Rogers, three years; Charles R. Burdick, four years.

Rev. Elijah H. Bonney, the present pastor, commenced his labors here January 16th, 1876. The church membership at present numbers one hundred and thirty-five.

January 20th, 1838, the church voted to establish a Sabbath-school, to be held during recess on the Sabbath, and chose O. P. Wilcox superintendent. There were eighty-nine members of the school in 1839, and one hundred and thirty-one in 1841. The school at present numbers one hundred and eighteen.

BRIEF BIOGRAPHIES.

The post-office address of the residents here sketched is Somerset where none is given.

C. H. Akley came from Edinburgh, Saratoga county, N. Y., where he was born May 6th, 1817, and located in the fertile plains of Somerset, January 7th, 1845. He was married in 1844 to Mary Ann, daughter of Benjamin and Polly Smith. Mrs. A. died May 25th, 1839. Mr. Akley was again married in 1859, to Cynthia Nash. He is a farmer and located in the west part of the town. Post-office, West Somerset. Jane Akley was born January 24th, 1846; Helen M. died November 5th, 1846; Smith C. died November 5th, 1846.

F. Newton Albright, one of the pioneers of this part of the county, was born in a log shanty in the town of Newfane, on the 28th of October, 1812. On the 16th of April, 1839, he was married to Miss Mary Ann, daughter of Jacob and Caty Haight, of Somerset. Mr. Albright is a farmer, and is secretary of the pioneer association of Niagara county. He has two children—Cecelia R., born November 26th, 1844, and Francis J., born May 2nd, 1848. His post-office address is Barker's.

William L. Atwater, of Somerset, was born October 8th, 1847, in Lockport. He is a surveyor and architect, and came to Somerset from Lockport about 1853. He was married November 11th, 1869, to Emily S., daughter of H. and D. Bennett, of Somerset.

Edwin E. Arnold was born in Benson, Vt., in 1826, located in Somerset in 1831, and was married in 1854 to Somerset. He is one of the enterprising men of the town; is a farmer by occupation, and fully identified with the temperance and religious interests of the town.

J. M. Badgley, a native of the town, was born in 1841. Caroline M., daughter of Jesse and Sarah Keeler, of His parents, George and Phebe Badgley, came here in the early history of the town. J. M. Badgley was married in 1864, to Miss Philura, daughter of R. and M. Storer, who reside in Dutchess county, N. Y. Mr. Badgley is one of the enterprising men of Somerset.

David Barker, a native of Charlotte, Clinton county, Vt., was born June 23d, 1794, and was married, October 18th, 1820, to Miss Vania Herendeen, of Farmington, N.Y., who was born April 10th, 1796. Mrs. Barker died October 10th, 1877. Mr. Barker came to Somerset, then part of Hartland, November 20th, 1815, from Charlotte, Vt. This town was then an almost unbroken forest, and Mr. Barker has done his full share in making it one of the garden spots of the world. He resides on the same farm on which he located in 1815. He has served his town as assessor, commissioner and inspector of common schools, and four terms as supervisor.

Samuel Barry was born at Seneca Falls, N. Y., on the 17th of March, 1813. His wife, Fidelia, was the daughter of Chester and Elsie Frost. Mr. B. located in Somerset in 1851, and engaged in farming. His son, Chester F. Barry, was the first man to enlist from this town, in defense of his country, during the late rebellion. He was at that time fifteen years of age, and served three years; he then re-enlisted, and served during the war. He occupied a union soldier's position for four months in the prison parlors of Belle Isle, Va.

Vernon D. Bateman, farmer, Somerset, was born January 3d, 1806, at Southbury, New Haven county, Conn., and removed to Cayuga county, N. Y., and subsequently, in June, 1834, to Somerset. He was married, September 16th, 1832, to Nancy Anderson, of Venice, Cayuga county, N. Y., and in February, 1859, to Kate Merryfield, of Benton Center, Yates county, N. Y.

William H. Hyde, one of the directors in the Farmers' Mutual Insurance Association of Orleans and Niagara Counties, was born January 22nd, 1822, at Pompey, Onondaga county, N. Y. He was married November 25th, 1853, to Eliza Jane Spalding, of Somerset. He removed from Yates, Orleans county, to West Somerset, where he has lived since 1842. He has served sixteen years as justice of the peace.

Barent Becker was born in Mayfield, Fulton county. N. Y. He was married in 1844 to Jane M., daughter of Barent and Hannah Dennie, of Mayfield. He located in the western part of Somerset in 1868, where he is engaged in farming. Post-office address, West Somerset.

Rev. Elijah H. Bonney was born November 4th, 1816, at Hadley, Mass. He was married to Miss Jane M. Jones, of Pawlet, Vt., on the 10th of July, 1848. He graduated at Amherst College in 1839, and at Union Theological Seminary, New York city, in 1844, and was licensed to preach in 1844, by the 3rd Presbytery of New

RES. OF P.W. BRIGHAM, TOWN OF SOMERSET

RES. OF WM H. HYDE, TOWN OF SOMERSET

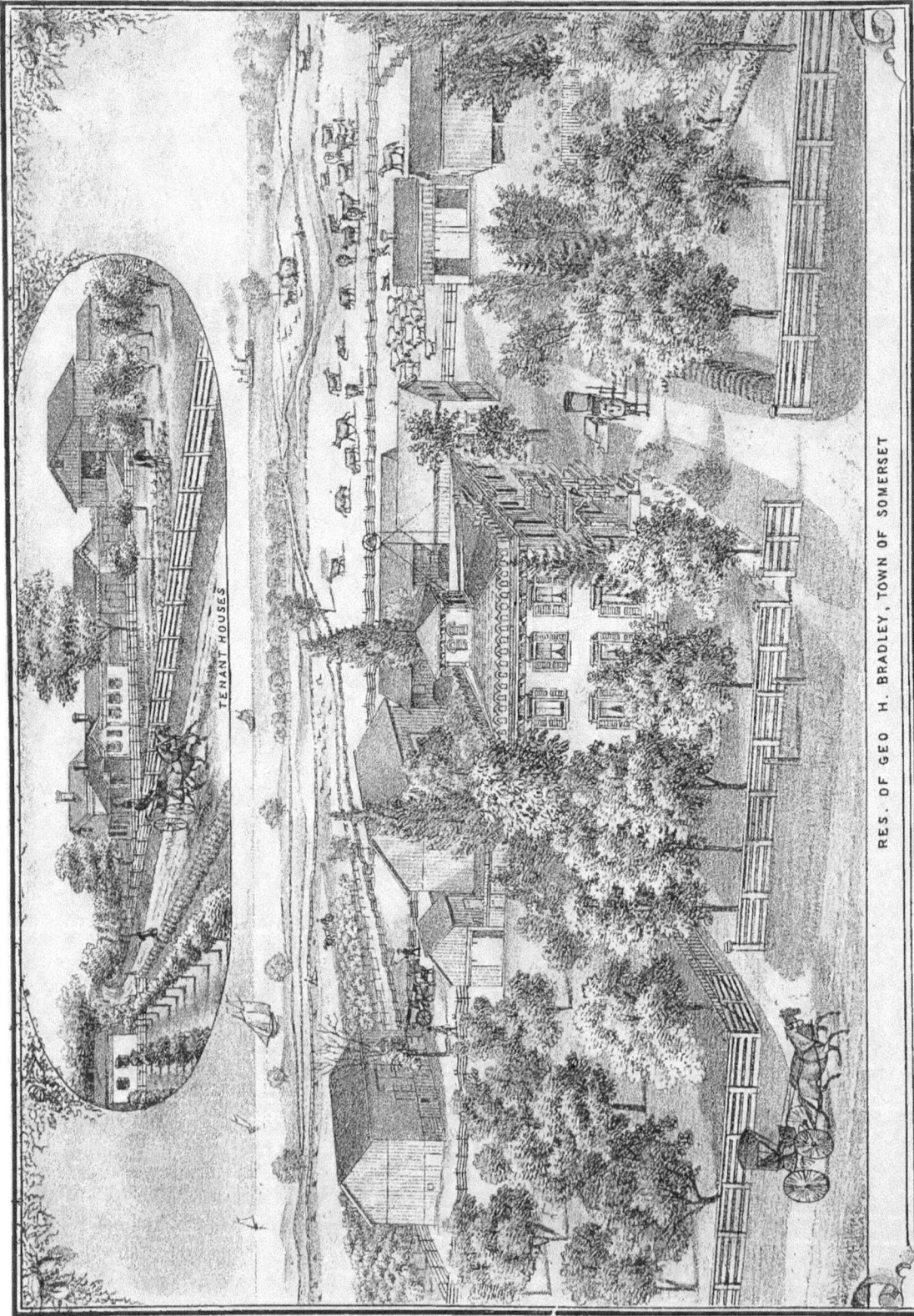

TENANT HOUSES

RES. OF GEO H. BRADLEY, TOWN OF SOMERSET

York. He was pastor at Vernon Center, N. Y., for seventeen years. He came from Lenox, N.Y., to Somerset in January, 1876, since which time he has been the pastor of the Presbyterian church at Somerset.

Henry Bowman was born in Herkimer county, N. Y., January 6th, 1806, and was married February 24th, 1832, to Sarah Ann Van Horne, of Cato, N. Y. Mr. Bowman is a farmer, and located in Somerset in 1843.

George H. Bradley is one of the successful farmers of this town, his farm containing 296 acres, located in the northwest part of the town. He was born in Arlington, Vt., in 1830, and moved to Hartland in 1835, and to Somerset in 1866. He was married in 1855, to Fanny, daughter of Louis and Ruth Mead, of Hartland. He was railroad commissioner in 1869. He has two sons, Lewis A. and Frank N. His post-office is Lake Road.

Hiram E. Briggs, postmaster at Barker's, was born at German Flats, N. Y., January 23d, 1817. He was married December 19th, 1844, to Harriet C., daughter of H. and P. Sharpsteen, of Somerset. He located here in 1834. He is a mechanic, and has been town collector for three years, and postmaster for two years.

P. W. Brigham, a native of Smithfield, N. Y., was born September 20th, 1806, and was married to Eunice Gray, also of Smithfield, in 1826. Mrs. Brigham died May 1st, 1874, and for his second wife Mr. Brigham married Mary A. Newell, of Newfane. Mr. B. came to this town in 1865, from Oneida county, N. Y., and is a farmer.

Henry Brown, a farmer by occupation, was born in Somerset on the 18th of May, 1832, and on the 3d of March, 1859, was married to Miss Mary F. Bickford, of Hartland. He resides at Somerset, which is his post-office address. His father, Dr. Asa B. Brown, was postmaster at Somerset for ten years, also a justice of the peace for several years.

Mrs. Huldah Bush was born in Cornwell, Vt., December 6th, 1813, and came with her parents to this town in 1815. She was married April 24th, 1831, to German Bush, of Shoreham, Vt.

Minor T. Cartwright is a farmer, located in the east part of the town. He was born January 8th, 1836, in Somerset, and was married to Fidelia M., daughter of Harry and Hannah Farrell, of Yates, N. Y. He has been town assessor for the last five years. Post-office, County Line.

Samuel Coates was born in the parish of Craike, Yorkshire, England, April 25th, 1828. He was married June 17th, 1855, to Martha, daughter of John and Jane Powell, of Lewiston, N. Y. He located in Somerset in 1833, and is a farmer by occupation.

John Coates, also a native of Craike parish, Yorkshire, England, was born May 5th, 1823. He emigrated to this country and settled in Somerset in 1833. He married November 22nd, 1852, Alice, daughter of Stephen Powell, of Lewiston. Mr. C. is a farmer.

Aaron, son of Samuel Coleman, who settled here in 1819, was born in Winsor, Mass., January 13th, 1814. His occupation is farming. He was married April 25th, 1838, to Sophia Nye, who died in January, 1839. His second marriage, which took place February 19th, 1843, was to Caroline L. Thurber, of Monroe county, N. Y. Mr. Coleman was one of the assessors of this town for fifteen years. Post-office, Barker's.

George Decker came from Boone county, Ill., and located in this town in 1862. He was born September 25th, 1824, in Greene, N. Y., and married February 28th, 1858, to Jane A., daughter of John and Sarah Williams, of Somerset. Farming is his occupation.

J. K. Denton, of South Somerset, is the son of Henry W. Denton, who settled in this town in 1816, cleared up a large farm, and raised a family of eight children. J. K. was born in this town in 1824, and was married to Paulina, daughter of John and Elsie Brewer, of Fulton county, N. Y., in 1852. Mr. D. is a farmer, and has been postmaster at South Somerset for the last four years. The births in Mr. D.'s family have been as follows: Anna M., July 6th, 1853; Henry W., March 25th, 1857; George William, October 25th, 1858; Mary E., July 20th, 1860; Cora B., December 2nd, 1862; James F., March 13th, 1866; Susan J., October 18th, 1867. Henry W. died March 31st, 1857.

Anson Dutcher resides at Somerset Corners, N. Y., and carries on a general blacksmithing and carriage ironing business. He is also a dealer in all kinds of agricultural implements. His post-office is Somerset. His father, Daniel P., was born in Bethlehem, N. Y., July 12th, 1822. He was married to Samantha Greenman, of Yates, N. Y., November 13th, 1844. She was born January 12th, 1821. Of their children, Chloe C. was born December 16th, 1846, and Alson D. and Anson N., twins, February 29th, 1848. Chloe C. died October 12th, 1853. Daniel P. Dutcher died in Somerset May 22nd, 1876.

Ephraim C. Ellis is a native of Champion, N. Y., where he was born January 7th, 1817. He left Jefferson county in 1837, and located in this town as a farmer. He was married February 26th, 1840, to Melissa, daughter of E. E. and Sarah Wilcox, of Somerset, N. Y. Mr. Ellis was one of the assessors of this town from 1866 to 1875.

Mrs. Eliza I. Fisk, mother-in-law of Sidney Smith, Esq., postmaster at Somerset, came to this town when it was a wilderness. She is probably the oldest woman, if not the oldest person, in the town, being over ninety, while her mental faculties remain as bright as when she was in her teens.

Alfred E. Fisk, a native of Wayne county, N. Y., was born in 1826, and came into Somerset in 1831. He was married November 26th, 1851, to Eliza J., daughter of Edward and Lydia Robinson, of Wayne county. They have one daughter, Anna C., born November 24th, 1854. Mr. Fisk was in the Mexican war for about one year.

Mrs. Mary S. Fisk was born in Greenfield, N. H., July 29th, 1795. She removed to Wayne county, N. Y., where she married James Fisk, of Arcadia, on the 3d day of March, 1814. They came to Somerset in 1831, and Mr. Fisk died in 1863. A son, Myron H. Fisk, was a soldier in the war of the rebellion, and was killed at the battle of Antietam, which was fought September 17th, 1862.

Hardy Fitts, a life-long resident of this town, was born May 27th, 1837. Mr. Fitts was married March 5th, 1862, to Sarah H., daughter of John and Sarah Williams of Greece, N. Y., who was born September 3rd, 1843. Mr. Fitts is a farmer. His children were born as follows: Bertha L. Fitts, January 27th, 1863; Frederick D. Fitts, February 8th, 1872; Almira S. Fitts, March 3rd, 1876.

Loran Fitts came to this town with his father in 1810. He was born in Mansfield, N. J., in 1800. His youthful pioneer life was one of exciting interest, of perils, hardships and sufferings, incident to a life in the wilderness wilds of western New York at an early date. He has lived to see the dense forests fade away before the sturdy pioneer, and in their stead, the waving fields of ripening grain, ready for the harvest. Volumes might be written of the transforming influences of civilization even in his day, but space will not permit. He has lived longer in this town than any other man. He is one of thirteen children, of whom there is only one other living. He has six children, three girls and three boys.

Prentice Fox, son of William B. Fox, was born in the town of Somerset in 1830, and is a farmer. He was married in 1850 to Marcia L., daughter of Robert and Mary Wisner, of Somerset. The births in the family have been as follows: Helen M., born May 3rd, 1852; George W., June 23rd, 1854; Evelena, September 8th, 1866; Charles L., May 22nd, 1872. Post-office, County Line, N. Y.

Alonzo D. Foote located in this town in 1842, and is at present engaged in farming. He has served as assessor in this town for two years. He was born in Harpersfield, N. Y., September 19th, 1815, and married September 30th, 1841, to Lucy R. Lum, of Somerset. Post-office, County Line.

Henry H. Frost, a native of Rensselaerville, N. Y., was born March 30th, 1816, and came to Somerset from Pittstown, N. Y., in 1835. He was married to Julia A. Wilcox, of Somerset, September 27th, 1843. Mr. Frost is a farmer, also the principal dry goods and grocery dealer in the village or town of Somerset. He has served his town as superintendent of common schools, and is notary public, public conveyancer, and is at present and has been for ten or twelve years town clerk. He is one of the active promoters of religion and temperance in his town.

Ira J. Gardner, farmer, was born in Cayuga county on the 2nd of November, 1825, and in 1835 located in this town, where he has since lived. He was married February 26th, 1857, to Harriet, daughter of Isaac and Rebecca Starbuck, of Somerset. Births of children have occurred in his family as follows: Fred D., May 10th, 1858; Lyman S., September 26th, 1859; Amos H., May 26th, 1864. Mary R., an adopted child, was born February 2nd, 1871. Lyman S., died April 8th, 1869.

Jacob S. Haight has been assessor for his town for three years. He is a farmer by occupation. He was born in Somerset in 1825, and was married to Angeline, daughter of Stephen and Mary Sharpsteen of Cayuga county, N. Y. He has one son, John Jay, born April 14th, 1851.

Joshua Haight, a former resident of Cayuga county, N. Y., was born there in 1808, and located here in 1820.

In 1835 Mr. Haight was married to Dorcas, daughter of David Dutcher. She died in 1875. In December, 1875, Mr. Haight was wedded to his second wife, Ann Eliza Townsend, of Somerset. Mr. H. is a farmer, and his post-office West Somerset.

Mrs. Louisa Haight was born in Bergen, Genesee county, N. Y., and married October 23rd, 1844, to Alfred, son of Jacob and Caty Haight of Somerset, N. Y., and came to this town in 1845. Mr. Haight died in Somerset, March 14th, 1871, aged 55 years, 3 months, 13 days. Mrs. H. owns and manages a farm of sixty-two acres. Her children have been: Ashbel, born June 8th, 1849; Mary O., April 3rd, 1851; Jacob C., September 1st, 1856; Caty S., April 1st, 1856. Jacob C., died May 26th, 1860.

Humphrey S. Haight, for fifty-eight years a resident of this town, was born in Cayuga county, N. Y., in 1813, and came to Somerset in 1820. He was married in 1840, to Mary Ann, daughter of Thomas W. and Hannah Merritt. Mrs. Haight died in 1874, and in 1875 Mr. H. was again united in matrimony, to Sarah, daughter of Obihial and Deborah Gardner, of Cayuga county. He is a farmer, and his post-office is Barker's. His children by his first wife were Willie J. T. and Merritt D. Mr. Haight was commissioner of highways for his town for thirteen years.

Peter Hess, who resides near the west line of the town, was born in Saratoga county in 1800. He settled here in 1821. His present farm was then a wilderness. He assisted in chopping and clearing the timber from what is now known as the "Hess road." Mr. Hess was married in 1828 to Martha, daughter of Jacob and Martha Shurtlief, of Saratoga. Post-office, West Somerset. His children are Elmon, born July 15th, 1831; Amanda, March 30th, 1834; Mary, May 3d, 1838.

Mrs. Barthena Hoag, relict of Philip Hoag, who died November 4th, 1876, came to Somerset about 1836. She is the mother of six children, viz.: Kate, born February 11th, 1836; Stephen C., October 22nd, 1837; Francis G., February 3d, 1840; Amy C., July 4th, 1844; William C., June 20th, 1851; and Thomas, February 2nd, 1853. Her post-office address is Lake Road.

Andrew M. Hoag came into this town in 1826, from Lockport. His occupation is that of a farmer and carpenter. He was born January 21st, 1826, in Lockport. He was married to Hannah Horsfall, December 2nd, 1853. Her parents lived in this town. His post-office address is Barker's.

James Hoffman is a farmer residing in the west part of the town. Post-office, West Somerset. He was born in 1810, in Steuben county, N. Y. He was married in 1833 to Miss Betsey Townsend, and removed to Somerset, where he has since lived. He is the father of six children, who were born in the years following: Phebe Jane, 1834; Benjamin F., 1836; Edwin M., 1841; Annette M., 1845; Newton L., 1847; Ida M., 1849.

Mrs. Olive M. Hood was born in Yates, Orleans county, N. Y., September 28th, 1827. She was married November 13th, 1849, to Daniel D. T., son of David and Elizabeth Hood, of Ridgeway, N. Y. They moved from Yates to Somerset October 1st, 1852. Mr. Hood died

MRS. ADAM PEASE.

ADAM PEASE.

RES. OF ADAM PEASE & Wm H. PEASE, QUAKER ROAD, TOWN OF SOMERSET, NIAGARA CO., N.Y.

October 11th, 1868, aged 48 years and 5 months. Of their two sons, Burroughs D. was born October 12th, 1853, and Wilber G., June 23d, 1857.

George K. Hood, farmer by occupation, was born in Otsego county, N. Y., in 1815, and came from that county to Somerset in 1837. He has been married three times, and as many times bereft of the sharer of his sorrows, and the partner of his joys. His first wife, Deliza Stockwell, died April 2nd, 1844; his second wife, Mary L. Nye, died June 30th, 1846; his third wife, Adriana M., daughter of Hon. Asa B. Brown, died March 23rd, 1871. Children have been born to him as follows: Harlan P., September 20th, 1837; Emma A., October 20th, 1840; George B., May 28th, 1850.

Rev. Jesse T. Humphrey, who was assigned to Somerset by the Genesee M. E. Conference in October, 1877, was born January 23rd, 1832, at Penn's Neck, Salem county, N. J. Early in life he joined the Methodist Episcopal church, and has passed through the different grades from a private member to a traveling preacher, having in the meantime graduated with honor to himself and the cause he represents. He has thus far been very successful on all the charges to which he had been assigned. He was married December 18th, 1855, to Miriam Mattson, of Penn's Neck, N. J.

Hon. Guy C. Humphrey, one of the honored men of the town, and of the second Assembly district, was born in Orwell, Vt., in 1821, and settled in Somerset in 1831. He was married in 1853 to Louisa, daughter of William M. Humphrey, of Somerset. Mr. H. owns and manages a farm of 238 acres. In 1871 he lost her whom he had chosen for his companion through life. The people of his Assembly district did him the honor of trusting their legislative affairs in his hands in the years 1865 and 1866, which trust he faithfully performed. His townsmen have also honored him with the office of supervisor of their town for the years 1858-61, and 1876-78.

Gurdon T. Huntingdon was born in Batavia, N. Y., December 15th, 1825. He came from Genesee county to Somerset in 1834, and was married September 17th, 1845, to Sally L., daughter of J. and E. Bloomer, of Somerset. Gurdon Huntingdon, sen., died September 15th, 1867, aged 83.

A. C. James, a fruit-farmer, was born in Morrison, Ill., in 1842. He married Mabel, daughter of John F. and Johana Wright, of Washington county, N. Y. Mr. James located in Somerset in 1876.

Benjamin G. Knowles came from Genesee county, N. Y., and located here in 1853. He was born in Connecticut in 1807, and was married July 4th, 1833, to Alice, daughter of Joel and Clarissa Phillips. Mr. K. is by occupation a gardner. Mrs. Alice Knowles died November 15th, 1874. Mr. K. was again married, to Mary J. Rolff, of Yates, Orleans county, by whom he has two sons. By his former wife he has one son, Albert, born December 31st, 1851. Post-office, County Line, N. Y.

Oscar E. Mann was born in 1833, in Oswego county, N. Y. On the 30th of January, 1855, he was married to Hannah E., daughter of I. E., and D. Merritt, of Somerset. He came to this town in 1834 with his parents. He was elected sheriff of Niagara county in 1869, and served three years from January 1st, 1870. He is engaged in farming, owns a steam saw-mill and manufactures lumber, barrel heading, staves, etc. His children are Willis T., who was born January 13th, 1857; Fred A., born February 13th, 1859, and Mertie M., born April 6th, 1876. His post-office is South Somerset.

Stephen Mead was born in Ovid, Seneca county, N. Y., in 1819. He located in Somerset in 1839, and was married in 1840 to Phebe, daughter of James and Betsey Prime of Allegany county, N. Y. He is a farmer and stock speculator.

Homer D. Mead was born in Somerset in 1842, and married in 1867 to Miss Julia Van Wagoner, of Lockport. Mr. Mead is a farmer by occupation and resides in the northwest part of the town. His post-office is Lake Road.

Marcus Noble, a farmer by occupation, has 237 acres of land, located in the western part of the town. He has been a resident of this town for thirty-eight years. He was born in Litchfield county, Conn., in 1808. He was married November 2nd, 1831, to Amelia Buckley, who departed this life September 9th, 1832. Mr. Noble was again married, October 3rd, 1833, to Abigail, daughter of Thomas and Jerusha Sherwood, of Somerset, N. Y. He has been justice of the peace in this town for four years. He has one son, Romeyn, married in 1867 to Miss Ellen Stewart. Post-office, West Somerset.

Adam Pease was born in the town of Groton, Cayuga county, N. Y., in 1808. His parents, John A. and Hannah Pease, were born and married in New Jersey. They removed in 1799 to Cayuga county, N. Y., where they raised a family of two boys and six girls. In the spring of 1817 they emigrated into the wilderness that then covered the town of Somerset. Here the pioneer died in August, 1848, having survived his wife some years. Adam Pease is now the only survivor of the large family to which he belonged. He has lived in Somerset sixty-one years. When twenty years old he bought of his father the farm on which he now lives. The log house and barn then on the place have, under Mr. Pease's management, given way to a good cobblestone house, fronted with lake stone of the first grade and finished in the most substantial manner, with out buildings to correspond. The farm is stocked with a plenty and variety of fruit. Mr. Pease's sister Polly was his housekeeper for nine years, during the last three of which he made six rather unpleasant journeys to New Jersey to settle up his father's affairs in that State. He never mourned over this business, however, for it made him acquainted with Margaret Patten, whom he married November 6th, 1836, and removed to his wilderness home. Six daughters and two sons have been born to them. Their daughter Permilla died at the age of one year and three months; all the others are living. Mrs. Pease died August 19th, 1871. To his oldest son, William H. H., Mr. Pease has sold his farm, after making certain reserves.

William Henry Harrison Pease was born in Somerset, December 24th, 1841. He was married March 13th, 1872, to Lucy Richmond, of Mount Morris, Livingston county, N. Y. Mr. Pease is one of the wide-awake, enterprising farmers of the town. Post-office, Barker's.

Lawton Pettit, Esq., who has been postmaster at Lake Road for about twelve years, was born in Saratoga, N. Y., in 1816. His occupation is farming. He was married February 16th, 1843, to Margaret, daughter of Nehemiah and Mary Whitlock. He has resided in Somerset since 1843. His children are: Joel, born January 5th, 1846, and Betsey Jane Jenks, adopted daughter, born June 24th, 1843.

H. W., son of William Randall, was born in Wheatfield April 29th, 1842. He located in Somerset in the spring of 1864 as a farmer. September 6th, 1869, he married Miss Susie, daughter of William and Susan Watts, of Hartland, N. Y.

Mrs. Sara Sawyer, whose maiden name was Curtis, was born in this town, and was married to William Sawyer, of Lockport, January 1st, 1870. Mr. Sawyer is a farmer by occupation. J. N. Curtis, father of Mrs. Sawyer, came to Niagara county in 1840, and died December 5th, 1875. Mrs. Sawyer has one child, Fred C., born October 29th, 1873. Post-office address, Lake Road.

Charles P. Schryver, a native of Hyde Park, N.Y., was born November 14th, 1814. He was married September 16th, 1840, to Amanda Still, and located in Somerset in 1845. His first wife died September 14th, 1865, and he married, March 3rd, 1866, Thomima, daughter of William and Maria Brass, of Yates, N. Y. Mr. Schryver is a mechanic and builder. Post-office, Barker's.

William M. Sharpsteen lives upon the farm on which he was born May 28th, 1828. He was married to Miss Louisa A. Hathaway, of Cambria, November 19th, 1865. He is a farmer, and lives near the center of the town. His post-office is Barker's. His father, Humphrey, came into this town in 1814, built a log cabin, suffered and endured with the other pioneers of this town.

John Sherwood is a native of Clarkson, Monroe county, N. Y. He was born in 1834; came to this town in the spring of 1835; and married in 1865 Miss Mary Hess, daughter of Peter and Martha Hess. He has four children, two sons and two daughters. He is located in the west part of the town, and carries on farming extensively. His post-office is West Somerset.

S. E. Smith is the owner of a farm of 200 acres in the west part of the town. He was born in 1814, in Haddam, Conn. In 1856 he was married to Ruth, daughter of Daniel Knowlton, of Oneida county, N. Y. He removed to Niagara county in 1836. Post-office, West Somerset.

George H. Taylor was born January 21st, 1837, in Yates, N. Y. He is a farmer, and was a justice of the peace from 1872 to 1877. He was married January 10th, 1861, to Harriet A., daughter of A. D. and Lucy Foote, of Somerset, N. Y. He located in this town in 1861. Post-office, County Line.

John P. Townsend came from Jefferson county, and settled in Somerset in 1865. He was born in Antwerp, December 3d, 1821. He was married March 8th, 1846, to Cynthia, daughter of Abram and Margaret Perkins. They have four children, two sons and two daughters. Mr. Townsend is a farmer. Post-office, Barker's. His father is still living, aged 82; his mother, 75; and mother-in-law, 86.

Robert R. Treat was born in Mendon, Monroe county, N. Y., in 1819, and married in 1849 to Betsey S., daughter of Benjamin and Catharine Vickery, who died May 14th, 1873. Mr. Treat located in Somerset in 1851, and was again married February 27th, 1878, to Delia, daughter of Asa and Olive Kenyon, of Somerset, N. Y. Mr. Treat is a carpenter and joiner, and manufacturing miller of the firm of Treat & Wickham. Post-office, Somerset, N. Y. He has three children: Elgie E., Flora A., and Ella M.

Cornelius Treat is a farmer by occupation, and located here in 1843, coming from Yates county, N. Y. He was born March 3rd, 1832, and married April 15th, 1862, to Mary L., daughter of Anson and Polly Robinson, of Somerset.

Andrew R. Webb was born in Hartland May 29th, 1846. He was married February 11th, 1868, to Annie, daughter of Adam and Elizabeth Miller, of the town of Yates, Orleans county, N.Y. He removed to Somerset in 1872, and is a farmer by occupation. His townsmen have honored him with the office of justice of the peace.

Jeremiah Wickham is a thirty-year resident of this town, having come here from Onondaga county in 1848. He is a carpenter and joiner by trade, and for the past nine years a manufacturing miller. He has been justice of the peace for the last eight years, and was re-elected in the spring of 1878 for another term. He was married in 1848 to Harriet Baker, who died in 1863. In 1865 Mr. Wickham was married to Sarah A., daughter of Ira and Betsey Wadsworth. He is the father of six children, four of whom are living, viz.: Francis O., Mary A., Edwin J., Leon W.

Charles W. Wilcox was born in Oneida county, N. Y., and settled here in 1837. He is a fruit farmer, owning one hundred acres. He was married December 8th, 1864, to Mary, daughter of Josiah and Mary Wilcox, of Orwell, Vt., who was a cousin of Hon. Alexander H Stevens, of Georgia.

Joseph W. Wing came to this town from Erie county, N. Y., in 1844. He was born in Duanesburg, N. Y., June 1st, 1839. He was married to Helen C., daughter of Marvin and Nancy Hess, of Somerset, N. Y., January 14th, 1864. His father, Daniel P. Wing, was one of the prominent men of this town, and was assessor for several years. He died April 12th, 1878. Mr. Wing is a farmer.

S. E. SMITH. RES. OF S. E. SMITH, TOWN OF SOMERSET, NIAGARA CO., N. Y. MRS. S. E. SMITH.

THE TOWN OF WHEATFIELD.

WHEATFIELD was taken from Niagara, May 12th, 1836, and named from the general character of the soil as a wheat producing section of the county. The first town meeting was held on the 6th of June, in the school-house of district No. 7, on the north line of the town. N. M. Ward was elected supervisor, and Edwin Cook town clerk; assessors, Isaac H. Smith, James Sweeney, Hiram Parks; justices of the peace, L. B. Warden, John Sweeney; commissioners of highways, Elias Parks, Matthew Gray; collector, Stewart Milliman; overseer of the poor, William Towsley; constables, Stewart Milliman, Daniel C. Jacobs, Calvin F. Champlin, Seth F. Roberts; commissioners of schools, Isaac L. Young, James Sweeney, Loyal E. Edwards.

"At a meeting of the school commissioners, August 10th, it was resolved that this school district be composed of the following territory: Lots 76, 77, 78 and 79, on the mile reservation, and lots 10, 12, 14 and 19 of township twelve, range eight, according to the Holland Company's survey, so-called; and that the same be known as school district No. 1, of said town of Wheatfield."

In the spring of 1845, it was voted that the town pay a bounty of twelve shillings for wild cat scalps, and five dollars for wolves' heads.

PIONEER SETTLEMENTS.

Evidence remains of worthy enterprise undertaken by such as broke into the wilderness as early as 1824, locating upon the higher ground and ridges without roads, neighbors or trading places. But few are left to consult; such of the early pioneers as have been consulted or can be traced, it is found interesting to make some mention of as witnesses in the siege of the forest, who stood in the front rank and made the most valiant attack.

Harvey Miller came from Rochester in January, 1824, and settled on the Lockport and Niagara Falls road, in the northern part of the town, purchasing 100 acres of the Holland Company at $5 per acre, on contract, advancing, as customary, twenty-five dollars for an article. His equipments for beginning were two yoke of steers, an ax and scant provisions and lodgings. Encouraged by a worthy young wife he commenced to labor for the success that has rewarded his efforts; they now look over three hundred acres of cultivated fields that afford homes for themselves and their children, who are their nearest neighbors. Mr. Miller was a pioneer in Rochester, where his father located before the wilderness had been subdued. In 1811 he took the job of clearing what is now Buffalo street in that city. He states that the first winter he lived in Wheatfield, with the assistance of a young man, he chopped twenty-five acres, which he cleared in the spring for suitable crops. During the summer he cleared the balance to sow eighteen acres of winter wheat; the piece produced eight hundred bushels, which he sold to other settlers as they came in at 75 cents per bushel, threshing it on a split log floor, during the winter, assisted by his wife in cleaning it. As a road commissioner he directed the opening of all the first roads in the town. Active in performing the public duties assigned him, he has not been without their honors. He is now acting as sole trustee of a large school district, No. 8, which has an average attendance of from fifty to sixty scholars, receiving for 1878 $160 of the public money. The first school in the district was taught by Ira Benedict, in 1826. Mr. Miller's age is 79; that of his wife, Matilda, 77. Mr. Miller credits N. M. Ward with raising the first wheat in the town.

Shawnee was named by Timothy Shaw, who, in connection with Volney Spalding, established a store and ashery in 1828. The hamlet contains a dry-goods and grocery store, blacksmith and wagon shop, a post-office, and a small, neatly constructed Methodist Episcopal church, erected in 1863. The earliest preaching was of that denomination, by the Rev. Messrs. Hoag and Cole.

The first religious organization was perfected by the Rev. Reuben Winchell, who also established the first Baptist church in Lockport. The Shawnee Baptist church was instituted in the barn of Harvey Miller, July 2nd, 1830. Removal of members and influx of a prevailing Lutheran population has given the latter the place of the former Baptist connection. The land for the church building was donated by Isaac Carl in 1847, and the church erected the same year.

John Grey located about a mile south of Shawnee in 1825, coming from Livingston county. He purchased of the Holland Company eighty-four acres at $5 per acre.

THE GERMAN NEIGHBORHOODS.

No better evidence can be produced of the certainty of cheering results from industry and frugality, than is afforded by the achievements of the Prussian population, who own the largest portion of the farming territory of this town. The character of a productive agricultural region, redeemed from swamps and marshes, is due to them.

Settlements in the different localities were simultaneous. In 1843 Carl Sack, Erdman Wurl and Fred Grosskopf purchased of William Vandervoote 400 acres, at $15 per acre, on the Tonawanda creek, in the southeast corner of the town, four miles east of Tonawanda village, at what is now known as the village of MARTINSVILLE. Lutheran religious antecedents caused the adoption of this name by the disciples of Martin Luther. The original purchase was divided into small lots of three acres and upward, as others were able to purchase, to provide for the location of thirty families the first season. They erected ten log houses in the autumn, each of which was occupied by three or four families during the winter and until joint efforts relieved the immigrants by building others. The families remained in Buffalo until the first houses were built, obtaining the best accommodations they could find. Forbidding as the prospect in the beginning must have been, it has been changed to the appearance of prosperity.

The church organization is the controling element in the government of the community, now consisting of one hundred families, connected with the two now existing, the result of divided feeling, but not an abandonment of the Lutheran faith. The first church building was erected in 1846. The present minister is the Rev. Mr. Stecholz. Connected with the church is a private school, taught by the minister, averaging twenty scholars.

The second church was built in 1861; minister, Rev. P. Heid. With this there is also a school sustained, managed by Albert Dornfeld, varying in regular attendance from seventy-five to one hundred scholars. The English and German are taught in both schools.

The business places and dwellings are located on one street, following the banks of the creek. A lively aspect of business is sustained by two establishments, in prosperous condition, connected with the manufacture of lumber. William Dornfeld and Christian Fritz in 1856 purchased the first saw-mill, which was built by Joseph Hewett. Christian Fritz built his saw-mill and planing-mill in 1860, with which is connected a dry kiln and lumber-yard of pine to supply the surrounding country.

William Dornfeld and Krull Brothers, proprietors of the planing-mill, sash, door and blind factory, erected in 1876, investing in buildings and machinery $8,000, connected a lumber yard for the sale of pine. They do an annual business of $10,000, supplying an extended section of country; an active business is transacted by them, affording steady employment to twenty-five or thirty mechanics and day laborers. Steam is the only power available.

William Dornfeld carries on the principal dry goods and general supply store, having begun business in 1851. To get a start in business, the canal was his first attraction. An abandoned and sunken canal boat was obtained on credit, which the purchaser raised and made profitable use of. The Martinsville Hotel is the only one in the village. In it the post-office is kept.

Of the early immigrants but few are left, bent in the attitude of old age. Christian Dornfeld located with others in 1843, purchased six acres of Vandervoote, and is still living, aged 79; his wife, Sophia, died in 1860, aged 56; his children living are William and Albert, and two other sons in the West.

NEW BERGHOLZ was settled in 1843 by a German Lutheran congregation, which emigrated from Prussia. It is named after the large village of Bergholz in Germany, from which a great number of families of this congregation came. Frederick Moll, John Williams and John Sy, as trustees, purchased the land for an association styled the Lutheran Evangelical, consisting of one hundred and twenty members. The land was conveyed in deeds, dated October 12th, 1843, by the Farmers' Loan and Trust Company, 820 acres, consideration, $5,748.50; by William L. Marcy and wife (Washington Hunt, attorney), 176½ acres, consideration, $1,765; by Washington Hunt for 118 acres, consideration, $2,000—near half of the village plot; by John J. De Graff, for 200 acres, consideration, $3,000, including the balance of the village; by Blundina Dudley, for 456 acres, consideration, $2,736; by the Farmers' Loan and Trust Company (November 14th, 1843), for 349 acres, consideration, $2,792.

The trustees caused a map to be made by W. S. Hains, designating 121 village lots, located upon parallel and diagonal streets, of convenient width, and an ample public square. By a general deed, executed by the trustees October 12th, 1843, they convey to Augustus Manske and one hundred and eighteen others, each a lot of one acre. The village has a present population of fifty families, occupying tenements.

A large barn that had been previously built—it is thought to accommodate lumber teams—was used to shelter the first population, in which they were stowed until houses could be built. In four weeks a sufficient number were got in readiness to take in four or five families in one house, relieving them from the more uncomfortable condition in the over-crowded store-house. Washington Hunt presented the community an ox team to aid them in building—the first they possessed in the country. The erection of log buildings was continued until one was, during the first season, placed upon nearly every lot that had been deeded.

The community had connected with them the necessary mechanics: a blacksmith, carpenter and joiner, mason, tailor, shoemaker, and cabinet-maker. The sale of wood for three and as high as five dollars per cord at Niagara Falls, Tonawanda and Buffalo, mostly transported by single horse teams, and the sale of ship timber and staves, were important aids to furnish means of subsistence and clearing the land. Potatoes and garden vegetables were the principal product for the first six or seven years.

John Salingre was a member of the community first locating; bringing with him a capital of $20,000. His benevolence and readiness to assist the less able and such as were without means were relied upon without disappointment of any who were industrious and worthy; he aiding them as a duty, often without any other returns than the gratification he experienced in doing others good. He died in January, 1871, aged 69. Two of the original trustees are still living. One is John Williams, who located upon the first purchase, one and a half miles from the village, where he now resides at the age of 70. One son, John, jr., lives in Wheatfield. The other surviving trustee is Frederick Moll, aged 71.

Christian Wolf located in 1843, purchasing forty acres of the trustees' land, and starting the first dry-goods and grocery store the same year. John Sy purchased in 1844, on the original tract, 102 acres, where his son Daniel now resides upon a highly cultivated farm. He died March 18th, 1861, aged 49; his wife, Justine, May 24th, 1873, aged 75. The first post-office was established in 1850, and John Sy was postmaster.

These Lutherans left their old country for conscience sake, as the King of Prussia, Frederick William III., introduced by force the union of the Lutheran and Reformed churches in his reign, and persecuted by distraining and imprisonment all those Lutherans who protested against such violation of their conscience and refused to accept the new church book, in which the Lutheran confession is altered and accommodated to the doctrines of the Reformed church. Many hundred families preferred to depart from their homes and fatherland rather than to deny their faith. Therefore a great number of families emigrated to Australia, and many others to America from 1839 until 1844.

For a year from the autumn of 1843, Rev. J. An. A. Grabau, from Buffalo, came to Bergholz from time to time, preached and administered the holy sacraments. When the Rev. Mr. Ehrenstroem, former pastor of the congregation, arrived from Germany, where he was imprisoned a year after the removal of his parishioners, he again became pastor, but he only remained for about one year, and was succeeded in 1845 by Rev. Henry von Rohr. This gentleman had been a captain in the Prussian army, and was a learned man. He remained as pastor until his death in 1874.

During the first years the new settlers had to combat with many difficulties, and could not build a church before 1846, for the lots which they had appointed for church grounds, as well as their own lots and farms, had to be cleared. Therefore they arranged and furnished a large barn as well as possible for a place of worship. But in 1846 the new church was dedicated and called "Holy Ghost Church."

The first school teacher was Mr. Stowasser, who emigrated with the others; and after he moved to Wisconsin Mr. G. Rehwald became his successor, remaining until 1857. From 1857 until 1874, Mr. Christian Goers was teacher.

In 1845 the Lutheran Synod of Buffalo was organized and the Holy Ghost congregation has belonged to this synod since its organization. But in 1866 a dissension arose in the synod, and it split into three parts.

In consequence of this dissension, the congregation at Bergholz also split into two parties in 1867. The one party, of about 52 families, joined with the Missouri Synod, renounced its old pastor, Mr. Von Rohr, and called Rev. W. Weinback; as this party had the majority of members and trustees, it remained in the possession of the whole church property, consisting of about 12 acres of land, with church, parsonage and school-buildings, and cemetery.

The other party, of about 37 families, remained with the pastor, Mr. Von Rohr, and held its services at first in a private house, and afterward it purchased about 3 acres of land, with dwelling, on the south side of Cayuga creek, arranged the house for a school, and built a new brick church, called "Trinity Church." In 1874 Rev. Mr. Von Rohr died, and that part of the Buffalo Synod whose president he was dissolved in May, 1877; about two-thirds of the Trinity congregation wished to unite again with the Buffalo Synod; but as the other part was not willing, and called the Rev. C. Schadow from Michigan, the two parties settled about the possession of the church property, so that the second party remained in possession of it and paid a corresponding sum of money to the first party, which organized the "Lutheran St. Jacob's Congregation," purchased one acre of land of Mr. Frederick Parchers, and built a new church, parsonage and school-house. The St. Jacob's organization took place in 1875, and a school-house and church were built in 1876, and the parsonage in 1877. Church wardens are Mr. William Devantier and Mr. Friedrich Goers. The trustees at present are the Messrs. W. Wendt, C. Meyer, William Zimmermann, Frederick Hellers and Christian Ferchen. The congregation consists of about forty families, or one hundred and fifty communicants. The school is attended by about thirty children. For two years from its organization, Rev. H. Stecholz, from Martinsville, preached to this congregation nearly every Sunday, but in September Rev. John A. Grabau, from Detroit, Mich., was called, and installed October 27th, 1877.

Divine service takes place every Sunday forenoon at 9 o'clock, and in the afternoon at two o'clock; also every Wednesday afternoon at one o'clock (except in the time of harvest) and on the days of the Apostles and other festival days.

ST. JOHNSBURG is an offspring of Bergholz, and situated on the 820 acres deeded by the Farmers' Loan and Trust Company. Advanced to the want of larger possessions than had first satisfied them, when only aspiring to a farm of one acre, some of the immigrants purchased from ten to one hundred acres apiece, rendering their new homes comfortable and amply provided for. The commodious brick church was built in 1846, now accommodating a congregation of eighty families. Rev. Frank W. Schmitt was the minister. A school attached was taught by J. Richdart, the number of scholars averaging 80. There is a general store, in which the post-office is kept, and blacksmith, wagon and harness shops. Though separation has taken place to form another neighborhood, the distinction is but slight—churches, schools and customs are sustained upon the same principle. No other school is tolerated than the Lutheran for children under fourteen years of age. At six years old both male and female are required to enter the church school, remaining up to the age of fourteen. The requirements of an undeviating confession of faith in the church ordinances are sealed by confirmation, when the restrictions become less absolute. The public schools are thus made available for further advance in obtaining an education in the English and German languages. The teachers are in most cases highly cultivated clergymen, and do not fail to insure an advance of the scholars equal if not superior to what could otherwise be obtained. The time for instruction is so divided that less hours of attendance are required during the summer term than in winter. The time required by the parents for the labor of the children is depended upon during the most favorable working season. Public school No. 5 is located in the village, and taught by C. F. Goers, averaging from fifteen to twenty pupils in attendance daily.

NEW WALMORE was named after a village in Prussia, from which the present inhabitants emigrated in 1843. Possessed of the requisite means to make an independent purchase and to locate on larger farms, they chose the above location, in the northwest corner of the town, purchasing from earlier settlers from Pennsylvania who had made considerable improvements. The last purchasers, from twenty to twenty-five in number, located at the same time, on farms varying from fifty to two hundred acres. Situated on somewhat higher land and commencing with the advantage of improvements, the successful growing of wheat has made a prosperous community and a wealthy farming district of the county. The location is adapted to the production of apples, but not peaches. The neighborhood and vicinity have erected a well planned brick Lutheran church, built in 1853.

SUPERVISORS OF WHEATFIELD.

The following gentlemen have been supervisors of the town:

In 1837, Benjamin McNitt; 1838, N. M. Ward; 1839, William Vandervoote; 1840, John Sweeney; 1842, Isaac L. Young; 1843, N. M. Ward; 1844, 1845, Lewis S. Payne; 1846, N. M. Ward; 1847, 1848, L. S. Payne; 1849, Sylvester McNitt; 1850, L. S. Payne; 1851, Seth F. Roberts; 1852, S. McNitt; 1853, 1854, Peter Greiner; 1855, Joseph Hawbecker; 1856, 1857, George W. Sherman; 1858, N. M. Ward; 1859-61, L. S. Payne; 1862, Peneuel Schmeck; 1863-66, George W. Sherman; 1867, H. H. Griffin; 1868, James Carney; 1869, H. H. Griffin; 1870, Edward A. Milliman; 1871-73, Joseph D. Loveland; 1874, 1875, Thomas C. Collins; 1876, L. S. Payne; 1877, 1878, Christian Fritz.

NORTH TONAWANDA.

Previous to the location and construction of the Erie Canal there appears to have been but little progress made in settling that portion of the town now embracing the large and rapidly advancing village of North Tonawanda. As at other localities, the canal was the impetus that moved capitalists to invest at this favorable point. The following original handbill shows the beginning of business enterprises:

"VILLAGE OF NIAGARA.

"This village is located at the confluence of the Niagara and Tonewanta rivers, where the Erie Canal from Buffalo enters the Tonewanta, and where boats pass from the canal into the Niagara river by a lock. At this junction of the rivers, and adjoining the village, is a safe and spacious harbor, as well for canal boats as for vessels navigating Lake Erie.

"These advantages cannot fail to render the village of Niagara the depot of the products of the West, destined to the city of New York, and of return cargoes of merchandise.

"A dam of four or five feet high will be thrown across the Tonewanta, at the village, so as to raise the river to the level of Lake Erie, and the river will be navigated for the distance of eleven miles, and be united with the canal between Niagara and Lockport. The surplus water from the dam will afford an abundant and steady supply for mills and other hydraulic works.

"The village is 12 miles from Buffalo, 8 from the Falls, 15 from Lewiston, and 16 miles from Lockport. A line of stages passes through from Buffalo to Lewiston daily, and another from Lockport to Buffalo every other day. Travelers to the Falls will leave the canal at this place.

"A bare inspection of Vance's or Lay's map of the western part of this State will at once show the advantageous position of the village for trade, market and manufactures.

"Building lots are now offered for sale to actual settlers. A map of the village may be seen by application to James Sweeney, at Buffalo, or to George Goundey, at the Land Office in Geneva; and the former will enter into contracts of sale.

"The title is indisputable, and good waranty deeds will be executed to purchasers.

"GEORGE GOUNDEY,
JAMES SWEENEY, } Proprietors.
JOHN SWEENEY,

"July 5th, 1824."

PIONEER RESIDENTS.

In 1809 George N. Burger erected a small frame house on the premises occupied by Vincent Koch & Co., in part as a lumber yard. No earlier settler has been found. Mr. Burger was a well known, prominent pioneer among the earliest settlers in the city of Lockport.

Joshua Pettit located in 1810, on the premises now occupied by Mr. Reid, on the Niagara river, near the Niagara Iron Works, where he opened a log tavern; the stream near by has long been known as Pettit creek. He remained until 1835, when he moved to Allegany county. He died May 2nd, 1857, aged 76. Two of his daughters, Hannah, wife of Whitman Jacobs, aged 71, and Polly, wife of Daniel C. Jacobs, aged 68, as far as is known are the oldest living settlers in the village of North Tonawanda, which has been their home from childhood.

Stephen Jacobs located in March, 1817, on the river, two miles below Tonawanda, purchasing of Augustus Porter

196 acres, at $8 per acre, when it lay in the wilderness, and improved it as a farm. The timber for building the first guard-lock where the Erie Canal enters the river was furnished by him. He died at Niagara Falls in January, 1840. He was in the battle of Bunker Hill at the age of seventeen. His children living are Daniel C., Whitman, Dana and Hiram, residents of Tonawanda.

Mrs. D. C. Jacobs states that when the alarm reached them of the burning of Lewiston, and descent of the enemy upon the few scattered settlers, in 1813, the consternation could not be described; the terrified men and women, in confusion, were at a loss where to seek a refuge, while children clung to their mothers' garments for protection. Ox teams were used to land them beyond the immediate scene of danger.

William Vandervoote located in 1825, occupying a log house, the only one that then existed. He had in view the transaction of mercantile business, and the purchase of staves and oak timber for the Boston market. The first public house, called the Niagara, was completed by him in 1828, and burnt in 1844. Mr. Vandervoote subsequently purchased of the Holland Company seventeen hundred acres of land, and sold to the Prussians the tract including the largest part of their possessions, on the Tonawanda creek and in its vicinity. He was a partner in a store established by the Boston Company, then floating in the full tide of prosperity, on Grand Island. He established the first bank in the place in 1836. His mother and his sister Sarah located with him, the latter of whom occupied a brick residence erected by her brother, the first of the kind in the place.

James Sweeney located first in Buffalo in 1811. As one of the proprietors in the original purchase of the land upon which the village of North Tonawanda has been erected, he located on it in 1828, and built the first frame dwelling. The clearing of the land was commenced for the purpose of furnishing timber for the Buffalo pier, and to prepare the way for the sale of village lots. He pursued a liberal policy in advancing his individual interests, or those of others whom he sought to interest in becoming citizens. The lots for the first Methodist church, built in 1837, and the first school-house, were donated by him. Not alone in these generous public benefits was he conspicuous as a citizen. As the advance of landed property added to his means, his benefactions increased, and he aided worthy objects wherever aid was needed. He worked earnestly to extend the benefits of local schools, manifesting the interest he felt by furnishing books and often clothing to destitute children, placing them in a condition to be benefitted by them. Leaving to posterity the legacy of a respectable name as a valuable citizen and man of integrity, he died January 13th, 1850, aged 57. His son John, who died in the midst of a career of business enterprises, managed the building of the first railroad depot, and was the first, and for several years the station manager at this point. He caused the first dock to be built on the creek, next to the bridge, afterwards extending it 250 feet along the bank of the creek in the direction of the river; employ-ing Elijah V. Day to supply the foundations and planking. He built the first and only grist-mill, which was afterwards destroyed by fire. Colonel John Sweeney built a saw-mill on the dam at the present position of the waste gates, the only one existing in this section of the country.

James Carney was a pioneer in the town as early as 1819, locating with his father, Edward Carney, who was one of the earliest settlers in Avon, Livingston county, in 1791 on Tonawanda Island (for many years and now more frequently designated Carney Island). His object in settling was to gain a pre-emption right if the boundary line, when settled, left the island in the territory of the United States. In 1824 the State of New York caused a survey to be made, ordering an assessed valuation of $4.50 per acre. During the following year the island was ordered to be sold at public auction in the city of Albany, requiring one-eighth of the purchase money to be paid down. James Carney, furnishing the required amount, placed it in the hands of Judge Samuel Wilkinson to purchase at the sale, but speculation had been stimulated by the purchase that had been made on Grand Island, opposite, by the Jews, to found the "City of Ararat" and concentrate the scattered tribes of Israel; and Samuel Leggate, of the city of New York, became the purchaser at $23 per acre. Mr. Carney set out in the effort to attain, by buying and clearing land, the position of affluence he now enjoys at an age of seventy-eight years. At seventeen he was an ox-teamster in the employ of Porter, Barton & Co., slowly plodding through the woods from Lewiston to Schlosser. He was a subject of pioneer life, doing milling, floating a canoe down the river for a harbor in Porter's mill race at the Falls; returning by applying his shoulder to a setting pole in the way he had learned in propelling scow-boats from Schlosser to Black Rock, often loaded with three hundred and fifty barrels of salt.

INCORPORATION AND VILLAGE INSTITUTIONS.

The village of North Tonawanda was incorporated May 8th, 1865. The first trustees were David Robinson, Jacob Bocker, George W. Sherman, Alexander Kent, Clark Ransom, and J. D. Vandervoote. The board for 1878 consists of F. J. Fellows, H. O. Nightingale, Augustus Brown, Alexander McBean (president) and W. H. Upson (clerk). A well constructed brick building centrally located, accommodates the common council room and clerk's office, fire engine, firemen's implements, and a safe jail, under the same roof. A well regulated police controls the diversified elements of a mixed population, that is brought together to perform the immense amount of labor required to handle daily the arrivals of lumber, in the yards that stretch along the banks of the town for over two miles. The village is a lumber mart of the largest extent, enjoying the best mechanical advantages. Mercantile pursuits are but little engaged in, except provision stores and groceries.

The private banking house of Evans, Schwingers & Co., was established May 1st, 1877, with James H. De

Graff president; E. Evans, vice president; William Savere, cashier; share holders: J. Simpson, E. Evans, J. H. DeGraff, C. Schwinger, A. G. Kent, L. S. Payne, J. A. Bliss, George P. Smith, H. B. Smith, E. H. Rogers, W. M. Larew and B. L. Hand, representing a capital of a quarter of a million.

The North Tonawanda Union School has four departments and four teachers. The last winter term averaged 190 scholars and the summer term 125, J. W. Brown is principal, with Libbie M. Pugsley, Hannah Densmore, and Nellie Becker as assistants. The whole number of scholars of school age is 674. The school-house was erected in 1866. The board of education consists of Benjamin F. Felton, president; H. O. Nightingale, clerk; Dr. C. Backer, Giles Schell and John Chadwick.

The school building is a substantial stone edifice, located at one of the most pleasant points in the village. The yards in front and play grounds are kept in good condition.

The *Tonawanda Herald*, established by J. Densmore July 19th, 1875, passed into the proprietorship of George W. Warren and T. M. Chapman October 14th, 1877. It is a well conducted paper, earnestly devoted to the interests of the business community, and enjoys a patronage creditable alike to itself and its patrons.

The iron bridge spanning the Tonawanda creek is the successor of three others; one was erected by the United States in 1800 or 1801, for military purposes. It was temporary in construction and was of short duration. After it fell, the crossing was done by a ferry until 1824, when a toll bridge was erected, in pursuance of a charter for twenty-one years; previous to the expiration of the charter, the interests of the stock-holders were purchased by the Buffalo and Niagara Falls Railroad Company, who rebuilt the bridge, with a roadway and side tracks for their road. The period of the charter expiring, the bridge became a county and town charge. Niagara and Erie counties erected the third, which remained until superseded in 1875 by the present wrought iron structure, which was built by the "Wrought Iron Bridge Company of Canton, Ohio." Fifty tons of iron were used in its construction. It is three hundred feet in length, with a twenty-six-foot roadway, and sidewalks on both sides seven feet wide.

The village has a cemetery, which was organized under the statute, in the year 1868. The incorporators were: Benjamin F. Felton, Garwood L. Judd, Franklin Warren, Hiram Hewell, Selden G. Johnson and John Simpson. Mr. Hewell was the first president, and Mr. Felton the first secretary of the board of organization.

At the first meeting of the board of trustees, Mr. Felton presented the corporation with a splendid book for the keeping of the records. Much credit is due to Messrs. Felton, Warren and Judd for the labor and interest they took in organizing the enterprise.

Mr. Judd drew up the articles of association; and being an attorney, obtained the requisite order from court, sanctioning the articles of incorporation, which were duly recorded in the office of the county clerk.

Many of the citizens have purchased lots in the cemetery and beautified them. Among the number are Hon. Henry J. Smith, Hon. John Simpson, Franklin Warren, Benjamin F. Felton, Hon. Lewis S. Payne, Garwood L. Judd, James Carney, Asa Ransom, Frederick Sommer, James G. Primer and others. The cemetery is situated on the easterly side of Payne avenue.

THE LUMBER TRADE.

The lumber trade is the prevailing feature of business, while other interests are to be included, as in a prosperous condition. At the various lumber yards is seen every necessary arrangement and skillful appliance to transact business with dispatch and economy. The capital employed and energy displayed can not fail of success. To detail the business would exceed our limits, but an account of a few of the leading concerns will not fail to interest the reader.

The firm of McGraw & Co. established themselves in the business over eight years since. Their yards and docks cover an area of six and one fourth acres, on Manhattan street. The main dock, facing on the Niagara river, is 400 feet long, with two slips, 600 feet each, making 1,600 feet of docking, with capacity to store 10,000,000 feet of rough lumber, 500,000 feet of dressed ceiling, siding and flooring, and a full stock of shingles and lath. Aside from the water front occupied by this firm, they also have the facilities for shipping on a branch of the Central railroad passing through their premises, loading cars directly from lake barges. Convenient access to the canal also places them in a favorable business position. The members of the firm are: John McGraw, T. H. McGraw, C. B. Curtiss and Ira D. Bennett. The last is the general manager, and A. J. Hathaway foreman on the yard.

Extensive as are the other yards and docks, astonishment is still further excited upon the premises of W. H. Gratwick & Co., one and a half miles down the river on the Central railroad. The office for the transaction of their business could not be more conveniently and comfortably arranged for employees and customers. W. H. Gratwick, formerly residing in Albany, is now a resident of Buffalo, acting as the local representative of the firm at that point; the other members associated are Robert S. Fryer, in Albany, under the name of Gratwick, Fryer & Co., and Edward Smith, in Michigan, representing the firm of Smith, Gratwick & Co. The capital they employ in the prosecution of their business is $500,000; in the various localities and departments they employ four hundred and fifty men. They own a tract of 31,000 acres of pine land in the northern part of Michigan, where they have two mills that annually turn out 28,000,000 feet, which is transported in barges to Tonawanda and forwarded by rail and canal to eastern markets; they deal exclusively in their own production. Their docks have a river frontage of 803 feet, with a water slip, doubling the means of storage, and an additional dock in the rear, 600 feet long; in all, 2,200 feet. Tramways have been built for wagon roads, and tracks to receive the cars from the

LEWIS T. PAYNE.

LEWIS S. PAYNE.

RESIDENCE OF COL. L. S. PAYNE, TONAWANDA, NIAGARA COUNTY, N.Y.

Central and Erie railroads, to be loaded directly from vessels or piles on the docks. The docks, 300 feet out in the river, reach thirteen feet depth of water, sufficient to float the largest craft on the lakes. The cost of land, docks and buildings was $25,000. The stock on hand of planed and dressed lumber averages from 4,000,000 to 8,000,000 feet, with a proportionately large supply of shingles and laths. About four years since, Gratwick & Co. became the pioneers in occupying lots far down the river, an example that others have thought worthy of imitation.

IRON WORKING ESTABLISHMENTS.

Where the Niagara River Iron Works are situated on the Niagara river, in 1810 a small opening was made in the woods for the erection of a rude log house, by Joshua Pettit. But a little over half a century has passed, and where stood the lowly log house noble structures rise to indicate the progress that has been made from a primitive to a more advanced condition.

The Niagara River Iron Company was formed in pursuance of the general manufacturing law, in 1872, with a paid-up capital of $400,000. The first purchase of real estate was of 165 acres from M. Bush. The buildings were erected in 1873, and manufacturing operations commenced the same year. The engine house stands in a prominent position, and by one not knowing its design might be taken for an elegant mansion or villa; the building is 68 by 74 feet, with a proportionate elevation, and finished in tasteful style. The boiler house, judiciously separately located, 45 feet by 70, contains ten ponderous boilers, four feet in diameter and sixty feet long; an octagon chimney eighty feet high rises in front. The blast furnace was constructed to run out fifty tons of pig iron per day, and is 60 by 200 feet and two stories high; a tower rising above one hundred feet contains the machinery for elevating ore and brick by steam power. The oven is 30 by 41 feet, with iron-bound exterior. The buildings named are massive and substantial brick erections, upon stone foundations. The stock house is a frame building, 72 by 500 feet and two stories high.

The dock fronting on the river is 500 feet in length, reaching ten feet depth of water. Located upon the dock is an engine for raising freight from the vessels.

Two branch tracks of the Central railroad pass over the docks and into the stock house, to deposit and remove material. The buildings cover an area of four acres.

The trustees are P. P. Pratt, president; Josiah Jewett, vice-president; S. S. Jewett, H. H. Gleney, George B. Hays, F. L. Danforth and B. F. Felton. During the present general depression in business the works are not operated; but as they are controlled by men of permanent wealth, willing to use it and able to hold their own until the day dawns upon brighter prospects, the advantages of this great concern will yet be felt by the community that has clustered about it in anticipation. The premises and machinery are kept in the most perfect order and neatness under the care of Alexander Reid.

The Tonawanda Engine and Machine Company's extensive machine shops are located in the rear of the Erie railway depot on Olive street, occupying a square of 150 feet. They manufacture steam engines and boilers, and furnish castings for all discriptions of agricultural implements. The firm consists of James Armitage, Allen Herschell, George C. Herschell and George A. Gillis.

The Pickard & Simpson Manufacturing Company, in connection with the above mentioned, organized for the manufacture of Pickard's patent vehicle axle boxes. The following gentlemen are connected with the firm: R. F. Pickard, John Simpson, E. B. Simpson, A. H. Pickard, E. H. Hewitt and H. H. Pickard.

BRIEF SKETCHES OF WHEATFIELD CITIZENS.

HON. LEWIS S. PAYNE.

Lewis S. Payne was born in the town of Bergen, Genesee county, N. Y., in 1819. His parents being poor he had no advantages of education, except the imperfect common schools which then existed, and the academies of Monroe and Genesee counties.

When sixteen years of age, he left his home and found employment at Tonawanda, N. Y., as clerk in a store. At the age of twenty-one he succeeded his employers in the mercantile business, and afterward became engaged in the lumber business, and in 1847 built the first steam saw-mill in Tonawanda. In 1855 Mr. Payne engaged in the forwarding, shipping and commission business, with the extensive elevator and docks at Tonawanda, and in 1858 turned his attention to farming, which is his present occupation.

In 1841 he changed his place of residence, from the Erie county to the Niagara county side of the Tonawanda creek, in the village of North Tonawanda, town of Wheatfield, where he still resides. In 1844 he was elected supervisor of his town, and for many years afterward represented the town in that capacity.

In 1849 he was appointed collector of canal tolls at Tonawanda, his being the first appointment made at that place; and in 1850 was re-appointed to the same position.

In the fall of 1850 he was elected clerk of Niagara county, and in 1854, at the end of his term, retired with the approbation of the citizens of the county universally, for the courteous manner in which he had discharged the duties of the office.

In politics Mr. Payne was formerly a national Whig; but on the dissolution of that party he became a Douglas Democrat, and in 1859 was nominated by that party for the office of State Senator for the 29th district.

In the fall of 1861 he raised, at his own expense, a company of volunteers, and formed a part of the one hundredth regiment, which was recruited from western New York at Buffalo. In April, 1862, with his regiment he landed at Newport News, and formed a part of Casey's division of McClellan's army in his famous campaign on the Peninsula. With his regiment he was second to cross the Chickahominy and the first to take up position at White Oak Station. Colonel Payne was in the battles of Williamsburg and Seven Pines, and afterward was in the seven days' retreat. He participated in the battles of White Oak Swamp and Malvern Hill; and in August returned to Gloucester Point, after a severe campaign of less than four months, in which he lost forty-two out of his company of one hundred and four men. In the winter following he was in North Carolina, in General Foster's army corps. Early in the spring of 1863 he was sent to Hilton Head; thence to St. Helena Island, in General Hunter's department; thence up to Cole's Island, with his regiment as a corps of observation in the vicinity of Charleston. It was from this point that he was ordered out, and made his many bold and daring expeditions and scouts with his company, and learned the nature and character of the whole country, the positions, situations and strength of the enemy in their various localities and stations. Some of his adventures during these expeditions are related in an article by John S. C. Abbott, entitled "Heroic Deeds of Heroic Men," published in Harper's Magazine in April, 1867.

On the nights of the 5th and 6th of April, 1863, he led the advance up Folly Island, under General Seymour, to support the attack of Admiral Dupont on Fort Sumter, made with his iron monitors on the 7th of April, 1863. On the 10th of May he led the advance, piloted and conducted up Folly river, and across Light-house Inlet, our forces, 4,500 men, all in small boats, to the point of attack on Morris Island, and was the first to land and first in the engagement. The party carried and took possession, under heavy fire, of the south end of Morris Island; and soon Colonel Payne with his company succeeded in reaching and burning the steamer Marrigault in Charleston harbor, which was engaged in supplying the enemy's forces at Forts Sumter, Moultrie, Johnson, Battery Wagner and Cummings Point.

On the night of the third of August, 1863, while engaged in intercepting communications of the enemy with Fort Sumter and other points, he was attacked by a superior force, and after a most desperate engagement was wounded and taken prisoner, conveyed to Charleston and confined in the Queen-street Hospital until sufficiently recovered from his wounds to be removed, when he was taken to Columbia, S. C., and there kept in close confinement until the 14th of February, 1865, when with others he was moved north for exchange.

On the fifth of March, 1865, he was exchanged at Wilmington, N. C., and reached home on the first of April, after an absence of three years and three months.

In the fall following (1865) he was again nominated and elected county clerk, though in a county giving several hundred Republican majority.

He served his term of three years, and in the fall following (1869) was elected member of Assembly from his district, and in the Assembly was made chairman of the committee on claims, and was also a member of the committees on canals and military affairs.

In November, 1877, he was again nominated for senator for the 29th district, and was elected over his opponent, the Republican nominee, being the first Democrat ever elected in the 29th senatorial district.

William L. Allen, M. D., was born at Ovid, N. Y., February 6th, 1847, and was educated at the New York State Normal School, Ovid Academy and Buffalo Medical College. He came to Tonawanda April 10th, 1876.

Heman A. Barnum was born March 27th, 1831, in the town of Wheatfield. Mr. Barnum is a farmer. His post-office address is Sanborn.

Theodore Bennett was born in Newstead, Erie county, December 17th, 1845. Residence, North Tonawanda. Business, school-teacher and fire-insurance agent.

James A. Betts, son of William C. Betts, was born in Upper Canada, October 19th, 1828, and came to Niagara county in 1835. He was married August 21st, 1867, to Mrs. B. G. Sturges, of Wheatfield. Mr. Betts enlisted in the nineteenth Illinois volunteers in May, 1861, and served three years, after which he re-enlisted, was transferred to the navy and served till the close of the war.

James Carney was born March 23rd, 1800, at Black Creek, Upper Canada, and was married to Sally Martin, of the town of Niagara, March 17th, 1825. Mr. Carney, who is now a retired farmer, has been supervisor and justice of the peace in Tonawanda, Erie county, and supervisor of the town of Wheatfield.

Wilhelm Dornfeld was born September 11th, 1826, in Prussia, and came to Martinsville, Niagara county, in 1843. Mr. Dornfeld is a farmer and merchant, and one of the firm of Krull Brothers & Dornfeld, proprietors of the lumber yard, planing-mill, and sash and door factory at Martinsville. He was postmaster from 1852 to 1865.

Albert Dornfeld was born January 5th, 1831, in Prussia, and came to Niagara county in 1843. Mr. Dornfeld, who is a teacher, has been justice of the peace for eight years, and was formerly proprietor of the dry dock sawmill at Martinsville.

C. F. Goers, whose post-office is Bergholz, has always lived in Wheatfield, having been born in the town January 2nd, 1850. He is a farmer and school-teacher, and has been a notary public over four years.

Charles Hagen, hotel-keeper and town clerk at North Tonawanda, was born in the Kingdom of Hanover, Germany, February 28th, 1839, and came to Niagara county on the 4th day of August, 1861. Mr. Hagen has been clerk of the town of Wheatfield six terms, and he served as clerk of Payne's Company D., 100th N. Y. regiment, and as clerk of the 3rd brigade, 1st division, 10th army corps, before Richmond, during the late war.

Garwood L. Judd was born at Augusta Centre, Oneida county, N. Y., July 4th, 1823. He studied law and was admitted to the bar, after having received a good education. Shortly after his admission, he was admitted to practice in the Supreme Court of the United States as a proctor and advocate in admiralty. He was married to Maria A. Pryne, eldest daughter of Francis P. Pryne. He practiced at Frankfort, Herkimer county, till 1853, and then removed to North Tonawanda, where he has since resided. He has been a justice of the peace in Wheatfield twenty-four years in succession.

Christian George Krull was born January 15th, 1846, at Bergholz. He was married September 17th, 1869, to

MR. G. L. JUDD.

MRS. G. L. JUDD.

RESIDENCE & OFFICE OF GARWOOD L. JUDD, ESQ. TONAWANDA, N.Y.

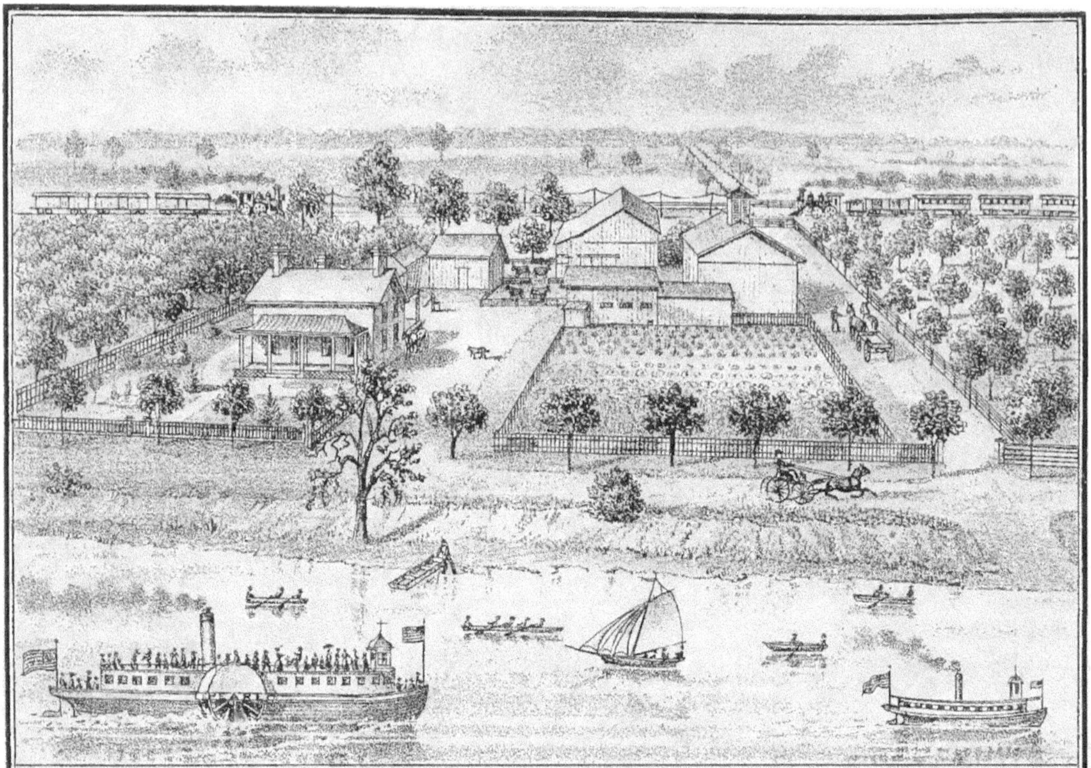

FARM RES. OF E.A. MILLIMAN, ESQ., TOWN OF WHEATFIELD, NIAGARA CO., N.Y.

FARM RES. OF NELSON ZIMMERMAN, ESQ, TOWN OF WHEATFIELD N.Y.

Ernstine Bettac, from Fahrenwalde, Prussia. In November he removed to Martinsville, where he now lives, engaged in farming and holding a partnership in the Centennial Planing-mill. He has been nine years a school trustee in the town, and was a commissioner of highways in 1872, 1873 and 1874.

Edward A. Milliman was born April 16th, 1832, in Wheatfield, and was married November 14th, 1854, to Susan E. Teal, of Lewiston. He removed to the town of Wheatfield September 21st, 1868. He is engaged in farming and in contracting and jobbing. Post-office, Tonawanda, N. Y. Mr. Milliman has been extensively engaged in railroad contracting, having constructed portions of many leading railroads throughout the United States, and he has held a number of official positions, among them those of commissioner of highways, deputy collector of customs, and supervisor.

Seth F. Roberts was born in Bloomfield, Ontario county, N. Y., December 5th, 1809, and came to Wheatfield in 1822, from Henrietta, Monroe county, N. Y. Mr. Roberts has been variously engaged during a long and busy life, having chopped, logged, taught district school seven winters, and served as supervisor, town clerk, school commissioner and justice of the peace for fifteen or twenty years. He holds the office of justice of the peace at the present time.

One of the thrifty farmers of Wheatfield is Herman F. Stieg, residing at St. Johnsburgh. He was born February 23rd, 1839, in Prussia, and came to this county with the German colony in 1843. He has served twelve years as assessor and four years as highway commissioner in his town.

George M. Warren was born in the town of Wheatfield, January 24th, 1847, and has been a life-long resident of Tonawanda, where, as a member of the firm of Warren & Clapham, he is engaged in editing and publishing the *Tonawanda Herald*. Mr. Warren was elected on the Democratic ticket in 1875 one of the school commissioners of Niagara county for a term of three years.

Nelson Zimmerman was born November 4th, 1831, at Tonawanda. Mr. Zimmerman, who is a prominent farmer of the town of Wheatfield, held the office of assessor in 1875, 1876 and 1877.

Others of the principal inhabitants of the town, with their post-offices, are: O. C. Thompson and B. F. Felton, of Tonawanda; Hon. J. D. Loveland, farmer, Beech Ridge; Harvey Miller, farmer, Shawnee; L. C. Koover, farmer, Sanborn; Daniel Sy, town assessor, farmer, Bergholz; William Clark, town and village assessor, carpenter and joiner, Tonawanda; G. W. Bush, lumber dealer and manufacturer, Tonawanda; Martin Reisterer, farmer and merchant, Tonawanda; H. O. Nightingale, village and school trustee, Tonawanda; Calvin Jacobs, farmer and boat-builder, Tonawanda; John Poinds, farmer, Tonawanda; Wilhelm Krull, farmer and lumber manufacturer, Martinsville; J. S. Tompkins, farmer, La Salle; W. H. Nash, farmer, Sanborn; S. D. Compton, farmer, Shawnee; Sebastian May, farmer, Tonawanda; Lyman Bruce, farmer, Tonawanda; B. C. Shuman, farmer, Tonawanda; J. F. Hoover, Tonawanda; Rev. John W. Weinback, clergyman, New Bergholz; John Simson, farmer and lumber dealer, Tonawanda; Dr. C. Backer, proprietor of the Backer Hotel, Tonawanda; Thomas Collins, farmer, La Salle; Daniel Treichler, farmer, Sanborn; F. D. Habecker and Peneuel Schmeck, farmers, Sanborn; A. B. Williams, saw and planing-mill, Tonawanda; Dr. Clinton A. Sage, Pekin; Emil Schmitze, restaurant and hotel keeper, Tonawanda; Jacob Nagel, carriage-maker, Tonawanda.

THE TOWN OF WILSON.

On April 10th, 1818, by special act of the Legislature, the town of Porter was divided, north and south, near its center, and a new town constituted from the eastern part, and named Wilson, in honor of Reuben Wilson, one of the first and most prominent pioneers of that section. This town was sub-divided in March, 1824, to furnish a portion of Newfane. Its organization was fully completed by the election of its first officers at a town meeting held at the house of David Porter, April 6th, 1819. They were: Reuben Wilson, supervisor; Daniel Holmes, town clerk; David Burgess, John Carter, and Henry Lockwood, assessors; Oramel Hartwell, collector; Abner Crossman and Burgoyne Kemp, overseers of the poor; James McKinney, Joshua Williams and John Carter, commissioners of highways; Oramel Hartwell and Joshua D. Coller, constables; Alexander Douglas, Reuben Wilson and Joshua Williams, excise commissioners; Jeremiah Whipple, Hul Bixby and Burgoyne Kemp, fence-viewers; Elisha Stevens, pound-master; and twelve overseers of highways. Reuben Wilson was the presiding justice at this election.

The town also voted a tax of $250 for the support of of bridges, and $25 for the benefit of the poor for the ensuing year, and a bounty of five dollars was pledged for every wolf killed in the town. The first school commissioners and inspectors were not elected until the spring of 1821. They were: Reuben Wilson, David Bixby and Alexander Butterfield, commissioners; and Andrew Brown, John U. Pease and Gideon B. Roys, inspectors. In May following the town was divided into five school districts by the above commissioners, and in July of the same year district No. 1 was subdivided. School children at that time could not have been very numerous, for the entire population of the town—which then included the western portion of Newfane—was but 680, and the entire vote cast for governor at the election held in April of that year was 32, of which DeWitt Clinton had 24 and Daniel D. Tompkins 8.

The town now contains one union and thirteen other school districts, with seventeen school-houses and 1088 scholars between the ages of five and twenty-one. The amount of public school money raised in 1878 was $2,484.

SUPERVISORS.

The following is a complete list of supervisors since the organization of the town:

In 1819-29, Reuben Wilson; 1830-32, John Carter; 1833-42, Luther Wilson; 1843-45, Robert L. McChesney; 1846, 1847, Samuel R. Merwin; 1848, Alexander Pettit; 1849, Russell Robinson; 1850, R. L. McChesney; 1851, Reuben F. Wilson; 1852, Curtis Pettit; 1853, Alexander Pettit; 1854, Orsemus Ferris; 1855, 1856, Luther Wilson; 1857, Orsemus Ferris; 1858, Henry N. Johnson; 1859-61, Ralph Stockwell; 1862, 1863, Tunis Outwater; 1864, David O. Jeffery; 1865, Benjamin Farley; 1866, Alexander Pettit; 1867, Richard C. Holmes; 1868-70, William Hamblin; 1871-74, Benjamin Dearborn; 1875-77, Ralph Stockwell; 1878, Edward Barker.

STATISTICAL FACTS.

The town had a voting population in 1875 of 785, and 2,835 inhabitants. Its area is 3,037 acres, three-fourths of which is in an excellent state of cultivation. It is bounded on the north by Lake Ontario, east by Newfane, south by Cambria and west by Porter. Its surface is very level and elevated about 15 feet above the lake. The soil is principally a dark, rich loam, mixed with clay on the west, and is well adapted to the raising of most cereals. Wheat, corn, oats and beans are the chief grain products. Fruit is also raised in abundance, apples, pears and grapes being the staple fruit products. The principal streams are the east and west branches of the Twelve-mile creek, so called because its mouth is that distance from Fort Niagara. At the mouth of this creek there is a peninsula forming a natural bay. Just inland from the lake the stream, widens, and forms a basin about twenty rods across. The basin and creek, for a mile or more up stream are of sufficient depth and width to float any ordinary vessel.

PIONEER EXPERIENCES.

The first settlements in the town were made along the lake shore, principally by Americans who had previously emigrated to Canada. But very few located to any considerable distance inland until after the close of the war of 1812. The only road which had been opened in the town up to this time was along the lake shore from Fort Niagara, through Wilson to Somerset, and from one side of the town to the other along this line the inhabitants suffered from the effects of the British raid made from the fort to Van Horn's mill on December 24th, 1813. But two or three houses escaped destruction. Some lost all their provision, stock and household effects, while a few were allowed to save a portion to prevent immediate starvation.

Henry Lockwood was probably the first white man who located within the present limits of Wilson. He came from Canada West in 1808, and obtained possession, by article from the Holland Land Company, of 100 acres of land on lot No. 77, in the extreme northeast corner of the town. Near the mouth of the creek which still bears his name he erected the pioneer house. It was constructed of logs, with split slabs for a floor and bark for a roof. Around this solitary house he made the first opening in the forest, which has long ago yielded to the pioneer's ax throughout the entire town. He remained here until the breaking out of the war, when he removed to Canada, and never returned. At the close of the war the title to this land was transferred to John Cudaback, and it is now occupied by J. S. Cudaback. Robert Waterhouse, from Connecticut, settled the same year in the extreme south part of the town, on lot No. 1. The only man to settle in 1809 was Stephen Sheldon. He came from Jefferson county, N. Y., bringing a large family with him, and located on the west bank of the east branch of Twelve-mile creek, about half a mile from its mouth, where he put up a rude log shanty for the temporary accommodation of his family. Lots number eight and nine had been previously "booked" to him by the Holland Company, giving him possession of 720 acres of land. In the spring of 1811 he erected a house at the mouth of the creek and removed thither, where in the fall of 1812 he died. His family remained here until their house was burned by the British. They afterward built a house near the locality of their first one, where they lived many years. In the summer of 1814 Smith Sheldon, the third son, was taken prisoner by some British troops. He with four others was harvesting for a Captain Brown near the Four-mile creek, when the captain and all his help were surprised and captured. They were taken to Quebec, where Sheldon died on a prison ship. The others were afterward exchanged and returned home.

The year 1810 witnessed quite an influx to this town. The first to come in that year were Reuben Wilson, John Eastman and Gilbert Purdy, who left the Canadian shore, near Toronto, together, in April—the two former with their families and a few household effects and farming utensils, and the latter as boatman. In two open batteaux, one laden with freight and the other with passengers, sailing and rowing around the head of Lake Ontario, and camping on its shores at night, they arrived at the mouth of Twelve-mile creek in the early part of June. A mile and a half east of this they unloaded their boats, drew them upon shore, and by setting them bottom upward, upon stakes, and closing the sides with boughs and bark, they speedily constructed for themselves summer residences. Their kitchen was spacious, being all out-doors. Their cooking was done by a fire over which hung the dinner pot, suspended from a pole supported by two crotches. In these airy castles they dwelt for three months, during which time Wilson and Eastman, assisted by Purdy, had each erected a substantial log house. John Eastman was a native of New Hampshire, but for a few years previous to his emigration to Wilson had resided at Coburg, Canada West. He had in 1809 obtained an article for 100 acres of land on lot No. 82, now occupied by A. A. Dailey. Here he remained until about 1818, when he exchanged places with James Cole and removed into the eastern part of Hartland, and subsequently to Chautauqua county, where he died.

Reuben Wilson was born in Massachusetts, from which State he emigrated to Otsego county, N. Y., in 1805, and from thence to Coburg, Canada, in 1807. After his arrival in Wilson he took up 170 acres of land on lot No. 82, at $2.50 per acre, paying nothing down, but promising to pay five per cent. in a few months. Upon this he at once commenced improvements. Besides building his house he cleared ten acres the first year, and the second year raised a crop of wheat more than sufficient for the use of his family, which then consisted of seven persons. His provisions for the first year were obtained in Canada. When he began to raise his own grain, he was obliged to go across the lake to Port Hope or Hamilton to get his grinding done. Niagara in those days was the nearest trading point. In 1816 Mr. Wilson purchased a saw-mill which had been built the previous year on Twelve-mile creek, his son Luther taking charge of it. In 1818 he sold his farm and moved into a dwelling which he had erected near the saw-mill. In 1825 he associated his son Luther with him in business, and the same year the new firm erected the first grist-mill in the town, near the site of the saw-mill. It was a frame, water power mill, 2½ stories high, 20 by 35 feet in size, and contained two run of stones. They also engaged in the mercantile business the same year in the same locality. Reuben Wilson may truthfully be called *the* pioneer of the present town of Wilson, for while the two or three who preceded him remained but a very few years, he was for forty years prominently identified with its political, agricultural and business developments; liberal toward religious societies and interested in educational matters.

At the time of the British raid along the Lake road, George Ash, who, with his family, was staying at Mr. Wilson's house, going that day out on horseback to his farm in Porter, unexpectedly met the enemy about six miles west of Wilson's. His horse, which he was leading at the time, took fright and escaped from him, but he fled on foot and arrived home in time to notify a portion of the neighborhood. The few cattle in the immediate vicinity—about 25 head—were speedily collected and started down the lake, driven by Reuben Wilson, then a boy of about fifteen years, who pressed them on in advance, passing Van Horn's about sundown with the enemy then in sight. A few of the cows had on bells, which Reuben, fearing they might be overheard, stuffed with dried leaves and continued on five miles beyond, where he rested for the night. The next day he returned, after the destruction of the mills and the retreat of the invaders. The British upon coming up to Mr. Wilson's made him their prisoner, but paroled him upon his word that he would remain at home until their return. Captain Scott who was in command of the troops, was a very humane officer, and seeing the scanty supplies of the settlers, and realizing the utter destitution which a strict fulfillment of his instructions would cause, sent his orderly sergeant, with George Ash, back from Mr. Wilson's to the fort, to portray to the officer in command there the situation of the inhabitants, and induce him to countermand the orders, in a measure at least, but he could not be influenced to relent. Mr. Ash was retained as a prisoner and the sergeant was sent back to his company, with word to Captain Scott to carry out his orders to the letter. On the return of the troops the next day, a small squad who were in advance of the main body, driving some cattle which had been picked up, called at Mr. Wilson's and forced him to go with them. The main body coming up, Mrs. Wilson had no little trouble in convincing the officers that her husband had not forfeited his word and voluntarily left. The officers remained at Mr. Wilson's house over night, partaking of food prepared by Mrs. W. For this hospitality, and the fact that the house stood about 20 rods from the main road, it was not burned by them. Mr. Wilson was kept at the fort about ten days, when he was released on parole and returned to his family. He afterward received many favors at the hands of the British officers at the fort.

Gilbert Purdy, after assisting Wilson and Eastman to erect their houses, went westward up the lake, and in the fall of 1810 obtained an article for one hundred acres of land on lot No. 26, now owned by Mrs. Daniel Dwight. The following winter he erected a house on his land, and in the spring moved his family from Coburg to his new home, where he died in 1813. His family were burned out by the British, and soon after returned to Canada, abandoning their land to the Holland Company.

Erastus Barnard came from Royalton in the summer of 1810, and lived for a time with his father-in-law, Stephen Sheldon. He took up land on lot No. 16, upon which he made some slight improvements, but soon after the war sold it and removed to Porter.

A German named May, from Schoharie, settled in the fall of the same year on lot No. 41, where the late Lawson Thompson resided. He remained until the summer of 1812, and then left through fear of the Indians, and never returned.

Dexter P. Sprague and Robert Edwards, from Vermont, located on lot No. 63 in the fall of 1810. At the commencement of the war, Sprague removed his family to the ridge in Hartland, and in 1815 sold his land to Adam Stevens, who was a permanent resident until his death. Edwards, who was a captain of militia, remained until the first day of the British raid, when he precipitately fled with his family to the house of his friend on the ridge. The place was soon after sold to David Porter, and is now occupied by J. M. Newman. James Meeker, from New Jersey, settled the same fall on 100 acres on lot No. 91, and Andrew Loys, from Canada, on lot No. 75, where Mrs. Sally Holmes now resides. Both of these pioneers, after erecting buildings and making two years' improvements, fled through fear and never returned.

Three Germans from the Mohawk valley, named, respectively, Vosbeck, Wood and Gray, came here together in the fall of 1810. They had each previously obtained an article for a quarter section of land, Vosbeck and Gray on lot No. 25 and Wood on lot No. 24, and each had a fine beginning at the breaking out of the war; but remembering the horrible cruelties perpetrated on their forefathers in the valley during the Revolution, they feared to remain. Their farms were afterward purchased by Stephen, John and David Tower, three brothers from Massachusetts, who moved on to them in 1818.

Elijah Mallory, from Coburg, Canada, became a resident on lot No. 82 in the spring of 1811. He was the owner of a horse team, and was required by the government to assist in the construction of the log causeway from Wright's to Warren's Corners, and was afterward detailed to haul supplies from Williamsville—which was then a military depot—to Buffalo, and died while in this service. His family remained in Wilson many years after his death.

The threatening prospect of war and its final outbreak caused an entire suspension of emigration to this town for nearly three years, and many of those who had previously located abandoned their new homes, through fear or otherwise, and sought safer and more thickly settled localities. It was not until 1815 that immigration to any extent was resumed.

Daniel and George Sheldon, the oldest sons of Stephen Sheldon, were residing in Kingston, Canada, at the commencement of the war. They were drafted into the British service, but succeeded in making their escape, and in 1814 came to Wilson. George afterward located on lot 17. Daniel in 1815, in company with Joshua Williams, built the first saw-mill in the town on the west bank of the Twelve-mile creek about half a mile from its mouth.

Richard and William Knowles also fled from Canada after being drafted into the English service, and in 1815 settled in Wilson, the former on the western part of lot No. 8—where his son, A. W. Knowles, still resides—and the latter on the north part of lot No. 7. David Porter, from Vermont, settled previous to the war in what is now Newfane. In 1815 he purchased and removed to the farm now owned by J. M. Newman.

Henry Barber and Nathan Pratt left Canada to avoid being drafted, and in 1815 located, the former on lot No. 89 and the latter on lot No. 7.

John Carter became a settler on the southwest part of lot No. 72 the same year. During the war he was residing at St. Catharines. At the time of the march of the American troops from Fort George to Stony creek he was accused by the British government of aiding and assisting them. He was arrested, and imprisoned for a time at Hamilton, where he and thirteen others were tried for treason, convicted and sentenced to be hung; but through the assistance of a British surgeon—a friend and former acquaintance—he succeeded in making his escape to the States. His comrades suffered the penalty of treason.

Abram Hutchings came from Avon, Livingston county, N. Y., in 1816, and took up his abode on lot No. 88, having obtained an article for the entire lot. He was a soldier in the war of 1812, previous to which he had served seven years in the English army, at the end of which time he had been re-enlisted through fraud or deceit. He, in 1813, with a company of thirty, was sent to Queenston, when, taking advantage of the opportunity, he deserted and joined the American army. At the battle of Black Rock he and a comrade named Berry, who had deserted with him, were taken prisoners by the British, and carried back to Queenston, Canada. After about three weeks captivity, he was smuggled across the Niagara river by a British surgeon named Anson Mary, who had been an old neighbor and friend in England. Berry was afterwards shot for desertion.

The following are among those who became settled in 1817: John Haze, from Coburg, located on lot No. 7; Nathan Sherwood, from Vermont, on the northeast part of lot No. 9, and James Cole, from Canada, who first settled on the ridge in 1814, afterwards removing to the east part of lot No. 82, on land formerly owned by John Eastman.

From this time on settlers began to increase rapidly, roads were laid out and bridges built, and the hardships of early pioneer life became comparatively easy in this section.

SUNDRY FIRST EVENTS.

The first tavern in the town was kept by T. T. Upton in 1818; it was located about west of Wilson village on Mrs. Delia Dwight's farm.

Benjamin Douglas built and worked the first ashery, in 1817, and also opened a store on a very small scale the same year, on the Twelve-mile creek, near the present grist-mill. He died soon after, and the business passed into the hands of R. & L. Wilson.

The first grist-mill in the town was for grinding corn. It was located on the Lake road, near the present residence of J. M. Newman, and consisted of a large oak stump, hollowed out on the top sufficiently to hold a half bushel or more of corn, which was ground or beaten into samp by a heavy wooden pestle supported by a spring pole, and worked with the foot. To this mill people for miles around would repair for their milling, each man doing his own grinding and taking his turn in the order in which he came. This mill was built about 1817, and was used for many years.

The first post-office in the town was established about 1824. Reuben Wilson was the first postmaster, his son Luther acting as deputy, and Daniel Holmes the first mail contractor. The route was from Olcott to Youngstown, once a week.

The first and only tannery in the town was built by Simon S. Sheldon, about 1825. It was a frame building, and stood on the northwest corner of lot No. 7. Mr. Sheldon operated it four or five years, when the business was suspended. Jeremiah Whipple built a distillery about 1826 on the "Ten-mile run," two miles west of Wilson village. This he worked three or four years, when it went down and the proprietor with it.

The first school in the town was an evening school for adults, taught by Luther Wilson during January and February, 1817, in a dwelling then standing on the farm of A. B. Arnold, one mile south of the village of Wilson.

The first school-house was built of hewed logs, in 1819. It was located on the south side of the Lake road, about one mile and a half east of Wilson village. Dr. Warner, who resided in Olcott, taught the first day-school here the same year, with an average attendance of about twelve scholars.

The first school-house at what is now Wilson village was built in 1820, of logs, and stood on the site now occupied by Luther Wilson's stone residence. Almira Welch taught the first school here, followed by David Murray.

Drs. Alvord and Smith, of Lewiston, the first physicians, were followed by Dr. Warner, of Olcott. The first physician to locate in the town was Jonathan Thayer, from Dutchess county, N. Y., who came in 1824, and purchased 100 acres of land of Reuben Wilson, on lot No. 73, where he remained and practiced his profession for many years.

The first lawyer was Sylvester Parsons, jr., whose parents came from Maine to Wilson village in 1840.

The first blacksmith to locate was Henry Johnson, who settled at the village of Wilson about 1824.

The first white child born in the town was Owen Wilson, a son of Reuben Wilson.

The first marriage was that of Luther Wilson to Sarah Stephens; and the first death was that of Stephen Sheldon.

The first mason to locate in the town was Peter Furrow, from Massachusetts, who came in 1824, and located on lot 25, Youngstown road. He did most of the mason work on all the early mills and other buildings in Wilson village up to 1840.

ROADS.

The first road opened in the town was that along the lake shore, running from Fort Niagara easterly into Somerset, and known as the Lake road. Most of it is still in use as originally cut through, in 1811.

The Youngstown road, extending from Youngstown to Van Horn's mill, was laid out in July, 1816, by Abner Crossman and George Sheldon, road commissioners, and surveyed by Joseph Aiken, who also ran most of the roads laid out previous to June, 1820.

The Town Line road, so called from the fact that it runs on the line between the seventh and eighth ranges of townships from Lake Ontario to the Pennsylvania line, was the first road opened running south from the lake. It was surveyed in May, 1816, and originally ran from the lake south two miles, and then took a southwest course to the southwest corner of the town. In November, 1819, it was straightened on the line, and the old road abandoned.

The Slash road, commencing at the lake road, between lots 72 and 82, and running due south to the Marsh road, was laid out in November, 1818. It received its name from the fact that the commissioners let the job to Daniel Holmes to "slash" through, or fall the timber, preparatory to burning. After being slashed, the road lay in this condition for some time, which gave it this appellation.

The Farley, Marsh, Daniels, Randall, Fitch and Palmer roads all took their names from the first settlers along their course.

THE LAST WOLF AND BEAR.

Mr. D. A. Jeffrey, of Ransomville, furnishes the following statement :

"I have a distinct recollection of the circumstances connected with the killing of the last two wolves known in this part of the country. The female—for there was one male and one female—was killed in the winter of 1837-8 by a boy by the name of Frank Brown (son of Nathaniel Brown), on the farm now owned by Moses Kinsler, then owned by ex-Governor W. Hunt, in the town of Wilson. The boy was about 17 or 18 years old. It had been known for some time that there but two wolves left in this part of the country by their tracks in the snow. Young Brown had a strong inclination for hunting, and had spent much of the winter hunting wolves, with no success. About the middle of February his efforts were crowned with success. He went to the woods about noon (it had been snowing all the forenoon), and had gone but a short distance when he struck a fresh wolf-track. Following it a few rods it went under a large elm tree that had blown up by the roots and lay about two feet from the ground on the root and top. He could find no place where the track left the tree, and on investigation he found the tree hollow, with an opening near the root large enough to admit his body with difficulty. Looking toward the top of the tree he discovered the eyes of some animal shining in the darkness. He then put his rifle into the tree, leveled it as well as he could, and discharged it. Letting the smoke clear away he found he had not killed his game, and repeated his tactics ; this time the animal biting the end of his gun. Having not yet killed the beast he again went through with the same process and killed his game. He then crawled into the log till he found the dead animal, dragged it out, and it proved to be a female wolf with young ones. On chopping the log open he found five pups, with their eyes not yet open.

"The male had but three feet (having probably lost one in a trap), and was killed, I think, the next winter, after a chase of two days and two nights, near the Barton saw-mill (built in a day by Solomon Hersey), on the Daniels road in the town of Wilson, by a man by the name of Miller. There was quite a large number of men shooting at him at the same time, and it was hard to tell who killed him ; but Miller claimed the honor and got the bounty. That was the last wolf I ever heard of in the county."

The wolves disposed of, a bear lurked for a much longer time, often seen in Wilson, Newfane and Porter and the outskirts of other towns, as believed from the most reliable data, up to about fourteen years ago. Parties were often on the track of and shot at the animal without success. Finally bruin was accidentally discovered in a brush heap by a man chopping, who gave the alarm to a party that dispatched him. This took place on the Raymond road, two miles from the turnpike.

THE VILLAGE OF WILSON.

This village, centrally located, near the shore of the lake at the mouth of the Twelve-mile creek, contains four churches, two hotels, three dry goods, one drug, one hardware, one jewelry, three grocery and three millinery stores, one grist-mill, two foundries, one planing-mill, a sash and blind factory, a proportionate number of merchants and traders' shops, and a population of about one thousand inhabitants. The place bears the name of its founders, whose grist-mill and store, built in 1825, formed the nucleus around which has grown a pleasant and prosperous village. The first plat was made by Luther Wilson in 1827. It consisted of a single tier of lots on the north side of Young street, from Lake street to the creek. This sufficed until 1847, when Mr. Wilson made the Hains addition—named from the surveyor, Jesse P. Hains—and the same year Simon Sheldon added the "Wood Plat," in the south part. Other additions were subsequently made by Andrew Brown and John Onderdonk.

On May 11th, 1858, the village was incorporated under the general act of the Legislature. Four hundred and sixteen acres were included in its corporate limits, embracing a total population at that time of 715. The first board of trustees consisted of Luther Wilson (president), Luren D. Wilson, Reuben F. Wilson, Henry S. McChesney and William P. Grout; John Hosmer was clerk. The present board consists of Oscar S. McChesney (president), Clinton D. Tabor, Oscar Tower, John E. Parcell and Alexander O. Bonesteel; clerk, Adelbert J. Clark.

The village is largely indebted to the public spirit and enterprise of Luther Wilson, Esq., for its early growth and development. He was for many years merchant and miller, in company with his father until 1837, afterward alone. In 1837 he enlarged the grist-mill, attached steam power and added two more run of stones. He was the first tavern-keeper in 1829, and in 1844 erected a large two-story stone hotel on the corner of Lake and Young streets, now owned and kept by R. S. Cheshire. In 1846 he obtained special permission from the Secretary of War, at Washington, to extend piers into the lake at the mouth of the Twelve-mile creek, and that year built two piers two hundred feet into the lake, and from that time until 1867 all the improvements at the harbor were made by his individual exertion.

By an act of the Legislature passed May 9th, 1867, the Wilson Harbor Company was formed, with a capital of $10,000, the object of which was the further improvement of the harbor. This company, however, was dissolved in 1870 and operations suspended. The government is now dredging the entrance to the harbor.

In 1846 Mr. Wilson built a store-house at the harbor

and begun buying and shipping grain and fruit, thus establishing a convenient market for the town. He also the same year opened a ship-yard at this point and constructed, for his own use, the vessel "R. F. Wilson," which afterward ran with produce and freight between this port and Oswego. Through his influence Congress, in 1848, made this a port of entry, and appointed Abram Vosburg collector. This port still continues, and at certain seasons yields a no inconsiderable income.

LODGES.

This village can boast of several well organized and flourishing secret orders and societies.

The masonic lodge was organized and chartered under the name of Ontario Lodge, No. 376, F. and A. M. of Wilson, July 8th, 1855, with seven charter members. The first officers were George L. Moote, master; R. L. McChesney, senior warden; Thomas Lyons, junior warden. Their first meetings were held in the 2nd story of the brick building on the northwest corner of Young and Catharine streets. An uninterrupted prosperity enabled them in April, 1866, to purchase this building, which they remodeled, fitting up convenient rooms for their accommodation, which they still occupy, renting the first floor for mercantile purposes. The present membership is 76. Regular meetings, first and third Wednesdays in each month. Annual election at the last meeting in December. Present officers: Henry Sanford, W. M.; John A. Strong, S. W.; E. E. Dox, jr., W.; Luther Wilson, treasurer; R. F. Wilson, secretary.

Lake Shore Lodge, No. 331, I. O. O. F. of Wilson was organized July 25th, 1872, by Konrad Fink, D.D.G. M. of Suspension Bridge, with eight charter members. The first officers were: R. L. B. McChesney, N. G.; Erastus McKnight, V. G.; J. Harvey Hutchings, secretary; John Darnoch, president. Their lodge room is in Pike's Hall, on Young street. Regular meetings, every Thursday evening. Semi-annual elections occur at the last meetings in June and December. The present number of members is 28. Present officers: G. N. Shears, N. G.; Roswell H. Sweet, V. G.; J. H. Hutchings, secretary; John Darnoch, president.

Douglas Lodge A. O. U. W. of Wilson was organized March 30th, 1878, with 23 charter members. The first and present officers are: O. S. McChesney, P. M. W.; H. Seeley, M. W.; E. Gardinier, general foreman; Hart Slocom, overseer; Arthur Barger, recorder. Regular meetings are held semi-monthly, and officers elected annually. They meet at present in Odd Fellows' Hall.

Crescent Council, No. 35, R. T. of T. of Wilson was organized March 4th, 1878, with 24 charter members. The first officers were C. D. Tabor, S. C.; B. D. Tabor, P. C.; A. F. Zeiter, V. C.; W. E. McChesney, secretary; E. E. Dox, treasurer; A. W. Story, chaplain. Meetings are held weekly at Good Templars' Hall. Officers are elected semi-annually.

Wilson Lodge, No. 527, I. O. of G. T. was formed by Stephen Hoag, February 10th, 1868, with 30 charter members. The leading officers were J. G. O. Brown, W. C. T.; Sarah M. Miller, W. V. T.; Rev. R. C. Brownlee, W. chaplain; W. H. Holmes, W. S. This lodge has ever since sustained its organization and is now in a flourishing condition, with 42 members in good standing.

Post Peter A. Porter, No. 126, G. A. R. of Wilson was organized with thirteen original members, January 7th, 1870, by Brigadier-General A. W. Brazee, of Lockport. The leading officers were: P. C. Bailey, post commander; John H. Gormley, S. V. C.; C. N. Arnold, J. V. C.; Harvey U. Pease, adjutant; L. D. LeVan, Q. M. Regular meetings are held weekly, on Tuesday evenings, at Grand Army Hall, Catharine street. Annual elections occur at the first meeting in December, and installation of officers at the first regular meeting in January. The present number of members is 29. The total number that have joined this post since its organization is 63. Lynford D. Le Van is the present post commander.

CEMETERIES.

The first depository for the dead near the village was made in 1812, on the east end of the peninsula northwest of the village. Another burial place was on the point of the hill just south of the present grist-mill, on Reuben Wilson's land. It was not until 1846 that a regular established and laid out burying ground was opened. It consisted of two acres of land lying on the east side of the Town Line road. The railroad now passes through it. These grounds were several years ago depopulated and the occupants transferred to the present cemetery; in the removal one body—that of Mrs. Eunice Wilson, who died ten or twelve years previous at the age of seventy-five—was found to be petrified and to weigh nearly four hundred pounds.

In 1851 Luther Wilson donated to a legally constituted board of trustees seven acres located upon a point of land extending into the bay of Twelve-mile creek, a short distance northwest of the village, to be used for burial purposes. Two acres more were afterwards purchased, opening the grounds to Harbor street. These grounds have been tastefully laid out and improved, and with the naturally picturesque scenery, constitute a beautiful spot for the use to which they have been appropriated. This cemetery is called Greenwood.

WILSON COLLEGIATE INSTITUTE.

In the early part of the year 1848 a few enterprising individuals, having a deep interest in the rising generation, conceived the idea of erecting at Wilson village a suitable building, and employing such talent as would not only accommodate the more advanced of their own children, but attract those of other localities. For this object a subscription paper was circulated, headed by the name of Luther Wilson, who gave $500. A sufficient amount was soon pledged, and that spring the construction of a large two-story cobble-stone structure was begun on a beautiful site, conveniently located and donated to the trustees for school purposes by Simon Sheldon. The building was completed the same year, and on February 19th, 1846, it was incorporated by the regents of the university, under the name of the Wilson Collegiate Institute. The first board of trustees consisted of Luther Wilson, Simon Sheldon, Morgan Johnson, Andrew Brown, Robert L. McChesney and Hiram V. Tabor. The institute was opened in the spring of 1846, with Benjamin Wilcox as principal and David H. Davis as assistant; the former remained at its head for nearly twelve years.

The institute was sustained from funds received for tuition; but, owing to the want of proper support, it became necessary to abandon this plan. Accordingly, in the fall of 1869, a union of four school districts in this vicinity was formed, called "Union School District No. 1, of the town of Wilson," and the Wilson Collegiate Institute was merged into

THE WILSON UNION SCHOOL.

The trustees of the former deeded the building, grounds and other property to the trustees of the latter, in accordance with legislative enactment, thus making it a free school. The first board of education of the Union School was composed of H. N. Johnson (president), Sylvester Parsons, Vincent Seeley, J. G. O. Brown, Jerome Gifford, Henry Sanford, Henry Perry, W. Richardson and Lorenzo Pratt.

An academic department, in connection with this school, was opened August 11th, 1870. The first principal was Professor S. C. Hall; his successors have been F. A. Green, A. M. Cooper, S. J. Pardee and A. H. Burdick. The academic department is subject to the visitation of the regents of the university. The school also comprises a grammar department and four primary departments. It has a well selected library of about 1,000 volumes, to which students have free access. It is also provided with a complete philosophical and chemical apparatus, a telescope, maps, charts, etc.

In accordance with an act of the Legislature, this school has been designated by the regents of the university to give instruction in the science and practice of common school teaching. Accordingly, a normal class is organized annually. The present board of education is composed of A. D. Pease (president), Charles W. Seeley (secretary), S. B. Miller, A. Hamlin, Peter Haner, George Griffin, A. B. Arnold, John Diez and H. B. Tabor.

SMALLER VILLAGES.

WILSON STATION, on the Lake Ontario Shore Railroad, is situated three-fourths of a mile south of Wilson village. There is here a fine large depot; also the warehouse and coal yard of E. A. Bickford, a hotel and a few dwellings.

EAST WILSON, or Beebe's Corners, in the southeast part of the town, contains a large steam saw-mill, a blacksmith and wagon shop, and ten or twelve dwellings, mostly of farmers. This vicinity is also known as the Marsh Settlement, Joseph Marsh having been one of the earliest settlers in this part of the town. He located on lot No. 65 about 1824. Those who followed him soon after were Reuben Streeter, William Woodcock, Potter Roberts, John Pollard and Barnabas Whitney.

CHURCH HISTORY OF THE TOWN.

PRESBYTERIAN CHURCH OF WILSON.

The first religious organization in the town of Wilson was in connection with the Presbyterian denomination, through the Christian zeal and influence of John Holmes and his son Daniel. On January 18th, 1819, a meeting was held at the house of John Holmes, who then resided near Hopkins's creek, in the present town of Newfane, at which Rev. David M. Smith, then pastor of the Presbyterian church at Lewiston, was present and acted as moderator. A Presbyterian church was then and there constituted, consisting of six members, viz.: John and Anna Holmes, Daniel and Sally Holmes, and Peter and Ruth Crosby. John Holmes and Daniel Holmes were elected ruling elders, and the latter was chosen church clerk. John Holmes was also appointed a delegate to represent the newly formed church at the next meeting of the Niagara Presbytery, which occurred in June following. On the next day (January 19th, 1819) "John and Daniel Holmes were set apart by prayer and ordained ruling elders in the church" by Rev. D. M. Smith. On Saturday, August 26th, 1820, Rev. D. M. Smith delivered a preparatory lecture, and on the following Sabbath the ordinance of the Lord's Supper was administered to this church for the first time. The first accessions to the church were received on June 15th, 1822, when ten persons joined. They were Henry Lockwood, David Bixby, Erastus Barnard, Mary Davis, Sophia Whitney, Sarah M. Davis, Phila Bixby, Mary Earl, Anna Barnes and Thankful Stout. The following day Amanda Coomer and Lydia Barnard united. The first regular pastor was Rev. Ebenezer Everett. His name appears for the first time February 12th, 1823, when he officiated as moderator of the session. He remained for two years, preaching here every alternate Sunday in connection with the church at Youngstown. The Niagara Presbytery met with this church for the first time on the last Tuesday in January, 1828.

In the latter part of 1828 the church engaged the services of Rev. Silas Parsons, who preached to them for nearly two years. Mr. Parsons was followed by Rev. Herman Holsey, who was regularly installed as pastor early in 1831. He divided his labors between this church and the church at Cambria, but did not remain over the year. During the year 1834 Rev. Andrew Rawson had the pastoral care of the church.

Up to this time public services had been held in school-houses and private dwellings, but principally in the school-house a mile and three-quarters south of Wilson village, on the Town Line road. In 1834 the church and society erected a church edifice in Wilson village, on a lot donated for that purpose by Reuben Wilson. The structure was of wood, and cost about $2,500. Ira Tompkins was the builder. It was completed in January, 1835, and on February 12th, following, it was dedicated by the Rev

Mr. Crawford of Albion. In the winter of 1849 and 1850, it was remodeled, reseated and improved internally at an expense of about $1,000. In 1854 twenty feet were added to the length of the building, and in 1870 a farther extension was made to form an orchestra, at a cost of about $400, and an organ, valued at $800, placed in it.

The dedication of the new church was immediately followed by a copious revival, and at a meeting of the session held February 25th, 1835, of which Rev. Mr. Mead was moderator, thirty-one persons applied for admission into the church. The annual report made to the presbytery for 1835 shows a membership of 117. The first minister to supply the pulpit regularly in the new church was Rev. John Eliott, who commenced his labors about the first of May and continued one year.

Although from its organization up to the year 1837 this church had been much of the time without a preacher, yet public services were regularly kept up. The church was frequently visited by ministers from the Home Missionary Society, but in the absence of a preacher Elder Daniel Holmes always conducted the services by prayer, singing and the reading of a sermon from approved authors. In the spring of 1837 Rev. Elisha B. Sherwood assumed the pastoral care of the church, to which he ministered regularly for four years.

Mr. Sherwood was moderator of the session for the last time on March 13th, 1841, and was soon after followed by Rev. George W. Lane, who remained two years. He was succeeded by Rev. Thomas Payne, from Somerset, who came in the fall of 1843, and resigned in June, 1847.

Daniel Holmes was clerk of the session from the organization of the church until 1845, a term of twenty-five years, during which time he was present at nearly every meeting.

Rev. Mr. Payne was followed in August, 1874, by Rev. E. B. Benedict, who remained about two years and a half, preaching his farewell sermon on March 10th, 1850. He was succeeded in May following by Rev. G. E. Delevan, who continued for six years, resigning his charge in May, 1856. The annual report for 1855 shows a membership of 225. After the resignation of Rev. G. E. Delevan, the pulpit was supplied irregularly from various sources, until November 1st, 1857, when Rev. G. F. Severance assumed the pastoral care of the church, and continued two years or more.

In April, 1860, Rev. G. W. Hubbard was engaged by the church as stated supply. Mr. Hubbard resigned in the spring of 1867, and removed to Michigan. He was succeeded by Rev. Jeremiah Odell, from Adrian, Michigan, in June following, who remained until December, 1869. On January 18th, 1869, the semicentennial anniversary of the organization of this church was celebrated with appropriate exercises, Rev. Mr. Odell preaching the anniversary sermon.

Mr. Odell was followed by Rev. F. H. Adams, who came in March, 1870, and remained five years. Rev. G. L. Hamilton assumed the pastoral charge of this church December 1st, 1875, and still holds it. On April 27th, 1878, this church adopted the "rotary system" of eldership. At the same time all the ruling elders under the former system tendered their resignation, to take effect when the new board of elders were elected, ordained and installed. The persons elected under the new system were A. B. Arnold and J. G. O. Brown, for three years; John Griffin and Andrew Hamlin, for two years; Richard C. Holmes and David L. Barnum, for one year. The following were elected to serve as deacons: R. C. Holmes, for three years; S. P. Case, for two years, and A. D. Pease, for one year. The present number of communicants is 166.

As an inducement to the early organization of churches, the Holland Land Company proposed to give one hundred acres of land in each township to the first regularly constituted orthodox church which should apply for it from that town. This church, soon after its organization, made application, and received a deed from the company to one hundred acres of land, situated near the center of the present town of Newfane. About 1833 the trustees of the church disposed of this land, and with the proceeds purchased a dwelling and one acre of land on the Town Line road, near the school-house, where their meetings were then held. This place was used as a parsonage until 1838, when it was sold, and a lot on Lake street, in Wilson village, purchased, upon which a cottage house was erected, for the use and accommodation of the pastor. In 1855 this place was also sold, and the present brick parsonage on Mechanics' street, adjoining the church, was purchased. It has since been repaired and remodeled, and is now valued at $2,000.

The Sunday-school in connection with this church was first organized in the summer of 1820, by Daniel Holmes, in the log school-house which stood near the Lake road, east of Wilson village. Daniel Holmes was the first superintendent. It continued to be held here until 1823, when it was removed to the school-house on the Town Line road. It has been regularly kept up since its first organization, and in August, 1870, its fiftieth anniversary was appropriately celebrated by a picnic, music, addresses and a historical oration by Rev. F. H. Adams.

Its superintendents have been Daniel Holmes, R. C. Holmes, John C. Brown, James Brown and J. G. O. Brown. The present number of scholars is 183.

BAPTIST CHURCH OF WILSON.

The initiatory steps towards the organization of a Baptist society were taken in December, 1833, by Russell Robinson, who called a meeting for prayer and conference at his house. The meetings were continued on Sabbath evenings until they grew in numbers and interest to such an extent that the school-house in district No. 4 was designated as the place for holding them, and Rev. Amos Reed, then pastor of the Newfane Baptist church, was induced to officiate occasionally. He was the first Baptist minister who ever preached in Wilson, and as a result of his labors here, during the early part of 1834, about forty experienced religion. In the meantime Russell Robinson and Stephen Millard and his wife had united by letter with the church at Newfane, and on March 24th, 1834, seven other persons from this neighborhood were immersed and joined the Newfane church. In the latter part of May following a branch of the Newfane church was formed by Rev. Amos Reed at the school-house in district No. 4, in Wilson, consisting of ten members: Russell Robinson, Stephen Millard, Abraham Pettit, Eunice Millard, Sarah Robinson, Jerusha Oliver, Sally D. Oliver, Electa Pettit and Curtis Pettit. Franklin Oliver was appointed standing clerk. At this meeting there were five additions made to the branch church, viz.: Alanson Robinson and wife, Alexander and Harvey Pettit, and Sally Robinson. The first regular covenant meeting was held on the third Saturday in June, 1834.

Rufus D. Purce, a licentiate of the Newfane church, was called to spend the summer of 1834 with this branch and preach to them. His salary was to consist of his board and clothing. Deacon Robinson obtained wool, and Mrs. Robinson picked and spun it. It being woven, she cut and made the young preacher's coat. Another member provided him with pants, another with a vest, still another purchased his boots. Mr. Purce "boarded around" a week in a place, and thus his salary was paid in full.

At the covenant meeting in September following it was decided to call a council for the purpose of being recognized as an independent church. This council, consisting of delegates from the Baptist churches of Porter, Lockport, Yates and Newfane, convened at the above-mentioned school-house, October 23d, 1834, at which time and place this branch was regularly constituted and recognized as an independent Baptist church, Rev. Arah Irons, of Yates, preaching the recognition sermon. The church at that time consisted of nineteen members.

About the 1st of January, 1835, Rev. Amos Reed was engaged to preach to this church a portion of the time and in the latter part of February following the sacrament was celebrated for the first time. About May 1st, 1835, Elder Reed, at his own request, was released from his engagement, and soon after publicly renounced his connection with the Baptist denomination.

On the 11th of June, 1835, the Baptist church of Wilson, consisting of twenty-one members, was received into the Niagara Baptist Association. After Elder Reed was dismissed the church was without a regular preacher until June, 1836, when Tracy Scott, a licentiate, was engaged for one year.

In May, 1837, an association was formed in connection with the church, called the "Religious Agricultural Society," of which Morgan Johnson was secretary, and R. Robinson, S. Millard and H. Pettit, directors. The object of this society was to cultivate certain lands, and appropriate the proceeds to benevolent purposes.

On December 24th, 1837, J. Halliday, a licentiate, accepted a call from this church, at a salary of $200 per year and a house and lot.

Up to 1838 public meetings had been held, for the most part, in the school-house in district No. 4, on the Slash road. On the 21st of April, 1838, the church met at the school-house at "Wilson Four Corners." This was the commencement of Baptist meetings at Wilson village. On the last Wednesday in September, 1838, Rev. J. Halliday was ordained and installed as pastor of this church. He continued his labors here until March 21st, 1840, when he resigned, and was followed, in May, by the Rev. G. C. Walker.

In March, 1847, a lot on the west side of Lake street was purchased of Luther Wilson, and the same year a dwelling for the pastor was erected upon it at a cost of about $800. In 1866 the church and society sold this place, and purchased a more commodious parsonage on Pettit street, in the west part of the village, which they still own.

By the end of 1842 the congregation had grown to such proportions that the church sorely felt the need of a larger building. Accordingly, in the early part of 1843, they commenced the erection of a church edifice on a lot donated for that purpose by Luther Wilson, located on the corner of Chestnut and Pettit streets. The structure is of cobble-stone, with a lecture room in the basement, and cost about $2,200. With the exception of its having been remodeled internally it remains the same as originally built.

Rev. Mr. Walker remained as pastor until April, 1845, and was succeeded on the 6th of May following by Rev. Arah Irons. The Niagara Baptist Association met with this church for the first time June 11th and 12th, 1845, and Mr. Irons was elected its moderator.

On June 13th, 1846, a meeting of the church and society was held, the object being, as the records show, "to reinstate the church property in the hands of the church and society in a legal form," the incorporation having been defective. Hence it would appear that upon this date the church was duly incorporated as the "First Baptist Church and Society of Wilson."

Elder Irons closed his labors as pastor of this church the last of October, 1846. His successor was Rev. B. F. Burr, who remained about one year, after which the church was destitute of a pastor a year or more. The records of October 7th, 1847, show the passage of a resolution "to give no minister a call that is in the usual habit of reading his sermons." On December 16th, 1848, a unanimous call was extended to Rev. J. H. Morrison, which he at once accepted, preaching his first sermon as pastor on the first Sabbath in January, 1849. Elder Morrison remained seven years and nine months, during which time there were 124 additions to the church, 77 of which were by baptism. He resigned September 28th, 1856.

Elder Morrison was followed, October 5th, 1856, by George M. Condron, a licentiate, who, on the 12th of November following, was ordained and installed pastor of this church. He resigned at the end of one year, and was succeeded in October, 1857, by Rev. L. C. Pattengill, of Akron, N. Y., at a salary of $500 per year. Under his ministrations, in the early part of 1858, eighty-five were added to the church by baptism. He remained nearly eight years, withdrawing in September, 1865, and in January, 1866, was succeeded by Rev. Warham Mudge.

As a result of a religious revival conducted by him in the early part of 1867, thirty-nine united with the church by baptism. His connection with this church was severed May 1st, 1869. The next pastor was Rev. B. F. Garfield, who came about the first of September, 1869, and remained one year, after which the pulpit was not regularly supplied until March 12th, 1871, when Rev. Mr. Reese accepted the pastorate. He surrendered it after a stay of less than three months, and was succeeded by Rev. Mr. Nordell as a supply. On August 27th, 1871, Rev. G. W. Divoll, from Akron, assumed the pastoral charge of the church, but, owing to failing health, was obliged to resign at the end of one year. He was followed on the 13th of October, 1872, by Rev. W. H. Dorward, who remained about two years, preaching his farewell sermon September 6th, 1874. His successor was Rev. E. Packwood, who came November 1st, 1874, at a salary of $800 per annum, and remained three years, resigning November 1st, 1877. The present pastor, Rev. S. S. Bidwell, from Morrisville, commenced his labors here May 1st, 1878.

A Sabbath-school was formed in connection with this church in 1834. Alexander Pettit was the first superintendent. It has been regularly kept up since its organization; H. S. Pettit has been and is at present the superintendent. The present number of scholars is 194, with a corps of 19 teachers and a library of about 400 volumes.

METHODIST EPISCOPAL CHURCH OF WILSON.

The exact date of the formation of a class of this denomination at this point is not known, but it was probably as early as 1820. The first quarterly meeting for Lewiston circuit, of which this class formed a part, was held in the town of Porter, August 23rd and 24th, 1823. The first quarterly meeting for the circuit held at Wilson was on July 8th, 1826, when Bishop Elijah Hedding presided. For a period of nineteen years Wilson continued to form a part of this circuit, during which time the society was served by the following preachers, in the order named: Revs. Ira Brownson, John Copeland, Andrew Prindle, Wilbur Hoag, John E. Cole, John Cozart, John B. Lankton, Henry F. Row, Philo Woodworth, Square W. Chase, George Wilkinson, Orrin Abbott, James H. Whallen, Josiah Brakeman, Alvin Waller, John B. Lankton, Judah S. Mitchell, Ira Brownson, John B. Lankton, S. R. Cook, James H. Whallen, William Warner, David Nichols, Lewis Coburn, William D. Buck, H. Ryan Smith, Daniel D. Buck, John Powell, J. B. Smith, Nelson Hoag and G. T. Witted. In addition to these regularly appointed ministers, there was employed from time to time a large number of local preachers of whom there is but slight record. By request of this society, and in accordance with a vote of the quarterly conference, held at Ransomville, August 27th, 1842, Wilson village was set apart as a station. It remained, however, in nominal connection with the Lewiston circuit until 1844, when the union was officially severed and it stood alone on the minutes of the conference.

The society was legally incorporated on the 28th of December, 1836, at which time the following trustees were elected: John Haze, Daniel Terry, Samuel R. Merwin Cyrus Case, Luther Wilson, Samuel Healy and Sylvester Hosmer. It was at the same time resolved "that this society build a house for divine worship." Accordingly, the erection of a frame church edifice was commenced in the early part of 1837. The site of the building, which is situated on the corner of Lake and High streets, was donated to the society by Andrew Brown for church purposes. Ira Tompkins was the builder. The structure was completed and appropriately dedicated the following year. Prior to the building of this church, private dwellings, barns, and district school-houses were used by the society for public worship.

The following is a list of the ministers who have served the church since Wilson became an independent station, in 1842: Revs. Nelson Hoag, Allen P. Ripley (two years), Sumner C. Smith, William H. De Puy (two years), Albert D. Wilber, D. B. Lawton, Zenas Hurd, James McEunin, C. S. Baker (two years), De F. Parsons (two years), Milo Scott (two years), J. McClelland, S. C. Church (two years), W. J. Nichols, R. S. Foot, Robert C. Brownlee (two years), Philo Woodworth (two years), William Barrett, H. Ryan Smith, H. L. Newton (two years), J. T. Humphrey (two years), and Ward B. Pickard, who is the present pastor.

The parsonage was built on the same lot with the church, fronting High street, during the pastorate of Rev. William H. De Puy, in the conference years of 1846 and 1847. The value of the property owned by the church and society is reported in the annual minutes at $5,300.

The Sunday-school connected with this church was among the first organized in this region of country, and has been sustained most of the time since its organization.

FREE METHODIST CHURCH OF WILSON.

A free Methodist class was organized at Wilson, as a branch of the Porter church, about the year 1865. The original members did not exceed fifteen in number, prominent among whom were John Billings, who was chosen the first class-leader; Albert A. Dailey, William Robinson, John Robinson and John Colbeth. Among the first ministers to preach to them were: Rev. Messrs. Freeland, Curry, William Cooley, Jones, and Burrett—mostly pastors of the church in Porter. Rev. William Cooley resided at Wilson, and preached regularly every two weeks in connection with the Porter church.

In the spring of 1874, William Allen, William Doyle, Ira Wilcox, and William Parish, who were members of the Porter church, but interested in the prosperity of the Wilson class, bought for $800 a lot in Wilson village, upon which were located a dwelling and a large building erected originally for a wagon and blacksmith shop. The latter they at once remodeled and converted into a meeting-house, which was dedicated in June, 1874, by Rev. B. T. Roberts, of Rochester. The free use of this building has been generously donated to this society ever since. Previous to this time the school-house at Wilson and often private dwellings were used by the society for public worship.

Since the fall of 1872, this class has been regularly supplied by ministers of the denomination. Rev. Mr. Partridge commenced his labors here at that time, in connection with the Porter church, and remained two years. He was followed by Rev. William Jackson for two years. Rev. Mr. Manning, of the Lockport church, assumed the pastoral charge of this church in the fall of 1876, and still retains it. This church belonged to what was known as the Porter and Wilson circuit until the fall of 1877, when it was set off to the Lockport and Newfane circuit. The present membership is about 18.

CHESTNUT STREET M. E. CHURCH.

The church edifice was erected in 1871. It is located on lot 56, Marsh road, in the southeast part of the town. Regular services are held here by M. W. Ayers, in connection with the M. E. church at Warren's Corners.

WILSON'S LEADING CITIZENS.

The post-office address of the persons here sketched is Wilson, N. Y., when not otherwise given.

Jared H. Ackerman was born in Saratoga county, N. Y., in 1820. He married Mary Perry, a native of the same county, in 1840. He removed to Wilson in 1845, and purchased and settled on his present farm in 1848. He was the first settler on lot 58, and caused the road to be opened by his place from the Slash to the Beebe road.

Hiram K. Burton was born in New Lebanon, Columbia county, N. Y., May 3rd, 1815. In 1837 he married Joannah Townsend, of Canaan, Columbia county. He came to Wilson in 1847 and purchased a partly improved farm of 100 acres on lot No. 30, Randall road, where he still resides. He has two sons and two daughters.

Edward Barker is a native of Norfolk, England, where he was born in 1828. He emigrated to Toronto, Canada West, in 1835. He removed to Lockport in 1838 and remained five years, when he purchased and located on fifty acres of land in Clarence, Erie county. Here, in 1851, he married Etsa Galloway. His estate increased in Clarence to 300 acres. In 1870 he removed to Wilson, and purchased 150 acres on the Town Line road, lot No. 3, where he now resides. He was elected supervisor of Wilson in the spring of 1878. Post-office address, South Wilson, N. Y.

Gilbert Brown was born in Saratoga county, N. Y., in 1800. He married Anna E. Olmstead in 1821, and came to Wilson in 1823, and settled on lot No. 72 on the Youngstown road, which was then only chopped through from Olcott to Wilson. He has had five children, three of whom are still living; his wife died in March, 1868.

Charles S. Birdsall was born in Lockport in 1832, where he learned the blacksmith's trade and followed that business. In 1864 he married Adelia A. Coulter, of Schenectady county, N. Y. He moved to Newfane and thence to Wilson in 1875, and purchased and settled on the farm on which he now resides. Post-office address, Olcott, N. Y.

Andrew Brown was born in Saratoga county in 1789. He is one of the early settlers of Wilson. Having purchased 100 acres on the north part of lot No. 90, where he now lives, he located there in 1816, since which time he has been identified with the growth and development of the town and village. He was for many years town clerk, also justice of the peace, and was one of the founders and first trustees of the Wilson Collegiate Institute. Several years ago he platted and added to the village of Wilson a portion of his farm.

Ozro Bachelder was born in Le Roy, Genesee county, N. Y., September 20th, 1823. In June, 1845, he came to Niagara county, stopping in Lockport until November following, when he located on lot No. 17 in Wilson, where he now resides. October 6th, 1853, he married Margaret Crawford, of Wilson.

William Burton was born in New Lebanon, Columbia county, N. Y., June 10th, 1810. In 1853 he emigrated to Wilson and located on lot No. 20, on the farm he still occupies, having cleared up a portion of it and planted all the fruit trees. Post-office address, Ransomville, N. Y.

F. F. Barnum was born in Penfield, Monroe county, N. Y., November 21st, 1820. At the age of two years he moved with his parents to Brighton, Monroe county, where he resided until June, 1862, when he came to Wilson and purchased a farm on lot No. 5, upon which he now resides. He erected all the fine buildings upon it, except one barn.

Elmer A. Bickford, of Wilson village, was born in Wilson, May 24th, 1849. He married Ada A. Eighme, of Cambria, November 27th, 1872. In 1876 he, in company with one Gifford, erected a warehouse and cider-mill at Wilson station, and began buying grain and produce. In the spring of 1877 Bickford bought Gifford's interest and now continues the business alone. In 1877 Mr. B. purchased and shipped over 100 car loads of grain from this station. He also deals in coal, handling from 500 to 800 tons annually.

Erwin Burton was born in Pembroke, Genesee county, N. Y., December 20th, 1825. When he was ten years of age his parents moved to Erie county. At the age of twenty he went to Rochester and was associated with the first established milk company of that city. In the spring of 1849 he removed to Wilson and purchased a new farm on lot No. 49, upon which he still resides, having made the improvements himself. Post-office address, Coomer, Niagara county, N. Y.

Calvin Bowker was born in Wilson October 7th, 1830. On December 31st, 1857, he married Elsie A. Tower, also a native of Wilson, and daughter of D. D. Tower. They have always resided in this town; own a farm on lot No. 15 which Mr. Bowker tills. They also own the American Hotel, a fine, large, two-story brick building in Wilson village, of which Frank Le Van is the present manager in chief.

Mrs. Lucy A. Campbell, a daughter of Sewall B. Miller, was born in the town of Wilson, May 2nd, 1855. In 1872 she was married to Frank B. Campbell, of Cambria, who died January 7th, 1875. She was again married, to Merrit L. Campbell, of Newfane, February 10th, 1876. They

MRS. N. C. WARD, NO. 1.   MR. N. C. WARD.   MRS. N. C. WARD NO. 2.

FARM RESIDENCE OF N. C. WARD ESQ. TOWN OF WILSON, NIAGARA COUNTY, N. Y.

have a fine farm of 62 acres, where they reside, and Mr. Campbell devotes his time to farming. Mrs. Campbell is a member of the M. E. church of Wilson.

Daniel Carter was born near St. Catharines, C. W., in 1811, and came to Wilson with his father in 1814. In 1831 he purchased 92 acres of land of John Brewer on lot No. 81, Slash road. In 1832 he married Elizabeth West, of Cazenovia, and settled on this farm, where he still remains. Mrs. Carter died in 1846, and in 1848 he was married to Louisa Gleason, of Coburg, C. W.

Richard Y. Chester was born in Harrison county, Ky., November 23d, 1833. He served four years in the rebel army as private in the 1st Kentucky regiment. He came to Wilson in December, 1867, from Paris, Bourbon county, Ky., and married Ella M. Howell, of Wilson, April 8th, 1868. He is a carpenter and joiner by trade, but is at present proprietor of the Ontario House, a large, two-story, cobble-stone hotel, in Wilson.

Grant Cuddeback is a native of Wilson; he was born in 1834, and married in 1853 to Eliza Bartlett, of Seneca county, N. Y. They have one son and one daughter. He purchased and in 1870 removed to the farm he now occupies, upon which there are about 500 fruit trees.

John J. Cushing was born in Hampshire county, Mass., April 13th, 1827. He came to Wilson in 1841. He married Elvira Covert, a native of Wilson, January 9th, 1851; both of them are members of the Baptist church of Wilson. They reside on lot No. 68, Slash road. Post-office address, Maple Street, N. Y.

John Diez was born in Wurtemburg, Germany, in 1835. He emigrated to America in 1853, and coming to Newfane he worked four years as a farm-hand, most of the time for Newell Farnham. In 1857 he married Christina Diez, also from Wurtemburg, who came to America at the same time with Mr. Diez. In 1858 he took a farm of Stephen Wilson to work on shares for five years, after which he rented another farm, of 70 acres, for one year, at the expiration of which time he purchased it. In 1865 he traded this farm for the one on which he now resides. It contains 167 acres of most excellent land, situated on the Youngstown road, and watered by the west branch of Twelve-mile creek. An illustration of his brick residence and surroundings may be seen on another page.

Mrs. Delia Dwight was born in Auburn, N. Y., August 5th, 1817. On March 20th, 1837, she was married to Daniel Dwight, of Dudley, Mass. She came from Le Roy, Genesee county, to Wilson in March, 1837, with her husband, who, for many years previous to his death, resided on lot No. 26, Lake road, where Mrs. D. still remains, conducting the farm.

J. W. Eggleston was born in Jordan, Onondaga county, N. Y., in 1826. At the age of four years he moved with his parents to Beaver Dam, Tioga county, where he remained until 1854, when he came to Porter, and in 1866 purchased and removed to the farm on lot No. 62 which he still occupies.

Daniel Farley was born June 26th, 1850, and married Mary Bradley, of Wilson, in February, 1872. He resides on a part of the old homestead and is employed in farming. His father, Benjamin Farley, was born in Salem, Mass., in 1810, and was of English extraction. He came to Wilson in 1842, and purchased a tract of wild land on lot No. 48, which he improved and resided on until his death, April 15th, 1876. He was supervisor of Wilson in 1865, and took an active part in filling the military quota of the town. He was elected sheriff of Niagara county in 1857, and was a member of Assembly in 1867 and 1868. Post-office address, Coomer, Niagara county, N. Y.

Orsemus Ferris was born at Ovid, Seneca county, May 5th, 1814. He moved to Ogden, Monroe county, in 1822, came to Wilson in 1836, and located on lot No. 14, where he now resides. This farm he cleared up and improved from a wilderness. He has long been a prominent member of the Baptist church, and for nearly 30 years a deacon. He was supervisor of Wilson in 1854, and again in 1857.

R. A. Ferris was born in Lester, Livingston county, N.Y., June 16th, 1833. He came to Niagara county in 1849, and located on his present farm, on lot No. 53, in 1868. He was a member of Company K, 151st regiment, and participated in the battle of Locust Grove, November 13th, 1862. Post-office address, Olcott, N. Y.

Enoch Fitch was born in Green River, Columbia county N. Y., February 12th, 1809. He came to Wilson and located November 20th, 1830, upon a new farm, which he still owns and occupies. He was married to Lucina Church, of Riga, Monroe county, August 29th, 1831. He is one of the earliest settlers in the western part of the town. His life-long occupation has been that of a farmer. Post-office address, Ransomville, N. Y.

Nathan Gallup was born in Schoharie county, N. Y., in 1815, and was married in 1841 to Julia Cook, of Utica. He came to Niagara county in 1843 and settled in Wilson. He has owned several farms, and located where he now resides, on lot No. 6, in 1874. When young he followed teaching several years, but latterly has pursued farming. His first wife died in June, 1870. He married Mary Small in December, 1870. He has been a member of the Presbyterian church nearly fifty years, and a member of the session six years.

Hiram H. Goodenough, a native of Wilson, was born in 1846. He enlisted in Company I, 2nd Mounted Rifles, under Captain Gould, of Lockport, and was at Petersburg, Mead's Station and Hatcher's Run, and present at the surrender of General Lee at Appomattox. He was discharged at Buffalo, August 31st, 1865. He married Harriet Jarvis, of Wilson, in August, 1867, and resides on the Randall road.

Hiram Gifford was born in Wilson in 1851. He married Hattie E. Scott, of the same town, in 1873. His father L. H. Gifford, born in Fulton county in 1815, came to Wilson in 1851 and purchased 160 acres on lot No. 3, on the Town Line road, where they still reside. He has been justice of the peace twelve years. Post-office address, South Wilson.

William Hamblin was born in Cornwall, Addison county, Vt., May 6th, 1821. He came to Wilson in 1834, and bought and cleared up a farm. He was in mercantile business in Wilson from 1854 to 1869. He purchased his present farm on lot No. 25 in 1867, and has since followed farming. He was supervisor of Wilson from 1867 to 1870, and has been railroad commissioner for the town since 1873. He was first married to Anna Tower, October 21st, 1842, and married the second time to Amoret E. Wood, of Wilson, April 30th, 1856.

Eli N. Hamblin, son of William Hamblin, was born in Wilson in 1842. He enlisted in Company K, 28th N. Y. regiment, under Captain Page, in May, 1861, and served two years, being at the battles of Antietam, Cedar Mountain, Chancellorsville, etc. He was discharged in June, 1863. He was married to Lydia, daughter of D. D. Tower, Esq., of Wilson, in 1864. He resides on the Youngstown road and is by occupation a farmer.

John Hill was born in Scotland in 1810, and emigrated to Canada in 1833. He took up arms against the British government under McKenzie in the revolt of 1837, for which he was arrested and imprisoned in Toronto, from December, 1837, to August, 1838, when he was banished at three days' notice, with penalty of death if ever caught on British soil of his own free will. He at once came to Lewiston, and in 1841 to Wilson, and located where he now resides in 1843. Having bought his farm when in a state of nature, he has cleared and improved it erected all the buildings and planted all the fruit and ornamental trees. One of his evergreens he brought sixty miles in his hand from Canada.

Mrs. Sally Holmes, relict of Daniel Holmes, and daughter of Judge John Taylor, of Saratoga county, was born in Charlton, Saratoga county, February 21st, 1792. She married Mr. Holmes February 12th, 1811, came with her husband to Wilson in an early day and experienced the hardships and privations attendant upon pioneer life. She is the only surviving original member of the Presbyterian church of Wilson, organized in 1819, and retains her health and faculties to a wonderful degree. Daniel Holmes was born in Saratoga county, July 3rd, 1789, where he remained until his marriage, when he removed to Schoharie county. In February, 1818, he emigrated with his father, John Holmes, to Wilson, moving his family and effects in a sled with an ox-team, and driving two cows Arriving here he purchased 160 acres of land on lot No. 73, on the Lake road, upon which there had once been a log house (burned in 1813 by the British), and a small clearing commenced by Andrew Lays, previous to the war. To this place Mr. Holmes, after erecting a log house, removed his family in June, and began life in earnest, clearing, making improvements and erecting buildings. His first orchard was raised from seeds which Mrs. Holmes brought in her pocket from her father's in Saratoga. These trees are still bearing fruit. Mr. Holmes was always an active, useful and influential man, both as a citizen and churchman. He was the first town clerk of Wilson, which office he held for many years. He was one of the founders of the Presbyterian church of Wilson, and a ruling elder in that church from its organization until his death. Much of his personal history will be found in connection with the history of that church. He was appointed captain of militia at the first military organization of the county in 1818, and was also contractor for the first mail to Wilson. The route was from Olcott to Youngstown, about 1825. He died at his residence May 26th, 1858, at the age of nearly 69 years. The portraits of this venerable and respected couple, together with a view of their home and surroundings, can be seen on another page.

Richard C. Holmes, son of Daniel and Sally Holmes, was born in 1813 at Carlisle, Schoharie county, N. Y., and came with his parents to Wilson in 1818. At the age of twelve years he was, by special permit from the Postmaster-General, made the first mail carrier through Wilson, going once a week on horseback from Olcott to Youngstown and back. This vocation he continued most of the time for five or six years. He was married in 1839 to Betsey C. Frost, of Millville, Orleans county, N. Y. At the age of twenty-one he received fifty acres of land on lot No. 72, Youngstown road, which he improved, and where after his marriage he located, remaining until 1870, when he purchased and moved on to his present farm of one hundred and twenty-five acres, on lot 31, Randall road. His first wife died in March, 1870, when he was again married, to Armista, daughter of Gay C. Loomis, in December, 1871. Mr. Holmes has from youth been a member of the Presbyterian church, and for many years a ruling elder; has always taken a deep interest in the Sunday-school cause, and was for twenty-five years superintendent of the Presbyterian school at Wilson. A view of his pleasant country home is given on another page.

J. C. Hopkins, born in Otsego county, N. Y., February 1st, 1818, moved to Wilson in 1835, and located on lot 38, where he still resides. His father, who came here at the same time with his son, died at the ripe old age of ninety-five. He had held the office of justice of the peace, and was also justice of the Court of Sessions one term.

John P. Hyde is a resident of Wilson, and a native of the county; he was born in Lewiston October 29th, 1855.

J. Harvey Htuchings, a resident of Wilson village, and by occupation a house painter, was born in this town May 17th, 1850. He is also a private detective in the employ of the U. S. Secret Service Company of Cincinnati. His father, Abram Hutchings, is one of the pioneers of this town, and was a soldier of 1812.

E. A. Johnson is a native of Wilson, and a farmer by occupation. He is a son of Joseph F. Johnson, who resides on lot No. 7, Town Line road, and who came to Wilson with his father, John Johnson, and family in 1837 from Schoharie county.

Levi L. Johnson, a son of John Johnson, was born in Schoharie county, N. Y., in 1823. He came to Wilson with his father's family in 1837. In May, 1844, he married Clarinda Wilson, a native of this town. He located on his present farm, of one hundred acres, on lot No. 6, Town Line road, in 1851.

Mrs. Maria Johnson, relict of Harvey N. Johnson, to whom she was married in 1844, is a native of Schoharie county, N. Y. Her husband was born in Schoharie

DANIEL HOLMES

MRS. DANIEL HOLMES

RES. OF MRS. DANIEL HOLMES TOWN OF WILSON

MRS. JAMES M. MORSE.

JAMES M. MORSE.

RES. OF JAMES M. MORSE, TOWN OF WILSON.

county in 1820. He was also a son of John Johnson, and came to Wilson in 1837. He located on lot No. 7, Town Line road, where he died in 1876. He was supervisor of Wilson in 1858, a member of the Baptist church of Wilson, and a warm friend of education.

Mrs. Levantia P. Johnson, born in Wilson in 1846, is the widow of Chester N. Johnson, to whom she was married in November, 1867, and who died in December, 1877, aged 33 years. He was a member of the Baptist church of Wilson. Mrs. Johnson and three children reside on the homestead of 80 acres, 17 acres of which is planted to fruit.

William A. Knowles is one of the oldest native citizens in the town of Wilson. He was born here March 27th, 1818. His father, Richard Knowles, came to Wilson in 1815, and in 1825 settled where William A. still resides on lot No. 8, Youngstown road. He married Sarah Robinson, of Madrid, St. Lawrence county, N. Y., October 24th, 1846. Mr. K. has been a life-long resident of the town, and has followed farming.

Lynford D. Le Van was born in Cambria, Niagara county, N. Y., September 28th, 1846. He removed with his father's family to Wilson village from Porter, in 1855. He enlisted as a private July 29th, 1862, in Company B, 129th regiment N. Y. volunteers, afterward the 8th heavy artillery, Captain J B. Baker. He was promoted in 1864, and discharged June 29th, 1865. He was married May 28th, 1867, to Mary E. Johnson, of Wilson. By occupation he is a painter and a moulder.

Oliver P. Lockwood is an enterprising farmer, located on lot 52, near the Youngstown road. He is a son of Samuel Lockwood, a native of Seneca county, N. Y., who settled in Newfane in 1828, where he died in 1876. Oliver P. was married in 1855, to Mary A. Cole, of Newfane, a native of New Jersey. Post-office address, Olcott, N. Y.

Guy W. Loomis was born in Litchfield county, Conn., in 1806. His father, Timothy, also a native of Connecticut, was born in 1779. He emigrated to Riga, Monroe county, in 1812, and was one of the volunteers to repel the British at the time of the burning of Buffalo. He died in Riga in 1842. His widow is still living, at the age of 95. Guy W. was married in 1831, to Calista Frost, of Columbia county, N. Y. He came to Wilson in 1836, and located on lot No. 70, just east of the Slash road, where he still resides.

James M. Morse was born in New York city, January 17th, 1817. He was the youngest of a family of eleven children. His father was a native of England, and came to New York when a young man, where he was employed in cabinet-making. Soon after the birth of his youngest son he went upon a voyage for his health and was lost at sea. In 1819 Mr. Morse's mother removed with her large family to Washington county, N. Y., and from there to Oneida in 1824, where they remained eleven years, after which they went to Orleans county. His mother subsequently went to Batavia, where she died in 1837, aged 54 years. In 1840 Mr. Morse came to Wilson, purchased 50 acres of land on lot 69, Slash road, and began making for himself a permanent home. To this he subsequently added 50 acres more. On May 11th, 1848, he married Sarah Lucor, of Rushville, Yates county, N. Y. The early life of Mr. Morse was one of hardships, privation and cruelty. Having been bound as an apprentice, to a cruel master, he was compelled to labor beyond his strength and suffer much unkind treatment, but hope and courage never failed him. His release at last came, he grew to be his own master, and by patient industry and economy has gained a fine home and a splendid competence in a pleasant and productive locality. His portrait, and that of his wife, together with an illustration of their beautiful residence and surroundings, may be seen elsewhere in this work.

Sewall B. Miller was born in Littleton, N. H., in 1825, and came to Wilson with his father's family in 1834. He married Caroline A. Newman, of Dutchess county, N.Y., in 1849. He purchased and located on his present farm on lot No. 81, Slash road, in 1850. He was commissioned lieutenant of militia by Governor King, in 1857, and promoted to a captaincy by Governor Fenton, in 1867.

David H. McDonald is by occupation a farmer, and is a native of Onondaga county, N. Y., where he was born in 1830. He came to Wilson in 1839. Post-office address, Olcott, N.Y.

William H. Miller was born in Jonesville, Mich., August 19th, 1849. He came to Wilson in 1851, and married Ella Colbath, of Wilson, February 21st, 1876. He is a farmer and resides near Wilson village.

William H. Mudge was born in Vermont, January 22nd, 1816, and emigrated to Niagara county in 1827. He now resides near Wilson village, and is engaged in farming.

S. Mix is a native of Wilson, and a life-long resident of the town. He was born July 21st, 1840. He lives on a fine farm on lot No. 79, Slash road.

James M. Newman was born in Romulus, Seneca county, in 1812. In 1815 his father, Nathaniel Newman, with his family, came to Niagara county, and located in Porter. Mr. Newman was married in 1848 to Ryanna Miller, of Vermont, who died in July, 1877. He has held several town offices. He was commissioned a lieutenant of militia in 1858, and promoted to the rank of captain by Governor Morgan in 1861. He is a farmer, and resides on lot No. 63, Lake road.

Curtis Pettit was born in Fulton county, N. Y., in 1806. He emigrated to Wilson in 1832, and in company with his brother Alexander purchased a farm of 139 acres on lot No. 71, Youngstown road. They afterward bought 100 acres more, adjoining. This farm was subsequently divided between them. Mr. Pettit built the first school-house frame in district No. 4, in 1834. He was married in 1844 to Harriet Starkweather, from Connecticut. He was elected supervisor of Wilson in 1852.

Alexander Pettit was born in Fulton county, in 1810, and came to Wilson in 1831, locating on lot No. 71, Youngstown road, where he still resides, having cleared up the farm from a wilderness. He was married to Maria B. Armstrong, of Onondaga county, N.Y., in 1836.

In 1832 Mr. Pettit built the first frame house in the neighborhood. He was elected supervisor of Wilson in 1848 and again in 1853, and has held other town offices. He has been a member of the Baptist church since 1834, and deacon since 1835.

Wm. O. Pettit was born in Broadalbin, Montgomery county (now in Fulton county), in 1820, and came to Wilson with his father, Samuel Pettit, and his family, in 1832. He was married to Nancy M. Newman in February, 1843. In 1852 he bought and located on the farm where he now resides, on lot No. 72, Youngstown road. He was first lieutenant of light artillery under the old military law, and is a member of the Wilson masonic lodge, of which he has been master.

George Pettit was born in Galway, Saratoga county, N. Y., February 6th, 1825. He came to Wilson in November, 1842, from Leonax, Madison county, N. Y., and was married to Ann L. Pease, of Wilson, February 6th, 1850. He has owned four different farms in this town. He was postmaster at Wilson under Filmore's administration. He was a commercial traveler from 1855 to 1875, since which he has followed farming.

George T. Parker was born June 10th, 1824, in Clarenden, Vt., removed to Wilson in 1844, and located where he now resides, on lot No. 21, Randall road, in 1865. Post-office address, North Ridge.

Lorenzo N. Pratt was born in Wilson, in 1831, and was married to Mary Jane Stickler, of Newfane, in 1856. He enlisted in August, 1861, in Company M, 1st N. Y. battery. He participated in 22 engagements, and was discharged in 1865. Mr. Pratt owns and occupies the farm where his father, Calvin Pratt, located in 1834, lot No. 82, Youngstown road. His grandfather, Nathan, settled on the Town Line road in 1817, cutting his own road to his new place.

Enoch Pease was born in Parsonsfield, Me., January 12th, 1795, came to Niagara county with his father's family in the winter of 1807, and settled in Newfane, near where Van Horn's mill was built, two years later. Here their house was burned by the British in 1813. Enoch's younger brother, Nathaniel, was the boy who rolled the barrels of flour out of the mill before it was destroyed. Mr. Pease settled in Wilson in May, 1836, on lot No. 91, on the lake shore, where he still resides.

Christopher Palmer was born in Hampton, Conn., September 7th, 1789, where he served an apprenticeship at wagon making. At the age of 18 he married Wealthy Johnson, a native of the same place, who was born March 16th, 1792. In 1808 he went to Exeter, Otsego county, worked at his trade a few years, and then purchased a farm in the same township and commenced farming. In 1834 he sold this farm and removed to Wilson, where he bought a farm on lot 38 upon which a small improvement had been commenced and a log house built, but only an opening cut through from the Youngstown road leading to it. Here he remained until the death of his wife, December 23rd, 1862, when he sold his farm to his son Reuben, and in June, 1864, again married and removed to Wilson village. At his early home in Wilson he established regular prayer meetings, which at length developed into meetings for public worship and preaching, followed by a general revival, which resulted in the establishment of a church in that vicinity. He was early in life elected to the office of deacon in the Baptist church, and as a christian and office bearer, he was always beloved, esteemed and respected. He was a member of the Wilson Baptist church at the time of his death, which occurred April 20th, 1878, and deeply mourned both by church and community.

Reuben Palmer, his son, was born in Exeter, Otsego county, N. Y., March 5th, 1812, and came to Wilson with his parents in 1834. He married Mary Jane Smithson April 8th, 1846, and in the spring of 1847 located on a farm of 71 acres on the north part of lot No. 39. His wife was born in Houdon, England, February 2nd, 1821, and came to this country in 1827. Soon after their arrival here both her parents died, being buried at the same time and in one grave, when she was adopted into the family of Jacob Moote, of Porter, Niagara county. Reuben Palmer remained on lot 39 two years, when he sold his farm and purchased 100 acres adjoining his father's farm on lot 38. In the spring of 1863 he bought of his father the old homestead of 166 acres, to which he immediately removed and where he still continues to reside. At the age of sixteen he made a public profession of religion and connected himself with the Baptist denomination. Soon after his arrival in Wilson he united with the Baptist church of Porter. In 1841 he voluntarily severed his connection with this denomination and joined the Presbyterian church at Youngstown, where he was soon after elected a ruling elder, in which capacity he still continues to serve. He has two sons and two daughters who still remain at their father's home, a comfort and support to their parents in their declining years. Mr. and Mrs. Palmer's portraits, together with a representation of their home and surroundings, may be seen on another page of this work.

Enoch Sanborn, son of Hon. L. R. Sanborn, was born in Sanborn, Niagara county, N. Y., June 6th, 1854. He married Addie M. Dodge, of Sanborn, October 28th, 1874, came to Wilson in the spring of 1875, and located on lot No. 14, Daniels road, where he erected the first and only cheese factory in the town, known as the "Wilson Cheese Factory." It is of wood, 24 by 56 feet in size, and 2 stories high. It contains two vats, heated by steam, and one gang press. Mr. Sanborn commenced the manufacture of cheese June 7th, 1875. He made 40,000 lbs. that season, 45,000 lbs. in 1876, 50,000 lbs. in 1877, and will turn out at least 75,000 lbs. for 1878. He is a practical cheese-maker and superintends the business in person. He also keeps a stock of family groceries and supplies in connection with his factory.

Silas P. Smith was born in Newfane in 1851, and married, in 1877, to Hattie E. Dutcher, of Newfane. He bought his present farm in Wilson of the Carlton heirs. It has eight acres of fruit on it.

Homer Swick was born in Covent, Seneca county, N. Y., January 22d, 1829. He moved to Tompkins county

REUBEN PALMER

MRS. REUBEN PALMER

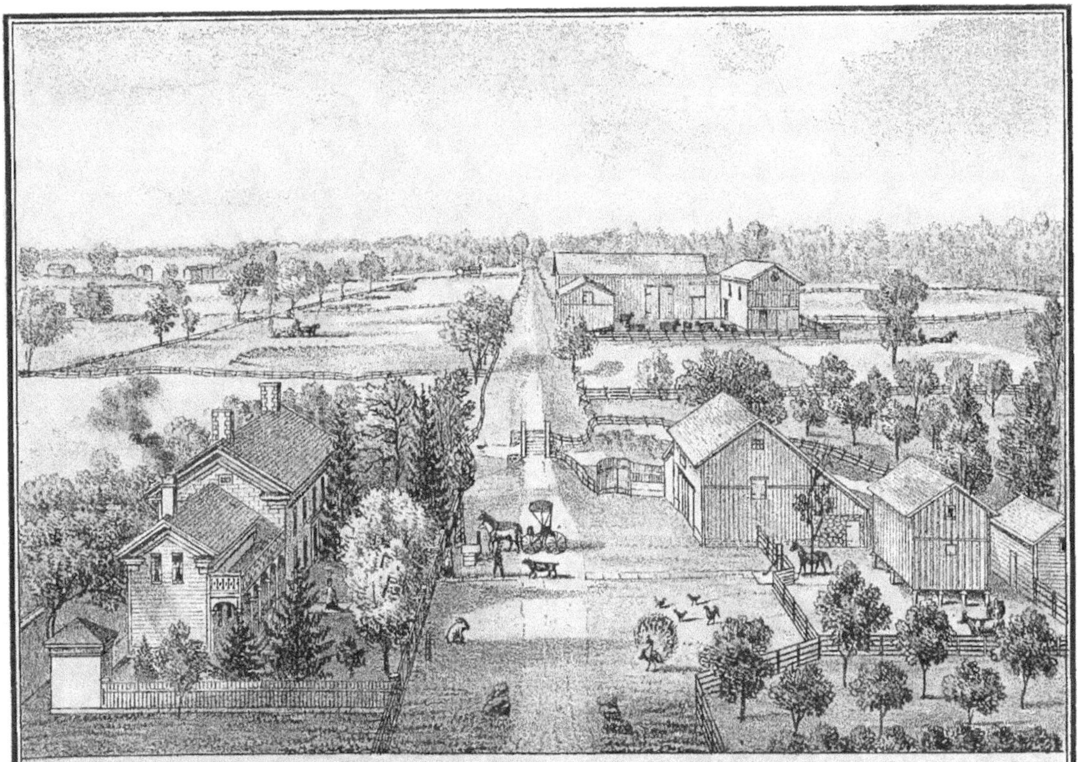

RES. OF REUBEN PALMER, TOWN OF WILSON

FARM RESIDENCE OF G. W. LOOMIS ESQ. TOWN OF WILSON, NIAGARA CO., N. Y.

with his parents in 1837, and came to Wilson in 1848, locating on a new farm, which he has since cleared and improved, and erected fine buildings, where he still resides, an enterprising and successful farmer.

H. B. Tabor, M.D., was born November 21st, 1814, in Orange county, Vt., whence he came to Wilson, arriving here August 1st, 1837, and located at the village, where he has since resided, practicing his profession, and is the leading physician of the place. He has always been a devoted friend of and a zealous worker in the cause of education, and was one of the founders of the Wilson Collegiate Institute.

Clinton D. Tabor was born October 5th, 1846, in Wilson and married, November 17th, 1870, to Kate E. Towner, of Wilson. Byron D. Tabor, born in Wilson, February 23d, 1842, married Helen J. McChesney, of Wilson, September 18th, 1873. These gentlemen compose the firm of Tabor Bros., manufacturers of and dealers in agricultural implements. They erected a suitable building and began business in the fall of 1874. In the spring of 1878 they enlarged their foundry and added steam power. They are the inventors and sole manufacturers of a gang plow and thill cultivator. They also manufacture a large variety of farming implements and do machine repairing. They are both practical mechanics and machinists, and superintend all branches of their business in person.

David D. Tower was born November 15th, 1814, at Cummington, Mass., and came to Wilson in 1837. He married, September 20th, 1838, Achsah E. Farrow, a native of St. Lawrence county, N. Y., born August 7th, 1820. He is the largest land owner in the town, possessing 1,000 acres, nearly all of which is under cultivation. The farm of 260 acres where he resides, on lot No. 25, Youngstown road, he cleared and improved from a state of nature.

John M. Tower was born in Cummington, Mass., in 1810. His father, John Tower, came to Wilson in 1814 and purchased 700 acres of land on lots 15, 16, 24 and 25, through which the west branch of Twelve-mile creek flows, upon which he built a saw-mill in 1827. He was married to Rebecca Pickard in 1840, and the same year settled on lot No. 25, where he still resides. His first wife died in 1849, and in 1853 he was married to Fannie Bells, of Chautauqua county.

De Witt Tower, born in Wilson, August 25th, 1848, married Sarah J. Cobb, of Newfane, June 29th, 1870. He has been a life-long resident of the town, and follows the vocation of farming and teaching.

Noah C. Ward was born in Vermont, September 30th, 1809, whence he moved to Orleans county in 1825, where in 1826 he "broke ground" for the first court-house at Albion. He married Betsey Robinson, of Gaines, Orleans county, in 1832, came to Wilson in 1835 and located on the Slash road, where he now resides. His first wife died in 1867. On March 24th, 1868, he married Paulina Ruggles, of Vermont; both are members of the Presbyterian church of Wilson.

Jefferson A. Webster was born in Ogden, Monroe county, May 26th, 1840, and came with his parents to Wilson in 1842. He married Mary F. Folger, of Wilson, January 11th, 1863, and settled on his present farm in 1869. He was seven years a member of the State militia.

C. D. Ward was born in Rutland county, Vt., in 1822. He removed to Orleans county in 1834, married and came to Wilson in 1843, and located on lot No. 53, Lake road. His occupation is farming and fruit-raising, he having fifty acres set out to fruit trees. Post-office address, Olcott, N. Y.

George E. Wilson, born February 13th, 1841, is a native of Wilson. He married Esther Wilson, of Wilson, April 2nd, 1863, and the same year located on lot No. 87 Town Line road, where he still resides.

H. H. Wright was born in Lockport, in 1840. He enlisted in Company M, 1st N. Y. light artillery, was in several engagements, and was discharged in 1863 for disability. He was married in 1863 to Catharine Starkey, of Niagara county. He resides where his father located in 1852.

George K. Wright is a native of Canaan, Columbia county, N. Y., whence he removed to Orleans county in October, 1831. He came to Wilson March 6th, 1843, and at once located on lot No. 13, Daniels road, on a new farm, which he cleared up and improved, and where he still resides.

James Williams has always been a resident of this county. He was born in Royalton, June 14th, 1816, where he remained until 1845, when he moved to Wilson, and located on a comparatively new farm on lot No. 28, Randall road, which he has subdued and brought under a high state of cultivation and erected magnificent buildings, and where he now resides, surrounded with all the conveniences and comforts of a farm house. A view of his country-seat may be seen on another page. He was married to Mary Jane Smith, of Royalton, July 23d, 1845. In 1839 he belonged to an independent rifle company, and at the time of the McKenzie or "patriot" war was warned out to defend his country against Canadian invasion. His company was mustered at the Falls December 31st, 1839, and on January 1st, 1840, they marched to Fort Schlosser, where the Canadians had seized the boat "Caroline," as elsewhere related, set her on fire, cut her loose, and pushed her out to drift over the falls. In 1841 Mr. Williams was commissioned a quartermaster in the colonel's staff, in the 216th regiment, 5th brigade, 24th division N. Y. State militia, which position he held until October, 1845, when he resigned.

Edward J. Williams, one of the prosperous farmers of Wilson, was born in the town January 25th, 1854, and has always lived in it; post-office, North Ridge.

To this list we may add the names of George H. Burch, M. S. Gifford, Ira W. Brown and Isaac Morse.

www.ingramcontent.com/pod-product-compliance
Lightning Source LLC
Chambersburg PA
CBHW051357070526
44584CB00023B/3198